THE REFUGEE IN INTERNATIONAL LAW

The Refugee in
International Law

Third Edition

GUY S. GOODWIN-GILL
and
JANE McADAM

OXFORD
UNIVERSITY PRESS

OXFORD
UNIVERSITY PRESS

Great Clarendon Street, Oxford OX2 6DP

Oxford University Press is a department of the University of Oxford.
It furthers the University's objective of excellence in research, scholarship,
and education by publishing worldwide in

Oxford New York

Auckland Cape Town Dar es Salaam Hong Kong Karachi
Kuala Lumpur Madrid Melbourne Mexico City Nairobi
New Delhi Shanghai Taipei Toronto

With offices in

Argentina Austria Brazil Chile Czech Republic France Greece
Guatemala Hungary Italy Japan Poland Portugal Singapore
South Korea Switzerland Thailand Turkey Ukraine Vietnam

Oxford is a registered trade mark of Oxford University Press
in the UK and in certain other countries

Published in the United States
by Oxford University Press Inc., New York

British Library Cataloguing in Publication Data

Data available

Library of Congress Cataloging-in-Publication Data

Goodwin-Gill, Guy S.
The refugee in international law / Guy S. Goodwin-Gill and Jane McAdam.—3rd ed.
  p. cm.
Includes bibliographical references and index.
ISBN 978–0–19–928130–5 (alk. paper)—ISBN 978–0–19–920763–3 (alk. paper)   1.
Refugees—Legal status, laws, etc. I. McAdam, Jane, 1974– II. Title.
K3230.G66 2007
342.08′3—dc22

2007003103

Typeset by Newgen Imaging Systems (P) Ltd., Chennai, India
Printed in Great Britain
on acid-free paper by
Antony Rowe Ltd., Chippenhan

ISBN 978–0–19–928130–5
ISBN 978–0–19–920763–3 (Pbk.)

1 3 5 7 9 10 8 6 4 2

Preface

The refugee in international law remains one of the most politically contested issues of our time. When the Office of the United Nations High Commissioner for Refugees (UNHCR) was established nearly sixty years ago, it was envisaged as a temporary institution with a lifespan of only three years. UNHCR continues, however, and today is responsible for over 20 million displaced people, of whom some 8.4 million are 'refugees' in the sense of the 1951 Convention/1967 Protocol. The agency's presence in 116 countries highlights the extent of forced migration as a national, regional, but ultimately international issue, which requires a cooperative international response. That response is to be found in the international laws and practices that have developed over the past century in particular, and which provide a comprehensive regime of rights and obligations for those in need of protection.

At a time when national governments seem focused on preventing asylum seekers from ever reaching their territories, devising creative, if questionable, 'non-arrival' policies and legal fictions to deny 'legal' presence in spite of 'physical' presence, the structures and content of the international protection regime have a heightened importance. States need to recall the legal obligations which they have voluntarily accepted in treaties and through their practice. In this respect, refugee law, human rights law, humanitarian law, international criminal law, and the law of the sea are all elements of an overarching protection framework.

In the last edition of this book, an apology was made for the increase in the size of the work and the gap in time between editions. We can only express this sentiment once again, but hope that the expanded work provides the reader with a comprehensive treatment of contemporary refugee law issues, set in their historical context and in the light of developments in a variety of jurisdictions. While the overall structure of this edition follows the pattern of the second, a number of significant changes have been introduced. A new introductory chapter outlines the legal framework, and situates both the refugee and protection in the practice of the United Nations and in the context of international and national law.

Chapters 2–5 look at how the refugee definition has evolved, analyse its constituent parts, and the circumstances leading to the cessation or denial of refugee status. The past ten or so years have seen a continuing expansion in the jurisprudence, references to which are used to illustrate areas of emerging consensus among national decision-makers and areas of divergent interpretation.

Part 2 on Asylum has been substantially revised as to structure and content. *Non-refoulement*—the principle that no State shall return a refugee to a territory in which he or she is at risk of persecution or other 'relevant harm'—remains the central feature in the international refugee protection regime. Chapter 5 looks closely at its scope and application in the context of the 1951 Convention/1967 Protocol, while a new Chapter 6, entitled 'Protection under Human Rights and General International Law', examines States' *non-refoulement* obligations beyond the 1951 Convention, in the area of 'complementary protection'. Chapter 7 then draws the analysis together in a re-examination of the concept of asylum, with due regard to practice as it affects the 'right to seek asylum' to which States lent their voice in the 1948 Universal Declaration of Human Rights.

Finally, Part 3 on Protection has been revised and updated to take account of the stronger emphasis now being given internationally to the plight of internally displaced persons, and to the legal responsibilities of international organizations in human rights matters.

Although their 'international' legal credentials may not be immediately apparent, the EU's harmonization initiatives are a recurring feature in this edition. For better or worse, they are likely to influence practice, not only within the territorial area of an expanded European Union now comprising twenty-seven States, but also more widely. New questions will arise regarding the separate responsibility of EU States party to international treaties such as the 1951 Convention/1967 Protocol, the responsibility of European institutions, the role of the European Court of Justice, and the complementarity of Europe's long-established human rights machinery. Some of these are touched on here, but it is to future practice that we must look for the signs of consistency or otherwise with international law.

European developments are also responsible in part for some of the omissions in the present edition. The Annexes have been trimmed in number, but expanded in content to include eight key EU instruments. Three earlier annexes (UNHCR Executive Committee Selected Conclusions on International Protection, Miscellaneous Texts, and Comprehensive Arrangements for Refugees) have been omitted, but are available and will be regularly supplemented on the companion web site to this volume, the *Online Resource Centre*, which is described more fully below.

We have attempted to state the law as it stood on 31 December 2006. Some more recent developments have been noted, although it was not possible to include a detailed analysis of a valuable judgment of the Third Section of the European Court of Human Rights in the case of *Salah Sheekh* v. *The Netherlands* (Application No. 1948/04), 11 January 2007. The judgment, which should be read subject to any later consideration by the Grand Chamber, contains an extensive review of country of origin information from a variety of national and international sources, and examines the risks faced by Somalis, members of minority groups without benefit of clan protection. The court emphasized that for an 'internal flight alternative' to exist, the person to be expelled must be able to travel to the area concerned, gain admittance, and be able to settle there. It also considered whether the applicant should be required to show specific facts or circumstances relating to him personally, in order to qualify for Article 3 ECHR50 protection (the '*Vilvarajah*' principle). Given the inhuman treatment already suffered and the continuing risk to the applicant as a member of an unprotected minority, it concluded that no such additional evidence was called for. It found further that the applicant had not failed to exhaust domestic remedies, as any appeal would have stood virtually no prospect of success, in view of the consistent jurisprudence on the question of specific acts and circumstances.

****

Our aim in this third edition remains the same as that of the first, namely, to describe the foundations and the framework of international refugee law by concentrating on three core issues: the definition of refugees, the principle of *non-refoulement*, and the protection of refugees. We hope that this edition provides a measured reminder of the importance of the international protection regime and of the inherent dignity of the individual in search of protection. We hope, too, that it will serve not only as an authoritative statement of the current law, but also as a pointer to the future, as a basis for further enquiry, the development of appropriate principles and solutions, and a world in which the *necessity* for flight, as a rational choice between alternative fates, may be reduced.

Guy S. Goodwin-Gill   Jane McAdam
All Souls College   Faculty of Law
Oxford   University of New South Wales, Sydney

Acknowledgements

Many individuals have contributed to this third edition, some by their persistent encouragement, others by their enthusiasm and readiness to share thinking and experience, to discuss developments, and to plan for the future. Although no financial grant has been received or employed in the preparation of this work, this new edition evidently draws upon a fair range of papers, opinions, and professional work, including legal advice and representation, undertaken for governments, international, and non-governmental organizations.

Both authors are grateful for their continuing association with, among others, the Refugee Studies Centre (RSC) at the University of Oxford and the Office of the United Nations High Commissioner for Refugees (UNHCR). At the RSC, the present Director, Professor Roger Zetter, and his predecessor, Professor Stephen Castles, provided support and opportunities for presentation and discussion, in the course of which we were able to benefit from the valuable contributions of Dr Matthew Gibney, Dr María-Teresa Gil-Bazo and, from the Law Faculty, of Professor Vaughan Lowe, Chichele Professor of Public International Law. At UNHCR, we both appreciate the chance to engage regularly with the Department of International Protection, for which we thank Erika Feller, its former Director and now Assistant High Commissioner for International Protection, as well as Jean-François Durieux, Anja Klug, Volker Türk, Udo Janz, and, in the remaining information and dissemination field (mainly *RefWorld*), Oldrich Andrysek and Jerome Sabety. Our Geneva experience has also been greatly assisted by colleagues at other UN agencies, including Sharon Rusu, currently at OCHA/ReliefWeb, and Mona Rishmawi at the Office of the UN High Commissioner for Human Rights. The Graduate Institute for International Studies (IUHEI) has provided a home from home, and we extend our thanks to Dr Daniel Warner, Professor Vera Gowlland, and Professor Andrew Clapham, as well as to Professor Walter Kälin of the University of Bern and now also, and appropriately, the Special Representative of the Secretary-General for the Human Rights of Internally Displaced Persons.

Non-governmental organizations (among them, Amnesty International, Liberty, the Immigration Law Practitioners' Association, the Refugee Legal Centre, and the European Council on Refugees and Exiles) play a critically important role in advocacy and refugee protection and here we have benefited from the support and friendship of Pia Oberoi, Per Baneke, Shami Chakrabarti, Chris Nash, Eve Lester, Alice Edwards, Barry Stoyle, and Nick Oakeshott.

Arthur Helton, who was killed in the attack on the UN Office in Baghdad in 2003, was a good friend and always ready to share his wealth of information and experience. He is greatly missed, as is Joan Fitzpatrick, whose acute and critical intelligence nailed many a misconception. We hope that the pages that follow do them both justice.

Each of us also has personal debts. Guy Goodwin-Gill has benefited from his continuing close relations with Canada, and from regular advice and talks with John Scratch, QC, formerly Head of the Human Rights Law Section of the Department of Justice. In recent years, he has also had the opportunity to represent UNHCR as intervener in three cases before United Kingdom courts (*El-Ali, European Roma Rights Centre*, and *Al Rawi*). Much of the research undertaken for these proceedings has helped to develop the analysis below (although the views and conclusions reached are those of the authors, and are not necessarily shared by UNHCR). Nevertheless, it was a pleasure to work with UNHCR's Representatives in London, Ann Dawson-Shepherd followed by Bemma Donkoh, and with Chooi Fong and Hannah Lily. UNHCR's solicitors, acting *pro bono*, provided strong and essential support in these proceedings, and particular thanks are due to Tom Cassels and his colleagues, Liz Williams, Emily Carlisle and Fiona Learmont, at Baker & McKenzie (in *El-Ali* and *Al Rawi*), and to Rebecca Money-Kyrle, Helen Moss, and Alex Wilks at SJ Berwin and Ania Slinn at Mayer, Brown, Rose & Maw (in *European Roma Rights Centre*). Blackstone Chambers likewise provided a solid base and excellent assistance; sound advice on many substantive and procedural issues was always available from colleagues there, including Ian Brownlie QC, Anthony Lester QC, Michael Fordham QC, Dinah Rose QC, Mark Shaw QC, and Robert Howe, and from Julia Hornor and Martin Smith. Nick Blake QC and Raza Husain from Matrix Chambers, Tim Otty QC from 20 Essex Street, Tim Eicke from Essex Court Chambers, and Rick Scannell from 57–60 Lincoln's Inn Fields, have also contributed in their own way. In Oxford, Lydia-Maria Bolani assisted with research on the international criminal tribunals, while All Souls College and the Codrington Library provided access to essential resources, as well as a congenial writing environment.

Finally, as so many of us who write will know, there is no way this edition would ever have been finished, had it not been for the love and support of family, and I am especially grateful to my wife Sharon for her endless encouragement, professionally but above all personally.

Jane McAdam was a number of the University of Sydney Faculty of Law at the time of writing this edition and would like to thank that Faculty for generously providing her with research funds from the Legal Scholarship Support Fund, and the University of Sydney College of Humanities and Social Sciences for awarding her a Writing Fellowship and Overseas Travel Grants. These awards enabled travel to Oxford to work on this edition, provided partial teaching relief to focus on writing; and, in particular, allowed for the engagement of two excellent research assistants, Anthony Levin and Emma Truswell, whose help was invaluable. She would also like to acknowledge the encouragement of her colleagues at the Sydney Law Faculty; in particular Associate Professor Mary Crock, the Dean, Professor Ron McCallum; and the former Challis Professor of International Law, now

Professor of International Law at the Australian National University, Professor Donald Rothwell.

Special thanks are also due to family and friends for their constant interest and support, especially when laptop and books got more time than they did. She is especially grateful to her parents, Peter and Jenanne McAdam, her partner, Ben Saul, and the Chartres, Bush and Dellow families.

****

Finally, we must both say that it has been a pleasure once again to work with the staff of Oxford University Press in the preparation of this edition, and our thanks go to John Louth, Alex Flach, Hugh Logue, and Geraldine Mangley, not only for unflagging patience, but also for solutions to problems. Notwithstanding the many who have contributed to our work over the years, we remain responsible, of course, for the views expressed herein, as also for such errors and omissions as occur.

Summary Table of Contents

Contents

Tables of Cases

PERMANENT COURT OF INTERNATIONAL JUSTICE/ INTERNATIONAL COURT OF JUSTICE

INTERNATIONAL CRIMINAL TRIBUNALS FOR FORMER
YUGOSLAVIA AND RWANDA

EUROPEAN COMMISSION AND EUROPEAN COURT
OF HUMAN RIGHTS

INTER-AMERICAN COURT AND COMMISSION
OF HUMAN RIGHTS

UNITED NATIONS COMMITTEE
AGAINST TORTURE

UNITED NATIONS HUMAN RIGHTS COMMITTEE

AUSTRALIA

FRANCE

IRELAND

NEW ZEALAND

UNITED KINGDOM

UNITED STATES OF AMERICA

MISCELLANEOUS

Table of Treaties and Other International and Regional Instruments

[The full text or relevant extracts of instruments marked with an asterisk can be found in the Annexes]

Selected Abbreviations

ACHR69	American Convention on Human Rights 1969
ACHPR81	African Charter of Human and Peoples' Rights 1981
AJIL	*American Journal of International Law*
ALR	Australian Law Reports
API	Protocol Additional to the Geneva Conventions of 12 August 1949, and relating to the Protection of Victims of International Armed Conflicts
APII	Protocol Additional to the Geneva Conventions of 12 August 1949, and relating to the Protection of Victims of Non-International Armed Conflicts
ArabCHR	Arab Charter of Human Rights 2004
ASEAN	Association of South East Asian States
Asyl	*Schweizerische Zeitschrift für Asylrecht und -praxis/Revue suisse pour la pratique et le droit d'asile*
AsylVfG	*Asylverfahrensgesetz* (Asylum Procedure Law—Germany)
AU	African Union (formerly OAU—Organization of African Unity)
AuslG	*Ausländergesetz* (Aliens Law—Germany)
Austrian J Public Intl L	*Austrian Journal of Public International Law*
Aust. YB Int'l Law	*Australian Yearbook of International Law*
BDIL	*British Digest of International Law*, vols. 2b-7, London, 1965, 1967 (C. Parry, ed.)
BGBl	*Bundesgesetzblatt* (published laws of Germany and/or Austria)
BHRC	Butterworths Human Rights Cases
BIA	Board of Immigration Appeals (USA)
BverfGE	*Entscheidungen des Bundesverfassungsgerichts* (decisions of the German Federal Constitutional Court)
BverwGE	*Entscheidungen des Bundesverwaltungsgerichts* (decisions of the German Federal Administrative Court)
BYIL	*British Yearbook of International Law*
Can. YIL	*Canadian Yearbook of International Law*
CAT84	Convention against Torture and Other Cruel, Inhuman or Degrading Treatment or Punishment 1984
CDR	Centre for Documentation on Refugees (UNHCR)
CEAS	Common European Asylum System

l   *Selected Abbreviations*

CETS	Council of Europe Treaty Series (formerly ETS)
CFR	Code of Federal Regulations (USA)
CIREA	Centre for Information, Discussion and Exchange on Asylum
CIREFCA	International Conference on Refugees in Central America
CLR	Commonwealth Law Reports (Australia)
CPA	Comprehensive Plan of Action for Indo-Chinese Refugees
CPRR	*Commission Permanente de Recours des Réfugiés* (Belgium)
CRC89	Convention on the Rights of the Child 1989
CRDD	Convention Refugee Determination Division (Immigration and Refugee Board, Canada; now Refugee Protection Division—RPD)
CRR	*Commission des recours des réfugiés* (France)
CSCE	Conference on Security and Co-operation in Europe (later the OSCE—Organization for Security and Co-operation in Europe)
CSR51	Convention relating to the Status of Refugees 1951
CTD	Convention Travel Document (issued under article 28 of the 1951 Convention relating to the Status of Refugees)
Cth	Commonwealth (Australia)
DHA	Department of Humanitarian Affairs (United Nations; now OCHA—Office for the Coordination of Humanitarian Affairs)
DIP	Department (formerly Division) of International Protection (UNHCR)
DISERO	Disembarkation Resettlement Offers
Doc. réf.	*Documentation réfugiés*
DORS Committee	Determination of Refugee Status Committee (Australia; see now Refugee Review Tribunal)
EC	European Community
ECHR50	European Convention for the Protection of Human Rights and Fundamental Freedoms 1950
ECOSOC	Economic and Social Council of the United Nations
ECOWAS	Economic Community of West African States
ECR	European Court Reports
ECRE	European Council on Refugees and Exiles
ECtHR	European Court of Human Rights
EEA	European Economic Area
EHRR	European Human Rights Reports
EJIL	*European Journal of International Law*

EJML	*European Journal of Migration and Law*
ELENA	European Legal Network on Asylum
ETS	*European Treaty Series* (now *CETS*)
EU	European Union
European HR L Rev	*European Human Rights Law Review*
EWCA	England and Wales Court of Appeal
FAO	Food and Agriculture Organization
FC	Federal Court (Canada)
FC-TD	Federal Court—Trial Division (Canada)
FCA	Federal Court of Australia or Federal Court of Appeal (Canada)
FCAFC	Federal Court of Australia Full Court
FCJ	Judgments of the Federal Court of Canada (Court of Appeal and Trial Division)
FCR	Federal Court Reports (Australia or Canada)
GCII	Second Geneva Convention for the Amelioration of the Condition of Wounded, Sick and Shipwrecked Members of Armed Forces at Sea 1949
GCIII	Third Geneva Convention relative to the Treatment of Prisoners of War 1949
GCIV	Fourth Geneva Convention relative to the Protection of Civilian Persons in Time of War 1949
Hackworth, *Digest*	Hackworth, G.H., *Digest of International Law*, 8 vols., Washington, 1940–4
Harv. ILJ	*Harvard International Law Journal*
HC	House of Commons
HC Deb.	Parliamentary Debates, House of Commons, 5th series
HCA	High Court of Australia
HL Deb.	Parliamentary Debates, House of Lords, 5th series
HRC	Human Rights Committee
HRLJ	*Human Rights Law Journal*
HRQ	*Human Rights Quarterly*
I&N Dec	Immigration and Nationality Decisions (USA)
IARLJ	International Association of Refugee Law Judges
ICCPR66	International Covenant on Civil and Political Rights 1966
ICERD66	International Convention on the Elimination of All Forms of Racial Discrimination 1966

ICESCR66	International Covenant on Economic, Social and Cultural Rights 1966
ICJ	International Court of Justice
ICLQ	*International and Comparative Law Quarterly*
ICTR	International Criminal Tribunal for Rwanda
ICTY	International Criminal Tribunal for the Former Yugoslavia
IDPs	Internally displaced persons
IFA	Internal flight alternative
IGCR	Inter-governmental Committee on Refugees
IJRL	*International Journal of Refugee Law*
ILA	International Law Association
ILC	International Law Commission
ILM	*International Legal Materials*
ILO	International Labour Organization
ILPA	Immigration Law Practitioners' Association
ILR	International Law Reports
IMCO	Inter-governmental Maritime Consultative Organization (renamed in 1982 as the International Maritime Organization—IMO)
Imm AR	Immigration Appeals Reports
IMO	See IMCO
IMT	International Military Tribunal
INA	Immigration and Nationality Act 1952 (USA)
INLR	Immigration and Nationality Law Reports
INS	Immigration and Naturalization Service (USA; now Citizenship and Immigration Services)
Int. Mig. Rev.	*International Migration Review*
IOM	International Organization for Migration
IRB	Immigration and Refugee Board (Canada)
IRO	International Refugee Organization
JRS	*Journal of Refugee Studies*
LN	League of Nations
LNTS	*League of Nations Treaty Series*
MEI	Minister of Employment and Immigration (Canada)
MIMA	Minister for Immigration and Multicultural Affairs (Australia)
MIMIA	Minister for Immigration, Multicultural and Indigenous Affairs (Australia)

Moore, *Digest*	Moore, J. B., *Digest of International Law*, 8 vols., Washington, 1906.
Moore, *Arbitrations*	Moore, J. B., *History and Digest of the International Arbitrations to which the United States has been a Party*, Washington, 1898.
NATO	North Atlantic Treaty Organization
Neth. QHR	*Netherlands Quarterly of Human Rights*
NGO	Non-governmental organization
NZAR	New Zealand Administrative Reports
NZLR	New Zealand Law Reports
NZSC	New Zealand Supreme Court
OAS	Organization of American States
OAU	Organization of African Unity (now AU—African Union)
OAU69	OAU Convention on the Specific Aspects of Refugee Problems in Africa 1969
OCHA	United Nations Office for the Coordination of Humanitarian Affairs
OFPRA	*Office français de protection des réfugiés et apatrides*
OJ	Official Journal
OMCT	World Organization against Torture
OSCE	See CSCE
PCIJ	Permanent Court of International Justice
RASRO	Rescue at Sea Resettlement Offers
RDDE	*Revue du droit des étrangers*
Rome Statute	Statute of the International Criminal Court 1998
RPD	Refugee Protection Division (Immigration and Refugee Board, Canada)
RRT	Refugee Review Tribunal (Australia)
RSAC	Refugee Status Advisory Committee (Canada—see now Immigration and Refugee Board)
RSQ	*Refugee Survey Quarterly*
SAR Convention	International Convention on Maritime Search and Rescue
SC res.	Security Council resolution
SCJ	Judgments of the Supreme Court of Canada
SOLAS Convention	International Convention on the Safety of Life at Sea
Sydney LR	*Sydney Law Review*
TPS	Temporary Protected Status (USA)
TPV	Temporary Protection Visa (Australia)

UDHR48	Universal Declaration of Human Rights 1948
UKHL	United Kingdom House of Lords
UKIAT	United Kingdom Immigration Appeals Tribunal (now Asylum and Immigration Tribunal)
UN	United Nations
UNCCP	United Nations Conciliation Commission for Palestine
UNCLOS82	United Nations Convention on the Law of the Sea 1982
UNDP	United Nations Development Programme
UNDRO	Office of the United Nations Disaster Relief Co-ordinator
UNGA	United Nations General Assembly
UNGA res.	United Nations General Assembly resolution
UNGAOR	United Nations General Assembly Official Records
UNHCR	Office of the United Nations High Commissioner for Refugees
UNHCR, *Conclusions*	UNHCR, *Conclusions on International Protection adopted by the Executive Committee of the Programme of the High Commissioner*, Geneva, 1979–
UNHCR, *Handbook*	UNHCR, *Handbook on Procedures and Criteria for Determining Refugee Status*, Geneva, 1979 (re-edited 1992)
UNICEF	United Nations Children's Fund
UNKRA	United Nations Korean Reconstruction Agency
UNPROFOR	United Nations Protection Force in Former Yugoslavia
UNRIAA	Reports of International Arbitral Awards
UNRRA	United Nations Relief and Rehabilitation Administration
UNRWA	United Nations Relief and Works Agency for Palestine Refugees in the Near East
UNTS	*United Nations Treaty Series*
USC	United States Code
USCRI	United States Committee for Refugees and Immigrants
VG	*Verwaltungsgericht* (Administrative Court, Germany)
Virg. JIL	*Virginia Journal of International Law*
WFP	World Food Programme
Whiteman, *Digest*	Whiteman, M. M., *Digest of International Law*, 15 vols., Washington, 1963–73
WHO	World Health Organization
YB ILC	Year Book of the International Law Commission
ZaöRV	*Zeitschrift für ausländisches und öffentliches Recht und Völkerrecht*

Online Resource Centre

<http://www.oup.com/uk/refugeelaw>

As noted above, the expansion in the text of this edition has necessitated cuts in the number of annexes. However, the Online Resource Centre (ORC), now made available by Oxford University Press at the address above, means that the relevant texts can continue to be available.

The ORC accompanying this publication will therefore contain, first, the full text of all the Annexes included in the present edition (Annexes 1–3). In addition, an updated collection of UNHCR Executive Committee Conclusions on international protection will be included, together with collections of miscellaneous texts and historical material. Initially, these will be provided in PDF form, for which a copy of the free Adobe Acrobat Reader will be required. Eventually, we hope to make these collections available also in HTML format, so as to be readily searchable online and organized with appropriate hyperlinks.

The ORC will also provide links to relevant web-based resources, including international organizations, regional organizations, non-governmental organizations, case law collections, national law sources, publications, and national refugee support organizations; a first list of such links is provided below.

From time to time, we hope to be able to highlight new cases of importance and to direct the reader to the original source; however, given the ready availability of judgments and decisions in their original format, we will not be proposing our own collection of judgments, or attempting to provide summaries or abstracts.

We hope that this Online Resource Centre will enable readers of *The Refugee in International Law* to keep up with developments, as they occur, and also to have various 'historical' resources available, either directly through the internet, or in downloadable form for consultation at convenience.

Websites

United Nations system and other international organizations

Food and Agriculture Organization: <http://www.fao.org>

International Committee of the Red Cross: <http://www.icrc.org>

International Court of Justice: <http://www.icj-cij.org>

International Criminal Court (Statute): <http://www.un.org/law/icc/statute/romefra.htm>

International Criminal Tribunal for Rwanda: <http://www.ictr.org>

International Criminal Tribunal for the Former Yugoslavia (Statute and reports of judgments): <www.un.org/icty>

International Federation of Red Cross and Red Crescent Societies: <http://www.ifrc.org>

International Labour Organization: <http://www.ilo.org>

International Law Commission: <http://untreaty.un.org/ilc/ilcintro.htm>

International Maritime Organization: <http://www.imo.org>

International Organization for Migration: <http://www.iom.int>

Inter-Parliamentary Union: <http://www.ipu.org>

Office of the Special Representative of the Secretary-General for Children and Armed Conflict: <http://www.un.org/special-rep/children-armed-conflict>

Office of the United Nations High Commissioner for Human Rights: <http://www.ohchr.org>

ReliefWeb (OCHA)—Information on complex emergencies: <http://www.reliefweb.int>

United Nations Action to Counter Terrorism: <http://www.un.org/terrorism>

United Nations Children's Fund (UNICEF): <http://www.unicef.org>

United Nations Documentation Centre: <http://www.un.org/documents>

United Nations Emergency Relief Coordinator (ERC) and Office for the Coordination of Humanitarian Assistance (OCHA): <http://ochaonline.un.org>

United Nations High Commissioner for Refugees (UNHCR): <http://www.unhcr.org>

United Nations Information System on the Question of Palestine (UNISPAL): <http://domino.un.org/unispal.nsf>

United Nations Inter-Agency Standing Committee (IASC): <http://www.humanitarianinfo.org/iasc>

United Nations Relief and Works Agency for Palestinian Refugees in the Near East (UNRWA): <http://www.un.org/unrwa>

United Nations Treaty Collection: <http://untreaty.un.org>

World Food Programme: <http://www.wfp.org>

World Health Organization: <http://www.who.int>

Regional organizations

African Union: <http://www.africa-union.org>

Asian–African Legal Consultative Organization: <http://www.aalco.org>

Council of Europe: <http://www.coe.int>

Council of Europe Treaty Collection: <http://conventions.coe.int>

European Community Humanitarian Office (ECHO): <http://ec.europa.eu/echo>

European Court of Human Rights: <http://www.echr.coe.int>

European Court of Justice (EU): <http://curia.europa.eu/en>

European Parliament: <http://www.europarl.eu.int>

European Union: <http://europa.eu.int>

Office for Cooperation and Security in Europe (OSCE): <http://www.osce.org>

Inter-American Court of Human Rights: <http://www.corteidh.or.cr/index.cfm>
Organization for Economic Cooperation and Development (OECD): <http://www.oecd.org>
Organization of American States (OAS): <http://www.oas.org>

National legal sources

Australian law: <http://www.comlaw.gov.au>
French law: <http://www.legifrance.gouv.fr>
German law: <http://bundesrecht.juris.de>
German Law Archive (German law in English translation): <http://www.ius-comp.org/gla>
Swiss law: <http://www.admin.ch/ch/f/rs>
United Kingdom Statute Law Database: <http://www.statutelaw.gov.uk>
United States Code and Code of Federal Regulations: <http://www.gpoaccess.gov>

National jurisprudence

Asylum and Immigration Tribunal (United Kingdom): <http://www.ait.gov.uk>
Australasian Legal Information Institute (Aust LII): <http://www.austlii.edu.au>
Board of Immigration Appeals (BIA) (United States of America): <http://www.usdoj.gov/eoir>
British and Irish Legal Information Institute (BAILII): <http://www.bailii.org>
Bundesamt für Migration und Flüchtlinge/Federal Office for Migration and Refugees (Germany): <http://www.bamf.de>
Canadian Legal Information Institute (CanLII): <http://www.canlii.org>
Commission des recours des réfugiés/Refugee Appeals Commission (France): <http://www.commission-refugies.fr>
Commission suisse de recours en matière d'asile, Swiss Asylum Appeals Commission (Switzerland): <http://www.vpb.admin.ch>
Conseil d'Etat (France): <http://www.conseil-etat.fr>; for jurisprudence, see also <http://www.legifrance.gouv.fr>
Executive Office for Immigration Review (EOIR) (United States of America): <http://www.usdoj.gov/eoir>
Immigration and Refugee Board (Canada): <http://www.irb-cisr.gc.ca>
Office française pour la protection des réfugiés et apatrides/French Office for the Protection of Refugees and Stateless Persons (OFPRA): <http://www.ofpra.gouv.fr>
Refugee Review Tribunal (Australia): <http://www.rrt.gov.au>
Refugee Status Appeals Authority (New Zealand): <http://www.nzrefugeeappeals.govt.nz>

Refugee and asylum seeker information sources

Amnesty International: <http://www.amnesty.org>
Article 19: <http://www.article19.org>

Child Rights Information Network (CRIN): <http://www.crin.org>
European Bureau for Conscientious Objection: <http://www.ebco-beoc.org>
European Country of Origin Information Network (ECOI): <http://www.ecoi.net>
Human Rights First: <http://www.humanrightsfirst.org>
Human Rights Watch: <http://www.hrw.org>
Interights: <http://www.interights.org>
International Crisis Group: <http://www.intl-crisis-group.org>
Refugee Law Project (Makerere University, Uganda): <http://www.refugeelaw-project.org>
Refugee Legal Centre (United Kingdom): <http://www.refugee-legal-centre.org.uk>
Statewatch: <http://www.statewatch.org>
United States Department of State Human Rights Reports: <http://www.state.gov/g/drl/rls/hrrpt>
University of Essex Children and Armed Conflict Unit: <http://www.essex.ac.uk/armedcon>
War Resisters International: <http://www.wri-irg.org>

Non-governmental organizations

AIRE Centre: <http://www.airecentre.org>
B'Tselem: <http://www.btselem.org>
BADIL: <http://www.badil.org>
British Refugee Council: <http://www.refugeecouncil.org.uk>
Canadian Council for Refugees: <http://www.web.ca/ccr>
Crimes of War Project: <http://www.crimesofwar.org>
European Council for Refugees and Exiles (ECRE): <http://www.ecre.org>
Forum des réfugiés (France): <http://www.forumrefugies.org>
Norwegian Refugee Council: <http://www.nrc.no>
Refugee Council of Australia: <http://www.refugeecouncil.org.au>
Refugee Law Centre (Boston, USA): <http://www.refugeelawcenter.org>
United States Committee for Refugees and Immigrants: <http://www.refugees.org>

Refugee and related legal studies

American Society of International Law: <http://www.asil.org>
Avalon Project (Yale University): <http://www.yale.edu/lawweb/avalon/avalon.htm>
Electronic Information System for International Law: <http://www.eisil.org>
European Journal of International Law: <http://www.ejil.org>
Forced Migration Online (University of Oxford): <http://www.forcedmigration.org>
International Journal of Refugee Law: <http://ijrl.oxfordjournals.org>
Journal of Refugee Studies: <http://jrs.oxfordjournals.org>

Migration Policy Institute: <http://www.migrationpolicy.org>
Refugee Law Reader: <http://www.refugeelawreader.org>
Refugee Studies Centre (University of Oxford): <http://www.rsc.ox.ac.uk>
Refugee Law at the Refugee Studies Centre: <http://refugeelaw.qeh.ox.ac.uk>
University of Minnesota Human Rights Library: <http://www.umn.edu/humanrts>

Miscellaneous

British Broadcasting Corporation (BBC)—News: <http://news.bbc.co.uk>

1

The Refugee in International Law

1. Introduction

The refugee in international law occupies a legal space characterized, on the one hand, by the principle of State sovereignty and the related principles of territorial supremacy and self-preservation; and, on the other hand, by competing humanitarian principles deriving from general international law (including the purposes and principles of the United Nations) and from treaty. Refugee law nevertheless remains an incomplete legal regime of protection, imperfectly covering what ought to be a situation of exception. It goes some way to alleviate the plight of those affected by breaches of human rights standards or by the collapse of an existing social order in the wake of revolution, civil strife, or aggression; but it is incomplete so far as refugees and asylum seekers may still be denied even temporary protection, safe return to their homes, or compensation.[1]

The international legal status of the refugee necessarily imports certain legal consequences, the most important of which is the obligation of States to respect the principle of *non-refoulement* through time. In practice, the (legal) obligation to respect this principle, independent and compelling as it is, may be difficult to isolate from the (political) options which govern the availability of solutions. The latter necessarily depend upon political factors, including whether anything can be done about the conditions which gave rise to the refugee's flight. For any solution to be ultimately satisfactory, however, the wishes of the individual cannot be entirely disregarded, for example the connections which he or she may have with one or another State.

The existence of the class of refugees in international law not only entails legal consequences for States, but also the entitlement and the responsibility to exercise protection on behalf of refugees. The Office of the United Nations High Commissioner for Refugees (UNHCR) is the agency presently entrusted with this function, as the representative of the international community, but States also have a protecting role, even though their material interests are not engaged, and

---

[1] To what extent one should seek to fill every gap is a moot point, and indeed may compromise another objective, namely, the right of everyone 'to belong—or alternatively to move in an orderly fashion to seek work, decent living conditions and freedom from strife': Sadruddin Aga Khan, *Study on Human Rights and Mass Exoduses*: UN doc. E/CN.4/1503, para. 9.

notwithstanding their common reluctance to take up the cause.[2] Moreover, the
'interest' of the international community is expanding, and this is raising new
legal and institutional questions on issues such as internal displacement, complex
humanitarian emergencies, and the 'responsibility to protect'.

The study of refugee law invites a look not only at States' obligations with
regard to the admission and treatment of refugees after entry, but also at the
potential responsibility in international law of the State whose conduct or omissions cause an outflow. It is easy enough to prescribe a principle of responsibility
for 'creating' refugees, but considerably harder to offer a more precise formulation
of the underlying rights and duties. Writing nearly seventy years ago, Jennings
posited liability on the repercussions which a refugee exodus has on the material
interests of third States. In his view, conduct resulting in 'the flooding of other
States with refugee populations' was illegal, ' . . . *a fortiori* where the refugees are
compelled to enter the country of refuge in a destitute condition'.[3]

With developments since 1939, the bases for the liability of source countries
now lie not so much in the doctrine of abuse of rights, as Jennings then suggested,
as in the breach of original obligations regarding human rights and fundamental
freedoms. Legal theory nevertheless remains imperfect, given the absence of
clearly correlative rights in favour of a subject of international law competent to
exercise protection, and the uncertain legal consequences which follow where
breach of obligations leads to a refugee exodus.[4] States are under a duty to
co-operate with one another in accordance with the UN Charter, but the method
of application of this principle in a given refugee case requires care. The promotion of 'orderly departure programmes', as an example of cooperation, supposes a
degree of recognition of the right to leave one's country *and* to enter another
which is not generally and currently justified by State practice.[5] Principles of
reparation for loss suffered by receiving States also remain undeveloped.

The practice of States certainly appears to permit the conclusion that States are
bound by a general principle not to create refugee outflows and to cooperate with
other States in the resolution of such problems as emerge. First, by analogy with

---

[2] Cf. *R (on the application of Al Rawi and others)* v. *Secretary of State for Foreign and Commonwealth Affairs (UNHCR intervening)* [2006] EWCA Civ 1279.

[3] Jennings, R. Y., 'Some International Law Aspects of the Refugee Question', 20 *BYIL* 98, 111 (1939); see also at 112–13: 'Domestic rights must be subject to the principle *sic utere tuo ut alienum non laedas*. And for a State to employ these rights with the avowed purpose of saddling other States with unwanted sections of its population is as clear an abuse of right as can be imagined.'

[4] The extent to which 'traditional' rules of State responsibility are, or can be made, relevant to refugee issues, particularly flight, is open to debate. Even with regard to the protection of those who have already left their country, theoretical and practical problems remain, as the discussion through-out this book will show.

[5] The Director of the Intergovernmental Committee established by the 1938 Evian Conference was charged with undertaking 'negotiations to improve the present conditions of exodus (of refugees from Germany and Austria) and to replace them by orderly emigration'. Orderly departure was also proposed (and adopted, though with some slow starts), as an alternative to the departure of refugees from Vietnam by boat. See further below on Indochinese refugees and the Comprehensive Plan of Action.

the rule enunciated in the *Corfu Channel* case, responsibility may be attributed whenever a State, within whose territory substantial transboundary harm is generated, has knowledge or means of knowledge of the harm and the opportunity to act.[6] Secondly, even if at a somewhat high level of generality, States now owe to the international community the duty to accord to their nationals a certain standard of treatment in the matter of human rights. Thirdly, a State owes to other States at large (and to particular States after entry), the duty to re-admit its nationals. Fourthly, every State is bound by the principle of international cooperation.

A *rule* to the effect that 'States shall not create refugees' is too general and incomplete. An ambulatory principle nevertheless operates, obliging States to exercise care in their domestic affairs in the light of other States' legal interests,[7] and to cooperate in the solution of refugee problems. Such cooperation might include, as appropriate, assisting in the removal or mitigation of the causes of flight, contributing to the voluntary return of nationals abroad, and facilitating, in agreement with other States, the processes of orderly departure and family reunion. Where internal conflict or non-State actors are the primary cause of flight, the theoretical application of rules and principles may be as difficult to achieve as practical and political solutions.

Given the uncertain (and perhaps unpromising) legal situation that follows flight, increasing attention now focuses on the ways and means to *prevent* refugee outflows.[8] The enjoyment of human rights and fundamental freedoms is conditioned, in part at least, upon the opportunity of individuals and groups to participate in and benefit from the nation and body politic, and from the sensible premise that the authority to govern derives from the will of the people as expressed in periodic and genuine elections. The responsibility of States, in turn,

---

[6] Cf. Stockholm Declaration: 'States have . . . the responsibility to ensure that activities within their jurisdiction or control do not cause damage to the environment of other States or of areas beyond the limits of national jurisdiction': *Report* of the UN Conference on the Human Environment: UN doc. A/CONF.48/14/Rev. 1 and Corr. 1, Principle 21, 5. To compare the flow of refugees with the flow of, for example, noxious fumes may appear invidious; the basic issue, however, is the responsibility which derives from the fact of control over territory, a point clearly made by the International Court of Justice in its Advisory Opinion in the *Namibia* case, ICJ *Rep.*, (1971), 16, at 54 (para. 118).

[7] Cf. International Law Commission, 'International Liability for Injurious Consequences arising out of acts not prohibited by international law': UN doc. A/36/10, 334ff (1981).

[8] A number of attempts have been made to devise more 'equitable' systems for dealing with the effects of refugee movements, for example, by the allocation of refugees to States in light of their relative well-being, space and capacity; see, for example, Grahl-Madsen, A., *Territorial Asylum*, (1980), 102–14; Hathaway, J., 'A Reconsideration of the Underlying Premise of Refugee Law', 31 *Harv. Int.L.J.* 129 (1990). See also State-sponsored initiatives include the United Kingdom's 2003 proposal for 'regional protection areas' (Home Office, 'New International Approaches to Asylum Processing and Protection', Mar. 2003) and Denmark's similar 1986 proposal to link a global resettlement scheme with annual quotas offered by UN Member States: 'International Procedures for the Protection of Refugees': UN doc. A/C.3/41/L.51, 12 Nov. 1986. None of these proposals has struck a responsive chord with States generally or with other actors, and it may be that this general unreadiness or unwillingness to cooperate in this direction is a factor in individual and 'bloc' efforts to regulate the movements of people by other means.

springs from the fact of control over territory and inhabitants. *A priori*, individuals and groups ought to be free to enjoy human rights in the territory with which they are connected by the internationally relevant social fact of attachment; and it is probably self-evident that this is most likely to be attained, not by imposition from outside, but where democratic and representative government, civil society, and the rule of law flourish locally.

Essential as it is to the preservation of life and liberty, the right to seek asylum from persecution and the threat of torture or other relevant harm is no substitute for the fullest protection of human rights at home. Population pressure is not just a matter of numbers, but also of rural-urban migration, military and social conflict, under-development, deficient or faltering democratization, and people's perception that they are not or no longer able to influence their own life-plans. Equally clearly, however, the responses of the more developed world seem frequently limited to measures at their own front or back door; hence, the concentration on adding locks and bolts, on building higher walls and stronger fences, on palliatives and not remedies.

This all adds up to a less than healthy background against which to portray the panorama of rules and principles that do comprise the international legal regime of refugee protection. The sceptic may consider the ambition entirely quixotic, finding the field of population displacement dominated by narrow national ideologies and the play of market forces. The preface to the first edition of this book in 1983 looked forward to a time when human rights and basic freedoms might be attainable, 'on behalf of every man, woman, and child who has not yet chosen flight from their homeland'. Two editions and twenty-five or so years later, this implicit optimism, premised on a profound belief in the human capacity to resolve problems, is certainly harder to sustain. No international lawyer, however, can help but be impressed by the extent to which human rights and individual welfare are now higher on the political and legal agenda, and by the commitment, particularly among non-governmental organizations and in regional supervisory mechanisms, to ensure that rules are followed and standards maintained. The legal and institutional challenges to fundamental principles should not be underestimated, however, and there is a continuing need to show both the continuing relevance of the rules and their necessity, in face of the social realities of displacement.

The community of nations is responsible in a general sense for finding solutions and in providing international protection to refugees. This special mandate was entrusted to UNHCR in relatively unambiguous terms in 1950, and as an actor on the international plane its practice has contributed greatly to the formation of legal structures and the development and consolidation of rules and standards. Since the early 1990s, however, UNHCR has often given the impression of an agency in search of a purpose, anxious to be seen to be active and to claim turf in the 'humanitarian space', particularly in relation to other international organizations. This has led at times to a loss of priority for its special responsibility for the protection of refugees, although some of the ground has been made up recently through the Global Consultations process and other promotional work. The backing of key players, both donors and members generally of the UNHCR Executive Committee, will be essential if protection is once again to acquire primary importance, although there is a danger it may be overcome by concerns of the moment or longer, including security, migration, and globalization. In addition, the UN's capacity to respond effectively to complex and other humanitarian emergencies, including both internal and external displacement, is under review, and both UNHCR and other bodies, such as the Office of the United Nations High Commissioner for Human Rights, will need to ensure that protection principles are effectively integrated into policy planning and implementation.[9]

2. The refugee in international law and the practice of the United Nations Security Council

Cross-border movements of refugees trigger legal principles like protection and *non-refoulement*, or activate the institutional responsibilities of organizations such as the United Nations High Commissioner for Refugees. Increasingly, however, such facts are acquiring another juridical relevance in the practice of the United Nations, and may come to influence the conduct of States and the development of the law. For example, the Security Council has turned its attention not only to internal and inter-State conflict, but also to genocide, massive violations of human rights, and crimes against humanity in formulating a variety of resolutions, measures, and actions, including under Chapter VII of the UN Charter. The actual displacement of populations has also been seen as a threat to international peace and security, or as contributing to such a threat.

In resolution 688 (1991) on Iraq, the Council did not proceed to Chapter VII action, but nevertheless expressed its grave concern at events which had led 'to a massive flow of refugees towards and across international frontiers and to cross-border incursions, which threaten international peace and security in the region'. In resolution 841 (1993) on Haiti, it recalled that it had earlier 'noted with concern' how humanitarian crises, including mass displacements, became or aggravated threats to international peace and security. In the particular circumstances, the persistence of the situation in Haiti was contributing to a climate of fear of persecution and economic dislocation which could increase the numbers seeking refuge in the region, and 'in these unique and exceptional circumstances', its continuation threatened international peace and security in the region.

---

[9] See Goodwin-Gill, G. S. 'Protection and Assistance for Refugees and the Displaced: Institutional Dimensions, Institutional Challenges', Paper presented at a Workshop on 'Refugee Protection in International Law: Contemporary Challenges', Refugee Studies Centre, University of Oxford, 24 Apr. 2006 <http://refugeelaw.qehlox.ac.uk>.

In resolution 819 (1993) on Bosnia and Herzegovina, the Council, this time acting under Chapter VII, condemned as unlawful any taking or acquisition of territory by threat or use of force, including through the practice of 'ethnic cleansing', as well as the forced evacuation of the civilian population and all violations of international humanitarian law. The Council repeated its views in resolution 836 (1993), adding that a lasting solution must depend on reversing the consequences of 'ethnic cleansing' and on recognition of the right of all refugees to return to their homes.

In resolution 1199 (1998), the Security Council condemned the actions of police and military in Kosovo, that is, within the territory of a sovereign State. These, said the Council, 'have resulted in numerous civilian casualties and . . . the displacement of over 230,000 persons from their homes'. It expressed concern at the resulting flows of refugees into neighbouring and other European countries, 'as a result of the use of force in Kosovo, as well as by the increasing numbers of displaced persons within Kosovo'. Again, it reaffirmed the right of refugees to return,[10] and the right of humanitarian organizations to access. The right of 'safe and free' return has also been emphatically repeated in later resolutions, such as resolutions 1239 and 1244 (1999), and in those adopted in respect to East Timor.

This involvement of the Security Council in forced migration, refugee flows and population displacement—as well as in the frequently related issues of genocide, war crimes, and crimes against humanity—invites attention to the nature of its role, and to whether it ought to be an actor in the field, and whether it can indeed exercise a 'responsibility to protect'. In addition, States need to consider the legal implications for themselves, both as Members of the United Nations and as directly affected by decisions and developments in these areas. It is not always clear to what extent law plays a part in Security Council deliberations and practice, and whether principles such as *non-refoulement* and asylum are given any weight when set alongside the overall goal of restoring or maintaining international peace and security. Nevertheless, a review of recent practice may identify some of the elements of an emerging international community interest—the international *ordre public* of which Judge Lauterpacht spoke, in another context, in the *Guardianship of Infants* case.

First, the right of refugees and the displaced to return to their homes has been clearly and emphatically affirmed, together with the responsibility of the State of origin to ensure the conditions which will allow such return in freedom and dignity. The obligations of the State are clearer, and presumably their non-fulfilment is now more likely to be the subject of sanctions or other appropriate measures. Secondly, the responsibility of individuals who have contributed to or caused flight by their involvement in genocide, war crimes, or crimes against humanity, has been progressively and substantially developed in principle and in the practice

---

[10] In SC res. 1203 (1998), the Security Council also underlined the responsibility of the Federal Republic of Yugoslavia for creating the conditions which would allow refugees to return.

of the International Criminal Tribunals for the former Yugoslavia and Rwanda, and in the adoption and entry into force of the 1998 Statute of the International Criminal Court. Thirdly, the right of access to refugees and civilian populations at risk, including the internally displaced, is now regularly insisted upon, with obvious implications for both refugee-receiving and refugee-producing countries.

3. The refugee in national and international law

Refugee protection is not only about the rules governing the relation between States, but also about how States themselves treat those in search of asylum. The substantial growth and elaboration of refugee determination procedures in the developed world, and the equally substantial body of jurisprudence that has accompanied it at various levels of appeal, have exposed the words of the 1951 Convention to close scrutiny, often apparently at one or more removes from its protection objectives. Besides questions of evidence and proof, national determination bodies have also considered the questions of attribution and causation—whether a claimant, for example, in fact fears persecution for reasons of or on account of his or her political opinion, given the motives of the persecutor, if any; whether prosecution and punishment under a law of general application can amount to persecution, in the absence of evidence of discriminatory application; whether a single act of an otherwise non-political claimant should be characterized as (sufficiently) political to qualify the resulting treatment or punishment as persecution within the meaning of the Convention; whether the refugee definition implies and requires 'good faith' conduct on the part of the claimant; whether conscientious objection to military service can form a sufficient basis for a refugee claim, and if so, in what circumstances; whether 'political offenders' are refugees; whether the notion of 'particular social group' is flexible enough to encompass any number of groups and categories in search of protection; and whether and to what extent human rights law contributes to or complements protection in refugee and analogous claims.

No treaty is self-applying and the meaning of words, such as 'well-founded', 'persecution', 'expel', 'return' or '*refouler*', is by no means self-evident. The Vienna Convention on the Law of Treaties confirms that a treaty 'shall be interpreted in good faith in accordance with the ordinary meaning to be given to the terms of the treaty in their context and in the light of its object and purpose'.[11] For the 1951 Convention relating to the Status of Refugees, this means interpretation by

---

[11] Art. 31(1), 1969 Vienna Convention on the Law of Treaties: UN doc. A/CONF.39/27; Brownlie, I., *Basic Documents in International Law*, (5th edn., 2004), 270. Art. 31(2) defines 'context' as follows: 'The context for the purpose of the interpretation of a treaty shall comprise, in addition to the text, including its preamble and annexes: (a) any agreement relating to the treaty which was made between all the parties in connection with the conclusion of the treaty; (b) any instrument which was made by one or more parties in connection with the conclusion of the treaty and accepted by the other parties as an instrument related to the treaty.'

reference to the object and purpose of extending the protection of the international community to refugees, and assuring to 'refugees the widest possible exercise of . . . fundamental rights and freedoms'.[12]

Article 31(3) of the Vienna Convention provides further that account shall also be taken of any subsequent agreement between the parties, or any subsequent practice bearing on the interpretation of the treaty, as well as 'any relevant rules of international law applicable in the relations between the parties'. This subsequent agreement and practice can be derived or inferred, amongst others, from the actions of the States parties at diplomatic level, including the adoption or promulgation of unilateral interpretative declarations; and at the national level, in the promulgation of laws and the implementation of policies and practices. The rules of treaty interpretation permit recourse to 'supplementary means of interpretation' (including the preparatory work, or *travaux préparatoires*) only where the meaning of the treaty language is ambiguous or obscure; or leads to a result which is manifestly absurd or unreasonable.[13] If the meaning of the treaty is clear from its text when viewed in light of its context, object and purpose, supplementary sources are unnecessary and inapplicable, and recourse to such sources is discouraged.[14]

During the Conference leading up to the Vienna Convention on the Law of Treaties, the United States and the United Kingdom adopted opposing positions on resort to preparatory works, the former favouring their use and the latter, together with France, arguing against the practice. The United Kingdom objected that:

preparation work was almost invariably confusing, unequal and partial: confusing because it commonly consisted of the summary records of statements made during the process of negotiations, and early statements on the positions of delegations might express the intention of the delegation at that stage, but bear no relation to the ultimate text of the treaty; unequal, because not all delegations spoke on any particular issue; and partial because it excluded the informal meetings between heads of delegations at which final compromises were reached and which were often the most significant feature of any negotiation.[15]

Or as the French put it, 'It was much less hazardous and much more equitable when ascertaining the intention of the parties to rely on what they had agreed in

---

[12] 1951 Convention, Preamble.

[13] Art. 32 of the 1969 Vienna Convention, above n. 11, provides: 'Recourse may be had to supplementary means of interpretation, including the preparatory work of the treaty and the circumstances of its conclusion, in order to confirm the meaning resulting from the application of article 31, or to determine the meaning when the interpretation according to article 31: (a) leaves the meaning ambiguous or obscure; or (b) leads to a result which is manifestly absurd or unreasonable.'

[14] This principle has long been established in international law; see, for example, *Interpretation of Article 3(2) of the Treaty of Lausanne*, (1925) PCIJ (Ser. B) No. 12, at 22; *The Lotus* case, 1927 PCIJ (Ser. A) No. 10, at 16; *Admission to the United Nations* case, ICJ *Rep.* (1950), 8. See generally, American Law Institute, *Restatement of the Law, Third, Foreign Relations Law of the United States*, (1987), vol. 1, §325; McNair, *The Law of Treaties*, (1961), Ch. XXIII.

[15] Vienna Conference Records: UN doc. A/CONF.39/11, (1968), 178.

writing, rather than to seek outside the text elements of intent which were far more unreliable, scattered as they were through incomplete or unilateral documents.'[16]

International courts occasionally resort to the preparatory works, but within fairly well defined limits. In *Interpretation of Article 3(2) of the Treaty of Lausanne*, for example, the Permanent Court of International Justice noted:

Since the Court is of opinion that Article 3 is in itself sufficiently clear to enable the nature of the decision to be reached by the Council under the terms of that article to be determined, the question does not arise whether consideration of the work done in the preparation of the Treaty of Lausanne (*les travaux préparatoires*) would also lead to the conclusions set out above.[17]

The International Court of Justice has adopted the same reasoning:

When the Court can give effect to a provision of a treaty by giving to the words used in it their natural and ordinary meaning, it may not interpret the words by seeking to give them some other meaning.[18]

For better or worse, refugee status decision-makers (and commentators ...) make frequent use of the *travaux préparatoires* to the 1951 Convention. Many key terms are vague, undefined and open to interpretation, but the results of inquiry into the background, as the present analysis shows, can be rather mixed. On the one hand, clear statements of drafting intentions are rare; yet on the other hand, the debates in the General Assembly, the Third Committee, the Economic and Social Council and, to a lesser extent, at the 1951 Conference itself, provide a fascinating insight into the politics of a highly sensitive and emotive issue. If some sentiments and statements seem frozen in time, others show the continuity of concern and, perhaps too rarely, confirmation of a pervasive humanitarianism.

4. Protection

The jurisprudence which has developed around the 1951 Convention in many national jurisdictions, while it has often taken the drafting history into account, has also contributed to a theoretical appreciation of the rationale for refugee law; whether the influence is always actually or potentially positive (for refugees), certainly deserves further inquiry, as the example of 'surrogacy' or 'surrogate protection' may show.

[16] Ibid., 176.
[17] *Interpretation of Article 3(2) of the Treaty of Lausanne*, (1925) PCIJ, Ser. B, No. 12, (1925), 22. See also *The Lotus* case, (1927) PCIJ, Ser. A, No. 10, (1927), 16: '... there is no occasion to have regard to preparatory work if the text of a convention is sufficiently clear in itself.'
[18] *Admission to the United Nations* case, ICJ *Rep.*, (1950), 8. See also *State of Arizona* v. *State of California* (1934) 292 US 341, at 359, 360, in which the US Supreme Court said that the rule permitting resort to preparatory work 'has no application to oral statements made by those engaged in negotiating the treaty which were not embodied in any writing and were not communicated to the government of the negotiator or to its ratifying body'.

Like many glosses on the meaning of words, the notion of 'surrogacy' can serve as a useful introduction to the system of international protection. It describes, succinctly, what happens when an international organization or a State steps in to provide the protection which the refugee's own State, by definition, cannot or will not provide. However, 'surrogacy' can also be misleading. While it owes its origins, in descriptive use, to the surrogate as someone who acts for or takes the place of another, in practice in the refugee context it has tended to displace the individual and his or her well-founded fear of persecution. In one of the leading 'social group' cases, *Ward*, the Federal Court of Canada identified as a 'fundamental principle', that international protection is to serve as 'surrogate protection' when national protection cannot be secured.[19] On appeal, the Supreme Court of Canada also noted:

> Except in situations of complete breakdown of the state apparatus, it should be assumed that the state is capable of protecting a claimant. This presumption, while it increases the burden on the claimant . . . reinforces the underlying rationale of international protection as a surrogate, coming into play where no alternative remains to the claimant.[20]

Instead of protection being driven, as it might be, by a focus on the individual at risk, the shift is to the State of origin and its capacity, actual or supposed, to provide protection; and then, in a corollary move, to the State of refuge and the extent of its obligations, if any, to provide protection instead.[21] The object and purpose of the 1951 Convention/1967 Protocol and the regime of protection are thus one step further removed from the individual human being, considered in social and political context.

The Convention definition begins with the refugee as someone with a well-founded fear of persecution, and only secondly, as someone who is unable or unwilling, by reason of such fear, to use or take advantage of the protection of their government. In our view, the Convention's first point of reference is the individual, particularly as a rights-holder, rather than the system of government and its efficacy or intent in relation to protection, relevant as these elements are to the well-founded dimension. Historically, the references to protection in article 1 were seen primarily as references to diplomatic and consular protection, rather than to the effectiveness of a State and its system of government to ensure rights at home. With the progressive evolution of refugee law and doctrine comes authority for the view today that such local or territorial protection has become an integral part of the refugee definition and the determination that a well-founded fear of persecution exists.[22]

[19] *Attorney General* v. *Ward* [1990] 2 FC 667, 67 DLR (4th) 1.

[20] *Attorney General* v. *Ward* [1993] 2 SCR 689.

[21] In the words of La Forest J. in *Ward*: 'Refugee claims were never meant to allow a claimant to seek out better protection than that from which he or she benefits already.'

[22] See Lord Carswell in *Januzi and Others* v. *Secretary of State for the Home Department* [2006] UKHL 5, [2006] 2 WLR 397, §66, citing Fortin, A., 'The Meaning of "Protection" in the Refugee Definition', 12 *IJRL* 548 (2001), but finding a shift in meaning. On the 'accountability' and 'protection' approaches, see also Kälin, W., 'Non-State Agents of Persecution and the Inability of the State to Protect', 15 *Georgetown Immigration Law Journal* 415 (2001).

Under the influence of the notion of surrogacy, however, the balance of emphasis has shifted, and the major premise is substituted by the minor.[23] The words of article 1A(2) show that the fundamental question is that of risk of relevant harm, and in this context surrogacy is an unnecessarily distracting and complicating factor, adding yet one more burden to the applicant in an already complex process. Reading 'surrogacy' back into the refugee definition tends, as elements in the jurisprudence show, to downplay and even to trump the individual's fear of persecution, while giving preference to the State and its efforts to provide a reasonably effective and competent police and judicial system which operates compatibly with minimum international standards.[24] At one time, refugee advocates in the United Kingdom feared that this might indeed be the effect of the House of Lords' judgment in *Horvath*, a case arising out of minority fears of racial violence in a State newly emerging to a democratic system of representative and accountable government. Later interpretations have gone some way towards bringing the central issue of risk of relevant harm back into centre-frame,[25] focusing not on whether the legal and judicial system in the country of origin is doing its best and not generally inefficient or incompetent, but whether the applicant faces a reasonable likelihood of being persecuted for a Convention reason if returned to his or her country of origin.

In his recent study of the human rights obligations of non-State actors, Clapham is rightly critical of another recent UK House of Lords' judgment, *Bagdanavicius*. The Court there held (on what was argued finally as an article 3 ECHR50 appeal) that to avoid expulsion the applicant needed to establish not only that he or she would be at real risk of suffering serious harm from non-State agents, but also that the country of origin did not provide 'a reasonable level of protection against such harm' for those within its territory.[26] Clapham calls attention to the following 'conceptual point' in the judgment of Lord Brown,

---

[23] See Lord Hope's comment in *Horvath* v. *Secretary of State for the Home Department* on the analysis (by Lord Lloyd in *Adan* v. *Secretary of State for the Home Department* [1999] 1 AC 293, 304) of the refugee definition in terms of two tests, namely, the fear test and the protection test. In Lord Hope's view, 'the two tests are nevertheless linked to each other by the concepts which are to be found by looking to the purposes of the Convention. The surrogacy principle which underlies the issue of state protection *is at the root of the whole matter*': *Horvath* [2001] 1 AC 489, 497 (emphasis supplied). The refugee definition has been approached sequentially, whereas it perhaps ought to be approached disjunctively: a refugee is someone outside their country of origin because of a well-founded fear of persecution. It is a characteristic of the refugee's condition that he or she is unable or unwilling to avail themselves of the protection of their country of origin, but that is only a condition of recognition of status so far as the facts may show that the fear is not well-founded.

[24] The surrogacy approach also fits well within traditional perceptions of the nation-State/citizen relationship, where the individual is only with difficulty conceived of as a human rights holder, let alone as a subject of international law.

[25] See, for example, *Noune* v. *Secretary of State for the Home Department* [2001] INLR 526, 539–40, §28, [2000] EWCA Civ 306; *Svazas* v. *Secretary of State for the Home Department* [2002] 1 WLR 1891, [2002] EWCA Civ 74.

[26] *R. (Bagdanavicius)* v. *Secretary of State for the Home Department* [2005] 2 WLR 1359, [2005] UKHL 38, Lord Brown at para. 30.

which has also been employed in the determination of persecution in the refugee context:

Non-state agents do not subject people to torture or the other proscribed forms of ill-treatment, however violently they treat them; what, however, would transform such violent treatment into article 3 treatment would be the state's failure to provide reasonable protection against it.[27]

As Clapham points out, this is not how human rights treaty bodies approach the issue, even if it dominates refugee law.

The whole ethos of humanitarian protection argues against such a judgmental approach with regard to the receiving state . . . [T]he only criterion under human rights treaty law is whether the person will be subject to a substantial risk of harm from the non-state actor. If there is such a risk, the human rights treaty obligation on the sending state should prevent such a state from sending individuals into harm's way.[28]

There are still many serious questions here: How does one distinguish between fear of being murdered on grounds of race and a 'well-founded fear of being persecuted unto death' for the same reason?[29] Why should the victim or person at risk of persecution be protected through the grant of asylum (if that is the case), but not those who face other violations of human rights? Who should provide protection in the particular case, and in what form, and for how long?

Many of these issues are open, or being reopened. The status of the refugee in international law is not quite in flux, and it has always been precarious to a point, but the aim of the following chapters is to try to indicate with some precision the fundamental interests which *must* be protected as a matter of law, if the inherent worth and dignity of the individual in flight are to be upheld.

---

[27] Ibid., para. 24.

[28] Clapham, A., *Human Rights Obligations of Non-State Actors*, (2006), 335–41, 340ff. Applied to the asylum context, the 'receiving State' here is the State of origin, nationality, or transit, to which the 'sending State' proposes to remove the individual.

[29] In *Horvath*, above n. 23, 503, Lord Lloyd thought that, 'It is the severity and persistence of the means adopted, whether by the state itself, or factions within the state, which turns discrimination into persecution; not the absence of state protection.'

PART 1

REFUGEES

2

Refugees Defined and Described

1. Refugees

The term 'refugee' is a term of art, that is, a term with a content verifiable according to principles of general international law. In ordinary usage, it has a broader, looser meaning, signifying someone in flight, who seeks to escape conditions or personal circumstances found to be intolerable. The destination is not relevant; the flight is to freedom, to safety. Likewise, the reasons for flight may be many; flight from oppression, from a threat to life or liberty, flight from prosecution; flight from deprivation, from grinding poverty; flight from war or civil strife; flight from natural disasters, earthquake, flood, drought, famine. Implicit in the ordinary meaning of the word 'refugee' lies an assumption that the person concerned is worthy of being, and ought to be, assisted, and, if necessary, protected from the causes and consequences of flight. The 'fugitive' from justice, the person fleeing criminal prosecution for breach of the law in its ordinary and non-political aspect, is therefore often excepted from this category of refugees.[1]

For the purposes of international law, States have further limited the concept of the refugee. For example, 'economic refugees'—the term has long been disfavoured, but is beginning to come into use, perhaps as a consequence of globalization—are not included. The solution to their problem, if any, lies more within the provinces of managed migration and of international aid and development, rather than in the institution of asylum, considered as protection of whatever duration on the territory of another State.

Defining refugees may appear an unworthy exercise in legalism and semantics, obstructing a prompt response to the needs of people in distress. States have nevertheless insisted on fairly restrictive criteria for identifying those who benefit from refugee status and asylum or local protection. For the victims of natural calamities,[2] the very fact of need may be the sufficient indicator, but for the

---

[1] The *New Shorter Oxford English Dictionary* (1993) defines a refugee as 'a person driven from his or her home to seek refuge, esp. in a foreign country, from war, religious persecution, political troubles, natural disaster, etc.' and 'refuge' as 'shelter from danger or trouble; protection, aid . . .'

[2] On measures to strengthen the UN's capacity to respond to natural disasters, other disasters, and complex humanitarian emergencies (also including displacement of populations), see UNGA res.

victims of conditions or disasters with a human origin, additional factors are required. The purpose of any definition or description of the class of refugees will vary, depending on its function in any particular organizational or State context. On the one hand, the definition or description may facilitate and justify aid and protection, while satisfying the relevant criteria ought in practice to indicate entitlement to the pertinent rights or benefits. In determining the content in international law of the class of refugees, therefore, the traditional sources—treaties and the practice of States—must be examined, with account taken also of the practice and procedures of the various bodies established by the international community to deal with the problems of refugees.

2. Refugees defined in international instruments 1922–46

In treaties and arrangements concluded under the auspices of the League of Nations, a group or category approach was adopted. That someone was (a) outside their country of origin and (b) without the protection of the government of that State, were sufficient and necessary conditions. A Russian refugee, for example, was defined in 1926 to include 'any person of Russian origin who does not enjoy or who no longer enjoys the protection of the Government of the Union of Socialist Soviet Republics and who has not acquired another nationality'.[3] In this instance, presence outside the country of origin was not explicitly required, but was implicit in the objectives of the arrangements, namely, the issue of identity certificates for the purpose of travel and resettlement.[4] Later definitions applied this standard formula to other categories of refugees, often but not always defined by national group. Even when social and political upheaval was accepted as giving content and meaning to refugee definitions, these remained circumscribed by particular crises and linked to ethnic or national origin.

46/182, 19 Dec. 1991, establishing the Office of the Emergency Relief Coordinator. On the work of the ERC and the Office for the Coordination of Humanitarian Assistance, successor to the UN Department of Humanitarian Affairs set up in 1992, see <http://ochaonline.un.org/>; and for active information on complex humanitarian emergencies, see <http://www.reliefweb.int>.

[3] Arrangement relating to the issue of identity certificates to Russian and Armenian refugees, 12 May 1926: 84 *LNTS* No. 2004. The definition of 'Armenian refugee' was to like effect: ibid. 'Assyrian, Assyro-Chaldean, and assimilated refugee' was defined in the Arrangement concerning the Extension to other Categories of Refugees of certain Measures taken in favour of Russian and Armenian Refugees of 30 June 1928: 89 *LNTS* No. 2006. Cf. art. 1, 1933 Convention relating to the International Status of Refugees, and reservations thereto: 159 *LNTS* No. 3663; Beck, R. J., 'Britain and the 1933 Refugee Convention: National or State Sovereignty?' 11 *IJRL* 597 (1999). See also Marrus, M., *The Unwanted—European Refugees in the Twentieth Century*, (1985), 74–81, 119–21 (hereafter Marrus, *The Unwanted*); Hathaway, J., 'The Evolution of Refugee Status in International Law,' 33 *ICLQ* 348 (1984).

[4] Certificates ceased to be valid if the bearers returned to their country of origin; see form and wording of the certificate attached to the arrangement of 5 July 1922: 13 *LNTS* No. 355; Res. 9 of the arrangement of 30 June 1928: 89 *LNTS* No. 2005; certificate attached to the Convention concerning the Status of Refugees coming from Germany of 10 Feb. 1938: 192 *LNTS* No. 4461.

A similar approach was employed in 1936 arrangements for those fleeing Germany,[5] which were later developed by article 1 of the 1938 Convention, to cover:

(a) Persons possessing or having possessed German nationality and not possessing any other nationality who are proved not to enjoy, in law or fact, the protection of the German Government.

(b) Stateless persons not covered by previous conventions or agreements who have left German territory after being established therein and who are proved not to enjoy, in law or in fact, the protection of the German Government.[6]

Article 1(2) excluded from the definition persons who left Germany for reasons of purely personal convenience.

Nevertheless, in the practice of the League, determining whom to protect was a selective, political process.[7] In a 1926 report, the High Commissioner identified over 150,000 people from eight national categories in analogous circumstances to Russian and Armenian refugees: 150 Assyrians and a small number of Montenegrin in France; 19,000 Assyro-Chaldeans in the Caucasus and Greece; 9,000 Ruthenes in Austria and Czechoslovakia; 100,000 refugees in Central Europe (including 10,000 former Hungarians in Austria, France and Romania); 16,000 Jews in Romania; and 150 Turks in Greece.[8] In choosing to extend legal protection to only a fraction,[9] the space and the necessity for 'complementary protection' were created.[10] Protection gaps necessarily result when refugee definitions become divorced from events—the social and political reality—which actually produces refugees.[11]

The *ad hoc* expansion of protection during the time of the League of Nations was partly the result of concern not to arouse the hostility of certain members or potential members. Sjöberg argues that this attitude largely explains opposition to

---

[5] Art. 1, Provisional Arrangement concerning the Status of Refugees coming from Germany, 4 July 1936: 171 *LNTS* No. 3952.

[6] 1938 Convention concerning the Status of Refugees coming from Germany: 191 *LNTS* No. 4461. The Convention was expanded the following year to include Austrian refugees after the *Anschluss*; see the Additional Protocol, 14 Sept. 1939: 198 *LNTS* No. 4634.

[7] Sjöberg, T., *The Powers and the Persecuted: The Refugee Problem and the Intergovernmental Committee on Refugee; (IGCR) 1938–1947*, (1991) 38 (hereafter, Sjöberg, *The Powers and the Persecuted*).

[8] League of Nations, 'Russian and Armenian Refugees: Report to the Eighth Assembly', (1927), (A.48.1927.XIII) 14, cited in Skran, C., *Refugees in Inter-War Europe: The Emergence of a Regime*, (1995), 115 (hereafter, Skran, *Refugees in Inter-War Europe*); see also Doc XIII. Refugees. 1927. XIII.3.

[9] Minutes of the 43rd Session of the Council LN O.J. (February 1927), cited in Skran, *Refugees in Inter-War Europe*, 115.

[10] See further below, Ch. 6; and for a fuller account, McAdam, J., *Complementary Protection in International Law*, (2007).

[11] As late as 1938, Switzerland observed that it daily received refugees who had lost their nationality on account of events during the First World War, but who remained unprotected by any international refugee instrument; see International Conference for the Adoption of a Convention Concerning the Status of Refugees Coming from Germany 'Provisional Minutes: Third Meeting (Private)' (8 February 1938) CONF.CSRA/PV3 (8 Feb. 1938) 4.

the incorporation of Italian and Spanish refugees within the League's mandate.[12] The Italian government had strenuously opposed their inclusion, 'and most of the member states of the League Council were not willing to provoke Mussolini on such a comparatively minor issue'.[13]

Throughout the 1930s, one of the most contentious issues was the continuing and increasing exodus from Hitler's Germany. At a meeting in Evian in 1938, participating States resolved to establish an Inter-governmental Committee on Refugees with, as its primary objective, 'facilitating involuntary emigration from Germany (including Austria)'.[14] Included within the scope of the committee's activities were those who had yet to emigrate on account of their political opinions, religious beliefs, or racial origin, as well as those who had already left for these reasons and had not established themselves elsewhere.[15] A major review at the Bermuda Conference in April 1943 expanded the mandate to include 'all persons, wherever they may be, who, as a result of events in Europe, have had to leave, or may have to leave, their country of residence because of the danger to their lives or liberties on account of their race, religion or political beliefs'.[16]

---

[12] 'All political refugees were a source of political embarrassment to the organization': Sjöberg, *The Powers and the Persecuted*, 38; among others, Italian refugees fleeing Mussolini's Fascist government after 1922 were not protected by the League machinery. Melander offers an alternative view, and queries whether political factors are sufficient to explain the protection of some groups of refugees but not others. He suggests that Italian and Spanish refugees were seen rather as 'human rights refugees', in a period when human rights violations were considered matters of domestic, not international concern; as a result, granting protection on such grounds, 'was inconsistent with the principle of non-intervention in the internal affairs of sovereign states': Melander, G., 'Refugee Policy Options—Protection or Assistance', in Rystad, G., ed., *The Uprooted: Forced Migration as an International Problem in the Post-War Era*, (1990), 151.

[13] Sjöberg, *The Powers and the Persecuted*, 27. Although Melander acknowledges that some refugees protected by the League instruments were clearly fleeing human rights abuses, he considers this merely incidental to the humanitarian law justification for their protection, as victims of armed conflicts or communal violence: Melander, 'Refugee Policy Options', above note, 146–7.

[14] (1938) 19 (8–9) LNOJ 676–7. For a full account of the IGCR, see Sjöberg, *The Powers and the Persecuted*. Speaking in 1979 to the Geneva Conference on Refugees and Displaced Persons in Southeast Asia, US Vice-President Mondale characterized the 1938 Evian Conference as a failure: 'The civilized world', he said, 'hid in a cloak of legalism': UN Press Release SG/REF/3, 21 Jul. 1979. See also Marrus, *The Unwanted*, 166–70.

[15] Para. 8, Resolution adopted by the Intergovernmental Meeting at Evian, 14 Jul. 1938: LNOJ, 19, nos. 8–9: Aug.–Sept. 1938, 676–7. See also art. 1, Agreement relating to the issue of Travel Documents to Refugees who are the Concern of the Intergovernmental Committee on Refugees, 15 Oct. 1946: 11 *UNTS* 73; Marrus, *The Unwanted*, 170–7.

[16] Sjöberg, *The Powers and the Persecuted*, 16 and Ch. 4. The functions of the organization were also rewritten: IGCR was 'to undertake negotiations with neutral or Allied States or with organizations, and to take such steps as may be necessary to preserve, maintain and transport' refugees within its mandate. The United Nations Relief and Rehabilitation Administration (UNRRA), established in Nov. 1943 with forty-four governments signing the constituent agreement, was principally concerned with assistance to civilian nationals of the allied nations and to displaced persons in liberated countries, and with the repatriation and return of prisoners of war. It was not authorized to resettle the displaced or to deal with or find solutions for refugees, considered as those who, 'for any reason, definitely cannot return to their homes, or have no homes to return to, or no longer enjoy the protection of their Governments . . .'. See para. 22, proposal concerning refugees submitted by the United

Commenting on definitions, Simpson observed already in 1938 that they each had certain inherent deficiencies. He stressed the importance of keeping in view the 'essential quality' of the refugee as one 'who has sought refuge in a territory other than that in which he was formerly resident as a result of political events which rendered his continued residence in his former territory impossible or intolerable'.[17] This description is in turn something of an abstraction from what was known then about the 'political events' producing refugees. While the notion of the impossibility or intolerability of continued residence illustrates the problem of the refugee in broad strokes, after the Second World War more precise criteria emerged. This is evident first in the Constitution of the International Refugee Organization (IRO), then in the Statute of the Office of the United Nations High Commissioner for Refugees (UNHCR), and finally in the provisions of the 1951 Convention relating to the Status of Refugees. In a little less than five years, the preferred approach to refugee definition moved from a basis in flexible or open groups and categories, to an apparently more closed and legalistic one.

The Constitution of the IRO continued the practice of earlier instruments, and specified certain categories to be assisted. 'Refugees' thus included victims of the Nazi, Fascist, or Quisling regimes which had opposed the United Nations, certain persons of Jewish origin, or foreigners or stateless persons who had been victims of Nazi persecution, as well as persons considered as refugees before the outbreak of the Second World War for reasons of race, religion, nationality, or political opinion. The IRO was also competent to assist 'displaced persons', including those deported or expelled from their own countries, some of whom had been sent to undertake forced labour.[18] In addition, the IRO Constitution included as refugees those unable or unwilling to avail themselves of the protection of the government of their country of nationality or former residence. It expressly recognized that individuals might have 'valid objections' to returning to their country of origin, including 'persecution or fear based on reasonable grounds of persecution because of race, religion, nationality or political opinions,' and objections 'of a political nature judged by the [IRO] to be valid'.[19]

Kingdom: UN doc. A/C.3/5, annexed to GAOR, Third Committee, 1st Sess., 1st Part, 1946, Summary Records: UN doc. A/C.3/SR.1–11. UNRRA nevertheless increasingly faced these issues as east Europeans fled or refused to return to communism; see Salomon, K., *Refugees in the Cold War: Toward a New International Refugee Regime in the Early Postwar Era*, (1991), 46–54 and *passim*; Woodbridge, G., *The History of the United Nations Relief and Rehabilitation Administration*, 3 vols., (1950); Marrus, *The Unwanted*, 317–24.

[17] Simpson, J. H., *Refugees—A Preliminary Report of a Survey* (1938), 1.
[18] On the re-emergence of the term 'displaced persons' see further below, s. 3.2.
[19] For full text, see below, Annexe 1, No. 1. Generally, see Holborn, L. W., *The International Refugee Organization: A Specialized Agency of the United Nations. Its History and Work 1946–1952*, (1956); Salomon, K., *Refugees in the Cold War: Toward a New International Refugee Regime in the Early Postwar Era*, (1991). For a brief account of the politicized debates in the UN on refugee definition in the 1940s, see Goodwin-Gill, G. S., 'Different Types of Forced Migration Movements as an International and National Problem', in Rystad, G., ed., *The Uprooted: Forced Migration as an International Problem in the Post-War Era*, (1990), 15, 22–9.

In 1949, the UN began to look forward to a post-IRO period. Several States were opposed to the adoption of a broad approach, considering it essential clearly to identify refugees who were in need of international protection. The United States favoured a narrow definition of those who would fall within the competence of a new, temporary agency, a de-emphasis of resettlement, and concentration on 'legal protection' pending integration in countries of refuge, as opposed to assistance or similar activities; the main purpose was to prevent refugees becoming a liability to the international community. Other refugee categories, such as those created by population transfers, were mostly entitled to rights afforded by their countries of residence, and thus in no need of international protection.[20] Apart from those countries actually having to deal with large populations of 'national refugees',[21] a consensus emerged that such refugees were not 'an international problem', and did not require international protection.

3. Refugees for the purposes of the United Nations

The Office of the United Nations High Commissioner for Refugees (UNHCR) succeeded the IRO as the principal UN agency concerned with refugees; the scope and extent of its competence are considered more fully below, taking account of the impact of developments within the UN, including article 14(1) of the Universal Declaration of Human Rights,[22] the relation of 'asylum'[23] to persecution, the adoption of the 1967 Declaration on Territorial Asylum, and the emergence and consolidation of a human rights base for protection. The foundations for an international legal concept of the refugee are thus securely fixed in treaties, State and United Nations practice, and in the Statute of the UNHCR.[24]

3.1 STATUTE OF THE UNITED NATIONS HIGH COMMISSIONER FOR REFUGEES (UNHCR)

UNHCR was established by the General Assembly to provide 'international protection' and to seek 'permanent solutions for the problem of refugees'. According to

[20] GAOR, 5th Sess., Third Committee, Summary Records, 324th Meeting, 22 Nov. 1950, paras. 44–9; see also 326th Meeting, 24 Nov. 1950, para. 31ff (United States). At the 329th Meeting, 29 Nov. 1950, the US representative, Eleanor Roosevelt, criticised the UK proposal to include refugees requiring assistance, but not protection. She noted that refugees in Germany, India, Pakistan, and Turkey had serious problems of integration, but they enjoyed the rights of nationals. Any specific relief programmes should be formulated within the overall economic framework of the countries concerned, and were beyond the competence of the High Commissioner. Ibid., paras. 34–6.
[21] Cf. the views of India: ibid., 332nd Meeting, 1 Dec. 1950, paras. 26–7.
[22] 'Everyone has the right to seek and to enjoy in other countries asylum from persecution.'
[23] See below, Ch. 5.
[24] An understanding of the historical context of UNHCR's creation is also important; see Salomon, K., *Refugees in the Cold War: Toward a New International Refugee Regime in the Early Postwar Era*, (1991); Sjöberg, *The Powers and the Persecuted* (both reviewed by Goodwin-Gill, G. S. in

its Statute, the work of the Office shall be of an entirely non-political character—it is to be 'humanitarian' and 'social' and to relate, as a rule, to groups and categories of refugees.[25]

The Statute first brings within UNHCR's competence refugees covered by various earlier treaties and arrangements. It next includes refugees resulting from events occurring before 1 January 1951, who are outside their country of origin[26] and unable or unwilling to avail themselves of its protection, 'owing to a well-founded fear of being persecuted' or 'for reasons other than personal convenience'.[27] Finally, the Statute extends to:

> Any other person who is outside the country of his nationality, or if he has no nationality, the country of his former habitual residence, because he has or had a well-founded fear of persecution by reason of his race, religion, nationality or political opinion and is unable or, because of such fear, is unwilling to avail himself of the protection of the government of the country of his nationality, or, if he has no nationality, to return to the country of his former habitual residence.

This description is of universal application, containing neither temporal nor geographical limitations. The substantive or ideological criteria are nevertheless a significant restriction on the scope of refugees 'strictly so-called', who must establish a well-founded fear of persecution on one or more of the stated grounds. Whether they must also *prove* a lack of protection is debatable.[28]

UNHCR's statutory definition remains a critical point of departure in determining who is entitled to the protection and assistance of the United Nations, for it is the lack of *protection* by their own government which has traditionally distinguished refugees from ordinary aliens. In its influential 1949 Report, *A Study of Statelessness*, the United Nations treated refugees as more or less equivalent to 'stateless persons *de facto*', whom it identified as:

> ... persons who, having left the country of which they were nationals, no longer enjoy the protection and assistance of their national authorities, either because these authorities refuse to grant them assistance and protection, or because they themselves renounce the assistance and protection of the countries of which they are nationals.[29]

6 *IJRL* 311 (1994); Rystad, G., ed., *The Uprooted: Forced Migration as an International Problem in the Post-War Era*, (1990); Jaeger, G., 'Les Nations Unies et les réfugiés', *Revue belge de Droit international*, 1989/1, 18–120.

[25] UNGA res. 428(V), annex, paras. 1, 2; for full text, see below, Annexe 1, No. 3. For brief background, see Goodwin-Gill, G. S., 'Different Types of Forced Migration Movements as an International and National Problem,' in Rystad, G., ed., *The Uprooted: Forced Migration as an International Problem in the Post-War Era*, (1990), 15.

[26] The phrase 'country of origin' is used for convenience here and throughout the text; it signifies, as appropriate, the refugee's country of nationality or, if he or she has no nationality, his or her country of former habitual residence.

[27] This latter provision would cover the situation of a person who, by reason of persecution already suffered, remains unwilling to return even though the circumstances which gave rise to his or her refugee status have ceased to exist. Cf. art. 1C(5), (6), 1951 Convention; and below, Ch. 4, s. 2.

[28] See further below, Ch. 3, s. 6.   [29] United Nations, *A Study of Statelessness*, (1949), 9.

What distinguished such a person from another foreigner with a nationality was precisely the *assistance* of his or her government which the latter enjoyed, and the benefits of its 'collaboration' with the authorities of the foreign country. In this sense, protection by the national government only rarely takes the form of 'representations', but more often manifests itself, for example, in efforts to improve the status of citizens abroad, particularly through treaties; oversight of such conventions and action to ensure that the rights granted to citizens are actually respected; consular services, including recommending citizens to the authorities of the country concerned; the provision of passports enabling citizens to travel abroad; the provision and certification of the various documents essential to regular life; and the provision of emergency relief and repatriation. Seen from this perspective of diplomatic and consular protection and assistance, the stateless person is clearly at a disadvantage, and will likely also be viewed with distrust and suspicion.[30] In the face of this lacuna, 'international protection' was therefore seen primarily as something to be provided to refugees and stateless persons.[31] The UN Study also emphasized that:

The conferment of a status is not sufficient in itself to regularize the standing of stateless persons and to bring them into the orbit of the law; they must also be linked to an

---

[30] Ibid., 11. See also Fortin, A., 'The Meaning of "Protection" in the Refugee Definition', 12 *IJRL* 548 (2001); while the argument for a diplomatic and 'external' perspective on 'protection' has solid historical roots, the availability or otherwise of effective 'internal protection' has been increasingly adopted as an element in defining both refugee and persecution. See the judgment of the UK House of Lords in *Januzi* v. *Secretary of State for the Home Department* [2006] UKHL 5, where Lord Carswell was of the view that, 'Since the temporal provision in article 1A(2) was removed in 1967 it has not been so interpreted and . . . ongoing interpretation of the Convention as a living instrument and adaptation to modern conditions have brought about a shift in meaning': para. 66. The Court found, in a case involving the so-called internal flight alternative, that while the availability of (internal) protection was relevant to determining the well-foundedness of fear of persecution, the concept did not go so far as to require the effective provision of a range of civil, political, social and economic rights as a pre-condition to 'reasonable relocation', at least so far as failings in this regard did not amount to persecution; see the judgment of Lord Bingham at para. 5–19; and further below, Ch. 3, s. 5.6.1.

[31] See, for example, the resolution adopted on 30 September 1938, by the Assembly of the League of Nations, in which it decided to establish an office of High Commissioner to deal with refugees formerly within the competence of the Nansen International Office and the Office of the High Commissioner for Refugees coming from Germany. Operative paragraph 2 provided that the High Commissioner's duties would be: '(a) to provide for the political and legal protection of refugees, as entrusted to the regular organs of the League by paragraph 3 of the Assembly's decision of 30 September 1930; (b) to superintend the entry into force and the application of the legal status of refugees, as defined more particularly in the Conventions of 28 October 1933, and 10 February 1938; (c) to facilitate the co-ordination of humanitarian assistance; and (d) to assist the Governments and private organizations in their efforts to promote emigration and permanent settlement': Resolution adopted by the XIXth Session of the Assembly of the League of Nations on 30 September 1938, concerning international assistance to refugees: League of Nations, *Official Journal*, 1938, Special Supplement No. 183, 26–8. See also the June 1948 Agreement concluded between the IRO and the Government of Brazil, which provides that, 'the rights of protection pertaining to nations with regard to their subjects abroad will be exercised in Brazil by the IRO with regard to the refugees established in Brazil so long as they are stateless or for other reasons have lost the protection of their national State and are therefore included in the jurisdiction and precepts of the IRO in accordance with its Constitution'. For references to both sources, see *A Study on Statelessness*, 32–3, 36–7, 49–52.

independent organ which would to some extent make up for the absence of national protection and render them certain services which the authorities of a country of origin render to their nationals resident abroad.[32]

In its view, moreover, that 'independent organ' would need to work in close collaboration with the governments of reception countries, and as its functions would be of an official nature, so it should be inter-governmental in character.

In attempting to make good the deficiency of national protection, the international protection agency should therefore aim to protect the refugee's basic human rights, including the right to life, liberty, and security of the person.[33] Simultaneously, 'protection activities' will need to focus on specific issues peculiar to the refugee: for example, ensuring that no refugee is returned to a country in which he or she will be in danger; ensuring that asylum seekers have access to an informed procedure and that every refugee is recognized as such, that asylum is granted, that expulsion is prevented, that travel and identity documents are issued. It follows that any intervention with governments must have a sound jurisdictional base, especially when made in a political context that is hostile to asylum, or in which laws, regulations and practice may be oriented to summary dismissal.

3.2 DEVELOPMENT OF THE STATUTORY DEFINITION AND EXTENSION OF THE MANDATE[34]

The UNHCR Statute nevertheless contains an apparent contradiction. On the one hand, it affirms that the work of the Office shall relate, as a rule, to groups and categories of refugees. On the other hand, it proposes a definition of the refugee which is essentially individualistic, seeming to require a case-by-case examination of subjective and objective elements. The frequency of large-scale refugee crises over the last 55 years or so, together with a variety of political and humanitarian considerations, has necessitated flexibility in the administration of UNHCR's mandate. In consequence, there has been a significant broadening of what may be termed the concept of 'refugees of concern to the international community'.

A major role in these developments has been played by the United Nations General Assembly and the Economic and Social Council, whose policy directions the High Commissioner is required to follow,[35] and similar influence has been exercised by the Executive Committee of the High Commissioner's Programme. Established in 1957,[36] the Executive Committee's terms of reference include advising the High Commissioner, on request, in the exercise of the statutory functions;

---

[32] *A Study of Statelessness*, 68–71.   [33] See further below, Ch. 6.
[34] See Jackson, I. C., *The Refugee Concept in Group Situations*, (1999), 40–81, and generally; Kourula, P., *Broadening the Edges: Refugee Definition and International Protection Revisited*, (1997), 157–62, 177–83, and *passim*.   [35] UNHCR Statute, para. 3.
[36] UNGA res. 1166(XII), 26 Nov. 1957. In 2005, the General Assembly decided to increase Executive Committee membership from sixty-eight to seventy States (UNGA res. 60/127, 16 Dec. 2005), and by a further two States in 2006 (UNGA res. 61/136, 19 Dec. 2006), an increase of twenty-two over eleven years. For membership, see below, Annexe 3, No. 4.

and advising on the appropriateness of providing international assistance through UNHCR in order to solve such specific refugee problems as may arise.[37] Over the last 15 to 20 years, the Executive Committee has both expanded its membership and come to play a much closer role in budgetary and management issues.

It was also in 1957 that the General Assembly first authorized the High Commissioner to assist refugees who did not come fully within the statutory definition, but whose situation was 'such as to be of concern to the international community'.[38] The case involved large numbers of mainland Chinese in Hong Kong whose status as 'refugees' was complicated by the existence of two Chinas, each of which might have been called upon to exercise protection. Given the need for assistance, express authorization to the High Commissioner 'to use his good offices to encourage arrangements for contributions' was an effective, pragmatic solution.[39] Assistance to other specific groups was authorized in the years that followed.[40] Concurrently, the General Assembly developed the notion of the High Commissioner's 'good offices' as an umbrella idea under which to bring refugees who did not come within the competence, or 'immediate competence',[41] of the United Nations. The type of assistance which might be given was initially limited, often to the transmission of financial contributions, but that restriction was soon dropped.[42]

In 1959, in anticipation of World Refugee Year, the General Assembly called for special attention to be given 'to the problems of refugees coming within the competence' of UNHCR, while simultaneously authorizing the High Commissioner to use his good offices in the transmission of contributions for the

[37] On the conclusions of the Executive Committee and their role in setting protection standards, see further below, Ch. 8, s. 1.

[38] UNGA res. 1167(XII), 26 Nov. 1957. Cf. UNGA res. 1129(XI), 21 Nov. 1956, approving UNHCR action already taken to assist Hungarian refugees. In UNGA res. 1784(XVII), 7 Dec. 1962, the General Assembly again acknowledged that the situation of Chinese refugees was of concern to the international community, recognized the continuing need for emergency and long-term assistance, and requested UNHCR to use its good offices in the provision thereof.

[39] See Hambro, E., *The Problem of Chinese Refugees in Hong Kong*, (1955), for background; also, Jackson, *Refugee Concept in Group Situations*, 93–4, 210–13.

[40] For example, to Algerians fleeing to Tunisia and Morocco to escape the effects of the struggle for liberation: UNGA resolutions 1286(XIII), 5 Dec. 1958; 1389(XVI), 20 Nov. 1959; 1500(XV), 5 Dec. 1960; 1672(XVI), 18 Dec. 1961; and to Angolan refugees in the Congo: UNGA res. 1671(XVI), 10 Dec. 1961. Using declassified archival material in London, Paris and Washington, as well as interviews with officials (including August Lindt, the High Commissioner of the day), Ruthström-Ruin has shown that earlier explanations attributing UNHCR's involvement with Algerian refugees to a 'good offices' basis are 'incomplete, and partly incorrect': *Beyond Europe: The Globalization of Refugee Aid*, (1993), 103f; reviewed by Goodwin-Gill in 7 *IJRL* 168 (1995). Following an on-site investigation in Tunisia, the High Commissioner initially decided that the Algerians were indeed within his mandate as refugees with a well-founded fear of persecution, only to change tack later. UNHCR's inconsistent interpretation and application of its Statute satisfied client governments, including those who, while critical of French policy in Algeria, either did not want France accused of persecution or were themselves uncertain whether Algerians who fled were 'refugees'. See also, Jackson, *Refugee Concept in Group Situations*, 120–42.

[41] The term is employed but not defined in UNGA res 1499(XV), 5 Dec. 1960.

[42] Compare UNGA resolutions 1167(XII), 26 Nov. 1957 and 1784(XVII) 7 Dec. 1962.

assistance of refugees 'who do not come within the competence of the United Nations'.[43] On the same day, the General Assembly had no hesitation in recommending that the High Commissioner continue his efforts on behalf of refugees from Algeria in Morocco and Tunisia, pending their return to their homes.[44] As more than the mere transmission of contributions was involved, these refugees, who had fled a particularly violent national liberation struggle,[45] were clearly considered to fall within the competence of the United Nations. Indeed, there is little to distinguish the resolution in question from that adopted three years earlier on refugees from Hungary.[46] After the reference to 'good offices refugees' in the General Assembly's 1963 resolution on the report of UNHCR,[47] the term does not recur again until its final appearance in 1973.[48] The 1965 resolution referred generically to the protection of refugees and to solutions for the 'various groups of refugees within (UNHCR) competence'.[49] Thereafter the language changed, became more composite and began to reflect the notion of refugees 'of concern' to UNHCR.[50]

General Assembly resolutions are rarely consistent in their language, and their rationale, too, is often hidden. The nature of the activities in which UNHCR was involved, however, suggests that the class of refugees assisted were either clearly not within the Statute or else had not been specifically determined to be within the Statute, perhaps for political or logistical reasons.[51] At the same time, the situations in question shared certain factors in common: the people in need (a) had crossed an international frontier, (b) as a result of conflicts, or radical political, social, or economic changes in their countries of origin. The very size of refugee problems in Africa in the 1960s made individual assessment of refugee status

---

[43] UNGA res. 1388(XIV), 20 Nov. 1959.

[44] UNGA res. 1389(XIV), 20 Nov. 1959. See also UNGA resolutions 1286(XIII), 5 Dec. 1958; 1500(XV), 5 Dec. 1960; and 1672(XVI), 18 Dec. 1961.

[45] The details are well summarized in Ruthström-Ruin, C., *Beyond Europe: The Globalization of Refugee Aid*, (1993), 81–93.

[46] See UNGA resolutions 1129(XI), 21 Nov. 1956; 1499(XV), 5 Dec. 1960; res. 1673(XVI), 18 Dec. 1961; 1783(XVII), 7 Dec. 1962.

[47] UNGA res. 1959(XVIII), 12 Dec. 1963, requesting the High Commissioner to continue to afford international protection to refugees and to pursue efforts on behalf of refugees within his mandate and of those for whom he extends his good offices, by giving particular attention to new refugee groups, in conformity with relevant General Assembly resolutions and Executive Committee directives (para. 1).

[48] UNGA res. 3143(XXVIII), 14 Dec. 1973, requesting the High Commissioner to continue his assistance and protection activities in favour of refugees within his mandate as well as for those to whom he extends his good offices or is called up to assist in accordance with relevant resolutions of the General Assembly.   [49] UNGA res. 2039(XX), 7 Dec. 1965.

[50] UNGA resolutions 2197(XXI), 16 Dec. 1966; 2294(XXII), 11 Dec. 1967 (continuing UNHCR and requesting protection, assistance and efforts towards solutions for refugees who are UNHCR's concern); 2399(XXIII), 6 Dec. 1968 (to similar effect, calling also for 'special attention to new groups of refugees, particularly in Africa', in conformity with relevant General Assembly resolutions and Executive Committee directives); 2594(XXIV), 16 Dec. 1969 (noting results obtained in regard to the international protection of refugees within the mandate, and requesting continued protection and assistance for refugees who are UNHCR's concern); 2650(XXV), 30 Nov. 1970; 2789(XXVI), 6 Dec. 1971; 2956(XXVII), 12 Dec. 1972.   [51] Cf. Ruthström-Ruin, *Beyond Europe*, 96–123.

impractical, as did the absence of appropriate machinery. Moreover, the pragmatic, rather than doctrinal, approach to the new problems was almost certainly influenced by factors such as the desire to avoid the imputation carried by every determination that a well-founded fear of persecution exists;[52] and the feeling, not always made manifest, that while 'political conditions' had compelled the flight of the entire group in question, it might not be possible to establish a well-founded fear on an individual case-by-case basis. The 'group approach', by concentrating on the fact that those concerned are effectively without the protection of their own government, thus avoids the restrictions of the legal definition.[53]

From the mid-1970s, the General Assembly has spoken of and unanimously commended the High Commissioner's activities on behalf of 'refugees and displaced persons of concern' to the Office. The reference to 'displaced persons' dates at least from 1972, when the Economic and Social Council acted both to promote the voluntary repatriation of refugees to the Sudan, including measures of rehabilitation and assistance, and also to extend the benefit of such measures to 'persons displaced within the country'.[54] The ECOSOC lead was followed by the General Assembly[55] in the first of references to displaced persons which were soon to acquire a regularity and substance of their own. In 1974 and 1975 the General Assembly reiterated its recognition of refugees of concern to UNHCR, and acknowledged an additional category of 'special humanitarian tasks' undertaken by the High Commissioner.[56] ECOSOC took another consolidating step forward in 1976 when it recognized the importance of UNHCR's activities in 'the context of man-made disasters, in addition to its original functions'. The High Commissioner was commended for his efforts 'on behalf of refugees and displaced persons, victims of man-made disasters', and requested to continue his activities 'for alleviating the suffering of all those of concern to his Office'.[57] In November 1976 the General Assembly formally endorsed the ECOSOC resolution and recognized the need to strengthen further the international protection of refugees.[58]

In 1975, in a short resolution, the General Assembly approved continued humanitarian assistance to 'Indo-chinese displaced persons'.[59] Originally intended

[52] This was certainly a factor with respect to France and refugees from Algeria: Ruthström-Ruin, *Beyond Europe*, 96–109.

[53] Schnyder, F., 'Les aspects juridiques actuels du problème des réfugiés', Hague *Recueil* (1965-I) 339–450, at 426–43; Sadruddin Aga Khan, 'Legal Problems relating to refugees and displaced persons', Hague *Recueil* (1976-I) 287–352, at 306, 339–43. Jackson argues that, in the period 1961–75, the principal groups of refugees in Africa were dealt with, either under the Statute/Convention definition, or on the basis of a 'developed' good offices approach based on *prima facie* group determination: *Refugee Concept in Group Situations*, 176.

[54] ECOSOC resolutions 1655(LII), 1 Jun. 1972; 1705(LII), 27 Jul. 1972; 1741(LIV), 4 May 1973; 1799(LV), 30 Jul. 1973; 1877(LVII), 16 Jul. 1974; Jackson, *Refugee Concept in Group Situations*, 229–35.

[55] UNGA res. 2958(XXVII), 12 Dec. 1972.

[56] UNGA resolutions 3271(XXIX), 10 Dec. 1974; 3454(XXX), 9 Dec. 1975. UNHCR had meanwhile served as focal point for assistance operations in India/Bangladesh, and in Cyprus.

[57] ECOSOC res. 2011(LXI), 2 Aug. 1976.   [58] UNGA res. 31/35, 30 Nov. 1976.

[59] UNGA res. 3455(XXX), 9 Dec. 1975. Fong, C. 'Some Legal Aspects of the Search for Admission into other States of Persons leaving the Indo-Chinese Peninsular in Small Boats', 52 *BYIL*

as after the fact legislative approval for UNHCR activities *inside* Laos and Vietnam,[60] it has come to be seen as contributing an international dimension to the notion of displaced persons by its apparent recognition of the fact of *external* displacement. If the term was intended to cover groups, besides refugees, who had crossed international frontiers, then at the time it may have been something of a misnomer. 'Displaced persons' had a special meaning in the Constitution of the IRO, but had otherwise been commonly employed to describe those displaced within their own country, for example, by the effects of civil strife or natural disasters.[61]

Whatever its current dimensions, the 'displaced persons' category was initially introduced to deal with two problematic but related areas of activity. First, it was addressed to the situation of countries divided in fact, if not in law; this included countries split by civil war, such as the Sudan,[62] or Vietnam and, to a lesser extent, Laos prior to 1975. In the case of Vietnam, the legal situation was complicated by the respective constitutions and laws of the divided parts, each of which purported to acknowledge the existence of only one legitimate, truly representative entity. Again in the case of Vietnam, necessity required that UNHCR, as occasion demanded, deal with three different parties—the north Vietnamese, the south Vietnamese and the Provisional Revolutionary Government. The 'displaced persons' category, with its foundations in humanitarian necessity, was the natural successor to the 'good offices' approach; in its time, 'good offices' had accommodated the need for *prima facie* eligibility, while 'displaced persons' came in to describe UNHCR action on the ground—providing humanitarian assistance to those displaced within divided countries, by the effects of civil war or insurgency. In this practical context, protection was of secondary or incidental concern; there is indeed no necessary or inextricable link between protection and assistance, even if these notions have come to run together with the refugee and displaced persons categories in the General Assembly resolutions which succeeded and consolidated these developments.

The refugee crises in the period 1975–95 illustrate both the development in the refugee definition and the problems that arise in applying it consistently to large numbers of asylum seekers. Over one-and-a-half million people left Kampuchea,

53, 80–5 (1982)—discusses the meaning of 'displaced persons,' with particular reference to UNGA res. 3454(XXX) and the mandate of UNHCR.

[60] UNHCR had become involved in the region, at the request of the governments concerned, and was promoting assistance programmes for those displaced by the effects of war. See the High Commissioner's statement to the 25th Session of the Executive Committee (1974): UN doc. A/AC. 96/511, annex; *Report* of the High Commissioner to the General Assembly (1975): E/5688, Add. 1, paras. 34–43. Such assistance was undertaken 'within the framework of [UNHCR's] "good offices" function', and 'on a purely humanitarian basis'.

[61] See below, s. 3.3. In debate on the successor to the IRO in 1950, several countries, including India, Pakistan and Greece, argued for the inclusion of 'internal refugees', but it was the insistence on the absence of *legal* protection that prevailed; for a summary account, see Goodwin-Gill, 'Different Types of Forced Migration', 27.   [62] See above, n. 54.

Laos, and Vietnam, beginning in April 1975.[63] Already involved in the region, with the turn of events in the spring of 1975, UNHCR was called upon to assist many who had left their countries of origin, in particular by securing asylum, providing care and maintenance, and promoting resettlement; the Provisional Revolutionary Government in South Vietnam also requested UNHCR to promote voluntary repatriation.

Official documentation of the period reveals a reluctance to apply the term 'refugee' to those assisted by UNHCR. Instead, the papers refer, for example, to 'displaced persons from Indo-China outside their country of origin',[64] and to 'persons leaving the Indo-China peninsula in small boats'.[65] UNHCR's operations were never challenged on the basis that the persons concerned might not fall within the mandate of the Office, however, and assistance and protection continued to be extended on the basis of that somewhat ambiguous resolution adopted by the General Assembly in December 1975.[66] The Executive Committee, however, began to employ more specific language in its annual conclusions. In 1976, it spoke of 'asylum seekers' who had left their country in small boats,[67] and in 1977 referred expressly to the problems of refugees from Indo-China.[68]

In that year, the High Commissioner for Refugees also requested the Executive Committee to clarify the distinction between refugees and displaced persons. No formal advice was tendered, although there was considerable support for the view that refugees had crossed an international frontier, whereas displaced persons had not.[69] Notwithstanding the focus on *internally displaced persons* which began in

---

[63] A summary of the background is provided in *Report* of the Secretary-General on the Meeting on Refugees and Displaced Persons in South East Asia, Geneva, 20–21 July 1979, and Subsequent Developments: UN doc. A/34/627. See also Jackson, *Refugee Concept in Group Situations*, 316–46; Osborne, M., 'The Indochinese Refugees: Causes and Effects', *International Affairs*, 1980, 37–53; Grant, B., *The Boat People* (1980); Garcia Marquez, G., 'The Vietnam Wars', *Rolling Stone*, May 1980; 'Human Rights, War and Mass Exodus', *Transnational Perspectives*, (1982), 34–8.

[64] UN docs. A/AC.96/516/Add. 1; A/AC.96/INF.147. The High Commissioner's report to the General Assembly (1976) refers to 'special operations within the framework of the High Commissioner's good offices function' and to 'displaced persons who face problems analogous to those of refugees': E/5853, paras. 170ff.

[65] UN doc. A/AC.96/534, para. 57 (1976). 'Displaced persons' and 'boat people' terminology prevailed through 1977 and 1978 (see E/5987, paras. 6, 185, 207, 212, 214; A/AC.96/553/Add. 1), with the composite 'refugees and displaced persons' also appearing.

[66] UNGA res. 3455(XXX), 9 Dec. 1975, on humanitarian assistance to the Indo-Chinese displaced persons.   [67] UN doc. A/AC.96/534, para. 87(f).

[68] UN doc. A/AC.96/549, para. 36(b). In 1980, the General Assembly referred to 'boat and land cases in South East Asia' as 'refugees': UNGA res. 35/41, 25 Nov. 1980, para. 8. The causes of population displacements naturally change over time; a 1985 internal UNHCR survey of motivations for departure from Vietnam looked at ethnic and religious discrimination, amongst others, but found that severe economic conditions were mentioned by practically all as a factor in the decision to leave. A review of refugee claims carried out by several officials working independently found that some 8% of cases had a clear claim to refugee status; 31% could qualify on basis of a 'very liberal interpretation'; and that 61% 'clearly' did not qualify: UNHCR, 'Assessment of Current Arrivals in South East Asian Countries of Persons leaving the SRVN by Boat', Sept. 1985.

[69] See the High Commissioner's statement to the Executive Committee in 1977: UN doc. A/AC.96/549, annexe, and for summary of the views of States: ibid., paras. 21, 26. For more detailed

the 1990s, and which has been accompanied by the search for a jurisdictional base, a competent protecting and assisting agency, and an applicable body of rules and standards,[70] by 1977 UNHCR responsibilities for refugees and displaced persons had clearly established their place in the language of the General Assembly.[71] They have remained ever since, with the incremental recognition of others requiring protection, including returnees, women and children, asylum seekers, those in need of complementary protection, and even for the safe return of those determined not to be in need of international protection.[72]

The field of UNHCR competence, and thus the field of its responsibilities, has broadened considerably since the Office was established. Briefly, the movement has been from the Statute through good offices and assistance, to protection and solutions. The class of beneficiaries has moved from those defined in the Statute, through those outside competence assisted on a good offices basis, those defined in relevant resolutions of the General Assembly and directives of the Executive Committee, arriving finally at the generic class of refugees, displaced and other persons of concern to UNHCR.[73]

Apart from purely humanitarian considerations,[74] this tendency shows awareness of the difficulty of determining in the case of a massive exodus that each and everyone has a well-founded fear of persecution in the sense of the UNHCR

statements, see UN docs. A/AC.96/SR.284, paras. 13, 25 *bis*, 46; SR.287, paras. 26, 35; SR.288, paras. 30, 57; SR.291, para. 6. See also the High Commissioner's statement to the 31st Session of the Executive Committee (1980): UN doc. A/AC.96/588, annexe 5. At that session, the representative for Turkey expressed the view that 'the time had come to ensure that UNHCR did not, by virtue of precedents, become a body which cared for anyone compelled for whatever reason to leave his country or even to move to a different area inside his country': UN doc. A/AC.96/SR.319, paras. 12–15.

[70] See further below, s. 3.3 and Ch. 9, s. 2.

[71] In 1973, the General Assembly requested the High Commissioner 'to continue his assistance *and protection* activities in favour of refugees within his mandate as well as for those to whom he extends his good offices or is called upon to assist in accordance with relevant resolutions of the General Assembly': UNGA res. 3143(XXVIII), 14 Dec. 1973. UNGA res. 32/68, 8 Dec. 1977, continued UNHCR's mandate and noted 'the outstanding work... performed... in providing international *protection* to refugees and displaced persons'. UNGA res. 35/41, 25 Nov. 1980, refers to UNHCR's responsibilities 'for *protecting* and assisting refugees and displaced persons throughout the world'. Cf. paras. 28–32, CIREFCA Plan of Action; for text, see the 2nd edn. of this work, Annexe 5, No. 2, and the Online Resource Centre <http://www.oup.com/uk/refugeelaw>.

[72] See, for example, UNGA res. 60/129, 'Office of the United Nations High Commissioner for Refugees', 16 Dec. 2005.

[73] The incremental, 'after the event', and sometimes accidental growth in UNHCR's area of institutional responsibility might have been more efficiently organized had the General Assembly maintained the approach to 'competence' proposed in the 1949 draft statute: '... for the time being, refugees and displaced persons defined in [the IRO Constitution] and, thereafter, such persons as the General Assembly may from time to time determine, including any persons brought under the jurisdiction of the High Commissioner's Office under the terms of international conventions or agreements approved by the General Assembly': UNGA res. 319(IV), 3 Dec. 1949, Annex, para. 3.

[74] That is, a general sense that something must be done, even if those in need of protection or assistance do not fall squarely within the letter of legal regimes of competence or obligation. On the dangers of 'negative responsibility', however, see Goodwin-Gill, G. S., 'Refugee Identity and Protection's Fading Prospect', in Nicholson, F. & Twomey, P., eds., *Refugee Rights and Realities*, (1999), 220, 240–1 (hereafter, Nicholson & Twomey, *Refugee Rights and Realities*).

Statute. It also suggests that something more general, such as lack of protection, should serve as the criterion for identifying persons 'of concern' to the High Commissioner.[75] This is not immediately obvious from the resolutions themselves, but appears to be confirmed by UNHCR and international agency practice, for example, in Rwanda and Zaire, Northern Iraq, Somalia, and former Yugoslavia.

The lack of protection may occur as a matter of law, for example, in the case of stateless persons; or it may be evident from the facts, for example, where it is clear or may be inferred that individuals or groups are unable or unwilling to avail themselves of the protection of the government of their country. This may be due to a well-founded fear of persecution for reasons of race, religion, nationality or political opinion; or to some man-made disaster, such as conflict or violence resulting from a variety of sources. For example, in establishing a Group of Governmental Experts on International Co-operation to Avert New Flows of Refugees in 1981, the General Assembly reaffirmed its strong condemnation of 'policies and practices of oppressive and racist regimes, as well as aggression, colonialism, *apartheid*, alien domination, foreign intervention and occupation', which it identified among the root causes of refugee movements.[76] In its 1986 Report,[77] this Group avoided definitional problems, concentrating instead on 'coerced movements', where the element of compulsion 'was to be understood in a wide sense covering a variety of natural, political and socio-economic factors which directly or indirectly force people to flee . . . in fear for life, liberty and security'. Wars and armed conflicts were cited as a major cause of refugee flows, for flight was often the only way to escape danger to life or extensive restrictions of human rights.[78]

Lack of protection by the government of the country of origin is already an element in the statutory definition of the refugee. Given the impracticability of individual determinations in the case of large-scale movements of asylum seekers, that element acquires great significance. 'Protection' here implies both 'internal protection', in the sense of effective guarantees in matters such as life, liberty, and security of the person; and 'external protection', in the sense of diplomatic protection, including documentation of nationals abroad and recognition of the right of

---

[75] 'Lack of protection', in this context, is intended to reflect general, though well-informed assessments of situations on the ground in countries of origin, rather than the highly individualized test which has been adopted for the purposes of determination of status in some jurisdictions.

[76] UNGA res. 36/148, 16 Dec. 1981.

[77] UN doc. A/41/324 (May 1986); for text, see the Online Resource Centre <http://www.oup.com/uk/refugeelaw>.

[78] The Group separated man-made causes and factors, sub-divided into political causes and socio-economic factors, from natural causes. Within the man-made category were wars, colonialism, the treatment of minorities (for example, under *apartheid*), discrimination and internal conflict, violation of human rights and fundamental freedoms, and expulsions. Socio-economic factors relevant to these causes were those that threatened the physical integrity and survival of individuals and groups, underdevelopment, particularly the legacy of colonialism, the absence of adequate economic infrastructures, and the parlous state of the world economy. Although details in the world picture and in the politics may have changed in the twenty or so years since this *Report* was published, the overall analysis still repays attention.

nationals to return. The 'right to return', in particular, is accepted as a normal incident of nationality. In the case of those leaving Vietnam, however, that right was initially subject to significant qualification. Although in 1975 the Provisional Revolutionary Government of South Vietnam requested UNHCR to promote voluntary repatriation, it stressed at the time that authorization to return fell within its sovereign rights and that each case would need to be examined separately.[79] Many of those who left Chile following the 1973 coup were also 'listed' as prohibited from returning, although they retained their citizenship.[80] These factors alone may justify protection and assistance by UNHCR, particularly where, in individual cases, further evidence is available of measures seriously affecting certain racial, social, or political groups.[81]

Although no objection was raised to UNHCR's activities on behalf of persons leaving Indo-China, challenges to the Office's competence have arisen with respect to the status of other groups. For example, in 1979 and 1984, the Afghan representative objected to assistance and protection being given to Afghan refugees,[82] while further interventions have focused on, among others, the status of Bulgarians of Turkish origin, Romanians of Hungarian origin, Sahrawis, Iraqis, and Palestinians.[83]

---

[79] See statement by the observer for the Democratic Republic of Vietnam at the 26th Session of the Executive Committee (1975): UN doc. A/AC.96/521, para. 105.

[80] See further below, Ch. 4, s. 1.

[81] The failure or unwillingness to readmit nationals, or to provide relevant documentation, can also arise outside the refugee context, strictly so called, and is a matter of continuing concern among migrant receiving States; cf. UNGA res. 60/129, 16 Dec. 2005, emphasizing 'the obligation of all States to accept the return of their nationals . . .': para. 17.

[82] In discussion of the High Commissioner's report in the Third Committee in 1979, for example, the representative of Afghanistan referred to UNHCR's 'assistance to fugitive insurgents in Pakistan' UN doc. A/C.3/34/SR.46, para. 58f. At the Executive Committee in 1984 the observer for Afghanistan claimed that Afghans in Iran and Pakistan, if not insurgents, were nomads and migrant workers; this was roundly rejected by representatives of the receiving and other countries: see UN docs. A/AC.96/SR.371, paras. 92–7, 107; SR.372, para. 60; SR.373, paras. 34, 78; similar exchanges occurred in 1987: UN doc. A/AC.96/SR.416, paras. 38–41, 82.

[83] In 1984, Morocco objected to use of the word 'refugee' in describing UNHCR assistance to Sahrawis in the Tindouf: UN doc. A/AC.96/SR.376, paras. 2–7, claiming that not enough was being done by Algeria to encourage their voluntary repatriation; see further ibid., paras. 8–15; SR.377, paras. 55–61, 67–9; SR.378, paras. 77–81. The dispute continued in later years; see UN docs. A/AC.96/SR.394, 59–71; SR.399, paras. 46–8 (1985); SR.403, paras. 65–6; SR. 407, paras. 81–3, 91–4 (1986); SR.414, para. 29; SR.415, para. 73; SR.420, paras. 7–9, 53 (1987). In 1986, Iraq claimed that the 'Iraqi refugees' referred to by Iran were in fact Iranians who had been living in Iraq and who had been expelled for having committed acts of terrorism and threatening security: SR.409, paras. 34, 94–103. The following year, Iran claimed that most so-called Iranian refugees were 'members of rival political groups, supported from outside . . . , attempting to infiltrate Iranian territory in order to commit subversive acts': UN doc. A/AC.96/SR.418, para. 105. Israel objected when Palestinians began to appear in the annual Executive Committee General Conclusion on International Protection (usually expressing concern about the lack of adequate international protection); see *Report* of the 39th Session of the Executive Committee: UN doc. A/AC/96/721, 13 Oct. 1988, paras. 22, 36. The last express reference to Palestinians appears to have been recorded in the 1993 General Conclusion; see *Report* of the 44th Session of the Executive Committee: UN doc. A/AC.96/821, 12 Oct. 1993, para. 19(z); in contrast to its previous practice, Israel raised no

Despite the protests of individual governments, the international community at large has not hitherto demurred when UNHCR has exercised its protection and assistance functions in cases of large-scale movements of asylum seekers. This, together with other developments, permits the conclusion that the class of persons within the mandate of, or of concern to, UNHCR includes: (1) those who, having left their country, can, on a case-by-case basis, be determined to have a well-founded fear of persecution on certain specified grounds; and (2) those often large groups or categories or persons who, likewise having crossed an international frontier, can be determined or presumed to be without, or unable to avail themselves of, the protection of the government of their State of origin. This is the broad meaning of the term 'refugee' for the purposes of the United Nations, and this is the class for which UNHCR will in principle seek the immediate protection of temporary refuge or *non-refoulement* through time, treatment in accordance with minimum standards, and appropriate long-term solutions. The preceding *functional* description of the scope of UNHCR's responsibilities towards refugees and the displaced begs a number of key questions relating to the international obligations of States, which are dealt with more fully below. For the present, it is sufficient to note that both the activities of UNHCR and the responses of States with regard to refugees in the broad sense may be limited to the provision of refuge and material assistance, and the pursuit of voluntary repatriation. Only the refugee who has been determined to have a well-founded fear of persecution, perhaps, enjoys the full spectrum of protection and the expectation of a lasting solution in a country of asylum or resettlement,[84] although that presumption also may be questioned today in the light of recent State practice.[85]

3.3 RESPONSIBILITY FOR INTERNALLY DISPLACED PERSONS

For UNHCR to assume protection and assistance responsibilities for the internally displaced raises a number of institutional dilemmas,[86] including issues of

---

objection on this occasion, although it has commented on the Palestinian issue in general debate; see the statement during the 53rd Session of the Executive Committee on 30 Sept. 2002 by the Secretary-General of the League of Arab States in UN doc. A/AC.96/561, 20 Oct. 2002, paras. 34–7, and the Israeli response in UN doc. A/AC.96/SR.562, 9 Oct. 2002, paras. 85–6. For discussion of Turkey/Bulgaria, see UN docs. A/AC.96/SR.438, para. 81; SR.440, paras. 93–7; SR.441, paras. 60–4, 65, 66 (1989); on Hungary/Romania, see SR.440, paras. 49–51, 112 (1989); SR.457, paras. 49–57 (1990). 'Inclusion' claims are also made from time to time; regarding 'Russians living in other republics', see SR.466, paras. 47–8 (1991); similarly, for Ukrainians, see SR.484, para. 20 (1993), touching also on the plight of Crimean Tatars, Germans, Greeks, and Bulgarians deported from the Ukraine during the Second World War.

[84] Reservations about the implications of an expanded refugee definition were expressed at the 32nd Session of the Executive Committee in 1981: UN doc. A/AC.96/601, para. 48, and at the 35th Session in 1984: UN doc. A/AC.96/651, para. 81. See further below, s. 7.

[85] See below, Chs. 6, 7.

[86] See, for example, Goodwin-Gill, G. S., 'UNHCR and Internal Displacement: Stepping into a Legal and Political Minefield', in US Committee for Refugees, *World Refugee Survey 2000*, (2000), 26–31.

legal standing and conflict of interest.[87] As the action already taken by the United Nations and others shows, the situation of internal displacement presents serious challenges to the principles underlying the international community. In the case of refugees, the fact of having crossed a frontier brings their situation clearly onto the international plane, triggering a raft of rules, practices, expectations, institutional mechanisms, and legal tools. On the other hand and as a matter of international law, primary responsibility for the protection of and assistance to internally displaced persons rests with the territorial State, in virtue of its sovereignty and the principle of non-intervention. In practice, of course, internal displacement is commonly the result of conflict, where the authority of the central government is in dispute, or its capacity or willingness to provide protection and assistance are in doubt; in recent years, this has been no more evident than in the case of Darfur.[88] At this point, the governing premises of sovereignty and non-intervention stand potentially in opposition to other governing principles of international organization, including the commitment to human rights and to international co-operation in the resolution of humanitarian problems. Clearly, those who are internally displaced gain little from being advised to look to their own government for protection and assistance, while other States and constituencies increasingly feel that the situation of the displaced *is* a matter of concern to them, and that in appropriate cases, something ought to be done.[89]

Historically, UNHCR's involvement with the internally displaced was practical and non-controversial, involving the provision of assistance simultaneously to both returning refugees and their internally displaced 'neighbours', very much in a general, development-oriented approach. Faced with ever more frequent calls to get involved in the problems of internal displacement, UNHCR began to explore the conditions for engagement. In 1993, taking UN General Assembly resolution 47/105 as its lead,[90] it identified these as (1) a *specific request* from the Secretary-General or other competent UN organ; and (2) the *consent* of the State concerned. This generally cautious approach was endorsed by the General Assembly,[91] and by

---

[87] An independent evaluation of UNHCR's performance in the Kosovo crisis, for example, found that, 'The primary and compelling focus on internal victims of the Kosovo conflict...had shifted institutional preoccupation away from the possibility—however remote—that a large-scale outflow of refugees might result, to assistance for the IDPs. Had UNHCR been more focused on its traditional refugee-specific mandate, it might have been more ready to prepare for worst-case refugee scenarios simply because refugees were its primary concern. Instead, as the agency's constituencies and interests multiplied, institutional attention became divided and diffused': 'The Kosovo Refugee Crisis: An Independent Evaluation of UNHCR's Emergency Preparedness and Response', UNHCR Evaluation and Policy Analysis Unit, (EPAU/2000/001), February 2000, para. 95.

[88] See Rafiqul Islam, M., 'The Sudanese Darfur Crisis and Internally Displaced Persons in International Law: The Least Protection for the Most Vulnerable', 18 *IJRL* 354 (2006).

[89] This increasing 'internationalization' of issues, of course, has been helped on its way by the Security Council's practice under Chapter VII in relation to threats to international peace and security.

[90] UNGA res. 47/105, 'Office of the United Nations High Commissioner for Refugees', 16 Dec. 1992, para. 14.

[91] UNGA res. 48/116, 'Office of the United Nations High Commissioner for Refugees', 20 Dec. 1993, para. 12, in which the General Assembly reaffirms, 'its support for the High Commissioner's

the UNHCR Executive Committee, which also stressed that UNHCR should *only* become involved in situations that call for its special expertise, and that it should pay due regard to the complementary mandates of other organizations and the availability of resources.[92] The idea of providing protection at the same time was certainly mooted, but a proposal that UNHCR be accorded a general competence in this regard on behalf of IDPs in 'refugee-like and potential refugee-generating situations' was not taken up, either by UNHCR or other States. UNHCR's 1994 note on the protection aspects of its IDP activities was in fact more of an attempt to refine the criteria for engagement, than to set out how it might or ought to protect IDPs. Indeed, on this issue, UNHCR was distinctly sanguine, recognizing in essence that IDP protection had little if anything to do with 'legal norms and remedies'.[93]

Neither UNHCR nor any other UN agency has any legal authority to 'protect' persons within their own country. No treaty or rule of customary international law establishes legal standing, even if the standards according to which internally displaced persons ought to be treated have been substantially clarified by the Guiding Principles on Internal Displacement.[94] After considerable hesitation among many States,[95] the General Assembly now sees the protection of the internally displaced as having been 'strengthened by identifying, reaffirming and consolidating specific standards . . .', in particular through the *Guiding Principles*,[96] and has 'recognized' those principles as 'an important international framework for the protection of internally displaced persons'.[97] However, the competence of

efforts, on the basis of specific requests from the Secretary-General or the competent principal organs of the United Nations and with the consent of the concerned State, and taking into account the complementarities of the mandates and expertise of other relevant organizations, to provide humanitarian assistance and protection to persons displaced within their own country in specific situations calling for the Office's particular expertise, especially where such efforts could contribute to the prevention or solution of refugee problems. . . .'

[92] See UNHCR Executive Committee Conclusion No. 75 (XLV), 1994, 'Internally Displaced Persons', *Report* of the 45th Session: UN doc. A/AC.96/839, para. 20.

[93] UNHCR, 'Protection Aspects of UNHCR Activities on behalf of Internally Displaced Persons', UN doc. EC/1994/SCP/CRP.2, 4 May 1994. See also, Mooney, E. D., 'In-country protection: out of bounds for UNHCR?', in Nicholson & Twomey, *Refugee Rights and Realities*, 200; and for a more recent perspective from within the organization, see UNHCR, *The State of the World's Refugees 2006*, (2006), Ch. 7.

[94] See 'Report of the Representative of the Secretary-General, Mr. Francis M. Deng, submitted to the United Nations Commission on Human Rights, pursuant to Commission resolution 1997/39, Addendum': UN doc. E/CN.4/1998/53/Add.2; Kälin, W., 'Introduction to the Guiding Principles on Internal Displacement' submitted by Francis Deng, Special Representative of the Secretary-General, to the UN Commission on Human Rights', 10 *IJRL* 557 (1998); Kälin, W., *Guiding Principles on Internal Displacement: Annotations*, (2000); Phuong, C., *The International Protection of Internally Displaced Persons*, (2005).

[95] See Goodwin-Gill, G. S., 'Note on paragraph 20 of General Assembly resolution 55/74', 13 *IJRL* 255–8 (2001).

[96] UNGA res. 60/168, 'Protection of and assistance to internally displaced persons', 16 Dec. 2005, (adopted without a vote), preambular para. 6.

[97] Ibid., para. 8. See also UNGA res. 60/124, 'Strengthening of the coordination of emergency humanitarian assistance of the United Nations', 15 Dec. 2005, para. 6. Although earlier reservations regarding the *Guiding Principles* did not recur, Cuba challenged the notion of a 'culture of protection',

the UN and UNHCR to 'oppose' those principles to States will still depend on consent or acquiescence, either *ad hoc*, or because they are otherwise binding as a matter of treaty or customary international law; moreover, the critical *political* dimensions to situations of internal displacement are unlikely to be abated.[98]

4. Refugees in the sense of the 1951 Convention and the 1967 Protocol relating to the Status of Refugees

The States which acceded to or ratified the 1951 Convention agreed that the term 'refugee' should apply, first to any person considered a refugee under earlier international arrangements; and, secondly, to any person who, broadly speaking, qualifies as a refugee under the UNHCR Statute.[99] In discussions leading up to agreement on the definition in the *Ad hoc* committee on refugees and stateless persons, the United States remained concerned that 'too vague a definition' would entail unknowable (and excessive) responsibilities, and provoke disagreements between governments with respect to its interpretation and application.[100] However, the definition should not be narrow or the field of application of the Convention excessively restricted. The United States therefore proposed four categories of refugees outside their country 'because of persecution or fear of persecution',[101] which were intended also to include those who had fled since the beginning of the Second World War or 'who might be obliged to flee from their countries for similar reasons in the future'.[102] The United Kingdom proposed an alternative, general definition,[103] and a working group was set up within the *Ad hoc* committee to resolve differences. Its provisional draft identified a number of categories, such as the victims of the Nazi or Falangist regimes and by reference to previous international agreements, but also adopted the criterion of well-founded fear and lack of protection.[104] The drafters thus used the IRO Constitution as a

which States are called on to promote in para. 3; see UN GAOR, 60th sess., 63rd plenary meeting, 15 Dec. 2005: UN doc. A/60/PV.63, p. 6. The *Guiding Principles* are also 'recalled' in UNGA resolution 60/128, 'Assistance to refugees, returnees and displaced persons in Africa', 16 Dec. 2005, para. 26.

[98] See further below, Ch. 8, s. 1; Ch. 9, s. 2 on institutional developments in the provision of humanitarian assistance and protection.   [99] Art. 1A(2) of the Convention.
[100] UN doc. E/AC.32/SR.3, para. 40 (Mr Henkin).
[101] See United States of America, *Memorandum on the Definition Article of the Preliminary Draft Convention Relating to the Status of Refugees (and Stateless Persons)*: UN doc. E/AC.32/L.4 (18 Jan. 1950). The four categories were (1) refugees from the period of the first world war; (2) inter-war refugees; (3) 'neo-refugees'; and (4) displaced persons and unaccompanied minors.
[102] UN doc. E/AC.32/SR.3, para. 45 (Mr Henkin).
[103] The UK definition would have included 'a person who, having left the country of his ordinary residence on account of persecution or well-founded fear of persecution, either does not wish to return to that country for good and sufficient reason or is not allowed by the authorities of that country to return there and who is not a national of any other country'. See UN docs. E/AC.32/L.2 (17 Jan. 1950) and E/AC.32/L.2/Rev.1 (19 Jan. 1950).
[104] See UN doc. E/AC.32/L.6, 23 Jan. 1950 (provisional draft of parts of the definition article). Various exclusions and limitations, including geographical, temporal and nationality factors, were also mentioned.

model for the formulation of certain categories of existing refugees,[105] while the general criterion of persecution or fear of persecution, neither narrow nor excessively restricted, according to the US delegate, was considered broad enough for post-Second World War and future refugees.

Originally, the definition, like the first part of that in the Statute, limited application of the Convention to the refugee who acquired such status 'as a result of events occurring before 1 January 1951'. An optional geographical limitation also permitted States, on ratification, to limit their obligations to refugees resulting from 'events occurring in Europe' prior to the critical date.[106] Finally, the substantive or ideological basis for the essential 'well-founded fear of persecution' differs slightly from that in the UNHCR Statute, by including 'membership of a particular social group' among the reasons for persecution, in addition to race, religion, nationality, or political opinion. The differences between the two definitions are due to amendments accepted by the Conference of Plenipotentiaries which adopted the final draft of the Convention.[107] The reference to 'membership of a particular social group' is analysed more fully below;[108] it makes little practical difference in the respective areas of competence of UNHCR and States parties to the Convention.

From the outset, it was recognized that, given its various limitations, the Convention definition would not cover every refugee. The Conference of Plenipotentiaries therefore recommended in the Final Act that States should apply the Convention beyond its strictly contractual scope, to other refugees within their territory.[109] Many States relied upon this recommendation in the case of refugee crises precipitated by events after 1 January 1951, until the 1967 Protocol expressly removed that limitation. It may still be invoked to support extension of the Convention to groups or individuals who do not fully satisfy the definitional requirements.[110]

---

[105] For the IRO Constitution, see below, Annexe 1, No. 1.

[106] Art. 1B. The Convention is frequently criticised for its 'European bias', but another view was apparent in 1951. Mr Rochefort, the French representative, remarked that although more than eighty invitations had been sent out, the Conference gave the appearance of nothing more than a 'slightly enlarged' meeting of the Council of Europe. He observed that only a small fraction of the forty-one governments that had voted for art. 1 in the General Assembly had been willing to come to Geneva to sign the Convention and nearly all were European. In his view, those who argued for deletion of the geographical limitation, 'had done so without any feeling of definite responsibility'. The system of generalized protection had failed; because the non-European countries were absent and because of the attitudes of the immigration countries (they claimed to have no protection problems), there was no practical possibility of 'giving refugees in general, and European refugees in particular, a truly international status': UN doc. A/CONF.2/SR.3, 12.

[107] Cf. Grahl-Madsen, A., *The Status of Refugees in International Law*, vol. 1, (1966), 217.

[108] See further below, Ch. 3, s. 4.2.4.   [109] Recommendation E of the Final Act.

[110] However, see Jackson, *Refugee Concept in Group Situations*, 73–6, for the view that Recommendation E was only intended to apply to refugees affected by the geographical or temporal limits, and not to those who failed to meet the well-founded fear of persecution criterion but were in a 'refugee-like' situation. Although qualification as a Convention definition is often the sufficient condition for the grant of asylum (see further below, 325–30, regarding the asylum aspects of the EU Qualification Directive), States also generally claim the right to grant asylum to others, for example,

Convention refugees are thus identifiable by their possession of four elemental characteristics: (1) they are outside their country of origin; (2) they are unable or unwilling to seek or take advantage of the protection of that country, or to return there; (3) such inability or unwillingness is attributable to a well-founded fear of being persecuted; and (4) the persecution feared is based on reasons of race, religion, nationality, membership of a particular social group, or political opinion.[111]

5. Regional approaches to refugee definition

The 1951 Convention and the 1967 Protocol remain the principal international instruments benefiting refugees, and their definition has been expressly adopted in a variety of regional arrangements aimed at further improving the situation of recognized refugees. It forms the basis for article I of the 1969 AU/OAU Convention on Refugee Problems in Africa,[112] although it has there been realistically extended to cover those compelled to leave their country of origin on account of external aggression, occupation, foreign domination, or events seriously disturbing public order.[113]

Latin America has long been familiar with the practice of diplomatic asylum[114] and with the concept of *asilado*. The Montevideo Treaty of 1889 acknowledged that 'political refugees shall be accorded an inviolable asylum',[115] while other agreements have dealt expressly with asylum granted in diplomatic premises or

for 'humanitarian reasons'. Thus, art. 2 of the Declaration on Territorial Asylum adopted by the Committee of Ministers of the Council of Europe on 18 Nov. 1977, reaffirms the right to grant asylum in respect of Convention refugees 'as well as to any other person [considered] worthy of receiving asylum for humanitarian reasons'. For text, see the 2nd edn. of this work, Annexe 4, No. 6; and the Online Resource Centre <http://www.oup.com/uk/refugeelaw>.

[111] For recent critiques of the international protection regime and the Convention/Protocol, see Fitzpatrick, J., 'Revitalizing the 1951 Refugee Convention', 9 *Harvard Human Rights Journal* 229 (1996); Sitaropoulos, N., 'Refugee: A legal definition in search of a principled interpretation by domestic fora', 52 *Revue hellénique de droit international* 151–90 (1999); Sztucki, J., 'Who is a refugee? The Convention definition: universal or obsolete?', in Nicholson & Twomey, *Refugee Rights and Realities*, 55; Tuitt, P., 'Rethinking the refugee concept', ibid., 106.

[112] The Organization of African Unity first met in Cairo in July 1964; for text of the Charter, see Brownlie, I., *Basic Documents in International Law*, (5th edn., 2002), 56. It was succeeded by the African Union in 2000. See further, <http://www.africa-union.org>.

[113] Generally, see Arboleda, E., 'Refugee Definition in Africa and Latin America: The Lessons of Pragmatism,' 3 *IJRL* 185 (1991); Rwelamira, M., '1989—An Anniversary Year: The 1969 OAU Convention on the Specific Aspects of Refugee Problems in Africa,' 1 *IJRL* 557 (1989); also, OAU/UNHCR, 'The Addis Ababa Symposium 1994,' 7 *IJRL Special Issue—Summer 1995*, (1995); Durieux, J.-F. & Hurwitz, A., 'How Many is Too Many? African and European Legal Responses to Mass Influxes of Refugees', 47 *German Yearbook of International Law* 105, 116f (2005)—challenging the view that the OAU approach 'was specifically designed to address situations of mass influx'.

[114] See further below Ch. 7, s. 3.

[115] See art. 16, 1889 Montevideo Treaty on International Penal Law: *OAS Official Records* OEA/Ser.X/1. Treaty Series 34; revised by the 1940 Montevideo Treaty on International Penal Law: ibid., art. 20 of which excludes extradition for 'political crimes'. See also, Fischel de Andrade, J. H., 'Regional Policy Approaches and Harmonization: A Latin American Perspective', 10 *IJRL* 389 (1998).

other protected areas.[116] The beneficiaries are usually described as being sought 'for political reasons' or 'for political offences', although the 1954 Caracas Convention on Territorial Asylum expressly refers to persons coming from a State 'in which they are persecuted for their beliefs, opinions, or political affiliations, or for acts which may be considered as political offences'.[117]

The refugee crisis in Central America during the 1980s led in due course to one of the most encompassing approaches to the refugee question. The *1984 Cartagena Declaration* proposed a significant broadening, analogous to that of the OAU Convention.[118] But this *Declaration* emerged not from within a regional organization, but out of an *ad hoc* group of experts and representatives from governments in Central America, meeting together in a colloquium in Colombia.[119] It is not a formally binding treaty, but represents endorsement by the States concerned of appropriate and applicable standards of protection and assistance.[120] Moreover, it recommends that the definition of a refugee to be used in the region include, in addition to the elements of the 1951 Convention and the Protocol, persons who have fled their country, because their lives, safety or freedom have been threatened by generalized violence, foreign aggression, internal conflicts, massive violation of human rights or other circumstances seriously disturbing public order. At the same time, the Inter-American system of human rights protection has helped to entrench the basic principles of asylum, recognizing 'the fundamental right of the individual to seek asylum from persecution and to be heard in making that presentation'.[121]

[116] See, for example, 1954 Caracas Convention on Diplomatic Asylum; text below, Annexe 2, No. 4.

[117] Art. 2. Arboleda notes that despite the appearance of a broader definition, 'virtually all Latin American scholars equate the Caracas Convention with earlier treaties'; see Arboleda, E., 'The Cartagena Declaration of 1984 and its Similarities to the 1969 OAU Convention—A Comparative Perspective,' 7 *IJRL Special Issue—Summer 1995*, 87, n. 6 (1995). See also arts. 4, 5, 6, 1981 Inter-American Convention on Extradition; below, Annexe 2, No. 15. Extradition is commonly the background to these regional agreements, non-extradition of political offenders being one part of the wider topic of asylum. Developments in the legal concept of the refugee have likewise had a corresponding influence on extradition arrangements. On the one hand, there has been a tendency to expand protection beyond the limitations which afflict the notion of political offence; on the other hand, international action to suppress the hijacking of aircraft, to counteract terrorism, and to protect diplomats, has imposed new limitations upon the class of those entitled to international protection. See further below, Ch. 4, s. 4.2.   [118] For text see Annexe 2, No. 7.

[119] The Colloquium was co-sponsored by the University of Cartagena, the Regional Center for Third World Studies and the Office of the United Nations High Commissioner for Refugees, and held under the auspices of the Colombian Government; see *La Protección Internacional de los Refugiados en América Central, México y Panamá: Problemas Jurídicos y Humanitarios*, National University of Colombia, (1984), 42. See also Gros Espiell, H., Picado, S., & Valladares Lanza, L., 'Principles and Criteria for the Protection of and Assistance to Central American Refugees and Displaced Persons in Latin America', 2 *IJRL* 83 (1990); Cuellar, R., García-Sayán, D., Montaño, J., Dieguez, M., & Valladares Lanza, L., 'Refugee and Related Developments in Latin America: Challenges Ahead', 3 *IJRL* 484 (1991).

[120] The OAS General Assembly has consistently endorsed the Cartagena Declaration; see, for example, 1991 Legal Resolution of Situation of Refugees, Repatriated and Displaced Persons in the American Hemisphere, AG/RES.1103 (XXI-0/91) (7 Jun. 1991).

[121] Inter-American Commission on Human Rights, 'Report on the Situation of Human Rights of Asylum Seekers within the Canadian Refugee Determination System', OEA/Ser.L/V/II.106, Doc. 40

There are no corresponding treaties or declarations applicable in the Asia region, although the Bangkok Principles, which describe themselves as 'declaratory and non-binding', include the broader terms of the AU/OAU Convention in the revised text adopted in June 2001 at the 40th Session of the Asian-African Legal Consultative Organization in New Delhi.[122]

Over the years, many European States developed national asylum practices going beyond the strict requirements of the 1951 Convention/1967 Protocol, and the developing jurisprudence of the European Court of Human Rights also ensured a measure of 'human rights protection' for those whose removal might lead to treatment contrary to article 3 ECHR50 or to other violations of European Convention rights. Although the Court confirmed that Contracting States have a responsibility to safeguard an individual against treatment contrary to article 3 in the event of expulsion,[123] a regional commitment to provide complementary protection was nevertheless lacking.

For the Member States of the European Union, that situation has now changed. The Treaty of Amsterdam, which was adopted in 1997 and entered into force in May 1999, moved asylum and immigration out of the inter-governmental decision-making process, and into the area where legally binding instruments of harmonization can be legislated by the Council of Ministers and a measure of judicial control exercised by the European Court of Justice.[124] A new treaty Title IV, 'Visas, asylum, immigration and other policies related to freedom of movement of persons', established a number of objectives; in particular, within five years of the Treaty's entry into force, the Council was required 'to adopt measures on asylum, in accordance with the Geneva Convention of 28 July 1951 and the Protocol of 31 January 1967 relating to the status of refugees and *other relevant treaties*'.[125]

Article 63 of the Treaty establishing the European Community set out the framework for the development of EU minimum standards in regard to, among others, entitlement to protection (referred to as 'qualification'), and temporary protection for displaced persons and others in need of international protection ('who cannot return to their country of origin and for persons who otherwise need international protection').[126]

---

rev., 28 Feb. 2000, para. 118. The Commission noted also that the status of refugee, 'is one which derives from the circumstances of the person; it is recognized by the State rather than conferred by it': ibid.

[122] For text, see <http://www.aalco.org>; UNHCR, *Ref World*, (15th edn., 2006).

[123] *Chahal* v. *United Kingdom* (1996) 23 EHRR 413, para. 80.

[124] The extent of such control remains to be seen; see further below, 325–30, 396–403, 537–42.

[125] Art. 63 TEC (emphasis supplied); see also the 1999 Tampere Conclusions, which refer to 'other relevant human rights instruments'.

[126] Other aspects of the harmonization project, considered further below, include the criteria and mechanisms for determining which Member State is responsible for deciding an application for asylum; the reception of asylum seekers; family reunification (generally, but with particular reference to refugees); procedures for granting or withdrawing refugee status; and promoting a balance of effort among Member States in receiving refugees and displaced persons.

The 2001 'Temporary Protection' Directive[127] draws on European experience with large-scale movements of refugees out of Bosnia and Herzegovina and Kosovo during the 1990s. It establishes a mechanism to be triggered by a Council Decision adopted by a qualified majority on a proposal from the Commission, and lays down minimum standards for dealing with a mass influx; it is as an exceptional procedure which does not prejudge any individual's entitlement to Convention refugee status. The intended beneficiaries, 'displaced persons', are defined as:

... third-country nationals or stateless persons who have had to leave their country or region of origin, or have been evacuated, in particular in response to an appeal by international organisations, and are unable to return in safe and durable conditions because of the situation prevailing in that country, who may fall within the scope of Article 1A of the Geneva Convention or other international or national instruments giving international protection, in particular:

(i) persons who have fled areas of armed conflict or endemic violence;
(ii) persons at serious risk of, or who have been the victims of, systematic or generalised violations of their human rights ... [128]

For its part, the 2004 EU Qualification Directive[129] incorporates and interprets the 1951 Convention/1967 Protocol refugee definition,[130] and makes provision for subsidiary protection. A person entitled to such protection is defined as:

... a third country national or a stateless person who does not qualify as a refugee but in respect of whom substantial grounds have been shown for believing that the person concerned, if returned to his or her country of origin, or in the case of a stateless person, to his or her country of former habitual residence, would face a real risk of suffering serious harm as defined in Article 15, and to whom Article 17(1) and (2) do not apply, and is unable, or, owing to such risk, unwilling to avail himself or herself of the protection of that country.[131]

Article 15, in turn, defines serious harm as '(a) death penalty or execution; or (b) torture or inhuman or degrading treatment or punishment of an applicant in the country of origin; or (c) serious and individual threat to a civilian's life or person by reason of indiscriminate violence in situations of international or internal armed conflict.' This is clearly narrower than the approach adopted in Africa and Central America,[132] and also does not include all those who may be entitled to

---

[127] EU Council Directive 2001/55/EC on minimum standards for giving temporary protection in the event of a mass influx of displaced persons and on measures promoting a balance of efforts between Member States in receiving such persons and bearing the consequences thereof: *Official Journal* of the European Communities, 7.8.2001, L 212/12. For text, see below, Annexe 2, No. 14.
[128] Art. 2(c). See further below, Ch. 6, s. 6.2.
[129] EU Council Directive 2004/83/EC of 29 April 2004 on minimum standards for the qualification and status of third country nationals or stateless persons as refugees or as persons who otherwise need international protection and the content of the protection granted: *Official Journal* of the European Union 30.9.2004 L 304/12. For text, see below, Annexe 2, No. 19.
[130] See further below, Ch. 3, s. 3.1.   [131] Art. 2(e).
[132] The European Commission had in fact proposed a broader scope for subsidiary protection; see below, Ch. 6, s. 4.

protection against removal under the European Convention on Human Rights.[133] On the one hand, the Qualification Directive can certainly be seen as the most important instrument in the European asylum regime, and 'the most ambitious attempt to combine refugee law and human rights law ... to date',[134] but on the other hand, the complementary protection scheme adheres to a traditional, individualistic approach, requiring the claimant for protection to show that he or she is personally at risk.[135] One advantage of the EU scheme, at least, is to provide a *status* for those granted subsidiary protection, even if it is less than that accorded to Convention refugees.[136]

6. Refugees in municipal law: some examples

The municipal law practice of non-extradition of political offenders is one antecedent to current principles protecting refugees from return to a State in which they may face persecution. It remains doubtful whether the narrow principle of non-extradition reflects a rule of international law, despite its wide acceptance in municipal law, but apart from the extradition context, many States have nevertheless recognized in their legislation that the refugee is someone worthy of protection and assistance. In some countries, the principle of asylum for refugees is expressly acknowledged in the constitution.[137] In others, ratification of the 1951 Convention and the 1967 Protocol has direct effect in local law, while in still other cases, ratifying States may follow up their acceptance of international obligations with the enactment of specific refugee legislation or the adoption of appropriate administrative procedures.

The Federal Republic of Germany, for example, has both constitutional and enacted law provisions benefitting refugees, both of which were amended in 1992/1993. The 1949 Constitution prescribes that the politically persecuted enjoy the right of asylum,[138] and the 1992 Asylum Procedure Law provides that

[133] Gil-Bazo, M.-T., 'Refugee Status Subsidiary Protection and the Right to be Granted Asylum under EC Law', UNHCR, *New Issues in Refugee Research*, Research Paper No. 136, (Nov. 2006).
[134] Lambert, H., 'The EU Asylum Qualification Directive, its Impact on the Jurisprudence of the United Kingdom and International Law', 55 *ICLQ* 161, 162 (2006).
[135] Klug, A., 'Harmonization of Asylum in the European Union—Emergence of an EU Refugee System?' 47 *German Yearbook of International Law* 594, 618 (2004); Durieux, J-F. & Hurwitz, A., 'How Many is Too Many? African and European Legal Responses to Mass Influxes of Refugees', 47 *German Yearbook of International Law* 105, 135ff (2005). [136] See further below, Ch. 6.
[137] See, for example, the provisions listed in preparation for the 1977 Conference on Territorial Asylum: *A Select Bibliography on Territorial Asylum* (1977): UN doc. ST/GENEVA/LIB/SER.B/Ref.9, 68–74.
[138] See art. 16a (formerly art. 16(2)): *'Politisch Verfolgte geniessen Asylrecht'*. Interpretations of the constitutional provision have often been at variance with those of art. 1A(2) of the 1951 Convention, and were arguably part of the problem with Germany's failure to accept non-State agents of persecution until a change in the law was required by the EU's harmonizing 'Qualification Directive'; see further below, Ch. 3, ss. 3.1, 5.3. For details of the constitutional and legal changes, see Federal Ministry of the Interior, 'Recent Developments in the German Law on Asylum and Aliens,' 6 *IJRL*

those recognized shall enjoy the status provided for by the 1951 Convention, as a minimum standard.[139] The recent amendments, however, establish a geographical limitation by prescribing that the right to asylum may not be invoked by one who enters from a European Union State or from a third country where application of the 1951 Convention and of the 1950 European Convention on Human Rights is guaranteed.[140]

An applicant for refugee status in Australia applies for the grant of a 'protection visa' under section 65 of the Migration Act 1958. Section 36 lays down the criteria and provides that the applicant must be a non-citizen in Australia to whom the Minister is satisfied that Australia has 'protection obligations' under the 1951 Convention/1967 Protocol.[141] The concept of 'protection obligations' does not appear in the 1951 Convention; subject to certain exceptions, it excludes anyone 'who has not taken all possible steps to avail himself or herself of a right to enter and reside in, whether temporarily or permanently and however that right arose or is expressed, any country apart from Australia, including countries of which the non-citizen is a national'.[142]

The Preamble to the 1946 Constitution of France, confirmed in the Constitution of 1958, declares that, 'Tout homme persécuté en raison de son action en faveur de la liberté a droit d'asile sur les territoires de la République'.[143] The 1952 law establishing the *Office français de protection des réfugiés et apatrides* (OFPRA), amended with effect from 1 January 2004, states that it, 'exerce la protection juridique et administrative des réfugiés et apatrides ainsi que celle des bénéficiaires de la protection subsidiaire'. It goes on to provide a comprehensive description of

---

265 (1994); Ablard, T. & Novak, A., 'L'évolution du droit d'asile en Allemagne jusqu'à la réforme de 1993', 7 *IJRL* 260 (1995); Blay, S. & Zimmermann, A., 'Recent Changes in German Refugee Law: A Critical Assessment', 88 *AJIL* 361 (1994).

[139] 'Asylberchtigte genießen im Bundesgebiet die Rechtstellung nach dem Abkommen über die Rechtstellung der Flüchtlinge vom 28. June 1951 . . .' Art. 2(1), *Asylverfahrensgesetz (AsylVfG)* vom 26. Juni 1992: *BGBl.* I S.1126; amended 30 Jun. 1993: *BGBl.* I S.1062 and subsequently. For detailed analysis and commentary, see Marx, R., *Kommentar zum Asylverfahrensgesetz*, (6. Aufl., 2005). See also art. 60 on the prohibition of removal in the 'Immigration Law' (*Gesetz über den Aufenthalt, die Erwerbstätigkeit und die Integration von Ausländern im Bundesgebiet vom 30. Juli 2004*): BGBl. I S. 1950, as amended to 2005: *Artikel 23 des Gesetzes vom 21. Juni 2005*: BGBl. I S. 1818. Access to German law is available at <http://bundesrecht.juris.de/>; a certain amount in English translation can be accessed at the German Law Archive: <http://www.iuscomp.org/gla/>.

[140] The latter countries are to be determined by law and approved by the *Bundesrat*, which is also empowered to list States which will be presumed not to engage in political persecution or inhuman or degrading treatment or punishment. A claimant from such a State has the additional evidentiary burden of overcoming that presumption: art. 16a(2),(3).

[141] Migration Act, s. 5(1); see also Parts 785 and 866 of Schedule 2 to the Migration Regulations,

[142] Migration Act, s. 36(3)–(5).

[143] La Constitution du 4 octobre 1958: <http://www.legifrance.gouv.fr/html/constitution/constitution2>. See also Article 53–1, a 1999 amendment, which permits agreements between France and other countries on respective competences in the determination of asylum claims. However, the constitutional position is protected: 'Toutefois, même si la demande n'entre pas dans leur compétence en vertu de ces accords, les autorités de la République ont toujours le droit de donner asile à tout étranger persécuté en raison de son action en faveur de la liberté ou qui sollicite la protection de la France pour un autre motif.'

those who will be recognized as refugees, or to whom subsidiary protection will be granted:

II.—L'office statue sur les demandes d'asile dont il est saisi. Il convoque le demandeur à une audition....

Au terme d'une instruction unique au cours de laquelle le demandeur d'asile aura été mis en mesure de présenter les éléments à l'appui de sa demande:

1— L'office reconnaît la qualité de réfugié à toute personne persécutée en raison de son action en faveur de la liberté ainsi qu'à toute personne sur laquelle le haut-commissariat des Nations unies pour les réfugiés exerce son mandat aux termes des articles 6 et 7 de son statut tel qu'adopté par l'Assemblée générale des Nations unies le 14 décembre 1950 ou qui répond aux définitions de l'article 1er de la convention de Genève du 28 juillet 1951 relative au statut des réfugiés. Ces personnes sont régies par les dispositions applicables aux réfugiés en vertu de la convention de Genève susmentionnée...[144]

Subsection 2 provides for the grant of subsidiary protection in terms drawn from the EU Qualification Directive cited above.

The United States Refugee Act 1980 abandoned the earlier ideologically and geographically based definition of refugees[145] in favour of that offered by the Convention and Protocol.[146] At the same time, it went beyond international instruments by offering 'resettlement' opportunities to those who might qualify as Convention refugees, save for the fact that they have not yet left their country of origin.[147] Canada also adopted the Convention definition in the 1976 Immigration Act,[148] where it served both as a criterion for selection under admission programmes and as the basis for formal recognition of refugee status and the grant of residence to those already in Canada.[149] Section 2(1) of the 2001 Immigration and Refugee Protection Act (IRPA) now contains express references, not only to the 1951 Convention and 1967 Protocol, but also to the 1984 Convention

---

[144] *Loi no. 52–893*, 25 Jul. 1952, art. 2, modifié par *Loi no*. 2003–1176 2003–12-10, art. 1, *Journal Officiel*, 11 décembre 2003 (en vigueur le 1er janvier 2004). French law can be accessed at <http://www.legifrance.gouv.fr/>. See now, in particular, the *Code de l'entrée et du séjour des étrangers et du droit d'asile*, in force since 1 March 2005. This new Code brings together under a single title the provisions of the *loi du 25 juillet 1952 relative à l'asile* and the *ordonnance du 2 novembre 1945 sur le droit commun des étrangers*.

[145] Refugees were limited to those fleeing from the Middle East or from Communist or Communist-dominated countries.

[146] See s.101(a)(42), Immigration and Nationality Act, as amended: 8 USC §1101(a)(42); also 8 CFR §§207.1, 208.13. For United States law (US Code and Code of Federal Regulations), see <http://www.gpoaccess.gov/>; also collected at <http://www.law.cornell.edu/uscode>. See also Fitzpatrick, J., 'The International Dimension of U.S. Refugee Law', 15 *Berkeley Journal of International Law* 1 (1997); and for a comprehensive account of US law, Legomsky, S., *Immigration and Refugee Law and Policy*, (4th edn., 2005).

[147] 8 USC §1101(a)(42)(B). This expanded category is dependent upon 'appropriate consultations' taking place between the President and Congress: ibid., and 8 USC §1157(e). For background to US refugee resettlement processing, see also Immigration and Naturalization Service, Department of Justice, *Worldwide Guidelines for Overseas Refugee Processing*, (Aug. 1983), 59–62, identifying, among others, certain general characteristics qualifying applicants for refugee status.

[148] S. 2(1).   [149] See now Part 2 of the Immigration and Refugee Protection Act, ss. 95–116.

against Torture. Section 3(2) of IRPA includes the following objectives, among several related to refugee matters:

(d) to offer safe haven to persons with a well-founded fear of persecution based on race, religion, nationality, political opinion or membership in a particular social group, as well as those at risk of torture or cruel and unusual treatment or punishment...

(h) to promote international justice and security by denying access to Canadian territory to persons, including refugee claimants, who are security risks or serious criminals. In addition, Canadian law makes provision for the designation of other classes who may be admitted to Canada, 'taking into account Canada's humanitarian tradition with respect to the displaced and the persecuted'.[150]

In other countries, the admission of refugees and special groups is often decided by the government in the exercise of broad discretionary powers. Although the Convention and Protocol have not been expressly incorporated in the United Kingdom, the effect of successive legislative references and the content of the rules adopted for implementation of immigration and asylum law have led the courts to conclude that, to all intents and purposes, they are indeed now part of domestic law.[151] Section 2 of the Asylum and Immigration Appeals Act 1993, for example, is entitled 'Primacy of the Convention'; it provides that, 'Nothing in the immigration rules...shall lay down any practice which would be contrary to the Convention.' Section 18(3) of the Nationality, Immigration and Asylum Act 2002 provides in turn that:

(3) A claim for asylum is a claim by a person that to remove him from or require him to leave the United Kingdom would be contrary to the United Kingdom's obligations under—
    (a) the Convention relating to the Status of Refugees done at Geneva on 28th July 1951 and its Protocol, or
    (b) Article 3 of the Convention for the Protection of Human Rights and Fundamental Freedoms agreed by the Council of Europe at Rome on 4th November 1950.[152]

Article 25 of the Swiss Constitution, in the 1999 version, provides that 'Les réfugiés ne peuvent être refoulés sur le territoire d'un Etat dans lequel ils sont persécutés ni remis aux autorités d'un tel Etat...Nul ne peut être refoulé sur le

---

[150] IRPA, ss. 12, 14. The following 'designated classes' have been identified at various times since 1978: *Indo-Chinese* (SOR/78–931), *Latin Americans* (SOR/78–932), *Self-exiled Persons* (SOR/78–933), and *Political Prisoners and Oppressed Persons* (SOR/82–977). Membership of a designated class does not ensure protection against *refoulement* under IRPA, s. 115(1): *Kim* v. *MCI* [2005] FC 437, 1 Apr. 2005.

[151] See *R. (European Roma Rights Centre)* v. *Immigration Officer at Prague Airport (UNHCR intervening)* [2005] 2 AC 1, [2004] UKHL 55, per Lord Bingham at paras. 6–9.

[152] See now also s. 12, Immigration, Asylum and Nationality Act 2006, amending s. 113(1) of the 2002 Act; Harvey, A. 'Immigration, Asylum and Nationality Act explained', *Legal Action*, Sept. 2006, 23. On the relevance and importance of refugee status, see *Saad* v. *Secretary of State for the Home Department* [2001] EWCA Civ 2008; *Secretary of State for the Home Department* v. *K* [2006] UKHL 46 per Lord Hope (para. 35), Lord Brown (para. 121).

territoire d'un Etat dans lequel il risque la torture ou tout autre traitement ou peine cruels et inhumains.'[153] Article 3 of the 1998 Swiss law on asylum elaborates slightly on the Convention refugee definition:

1. Sont des réfugiés les personnes qui, dans leur Etat d'origine ou dans le pays de leur dernière résidence, sont exposées à de sérieux préjudices ou craignent à juste titre de l'être en raison de leur race, de leur religion, de leur nationalité, de leur appartenance à un groupe social déterminé ou de leurs opinions politiques.

2. Sont notamment considérées comme de sérieux préjudices la mise en danger de la vie, de l'intégrité corporelle ou de la liberté, de même que les mesures qui entraînent une pression psychique insupportable. Il y a lieu de tenir compte des motifs de fuite spécifiques aux femmes.[154]

Many other similar instances can be cited.[155] Botswana's 1968 Refugees (Recognition and Control) Act, for example, defines the refugee in Convention terms,[156] as do the laws of Japan[157] and Spain.[158] Section 3 of Lesotho's 1983 Refugee Act adopts both 1951 Convention and 1969 OAU criteria with respect to individuals, and likewise as to classes so declared by the Minister. The 1983 Zimbabwe Refugee Act, section 3, is very similar, containing particularly detailed provision for class determinations. Despite its Central American location, the 1991 Belize Refugees Act incorporates the 1951 Convention definition and not the Cartagena Declaration extensions, as might have been expected, but the broader terms of the 1969 OAU Convention (section 4). Article 15 of Norway's Immigration Act extends protection to refugees having a fear of persecution, as well as to foreign nationals who, 'for reasons similar to those given in the definition of a refugee are in considerable danger of losing their lives or of being made to suffer inhuman treatment'.[159] Bolivian law provides also for both Convention

---

[153] *Constitution fédérale de la Confédération suisse du 18 avril 1999*, Art. 25, RO 1999 2556.

[154] *Loi sur l'asile du 26 juin octobre 1998*: RO 1999 2262; Swiss law can be viewed at <http://www.admin.ch>, and some is available in English. For discussion of earlier law and practice, see Kälin, W., 'The Legal Condition of Refugees in Switzerland', 24 *Swiss Reports presented at the XIVth International Congress of Comparative Law*, 57–73 (1994); Achermann, A. & Hausammann, C., *Handbuch des Asylrechts*, (1991), 71ff; Bersier, R., *Droit d'asile et statut de réfugié*, (1991), 43ff; Kälin, W., *Grundriss des Asylverfahrens*, (1990), 23ff. Peruvian law uses almost identical terminology; see, for example, art. 11, *Decreto Pres. No.1 Situation Juridica De Los Refugiados*: 'Para los efectos dispuestos en el artículo 7, se considera particularmente como serios perjuicios el hallarse en peligro la vida, la integridad física o la libertad personal, al igual que las medidas que acarrean una presión psíquica intolerable'.

[155] The following and further examples are available on the UNHCR CD-ROM/DVD collection, *RefWorld*, (15th edn., 2006); see also Messina, C., 'Refugee definitions in the countries of the Commonwealth of Independent States', in Nicholson & Twomey, *Refugee Rights and Realities*, 136.

[156] 'Political refugee' is defined in the Schedule to the Refugees (Recognition and Control) Act, Cap. 25:03.   [157] Immigration Control and Refugee Recognition Act, art. 2(3)-2.

[158] Ley 5/1984 (as modified by Ley 9/1994) Reguladora del Derecho de Asilo y de la Condicion de Refugiado, art. 3 (Causas que justifican la concesión de asilo y su denegación). The law provides that asylum will be granted to any person who meets the requirements of international treaties to which Spain is party, especially the 1951 Convention and 1967 Protocol.

[159] Immigration Act, 24 June 1988 No. 64 (amended to 28 July 2002).

and extended definitions.[160] The 1999 asylum law of the Czech Republic adopts the 1951 Convention approach in section 12, while section 14 provides that asylum may also be granted for humanitarian reasons.[161] The Danish Aliens Act provides for the issue of a residence permit to a person who falls within the terms of the 1951 Convention, or who risks torture or the death penalty in the case of return to their country of origin.[162]

This far from comprehensive selection illustrates the extent to which certain States have translated their concern for the international problem of refugees into action on the municipal level. Many immigration and non-immigration countries have incorporated the Convention definition, with occasional modifications, into their laws and policies. That definition may be used both as a basis for overseas selection and for the purposes of determining claims to asylum and/or refugee status raised by persons physically present or arriving in their territory. A further notable feature is the tendency of States to take account of the plight of others, who are either not recognized or not strictly refugees in the sense of the Convention, but who have valid humanitarian reasons for being offered resettlement opportunities or protection.[163] The tension between obligation and discretion nevertheless contributes a measure of uncertainty to the debate, which is amplified by the now established practice among many States effectively to qualify the refugee definition by reference to other, exclusionary criteria, such as a continuing need for protection, or the absence of another State with actual or assumed protection responsibilities.[164]

[160] See Decreto Presidencial No. 19640 (in force 4 July 1983), art. 1 and the extended definition in art. 2: 'Se considerará también refugiados por razones humanitarios a todas aquellas personas que se hayan visto forzadas a huir de su país a causa de conflictos armados internos; agresión, ocupación o dominación extranjeras, violación masiva de los derechos humanos; o en razón de acontecimientos de naturaleza política que alteren gravemente el orden público en el país de origen o procedencia'.

[161] Act 325/1999 Coll. on Asylum, as amended to 2002, ss. 12–14; s. 13 provides for asylum to be granted to certain of a recognized refugee's family members. See also Nagy, B., 'Asylum Seekers and Refugees: Hungarian Dilemmas,' 34 *Acta Juridica Hungarica*, (1992), No. 1–2, 27—s. 65 of the Hungarian Constitution refers to persecution for 'linguistic' reasons, in addition to racial, religious, national and political grounds; Nagy, B., 'Before or After the Wave? The Adequacy of the New Hungarian Refugee Law', 3 *IJRL* 529 (1991).

[162] Danish Ministry of Refugee, Immigration and Integration Affairs, Consolidation Act No. 685 of 24 July 2003, articles 7, 31.

[163] See Weis, P., 'The Legal Aspects of the Problems of *de facto* Refugees', in International University Exchange Fund, *Problems of Refugees and Exiles in Europe*, (1974). The notion of 'valid reasons' is expanded at 3–5 and would include (1) a person's reasonable belief that he or she would be prejudiced in the exercise of human rights, would suffer discrimination, or be compelled to act against conscience; and (2) war or warlike conditions, foreign or colonial occupation, or serious disturbance of public order in part or all of the person's country of origin. See also UNHCR, 'Note on Consultations on the Arrivals of Asylum-seekers and Refugees in Europe': UN doc. A/AC.96/INF.174 (July 1985), Annexe V.

[164] As noted above, Australian legislation seeks to incorporate the notion of 'person to whom Australia owes protection obligations' into the very definition of 'refugee'.

7. Institutional responsibilities and international obligations

Notwithstanding the concerns expressed regarding the viability of the international refugee protection regime in the face of today's challenges, voting patterns in the General Assembly on UNHCR and related topics confirm that the majority of States clearly want the United Nations to assume responsibilities for a broad category of persons obliged to flee their countries for a variety of reasons. Indeed, as has been briefly shown above, the scope of those who might count on international protection is expanding to include the internally displaced, at least in certain circumstances. In each case, however, there is a clear gap between what may be called *functional* responsibilities and expectations, on the one hand, and the legal obligations of States, on the other hand.

That UNHCR's competence and responsibility have evolved is beyond question,[165] and neither the Executive Committee nor the General Assembly has resiled from this position.[166] However, as States endorsed a wider role for UNHCR, so they began also to express their reservations about a general widening of the refugee definition.[167] At the UNHCR Executive Committee in 1985, for example, several States expressed concern about abuse of asylum procedures, but still agreed that those fleeing armed conflict or internal disturbances deserved protection.[168] One State suggested that protection in such cases was based not so much on international obligations, as on national asylum policies; and that

[165] As long ago as 1980, the UNHCR Executive Committee noted continuing large-scale movements from man-made disasters; it stressed the necessity for coordination among UN bodies concerned with such emergencies and those involving refugees and displaced persons in refugee-like situations, and 'emphasized...the leading responsibility of (UNHCR) in emergency situations which involve refugees in the sense of its Statute or of General Assembly resolution 1388(XIV) and its subsequent resolutions': *Report* of the 31st Session: UN doc. A/AC.96/588, paras. 29.A(c), 29.B(c)(e)(f). On developments in relation to humanitarian assistance, see further below, Ch. 8, s. 1.

[166] In its 2005 General Conclusion on International Protection, the Executive Committee acknowledged the range of causes, expressing its concern at 'instances of persecution, generalized violence and violations of human rights which continue to cause and perpetuate displacement within and beyond national borders...': Executive Committee Conclusion No. 102 (LVI)—2005, *Report* of the 56th Session, UN doc. A/AC.96/1021, 7 Oct. 2005, para. 20(f).

[167] Already in 1982 some States were emphasizing that UNHCR's mandate was 'sufficiently flexible and adaptable to changing requirements', that no change there or in the refugee definition was called for; see *Report* of the 33rd Session: UN doc. A/AC.96/614 (1982), para. 43(f); also UN doc. A/AC.96/SR.344, para. 11 (USA); SR.352, paras. 60–2 (UK).

[168] See Summary Records, 36th Session (1985): UN doc. A/AC.96/SR.391, paras. 50–1 (Switzerland); also para. 42 (Australia), confirming UNHCR's protecting role for the broader class, but considering it 'undesirable to define those groups of persons as "refugees" and to grant them the full range of protection available to victims of individual persecution'; also SR.464, para. 14 (1991), where Australia suggested priority for those in the broader class should be 'relief and humanitarian assistance and repatriation when that is possible in reasonably safe conditions'. Compare the contrasting positions of Tunisia and France in 1984: A/AC.96/SR.374, paras. 57–60.

48 *Refugees*

the universally accepted definition of a refugee should not be applied, lest this diminish the readiness of governments to grant asylum.[169]

When in 1986 the High Commissioner opened that year's Executive Committee with the suggestion that perhaps the concept of individual persecution had been overtaken by forced mass migration, and that, while still useful, the 1951 Convention no longer fully matched realities,[170] the reaction was largely negative, particularly among developed States.[171] Nevertheless, in due course a working group was established by UNHCR, which identified some seven categories of persons falling, in various degrees, within the Office's area of operations.[172] A discussion paper on 'persons of concern' to the Office was submitted to an intersessional meeting of the Executive Committee in April 1992,[173] which noted the disjuncture between the 'obligation' of the international community to provide protection, and the discretionary responses of States. The debate revealed general recognition of the need to deal with the protection issues, but no great willingness to move speedily in the direction of a separate regime, for example in Europe, that would combine criteria, burden sharing, identification of safe countries or areas, and evaluation of safe return possibilities.[174]

UNHCR's 1994 *Note on International Protection* concluded that, while there was broad consensus on the need to provide protection, States had little inclination to adopt a new Convention; instead, it proposed 'the adoption of guiding principles embodied in a global or regional declaration'.[175] Although this idea received support from many States in the Executive Committee in 1994 and

[169] Ibid., para. 72 (The Netherlands). Not many States recognized the distinction between the *functional* responsibilities of UNHCR, which they themselves have determinedly enlarged, and the precise scope of their own *legal* obligations, which are to be assessed in the light of treaty and customary international law.

[170] See *Report* of the 37th Session, Annex, 2–3: UN doc. A/AC.96/688 and /Corr.1.

[171] For reactions at the 37th Session (1986), see UN doc. A/AC.96/SR.401, para. 70 (United Kingdom); SR.403, para. 19 (Belgium); para. 22 (Norway); UN doc. A/AC.96/SR.402, para. 32 (Germany); at the 38th Session (1987), see UN doc. A/AC.96/SR.414, para. 39 (Sweden); para. 49 (Switzerland); SR.417, para. 83 (United Kingdom); paras. 84–5 (Sweden); and at the 39th Session (1988), see UN doc. A/AC.96/SR.426, para. 81 (Norway); para. 88 (Belgium); SR.430, para. 41 (Switzerland); para. 51 (United Kingdom). For further details on the debate in this period, see the 2nd edn. of this work, 26–8.

[172] Convention/Protocol refugee, OAU/Cartagena refugees, refugees from man-made disasters, persons in flight from natural disasters, rejected cases, internally displaced persons, stateless persons: *Report* of the Working Group on Solutions and Protection: UN doc. EC/SCP/64 (12 Aug. 1991), paras. 8–53. The *Report* was 'accepted with appreciation', rather than adopted by the Sub-Committee of the Whole on International Protection, which recommended further discussions: *Report* of the Sub-Committee: UN doc. A/AC.96/781 (9 Oct. 1991), paras. 2–18.

[173] 'Protection of Persons of Concern to UNHCR who fall outside the 1951 Convention: A Discussion Note': EC/SCP/1992/CRP.5; the African Group and the Latin America Group also submitted a paper on the scope, respectively, of the OAU Convention and the Cartagena Declaration: EC/SCP/1992/CRP.6.

[174] *Report* of the 13–14 April Meeting: UN doc. EC/SCP/71 (7 Jul. 1992), paras. 31–44.

[175] UNHCR, *Note* on International Protection: UN doc. A/AC.96/830 (7 Sept. 1994), paras. 19–43, 54–7; published also in 6 *IJRL* 679 (1994).

1995,[176] in 1999 the Executive Committee expressly recognized the need to develop complementary forms of protection, alongside the 1951 Convention/ 1967 Protocol. Six years later, it adopted Conclusion No. 103 (LVI), precisely on the provision of international protection including through complementary forms of protection.[177]

8. 'Refugees' for the purposes of general international law

Refugees within the mandate of UNHCR, and therefore eligible for protection and assistance by the international community, include not only those who can, on a case-by-case basis, be determined to have a well-founded fear of persecution on certain grounds (so-called 'statutory refugees'); but also other often large groups of persons who can be determined or presumed to be without the protection of the government of their State of origin. In principle, it is still essential that the persons in question should have crossed an international frontier and that, in the case of the latter group, the reasons for flight should be traceable to conflicts, human rights violations, breaches of international humanitarian law, or other serious harm resulting from radical political, social, or economic changes in their own country. With fundamental human rights at issue, a central feature triggering the international protection regime remains violence, or the risk or threat of violence; those who move because of pure economic motivation, pure personal convenience, or criminal intent are excluded.

As also noted above, UNHCR may also assist persons displaced *within* their own countries and contribute to the rehabilitation and reintegration of returning refugees and 'externally' displaced persons.[178] The extent to which UNHCR (or any other international agency) may exercise a protection function with respect to the internally displaced is less certain.[179]

On the basis of State and international organization practice, the above core of meaning represents the content of the term 'refugee' in general international law. Grey areas nevertheless remain. The class of persons 'without the protection of the government of their State of origin' begs many questions. Moreover, the varying content of the term 'refugee' may likewise import varying legal consequences, so that the obligations of States in matters such as *non-refoulement*, non-rejection at the frontier, temporary refuge or asylum, and treatment after entry will depend

---

[176] *Report* of the Sub-Committee of the Whole on International Protection: UN doc. A/AC.96/ 837 (4 Oct. 1994), para. 19, Executive Committee General Conclusion on International Protection, *Report* of the 45th Session: UN doc. A/AC.96/839 (11 Oct. 1994), para. 19(k)–(q); UN doc. A/AC.96/SR.490, para. 8 (Canada); SR.491, para. 35 (Norway); SR.492, para. 16 (Switzerland); see also UNGA res. 49/169, 23 Dec. 1994, paras. 6, 7.   [177] See further below, Ch. 6.
[178] The facilitation and promotion of voluntary repatriation are prescribed functions of UNHCR (paras. 1 and 8(c) of the Statute), which may extend to a period after initial return, when technically the persons in question will have ceased to be refugees; see further below Ch. 9, s. 3.2.
[179] See further below, Ch. 9, s. 3.2.

upon the precise status of the particular class. In many situations, UNHCR's institutional responsibilities will be complemented by the obligations of States under the 1951 Convention/1967 Protocol, or supplemented by regional arrangements. This is by no means a complete legal regime, however. The disjuncture between the obligations of States and the institutional responsibilities of UNHCR is broadest and most clearly apparent in regard to refugees, other than those having a well-founded fear of persecution or falling within regional arrangements. The disjuncture is compounded by differences as to the criteria determining the limits of the class, and as to the applicability of certain basic principles of human rights, including rights to refuge and protection.[180] UNHCR has been accorded a functional role and responsibility by the international community, but it remains dependent upon the resources and the political will of States to work out the practical problems of protection, assistance and solutions. UN General Assembly resolutions may impose obligations on UNHCR, its subsidiary organ, but they do not thereby directly impose obligations on States.[181]

As shown below, however, the principle of *non-refoulement* (in its generic form of 'refuge') is the foundation stone of international protection and applies across a broad class, even if the resulting regime of law and practice is far from adequate either for States or individuals. Certain factual elements may be necessary before the principle is triggered—for example, mass movement to or across an international frontier and some evidence of relevant and valid reasons for flight, such as human rights violations in the country of origin—but it would not be permissible for a State to seek to avoid its obligations, either by declining to make a formal determination of refugee status or by ignoring and acting in disregard of the development of the refugee concept in State and international organization practice.

While States are conscious of the potential threat to their own security that a massive influx can pose, none claims an absolute right to return a refugee, as such, to persecution. A State may try to assert for itself greater freedom of action, however, by avoiding any use of refugee terminology. Asylum seekers are thus classified as 'displaced persons', 'illegal immigrants', 'economic migrants', 'quasi-refugees', 'aliens', 'departees', 'boat-people', or 'stowaways'. Similarly, the developed world, in particular, expends considerable energy in trying to find ways to prevent claims for protection being made at their borders, or to allow for them to be summarily passed on or back to others. 'Interdiction', 'pre-inspection', 'visa requirements', 'carrier sanctions', 'safe third country' concepts, 'security zones', 'international zones', and the like are among the armoury of measures currently employed. The intention may be either to forestall arrivals, or to allow those arriving to be dealt with at discretion, but the clear implication is that, for States at large, refugees are protected by international law and, as a matter of law, entitled to a better and higher standard of treatment.

[180] Cf. the differences noted above between the scope of 'subsidiary protection' in the EU, and that of the AU/OAU Convention and the Cartagena Declaration.
[181] See also Goodwin-Gill, G. S., 'The Language of Protection,' 1 *IJRL* 6 (1989); and 'Refugees: The Functions and Limits of the Existing Protection System,' in Nash, A., ed., *Human Rights and the Protection of Refugees under International Law*, (1988), 149–82.

3

Determination of Refugee Status:
Analysis and Application

The legal consequences[1] which flow from the formal definition of refugee status are necessarily predicated upon determination by some or other authority that the individual or group in question satisfies the relevant legal criteria.[2] In principle, a person becomes a refugee at the moment when he or she satisfies the definition, so that determination of status is declaratory, rather than constitutive;[3] problems arise, however, where States decline to determine refugee status, or where States and UNHCR reach different determinations.[4]

1. Respective competence of UNHCR and of States parties to the Convention and Protocol

The UNHCR Statute and the 1951 Convention contain very similar definitions of the term 'refugee'. It is for UNHCR to determine status under the Statute and

---

[1] To the drafters of the 1951 Convention, at least initially, the absence of a clear legal status necessarily had repercussions on the refugee's right to recognition as a person before the law, as required by art. 6 UDHR48, while such status was also essential in order to enable the refugee 'to lead a normal and self-respecting life'. See UN doc. E/AC.32/2, 3 Jan. 1950, *Ad hoc* Committee on Statelessness and Related Problems. Memorandum by the Secretary-General. Annex. Preliminary Draft Convention, para. 13. These references were dropped from the final version of the Preamble; today, although 'refugee status' is understood more as the formal confirmation of entitlement to international protection or asylum in the sense of solution, than as a particular civil quality, its absence or denial may well entail the marginalization of substantial numbers of individuals otherwise in need of refuge.

[2] See Steinbock, D. J., 'The refugee definition as law: issues of interpretation', in Nicholson, F. & Twomey, P., eds., *Refugee Rights and Realities*, (1999), 13 (hereafter, Nicholson & Twomey, *Refugee Rights and Realities*).

[3] See UNHCR, *Handbook on Procedures and Criteria for Determining Refugee Status*, (1979, re-edited 1992) (hereafter, UNHCR, *Handbook*), para. 28; Grahl-Madsen, A., *The Status of Refugees in International Law*, vol. 1, (1966), 340; Tribunal civil, Verviers, 15 nov. 1989, *X c/ Etat belge:* 55 *Revue du droit des étrangers* (RDDE), sept.–oct. 1989, 242; Inter-American Commission on Human Rights, 'Report on the Situation of Human Rights of Asylum Seekers within the Canadian Refugee Determination System', OEA/Ser.L/V/II.106, Doc. 40 rev., 28 Feb. 2000, para. 118.

[4] See generally, Grahl-Madsen, *Status of Refugees*, vol. 1, (1966); Weis, P., 'The Concept of the Refugee in International Law', *Journal du droit international*, (1960) 1; Schnyder, F., 'Les aspects

any relevant General Assembly resolutions, and for States parties to the Convention and the Protocol to determine status under those instruments.[5] Given the differences in definition, an individual may be recognized as both a mandate,[6] and a Convention[7] refugee; or as a mandate refugee but not as a Convention refugee.[8] The latter can arise, for example, where the individual is in a non-contracting State or a State which still adheres to the temporal or geographical limitations permitted under the Convention.[9] Divergence between mandate and Convention status can also result from differences of opinion between States and UNHCR, although a number of factors ought in principle to reduce that possibility. UNHCR, for example, has the statutory function of supervising the application of international conventions for the protection of refugees,[10] and States parties to the Convention and Protocol formally undertake to facilitate this duty.[11] Moreover, many States accept direct or indirect participation by UNHCR in procedures for the determination of refugee status, so that the potential for harmonization of decisions is increased. The problem of divergent positions is more likely, however, where States decline to determine refugee status for any reason; or where refugees whose claims are well-founded under a regional regime move elsewhere.

juridiques actuels du problème des réfugiés', Hague *Recueil* (1965-I) 339; Sadruddin Aga Khan, 'Legal Problems relating to Refugees and Displaced Persons', Hague *Recueil* (1976-I) 287; Anker, D. A., *Law of Asylum in the United States*, (3rd edn., 1999), and 'Law and Procedures Supplement 2002'; Hathaway, J. C., *The Law of Refugee Status*, (1991); Kälin, W., *Grundriss des Asylverfahrens*, (1990); Germov, R. & Motta, F., *Refugee Law in Australia*, (2003); Stevens, D., *UK Asylum Law and Policy*, (2004); Alland, D. & Teitgen-Colly, C., *Traité du droit d'asile*, (2002); Marx, R., *Kommentar zum Ausländer- und Asylrecht*, (2. Aufl., 2005); *Kommentar zum Asylverfahrensgesetz*, (6. Auflag, 2005); Tiberghien, F., *La protection des réfugiés en France*, (2e ed., 1988).

[5] The situation of refugees acknowledged under earlier arrangements and formally included in both Statute and Convention is not examined further; cf. Statute, para. 6(a)(1) and 1951 Convention, art. 1A(1): below, Annexe 1, Nos. 3 & 4; Grahl-Madsen, *Status of Refugees*, vol. 1, 108–41; Tiberghien, *La protection des réfugiés*, 401–41.

[6] The term 'mandate refugee' will signify a refugee within the competence of UNHCR according to its Statute, or according to specific General Assembly resolutions. French law recognizes as refugees 'toute personne persécutée en raison de son action en faveur de la liberté ainsi qu'à toute personne sur laquelle le haut-commissariat des Nations unies pour les réfugiés exerce son mandat aux termes des articles 6 et 7 de son statut...ou qui répond aux définitions de l'article 1er de la convention de Genève du 28 juillet 1951...': see art. 2, Loi n° 52-893 du 25 juillet 1952, relative au droit d'asile (modifié 2003); art. L711–1, Code de l'entrée et du séjour des étrangers et du droit d'asile. <http://www.legifrance.gouv.fr/>. See also CRR, 16 mai 1988, 38.367, *Kazilbash, Doc. réf.* no. 79, 4/13 juill. 1989, Suppl., JC, 1—Afghan asylum seeker received UNHCR protection in India, but claim in France rejected. CRR held that OFPRA was required not only to determine whether claimant was within the Convention, but also whether within mandate of UNHCR.

[7] The term 'Convention refugee' will signify a refugee within the meaning of the 1951 Convention and/or 1967 Protocol.

[8] Recognition as a Convention, but not as a mandate refugee would import no consequences of significance.

[9] These optional limitations are not discussed further; see Grahl-Madsen, *Status of Refugees*, vol. 1, 164–72. States parties maintaining the limitations are listed below in Annexe 3, No. 1.

[10] Para. 8(a).   [11] Art. 35 of the Convention; art. II of the Protocol.

2. Determination of refugee status by UNHCR

The basic elements of the refugee definition are common to States and to UNHCR and are examined more fully in Section 3. UNHCR itself will be concerned to determine status (1) as a condition precedent to providing international protection (for example, intervention with a government to prevent expulsion); or (2) as a prerequisite to providing assistance to a government which requests it in respect of certain groups within its territory. Except in individual cases, formal determination of refugee status may not be necessary. Intervention to secure refuge or protection as a matter of urgency, for example, can be based on prima facie elements in the particular case—the fact of flight across an international frontier, evidence of valid reasons for flight from the country of origin, and the material needs of the group in question. Where assistance is expressly requested by a receiving country, that invitation alone would justify UNHCR's involvement in the absence of hard evidence that those to be helped were not refugees or displaced persons, or of any coherent, persuasive opposition by the country of origin or other members of the international community.[12]

Formal determination of mandate status, however, is often necessary in individual cases.[13] In States which have not yet instituted procedures for assessing refugee claims, intervention by UNHCR on the basis of a positive determination of refugee status may be required to protect the individual. Occasionally, access to national refugee resettlement programmes may be conditional upon certification by the UNHCR office in the country of first admission that the individuals in question fall within the mandate of the High Commissioner.[14] In each scenario, UNHCR's approach to the determination of status in recent years has attracted considerable criticism, particularly in matters of due process and appeal or review.[15]

3. Determination of refugee status by States

The 1951 Convention defines refugees and provides for certain standards of treatment to be accorded to refugees. It says nothing about procedures for determining

[12] Cf. various State objections, cited above, Ch. 2, s. 3.2.

[13] In its 2005 'Note on International Protection', UNHCR reported that during 2004 it had been involved in refugee status decision-making in one way or another in 87 countries, affecting some 50,000 people; a minority of such determinations were for resettlement purposes, with others taken to determine eligibility for mandate protection and assistance and/or to facilitate a durable solution: UN doc. A/AC.96/1008, 4 July 2005, para. 20.

[14] UNHCR's determination operates as a filter in such cases, although the final decisions on both status and acceptance are increasingly taken by governments themselves.

[15] See Alexander, M., 'Refugee Status Determination Conducted by UNHCR', 11 *IJRL* 251 (1999); Kagan, M., 'The Beleaguered Gatekeeper: Protection Challenges Posed by UNHCR Refugee Status Determination', 18 *IJRL* 1 (2006). To meet these concerns, UNHCR drafted and circulated a detailed handbook, *Procedural Standards for Refugee Status Determination under UNHCR's Mandate*, (2004).

refugee status, and leaves to States the choice of means as to implementation at the national level.[16] Given the nature of the definition, the assessment of claims to refugee status thus involves a complex of subjective and objective factors, while the context of such assessment—interpretation of an international instrument with fundamentally humanitarian objectives—implies certain ground rules.[17]

Clearly, the onus is on the applicant to establish his or her case, but practical considerations and the trauma which can face a person in flight, impose a corresponding duty upon whomever must ascertain and evaluate the relevant facts and the credibility of the applicant.[18] Given 'protection' of refugees as one of the Convention's objectives, a liberal interpretation of the criteria and a strict application of the limited exceptions are called for. Moreover a decision on the well-foundedness or not of a fear of persecution is essentially an essay in hypothesis, an attempt to prophesy what might happen to the applicant in the future, if returned to his or her country of origin. Particular care needs to be exercised, therefore, in applying the correct standard of proof.

In civil and criminal cases, two 'standards of proof' are commonly advanced: 'proof on a balance of probability' for the former, and 'proof beyond a reasonable doubt' for the latter. In practice, there can be no absolute standard in either case, and it will vary with the subject-matter. In the United Kingdom, for example, in habeas corpus proceedings, the applicant must cast some doubt on the validity of his or her detention. But in matters of fact, it is enough that the applicant presents such evidence as raises the possibility of a favourable inference. It then falls to the respondent, the detaining authority, to rebut that inference.[19] It might be argued that, in a refugee status case, the 'likelihood of persecution' must be established on a balance of probabilities. In civil cases, the typical issue is whether a close, legally relevant relation exists between past causes and past effects.[20] The applicant for refugee status, however, is adducing a future speculative risk as the basis for a claim

---

[16] See further below, Ch. 10, ss. 2–4.

[17] Cf. art. 31(1), Vienna Convention on the Law of Treaties. The UNHCR *Handbook on Procedures and Criteria for Determining Refugee Status* was prepared at the request of States members of the Executive Committee of the High Commissioner's Programme, for the guidance of governments: UNHCR Executive Committee, *Report of the 28th Session*: UN doc. A/AC.96/549 (1977), para. 53.6(g). First published in 1979, it has been reprinted several times in many languages, generally with a new foreword by the current Director of International Protection and updated lists of States parties. The content, however, is unchanged, being based on material and analysis available at the date of preparation, including UNHCR experience, State practice in regard to the determination of refugee status, exchanges of views between the Office and the competent authorities of Contracting States, and relevant literature. The *Handbook* has been widely circulated and approved by governments and is frequently referred to in refugee status proceedings throughout the world; however, courts citing it, even with approval, commonly note that it is not binding. The *Handbook* has been supplemented recently by the publication of UNHCR 'Guidelines' on selected issues of interpretation, which are referred to below. See also, UNHCR, 'Interpreting Article 1 of the 1951 Convention relating to the Status of Refugees', Geneva, Apr. 2001.

[18] UNHCR, *Handbook*, paras. 195–205.

[19] *R. v. Governor of Brixton Prison, ex p. Ahsan* [1969] 2 QB 222 per Goddard L.C.J. at 233.

[20] For example, did war service cause or contribute to cancer of the gullet leading to death? Cf. *Miller v. Minister of Pensions* [1947] 2 All ER 372.

to protection. Analogous issues were considered as long ago as 1971 in the United Kingdom by the House of Lords in an extradition case, *Fernandez* v. *Government of Singapore*.[21] Here, Lord Diplock noted that the phrase 'balance of probability' was 'inappropriate when applied not to ascertaining what has happened, but to prophesying what, if it happens at all, can only happen in the future'.[22] He went on to note that the relevant provision of the Fugitive Offenders Act:

... calls upon the court to prophesy what will happen to the fugitive in the future if he is returned ... The degree of confidence that the events specified will occur which the court should have to justify refusal to return the fugitive ... should, as a matter of common sense and common humanity, depend upon the gravity of the consequences contemplated on the one hand of permitting and on the other hand of refusing, the return of the fugitive if the court's expectation should be wrong. The general policy of the Act, viz. that persons against whom a prima facie case is established that they have committed a crime ... should be returned to stand their trial ..., is departed from if the return of a person who will not be detained or restricted for any of the reasons specified in paragraph (c) is refused. But it is departed from only in one case. On the other hand, detention or restriction in his personal liberty, the consequence which the relevant words are intended to avert, is grave indeed to the individual fugitive concerned.[23]

One significant difference between the principle of non-extradition and that of protection of refugees lies in the risk to society if return is refused when, in fact, persecution would not have occurred.[24] On the one hand, a suspected or actual criminal is allowed to remain, while on the other hand, someone who is innocent and against whom no allegations are made is not allowed to remain. The attitude to the asylum seeker should be at least as benevolent as that accorded to the fugitive from justice. Lord Diplock took account of the relative gravity of the consequences of the court's expectations proving wrong either one way or the other, and concluded that the appellant need not show that it was more likely than not that he or she would be detained or restricted if returned. A lesser degree of likelihood sufficed such as 'a reasonable chance', 'substantial grounds for thinking', or 'a serious possibility'.[25] Considered in isolation, these terms lack precision. In practice,

---

[21] [1971] 1 WLR 987. The Court considered and applied s. 4(1)(c) of the Fugitive Offenders Act 1967 which provides: 'A person shall not be returned under this Act ... if it appears ... that he might, if returned, be prejudiced at his trial or punished, detained or restricted in his personal liberty by reason of his race, religion, nationality or political opinion.' See now, UK Extradition Act 2003, ss. 13, 81.

[22] [1971] 1 WLR 987, at 993–4. Cf. the quantification of future losses, both pecuniary and non-pecuniary, which courts undertake in personal injury claims; see for example, *Davies* v. *Taylor* [1972] All ER 836, *Jefford* v. *Gee* [1970] 2 QB 130.   [23] [1971] 1 WLR 987, 994.

[24] This point is made in somewhat different fashion in *T* v. *Secretary of State for the Home Department* [1996] AC 742, per Lord Mustill at 755.

[25] [1971] 1 WLR 987, 994. Cf. art. 2, Draft Convention on Territorial Asylum, proposing a 'definite possibility of persecution' as the criterion for the grant of asylum; also art. 3, CAT84; art. 3, ECHR50. For texts, see below, Annexe 1, Nos. 6 & 7; Annexe 2, No. 8. See also Jackman, B., 'Well-founded fear of persecution and other standards of decision-making: A North American perspective', in Bhabha, J. & Coll, G., eds., *Asylum Law and Practice in Europe and North America*, (1992), 44.

however, they are appropriate, beyond the context of municipal law, for the unique task of assessing a claim to refugee status. While the facts on which the claimant relies may be established on a balance of probability, the decision-maker must then make a reasoned guess as to the future, taking account also of the element of relativity between the degree of persecution feared (whether death, torture, imprisonment, discrimination, or prejudice, for example), and the degree of likelihood of its eventuating.[26]

In 1984, UNHCR submitted an *amicus curiae* brief to the US Supreme Court in the *Stevic* case, arguing against the balance of probability, or clear probability, test as the criterion for the grant of asylum. The Court concluded that the well-founded fear standard, which is incorporated into the Refugee Act 1980 as the criterion for the grant of asylum, does not apply to applications for relief from deportation under section 243(h) of the Immigration and Nationality Act;[27] in such cases, relief is conditional on the applicant showing 'a clear probability' of persecution. However, the Court also emphasized that eligibility for asylum under section 208 of the Act remained an entirely separate issue.[28]

Following this ruling, courts and administrative authorities were divided. Officials insisted that well-founded fear requires applicants to show that it is more likely than not that they will be singled out for persecution, a view also followed by the Immigration and Naturalization Service and the Board of Immigration Appeals.[29] In *Acosta*, for example, the applicant appealed against denial both of his application for asylum and for withholding of deportation to El Salvador.[30] His claim was based on active participation in a co-operative organization of taxi-drivers, threatened by anti-government forces seeking to disrupt transportation; a number of taxis were burnt and drivers killed, and the applicant testified to having received a beating and various threats. The Board of Immigration Appeals (BIA) found the applicant's testimony, which was corroborated by other objective evidence in the record, to be worthy of belief; however, it considered this insufficient to meet the statutory standards of eligibility for asylum and withholding of deportation.

The Board referred to the *Stevic* case, but remarked that, 'as a practical matter the showing contemplated by the phrase "a well-founded fear" of persecution converges with the showing described by the phrase "a clear probability" of persecution'. The asylum seeker's fear must be *well-founded* in the sense that, 'an individual's fear of persecution must have its basis in external, or objective, facts that show there is a realistic likelihood he will be persecuted on his return':

---

[26] This approach should not be confused with 'balancing' (on which see further below, 180–4), but reflects the inherent uncertainties in the nature of refugee claims and in the assessment of both personal and background information.   [27] See further below, n. 36.

[28] *INS* v. *Stevic* 467 US 407 (1984); Weinman, S.C., '*INS* v. *Stevic*: A Critical Assessment', 7 *HRQ* 391 (1985).

[29] The Board of Immigration Appeals (BIA) hears appeals, among others, against the decisions of asylum officers; it is housed under the Department of Justice, Executive Office for Immigration Review. Decisions by the BIA and the Attorney-General can be accessed at <http://www.usdoj.gov/eoir>— the 'Virtual Law Library'.   [30] *Acosta*, 19 *I&N Dec.* 211 (BIA, 1985).

... the evidence must demonstrate that (1) the alien possesses a belief or characteristic a persecutor seeks to overcome in others by means of punishment of some sort; (2) the persecutor is already aware, or could easily become aware, that the alien possesses this belief or characteristic; (3) the persecutor has the capability of punishing the alien; and (4) the persecutor has the inclination to punish the alien.[31]

Subjective fears alone were not enough; they must 'have a sound basis in personal experience or in other external facts or events'. The various competing standards of proof (likelihood of persecution, clear probability of persecution, persecution as more likely than not), did not reflect meaningful distinctions in practice.

Although the Board's reasoning is well thought-out and retains a persuasive and pervasive logic, yet it finally demands too much of the asylum seeker, as other courts and other jurisdictions have found, and pays too little attention to the essentially future-oriented and hypothetical assessment attaching to the determination that a well-founded fear of persecution exists.[32]

In due course, the US Supreme Court was called on to rule precisely on the difference, if any, between a 'well-founded fear', and a 'clear probability' of persecution. UNHCR's *amicus curiae* brief in *INS* v. *Cardoza-Fonseca*[33] examined the negotiating history of article 1 of the Convention, and demonstrated that the status of refugee had been intended for a person who has been persecuted or who has 'good reason' to fear persecution, and that the subjective fear should be based on an objective situation, which in turn made that fear plausible and reasonable in the circumstances. It concluded:

No statistical definition is... appropriate to determine the reasonableness of an applicant's fear, given the inherently speculative nature of the exercise. The requisite degree of probability must take into account the intensity of the fear, the nature of the projected harm (death, imprisonment, torture, detention, serious discrimination, etc.), the general history of persecution in the home country, the applicant's personal experience and that of his or her family, and all other surrounding circumstances.[34]

The Supreme Court confirmed its earlier judgment in *Stevic*, but rejected the Government's argument that the clear probability standard also controlled

---

[31] Ibid., 226.

[32] Cf. *Bolanos-Hernandez* v. *Immigration and Naturalization Service*, 749 F.2d 1316 (9th Cir., 1984). The Court of Appeals held that while evidence of a general level of violence was not alone enough, the uncontroverted evidence of a threat to the applicant's own life was sufficient to establish a likelihood of persecution. The documentary evidence submitted also illustrated the likely fate of those who refused to cooperate with the non-governmental forces, and that the guerrillas had both the ability and the will to carry out their threats; to require further corroborative evidence would impose an impossible burden. See also *Hernandez-Ortiz* v. *INS* 777 F.2d 509 (9th Circ., 1985); *Kiala*, 16.580, Commission des recours, 7 Jan. 1983—documentary evidence of the general situation in the country of origin and without specific reference to the claimant is insufficient: cited in Tiberghien, *La protection des réfugiés*, 377.   [33] 480 US 421 (1987).

[34] See UNHCR, *Handbook*, para. 42: 'In general, the applicant's fear should be considered well-founded if he can establish, *to a reasonable degree*, that his continued stay in his country of origin has become intolerable to him for the reasons stated in the definition, or would for the same reasons be intolerable if he returned there.' (Emphasis supplied.) See also, Gibney, M., 'A "Well-founded Fear" of Persecution', 10 *HRQ* 109 (1988).

applications for asylum. The 'ordinary and obvious meaning' of the words used in the Refugee Act, its legislative history and the provisions of the Convention and Protocol, showed that Congress intended to establish a broad class of refugees eligible for the discretionary grant of asylum, and a narrower class with the statutory right not to be deported.[35] Giving the judgment of the Supreme Court, Justice Stevens emphasized the role of discretion. There is no entitlement to asylum, although its benefits once granted are broader than simple relief under 'withholding of removal';[36] the latter is 'country-specific', and merely prohibits deportation to the country or countries in which life or freedom would be threatened. Moreover, while it constrains discretion in the matter of *non-refoulement*, 'the Protocol does not require the granting of asylum to anyone'.[37] The Court found very different meanings in the statutory language. The 'would be threatened' criterion of the withholding of removal provision (and article 33 of the Convention) contains no subjective element; objective evidence showing persecution as more likely than not is therefore required. By contrast, the reference to fear in section 208(a), 'obviously makes the eligibility standard turn to some extent on the subjective mental state' of the applicant.[38] The 'well-founded' qualifier does not entail a clear probability standard: 'One can certainly have a well-founded fear of an event happening when there is a less than 50% chance of the occurrence taking place.'[39]

The Court did not elaborate the standard of proof more precisely, being of the view that a term like 'well-founded fear' is ambiguous to a point, and can only be given concrete meaning through a process of case-by-case adjudication; abstract speculation on the differences between the two standards has its limits, and it remains for the responsible authorities to develop a standard whose 'final contours are shaped by application to the facts of specific cases'.[40]

The debate regarding the standard of proof reveals some of the inherent weaknesses of a system of protection founded upon essays in prediction. It is no easy task to determine refugee status; decision-makers must assess credibility and will look to the demeanour of the applicant. Information on countries of origin may be lacking or deficient, so that it is tempting to demand impossible degrees of corroboration. The applicant's testimony may seem unduly self-serving, though it

---

[35] 480 US 421, 431 (1987).

[36] Ibid., 428–9. The '*non-refoulement*' provision of US law has been changed on a number of occasions. Section 243(h) of the INA initially simply empowered the Attorney General to withhold deportation if of the opinion that the individual would be subject to persecution. This was amended by the 1980 Refugee Act to require that the Attorney General, 'shall not deport or return' any such individual, if he or she determines that that person would be persecuted. However, s. 241(b)(3)(A) now reverts to discretionary mode, to provide that the Attorney-General, 'may not remove an alien to a country if the Attorney-General decides that the alien's life or freedom would be threatened in that country because of race, religion, nationality, membership in a particular social group or political opinion': INA §241(b)(3), 8 USC §1231(b)(3).

[37] 480 US 421, 429, n. 8 (1987).   [38] Ibid., 430–1.   [39] Ibid., 431.

[40] Ibid., 452.

could scarcely be otherwise, absent anyone else to speak on his or her behalf.[41] The onus of establishing a well-founded fear of persecution is on the applicant, and some objective evidence is called for; but documentary corroboration is frequently unavailable or too general to be conclusive in the individual case.

Credibility remains problematic, but the nature of the exercise in prediction and the objective of protection call for account to be taken of consequences, and of degrees of likelihood far short of any balance of probability.[42] This indeed seems now to have been recognized in most jurisdictions involved in individual refugee determination, if not in the assessment of claims to be protected against return to the risk of torture.[43] In *Adjei* v. *Minister of Employment and Immigration*, for example, the Canadian Federal Court of Appeal approved 'good grounds for fearing persecution' as a description of what the evidence must show to support a claim to be a Convention refugee, posing the question, 'Is there a reasonable chance that persecution would take place were the applicant returned to his country?'[44] Swiss law provides that the asylum seeker, 'doit prouver ou du moins rendre vraisemblable qu'il est un réfugié', although 'vraisemblable' appears to mean more than what is merely plausible.[45] The Australian High Court has applied the notion

---

[41] In their own way, both *Acosta* and *Bolanos-Hernandez* underline the importance of personal testimony and documentary evidence.

[42] Cf. Inter-American Court of Human Rights, *Velasquez Rodriguez*, (Forced Disappearance and Death of Individual in Honduras, 29 Jul. 1988): 28 *ILM* 291 (1989)—with respect to the standard of proof, international jurisprudence recognizes the power of the courts to weigh the evidence freely. The standard adopted should take into account the seriousness of the finding; not only direct, but also circumstantial evidence, indicia and presumptions may be considered, and are especially important where the type of repression is characterized by attempts to suppress all information and the State controls the means to verify acts occurring within territory. The object of the proceedings is not to punish, 'but to protect the victims and to provide for the reparation of damages'.

[43] See s. 97, Immigration and Refugee Protection Act 2001, which applies the 'substantial grounds for believing' test; *Li* v. *Minister for Citizenship and Immigration* [2005] 3 FCR 239 (Federal Court of Appeal); *V.N.I.M.* v. *Canada*, UN doc. CAT/C/29/D/119/1998, 19 Dec. 2002, para. 8.3: 'the risk of torture must be assessed on grounds that go beyond mere theory or suspicion. However, the risk does not have to meet the test of being highly probable.' The European Court of Human Rights uses a 'real risk' test for art. 3 ECHR50 purposes: *Soering* v. *United Kingdom* (1989) 11 EHRR 439, para. 27; *Vilvarajah* v. *United Kingdom* (1991) 14 EHRR 248, para. 111.

[44] [1989] 2 FC 680, 683. Speaking for the Court, MacGuigan J. said, 'It was common ground that the objective test is not so stringent as to require a probability of persecution.' In other words, *although an applicant has to establish his case on a balance of probabilities, he does not nevertheless have to prove that persecution would be more likely than not* ... We would adopt that phrasing, which appears to us to be equivalent to that employed by Pratte J. A. in *Seifu* v. *Immigration Appeal Board* [1983] FCJ No. 34 QL; A-277–822, 12 Jan. 1983: '[I]n order to support a finding that an applicant is a Convention refugee, the evidence must not necessarily show that he "has suffered or would suffer persecution"; what the evidence must show is that the applicant has good grounds for fearing persecution for one of the reasons specified in the Act.' (Emphasis supplied.) See also *Salibian* v. *MEI* [1990] 3FC 250; *Arrinaj* v. *Minister for Citizenship and Immigration* [2005] FC 773; *Li* v. *Minister for Citizenship and Immigration* [2003] FC 1514; *Begollari* v. *Minister for Citizenship and Immigration* [2004] FC 1340.

[45] Loi sur l'asile 1999, art. 7(1), 'Preuve de la qualité de réfugié'. The article continues, '2. La qualité de réfugié est vraisemblable lorsque l'autorité estime que celle-ci est hautement probable. 3. Ne sont pas vraisemblables notamment les allégations qui, sur des points essentiels, ne sont pas suffisamment fondées, qui sont contradictoires, qui ne correspondent pas aux faits ou qui reposent de manière déterminante sur des moyens de preuve faux ou falsifiés.'

of a 'real chance', understood to mean a less than fifty per cent possibility,[46] while the United Kingdom House of Lords has confirmed the approach initiated in *Fernandez*: The 'well-founded' requirement, 'means no more than that there has to be demonstrated a reasonable degree of likelihood of . . . persecution . . .'[47]

3.1 THE 2004 EUROPEAN UNION QUALIFICATION DIRECTIVE[48]

Adopted as part of the EU's harmonization drive and efforts to reach a common asylum policy, the Qualification Directive in its final form combines disparate elements, some mandatory, others optional. Differences of approach among EU Member States are likely to remain, but whether as 'higher standards' is questionable, and certain key elements are still unclear, for example, the relationship of the Directive to the 1951 Convention/1967 Protocol and to fundamental rights.[49] The recital's statement of the goals to be achieved is only partially matched by the content which follows, and inconsistencies with governing, emerging or consolidating international standards are apparent.

3.1.1 *The goal of 'common criteria'*

As has been noted above in Chapter 2, the Qualification Directive has a place in an overall, post-Treaty of Amsterdam scheme to establish a 'common policy on asylum', including a Common European Asylum System. This in turn is to be based on 'the full and inclusive application' of the 1951 Convention and the 1967 Protocol, which are recognized as the 'cornerstone of the international legal regime for the protection of refugees'.[50] The main objective is to ensure that Member States 'apply common criteria' for the identification of those generally in

---

[46] *Chan* v. *Minister for Immigration and Ethnic Affairs* (1989) CLR 379—real, that is, substantial chance includes less than 50% likelihood.

[47] *R.* v. *Secretary of State for the Home Department, ex p. Sivakumaran et al.* [1988] 1 AC 958, 1000 (Lord Goff); 994 (Lord Keith). In a 1990 decision, the Administrative Appeals Court of Hesse in the Federal Republic of Germany ruled that the test of persecution was a 'reasonable likelihood': *Hessischer Verwaltungsgerichtshof,* 13 UE 1568/84, 2 May 1990. In a 1989 judgment, the *Tribunal Supremo* of Spain ruled that asylum seekers coming from countries in turmoil need only establish a *prima facie* case in order to qualify for asylum or be granted refugee status: *Tribunal Supremo, Recurso de apelación 2403/88: La Ley,* vol. X, No. 2276 (1989); *Aranzadi,* Tomo LVI, v. III, (1989). The standard of proof for art. 3 claims before the European Court of Human Rights is considerably higher, however; see further below, Ch. 6, s. 3.4.1.   [48] For text, see below, Annexe 2, No. 19.

[49] See Lambert, H., 'The EU Asylum Qualification Directive, its Impact on the Jurisprudence of the United Kingdom and International Law', 55 *ICLQ* 161 (2006); Klug, A., 'Harmonization of Asylum in the European Union—Emergence of an EU Refugee System?' 47 *German Yearbook of International Law* 594 (2004); also, Gil-Bazo, M-T., 'Refugee Status, Subsidiary Protection and the Right to be granted Asylum under EC Law', (2006).

[50] Qualification Directive, Recital, paras. 2, 3. These words are taken from the Presidency Conclusions, Tampere European Council 15 and 16 October 1999, (Tampere Conclusions) para. 13; text in 11 *IJRL* 738 (1999). The Conclusions also identified the aim of 'an open and secure European Union, *fully committed to the obligations of the Geneva Refugee Convention and other relevant human rights instruments,* and able to respond to humanitarian needs on the basis of solidarity . . .' Ibid., para. 4.

need of protection. However, so far as the Directive is about minimum standards, 'so Member States should have the power to introduce or maintain more favourable provisions'.[51]

The goal of common criteria in the determination of Convention refugee status is to be realized in regard to the recognition of refugees through the introduction of 'common concepts of protection needs' in regard to applications *sur place*, sources of harm and protection, internal protection, and persecution, including the reasons for persecution and particularly membership of a particular social group. In keeping with the times, the Directive also deals with the terrorism dimension, endorsing the Security Council view on the purposes and principles of the United Nations, and embracing a concept of *national* security and public order which encompasses *international* terrorism.[52]

While making provision for subsidiary protection, on the one hand,[53] the Directive also draws the line against providing protection against 'risks to which a population . . . or section of the population is generally exposed'.[54] It is doubtful whether this is enough. International law and the legal protection of refugees are in constant development, and evaluation at regular intervals is therefore proposed, with account to be taken 'in particular' of the evolution of international obligations regarding *non-refoulement*;[55] presumably, this would not exclude consideration of other protecting norms and standards. A number of commentators have already called attention to provisions of the Directive which appear to be behind the international standard or otherwise inconsistent with the 1951 Convention/ 1967 Protocol and customary international law.[56]

Alternative terminology and efforts to describe international legal concepts in other words are sometimes harmless and sometimes helpful, but they can also be misleading. For example, the variation between the words chosen to define the refugee in article 2(c) of the Qualification Directive and those in article 1A(2) of the 1951 Convention is mostly harmless, and in one respect correctly clarifies an occasionally recurring misunderstanding in relation to stateless refugees.[57] The definition of 'family members' in article 2(f) chimes with EU law and the practice of many European States, but not necessarily with the international concept.

The first major point of contention to which UNHCR and others have called attention is the Directive's limitation to 'third country nationals', that is, to individuals who are not EU citizens. This is prima facie incompatible with the Convention, so far as article 42 CSR51 permits no reservation to the refugee

---

[51] Qualification Directive, Recital, paras. 6, 8; arts. 1, 3.
[52] Ibid., Recital, paras. 17, 18, 20, 28.   [53] On which see further below, Ch. 6.
[54] Qualification Directive, Recital, para. 26; cf. the scope of human rights protection described below in Ch. 6.   [55] Ibid., para. 36.
[56] See above, n. 49; also UNHCR, 'Observations on the European Commission's Proposal for a Council Directive on Minimum Standards for the Qualification and Status of Third Country Nationals and Stateless Persons Who Otherwise need International Protection', 14109/01 ASILE 54 (16 Nov. 2001).   [57] See further below, s. 4.1.2.

definition in article 1, while article 45 CSR51, which provides that 'Any Contracting State may request revision of this Convention at any time' by way of notification to the UN Secretary-General, has not been exercised.

The revision of multilateral treaties is also governed by established rules of general international law, in particular, those set out in articles 40 and 41 of the 1969 Vienna Convention on the Law of Treaties. Article 41, dealing with modification between certain parties only, confirms that an agreement to modify is permissible only where provided for by the treaty or where, such modification not being prohibited by the treaty, it 'does not affect the enjoyment by the other parties of their rights under the treaty or the performance of their obligations', and 'does not relate to a provision, derogation from which is incompatible with the effective execution of the object and purpose of the treaty as a whole'.[58] In its commentary, the International Law Commission stated that 'the very nature of the legal relation established by a treaty requires that every party should be consulted in regard to any amendment or revision . . . '[59]

Specifically with regard to article 41, the International Law Commission recorded its doubts regarding '*inter se* agreements' for modification, which, history showed, were more likely to be incompatible with the object and purpose of the treaty.[60] Paragraph 2 of article 41 was therefore intended as a further protection for all the parties against 'illegitimate modification';[61] while it does not appear that other parties to the 1951 Convention/1967 Protocol have been so notified,[62] it is also uncertain to what extent the EU modification will affect the rights of other States party or the performance of their obligations, at least so long as no EU State generates refugees. If mainly at present at the theoretical level, this raises issues of importance and interest to general international law which are worthy of further exploration at another time. In particular, the implicit logic of a single European territory without internal borders (if such is ever achieved) challenges certain basic assumptions regarding, among others, the territorial scope of international obligations accepted by the territory's constituent elements, namely, States.[63]

---

[58] 1969 Vienna Convention on the Law of Treaties, art. 41(1)(b).

[59] *Report* of the International Law Commission on its 18th Session, 4 May–19 July 1966, 63, para. (9)—comment to draft art. 35, later art. 40; in its view, this requirement flowed 'directly from the obligation assumed by the parties to perform the treaty in good faith . . . '

[60] *Report* of the International Law Commission on its 18th Session, 4 May–19 July 1966, 65, paras. (1)–(3).

[61] Art. 41(2) provides: 'Unless . . . the treaty otherwise provides, the parties in question shall notify the other parties of their intention to conclude the agreement and of the modification to the treaty for which it provides.'

[62] The earlier 'Spanish Protocol' purported not to amend the Convention, but to establish a rebuttable presumption that all Member States are 'safe countries of origin': Declaration relating to the Protocol on asylum for nationals of Member States of the European Union: *OJ* C 340, 10/11/1997, 141; see also the declaration by Belgium at 144. Bribosia, E. & Weyembergh, A., 'Extradition et asile: vers un espace judiciaire européen?' (1997) *Rev. belge dr.int.* 69.

[63] Among others, the 'logic' would seem to imply EU-wide recognition of status granted in any of its parts, and effective implementation of Convention rights and standards within the Community as a whole.

The Directive/Convention link is unclear in other respects. Article 3, for example, accepts that Member States may introduce or retain more favourable standards for determining who is a refugee, 'in so far as these standards are compatible' with the Directive. The possibility that the Directive, now or in the future, may be incompatible with or lag behind the Convention or other relevant international protection standards is not addressed.[64]

4. The refugee definition and the reasons for persecution

4.1 GENERAL MATTERS

A claimant to refugee status must be 'outside' his or her country of origin,[65] and the fact of having fled, of having crossed an international frontier, is an intrinsic part of the quality of refugee, understood in its ordinary sense. Certain States may provide for those who would be considered as refugees once they took flight,[66] and a growing body of practice aims to bring some measure of protection and assistance to the internally displaced, but this in no way alters the basic international rule.[67]

The Convention requires neither that the putative refugee shall have fled by reason of fear of persecution, nor that persecution should have actually occurred. The fear may derive from conditions arising during an ordinary absence abroad (for example, as student, diplomat or holiday-maker), while the element of well-foundedness looks more to the future, than to the past. Subjective and objective factors are thus combined. Fear, reflecting the focus of the refugee definition in part at least on factors personal to the individual, and the degree to which it is felt,

[64] On the question of the 'primacy' of the Convention and the international obligations of Member States, see Lambert, H., 'The EU Asylum Qualification Directive, its Impact on the Jurisprudence of the United Kingdom and International Law', 55 *ICLQ* 161, 183–90 (2006); Gil-Bazo, M-T., 'Refugee Status, Subsidiary Protection and the Right to be granted Asylum under EC Law' (2006).

[65] Strictly speaking, the refugee must also be without the protection of any other nationality which he or she may possess, or be able to 'activate'; see *Minister of Citizenship and Immigration* v. *Williams* [2005] FCA 126, (2005) 253 DLR (4th) 449—in s. 96 of the Canadian Immigration and Refugee Protection Act, the phrase 'countries of nationality' includes a country were the claimant can obtain citizenship. Cf. *NAFV* v. *MIMIA* (2005) 79 ALJR 609; [2005] HCA 6, in which the High Court rejected the argument that, because they could enter and reside in another country (Israel, under the 'right of return') Australia had no 'protection obligations' to the claimants. See also Taylor, S., 'Protection Elsewhere/Nowhere', 18 *IJRL* 283 (2006).

[66] See United States law: 8 USC §1101(a)(42)(B). UK immigration rules on asylum have been held not to apply to a refugee in a third country (*Secretary of State* v. *Two citizens of Chile* [1977] Imm AR 36) or to a would-be refugee in his or her country of origin (*Secretary of State* v. *X. (a Chilean citizen)* [1978] ImmAR 73). The lawfulness of immigration controls applied by UK officials in a foreign country with a view to preventing travel to the UK of potential asylum seekers was considered by the House of Lords in *R. (European Roma Rights Centre)* v. *Immigration Officer at Prague Airport (UNHCR Intervening)* [2005] 2 AC 1; see further below, 378–89.

[67] On the question of *non-refoulement* and the rejection of refugees at the frontier, see further below, Ch. 5, s. 2.

are incapable of precise quantification.[68] Fear may be exaggerated or understated, but still be reasonable.[69] It is by no means clear, however, whether from the definition, jurisprudence or commentary, how much of a role the subjective element is expected to play in a determination process that is practically oriented to the assessment of *risk*. If the applicant's statements in regard to his or her fear are consistent and credible, then little more can be required in the way of formal proof.[70] What seems to be intended, however, is not so much evidence of subjective fear, as evidence of the subjective aspects of an individual's life, including beliefs and commitments. These help not only to locate the claimant in a social and political context, but also go to the double issue of personal credibility and credible, reasonable fear.[71] For the heart of the question is whether that 'subjective' fear is well-founded; whether there are sufficient facts to permit the finding that this applicant, in his or her particular circumstances, faces a serious possibility of persecution.[72]

Problems of assessment cannot be pursued very far in the abstract. All the circumstances of the case have to be considered, including the relation between the nature of the persecution feared and the degree of likelihood of its happening. At each stage, hard evidence is likely to be absent, so that finally the asylum seeker's own statements, their force, coherence, and credibility must be relied on, in the light of what is known generally, from a variety of sources, regarding conditions in the country of origin.[73]

---

[68] The relevance or value of such an exercise is questionable in cases involving minority or mental disturbance. On children, see further below, s. 5.7.   [69] UNHCR, *Handbook*, paras. 37–41.

[70] Hathaway, *Law of Refugee Status*, 65–97, argues that 'Well-founded fear has nothing to do with the state of mind of the applicant for refugee status . . .', save so far as the claimant's testimony may be evidence of conditions in the country of origin, and that, 'The concept of well-founded fear is rather inherently objective, and was intended to restrict the scope of protection to persons who can demonstrate a present or prospective risk of persecution irrespective of the extent or nature of mistreatment, if any, that they have suffered in the past.' This argument, and the not unreasonable view that what is meant is not so much 'fear' as 'apprehension' or 'anticipation' regarding future events, is developed at some considerable length in Hathaway, J. C. & Hicks, W. S., 'Is there a Subjective Element in the Refugee Convention's Requirement of "Well-founded Fear"?' 26 *Michigan Journal of International Law* 505 (2005); 10, s. 4.; in practice, however, decision-makers do not tend to make much of the subjective issue.   [71] On the assessment of claims, see further below, Ch. 10, s. 4.

[72] The *Ad hoc* Committee referred to a refugee as a person who 'has either actually been a victim of persecution or can show good reasons why he fears persecution': UN doc. E/1618, 39. Evidence of past persecution alone has been considered sufficient in some circumstances; for example, in *Chen*, 20 *I&N Dec.* 16 (BIA, 1989), the Board of Immigration Appeals held that past persecution established a rebuttable presumption of reason to fear future persecution. This position is now part of US asylum regulations; see 8 CFR §208.13(b), which provides that an applicant, 'may qualify as a refugee either because he or she has suffered past persecution or because he or she has a well-founded fear of future persecution', and that an 'applicant who has been found to have established such past persecution shall also be presumed to have a well-founded fear of persecution on the basis of the original claim'. The presumption is rebuttable if it is found, by a preponderance of the evidence, that a fundamental change of circumstances has occurred, or that the applicant could relocate to another part of the country. Cf. *Fernandopulle v. Minister of Citizenship and Immigration* (2005) FCA 9, (2005) 253 DLR (4th) 425—no presumption that past persecution establishes well-founded fear as to the future.

[73] Art. 4(3) of the EU Qualification Directive emphasizes that an application for protection is to be carried out on an individual basis, with account taken of, among others, relevant country of origin

4.1.1 *'Good faith' and activities in the country of refuge*

The UK Court of Appeal decision in *Danian*[74] is a fairly typical example of a small number of cases which periodically raise the question, whether an individual who has engaged in activities in the country of refuge with a view to building a refugee case can nonetheless come within the terms of the 1951 Convention, or whether his or her claim is defeated by lack of 'good faith'. As has been reiterated on many occasions already, the Convention's central premise is that protection should be granted to a person with a well-founded fear of being persecuted for a Convention reason. In the determination of status, the credibility of the claimant and of information relating to his or her country of origin are of critical importance, but the Convention makes no provision as to character, and the essential question remains that of risk of relevant harm if returned. There is no doubt that a person may become a refugee after leaving their country of origin, and the UNHCR *Handbook* recognizes that:

A person may become a refugee 'sur place' as a result of his own actions, such as associating with refugees already recognized, or expressing his political views in his country of residence. Whether such actions are sufficient to justify a well-founded fear of persecution must be determined by a careful examination of the circumstances. Regard should be had in particular to whether such actions may have come to the notice of the authorities of the person's country of origin and how they are likely to be viewed by those authorities.[75]

In deciding that the claimant in *Danian* fell outside the 1951 Convention,[76] the United Kingdom Immigration Appeal Tribunal relied on a number of decisions by the New Zealand Refugee Status Appeals Authority (RSAA), the administrative body responsible for hearing appeals from initial decisions by officials.[77] In one case in particular, the RSAA had concluded that there was indeed a 'good faith' requirement imposed on asylum seekers, although no legal authority was offered in support of the proposition. Nevertheless, in its view, 'without the good

---

information and the applicant's position and personal circumstances, as it were, in context. Previous persecution or threats of harm are 'a serious indication' of well-founded fear, 'unless there are good reasons to consider' that they will not be repeated: art. 4(4). See also art. 4(5), on the benefit of the doubt. The UNHCR *Handbook* suggests that 'Determination of refugee status will...primarily require an evaluation of the applicant's statements rather than a judgement on the situation prevailing in the country of origin' (paras. 37, 42). This apparent attempt to 'depoliticize' the process in no way reflects the practical reality of refugee determination, however, which is precisely an essay in the assessment and evaluation of the situation prevailing in the country of origin. On the sources and uses of documentary information, see further below, Ch. 10, s. 4.2.

[74] [1999] EWCA Civ 3000; see further, see Goodwin-Gill, G. S., 'Comment: Refugee Status and 'Good Faith', 12 *IJRL* 663 (2000). On political activity, see also below, 87–90.

[75] UNHCR, *Handbook*, para. 96.

[76] Decision of the Special Adjudicator in the appeal of Thomas Ataghauma Danian and Secretary of State for the Home Department, Appeal No. CC/30274/97, 29 Oct. 1997; decision of the Immigration Appeal Tribunal in the further appeal in the same matter, Appeal No. CC 30274/97 (16494), 28 May 1998.

[77] *Refugee Appeal: 2254/94 Re HB* (21 Sept. 1994). The 'good faith requirement' does not appear to have come before a New Zealand court.

faith requirement, individuals may unilaterally determine the grant of refugee status to themselves'. This somewhat surprising statement seems to ignore both the criteria set out in article 1A(2) and the particular responsibility of decision-makers in the determination of refugee status, which requires them to assess the personal experiences and credibility of the individual claimant in context, and to assess the likely behaviour of the State of origin or other putative persecutor if the claimant were to be returned. To give primary weight to any less than creditable actions of the individual leaves half the question begging. In addition, even a 'good faith claimant', such as one moved by a sincere change of faith,[78] in effect 'unilaterally' determines the conditions that justify the grant of refugee status.

In fact, the RSAA's views on good faith were unnecessary to the decision, the tribunal finding that the risk of persecution was non-existent. The UK Immigration Appeals Tribunal also found that the claimant did not have a well-founded fear of persecution, but it took the RSAA's views one step further:

the appellant falls within the category of person who is a refugee *sur place*, but who has acted in bad faith. As he has acted in bad faith, he falls outwith the Geneva Convention. He is not a person to whom the Convention applies; this would be our view regardless of whether his activities post 1995 may have brought him to the attention of the Nigerians and *regardless of whether his fear of persecution may be well founded*. (Emphasis supplied)

Both the RSAA and the IAT relied heavily on Grahl-Madsen,[79] but also appear to have misconstrued Hathaway,[80] and were unable to show any more specific authority for their respective positions. Following the decision in *Re HB*, 'good faith' was invoked in a number of other decisions, although on each occasion the (negative) decision itself was based on the absence of a well-founded fear.[81] Australian decision-makers also flirted with the good faith requirement,[82] but in *Mohammed* v. *Minister for Immigration and Multicultural Affairs*, the Federal Court of Australia emphasized that, 'At all times . . . the determination to be made is whether there is a genuine fear of persecution and whether that fear is well-founded . . . [and that] . . . recognition of refugee status cannot be denied to a person whose voluntary acts have created a real risk that the person will suffer persecution occasioning serious harm if that person is returned to the country of nationality.'[83]

---

[78] As recognized by the RSAA in *Refugee Appeal: 70720/97*, 30 Jul. 1998.

[79] Grahl-Madsen, A., *The Status of Refugees in International Law*, vol. 1, (1966), 248, 251–2.

[80] Hathaway, J. C., *The Law of Refugee Status*, (1991), 35, 38, 59; for more detailed analysis, see Goodwin-Gill, above n. 74. See also US practice: Anker, D., *Law of Asylum in the United States*, (3rd edn., 1999), 35–40.

[81] See, for example, *Refugee Appeal No. 70100/96*, 28 Nov. 1997; see also *Refugee Appeal No. 2226/94*, 16 Oct. 1996.

[82] See *Somaghi* v. *Minister for Immigration, Local Government and Ethnic Affairs* 102 ALR 339 (1991); also the following decisions of the Refugee Review Tribunal: *RRT Reference: N98/23213* (11 Nov. 1998); *RRT Reference: V96/04847* (4 Dec. 1996).

[83] [1999] FCA 868, especially paras. 27–8, 31; *MIMA* v. *Mohammed* (2000) 98 FCR 405; [2000] FCA 576-FCA FC; *MIMA* v. *Farahanipour* (2001) 105 FCR 277; [2001] FCA 82—FCA FC.

In *M v. Secretary of State for the Home Department*,[84] the United Kingdom Court of Appeal was concerned, not with the claimant's self-serving actions, but with the question, whether 'a person who puts forward a fraudulent and baseless claim for asylum . . . is not . . . able to bring himself within [the 1951 Convention]'. The Court was unanimously of the view that such a proposition could not be supported. Millett L.J. noted that such a person:

> . . . may be guilty of an attempt to pervert the course of justice and, in theory at least, at risk not only of having his claim dismissed but of finding himself the subject of criminal proceedings. But he *is not thereby deprived of the protection of the convention*. . . . Express exceptions are provided for in the convention itself; they do not include the case where the applicant for asylum has made a previous claim which has been found to be fraudulent and baseless. If, therefore, despite having made such a claim and having had it rejected he can nevertheless at any time thereafter and on whatever basis satisfy the authorities that he has a well-founded fear of persecution for a convention reason if he is returned to the country of his nationality, it would be a breach of the United Kingdom's international obligations under the convention to return him to face possible death or loss of freedom . . .

In his Lordship's view, the asylum seeker still faced the hurdle of establishing a well-founded fear: 'Whether he can do so or not will largely turn on his credibility, and an applicant who has put forward a fraudulent and baseless claim for asylum is unlikely to have much credibility left.'[85]

4.1.2 Statelessness

Article 1A(2) of the Convention makes separate provision for refugees with a nationality and for those who are stateless. For the former, the relevant criterion is that they should be unable or unwilling to avail themselves of the protection of their State of nationality, while the latter should be unable or unwilling to return to their State of former residence.[86] In cases of dual or multiple nationality, refugee status will only arise where the individual in question is unable or unwilling, on the basis of well-founded fear, to secure the protection of any of the States of nationality. In this context, whether the link of nationality is effective in the sense of general international law will be a relevant consideration.[87]

---

[84]   [1996] 1 WLR 507.

[85]   Ibid, 513; see also the judgment of Ward L.J. at 516–17.

[86]   See report of the *Ad hoc* Committee: UN doc. E/1618, 39: 'The Committee agreed that for the purposes [of this provision], and therefore the draft Convention as a whole, "unable" refers primarily to stateless refugees but includes also refugees possessing a nationality who are refused passports or other protection by their own government. "Unwilling" refers to refugees who refuse to accept the protection of the government of their nationality.' A number of decisions, particularly in Canada, have recognized that 'inability' also describes the situation of claimants who cannot obtain protection, for example, because the government or authorities of their country are non-existent, ineffective, or in active or passive collusion with the persecutors; see *Zalzali v. Minister of Employment and Immigration* [1991] FCJ No. 341.

[87]   Cf. Goodwin-Gill, G.S., *International Law and the Movement of Persons between States*, (1978), 46–9; Piotrowicz, R., '*Lay Kon Tji v. Minister for Immigration and Ethnic Affairs*: The Function and Meaning of Effective Nationality in the Assessement of Applications for Asylum', 11 *IJRL* 544 (1999).

Statelessness and refugee status are by no means identical phenomena.[88] On occasion, those fleeing may be deprived of their nationality, but it is quite common also for the formal link to remain. Following the Russian revolution in 1917, large numbers of citizens were stripped of their status and for years Soviet Jews leaving the country permanently were required to renounce their citizenship. Refugee status in such cases might appear determinable in the light of the situation prevailing in the country of origin as the 'country of former habitual residence'.[89] However, in addition to internal repressive measures applied to those seeking to leave that country,[90] the denationalization itself provided compelling testimony of denial of protection. Whether it severs the effective link for all purposes of international law, including the responsibility of States, is less clear, but the expulsion of an unwanted minority could not justifiably be predicated upon the municipal act of deprivation of citizenship.[91]

One question which has arisen is whether a stateless person unable to return to his or her country of former habitual residence may qualify as a Convention refugee without having to show that he or she is outside such country by reason of a well-founded fear of persecution. The possibility that a different standard of protection was intended for stateless refugee claimants arises from a grammatical 'anomaly' in article 1A(2), which appears not to apply the 'well-founded fear' requirement in the same way to those with and those without a nationality. If interpreted literally, as Cooper J. said in *Rishmawi* v. *Minister for Immigration and*

---

[88] A stateless person has been defined as 'a person who is not considered as a national by any State under the operation of its law' in art. 1, 1954 Convention relating to the Status of Stateless Persons: 360 *UNTS* 117. By 16 votes to 1 with 4 abstentions the Conference preceding the Convention adopted a recommendation that each contracting State 'when it recognises as valid the reasons for which a person has renounced the protection of the State of which he is a national' should consider sympathetically extending the Convention to such persons. See also the 1961 Convention on the Reduction of Statelessness: UN doc. A/CONF.9/15, Final Act, where the Conference recommended that 'persons who are stateless *de facto* should as far as possible be treated as stateless *de jure* to enable them to acquire an effective nationality'; text in Brownlie & Goodwin-Gill, *Basic Documents on Human Rights*, (5th edn., 2006), 329. Cf. Weis, who for long criticized the terminology of *de facto* and *de jure* statelessness, for example, in 72 *AJIL* 680–1 (1978), reviewing Mutharika, *The Regulation of Statelessness under International and National Law: Texts and Documents* (1977); Weis, P., 'The Convention relating to the Status of Persons', 10 *ICLQ* 255 (1961); 'The UN Convention on the Reduction of Statelessness', 11 *ICLQ* 1073 (1962); Batchelor, C., 'Statelessness and the Problem of Resolving Nationality Claims', 10 *IJRL* 156 (1998).

[89] There is no historical, textual or commonsensical basis for one commentator's view that because a stateless person is not 'returnable' to his or her country of former habitual residence, so he or she is not in danger of being *refouled* and therefore is not a refugee: Hathaway, *Law of Refugee Status*, 59–63. None of the citations or references to the *travaux préparatoires* provides any support for the 'returnability' gloss. Although this notion was adopted by some members of Canada's Convention Refugee Determination Division, principally as a ground for denying protection to Palestinians expelled from the Gulf States after the first Gulf War in 1991, it has since been categorically rejected by the Federal Court; see, for example, *Desai* v. *Canada (Minister of Citizenship and Immigration)* [1994] FCJ No. 2032; also, New Zealand, RSAA, *Refugee Appeal No. 73861*, 30 Jun. 2005, likewise rejecting the attempt of another panel (in *Refugee Appeal No. 72635*, 6 Sept. 2002) to 'rehabilitate' the returnability test.

[90] For details of practice in an earlier period, see *Religious Minorities in the Soviet Union*, (Minority Rights Group, report no. 1, rev. ed. 1977), 18–20.

[91] See Fisher Williams, J., 'Denationalization', 8 *BYIL* 45 (1927).

Multi-Cultural Affairs, the effect would be that 'a stateless person outside his or her country of former habitual residence for a reason other than a Convention reason and unable to return to it for whatever reason other than a Convention reason would by definition be a refugee'.[92] That there are indeed certain practical differences between stateless and other refugees has been recognized in a number of judicial decisions. Courts in Austria and Germany, for example, have found in favour of refugee claimants outside their country of former habitual residence and unable to obtain its protection or to return there.[93] In Canada, the law imposes the requirement of well-founded fear on both categories, as a condition of presence outside the country of nationality/country of former habitual residence,[94] but the stateless person's particular lack of protection has been recognized by Canadian courts. In *Thabet* v. *Minister of Citizenship and Immigration*, the Federal Court of Appeal said that:

... it is important to note the key distinction between the two groups of people so that neither advantages nor disadvantages are created. The distinction is contained in the wording of the refugee definition itself. In the case of nationals it talks of the claimant being 'unwilling to avail himself of the protection of that country'. In the case of stateless persons it talks only of an unwillingness to return to that country. In this latter case the question of the availment of protection does not arise... The definition takes into account the inherent difference between those persons who are nationals of a state, and therefore are owed protection, and those persons who are stateless and without recourse to state protection. Because of this distinction one cannot treat the two groups identically, even though one should seek to be as consistent as possible.[95]

The view now generally accepted, and which makes sense in pursuit of a 'single test' for refugee status, is that no substantial difference is intended between stateless and other refugees, and that the Convention aims to provide protection to a

---

[92] [1997] 77 FCR 421, 428 (Federal Court of Australia). For recognition of a similar anomaly during the 1951 Conference and an amendment to ensure equality of treatment by reference to the relevant causal events, namely, 'events occurring before 1 January 1951', see Summary Record of the 34th Meeting, 25 July 1951: UN doc. A/CONF.2/SR.34, 12 (Mr Hoare); the British amendment was adopted by 17 votes to none, with 3 abstentions.

[93] See, for example, Decision of the Austrian Administrative Appeals Court, in *A.* v. *Ministry of Internal Affairs*, Verwaltungsgerichtshof = (Austrian) Administrative Appeals Court, 29 Jan. 1986. 84/01/0106. SlgNF 12.005(A) = Sammlung der Erkentnisse und Beschlüsse des Verwaltungsgerichtshofes, Neue Folge, Administrativrechtlicher Teil = Collection of Decisions pp. 47–50. Also, Decision of the Administrative Court of Berlin of 3 Nov. 1989: Verwaltungsgericht Berlin = Administrative Court Berlin. 3 Nov. 1989. No. VG 10 A 4.88.

[94] See now s. 2(1), Immigration and Refugee Protection Act 2001 (formerly s. 2(1)(a)(i), (ii), Immigration Act 1976).

[95] *Thabet* v. *Canada (Minister of Citizenship and Immigration)* [1998] 4 FC 21, para. 17. See also *Pachkov* v. *Minister*, IMM-2340–98, Federal Court of Canada—Trial Division, 8 Jan. 1999, per Teitelbaum J. at para. 20.'The main difference in the application of [the legislation] is that people who have a nationality are required to demonstrate a lack of State protection in the country of their nationality. This obligation is not imposed on stateless persons, who have to demonstrate that they are unable, or by reason of their fear, unwilling to return.' For further litigation arising out of the same case, though on a different matter, see *Pachkov* v. *Minister of Citizenship and Immigration*, IMM-5449–99, 28 Jun. 2000. See also *Al-Anezi* v. *Minister for Immigration & Multicultural Affairs* (1999) 92 FCR 283; [1999] FCA 355 (Federal Court of Australia).

person, whether outside their country of nationality, or, not having a nationality and outside their country of former habitual residence, who has a well-founded fear of being persecuted on Convention grounds.[96]

4.2 REASONS FOR PERSECUTION

The Convention identifies five relevant grounds of persecution, all of which, in varying degrees, have been correspondingly developed in the field of non-discrimination.[97] The linkage to discrimination has been taken up in many leading decisions in different jurisdictions, although the extent to which discrimination is always a *necessary* element of persecution raises some theoretical issues which are briefly discussed below.[98]

4.2.1 Race

With regard to *race* for example, account should be taken of article 1 of the 1966 Convention on the Elimination of All Forms of Racial Discrimination which defines that practice to include distinctions based on 'race, colour, descent, or national or ethnic origin'.[99] Given legal developments over the last forty or so years, the broad meaning can be considered valid also for the purposes of the 1951 Convention, although interpretative challenges may still occur. Verdirame, for example, reviewing the jurisprudence of the International Criminal Tribunals, notes a shift towards the greater use of 'subjective criteria', including self-perception and the perception of others: 'The Tribunals are . . . beginning to acknowledge that collective identities, and in particular ethnicity, are by their very nature social constructs, "imagined" identities entirely dependent on variable and contingent perceptions, and *not* social facts, which are verifiable in the same manner as natural phenomena or physical facts.'[100]

Persecution on account of race is all too frequently the background to refugee movements in all parts of the world.[101] The international community has

---

[96] *Revenko* v. *Secretary of State for the Home Department* [2001] QB 601, [2000] 3 WLR 1519, per Pill L.J., §§1–75. No consideration of the interpretation of art. 1A(2) with regard to stateless persons would be complete without a reading of the judgment of Katz J in *Savvin* v. *Minister for Immigration and Ethnic Affairs* [2000] 171 ALR 483. See now also art. 2(c), EU Qualification Directive.

[97] See generally, UNHCR, *Handbook*, paras. 66–86; Grahl-Madsen, *Status of Refugees*, vol. 1, (1966), 217–53; Hathaway, *Law of Refugee Status*, 135–88. The substantive linkage to non-discrimination was recognized by the Canadian Supreme Court in *Attorney-General* v. *Ward* [1993] 2 SCR 689. On the specific issue, see also Vierdag, E. W., *The Concept of Discrimination in International Law*, (1973); McKean, W. A., 'The Meaning of Discrimination in International and Municipal Law', 44 *BYIL* 177 (1970); Goodwin-Gill, *Movement of Persons*, 75–87.   [98] See further below, 90–2, 128–9.

[99] See also art. 10(1)(a), Qualification Directive.

[100] See Verdirame, G., 'The Genocide Definition in the Jurisprudence of the *Ad Hoc Tribunals*', 49 *ICLQ* 578, 592–4 (2000).

[101] For example, Ugandan citizens of Asian origin were persecuted and expelled in 1972: see Goodwin-Gill, *Movement of Persons*, 212–16. The same year, large numbers of Burundi citizens of the Hutu tribe were massacred, while many others fled into neighbouring countries: *Selective Genocide in*

expressed particular abhorrence at discrimination on racial grounds, as evidenced by repeated resolutions of the General Assembly, but the point at which such practices amount to persecution of themselves is more controversial.[102]

4.2.2 Religion

Religion has long been the basis upon which governments and peoples have singled out others for persecution. In 1685, thousands of Huguenots fled from France to England and Prussia after revocation of the Edict of Nantes opened the way to massacre and oppression. The late nineteenth century witnessed pogroms of Jews in Russia and of Armenian Christians in Ottoman Turkey. The past century likewise saw large-scale persecution of Jews under the hegemony of Nazi and Axis powers up to 1945, with later targets in other regions including Jehovah's Witnesses in Africa and among the Commonwealth of Independent States, Muslims in Burma, Baha'is in Iran, Ahmadis in various Islamic countries, and believers of all persuasions in totalitarian and self-proclaimed atheist States.[103]

Article 18 of the 1966 Covenant on Civil and Political Rights, elaborating article 18 of the Universal Declaration of Human Rights, prescribes that everyone shall have the right to freedom of thought, conscience, and religion, which shall include the freedom to have or adopt a religion or belief of choice and the freedom to manifest such religion or belief.[104] Moreover, no one is to be subject to coercion

---

Burundi, Minority Rights Group, report no. 20, 1974; cf. US Committee for Refugees, 'Transition in Burundi: The Context for a Homecoming,' Sept., 1993. The combination of genocidal massacres in Rwanda in 1994 and successful military resistance caused the internal and external displacement of many thousands of both Hutu and Tutsi citizens: Prunier, G., 'La crise rwandaise: structures et déroulement', 13 *RSQ*, Nos. 2 & 3, 13 (1994); Degni-Ségui, R., 'Rapports sur la situation des droits de l'homme au Rwanda du 28 juin 1994 et du 12 août 1994', ibid., 116. After 1975 thousands of Vietnamese citizens of Chinese ethnic origin felt compelled, along with many others, to seek protection in the countries of South East Asia: see above, Ch. 2, n. 63, and sources cited. In apartheid South Africa, institutionalized discrimination and its politics of repression likewise contributed to large-scale exodus: 'Human Rights, War and Mass Exodus', *Transnational Perspectives* (1982), 11, 14. See also Tiberghien, *La protection des réfugiés*, 87f, 329–35.

[102] See further below, s. 5.2. In the view of the European Commission on Human Rights, discrimination on racial grounds could, in certain circumstances, constitute degrading treatment within the meaning of art. 3 ECHR50: Decision on Admissibility, *Patel*, Application No. 4403/70 *et al.* v. *United Kingdom* Oct. 1970, 30. Cf. *Ali* v. *Secretary of State* [1978] ImmAR 126 (discrimination likely to be faced by Kenyan citizen of Asian origin did not amount to persecution).

[103] For summary accounts of the treatment of religious minorities in different States, see the Country Reports on Human Rights Practices, submitted annually by the US Department of State to the US Congress: <http://www.state.gov/g/drl/rls/hrrpt/>. See also Forum 18, an NGO based in Oslo, Norway, which promotes the implementation of art. 18 UDHR48: <http://www.forum18.org/>.

[104] Art. 9 ECHR50 likewise recognizes the freedom to change religion or belief, although a distinction may be drawn between the freedom to practise religious belief and the right to proselytize; see *Kokkinakis* v. *Greece* (1994) 17 EHRR 397, paras. 33, 44, 48–9. For a studied critique of the Court's jurisprudence, see Evans, eds., C., *Freedom of Religion under the European Convention on Human Rights*, (2001); also, Janis, M. & Evans, C., eds., *Religion and International Law*, (2004). On interference with the manifestation of religion, see *R. (SB)* v. *Governors of Denbigh High School* [2006] 2 WLR 719, [2006] UKHL 15.

which would impair the freedom to have or adopt a religion or belief of choice.[105] In 1962, the General Assembly requested the Commission on Human Rights to draw up a draft declaration and draft convention on the elimination of all forms of intolerance based on religion or belief,[106] and in 1967 it took note of the Preamble and article 1 of a proposed convention,[107] in which the Third Committee had suggested that the expression 'religion or belief' should include 'theistic, non-theistic and atheistic beliefs'.[108] The Declaration on the Elimination of All Forms of Intolerance and of Discrimination Based on Religion or Belief, adopted in 1981, indicates the interests to be protected, the infringement of which may signal persecution.[109] Religion-based claims nevertheless present their own challenges, both for advocates and decision-makers,[110] and the 'content' of the right to freedom of thought, conscience, and religion continues to be the subject of enquiry.[111]

4.2.3 Nationality

The reference to persecution for reasons of *nationality* is somewhat odd, given the absurdity of a State persecuting its own nationals on account of their membership of the body politic. Those who possess the nationality of another State will, in normal circumstances, be entitled to its protection and so fall outside the refugee definition. Conceivably, the nationals of State B resident in State A could find themselves persecuted on account of their nationality, driven out to a neighbouring

[105] In *NABD* v. *MIMIA* (2005) 79 ALJR 1142, the High Court of Australia noted that the right legal question to ask was not whether it was possible for the claimant to live in Iran in such a way as to avoid adverse consequences, but whether the claimant had a well-founded fear of persecution in Iran on the ground of religion. See also *Wang* v. *MIMA* (2000) 105 FCR 548; [2000] FCA 1599, in which the Full Court of Federal Court of Australia held that 'religion' includes the practice of a religious faith in community with others, and that a law regulating such practice, or applying only to those practising religion, is not a law of general application. Fear of prosecution or punishment for breach of such laws can therefore give rise to a well-founded fear of persecution for a Convention reason. The fact that an applicant has brought or intends to bring into existence circumstances that give rise to a fear of persecution by an unnecessary or unreasonable voluntary act (such as worshipping at a non-registered church) may be relevant to assessing the genuineness of the claim but is not determinative of whether the fear is well-founded.　　　　[106] UNGA res. 1781(XVII), 7 Dec. 1962.
[107] UNGA res. 2295(XXII), 11 Dec. 1967.
[108] Article reproduced in *Elimination of All Forms of Religious Intolerance, Note by the Secretary-General*: UN doc. A/8330, 8. This article, which includes definitions of discrimination on religious grounds and of religious intolerance, was adopted by 91 votes in favour, 2 against, with 6 abstentions. See also art. 10(1)(b), Qualification Directive.
[109] Declaration adopted without vote by UNGA res. 36/55 of 25 Nov. 1981; text in Brownlie, I. & Goodwin-Gill, G. S., *Basic Documents on Human Rights*, (5th edn., 2006), 74.
[110] See Akram, S. M., 'Orientalism Revisited in Asylum and Refugee Claims', 12 *IJRL* 7 (2000); Good, A., 'Persecution for Reasons of Religion under the 1951 Refugee Convention: An Anthropological Approach', 2006 Elizabeth Colson Lecture, Refugee Studies Centre, Oxford; UNHCR, Guidelines on International Protection: 'Religion-Based Claims under Article 1A(2) of the 1951 Convention and/or the 1967 Protocol relating to the Status of Refugees', HCR/GIP/04/06, 28 Apr. 2004; Helton, A. C. & Münker, J., 'Religion and Persecution: Should the United States provide Refuge to German Scientologists?' 11 *IJRL* 310 (1999); Musalo, K., 'Claims for Protection based on Religion or Belief', 16 *IJRL* 165 (2004).
[111] See the annual reports of the Special Rapporteur on freedom of religion, appointed by the Commission on Human Rights in 1986; for example, UN docs. E/CN.4/2005/61, 20 Dec. 2004; E/CN.4/2006/5, 9 Jan. 2006; see also *Report* on the Situation of Human Rights in the Sudan: UN doc. E/CN/.4/1994/48 (1 Feb. 1994), para. 79—apostasy; see also UN doc. E/CN.4/1992/52.

country and yet still denied the protection of State B, particularly that aspect which includes the right of nationals to enter their own State.[112] However, nationality in article 1A(2) of the 1951 Convention is usually interpreted more loosely, to include origins and the membership of particular ethnic, religious, cultural, and linguistic communities.[113] It is not necessary that those persecuted should constitute a minority in their own country, for oligarchies traditionally tend to resort to oppression.[114] Nationality, interpreted in this way, illustrates the points of distinction which can serve as the basis for the policy and practice of persecution.[115] There may be some overlap between the various grounds and, likewise, factors derived from two or more of the criteria may contribute cumulatively to a well-founded fear of persecution.

4.2.4 Membership of a particular social group[116]

Further potential overlap lies in the criterion, *membership of a particular social group*.[117] The 1951 Convention is not alone in recognizing 'social' factors as a

---

[112] Such denial of protection could easily arise through the haphazard workings of citizenship and immigration laws; cf. the situation of citizens of the United Kingdom and Colonies resident in East Africa, discussed in Goodwin-Gill, *Movement of Persons*, 101–3, 164–7. See also the following decisions of the Commission des recours des réfugiés: *Huang*, 12,935 and 13,451, 26 janv. 1982, cited by Tiberghien, *La protection des réfugiés*, 318.

[113] See art. 10(1)(c), Qualification Directive, which adds 'common geographical or political origins or [a group's] relationship with the population of another State'. Cf. *London Borough of Ealing* v. *Race Relations Board* [1972] AC 342, in which the court *excluded* nationality from the generic term 'national origin'. Note art. 27 ICCPR 66: 'In those States in which ethnic, religious or linguistic minorities exist, persons belonging to such minorities shall not be denied the right, in community with the other members of their group, to enjoy their own culture, to profess and practise their own religion, or to use their own language.' See also Grahl-Madsen, *Status of Refugees*, vol. 1, (1966), 218–19; Report of the independent expert on minority issues, Gay McDougall, UN doc. E/CN.4/2006/74, 6 Jan. 2006; Capotorti, F., *Study on the Rights of Persons belonging to Ethnic, Religious and Linguistic Minorities* (1978): UN doc. E/CN/4/Sub. 2/384/Rev. 1, 5–15, 95–6; Rights of Persons belonging to National and Ethnic, Religious and Linguistic Minorities: UN doc. E/CN.4/1994/72 (13 Dec. 1993); Pejic, J., 'Minority Rights in International Law', 19 *HRQ* 666 (1997); Pentassuglia, G., *Minorities in International Law*, (2002). Cf. Report of the Special Rapporteur on the situation of human rights and fundamental freedoms of indigenous people, Rodolfo Stavenhagen, UN doc. E/CN.4/2006/78, 16 Feb. 2006; Martinez Cobo, *Study of the Problem of Discrimination against Indigenous Populations* (1979): UN doc. E/CN.4/Sub. 2/L. 707; Elles, *International Provisions Protecting the Human Rights of Non-Citizens* (1980): UN doc. E/CN.4/Sub. 2/392/Rev. 1, 25f.

[114] *Selective Genocide in Burundi*, above, n. 101; see also the analysis in *The Two Irelands—the Double Minority*, (Minority Rights Group, report no. 2, rev. ed., 1979).

[115] Grahl-Madsen notes that persecution for reasons of nationality is also understood to include persecution for lack of nationality, that is, by reason of statelessness: *Status of Refugees*, vol. 1, 219. See further on the particular situation of Palestinians, below, Ch. 4, s. 3.2.

[116] See UNHCR, Guidelines on International Protection: ' "Membership of a Particular Social Group" within the Context of Article 1A(2) of the 1951 Convention and/or its 1967 Protocol Relating to the Status of Refugees': HCR/GIP/02/02, 7 May 2002 (hereafter, UNHCR *Guidelines No. 2*, 'Membership of a Particular Social Group'); Aleinikoff, T. A., 'Protected characteristics and social perceptions: An analysis of the meaning of "membership of a particular social group",' in Feller, Türk, & Nicholson, *Refugee Protection in International Law*, 263; Summary Conclusions on membership of a particular social group, ibid., 312;

[117] Henri Tajfel, in *The Social Psychology of Minorities*, (Minority Rights Group, report no. 38, 1978), cites at p. 3 Simpson and Yinger, *Racial and Cultural Minorities*, (1965), 17, for the following

potential irrelevant distinction giving rise to arbitrary or repressive treatment. Article 2 of the 1948 Universal Declaration of Human Rights includes 'national or social origin, property, birth or other status' as prohibited grounds of distinction,[118] a form of words repeated in article 2 of the 1966 Covenants on Economic, Social, and Cultural Rights and Civil and Political Rights; it also appears in article 26 of the latter Covenant, which calls for equality before and equal protection of the law.

The *travaux préparatoires* provide little explanation for why 'social group' was included. The Swedish delegate to the 1951 Conference simply stated that social group cases existed, and that the Convention should mention them explicitly.[119] The lack of substantive debate on the issue suggests that contemporary examples of such persecution may have been in the minds of the drafters, such as resulted from the 'restructuring' of society then being undertaken in the socialist States and the special attention reserved for landowners, capitalist class members, independent business people, the middle class and their families.

The initial intention may thus have been to protect known categories from known forms of harm; less clear is whether the notion of 'social group' was expected or intended to apply generally to then unrecognized groups facing new forms of persecution. The answer to that question will never be found, but there is no reason in principle why this ground, like every other, should not be progressively developed.[120] The experience of 1951 is also illustrative, for its implicit reference to the perception or attitude of the persecuting authority. It is still not unusual for governments publicly to write off sections of their population—the petty bourgeoisie, for example, or the class traitors; and even more frequent will be those occasions on which the identification of groups to be neutralized takes place

---

set of definitional criteria appropriate for the identification of social minorities: '(1) Minorities are subordinate segments of complex state societies; (2) minorities have special physical or cultural traits which are held in low esteem by the dominant segments of the society; (3) minorities are self-conscious units bound together by the special traits which their members share and by the special disabilities which these bring; (4) membership in a minority is transmitted by a rule of descent which is capable of affiliating succeeding generations even in the absence of readily apparent special cultural or physical traits; (5) minority peoples, by choice or necessity, tend to marry within the group'.

[118] During debate on the Universal Declaration, the USSR stressed the importance of abolishing 'differences based on social conditions as well as the privileges enjoyed by certain groups in the economic and legal fields'.

[119] UN docs. A/CONF.2/SR.3, p.14—Mr Petren (Sweden): 'experience had shown that certain refugees had been persecuted because they belonged to particular social groups. The draft Convention made no provision for such cases, and one designed to cover them should accordingly be included'; also SR.19, p.14; SR.23, p.8—Swedish amendment adopted by 14–0-8; A/CONF.2/9—text of amendments.

[120] See *Islam v. Secretary of State for the Home Department* [1999] 2 AC 629, 651 per Lord Hoffmann: 'the concept of a social group is a general one and its meaning cannot be confined to those social groups which the framers of the Convention may have had in mind. In choosing to use the general term "particular social group" rather than an enumeration of specific social groups, the framers of the Convention were in my opinion intending to include whatever groups might be regarded as coming within the anti-discriminatory objectives of the Convention.' See also Lord Hope at 657. This case involved the consolidated appeals, *Islam v. Secretary of State for the Home Department* and *R. v. Immigration Appeal Tribunal, ex p. Shah*.

covertly. In eastern Europe in the late 1940s and the 1950s, groups and classes and their descendants were *perceived* to be a threat to the new order, whatever their individual qualities or beliefs. In Vietnam in the late 1970s, the bourgeoisie were similarly seen as an obstacle to economic and social restructuring (in circumstances in which class and ethnicity happened to combine). The *characteristics* of the group and its individual members were what counted. More recently, attention has focused on other discrete candidate groups, including women, homosexuals, and those with HIV/AIDs, among others. As paragraph 78 of the UNHCR *Handbook* puts it:

> Membership of a particular social group may be at the root of persecution because there is no confidence in the group's loyalty to the government or because the political outlook, antecedents or economic activity of its members, or the very existence of the social group as such, is held to be an obstacle to the Government's policies.

Especially important is the conjunction of 'internal' characteristics and 'external' perceptions.[121] *Linking*, rather than unifying, characteristics, more accurately represent social reality, while circumstances external to the group may have isolated it from the rest of society, or may lead to its separate treatment.

A superficial linguistic analysis suggests people in a certain relation or having a certain degree of similarity, or a coming together of those of like class or kindred interests. A fully comprehensive definition is impracticable, if not impossible, but an essential element in any description would be a combination of matters of choice with other matters over which members of the group have no control. In determining whether a particular group of people constitutes a 'social group' within the meaning of the Convention, attention should therefore be given to the presence of linking and uniting factors such as ethnic, cultural, and linguistic origin; education; family or other background; economic activity; shared values, outlook, and aspirations.[122] Also highly relevant are the attitude to the putative social group of other groups in the same society and, in particular, the treatment accorded to it by State authorities. The importance, and therefore the identity, of a

---

[121] Cf. *Prosecutor* v. *Jelisic*, Case No. ICTY-I-95-10, 14 Dec. 1999, Trial Chamber, para. 70: '... it is more appropriate to evaluate the status of a national, ethnical or racial group from the point of view of those persons who wish to single out that group from the rest of the community ... It is the stigmatisation of a group as a distinct national, ethnical or racial unity by the community which allows it to be determined whether a targeted population constitutes a national, ethnical or racial group in the eyes of the alleged perpetrators.' Quoted in Verdirame, G., 'The Genocide Definition in the Jurisprudence of the *Ad Hoc Tribunals*', 49 *ICLQ* 578, 593–4 (2000).

[122] The US Board of Immigration Appeals adopted very similar language in *Acosta*, 19 *I&N Dec.* 211 (BIA, 1985); applying the *ejusdem generis* rule, the BIA limited its understanding of the term 'social group' to reflect a common, immutable characteristic, that is, one which it is either beyond the power of an individual to change, or which is so fundamental to individual identity or conscience that changing it should not be required. This might include sex, class, kinship or even shared past experience, but membership of a taxi-drivers' co-operative, or a particular manner of wage-earning, did not fall within such a class of characteristics. For an alternative view on the inappropriateness of the *ejusdem generis* rule in this context, see Goodwin-Gill, G. S., 'Judicial Reasoning and "Social Group" after *Islam* and *Shah*', 11 *IJRL* 528 (1999); see also McHugh J., in *Applicant A* v. *MIEA* [1997] HCA 4, 71 ALJR 381, 401.

social group may well be in direct proportion to the notice taken of it by others—
the view which others have of us—particularly at the official level. The notion of
social group thus possesses an element of open-endedness capable of expansion, as
the jurisprudence shows, in favour of a variety of different classes susceptible to
persecution.[123]

4.2.4.1 The concept develops[124]

The 1986 United States case of *Sanchez-Trujillo* v. *INS* illustrates some of the
problematic issues that arise in identifying a social group at risk of persecution.
The asylum applicants from El Salvador based their claim on membership of a
class that included young, urban, working-class males, who were further identified
as unwilling to serve in the armed forces of their country.[125] Anticipating the need
to 'identify a cognizable group', the claimants adduced fairly cogent statistical
evidence showing the numbers of such young, urban non-combatant males who
figured among the disappeared and the dead, to which they added personal
testimony and experience. The court found little guidance in the UNHCR
Handbook reference to 'persons of similar background, habits or social status',[126]
considering instead that a social group implied 'a collection of people closely affil-
iated with each other who are actuated by some common impulse or interest'.
Moreover, 'a voluntary associational relationship' was also required, 'which imparts
some common characteristic that is fundamental to their identity'. In the court's
view, 'family members' were a prototypical example, conveniently meeting its criteria of affiliation, common interest, or association. The family also has the advantage of being finite; it is usually small, readily identifiable, and terminable with
difficulty. Potentially larger categories, including so-called statistical groups, such
as the red-headed, the blue-eyed, or the over six-feet tall,[127] were dismissed, even

---

123 Many commentators have favoured a broad approach; cf. Grahl-Madsen, *Status of Refugees*,
vol. 1, (1966), 219—'the notion . . . is of broader application than the combined notions of racial,
ethnic and religious groups . . .'; Helton, A. C., 'Persecution on Account of Membership in a Social
Group as a Basis for Refugee Status', 15 *Col. Hum. Rts.L.R.* 39 (1983). It is not, however, a 'catch-all'
provision: Hathaway, *The Law of Refugee Status*, 159. Cf. Council of Europe Committee of Ministers
Recommendation Rec(2004)9 on the concept of 'membership of a particular social group', 30 Jun.
2004, which recommends that the concept 'should be interpreted in a broad and inclusive manner in
the light of the object and purpose of the 1951 Convention', although not so as to 'extend the scope of
the Convention to impose upon states obligations to which they have not consented . . .'
124 For earlier cases, cf. Grahl-Madsen, *Status of Refugees*, vol. 1, 219–20; *Lai* v. *Minister of
Employment and Immigration* [1989] FCJ No. 826—capitalist background in China resulted in persecution due to family's social position; *De Valle* v. *INS* 901 F.2d 787 (9th Cir., 1990)—family members of deserters manifest diverse and different life-styles and varying interests and therefore do not
constitute a social group; *Ramirez-Rivas* v. *INS* 899 F.2d 864 (9th Cir., 1990)—name association
with family subject to persecution sufficient to support social group claim.
125 801 F.2d 1571 (9th Cir. 1986).
126 UNHCR, *Handbook*, para. 77; *Secretary of State for the Home Department* v. *K* [2006] UKHL
46, para. 98.
127 Cf. Helton, A. C., 'Persecution on Account of Membership in a Social Group as a Basis for
Refugee Status', 15 *Col. Hum. Rts. L.R.* 39 (1983).

though such arbitrary classifications have been the basis for persecutory practices in the past. Like others before and since, this court was evidently anxious to guard against 'sweeping demographic divisions' that encompass a plethora of different lifestyles, varying interests, diverse cultures, and contrary political leanings. Thinking and application have progressed substantially in the subsequent practice of States and tribunals, if not always without difficulty.

During the 1990s, the social group category produced several, not always easily reconcilable, judgments in different jurisdictions and particularly in Canada. The cases there involved China's 'one-child policy', so far as it was claimed that the parents of one or more children might run the risk of forcible sterilization and whether a social group could be based on sexual orientation, or on a fear of 'domestic' violence in their own country by women unable to obtain protection locally. One leading case concerned a former terrorist group member, who feared retribution at the hands of the group.[128]

In *Cheung*, the Canadian Federal Court of Appeal held that 'women in China who have (more than) one child and are faced with forced sterilization satisfy enough of the . . . criteria to be considered a particular social group'.[129] In *Chan*, another case based on fear of forced sterilization (this time by a father), a majority of the Supreme Court dismissed the appeal on the ground that the appellant had not discharged the burden of proof, with respect either to the subjective or objective elements.[130]

Ward concerned a resident of Northern Ireland who had voluntarily joined the Irish National Liberation Army (INLA), a terrorist group dedicated to the political union of Ulster and the Irish Republic. Detailed to guard innocent hostages, he facilitated their escape on learning that they were to be executed. The INLA in

---

[128] See, among others, *Cheung* v. *MEI* [1993] 2 FC 314 (Federal Court of Appeal); *Attorney-General* v. *Ward* [1993] 2 SCR 689 (Supreme Court of Canada; hereafter *Ward*); and *Chan* v. *MEI* [1993] 3 FC 675 (Federal Court of Appeal), [1995] 3 SCR 593 (Supreme Court of Canada; hereafter *Chan*). Daley, K. & Kelley, N., 'Particular Social Group: A Human Rights Based Approach in Canadian Jurisprudence', 12 *IJRL* 148 (2000); Kelley, N., 'The Convention Refugee Definition and Gender-Based Persecution: A Decade's Progress', 13 *IJRL* 559 (2001).

[129] [1993] 2 FC 314, 320; the court in *Chan* considered that the bracketed words 'more than' had been omitted accidentally.

[130] [1993] 3 FC 675, 692–3; [1995] 3 SCR 593. See the High Court of Australia's review of case law from different jurisdictions in *Applicant A* v. *MIEA* [1997] HCA 4, 71 ALJR 381, 401. See also, US Board of Immigration Appeals, *Chang*, 20 *I&N Dec.* 38 (BIA, 1989), finding the birth control policy not persecutory on its face, but a matter for case-by-case evaluation. The ruling in practise was significantly modified by policy instructions and later by legislation locating the issue in 'political opinion', not social group. In 1996, the refugee definition section of the Immigration and Nationality Act was amended to insert at the end: ' . . . a person who has been forced to abort a pregnancy or to undergo involuntary sterilization, or who has been persecuted for failure or refusal to undergo such a procedure or for other resistance to a coercive population control program, shall be deemed to have been persecuted on account of political opinion, and a person who has a well founded fear that he or she will be forced to undergo such a procedure or subject to persecution for such failure, refusal, or resistance shall be deemed to have a well founded fear of persecution on account of political opinion': 8 USC §1101(a)(42)(B). Dauvergne, C., 'Chinese Fleeing Sterilisation: Australia's Response against a Canadian Background', 10 *IJRL* 77 (1998).

turn 'court-martialled' and tortured him and decided that he should be killed. Amongst other grounds, he claimed to fear persecution by reason of membership in the particular social group constituted by the INLA. The Supreme Court of Canada held that the group of INLA members were not a 'particular social group'; its membership was not characterized by an innate characteristic or an unchangeable historical fact, while its objectives also could not be said to be so fundamental to the human dignity of its members.[131]

The Supreme Court in *Ward* recognized also that the process of interpreting particular social group should reflect certain themes, namely, human rights and anti-discrimination. It considered that there were three possible categories of social group: (1) those defined by an innate or unchangeable characteristic, for example, individuals fearing persecution by reason of gender, linguistic background and sexual orientation; (2) those whose members voluntarily associate for reasons so fundamental to their human dignity that they should not be forced to forsake the association, for example, human rights activists;[132] and (3) those associated by a former voluntary status, unalterable due to its historical permanence. Given that 'one's past is an immutable part of the person',[133] the third category belongs essentially to the first.

4.2.4.2 The categories of association

The *Ward* judgment is of major importance on a variety of issues, but the analysis of the social group question raises a number of concerns. What is meant by 'groups associated by a former voluntary status', is far from clear. The Court said that this sub-category was included 'because of historical intentions'. However, there is no evidence to suggest that those apparently intended to benefit from the social group provision, the former capitalists of eastern Europe, were ever formally associated one with another. They may have been, but equally they may not. What counted at the time was the fact that they were not only *internally* linked by having engaged in a particular type of (past) economic activity, but also *externally* defined, partly if not exclusively, by the perceptions of the new ruling class.[134]

As the Supreme Court in fact recognized, capitalists were persecuted historically, 'not because of their contemporaneous activities but because of their past

---

[131] Why the refugee claim was based on social group was never clear. The claimant's fear was not based on membership, but on his actions in a political context, motivated by conscience; political opinion was first raised by UNHCR in its intervenor brief; see *Ward*, [1993] 2 SCR 689, 740. Also, Bagambiire, D., 'Terrorism and Convention Refugee Status in Canadian Immigration Law: The Social Group Category according to *Ward* v. *Canada*', 5 *IJRL* 183 (1993), which considers the earlier Federal Court of Appeal decision.

[132] In *Cheung*, particular weight was attached to a woman's reproductive liberty as a basic right fundamental to human dignity. Women in China who have more than one child were 'united or identified by a purpose which is so fundamental to their human dignity that they should not be required to alter it': [1993] 2 FC 314, 322.   [133] *Ward* [1993] 2 SCR 689, 739.

[134] New ruling *social group*? Thus, in the sense of the text, the government of the Socialist Republic of Vietnam announced its intention to 'restructure' society and abolish the 'bourgeoisie': Foreign Language Press, *The Hoa in Vietnam*, (1978).

status *as ascribed to them by the Communist leaders*'.[135] In this sense, they were persecuted not because they were *former* capitalists, but because they *were* former capitalists; not because of what they had done in the past, but because of what they were considered to be today; not because of any actual or imagined voluntary association, but because of the perceived threat of the class (defined *incidentally* by what they had once done) to the new society. The approach of the new ruling class to the capitalist class reveals a clear overlap between *past* activity and/or status and the perception of a *present* threat to the new society.[136]

Having proposed a 'limiting' approach to social group,[137] it is hardly surprising that the Supreme Court at first seems conservative in its list of innate or unchangeable characteristics: 'such bases as gender, linguistic background and sexual orientation'.[138] In fact, this approach is not as restrictive as might appear; the list is clearly illustrative, and in principle other innate or unchangeable factors relevant to non-discrimination in the enjoyment of fundamental rights may also be included, such as ethnic or cultural factors, education, family background, property, birth or other status, national or social origin;[139] in short, the very sorts of *social* factors that are or ought to be irrelevant to the enjoyment of fundamental human rights.

Economic activity, shared values, outlook and aspirations should not be excluded, because either they are part of the unchangeable past,[140] or they describe, if only generally, the idea of individuals associated for reasons fundamental to their human dignity, and the sort of 'value' association which voluntary participants ought not to be required to forsake.

4.2.4.3 Common victimization

In *Ward*, the Supreme Court was clearly of the view that an association of people should not be characterized as a particular social group, 'merely by reason of their

---

[135] *Ward* [1993] 2 SCR 689, 731, emphasis supplied.

[136] In one sense, the 'grouping' will often be independent of will, so that the requirement of voluntary associational relationship, if adopted in all cases, not only introduces an unjustified, additional evidential burden on the claimant (under the guise of interpretation), but also departs from the jurisprudence of earlier years, admittedly sparse, which nonetheless recognized the existence of a social group among individuals, who displayed little if any *voluntary* association relationship with others similarly situated. See, however, La Forest J., diss., in *Chan* [1993] 3 FC 675, para. 87, also quoting Macklin, 'Review Essay', at 375.

[137] 'Foreign governments should be accorded leeway in their definition of what constitutes anti-social behaviour of their nationals. Canada should not overstep its role in the international sphere by having its responsibility engaged whenever any group is targeted': *Ward* [1993] 2 SCR 689, 738–9. See also *Chan* [1995] 3 FC 675, La Forest J., diss., para. 65.

[138] *Ward* [1993] 2 SCR 689, 739.

[139] In *C-A-*, 23 *I&N Dec.* 951 (BIA, 2006), the Board of Immigration Appeals affirmed that 'sex' and 'family membership' are obvious examples of characteristics which define a social group, and that 'social visibility' can help to define other particular social groups. On the 'family' see also the judgment of Lord Hope in *Secretary of State for the Home Department* v. *K(FC)* [2006] UKHL 46 (decided jointly with *Fornah*), paras. 39–52; Lord Rodger, paras. 61–8; Baroness Hale, paras. 104–7.

[140] In which case it is irrelevant that economic activity is not a matter of fundamental human rights; what counts is that the activity 'links' people who then, on the basis of perceptions among the ruling class or society at large, are subject to treatment amounting to persecution.

common victimization as the objects of persecution';[141] on this point, it has been joined by courts in other jurisdictions.[142] The essential question, however, is whether the persecution feared is the *sole* distinguishing factor that results in the identification of the particular social group. Taken out of context, this question is too simple, for wherever persecution under the law is the issue, legislative provisions will be but one facet of broader policies and perspectives, *all* of which contribute to the identification of the group, adding to its pre-existing characteristics.

For example, parents with one or more children can be considered as an identifiable social group because of (1) their factual circumstances and (2) the way in which they are treated in law and by society. Arbitrary laws might subject red-headed people, mothers of one or more children, and thieves to a variety of penalties, reflecting no more than the whims of the legislator. Where such laws have a social and political context and purpose, and touch on fundamental human rights, such as personal integrity or reproductive control, then a rational basis exists for identifying red-headed people and mothers of one or more children as a particular social group, *in their particular circumstances*, while excluding thieves.[143] For the purposes of the Convention definition, internal linking factors cannot be considered in isolation, but only in conjunction with external defining factors, such as perceptions, policies, practices, and laws.

Treatment amounting to persecution thus remains relevant in identifying a particular social group, where it reflects State policy or civil society attitudes towards a particular class.[144] As the penal law embodies State policy on criminals, so other laws and practices may illustrate policy towards individuals or groups who assert fundamental rights, for example, with respect to family life or conscience.[145] In both cases, the penalties help to identify the group at risk; so far as they also exceed the limits of reasonableness and proportionality, they may also cross the line from permissible 'sanction' for contravention of a particular social policy into impermissible persecution.

[141] *Ward* [1993] 2 SCR 689, 729; also *Chan* [1993] 3 FC 675 (FCA).
[142] See *Islam* v. *Secretary of State for the Home Department* [1999] 2 AC 629, per Lord Steyn at 634; Lord Hope at 656; *Applicant A* v. *MIEA* [1997] HCA 4, 71 ALJR 381, 401 (McHugh J.).
[143] See Macklin, 'A Review Essay', at 371–8.
[144] As McHugh J. remarked in *Applicant A* v. *MIEA* [1997] HCA 4, 71 ALJR 381, 402, 'while persecutory conduct cannot define the social group, the actions of the persecutors may serve to identify or even cause the creation of a particular social group in society...' For that reason also, 'To identify a social group, one must first identify the society of which it forms a part': Lord Hoffman, *Islam* v. *Secretary of State for the Home Department* [1999] 2 AC 629, 652; Lord Hope: 'The word "social" means that we are being asked to identify a group of people which is recognised as a particular group by society. As social customs and social attitudes differ from one country to another, the context for this inquiry is the country of the person's nationality. The phrase can thus accommodate particular social groups which may be recognisable as such in one country but not in others or which, in any given country, have not previously been recognised': ibid., 657.
[145] See below, s. 5.5.1, on conscientious objection to military service.

4.2.4.4 Women, social group, and refugee status[146]

Although the principle of non-discrimination on the ground of sex is now well established in international law, gender was not included in article 1A(2) as the basis for a well-founded fear of persecution. The need for protection in this field has nevertheless been recognized, as claims began to be made by women seeking refuge from 'domestic' violence and from violence against women in society. From the perspective of the 1951 Convention, however, the problem with much of the violence against women is precisely that it is perceived, either as 'domestic', or as individual and non-attributable to the State or other political structure.[147] The term 'domestic violence' is commonly used to describe spousal violence applied in a domestic setting, out of the public eye, and for reasons personal to the aggressor. It is 'private', unlike the 'public' dimension to so much political, ethnic, or religious persecution, and it tends to serve individual, usually male, ends, such as aggression, sadism, oppression, or subjection.[148] Violence has been considered as non-attributable to the State, when perpetrated by random individuals for personal reasons, including soldiers, policemen, or other holders of public authority, such as civil officials or State religious leaders, when acting outside or beyond authority.

Many societies have long turned a blind eye to domestic violence, on the ground that unless it was 'excessive', it was not a proper matter for State involvement or State penalties. The *policy* implicit in such a laissez-faire approach, not surprisingly, has found its reaction in the proposition that *all* violence against women is political, or in its slightly less radical variant, that all violence against women should be presumed to be political unless and until the State is shown to provide effective protection. Thus, it is argued, being a woman is a sufficiently political statement in itself, so far as violence against women, domestic, sexual or public, is part of the process of oppression.

Within the scheme of international protection offered by the 1951 Convention relating to the Status of Refugees and its national counterparts, such an approach

---

[146] See UNHCR, Guidelines on International Protection: 'Gender-Related Persecution within the Context of Article 1A(2) of the 1951 Convention and/or its 1967 Protocol Relating to the Status of Refugees': HCR/GIP/02/01, 7 May 2002.

[147] See generally, Crawley, H., *Refugees and Gender: Law and Process*, (2001); Anker, D., Gilbert, L. & Kelly, N., 'Women whose governments are unable or unwilling to provide reasonable protection from domestic violence may qualify as refugees under United States asylum law', 11 *Georgetown Immigration Law Journal* 709 (1997).

[148] See generally, Castel, J. R., 'Rape, Sexual Assault and the Meaning of Persecution', 4 *IJRL* 39 (1992); Thomas, D. Q. & Beasley, M. E., 'Domestic Violence as a Human Rights Issue', 15 *HRQ* 36 (1993); *Prosecutor* v. *Akayesu*, Case No. ICTR-96-4-T, paras. 687-8; Anker, D., 'Rape in the Community as a Basis for Asylum: The Treatment of Women Refugees' Claims to Protection in Canada and the United States', 2 *Bender's Immigration Bulletin*, No. 12 (15 June 1997), Part I—Canada, 476-84; No. 15 (1 August 1997), Part II—The United States, 608-22; Heyman, M. G., 'Domestic Violence and Asylum: Toward a Working Model of Affirmative State Obligations', 17 *IJRL* 729 (2005).

has not found support as such, and periodic proposals to add gender to the list of Convention reasons have not been taken up. Women claimants may yet come within the refugee definition, drawing by analogy on rights-based approaches in other circumstances, on increasing sensitivity to the frequently systemic character of denials of rights to women, and on underlying obligations incumbent on all States to protect the human rights of everyone within their territory and subject to their jurisdiction. Executive Committee Conclusion No. 39 (1985) was an early step towards better protection, although it simply recognizes that States, 'in the exercise of their sovereignty', may interpret 'social group' to include women who face harsh or inhuman treatment for having transgressed the social mores of their community.[149] The 1993 UN Declaration on the Elimination of Violence against Women,[150] moreover, acknowledges that all States have an obligation to work towards its eradication.

What might at first glance appear 'domestic' may enter the public arena and therefore the traditional refugee domain when it passes into the ambit of State-sanctioned or State-tolerated oppression. This raises evidential considerations of some magnitude, however, and at a certain point cases call rather for a value judgment, than a purely factual assessment of conditions in this or that country. Nevertheless, gender-related persecution will often have political purposes, including the enforcement of conformity to a particular religious, cultural, or social view of society;[151] such persecution has included torture or oppression by State agents at the individual level, as well as more generalized harassment by sections of the public.[152] Rape by a soldier, policeman, or person in authority, for example, may be characterized as the unauthorized private act of an individual, and therefore not persecution. An examination of the context in which the act takes place, however, may disclose a manifestation of public State authority; the conditions and the occasion may as much be the responsibility of the State, as the

---

[149] *Report* of the 36th Session: UN doc. A/AC.96/673, para. 115(4). The first edition of this work in 1983 suggested that it *may* be the case that the discrimination suffered by women in many countries on account of their sex alone, though severe, is not yet sufficient to justify the conclusion that they, as a group, have a fear of persecution within the meaning of the Convention. Times have changed, though the need for protection is no less.

[150] UNGA res. 48/104, 20 Dec. 1993. See also 1995 Beijing Declaration and Platform for Action; 1994 Inter-American Convention on the Prevention, Punishment and Eradication of Violence against Women: 33 *ILM* 1534 (1994); all texts in Brownlie & Goodwin-Gill, *Basic Documents on Human Rights*, 186, 205, 970

[151] See France, CRR, Sections réunies, 15 mars 2005, 489.014, *Mlle T*—accepted that in certain parts of Turkey the refusal to submit to forced marriage was regarded as unacceptable by the population and the authorities, and could lead to the risk of ill-treatment and so-called honour crimes without the possibility of local protection; women in this situation were consequently members of a particular social group.

[152] Art. 1 of the 1993 UN Declaration interprets violence against women widely: 'any act of gender-based violence that results in, or is likely to result in, physical, sexual or psychological harm or suffering to women, including threats of such acts, coercion or arbitrary deprivation of liberty, whether occurring in public or private life'. Such violence is seen not so much in terms of individual behaviour, but as a 'manifestation of historically unequal power relationships between men and women', which may occur in the family, in the general community, or be perpetrated or condoned by the State.

failure to provide an effective remedy. For women suffer particular forms of persecution *as women*, and not just or specifically because of political opinion or ethnicity. Even though men too may be sexually abused, their gender is not a
consideration. Women may be raped because of their politics, but they are also
raped because they are women and because rape inflicts a particular indignity and
promotes a particular structure of male power.[153]

Even if 'domestic' violence is given a public, political face, however, there is still
some distance between the act and the *reasons* in the Convention definition.[154]
The State is unwilling or unable to prevent or punish such violence as might otherwise amount to persecution, but *why* is the claimant so affected? The language
of political opinion does not readily fit, and the question is whether membership
of a particular social group will establish the sufficient link.

If it is assumed that gender, in principle, is a sufficient identifying factor held in
common, so that all women may comprise a social group, is this enough for
Convention purposes to show that the woman who faces domestic or even public
violence is persecuted *for reasons of* membership in that group?[155] The answer,
some have argued, lies in further sub-categorization, and in *Islam*, for example,
counsel argued that some three characteristics set the appellants apart from the
rest of society, namely, gender, suspicion of adultery, and unprotected status.[156] In
this case, the applicants, citizens of Pakistan otherwise unconnected with each
other, suffered violence in their country of origin after their husbands had falsely
accused them of adultery. They applied for asylum in the United Kingdom on the
ground that having been abandoned by their husbands, lacking any other male
protection and condemned by the local community for sexual misconduct, they
feared persecution if returned, in that they would be physically and emotionally

---

[153] See *Prosecutor* v. *Akayesu*, Case No. ICTR-96–4-T, paras. 687–688: 'Like torture, rape is used
for such purposes as intimidation, degradation, humiliation, discrimination, punishment, control or
destruction of a person. Like torture, rape is a violation of personal dignity, and rape in fact constitutes torture when it is inflicted by or at the instigation of or with the consent or acquiescence of a
public official or other person acting in an official capacity...' See also Haines, R., 'Gender-related
persecution', in Feller, Türk, & Nicholson, *Refugee Protection in International Law*, 319, 336: 'Women
are particularly vulnerable to persecution by sexual violence as a weapon of war', and citing also
Crawley, H., *Refugees and Gender: Law and Process*, 89–90; UNHCR, *Guidelines No. 1*, 'Gender-
Related Persecution', para. 24.

[154] See Musalo, K., 'Revisiting Social Group and Nexus in Gender Asylum Claims: A Unifying
Rationale for Evolving Jurisprudence', 52 *De Paul Law Review* 777 (2003); Kelly, N., 'Guidelines for
Women's Asylum Claims', 6 *IJRL* 517 (1994); Mawani, N., 'Introduction to the Immigration and
Refugee Board of Canada Guidelines on Gender-Related Persecution', 5 *IJRL* 240 (1993); 'IRB:
Guidelines on Gender-Related Persecution', 5 *IJRL* 278 (1993); Oosterveld, V. L., 'The Canadian
Guidelines on Gender-Related Persecution: An Evaluation', 8 *IJRL* 569 (1996).

[155] See *Secretary of State for the Home Department* v. *K* [2006] UKHL 46; *MIMA* v. *Khawar* (2002)
210 CLR 1, [2002] HCA 14—High Court of Australia; also, RSAA, *Refugee Appeal No. 75609*, 2
Jun. 2006, referring to the unequal status of women and 'a systemic failure by the state to protect victims of domestic violence': para. 75.

[156] *Islam* v. *Secretary of State for the Home Department* [1999] 2 AC 629, 643–4 (Lord Steyn);
652–3 (Lord Hoffmann); see also *Secretary of State* v. above note, paras. 27–31 (Lord Bingham); 53–8
(Lord Hope); 75–81 (Lord Rodger); 111–14 (Baroness Hale).

abused, ostracised and unprotected by the authorities, and might be liable to death by stoning. Three judges (Lord Steyn, Lord Hoffmann, and Lord Hope) considered that women in Pakistan constituted a particular social group, because they were discriminated against as a group in matters of fundamental human rights, because the state gave them no protection, and because they were perceived as not being entitled to the same human rights as men. Two judges (Lord Steyn and Lord Hutton) considered that the applicants also belonged to a more narrowly defined particular social group, the unifying characteristics of which were gender, being suspected of adultery, and lacking protection from the state and public authorities. Although not all members of the group were persecuted, the persecution feared by the applicants was sanctioned or tolerated by the State was for reasons of membership of a particular social group; they were accordingly entitled to asylum.[157]

As this case demonstrates, when taking account of conditions in a particular country, it may become clear that the group within the group is identifiable by reference to the fact of their liability, exposure or vulnerability to violence in an environment that denies them protection. Such a social group of women may be additionally identifiable by reference to other descriptors, such as race or class, which leads to their being denied protection in circumstances in which other women in the same society are not (so) affected or deprived. They face violence amounting to persecution, and other denials of rights, because of their gender, their race and their class and because they are unprotected.[158] Clearly, gender *is* used by societies to organize or distribute rights and benefits; where it is also used to deny rights or inflict harm, the identification of a gender-defined social group has the advantage of external confirmation.[159]

4.2.4.5 A social view of 'social group'
The jurisprudence of recent years shows courts and tribunals in different jurisdictions wrestling with the concept of particular social group, and a coherent, general

---

[157] For comment, see Vidal, M., ' "Membership of a particular social group" and the effect of *Islam* and *Shah*', 11 *IJRL* 528 (1999); Goodwin-Gill, G. S., 'Judicial Reasoning and "Social Group" after *Islam* and *Shah*', 11 *IJRL* 537 (1999).

[158] Laws of general application can operate similarly. The refugee sub-group, that is, the group within the larger group of those conforming or reluctantly conforming, is identified by the fact of prosecution and/or liability to sanction, considered together with the assertion by the sub-group of certain fundamental rights, such as those relating to conscience or belief. See *Wang* v. *MIMA* (2000) 105 FCR 548; [2000] FCA 1599—FCA FC.

[159] In *Applicant A* v. *MIEA* [1997] HCA 4, 71 ALJR 381, 401 n.120, McHugh J. referred to the Canadian court's finding in *Mayers* 97 DLR (4th) 729 (1992), that a Trinidadian woman who had been abused by her husband for many years was a refugee because she was a member of a particular social group. He noted that it seemed to have been common ground between the parties that the relevant group was 'Trinidadian women subject to wife abuse', but it did not follow 'that the applicant was abused because of her *membership* of that group' (emphasis in original). Macklin, however, identifies the 'risk factor' in both *Mayers* and *Cheung* (a forcible sterilization case; above n. 128) as one's identity as a woman: 'A Review Essay', at 377. Cf. Lord Millett, dissenting, in *Islam* v. *Secretary of State for the Home Department* [1999] 2 AC 629, 653–4.

approach is beginning to emerge.[160] Clearly, there are social groups other than those that share immutable characteristics, or which combine for reasons fundamental to their human dignity. Drawing the contours of such groups by reference to the likelihood of persecution confuses the issues of identity and risk, despite the fact that each is relevant to the other. The individualized approach of the Convention refugee definition requires attention to personal circumstances, time and place, all of which may combine to distinguish those at risk from others who may share similar characteristics and yet not be in danger. Although there will be policy pressures to limit refugee categories in periods of increased population displacement, there is no rational basis for denying protection to individuals who, even if divided in lifestyle, culture, interests and politics, may yet be linked across another dimension of affinity.

There is probably no single coherent definition, but rather a set of variables, a 'range of permissible descriptors'. These include, for example, (1) the fact of voluntary association, where such association is equivalent to a certain *value* and not merely the result of accident or incident, unless that in turn is affected by the way it is perceived; (2) involuntary linkages, such as family, shared past experience, or innate, unalterable characteristics; and (3) the perception of others.[161]

In the cases considered above, the courts inclined towards relatively simple bases of categorization, relying on innate or unchangeable characteristics and notions of association for reasons fundamental to human dignity. There are many 'natural' meanings of 'social', however, which have received little or no attention, but which may also prove a sufficient and appropriate basis for defining or describing social groups for the purposes of the Convention. Beyond the ideas of individuals associated, allied, or combined, characterized by mutual intercourse, united by some common tie,[162] stand those who, in simple sociological terms, are *groups in society*, in the ordinary, everyday sense which describes the constitution or make-up of the community at large. This is most evident in the use of language to describe, for example, the landlord class, the working class, the ruling class, the bourgeoisie, the middle class, even the criminal class. For this reason it helps to emphasise, not so much that the group is, as it were, 'set apart from society', as that it is essentially a group *within* society which is faced with persecution within the

---

[160] UNHCR, Guidelines on International Protection: '"Membership of a Particular Social Group" within the Context of Article 1A(2) of the 1951 Convention and/or its 1967 Protocol Relating to the Status of Refugees': HCR/GIP/02/02, 7 May 2002. These *Guidelines* were expressly approved by the House of Lords in *Fornah* [2006] UKHL 46.

[161] Cf. Council of Europe Committee of Ministers Recommendation Rec(2004)9 on the concept of 'membership of a particular social group' in the context of the 1951 Convention relating to the status of refugees, 30 Jun. 2004, for the position that 'a "particular social group" is a group of persons who have, or are attributed with, a common characteristic other than the risk of being persecuted and who are perceived as a group by society or identified as such by the state or the persecutors. Persecutory action towards a group may however be a relevant factor in determining the visibility of a group in a particular society'.

[162] 'Cohesiveness', however, is not required: *Islam v. Secretary of State for the Home Department* [1999] 2 AC 629, 632, 640–3 (Lord Steyn); 651 (Lord Hoffmann); 657 (Lord Hope); 662 (Lord Millett).

social context of that very society (including its attitudes, prejudices and actions).[163] The principle of non-discrimination, linked to fundamental rights, serves to distinguish between those deserving protection, because their social origins or situation now put them at risk; and those who do not, such as those who are liable to penalties for breach of the law, considered in its ordinary, common law sense.[164]

If a sociological approach is adopted to the notion of groups in society, then apparently unconnected and unallied individuals may indeed satisfy the criteria: mothers; mothers and families with two children; women at risk of domestic violence; capitalists; former capitalists, homosexuals,[165] and so forth. Whether they then qualify as refugees having a well-founded fear of persecution by reason of their membership in a particular social group will depend on answers to related questions, including the perceptions of the group shared by other groups or State authorities, policies and practices vis-à-vis the group, and the risk, if any, of treatment amounting to persecution. It can be difficult to recognize when discrimination shades into persecution, particularly where minority or even majority groups are systematically treated less favourably than others. One defining moment may occur when the individual group member chooses to oppose the system, by overt action or simply by non-conformity, actual or perceived. The proximate cause may be action or non-conformity, but the underlying *reason for* the persecution can often clearly be elsewhere; so with the social group, women, particularly in societies in which the attitudinal dimension indicates necessary conformity with another's particular image of herself.[166]

4.2.5 Political opinion

Finally, the Convention adduces fear of persecution for reasons of political opinion. Article 19 of the 1948 Universal Declaration of Human Rights provides

---

163 See above, n. 144.

164 Cf. art. 10(1)(d), EU Qualification Directive, which prescribes in part that, 'a group shall be considered to form a particular social group where in particular:—members of that group share an innate characteristic, or a common background that cannot be changed, or share a characteristic or belief that is so fundamental to identity or conscience that a person should not be forced to renounce it, and—that group has a distinct identity in the relevant country, because it is perceived as being different by the surrounding society . . . ' The axiomatic linkage of innate characteristics *and* social perception is somewhat dogmatic and out of touch with much of the doctrine described above, while the accompanying language on gender and sexual orientation ('might include', 'might be considered') is equivocal, to say the least. In *Fornah* [2006] UKHL 46 several of the judgments emphasize that this provision must be interpreted as if the criteria were *alternatives*, and that the Directive should be applied accordingly; Lord Bingham, para. 15; Lord Brown, para. 118. For full text of art. 10 and the Directive, see below, Annexe 2, No. 19.

165 See *Navaez* v. *Canada (Minister of Citizenship and Immigration)* [1995] FCJ No. 219; *Hernandez-Montiel* v. *INS*, 225 F.3d 1084, 1094 (9th Cir. 2000)—recognizing as a distinct social group 'gay men with female sexual identities in Mexico'.

166 Note, however, the caveat sounded by McHugh J. in *Applicant A* v. *MIEA* [1997] HCA 4, 71 ALJR 381, 401, concluding that the simple fact of opposition to policy or law is not itself sufficient to link individuals and that there is nothing external in the way of social attribute or characteristic to allow them to be perceived as a social group.

that: 'Everyone has the right to freedom of opinion and expression; the right includes freedom to hold opinions without interference and to seek, receive and impart information and ideas through any media and regardless of frontiers.' The basic principle is restated in article 19 ICCPR66, but the right to freedom of expression is qualified there by reference to 'special duties and responsibilities'. Certain types of opinion may therefore be judged unacceptable.[167]

In the 1951 Convention, 'political opinion' should be understood in the broad sense, to incorporate, within substantive limitations now developing generally in the field of human rights, any opinion on any matter in which the machinery of State, government, and policy may be engaged.[168] The typical 'political refugee' is one pursued by the government of a State or other entity on account of his or her opinions, which are an actual or perceived threat to that government or its institutions, or to the political agenda and aspirations of the entity in question.[169] Political opinions may or may not be expressed, and they may be rightly or wrongly attributed to the applicant for refugee status.[170] If they have been expressed, and if the applicant or others similarly placed have suffered or been threatened with repressive measures, then a well-founded fear may be made out. Problems arise, however, in assessing the value of the 'political act', particularly if the act itself stands more or less alone, unaccompanied by evident or overt expressions of opinion.[171] Political activity undertaken in the country of (potential) refuge also poses

---

[167] Cf. art. 4 ICERD66; art. 10 ECHR50; *Handyside* v. *U.K.*, (1976) 1 EHRR 737; *Sunday Times* v. *U.K.*, (1979) 2 EHRR 245; *Arrowsmith* v. *U.K.* (1978) 3 EHRR 218.

[168] This wording was adopted and endorsed by the Supreme Court of Canada in *Attorney General* v. *Ward* [1993] 2 SCR 689; see also *Klinko* v. *Minister of Citizenship and Immigration (T.D.)* [2000] 3 FC 327, (2000), 184 DLR (4th) 14, §22, further approving the above interpretation.

[169] The approach to political opinion in art. 10(1)(e) of the Qualification Directive is tied to the potential 'actors of protection' identified in art. 7, not just to State and government, while art. 10(2) rightly recalls that it is immaterial whether the applicant for protection actually possesses the relevant characteristic, provided it is attributed to him or her by the persecutor.

[170] In *Ward*, the Supreme Court of Canada held that circumstances should be examined from the perspective of the persecutor, since this perspective is determinative in inciting the persecution: [1993] 2 SCR 689, 747. Cf. *S-P-*, 21 *I&N Dec.* 486, 487 (BIA, 1996), discussing and reaffirming *B-*, 21 *I&N Dec.* 66 (BIA, 1995), and noting that in the latter, the Board 'did not become entangled in the impossible task of determining whether harm was inflicted because of the applicant's acts or because of his beliefs underlying those acts'.

[171] It may not always be appropriate to view the (objective) political act as equivalent to the (subjective) notion of political opinion, for the asylum seeker's actual motivation can make such an approximation pure fiction. The same applies in the case of the individual who is likely to be persecuted for political opinions *wrongly* attributed to him or her, and the humanitarian aspects of such cases may be better accommodated in a liberal asylum practice, than in a forced interpretation of refugee status criteria. However, see Belgium, Conseil d'Etat, no. 135.838, *x c/ C.G.R.A.*, 8 oct. 2004: *RDDE*, 2004, No. 130, 591—the claimant's activities considered as political by his persecutors, though he himself had no significant political opinion; *Briones* v. *INS*, 175 F.3d 727, 729 (9th Cir., 1999), holding that 'activity as a confidential informer who sided with the... military in a conflict that was political at its core certainly would be perceived as a political act by the group informed upon.' Cf. *INS* v. *Elias-Zacarias*, 502 US 478 (1992), in which a majority of the US Supreme Court held that resisting forced recruitment by guerillas did not, on the facts, necessarily imply a political opinion. Musalo, K., 'Irreconcilable Differences? Divorcing Refugee Protections from Human Rights Norms', 15 *Mich. J. Int. Law* 1179 (1994).

evaluation challenges, some of which have been examined above in the context of 'good faith'.

In principle, there is no reason why a well-founded fear of persecution should not be based on activity after departure. French doctrine, for example, does not rule out this possibility, and the jurisprudence also does not discriminate against those who may even have left their country of origin for reasons of personal convenience. The cases summarized in one of the leading French commentaries nevertheless place emphasis on an *active* political role of the sort likely to give rise to a fear of persecution, and on whether the claimant is likely to have come to the attention of the authorities of his or her country of origin.[172]

Article 54 of the Swiss law on asylum comes to the issue from the perspective of 'subjective reasons arising after flight', and provides that asylum is not granted to a person who has only become a refugee by leaving his country of origin or by reason of their subsequent activities.[173] However, although 'asylum' may be refused in this limited class of case, the application of the principle of *non-refoulement* continues to be accepted.[174] Thus, in one case where knowledge of the individual concerned had likely come into the possession of the authorities of the country of origin (because of actions taken by the Swiss authorities), refugee status was upheld.[175] Although some European doctrine attaches particular importance to political activities *sur place* being a continuation of activities begun in the country of origin, this may be intended to go to the questions of credibility and 'well-foundedness', as the ordinary meaning of article 1A(2) would imply. Article 5 of the EU Qualification Directive, however, has failed to reconcile different approaches consistently with the Convention. On the one hand, post-departure activities 'may' be the basis for a well-founded fear of persecution; on the other hand, though 'without prejudice' to the 1951 Convention, Member States may decide not to grant refugee status in a subsequent application where the risk of persecution is based on circumstances which the applicant has created since

---

172 Tiberghien, F., *La protection des réfugiés en France*, (2ème éd., 1988, 389–92 ('Activités politiques entreprises durant le séjour en France'); see also Carlier, J-Y, Vanheule, D., Hullmann, K. & Peña Galiano, C., eds., *Who is a Refugee? A Comparative Case Law Study*, (1997), 384–5; also 70–1 (Belgium), 311–12 (Denmark).

173 Loi sur l'asile, 26 Jun. 1998, Art. 54—Motifs subjectifs survenus après la fuite. 'L'asile n'est pas accordé à la personne qui n'est devenue un réfugié au sens de l'article 3 qu'en quittant son Etat d'origine … ou en raison de son comportement ultérieur.'

174 'Aucune personne ne peut être contrainte, de quelque manière que ce soit, à se rendre dans un pays …' / 'No one may be compelled, in any manner whatsoever, to return to a country …' in which life or liberty may be at risk for a refugee-related reason: art. 5, loi sur l'asile. This article extends protection to include non-return to a country from which in turn the person may be sent to a country in which he or she would be at risk for the reasons mentioned in the refugee definition set out in art. 3.

175 Carlier, *et al.*, above n. 172, 134; see also *Minister of Citizenship and Immigration* v. *Asaolu* [1998] FCJ No. 1108, Court File No. IMM-237-98, Federal Court of Canada, Trial Division, 31 July 1998—Citizenship and Immigration Canada sent claimant's story and photograph to visa officer in Lagos, Nigeria to facilitate investigation of claim to refugee status; determination in favour of respondent as refugee *sur place* upheld, based on knowledge of human rights conditions in Nigeria and failure to explain how investigation conducted there.

leaving his or her country of origin. The drafting clearly discloses doubt as to correctness of such action in international law, and is also internally inconsistent; it supposes the existence in fact of a risk of persecution, but suggests discretion to disregard the individual's well-founded fear.[176]

If the central issue of risk of relevant harm for a Convention reason is kept in focus, then it will be seen that there is no rational basis for distinguishing between an individual whose opinions and activities in the country of refuge represent a continuation of opinions and activities begun in the country of origin, and one whose political engagement only begins when he or she has left their homeland. The notion of continuity, as an evidential requirement, may provide some assurance that the person concerned is indeed a person of sincerely held opinions, such as might attract the attention of a persecutor, but this is one aspect only of the issue of credibility. Equally, there is no rational basis for distinguishing in the matter of refugee status between the innocent bystander to whom political opinions are imputed by the persecutor, and the less than innocent bystander whose self-interested actions lead the persecutor also to impute political opinions to the person concerned.[177] The so-called good faith requirement seems to offer an answer to manipulation of the system, but it has no legal authority, is not mentioned in the Convention, and is not supported by any general principle of international law. What remains relevant in every case, however, is the question of credibility as it applies both to the claimant to and to evidence relating to the country of origin.[178]

It is equally no answer to a prospective refugee claim that the individual ought to cease to engage in or moderate the conduct[179] or political activities targeted by the authorities or by non-State actors. Although there are many recognized limitations attaching to human rights and fundamental freedoms, there is also commonly a 'core content' which, it has been held in related contexts, no one should be required to deny.[180] For example, the right to freedom of opinion, including political opinion, is invariably linked to freedom of expression, without which the

---

[176] The drafting reflects German practice in particular, and the doctrine of *Nachfluchtgründe*; the equivocation flows perhaps from the practice of other States, such as the United Kingdom, which do not consider the Convention refugee definition to include any requirement that the applicant act in 'good faith'. See above, 66–7.

[177] Cf. *Nejad* v. *Minister of Citizenship and Immigration* 1997 CanLII 5458 (F.C.): 'The new panel ... should consider ... whether the applicants became refugees *sur place* and whether it would be safe for them ... to return to Iran. They may not be very intelligent in their attending of the political rally in Canada; they are obviously not brave, but ... the law is not addressed only to save the brave, but also the weak, the timid and even the imprudent.'

[178] See further below, Ch. 10, s. 4.

[179] See New Zealand, RSAA, *Refugee Appeal No. 74665/03*, 7 Jul. 2004; *Appellant S395/2002* v. *Minister for Immigration and Multicultural Affairs* [2003] HCA 71; McHugh and Kirby JJ. held that 'persecution does not cease to be persecution for the purpose of the Convention because those persecuted can eliminate the harm by taking avoiding action within the country of nationality': para. 40.

[180] On freedom of opinion and expression as lying at the 'core' of ICCPR66, see Nowak, M., *UN Covenant on Civil and Political Rights: CCPR Commentary* (1993) 336.

former is practically meaningless.[181] Moreover, political opinion and political activity are inherently linked; 'activity' is implicit in the concept of freedom to hold opinions, and is directly related to the exercise of 'political rights' at large.[182] As the UNHCR *Handbook* observes with regard to a potential 'political' refugee,

There may...be situations in which the applicant has not given any expression to his opinions. *Due to the strength of his convictions, however, it may be reasonable to assume that his opinions will sooner or later find expression and that the applicant will, as a result, come into conflict with the authorities.* Where this can reasonably be assumed, the applicant can be considered to have fear of persecution for reasons of political opinion.[183]

5. Persecution: Issues of interpretation and application

'Persecution' is not defined in the 1951 Convention or in any other international instrument.[184] Articles 31 and 33 of the Convention refer to those whose life or freedom 'was' or 'would be' threatened,[185] and the 1984 UN Convention against Torture defines torture as covering:

any act by which severe pain or suffering, whether physical or mental, is intentionally inflicted on a person...It does not include pain or suffering arising only from, inherent in or incidental to lawful sanctions.[186]

Although discrimination may be a factor, torture, unlike Convention refugee status, need not necessarily be linked to specific indices such as race, religion, nationality, social group, or political opinion.[187] Other acts amounting to persecution on the particular facts of the case may include those covered by the prohibition of

---

[181] With regard to art. 19 ICCPR66, the Human Rights Committee has noted that para. 1 requires protection of the right to hold opinions without interference, to which the Covenant permits no exception or restriction; and that para. 2 requires protection of the right to freedom of expression, which includes not only freedom to 'impart information and ideas of all kinds', but also freedom to 'seek' and 'receive' them 'regardless of frontiers' and in whatever medium, 'either orally, in writing or in print, in the form of art, or through any other media of his choice': Human Rights Committee, General Comment 10—Article 19 (19th Session, 1983), Compilation of General Comments and General Recommendations by Human Rights Treaty Bodies HRI/GEN.1/Rev.8, 8 May 2006, 171.

[182] See Human Rights Committee, General Comment 25, Article 25 (57th Session, 1996), ibid., 207. [183] UNHCR, *Handbook*, para. 82, emphasis supplied.

[184] UNHCR, *Handbook*, paras. 51–65; Grahl-Madsen, *Status of Refugees*, vol. 1, 188–216; Hathaway, *Law of Refugee Status*, 99–134.

[185] Cf. UNHCR, *Handbook*, para. 51: '...it may be inferred that a threat to life or freedom on account of race, religion, nationality, political opinion or membership of a particular social group is always persecution. Other serious violations of human rights—for the same reasons—would also constitute persecution.'

[186] Art. 1; for full text, see below, Annexe 1, No. 7. The Convention requires a linkage between the act and a public official or other person acting in an official capacity.

[187] The Committee against Torture's practice in reviewing State action in matters of refusal of admission and removal of those whose return may lead them to face the risk of torture contributes significantly to the consolidation of 'human rights-based protection'; see further below, Ch. 6.

cruel, inhuman, or degrading treatment or punishment,[188] or punishment, or repeated punishment for breach of the law, which is out of proportion to the offence. In other respects, a margin of appreciation is left to States in interpreting this fundamental term, and the jurisprudence, not surprisingly, is sometimes inconsistent.[189] Specific decisions by national authorities are some evidence of the content of the concept, as understood by States, but comprehensive analysis requires the general notion of persecution to be related to developments within the broad field of human rights. Article 9 of the EU Qualification Directive, which sets out for Member States the 'common concept' of persecution, provides that the relevant acts *must* 'be sufficiently serious by their nature or repetition as to constitute a severe violation of basic human rights', in particular, those rights which are non-derogable under the European Convention on Human Rights; or they must amount to an accumulation of measures of equivalent severity. An illustrative list of 'acts of persecution' follows, ranging from the general (physical or mental violence, discrimination) to the particular ('prosecution or punishment for refusal to perform military service which would include crimes or acts falling under the exclusion clauses ... ').[190]

Australia's Migration Act also seeks to 'interpret' the Convention refugee definition. Persecution must involve 'serious harm' to the applicant, and systematic and discriminatory conduct. 'Serious harm', in turn, is described as including a threat to life or liberty, significant physical harassment or ill-treatment, or significant economic hardship or denial of access to basic services or denial of capacity to earn a livelihood, where such hardship or denial threatens the applicant's capacity to subsist.[191] Persecution also implies an element of 'motivation' on the part of those who persecute, in the sense that people are persecuted because of something perceived about them or attributed to them. It must be for reasons of a Convention ground, though that does not have to be the only ground provided a Convention

---

[188] See, for example, art. 16 CAT84; art. 7 ICCPR66; art. 3 ECHR50; art. 5 ACHR69; art. 5 ACHPR81; art. 8 ArabCHR04; all texts in Brownlie & Goodwin-Gill, *Basic Documents on Human Rights.*

[189] In *Acosta* 19 *I&N Dec.* 211 (BIA, 1985), the Board of Immigration Appeals described persecution as meaning, 'the infliction of suffering or harm in order to punish an individual for possessing a particular belief or characteristic the persecutor seeks to overcome'. Experience is not quite so mechanical. See also Tiberghien, F., 'Le champ d'application de l'article 1er, A, 2 de la Convention de Genève': *Doc. réf.* no. 49, Suppl., CJ, 1–24—an extensive review of decisions of the *Commission des recours*, mostly showing what is not persecution. For example, CRR, 26 nov. 1987, 56.191, *Avakian,* ibid., 6—injured by revolutionary guards for failure to respect islamic dress standards: not persecution; CRR, 23 nov. 1987, 58.649, *Skiba,* ibid., 15—left Poland for economic reasons and to join relative in France: not within Convention; CRR, 29 sept. 1987, 66.701, *Shan,* ibid., 17. PRC legislation on family planning is of a general character and it is not claimed that it was applied in a discriminatory manner linked to the grounds set forth in the Convention; CRR, 10 nov. 1987, 67.843, *Yu,* ibid., 17—similarly; CRR, 3 dec. 1987, 30.620, *Simon,* ibid., 11—Romanian adventist refused passport: not sufficient to amount to persecution; CRR, 30 avr. 1987, 49.936, *Tawileh,* ibid—similarly.

[190] The last-mentioned may be illustrative of the protection due to the conscientious objector but, in our view, it is not exhaustive; see further below, s. 5.5.1.

[191] Migration Act, s. 91R(2). Cf. *MIMA* v. *Ibrahim* (2000) 294 CLR 1, [2000] HCA 55—High Court of Australia: a single act may suffice and it is not necessary to show systematic persecution.

reason or reasons are the essential and significant motivation for the persecution feared.[192] Finally, the applicant must have a well-founded fear, that is, a fear based on a real chance of persecution, which is not remote, insubstantial or far-fetched; and be unable or unwilling, because of such fear, to avail him- or herself of the protection of their country of nationality or nationalities, or if stateless, to return to their country of former habitual residence.

Fear of persecution and lack of protection are themselves interrelated elements, as article 1A(2) of the 1951 Convention makes clear. The persecuted clearly do not enjoy the protection of their country of origin, while evidence of the lack of protection on either the internal or external level may create a presumption as to the likelihood of persecution and to the well-foundedness of any fear.[193] The core meaning of persecution readily includes the threat of deprivation of life or physical freedom.[194] In its broader sense, however, it remains very much a question of degree and proportion; less overt measures may suffice, such as the imposition of serious economic disadvantage, denial of access to employment, to the professions, or to education, or other restrictions on the freedoms traditionally guaranteed in a democratic society, such as speech, assembly, worship, or freedom of movement.[195] Whether such restrictions amount to persecution within the 1951 Convention will again turn on an assessment of a complex of factors, including (1) the nature of the freedom threatened, (2) the nature and severity of the restriction, and (3) the likelihood of the restriction eventuating in the individual case.

5.1 PROTECTED INTERESTS

The references to 'race, religion, nationality, membership of a particular social group, or political opinion' illustrate briefly the characteristics of individuals and groups which are considered worthy of special protection. These same factors have figured in the development of the fundamental principle of non-discrimination in

---

[192] Migration Act, s. 91R(1)(a).

[193] This passage (from the first edition of this work) was not clearly understood by Urie, J. A. in *Attorney General* v. *Ward* [1990] 2 FC 667 (Federal Court of Appeal). He said that it was important to avoid confusing 'the determination of persecution and ineffective protection', that 'the two concepts must be addressed and satisfied independently,' and that the absence of protection did not serve as a presumption of persecution (at 680–1). On appeal, the Supreme Court of Canada, quoting the passage in the text, stated that having established that the claimant has a fear, the decision-maker is 'entitled to presume that persecution will be *likely* and the fear *well-founded* if there is an absence of state protection. The presumption goes to the heart of the inquiry, which is whether there is a likelihood of persecution... The presumption is not a great leap... Of course, the persecution must be real—the presumption cannot be built on fictional events—but the *well-foundedness* of the fears can be established through the use of such a presumption': *Ward* [1993] SCR 689, 708 (emphasis in original). See also *Zalzali* v. *Minister for Employment and Immigration* [1991] FCJ No. 341.

[194] See Grahl-Madsen, *Status of Refugees*, vol. 1, 193, quoting Zink's 'restrictive' interpretation.

[195] Ibid., citing the liberal interpretations of Weis, P., in 'The concept of the refugee in international law,' 87 *Clunet* 928 (1960): 'other measures in disregard of human dignity'; and Vernant, J., *The Refugee in the Post-War World*, (1953), 8: 'severe measures and sanctions of an arbitrary nature, incompatible with the principles set forth in the Universal Declaration of Human Rights'.

general international law,[196] and have contributed to the formulation of other fundamental human rights. In its oft-quoted judgment in the *Barcelona Traction Case* in 1970, the International Court of Justice referred to the outlawing of genocide, slavery, and racial discrimination as falling within the emergent notion of obligations *erga omnes*.[197] The resulting rights, so far as they are embodied in international conventions, figure generally among those from which no derogation is permitted, even in exceptional circumstances.[198] These basic rights include: the right to life, to the extent that the individual is protected against 'arbitrary' deprivation;[199] the right to be protected against torture, or cruel or inhuman treatment or punishment;[200] the right not to be subjected to slavery or servitude;[201] the right not to be subjected to retroactive criminal penalties;[202] the right to recognition as a person before the law;[203] and the right to freedom of thought, conscience, and religion.[204] Although not included within the same fundamental class, the following rights are also relevant in view of the frequent close connection between persecution and personal freedom: the right to liberty and security of the person, including freedom from arbitrary arrest and detention;[205] and the right to freedom from arbitrary interference in private, home, and family life.[206]

Recognition of these rights is essential to the maintenance of the integrity and inherent human dignity of the individual. Persecution within the Convention thus comprehends measures, taken on the basis of one or more of the stated grounds, which threaten deprivation of life or liberty; torture or cruel, inhuman, or degrading treatment; subjection to slavery or servitude; non-recognition as a person (particularly where the consequences of such non-recognition impinge directly on an individual's life, liberty, livelihood, security, or integrity); and oppression, discrimination, or harassment of a person in his or her private, home, or family life.[207]

5.2 THE WAYS AND MEANS OF PERSECUTION

Persecution is a concept only too readily filled by the latest examples of one person's inhumanity to another, and little purpose is served by attempting to list all its

---

[196] Cf. Goodwin-Gill, *Movement of Persons*, 66–87.
[197] *Barcelona Traction* case, ICJ *Rep.* (1970) 3, at 32.
[198] Cf. art 15(2) ECHR50; art. 4 ICCPR66; art. 27 ACHR69; But see also Meron, T., 'On a Hierarchy of International Human Rights', 80 *AJIL* 1 (1987), with discussion of International Law Institute proposals for non-extradition 'where there is a well-founded fear of the violation of the fundamental human rights of an accused in the territory of the requesting State' (17–18); Weil, P., 'Towards Relative Normativity in International Law?' 77 *AJIL* 413 (1985).
[199] Art. 6 ICCPR66.   [200] Ibid., art. 7.   [201] Ibid., art. 8.   [202] Ibid., art. 15.
[203] Ibid., art. 16. See above, n. 1.   [204] Ibid., art. 18.   [205] Ibid., art. 9.
[206] Ibid., art. 17.
[207] Cf. Martin, D. A., 87 *AJIL* 348 (1993), review of Hathaway, *Law of Refugee Status*, criticising too tight a linkage with the Covenants, drafted without reference to asylum, noting discrepancies in the lists of non-derogable rights, and concluding that 'the concept of "persecution" simply does not implicate the full range of rights listed in the Covenants' (350).

known measures. Assessments must be made from case to case, taking account, on the one hand, of the notion of individual integrity and human dignity and, on the other hand, of the manner and degree to which they stand to be injured. A straightforward threat to life or liberty is widely accepted,[208] and the repeated condemnation of a wide range of activities involving violation of international humanitarian law, genocide, crimes against humanity and related offences should also be taken into account, given the recognition of responsibility at both State and individual level.

Certain measures, such as the forcible expulsion of an ethnic minority or of an individual, will clearly show the severance of the normal relationship between citizen and State, but the relation of cause and effect may be less clear in other cases. For example, expulsion may be encouraged indirectly, either by threats[209] or by the implementation of apparently unconnected policies. Thus, in Vietnam after 1978, State policies aimed at the restructuring of society and the abolition of the bourgeoisie[210] began to be implemented, giving rise among those affected to serious concern for their future life and security. Those in any way associated with the previous government of South Vietnam were already liable not only to 're-education',[211] but thereafter also to surveillance, to denial of access to employment and the ration system, or to relocation in a 'new economic zone'.[212] The situation of ethnic Chinese was exacerbated by the deterioration in relations and subsequent armed conflict with the People's Republic of China.[213] The net result was a massive exodus of asylum seekers by boat and land to countries in the region.

5.2.1 Persecution as a crime in international law

The jurisprudence of various international tribunals might provide insights, first, into the meaning of persecution; and secondly, into the present-day scope of war crimes as a basis for exclusion. Persecution was certainly acknowledged by the International Military Tribunal in a number of post World War Two trials,[214] and article 5 of the Statute of the International Criminal Tribunal for Former Yugoslavia authorised the prosecution of those responsible for 'persecutions on political, racial and religious grounds', 'when committed in armed conflict, whether international or internal in character, and directed against any civilian population'.[215]

---

[208] 'Enmity' or 'malignity' is not necessary: *S v. MIMA* (2004) 78 ALJR 854—High Court of Australia.   [209] As was done by President Amin in the case of the Ugandan expulsions in 1972.
[210] Foreign Language Press, *The Hoa in Vietnam*, (1978), 12.
[211] Cf. Amnesty International, *1980 Report*, 241–6; *1982 Report*, 249–52.
[212] Grahl-Madsen includes 'removal to a remote or designated place within the home country' in a list of measures which may amount to persecution: *Status of Refugees*, vol. 1, 201.
[213] Osborne, M., 'Indo-China's refugees: causes and effects', *International Affairs*, (1980) 37, 38–44.
[214] See, for example, the *Nuremberg Trial Proceedings*, vol. 1, Indictment: Count One; available at <http://www.yale.edu/lawweb/avalon/avalon.htm>.
[215] Art. 5(h). For the updated text of the ICTY Statute and reports of judgments, see <http://www.un.org/icty>. Art. 5 of the Statute, 'Crimes against humanity', also lists (a) murder; (b) extermination;

While the jurisprudence of the International Criminal Tribunal is replete with instances of persecution, its value for the purpose of interpreting the 1951 Convention is necessarily limited by its criminal law context and by the Tribunal's approach to persecution as a crime, rather than as protective principle in the form of well-founded fear. In *Blaskic* and other cases, for example, the Appeals Chamber has defined persecution as a crime against humanity that involves, 'an act or omission which... (1) discriminates in fact and which denies or infringes upon a fundamental right laid down in international customary or treaty law (the *actus reus*); and (2) was carried out deliberately with the intention to discriminate on one of the listed grounds, specifically race, religion or politics (the *mens rea*).'[216]

The Appeals Chamber has also held that acts of persecution, whether considered separately or together, should reach a certain level of severity, and that although discriminatory intent is essential,[217] it is not alone sufficient.[218] Nevertheless, among the various acts that may constitute persecution, it has accepted instances of serious bodily and mental harm, including rape and sexual assault; the destruction of property, depending on its nature and extent; attacks in which civilians are targeted;, and deportation, forcible transfer, and forcible displacement. In each case, the tribunal looks to the gravity of the crimes, when compared with those set out in article 5 of the ICTY Statute.[219]

(c) enslavement; (d) deportation; (e) imprisonment; (f) torture; (g) rape... and (i) other inhumane acts. See also Statute of the International Tribunal for Rwanda, art. 3: SC res. 955, 8 Nov. 1994, Annex.

[216] *Prosecutor v. Tihomir Blaskic*, Case IT-95–14-A, 29 Jul. 2004, Appeals Chamber, paras. 131–5. This formula has been repeated in a number of other decisions; see, for example, *Prosecutor v. Dario Kordic and Mario Cerkez*, Case IT-95–14/2-A, 17 Dec. 2004, Appeals Chamber, paras. 105–9; *Prosecutor v. Miroslav Kvocka, Mlado Radic, Zoran Zigic, Dragoljub Prcac*, Case IT-98–30/1-A, 28 Feb. 2005, Appeals Chamber, paras. 317–28. Cf. art. 3 of the Statute of the International Criminal Tribunal for Rwanda, which also provides for jurisdiction with regard to 'persecutions on political, racial and religious grounds'. However, it does not employ the language of 'armed conflict', but requires that crimes against humanity be 'committed as part of a widespread and systematic attack against any civilian population on *national, political, ethnic, racial or religious grounds*' (emphasis supplied): <http://www.ictr.org>.

[217] 'Discriminatory intent' is unique to the crime of persecution and is not an element in other crimes against humanity, such as murder; see *Prosecutor v. Tadic*, Case IT-94–1, 15 Jul. 1999, Appeals Chamber, paras. 287–92, 305. The same has been held by the International Criminal Tribunal for Rwanda; see *Prosecutor v. Akayesu*, ICTR-96–4, 1 Jun. 2001, Appeals Chamber, paras. 460–9. See also *Mugesera v. Canada* [2005] SCC 40, Supreme Court of Canada, 28 Jun. 2005, paras. 142–3.

[218] *Prosecutor v. Tihomir Blaskic*, above n. 216, para. 143. Although persecution generally refers to a series of acts, a single act can be enough: *Prosecutor v. Mitar Vasiljevic*, Case IT-98–32-A, 25 Feb. 2004, Appeals Chamber, para. 113; and while the 'gravity test' will only be met by gross or blatant denials of fundamental rights, the relevant acts must be considered in context and in light of their cumulative effect: *Prosecutor v. Radoslav Brdjanin*, IT-99–36-T, 1 Sept. 2004, Trial Chamber II, paras. 996–7, 1032–48.

[219] Ibid., paras. 149, 158, 167, 183, 185. For the other crimes listed in art. 5, see above n. 215. The Appeals Chamber in *Blaskic* also approved the finding by the Trial Chamber in *Kupreskic*, that the crime of 'persecutions' had developed in customary international law to encompass acts that include 'murder, extermination, torture, and other serious acts on the person such as those presently enumerated in Article 5': ibid., para. 149.

The Statute of the International Criminal Court appears to take a more restricted approach. On the one hand, it reiterates the necessity for a deprivation of fundamental human rights, emphasizes the element of discriminatory intent, and formally extends the range of impermissible grounds of distinction; but on the other hand, it also requires that persecution be committed in connection with another crime against humanity or crime within the jurisdiction of the Court:

Article 7—Crimes against humanity

1. For the purpose of this Statute, 'crime against humanity' means any of the following acts when committed as part of a widespread or systematic attack directed against any civilian population, with knowledge of the attack...

(h) Persecution against any identifiable group or collectivity on political, racial, national, ethnic, cultural, religious, gender as defined in paragraph 3,[220] or other grounds that are universally recognized as impermissible under international law, in connection with any act referred to in this paragraph or any crime within the jurisdiction of the Court...

2. For the purpose of paragraph 1...

(g) 'Persecution' means the intentional and severe deprivation of fundamental rights contrary to international law by reason of the identity of the group or collectivity...[221]

No asylum seeker is required to show that the crime of persecution has been or is likely to be committed, and certain of the elements of the crime, for example, in relation to 'intent', engage evidential issues far beyond the requirements of the well-founded fear test. The offences committed during the Yugoslavia conflict, including deportation and forcible transfer, were nevertheless frequently connected to the concept of 'ethnic cleansing'.[222] Here, the jurisprudence of the

---

[220] Para. 3 defines 'gender' as follows: 'For the purpose of this Statute, it is understood that the term "gender" refers to the two sexes, male and female, within the context of society. The term "gender" does not indicate any meaning different from the above.'

[221] For text of the ICC Statute, see <http://www.un.org/law/icc/statute/romefra.htm>. The *Elements of Crimes* in relation to art. 7(1)(h) emphasize, '1. The perpetrator severely deprived, contrary to international law, one or more persons of fundamental rights. 2. The perpetrator targeted such person or persons by reason of the identity of a group or collectivity or targeted the group or collectivity as such. 3. Such targeting was based on political, racial, national, ethnic, cultural, religious, gender as defined in article 7, paragraph 3 of the Statute, or other grounds that are universally recognized as impermissible under international law. 4. The conduct was committed in connection with any act referred to in article 7, paragraph 1, of the Statute or any crime within the jurisdiction of the Court. 5. The conduct was committed as part of a widespread or systematic attack directed against a civilian population. 6. The perpetrator knew that the conduct was part of or intended the conduct to be part of a widespread or systematic attack directed against a civilian population.' International Criminal Court, *Elements of Crimes*, doc. ICC-ASP/1/3, 122. In *Kupreskic*, the Trial Chamber considered that the art. 7(1)(h) limitation in the ICC Statute was 'not consonant with customary international law'; relying on art. 10 of the same Statute, it declined to adopt such an interpretation for the purposes of the ICTY: *Prosecutor* v. *Kupreskic et al.*, Case IT-95–16, 14 Jan. 2000, Trial Chamber II, paras. 580–1.

[222] Cf. SC res. 819 (1993), 16 Apr.1993, para. 5, in which the Security Council, '*Reaffirms* that any taking or acquisition of territory by threat or use of force, including through the practise of "ethnic cleansing", is unlawful and unacceptable'; and para. 7, in which it '*Reaffirms* its condemnation of all violations of international humanitarian law, in particular the practice of 'ethnic cleansing' and

Tribunal may be of greater assistance, so far as it illustrates and increases understanding of the ways and means of persecution. It also may be relevant, of course, to the question of *exclusion*. In the recent Canadian case of *Mugesera*, for example, the Supreme Court of Canada found the applicant to be inadmissible by reason of his having committed a crime against humanity outside Canada, namely, 'persecution by hate speech'.[223] In the case of *Krnojelac*, the Appeals Chamber took account of article 49 of the Fourth Geneva Convention, article 85 of Additional Protocol I and article 17 of Additional Protocol II, and found that these instruments 'prohibit forced movement within the context of both internal and international armed conflicts'. This prohibition is aimed at 'safeguarding the right and aspiration of individuals to live in their communities and homes without interference', and if forcible displacement is committed with the requisite discriminatory intent, it may constitute the crime of persecution.[224] In *Simic*, the Trial Chamber noted that displacement is only illegal when it is 'forced', but that this does not require physical force:

it may also include 'the threat of force or coercion, such as that caused by fear of violence, duress, detention, psychological oppression or abuse of power against such person or persons or another person, or by taking advantage of a coercive environment'. The essential element is that the displacement be involuntary in nature, that 'the relevant persons had no real choice'. In other words, a civilian is involuntarily displaced if he is 'not faced with a genuine choice as to whether to leave or to remain in the area' . . . [225]

The lack of genuine choice, in turn, may be inferred from, among others, threatening and intimidating acts, shelling of civilian objects, burning of civilian property, and the commission or threat to commit crimes 'calculated to terrify the population and make them flee the area with no hope of return'.[226]

---

reaffirms that those who commit or order the commission of such acts shall be held individually responsible in respect of such acts . . .'

[223] *Mugesera* v. *Minister of Citizenship and Immigration* [2005] 2 SCR 100, [2005] SCC 40 (paras. 146, 150). Referring to the importance of interpreting domestic law in accordance with the principles of customary international law and with Canada's international obligations, the Court noted the specific relevance of sources such as the jurisprudence of international criminal tribunals: para. 82. On exclusion generally, see further below, Ch. 4, s. 4.

[224] *Prosecutor* v. *Milorad Krnojelac*, IT-97–25, 17 Sept. 2003, Appeals Chamber, paras. 220–2. In *Brdjamin*, the Trial Chamber was careful to distinguish in its use of terms between 'deportation', which it considered to require crossing an international border; and 'forcible transfer', which did not: *Prosecutor* v. *Radoslav Brdjanin*, IT-99–36-T, 1 Sept. 2004, Trial Chamber II, paras. 541–4. It appears generally agreed that the illegality of deportation or transfer does not depend on removal to a particular destination: *Krnojelac*, above, para. 218; *Prosecutor* v. *Milomir Stakic*, IT-97–24-T, 31 Jul. 2003, Trial Chamber II, para. 677.

[225] *Prosecutor* v. *Simic et al.*, IT-95–9, 17 October 2003, Trial Chamber I, para. 125 (internal citations and references omitted). The Trial Chamber further observed that, 'what matters is the personal consent or wish of an individual, as opposed to collective consent as a group, or a consent expressed by official authorities, in relation to an individual person, or a group of persons': ibid., para. 128.

[226] Ibid., para. 126.

5.3 AGENTS OF PERSECUTION

Cause and effect are yet more indirect where the government of the country of origin cannot be immediately implicated. Refugees, for example, have fled mob violence or the activities of so-called 'death squads', while governments may be unable to suppress such activities, or unwilling or reluctant to do so, or even colluding with those responsible. In such cases, where protection is in fact unavailable, persecution within the Convention can result, for it does not follow that the concept is limited to the actions of governments or their agents.[227]

The term, 'agent of persecution', is somewhat misleading. An 'agent' usually acts for and on behalf of another, the 'principal'. In the law of contract, for example, an agent is empowered to represent and to conclude agreements that bind the principal. In some cases, the agent who acts beyond the bounds of specific authority may also bind the principal, and even on occasion one who, having no authority, holds him- or herself out as representing a principal may also bind the latter, unless the principal takes steps to avoid responsibility. In agency cases, therefore, the essential link is the actual or implied conferral upon another of authority to act.

Neither the 1951 Convention nor the *travaux préparatoires* say much about the source of the persecution feared by the refugee,[228] and no necessary linkage between persecution and government authority is formally required. On the other hand, the Convention does recognize the relation between protection and fear of persecution. A Convention refugee, by definition, must be *unable* or *unwilling*

---

[227] Türk, V., 'Non-State Agents of Persecution', in Chetail, V. & Gowlland-Debbas, V., eds., *Switzerland and the International Protection of Refugees*, (2002), 95; Kälin, W., 'Non-State Agents of Persecution and the Inability of the State to Protect', 15 *Georgetown Immigration Law Journal* 415 (2001); Wilsher, D., 'Non-State Actors and the Definition of A Refugee in the United Kingdom: Protection, Accountability or Culpability?' 15 *IJRL* 68 (2003); Yeo, C., 'Agents of the State: When is an Official of the State an Agent of the State?' 14 *IJRL* 509 (2002); Moore, J., 'From Nation State to Failed State: International Protection from Human Rights Abuses by Non-State Agents', 31 *Columbia Human Rights Law Review* 81 (1999). Persecution for reasons of race or religion will often spring from hostile sections of the populace, while that for reasons of political opinion will more commonly derive from direct, official action. See Cons. d'Etat, *Dankha*, 27 mai 1983, 42,074; CRR, *Duman*, 3 avr. 1979, 9,744, cited in Tiberghien, *La protection des réfugiés*, 247, 394, respectively; also CRR, Section réunies, 8 juin 1999, 315.503, *M. L*—refugee status recognized where authorities tolerated threats and attacks on Christians by Islamic extremists.

[228] See *MIMA* v. *Khawar* (2002) 210 CLR 1, [2002] HCA 14, the High Court of Australia noting that the Convention does not refer to any particular type of persecutor, but to persecution, that is, conduct of a certain character which may include the actions of non-State agents. The Convention also does not specify *where* the threat or persecution must take place. Tiberghien, F., 'Le lieu d'exercice des persecutions': *Doc. réf.* no. 67, 6/15 mars 1989, 1–5—notes acceptance of the idea that a threat or other act committed in France can be equated with persecution in the country of origin, for example, (1) where the authorities of the country of origin undertake their activities abroad through groups which they control or manipulate; (2) where the persecutor is the country of residence, and the country of origin does not protect. Cf. Conseil d'Etat, 4 dec. 1987, 61.376, *Urtiaga Martinez*, ibid., 3— Basque threatened in France by group tolerated or encouraged by Spanish authorities, and name found on list in possession of suspected counter-terrorist group member; refugee status upheld.

to avail himself or herself of the protection of the State or government.[229] This connection is echoed in the EU Qualification Directive, where articles 6 and 7 deal with 'actors of persecution or serious harm' and 'actors of protection', respectively. Persecutors include the State, parties or organizations controlling all or a substantial part of the State, and non-State actors, provided that the parties identified in article 7,[230] 'are unable or unwilling to provide protection against persecution or serious harm'. Protection, in turn, is said to be 'generally provided' when the responsible authorities 'take reasonable steps to prevent the persecution or suffering of serious harm, *inter alia,* by operating an effective legal system for the detection, prosecution and punishment of acts constituting persecution or serious harm, *and* the applicant has access to such protection'.[231]

Grahl-Madsen ties persecution 'to acts or circumstances for which the government (or, in appropriate cases, the ruling party) is responsible, that is,...acts committed by the government (or the party) or organs at its disposal, or behaviour tolerated by the government in such a way as to leave the victims virtually unprotected by the agencies of the State'.[232] The decisive factor, in his view, is the 'place' of the acts or atrocities in the general situation prevailing in the country of origin, for example, whether they are sporadic and rapidly terminated, or 'continue over a protracted period without the government being able to check them effectively', thereby amounting to a flaw in the organization of the State.[233]

5.3.1 *Agents of persecution and State responsibility*

The purpose is not to attribute responsibility, in the sense of State responsibility,[234] for the persecution. If it were, then qualifying as a refugee would be conditional on the rules of attribution, and protection would be denied in cases where, for any reason, the actions of the persecutors were not such as to involve the responsibility of the State.[235] As with the putative question of persecutory intent,

---

[229] In the view of the *Ad hoc* Committee in 1950, '..."unable" refers primarily to stateless refugees but includes also refugees possessing a nationality who are refused passports or *other* protection by their own government...' Report of the *Ad hoc* Committee: UN doc. E/1618, para. 39.

[230] Those identified as 'actors of protection' are the State and others, including international organizations, controlling the State or a substantial part thereof.

[231] Qualification Directive, art. 7(2), emphasis supplied. Cf. the decisions of the UK House of Lords in *Januzi* v. *Secretary of State for the Home Department* [2006] 2 WLR 397, [2006] UKHL 5 and *Horvath* v. *Secretary of State for the Home Department* [2001] 1 AC 489. See further above, Ch. 1, s. 4.

[232] Grahl-Madsen, *Status of Refugees,* vol. 1, 189; also Hathaway, *Law of Refugee Status,* 125–33.

[233] Grahl-Madsen, *Status of Refugees,* vol. 1, 192. For a brief discussion of earlier French doctrine on the source of persecution, see the second edition of this work, 72–3. The law has now been changed; see the *loi no. 2003–1176,* 10 déc. 2003; Code de l'entrée et de séjour des étrangers et du droit d'asile (Livre VII), *J.O.* du 25 nov. 2004, in force 1 Mar. 2005.

[234] By 'State responsibility' is understood the body of principles which determines when and how one State may be liable to another for breach of an international obligation deriving either from treaty or from customary law. See also, in particular, Clapham, A., *Human Rights Obligations of Non-State Actors,* (2006), generallity and at 335–41.

[235] See the International Law Commission, 'Articles on the Responsibility of States for Internationally Wrongful Acts', annexed to UNGA res. 56/83, 12 Dec. 2001; also Brownlie, I., *System of the Law of Nations: State Responsibility, Part I,* (1983), 159–79.

so the issue of State responsibility for persecution, relevant though it may be in other circumstances, is not part of the refugee definition. Analogous aspects may arise, however, in considering the availability and/or sufficiency of local protection. Here, the law of State responsibility provides some parallel illustrations; for example, if the acts of private groups or individuals are attributable to the State, then the lack of adequate local protection can be inferred. Likewise, where the State is either unable or unwilling to satisfy the standard of due diligence in the provision of protection, the circumstances may equally found an international claim, as provide a basis for fear of persecution within the meaning of the Convention. The correlation is coincidental, however, not normative. The central issue remains that of *risk of harm amounting to persecution*; the principles and practice of State responsibility can contribute to that assessment, for example, by confirming the level of protection and judicial or other guarantees that may be due under universal and regional human rights instruments.[236]

Moreover, while the inability in fact of a State to exercise control in certain circumstances may entail an absence of responsibility vis-à-vis the rights of other States,[237] there is no basis in the 1951 Convention, or in general international law, for requiring the existence of effective, operating institutions of government as a pre-condition to a successful claim to refugee status. In the same way, the existence or non-existence of governmental authority is irrelevant to the issue of individual responsibility for genocide, war crimes, or other serious violations of international humanitarian law.

5.4 FEAR, INTENT, MOTIVE, AND THE RATIONALE FOR PERSECUTION

Applications for refugee status are sometimes denied on the ground that the claimant has failed to prove either that the law was enacted with intent to persecute, or that the authorities in his or her country of origin themselves *intended* to persecute the individual for one or other Convention reason. Proof of legislative or organizational intent is notoriously hard to establish and while evidence of such motivation may be sufficient to establish a claim to refugee status, it cannot be considered a *necessary* condition.

Nowhere in the drafting history[238] of the 1951 Convention is it suggested that the motive or intent of the persecutor was ever to be considered as a *controlling*

---

[236] In *R (Bagdanavicius)* v. *Secretary of State for the Home Department* [2005] 2 WLR 1359, [2005] UKHL 38, the Court held that in an appeal against removal on art. 3 ECHR50 grounds it had to assess whether there was a 'real risk' of harm on return, and whether that harm amounted to prohibited ill-treatment. It held further that where non-State agents were the source of harm, it would not constitute art. 3 ill-treatment *unless* the State in addition failed to provide 'a reasonable level of protection': paras. 22–4.

[237] Note, however, that a successful insurrectional movement is liable for its activities *before* its assumption of power; see Borchard, E. M., *The Diplomatic Protection of Citizens Abroad*, 241; *Bolivár Railway Co. Case (Great Britain* v. *Venezuela)*, Ralston's *Report*, 388, 394, per Umpire Plumley.

[238] The 'drafting history' includes, in particular, debates in the United Nations Economic and Social Council (ECOSOC) in 1950, the two sessions of the *Ad hoc* Committee on Statelessness and

factor in either the definition or the determination of refugee status. The debate in the *Ad hoc* Committee regarding the 'precedent' of the IRO Constitution's approach to classification and description, considered in context, reveals itself as a debate, not about fear, intention, or motive, but one between those who, like the United Kingdom, France and Belgium, favoured a definition in general terms; and those who, like the United States, preferred a detailed statement of the various categories of refugees who should receive international protection.

As revised, the definition which emerged on 30 January 1950 was substantially that which was adopted in July 1951, at the Conference of Plenipotentiaries.[239] As the Israeli delegate observed at the time, 'All the *objective* factors which would make it possible to characterize a person as a refugee were now known ... (and) ... contained in paragraph 1.'[240] The only *subjective* elements of relevance, for this delegate, went to the 'horrifying memories' of past persecution which might justify non-return to the country of origin. The (subjective) state of the *persecutor's* mind was never mentioned. As the *Ad hoc* Committee stated to ECOSOC in its comments on the draft:

The expression 'well-founded fear of being the victim of persecution for reasons of race, religion, nationality or political opinion' means that a person has either been actually a victim of persecution or can show good reason why he fears persecution.[241]

Persecution for Convention reasons has sometimes been read to mean 'the infliction of suffering *because of or on account of* the victim's race, beliefs or nationality, etc'.[242] Such a seemingly innocuous change in the wording, however, distorts the natural meaning of the language and can create additional evidentiary burdens for the claimant. In particular, perhaps unwittingly, it may import a *controlling* intent on the part of the persecutor, as an element in the definition.

Of course, intent is relevant; indeed, evidence of persecutory intent may be conclusive as to the existence of well-founded fear, but its absence is not necessarily conclusive the other way. A persecutor may intend to harm an individual because of/for reasons of/on account of that person's race or religion.[243] Similarly,

---

Related Problems (in January–February and August 1950; the Committee was renamed the *Ad hoc* Committee on Refugees and Stateless Persons), and the Conference of Plenipotentiaries which settled the final text of the Convention in July 1951.

239 See UN doc. E/AC.32/L.6/Rev.1 (30 Jan. 1950).

240 See UN doc. E/AC.32/SR.18, para. 10 (31 Jan. 1950)—Mr. Robinson (emphasis supplied).

241 See UN doc. E/1618 (17 Feb. 1950), Annex.

242 For reasons that are not clear, US law employs 'on account of' in preference to 'for reasons of' in its statement of the refugee definition: 8 USC §1101(a)(42). This harkens back to one of the first US contributions to the definitions debate in 1950; see United States of America, *Memorandum on the Definition Article of the Preliminary Draft Convention Relating to the Status of Refugees (and Stateless Persons)*: UN doc. E/AC.32/L.4 (18 Jan. 1950).

243 This is the sense of *Acosta*, above n. 30 and accompanying text, in which the BIA emphasized the relevance of 'a belief or characteristic a persecutor seeks to overcome', and of the persecutor having 'the inclination to punish' the claimant. Referring to persecution for reasons of political opinion in the *Ward* case, the Supreme Court of Canada noted that the 'examination of the circumstances should be approached from the perspective of the persecutor, since that is the perspective that is determinative

a persecutor may intend to harm an individual because of an opinion expressed, or a decision or action taken, irrespective or regardless of that individual's actual motivation or conviction. If that opinion, decision, or action falls within the category of protected interests (freedom of religion, expression, opinion, conscience, and so forth), and *if* the harm visited or feared is in fact of a degree to amount to persecution, then a sufficient link may be inferred on which to base a well-founded fear of persecution within the meaning of the Convention. There are slight but important differences between the terms *on account of* and *for reasons of.* 'On account of', which is *not* the language of the Convention, implies an element of conscious, individualized direction which is often conspicuously absent in the practices of mass persecution.

The Convention definition offers a series of objective elements by which to describe the refugee. The *travaux préparatoires* suggest that the only relevant intent or motive would be that, not of the persecutor, but of the refugee or refugee claimant: one motivated by personal convenience, rather than fear, might be denied protection;[244] while one with horrifying memories of past persecution might yet continue to receive protection, notwithstanding a change of circumstances in the country of origin.[245] Otherwise, the governing criterion remains that of a serious possibility of persecution, not proof of intent to harm on the part of the persecutor.

5.5 PERSECUTION AND LAWS OF GENERAL APPLICATION

Applications for refugee status are often denied on the ground that the claimant fears not persecution, but prosecution under a law of general application. Experience shows, however, that the law can as well be the instrument of persecution as any other arbitrary measure. The question then is, if some laws can be the instruments of persecution, which are they?[246]

in inciting the persecution': [1993] 2 SCR 689, 740f. See also, Kälin, W., Comment on Bundesverfassungsgericht (BRD) v. 10.7.1989—2 BvR 502/86 u.a. (EuGRZ 1989, S.444–455): *Asyl,* 1990/4, 13; *INS* v. *Elias-Zacarias,* 502 US 478 (1992); 908 F.2d 1452 (9th Cir. 1990); Case Abstract No. *IJRL/0114:* 4 *IJRL* 263 (1992); Anker, D., Blum, C.P. & Johnson, K. R., '*INS* v. *Zacarias:* Is There Anyone Out There?' 4 *IJRL* 266 (1992); von Sternberg, Mark R., 'Emerging Bases of "Persecution" in American Refugee Law: Political Opinion and the Dilemma of Neutrality', 13 *Suffolk Transnat'l L.J.* 1 (1989).

[244] See the United States draft: UN doc. E/AC.32/L.4, para. B. Cf. the views of the United Kingdom: UN docs. E/AC.32/SR.6, para. 5; E/AC.32/L.2/Rev.1.

[245] See UN doc. E/AC.32/SR.18, paras. 10–16 (Mr. Robinson); art. 1C(5), (6) CSR51; and further below, Ch. 4, s. 1.

[246] In *Zolfagharkhani* v. *Minister for Employment and Immigration* [1993] FC 540, the Canadian Federal Court of Appeal offered the following propositions with respect to persecution and an ordinary law of general application: (1) the Convention refugee definition makes the intent or any principal effect of an ordinary law of general application, rather than the motivation of the claimant, relevant to the existence of persecution; (2) the neutrality of such law vis-à-vis the five Convention grounds must be judged objectively; (3) an ordinary law of general application, even in non-democratic societies, should be presumed valid and neutral, and it is for the claimant to show that the law is

This has been a controversial aspect of claims based in recent years on the alleged impact of China's 'one child policy', and in those involving conscientious objectors. Claimants in different jurisdictions argued that their being liable to forcible sterilization for breach of this policy amounted to persecution within the meaning of the Convention, and decisions in the matter have also been open to political considerations. In *Chang*, for example, the US Board of Immigration Appeals held that the policy is not persecutory and does not, by itself, create a well-founded fear of persecution, 'even to the extent that involuntary sterilization may occur'. To qualify for asylum, the claimant must show that he or she is at risk because the policy is being selectively applied on Convention grounds, or being used to punish for those reasons.[247]

Every government has the right to enact, implement, and enforce its own legislation, inherent in its sovereignty and in the principle of the reserved domain of domestic jurisdiction. Notwithstanding the presumption of legitimacy in the legislative field, the discriminatory application of law or the use of law to promote discrimination may tend to persecution.[248] In this sense, a human rights perspective can inform the approach to persecution, for example, by indicating which rights are absolute, which may be 'subject to such restrictions as are prescribed by law and reasonably necessary in a democratic society', whether restrictions are reasonably necessary, and whether any prohibition or penalty is proportional to the (social) objective that the legislation aims to achieve. The issues involved can be illustrated by reference to what has been called the offence of *Republikflucht*, arising out of the restrictions often imposed by totalitarian States on travel abroad by their nationals. When unauthorised border-crossing and absence abroad beyond the validity of an exit permit attract heavy penalties, the question is whether fear of prosecution and punishment can be equated with a well-founded fear of persecution on grounds of political opinion, especially where the claim to refugee status is based on nothing more than the anticipation of such prosecution and punishment.[249] On the one hand, the individual involved is simply treated according to

---

persecutory, either inherently or for some other reason; and (4) the claimant must show not that a particular regime is generally oppressive, but that the law in question is persecutory in relation to a Convention ground: ibid., paras. 20–3. See also *S v. MIMA* (2004) 78 ALJR 854—High Court of Australia: whether what results from the discriminatory implementation of a law of general application is persecution depends on whether the treatment is appropriate and adapted to achieving a national objective consistent with the standards of civilized society.

[247] 20 *I&N Dec.* 38 (BIA, 1989).

[248] Cf. CRR, 26 juillet 1990, *Gambini*, 93.031, *Doc. réf.* no. 145, 28 avr./7 mai 1991, Suppl., JC, 4—lack of legislative provision for transexuals in Argentina a situation of a general character and not discriminatory; CRR, 23 mai 1988, *Gungor*, 74.537—flight because of homosexuality did not fall within the Convention, for in Tiberghien's view (ibid.), 'un vide législatif n'est pas assimilable à une persécution, sauf si ce vide législatif est délibérément maintenu par un Etat pour persécuter une fraction de la population qu'il prive ainsi de protection.' Cf. *Toboso-Alfonso*, 20 *I&N Dec.* 819 (BIA, 1990), in which the BIA found that a Cuban homosexual was persecuted as a result of government's desire that all homosexuals be forced to leave their homeland.

[249] The issue is less relevant today, with the progressive spread of democratization. For examples of laws, see the first edition of this work. Amnesty International has often taken up the cases of those

law; on the other hand, the object and purpose of such laws might show that leaving or staying abroad is treated as a *political act*, either because it reflects an actual and sufficient political opinion, or because the state authorities may attribute dissident political opinion to the individual concerned.

5.5.1 Conscientious objectors

Issues of 'causation', attribution and the motives for treatment amounting to persecution are also raised by asylum seekers who base their claim upon the fear of prosecution and punishment for conscientious objection to military service, or upon fear of sanctions imposed by non-governmental armed opposition elements. Objectors may be motivated by reasons of conscience or convictions of a religious, ethical, moral, humanitarian, or philosophical nature;[250] they may be opposed to their own government, or to its policy on this occasion; they may object to all wars or to particular wars; they may consider the conflict to be contrary to international law, either in itself or because of the methods being employed; or they may simply not want to kill or be killed.[251] Against their claim to be refugees, it may be argued that they are punished not on account of their beliefs, but because of their failure to obey a law of universal application; that the 'right' to refuse to do military service is not a recognized human right; that punishment does not necessarily amount to persecution; and that there is no sufficiently close connection between refusal to serve and a Convention-based motivation.[252]

In our view, however, the fundamental issues in determining entitlement to protection by an applicant on the basis of objection to military service are the

punished under this rubric; see *1979 Report*, 123, 133; *1980 Report*, 255, 269f., 277f., 291, 303; *1982 Report*, 270f., 286f., and later *Reports*.

[250] See Human Rights Committee, General Comment No. 22 (48) on art. 18(1) ICCPR66—freedom of thought, conscience and religion. The Committee believes that a right of conscientious objection, 'can be derived from article 18, inasmuch as the obligation to use lethal force may seriously conflict with the freedom of conscience and the right to manifest one's religion or belief. When this right is recognized by law or practice, there shall be no differentiation among conscientious objectors on the basis of the nature of their particular beliefs': UN doc. HRI/GEN/1/Rev.8, 8 May 2006, 194, para. 11.

[251] UNHCR, *Handbook*, paras. 167–74; Grahl-Madsen, *Status of Refugees*, vol. 1, 231–8; Hathaway, *Law of Refugee Status*, 174–85.

[252] Reviewing jurisprudence of the French *Commission des recours* in 1993, Tiberghien concluded that if desertion or conscientious objection were not linked to a Convention reason, refugee status would not be upheld: Tiberghien, F., 'La crise yougoslave devant la Commission des recours', *Doc. réf.*, no. 223, 17/30 août 1993, Suppl., CJ, 1–10. What is required is either 'un motif politique ou de conscience qui soit personnel au requérant': cf. CRR, Sections reunies, 29 janv. 1993, 217.894, *Sporea*, ibid., 7—member of Romanian minority in Voivodina, opposed to ethnic and cultural hegemony and unwilling to serve for political reasons; appeal against refusal of refugee status upheld. An unwillingness to fight Croats ('fellow compatriots') is not enough, despite the fact that the UN has condemned the conflict: CRR, Sections réunies, 29 janv. 1993, 229.937, *Djukic*, ibid., 6. But the possibility of sanctions on family members in another State may support refugee status on the basis of a 'conscientious' objection to service; see CRR, Sections réunies, 29 janv. 1993, 229.956, *Dabetic*, ibid., 6: Claimant's family members resided in different States (Croatia and Montenegro); he left Croatia to avoid conscription, and if returned to Yugoslavia, was likely to be conscripted into the *federal* army with resulting sanctions on relations in Zagreb.

sincerity of the conviction which sets him or her in opposition to their government, and the risk of treatment amounting to persecution, by reason of such objection. Serious questions relating to cause and motive must nevertheless be addressed.

Over thirty years ago, in 1976, the United Kingdom's Immigration Appeal Tribunal found that, on the basis of the law and practice then applying in Greece,[253] punishment of conscientious objectors amounted to persecution. However, the Tribunal doubted that this was persecution for reasons of religion or political opinion. The 'immediate cause of the persecution', it said, 'is a refusal to obey the law of the land, and the fact that such refusal may be due to religious beliefs or political opinion is... only the secondary cause'. It also considered that the relevant law was not discriminatory, because 'other religious beliefs with similar views... and indeed persons with no religious beliefs at all ..., would all be treated in the same way'.[254]

5.5.1.1 The 'right' of conscientious objection

No international human rights instrument yet recognizes the right of conscientious objection to military service, even though the right to freedom of conscience itself is almost universally endorsed.[255] The *exercise* of that latter right, however, may be subject to certain legal limitations, such as those necessary to protect the rights or freedoms of others, and a conflict of competing interests is perhaps inevitable.[256] The international community nevertheless appears to be moving

---

[253] Art. 13 of the Constitution of the Republic of Greece, which deals with freedom of conscience, provides in para. 4 that 'No person shall, by reason of his religious convictions, be exempt from discharging his obligations to the State, or refuse to comply with the laws.' Art. 4(6) obliges every Greek able to bear arms to assist in the defence of the nation. Practice at various periods has often resulted in conscientious objectors being sentenced to repeated terms of imprisonment throughout the period of military age. See generally Amnesty International, *5000 years in prison: Conscientious objectors in Greece*, Mar. 1993; also, Amnesty International, *Report 1994*, 140–2. For more recent developments, see, in addition to reports by Amnesty International, the websites of War Resisters International: <http://www.wri-irg.org/> and the European Bureau for Conscientious Objection: <http://www.ebco-beoc.org/>.

[254] *Dounetas* v. *Secretary of State*, approved and applied in *Atibo* v. *Immigration Officer, London (Heathrow) Airport* [1978] ImmAR 93. The Tribunal in *Dounetas* also suggested that 'If the Jehovah's Witnesses in Greece were being persecuted for reasons of religion, we would expect that their teachings and meetings would be proscribed. This is evidently not the case...' Cf. *Kokkinakis* v. *Greece* (1994) 17 EHRR 397.

[255] See art. 18 UDHR48; art. 18 ICCPR66; art. 12 ACHR69; art. 9 ECHR50. The following analysis draws in part on the *amicus curiae* brief submitted by UNHCR in 1989 to the US Court of Appeals for the Ninth Circuit in *Cañas-Segovia* v. *Immigration and Naturalization Service*, 902 F.2d 717 (9th Cir, 1992), in the drafting of which Guy Goodwin-Gill participated together with Susan Timberlake and Ralph Steinhardt; for the brief in full, see 2 *IJRL* 341 (1990). It also takes into account Goodwin-Gill's more recent work in connection with proceedings in the case of *Sepet & Bulbul* v. *Secretary of State for the Home Department* [2003] 1 WLR 856; see further below, s. 5.5.1.4.

[256] Note also art. 4 ECHR50, prohibiting slavery, servitude, forced or compulsory labour. Art. 4(3)(b) provides that the term 'forced or compulsory labour' shall not include 'any service of a military character or, in case of conscientious objectors in countries where they are recognized, service exacted instead of compulsory military service'. Art. 4(3) also excludes work required to be done during detention, or service exacted in emergencies, or as part of normal civic obligations. Fawcett has observed that this 'implies that such conscientious objection is an exercise of freedom of conscience under art. 9, but that a State may restrict it by allowing no exemption from military service, if it is

towards acceptance of a right of conscientious objection, particularly as a result of the standard-setting activities of United Nations and regional bodies.[257] It is increasingly accepted in a variety of different contexts that it may be unconscionable to require the individual to change, or to exercise their freedom of choice differently.

In reviewing the reports of States, the Human Rights Committee has continued to express its concern at the treatment of conscientious objectors in a number of countries. In its report on Georgia in 2002, for example, it referred to 'the discrimination suffered by conscientious objectors owing to the fact that non-military alternative service lasts for 36 months compared with 18 months for military service; it regrets the lack of clear information on the rules currently governing conscientious objection to military service'.[258] The Commission on Human Rights has also expressed its concern at the repeated incarceration of conscientious objectors.[259]

The Parliamentary Assembly of the Council of Europe has had conscientious objection on its agenda for over forty years,[260] and it has recently been examined in other European forums, not usually associated with the issue. For example, the character of the provisions adopted in regard to alternative service came before the European Committee of Social Rights, in its review of State compliance with article 1.2 of the European Social Charter which obliges the Contracting parties, with

---

necessary for the public safety . . . ' Fawcett, J., *The Application of the European Convention on Human Rights*, (2nd edn., 1987), 64. Nevertheless, this leaves open the question, whether the national system of military and alternative service is otherwise compatible with the State's other obligations under international law.

[257] For background, see *Conscientious Objection to Military Service*: UN doc. E/CN.4/Sub.2/1983/30/Rev.1 (the Eide/Mubanga-Chipoya report); *Report of the Secretary-General, The Role of Youth in the Promotion and Protection of Human Rights, including the Question of Conscientious Objection to Military Service*: UN doc. E/CN.4/1989/30 (20 Dec. 1988); *Report of the United Nations Commission on Human Rights*: UN doc. E/CN.4/1989/L.10/Add.15 (9 Mar. 1989); Commission on Human Rights res. 1998/77, 22 Apr. 1998, 'Conscientious Objection to Military Service' (adopted without a vote); recalled in CHR res. 2000/34, 20 Apr. 2000; see also CHR resolution 1995/83, which clarified that the religious, ethical or similar motives that may be the basis for conscientious objection also included humanitarian motives, and that the principle was equally applicable to those already serving in the armed forces.

[258] Human Rights Committee, UN doc. CCPR/CO/74/GEO, 19 Apr. 2002, Concluding observations on the second periodic report of Georgia: para. 18. See also Human Rights Committee, UN doc. CCPR/CO/73/UKR, 12 Nov. 2001, Concluding observations of the Human Rights Committee: para. 20 (noting with concern that 'conscientious objection was accepted only in regard to objections for religious reasons and only with regard to certain religions, which appear in an official list').

[259] Report of the Working Group on Arbitrary Detention, UN doc. E/CN.4/2001/14, 20 Dec. 2000, paras. 91–4.

[260] See, among others, Council of Europe, Parliamentary Assembly, Recommendation 1518 (2001), 23 May 2001, 'Exercise of the right of conscientious objection to military service in Council of Europe member states'. CE Doc. 9379, 1 Mar. 2002, Reply from the Committee of Ministers to Parliamentary Assembly Recommendation 1518 (2001); Committee of Ministers Recommendation No. R(87)8 (9 Apr. 1987); Council of Europe, Conscientious Objection to Military Service, Explanatory Report: CE Doc. 88.C55 (1988).

a view to ensuring effective exercise of the right to work, 'to protect effectively the right of the worker to earn his living in an occupation freely entered upon'.[261] In 2001, on a complaint by the Quaker Council for European Affairs, the Committee found that the situation in Greece was not in conformity with that article. Taking account of article 4(3)(b) ECHR50, to the effect that military service and alternative civilian service, 'cannot, *as such*, be considered a form of forced labour', it nevertheless concluded that alternative civilian service may indeed amount to a restriction on the freedom to earn one's living in an occupation freely entered upon. While accepting that to require a longer period of civilian service fell within the State's margin of appreciation, the Committee considered that a period of eighteen additional months was unreasonable and a disproportionate restriction on the right of the worker.[262]

The European Court of Human Rights, however, has not so far considered the basic issue of recognition of the right to conscientious objection. In *Thlimmenos* v. *Greece*,[263] it found a violation of article 14 ECHR50 in conjunction with article 9, in relation to a Jehovah's Witness convicted under the Military Code for insubordination for refusing to wear the military uniform; this conviction prevented him from subsequently becoming an accountant. Because the Court found a violation of article 14, it did not consider whether, notwithstanding article 4(3)(b) ECHR50, the imposition of such sanctions on conscientious objectors to compulsory military service may in itself infringe the right to freedom of thought, conscience and religion guaranteed by article 9(1) ECHR50.[264] However, in ruling on the article 14 issue and finding that the refusal of the Greek Government to allow the applicant to practice as an accountant was discriminatory, the Court emphasized that this was because the Respondent 'failed to treat differently persons whose situations are significantly different'.[265] This approach echoes that

---

[261] 1961 European Social Charter, ETS No. 35, 529 UNTS 89; text in Brownlie & Goodwin-Gill, *Basic Documents on Human Rights*, 645.

[262] Complaint No. 8/2000 (*The Quaker Council for European Affairs* v. *Greece*, decision on the merits, 25 April 2001), paras. 22–5. <http://www.coe.int/T/E/Human_Rights/Esc/>. The Committee of Ministers has taken note of the measures taken by the Greek Government, 'to bring the situation into conformity with the Charter in good time': Council of Europe, Committee of Ministers Resolution ResChs(2002)3, Collective Complaint No. 8/2000, 6 Mar. 2002.

[263] (2001) 31 EHRR 15.

[264] Ibid, para. 53. A majority of the European Commission on Human Rights had nevertheless found that, as no substitute service was available, 'Jehovah's Witnesses were faced with the choice of either serving…or being convicted. In these circumstances, the Commission considers that the applicant's conviction amounted to an interference with his right to manifest his religion.' A minority of the Commission went further, casting doubt on earlier jurisprudence, such as *Grandrath* v. *Federal Republic of Germany*, Application No. 2299/64, 12 Dec. 1966, (1967) 10 *Yearbook* 626.

[265] Ibid., para. 44. See also *Dian Dimitrov, Krassimir Savov and Atanas Vishanov* v. *Bulgaria*, Decision as to the Admissibility of Applications Nos. 37358/97, 37988/97, and 39565/98, 10 April 2000; and *Stefanov* v. *Bulgaria*, Application no. 32438/96, judgment of the European Court of Human Rights (friendly settlement), 3 May 2001.

adopted by the Special Rapporteur of the Sub-Commission on the Prevention of Discrimination and the Protection of Minorities in his 1960 report:

> Since each religion or belief makes different demands on its followers, a mechanical approach of the principle of equality which does not take into account the various demands will often lead to injustice and in some cases even to discrimination.[266]

5.5.1.2 The 'right' to object to participation in conflict 'condemned by the international community'

The context in which the individual exercises his or her freedom of conscience is determined not only by personal motivation and sincerity of belief, but also by the particular facts and broader political issues. This, in turn, may include positions taken by external actors, such as the Security Council, the General Assembly, other States, regional organizations, and so forth. 'International public policy' may be confirmed, for example, where the military operation objected to is 'condemned by the international community as contrary to basic rules of human conduct'.[267] However, 'international condemnation' is not a term of art and evidence of such views may be obtained from a variety of sources. In April 1991, for example, the Security Council expressed its concern at the 'repression of the Iraqi civilian population in many parts of Iraq, including most recently in Kurdish population areas'.[268] In December 1992, it demanded that all parties, movements, and factions in Somalia 'immediately cease and desist from all breaches of international humanitarian law . . . ',[269] and in April 1993, it reaffirmed that the acquisition of territory by threat or use of force, including through 'ethnic cleansing', was unlawful and unacceptable, condemned such practices and all violations of international humanitarian law, and reaffirmed the principle of individual responsibility for such acts.[270]

Courts have recognized that a person who objects to participating in an internationally condemned conflict can claim that the risk of prosecution amounts to persecution,[271] and in *Sepet and Bulbul*, Lord Bingham said:

> There is compelling support for the view that refugee status should be accorded to one who has refused to undertake compulsory military service on the grounds that such service would or might require him to commit atrocities or gross human rights abuses or participate in a conflict condemned by the international community, or where refusal to serve would earn grossly excessive or disproportionate punishment.[272]

---

[266] 'Study of Discrimination in the Matter of Religious Rights and Practices', UN doc. E/CN.4/Sub.2/300/Rev.1 (1960), 15.   [267] See UNHCR, *Handbook*, para. 171.

[268] SC res. 688, 5 Apr. 1991.   [269] SC res. 794, 3 Dec. 1992.

[270] SC res. 819, 16 Apr. 1993 (Bosnia and Herzegovina).

[271] Cf. *Adan* v. *Secretary of State for the Home Department* [1997] 1 WLR 1107, 1127, per Hutchison L. J.

[272] *Sepet & Bulbul* v. *Secretary of State for the Home Department* [2003] 1 WLR 856, [2003] UKHL 15, para. 8; see also *Krotov* v. *Secretary of State for the Home Department* [2004] 1 WLR 1825, [2004] EWCA Civ 69; *Zolfagharkhani* v. *Minister of Employment and Immigration* [1993] 3 FC 540;

The EU Qualification Directive includes in its list of 'acts of persecution', 'prosecution or punishment for refusal to perform military service in a conflict, where performing military service would include crimes or acts falling under the exclusion clauses...'[273] Moreover, the New Zealand Refugee Status Appeals Authority has stressed that there is, 'no need for the particular conflict to have been the subject of a formal condemnation by resolution of a supranational body, although plainly the existence of such condemnation would be relevant to the inquiry. Rather, what is happening on the ground as to observance of the laws of war by parties to the conflict is key.'[274]

5.5.1.3 The nature of the dispute between the individual and the State

The manner in which some courts have approached the question of conscientious objection suggests doubts as to the appropriate theoretical basis on which to distinguish between those opponents of State authority who do, and those who do not, require international protection. For sincerely held reasons of conscience may motivate the individual who refuses to pay such proportion of income tax as is destined for military expenditures;[275] or the shopkeeper who wishes to trade on Sundays; or the parents who, on grounds of religious conviction, refuse to send their children to public schools.

To a degree, the conflict between these individuals and the State is attributable to the 'choice' of the individual, who elects to place matters of principle or belief over obligations in law. The unrecognized conscientious objector to military service is constrained, in a direct physical sense, to act either in a way contrary to conscience or to face punishment. The objector must choose either to participate in the violence opposed, or to suffer the sanction. The reluctant taxpayer, on the

Ciric v. *Minister of Employment and Immigration* [1994] 2 FC 65. Cf. *Hinzman* v. *Canada (Minister of Citizenship and Immigration)*, 2006 FC 420, 2006-03-31 (US conscientious objector in Canada, and whether in the case of 'mere foot soldier', the lawfulness of the military conflict in question is relevant to the question of refugee status).

273 Art. 9(2)(e), Qualification Directive. As argued here, this does not exhaust the category of persecution by reason of conscientious objection. It is also considerably narrower than the Commission's original proposal, which would have specifically mentioned 'prosecution or punishment for refusal to meet a general obligation to perform military service on the grounds of race, religion, nationality, political opinion or membership of a particular social group', and, 'in situations of war or conflict, if the person can establish that performance of military service will require his or her participation in military activities which are irreconcilable with the applicant's deeply held moral, religious or political convictions, or other valid reasons of conscience': European Commission, Proposed draft for the qualification directive (2002/C 51 E/17) COM(2001) 510 final 2001/0207(CNS) (Submitted by the Commission on 30 October 2001), *Official Journal* of the European Communities C 51 E/325, 26.2.2002.
274 New Zealand, RSAA, *Refugee Appeal No. 73578*, 19 Oct. 2005, para. 87; the tribunal, recognizing refugee status, held that there was indeed a risk of violation of the laws of war, and that the applicant's position was 'political'. See also *Krotov*, above n. 272.
275 See Grief, N., 'British Quakers, the Peace Tax and International Law', in Janis, M. W. & Evans, C., eds., *Religion and International Law*, (1999), 339, referring to the campaign for a conscientious objector status for taxpayers.

other hand, has only to tolerate the use of funds for military purposes,[276] while the would-be Sunday trader is restrained from transacting business at will.[277] Again, the conscientious objector is distinguishable because the State requires his or her *active* complicity in military service, not just tolerance or restraint or restrictions on certain conduct.

A 1988 Council of Europe report emphasized the centrality of 'compelling reasons of conscience' in this context, in preference to a listing of 'acceptable' reasons for objection.[278] Leaving aside any cumulative factors supporting refugee status (such as personal, social, religious or political background), the conscientious objector is also distinguishable from the 'mere' draft evader or deserter by the sincerely-held opinion. This locates the conflict of individual and State within the realm of competing (but nonetheless lawful) rights or interests, and separates out others whose motivations may be purely self-regarding and devoid of any recognized human rights basis.

Nor, as discussion above on internationally condemned conflicts has illustrated, does it matter that the individual seeking protection is a 'partial objector'. As Eide and Mubanga-Chipoya noted many years ago:

Partial conscientious objection to military service . . . is built on the conviction that armed force may be justified under limited circumstances, derived from standards of international or national law or morality. Objection based on reference to standards of international law

---

[276] In *Prior* v. *Canada* [1988] FCJ No. 107, a claim by a taxpayer who objected on grounds of conscience to contributing to military expenditure, was struck out, the court finding no 'offence to conscience', no being 'forced to act in a way contrary to . . . beliefs'. The Canadian Constitution does not guarantee that the State will not act inimically to a citizen's standards of proper conduct, but merely that a citizen will not be required to do something contrary to those standards, subject to the reasonable limitations recognized by s. 1 of the *Canadian Charter of Rights and Freedoms*.

[277] See *R.* v. *Big M Drug Mart* [1985] 1 SCR 295; *Edwards Books and Art Limited* v. *The Queen et al.* [1986] 2 SCR 713. In *Jones* v. *The Queen* [1986] 2 SCR 284, the issue of compulsory school attendance was examined, in a context closer to the experience of the conscientious objector. The legislation in question was held to be a reasonable limitation on a parent's religious convictions regarding the education of children. The authorities did not purport to exercise absolute control, and there was no absolute obligation to attend public schools. Instruction could be given elsewhere, including at home, provided it was certified as efficient; the appellant objected, again on religious grounds, to seeking such certification, but the court found this to be demonstrably justifiable under Canadian law.

[278] 'Compelling' here being used in the sense of 'impossible to resist': Council of Europe, *Explanatory Report*, above n. 260, paras. 15–17. In a 1985 report on *Conscientious Objection to Conscripted Military Service*, the Australian Senate Standing Committee on Constitutional and Legal Affairs referred to the individual's right not to be compelled by law to act contrary to a conscientiously held position in such a way that this would 'fundamentally impair his sense of integrity as a human being'. The Committee also rejected a 'list approach' to the bases for conscientious objection (paras. 2.2, 2.4, 2.29). In describing what was meant by conscientious belief, the Committee placed particular weight on the following analysis: ' . . . the only possible definition of a conscientious belief is a belief based on a seriously held moral conviction. That is, of course, very broad and it is perhaps best understood if we see what it leaves out. What it leaves out most clearly are beliefs based on selfish desires of one sort or another, personal interest, belief based on emotions like fear or ambition . . . beliefs which are whimsical or based on impulse.' Testimony of Prof. Peter Singer, Professor of Philosophy, Monash University: quoted ibid., para. 2.13.

may concern the purpose for which armed force is used, or it may concern the means and methods used in armed conflict ... [279]

The fundamental issue in determining entitlement to protection as a refugee on the basis of objection to military service remains the sincerity of the conviction which sets the individual in opposition to their government, and the risk of treatment amounting to persecution. Military service and objection thereto, seen from the point of view of the State, are also issues which go to the heart of the body politic. Refusal to bear arms, however motivated, reflects an essentially political opinion regarding the permissible limits of State authority; it is a political act.[280] The 'law of universal application' can thus be seen as singling out or discriminating against those holding certain political views.[281] While the State has a justifiable interest in the maintenance of its own defence,[282] the measures taken to that end should at least be 'reasonably necessary in a democratic society';[283] specifically, there ought to exist a reasonable relationship of proportionality between the end and the means.[284] The element of proportionality is especially important in

[279] The Eide/Mubanga-Chipoya Report, above n. 257, 3–4.

[280] This approach was cited with approval by the Canadian Federal Court of Appeal in *Zolfagharkhani* v. *Minister for Employment and Immigration* [1993] 3 FC 540, para. 36; see also *Erduran* v. *MIMA* (2002) 122 FCR 150; [2002] FCA 814 (Federal Court of Australia). Cf. *Mehenni* v. *Minister for Immigration and Multicultural Affairs* (1999) 164 ALR 192, [1999] FCA 789, in which the court had no doubt that both full and partial objectors could be a particular social group, but considered that a law of general application applied in a non-discriminatory way would not amount to persecution 'for reasons of' such membership. In our view, analysis along the spectrum of political opinion, which 'necessarily' opposes the individual to the authority of the State, is capable of bridging that gap.

[281] Cf. Hill J. in *Applicant N 403* v. *Minister for Immigration and Multicultural Affairs* [2000] FCA 1088 (23 Aug. 2000), para. 23, referring to Australia's draft laws during the Vietnam War, which allowed those with 'real conscientious objections' to serve in non-combatant roles: 'Without that limitation a conscientious objector could have been imprisoned. The suggested reason for their imprisonment would have been their failure to comply with the draft law, a law of universal application. But if the reason they did not wish to comply with the draft was their conscientious objection, one may ask what the real cause of their imprisonment would be. It is not difficult ... to argue that in such a case the cause ... would be the conscientious belief, which could be a political opinion, not merely the failure to comply with a law of general application. It is, however, essential, that an applicant have a real, not a simulated belief.'

[282] The converse is that no State has the right to wage a war of aggression, or to employ unlimited choice of weapons. In *Zolfagharkhani*, above n. 280, the court found that, 'The probable use of chemical weapons ... is clearly judged by the international community to be contrary to basic rules of human conduct, and consequently the ordinary Iranian conscription law of general application, as applied in a conflict in which Iran intended to use chemical weapons, amounts to persecution for political opinion': para. 34.

[283] Cf. *Akar* v. *Attorney General of Sierra Leone* [1970] AC 853, in which the Privy Council declined to accept that a law dealing with citizenship was *by that fact alone* 'reasonably necessary in a democratic society' so as to avoid constitutional limitations, including provisions on discrimination. The European Court of Human Rights interprets this phrase to mean 'justified by a pressing social need and, in particular, proportionate to the legitimate aim pursued'; see *Moustaquim* v. *Belgium* (1991) 13 EHRR 802, para. 43; *Beldjoudi* v. *France* (1992) 14 EHRR 801; *Berrehab* v. *The Netherlands* (1989) 11 EHRR 322, paras. 25, 29.

[284] In the United Kingdom, throughout the Second World War, conscientious objectors were permitted the alternative of civilian service. Exemption from that was also permitted if reasons of

this context of competing interests, where the right in question has not yet been generally accepted by States as falling within the corpus of fundamental human rights.[285]

Alternative service can help to reconcile the situation in a way that promotes community interests in defence and equality of treatment, and the individual's interest in his or her own conscience. Whether alternative service meets international standards is a question of fact in each case, having regard to conditions, nature, and duration.[286] In the absence of alternative service, or where insufficient weight is given to a sincerely held belief going to conscience, the likelihood of prosecution and punishment must be examined in order to determine whether they amount to persecution. This may be the case where the treatment is disproportionate, excessive or arbitrary, and whether it derives from official or unofficial sources.

5.5.1.4 *Sepet and Bulbul*

The United Kingdom case of *Sepet and Bulbul* involved applications for asylum by Turkish citizens, members of the Kurdish minority, who objected to serving in the Turkish military.[287] Lord Bingham and Lord Hoffmann made three findings in particular. First, the treatment feared by the claimants, even if severe enough to amount to persecution, was not 'caused' by their belief, but by their refusal to obey a law of general application. Secondly, there was no 'core human right' called conscientious objection to military service which could be shown to be violated. Thirdly, in Lord Hoffmann's view, freedom of conscience ends where manifestation of conscience begins.

In the judgment of Lord Bingham, when deciding whether a person would be persecuted for a Convention reason, the 'real reason' had to be assessed; this was the

religion or conscience demanded, while the criterion for exemption was the honesty or sincerity, rather than the 'validity' of the views held. See Barker, R., *Conscience, Government and War*, (1982); Hayes, D., *Challenge of Conscience. The Story of the Conscientious Objectors of 1939–1949*, (1949). Some 60,000 conscientious objectors were registered in the United Kingdom during the Second World War, that is, some 1.2 % of the total conscripted: Barker, above, 115.

[285] In a case in the Federal Republic of Germany in 1976 (*Verwaltungsgericht, Ansbach Nr.* AN3220-II(IV)/73, cited with approval by the same court in 1977: *VG Ansbach Nr.* AN8341-IV/76), the court expressly conceded the widest discretion to other States in the regulation of military service, which it considered to fall within the reserved domain of domestic jurisdiction (*innerstaatliche Rechtsordnung*). The court declined to apply the standard of exemption recognized by art. 4 of the 1949 Constitution of the Federal Republic; its reasoning would not appear wholly consistent with that adopted in cases of *Republikflucht*, but seems well established. See also *BVerwGE*, Bd. 62. 5. 123 (1981).

[286] See on alternative service, Sub-Commission on the Prevention of Discrimination and the Protection of Minorities, *Conscientious Objection to Military Service*: UN doc. E/CN.4/Sub.2/1983/30/Rev.1, paras. 104–15, 150–3; but see also *Hendens* v. *Belgium* App. No. 24630/94, 22 May 1995, in which the European Commission on Human Rights declared inadmissible an application by a Jehovah's Witness imprisoned for refusal to do either military or alternative service; and *JPK* v. *Netherlands*, Communication no. 401/1990, CCPR/C/143/0/401/1990, 7 Nov. 1991, Human Rights Committee—requirement to do military service does not violate arts. 6, 7 ICCPR66.

[287] *Sepet and Bulbul* v. *Secretary of State for the Home Department* [2003] 1 WLR 856.

reason operating in the mind of the persecutor, and treatment was not persecutory if it was meted out to all and was not discriminatory. In his view, the applicants were not being persecuted for their political opinions, since it was clear that anyone refusing to perform military service would be treated in the same way, whatever his personal grounds for doing so.[288] Lord Hoffmann took a similar view:

If the applicants refuse to serve, the state is entitled to punish them, not for their political opinions but for failing to enlist. Their political opinions may be the reason why they refuse to serve but they are not the reason why they will be punished . . . . [I]mposing a punishment for failing to comply with a universal obligation of this kind is not persecution.[289]

In our view, this approach to causation is insufficient; it does not take adequate account of relevant difference, a point already stressed above and cogently made over forty years ago:

Since each religion or belief makes different demands on its followers, a mechanical approach of the principle of equality which does not take into account the various demands will often lead to injustice and in some cases even to discrimination.[290]

In the matter of human rights, matters of conscience (beliefs sincerely held in the exercise of this freedom) are matters of *relevant difference*, which is why freedom of conscience is a fundamental human right not subject to derogation, even in time of national emergency.

Having accepted that 'there could be no persecution for Convention reasons without discriminatory infringement of a recognized human right',[291] the Court examined whether the treatment feared by the applicants would indeed violate a recognized human right. It answered this question in the negative, because the right it wanted and failed to find was the human right to conscientious objection to military service, rather than freedom of conscience itself or the 'relevant difference' to which the exercise of freedom of conscience might give rise.

Although it had before it a considerable body of material showing the evolution of State practice in support of such a right, the Court was impressed more by the lack of formal recognition and by the fact that key human rights instruments expressly maintained that the prohibition of 'forced or compulsory labour' should *not* include either military service or substitute service. What the Court did not note was that this formulation leaves open the possibility that (permissible) military service may still infringe human rights other than the prohibition on forced labour.[292] For example, it is by no means inconceivable that the conditions of compulsory military service might violate the prohibition of inhuman or

---

[288] Ibid., 871–2, para. 22.

[289] Ibid., 873, para. 27. This rather recalls the words of Anatole France: 'The law, in its majestic equality, forbids the rich as well as the poor to sleep under bridges, to beg in the streets, and to steal bread': *The Red Lily* (1894).

[290] United Nations, 'Study of Discrimination in the Matter of Religious Rights and Practices', UN doc. E/CN.4/Sub.2/300/Rev.1 (1960), 15.   [291] Ibid., 863–4, para. 9.

[292] See above, 105–7.

degrading treatment,[293] or, as the European Committee of Social Rights found, 'the right of the worker to earn his living in an occupation freely entered upon'.[294]

The confusion of the Court arises from the perceived need to establish that the right of conscientious objection to military service exists and is recognized as a fundamental human right or 'core entitlement', *before* it can form the basis for a refugee claim and a well-founded fear of persecution within the meaning of the 1951 Convention. In our view, this is incorrect and not required by the terms of the 1951 Convention or impliedly by reference to its object and purpose. The right to freedom of conscience is the central right at issue, and freedom of conscience which is violated in the public political sphere when a person is compelled to do military service contrary to their sincerely held belief. That violation may take many forms, for example, from physical compulsion to penalties for non-compliance of varying severity. Whether the treatment amounts to persecution within the meaning of the Convention will depend on a number of factors, including the availability of alternative service and the frequency and extent of punishment.

Just as the right to freedom of expression ensures the protection of opinions from right to left, so the right to freedom of conscience protects beliefs and the manifestation of belief. However, in *Sepet and Bulbul* this simple point got lost in the hunt for just one specific manifestation, namely, the 'lesser' right of objection to military service. In Lord Hoffmann's view, what counted was the fact that the 'absolute' right to freedom of conscience is qualified at the point where it is made 'manifest', whereupon it may be limited so far as 'necessary to protect public safety, order, health, or morals, or the fundamental rights and freedoms of others'. In his view, 'The framers of the covenants appear to have believed ... that public safety was a legitimate reason for not allowing a religion or belief to be manifested by refusal to do military service.'[295]

What the framers did in fact was to leave it to States to determine how to regulate military service, should they opt for conscription, within the limits of the Covenant and international law. There is nothing in the Covenant that requires eternal passive submission on the part of those seeking to exercise their freedom of conscience, but whether those who object on that account to military service are refugees within the meaning of the Convention depends on how the State responds. If objectors are persecuted, then they are persecuted for a Convention reason.

The judgment in *Sepet and Bulbul* also appears to be internally inconsistent. Neither Lord Hoffmann's view of conscience nor his and Lord Bingham's view of

[293] Cf. *Krotov v. Secretary of State for the Home Department* [2004] 1 WLR 1825, [2004] EWCA Civ 69.

[294] Complaint No. 8/2000 (*The Quaker Council for European Affairs v. Greece*, decision on the merits, 25 April 2001); Council of Europe, European Social Charter, European Committee of Social Rights, *Conclusions XVI–1*, Vol. 1, July 2001–June 2002; above, 106–7.

[295] *Sepet and Bulbul* [2003] 1 WLR 856, 877–8, para. 46.

causation sits easily with the Court's earlier finding that refugee status can indeed be accorded to one who refuses military service, if such service might require him to commit atrocities or gross human rights abuses, *or* where refusal to serve would earn grossly excessive or disproportionate punishment. As a matter of logic, grossly excessive or disproportionate punishment cannot turn non-Convention persecution into Convention persecution. Even if 'disproportionate punishment' is presumed to be discriminatory, still the question remains, on what Convention ground? The degree of punishment may be evidence of persecution, but the link to the Convention must lie somewhere else; and in our view, that can only be through the political opinion that is reflected in the exercise of freedom of conscience.

From recognition of the protected interest of freedom of conscience, it is but a short step to the critical issue, namely, the circumstances under which the punishment or treatment, legal or extra-legal, feared by the claimant amounts to persecution. As a matter of principle, States are free to recognize conscientious objection *in itself* as a sufficient ground upon which to base recognition of refugee status. In this sense, they are free to attribute such value to the fundamental right to freedom of conscience that *any* measures having as their object to compel the individual to act contrary to sincerely held belief, or any punishment, such as deprivation of liberty, imposed to that end, amounts to persecution within the meaning of the 1951 Convention, regardless of its duration.

As a matter of practice, however, States determining refugee status hold back from such absolute positions, in favour of taking full account of all the circumstances. International human rights law attaches special importance to the individual's freedom of conscience. The standards of reasonableness and proportionality must be applied to the particular facts of each case. Whether prosecution and punishment amount to persecution in the sense of the Convention will depend on the object and purpose of the law, the precise motivation of the individual who breaches such law, the 'interest' which such individual asserts and the nature and extent of the punishment. This in turn invites attention to (1) the genuineness of the applicant's beliefs, as a manifestation of freedom of conscience; (2) the nature of the individual's objection, so far as it may be relevant to the nature of the military conflict at issue (if any), or the way in which war is being waged; (3) the legality of the military action (if any), for which conscription is employed; (4) the scope and manner of implementation of military service laws; (5) the selective conscription of particular groups within society, and the bases of such distinctions; (6) the extent to which the right of conscientious objection is recognized, if at all; (7) the type of alternative service available, if any, its length and conditions by comparison with military service, and the treatment of conscientious objectors performing such service; (8) the manner of prosecution and the proportionality and likelihood of punishment of conscientious objectors in the absence of alternative service; (9) the treatment of conscientious objectors subject to such punishment, including the extra-legal activities of paramilitary groups or sections of the populace; and (10) the extent to which penalties for conscientious objection may be employed selectively, against specific racial, religious, social, or political groups.

5.5.2 Political and non-political offenders

Similar considerations apply to the related question of non-extradition of political offenders. The IRO Constitution excluded 'ordinary criminals who are extraditable by treaty' as well as 'war criminals, quislings, and traitors' and a variety of other 'undeserving' groups; the UNHCR Statute and the 1951 Convention contain equivalent provisions.[296] The exception in favour of political offenders developed in the nineteenth century in the context of bilateral extradition arrangements, and is not the consequence of any rule of general international law. No duty obliges States to surrender fugitive criminals and extradition itself has traditionally been seen as a gloss upon the rule which permits the grant of territorial asylum.[297] In practice, characterization of an offence as 'political' is left to the authorities of the State from which extradition is requested, and the function of characterization itself is evidently one in which political considerations will be involved, including the self-interest of the requested State as reflected in its military and other alliances.[298] Not surprisingly, divergent attitudes are revealed in municipal law. For example, the political offence exception did not figure in the extradition arrangements existing between eastern European socialist States,[299] although their constitutions commonly recognized the institution of asylum.[300] In contrast, certain Western European States developed an elaborate comprehensive approach to purely political offences, complex political offences, and related political offences, all of which might justify non-extradition.[301] Nevertheless, the weight to be accorded to the motives of the offender varied from jurisdiction to jurisdiction,[302] as did the practice on substantive limitations to the political

---

[296] Para. 7(d) and art. 1F, respectively. See further below, Ch. 4, s. 4.

[297] O'Connell, D. P., *International Law*, (2nd edn., 1970), 720; *Asylum* case, ICJ *Rep.*, 1950, 266, at 274; Lauterpacht, H., 'The Law of Nations and the Punishment of War Crimes', 21 *BYIL* (1944); Bassiouni, M. C., *Crimes against Humanity in International Criminal Law*, (1992).

[298] Goodwin-Gill, *Movement of Persons*, 143ff, 226–8; Corey, J. M., 'INS v Doherty: The Politics of Extradition, Deportation and Asylum', 16 *Maryland J. Int'l. L & Trade* 83 (1992).

[299] See Shearer, I. A., *Extradition in International Law* (1971) 65–6; Epps, V., 'The Validity of the Political Offence Exception in Extradition Treaties in Anglo-American Jurisprudence', 20 *Harv. ILJ* (1979) 61, 86; Gold, M. E., 'Non-extradition for political offences: the Communist perspective', 11 *Harv. ILJ* (1970) 191.

[300] See the provisions listed in *A Selected Bibliography on Territorial Asylum* (1977): UN doc. ST/GENEVA/LIB.SER.B/Ref.9, 68–74.

[301] See, in particular, the Swiss cases: *Pavan*, Ann. Dig., 1927–8, 347 (in which the theory of predominance is advanced); *Ficorilli*, 18 ILR 345 (1951); *Kavic*, 19 ILR 371 (1952); also, Whiteman, M., *Digest of International Law*, vol. 6, 799ff.

[302] In *Giovanni Gatti*, Ann. Dig. 1947 case no. 70: Kiss, *Répertoire de la pratique française en matière de droit international public*, (1966), vol. 2, 213–14, the Court of Appeal of Grenoble took the view that motive alone does not give a common crime the character of a political offence; such offence springs from the nature of the rights of the State which are injured. Cf. *Public Prosecutor* v. *Zind*, 40 ILR 214.

offence exception. Some States have long excluded assassination of the head of State, while others have explicitly excluded acts of barbarism or offences the suppression of which is required under international obligations.[303] Moreover, appreciation of the political character of offences is clearly likely to vary according to the particular perspective of the requested State.[304]

Much of the early debates and the jurisprudence concentrated on acts committed during the course of an insurrection,[305] and successive decisions of courts in the United Kingdom have limited the exception to offences committed in the context of parties in opposition and conflict.[306] To a significant extent, and taking account also of recent internationally agreed limitations, this approach is confirmed in the jurisprudence of the United States and other countries. The offence should have been committed in the course of some political dispute or conflict, and have been related to the promotion of political ends. Intention or motive is not conclusive, however, and there is a presumption against classifying as political those offences which may be loosely described as common law crimes, such as murder and robbery. Inherent limitations on the category of political offences, by reference to their nature and circumstances, are increasingly accepted.

In the Federal Republic of Germany, for example, the extradition law expressly excludes murder and attempted murder, unless they occur in open combat.[307] Judicial decisions confirm that to qualify as political offences, the actions in question must be directed against the organization of the State (*unmittelbar*

---

[303] Kiss, *Répertoire de la pratique française*, vol. 2, 210, 212, 216–17; cf. art. 3, 1957 European Convention on Extradition.

[304] See *VerwRspr*, Bd. 20, S. 332 (OVG Münster, 1968). A Belgian was sentenced to 12 years imprisonment for having served in the *Wehrmacht* during the Second World War. Released on parole, he was subsequently sentenced to serve the remainder of his sentence. He fled to the Federal Republic of Germany where the court upheld his appeal against expulsion and noted that he would in any event be immune from extradition by reason of the political character of his offence. Cf. *In re Pohle*, 46 *BVerfGE*, 214, noted 73 *AJIL* 305–6 (1979), where the Federal Constitutional Court, in an appeal by a convicted member of the Baader-Meinhof group subsequently extradited from Greece, maintained the traditional rule that extradition treaties confer no rights on individuals, save if expressly mentioned. It construed the treaty with Greece as neither conferring rights on political offenders nor as barring a request for surrender of an offender who might be covered by an exception clause. It further held that membership in a 'criminal organization', even if politically motivated, did not constitute a political offence from the perspective of the German legal system.

[305] See, for example, debates in the United Kingdom, summarised in 6 *British Digest of International Law*, 661ff.

[306] In the leading cases, *Re Castioni* [1891] 1 QB 149 and *Re Meunier* [1894] 2 QB 415, the court emphasized that, to qualify for non-extradition, the offences in question must be 'incidental to and...part of political disturbances', involving two or more parties. In *R. v. Governor of Brixton Prison, ex p. Schtraks* [1964] AC 556, it was suggested that the word 'political', 'indicate[s]...that the requesting State is after [the fugitive] for reasons other than the enforcement of the criminal law in its ordinary,...common or international aspect'. In each case, the fundamental requirement was that of political disturbance and opposition. See also *Cheng v. Governor of Pentonville Prison* [1973] 2 All ER 204, at 209; Lord Diplock said that an offence could not be considered political 'unless the only purpose sought to be achieved by the offender...were to change the government of the *state in which it was committed*...' (emphasis supplied); and the more recent detailed analysis in *T v. Secretary of State for the Home Department*, discussed below at 120–2.

[307] Art. 3(3), *Deutsches Auslieferungsgesetz 1929:* '...im offenen Kampf'.

gegen...).[308] The Federal Administrative Court has also ruled against the grant of asylum to those who commit offences in a fight against democracy in other countries, and, in the absence of any evidence of persecution, face prosecution for such offences.[309]

The French Extradition Law of 1927 provides that there shall be no extradition, 'Lorsque le crime ou délit a un caractère politique ou lorsqu'il résulte des circonstances que l'extradition est demandée dans un but politique...'[310] Acts committed during civil war or insurrection may benefit, unless they amount to 'odious barbarism'.[311] Decisions on claims to asylum and refugee status have been founded on a similar principle. In a 1958 decision, for example, the *Office français de protection des réfugiés et apatrides* (OFPRA) applied the rule that:

Par crime de droit commun... il y a lieu d'entendre toute infraction qui n'est pas commise à l'occasion de la lutte de l'intéressé contre les autorités responsables des persécutions dont l'intéressé est ou a été victime, sans d'ailleurs qu'il y ait lieu de donner au mot 'crime' le sens précis que lui prête le droit interne français.[312]

Homicides and, in particular, the deaths of civilians or even State officials chosen at random, have been consistently found to fall outside the protection of the political offence.[313] Commenting on exclusion jurisprudence in 1988, Tiberghien concluded:

... dans toutes les affaires jugées jusqu'ici par la Commission des recours et par le Conseil d'Etat, les assassinats et les attentats visaient soit des civils innocents, soit des représentants

---

[308] See the following two extradition cases: OLG Frankfurt, 8.6.1973; *NJW* 1973, 1568: neither attacks on banks nor explosives offences are political offences as such, and do not become political because committed by radical anarchists with the aim of altering society and having the intention to combat with force all manifestations of State authority. See similarly, BGH, 17.8.1978, a case involving the Croatian Revolutionary Brotherhood, whose goals and methods included bomb attacks on innocent civilians: '... sind als politisches Taten aber nur strafbare Angriffe anzusehen, die sich *unmittelbar* gegen den Bestand oder die Sicherheit des Staates richten, soweit sie nicht im offenen Kampf begangen worden sind'. ('Unless they occur during open combat, criminally punishable acts are only to be considered as political offences if they are *directly* targeted on the organization and security of the State.' Authors' translation). The court also ruled that for extradition purposes, more than mere membership in such a terrorist organization is required before an individual can be returned on the ground of involvement in an offence against life.

[309] BVerwG 17.5.1983; *BVerwGE* 76, 184; the Federal Administrative Court confirmed the interpretations of art. 3 of the extradition law described above. In *Quinn* v. *Wren* [1985] IR 322 the court refused to accord immunity from extradition to those whose objectives included the destruction of the very constitution under which they now claimed protection. In a later decision of the Supreme Court, the Chief Justice ruled that personal, mental reservations regarding the overthrow of the Irish Constitution were insufficient to allow the appellant thereby to rely on the principle of non-extradition for political offences: *Russell* v. *Fanning* [1988] IR 333, 340.

[310] Art. 5(2), loi du 10 mars 1927; Kiss, *Répertoire de la pratique française en matière de droit international public*, vol. 2, 204.

[311] Such as killing a wounded policeman, 'un crime de droit commun... un acte de barbarie odieux contraire aux lois de l'honneur et de la guerre, depuis longtemps indiscutées par les nations civilisées': *Morelli*, Cour d'Aix, arrêt du 15 nov. 1928: *Clunet 1930*, 108–9.

[312] *Gardai*, 2.800, 7 fév. 1958; cited in Tiberghien, *La protection des réfugiés*, 104.468. So far, no decision has 'upheld' an offence committed against the authors of persecution.

[313] Cf. *McMullen* v. *INS* 788 F.2d 591, 597 (9th Cir., 1986): 'There is a meaningful distinction between terrorist acts directed at the military or official agencies of the State, and random acts of

de l'ordre public choisis au hasard et non pas pour leur qualité de responsables de persécutions infligées aux auteurs des assassinats.[314]

The case of *Urizar-Murgoitio*, decided by the *Conseil d'Etat* on 14 December 1987, is illustrative. The appellant, from the Basque country in Spain, was accused of the death by shooting of a naval officer and a bar-owner, a suspected informer, and of a bomb attack against the police, which left two children victims, one dead, and the other disabled and blind. The *Conseil d'Etat* noted:

... la circonstance que ces crimes, qui ne sont pas politiques par leur nature, auraient été commis dans le cadre d'une lutte pour l'indépendance du pays basque et au sein d'une organisation armée, ne suffit pas, compte tenu de leur gravité, à les faire regarder comme ayant un caractère politique.[315]

Neither intention, nor the presence or absence of political motives will determine the characterization of the offence.[316] In *McMullen* v. *INS*, the US Court of Appeals for the Ninth Circuit expressly rejected 'the argument that places the determination... on the alien's state of mind. The law focuses on the circumstances surrounding the acts.'[317] Quoting the first edition of this work,[318] among other sources, the court further observed:

Of course, for a criminal act to be 'political', the individual must have been motivated by political reasons... However, 'motivation is not itself determinative of the political character of any given act.' ... The critical issue is 'whether there is a close and direct causal link between the crime committed and its alleged political purpose and object.'

Notwithstanding certain contradictory elements, United States jurisprudence generally supports the view that indiscriminate violence is not a protected political act.[319]

---

violence against ordinary citizens that are intended only "to promote social chaos".' Also, *T* v. *Secretary of State for the Home Department*, below, 120–2.

[314] Tiberghien, F., *Doc. réf.*, No. 43, 9/18 juillet 1988, Supp., pp. 3–4.

[315] *Rec. Dalloz Sirey*, 1988, Inf. rap., 20; extract of decision in *Documentation réfugiés, Doc. réf*, No. 43, 9/18 juillet 1988, Supp., 6. To similar effect, *Lujambio Galdeano*, Conseil d'Etat (CE), 25 sept. 1984, 62.847: *Rec. Lebon*, 308; Tiberghien, *La protection des réfugiés*, 254f. This case involved 'assassinat par groupes armées'; such crimes were not inherently political and did not become so, merely by reason of their commission in the context of an independence struggle. See also *Croissant*, CE, 7 juillet 1978, 10.079: *Rec. Lebon*, 292; *(Gabor) Winter*, CE, 15 fév. 1980, 17.224: *Rec. Lebon*, 87. The application of art. 1F(b) to those who commit serious non-political crimes *in* France has been controversial for some years: Tiberghien, 102–3, 468; also the case of presumed ETA leader, Santiago Arrposide Sarasola (Santi Potros), *Doc. réf.* no. 126: 20/29 oct. 1990; and below,

[316] Cf. *Giovanni Gatti*, in which the Cour de Grenoble in 1947 observed, 'Le caractère politique d'un acte ne dépend pas de l'existence ou de la non-existence de motifs politiques, qui sont le secret de la pensée de l'auteur, mais uniquement de l'acte considéré en lui-même...': Ch. des mises en accusation, arrêt de 13 janv. 1947; Kiss, *Répertoire de la pratique française en matière de droit international public*, vol. 2, 213.   [317] *McMullen* v. *INS*, 788 F.2d 591, 597.

[318] At 60–1; see now below, Ch. 4, s. 4.2.

[319] In *Eain* v. *Wilkes*, 641 F.2d 504 (7th Cir., 1981), a member of the PLO who planted a bomb in a market-place, which killed two young boys and wounded many other people, was extradited precisely on this ground. See *O'Cealleagh*, 23 *I&N Dec.* 976 (BIA, 2006), in which the BIA interpreted the 'purely political offense' exception to inadmissibility under 8 USC §1182(a)(2)(A)(i)(I), holding that the offence must be completely or totally political.

McMullen concerned a former member of the Provisional IRA, who had successfully resisted extradition from the United States, and who now sought asylum
and withholding of deportation to the Republic of Ireland.[320] The Ninth Circuit
addressed precisely the issue, whether the petitioner was ineligible for asylum by
reason of there being serious reasons to consider that he had committed a serious
non-political crime. Emphasizing the asylum context, the court favoured the use
of a balancing approach to the alleged serious non-political crime, in which the
proportionality of the act to its objective and the degree of atrocity would be taken
into account. It noted that terrorist activities were involved, including indiscriminate bombing campaigns, murder, torture, and maiming of innocent civilians
who disagree with the objectives and methods of the Provisional IRA. In the view
of the court, 'such acts are beyond the pale of protectable "political offence" '.
There was no sufficient link between the acts and the political objective; they
were so barbarous, atrocious, and disproportionate as to amount to serious non-
political crimes. At several places, the court stresses the civilian targets of PIRA
terrorist activities, in a manner that recalls the special protection accorded to civilians under the laws of war, and presents an analogy with the mandatory exclusion
from the Convention of those who have committed war crimes.[321]

At one time, Irish courts tended to disregard the nature of the offences that
were the subject of extradition requests by the British authorities;[322] that position
changed as it came to be recognized that not every charge connected with armed
struggle is to be considered a political offence. In *McGlinchey* v. *Wren*, for example,
the murder of an elderly postmistress by the PIRA was ruled not to fall within the
political offence exception.[323] This was followed in *Shannon* v. *Fanning*, which
involved the murder of a former Speaker of the Northern Ireland House of
Commons, and of his son, a former MP. In the view of the court:

> ... the circumstances of the murders ... were so brutal, cowardly and callous that it would
> be a distortion of language if they were to be accorded the status of political offences or
> offences connected with political offences.[324]

In one of the few relatively recent cases to consider the question, *T* v. *Secretary of
State for the Home Department*, the House of Lords divided over the correct
approach to 'political offence'. Lords Keith, Browne Wilkinson and Lloyd were of

---

[320] The facts are set out in full in 658 F.2d 1312 (1981).

[321] In a 1989 extradition case, the Court ruled that an act properly punishable even in the context
of declared war, or in the heat of open military conflict, cannot fall within the political offence exception: *Mahmoud Abed Atta*, 706 F. Supp. 1032 (D.Ct., EDNY, 1989). The case involved an attack in
Israel on a bus, in which the driver was killed and a passenger wounded. The court opted for a quali-
tative standard, that takes account of 'our own notions of civilised strife'. It also ruled that, even if one
or more of the passengers might have been a non-civilian, this did not make the bus a military vehicle
at the time of the attack, so exposing it to indiscriminate attack. Cf. *Gonzalez* v. *Minister of
Employment and Immigration* [1994] FCJ No. 765.

[322] See, for example, *O'Neill* v. *Attorney-General*, *The Times*, 30 Jul. 1974 (deaths of passers-by in
bombing attack on police station).   [323] [1982] IR 154.

[324] [1984] IR 569, 581.

the view that there must be both a political purpose and a sufficiently close and direct link between the crime and the purpose; they further considered that the means employed, including the target and the likelihood of indiscriminate killing of members of the public, may 'break' the link and make the connection too remote. For Lords Mustill and Slynn, however, acts of violence such as the indiscriminate killing of persons unconnected with the government could not, by definition, amount to political crimes, and in their view, both causation and remoteness as tests of the 'political' raised too many problems.

The gravity of the offence is relevant to the question whether it is 'serious' for the purposes of article 1F(b). But the crime either is or is not political when committed, and its character cannot depend on the consequences which the offender may afterwards suffer if he is returned.[325]

In the absence of any definition or list of political crimes, national or international, this reasoning appears to beg the question, for experience shows that a crime may indeed be 'political' *precisely* because of the consequences which await the offender. Lord Mustill's query of the approach adopted in *McMullen* to questions of means and ends and proportionality also misses the point:

. . . why should a crime which would have been political in nature be turned into one which is not political, simply because the judge deems the offender to have gone too far?[326]

The short answer is because that is how different jurisdictions have in fact placed limitations on the extent of immunity from extradition, and because few crimes are necessarily and inherently 'political', and because any crime ought to be considered in context; and finally, because the decision to be made itself has an inherently 'political' dimension. The idea that an offence 'either is or is not political when and where committed' may be appropriate from the single perspective of the criminal, but that view alone has not been accepted as sufficient by the courts. Lord Mustill suggested writing 'terrorism' into the modern concept of the political crime, and took the League of Nations definition ('criminal acts directed against a State and intended or calculated to create a state of terror in the minds of particular persons, or a group of persons or the general public'[327]) as an appropriate, objective model.

Lord Lloyd, on the other hand (who cited the approval in *McMullen* of the test proposed in the first edition of the work), was of the view that a definitive answer to the political crime question was unlikely: 'The most that can be attempted is a description of an idea.' Nevertheless, that could still be done:

A crime is a political crime for the purposes of art. 1F(b) . . . if, and only if; (1) it is committed for a political purpose, that is to say, with the object of overthrowing or subverting or changing the government of a state or inducing it to change its policy; and (2) there is a

[325] *T* v. *Secretary of State for the Home Department* [1996] AC 742, 769.   [326] Ibid., 770.
[327] Ibid., 762, 773.

sufficiently close and direct link between the crime and the alleged political purpose. In determining whether such a link exists, the court will bear in mind the means used to achieve the political end, and will have particular regard to whether the crime was aimed at a military or governmental target, on the one hand, or a civilian target on the other, and in either event whether it was likely to involve the indiscriminate killing or injuring of members of the public.[328]

In the European context, the development, or consolidation, of a restrictive approach to the political offence has reflected regional developments, such as the 1977 European Convention on the Suppression of Terrorism, as well as recognition of the new dimension of terrorist violence introduced by military and paramilitary organizations. From an international legal perspective, this progression is by no means new; already in 1948, States had agreed that genocide should not be considered a political offence for extradition purposes, and subsequent years have seen broad agreement on the depoliticization of other offences, such as hijacking, hostage-taking, and offences against diplomats.[329]

In general, it may be concluded that an offence will not be considered political if (1) it is *remote*, in the sense that there is no sufficient 'close and direct causal link between the crime committed and its alleged political purpose'; and (2) if it is *disproportionate* in relation to the political aims.

In one British case, Lord Diplock explained that the political offence exception had the dual purpose of avoiding the United Kingdom's involvement in the internal political conflicts of foreign States; and preventing, on humanitarian grounds, the surrender of an offender to a jurisdiction in which trial and punishment might be unfairly prejudiced by political considerations.[330] As regards the latter, international legal principles relating to the protection of refugees are immediately involved. Not only must the offence in respect of which extradition is requested be examined, but also the broader context, with due consideration given to humanitarian issues and the fundamental rights of the individual. The good faith and motives of the requesting State may require investigation, and although some courts are wary of this highly political arena,[331] others have been prepared to apply 'persecution criteria' more generously. State practice suggests, at the least,

---

[328] Ibid., 786–7.

[329] The 1977 European Convention on the Suppression of Terrorism (*ETS* No. 196), for example, provides that the following offences shall not be considered as political offences: offences against internationally protected persons; kidnapping; hostage-taking; the use of explosives or automatic firearms, if such use endangers persons; and attempts to commit any of the above. Other offences may also be excluded if they involve collective danger to the life, physical integrity, or liberty of persons; if those affected are foreign to the motives of those responsible; and if cruel or vicious means are employed. For text, see below, Annexe 2, No. 12; see also art. 1 and Appendix, 2005 European Convention on the Prevention of Terrorism: *CETS* No. 196.

[330] *Cheng* v. *Governor of Pentonville Prison* [1973] 2 All ER 204, at 209. Cf. United Kingdom Extradition Act 2003, ss. 13, 21.

[331] See, for example, *Re Arton* [1896] 1 QB 108, 110, 115; *R.* v. *Governor of Brixton Prison, ex p. Kotronis* [1971] AC 250; *Zacharia* v. *Cyprus* [1962] 2 All ER 438; *R.* v. *Governor of Brixton Prison, ex p. Keane* [1971] 2 WLR 1243; similarly in the United States of America, see *Re Lincoln* 228 F. 70 (1915); *Re Gonzalez* 217 F. Supp. 717 (1963).

that these factors should be taken into account at some level, either judicial or executive.

At one time it might have been fashionable to argue that the international community did not exist for the purpose of preserving established governments, and that the political offence exception was therefore valuable for the dynamic quality it brought to the relations between States, on the one hand, and between States and their citizens, on the other hand.[332] International law, however, provided no guidance on the substance of the concept of political offence, other than its outermost limits, and States retained the broadest discretion. Given the range now of agreements restricting the concept of political offence, as well as the increasingly common rejection of political violence, particularly where innocent lives are taken or put at risk, it is increasingly open to question whether much remains in the way of core content. The underlying humanitarian issues—protection against persecution, torture, inhuman treatment, and so forth—and what might be termed the expanding responsibilities of States in regard to an international *ordre public*, are presently in tension.[333] Arguably, the mere commission of a political offence is not sufficient to qualify a person for refugee status, which arises only where the anticipated punishment shades into persecution. Alternatively, it may be that certain offences are inherently political, that their commission reflects the failure of a State to protect a greater and more valued interest, so that any punishment would be equivalent to persecution.

5.6 PERSECUTION AND SITUATIONS OF RISK

5.6.1 *Internal flight alternative*

There is no reason in principle why an asylum seeker's fear of persecution should relate to the whole of his or her country of origin;[334] for various reasons, it may be

---

[332] Many earlier treaties, however, were intended precisely to ensure the survival of rulers. See, for example, art. 3, 1765 Treaty between the Nabob Shujah-ul-Dowla, the Nabob Nudjum-ul-Dowla, and the English Company, executed at Illiabad: 'His Highness solemnly engages never to entertain or receive Cossim Ally Khan, the late Soubahday of Bengal, etc., Sombre, the assassin of the English, nor any of the European deserters, within his dominions, nor to give the least countenance, support, or protection to them. He likewise solemnly engages to deliver up to the English whatever Europeans may in future desert from them into his country': Aitchison, C.U., *A Collection of Treaties, Engagements and Sanads Relating to India and Neighbouring Countries*, (4th edn., 1909), vol. I., 89–91. Also, 1816 Treaty of Perpetual Defensive Alliance between the Honorable English East India Company and His Highness Maharajah Pursojee Bhooslah, his heirs and successors, which, after providing in art. 1 that 'The friends and enemies of either shall be the friends and enemies of both . . .', continues in art. 14: 'The British Government agrees not to give aid or countenance to any discontented subjects or dependants of the Maharajah, or any members of His Highness' family or relations or servants of His Highness, who, in like manner, engages to refuse protection to any persons who may be in a state of rebellion against the British Government or its allies, or to any fugitives from their respective territories': ibid., vol. I, 419–24.

[333] Cf. Goodwin-Gill, G. S., 'Crimes in International Law: Obligations *Erga Omnes* and the Duty to Prosecute', in Goodwin-Gill, G. S. & Talmon, S., eds., *The Reality of International Law: Essays in Honour of Ian Brownlie*, (1999), 199.

[334] In *Acosta*, 19 *I&N Dec.* 211 (BIA, 1985), however, the US Board of Immigration Appeals saw the requirement of international protection as inherent in the refugee concept, because the claimant's

impossible or impracticable for the asylum seeker to move internally, rather than to cross an international frontier.[335] There is also authority for the principle that it should be *reasonable* for the potential refugee to relocate to a safe area, although that apparently simple notion has given rise both to extensive discussion and to a range of not always consistent applications.[336] While different jurisdictions have held that the principal criterion is the availability in fact of effective protection against persecution in another region,[337] decisions have varied in regard to the requisite level of protection of other rights, such as those necessary to maintaining some sort of social and economic existence.[338] In *ex parte Robinson*, a 1997 decision of the UK Court of Appeal,[339] it was said that all the circumstances should be considered, 'against the backcloth that the issue is whether the claimant is entitled to refugee status'. The court referred to various tests, including the reasonable

country of origin was no longer safe. The criterion of inability or unwillingness to return to a particular 'country' implied further that the claimant 'must do more than show a well-founded fear of persecution in a particular place ... within a country; he must show that the threat of persecution exists for him country-wide'.

[335] Cf. art. I(2) OAU69; see also Köfner, G. & Nicolaus, P., *Grundlagen des Asylrechts in der Bundesrepublik Deutschland*, 360–84; Marx, R., *Kommentar zum Asylverfahrensgesetz*, (6. Aufl. 2005). Cf. UNHCR, *Handbook*, para. 91; Kelley, N., 'Internal Flight/Relocation/Protection Alternative: Is it Reasonable?' 14 *IJRL* 4 (2002); Marx, R., 'The Criteria of Applying the "Internal Flight Alternative" Test in National Refugee Status Determination Procedures', 14 *IJRL* 179 (2002); Storey, H., 'The Internal Flight Alternative Test: The Jurisprudence Re-examined', 10 *IJRL* 499 (1998).

[336] For early examples, see *R. v. Immigration Appeal Tribunal, ex p. Jonah* [1985] ImmAR 7 (QBD, Nolan J.)—finding that protection available elsewhere in country of origin reversed on ground that to obtain same would have required claimant to live in a remote village away from wife and to give up trade union activities, which was unreasonable; *R. v. Secretary of State for the Home Department, ex p. Yurekli* [1990] ImmAR 334 (QBD, Otton J.)—a Kurd persecuted in his own village moved to Istanbul, leaving wife and children behind. Although safe from persecution, he was not able to find secure employment, apparently because of ethnic origin. The Secretary of State's argument that such harassment did not amount to persecution upheld as not manifestly unreasonable. The United States Asylum Regulations provide: 'An applicant does not have a well-founded fear of persecution if the applicant could avoid persecution by relocating to another part of the applicant's country ... if under all the circumstances it would be reasonable to expect the applicant to do so.': 8 CFR §208.13(b)(2)(ii).

[337] See decision of the Bundesverfassungsgericht = Federal Constitutional Court, 10 Jul. 1989, *BVerfGE* 2 BvR 502/86, 2 BvR 1000/86, 2 BvR 961/86, noting that an internal flight alternative presupposes that the territory in question offers the asylum seeker reasonable protection against persecution: Case Abstract No. *IJRL/0084*: 3 *IJRL* 343 (1991).

[338] According to art. 8 of the Qualification Directive, Member States may determine that there is no need for international protection if, in a part of his or her country of origin, the applicant has no well-founded fear *and* he or she can reasonably be expected to stay there. Member States are to have regard to 'the general circumstances prevailing in that part of the country and to the personal circumstances of the applicant', but questions of access and when a person may 'reasonably be expected' to stay in the particular location are left open. See Belgium, Commission permanente de recours des réfugiés, No. 04-0511/F1652, *X c/C.G.R.A.*, 20 oct. 2004: *RDDE*, 2004, 130, finding an absence of internal flight in the case of a former resident of Kosovo and citizen of Serbia and Montenegro; if removed to Serbia, 'elle s'y trouverait ... reprise parmi une catégorie de personnes n'ayant pas le droit d'être enregistrées comme "personnes déplacées", ce qui le placerait dans une extrême précarité et la priverait d'accès aux droits sociaux élémentaires'. The Commission also took into account her situation as a woman alone with three children. See also France, CRR, SR, 24 juin 2004, 446.177, *M.B.*

[339] [1997] 3 WLR 1162. See also, Storey, H., 'The Internal Flight Alternative Test: The Jurisprudence Re-examined', 10 *IJRL* 499 (1998).

accessibility of the safe place, whether great physical danger or undue hardship had to be faced getting or staying there, and whether the 'quality of the internal protection' met 'basic norms of civil, political and socio-economic human rights'. In the end, however, having listed the various tests, Woolf L. J. opted for that proposed by Linden J. A. in the Canadian case of *Thirunavukkarasu*,[340] namely, 'would it be unduly harsh to expect this person . . . to move to another less hostile part of the country?' This was particularly helpful, so far as the words 'unduly harsh' fairly reflect that what is in issue is whether a person claiming asylum can reasonably be expected to move to a particular part of the country.[341]

The United States Asylum Regulations provide, for example, that consideration should be given to the following factors:

whether the applicant would face other serious harm in the place of suggested relocation; any ongoing civil strife within the country; administrative, economic, or judicial infrastructure; geographical limitations; and social and cultural constraints, such as age, gender, health, and social and familial ties. Those factors may, or may not, be relevant, depending on all the circumstances of the case, and are not necessarily determinative of whether it would be reasonable for the applicant to relocate.[342]

Exactly how to apply the 'reasonableness test' was examined by the UK House of Lords in *Januzi* v. *Secretary of State for the Home Department*.[343] The Court considered but soundly rejected the argument that the 'reasonableness' of relocation is to be judged by 'whether the quality of life in the place of relocation meets the norms of civil, political and socio-economic human rights'.[344] Lord Bingham based his judgment firmly in the words of the 1951 Convention, beginning with the requirement that refugee status be based on a well-founded fear of persecution; if there is a place in which there is no fear of persecution and protection is available, and if the claimant could reasonably be expected to relocate there, then he or she cannot be said to be outside their country of origin by reason of well-founded fear.[345] Moreover, the Convention provided no justification for such an extensive

---

[340] 109 DLR (4th) 682, 687. In the particular circumstances of the appellant, a Sri Lankan Tamil, the court found that Colombo did *not* constitute an internal flight alternative, and he was declared to be a Convention refugee: ibid., paras. 14–15. See also *Rasaratnam* v. *Minister of Employment and Immigration* [1992] 1 FC 706; Case Abstract No. *IJRL/0099*: 3 IJRL 95 (1992).

[341] [1997] 3 WLR 1162, 1169–70, 1172–3.

[342] 8 CFR §208.13(b)(3)—asylum: reasonableness of internal location; 8 CFR §208.18(b)(3)— withholding. The Regulations also make the following distinctions in relation to the burden of proof: Where the applicant has not shown past persecution, then he or she has the burden of establishing that it would not be reasonable to relocate, unless the persecution is by a government or is government-sponsored; in the latter case, or if the applicant has shown past persecution, the burden is on the authorities to show, 'by a preponderance of the evidence that, under all the circumstances, it would be reasonable for the applicant to relocate': 8 CFR §208.13(b)(3)(i), (ii).

[343] *Januzi* v. *Secretary of State for the Home Department* [2006] UKHL 5, [2006] 2 WLR 397.

[344] Ibid., per Lord Hope, §45, concurring with Lord Bingham, rejecting the 'Hathaway/New Zealand rule', at paras. 15 and following. The Court preferred the approach adopted by the Court of Appeal in *E* v. *Secretary of State for the Home Department* [2004] QB 531.

[345] Ibid., per Lord Bingham, para. 7.

'human rights test', which could also not be implied, for the Convention's essential purpose was 'to ensure the fair and equal treatment of refugees in countries of asylum'.[346] In further support, he noted that the rule was not expressed in article 8 of the EU Qualification Directive, that it was not sufficiently supported in the practice of States as to give rise to a rule of customary international law, and that it would lead to anomalous consequences.[347] Instead, the Court found assistance in UNHCR's Guidelines on internal flight, in particular, for their focus on the standards prevailing generally in the country of nationality and for the manner in which the reasonableness question is framed: 'Can the claimant, in the context of the country concerned, lead a relatively normal life without facing undue hardship? If not, it would not be reasonable to expect the person to move there.'[348] As expressed by Lord Hope, 'the words "unduly harsh" set the standard that must be met', if relocation is to be considered unreasonable.[349]

5.6.2 Flight from civil war

The fact of having fled from civil war is not incompatible with a well-founded fear of persecution in the sense of the 1951 Convention.[350] Too often, the existence of civil conflict is perceived by decision-makers as giving rise to situations of general insecurity that somehow exclude the possibility of persecution.[351] A closer look at the background to the conflict, however, and the ways in which it is fought, will often establish a link to the Convention. As the Canadian Federal Court of Appeal stated in one case, 'a situation of civil war . . . is not an obstacle to a claim provided that the fear is not that felt indiscriminately by all citizens as a consequence . . . ,

[346] Ibid., paras. 15–16.   [347] Ibid., paras. 17–19.
[348] Ibid., paras. 20–1; UNHCR, 'Guidelines on Internal Flight or Relocation Alternative within the Context of Article 1A(2) of the 1951 Convention and/or 1967 Protocol relating to the Status of Refugees', HCR/GIP/03/04, 23 Jul. 2003, paras. 7, 28–30.
[349] Ibid., para. 47. According to the Canadian Federal Court of Appeal in *Ranganathan* v. *Minister of Citizenship and Immigration* [2001] 2 FC 164, this is a 'very high threshold'; cited in *Januzi*, para. 12. Cf. the jurisprudence on expulsion and art. 3 ECHR50, for example, *Bensaid* v. *United Kingdom*, (2001) 33 EHRR 205 paras. 37–40; *Arcila Henao* v. *The Netherlands*, Application No. 13669/03, 24 Jun. 2003; *D* v. *United Kingdom* (1997) 24 EHRR 423.
[350] See generally, UNHCR, *Handbook*, paras. 164–66; also Kälin, W., 'Flight in times of war', 83 *International Review of the Red Cross*, No. 843, 629–50 (2001); Bodart, S., 'Les réfugiés apolitiques: guerre civile et persécution de groupe au regard de la Convention de Genève', 7 *IJRL* 39 (1995); Hathaway, *Law of Refugee Status*, 185–8; von Sternberg, M. R., *The Grounds of Refugee Protection in the Context of International Human Rights and Humanitarian Law*, (2002); von Sternberg, M. R., 'Political Asylum and the Law of Internal Armed Conflict: Refugee Status, Human Rights and Humanitarian Law Concerns,' 5 *IJRL* 153 (1993); Kälin, W., 'Refugees and Civil Wars: Only a Matter of Interpretation?' 3 *IJRL* 435 (1991).
[351] See CRR, 21 fev. 1984, *Waked*, 21.951, *Doc. réf.*, no. 7, 15/24 juillet 1987, Suppl., CJ., 2—'les faits ainsi allégués sont des conséquences de la guerre civile qui déchire le Liban depuis de longue années et ne constituent pas des persécutions émanant directement des autorités publiques ou exercées par des particuliers avec l'encouragement ou la tolérance volontaires de ces autorités . . .' CRR, 15 sept. 1986, *Chahine*, 33.958, *Doc. réf.*, no. 7, 15/24 juillet 1987, Suppl., CJ., 4—'la requérante décrit une situation générale d'insécurité et ne fait état d'aucun mauvais traitement dont elle aurait été victime personnellement . . .'.

but that felt by the applicant himself, by a group with which he is associated, or, even by all citizens on account of a risk of persecution based on one of the reasons stated...'.[352] It nevertheless remains for the applicant to show that he or she is unable to obtain the protection of the State, and to establish the requisite Convention link.[353]

In other situations, it may be argued that the Convention does not and cannot apply to a conflict between two competing groups, or when there is no effective government responsible for the implementation of international obligations relating to human rights. A number of earlier German and French decisions and commentators, for example, drew distinctions between the civil war in Liberia and that in Somalia, finding for refugee status in the former (where rival factions had divided power between themselves and were competing for supremacy);[354] and denying it in the latter (where clans, sub-clans and factions competed amongst themselves, but none emerged as an authority in fact, controlling territory and possessing a minimum of organization).[355] This reasoning, which draws on the 'old' legal history of civil war and recognition of belligerency, has no obvious relevance to the 1951 Convention.

Likewise, in our view, both the reasoning and the result in the UK case of *Adan* v. *Secretary of State for the Home Department*[356] disclose a number of problems. The House of Lords found, *inter alia*, that the appellant was not a refugee from Somalia, then in a situation of clan-based civil war, in that he could not show a well-founded fear of persecution for a Convention reason. Lord Lloyd referred to 'the principle that those engaged (sic) in civil war are not, as such, entitled to the protection of the Convention so long as the civil war continues, even if the civil war is being fought on religious or racial grounds'.[357] Referring to the Immigration Appeal Tribunal's conclusion that all sections of society in northern Somalia were equally at risk so long as the civil war continued, Lord Lloyd considered that there

[352] *Salibian* v. *Minister for Employment and Immigration* [1990] 3 FC 250, 258; also, Conseil d'Etat, 26 mai 1993, No. 43.082 (3è ch.), *Muric c/ Etat belge*, 74 *Revue du droit des étrangers*, jan.–avr. 1993, 336. Shoyele, O., 'Armed Conflicts and Canadian Refugee Law and Policy', 16 *IJRL* 547 (2004).
[353] See *Isa* v. *Canada (Secretary of State)* [1995] FCJ No. 254 (FC-TD); *Rizkallah* v. *Minister of Employment and Immigration* [1992] FCJ No. 412 (FCA); *Zalzali* v. *Canada (Minister of Employment and Immigration)* [1991] 3FC 605 (FCA); *Attorney General* v. *Ward* [1993] 2 SCR 689.
[354] See for example, CRR, 4 sept. 1991, *Freemans*; CRR, 30 sept. 1991, *Togbah*, discussed in Tiberghien, F., 'Les situations de guerre civile et la reconnaissance de la qualité de réfugié', *Doc. réf.*, no. 181, 21/30 avr. 1992, Suppl., CJ, 4. See also *Ahmed* v. *Austria* (1996), 24 EHRR 278, finding that because of the civil war and disintegration of State authority in Somalia, 'there was no indication that... any public authority would be able to protect' the claimant: para. 44.
[355] CRR, Sections reunies, 26 nov. 1993, *Ahmed Abdullah*, 229.619, *Doc. réf.*, no. 237, 1er/14 mars 1994, Suppl., CJ, 1. See also Hailbronner, K., 'Rechtsfragen der Aufnahme von "Gewaltflüchtlingen" in Westeuropa—am Beispiel Jugoslawien', (1993) *Schweizerische Zeitschrift für internationales und europäisches Recht* 517, 527–9, citing decisions of the Federal Constitutional Court, and arguing that protection against violations of human rights in open civil war does not come within the scheme of protection of the 1951 Convention, unless a government responsible for the implementation of international obligations can still be identified.   [356] [1999] AC 293.
[357] Ibid., 311.

was 'no ground for differentiating between Mr. Adan and the members of his own or any other clan'.[358] It is not clear why, in the passage quoted above, Lord Lloyd referred to those 'engaged' in civil war, as opposed to those affected or potentially affected by it.[359] The claimant's case was not based on his active involvement in the conflict, but on the risk faced from the conflict, by reason of his clan membership. Indeed, any 'involvement' in such a conflict might well justify exclusion under article 1F(a), particularly if persecution or other war crimes are committed.

Secondly, the logic of denying refugee status to those affected by a civil conflict which itself engages or is driven by one or other Convention ground is not clear, and indeed, is not supported by authority; in our view, it is wrong.[360] The idea of 'differential risk' or 'differential impact', also relied on by Lord Lloyd, may well be a misreading of an academic gloss,[361] but in cases such as these it is hardly necessary to go beyond the words of the Convention.[362]

5.6.3 The individual and the group

Wherever large numbers of people are affected by repressive laws or practices of general or widespread application, the question arises whether each member of the group can, by reason of such membership alone, be considered to have a

[358] Ibid., 312.

[359] Lord Lloyd twice used the same word earlier in his judgment, first as a description in the passive voice: 'the local clans are engaged in civil war': ibid., 303; and secondly, in an adjectival phrase: 'fighting between clans engaged in civil war is not what the framers of the Convention had in mind by the word persecution': ibid., 308.

[360] Presumably if the conflict had become genocidal, refugee status would also have been denied; which cannot be right. Compare the decision of the US Board of Immigration Appeals in *H-*, 21 *I&N Dec.* 337 (BIA 1996), holding, first, that membership in a clan can constitute membership in a 'particular social group', and that the Marehan subclan of Somalia, the members of which share ties of kinship and linguistic commonalities, is such a group; and secondly, that while inter-clan violence may arise during the course of civil strife, such circumstances do not preclude the possibility that harm inflicted during the course of such strife may constitute persecution.

[361] See Kagan, M. & Johnson, W. P., 'Persecution in the Fog of War: The House of Lords' Decision in *Adan*', 23 *Michigan Journal of International Law* 247 (2002)—the authors' proposal for the alternative terminology of 'differential victimization' would seem to add little or anything to a commonsense assessment of the risk of harm. See also Shah, P., 'Rewriting the Refugee Convention: The *Adan* Case in the House of Lords', 12 *Immigration & Nationality Law & Practice* 100 (1998).

[362] A point made succinctly by Wilcox J. in the Australian case, *MIMA* v. *Abdi* [1999] FCA 299 (Full Court, 26 Mar. 1999), para. 37, adding at para. 39: 'It is difficult, with respect, to see the basis on which a superadded requirement of "greater risk", "differential risk" or "risk over and above that arising from clan warfare" can be derived as a criterion for application of the Convention definition where the war is based on race or religion rather than for example a quest for property, power or resources. For example, once it is established that a person is at risk of being killed or tortured in a war by reason of clan membership, in circumstances where that is one of the objectives of the war one might properly ask what further degree of danger or exposure needs to be established before the required nexus with a Convention reason is made out? Given the purpose of the Convention and the well-settled principle that a broad, liberal and purposive interpretation must be given to the language, it is difficult to see the reason why a "second tier" of "differential" or superadded persecution should be imposed on an applicant for refugee status.' See also *MIMA* v. *Ibrahim* (2000) 294 CLR 1—High Court of Australia; RSAA, *Refugee Appeal No. 71462/99*, 27 Sept. 1999.

well-founded fear of persecution; or does persecution necessarily imply a further act of specific discrimination, a singling out of the individual?[363] Where large groups are seriously affected by a government's political, economic, and social policies or by the outbreak of uncontrolled communal violence, it would appear wrong in principle to limit the concept of persecution to measures immediately identifiable as direct and individual.[364] General measures, aimed as often at 'restructuring' society as at maintaining the *status quo*,[365] will frequently be directed at groups identifiable by reference to the Convention reasons for persecution, and carried through with the object, express or implied, of excluding them from or forcing them into the mainstream of the new society. Where individual or collective measures of enforcement are employed, such as coercion by denial of employment or education, restrictions on language and culture, denial of access to food supplies, expropriation of property without compensation, and forcible or involuntary relocation, then fear of persecution in the above sense may exist; mere membership of the affected group can be sufficient. Likewise, where punishment under a law of general application may result, any necessary condition of singling out would be met by the decision to prosecute in a given case. Already in 1990, the US Asylum Regulations had explicitly dispensed with the 'singling out' or 'targeting' requirement, which now extends if the applicant can show 'a pattern or practice . . . of persecution of a group persons *similarly situated* to the applicant', and his or her 'own inclusion in, and identification with, such group of persons such that his or her fear of persecution upon return is reasonable'.[366] Whether a well-founded fear of persecution exists will depend upon an examination of the class of persons in fact affected, of the interests in respect of which they stand to be punished, of the likelihood of punishment, and the nature and extent of the penalties.

[363] See Crawford, J. & Hyndman, P., 'Three Heresies in the Application of the Refugee Convention', 1 *IJRL* 152 (1989).

[364] Grahl-Madsen, *Status of Refugees*, vol. 1, 213. In *R. v. Secretary of State for the Home Department, ex p. Jeyakumaran*, No. CO/290/84, QBD, unreported, 28 Jun. 1985, Taylor J. referred to the singling out requirement as a 'startling proposition. It can be little comfort to a Tamil family to know that they are being persecuted simply as Tamils rather than as individuals. How can this dismal distinction bear upon whether the applicant has a well-founded fear of persecution?' The court held that 'the evidence clearly shows the reason for oppression to have been simply membership of the Tamil minority'.

[365] Economic reasons or motivation alone will not entitle a person to refugee status; but a government's 'economic measures' may well be the cloak for action calculated to destroy the economic livelihood of specific groups; in such cases, a fear of persecution can be well founded. Cf. Palley, C., *Constitutional Law and Minorities* (Minority Rights Group, report no. 36, 1978) on the subject of laws and administrative action designed to remedy economic imbalances, at 10: 'If the emphasis is on remedying disadvantage and lack of opportunity (such as special educational programmes, special technical assistance programmes, special loan programmes in setting up co-operatives) or is protective (protection of native land against sale to capitalist entrepreneurs) it can be more readily tolerated by non-recipients. If it becomes an instrument of economic attack on other communities by denial of the right to engage in their traditional occupations, then it is proper to describe the technique as one of domination.'

[366] 8 CFR §208.13(b)(2)(iii)—asylum (emphasis supplied); §208.16(b)92)—withholding.

5.7 CHILDREN AS ASYLUM SEEKERS AND REFUGEES

A preliminary issue in all cases involving children and young persons, is whether they are accompanied. In principle, this has no bearing on whether they are refugees, but may affect how their claims are dealt with, as well as the solutions which may be proposed. Unaccompanied children, in particular, need special attention, and a guardian or other person competent to protect their interests.[367] The UNHCR *Handbook* locates the refugee status of accompanied dependants, including children, in the context of family unity. If the head of the family is recognized as a refugee then, all things being equal,[368] the 'dependants are normally granted refugee status according to the principle of family unity'.[369] Practical reasons and procedural convenience subordinate individual claims to an alternative principle, and the child's status is relegated to that of dependency.[370] Whereas this may be sufficient and reflect social realities in the case of accompanied children, a more comprehensive approach is required for the unaccompanied in search of protection. The UNHCR *Handbook*, drafted some ten years before the Convention on the Rights of the Child, focuses on refugee status as a primary consideration. With this underlying premise, the *Handbook* somewhat misleadingly invokes 'mental development and maturity' as the criterion for determining the existence of a well-founded fear of persecution.[371] The approach to refugee status in terms of maturity is misguided for several reasons. First, there is no necessary connection between any particular level of maturity and the existence of a well-founded fear of persecution. Secondly, and in so far as the subjective dimension remains relevant, children are as capable as adults of feeling fear; their maturity may affect merely their capacity to understand the events or conditions which are the basis of that fear. Thirdly, a child's maturity is irrelevant to the question

---

[367] Cf. art. 22(1), 1989 Convention on the Rights of the Child (CRC89): 'States Parties shall take appropriate measures to ensure that a child who is seeking refugee status ... shall, whether unaccompanied or accompanied by his or her parents or by any other person, receive appropriate protection and humanitarian assistance in the enjoyment of applicable rights set forth in the present Convention and in other international human rights or humanitarian instruments to which the said States are Parties.' Bhabha, J. & Young, W., 'Not Adults in Miniature: Unaccompanied Child Asylum Seekers and The New U.S. Guidelines', 11 *IJRL* 84 (1999); Russell, S., 'Unaccompanied Refugee Children in the United Kingdom', 11 *IJRL* 126 (1999).

[368] Provided, for example, that the dependant is not excludable, or a citizen having the protection of another country.   [369] UNHCR, *Handbook*, paras. 181–8, 184.

[370] The *Handbook* nevertheless leaves open the possibility of individual entitlement: 'the principle of family unity operates in favour of dependants, and *not against them*': ibid., para. 185 (emphasis added).

[371] Ibid., para. 214. Cf. para. 215: 'It can be assumed that—in the absence of indications to the contrary—a person of 16 or over may be regarded as sufficiently mature to have a well-founded fear of persecution. Minors under 16 years of age may normally be assumed not to be sufficiently mature.' See Commission permanente de recours des réfugiés, (Belgium), 12 mai 1993, No. 93/021/R1115(Iè ch.franc.), holding that a sixteen-year-old was sufficiently mature to claim refugee status in his own right: *RDDE*, No. 77, jan.–fev. 1994, 41. See also 'Note on Refugee Children': UN doc. EC/SCP/46 (31 Aug. 1987), paras. 14–16.

whether he or she may be persecuted. Fourthly, and above all, the principle of the *best interests of the child* requires that decisions on behalf of the child be taken on the basis of all the circumstances, including his or her personal situation and the conditions prevailing in the child's country of origin. The welfare of the child, and the special protection and assistance which are due in accordance with international standards, prevail over the narrow concerns of refugee status. What is required is a decision for and on behalf of the unaccompanied child, which takes account of the best interests of the child and effectively contributes to his or her full development, preferably in the environment of the family. To channel children in flight into refugee status procedures will often merely interpose another obstacle between the child and a solution.[372]

That being said, however, in some jurisdictions a successful refugee claim may be the only way by which to access child welfare services. The United Kingdom immigration rules, for example, appear to be premised on the assumption that a child arriving alone is in need of protection and assistance. So far as such child may apply for asylum, the rules require priority treatment, close attention to welfare needs, and care in interviewing.[373] Nevertheless, the child's best interests are a primary concern. The likelihood of risk of harm in his or her country of origin must be factored in, but in many cases the most appropriate solution may still be reunion with family members who have remained behind.[374] Equally, prolonged detention in a closed camp has a serious negative effect on any child's development, and needs to be avoided through prompt and appropriate decision-making.[375]

6. Persecution and lack of protection

Persecution under the Convention is thus a complex of reasons, interests, and measures. The measures affect or are directed against groups or individuals for reasons of race, religion, nationality, membership of a particular social group, or political opinion. These reasons in turn show that the groups or individuals are identified by reference to a classification which ought to be irrelevant to the enjoyment of fundamental, protected interests. Persecution results where the measures

---

[372] See now UNHCR, 'Guidelines on Policies and Procedures in dealing with Unaccompanied Children seeking Asylum', Feb. 1997.

[373] UK Immigration Rules, paras. 350–2. For a particularly clear guide to United Kingdom law and procedure, see Guedalla, V., 'Representing unaccompanied refugee children in the asylum process', *Childright*, Dec. 1994, No. 112. Also, Carlier, J.-Y., 'La demande d'asile introduite par un mineur non accompagné', *RDDE*, 19–20 mai 1994, 94–102.

[374] Some two-thirds of the 'best interests' decisions by the Special Committees established under the CPA were for reunion with family members still in Vietnam; see 'Programming for the Benefit of Refugee Children': UN doc. EC/SC.2/CRP.15 (25 Aug. 1993), para. 15; cf. O'Donnell, D., 'Resettlement or Repatriation: Screened-out Vietnamese Child Asylum Seekers and the Convention on the Rights of the Child', 6 *IJRL* 382 (1994).

[375] See McCallin, M., 'Living in detention: A review of the psychological well-being of Vietnamese children in the Hong Kong detention centres', (1992).

in question harm those interests and the integrity and inherent dignity of the human being to a degree considered unacceptable under prevailing international standards or under higher standards prevailing in the State faced with determining a claim to asylum or refugee status.[376] An element of relativity is perhaps inherent and inescapable in determining the value to be attributed to the protected interest (for example, life and freedom of conscience), and the nature or severity of the measure threatened (for example, death and some lesser interference).

Although persecution itself is undefined by any international instrument, an approach in terms of *reasons, interests,* and *measures* receives support by analogy from the human rights field. The International Convention on the Suppression and Punishment of the Crime of Apartheid,[377] for example, identifies the 'crime of apartheid' very much in these terms. The *reasons* are self-evident—race and racial domination; the *interests* threatened and in need of protection include the right to life; liberty of the person; freedom; dignity; participation in political, social, economic and cultural rights; the right to work; the right to form trade unions; the right to education; the right to a nationality; freedom of movement and residence; freedom of opinion and expression; freedom of peaceful assembly and association; and non-discrimination. The measures that were used to defend apartheid and achieve its objectives included inhuman acts; systematic oppression; denial of rights; murder; infliction of serious bodily or mental harm; torture; cruel, inhuman or degrading treatment or punishment; arbitrary arrest; illegal imprisonment; deliberate imposition of substandard living conditions; legislative measures denying participatory rights; denial of development; segregation on

---

[376] For details of 'ethnic cleansing' and other events in former Yugoslavia, see the reports by Tadeusz Mazowiecki, Special Rapporteur of the UN Commission on Human Rights: UN docs. E/CN.4/1992/S-1/9 (28 Aug. 1992); E/CN.4/1992/S-1/10 (27 Oct. 1992). The following historical examples provide illustrations of persecution: the treatment accorded to those returned to the USSR after the Second World War: Bethell, N., *The Last Secret* (1974); Tolstoy, N., *Victims of Yalta* (rev. edn. 1979); relocation of national minorities in the USSR: *The Crimean Tatars, Volga Germans and Meskhetians* (Minority Rights Group, Report No. 6, rev. edn. 1980); mob and institutionalized attacks on members of the Baha'i faith in Iran: *The Baha'is in Iran* (Baha'i International Community, June 1981 and updates); measures taken against ethnic minorities: McCarthy, J., *Death and Exile: The Ethnic Cleansing of Ottoman Muslims, 1821–1922,* (1995); *Selective Genocide in Burundi* (Minority Rights Group, Report No. 20, 1974); *What future for the Amerindians of South America?* (Minority Rights Group, Report No. 15, rev. edn. 1977); institutional and individual measures of repression against religious groups: *Religious Minorities in the Soviet Union* (Minority Rights Group, Report No. 1, rev. edn. 1977); *Jehovah's Witnesses in Central Africa* (Minority Rights Group, Report No. 29. 1976); economic measures affecting Asians in East and Central Africa: *The Asian Minorities of East and Central Africa* (Minority Rights Group, Report No. 4, 1971); *Problems of a Displaced Minority: The new position of East Africa's Asians,* (Minority Rights Group, Report No. 16, rev. edn. 1978); the complex of measures aimed or calculated to deny self-determination: *The Kurds* (Minority Rights Group, Report No. 23, rev. edn. 1981); *The Namibians of South West Africa* (Minority Rights Group, Report No. 19, rev. edn. 1978); *The Palestinians* (Minority Rights Group, Report No. 24, rev. ed. 1979).

[377] Adopted by the UN General Assembly on 30 Nov. 1973: res. 3068(XXVIII); by 31 Jan. 2007, 107 States were parties to the Convention. Text in Brownlie & Goodwin-Gill, *Basic Documents on Human Rights,* 382.

racial lines; prohibition of mixed marriages; expropriation of landed property; forced labour; and denial of rights to political opponents.

The criteria for refugee status posited by article 1 of the 1951 Convention have the individual asylum seeker very much in mind. In the case of large numbers of asylum seekers, establishing a well-founded fear of persecution on a case-by-case basis can be impossible and impracticable. A *prima facie* or group determination, based on evidence of lack of protection but without prejudice to status as refugees, may therefore be the answer.[378] This solution is implied by the second leg of the refugee definition adopted in the 1969 OAU Convention and by the Cartagena Declaration, which extends to 'every person who, owing to external aggression, occupation, foreign domination, or events seriously disturbing public order in either part or the whole of his country of origin or nationality', is compelled to seek refuge in another country.[379] Certainly, a group determination may be called for in the initial stages of any movement where protection and material assistance are the first priorities. It may also be appropriate in other contexts, for example, either where the need for protection is expected to be short-term and prospects for return in security are good; or, on the contrary, where the situation in the country of origin is so bad that practical realities dictate a prompt move in the direction of local asylum or resettlement. Establishing that civil war has broken out, that law and order have broken down, or that aggression is under way is relatively simple. The notion of lack of protection, however, is potentially wider and invites attention to the general issue of a State's duty to protect and promote human rights. Clearly, not every failure by the State to promote and protect, for example, the various rights recognized by the 1966 Covenants, will justify flight across an international frontier and a claim to refugee status.[380] Not all the rights are fundamental, some are subject to progressive implementation only, while others may in turn be the subject of permissible derogations.[381]

---

[378] Durieux, J.-F. & Hurwitz, A., 'How Many is Too Many? African and European Legal Responses to Mass Influxes of Refugees', 47 *German Yearbook of International Law* 105, 120 (2005); Hyndman, J, & Nylund, B. V., 'UNHCR and the Status of Prima Facie Refugees in Kenya', 10 *IJRL* 21 (1998).   [379] For full texts, see Annexe 2, Nos. 1 and 7.

[380] See *Amare* v. *Secretary of State for the Home Department* [2005] EWCA Civ 1600, paras. 28–31; also, Lord Justice Laws, 'Asylum—a Branch of Human Rights Law?', Paper presented at the Asylum and Immigration Tribunal Conference, June 2006; *Januzi* v. *Secretary of State for the Home Department* [2006] UKHL 5, per Lord Bingham at paras. 4–6.

[381] Both the protection due to certain rights and the circumstances of permitted derogation are of course subject to development in international law. See, for example, the 1994 OAS Inter-American Convention on the Forced Disappearance of Persons: 22 *ILM* 1529 (1994); the preamble characterizes the act as a crime against humanity; art. II links the concept to 'agents of the State or . . . persons or groups of persons acting with the authorization, support, or acquiescence of the State', and art. X provides that exceptional circumstances do not justify forced disappearance, and that effective judicial procedures must be retained. Also, Inter-American Court of Human Rights, Advisory Opinion, *Habeas Corpus in Emergency Situations*, 30 Jan. 1987, AO OC-8/87: 27 *ILM* 512 (1988), noting that 'essential judicial remedies' should remain in force: paras. 27–30.

The list of fundamental protected interests proposed above can be expanded in the future, as hitherto unrecognized groups and individuals press their claims, and as the value of certain economic and social rights is increasingly accepted. Although States generally do not appear willing to accept any formal extension of the 1951 Convention refugee definition, their practice commonly reflects recognition of the protection needs and entitlements of a broader class. Nevertheless, one legal implication of developments in favour of refugees and of human rights generally is that there are limits to the legitimate or permissible extent of State power. If individuals, social groups, and classes are at the absolute disposal of the State, then repression, re-education, relocation or even expulsion aimed at the restructuring of society can be considered comprehensible, even acceptable. But where there are limits to State power, and individuals and groups have rights against the State or interests entitled to recognition and protection, then such measures may amount to persecution. The traditional response to those who flee in fear of persecution has been to grant protection; increasingly, the international community now focuses its attention on the possibility of dealing with causes at source.

4

Loss and Denial of Refugee Status and its Benefits

Most recent international instruments not only define refugees, but also provide for the circumstances in which refugee status shall terminate or in which the benefits of status shall be denied or withdrawn.[1] The IRO Constitution, for example, described the circumstances in which refugees and the displaced would 'cease to be the concern' of the organization, and excluded various others, including 'war criminals, quislings and traitors', and 'ordinary criminals...extraditable by treaty'.[2] Article 14 of the Universal Declaration of Human Rights prohibits invocation of the right of asylum 'in the case of prosecutions genuinely arising from non-political crimes or from acts contrary to the purposes and principles of the United Nations'. These categories have been expanded in other instruments and in State practice so that, broadly, there are four sets of circumstances in which refugee status may be lost or denied: (1) by reason of voluntary acts of the individual; (2) by reason of change of circumstances; (3) by reason of protection accorded by other States or international agencies; and (4) in the case of criminals or other undeserving cases.

1. Voluntary acts of the individual

Both the UNHCR Statute and the 1951 Convention provide for loss of refugee status where the individual, by his or her own actions, indicates that a well-founded fear of persecution no longer exists or that international protection is no longer required.[3] The circumstances include voluntary re-availment of the protection of the country of origin, voluntary reacquisition of nationality, acquisition

---

[1] See generally, Grahl-Madsen, A., *The Status of Refugees in International Law*, vol. 1, (1966), 262–304, 367–412; UNHCR, *Handbook on Procedures and Criteria for Determining Refugee Status*, (1979), paras. 111–63; Weis, P., 'The Concept of the Refugee in International Law', *Journal du dr. inter.*, (1960) 1, at 25–30; Tiberghien, F., *La protection des réfugiés en France* (2e. éd., 1988), 101–34, 441–76; Hathaway, J., *The Law of Refugee Status*, (1991), 189–229; Fitzpatrick, J., 'The End of Protection: Legal Standards for Cessation of Refugee Status and Withdrawal of Temporary Protection', 13 *Georgetown Immigration Law Journal* 343 (1999).   [2] IRO Constitution, Section D; Part II.
[3] Statute, para. 6(a)–(d); Convention, art. 1 C (1)–(4). The French *Commission des recours* has held that withdrawal in cases of fraud is also permitted: CRR, 2 mai 1988, *Dogan*, 59.037, *Doc. réf.* no. 79, 4/13 juill. 1989, Suppl., JC, 2.

of a new nationality and the protection which derives therefrom, and voluntary re-establishment in the country of origin.

For the purposes of *re-availment of protection*, the refugee must not only act voluntarily, but must also intend to and actually obtain protection.[4] Protection comprises all such actions by the refugee as indicate the establishment of normal relations with the authorities of the country of origin, such as registration at consulates or application for and renewal of passports or certificates of nationality. Sometimes, however, a refugee may be unwillingly obliged to seek a measure of protection from those authorities, as where a passport or travel document is essential to obtain the issue of a residence permit in the country of asylum.[5] Being involuntary, the protection obtained should not bring refugee status to an end.

In other cases of application for and obtaining a national passport or the renewal of a passport, it may be presumed, in the absence of evidence to the contrary, that re-availment of protection is intended. The presumption may be strengthened where the refugee in fact makes use of the passport for travel, or for return to the country of origin, or in order to obtain some advantage in the country of asylum that is dependent on nationality. Possession of a national passport and a visit to the country of origin would seem conclusive as to cessation of refugee status. Grahl-Madsen, however, suggests that 'physical presence in the territory of the home country does not *per se* constitute reavailment of protection . . . it is the conscious subjection under the government of that country . . . the normalization of the relationship between State and individual which matters'.[6] Indeed, on leaving the country of origin for the second time, the individual in question may well be able to show that he or she, still or once again, has a well-founded fear of persecution within the Convention.[7]

---

[4] UNHCR, *Handbook*, paras. 118–25.

[5] Abstracts of earlier French decisions can be found in *Jurisprudence de la Commission de Recours des Réfugiés* (1961) and in Tiberghien, F., *La protection des réfugiés en France*, (2e. éd., 1988). See, for example, *Chimeno*, 1.208, 1.209, 25 oct. 1956—nationality certificate obtained at request of French authorities but not used to obtain any advantage not re-availment; *Grunberg*, 185, 19 janv. 1954—passport for journey to third country obtained from consular authorities at invitation of *Préfecture de Police* not re-availment: Tiberghien, *La protection des réfugiés*, 442–8; also at 396–8. See *Jagir Singh*, TH. 60274/92, 16 Jun. 1994, where the UK adjudicator held that renewal of passport during the asylum process for purpose of travel to a third State amounted to re-availment of protection; and similarly in Belgium: C.P.R., 2 ch., 11 déc. 1991, R226; V.B.C., 2 ch., 1er juin 1992, W526; cf. Conseil d'Etat, 13 janv. 1989, *Thevarayan*, 78.055, *Doc. réf.* no. 79, 4/13 juill. 1989, Suppl., JC, 6—fact of requesting issue or renewal of passport from diplomatic or consular authorities generally sufficient to raise presumption that the individual has re-availed himself or herself of the protection of their country of origin, but such presumption can be rebutted; it is error of law not to enquire into the reasons why. More recent decisions are now available on the web; for OFPRA, see <http://www.ofpra.gouv.fr>; for the Commission des recours: <http://www.commission-refugies.fr/>; and for the Conseil d'Etat: <http://www.legifrance.gouv.fr>.

[6] *Status of Refugees*, vol. 1, 384f. See also *Dominquez del Rey*, 593, 29 janv. 1955—brief, clandestine return journeys to the country of origin not re-availment of protection; *Vallejo Leon*, 15.683, 26 août. 1982—return to country of origin following death of mother and to assist father, himself in ill health, also not re-availment: Tiberghien, *La protection des réfugiés*, 447; UNHCR, *Handbook*, para. 125.

[7] Note that art. 1C(4) of the Convention, which provides for cessation of refugee status on 'voluntary re-establishment' in the country of origin, clearly implies something more than mere presence.

All the circumstances of the contact between the individual and the authorities of the country of origin must be taken into account. It is therefore relevant to consider the age of the refugee,[8] the object to be attained by the contact,[9] whether the contact was successful,[10] whether it was repeated,[11] and what advantages were actually obtained.[12] In cases involving passports, it will be relevant if the refugee's country of residence is a party to the 1951 Convention and/or the 1967 Protocol, and so bound under article 28 to issue travel documents to refugees lawfully staying in its territory.[13] If not a party, that State may yet issue aliens passports or certificates of identity which enable the refugee to avoid recourse to his or her national authorities. In addition, it will be necessary to determine whether the national passport which the refugee obtains in fact reflects the full measure of national protection, for example, by enabling him or her to return freely to the country of issue.

These various issues were illustrated in the late 1970s when many Chilean refugees were found to be obtaining and renewing national passports, apparently without difficulty. In 1976 the Chilean Government had decided that passports might be issued or renewed for citizens abroad, even if they had refugee status and asylum in their country of residence. However, under a 1973 legislative decree,[14] persons who had left Chile to seek asylum, who had left illegally or been expelled

---

[8] See *Ibanez bel Ramon*, 4.145, 18 oct. 1960; *Lopez Perez*, 2.049 et 2.423, 7 fév. 1958—only from age 18 should the individual be considered as understanding the nature of their acts: Tiberghien, *La protection des réfugiés*, 463, 471. The fact that the contact has been made on behalf of the refugee by a third party is not generally sufficient to rebut a finding of re-availment of protection; see *Morales*, 135, 19 janv. 1954: ibid., 443, 448.

[9] See *Borensztajn*, 3.355, 3 déc. 1959—passport renewed in order to obtain foreign visas for urgent journeys for professional purposes not re-availment: Tiberghien, *La protection des réfugiés*, 472; *Mendez Perez*, 1.486, 26 mars 1957—passport obtained and renewed by seaman for whom such document essential to pursue his profession not re-availment, particularly as document not valid for return to home country: ibid., 444.

[10] See *Bata Lojos*, 1.727, 24 oct. 1957—unsuccessful approach to consular authorities with view to repatriation not considered re-availment; *Kjosev*, 534, 29 janv. 1955—repatriation requested and passport permitting return obtained amounted to re-availment in absence any proof that refugee acted in moment of severe depression; *Michalska*, 6.681, 16 déc. 1969—single reference to consular authorities by mistake, in order to obtain renewal of residence permit in France not re-availment: Tiberghien, *La protection des réfugiés*, 443, 445.

[11] See *Llesta Escanilla*, 288, 21 juin 1954—nationality certificate obtained, apparently to facilitate reunion with minor daughter, but twice renewed and considered re-availment of protection; *Rebay Lazlo*, 55, 16 oct. 1953—unsuccessful application for passport but stated intention to apply again indicative of absence of fear, thus justifying refusal of recognition of refugee status; *Caballero Martin*, 133, 19 janv. 1954—obtaining and renewing passport amounted to re-availment of protection: Tiberghien, *La protection des réfugiés*, 209, 471.

[12] See *Roldan*, 271, 21 juin 1954—nationality certificate obtained to complete sale of property in country of origin, but not renewed or used to obtain any other advantage, not considered re-availment. Cf. *Rodriguez Martin*, 291, 21 juin 1954—nationality certificate obtained and used to renew residence permit amounted to re-availment; *Callado Sierra*, 562, 29 janv. 1955—similarly; *Codina Bea*, 941, 12 avr. 1956—initial reference to consular authorities with agreement of *Office français de protection des réfugiés et apatrides* followed by second reference with object of benefitting from advantages granted to those of applicant's nationality considered re-availment of protection: Tiberghien, *La protection des réfugiés*, 442, 444, 446.   [13] See further below, Ch. 10, s. 1.2.3.

[14] Art. 3 of Decree Law no. 81 of 11 Oct. 1973; *Diario Oficial*, no. 28694, 6 Nov. 1973.

or forced to leave, were prohibited from returning without express authorization by the Minister of the Interior. Moreover, those returning without such permission were liable to prosecution.[15] Holding a Chilean passport could thus still be compatible with refugee status, although the holder might reasonably be required to explain why alternative documentation had not been obtained.[16]

Voluntary action is also explicitly required in respect of *re-acquisition of nationality*.[17] Such an act is more immediately verifiable than the notion of re-availment of protection, yet perhaps constitutes the supreme manifestation of the latter. There is less scope for explanation of extenuating circumstances: the intention of the individual and the effectiveness of the act will suffice in most cases.[18]

In the case of *acquisition of a new nationality*,[19] however, the individual must also enjoy protection in virtue of that status. The new nationality must be effective, in that at least the fundamental incidents of nationality should be recognized, including the right of return and residence in the State.[20] In a number of decisions in the 1950s, the French *Commission des recours* considered the refugee status of Jews who had travelled to and resided in Israel. The general view was that acquisition of Israeli nationality under the provisions of the Law of Return brought the individuals within the scope of article 1C(3), particularly where Israeli passports were later used.[21] In one case, the Commission held that the 'très graves difficultés d'existence' which had motivated the individual to leave Israel were not attributable

---

[15] Cf. Amnesty International *1978 Report*, 111; *1980 Report*, 118; *1981 Report*, 122–3.

[16] See *Petrow*, 637, 1er avr. 1955, where the *Commission des recours* took the view that use of a 'passport of convenience' issued by a third State had no effect on the holder's true nationality such as to remove the basis for her claim to refugee status; see also *Berline*, 577, 25 fév. 1955; *Ekmekdjian*, 313, 3 mars 1954: Tiberghien, *La protection des réfugiés*, 313, 474. In a series of cases in 1980, the Australian DORS Committee considered the weight to be accorded to Taiwanese passports held by Indo-Chinese seeking refugee status in Australia. The Committee noted that the Taiwanese authorities issued two types of passport, only one of which (the so-called 'MFA' passport) enabled the holder to return to and reside in Taiwan. Other passports, issued freely to 'overseas Chinese', amounted to no more than a travel facility and could not be equated with the full protection normally accorded to passport holders by the State of issue. Cf. *Hong*, 11.517, 21 avr. 1981—claimant, born in Vietnam of Chinese parents issued with passport by authorities in Taiwan where he had lived one year with his parents after leaving Vietnam. It was not alleged that the passport had been obtained by fraud or that it was a mere passport of convenience. Moreover, the document carried the mention, 'Overseas Chinese who has resided in the mother country', indicating that he was recognized as a Chinese national, having the right to reside in Taiwan and otherwise entitled to its protection: Tiberghien, at 473. See generally, Goodwin-Gill, *Movement of Persons*, 24–50; and on the nationality question, Tang Lay Lee, 'Stateless Persons and the Comprehensive Plan of Action-Part 1: Chinese Nationality and the Republic of China (Taiwan)', 7 *IJRL* 201 (1995).

[17] Statute, para. 6(b); Convention, art. 1C(2); UNHCR, *Handbook*, 126–8.

[18] Cf. *Gorbatcheff*, 772, 8 mars. 1955—nationality acquired on marriage lost following remarriage with refugee after divorce from first husband: Tiberghien, *La protection des réfugiés*, 450.

[19] Statute, para. 6(c); Convention, art. 1C (3); UNHCR, *Handbook*, 129–32.

[20] Cf. Goodwin-Gill, *Movement of Persons*, 45–9.

[21] See *Breitholz*, 208, 30 avr. 1954; *Schapira*, 237, 31 mai 1954—no steps taken to avoid the acquisition of nationality; 473 *Mincu*, 432, 21 juill. 1954—similarly, and no evidence that the individual applied for or was refused a Convention Travel Document: Tiberghien, *La protection des réfugiés*, 432, 449–51, 474.

to the political or administrative authorities and could not be equated with persecution or lack of protection.[22]

Finally, refugee status may be lost by *voluntary re-establishment in the country of origin*.[23] Something more than a visit or mere presence is required; the individual must have settlement on a permanent basis in view, with no evident intention of leaving.[24] Should the individual leave again and claim refugee status, the case will need to be considered in the light of events subsequent to re-establishment.

2. Change of circumstances[25]

Article 1C of the 1951 Convention provides that it shall cease to apply if, because the circumstances in connection with which the refugee was recognized have ceased to exist, he or she can no longer continue to refuse to avail him- or herself of the protection of the country of nationality. However, cessation is not to apply to a refugee under article 1(A)(1)—so-called 'statutory refugees'—who is able to invoke 'compelling reasons arising out of previous persecution' for refusing to avail themselves of the protection of their country of nationality.[26] The 'change of circumstances' anticipated is clearly intended to comprehend fundamental changes in the country which remove the basis of any fear of persecution. The replacement of a tyrannical by a democratic regime is an obvious example,[27] but the process of change may be more subtle and reflected over a number of years by legal reforms and gradual improvements in human rights.

Cessation, however, involves loss of status and the rights that accompany that status; it may also result in the return of persons to their countries of origin. Refugee status is essentially an individualized status, and the principle of case-by-case assessment is as essential to the proper determination of claims, as it is to procedures and due process in the matter of cessation. Cessation, too, is described in individual terms, with article 1C(5) referring not to general political or human rights conditions, but to 'the circumstances in connection with which [the

---

[22] See *Arbusoff*, 11.898, 12 fév. 1981: Tiberghien, *La protection des réfugiés*, 239, 473.

[23] Statute, para. 6(d); Convention, art. 1C(4); UNHCR, *Handbook*, 133–4. Cf. IRO Constitution, part I D, below, Annexe 1, No. 1.

[24] See *Maqueda*, 59, 1er oct. 1953—two years' clandestine but voluntary residence amounted to voluntary re-establishment; cf. *Dominquez del Rey*, 593, 29 jan. 1955—short, clandestine visits to help family leave for France not re-availment: Tiberghien, *La protection des réfugiés*, 451, 447.

[25] See Fitzpatrick, J. & Bonoan, R., 'Cessation of refugee protection', in Feller, Türk, & Nicholson, *Refugee Protection in International Law*, 491; UNHCR, Guidelines on International Protection: 'Cessation of Refugee Status under Article 1C(5) and (6) of the 1951 Convention relating to the Status of Refugees', HCR/GIP/03/03, 10 Feb. 2003 (hereafter, 'UNHCR *Guidelines No. 3*, 'Cessation'); Zambelli, P., 'Procedural Aspects of Cessation and Exclusion: The Canadian Experience', 8 *IJRL* 144 (1996).

[26] Art. 1C(5), (6) CSR51; UNHCR Statute, para. 6(e), (f). The difference in the wording of the two paragraphs reflects that between refugees with and refugees without a nationality.

[27] Cf. IRO Constitution, Annexe 1, No. 1, below, part 1 C 2.

individual] has been recognized as a refugee', and to whether he or she 'can no longer . . . refuse to avail [themselves] of the protection' of their State of origin.

In a cessation proceeding, therefore, the central questions will be related to the causes of the individual's flight, whether later changes have removed the risk of persecution, and whether effective protection is now available in fact from the State of origin. For only if such conditions exist will it be 'unreasonable' for the refugee to continue to refuse national protection. The individualized approach also enables the decision-maker to determine whether the refugee is eligible for an exemption from cessation.[28]

A UNHCR paper on change of circumstances, presented to the Sub-Committee on International Protection in January 1992, noted that the cessation clauses were exhaustive, and that a strict approach to their application was called for.[29] This was endorsed by the Executive Committee later that year, when it that:

> . . . a careful approach to the application of the cessation clauses using clearly established procedures is necessary so as to provide refugees with the assurance that their status will not be subject to unnecessary review in the light of temporary changes, not of a fundamental character, in the situation prevailing in the country of origin,
>
> (a) . . . States must carefully assess the fundamental character of the changes in the country of nationality or origin, including the general human rights situation, as well as the particular cause of fear of persecution, in order to make sure in an objective and verifiable way that the situation that justified the granting of refugee status has ceased to exist;
>
> (b) . . . [A]n essential element in such assessment by States is the fundamental, stable and durable character of the changes, making use of appropriate information available in this respect, *inter alia*, from relevant specialized bodies, including particularly UNHCR . . .[30]

UNHCR had argued that special weight should be attached to 'the level of democratic development in the country, its adherence to international human rights (including refugee) instruments and access allowed for independent national or international organizations freely to verify and supervise the respect for human rights'. Other, more specific factors might include declarations of amnesty, the

---

[28] In *Minister for Immigration, Multicultural and Indigenous Affairs* v. *QAAH* [2006] HCA 53, (Kirby J., diss.), the majority of the High Court of Australia misunderstood the centrality of *status* in the Convention scheme of protection; in applying domestic law without regard to international law and practice, they supposed that cessation was somehow automatic and thereby failed to do justice to the individual dimensions of a case involving a refugee subject to Australia's 'temporary protection visa' scheme.

[29] 'Discussion Note on the Application of the "ceased circumstances" Cessation Clause in the 1951 Convention': UN doc. EC/SCP/1992/CRP.1 (20 Dec. 1991). The inelegant phrase, 'ceased circumstances', is somewhat misleading in its reference to the Convention provisions, which predicate the end or 'cessation' of refugee status on a sufficient change *in the factual base for a well-founded fear of persecution*.

[30] Executive Committee Conclusion No. 69 (1992) on Cessation of Status; for full text see *Report* of the 43rd Session, UN doc. A/AC.96/804, para. 22. The draft conclusion was revised in two earlier

repeal of repressive legislation, the annulment of judgments against political opponents and the general re-establishment of legal protection and guarantees. UNHCR emphasized 'that a minimum period of 12 to 18 months (always depending on the circumstances) should normally elapse before a judgment... can be considered reliable'. Executive Committee Conclusion No. 69, however, emphasizes that application of the cessation clauses is a matter 'exclusively' for States, although the High Commissioner should be appropriately involved.[31] States also considered that no particular time frame could be laid down as a condition of durable change,[32] but they accepted that every refugee affected by a cessation decision should be able 'to have such application in their cases reconsidered on grounds relevant to their individual case'.[33] UNHCR noted that voluntary repatriation, as a matter of fact, often does away with the need for formal decisions by the Office on cessation, which had anyway been relatively rare.[34] At the same time, however, the Executive Committee acknowledged that a declaration by UNHCR that its statutory competence with regard to certain refugees had ceased to apply might be useful to States in applying the clauses.[35]

UNHCR's 2003 *Guidelines* reaffirm and develop its position, emphasizing that, for cessation to apply, the changes in the conditions in the country of origin, need to be of a fundamental nature, such that the refugee 'can no longer... continue to refuse to avail himself of the protection of' his country of origin; that is, the changes themselves must have addressed the causes of displacement and thus the decision to recognize the individual as a refugee. As examples, the guidelines suggest, 'an end to hostilities, a complete political change and return to a situation of peace and stability...'[36] Developments which appear to evidence

inter-sessional meetings; see 'Report of the 13–14 April Meeting': UN doc. EC/SCP/71 (7 Jul. 1992), paras. 6–11; 'Report of the 25 June Meeting': UN doc. EC/SCP/76 (13 Oct. 1992), paras. 20–2.

[31] UNHCR's offer to share its country of origin information with States was generally welcomed: 'Report of the 23 January Meeting': UN doc. EC/SCP/70 (7 Jul. 1992), para. 20; Executive Committee Conclusion No. 69, para. (b).

[32] 'Report of the 23 January Meeting': UN doc. EC/SCP/70, para. 20; see also generally paras. 11, 12, 14, 15.

[33] Executive Committee Conclusion No. 69, para. (d). A parallel paper introduced by the Swiss government in the Sub-Committee also emphasized the right to request reconsideration; see 'Report of the 23 January Meeting': UN doc. EC/SCP/70, para. 8.

[34] 'Discussion Note': UN doc. EC/SCP/1992/CRP.1, para. 19. UNHCR cited the following examples of formal determinations of cessation: Zimbabweans (1981), Argentinians (1984), Uruguayans (1985), Czechs (1991), Hungarians (1991), and Poles (1991).

[35] Executive Committee Conclusion No. 69, Preamble, third paragraph; see also 'Discussion Note': UN doc. EC/SCP/1992/CRP.1, para. 3.

[36] UNHCR *Guidelines No. 3*, 'Cessation', paras. 10, 11. See *NBGM* v. *MIMIA* (2004) 84 ALD 40, [2004] FCA 1373, considering whether the removal of the Taliban in Afghanistan amounted to a 'substantial, effective and durable' change; also *WAHK* v. *MIMIA* (2004) 81 ALD 322, [2004] FCAFC 12, finding, again on the effects of the Taliban's removal, that the tribunal erred in focusing on risk of persecution by government, and remitting for consideration of whether the interim government was able and willing to protect the appellant from acts of persecution in Ghazani province.

significant and profound changes should be given time to consolidate. The question is whether protection is now available:

15. ...Such protection must...be effective and available. It requires more than mere physical security or safety. It needs to include the existence of a functioning government and basic administrative structures, as evidenced for instance through a functioning system of law and justice, as well as the existence of adequate infrastructure to enable residents to exercise their rights, including their right to a basic livelihood...

16. An important indicator in this respect is the general human rights situation in the country...There is no requirement that the standards of human rights achieved must be exemplary. What matters is that significant improvements have been made, as illustrated at least by respect for the right to life and liberty and the prohibition of torture; marked progress in establishing an independent judiciary, fair trials and access to courts: as well as protection amongst others of the fundamental rights to freedom of expression, association and religion...[37]

In practice, States have rarely had recourse to cessation, particularly if recognition of refugee status has exhausted itself in the grant of permanent or indefinite residence, but provision for termination is often included in municipal legislation and the policy re-alignment in some States towards refugee protection as a *temporary* mechanism may see this increase. Swiss law, for example, incorporates article 1C by reference,[38] while Canadian law expressly includes the substance of that article as a basis both for rejection of an application and for later cessation; with regard to 'changed circumstances', it declares that a person ceases to be a refugee when 'the reasons for which the person sought refugee protection have ceased to exist', and authorises the Minister to apply for a determination to that effect.[39] The legislative approach locates the issue firmly in a *procedural* context.

The question frequently asked is whether there is a *prescriptive* sense to adjectives such as 'significant', 'effective', and 'durable' so that cessation is contingent on their existence; or whether they are merely *illustrative*.[40] In practice, the problem is essentially procedural, and goes to the burden and standard of proof: Who

---

[37] Ibid., paras. 15, 16.   [38] *Loi sur l'asile*, 28 juin 1998, *Art. 63 Révocation*.

[39] *Immigration and Refugee Protection Act 2001*, s. 108. French law does not permit the use of 'cessation' for purposes of initial refusal: Conseil d'Etat, 25 nov. 1998, 184.740, *Mlle I*.

[40] The change of circumstances cessation clause was first proposed by the French representative in the Third Committee: UN doc. A/C.3/L.123 (27 Nov. 1950), and was incorporated, apparently without debate, in a revised draft drawn up by an informal working group: UN doc. A/C.3/L.131/Rev.1, 1 Dec. 1950, and duly adopted in UNGA res. 429(V), 14 Dec. 1950, Annex, recommending the draft definition to the Conference of Plenipotentiaries to be held in July 1951. Apart from isolated references to the restoration of democracy, the *travaux préparatoires* do not deal with how or when change of circumstances should result in cessation of refugee status. France, for example, simply thought that a country which had 'returned to democratic ways' should 'take over the burden' of its nationals: UN doc. A/CONF.2/SR.28, pp. 12, 13. It had earlier explained this proposal by 'its desire to allow only persons who were still refugees to keep that status', while accepting that, 'in no case could the victims of racial persecution be compelled to resume their former nationality or resettle in countries where they had suffered so bitterly': ECOSOC, 406th Mtg., UN doc. E/OR(XI), p. 276, para. 58. Cf. Israel's view: UN doc. A/CONF.2/SR.23, pp. 20–1.

must prove what, and when? The burden of proof concerning a fundamental change of circumstances is on the authority which seeks to bring refugee status to an end. Cessation or change of circumstances acquires meaning only in context, that is, firstly, where the claimant seeks to show today that he or she has a well-founded fear of persecution; or secondly, where the appropriate authority seeks to show that a previously recognized refugee should no longer be considered as such.

In the first instance, the burden of proof is on the claimant, and the standard of proof remains that of showing that the changes in question nevertheless leave open the existence of a serious risk or possibility of persecution. In the second instance, the burden is on the authority concerned, and the standard of proof for bringing refugee status to an end is the balance of probabilities: Is the nature of the changes such that it is more likely than not that the pre-existing basis for fear of persecution has been removed? In either case, change alone may be insufficient; it is relevant only in relation to the claim, as part of the evidence of the existence or non-existence of risk. The central issue remains that of risk, the assessment of which is a matter of fact; no other *legal* condition is required, such as any degree of permanence, or the holding of elections.[41] Whether the change is significant, effective, durable or substantial is merely another way of describing its evidential weight.

In brief, therefore, (1) the *burden* of proof is on the State of refuge to show that there has been a fundamental, stable and durable change in the country of origin and that cessation is appropriate; (2) the *standard* of proof is the balance of probabilities, that is, in assessing the situation the country of origin, the State or its decision-making authority must 'make sure in an objective and verifiable way that the situation which justified the granting of refugee status has ceased to exist';[42] and (3) given the potential impact of cessation on individuals and families, the person concerned should be given an opportunity to show why, either generally or in his or her particular situation, cessation should not apply.

2.1 CONTINUING STATUS IN EXCEPTIONAL CIRCUMSTANCES

The UNHCR Statute and the 1951 Convention deal somewhat differently with those who, having fled, may still be considered as having valid reasons for

---

[41] In *Yusuf* v. *Canada (Minister of Employment and Immigration)* (1995), 179 N.R. 11, para 2, the Federal Court of Appeal of Canada noted that 'the issue of so-called "changed circumstances" seems to be in danger of being elevated, wrongly in our view, into a question of law when it is, at bottom, simply one of fact'. The fundamental issue is the possibility or risk of persecution: 'there is no separate legal "test" by which any alleged change in circumstances must be measured. The use of words such as "meaningful", "effective" or "durable" is only helpful if one keeps clearly in mind that the only question, and therefore the only test, is ... does the claimant now have a well founded fear of persecution?' To similar effect, see Conseil d'Etat, 10/9 SSR, 19 déc. 1986, 72.149, *Zapirain Elisalde*, recognizing the relevance of country conditions generally, but emphasizing the central focus on whether the individual's fear was well-founded.

[42] Executive Committee Conclusion No. 69 (XLIII) (1992), above n. 30, para. (a).

continuing to enjoy the status of refugee, any change in their country of origin notwithstanding. The Convention expressly acknowledges the weight to be accorded to 'compelling reasons arising out of previous persecution',[43] yet perversely limits the right to invoke such reasons to refugees recognized under earlier agreements.[44] The Statute refers to 'grounds other than those of personal convenience' as justifying a refusal to have recourse to the protection of the country of origin, but without limiting their availability.[45] One early commentator on the Convention suggested that the provision is 'mainly intended to cover the case of victims of racial persecution where, unlike political persecution, the population as well as the government often took an active part'.[46]

The rationale for restricting application of the limited exception is not entirely clear from the *travaux préparatoires*, but can best be understood in the light of a summary account of the drafting history. As has been noted already, many of the States participating in negotiations for the new convention in 1950–51 were unwilling to assume obligations towards unknown numbers of future refugees. In discussing the limits of the refugee definition, it was accepted that a refugee might have grounds for retaining status after a change of circumstances, but some States were concerned at how that entitlement should be worded. To express the refugee's unwillingness to avail him- or herself of the protection of their State in terms of 'reasons other than personal convenience' was too vague, and also 'appeared to oblige governments to accept the possibility of receiving an unknown number of persons who might become refugees after 1 January 1951 as a result of events occurring before that date'.[47] The Israeli delegate suggested the phrase, 'compelling family reasons or reasons arising out of previous persecution' clause, which had been used by the IRO, and also that it should be limited in application to statutory refugees, 'where to all intents and purposes the obligations were known'.[48] The French delegate continued to have reservations, particularly in regard to the 'burden' of assistance to such refugees which, he said, should be borne by the country of nationality.[49] The proposal was subject to further amendment, and the exception was reduced to the single ground of 'compelling reasons arising out of previous persecution'. The UK delegate, Mr Hoare, regretted that the proposal was to be limited to so-called statutory refugees, while the equivalent

---

[43] Cf. IRO Constitution, Annexe 1, No.1, below, Part 1 C (a) (iii).

[44] In *R (Hoxha)* v. *Special Adjudicator* [2005] 1 WLR 1063, [2005] UKHL 19, para. 70, Lord Brown, referring to this assessment in the 2nd edition, considered that 'perverse' was putting it too high, and that it was understandable why some States wanted (still) to limit the proviso; he cited EU Member States' failure to incorporate the Commission's proposal in the Qualification Directive. See further below, 146.

[45] The precise relationship between the various parts of para. 6 is far from clear.

[46] Pompe, C. A., 'The Convention of 28 July 1951 and the international protection of refugees', HCR/INF/42 (May 1958) 10, n. 3; originally published in Dutch in *Rechtsgeleerd Magazyn Themis*, (1956), 425–91.

[47] See UN doc. A/CONF.2/SR.23, 26 Nov. 1951, 20–1 (Mr Robinson, Israel).

[48] UN doc. A/CONF.2/SR.23, 20–1.

[49] UN doc. A/CONF.2/SR.28, 28 Nov. 1951, 16 (Mr Rochefort, France).

provision in the UNHCR Statute was of general application;[50] he therefore proposed to abstain.[51]

2.1.1 Interpretation and application

Since the adoption of the 1951 Convention, both UNHCR itself and the UNHCR Executive Committee have set out their position on interpretation of the exception to article 1C(5). In its 1979 *Handbook*, for example, UNHCR noted that when the Convention was drafted, the majority of refugees were statutory refugees, but that the exception reflects 'a more general humanitarian principle' which could be applied to other refugees.[52]

In Executive Committee Conclusion No. 69, referred to above, the Committee:

(e) Recommend[ed], so as to avoid hardship cases, that States seriously consider an appropriate status, preserving previously acquired rights, for persons who have compelling reasons arising out of previous persecution for refusing to re-avail themselves of the protection of their country, and recommends also that appropriate arrangements, which would not put into jeopardy their established situation, be similarly considered by relevant authorities for those persons who cannot be expected to leave the country of asylum, owing to a long stay in that country resulting in strong family, social and economic links there;[53]

Many States have also either legislated or otherwise adapted their practice to avoid the arbitrary distinction between refugees which would flow from the literal application of the second paragraph of that article. For example, in the area of State legislative practice, the Canadian *Immigration and Refugee Protection Act* now extends the continuing protection first incorporated for the benefit of *all* refugees by the earlier legislation.[54] Taking account of practice and particularly of the need to ensure the full implementation of obligations assumed under other international instruments, such as article 7 ICCPR66 and article 3 CAT84, as well as the widely recognized prohibition on cruel and inhuman treatment, cessation now does not apply when the reasons for which the person sought refugee protection have ceased to exist, but where that person:

... establishes that there are compelling reasons arising out of *previous persecution, torture, treatment or punishment* for refusing to avail themselves of the protection of the country

---

[50] Para. 6A(ii)(e) of the Statute provides that the competence of the High Commissioner shall cease to apply to any refugee if, 'He can no longer, because the circumstances in connection with which he has been recognized as a refugee have ceased to exist, claim grounds other than those of personal convenience for continuing to refuse to avail himself of the protection of the country of his nationality. Reasons of a purely economic character may not be invoked...'

[51] UN doc. A/CONF.2/SR.28, 28 Nov. 1951, 15–16.

[52] UNHCR *Handbook*, para. 136: 'Even though there may have been a change of regime in his country, this may not always produce a complete change in the attitude of the population, nor, in view of his past experiences, in the mind of the refugee.' See also, UNHCR, *Guidelines No. 3*, 'Cessation', paras. 20–1.

[53] Executive Committee Conclusion No. 69 (XLIII)—1992 'Cessation of Status': *Report* of the 43rd Session: UN doc. A/AC.96/804, para. 22.

[54] See subs. 2(3) of the *Immigration Act*, as amended by R.S.C., 1985, (4th Supp.), c. 28, s. 1.

which they left, or outside of which they remained, due to such previous persecution, torture, treatment or punishment.[55]

United States law provides that asylum may be granted in the exercise of discretion to an applicant who, although able to show past persecution, does not have a well-founded fear of future persecution, if he or she 'has demonstrated compelling reasons for being unwilling or unable to return to the country arising out of the severity of the past persecution; or . . . has established that there is a reasonable possibility that he or she may suffer other serious harm upon removal to that country'.[56]

The European Commission's original qualification directive proposal noted in relation to cessation on the basis of changed circumstances, without distinction between categories of refugees, that 'The Member State invoking this cessation clause should ensure that an appropriate status, preserving previously acquired rights, is granted to persons who are unwilling to leave the country for compelling reasons arising out of previous persecution or experiences of serious and unjustified harm . . .'[57] The final version, while it incorporates most of the provisions of article 1C of the Convention more or less verbatim, failed to include the humanitarian exception.[58] On the other hand, the essentials of this 'humanitarian principle' *are* included in article 22 of the EU Temporary Protection Directive, which provides that, in cases of forced return following the end of such measures, 'Member States shall consider any compelling humanitarian reasons which may make return impossible or unreasonable in specific cases.'[59]

The practice reflected in legislation is also matched in the case law of courts and tribunals in a number of different jurisdictions. For example, the refugee board in Belgium noted in regard to the case of a member of the Eritrean People's Liberation Front, who had been tortured and sexually abused on two occasions by members of the Ethiopian army, that, 'the facts, to which [the claimant] had been subjected, have marked her permanently . . . moreover, it is plausible that these facts will lead to her social exclusion from the Eritrean society upon her return'.[60] A similar

---

[55] Immigration and Refugee Protection Act 2001, s. 108(4) (emphasis supplied).

[56] 8 CFR § 208.13(b)(iii), 'Establishing asylum eligibility'.

[57] Commission of the European Communities, Proposal for a Council Directive laying down minimum standards for the qualification and status of third country nationals and stateless persons as refugees, in accordance with the 1951 Convention, doc. COM(2001) 510, 12 Sept. 2001, Explanatory Memorandum, comments to draft article 13.

[58] See arts. 11, 14(1), Qualification Directive. Cf. art. 28(2), Temporary Protection Directive. Within the European system, there may be other bases for protection, for example, under art. 8 ECHR50. See *R. (on the application of K)* v. *Secretary of State for the Home Department* [2006] EWHC 1208 (Admin), in which the court decided (though without getting to the merits), that where the suffering of an asylum seeker had been appalling and extreme and she had an extremely close bond of dependency on her brother, her only known relative who had been granted asylum in the United Kingdom, it was wrong to certify her art. 8 ECHR50 human rights claim as clearly unfounded under s. 93(2)(b) of the Nationality, Immigration and Asylum Act 2002.

[59] Art. 22(2), Temporary Protection Directive; for full text see below, Annexe 2, No. 14.

[60] V.B.C. (2 ch.), 3 oct. 1994, E84, cited in Carlier, J.-Y., Vanheule, D., Hullmann, K. & Peña Galiano, C., eds., *Who is a Refugee? A Comparative Case Law Study*, (1997), 106.

approach has been endorsed in France, where it has been confirmed that, 'Because of the general humanitarian principle from which they proceed, the stipulations of the second sub-paragraph of Article 1C(5) must be considered as applicable not only to the refugees covered by Article 1A(1) of the Geneva Convention, but also to refugees covered by Article 1A(2).'[61]

National case law also provides a substantial measure of consistent guidance on how the 'compelling reasons' requirement is to be applied. The decisions of the courts in Canada, applying, of course, a clear and undifferentiated legislative intent, are particularly instructive. In the leading case of *Obstoj*, the Federal Court of Appeal held that the exception was to be read as requiring the recognition of refugee status on humanitarian grounds in the case of those who have suffered such appalling persecution that they ought not to be returned, even though there was no reason to fear further persecution.[62] In *Biakona*, Teitelbaum J. considered that 'only exceptional circumstances will give rise to the exemption', and that 'the issue of whether a person's experience amounts to "compelling reasons"... is a question of fact'.[63] He cited with approval the decision of Noël J. in *Shahid* and, in particular, the guidance given to the Immigration and Refugee Board which, 'once it embarked upon the assessment of the applicant's claim... had the duty to consider the level of atrocity of the acts inflicted upon the applicant, the repercussion upon his physical and mental state, and determine whether this experience alone constituted a compelling reason not to return him to his country of origin'.[64]

Thus, the benefit of article 1C(5) CSR51 is capable of extending to *all* Convention refugees, notwithstanding that it is limited by its express words to so-called 'statutory' refugees. Whether it ought now so to apply as a matter of treaty interpretation, however, is another matter. The selected practice reviewed above is clearly driven by, among others, the essentially humanitarian and necessary nature of the provision, by recognition that to all intents and purposes, the class of refugees within article 1A(1) of the Convention is largely obsolete, by Recommendation E of the Final Act adopted the Conference of Plenipotentiaries, expressing 'the hope that the Convention... will have value as an example exceeding its contractual

---

[61] Commission des recours des réfugiés, 28 Feb. 1984, 10.884, cited in Carlier, *et al.*, *Who is a Refugee?*, above note, 431.

[62] *Minister of Employment and Immigration* v. *Obstoj* [1992] 2 FC 739.

[63] *Biakona* v. *Minister of Citizenship and Immigration* [1999] FCJ No. 391 (Trial Division), Teitelbaum J., paras. 32, 35.

[64] *Shahid* v. *Canada (Minister of Citizenship and Immigration)* (1995) 28 Imm. L.R. (2d) 130, 138. See also *Arguello-Garcia* v. *Minister of Employment and Immigration* (1993) 21 Imm. L.R. (2d) 285. For other instances of 'raisons impérieuses justifiant la maintien du statut de réfugié', including the case of a Rwandese whose family and companion had been victims of the genocide (CRR, 13 fév. 1995, 258.697, *Nzabonimana*), see Tiberghien, F., *Le droit des réfugiés en France*, 1998, 296–8; see also *Skalak* v. *INS* 944 F.2d 364, 365 (7th Cir., 1991): 'The experience of persecution may so sear a person with distressing associations with his native country that it would be inhumane to force him to return there, even though he is in no danger of further persecution.'

scope...', and by the need to ensure fulfilment of international obligations prohibiting cruel and inhuman treatment.[65]

Arguably, and in the light of the above and the practice of States, the interpretation proposed comes within the scope of the 1969 Vienna Convention on the Law of Treaties. After confirming that a treaty shall be interpreted in good faith in accordance with the ordinary meaning to be given to its terms in their context and in the light of its object and purpose, article 31 provides that, 'There shall be taken into account, together with the context: (a) any subsequent practice in the application of the treaty which establishes the agreement of the parties regarding its interpretation...'[66] Both legislation and judicial decisions constitute 'State practice',[67] and in assessing the legal weight to be attached to such practice in international law, it is relevant to consider not only its extent, uniformity and consistency, but also which States are involved. For present purposes, the practice of major asylum and refugee resettlement countries is particularly important, and Canada, the United States of America, France, and Belgium are significant actors in the field;[68] it is certainly not necessary that there should be universal agreement.[69] The interpretation was not accepted, however, when the issue came up in the case of *Hoxha* in the United Kingdom House of Lords in 2005.[70] After extensively reviewing the argument and materials, the Court considered that the evidence 'does not establish a clear and widespread state practice sufficient to override the express words', and that to hold otherwise would be 'to create a new entitlement to refugee status'.[71] As will be evident from the above, in our view it is open to States parties, in the light of that practice and consistently with their obligations under the 1951 Convention, to apply the humanitarian exception to all Convention refugees; this does not create a 'new entitlement' to refugee status,

---

[65] See also the summary conclusions of the Expert Roundtable of the Global Consultations on International Protection, Lisbon, 3–4 May 2001, which include the following: '(18) Application of the "compelling reasons" exception to general cessation contained in Article 1C(5)–(6) is interpreted to extend beyond the actual words of the provision and is recognized to apply to Article 1A(2) refugees. This reflects a general humanitarian principle that is now well-grounded in State practice': UNHCR, *Global Consultations*, Second Track, Expert Meetings: Summary Conclusions on cessation in Feller, Türk, & Nicholson, *Refugee Protection in International Law*, 545.

[66] Art. 31(3), 1969 Vienna Convention on the Law of Treaties; text in Brownlie, I., *Basic Documents in International Law*, 270.

[67] Brownlie, I., *Principles of Public International Law*, (6th edn., 2003), 2.

[68] Note also the UK's abstention in 1951, as a matter of principle, on the proposal to limit the exception; above, n. 51.

[69] 'A practice can be general even if it is not universally accepted; there is no precise formula to indicate how widespread a practice must be, but it should reflect wide acceptance among the states particularly involved in the relevant activity': *Restatement (Third) of Foreign Relations Law of the United States*, 102, Reporters' note b, (1987); Malanczuk, P., ed., *Akehurst's Modern Introduction to International Law*, 7th rev. edn., 42–3.

[70] This section draws in part on Goodwin-Gill's report in support of one appellant, prepared at the request of solicitors, White Ryland, London, at an earlier stage of proceedings.

[71] *R. (Hoxha)* v. *Special Adjudicator* [2005] 1 WLR 1063. See, in particular, the judgment of Lord Hope (paras. 3–26), including comments (paras. 23–4) on Goodwin-Gill's evidence to the House of Lords Select Committee on the European Union when it reviewed the draft Qualification Directive in 2002; also, Lord Brown (paras. 69–88). Milner, D., 'Exemption from Cessation of Refugee Status in the Second Sentence of Article 1C(5)/(6) of the 1951 Refugee Convention', 16 *IJRL* 91 (2004).

but provides a legal basis on which to continue to treat someone as if they were still a refugee, where the humanitarian considerations are particularly strong.

3. Protection or assistance by other States or United Nations agencies

3.1 THE COUNTRY OF FIRST ASYLUM PRINCIPLE[72]

At the universal level, States have so far not accepted an obligation to grant asylum to refugees, and, otherwise than on a regional basis, have likewise failed to agree upon principles which would establish the appropriate State to consider applications in any given case. Article 31 of the 1951 Convention relating to the Status of Refugees requires refugees present or entering illegally not to be penalized, but is limited to those 'coming directly from a territory where their life or freedom was threatened'.[73] In discussions on this issue at the 1951 Conference of Plenipotentiaries, the then High Commissioner for Refugees, Mr van Heuven Goedhart, expressed his concern about the occasions when transit was necessary. Recalling that he himself had fled the Netherlands in 1944 to escape persecution, he told how, still at risk, he had been helped by the resistance to move on from Belgium to France, then Spain and finally to safety in Gibraltar. It would be unfortunate, said the High Commissioner, if refugees in similar circumstances were penalized for not proceeding 'directly' to a country of refuge.[74] At the time, however, a number of States were concerned that refugees 'who had settled temporarily in a receiving country' or 'found asylum', should not be accorded a 'right of immigration' that might be exercised for reasons of mere personal convenience.[75] The final wording of article 31 is in fact something of a compromise, limiting the benefits of non-penalization to refugees 'coming directly', but without further restricting its application to the country of origin.

With the background of this somewhat ambiguous reference, a practice developed in certain States of excluding from consideration the cases of those who have found or are deemed to have found asylum or protection elsewhere, or who are considered to have spent too long in transit.[76] Asylum and resettlement policy

---

[72] On identification of the State responsible to determine an asylum claim and the broader context of non-admission policies, see below, Ch. 7, s. 6. [73] For text, see below, Annexe 1, No. 4.

[74] UN doc. A/CONF.2/SR.14, 4–5.

[75] France first favoured a limitation to refugees coming directly from their *country of origin*, objecting to the first draft which would have allowed the refugee, 'to move freely from one country to another without having to comply with frontier formalities': UN doc. A/CONF.2/SR.13, 13. This position was moderated in acceptance of the present wording, which is capable also of covering unsafe transit countries. What remains unclear is whether the refugee is entitled to invoke art. 31 when continued flight has been dictated more by the refusal of other countries to consider the claim or to grant asylum, for example, because of time limits, or exclusionary provisions such as those on safe third country, or safe country of origin.

[76] In the Federal Republic of Germany, asylum may not be claimed where the applicant comes from a safe third State, or has already found protection against persecution: *AsylVfG* 1993,

tends to concentrate on refugees 'still in need of protection'. Consequently, a refugee formally recognized by one State, or who holds an identity certificate or travel document issued under the 1951 Convention,[77] generally has no claim to transfer residence to another State, otherwise than in accordance with normal immigration policies. Much the same approach has also been applied to refugees and asylum seekers who, though not formally recognized, have found protection in another State.[78] In resettlement countries, too, eligibility for special entry programmes may be conditional upon the refugee not otherwise having found a durable solution. Under United States law, a refugee has long been liable to refusal of admission if already established in another State.[79] A temporary refuge may not prejudice the claim to resettlement, but this will depend on all the circumstances, including whether the individual has established any business, or held an official position inconsistent with status, and the duration of stay.[80] This limitation was introduced by the United States 1980 Refugee Act,[81] and has also been used as a criterion for qualification in Canada's designated classes.[82]

art. 26a. Residence for three months or more raises a presumption that protection has been found, which can be rebutted by credible evidence of a risk of expulsion to a State in which the claimant fears persecution: ibid., art. 27. In other countries, an applicant for refugee status may be barred from submitting or pursuing a claim if it is not made within a determined period after departure from the country of origin, or after the occurrence of events there which give rise to the fear of persecution, or after entry to the potential asylum country. For earlier accounts of the problem, see Melander, G., *Refugees in Orbit*, (1978); also, Grahl-Madsen, A., *Territorial Asylum*, (1980), 95–101.

[77] 1951 Convention, arts. 27, 28; see further below, Ch. 10, s. 1.2.3.

[78] On 'effective protection', see below, Ch. 7, s. 6.3.

[79] *Rosenberg* v. *Yee Chien Woo* 402 US 49 (1971): 65 *AJIL* 828 (1971): US Supreme Court held that presence in the United States must be a consequence of the flight in search of refuge, 'reasonably proximate to the flight and not following a flight remote in point of time or intervening residence in a third country reasonably constituting a termination of the original flight in search of refuge'. For early United Kingdom practice, see 469 HC Deb. col. 811 (1949).

[80] In 1979, the Australian DORS Committee disregarded the fact that various Indo-Chinese applicants had spent some time in camps in Malaysia and Thailand before travelling on by boat to Australia, on the ground that the 'transit' States could not be considered as potential countries of asylum. Policy and practice more recently has actively sought to ensure that refugees and asylum seekers do not move on from countries to the north; see further below, Ch. 7, s. 6. The Conseil d'Etat in France has held on several occasions that the mere fact of having resided in an intermediate country is not alone sufficient to justify refusal of refugee status; see *Conté*, 20.527, 16 janv. 1981; *Chin Wei*, 21.154, 27 mars 1981: Tiberghien, *La protection des réfugiés*, 238, 239, 466–7.

[81] See now 8 USC §1158(b)(2)(vi)—asylum; 8 USC §1157(c)—admission of refugees from abroad; 8 CFR §208.18—definition of 'firm resettlement'. The combined effect of statute and regulations is to disqualify refugees 'firmly resettled' in third countries from both asylum and overseas admission. The individual will be considered 'firmly resettled' if, before seeking admission, he or she entered another State with, or received while there, an offer of permanent residence, citizenship or other type of permanent resettlement. The person concerned will not be considered firmly resettled, however, if he or she can show, either that entry into the other State was a necessary consequence of flight, that he or she remained there only so long as was necessary to arrange onward travel, and that no significant ties were established; or that the conditions of residence there were 'so substantially and consciously restricted by the authority of the country of refuge', that he or she was not in fact resettled. Relevant factors for consideration by the decision-maker include the living conditions of residents, type of housing and employment available, property and other rights and privileges, such as travel documents, rights of entry and return, education, and public relief.

[82] The Indo-Chinese and Self-Exiled Designated Classes regulations (SOR/78-931 and 933) referred to persons who 'have not become permanently resettled'.

Article 31 contains an obligation of essentially negative scope, prescribing what States shall *not* do with respect to certain refugees. Today, the problem is no longer non-penalization, but that of identifying which State is 'responsible' for determining a claim to asylum and ensuring protection for those found eligible. The 1951 Convention as a whole is silent with respect to such positive obligations, save so far as article 31 has come to be seen by some States parties as implicitly endorsing a concept of 'first country of asylum' and various legal consequences.

Problems arise, however, where the candidate for refugee status has not been formally recognized, has no asylum or protection elsewhere, but is nevertheless unilaterally considered by the State in which application is made to be some other State's responsibility. Individuals can end up in limbo, unable to return to the alleged country of asylum or to pursue an application and regularize status in the country in which they now find themselves. The absence of any convention or customary rule on responsibility in such cases, the variety of procedural limitations governing applications for refugee status and asylum, as well as the tendency of States to interpret their own and other States' duties in the light of sovereign self-interest, all contribute to a negative situation potentially capable of leading to breach of the fundamental principle of *non-refoulement*.

At the abortive 1977 United Nations Conference on Territorial Asylum, States reached a measure of agreement on the principle that:

> Asylum should not be refused . . . solely on the ground that it could be sought from another State. However, where it appears that a person before requesting asylum from a Contracting State already has a connection or close links with another State, the Contracting State may, if it appears fair and reasonable, require him first to request asylum from that State.[83]

The UNHCR Executive Committee adopted much the same approach in its 1979 Conclusion No. 15 on refugees without an asylum country, stressing the need for agreement on criteria to allow positive identification of the responsible State, taking account of the duration and nature of any stay in another country, as well as of the asylum seeker's intentions.[84]

3.2 REFUGEES RECEIVING UNITED NATIONS PROTECTION AND ASSISTANCE[85]

Palestinians are the only group effectively placed outside the protection regime established by the UNHCR Statute and the 1951 Convention.[86] UNHCR's competence under paragraph 6 of its Statute was limited by paragraph 7(1), which

---

[83] See Additional Paragraph to Draft Article 1, 'Report of the United Nations Conference on Territorial Asylum, UN doc. A/CONF.78/12, 21 Apr. 1977; see the Online Resource Centre.

[84] *Report* of the 30th Session, UN doc. A/AC.96/572, para. 72(2); see the Online Resource Centre.

[85] See, in particular, BADIL, *Closing Protection Gaps: Handbook on Protection of Palestinian Refugees in States signatories to the 1951 Refugee Convention,*(2005); Takkenberg, L., *The Status of Palestinian Refugees in International Law,* (1998).

[86] The competence of the High Commissioner in the political issues surrounding the Palestinian question was once thought incompatible with the proclaimed non-political character of UNHCR's work: UN doc. E/AC.7/SR.172.

provides that such competence shall not extend to a person, 'who continues to receive from other organs or agencies of the United Nations protection or assistance'.[87] At the 1951 Conference of Plenipotentiaries it was likewise decided to disqualify Palestinians from the application of the Convention, as 'persons who are at present receiving from organs of the United Nations other than the United Nations High Commissioner for Refugees protection or assistance'.[88] Although political reasons were again involved, the pertinent issue this time was not that of inter-agency competence, but the continuity of rights and status. Article 1D was therefore qualified, as follows:

When such protection or assistance has ceased for any reason, without the position of such persons being definitively settled in accordance with the relevant resolutions adopted by the General Assembly of the United Nations, these persons shall *ipso facto* be entitled to the benefits of this Convention.[89]

Article 1D is not free from ambiguity, however. On the one hand, it premises disqualification from the Convention regime on the continuing receipt of protection *or* assistance; on the other hand, it premises entitlement to the benefits of the Convention on the cessation *ipso facto* of protection *or* assistance, without the situation of such persons having been resolved, for example, through legal provision for and recognition of a separate nationality. For States party to the 1951 Convention, the question arises whether article 1D is limited to those Palestinian refugees who were receiving protection or assistance on 28 July 1951 (the date on which the 1951 Convention was opened for signature), or some other contemporaneous date; or whether it also includes the descendants of such Palestinian refugees and Palestinians displaced by later events; and, if it does so apply, with what legal consequences.[90]

---

[87] GAOR, 5th Sess., Plenary, Summary Records, 328th Meeting, 27 Nov. 1950, paras. 37 (Egypt), 45–7 (Lebanon), 54–5 (Saudi Arabia). See also GAOR, 5th Sess., Plenary, Summary Records, 325th Meeting, 14 Dec. 1950, paras. 187–92 (Iraq). As early as 1946, in the Third Committee, the Egyptian, Iraqi and Lebanese representatives wanted a clear distinction to be made between 'the political and humanitarian aspects of the Jewish question': UN doc. A/C.3/SR.7, pp. 18–20, (4 Feb. 1946). Support for this approach was by no means limited to Arab States; the United States, for example, endorsed the exclusion of certain groups, such as Palestinians, for whom the UN had made special arrangements. See for example, *Ad hoc* Committee on Statelessness and Related Problems: UN doc. E/AC.32/SR.3, paras. 35–48 (26 Jan. 1950). The limitation also had a functional aspect and served to delimit the respective areas of responsibility of UNHCR, UNRWA, and the United Nations Conciliation Commission for Palestine (UNCCP).   [88] Art. 1D CSR51.

[89] In practice, assistance has been provided to Palestinian refugees by UNRWA, within the area of its operations and subject to the conditions of entitlement and registration; see further below, Ch. 8, s. 1.2. No international agency has been charged with providing protection to Palestinian refugees, although elements of that function were entrusted to UNCCP, but cf. Takkenberg, L., 'The Protection of Palestine Refugees in the Territories Occupied by Israel', 3 *IJRL* 414 (1991).

[90] Cf. UNHCR, *Handbook*, para. 143: a refugee from Palestine outside the UNRWA area 'may be considered for determination of refugee status under the criteria [sc. well-founded fear of persecution] of the 1951 Convention. It should normally be sufficient to establish that the circumstances which originally made him qualify for protection or assistance from UNRWA still persist and that he has neither ceased to be a refugee under one of the cessation clauses nor is excluded from the application

Palestinian refugees who leave UNRWA's area of operations, being without protection and no longer in receipt of assistance, would seem to fall by that fact alone within the Convention,[91] irrespective of any determination that they qualify independently as refugees with a well-founded fear of persecution. In practice, however, many States have resisted providing automatic Convention protection, and consider that the key issue is not so much the status of Palestinians as refugees, but whether they are able to return to their (former) State of residence, or are, as stateless persons, claiming to be refugees as against that country. Article 1D in fact should be seen not so much an 'exclusion' clause, as a contingent inclusion clause; it recognizes the refugee character of Palestinian refugees as a group, but makes their inclusion within the Convention regime contingent upon certain events and ensures that such protection or assistance will continue automatically, although in what circumstances is not entirely clear.[92]

3.2.1 Historical background

It is against the historical background to the UN's institutional arrangements, programmes and policies[93] that the various provisions touching on Palestinian refugees in the UNHCR Statute, the 1951 Convention relating to the Status of Refugees and the 1954 Convention relating to the Status of Stateless Persons have to be understood, each being drafted at a time when the Palestine refugee problem was high on the international agenda and an early solution was still expected. For political and practical reasons, States decided not to extend the UNHCR Statute or to apply the 1951 and 1954 Conventions to Palestine refugees.[94] The primary

---

of the Convention under one of the exclusion clauses.' See now, UNHCR, 'Note on the Applicability of Article 1D of the 1951 Convention relating to the Status of Refugees to Palestinian refugees', Geneva, Oct, 2002, paras. 5–8; text in 14 *IJRL* 450 (2002).

[91] See Grahl-Madsen, *Status of Refugees*, vol. 1, 140–2, who is of the opinion that the words '*ipso facto*' in art. 1D imply that 'no new screening is required for the persons concerned to become entitled to the benefits of the Convention', and that on the cessation of UNRWA assistance and/or protection, those concerned 'will become a kind of "statutory refugees"...' Statutory refugees are those within the scope of art. 1A(1) of the Convention, having qualified or been treated as refugees under earlier treaties and arrangements. Grahl-Madsen also suggests that the cessation of protection or assistance may result from departure from UNRWA's area of operations: ibid., 263–5.

[92] See, for example, the views of the French representative at the 1951 Conference: UN doc. A/CONF.2/SR.19, pp. 11–12; and of the Egyptian and Iraqi representatives: ibid., 16–17. Egypt proposed an amendment to the initial draft of art. 1D, with the expressed object of ensuring that 'Arab refugees from Palestine who were still refugees when the organs or agencies of the United Nations at present providing them with protection or assistance ceased to function, would automatically come within the scope of the Convention'. See ibid., SR.29, 5–9. The question is whether, without those organs or agencies ceasing to function as such, the requisite protection or assistance should be deemed to have terminated, either because of voluntary removal from the jurisdiction of UNRWA, or because of expulsion or denial of return to a country of residence, such as Lebanon.

[93] See further below, Ch. 8, s. 1.2.

[94] Art. 1(2)(i) of the 1954 Convention relating to the Status of Stateless Persons, which is not considered further, provides that the Convention shall not apply 'to persons who are at present receiving from organs or agencies of the United Nations other than the United Nations High Commissioner for refugees protection or assistance so long as they are receiving such protection or assistance...'.

consideration was the desire of Arab States, concurred in by other States, to maintain the special status of Palestinian refugees. A secondary consideration, confirmed in the drafting of the relevant international instruments, was to provide a
protection safety net for such refugees, should protection or assistance otherwise
cease. Representatives of Arab States were nevertheless concerned that the protection of the High Commissioner *should* be available if the other relevant UN agencies ceased to function; it was essential that the *continuity* of protection be
ensured.[95]

The Third Committee, which drafted both the UNHCR Statute and a refugee
definition for the 1951 Conference, included a provision stating that 'The
Convention shall not apply to persons who are at present receiving from other
organs or agencies of the United Nations protection or assistance'.[96] For reasons
which are not clear (but which may have been dictated by time constraints), the
draft Convention refugee definition was not amended to bring it into line with the
UNHCR Statute before being was sent on to the Conference of Plenipotentiaries.

In Geneva, however, the Palestine refugee issue was raised almost at once, when
the Egyptian delegate remarked that his Government, 'considered that *so long as
the problem of the Palestine refugees continued to be a United Nations responsibility*,
the Convention should not be applicable to them. Once United Nations assistance ceased, the Palestine refugees should automatically enjoy the benefits of the
Convention. The Egyptian Government had no doubt at all that such refugees
came under the terms of article 1.'[97] He therefore proposed an amendment, the
aim being 'to grant to all refugees the status for which the Convention provided'.[98] The goal, he said, 'was to make sure that Arab refugees from Palestine
who were still refugees when the organs or agencies of the United Nations at present providing them with protection or assistance ceased to function, would automatically come within the scope of the Convention'. The representative of Iraq

---

Clearly, the composition of this group would have changed in the three years since the equivalent
provision was adopted in the 1951 Convention, as a result of births, deaths and other displacement.
For this reason alone, it is reasonable and consistent with history to see the group in question, the
Palestinian refugees, as identified by the events of 1948–49, as receiving protection or assistance both
in 1951 and 1954, and as likely to continue to receive protection or assistance thereafter.

[95] GAOR, Fifth Session, 344th Meeting, 11 Dec. 1950, para. 13 (Mr Raafat, Egypt); paras. 24–5
(Mr Baroody, Saudi Arabia); para. 28 (Mr Lesage, Canada); paras. 29–30 (Mr Davin, New Zealand);
para. 39 (Mr Noriega, Mexico); para. 42 (Mr Raafat, Egypt).
[96] Report of the Third Committee: UN doc. A/1682: GAOR, Fifth Session, Annexes, 26,
Recommendations of the Third Committee, B; UNGA res. 429 (V), 14 Dec. 1950.
[97] 1951 Conference of Plenipotentiaries, Summary Record of the 2nd Meeting: UN doc.
A/CONF.2/SR.2, 22 Mostafa Bey (Egypt) (emphasis added); see also the Egyptian delegate's remarks
at the 20th Meeting: UN doc. A/CONF.2/SR.20, 8–9; and the views of Mr Rochefort (France):
ibid., Summary Record of the 2nd Meeting: UN doc. A/CONF.2/SR.2, 27, and Summary Record of
the 3rd Meeting: UN doc. A/CONF.2/SR.3, 10.
[98] Ibid., Summary Record of the 19th Meeting: UN doc. A/CONF.2/SR.19, 16–17; UN doc.
A/CONF.2/13. See also comments of the British representative, Mr Hoare: Summary Record of the
19th Meeting: UN doc. A/CONF.2/SR.19, 18; also, Summary Record of the 19th Meeting: UN
doc. A/CONF.2/SR.19, 26–7 (Mr Habicht, International Association of Penal Law).

added 'that the amendment represented an agreed proposal on the part of all the Arab States... It was obvious that, if the Egyptian amendment was rejected, the refugees it was designed to protect might eventually find themselves deprived of any status whatsoever.'[99]

The *travaux préparatoires* of paragraph 7(c) of the UNHCR Statute and article 1D of the 1951 Convention confirm the agreement of participating States that Palestine refugees were in need of international protection, and that there was no intention to *exclude* them from the regime of international protection. What was important was continuity of protection; the non-applicability of the 1951 Convention was intended to be temporary and contingent, postponing or deferring the incorporation of Palestine refugees until certain preconditions were satisfied.[100] Those to whom the Convention is not to apply are those 'at present receiving... protection or assistance'/'qui bénéficient actuellement d'une protection ou d'une assistance', and only until such time as protection or assistance shall have ceased 'for any reason', without their position having been definitively settled in accordance with the relevant General Assembly resolutions. In those circumstances, these persons 'shall *ipso facto* be entitled to the benefits of this Convention'/ 'bénéficieront de plein droit du régime de cette Convention'.

States expected that the Palestine refugee problem would be resolved on the basis of the principles laid down in UNGA resolution 194 (III), particularly through repatriation and compensation in accordance with paragraph 11, and that protection under the 1951 Convention would ultimately be unnecessary. However, they also sought to provide for a situation of no settlement, and to avoid a lacuna in the provision of international protection.[101] The refugee character of the protected constituency was never in dispute; in the absence of settlement in accordance with relevant General Assembly resolutions, no new determination of eligibility for Convention protection would be required, and Palestinians would '*ipso facto*/de plein droit' benefit from the Convention regime.

[99] The Egyptian amendment was adopted by 14 votes to 2, with 5 abstentions, and the relevant paragraph, as amended, was adopted by 18 votes to none, with 5 abstentions: Summary Record of the 29th Meeting: UN doc. A/CONF.2/SR.29, 6, 8, 9.

[100] Mr Rochefort, France, noted: '... as the representative of Egypt had pointed out, the effect of [the] paragraph... would be *merely to postpone* the inclusion of the Palestinian refugees' (emphasis supplied); he was nevertheless concerned lest Contracting States bind themselves to 'include a new, large group of refugees, not as the result of a decision freely arrived at, but through the operation of United Nations policy—or in other words, by the withdrawal of assistance which various United Nations bodies were at present giving to the Arab refugees in Palestine': Summary Record of the 19th Meeting: UN doc. A/CONF.2/SR.19, 11–12. See also Summary Record of the 19th Meeting: UN doc. A/CONF.2/SR.19, 16 (Mostafa Bey, Egypt); Summary Record of the 20th Meeting: UN doc. A/CONF.2/SR.20, 8–9 (Mostafa Bey, Egypt).

[101] See also UNGA res. 56/56, 10 Dec. 2001, preamble, expressing awareness 'of the *continuing* needs of Palestine refugees throughout the Occupied Palestinian Territory and in the other fields of operation, namely, in Lebanon, Jordan and the Syrian Arab Republic...' (emphasis supplied); UNGA res. 56/56, 10 Dec. 2001, para. 10, requesting the UNRWA Commissioner-General, 'to proceed with the issuance of identification cards for *Palestine refugees and their descendants* in the Occupied Palestinian Territory...' (emphasis supplied); also, UNGA res. 56/54, 10 Dec. 2001, 'Persons displaced as a result of the June 1967 and subsequent hostilities'.

3.2.2 Interpretation and application

In practice, article 1D continues to give rise to problems of interpretation and application, particularly at the individual case level, when Palestinians seek refuge outside UNRWA's operational area; these are well illustrated by the judgment of the United Kingdom Court of Appeal in *El-Ali and Daraz v. Secretary of State for the Home Department.*[102] Because of the way in which UK immigration and refugee law is structured, the case came before the court as an appeal against refusal of asylum. The Court therefore proceeded on the assumption that what was being argued was that article 1D, properly applied, entitled an individual 'to enter and remain in the United Kingdom as a refugee'; in fact, this is not what the Convention requires, but it may explain in part why a restrictive approach to the interpretation of article 1D has been adopted in this and other cases.

The Court focused its attention on the words and organization of the article. With regard to the meaning of the words 'at present', Laws L.J. rejected the case for 'continuing' effect set out above, and the argument that article 1D applied both to Palestinians receiving protection or assistance in 1951, and to Palestinians who have become the concern of UNRWA thereafter, either by birth or subsequent events and decisions of competent bodies, such as the UN General Assembly.[103] To interpret article 1D as applying also to Palestinian refugees who began to receive protection or assistance after 28 July 1951 (the date on which the Convention was opened for signature), would be 'a very considerable distortion' of the language; he rejected UNHCR's submission that the words should be read to include 'persons who were and/or are now receiving' protection or assistance which, he said, would 'substitute what is really an entirely different provision'.[104] Moreover, the words, 'such protection or assistance has ceased for any reason', could only mean 'the cessation of UNRWA assistance' overall. They did not include the cessation of assistance consequent on a Palestinian refugee leaving a

---

[102] [2002] EWCA Civ. 1103 (26 Jul. 2002). UNHCR intervened in this appeal with the permission of the Court, and was represented by Guy Goodwin-Gill; the views expressed below are the authors' and are not necessarily shared by UNHCR or the United Nations. See also *MIMA* v. *WABQ* (2002) 121 FCR 251, [2002] FCAFC 329 (Federal Court of Australia, Full Court); *Al-Khateeb* v. *MIMA* (2002) 116 FCR 261, [2002] FCA 7 (Federal Court of Australia); Akram, S. M. & Rempel, T., 'Temporary Protection as an Instrument for Implementing the Right of Return of Palestinian Refugees', 22 *Boston University International Law Journal* 1, 57–63 (2004).   [103] Paras. 28–43.

[104] Lord Phillips M.R. on the other hand, thought that if it were indeed a distortion, it was not 'beyond the bounds of what can be achieved by the type of purposive interpretation that is applied to international conventions'; what counted, however, was what the parties had agreed in 1951: paras. 63, 66. Other reasons given by Laws L.J. for rejecting this interpretation included the fact that art. 1D had not been amended by the 1967 Protocol; that it was unlikely that the 'highly preferential and special treatment' provided for under the second sentence of art. 1D would have been intended to apply to others, including those not yet born; that General Assembly resolutions expanding the mandate of UNRWA 'are not legally capable of effecting an amendment to the Convention' and do not constitute 'practice in the application of the treaty'; and because, in his view, the court's interpretation, 'yields a proper balance between the special claims of those Palestinians who were actually displaced in 1948–49 and the rights of other persons, including Palestinians not members of the original group, to claim protection under Article 1A(2) of the Convention': paras. 34, 36–7, 40, 42.

territory in which he or she is registered and receiving assistance, except in an 'exceptional circumstance', for example, where the refugee is actually prevented from returning there by the relevant authorities.[105] Laws L.J. nevertheless agreed that the effect of the phrase, 'these persons shall *ipso facto* be entitled to the benefits of the Convention', is automatic, but thought that 'so great a parcel of rights would not likely be conferred ... unless the class of its recipients were clear and certain ...'.[106]

3.2.3 An alternative interpretation

The Court's ruling is based on a hard and serious look at a complex background,[107] but finally it does not take sufficient account of the historical context and the intent of States, or of the consequences in fact and in law of the alternative approach. The Court recognizes that the words 'at present' are capable of bearing the meaning argued for here, but by not giving them that meaning, it effectively defeats the object and purpose of the provision.

First, the extent of UNRWA's mandate is central to understanding the personal scope of article 1D.[108] The endorsement or extension of UNRWA mandate activity by the UN General Assembly over the years has necessarily involved all the Member States of the United Nations, and therefore also the States party to the 1951 Convention. The relevant General Assembly resolutions are therefore evidence of a policy and practice indicating, on the part of Member States, how the notion of Palestinian refugee and the scope of UNRWA's mandate are to be understood. Indeed, on any interpretation, it would not be possible to ascertain the reach of article 1D *without* examining the practice of UNRWA in general and in specific instances, such as registration.

Secondly, the background described above and, in particular, the object and purpose of the 1951 Convention in its application to Palestinian refugees, require that the phrase 'at present receiving' be interpreted in historical context, with due regard to the fact that States in 1951 did not anticipate a protracted refugee situation, but also with a view to adopting the interpretation most likely to result in effective protection for the one group of refugees which the United Nations and its Member States have consistently recognized over time as their special responsibility.

The words 'persons at present receiving' should therefore be understood to mean 'persons who were and/or are now receiving' protection or assistance. This interpretation, which is descriptive rather than definitive, effectively reconciles

---

[105] But see *AK* v. *Secretary of State for the Home Department* [2006] EWCA Civ. 1117, considering the possibility of refusal of re-entry to the Occupied Palestinian Territories and whether denial of entry could constitute 'persecution': Richards L.J., paras. 46–8.

[106] *El-Ali* [2002] EWCA Civ. 1103, paras. 44–50.

[107] See also *MIMA* v. *WABQ* (2002) 121 FCR 251, [2002] FCAFC 329, in which the Federal Court of Australia—Full Court also engaged in an extensive examination of the issues, while nevertheless reaching similar conclusions ... (Hill J., at paras. 68–9).

[108] On which, see further below, Ch. 8, s. 1.2.

any apparent discrepancy between the first and second paragraphs of article 1D, minimizes ambiguity, avoids arbitrary distinctions, and is most consistent with the original intentions of States and with later General Assembly resolutions.[109]

The date on which the Convention was opened for signature (28 July 1951) is not mentioned in the Convention for the purpose of delimiting its scope.[110] Its use for such purposes will lead precisely to the consequence which the drafters sought to avoid, namely, the denial of the special character and status of Palestinian refugees as a group, and the submerging of individual Palestinian refugees in the general problem. The dangers of inconsistency become especially apparent when considering the variety of other potential cut-off dates potentially applicable to Palestinians.[111] The adoption of such an approach, as opposed to an interpretation oriented to object and purpose, means that the category of 'persons receiving protection or assistance from organizations other than UNHCR' will vary according to the instrument in question, and that the same individual may receive different answers, depending on an arbitrarily selected date, rather than on whether he or she is in fact a Palestinian refugee.

Thirdly, the applicability of article 1D depends, first, on whether the individual is eligible for protection or assistance. If he or she is so eligible, the question whether such protection or assistance has ceased is a matter of fact to be decided in the light of the individual's personal history. The Court of Appeal in *El-Ali* held that cessation of protection or assistance should be considered 'institutionally', in the sense of UNRWA or another competent agency ceasing to exist, and this

---

[109] See, for example, UNGA res. 2252 (ES-V), 4 Jul. 1967, para. 6; UNGA res. 2341 (XXII) B, para. 2, 19 Dec. 1967; UNGA res. 56/54, 10 Dec. 2001, para. 3; UNGA res. 56/56, 10 Dec. 2001, para. 10.

[110] If, on the other hand, it is thought that art. 1D should be governed by the only operative date specifically mentioned in art. 1 CSR51 (1 January 1951), then the following comments may be relevant. At the 29th Meeting of the Conference of Plenipotentiaries, the French representative called attention to the impact on the interpretation of art. 1D of the option, which had then been agreed, enabling Contracting States at time of signature, ratification or accession to indicate whether they understood the words 'events occurring before 1 January 1951' to mean 'events occurring in Europe' or 'events occurring in Europe or elsewhere ...'. In his view, the adoption of the Egyptian amendment, 'could not be allowed to conflict with the specification by each of the Contracting States for which article 1 now provided...'. The United Kingdom representative agreed; if the Egyptian amendment were adopted, 'it would be subject in its operation to the decision taken by the Conference on sub-paragraph (2) of paragraph A, and would take effect only for those States which had adopted the wider geographical alternative in the definition of the term "refugee"'. UN doc. A/CONF.2/SR.29. It may reasonably be inferred from this interpretation that, if art. 1D were indeed subject both to the (optional) geographical limitation and to the time limited reference to 1 January 1951, then it was freed from both such limitations by operation of art. I(2) of the 1967 Protocol: 'For the purpose of the present Protocol, the term "refugee" shall ... mean any person *within the definition of Article 1 of the Convention* as if the words "As a result of events occurring before 1 January 1951 and ..." the words "... a result of such events", in Article 1A(2) were omitted' (emphasis added).

[111] For example, the UNHCR Statute was adopted by the General Assembly on 14 December 1950, and the High Commissioner's Office came into being on 1 January 1951; the 1951 Convention was signed on 28 July 1951 and came into force on 22 April 1954; the 1954 Convention on Stateless Persons was opened for signature on 23 September 1954 and came into force on 6 June 1960.

certainly has some support in the *travaux préparatoires*.[112] Nevertheless, the words 'for any reason' are equally capable of bearing another meaning, and there are many other relevant reasons why protection or assistance can come to an end, as events have shown. These have included military occupation of the territory in which UNRWA operates and the interruption of its programmes, or further flight because of well-founded fear of persecution, violation of human rights, or violence. Where protection or assistance has so ceased, then absent definitive settlement, such persons ought automatically to be entitled to the benefits of the Convention and no separate determination of well-founded fear is required.

Finally, the Court of Appeal in *El-Ali* correctly understood the meaning and effect of the second sentence of article 1D: *ipso facto* entitlement amounts in effect to the automatic entitlement of Palestinian refugees to be treated in accordance with the 1951 Convention.[113] 'Automatic entitlement' does *not* mean that the individual Palestinian refugee arriving in a Contracting State is thereupon entitled to asylum and residence;[114] it does mean, however, that he or she should be treated as a refugee, and that the State is required to seek an appropriate solution in light of that status, and in cooperation with UNHCR and UNRWA.

3.2.4 Article 1D and the future

Since the *El-Ali* case was decided, UNHCR has clarified its own position and described two groups who fall within the scope of article 1D.[115] These are, first, 'Palestine refugees' within the meaning of General Assembly resolution 194 (III) and other relevant resolutions, who were displaced from that part of Palestine which became Israel, and who have been unable to return there; and secondly, Palestinians who are 'displaced persons' within the sense of General Assembly resolution 2252 (ES-V) and later resolutions, and who have been unable to return to the Palestinian territories occupied by Israel since 1967. In each case, the relevant group includes not only those who were displaced, but also their descendants. With regard to the application of the Convention, UNHCR considers that:

6. If the person concerned is inside UNRWA's area of operations and is registered, or is eligible to be registered, with UNRWA, he or she should be considered as receiving protection or assistance within the sense of Article 1D, and hence is excluded from the benefits of the 1951 Convention and from the protection and assistance of UNHCR.

7. If, however, the person is outside UNRWA's area of operations, he or she no longer enjoys the protection or assistance of UNRWA and therefore falls within paragraph 2 of

---

[112] [2002] EWCA Civ. 1102, per Laws L.J. at paras. 44–8; see also para. 25, where Laws L.J. suggests that to allow cessation of protection or assistance to be driven by 'individual events', such as a decision to leave the area, would leave the individual more or less free to move 'between the first and second sentence' of art. 1D. On 'institutional failure', see above, n. 92.

[113] Ibid., per Laws L.J., paras. 49–50.

[114] Contrary to what is implied by Laws L.J., ibid., para. 26.

[115] UNHCR, 'Note on the Applicability of Article 1D of the 1951 Convention relating to the Status of Refugees to Palestinian refugees', Oct. 2002, para. 3, footnotes omitted.

Article 1D, providing ... that Articles 1C, 1E and 1F do not apply. Such a person is automatically entitled to the benefits of the 1951 Convention and falls within the competence of UNHCR. This would also be the case even if the person has never resided inside UNRWA's area of operations.

8. The fact that such a person falls within paragraph 2 of Article 1D does not necessarily mean that he or she cannot be returned to UNRWA's area of operations, in which case, once returned, the person would fall within paragraph 1D and thereby cease to benefit from the 1951 Convention.[116]

In the last-mentioned situation, UNHCR nevertheless recognizes that there may be reasons why the individual concerned cannot be returned to UNRWA's area of operations, for example, because of threats to physical safety or freedom, or other serious protection-related problems; or when he or she is unable to return because the authorities of the country concerned refuse re-admission or the renewal of travel documents.[117]

The above interpretation of article 1D is consistent with the ordinary meaning of the words and with the intentions of the drafters, as disclosed in the *travaux préparatoires*. Its construction is in harmony with the object and purpose of the Convention and with the complementary measures undertaken to ensure the protection of Palestinian refugees, pending a definitive settlement of their situation. Such a purposive approach to the interpretation of the Convention is not only possible, but also justified by the goal of protection and assistance pending a lasting solution.[118] The *non-applicability* of article 1D might at first seem an attractive proposition for many Palestinian refugees, opening up to them the possibility of applying for refugee status or asylum on the basis a well-founded fear of persecution within the meaning of article 1A(2). This might indeed be the case for certain groups of Palestinians, such as members of the diaspora outside UNRWA's area of operations who were targeted for persecution or expelled from and denied re-entry to their State of former habitual residence.[119] For reasons explained above, however, even for the Palestinian refugee twice over, the necessity to go through the article 1A(2) gateway can and should be avoided by the correct interpretation and application of article 1D.

In many respects, the legal situation of Palestinians with respect to the 1951 Convention has become more complex, first, as a result of the 1993 *Declaration of*

---

[116] Ibid., paras. 5–8.

[117] Given its supervisory role in relation to the Convention, as well as its status as a subsidiary organ of the UN General Assembly, this statement of position needs to be considered seriously and in good faith when interpreting and applying art. 1D; see further below, Ch. 10, s. 1.

[118] As already noted, Lord Phillips M.R. recognized that if the interpretation proposed were indeed a distortion, it was not 'beyond the bounds of what can be achieved by the type of purposive interpretation that is applied to international conventions': *El-Ali v. Secretary of State for the Home Department* [2002] EWCA Civ. 1102, para. 63.

[119] This was the fate of many Palestinians long resident in the Gulf States, for example, following Yasser Arafat's decision to support Saddam Hussein's invasion of Kuwait. Laws L.J. suggests in *El-Ali* that if the identity of those 'excluded' under art. 1D is fixed at, say, 28 July 1951, then a Palestinian Arab who does not come within its terms is not 'disqualified', but is free to apply for refugee status: ibid., paras. 24, 35.

Principles on Interim Self-Government Arrangements in the West Bank and Gaza;[120] secondly, because of the withdrawal from Gaza and the continuing uncertainty regarding the international standing of that territory, the West Bank, and the inhabitants; and thirdly, by reason of the evident lack of progress towards statehood. Notwithstanding the changed and changing political situation, UNRWA retains competence with respect to those who left Palestine as a result of the 1948 conflict, their dependants and descendants, as well as those who fled by reason of later conflicts.[121] UNHCR, too, will likely maintain a protection role for Palestinians outside UNRWA's operational area, and article 1D and the extent of State obligations under the 1951 Convention will continue to raise problems of interpretation and application.[122]

3.3 OTHER REFUGEES NOT CONSIDERED TO REQUIRE INTERNATIONAL PROTECTION

Finally, the Statute and the Convention disqualify from any entitlement to protection those who, in their country of residence, are considered by the competent authorities 'as having the rights and obligations which are attached to the possession of the nationality of that country'.[123] The reference is clearly intended to take account of an effective nationality, such as that enjoyed by the so-called *Volksdeutsche*, or ethnic Germans, under article 116 of the Constitution of the Federal Republic of Germany.[124] The constitution of the IRO excluded Germans by name,[125] as did earlier drafts of the 1951 Convention,[126] but the general scope of the later provision is capable of extending to many other groups. Section 1(2) of the British Nationality Act 1948, for example, declared the citizens of independent Commonwealth countries to be British subjects or Commonwealth citizens, the expressions having the same meaning. The assimilation of Commonwealth citizens to United Kingdom nationals strictly so-called was most fully realized in the years up to 1962, when all British subjects (Commonwealth citizens) had the unrestricted right of entry into the United Kingdom, whatever their country of origin. They were free to settle, they enjoyed the right to work and the right to vote, and they were not subject to removal; they also enjoyed the right after twelve

---

[120]   For text see 32 *ILM* 1520 (1993).

[121]   By UNGA res. 2252(ES-V), 4 Jul. 1967, the mandate for assistance was extended to other persons in the area in serious need as a result of the June 1967 war; operations were extended to Egypt on behalf of those displaced from the Gaza Strip.   [122]   See further below, Ch. 8, s. 3.

[123]   Statute, para. 7(b); Convention, art. 1E.

[124]   See further, Goodwin-Gill, *Movement of Persons*, 16–20. The agency responsible for refugees in the Federal Republic of Germany was for many years correspondingly known as the *Bundesamt für die Anerkennung ausländischer Flüchtlinge* = Federal Office for the Recognition of *Foreign* Refugees; it was not competent for German 'refugees', whether they fled from the German Democratic Republic before reunification, or from German minority communities elsewhere in eastern Europe. The Office is now named the *Bundesamt für Migration und Flüchtlinge* = Federal Office for Migration and Refugees: <http://www.bamf.de>.

[125]   Annexe I, part II, s. 4; see below, Annexe 1, No. 1. See also de Zayas, A., *Die Anglo-Amerikaner und die Vertreibung der Deutschen*, (1977); published in English as *Nemesis at Potsdam: the Anglo-Americans and the Expulsion of the Germans*, (1977).

[126]   See, for example, Second Report of the Social Committee to ECOSOC: UN doc. E/1814, para. 4 (10 Aug. 1950).

months of residence to register as citizens of the United Kingdom. However, the most important of these indices of nationality have now been specifically removed, namely, the right to enter freely and the right not to be expelled. The distinction between non-patrial Commonwealth citizens and patrial citizens of the United Kingdom and Colonies is stated clearly in the Immigration Act 1971 which limits the 'right of abode' to the latter.[127] Simply describing non-patrial Commonwealth citizens as 'British subjects' did not constitute them nationals of the United Kingdom for the purposes of international law generally or article 1E of the 1951 Convention in particular. The term was a matter of internal law, from which the United Kingdom derived none of the rights (such as that of protection) or obligations (such as the duty of admission) that are the normal attributes of nationality in international law.[128] In 1981, a new 'British citizenship' was introduced, which became the sole criterion for the right of entry and residence in the United Kingdom.[129]

Article 1E of the Convention and the corresponding provision in the UNHCR Statute do not require that the individuals in question should enjoy the full range of rights incidental to citizenship. Given the fundamental objective of protection, however, the right of entry to the State and freedom from removal are to be considered essential.[130]

4. Exclusion from refugee status[131]

A different drafting approach is used in the Statute and the Convention to describe those whose personal conduct is considered to exclude them from the protection of refugee status,[132] but without great differences of substance.[133]

---

[127] See ss. 1 and 2. Non-patrials are liable to deportation; ibid. s. 3(5), with exemptions from deportation for those ordinarily resident in the United Kingdom on 1 Jan. 1973: s. 7. See now also s. 57, Immigration, Asylum and Nationality Act 2006, adding a new s. 2A, 'Deprivation of right of abode'.   [128] See Goodwin-Gill, *Movement of Persons*, 174–5.

[129] The British Nationality Act 1981 abandoned use of the term 'British subject' as a common description of all Commonwealth citizens, with certain savings. In 1979, changes in the UK immigration rules provided for the first time for the recognition of refugees from Commonwealth countries, who even if granted asylum had not previously been accepted under the Convention, because of their status as 'British subjects'; see 967 HC Deb. cols. 1379–80 (1979).

[130] Cf. *Kola* v. *MIMA* (2002) FCA 265, [2002] FCAFC 59—FCA FC, finding that ethnic Albanians from Serbia were able to enter and reside in Albania where they enjoyed effective protection and faced no risk of *refoulement* to Serbia. See also *NAFV* v. *MIMIA* (2005) 79 ALJR 609, [2005] HCA 6—High Court of Australia.

[131] See Gilbert, G., 'Current issues in the application of the exclusion clauses', in Feller, Türk, & Nicholson, *Refugee Protection in International Law*, 425; Summary Conclusions on exclusion, ibid., 479; 'Exclusion from Protection', 12 *IJRL* (2000), Special Supplementary Issue; UNHCR, Guidelines on International Protection: 'Application of the Exclusion Clauses: Article 1F of the 1951 Convention relating to the Status of Refugees', HCR/GIP/03/05, 4 Sep. 2003 (hereafter, 'UNHCR *Guidelines No. 5*, 'Exclusion').

[132] Statute, para. 7(d); Convention, art. 1F; UNHCR, *Handbook*, paras. 147–63, 175–80.

[133] Traditionally, States have applied art. 1F during the initial determination procedure, and relied on arts. 32 or 33(2) in cases involving serious security or criminality concerns arising after

4.1 CRIMES AGAINST PEACE, WAR CRIMES, AND CRIMES AGAINST HUMANITY

4.1.1 The drafting history of article 1F(a)

The Constitution of the International Refugee Organization, adopted by the UN General Assembly in 1946, explicitly excluded 'war criminals, quislings and traitors', those who had assisted the enemy in persecuting civilian populations, ordinary criminals extraditable by treaty, and those who had participated in any organization having the purpose of overthrowing by force the government of a UN Member State, or who had participated in any terrorist organization.[134] The exclusion of war criminals from the benefits of the 1951 Convention was first considered by the *Ad hoc* Committee on Statelessness and Related Problems at its initial session in January-February 1950, when article 14(2) of the Universal Declaration of Human Rights was cited.[135]

France submitted an alternative draft convention which would have denied recognition as a refugee to any person to whom article 14(2) applied.[136] 'War criminals', noted the French representative, 'would naturally be excluded'.[137] The representative for the United States, on the other hand, thought that as there were no longer any unpunished war criminals, there was no need to exclude them; common law criminals subject to extradition, however, should be excepted.[138] Not surprisingly, the US position was challenged as premature by the Israeli delegate, who suggested that those guilty of persecuting others should also be expressly mentioned.[139] The draft duly prepared by an *Ad hoc* Committee Working Group proposed to frame exclusion by reference to the commission of crimes 'specified in Article VI of the London Charter of the International Military Tribunal or any other act contrary to the purposes and principles of the United Nations'.[140] Again, the United States had reservations regarding mandatory exclusion, preferring that each receiving State retain discretion in the matter.[141]

---

admission. UNHCR's 2003 Guidelines recognize that conduct falling within art. 1F(a) and 1F(c) can trigger *revocation* of refugee status in appropriate cases, but emphasize that, '. . . it is essential that rigorous procedural safeguards are built into the exclusion determination procedure. Exclusion decisions should in principle be dealt with in the context of the regular refugee status determination procedure and not in either admissibility or accelerated procedures': UNHCR, *Guidelines No. 5*, 'Exclusion', paras. 4, 5, 31. See on the EU Qualification Directive, below, s. 4.4.

134 IRO Constitution, Annex I, Pt. II.

135 See *Memorandum by the Secretary-General*: UN doc. E/AC.32/2, 2 Jan. 1950, pp. 15–8, 22–3. 'Exclusion' was not mentioned as such. Art. 14(2), which provides that the right to seek and to enjoy asylum 'may not be invoked in the case of prosecutions genuinely arising from non-political crimes or from acts contrary to the purposes and principles of the United Nations', was cited in the context of admission of refugees.   136 UN doc. E/AC.32/L.3, 17 Jan. 1950, 3.

137 UN doc. E/AC.32/SR.4, 26 Jan. 1950, para. 25.

138 UN doc. E/AC.32/SR.5, 26 Jan. 1950, para. 16.

139 Ibid., para. 45. The French representative concurred: para. 73.

140 UN doc. E/AC.32/L.6, 23 Jan. 1950.

141 UN doc. E/AC.32/SR.17, 6 Feb. 1950, para. 37

This also produced a reaction,[142] leading France to counter with an amendment confirming an *obligation* not to apply the Convention to war criminals.[143]

In August 1950, the Economic and Social Council and the Third Committee each revised the exclusion provisions of the refugee definition, which now included references both to the IMT Charter and the Universal Declaration:

The provisions of this Convention shall not apply to any person with respect to whom there are serious reasons for considering that (a) he has committed a crime specified in article VI of the London Charter of the International Military Tribunal; or (b) he falls under the provisions of article 14, paragraph 2, of the Universal Declaration of Human Rights.[144]

In December 1950, this was duly recommended by the General Assembly to the Conference of Plenipotentiaries scheduled to meet in July 1951.[145]

At the 1951 Conference, the representative of the Federal Republic of Germany suggested referring to the 1949 Geneva Conventions as an alternative to the IMT Charter. 'By associating the Geneva Conventions with the work of the Conference, the humanitarian aims which should govern the Convention would be stressed.'[146] He emphasized nonetheless that all war criminals should be excluded from the Convention, and objected essentially to the *source* of the applicable rules.[147]

The issue was referred to a working group,[148] which recommended the phrasing now found in article 1F(a).[149] It was adopted by twenty votes to one against,

---

[142] See UN doc. E/AC.32/SR.17, para. 38 (Israel); ibid., SR.18, para. 4 (France).

[143] The proposed French amendment provided that, 'The High Contracting Parties shall not apply the present convention in the case of a person they consider a war criminal . . .' UN doc. E/AC.32/SR.18, para. 5. It was adopted by the Committee: UN doc. E/AC.32/L.20/Rev.1.

[144] See UN docs. E/1814; A/1682. The Third Committee took note also of the Second Session of the *Ad hoc* Committee (UN docs. E/1850 and E/1850/Annex).

[145] UNGA res. 429(V), 14 Dec. 1950. The text of the draft convention was submitted to the Conference of Plenipotentiaries by the Secretary-General: UN doc. A/CONF.2/1, 12 Mar. 1951. It comprised the Preamble, adopted by ECOSOC in res. 319(XI)B II, 11 Aug. 1950; art. 1, the definition, adopted by the General Assembly; and the text of the remaining articles and annex, prepared by the *Ad hoc* Committee: *Report* of the Second Session, 14–25 Aug. 1950: UN doc. E/1850 and Annex.

[146] Conference of Plenipotentiaries on the Status of Refugees and Stateless Persons: UN doc. A/CONF.2/SR.19, p. 26; the German proposal is in UN doc. A/CONF.2/76.

[147] See A/CONF.2/SR.24, p. 7. As the representative for Germany pointed out, even art. 6 mentioned crimes committed 'before or during *the war*' (emphasis supplied). The representative of the Consultative Council of Jewish Organizations argued strongly against deletion of the reference to the London Charter, on the ground that its principles had since been twice confirmed by the UN General Assembly, and formulated by the International Law Commission (see UNGA resolutions 95(I), 11 Dec. 1946, and 177(II), 21 Nov. 1947); neither the Geneva Conventions nor the UN Genocide Convention had the same 'solid foundation': UN doc. A/CONF.2/SR.21, 7–11, a view later reiterated by the Israeli delegate: A/CONF.2/SR.24, 14–15. The Federal Republic of Germany replied that the objective would be as well met by a provision excluding anyone who had committed non-political crimes or acts contrary to the purposes and principles of the United Nations: A/CONF.2/SR.24, 6–8.

[148] Ibid., 16. The Canadian representative suggested that the working group might consider including a suitable reference to art. 30 UDHR48; in his view, one serious problem was that of refugees, or presumed refugees, who presented themselves and attempted then to subvert the country of refuge.   [149] UN docs. A/CONF.2/SR.29, 9; A/CONF.2/92.

with two abstentions, the Israeli representative explaining that his negative vote was due to the omission of all reference to the London Charter, and to its possible political and moral implications.[150]

4.1.2 The scope of article 1F(a)

Even though the final text of article 1F(a) omitted all mention of the IMT Charter, the participating States clearly saw it as an appropriate and relevant source of international law.[151] Excluded are those 'with respect to whom there are *serious reasons* for considering' that they have committed a crime against peace, a war crime or a crime against humanity, which has been interpreted to require a lower standard of proof on matters of fact than a balance of probabilities.[152] As Canadian courts have described it, the standard is more than mere suspicion, but less than the balance of probabilities,[153] and it is for the Minister to show serious reasons for considering that the individual concerned has committed the crime or act in question.[154] Arguably also the crimes mentioned in article 1F(a) are necessarily extremely serious, to the extent that there is no room for any weighing of the severity of potential persecution against the gravity of the conduct which amounts to a war crime, a crime against peace or a crime against humanity. Being integral to the refugee definition, if the exclusion applies, the claimant cannot be a Convention refugee, whatever the other merits of his or her claim.[155]

4.1.2.1 Crimes against peace

Article VI of the IMT Charter provided for individual responsibility in the case of crimes against peace, defined to include 'planning, preparation, initiation or waging of a war of aggression or a war in violation of international treaties, agreements, or assurances or participation in a common plan or conspiracy for any of the foregoing'.[156] Control Council Law No. 10, from which the Allied Military

---

[150] A commentary published shortly after the 1951 Conference suggested that the agreed formulation of art. 1F(a) was broader than the corresponding reference to the London Charter in the UNHCR Statute, and took account of continuing work on the subject: Robinson, N., *Convention relating to the Status of Refugee: A Commentary*, (1953); see also, Weisman, N., 'Article 1F(a) of the 1951 Convention relating to the Status of Refugees', 8 *IJRL* 111 (1996).

[151] 1946 London Agreement for the Establishment of an International Military Tribunal: 82 *UNTS* 279; confirmed by UNGA resolutions 3(I), 13 Feb. 1946 and 94(I), 11 Dec. 1946.

[152] *Moreno* v. *Minister of Employment and Immigration* [1994] 1 FC 298 (FCA), para. 16—the criteria are not satisfied if there are serious reasons for considering that an act *could* be classified as a crime against humanity; it *must* be established that, in law, it definitely was. Art 1F(a) CSR51 is now incorporated by s. 98 of the Canadian *Immigration and Refugee Protection Act 2001*.

[153] *Lai* v. *Minister of Immigration and Citizenship* [2000] FCA 125, para. 25; see also *Arquita* v. *MIMA* [2000] FCA 1889 (Federal Court of Australia)—the evidence must be capable of being regarded as 'strong', but not up to either the 'beyond reasonable doubt' or 'balance of probability' test.

[154] *Ramirez* v. *Minister of Employment and Immigration* [1992] 2 FC 306 (FCA), para. 5; *Xie* v. *Minister of Citizenship and Immigration* [2004] FCA 250, (2004) 243 DLR (4th) 395; *Sing* v. *Minister of Citizenship and Immigration* [2005] FCA 125, (2005) 253 DLR (4th) 606, para. 23.

[155] *Gonzalez* v. *Minister of Employment and Immigration* [1994] 3 FC 646 (FCA); New Zealand, RSAA, *Refugee Appeal No. 74796*, 10 Apr. 2006.

[156] See Brownlie, I., *International Law and the Use of Force by States*, (1963), Ch. IX.

Tribunals in Germany derived their jurisdiction to try other war criminals, similarly provided that crimes against peace included the 'initiation of invasions of other countries and wars of aggression in violation of international law and treaties...'. Here and in domestic war trials, as in the trials of the major war criminals, those accused were 'almost exclusively leading members of the governments and High Commands of the Axis States and those convicted on such charges were principally the "policy-makers"'.[157] Brownlie notes that neither the soldier in the field, nor the civilian who supported the war effort, were intended to be punished under these provisions.[158]

Article 5 of the Rome Statute of the International Criminal Court includes the 'crime of aggression' within the jurisdiction of the Court, subject to the adoption of a provision in accordance with articles 121 and 123 of the Statute, defining the crime and setting out the conditions under which jurisdiction is to be exercised.[159]

4.1.2.2 War crimes

'War crimes' are defined as violations of the laws or customs of war, including 'murder, ill-treatment or deportation to slave labour or for any other purpose of civilian population of or in occupied territory, murder or ill-treatment of prisoners of war or persons on the seas, killing of hostages, plunder of public or private property, wanton destruction of cities, towns or villages, or devastation not justified by military necessity'. Just as the International Military Tribunal succeeded to an existing body of law, so article 1F(a) today must be interpreted in the light of more recent developments and the 'relevant international instruments' referred to have been considerably supplemented since 1951. The principles of the IMT Charter have been strengthened by the 1949 Geneva Conventions and the 1977 Additional Protocols, through the jurisprudence of the international tribunals for former Yugoslavia and Rwanda, and by the adoption of the Statute of the International Criminal Court (ICC).

'War crimes' thus also encompass the 'grave breaches' of the Geneva Conventions,[160] now summarized in the 1998 ICC Statute to include any of the following acts: wilful killing; torture or inhuman treatment, including biological

---

[157] Ibid., 176, 197.   [158] Ibid., 195.

[159] ICC Statute, art. 5; on the international crime of aggression and municipal law, see *R. v. Jones* [2006] UKHL 16.

[160] Art. 50, 1949 Geneva Convention for the Amelioration of the Condition of Wounded and Sick in Armed Forces in the Field (GCI); see also arts. 50, 51, 1949 Geneva Convention for the Amelioration of the Condition of Wounded, Sick and Shipwrecked Members of the Armed Forces at Sea (GCII); arts. 129, 130, 1949 Geneva Convention relative to the Treatment of Prisoners of War (GCIII); arts. 146, 147, 1949 Geneva Convention relative to the Protection of Civilian Persons in Time of War (GCIV); arts. 11, 85, Additional Protocol I (API). The term 'war crimes' is not used in the Conventions, but art. 85 API provides that grave breaches shall be considered as such: art. 85(5). International humanitarian law also identifies certain 'terrorist' crimes; see GCIV, art. 33(1), prohibiting measures of terrorism; API, art. 51(2), prohibiting spreading terror among civilians. See generally, Rikhof, J., 'War Crimes, Crimes against Humanity and Immigration Law', 19 *Imm. L.R.* (2d) 18; and for a detailed analysis of sources relevant to art. 1F(a), and discussion of superior orders, see *SRYYY v. Minister for Immigration of Multicultural of indigenous Affairs* [2005] FCAFC 42.

experiments; wilfully causing great suffering or serious injury to body or health; extensive destruction and appropriation of property, not justified by military necessity and carried out unlawfully and wantonly; compelling a prisoner of war or other protected person to serve in the forces of a hostile power; wilfully depriving a prisoner of war or other protected person or the rights of fair and regular trial; unlawful deportation or transfer or unlawful confinement of a civilian; and taking hostages.[161]

Like the 1993 Statute of the International Criminal Tribunal on Yugoslavia, the ICC Statute also provides for jurisdiction to prosecute persons who have committed other 'serious violations of the laws and customs applicable in international armed conflict';[162] and following the Statute of the International Criminal Tribunal for Rwanda, it includes jurisdiction with regard to 'serious violations of article 3 common to the four Geneva Conventions of 12 August 1949'.[163]

4.1.2.3 Crimes against humanity

Crimes against humanity, as is clear from the definition provided by the IMT Charter, are akin to war crimes, save on a larger scale; the concept led directly to the Genocide Convention,[164] and inspired the 1976 International Convention on the Suppression and Punishment of the Crime of Apartheid.[165] The crime

---

[161] ICC Statute, art. 8. para. 1 provides that, 'The Court shall have jurisdiction in respect of war crimes in particular when committed as part of a plan or policy or as part of a large-scale commission of such crimes.'

[162] ICC Statute, art. 8(2)(b). Additional Protocol I includes attack on or indiscriminate attack affecting the civilian population; attack on those known to be *hors de combat*; population transfers, either of the State's own population into occupied territory, or of the local population out of occupied territory; and other inhuman and degrading practices involving outrages on personal dignity based on racial discrimination; and attacking non-defended localities and demilitarized zones. Cf. 1993 Statute of the International Tribunal on Yugoslavia, art. 3: Text in *Report* of the Secretary-General pursuant to para. 2 of Security Council Resolution 808 (1993): UN doc. S/25704, 3 May 1993, Annex; see Akhavan, P., 'Punishing War Crimes in the Former Yugoslavia: A Critical Juncture for the New World Order', 15 *HRQ* 262 (1993). See also the International Law Commission's 1994 Draft Statute of the International Criminal Court, which proposed jurisdiction with respect to certain other crimes established under treaty, including the 1984 UN Convention against Torture (art. 20 and Annex): Text in *Report of the International Law Commission*, (1994), UN GAOR, 49th Sess., Suppl. No. 10 (A/49/10). See UNHCR, *Handbook*, Annex VI, for an earlier list of the main international instruments relating to art. 1F(a).

[163] ICC Statute, art. 8(2)(c). Art. 4 of the 1994 Statute of the International Tribunal on Rwanda also referred to serious violations of Additional Protocol II: Text in SC res. 955 (8 Nov. 1994), Annex. ICC Statute, art. 8(2)(e) nevertheless addresses 'other serious violations of the laws and customs applicable in armed conflicts not of an international character', providing a comprehensive list of such acts.

[164] 78 *UNTS* 277; text in Brownlie & Goodwin-Gill, *Basic Documents on Human Rights*, 283.

[165] UNGA res. 3068(XXVIII), 30 Nov. 1973; text in Brownlie & Goodwin-Gill, *Basic Documents on Human Rights*, 382. Under art. 1, States parties declare apartheid to be a crime against humanity, undertake to adopt appropriate legislative and administrative measures to prosecute and punish those responsible, and agree that the acts constituting the crime shall not be considered political crimes. On the relation between war crimes, crimes against humanity, genocide, and apartheid, see generally Ruhashyankiko, N., 'Study of the Question of the Prevention and Punishment of the Crime of Genocide': UN doc. E/CN.4/Sub. 2/416, (1978), paras. 377–408.

of genocide is expressly included within the jurisdiction of the International Criminal Court,[166] while crimes against humanity are defined extensively in article 7 to include murder, extermination, enslavement, deportation, imprisonment, torture, rape, persecution against any identifiable group or collectivity, on 'political, racial, national, ethnic, cultural, religious, gender... or other grounds... universally recognized as impermissible', enforced disappearance, apartheid, and other inhumane acts.[167] Article 7 further clarifies some of the terminology, providing among others that persecution. 'means the intentional and severe deprivation of fundamental rights contrary to international law by reason of the identity of the group or collectivity...'.[168]

4.1.3 *Individual responsibility*

The International Military Tribunal had no hesitation on the issue of individual criminal responsibility; that a soldier was ordered to kill or torture in violation of the international law of war had never been recognized as a defence.[169] This responsibility derives ultimately from international law, whether it is established by an international tribunal, or by a domestic court whose competence itself is based on international law. The Tribunal rejected the argument that international law was concerned only with the actions of sovereign States, and that those who carried out such actions might be protected by the doctrine of State sovereignty:

individuals have international duties which transcend the national obligations of obedience imposed by the individual State. He who violates the laws of war cannot obtain

[166] ICC Statute, art. 6.

[167] ICC Statute, art. 7 opens with the qualification, 'when committed as part of a widespread or systematic attack directed against any civilian population, with knowledge of the attack'. The same terminology was used in art. 5, 1993 Statute of the International Tribunal on Yugoslavia (crimes 'committed in armed conflict, whether international or internal in character, and directed against any civilian population'); and art. 3, 1994 Statute of the International Tribunal on Rwanda (crimes 'committed as part of a widespread or systematic attack against any civilian population on national, political, ethnic, racial or religious grounds'). Cf. *Mugesera v. Minister of Citizenship and Immigration* [2005] 2 SCR 100—persecution by hate speech; *A-H-*, 23 *I&N* Dec. 774 (A.G. 2005)—incitement to the persecution of others; *Gonzalez v. Minister of Employment and Immigration* [1994] 3 FC 646 (FCA)—killing of civilians during the course of armed action found not to be a war crime or crime against humanity; *Equizabal v. Minister of Employment and Immigration* [1994] 3 FC 514 (FCA)—claimant, deserter from the Guatemalan army admitted torturing civilians; excluded on ground of crime against humanity and defence of superior orders not made out; New Zealand, RSAA, *Refugee Appeal No. 74302*, 26 Jun. 2006; *Refugee Appeal No. 74273*, 10 May 2006—informant for security forces, 'with full knowledge... that the killings and torture would in all likelihood continue', excluded.

[168] ICC Statute, art. 7(2)(g). On the interpretation and application of the elements of the crime of persecution, see above, Ch. 3, s. 5.2.1.

[169] See generally *Attorney-General of Israel v. Eichmann* 36 *ILR* 277 (Supreme Court of Israel, 1962); *R. v. Finta* [1994] 1 SCR 701; *In Matter of Demjanjuk*, 603 F. Supp. 1468; aff'd 776 F.2d 571; *Barbie* [1983] *Gaz. Pal. Jur.* 710 (Cass. crim., 6 Oct. 1983); *Barbie* (1988) *Sem. Jur. II*, 21149 (Cass. crim., 3 juin 1988). In *Barbie*, the court confirmed the non-applicability of any limitations period with respect to crimes against humanity.

immunity while acting in pursuance of the authority of the State, if the State in authorising action moves outside its competence under international law.[170]

The 1949 Geneva Conventions specifically provide for individual responsibility. Each Convention, for example, requires of each party that it search out persons, regardless of nationality, who are alleged to have committed, or ordered to be committed, a grave breach of a Convention, and to prosecute them.[171] The applicability of the principle of individual responsibility is widely recognized in the manuals of military law issued by States to their armed forces.[172] It is clarified further in the Statute of the International Criminal Court, which stresses that 'official capacity as a Head of State or Government, a member of a Government or parliament, an elected representative or a government official shall in no case exempt a person from criminal responsibility under this Statute, nor shall it, in and of itself, constitute a ground for reduction of sentence'.[173] A superior may also be responsible for the actions of a subordinate,[174] but the orders of a superior may relieve the individual of responsibility if:

(a) The person was under a legal obligation to obey orders of the Government or the superior in question;
(b) The person did not know that the order was unlawful; and
(c) The order was not manifestly unlawful.

However, orders to commit genocide or crimes against humanity are manifestly unlawful.[175]

A distinction must nevertheless be drawn between 'mere' membership of an organization which engages in international crimes, and actual complicity. The International Military Tribunal accepted that such membership was not sufficient to establish liability,[176] and jurisprudence has also required 'personal and knowing

---

[170] Judgment of the Nuremburg International Military Tribunal, 41 *AJIL* 172 (1947). In *Sivakumar v. Minister of Employment and Immigration* [1994] 1 FC 433, (1993) 163 NR 197, a senior member of the Sri Lankan LTTE was held excluded, the court ruling in a comprehensive judgment that non-governmental entities can commit crimes against humanity. A challenge to removal was upheld on the ground that it would breach the claimant's rights under ss. 7, 12 of the Canadian Charter of Fundamental Rights and Freedoms: [1996] 2 FC 872 (FCA).

[171] See, for example, art. 49, 1949 Geneva Convention for the Amelioration of the Condition of the Wounded and Sick in Armed Forces in the Field.

[172] See, for example, the UK Ministry of Defence, *The Manual of the Law of Armed Conflict*, (2005). Grahl-Madsen is also of the view that it is reasonable to include within art. 1F(a) anyone guilty of any of the grave breaches identified in the Geneva Conventions: *Status of Refugees*, vol. 1, 276.

[173] ICC Statute, art. 27. To similar effect, see art. 7(2), 1993 Statute of the International Tribunal on Yugoslavia; art. 6(2), 1994 Statute of the International Tribunal on Rwanda.

[174] ICC Statute, art. 28. Responsibility is contingent on the superior knowing or having reason to know that the subordinate was about to commit or had committed the crimes in question, and having failed to take reasons measures to prevent their commission or to punish the perpetrators. See also arts. 7(3) and 6(3) of the Statutes for Yugoslavia and Rwanda, respectively.

[175] ICC Statute, art. 33; cf. art. 6(4), Statute for Rwanda. There was no equivalent provision in the Statute for Yugoslavia; see art. 7.

[176] See Grahl-Madsen, *Status of Refugees*, vol. 1, 277.

participation'.[177] In the recent Canadian case of *Valère*, the Court recalled the principles regarding the level of participation required to establish complicity (personal and knowing participation, association, shared common purpose), laid down in earlier judgments:

... mere membership in an organization which from time to time commits international offences is not normally sufficient to bring one into the category of an accomplice. At the same time, if the organization is principally directed to a limited, brutal purpose, such as secret police activity, mere membership may indeed meet the requirements of personal and knowing participation. The cases also establish that mere presence at the scene of an offence, for example, as a bystander with no intrinsic connection with the persecuting group will not amount to personal involvement. Physical presence together with other factors may however qualify as a personal and knowing participation... [A] person who is a member of the persecuting group and who has knowledge that activities are being committed by the group and who neither takes steps to prevent them from occurring (if he has the power to do so) nor disengages himself from the group at the earliest opportunity (consistent with safety for himself) but who lends his active support to the group will be considered to be an accomplice. A shared common purpose will be considered to exist... [T]he situation envisaged... is not one in which isolated incidents of international offences have occurred but where the commission of such offences is a continuous and regular part of the operation.[178]

The Court added that 'passive acquiescence' is not sufficient to establish the basis for exclusion, that the rank of the individual concerned is relevant, and that whereas the law does not expect 'people to place themselves in grave peril in order to extricate themselves from the organization in question, [n]either... can they be "amoral robots"'.[179]

---

[177] See *Ramirez* v. *Minister of Employment and Immigration* [1992] 2 FC 306—proposing a three-part test for complicity: (1) membership in an organization which committed international offences as a continuous and regular part of its operation; (2) personal and knowing participation; and (3) failure to disassociate from the organization at the earliest safe opportunity. Mere presence at the scene of crimes was insufficient, although being an associate of principal offenders may be. Although he had not personally tortured anyone, the applicant was excluded, as a participating and knowing member. Cf. *Moreno* v. *Minister of Employment and Immigration* [1994] 1 FC 298 (FCA)—witness of torture incident by forcible conscript in El Salvador not sufficient to exclude.

[178] *Valère* v. *Minister of Citizenship and Immigration* [2005] FC 524, para. 21, citing *Zazai* v. *Minister of Citizenship and Immigration* [2004] FC 1356, paras. 27–8 (Layden-Stevenson J.), in turn citing *Penate* v. *Minister of Employment and Immigration* [1994] 2 FC 79, 88–9 (Reed J.).

[179] *Valère* v. *Minister of Citizenship and Immigration*, above note, paras. 22–4. In the instant case, the Court ruled that there was no evidence that the appellant had ever committed a crime against humanity, that he had assisted others, or, even if he was aware of crimes being committed, that he shared a common purpose. Cf. *SHCB* v. *Minister for Immigration and Multicultural Affairs* (2003) 133 FCR 561, [2004] FCAFC 308; also CRR, Sections réunies, 19 juin 1996, 28.2004, *M.N.*— 'M.N. a exercé des fonctions ministérielles au sein du gouvernement intérimaire... dont il est notoire qu'il a toléré et même encouragé des actes qualifiés par la communauté internationale de crimes de génocide... les pièces du dossier ne permettent pas de tenir pour vraisemblable qu'en tant que ministre, son action d'avril au juillet 1994 ait été consacrée à défendre la paix et à s'y opposer au génocide qui y a été perpetré...'; also, CRR, 25 mai 2004, 451.355, *M.K.*: Commission des recours des

A different approach may be called for, however, with regard to crimes alleged to have been committed by child soldiers. Although the recruitment and use in combat of those under fifteen is a war crime in itself,[180] and although the 2000 Optional Protocol to the Convention on the Rights of the Child raises the permissible age of recruitment and conscription to eighteen,[181] the participation of children and young people in armed conflict continues to be a major problem.[182] Some of the issues relating to criminal liability are discussed in the Secretary-General's 2002 Report on the establishment of a Special Court for Sierra Leone, where the possibility of responsibility at age fifteen is suggested, but with an attempt also to achieve a working balance with child rehabilitation and other programmes.[183] The French *Commission des recours* has recognized that children who have committed offences which make them liable to exclusion may be exonerated, if they were in a particularly vulnerable situation.[184]

4.2 SERIOUS NON-POLITICAL CRIMES

Article 1F(b) is the only paragraph to apply expressly to offences committed *outside* the country of refuge, and prior to admission to that country as a refugee. This requirement has not always been followed in the practice of States, and earlier French jurisprudence sought also to apply it to resident refugees. The High Court of Australia, while recognizing that the qualification describes both where and when the offence in question should have been committed, nevertheless was prepared to interpret 'admission' also to include 'putative admission'.[185] The EU Qualification Directive takes a similar approach.[186]

---

réfugiés, *Contentieux des réfugiés: Jurisprudence du Conseil d'Etat et de la Commission des recours des réfugiés*, Année 2004, 72–3; CRR, 13 avril 2005, 375214, *M.S.*, ibid., Année 2005, 92.

[180] ICC Statute, art. 8(2)(b)(xxvi)–(e)(vii); Statute of the Special Court of Sierra Leone, art. 4(c)

[181] Art. 3; text in Brownlie & Goodwin-Gill, *Basic Documents on Human Rights*, 448.

[182] Among others, see the work of the Office of the Special Representative of the Secretary-General for Children and Armed Conflict: <http://www.un.org/special-rep/children-armed-conflict/>; the Child Rights Information Network: <http://www.crin.org/>; the University of Essex Children and Armed Conflict Unit: <http://www.essex.ac.uk/armedcon/>. For background, see Happold, M., *Child Soldiers in International Law*, (2005); Brett, R. & McCallin, M., *Children: The Invisible Soldiers*, (2nd edn., 1998); Cohn, I. & Goodwin-Gill, G. S., *Child Soldiers: The Role of Children in Armed Conflict*, (1994).

[183] Report of the Secretary-General on the establishment of a Special Court for Sierra Leone, UN doc. S/2000/915, 4 Oct. 2000, 7–8; Statute of the Special Court, arts. 7, 15(5): ibid., 21–9. For further discussion of the 'age issue', see Happold, M., 'Excluding Children from Refugee Status: Child Soldiers and Article 1F of the Refugee Convention', 17 *American University International Law Review* 1131, 1148–57 (2002); also, Gallagher, M. S., 'Soldier Boy Bad: Child Soldiers, Culture and Bars to Asylum', 13 *IJRL* 310 (2001).

[184] CRR, 28 avril 2005, 459358, *M.V.* (Colombie—mineur contraint par les FARC de participer à différentes actions); CRR, 28 janvier 2005, 448119, *M.C.* (Sierra Leone). See also ICC Statute, art. 33 (defence of duress).

[185] *Minister for Immigration & Multicultural Affairs* v. *Singh* (2002) 209 CLR 533, [2002] HCA 7. Cf. Conseil d'Etat, 25 sept. 1998, 165.525, *M.R.*—crimes committed in France do not permit exclusion under art. 1F(b).   [186] See below, s. 4.4.

4.2.1 *The drafting history of article 1F(b)*

Criminal and other undesirable refugees received little attention in the instruments and arrangements of the inter-war and immediate post-war period.[187] The IRO Constitution excluded refugees who were 'ordinary criminals... extraditable by treaty',[188] in terms to be recalled by the UNHCR Statute;[189] and article 14(2) of the Universal Declaration of Human Rights seems to rule out asylum 'in the case of prosecutions genuinely arising from non-political crimes'. Apart from the immediate concern of States with the exclusion of war criminals and their surrender to prosecution, the *travaux préparatoires* of the 1951 Convention disclose many unanswered questions relating to the general exclusion of criminals from the benefits of refugee status. The Convention finally uses the deceptively simple phrase, 'serious non-political crime',[190] as the basis, and limits such crimes to those committed 'outside the country of refuge prior to... admission... as a refugee'.

The British representative at the 1951 Conference objected to article 14(2) of the Universal Declaration as a reference for exclusion, arguing that it was arbitrary and unjust to place beyond protection all who might be caught by the notion of 'prosecutions genuinely arising from non-political crimes'.[191] France in turn objected that it was impossible to drop the limiting clause with respect to common law criminals, who should be eliminated from the definition.[192] The British concern remained not to prejudice those guilty of minor crimes; that of France, to retain discretion to grant asylum to minor criminals, but without being obliged to recognize refugee status; and that of other States, to avoid a clash of obligations between the Convention and extradition treaties.[193] One representative also suggested that it would be necessary to balance the seriousness of the crime against the degree of inconvenience or persecution feared.[194]

In later debate, the British representative expressed his concern that such a provision might be used to revoke the refugee status or asylum of one who committed

---

[187] The 1936 provisional agreement on German refugees, for example, proposed limiting expulsion to reasons of national security or public order: art. 4(2); text in 171 *LNTS* No. 3952; see also art. 5, 1938 Convention concerning the Status of Refugees coming from Germany: 192 *LNTS* No. 4461. The UK made a reservation to the effect that refugees subject to extradition proceedings commenced in the UK were not to be regarded as entitled to claim protection; and declared that 'public order' included matters relating to crime and morals.

[188] The IRO's *Eligibility Manual* included the following extradition crimes: murder, poisoning, rape, arson, forgery, issuing counterfeit money, perjury, theft, bankruptcy, receiving stolen goods, embezzlement, bigamy, assault, grave injury, and malicious destruction. Cf. Shearer, I. A., *Extradition in International Law*, (1971), Ch. 5.

[189] Para. 7(d) excludes those whom there are serious reasons for considering have 'committed a crime covered by the provisions of treaties of extradition'.

[190] See Rasulov, A., 'Criminals as Refugees: The "Balancing Exercise" and Article 1F(b) of the Refugee Convention', 16 *Georgetown Immigration Law Journal* 815, 817–8 (2002), who wonders, not unreasonably but too late, whether art. 1F(b) is so ambiguous as to justify recourse to the *travaux préparatoires*.   [191] See UN doc. A/CONF.2/SR.24, 4.

[192] Ibid., 5.   [193] Ibid., 9–6.   [194] Denmark, ibid., 13.

a crime *after* entry, in circumstances in which the exceptional limitations on *non-refoulement* did not apply.[195] The Conference eventually agreed that crimes committed before entry were at issue, and that the word 'crime' should be qualified by the word 'serious',[196] thus moving the exclusion clause nearer to the *non-refoulement* exception.[197]

4.2.1.1 The relation to extradition

Although the drafters elected to make no formal connection, it is perhaps unclear whether this exclusion clause was intended to have any more than an incidental role in the extradition process, or whether the 'doctrine' of extradition was to play some role in the interpretation of the Convention.[198] In addition, the *travaux préparatoires* do not reveal whether the commission of a serious crime outside the country of refuge was to be a permanent bar to refugee status; or whether the exclusion might be expunged by the lapse of time, by prosecution and conviction, by the serving of a sentence duly imposed, or by amnesty or pardon. The UNHCR *Handbook* notes:

In evaluating the nature of the crime presumed to have been committed, all the relevant factors—including any mitigating circumstances—must be taken into account. It is also necessary to have regard to any aggravating circumstances as, for example, the fact that the applicant may already have a criminal record. The fact that an applicant convicted of a serious non-political crime has already served his sentence or has been granted a pardon or has benefited from an amnesty is also relevant. In the latter case, there is a presumption that the exclusion clause is no longer applicable, unless it can be shown that, despite the pardon or amnesty, the applicant's criminal character still predominates.[199]

This statement of position also is unclear. Its foundation on a principle of liberal interpretation is unexceptional in a commentary on a humanitarian instrument such as the 1951 Convention.[200] On the one hand, however, it seems to confirm

---

[195] UN doc. A/CONF.2/SR.29, 11–12.

[196] UN doc. A/CONF.2/SR.29, 17–24. Overall, the summary records reveal shared concerns, but little consensus. The Netherlands thought it illogical to exclude common criminals from the benefits of the Convention, but appropriate that they should not enjoy the right of asylum. Belgium thought there should be no denial of refugee status to a person simply because of conviction for a criminal offence, but that some reference to extradition was called for: ibid., 12–14.

[197] On art. 33(2), see further below, Ch. 5, s. 3.2.

[198] Whatever may have been the legal situation in 1951, later developments in treaty law and the practice of States have confirmed that the principle of *non-refoulement*, which covers expulsion or return 'in any manner whatsoever', also includes extradition; and that a refugee should not be extradited to a country in which he or she may be persecuted for Convention reasons. See Ch. 5, s. 3.3.3.

[199] UNHCR, *Handbook*, paras. 151–161, at 157; see now also UNHCR, Guidelines on International Protection: 'Application of the Exclusion Clauses: Article 1F of the 1951 Convention relating to the Status of Refugees', HCR/GIP/03/05, 4 Sept. 2003 (hereafter, 'UNHCR *Guidelines No. 5*, 'Exclusion'), para. 23.

[200] Cf. *Handbook*, para. 149: 'Considering the serious consequences of exclusion for the person concerned, . . . the interpretation of these exclusion clauses must be restrictive'. This position is determined by the overall approach to the refugee definition, which supposes that a person must first be found to satisfy the 'inclusion' provisions of art. 1A(2) (that is, to have a well-founded fear of

that the role of article 1F(b) is not confined to extradition and prosecution as an immediate, or present process; on the other hand, it suggests that continuing exclusion may be justified by continuing criminal character, in a manner reminiscent of article 33(2).

Referring to the IRO Constitution, the Universal Declaration of Human Rights and the UNHCR Statute, Grahl-Madsen emphasized the objective of exclusion as ensuring that international instruments are not abused by 'fugitives from justice', and do not interfere with the law of extradition.[201] This led him to conclude that, given the non-applicability of extradition where the individual has already been convicted and punished, pardoned or amnestied, or has benefited from a statute of limitations, any such crimes as may have been committed 'should not be held against persons seeking recognition as refugees'.[202] This is not what the words of article 1F(b) actually say, and it has also never been very clear exactly what role the extradition analogy is supposed to play. It might be argued that evidence of any extradition crime as defined in the relations between the parties would be a proper basis for exclusion, irrespective of individual circumstances; or that the range of 'excludable crimes' should develop as extradition practice also develops; or that States should be guided by their extradition laws and agreements when applying the notions of 'serious' and 'non-political'.

Extradition practice has indeed developed over the last one-and-a-half centuries or so; the range of offences has broadened, but so too has the scope of protection.[203] It might be argued that the numbers of those to be excluded under article

persecution), before he or she can be considered as excluded under any of the subsequent provisions. In practice, the two issues frequently run together, and separation becomes quite arbitrary.

[201] A similar view is advanced by Tiberghien, *La protection des réfugiés en France*, (2e. éd., 1988), 103: 'L'article 1er F, b répond uniquement au désir des auteurs de la Convention d'exclure de son bénéfice les criminels qui cherchaient à obtenir le statut de réfugié dans un pays tiers pour échapper à une condamnation de droit commun dans leur pays d'origine'. The French representative at the 1951 Conference, however, seems to have been pressing for a wider discretion to deny refugee status to common criminals. In *Attorney General* v. *Ward* [1993] 2 SCR 689, the Supreme Court of Canada inclined to the view that art. 1F(b) was confined to accused persons who are fugitives from prosecution, as consistent with the *travaux préparatoires*. Rikhof doubts that this interpretation stands scrutiny, a reading of the *travaux* showing that they are nebulous at best: Rikhof, J., 'War Crimes, Crimes against Humanity and Immigration Law', 19 *Imm. L.R.* (2d) 18. See now *Zrig* v. *Minister of Citizenship and Immigration* [2003] 3 FC 761, (2003) 229 DLR (4th) 235 (Federal Court of Appeal).

[202] Grahl-Madsen, *Status of Refugees*, vol. 1, (1966), 291ff.

[203] For example, the 1843 treaty between France and Great Britain dealt with 'Murder (comprehending the Crimes designated in the *French* Penal Code by the Terms Assassination, Parricide, Infanticide, and Poisoning), or of an Attempt to commit Murder, or of Forgery, or of fraudulent Bankruptcy...': Extradition Act 1843. The 1870 Extradition Act, in force when the 1951 Convention was drafted, contained a longer list of offences, with more financial crimes, such as embezzlement, obtaining money by false pretences, crimes against bankruptcy law, and fraud, but also adding, among others, rape, abduction, child stealing, burglary, arson, robbery with violence, threats with intent to extort, piracy, and various other offences on the high seas: Schedule 1; bribery was added in 1906. With the Extradition Act 1989, extraditable offences came to be defined in terms of liability to imprisonment for twelve months or more: s. 2; and under the Extradition Act 2003, s.148, an extradition offence in relation *to* the United Kingdom includes one in respect of which a 'sentence of imprisonment or another form of detention for a term of 4 months or a greater punishment' has been

1F(b) have also grown, but that potentially deprives the word 'serious' of any independent, 'international' content. Whereas an implied reference to extradition in the past might have helped to concentrate attention in matters of exclusion on only the most serious of crimes, the irony today is that this has led precisely in the opposite direction, namely, to a broadening by some States of the scope for exclusion, through the use of ever more expansive extradition provisions, increased use of 'certification' and warrants procedures between 'like-minded' States, and a very substantial diminution in the space to review the individual characteristics of the particular case. These developments are nowhere more clearly in evidence than in the recent practice of the United Kingdom—the original defender of the 'minor' criminal refugee.[204]

Although legislative and executive challenges to the ordinary meaning of words seem likely to continue,[205] the 'fugitives from justice' thesis appears to be on the wain, as being inconsistent with the ordinary meaning of the words. It is one thing to say that those seeking to escape prosecution for serious non-political crimes should not be recognized as refugees; but quite another to say that *only* such fugitives come within the scope of article 1F(b). In *Ovcharuk* v. *Minister for Immigration and Multicultural Affairs*, for example, the Full Court of the Federal Court of Australia concluded that there was nothing there to suggest any such limitation.[206] In *Zrig* v. *Minister of Citizenship and Immigration*, the Canadian Federal Court of Appeal agreed, and observed that a passing remark in an earlier Supreme Court case was not to be read as intending that the serious non-political crimes covered by article 1F(b) were limited to those extraditable under treaty.[207] The primary emphasis is on 'seriousness', such as was illustrated, but not limited, by crimes associated with extradition.[208]

Although the *travaux préparatoires* provide no hard answers, a more principled approach may be justified. Historically, States were determined to limit the discretion to accord refugee status to war criminals.[209] Since the Convention was drafted, they have also acted, both internationally and regionally,[210] to ensure that

imposed. See also Australia, Extradition Act 1988, s. 5—offences for which the maximum penalty is death or imprisonment or other deprivation of liberty for not less than 12 months; 1957 European Convention on Extradition, art. 2—at least one year; 1981 Inter-American Convention on Extradition, art. 3(1)—not less than two years of deprivation of liberty.

[204] See further below, s. 4.2.2.
[205] Exclusion from refugee status still leaves open the very real possibility of human rights protection; see below, Ch. 6.
[206] *Ovcharuk* v. *Minister for Immigration and Multicultural Affairs* (1998), 158 ALR 289 (Branson, J.A. at 300; Whitlam, J.A. at 294—both referring to 'ordinary meaning'; Sackville J.A. at 302–4).
[207] *Zrig* v. *Minister of Citizenship and Immigration* [2003] 3 FC 761, (2003) 229 DLR (4th) 235, Nadon J.A., paras. 65–7, referring to obiter remarks by Bastarache J. in *Pushpanathan* v. *Minister of Citizenship and Immigration* [1998] 1 SCR 982, para. 73; see also paras. 83–4 and Décary J. at paras. 123–4, referring to and agreeing with the 2nd edition of this work.
[208] Ibid., paras. 67, 125–6.   [209] See above, s. 4.1.
[210] See 1968 Convention on the Non-Applicability of Statutory Limitations of War Crimes and Crimes against Humanity: UNGA res. 2391 (XXIII), 26 Nov. 1968; in force Nov. 1970; also, art. 1, 1975 Additional Protocol to the European Convention on Extradition: below, Annexe 2, No. 11.

statutes of limitation shall not run in favour of war criminals, and the notion of serious non-political crime has increasingly come to be associated with many offences against the laws of war, and with the emerging concept of 'terrorism'. Although it needs careful oversight, the related concept of 'security' now also occupies a more dominant place in controlling the movement of people between States, whether refugees or not; provided it can be kept within a framework of accountability,[211] security may offer the necessary theoretical basis for the application of article 1F(b) in a context which also ensures the integrity of the international system of protection. The commission of a serious non-political crime may be sufficient reason for exclusion because it is indicative of some future danger to the community of the State of refuge; or because the very nature and circumstances of the crime render it a basis for exclusion in itself, regardless of extradition, prosecution, punishment or non-justiciability.

4.2.1.2 'Serious' and 'non-political'
That the individual who had committed a political crime was to be distinguished from the 'common criminal'[212] is illustrated well by the equally authoritative French text of article 1F(b):

Les dispositions de cette convention ne seront pas applicables aux personnes dont on aura des raisons sérieuses de penser:

. . .

(b) Qu'elles ont commis *un crime grave de droit commun* en dehors du pays d'accueil avant d'y être admises comme réfugiés. (Emphasis supplied.)

Each State must determine what constitutes a serious crime, according to its own standards up to a point, but on the basis of the ordinary meaning of the words considered in context and with the objectives of the 1951 Convention. Given that the words are not self-applying, each party has some discretion in determining whether the criminal character of the applicant for refugee status in fact outweighs his or her character as *bona fide* refugee, and so constitutes a threat to its internal order.[213] Just as the 1951 Conference rejected 'extradition crimes' as an *a priori* excludable category, so *ad hoc* approaches founded on length of sentence are of

---

[211] The difficulty of supervising security-driven measures should not be underestimated; see, for example, *A* v. *Secretary of State for the Home Department* [2005] 2 AC 68, [2004] UKHL 56; *Secretary of State for the Home Department* v. *M* [2004] EWCA Civ 324; *Suresh* v. *Minister of Citizenship and Immigration* [2002] 1 SCR 3, (2002) 208 DLR (4th) 1; *Ahani* v. *Minister of Citizenship and Immigration* [2002] 1 SCR 72, (2002) 208 DLR (4th) 57; Barak, A., 'A Judge on Judging: the Role of a Supreme Court in a Democracy', 116 *Harv. LR* 16, 158 (2002); Türk, V., 'Forced Migration and Security', 15 *IJRL* 113 (2003).

[212] See, for example, UN docs. A/CONF.2/SR.24, 5, 10 (France); SR.29, 12 (The Netherlands).

[213] At the Conference of Plenipotentiaries, the President, Mr Larsen, said that it would be 'for the country of refuge to strike a balance between the offences committed . . . and the extent to which [the] fear of persecution was well-founded': UN doc. A/CONF.2/SR.29, 23; cf. Weis, P., 'The concept of the refugee in international law', *Journal du dr. inter.* (1960), 1, 30.

little help,[214] unless related to the nature and circumstances of the offence.[215] Commentators and jurisprudence seem to agree, however, that serious crimes, above all, are those against physical integrity, life, and liberty.[216]

The problem of determining whether a crime is political has already been considered.[217] The nature and purpose of the offence require examination, including whether it was committed out of genuine political motives or merely for personal reasons or gain, whether it was directed towards a modification of the political organization or the very structure of the State, and whether there is a close and direct causal link between the crime committed and its alleged political purpose and object. The political element should in principle outweigh the common law character of the offence, which may not be the case if the acts committed are grossly disproportionate to the objective, or are of an atrocious or barbarous nature.[218] The tendency to 'depoliticize' certain offences, such as hijacking, hostage-taking, offences against diplomats, and terrorism, is a potential source of difficulties[219] which are not entirely resolved by inclusion in some of the conventions of the principle, *aut dedere aut judicare*. Although certain States have been prepared to prosecute the 'extra-territorial criminal' or suspected terrorist, the

---

[214] Cf. Grahl-Madsen, *Status of Refugees*, vol. 1, (1966), 294.

[215] Cf. Canadian *Immigration and Refugee Protection Act*, s. 101(1)(f), (2). Broadly, this excludes from the refugee status procedure any individual who has been convicted in Canada of an offence punishable with a term of imprisonment of ten years or more and a sentence of at least two years has been imposed; and, in the case of convictions outside Canada, where the Minister is of the opinion that the person is a danger to the public in Canada and the conviction is for an offence which, if committed in Canada, would be punishable by a maximum sentence of at least ten years' imprisonment. See *Minister of Citizenship and Immigration* v. *Ragupathy* [2006] FCA 151 (application for judicial review of a 'danger opinion').

[216] Cf. Tiberghien, *La protection des réfugiés*, 104; Kälin, *Prinzip*, 124; Grahl-Madsen, *Status of Refugees*, vol. 1, 294ff; Köfner & Nicolaus, *Grundlagen des Asylrechts in der Bundesrepublik Deutschland*, 327; Alland & Teitgen-Colly, *Traité du droit d'asile*, 523–31.   [217] See above, Ch. 3, s. 5.5.2.

[218] The approach in the text was cited with approval by the Court of Appeals in *McMullen* v. *INS*, 788 F.2d 591, 597 (9th Cir. 1986). See CRR, Sections réunies, 9 janvier 2003, 362.645, *M.A.*—founding member of the PKK excluded on ground of serious reasons to consider he had participated in decisions leading to the commission of serious non-political crimes, including the use of terrorist methods against the civilian population and in the absence of evidence of disassociation from the aims and methods of the organization; Conseil d'Etat, 28 février 2001, 195.356, *M.D.*—LTTE member excluded by reason of personal participation in an attack on a military camp resulting in more than 100 deaths; also *Rodriguez Martinez Manuel* (1941) cited by Kiss, *Répertoire de la pratique française en matière de droit international public*, vol. 2, (1966), 216; and *Morelli*, ibid., 217.

[219] See, for example, art. 16, 1963 Tokyo Convention on Offences and Certain other Acts committed on board Aircraft; art. 7, 1970 Hague Convention for the Suppression of Unlawful Seizure of Aircraft; art. 7, 1971 Montreal Convention for the Suppression of Unlawful Acts against the Safety of Civil Aviation; art. 7, 1973 Convention on the Prevention and Punishment of Crimes against Internationally Protected Persons, including Diplomatic Agents; art. 3, 1957 European Convention on Extradition; art. 5, 1977 European Convention on the Suppression of Terrorism; art. 9, 1979 United Nations Convention on the Taking of Hostages; art. 9, 1971 OAS Convention to prevent and punish Acts of Terrorism taking the form of Crimes against Persons and related Extortion that are of International Significance; art. 5, 1981 OAS Inter-American Convention on Extradition. See further below, s. 4,5, on recent action with regard to terrorism and its impact on refugees and asylum seekers.

possibility of *refoulement* to persecution cannot be excluded in the present climate.[220]

The political aspect apart, the phrase 'serious non-political crime' is not easy to define given the different connotations of the term 'crime' in different legal systems.[221] The standard finally to be applied is an international standard, in that a provision of a multilateral treaty is involved, but standards relating to criminal prosecution and treatment of offenders current in the potential country of asylum are also relevant. Each case will require examination on its merits, with regard paid to both mitigating and aggravating factors, and to the level of individual responsibility. This point is commonly overlooked by advocates against 'balancing'—that in any criminal process, justice requires consideration of more than the particular label which the legislature or the executive may attach to an offence.[222]

Article 1F excludes 'persons', rather than 'refugees' from the benefits of the Convention, suggesting that the issue of a well-founded fear of persecution is irrelevant and need not be examined at all if there are 'serious reasons for considering' that an individual comes within its terms. In practice, the claim to be a refugee can rarely be ignored, for account must be taken of the nature of the offence presumed to have been committed, the context in which it is alleged to have occurred, and the surrounding circumstances, including the treatment likely to be faced on return. This is implicit in the regime of international protection, whether refugee or human rights law is concerned, and is also required by the 'new' standards applicable in extradition.

There are three points at which assessments have to be made when deciding exclusion under article 1F(b): first, whether there are serious reasons for considering that the individual in question has committed the offence; secondly, whether the crime is serious, considered with due regard to context and individual circumstances; and thirdly, whether it is non-political. None of these points of assessment is sealed off from any other, and each impacts on every other, for no serious non-political crime exists in a vacuum, whatever national legislation or executive certification may provide. This is why it is relevant to consider not only the nature of the crime or crimes in question, but also the persecution feared, and whether criminal character in fact outweighs the applicant's character as a *bona fide* refugee.[223]

---

[220] See generally, Goodwin-Gill, G. S., 'Crimes in International Law: Obligations *Erga Omnes* and the Duty to Prosecute', in Goodwin-Gill, G. S. & Talmon, S., eds., *The Reality of International Law: Essays in Honour of Ian Brownlie*, (1999), 199.

[221] Cf. Grahl-Madsen, *Status of Refugees*, vol. 1, 289–99.

[222] On context and proportionality, see below, s. 4.2.2.

[223] See *Prosecutor* v. *Kupreskic*, ICTY, Case No. IT-95-16, Trial Chamber, 14 Jan. 2000, para. 852: 'The determination of the gravity of the crime requires a consideration of the particular circumstances of the case, as well as the form and degree of the participation of the accused in the crime'. Cited in Rasulov, A., 'Criminals as Refugees: The "Balancing Exercise" and Article 1F(b) of the Refugee Convention', 16 *Georgetown Immigration Law Journal* 815, 819 (2002).

In 1980, following the arrival of some 125,000 Cuban asylum seekers in the United States, UNHCR was requested by the authorities to advise on asylum applications which were likely to be refused on account of the applicants' criminal background.[224] The size of the influx made individual case-by-case assessment difficult, and it was later decided to accord the majority an interim status in anticipation of their situation being regularized by special legislation.[225] Suspected criminal cases, however, were examined in a joint UNHCR/State Department exercise, in which one of the authors was closely involved during June and July 1980.

With a view to promoting consistent decisions, UNHCR proposed that, in the absence of any political factors, a presumption of serious crime might be considered as raised by evidence of commission of any of the following offences: homicide, rape, child molesting, wounding, arson, drugs traffic, and armed robbery.[226] However, that presumption should be capable of rebuttal by evidence of mitigating factors, some of which are set out below. The following offences might also be considered to constitute serious crimes, provided other factors were present: breaking and entering (burglary); stealing (theft and simple robbery); receiving stolen property; embezzlement; possession of drugs in quantities exceeding that required for personal use; and assault. Factors to support a finding of seriousness included: use of weapons; injury to persons; value of property involved; type of drugs involved;[227] evidence of habitual criminal conduct. With respect to all cases, the following elements were suggested as tending to rebut a presumption or finding of serious crime: minority of the offender; parole; elapse of five years since conviction or completion of sentence; general good character (for example, one offence only); offender was merely accomplice; other circumstances surrounding commission of the offence (for example, provocation and self-defence).[228]

---

[224] The text of the United States request for assistance is in 19 *ILM* 1296. The 1980 Refugee Act incorporated the substance of art. 1F(b) CSR51 as an exception to the prohibition on the deportation or return of an alien to a country in which his or her life or freedom may be threatened. However, the legislative position has now changed radically; see further below, s. 4.2.2.

[225] See 'Cuban-Haitian Arrivals in US', *Current Policy no. 193*, 29 Jun. 1980, statement by Victor H. Palmieri, US Co-ordinator for Refugee Affairs.

[226] This list, of course, is by no means exclusive, but draws on the sorts of offences in fact admitted. The evidence in question was provided by the asylum seekers themselves, in interviews with US officials.

[227] Mere possession of marijuana for personal use was not considered to amount to a serious non-political crime. Cf. Gottwald, M., 'Asylum Claims and Drug Offences: The Seriousness Threshold of Article 1F(b) of the 1951 Convention relating to the Status of Refugees and the UN Drug Conventions', 18 *IJRL* 81 (2006).

[228] There was ample evidence in statements by convicts from different jails that an incentive to leave Cuba had been the threat by officials of a further term of imprisonment. Others, particularly former convicts, were threatened with up to four years' jail under Cuba's *Ley de Peligrosidad*, while some were issued with passports on simple production of their release certificates at local police stations. During a period of some seven weeks, 1,021 cases were examined and most provided few problems, in that the commission of serious crimes was clearly indicated. A number of cases, however, were discussed at length, resulting in general agreement on the serious or non-serious nature of the

These criteria may still be of general value in the interpretation of the Convention and the Statute, bearing in mind that the objective of such provisions is to obtain a humanitarian balance between a potential threat to the community of refuge and the interests of the individual who has a well-founded fear of persecution.

4.2.2 Context and proportionality

In its 2003 *Guidelines* on exclusion, UNHCR argues that, 'As with any exception to a human rights guarantee, the exclusion clauses must . . . be applied in a manner proportionate to their objective, so that the gravity of the offence in question is weighed against the consequences of exclusion.' It suggests that, given the implicit gravity of the offences, such an approach would not normally be required with regard to article 1F(a) or 1F(c), but that it is appropriate for article 1F(b) and 'less serious' war crimes.[229] There is nothing in the words of the exclusion clause to rule out such an approach, which found favour with certain delegates at the 1951 Conference,[230] and which also has some support in the jurisprudence. In *Pushpanathan*, for example, the Supreme Court of Canada noted specifically that:

Article 1F(b) contains a balancing mechanism in so far as the specific adjectives 'serious' and 'non-political' must be satisfied, while Article 33(2) as implemented in the Act by ss. 53 and 19 provides for weighing of the seriousness of the danger posed to Canadian society against the danger of persecution upon *refoulement*. This approach reflects the intention of the signatory states to create a humanitarian balance between the individual in fear of persecution on the one hand, and the legitimate concern of states to sanction criminal activity on the other . . .[231]

There seems to have been little rational explanation for why courts in several jurisdictions have rejected the principle of individualized determination,[232] even as 'extradition law' itself has evolved, particularly at the regional level, precisely to incorporate 'refugee' protection. Already in 1957 the European Convention on Extradition provided that extradition shall not be granted where the requested party had substantial grounds to believe that the request was made for the purpose

crime, or in deferral for further inquiries and reinterview regarding either the circumstances of the offence or political and refugee elements. In December 1984 the US and Cuba agreed on the return of some 2,746 inadmissible Cuban nationals and for the resumption of immigration processing in Havana by the US authorities: 24 *ILM* 32 (1985). Only a few had in fact been returned when Cuba suspended the agreements on commencement of broadcasting by a Florida-based station, Radio Marti, considered hostile to the government. It has not been possible to determine with certainty whether any of the cases considered non-serious in 1980 were in fact scheduled for deportation in 1984/85 and, if so, on what grounds. For related litigation, see the various decisions entitled *Fernandez-Roque* v. *Smith* 535 F. Supp. 741 (1981); 671 F.2d 426 (1982); 539 F. Supp. 925 (1982); 557 F. Supp. 690 (1982); 567 F. Supp. 1115 (1983); 734 F.2d 576 (1984).

[229] UNHCR *Guidelines No. 5*, 'Exclusion', para. 24.   [230] See above, 172.

[231] *Pushpanathan* v. *Canada (Minister of Citizenship and Immigration)* [1998] 1 SCR 982, para. 73. On the interpretation and application of the exceptions to *non-refoulement* in art. 33(2), see below, Ch. 5, s. 3.2.

[232] For reasons set out below, this terminology perhaps describes more accurately than 'balancing' what ought to occur in certain exclusion hearings.

of prosecuting or punishing a person, 'on account of his race, religion, nationality or political opinion, or that that person's position may be prejudiced for any of these reasons'.[233] Current UK legislation prohibits extradition for what the Act now calls 'extraneous reasons';[234] it is also barred if incompatible with Convention rights within the meaning of the Human Rights Act 1998, and if the individual sought, 'could be, will be or has been sentenced to death'.[235] On the other hand, in the refugee and asylum context, UK legislation adopts another approach—presumptive exclusion. Section 72 of the Nationality, Immigration and Asylum Act 2002 purports to apply 'for the purpose of the construction and application of Article 33(2) of the Refugee Convention (exclusion from protection)'.[236] It provides that, 'a person shall be presumed to have been convicted by a final judgment of a particularly serious crime *and* to constitute a danger to the community of the United Kingdom' (emphasis supplied), if he or she has been convicted of an offence and sentenced to imprisonment for at least two years.[237] Sections 72(3) and 72(4) provide for equivalent presumptions in relation to conviction and sentence outside the United Kingdom, and in relation to such other offences as may be specified or certified by the Secretary of State. While the presumption may be rebutted, section 72(8) extends and applies the obligation, when making the assessment, to disregard the gravity of fear or threat of persecution, which was first introduced by section 34(1) of the Anti-Terrorism, Crime and Security Act 2001.[238] In 2004, the House of Commons/House of Lords Joint Committee on Human Rights concluded that section 72 was incompatible with the UK's obligations under the 1951 Convention,[239] and that the crimes included in the 2004 Order 'go far beyond what can be regarded as "particularly serious crimes" for the purposes of Article 33(2)'.[240]

In the United States, the 'aggravated felony' provisions make certain individuals ineligible for asylum or withholding of removal; certain conduct is considered too serious to justify exceptions, and no consideration is given to relief in the

---

[233] Art. 3; see also art. 4(4), 1981 Inter-American Convention on Extradition—denial of extradition when, 'from the circumstances of the case, it can be inferred that persecution for reasons of race, religion, or nationality is involved, or that the position of the person sought may be prejudiced for any of these reasons'. Cf. *Fernandez* v. *Government of Singapore* [1971] 1 WLR 987, discussed above in Ch. 2, s. 3, s. 3   [234] Extradition Act 2003, ss. 13, 81,
[235] Ibid., ss. 21, 87, 94.
[236] Art. 33(2) CSR51, of course, is not in fact about 'exclusion', an art. 1F matter, but about a limited exception to the principle of *non-refoulement*; see further below, Ch. 5, s. 3.2. Cf. EU Qualification Directive, arts. 12, 14, and below, s. 4.4.
[237] S. 72(2); ss. 72(3) and 72(4) provide for equivalent presumptions in relation to conviction and sentence outside the UK, and in relation to such other offences as may be specified or certified by the Secretary of State. At no time has the UK Government shown any empirical justification for the additional penalization of refugees, for example, by reference to above average criminality.
[238] The government admitted at the time that the legislation was intended to do away with the proportionality test: Lord Rooker, *Hansard*, HL 629, col. 1253.
[239] Joint Committee on Human Rights, *The Nationality, Immigration and Asylum Act 2002 (Specification of Particularly Serious Crimes) Order 2004*, HL Paper 190/HC1212, 2004, 14–5; see also at 8–12 on the 'proper interpretation' of art. 33(2) CSR51.   [240] Ibid., 11.

alternative.[241] An aggravated felony is a 'particularly serious crime' which 'constitutes a danger to the community', and thus bars asylum.[242] In the case of withholding, aggravated felony convictions which involve a sentence of more than five years are considered particularly serious crimes and are an automatic bar,[243] while the Attorney-General has also determined that drug trafficking offences are presumed to be particularly serious crimes, in the absence of specifically listed extraordinary and compelling circumstances.[244]

The Illegal Immigration and Immigrant Responsibility Act 1996 eliminated the two part analysis which had previously conditioned denial of asylum on (a) involvement in terrorist activity, and (b) reasonable grounds to believe that the individual was a danger to the security of the United States.[245] The statutory language now provides that the individual is ineligible for asylum if the Attorney-General determines that 'there are reasonable grounds for regarding' him or her as such a danger, *or* if the individual meets the statutory criteria relating to terrorist activity.[246] The political offence exception does not apply to 'terrorist activity', but only to the sections of the Immigration and Nationality Act in which it is specifically mentioned.[247] In addition, where the Attorney-General has determined that an individual has engaged in terrorist activities, then 'there are reasonable grounds for regarding [him or her] as a danger to the security of the United States'.[248]

[241] See the Anti-Terrorism and Effective Death Penalty Act 1996, Pub. L. No. 104–32, 110 Stat. 1214 (1996); and the Illegal Immigration Reform and Immigrant Responsibility Act 1996, Pub. L. No. 104–208, 110 Stat. 3009-546 (1996).

[242] 8 USC § 1158(b)(2)(A)(ii), 8 USC § 1158(b)(2)(B)(i).

[243] 8 USC § 1231(b)(3)(B). See *L-S-*, 22 *I&N Dec.* 645 (BIA 1999), holding that an individual examination of the nature of the conviction, the sentence imposed, and the circumstances and underlying facts of the conviction is required, and finding that an alien convicted of bringing a foreign national illegally into the country and sentenced to three-and-a-half months' imprisonment had not, in the circumstances, been convicted of a particularly serious crime and was eligible to apply for withholding of removal.   [244] *Y-L-, A-G-, R-S-R-*, 23 *I&N Dec.* 270 (BIA, 2002).

[245] In *A-H-*, 23 *I&N Dec.* 774 (A.G. 2005), the Attorney General ruled that the phrase 'danger to the security of the United States' means any non-trivial risk to the nation's defence, foreign relations, or economic interests.

[246] 8 USC § 1227(a)(4)(B), dealing with 'terrorist activities', states that any alien described in 8 USC § 1182(a)(3) is deportable. This in turn provides in part that 'terrorist activity' is 'any activity which is unlawful...which involves...[using an] explosive, firearm, or other weapon or dangerous device (other than for mere personal monetary gain), with intent to endanger, directly or indirectly the safety of one or more individuals or to cause substantial damage to property': 8 USC § 1182(a)(3)(B)(iii)(V)(b). In *McAllister* v. *Attorney General* 2006 U.S. App. Lexis 8701, (3rd Cir., 2006), the Court considered that, while 'certainly broad', the definition was 'neither vague nor overbroad in that it does not infringe on constitutionally protected behavior': 14. Moreover, the qualification 'personal monetary gain' removed common crimes from the category, while further protection of individuals lay in the requirement of specific intent to endanger the safety of individuals or to cause substantial damage to property.   [247] 8 USC § 1101(a)(43)(F); 1182(a)(2)(A)(i)(I), and 1182(a)(2)(B).

[248] 8 USC § 1231(b)(3)(B). In a concurring opinion in *McAllister* v. *Attorney General*, above note, App., Barry J. strongly regretted that the law was drawn too broadly, bearing 'no relation to any common-sense understanding of what "terrorist activity" really is or should be', and that it did not allow consideration to be given to whether the Appellant was now a threat to anyone or to national security: 30.

The problem with the dogmatic rejection of such factors in favour of the mechanistic approach now required by some national legislation, is precisely that it leaves that individual dimension to chance consideration in the country of potential persecution.[249] In our opinion, in a potential article 1F(b) exclusion case in which there *is* credible evidence of likely persecution, the court or reviewing authority should subject the other evidential requirements of article 1F to the most anxious scrutiny: Are there indeed 'serious reasons to consider' that the applicant has committed the crime? Is the seriousness of the offence not so much inherent, as a consequence of the circumstances in which it was committed or is alleged to have been committed, and how do those circumstances bear on the 'guilt' or liability of the applicant? An approach in terms of the individual will better serve the protection objectives of the Convention, ensure the restrictive application of an exception to the Convention, avoid mechanical application of pre-conceptions, do justice, and work no disservice to the potential State of refuge. The failure to incorporate these elements into the determination of excludability under article 1F(b) necessarily means that, as a matter of international obligation, they must nevertheless be examined at a later date, in another hearing. Although there may be scope for harmonizing and prioritizing extradition and refugee status procedures, there is no obvious reason why the latter should not deal both with the question of serious non-political crime, and with that of liability to persecution.

The rebuttable presumption and the process of 'certification' introduced by the legislation described above,[250] not only reverse the burden of proof in the withdrawal of protection, but also contradict the object and purpose of the 1951 Convention in general. Just as the Convention makes refugee status contingent upon the individual satisfying the well-founded fear of persecution test in article 1A(2), so it also requires that the Convention 'shall not apply to any person with respect to whom there are serious reasons for considering' that he or she, *individually*, has committed one or other of the acts mentioned in article 1F. Equally, the Convention makes the application of exceptions to the cardinal principle of *non-refoulement* contingent upon a finding that the *individual refugee* is someone 'whom there are reasonable grounds for regarding as a danger to the security of the country'; or who, 'having been convicted ... of a particularly serious crime, constitutes a danger to the community of that country'.

Whether a refugee is a danger to security or a danger to the community, or has committed a 'serious non-political crime', can only be determined on the basis of

---

[249] The reluctance of courts in some jurisdictions to apply the proportionality test may reflect a measure of deference in national security matters, and recognition also that, in matters of judicial review, there is little opportunity to re-assess findings and matters of fact; however, that does not except first instance decision-makers from examining all the circumstances.

[250] And now extended in the UK by the Immigration, Asylum and Nationality Act 2006, ss. 54, 55; in force 31 Aug. 2006: 'The Immigration, Asylum and Nationality Act 2006 (Commencement No. 2) Order, SI 2006/2226 (C.75), 13 Aug. 2006.

the evidence relating to that individual.[251] In either case, presumptions based on legislative classification or executive certification will tend to disregard the nature and the circumstances of the offence and to distort the process of individual assessment. The simplistic approach—here is a serious non-political crime, there is exclusion—will likely appeal to administrations and others adverse to a rights approach. The failure to consider all the circumstances, however, does an injustice to the words of article 1F(b), none of which is self-applying, to the object and purpose of the 1951 Convention, but also and most seriously, to the individual claimant. Courts which have declined to look at context have either applied the wrong test, or have applied their minds to the wrong question, while legislation which seeks to establish an 'automatic' link between exclusion and a particularly labelled offence undermines the principles of protection implicit even in article 1F(b) and no less apparent in extradition law.

4.3 ACTS CONTRARY TO THE PURPOSES AND PRINCIPLES OF THE UNITED NATIONS

4.3.1 *The drafting history of article 1F(c)*

The principle of exclusion from the Convention by reason of acts contrary to the purposes and principles of the United Nations appears in embryonic form in the IRO Constitution, which excluded those who, since the end of the Second World War, had participated in any organization seeking the overthrow by armed force of a government of a UN member State, or in any terrorist organization; or who were leaders of movements hostile to their government or sponsors of movements encouraging refugees not to return to their country of origin.[252]

The present text of article 1F(c) was adopted on the basis of a draft submitted by the Yugoslav representative,[253] notwithstanding doubts about using the terminology of article 14(2) of the Universal Declaration as a basis for exclusion. The British representative had in fact supposed that 'acts contrary to the purposes and principles of the United Nations' covered 'war crimes, genocide and the subversion or overthrow of democratic régimes', with other possibilities being suggested by various States.[254]

---

[251] Cf. art. 28(2), EU Directive on Temporary Protection, requiring that the grounds for exclusion, 'shall be based solely on the personal conduct of the person concerned. Exclusion decisions or measures shall be based on the principle of proportionality'. Text below, Annexe 2, No. 14.

[252] IRO Constitution, Annex I, Part II. See also Annex I, General Principles, para. 1(d): 'It should be the concern of the Organization to ensure that its assistance is not exploited in order to encourage subversive or hostile activities directed against the Government of any of the United Nations.' IRO, *Manual for Eligibility Officers*, (s.d.), 39. IRGUN, for example, was classified as a terrorist organization: ibid., para. 64. With respect to the second category of excludables, the practice was to concentrate on leaders, not subordinates or followers: ibid., 40.

[253] UN doc. A/CONF.2/SR.29, 20–1, 27.

[254] UN doc. A/CONF.2/SR.24, 5; SR.29, 11–12. In debate in the Social Committee, the French representative also considered that those guilty of genocide were covered: UN doc. E/AC.7/SR.160, 15. He later added that the provision was not aimed at the ordinary individual, 'but at persons

4.3.2 The 'purposes and principles of the United Nations'

The purposes and principles of the United Nations are set out in the Preamble and articles 1 and 2 of the United Nations Charter.[255] The main objectives are to prevent war, to reaffirm faith in fundamental human rights, to establish the conditions under which justice and respect for obligations can be maintained, and to promote social progress and better standards of life in larger freedom. To these ends, the purposes and principles include collective measures to prevent and remove threats to the peace and acts of aggression; the peaceful settlement of disputes; the development of friendly relations between States; respect for the equal rights and self-determination of peoples; international cooperation in economic, social, cultural, and humanitarian matters; and the promotion and encouragement of respect for human rights for all without distinction. Specifically, article 2 addresses both the Organization and its Members, laying down principles which should govern relations between them. These include recognition of the principle of sovereign equality of nations; the fulfilment in good faith of international obligations; the settlement of disputes by peaceful means; the obligation to refrain from the threat or use of force; and the duty of the United Nations not to intervene in the domestic jurisdiction of any State.

The statement of purposes and principles is essentially organizational, establishing what shall be done by States Members working together within the UN; and how they should conduct relations between themselves. But like most constituent documents, the UN Charter also has a dynamic aspect, and in certain areas the practical content of the declared purposes and principles must be determined in the light of more general developments.

For example, the principle of respect for human rights has been developed through the Universal Declaration, the 1966 Covenants, regional treaty arrangements, and customary law. Thus, an individual who has denied or restricted the human rights of others arguably falls within the exception. Those who had persecuted others were indeed expressly excluded from the IRO's mandate, and a similar provision was introduced by the United States Refugee Act[256] and Canada's Immigration and Refugee Protection Act 2001.[257] Also relevant are the individual's

---

occupying government posts, such as heads of State, Ministers and high officials . . .': SR.166, 6. The US representative mentioned collaborators: SR.160, 16; and the representative of the UN Secretariat was of opinion that it referred to those who violated human rights without committing a crime: SR.166, 9.

[255] Text in Brownlie, I., *Basic Documents in International Law*, (5th edn., 2002), 3–4; Simma, B. ed., *The Charter of the United Nations: A Commentary*, (2nd edn., 2002), 39–47, 63–171.

[256] See now 8 USC §1231(a)(3)(B)(i), which provides that the benefit of *non-refoulement* shall not apply if the Attorney-General decides that, 'the alien ordered, incited, assisted, or otherwise participated in the persecution of an individual because of the individual's race, religion, nationality, membership in a particular social group, or political opinion'. Also, 8 CFR §208.13(c)(2)(E), which includes such involvement in persecution as a basis for mandatory denial of asylum.

[257] *Immigration and Refugee Protection Act*, s. 35, provides for inadmissibility on grounds of violating human or international rights in the case of, among others, a permanent resident or foreign

186 Refugees

duties to the community, and the limitations inherent in human rights.[258] Article 17 of the European Convention on Human Rights, for example, provides:

Nothing in this Convention may be interpreted as implying for any State, group or person any right to engage in any activity or perform any act aimed at the destruction of any of the rights and freedoms set forth herein or at their limitation to a greater extent than is provided for in the Convention.

Such a principle is sometimes incorporated or reflected in municipal law.[259]

4.3.2.1 Individuals acting on behalf of the State

Although the purposes and principles focus on the conduct of, and the relations between, States, article 1F(c) clearly contemplates an area of individual responsibility. The question is, whether such responsibility is limited to those who control and implement the policies of States; or whether it also covers the relationship of one individual to another. The UNHCR *Handbook* sees article 1F(c) as overlapping with the preceding exclusion clauses, without introducing 'any specific new element'; it infers that for an individual to fall within this exclusion clause, he or she '*must* have been in a position of power . . . and instrumental' in the State's violation of the principles.[260]

Many commentators share a similar view, and would limit this exclusion clause to heads of State and high officials, while reserving its exceptional application to individuals not necessarily connected with government, such as torturers and others guilty of flagrant violation of human rights.[261] Up until the mid-1990s, the jurisprudence in different countries revealed two broad streams; one focused almost exclusively on State officials and others similarly situated, while the other sought to extend the scope of individual responsibility. In two early cases, the French *Commission des recours* confirmed the denial of refugee status to individuals who, during the Second World War, denounced people to the occupation forces.[262] In a prescient move, the individual dimension was also upheld in a 1972 German decision, where the court held that bomb and terrorist attacks resulting

national who has committed an offence outside Canada referred to in ss. 4–7 of the Canadian *Crimes Against Humanity and War Crimes Act*; or who is a 'prescribed senior official' in a government that, 'in the opinion of the Minister, engages or has engaged in terrorism, systematic or gross human rights violations, or genocide, a war crime or a crime against humanity . . .' Inadmissibility in the second case may be waived if the individual satisfies the Minister that their presence in Canada would not be detrimental to the national interest.

[258] Art. 29 UDHR48; see generally Daes, E.-I., 'Study of the Individual's Duties to the Community and the Limitations of Human Rights and Freedoms under Article 29 of the Universal Declaration of Human Rights': UN doc. E/CN.4/Sub.2/432/Rev.1 (1980).

[259] See, for example, art. 16, *Grundgesetz 1949* (Constitution of the Federal Republic of Germany); also the Irish cases cited above, 120.

[260] Paras. 162–3; also, UNHCR, *Guidelines No. 5*, 'Exclusion', para. 17.

[261] Cf. Grahl-Madsen, *Status of Refugees*, vol. I, 282–3, 286; Kälin, *Prinzip*, 127–9; Köfner & Nicolaus, *Grundlagen*, 330.

[262] See *Milosek*, 304, 7 juill. 1954: Tiberghien, *La protection des réfugiés*, 470; *Kamykowski*, 858, 8 déc. 1955: ibid.

in deaths in various countries were contrary to the purposes and principles of the United Nations.[263] In a 1973 case, the court found that continual terrorist and sabotage activities from Lebanese territory against Israel revealed a basis for exclusion under article 1F(c).[264] Decisions after 1975, however, stressed that articles 1 and 2 of the UN Charter were concerned with international, not individual relations; and that only if inter-State peace or inter-State understanding is affected, will the exclusion clause apply.[265]

If German jurisprudence in this period tended to restrict the potential area of individual responsibility, decisions in France showed a different emphasis. In *Shakeri Noori*, where the negative decision was ultimately based on the absence of a fear of persecution for Convention reasons, the *Commissaire du gouvernement*[266] argued that article 1F(c), 'ne pouvait viser que les agissements commis par les Etats et par les détenteurs du pouvoir au sein de l'Etat'.[267] That approach was exemplified in the *Duvalier* case, in which an application for refugee status by the former dictator of Haiti was rejected. The *Commission des recours* found that respect for human rights and fundamental freedoms was among the purposes and principles of the United Nations. It observed further that article 1F(c):

... se rapporte notamment à l'action contraire aux droits de l'homme et aux libertés fondamentales que la personne en cause a pu exercer dans son pays, ... que (M. Duvalier) a exercé ... les fonctions de président de la République de Haïti; ... que de graves violations des

---

[263] VG Ansbach, 17.10.1972, Nr. 2735-II/72, cited in Köfner & Nicolaus, *Grundlagen*, 330, n. 75. See also Grahl-Madsen, *Status of Refugees*, vol. I, 287–9 (criticizing a 1962 German decision excluding a former official in the Czech censor's office, notwithstanding his change of beliefs and later anti-government activities).

[264] VG Ansbach, 18.4.1973, Nr. 2907-II/72, cited in Köfner & Nicolaus, *Grundlagen*, 330f, n. 75. The applicant had been involved in transporting arms for the PFLP. In the view of the court, this had supported his organization in the escalation of the conflict with Israel. It found further that this organization was involved in terror and sabotage from Lebanon into Israel, and that this was contrary to the purposes and principles of the United Nations, specifically, peaceful co-existence and peaceful settlement of disputes. See also VG Ansbach, 31.10.1972, Nr. 7357-IV/71: ibid.; the applicant had been involved in the private wars of exile groups, and in various incidents, including fighting and threats. In the view of the court, his conviction for possession of weapons excluded him under art. 1F(c).

[265] BverwG, 1.7.1975, I C 44.68. The applicant illegally purchased two loaded pistols for two fellow nationals; he ought to have known that they might have been used for political killings in Croatia. He was convicted and fined, and his application for asylum was initially refused on the ground that his offence had been contrary to the purposes and principles of the United Nations, in that it was likely to disturb German/Yugoslav relations. The Federal Administrative Court ruled, however, that art. 1F(c) did not apply. Art. 1 of the UN Charter was concerned with inter-State, that is, international relations; and art. 2 was directed to the UN Organization and its Members; neither of these areas was affected by the applicant's offence.

[266] The *Commissaire du gouvernement* is an official of the court, not a representative of the government as such, who reviews the dossier of each case, explores matters which the *rapporteur* may have overlooked, and then prepares a report or 'conclusions'. The purpose of the conclusions is to sum up the case as clearly as possible and 'to relate the proposed solution to the general pattern of the case-law and, if possible, to foreshadow its future development'. Brown, L. N. & Bell, J., *French Administrative Law*, (5th edn., 1998), 104–6.

[267] Cons. d'Etat, 12 Oct. 1994, 47.706, cited in Tiberghien, *La protection des réfugiés*, 106, 256.

droits de l'homme ont été commises dans ce pays pendant ce période;... que (M. Duvalier) était, en sa qualité de président... le chef des forces armées, de la police, et des volontaires de la sécurité nationale qui se sont livrés à de graves violations des droits de l'homme; *qu'alors même qu'il ne résulte pas de l'instruction que le requérant ait personnellement commis de tels agissements, il les a nécessairement couverts de son autorité*... [268] (emphasis supplied).

Later decisions, however, have looked for evidence of personal involvement in activities contrary to the purposes and principles of the United Nations.[269] The formal exclusion of those who have persecuted others is justified, both historically and in the light of recent practice. In *Pushpanathan*, for example, the Supreme Court of Canada noted, while holding that conspiring to traffic in a narcotic does not fall within article 1F(c):

The rationale of Art. 1F of the Convention is that those who are responsible for the persecution which creates refugees should not enjoy the benefits of a Convention designed to protect those refugees. In the light of the general purposes of the Convention and the indications in the *travaux préparatoires* as to the relative ambit of Arts. 1F(a) and 1F(c), *the purpose of Art. 1F(c) is to exclude those individuals responsible for serious, sustained or systemic violations of fundamental human rights which amount to persecution* in a non-war setting... Article 1F(c) will thus be applicable where there is *consensus in international law that particular acts constitute sufficiently serious and sustained violations of fundamental human rights* as to amount to persecution, or are explicitly recognized as contrary to the UN purposes and principles.[270]

This finding rightly emphasizes the importance, in international law, of agreement among States on what acts are sufficiently serious and sustained violations of human rights as to fall within the terms of article 1F(c).

In a 1982 Australian case, the Determination of Refugee Status Committee examined an application by an Iranian who had been present for some of the time at the occupation of the United States Embassy in Tehran, when diplomatic and consular staff were held hostage. In 1980, the International Court of Justice characterized the detention of the hostages as 'manifestly incompatible' with the

---

[268] *Duvalier*, 50.265, 19 juill. 1986: Tiberghien, *La protection des réfugiés*, 262–3. The Conseil d'Etat agreed: *Duvalier*, 10/3 SSR, 31 juillet 1992, 81.963; see also Conseil d'Etat, *Mme. Duvalier*, 10/ 3 SSR, 31 juillet 1992, 81.962—it was not error of law for CRR to find that the claimant's fear of persecution was the consequence of the serious human rights violations committed by security forces under the responsibility of her husband, and not to any political opinion of her own or to any other Convention reason.

[269] See Conseil d'Etat, 25 mars 1998, 170.172, *M.M.*, finding error of law where the Commission des recours excluded a former official, 'du seul fait de l'adhésion à un régime politique qu'aurait impliqué l'exercice de certaines fonctions publiques... sans rechercher si l'intéressé s'était personnellement rendu coupable d'agissements contraires aux but et principes...' Cf. *Aghel*, Nos. 14.793–14.795, 14.909, 22 juin 1982—the head of recruitment for the political police was excluded, on the ground that he must have known of the organization's various activities; also *Mohavedi*, No. 13.690, 4 fév. 1982; *Engabe*, No. 25.229, 31 août 1984; decisions of the *Commission des recours*, cited in Tiberghien, *La protection des réfugiés*, 470.

[270] *Pushpanathan* v. *Canada* [1998] 1 SCR 982 (L'Heureux-Dubé, Gonthier, McLachlin, and Bastarache J.J.; emphasis supplied).

purposes and principles of the United Nations.[271] Relying upon this, some members of the Committee argued that the mere fact of presence or involvement was sufficient to bring the applicant within article 1F(c). Others took the view that the Court's judgment was principally concerned with issues of State responsibility; its views on the initially independent actions of individuals[272] should not be taken as excluding an applicant for all time and all purposes from the benefits of refugee status. The nature and extent of the individual's role in the occupation should be examined, as well as his motives and intentions and current situation vis-à-vis his country of origin. A majority of the Committee recommended that the applicant be excluded by reason of the degree of his involvement in the hostages incident.[273]

From the jurisprudence developed to the mid-1990s, it could be inferred that article 1F(c) may exclude high officials of State responsible for the implementation of policies that violate human rights or are otherwise contrary to the purposes and principles of the United Nations. In appropriate circumstances, however, it might also apply to individuals at some remove from political responsibility, who were party to human rights violations, either individually, or as members of organizations engaged in such activities. The application of article 1F(c) to individuals acting on behalf of unrecognized entities, belligerent or 'terrorist' groups must now be read subject to international action in regard to terrorism, considered below. The IRO's exclusion clauses were for the most part aimed specifically at individuals and members of non-State entities, such as terrorist organizations and other organizations seeking the overthrow of the government of a Member State; in principle, there is no reason why such actions should not fall within article 1F(c), although the question may be somewhat academic, so far as an individual whose actions outside the organization of a State give rise to the issue of exclusion will likely fall within article 1F(a) or (b).

4.3.3 Article 1F(c) in brief

The legislative history of article 1F(c), considered together with the judicial and administrative decisions and the practice of States and the United Nations, establishes that the following general categories, in particular, may be excluded from the benefits of the 1951 Convention: (1) policy-makers and those holding positions of political responsibility, in situations where, for example, violations of human rights or other activities contrary to the purposes and principles of the United Nations have occurred, and where they may be considered to have covered such activities with their authority; (2) the agents of implementation of such

---

[271] *United States Diplomatic and Consular Staff in Tehran* (USA v. Iran), ICJ *Rep.*, (1980), 3 at 42 (para. 91). [272] Ibid., 35 (para. 74); 29–30 (paras. 58–9).
[273] *M.R.* The account of this case is drawn from Goodwin-Gill's participation as UNHCR observer in the proceedings. In the event, the Minister for Immigration, who is finally responsible for decisions on refugee status, chose to disregard the DORS Committee recommendation, and accepted the applicant as a refugee. The principles relating to assessment of the degree of involvement, however, are considered to be generally valid.

policies, including, for example, officials in government departments or agencies who knew or ought to have known what was going on; and the members of government and other organizations engaged in activities, such as persecution, contrary to the purposes and principles of the United Nations; (3) individuals, whether members of organizations or not, who, for example, have personally participated in the persecution or denial of the human rights of others;[274] and (4) those individuals, whether connected with the organization of a State or not, who are considered to have committed 'terrorist' or 'terrorist-related' acts.

Article 1F(c) of the Convention is potentially very wide. Besides the examples mentioned above, the United Nations has also taken action to combat the narcotics traffic, to promote democratic and representative forms of government, and to recognize the international standing of certain liberation movements. This may imply that those involved in the drugs trade,[275] who displace or obstruct the democratic process, or who are responsible for maintaining colonial and colonial-style regimes should not subsequently be entitled to recognition of refugee status. Once rarely mentioned, the exception is now frequently cited in the context of anti-terrorism measures, although its application in individual cases continues to be infrequent; apart from the terrorism context, its interpretation and development are likely to vary, however, given the disparate interests of the sovereign States members of the United Nations.

4.4 THE 2004 EUROPEAN UNION QUALIFICATION DIRECTIVE

The 'new' inclination towards exclusion is also illustrated by the approach adopted in the EU Qualification Directive, which mixes loyalty to the terms of the Convention with potentially problematic legal innovations. Article 12(1) incorporates articles 1D[276] and 1E of the Convention, while article 12(2) brings in article 1F. In relation to article 1F(b), the Directive defines 'prior to . . . admission as a refugee' to mean before the issue of a residence permit, 'based on the granting of refugee status'; and it adds, consistently with the doctrine described above, that 'particularly cruel actions, even if committed with an allegedly political objective, may be classified as serious non-political crimes'.

The exclusion theme is further developed in article 14, on the revocation, ending or refusal to renew refugee status. Some aspects, such as article 14(1) and (2) on cessation and review, are non-controversial, if poorly drafted, while other provisions tread close to the line laid down by the Convention. Article 14(3), for

[274] In principle, exclusion under art. 1F(c) may as well apply to State officials, as to others.
[275] But see *Pushpanathan*, above n. 270, per Bastarache J. at para. 74: 'Until the international community makes clear its view that drug trafficking, in one form or another, is a serious violation of fundamental human rights amounting to persecution, then there can be no rationale for counting it among the grounds of exclusion. The connection between persecution and the international refugee problem is what justifies the definitional exclusions in Article 1F(a) and F(c).'
[276] The Directive thus misses the opportunity of clarifying art. 1D CSR51, and of ensuring the fuller and better protection of Palestinian refugees which is still need; see above, s. 3.2.

example, requires ('Member States shall') the termination of refugee status if the individual in question 'should have been or is excluded'; or if misrepresentation or omission of facts were decisive for a positive determination. Paragraphs 4 and 5, however, have a less solid basis in the Convention scheme of protection. In broad terms, these provisions seek to transform the article 33(2) CSR51 exceptions to *non-refoulement* into grounds for termination or denial of refugee status.[277] By comparison with the first three paragraphs of article 14, however, the language chosen for paragraph 4 is equivocal: Member States 'may', but not 'shall', act; and it is not 'refugee status' that is ended, but 'the status granted to a refugee'. The resulting situation in law is further complicated by paragraph 6, which provides that those affected by paragraphs 4 and 5 are nevertheless entitled to the benefit of Convention articles 3, 4, 16, 22, 31, and 33 (non-discrimination, freedom of religion, access to the courts, public education, non-penalization for illegal entry, limited grounds of expulsion, and *non-refoulement*); it is tempting to surmise that nothing happens.

4.5 TERRORISM, REFUGEES, AND THE PURPOSES AND PRINCIPLES OF THE UNITED NATIONS

There is nothing new about terrorism and the dangers it poses to human rights. When States adopted the Universal Declaration of Human Rights in 1948, they agreed that nothing in it 'may be interpreted as implying for any State, group or person any right to engage in any activity or to perform any act aimed at the destruction of any of the rights and freedoms set forth herein'.[278] Following the lead of the Universal Declaration, the European Convention prohibits abuse of rights ('any activity or . . . act aimed at the destruction of any of the rights and freedoms . . . or at their limitation to a greater extent than is provided for': article 17 ECHR50; also article 18), in an approach adopted also in article 5 of the 1966 International Covenant on Civil and Political Rights.[279] In June 2003, however, UN special rapporteurs and independent experts meeting in Geneva expressed their 'alarm' at the growing threats against human rights, and their concern at the indiscriminate use of the term 'terrorism',[280] and 'at the multiplication of policies,

---

[277] See also art. 21(3).   [278] Art. 30 UDHR48; see also art. 29.

[279] See also Vienna Declaration and Programme of Action, adopted by the World Conference on Human Rights on 25 June 1993, UN doc. A/CONF.157/23, 12 Jul. 1993, section I, para. 17, which states that acts, methods and practices of terrorism in all its forms and manifestations are activities aimed at the destruction of human rights, fundamental freedoms and democracy, threatening territorial integrity, security of States and destabilizing legitimately constituted Governments; text in Brownlie & Goodwin-Gill, *Basic Documents on Human Rights*, 138.

[280] The Policy Working Group on the United Nations and Terrorism has also noted (2002): 'The rubric of counter-terrorism can be used to justify acts in support of political agendas, such as the consolidation of political power, elimination of political opponents, inhibition of legitimate dissent and/or suppression of resistance to military occupation. Labelling opponents or adversaries as terrorists offers a time-tested technique to de-legitimize and demonize them. The United Nations should beware of offering, or be perceived to be offering, a blanket or automatic endorsement of all measures

legislation and practices being adopted by many countries in the name of the fight against terrorism which affect negatively the enjoyment of virtually all human rights—civil, cultural, economic, political and social'.[281]

In 1994, the General Assembly had adopted the Declaration on Measures to Eliminate International Terrorism, in which it described terrorism as including 'criminal acts intended or calculated to provoke a state of terror in the general public'.[282] This clearly left many questions unanswered, and the United Nations has since maintained its focus on the issue and on what States can and should do to combat the threat. An agreed general definition of the phenomenon is still lacking,[283] however, for reasons which are usefully summarized in the 2001 report, 'Terrorism and human rights', by the Special Rapporteur of the Sub-Commission on the Promotion and Protection of Human Rights on Terrorism:

> ... the international community has addressed terrorism only in a piecemeal fashion (i.e. crime by crime/issue by issue) rather than comprehensively. The controversial issue of terrorism has thus been approached from such different perspectives and in such different contexts that it has been impossible for the international community to arrive at a generally acceptable definition to this very day ... Indeed, it may be that the definitional problem is the major factor in the controversy regarding terrorism. This is all the more true when considering the high political stakes attendant upon the task of definition. For the term terrorism is emotive and highly loaded politically. It is habitually accompanied by an implicit negative judgement and is used selectively ... [284]

Notwithstanding, or because of, the difficulty in reaching international agreement on a general definition, many States adopted their own laws and definitions, at the same time as they developed or consolidated, through regular law-making processes, a network of treaty regimes and obligations to deal with particular incidents or aspects of 'terrorism', such as hijacking, hostage-taking, bombing, financing,

taken in the name of counter-terrorism.' Report of the Policy Working Group on the United Nations and Terrorism: UN doc. A/57/273, S/2002/875, para. 14; for membership of the Working Group, see para. 3.

[281] UN doc. E/CN.4/2004/4, Annex 1 (June 2003).

[282] UNGA res. 49/60, 'Measures to eliminate international terrorism', 9 Dec. 1994, Section I, para. 3; see also UNGA res. 51/210, 'Measures to eliminate international terrorism', 17 Dec. 1996, Annex: 'Declaration to Supplement the 1994 Declaration on Measures to Eliminate International Terrorism'.

[283] See generally, Saul, B., *Defining Terrorism in International Law*, (2006); *Gurung v. Secretary of State for the Home Department* [2002] UKIAT 04870, para. 100.

[284] Sub-Commission on the Promotion and Protection of Human Rights, 'Terrorism and human rights', Progress report prepared by Ms Kalliopi K. Koufa, Special Rapporteur: UN doc. E/CN.4/ Sub.2/2001/31, paras. 24, 25. See also debate in the UN General Assembly Sixth Committee in 1996; several States stressed the need to arrive at an agreed definition of terrorism which distinguished it from the 'legitimate defence' of rights. Among others, Liechtenstein emphasized the importance of striking 'a balance between the effectiveness of measures to combat terrorism and the protection of human rights and freedoms': UN Press Release GA/L/3008, 4 Oct. 1996. The difficulty in drawing the line between political protest and terrorism is implicit in the third paragraph of the preamble to UDHR48: 'It is essential, if man is not to be compelled to have recourse, as a last resort, to rebellion against tyranny and oppression, that human rights should be protected by the rule of law.'

offences against diplomats, and 'nuclear terrorism'.[285] The regular law-making processes remain essential elements in the more precise identification of acts amounting to terrorism, and in the eventual development of a comprehensive legal framework, and while resolutions and declarations adopted by the General Assembly or the Security Council are relevant to understanding the sense of members regarding matters of international concern, there are clear Charter limitations on the extent to which either body can 'legislate' for States or determine the bounds of existing treaty relations.[286]

There being no definition of terrorism, the General Assembly 'encourages' States towards a comprehensive legal framework, and 'urges' them 'to consider... becoming parties to... international conventions and protocols...'[287] The General Assembly also emphasizes the need for States to ensure that, in combatting terrorism, they comply fully with their international obligations generally and in relation to human rights, including the 1951 Convention and the principle of *non-refoulement*.[288]

The Security Council, which has primary responsibility for the maintenance of international peace and security,[289] is obliged itself to act in accordance with the purposes and principles of the Organization. Member States agree 'to accept and carry out the decisions of the Security Council in accordance with the... Charter',[290] but not everything in a Security Council resolution is a decision having binding effect. Moreover, given the Charter's constraints on the Security Council itself, there are obviously certain, if undefined, limitations on how far it can lawfully interfere with States' international obligations generally.[291] In

---

[285] The Report of the Policy Working Group mentioned above lists some nineteen global or regional treaties relating to the subject: UN doc. A/57/273, S/2002/875, Appendix. See also UNGA res. 59/290, 'International Convention for the Suppression of Nuclear Terrorism', 13 Apr. 2005.

[286] For example, the General Assembly has a broad competence to discuss matters falling under the Charter, but a power only to make recommendations to Member States: art. 10, United Nations Charter. Declarations attached to resolutions, such as UDHR48, or the Declaration on Measures to Combat International Terrorism 1994, have no more authority than the resolution itself, unless or until they are transformed by treaty, or are recognized in the practice of States as authoritative statements of customary international law.

[287] UNGA res. 49/60, 9 Dec. 1994, 'Declaration on Measures to Eliminate International Terrorism', paras. 7, 8.

[288] UNGA res. 51/210, 17 Dec. 1996, 'Declaration to Supplement the 1994 Declaration on Measures to Eliminate International Terrorism', Preamble.

[289] Art. 24, United Nations Charter: '1. In order to ensure prompt and effective action by the United Nations, its Members confer on the Security Council primary responsibility for the maintenance of international peace and security, and agree that in carrying out its duties under this responsibility the Security Council acts on their behalf. 2. In discharging these duties the Security Council shall act in accordance with the Purposes and Principles of the United Nations...'

[290] Art. 25, United Nations Charter: 'The Members of the United Nations agree to accept and carry out the decisions of the Security Council in accordance with the present Charter.'

[291] To take an extreme example, the Security Council could not lawfully authorize genocide; see Judge Sir Elihu Lauterpacht, Dissenting Opinion, *Case concerning the Application of the Convention on the Prevention and Punishment of Genocide (Bosnia & Herzegovina v Yugoslavia (Serbia and Montenegro))*, *(Further Request for the Indication of Provisional Measures)* (1993) ICJ *Reports* 325, 440, §100.

practice, however, the Security Council's approach reflects recognition that it is not a legislative body as such, and it is careful to locate its actions within the existing legal environment. Thus, while the Security Council may decide and indeed has decided that 'terrorism, like aggression, is contrary to the purposes and principles of the United Nations', it has not chosen to determine, at the 'legislative' level, the generally constituent elements of the act; nor has it at any time proclaimed that 'terrorism', as such and apart from the conventions making specific provision in particular respects, is an international crime.

Over the last fifteen years or so, in exercising its responsibilities under article 24 and Chapter VII, the Security Council's determinations of threats to international peace and security have taken account of factors beyond conflict between States in its simplest sense. They have included the overthrow of a democratically elected president in Haiti, the humanitarian crisis in Somalia, Libya's refusal to surrender suspects in the Lockerbie bombing, violations of the laws of war in Rwanda, and refugee flows and population displacements in Kosovo and elsewhere. It has also increasingly factored terrorism into its assessments. In 1996, for example, it noted that the continuation of conflict in Afghanistan provided 'fertile ground for terrorism and drug trafficking which destabilize the region and beyond...'[292] Following the bombings in Nairobi and Dar-es-Salaam, it stressed the duty of every Member State 'to refrain from organizing, instigating, assisting or participating in terrorist acts in another State or acquiescing in organized activities within its territory directed towards the commission of such acts'.[293]

In October 1999, the Security Council adopted a general resolution on international terrorism, which appeared to identify refugees and asylum seekers as potential participants in terrorism.[294] A comprehensive agenda for 'all States' followed the events of 11 September 2001 with the unanimous adoption by the Security Council, acting under Chapter VII, of resolution 1373.[295] To a significant extent, the language of this particular resolution is not exhortatory, but mandatory: the Security Council decides that 'all States *shall* . . .', and the ends to be achieved will require an extensive legislative programme (see paragraphs 1 and 2, in particular). In other matters, some margin of appreciation is allowed, and following resolution 1269, the Security Council 'calls' upon all States to take 'appropriate measures' to ensure that asylum seekers have not 'planned, facilitated or participated in the commission of terrorist acts', and to 'ensure . . . that refugee status is not abused by the perpetrators, organizers or facilitators of terrorist acts,

---

[292] SC res. 1076, 22 Oct. 1996, para. 5.
[293] SC res. 1189, 13 Aug. 1998, preamble; SC res. 1193, 28 Aug. 1998; SC res. 1214, 8 Dec. 1998.
[294] SC res. 1269, 19 Oct. 1999.
[295] SC res. 1373, 28 Sept. 2001; see also SC res. 1368, 12 Sept. 2001, SC res. 1390, 16 Jan. 2002.

and that claims of political motivation are not recognized as grounds for refusing requests for the extradition of alleged terrorists'.[296] It also declares that:

Acts, methods and practices of terrorism are contrary to the purposes and principles of the United Nations and that knowingly financing, planning and inciting terrorist acts are also contrary to the purposes and principles of the United Nations.[297]

These and other resolutions disclose both an agenda which includes the promotion of an international legal and cooperative regime to combat terrorism, linked in turn to various recent treaties, such as those on terrorist bombing and terrorist financing.[298] Given the premise that terrorism constitutes a threat to international peace and security, the measures required of States may appear unexceptional (though nonetheless innovative and far-reaching in light of earlier Security Council practice). Potential problems emerge, however, when this political organ assumes executive and legislative functions simultaneously, especially when its resolutions affect the legal rights of States,[299] or are 'incompatible with general international law or the normal application of multilateral standard-setting treaties'.[300] The impact of these resolutions on the international protection of refugees is a case in point.

International standards are well-established in this area under the regime of the 1951 Convention/1967 Protocol and, as shown above, specific rules already govern the definition of a refugee and the circumstances in which an individual may be denied refugee status or the benefits of protection. Arguably, they were already adequate to the purpose of combatting terrorism and ensuring the exclusion from protection as refugees of those who had engaged in 'terrorist acts'. Both the measures which States are now required to take and the Security Council's executive pronouncement on the meaning of terms (specifically, what is contrary to the purposes and principles of the United Nations) will potentially have an impact not only on the substantive content of international protection, but also on the procedural entitlements hitherto recognized as essential to a fair regime and the effective implementation of international obligations.

---

[296] SC res. 1373, para. 3(f),(g). See also the 2002 Inter-American Convention against Terrorism; 2005 European Convention for the Prevention of Terrorism: *CETS* No. 196; 2001 EU Common Position on Combating Terrorism, arts. 16, 17, below, Annexe 2, No. 15; 2004 EU Qualification Directive, Recital, paras. 22, 38, art. 12(2)(b), 14(4), below, Annexe 2, No. 19; EU Commission, 'The Relationship between Safeguarding Internal Security and Complying with International Protection Obligations and Instruments', COM(2001) 743 final, 5 Dec. 2001; *Human Rights and the fight against terrorism—The Guidelines of the Council of Europe*, 2002, 2005.

[297] SC res. 1373, para. 5; see also SC res. 1377, 12 Nov. 2001—Declaration on the global effort to combat terrorism.

[298] For information on developments in the UN, see <http://www.un.org/terrorism/>.

[299] Bowett, D., 'The Impact of Security Council Decisions on Dispute Settlement Procedures', 5 *EJIL* 89, 93 (1994).   [300] Brownlie, I., *The Rule of Law in International Affairs*, (1999), 219.

In 2001, for example, the United Kingdom enacted the Anti-Terrorism, Crime and Security Act. Following up on the Terrorism Act 2000 and avowedly on the above Security Council resolutions, its various provisions include a power in favour of the Secretary of State to 'certify' a suspected international terrorist.[301] Section 33 allows the Secretary of State, in an asylum appeal, to certify that the 1951 Convention does not apply, that is, that the appellant is not entitled to the protection of *non-refoulement* because article 1F or article 33(2) apply, and that the removal of the appellant from the United Kingdom would be conducive to the public good.[302] Moreover, as noted above, section 34 requires that in any appeal, no account be taken of the gravity of the events or fear which may be relevant to an individual's claim to refugee status, or of any threat to his or her life or freedom; rights of appeal and review are also restricted.

The significant number of treaties covering different aspects of terrorism, and the absence to date of any agreed general definition, allow for a number of inferences in relation to the legal situation of refugees and asylum seekers. Among them, it is arguable that only if a particular act falls within the category of acts covered by one or other of the nineteen global and regional treaties mentioned above,[303] can it or should it be characterized as 'terrorist', as a matter of international law. In the absence of express treaty coverage, customary international law may also allow an act to be characterized as 'terrorist', where it reaches a certain level of seriousness (death or injury to persons), *and* is intended to provoke a state of terror for political purposes. As the Canadian Supreme Court found in *Pushpanathan*, above, the existence of international consensus (in the sense of customary international law), must still be shown.[304]

It is one thing to state as a matter of policy that terrorism is contrary to the purposes and principles of the United Nations, but quite another to translate that policy into a rule of law. Justifiable concerns remain in many quarters about where to draw the line between political acts and protest, on the one hand, and 'terror', on the other. Too often, political acts themselves may be 'criminalized', and

---

[301] This power may be exercised, 'if the Secretary of State reasonably ... (a) believes that the person's presence in the UK is a risk to national security, and (b) suspects that the person is a terrorist': s. 21(1). A terrorist in turn is defined as a person who is or has been concerned in the commission, preparation or instigation of acts of international terrorism, is a member of or belongs to an international terrorist group, or has links with an international terrorist group, but only if he or she supports or assists it: ss. 21(2), 21(4). 'Terrorism' is defined in the Terrorism Act 2000, s. 1, as amended by the Terrorism Act 2006, s. 34. The 2000 Act provides for the proscription of terrorist organizations and creates offences relating to membership, support, uniforms and fund raising: ss. 3, 11, 12, 13, 15. An international terrorist group is one that is subject to the control or influence of persons outside the UK, and the Secretary of State suspects that it is concerned in terrorist acts: s. 21(3).

[302] S. 33, now replaced by s. 55, Immigration, Asylum and Nationality Act 2006; cf. Bruin, R. & Wouters, K., 'Terrorism and the Non-Derogability of *Non-refoulement*'. 15 *IJRL* 5 (2003).

[303] Or is a matter of customary international law.

[304] See above, n. 270 and accompanying text.

'counter-terrorism' can be and often is used to consolidate political power, eliminate political opponents, and inhibit dissent.

In resolution 1624, adopted on 14 September 2005, the Security Council again placed particularly strong emphasis on the conformity of anti-terrorist measures with States' obligations generally under international law and particularly under international human rights law, refugee law, and humanitarian law.[305] While 'terrorism' may indeed be contrary to the purposes and principles of the United Nations and therefore a basis for exclusion under article 1F(c), conformity with international obligations requires that decisions to exclude or subsequently to annul a decision on refugee status be taken in accordance with appropriate procedural guarantees. Article 1F(c) ought only to be applied, therefore, where there are serious reasons to consider that the individual concerned has committed an offence specifically identified by the international community as one which must be addressed in the fight against terrorism, and only by way of a procedure conforming to due process and the State's obligations generally in international law.

---

[305] SC res. 1624, 14 Sept. 2005. The Security Council also recalled art. 14 UDHR48 and the right to seek asylum, as well as States' *non-refoulement* obligations: Preamble and para. 4. The requirement of 'consistency' or 'compatibility' is well established, and is as applicable in times of emergency as in normal times. Art. 15 ECHR50 provides a clear statement of the principle: 'In time of war or other public emergency threatening the life of the nation any High Contracting Party may take measures derogating from its obligations under this Convention to the extent strictly required by the exigencies of the situation, *provided that such measures are not inconsistent with its other obligations under international law* (emphasis supplied). The UK's recent legislation appears to have gone beyond what was required, and to have been framed in disregard of the important qualifications recognized by the Security Council.

PART 2

ASYLUM

5

Non-Refoulement in the 1951
Refugee Convention

The principle of *non-refoulement* prescribes, broadly, that no refugee should be returned to any country where he or she is likely to face persecution, other ill-treatment, or torture. In this chapter, the scope of the principle is examined against the background of a number of recurring issues: the question of 'risk'; the personal scope of the principle, including its application to certain categories of asylum seekers, such as stowaways or those arriving directly by boat; exceptions to the principle; extraterritorial application; extradition; and the 'contingent' application of the principle in situations of mass influx.

1. Evolution of the principle

The term *non-refoulement* derives from the French *refouler*, which means to drive back or to repel, as of an enemy who fails to breach one's defences. In the context of immigration control in continental Europe, *refoulement* is a term of art covering, in particular, summary reconduction to the frontier of those discovered to have entered illegally and summary refusal of admission of those without valid papers.[1] *Refoulement* is thus to be distinguished from expulsion or deportation, the more formal process whereby a lawfully resident alien may be required to leave a State, or be forcibly removed.

The idea that a State ought not to return persons to other States in certain circumstances is of comparatively recent origin. Common in the past were formal

---

[1] Historically, many bilateral agreements have institutionalized the practice; see the 'conventions de prise en charge à la frontière' discussed in Batiffol and Lagarde, *Droit international privé* (5th edn., 1970) i.198; and the 'Übernahme-' or 'Schubabkommen' discussed in Schiedermair, *Handbuch des Ausländerrechts der Bundesrepublik Deutschland*, (1968), 178, 227–30. For their more modern counterparts, see UNHCR, 'Overview of Re-Admission Agreements in Central Europe', (Sept. 1993); Inter-Governmental Consultations, 'Working Paper on Readmission Agreements', (Aug. 1994); van Selm, J., 'Access to Procedures: "Safe Third Countries", "Safe Countries of Origin" and "Time Limits"' (Global Consultations Background Paper, 2001), section 1.A.7; Legomsky, S. H., 'Secondary Refugee Movements and the Return of Asylum Seekers to Third Countries: The Meaning of Effective Protection', 15 *IJRL* 567 (2003).

agreements between sovereigns for the reciprocal surrender of subversives, dissidents, and traitors.[2] Only in the early- to mid-nineteenth century do the concept of asylum and the principle of non-extradition of political offenders begin to concretize, in the sense of that protection which the territorial sovereign can, and perhaps should, accord. At that time, the principle of non-extradition reflected popular sentiment that those fleeing their own, generally despotic governments, were worthy of protection.[3] It was a period of political turmoil in Europe and South America, as well as of mass movements of populations occasioned by pogroms against Jewish and Christian minorities in Russia and the Ottoman Empire.

A sense of the need to protect the persecuted can be gathered from the UK's 1905 Aliens Act, where section 1 made an exception to refusal of entry for want of means in respect of those 'seeking to avoid prosecution or punishment on religious or political grounds or for an offence of a political character, or persecution involving danger of imprisonment or danger to life or limb on account of religious belief'. Not until after the First World War, however, did international practice begin to accept the notion of non-return, and only in 1933 does the first reference to the principle that refugees should not be returned to their country of origin occur in an international instrument.[4] In article 3 of the 1933 Convention relating to the International Status of Refugees, the contracting parties undertook not to remove resident refugees or keep them from their territory, 'by application of police measures, such as expulsions or non-admittance at the frontier (*refoulement*)', unless dictated by national security or public order.[5] Each State undertook, 'in any case not to refuse entry to refugees at the frontiers of their countries of origin'. Only eight States ratified this Convention, however; three of them, by reservations and declarations, emphasized their retention of sovereign competence in the matter of expulsion, while the United Kingdom expressly objected to the principle of non-rejection at the frontier.

Agreements regarding refugees from Germany in 1936 and 1938 also contained some limitation on expulsion or return.[6] They varied slightly: broadly,

---

[2] Goodwin-Gill, G. S., *International Law and the Movement of Persons between States*, (1978), 143, n. 2.

[3] See, for example, 6 *BDIL*, 53–4, 64–5.

[4] Under a 1928 arrangement (89 *LNTS* No. 2005), States had adopted a recommendation (no. 7), 'that measures for expelling foreigners or for taking such other action against them be avoided or suspended in regard to Russian and Armenian refugees in cases where the person concerned is not in a position to enter a neighbouring country in a regular manner'. The recommendation was not to apply to a refugee who had entered a State in intentional violation of national law.

[5] 159 *LNTS* No. 3663; official text in French.

[6] Art. 4, Provisional Arrangement concerning the Status of Refugees coming from Germany, 1936: 171 *LNTS* No. 3952; official text in English and French. The arrangement was signed by seven States; the United Kingdom excluded refugees subject to extradition proceedings from the ambit of art. 4, and likewise, for most purposes, refugees admitted for a temporary visit or purpose. See also art. 5, Convention concerning the Status of Refugees coming from Germany, 1938: 192 *LNTS* No. 4461; official texts in English and French. The Convention was ratified by only three States; the United Kingdom repeated its 1936 reservations.

refugees required to leave a contracting State were to be allowed a suitable period to make arrangements; lawfully resident refugees were not to be expelled or sent back across the frontier[7] save 'for reasons of national security or public order'; and even in such cases, governments undertook not to return refugees to the German Reich,[8] 'unless they have been warned and have refused to make the necessary arrangements to proceed to another country or to take advantage of the arrangements made for them with that object'.

Action in the inter-war period focused principally on improving administrative arrangements to facilitate resettlement and relieve the burden on countries of first asylum. The need for protective principles for refugees began to emerge, but limited ratifications of instruments containing equivocal and much qualified provisions effectively prevented the consolidation of a formal principle of *non-refoulement*. Nevertheless, the period was also remarkable for the very large numbers of refugees not in fact sent back to their countries of origin, whether they fled Russia after the revolution, Spain, Germany, or the Ottoman Empire.[9]

Following the Second World War, a new era began. In February 1946, the United Nations expressly accepted that 'refugees or displaced persons' who had expressed 'valid objections' to returning to their country of origin should not be compelled to do so.[10] The International Refugee Organization was established the same year, charged with resolving the problems of displacement left over from the war; some 1,620,000 refugees were assisted with resettlement and integration, while many others fleeing political developments in Eastern Europe were readily admitted to western countries.[11]

In 1949, the United Nations Economic and Social Council (ECOSOC) appointed an *Ad hoc* Committee to 'consider the desirability of preparing a revised and consolidated convention relating to the international status of refugees and stateless persons and, if they consider such a course desirable, draft the text of such a convention'.[12] The *Ad hoc* Committee on Statelessness and Related Problems

[7] The 1938 Convention substituted 'measures of expulsion or reconduction . . .'

[8] The 1936 arrangement read: 'refugees shall not be sent back across the frontier of the Reich'; the 1938 Convention provided that States parties 'undertake' not to reconduct refugees to German territory.

[9] Kiss notes, for example, that in 1939 France admitted 400,000 refugees from Spain in just ten days: *Répertoire de la pratique française en droit international public*, (1966), vol. 4, 433–5.

[10] UNGA res. 8(1), 12 Feb 1946, para. (c)(ii).

[11] On IRO and post Second World War practice, see Marrus, M. R., *The Unwanted: European Refugees from the First World War through the Cold War* (2nd edn., 2002); Rystad, G., ed., *The Uprooted: Forced Migration as an International Problem in the Post-War Era*, (1990); Skran, C., *Refugees in Inter-War Europe: The Emergence of a Regime*, (1995). State practice of the immediate post-war period, however, is somewhat inconclusive. Writing in 1954, Weis found that *refoulement* was rare, save 'in the case of some Russians and Ukrainians covered by certain wartime agreements': Weis, P., 'The International Protection of Refugees', 48 *AJIL* 193, 196 (1954). The later release of relevant documents to public scrutiny showed the full extent of a forcible repatriation policy which meant death or horrific treatment for well over two million, by no means all of them covered by those wartime agreements: see Tolstoy, N., *Victims of Yalta* (1977, rev. edn. 1979); Bethell, N., *The Last Secret* (1974); also, Corsellis, J. & Ferrar, M., *Slovenia 1945: Memories of Death and Survival*, (2005).

[12] ECOSOC res. 248(IX)B, 8 Aug. 1949.

met twice in New York in January–February and August 1950,[13] and drew up the following provision, considered so fundamental that no exceptions were proposed:

No contracting State shall expel or return a refugee in any manner whatsoever to the frontiers of territories where his life or freedom would be threatened on account of his race, religion, nationality or political opinion.[14]

During this same period, however, States resisted inclusion of a right to be granted asylum, both in the 1948 Universal Declaration of Human Rights and in the 1951 Convention. The 1951 Conference of Plenipotentiaries also had concerns regarding the absoluteness of *non-refoulement*, adding the following paragraph to what was to become article 33:

The benefit of the present provision may not, however, be claimed by a refugee whom there are reasonable grounds for regarding as a danger to the security of the country in which he is, or who, having been convicted by a final judgment of a particularly serious crime, constitutes a danger to the community of that country.[15]

Apart from certain situations of exception, the drafters of the 1951 Convention clearly intended that refugees not be returned, either to their country of origin or to other countries in which they would be at risk.[16]

[13] The Committee decided to focus on the refugee, and duly produced a draft convention. In August 1950, ECOSOC returned the draft for further review, before consideration by the General Assembly, and finalized the Preamble and refugee definition. In December 1950, the General Assembly decided to convene a Conference of Plenipotentiaries to complete the draft: UNGA res. 429(V), 14 Dec. 1950. See generally *Report* of the *Ad hoc* Committee on Refugees and Stateless Persons, Second Session: UN doc. E/1850. The Committee had been renamed in the interim. The most important United Nations documents from this period are usefully collected in Takkenberg, A. and Tahbaz, C. C., *The Collected Travaux Préparatoires of the 1951 Convention relating to the Status of Refugees*, 3 volumes, (1988). The full *travaux préparatoires* may be found online at <http://www.unhcr.org/research.html> and in UNHCR, *RefWorld*, DVD-CD Rom, (15th edn., 2006).

[14] UN doc. E/1850, para. 30. Cf. Louis Henkin, United States delegation, 'Whether it was a question of closing the frontier to a refugee who asked admittance, or of turning him back after he had crossed the frontier, or even of expelling him after he had been admitted to residence in the territory, the problem was more or less the same ... Whatever the case might be ... he must not be turned back to a country where his life or freedom could be threatened. No consideration of public order should be allowed to overrule that guarantee, for if the State concerned wished to get rid of the refugee at all costs, it could send him to another country or place him in an internment camp': *Ad hoc* Committee on Statelessness and Related Problems: UN doc. E/AC.32/SR.20, paras. 54–5 (1950). The Israeli delegate reiterated that the prohibition on return 'must, in fact, apply to all refugees, whether or not they were admitted to residence; it must deal with both expulsion and non-admittance'; he concluded that '[t]he Committee had already settled the humanitarian question of sending any refugee whatever back to a territory where his life or liberty might be in danger', ibid., paras. 60–1. The British delegate also concluded from the discussion that the notion of *refoulement* 'could apply to ... refugees seeking admission': UN doc. E/AC.32/SR.21, para. 16 (1950).

[15] The change in the international situation between the meeting of the *Ad Hoc* Committee in Aug. 1950 and the Conference in July 1951 is usually cited as the reason for the introduction of exceptions; see UN doc. A/CONF.2/SR.16, 8 (1951) (views of the United Kingdom).

[16] The *Ad hoc* Committee reported in its comments that the draft article referred 'not only to the country of origin but also to other countries where the life or freedom of the refugee would be threatened': see UN doc. E/AC.32/SR.20, 3 (1950), for the UK's proposal and views; UN doc. E/1618,

As expressed in article 33, the principle of *non-refoulement* raises questions as to its personal scope and relation to the issues of admission and non-rejection at the frontier. It is a rule clearly designed to benefit the refugee, the person who, in the sense of article 1 of the Convention, has a well-founded fear of being persecuted on grounds of race, religion, nationality, membership of a particular social group, or political opinion. In principle, its benefit ought not to be predicated upon formal recognition of refugee status which, indeed, may be impractical in the absence of effective procedures or in the case of a mass influx.[17] Likewise, it would scarcely be consonant with considerations of good faith for a State to seek to avoid the principle of *non-refoulement* by declining to make a determination of status.

From the point of general, as opposed to treaty-based international law, the issue is rendered more problematic by developments in the refugee definition, as well as by uncertainties as to the scope and standing of *non-refoulement* outside the relevant international instruments. Extensions of UNHCR's mandate might be interpreted as purely functional, in that they authorize the channelling of material assistance but do not justify insistence on the provision of protection through *non-refoulement*. States have argued in the not so recent past that, in regard to the expanded class, their obligations are humanitarian rather than legal, but that view clearly requires reconsideration in light of the consolidation of human rights protection.[18] As shown below, State practice in cases of mass influx offers some support for the view that *non-refoulement*, or an analogous principle of refuge, applies both to the individual refugee with a well-founded fear of persecution, and to the frequently large groups of persons who do not in fact enjoy the protection of the government of their country of origin in certain fairly well-defined circumstances.

E/AC.32/5, 61, for the *Ad hoc* Committee's comment. Sweden proposed a more specific rule against the return of a refugee to a country 'where he would be exposed to the risk of being sent to a territory where his life or freedom' would be threatened, for example, by extradition or expulsion: see UN docs. A/CONF.2/70, A/CONF.2/SR.16, 9 (1951). This was withdrawn, on the assumption that art. 33 covered at least some of the ground. The Danish representative noted that a government expelling a refugee to an intermediate country could not foresee how that State might act. But if expulsion presented a threat of subsequent forcible return to the country of origin, then the life or liberty of the refugee would be endangered, contrary to the principle of *non-refoulement*: see UN doc. A/CONF.2/SR.16, 9f. In *Re Musisi* [1987] 2 WLR 606, at 620, the UK House of Lords struck down a decision to deny asylum to a Ugandan refugee and return him to Kenya, his country of first refuge. The reasons given by the Secretary of State indicated that he had failed to take into account, or to give sufficient weight to, a relevant consideration, namely, that on a number of occasions Kenya had handed over Ugandan refugees to the Ugandan authorities.

[17] Executive Committee Conclusion No. 6 (1977), para. (c), Executive Committee Conclusion No. 79 (1996), para. (j), Executive Committee Conclusion No. 81 (1997), para. (i), Executive Committee Conclusion No. 82 (1997), para. (d)(i) reaffirm the principle of *non-refoulement*, irrespective of formal recognition of refugee status. The 1979 Arusha Conference on the Situation of Refugees in Africa observed, among other matters, that refugee status procedures might be impractical in the case of large-scale movements of asylum seekers in Africa, and that special arrangements might be necessary. As a minimum, however, the conference recommended that the protection of individuals by virtue of the principle of *non-refoulement* be ensured: UN doc. A/AC.96/INF.158 at 9; see also Executive Committee Conclusion No. 19 (1980), para. (a).

[18] See above, Ch. 2, s. 8 and below, Ch. 6.

2. Relation of the principle of *non-refoulement* to particular issues

2.1 ADMISSION AND NON-REJECTION AT THE FRONTIER

Those who argue in favour of the restrictive view of the obligations of States under article 33 sometimes rely on comments made by the Swiss and Dutch delegates to the Conference of Plenipotentiaries in 1951. The Swiss interpretation of *non-refoulement* would have limited its application to those who had already entered State territory, but they spoke *only* about mass migrations, saying nothing about the non-applicability of article 33 outside that context.[19] The Dutch delegate considered that the word 'return' related only to refugees already within the territory, and that mass migrations were not covered.[20] This narrow view did not fully square with the meaning of *refoulement* in European immigration law or with the letter of article 3 of the 1933 Convention, at least in their individual dimension. The words 'expel or return' in the English version of article 33 also have no precise meaning in general international law. The former may describe any measure, judicial, administrative, or police, which secures the departure of an alien, although article 32 possibly implies that measures of expulsion are reserved for lawfully resident aliens. The word 'return' is even vaguer; to the Danish representative it suggested such action as a State might take in response to a request for extradition.[21] The Dutch delegate's comments, however, primarily reflected concern that the draft article would require his government to grant *entry* in the case of a mass migration.[22]

Probably the most accurate assessment of States' views in 1951 is that there was no unanimity, perhaps intentionally so. At the same time, however, States were not prepared to include in the Convention any article on admission of refugees;

---

[19] UN doc. A/CONF.2/SR.16, 6 (1951); see also Weis, P., 'Legal Aspects of the Convention of 28 July 1951 relating to the Status of Refugees,' 30 *BYIL* 478, 482 (1953).   [20] See below, n. 22.

[21] UN doc. A/CONF.2/SR.16, 10 (1951). On extradition and *non-refoulement*, see below, s. 3.3.3.

[22] For the Dutch delegate's comments, see UN doc. A/CONF.2/SR.35 at 21 (1951): Baron van Boetzelaer of the Netherlands, 'recalled that at the first reading the Swiss representative had expressed the opinion that the word "expulsion" related to a refugee already admitted into a country, whereas the word "return" ("*refoulement*") related to a refugee already within the territory but not yet resident there...At the first reading the representatives of Belgium, the Federal Republic of Germany, Italy, the Netherlands and Sweden had supported the Swiss interpretation...In order to dispel any possible ambiguity and to reassure his Government, he wished to have it placed on record that the Conference was in agreement with the interpretation that the possibility of mass migrations across frontiers or of attempted mass migrations was not covered by article 33...There being no objection, the PRESIDENT ruled that the interpretation given by the Netherlands representative should be *placed on the record*' (Emphasis added.) Earlier, the Dutch delegate explained that his concern was that of 'a country bordering on others...about assuming unconditional obligations as far as mass influxes of refugees were concerned...*unless international collaboration was sufficiently organized to deal with such a situation*': UN doc. A/CONF.2/SR.16, 11 (emphasis added). The Dutch comments are thus neither an 'official' interpretation of the Convention, nor a binding limitation on the plain language.

non-refoulement in the sense of even a limited obligation to allow entry may well have been seen as coming too close to the unwished-for duty to grant asylum.

Since then, the views of commentators on the scope of article 33 have varied,[23] and little is to be gained today by further analysis of the motives of States or the meaning of words in 1951. Likewise, it is fruitless to pay too much attention to moments of entry or presence, legal or physical. As a matter of fact, anyone presenting themselves at a frontier post, port, or airport will already be within State territory and jurisdiction; for this reason, and the better to retain sovereign control, States have devised fictions to keep even the physically present alien technically, legally, unadmitted.[24] Similarly, no consequence of significance can be derived from repeated reliance on the proposition that States have no duty to admit refugees, or indeed, any other aliens. 'No duty to admit' begs many questions; in particular, whether States are obliged to protect refugees to the extent of not adopting measures which will result in their persecution or exposure to danger. State practice in fact attributes little weight to the precise issue of admission, but far more to the necessity for *non-refoulement* through time, pending the

[23] Cf. Robinson: *Commentary*, (1953), 163—art. 33 'concerns refugees who have gained entry into the territory of a contracting State, legally or illegally, but not refugees who seek entrance into this territory'; Weis, P.: 'Legal Aspects of the Convention of 28 July 1951 relating to the Status of Refugees', 30 *BYIL* 478 (1953) at 482–3—*non-refoulement* 'leads the way to the adoption of the principle that a State shall not refuse admission to a refugee, i.e. it shall grant him at least temporary asylum...if non-admission is tantamount to surrender to the country of persecution'; (High Commissioner for Refugees) Schnyder, F., 'Les aspects juridiques actuels du problème des réfugiés', Hague *Recueil* (1965-I) 339, at 381—the principles of non-rejection and temporary asylum are becoming more and more recognized; (High Commissioner for Refugees) Sadruddin Aga Khan, 'Legal Problems Relating to Refugees and Displaced Persons', Hague *Recueil* (1976-I) 287, at 318–22—concluding that States do not accept the rule of non-rejection. See also Weis, P., 'Territorial Asylum', 6 *Indian Journal of International Law* (1966) 173, 183—arguing for extension of the principle to non-rejection at the frontier, otherwise protection becomes dependent on 'the fortuitous circumstance' that the refugee has successfully entered State territory. Grahl-Madsen consistently argued that art. 33 is limited to those present, lawfully or unlawfully, in the territory of contracting States, that protection depends upon having 'set foot' in that territory: *The Status of Refugees in International Law*, (1966), vol. 2, 94–9; *Territorial Asylum*, (1980), 40ff. In the most recent and comprehensive analysis, Lauterpacht & Bethlehem argue that *non-refoulement* encompasses non-rejection at the frontier, noting that: 'where States are not prepared to grant asylum to persons who have a well-founded fear of persecution, they must adopt a course that does not amount to *refoulement*. This may involve removal to a safe third country or some other solution such as temporary protection or refuge. No other analysis, in our view, is consistent with the terms of Article 33(1)': Lauterpacht, E. & Bethlehem, D., 'The Scope and Content of the Principle of *Non-Refoulement*: Opinion' in Feller, E., Türk, V. and Nicholson, F., eds., *Refugee Protection in International Law: UNHCR's Global Consultations on International Protection* (2003), 113, para. 76 (hereafter, Lauterpacht & Bethlehem, '*Non-refoulement*: Opinion').

[24] See, for example, the elaborations of Lord Denning in *R. v. Governor of Brixton Prison, ex p. Soblen* [1963] 2 QB 243; also the United States decisions cited by Pugash, J. Z., 'The Dilemma of the Sea Refugee: Rescue without Refuge,' 18 *Harv. ILJ* 577, at 592ff (1977); *A Study on Statelessness* (UN doc. E/1112 and Add. 1, 60 (1949)) defines *reconduction* as 'the mere physical act of ejecting from the national territory a person who has gained entry or is residing therein irregularly' and *expulsion* as 'the juridical decision taken by the judicial or administrative authorities whereby an individual is ordered to leave the territory of the country'. The study observes that terminology varies, but for its purposes the term *refoulement* (reconduction) was not used to signify the act of preventing a foreigner present at the frontier from entering the national territory. See below, s. 3.3.2 ('International zones').

obtaining of durable solutions. For this reason, Noll describes *non-refoulement* in this context as 'a right to transgress an administrative border.'[25]

Let it be assumed that, in 1951, the principle of *non-refoulement* was binding solely on the conventional level, and that it did not encompass non-rejection at the frontier. Analysis today requires full account of State practice since that date,[26] as well as that of international organizations. Over the last fifty-five or so years, the broader interpretation of *non-refoulement* has established itself. States have allowed large numbers of asylum seekers not only to cross their frontiers, for example, in Africa, Europe, and South East Asia, but also to remain pending a solution.[27] State practice, individually and within international organizations, has contributed to further progressive development of the law. By and large, States in their practice and in their recorded views, have recognized that *non-refoulement* applies to the moment at which asylum seekers present themselves for entry, either within a State or at its border.[28] Certain factual elements may be necessary before the principle is triggered, but the concept now encompasses both non-return and non-rejection. A realistic appraisal of the normative aspect of *non-refoulement* in turn requires that the rule be examined not in isolation, but in its dynamic sense and in relation to the concept of asylum and the pursuit of durable solutions.

2.2 CONVENTIONS AND AGREEMENTS

In addition to the 1951 Convention/1967 Protocol, the principle of *non-refoulement* is powerfully expressed in article 3 of the 1984 UN Convention against Torture (CAT84):

1. No State Party shall expel, return ('refouler') or extradite a person to another State where there are substantial grounds for believing that he would be in danger of being subjected to torture.

2. For the purpose of determining whether there are such grounds, the competent authorities shall take into account all relevant considerations including, where applicable, the existence in the State concerned of a consistent pattern of gross, flagrant or mass violations of human rights.

Article 7 of the 1966 International Covenant on Civil and Political Rights (ICCPR66), which provides that '[n]o one shall be subjected to torture or to cruel, inhuman or degrading treatment or punishment', has been interpreted as

---

[25] Noll, G., 'Seeking Asylum at Embassies: A Right to Entry under International Law?' 17 *IJRL* 542, 548 (2005).

[26] Cf. arts. 31 (1), (2), 1969 Vienna Convention on the Law of Treaties.

[27] In 1953 the French Minister of the Interior, advising the Parliament that asylum seekers from Spain were still arriving, gave assurances that none was refused admission; all were allowed to remain pending determination of refugee status, when those not recognized were invited to return to their country: Kiss, *Répertoire de la pratique française*, vol. 4, 434–5. In 1956, following the Hungarian crisis, some 180,000 were granted immediate first asylum in Austria, and a further 20,000 in Yugoslavia: UNHCR, *A Mandate to Protect and Assist Refugees*, (1971), 67–77.

[28] *R. (European Roma Rights Centre and others) v. Immigration Officer at Prague Airport (UNHCR Intervening)* [2005] 2 AC 1, [2004] UKHL 55, para. 26 (Lord Bingham).

containing an implied prohibition on *refoulement*.[29] It is broader than the prohibition under the Convention against Torture, since it extends to cruel, inhuman or degrading treatment or punishment as well. This obligation arises out of the combination of articles 7 and 2(1), which requires States to guarantee the Convenant rights 'to all persons who may be within their territory and to all persons subject to their jurisdiction',[30] including asylum seekers and refugees. This also entails a duty 'not to extradite, deport, expel or otherwise remove a person from their territory, where there are substantial grounds for believing that there is a real risk of irreparable harm, such as that contemplated by articles 6 and 7 of the Covenant, either in the country to which removal is to be effected or in any country to which the person may subsequently be removed'.[31] International humanitarian law provides additional support. The 1949 Geneva Convention relative to the Protection of Civilian Persons in Time of War defines 'protected persons' as 'those who, at a given moment and in any manner whatsoever, find themselves, in case of a conflict or occupation, in the hands of a Party to the conflict or Occupying Power of which they are not nationals'.[32] Article 45 provides in part:

Protected persons shall not be transferred to a Power which is not a party to the Convention...

In no circumstances shall a protected person be transferred to a country *where he or she may have reason to fear persecution for his or her political opinions or religious beliefs.* (Emphasis added.)

Non-refoulement is also embodied in regional instruments. Article II(3) of the 1969 OAU Convention Governing the Specific Aspects of Refugee Problems in Africa (OAU69)[33] declares that:

[n]o person shall be subjected... to measures such as rejection at the frontier, return or expulsion, which would compel him to return to or remain in a territory where his life, physical integrity or liberty would be threatened.

The central features of *non-refoulement* are present in article 22(8) of the 1969 American Convention on Human Rights (ACHR69):

In no case may an alien be deported or returned to a country, regardless of whether or not it is his country of origin, if in that country his right to life or personal freedom is in danger of being violated because of his race, nationality, religion, social status, or political opinions.[34]

---

[29] Human Rights Committee, General Comment No. 31 (2004), para. 12. The Committee's comments and those of other treaty-monitoring bodies are collected in UN doc. HRI/GEN/Rev.8 (8 May 2006).

[30] Ibid., para. 10; see also Human Rights Committee, General Comment No. 15 (1986).

[31] Human Rights Committee, General Comment No. 31 (2004), para. 12; see also Human Rights Committee, General Comment No. 20 (1992), para. 9.

[32] Art. 4, Geneva Convention Relative to the Protection of Civilian Persons in Time of War (Fourth Convention of 12 August 1949).

[33] 1001 *UNTS* 45; below Annexe 2, No. 1. In July 2004, the African Union Summit of Heads of State confirmed the OAU Convention's continuing relevance.

[34] *OAS Official Records*, OEA/Ser.K/XVI/1.1.

Article 12(3) of the 1981 African Charter of Human and Peoples' Rights (ACHPR81) focuses specifically on asylum:

Every individual shall have the right, when persecuted, to seek and obtain asylum in other countries in accordance with the law of those countries and international conventions.

In the Americas, regional protection of asylees goes back to the 1889 Montevideo Treaty on International Penal Law;[35] article 16 proclaims that, 'Political refugees shall be afforded an inviolable asylum', and article 20 excludes extradition for political crimes.[36] Each of these regional instruments has been widely accepted, with no reservations recorded or attempted in respect of the basic principle of non-return.

The principle of *non-refoulement* is also reflected in article 3 of the 1950 European Convention on Human Rights, which prohibits removal to torture, or cruel, inhuman or degrading treatment or punishment.[37] The European Court of Human Rights has held that the extradition[38] or expulsion[39] of a person will breach article 3 where there are substantial grounds for believing that he or she faces a real risk of being subjected to torture or to inhuman or degrading treatment or punishment in the receiving State. This illustrates the general issue of State responsibility with regard to the removal of persons from State territory, and is founded on the unqualified terms of article 3, read in conjunction with article 1, requiring contracting States to protect everyone within their jurisdiction from the real risk of such treatment, in the light of its irremediable nature.[40] By contrast to

---

[35] *OAS Official Records*, OEA/Ser.X/1. Treaty Series 34. See also art. 20, 1940 Montevideo Treaty on International Penal Law; art. 3, 1954 Caracas Convention on Territorial Asylum ('No State is under the obligation to surrender to another State, or to expel from its own territory, persons persecuted for political reasons or offenses'); below, Annexe 2, No. 3.

[36] Other relevant provisions include art. 4(5), 1981 Inter-American Convention on Extradition; art. 3(2), 1957 European Convention on Extradition; below, Annexe 2, No. 10.

[37] From the 1960s, the European Commission on Human Rights interpreted art.3 ECHR50 as encompassing the principle of *non-refoulement*: see, for example, *X v. Belgium* (984/61), 29 May 1961, 6 CD 39–40; *X v. Federal Republic of Germany* (1963) 6 *Yearbook* 462, 480; Recommendation 434 (1965) concerning the Granting of the Right of Asylum to European Refugees; see also *Kirkwood v. United Kingdom* (1984) 6 EHRR 373; *Chahal v. United Kingdom* (1996) 23 EHRR 413. See further below, Ch. 6   [38] *Soering v. United Kingdom* (1989) 11 *EHRR* 439, para. 91.

[39] *Chahal*, above note, para. 80. See also *Cruz Varas v. Sweden* (1991) 14 EHRR 1; *Vilvarajah v. United Kingdom* (1991) 14 EHRR 248; *D v. United Kingdom* (1997) 24 EHRR 423; *HLR v. France* (1997) 26 EHRR 29; *Dehwari v. Netherlands* (2000) 29 EHRR CD 74; *Hilal v. United Kingdom* (2001) 33 EHRR 31. These decisions, based on *Chahal*, are being challenged in the European Court of Human Rights by Lithuania, Portugal, Slovakia, and the United Kingdom (as interveners) in the matter of *Ramzy v. The Netherlands*: see 'Observations of the Governments of Lithuania, Portugal, Slovakia and the United Kingdom intervening in Application No. 25424/05: *Ramzy v. The Netherlands*' (22 Nov. 2005).

[40] Art. 3 ECHR50 has been interpreted as an obligation to afford humanitarian assistance in cases of gross violations of human rights by other States, although it has been argued that this gives rise to no general right of 'temporary refuge', and that the article's focus on conduct of particular gravity attracts a heavy evidential burden ('substantial grounds to fear', 'actual concrete danger'): Hailbronner, K., '*Non-refoulement* and "Humanitarian" Refugees: Customary International Law or Wishful Legal Thinking?' 26 *Virg J.I.L.* 857 (1986); also published in Martin, D., *The New Asylum-Seekers*, (1988).

the exceptions to *non-refoulement* in articles 32 and 33 of the 1951 Convention, article 3 is absolute, preventing removal no matter how 'undesirable or dangerous' an individual's conduct.[41]

In the European Union, the 2004 Qualification Directive prohibits Member States from returning individuals to the death penalty or execution; to torture or inhuman or degrading treatment or punishment in the applicant's country of origin; or to a 'serious and individual threat to a civilian's life or person by reason of indiscriminate violence in situations of international or internal armed conflict'.[42] While these provisions are based on Member States' existing *non-refoulement* obligations under international and EU law, the Qualification Directive is the first binding supranational agreement by States concerning the determination of eligibility and status of individuals with 'complementary protection' needs—that is, international protection needs falling outside the scope of the 1951 Convention.

2.3 DECLARATIONS AND RESOLUTIONS

Besides the range of obligations formally undertaken by States, the standing of the principle of *non-refoulement* in international law must also be assessed by reference also to non-binding declarations and resolutions. States are able to express their views and policies in a variety of international fora; if their practice in turn conforms to such statements, this may give further support to the concretization of a norm of customary international law.

The most recent declaration by States on the importance of the principle was adopted on 13 December 2001, when States party to the Convention and/or Protocol affirmed those instruments' enduring importance, called for universal adherence to them, and noted 'the continuing relevance and resilience of this international regime of rights and principles, including at its core the principle of *non-refoulement*, whose applicability is embedded in customary international law'.[43]

Earlier declarations reveal States' understanding of the meaning and scope of *non-refoulement*. Thus, the 1967 Declaration on Territorial Asylum, adopted unanimously by the General Assembly, recommends that States be guided by the principle that no one entitled to seek asylum 'shall be subjected to measures such as rejection at the frontier or, if he has already entered the territory in which he

So far as this is indeed borne out by the case law, art. 3 may fail to offer any *additional* protection to the refugee, while it nevertheless strengthens the basic principle of non-return to certain specifically threatening situations. See Ch. 6 below on complementary protection.

[41] *Chahal* (1996) 23 EHRR 413, para. 80; *Soering* (1989) 11 EHRR 439, para. 88.

[42] Art. 15, Council Directive 2004/83/EC of 29 April 2004 on Minimum Standards for the Qualification and Status of Third Country Nationals or Stateless Persons as Refugees or as Persons Who Otherwise Need International Protection and the Content of the Protection Granted [2004] O.J. L304/12; for text see below, Annexe 2, No. 19.

[43] Declaration of States Parties to the 1951 Convention and/or its 1967 Protocol relating to the Status of Refugees, UN doc. HCR/MMSP/2001/09 (16 Jan. 2002), para. 4, contained in UNHCR, *Agenda for Protection*.

seeks asylum, expulsion or compulsory return to any State where he may be subjected to persecution'.[44]

Very similar language was used in article III(3) of the Principles concerning Treatment of Refugees, adopted by the Asian–African Legal Consultative Committee in Bangkok in 1966.[45] A resolution adopted by the Committee of Ministers of the Council of Europe the following year acknowledged that States should 'ensure that no one shall be subjected to refusal of admission at the frontier, rejection, expulsion or any other measure which would have the result of compelling him to return to, or remain in, a territory where he would be in danger of persecution...'[46] The Committee of Ministers reiterated this principle in 1984, 'regardless of whether [the] person has been recognized as a refugee...'[47] and again in 1998.[48] The 1984 Cartagena Declaration is yet more categoric, not only endorsing a broader, regionally specific refugee definition, but also reiterating the importance of *non-refoulement* and non-rejection at the frontier as a 'corner-stone' of international protection, having the status of *jus cogens*.[49] The 2004 Mexico Declaration, adopted on the 20th anniversary of the Cartagena Declaration, echoes this position, recognizing 'the commitment of Latin American countries to keep their borders open in order to guarantee the protection and security of those who have a right to enjoy international protection'.[50] A Declaration on Refugees was adopted in January 2004 by the Eminent Persons Group, comprising leading figures from five South Asian States, and called for States in that region to ratify the Convention and Protocol and develop national asylum legislation in accordance with a model law.[51]

In June 2001, the Asian–African Legal Consultative Organization agreed on principles on the treatment of refugees,[52] which revised and consolidated the

---

[44] Art. 3(1); below, Annexe 1, No. 6. Note that art. 3(2) provides that an exception may be made to the basic principle, 'only for overriding reasons of national security or in order to safeguard the population, as in the case of a mass influx of persons'. In such circumstances, the State contemplating such exception, 'shall consider the possibility of granting to the person concerned, under such conditions as it may deem appropriate, an opportunity, whether by way of provisional asylum or otherwise, of going to another State': art. 3(3).

[45] *Report of the Eighth Session of the Asian–African Legal Consultative Committee*, Bangkok (8–17 Aug. 1966), 355 A revised text was adopted in 2001; see below, n. 52.

[46] Res. (67) 14 on Asylum to Persons in Danger of Persecution, 29 Jun. 1967; cf. art. II(3) OAUR69.

[47] Rec. No. R (84) 1, Recommendation on the Protection of Persons satisfying the Criteria in the Geneva Convention who are not Formally Recognized as Refugees.

[48] Rec. No. R (98) 15 of the Committee of Ministers to Member States on the Training of Officials Who First Come into Contact with Asylum Seekers, in Particular at Border Points.

[49] Cartagena Declaration, Conclusions and Recommendations, III, 5; below, Annexe 2, No. 7.

[50] Mexico Declaration and Plan of Action to Strengthen the International Protection of Refugees in Latin America (Mexico City, 16 Nov. 2004). Note also the Declaration adopted on the 10th anniversary of the Cartagena Declaration: San Jose Declaration on Refugees and Displaced Persons (San Jose, 5–7 Dec. 1994).

[51] UNHCR, 'Note on International Protection', UN doc. A/AC.96/989 (7 Jul. 2004), para. 10.

[52] Final Text of the Asian–African Legal Consultative Organization's 1966 Bangkok Principles on Status and Treatment of Refugees, 40th Session, New Delhi (adopted 24 June 2001); see also RES/ 40/3 (24 June 2001): <http://www.aalco.org>.

Bangkok Principles. For many Asian States, these are the only agreed statements of refugee protection principles which are applied throughout the region.

In September 2001, the Council of the International Institute of Humanitarian Law adopted a Declaration stating that: 'The Principle of Non-Refoulement of Refugees incorporated in Article 33 of the Convention relating to the Status of Refugees of 28 July 1951 is an integral part of Customary International Law.'[53] In an explanatory note, the Council described as a 'telling point' the fact that in the last half-century, no State had returned a refugee 'using the argument that refoulement is permissible under contemporary international law. Whenever *refoulement* occurred, it did so on the grounds that the person concerned was not a refugee (as the term is properly defined) or that a legitimate exception applied.'[54]

In 2002, the International Law Association noted 'the fundamental obligation of States not to return (*refouler*) a refugee in any manner whatsoever to a country in which his or her life or freedom may be threatened', and declared:

1. Everyone seeking international protection as a refugee outside his or her country of origin and in accordance with the relevant international instruments should have access to a fair and effective procedure for the determination of his or her claim . . .

5. No one who seeks asylum at the border or in the territory of a State shall be rejected at the frontier, or expelled or returned in any manner whatsoever to any country in which he or she may be tortured or subjected to inhuman, cruel or degrading treatment or punishment, or in which his or her life or freedom may be endangered.[55]

The United Nations has also recognized the relationship between *non-refoulement* and the protection of human rights.[56] For example, the Principles on the Effective Prevention and Investigation of Extra-Legal, Arbitrary and Summary Executions, endorsed by the General Assembly in 1989, provide that 'no one shall be involuntarily returned or extradited to a country where there are substantial grounds for believing that he or she may become a victim of extra-legal, arbitrary or summary execution in that country'.[57] In 1992, the General Assembly adopted the Declaration on the Protection of All Persons from Enforced Disappearance, article 8(1) of which declares that: 'No State shall expel, return (*refouler*) or extradite a person to another State where there are substantial grounds to believe that he would be in danger of enforced disappearance'.[58] The two Protocols to the Convention against Transnational Organized Crime operate subject to 'the rights,

---

[53] San Remo Declaration on the Principle of Non-Refoulement, (Sept. 2001).

[54] Ibid., 'Explanatory Note on the Principle of Non-Refoulement of Refugees as Customary International Law'.   [55] International Law Association, Res. 6/2002 (Apr. 2002).

[56] See also UNHCR's statement that: 'The entry into force in January 2004 of the Protocol establishing the African Court on Human and Peoples' Rights is particularly welcome in view of the many linkages between human rights and refugee issues': UNHCR, 'Note on International Protection', UN doc. A/AC.96/989 (7 Jul. 2004), para. 20.

[57] UNGA res. 44/162, 15 Dec. 1989, para. 5. See also ECOSOC res. 1989/65, 24 May 1989, recommending that the principles annexed to the resolution be taken into account and respected by governments.

[58] UNGA res. 47/133, 18 Dec. 1992, adopted without a vote. Art. 8(2) reproduces art. 3(2) CAT84.

214   *Asylum*

obligations and responsibilities of States and individuals under international law... in particular, where applicable, the 1951 Convention and the 1967 Protocol relating to the Status of Refugees and the principle of non-refoulement as contained therein',[59] echoed in the 2005 Council of Europe Convention on Action against Trafficking in Human Beings.[60] These provisions contribute to and confirm the meaning of persecution, and even if they do not expand the substantive scope of protection, nevertheless consolidate the legal standing of the principle of *non-refoulement* in general international law.

More generally, the General Assembly has repeatedly affirmed the importance of full respect for the principle of *non-refoulement* and urged States to observe it.[61] Similarly, both the Commission on Human Rights[62] and the Sub-Commission on Human Rights[63] have called upon States to ensure the effective protection of refugees by respecting the principle of *non-refoulement*.

There has been increased attention to the principle of *non-refoulement* by other branches of the UN as well. The Special Rapporteur on Extrajudicial, Summary or Arbitrary Executions, the Special Rapporteur on the Human Rights of Migrants, and the Special Rapporteur on the Question of Torture have all expressed concern about, and reported on, cases of alleged *refoulement* of asylum seekers by various States.[64] In

---

[59] Protocol to Prevent, Suppress and Punish Trafficking in Persons, Especially Women and Children, supplementing the United Nations Convention against Transnational Organized Crime, UNGA res. 55/25 (15 Nov. 2000), art. 14(1); Protocol against the Smuggling of Migrants by Land, Sea and Air, supplementing the United Nations Convention against Transnational Organized Crime, UNGA res. 55/25 (15 Nov. 2000), art. 19(1).

[60] *CETS* No. 197 (opened for signature 16 May 2005). The treaty will enter into force when it has been ratified by ten States, of which at least eight must be Member States of the Council of Europe.

[61] UNGA res. 32/67 (8 Dec. 1977), para 5(c); UNGA res. 33/26 (29 Nov. 1978), para. 6; UNGA res. 34/60 (29 Nov. 1979), para. 3(a); UNGA res. 35/41 (25 Nov. 1980), para. 5(a); UNGA res. 36/125 (14 Dec. 1981), para. 5(a); UNGA res. 37/195 (18 Dec. 1982), para. 2; UNGA res. 38/121 (16 Dec. 1983), para. 2; UNGA res. 39/140 (14 Dec. 1984), para. 2; UNGA res. 40/118 (13 Dec. 1985), para. 2; UNGA res. 41/124 (4 Dec. 1986), para. 2; UNGA res. 42/109 (7 Dec. 1987), para. 1; UNGA res. 43/117 (8 Dec. 1988), para. 3; UNGA res. 44/137 (15 Dec. 1989), para. 3; UNGA res. 45/140 (14 Dec. 1990), para. 3; UNGA res. 46/106 (16 Dec. 1991), para. 4; UNGA res. 47/105 (16 Dec. 1992), para. 4; UNGA res. 48/116 (20 Dec. 1993), para. 3; UNGA res. 49/169 (23 Dec. 1994), para. 4; UNGA res. 50/152 (21 Dec. 1995), para. 3; UNGA res. 51/75 (12 Dec. 1996), para. 3; UNGA res. 52/103 (12 Dec. 1997), para. 5; UNGA res. 52/132 (12 Dec. 1997), para. 16; UNGA res. 53/125 (9 Dec. 1998), para. 5; UNGA res. 54/146 (17 Dec. 1999), para. 6; UNGA res. 55/74 (4 Dec. 2000), para. 6; UNGA res. 56/137 (19 Dec. 2001), para. 3; UNGA res. 57/187 (18 Dec. 2002), para. 4; UNGA res. 58/151 (22 Dec. 2003), para. 3; UNGA res. 59/170 (20 Dec. 2004), para. 3; UNGA res. 60/129 (16 Dec. 2005), para. 3.

[62] CHR res. 2005/48 'Human Rights and Mass Exoduses', para. 7; CHR res. 2005/80 'Protection of Human Rights and Fundamental Freedoms while countering Terrorism', para. 5; CHR res. 2003/52 'Human Rights and Mass Exoduses', para. 6; CHR res 2000/55 'Human Rights and Mass Exoduses', para. 6; CHR res. 1998/49 'Human Rights and Mass Exoduses', para. 6; CHR res. 1997/75 'Human Rights and Mass Exoduses', para. 1.

[63] See the following resolutions of the Sub-Commission: E/CN.4/Sub.2/Res/2002/23, paras. 1, 2; E/CN.4/Sub.2/Res/2001/16, paras. 1, 2; E/CN.4/Sub.2/Res/2000/20, para. 1; E/CN.4/Sub.2/Res/1997/29, para. 6; E/CN.4/Sub.2/Res/1996/9, para. 4.

[64] See the following reports: E/CN.4/2004/7, paras. 64–5; E/CN.4/2003/85, paras. 22–5; E/CN.4/2004/76/Add.1, paras. 1–9, 89–91, 123–35; E/CN.4/2003/85/Add.1, paras. 1–4, 95–7,

2004, the Special Rapporteur on Extrajudicial, Summary or Arbitrary Executions sent communications to Malaysia, Sweden, the United States, and Zimbabwe regarding cases of expulsion, *refoulement*, or returns of people to countries or places where their lives were in danger.[65]

2.4 THE UNHCR EXECUTIVE COMMITTEE CONCLUSIONS ON INTERNATIONAL PROTECTION

The UNHCR Executive Committee[66] has consistently endorsed the fundamental character of the principle of *non-refoulement* in its annual general and specific conclusions. In 1977, for example, the Executive Committee noted that the principle was 'generally accepted by States', expressed concern at its disregard in certain cases, and reaffirmed:

the fundamental importance of the observance of the principle of *non-refoulement*—both at the border and within the territory of a State—of persons who may be subjected to persecution if returned to their country of origin irrespective of whether or not they have been formally recognized as refugees.[67]

Later Conclusions have stressed that the principle of non-rejection at the frontier requires 'access to fair and effective procedures for determining status and protection needs'.[68] Thus, although *non-refoulement* is not synonymous with a right to admission, the principle of non-rejection at the frontier implies at least temporary admission to determine an individual's status.[69] Only in this way can a State ensure that it does not send back an individual to persecution or torture. Hathaway describes this as a 'de facto duty to admit the refugee', although he is careful to emphasize its narrow application to cases where there is a real risk that

148, 261; E/CN.4/2001/83, paras. 77–8; also E/CN.4/2004/56; E/CN.4/2003/68/Add.1; E/CN.4/2002/76/Add.1; E/CN.4/2001/66; E/CN.4/2000/9; E/CN.4/1999/61; E/CN.4/1998/38/Add.1; E/CN.4/1997/7/Add.1; E/CN.4/1996/35/Add.1; E/CN.4/1995/34; E/CN.4/1994/31.

[65] Commission on Human Rights, 'Civil and Political Rights, including the Questions of Disappearances and Summary Executions: Extrajudicial, Summary or Arbitrary Executions: Report of the Special Rapporteur, Philip Alston', UN doc. E/CN.4/2005/7 (22 Dec. 2004), para. 19(g).

[66] On which see further below, Ch. 8, s. 1.1.1.

[67] Executive Committee Conclusion No. 6 (1977). Importantly, this Conclusion was adopted *after* the 1977 Conference on Territorial Asylum. States' failure to agree on a Convention on Territorial Asylum was not due to any rejection of the principle of *non-refoulement* and its extension to non-rejection at the frontier, as was erroneously suggested by the UK Court of Appeal in *R. (European Roma Rights Centre)* v. *Immigration Officer at Prague Airport* [2003] EWCA Civ 666, [2004] QB 811, para. 44 (Simon Brown L.J.) and apparently accepted by Lord Bingham in *R. (European Roma Rights Centre)* v. *Immigration Officer at Prague Airport* [2005] 2 AC 1, [2004] UKHL 55, para. 17, but rather because States were not prepared at that time to accept an individual right to asylum.

[68] Executive Committee Conclusion No. 85 (1998) and No. 99 (2004).

[69] The Human Rights Committee has noted that although ICCPR66 does not recognize the right of aliens to enter or reside in the territory of a State party, 'in certain circumstances an alien may enjoy the protection of the Covenant even in relation to entry or residence, for example, when considerations of non-discrimination, prohibition of inhuman treatment and respect for family life arise': General Comment No. 15 (1986).

rejection will expose an individual to persecution for a Convention reason.[70] In particular, *non-refoulement* is not commensurate with a right to asylum.[71]

Non-refoulement as a paramount consideration has also been reiterated in specific contexts. For example, 'in the case of large-scale influx, persons seeking asylum should always receive at least temporary refuge';[72] similarly, 'in situations of large-scale influx, asylum seekers should be admitted to the State in which they first seek refuge... In all cases the fundamental principle of *non-refoulement*— including non-rejection at the frontier—must be scrupulously observed'.[73]

In its 1982 General Conclusion on protection, the Executive Committee expressed the view that the principle 'was progressively acquiring the character of a peremptory rule of international law'.[74] Reported instances of breach of the principle have been consistently deplored,[75] and in 1989, after the matter was raised expressly by UNHCR in its annual Note on International Protection,[76] the Executive Committee expressed its deep concern 'that refugee protection is seriously jeopardized in some States by expulsion and *refoulement* of refugees or by measures which do not recognize the special situation of refugees'.[77] The same year, when dealing with the problem of irregular movements, the Executive Committee affirmed that 'refugees and asylum seekers [who] move in an irregular manner from a country where they have already found protection... may be returned to that country if... they are protected there against *refoulement*'; but if, in exceptional circumstances, the physical safety or freedom of such refugee or asylum seeker may be at risk, or he or she has good reason to fear persecution there, then their cases should be considered favourably.[78]

Similar language occurs in later Conclusions. In 1991, the Executive Committee emphasized 'the primary importance of *non-refoulement* and asylum as cardinal principles of refugee protection', while indirectly stressing the protective purpose of the principle by reference to the need for refugees to be able to 'return in safety and dignity to their homes without harassment, arbitrary detention or physical threats during or after return'.[79]

[70] Hathaway, J. C., *The Rights of Refugees under International Law*, (2005), 301 (hereafter, Hathaway, *Rights of Refugees*, (2005)).   [71] See below, Ch. 7.

[72] Executive Committee Conclusion No. 19 (1980).

[73] Executive Committee Conclusion No. 22 (1981).

[74] *Report* of the 33rd Session: UN doc. A/AC.96/614, para. 70.

[75] See, for example, Executive Committee Conclusions Nos. 3 (1977); 11 (1978); 14 (1979); 16 (1980); 21 (1981); 25 (1982); 33 (1984); 41 (1986); 46 (1987); 50 (1988); 61 (1990); 68 (1992); 71 (1993); 74 (1994); 79 (1996); 85 (1998); 89 (2000); 102 (2005).

[76] UN doc. A/AC.96/728 (2 Aug. 1989), para. 19.

[77] Executive Committee Conclusion No. 55, *Report* of the 40th Session: UN doc. A/AC.96/737 (19 Oct. 1989), para. 22(d).

[78] Executive Committee Conclusion No. 58 (1989), paras. (f), (g).

[79] Executive Committee Conclusion No. 65 (1991), *Report* of the 42nd Session: UN doc. A/AC.96/783 (21 Oct. 1991), para. 21(c), (j).

In 1992, the Executive Committee maintained this traditional language, but emphasized also that UNHCR's involvement with internally displaced persons and related approaches, 'should not undermine the institution of asylum, as well as other basic protection principles, notably the principle of *non-refoulement*'.[80] More recently, the Executive Committee reiterated that the principle applies to asylum seekers 'whether or not they have been formally granted refugee status', and extends to 'persons in respect of whom there are substantial grounds for believing that they would be in danger of being subjected to torture, as set forth in the 1984 Convention against Torture and Other Cruel, Inhuman, or Degrading Treatment or Punishment'.[81] In 2005, the Executive Committee adopted a Conclusion on complementary forms of protection, affirming that 'relevant international treaty obligations, where applicable, prohibiting *refoulement* represent important protection tools to address the protection needs of persons who are outside their country of origin and who may be of concern to UNHCR but who may not fulfil the refugee definition under the 1951 Convention and/or its 1967 Protocol; and *call[ing] upon* States to respect the fundamental principle of *non-refoulement*'.[82] The Conclusion itself deals with the protection of individuals whose removal is prohibited by the principle of *non-refoulement* under human rights law.

The Conclusions adopted by the UNHCR Executive Committee do not have force of law and do not, of themselves, create binding obligations. They may contribute, however, to the formulation of *opinio juris*—the sense of legal obligation with which States approach the problems of refugees. Some Conclusions seek to lay down standards of treatment, or to resolve differences of interpretation between States and UNHCR, while others are more hortatory, repeating and reaffirming basic principles without seeking to expand their field of application.[83] They must therefore be reviewed in the context of States' expressed opinions, and in light of what they do in practice.

---

[80] Executive Committee Conclusion No. 68 (1992), *Report* of the 43rd Session: UN doc. A/AC.96/804, (15 Oct. 1992), para. 21(e), (f), (r). See also Executive Committee Conclusions No. 74 (1994), *Report* of the 45th Session: UN doc. A/AC.96/839, para. 19; No. 77 (1995), *Report* of the 46th Session: UN doc. A/AC.96/860, para. 19.

[81] Executive Committee Conclusion No. 81 (1997), para. (i); Executive Committee Conclusion No. 82 (1997), para. (d)(i); see also UNHCR, 'Note on International Protection' UN doc A/AC.96/882 (2 Jul. 1997), para. 17.

[82] Executive Committee Conclusion No. 103 (2005), para. (m). Complementary protection is discussed in Ch. 6 below. See also Executive Committee Conclusion No. 99 (2004), which refers to the importance of respecting the 'fundamental principle of *non-refoulement*' in the broader context of persecution, generalized violence, and violations of human rights causing and perpetuating displacement.

[83] See Sztucki, J., 'The Conclusions on the International Protection of Refugees adopted by the Executive Committee of the UNHCR Programme', 1 *IJRL* 285 (1989); Lewis, C., 'UNHCR's Contribution to the Development of International Refugee Law: Its Foundations and Evolution', 17 *IJRL* 67 (2005).

2.5 STATE VIEWS AND STATE PRACTICE

2.5.1 *State views*

The views and comments of States in the Executive Committee fall into two broad categories: first, general endorsements of the principle of *non-refoulement*, which usually say little about content or scope; and secondly, more focused comments, by which States seek to show where, in their opinion or practice, the limits of obligation lie.

One of the clearest general statements in support of the principle of *non-refoulement* was made by Ambassador Jonathan Moore, United States Co-ordinator for Refugee Affairs, at the Executive Committee in 1987.

Forced repatriation had occurred in almost every region of the world during the past year, resulting in death, serious injury and imprisonment. Considering that the most important element of a refugee's protection was the obligation of *non-refoulement*, it was tragic that refugees had been forced to return to their countries against their will and without assurances that they would not face persecution on their return, especially when such violations were committed by, or with the concurrence of, States parties to international instruments prohibiting such acts. The threat to a country posed by influxes of economic migrants should not serve as an excuse for refusing asylum.[84]

Other comments in the years since 1987 have ranged from support for the idea that *non-refoulement* is a long-standing rule of customary international law[85] and even a rule of *jus cogens*,[86] to regret at reported instances of non-observance of fundamental obligations,[87] to its fundamental importance in situations of mass influx,[88] to concern at current challenges to the related 'principle of first asylum',[89] to the need, before implementing any form of compulsory return, to define objective criteria 'to determine whether security concerns had been fully met', and further, with respect to the cessation clauses, 'to ensure that refugees were not forced to return to unsafe countries'.[90]

More focused comments have addressed issues of specific application. In 1987, the Turkish representative raised a particularly serious question:

The principle of *non-refoulement* . . . had to be scrupulously observed. Nevertheless, . . . countries of first asylum or transit . . . , faced with the difficulties of repatriation and the

---

[84] UN doc. A/AC.96/SR.415, para. 16 (1987).

[85] Mr Noirfalisse (Belgium): UN doc. A/AC.96/SR.552, para. 50 (2001).

[86] Mr Mponda (Observer for Malawi): UN doc. A/AC.96/SR.431, para. 32 (1988).

[87] 'The *refoulement* of refugees must not be allowed to occur under any circumstances:' Mr Ceska (Austria): UN doc. A/AC.96/SR.439, para. 9 (1989).

[88] Mr de Courten (International Committee of the Red Cross): UN doc. A/AC.96/SR.522, para. 8 (1997); Ms Nielsen (Switzerland): UN doc. A/AC.96/SR.541, para. 13 (1999); on flexibility of the Convention in mass influx, see remarks of Mrs Kunadi (India): UN doc. A/AC.96/SR.545, para. 6 (2000); Mr Shen (China): UN doc. A/AC.96/SR.563, para. 17 (2002).

[89] Mrs Lafontant (USA): UN doc. A/AC.96/SR.437, para. 49 (1989). Mrs Lafontant had succeeded Jonathan Moore, and was Ambassador-at-Large and US Coordinator for Refugee Affairs.

[90] Mr de Sa Barbuda (Brazil): UN doc. A/AC.96/SR.475, para. 83 (1992), commenting on temporary protection and its eventual termination as a possible alternative to asylum in mass influx situations.

progressively more restrictive practices of host countries, might find themselves unable to continue bearing the burden and, for want of any other solution, come to regard *refoulement* as the only possible way out. If that should occur, they would not be the only ones at fault, since the responsibility for ensuring the conditions necessary for observance of the *non-refoulement* principle rested with the international community as a whole.[91]

This precise point emerged again in 1989, when the Turkish representative remarked that the refugee problem, 'was such that it was no longer possible to disassociate international protection from international co-operation and assistance'.[92] Commenting on developments in Iraq in April 1991 and the arrival on the border of some half-million Kurdish asylum seekers, the Turkish representative noted that while his country had tried to meet the needs of those concerned, '[t]he scale of the operation had... been prohibitive, and Turkey had been compelled to call for urgent international assistance... As a result of the subsequent international cooperation, virtually all those displaced persons had now been resettled in the security zone established in the north of Iraq.'[93] If the reference to 'security' can be taken as controlling, then the rather unique situation of the Kurdish people in search of refuge might still be interpreted consistently with a variant of *non-refoulement* that permits only limited exceptions, conditioning return or rejection in situations of mass influx on the availability of alternative forms of safety. This is not particularly persuasive, but the 'solution' imposed on northern Iraq remains unique.[94] In cases not involving 'mass migrations', no such exception could apply,[95] although the 'internal flight alternative' is a variant of the safe haven concept which may be lawful in limited circumstances.[96]

---

[91] Mr Yavuzalp (Turkey): UN doc. A/AC.96/SR.418, para. 74 (1987).

[92] Mr Demiralp (Turkey): UN doc. A/AC.96/SR.442, para. 92 (1989); see also Mr Cem Duna (Turkey): UN doc. A/AC.96/SR.456, para. 7 (1991). On several occasions, the Turkish representatives have both upheld the fundamental character of *non-refoulement* while simultaneously supporting the right of the asylum seeker to choose in which country to seek asylum, thereby staking a claim for a form of 'natural' burden-sharing. On 'mass influx' see further below, Ch. 6, s. 6.

[93] Mr Atkan (Turkey): UN doc. A/AC.96/SR.468, para. 18 (1991).

[94] See generally, Adelman, H., 'Humanitarian Intervention: The Case of the Kurds', 4 *IJRL* 4 (1992). Today, faced with an imminent refugee exodus, States are more likely to consider humanitarian intervention or containment, as in Kosovo, rather than waiting for people to flee. In 2004, the High Commissioner welcomed the Sudanese government's agreement to the idea of 'safe havens' for the internally displaced, since it indicated some commitment to the peace process; however, for many persons, 'such areas were more like prisons than safe areas': Mr Lubbers (High Commissioner): UN doc. A/AC.96/SR.581, para. 6 (2004).

[95] Although Turkey's formal reservations have focused on mass influx, its record on individual cases has not always been perfect; see Amnesty International, 'Turkey: Selective Protection. Discriminatory Treatment of Non-European Refugees and Asylum Seekers' (1994); Kirişçi, K., 'Asylum Seekers and Human Rights in Turkey', 10 *Neth.Q.H.R.* 447 (1992). Note, however, that Turkey maintains the geographical limitation to its obligations under the 1951 Convention/1967 Protocol.

[96] See above, Ch. 3, s. 5.6.1. See *Januzi v. Secretary of State for the Home Department* [2006] 2 WLR 397 for discussion of the application of the internal flight alternative. Coleman argues that returns to safe havens in Croatia in 1992 constituted *refoulement* because they were effected before

During the 1980s, a number of States stressed that *non-refoulement* did not apply to non-Convention refugees, although many accepted that protection needs were involved. In 1988, the Swiss representative was apprehensive that the 'dilution' of the refugee concept 'would...weaken the basic principle of *non-refoulement*'. While others might be allowed to remain for humanitarian reasons, this would not be based on a Convention obligation, so much as on 'considerations of humanitarian law or international solidarity, in other words, on a free decision by the State concerned'.[97] By the 1990s, however, there was increasing recognition of States' *non-refoulement* obligations beyond article 33 of the 1951 Convention. Several States called attention to the fact that they were parties to the 1984 United Nations Convention against Torture, and consequently also bound by that treaty's provision prohibiting the return of individuals to situations of torture, irrespective of the character or legal status of the individual concerned. Two delegations commented that 'any responsibility not to return non-refugees was far less clear-cut in situations that do not involve torture'.[98] In 1996, the United States described States' responsibility to protect persons from *refoulement* to persecution *and* torture as both a legal and moral duty.[99] The Swedish government expressed its eagerness 'to provide legal protection to the victims of armed conflict, torture and other inhumane treatment',[100] noting that a bill proposed in 1996 also addressed questions relating to victims of gender-related persecution, persecution due to sexual orientation, and environmental disasters. Similarly, the Egyptian delegation stated that '[f]lexibility should be shown in dealing with groups which did not come under the definition of refugees contained in the 1951 Convention relating to the Status of Refugees and its 1967 Protocol'.[101]

In 1998, Belgium stipulated for the first time that all asylum seekers' claims for protection be assessed according to article 3 ECHR50, in addition to article 1A(2) of the 1951 Convention.[102] In the same year, France gave legislative force to two new forms of asylum: 'constitutional asylum', for persecution based on 'actions intended to promote freedom, even if such persecution had not been State-instigated', and 'territorial asylum', a previously *ad hoc* French procedure, to be 'granted to an alien who risked being subjected to inhuman or degrading treatment

refugee status determination could occur: Coleman, N., '*Non-Refoulement* Revised: Renewed Review of the Status of the Principle of *Non-Refoulement* as Customary International Law', 5 *EJML* 23, 29 (2005) (hereafter, Coleman, '*Non-Refoulement* Revised').

[97] Mr Hadorn (Switzerland): UN doc. A/AC.96/SR.430, para. 42 (1988). For example, in 1997, Italy argued that the majority of Albanian asylum seekers that had fled to Italy had not qualified for asylum under the 1951 Convention, but the Italian government 'had decided to admit them temporarily on humanitarian grounds': Mr Baldocci (Italy): UN doc. A/AC.96/SR.518, para. 12 (1997).

[98] *Report* of the Sub-Committee of the Whole on International Protection: UN doc. A/AC.96/758, (2 Oct. 1990), para. 29.

[99] Ms Oakley (United States): UN doc. A/AC.96/SR.507, para. 60 (1996).

[100] Ms Andersson (Sweden): UN doc. A/AC.96/SR.508, para. 5 (1996).

[101] Mr Zahran (Observer for Egypt): UN doc. A/AC.96/SR.511, para. 6 (1996).

[102] Mr de Palichy (Belgium): UN doc. A/AC.96/SR.527, para. 40 (1998).

or whose personal safety would be in serious danger if he were to be refused entry to France'.[103] Meanwhile, the United Kingdom reiterated that States 'should offer protection in line with international human rights standards and obligations'.[104] Since 2000, the US, Canada and the Member States of the European Union have all adopted domestic legislation extending protection to certain persons encompassed by the prohibition on *refoulement* in international instruments like the Convention against Torture and the European Convention.[105]

During this period, Australia was the only State to express near-contempt for extended *non-refoulement* obligations under international law.[106] It described what it appeared to regard as audacious attempts by asylum seekers 'to prolong their stay in Australia indefinitely, in particular by submitting appeals to international bodies such as the Human Rights Committee on the basis of international instruments other than the [Refugee] Convention. The Government of Australia would not allow the increased complexity of procedures to undermine its system for determining refugee status.'[107] The Australian delegation conveniently ignored the fact that, due to Australia's ratification of the Convention against Torture, which provides for individual complaints under article 22, and the Optional Protocol to the International Convenant on Civil and Political Rights, it recognized that asylum seekers have a right to lodge such appeals. Furthermore, since complementary protection does not exist in Australian domestic law, complaints to international committees may in fact provide the first opportunity for asylum seekers to have evidence of human rights abuses not amounting to persecution taken into consideration.

On other occasions, States have described practices which, in their view, did not amount to *refoulement*, such as normal immigration controls, visa policies, and carrier sanctions. In 1988, the UK representative declared his country's intention to abide fully by the principle, but stated that this did not prevent the

---

[103] Mr Besancenot (France): UN doc. A/AC.96/SR.527, para. 44 (1998).

[104] Mr Manning (United Kingdom): UN doc. A/AC.96/SR.527, para. 9 (1998). For a review of European State practice with respect to non-Convention refugees, see Bouteillet-Paquet, D., 'Subsidiary Protection: Progress or Set-Back of Asylum Law in Europe? A Critical Analysis of the Legislation of the Member States of the European Union' in Bouteillet-Paquet, D., ed., *Subsidiary Protection of Refugees in the European Union: Complementing the Geneva Convention?* (2002).

[105] For the United States, see: 8 CFR §208.16, 8 CFR §208.17; Canada: Immigration and Refugee Protection Act 2001, s. 97(1); EU: the Qualification Directive 2004 (transposition required by 10 Oct. 2006; for text, see below, Annexe 2, No. 19).

[106] Australia and New Zealand are notable exceptions among western States, having no codified form of complementary protection. However, New Zealand's *non-refoulement* obligations under arts. 6 and 7 ICCPR66 and art. 3 CAT84 are reflected in ss. 8 and 9 of the Bill of Rights Act 1990 (see the government's acknowledgement of this in *Attorney-General* v. *Zaoui* [2005] NZSC 38, para. 76), and a codified system of complementary protection is proposed: New Zealand Dept. of Labour, 'Immigration Act Review: Discussion Paper', (Apr. 2006), s. 14. In Australia, Senator Andrew Bartlett of the Australian Democrats introduced a private member's bill into Parliament on 13 Sept. 2006, entitled the Migration Legislation Amendment (Complementary Protection Visa) Bill 2006, but it is unlikely that there will be sufficient support for it to pass.

[107] Mr Ruddock (Australia): UN doc. A/AC.96/SR.507, para. 71 (1996).

return of 'failed asylum seekers', or removals to 'safe third countries'.[108] The representative for Argentina, on the other hand, was careful to stress that practices such as 'the refusal of admission at a border for purely administrative reasons vitiated the principle of *non-refoulement*'.[109] UNHCR, however, considers denial of access to asylum procedures at airports, *refoulement* from 'safe third countries', and the extradition of foreigners without examining any asylum claims as examples of violations of the principle of *non-refoulement*.[110] The US Committee for Refugees and Immigrants has observed the constructive *refoulement* of refugees from Malaysia, who have 'volunteered' for deportation owing to the horrendous conditions in detention camps.[111] NGOs have criticized Denmark's accelerated procedures for denying asylum seekers a fair hearing, and accordingly subjecting many to *refoulement*. They argue that the system is being misused—having been designed for manifestly unfounded claims, by mid-2002 it was being used in 60 per cent of cases.[112]

Over the past decade in particular, States have sought to justify restrictive entry policies on account of the mixed character of migratory flows. Many States have invoked 'migration management' mechanisms as tools to prevent abuses of the asylum system and thereby preserve the integrity of international protection.[113] The Polish delegate stated in the Executive Committee that 'the increase in requests from individuals who clearly had no valid claim to refugee status' justified restrictive admission policies.[114] The Italian government noted that its geographical location exposed it to migratory flows which 'could entail the use of political asylum to achieve economic and migration-related aims'.[115] The delegation from Botswana argued that its policy not to accept all asylum seekers wishing to settle there was aimed at controlling immigration and did not 'question respect for the right of asylum'.[116] Similarly, the Venezuelan delegate affirmed her country's awareness of its international obligations and stated that it had always fulfilled them, but noted that 'a balance must be struck between compliance with international commitments and respect for national interests'.[117] She went on to say that while her government 'was of the opinion that persons fleeing violence had to be given protection, that protection did not necessarily have to be limited to asylum, but could also take the form of relocation in the country of origin in areas where those persons would not be in danger'.[118] By contrast, Norway recognized that '[p]reventing

---

[108] Mr Wrench (United Kingdom): UN doc. A/AC.96/SR.430, para. 53 (1988). This interpretation was reiterated the following year; see UN doc. A/AC.96/SR.442, para. 51 (1989).
[109] Mr Strassera (Argentina): UN doc. A/AC.96/SR. 442, para. 46 (1989).
[110] UNHCR, 'Note on International Protection' UN doc. A/AC.96/951, para. 20.
[111] US Committee for Refugees and Immigrants, *World Refugee Survey*, (2005).
[112] US Committee for Refugees and Immigrants, *World Refugee Survey*, (2003).
[113] Mr Bösenbacher (Hungary): UN doc. A/AC.96/SR.546, para. 18 (2000); Mr Perez-Villanueva (Spain): UN doc. A/AC.96/SR.546, para. 44 (2000).
[114] Mr Knothe (Poland): UN doc. A/AC.96/SR.545, para. 54 (2000).
[115] Mr Bruni (Italy): UN doc. A/AC.96/SR.581, para. 76 (2004).
[116] Mr Sesinyi (Observer for Botswana): UN doc. A/AC.96/SR.529, para. 24 (1998).
[117] Mrs Betancourt (Venezuela): UN doc. A/AC.96/SR.540, para. 61 (1999).
[118] Ibid..540, para. 63.

asylum-seekers from finding safety, or from obtaining access to procedures, negates their fundamental rights, and may amount to *refoulement* in breach of international law'.[119] It argued that although it was important to combat irregular migration, it was also important not to put pressure on asylum mechanisms, and in this respect a more generous interpretation of international instruments might assist.[120]

UNHCR repeatedly stressed the importance of ensuring that asylum seekers are able to voice their protection claims, noting that 'refugees do not lose their protection needs and entitlements just because they are part of a mixed flow'.[121] Similarly, it explained that refugees may resort to people smugglers to leave their countries of origin,[122] sometimes out of desperation and sometimes because there is no means of obtaining a visa to enter legally.

In its 2001 Note on International Protection, UNHCR framed the challenge as finding a way of controlling illegal migration 'in a manner which does not have the effect of enhancing opportunities for smugglers and traffickers, but which ensures that the needs of refugees and asylum-seekers, including access to protection, are properly met'.[123] UNHCR expressed concern that increased processes and regulations concerning entry were 'ever less compatible with the prevailing protection framework'.[124]

Security issues have also emerged as an excuse for denying protection. In 1997, the Turkish representative observed that: 'The right to seek asylum was a sacred right, but, like any category of human rights, it should also be protected from abuses that could impair the general welfare of host societies or destroy other rights and freedoms'.[125] Following the 11 September 2001 terrorist attacks, some States began casting 'terrorists' as likely abusers of the asylum system.[126] Just a month after the attacks, the High Commissioner expressed concern that certain States had already increased practices to counter irregular migration, 'resulting in non-admission, denial of access to asylum procedures and even cases of refoulement'.[127] The Indian delegation said that while the attacks on the United States should not dilute international protection, 'it was important to guard against abuse by States that, unwittingly or otherwise, sheltered terrorists'.[128]

---

[119] UNHCR, 'Note on International Protection', UN doc. A/AC.96/882 (2 Jul. 1997), para. 14. Norway took up the issue with the IMO, UNHCR, and in the UN General Assembly: UN docs. GA/9980, GA 9981; IMO Circular Letter No. 2337 (31 Aug. 2001); Note No. 110 (2 Sept. 2001) to UNHCR.

[120] Mr Skogmo (Norway): UN doc. A/AC.96/SR.549, para. 8 (2000).

[121] UNHCR, 'Note on International Protection', UN doc. A/AC.96/989 (7 Jul. 2004), para. 25; see also UNHCR, 'Note on International Protection', UN doc. A/AC.96/975 (2 Jul. 2003), para. 13.

[122] UNHCR, 'Note on International Protection', UN doc. A/AC.96/989 (7 Jul. 2004), para. 25.

[123] UNHCR, 'Note on International Protection', UN doc. A/AC.96/951 (13 Sept. 2001), para. 11.

[124] Ms Feller (UNHCR, Department of International Protection): UN doc. A/AC.96/SR.548, para. 78 (2000).   [125] Mr Uluçevik (Turkey): UN doc. A/AC.96/SR.518, para. 72 (1997).

[126] Mr Sungar (Turkey): UN doc. A/AC.96/SR.554, para. 36 (2001); see also Mr Sungar (Turkey): UN doc. A/AC.96/SR.563, para. 48 (2002).

[127] Mr Lubbers (High Commissioner): UN doc. A/AC.96/SR.561, para. 22 (2002).

[128] Ms Kunadi (India): UN doc. A/AC.96/SR.554, para. 38 (2001).

Where States claim not to be bound by any obligation, their arguments either dispute the status of the individuals in question, or invoke exceptions to the principle of *non-refoulement*, particularly on the basis of threats to national security. Such considerations were dominant in the March/April 1995 decision by Tanzania to close its border to Rwandan refugees;[129] in the *refoulement* of Rwandans carried out by Zaire in the following September; and in Turkey's response to Kurdish refugees in the aftermath of the first Gulf War.[130] It is in this vein that accusations of *refoulement* have been strongly refuted in the Executive Committee. In response to an Eritrean allegation that its nationals had been deported by Ethiopia, the Ethiopian delegation stated that it 'in fact abided strictly by the principles of international law, despite the challenge it was facing'.[131] While admitting that it had closed borders, the Congolese representative sought to blame UNHCR for failings in its own protection duties, rather than attempting to justify *refoulement*.[132]

States may deny the 'refugee' character of a flow in an effort to justify non-admittance or removal, even though an objective assessment based on international standards may disclose a violation of the principle of *non-refoulement*.[133] For example, the Tanzanian representative said that his State 'had always admitted genuine refugees and asylum-seekers, but it was not prepared to make concessions to illegal immigrants, wherever they were from', citing its right as a sovereign State to determine whom it admitted.[134] Similarly, the observer for Myanmar, while confirming Myanmar's respect for the principle of *non-refoulement*,[135] argued that '[e]very State was free to legislate as it wished on the question of economic immigration and ... international activities to help refugees and displaced persons should respect the sovereignty of States'.[136] Furthermore, even though he recognized the need to support 'illegal and irregular migrants on humanitarian grounds and international protection for the poor and vulnerable', he regarded stricter immigration policies as justified because of the difficulties of distinguishing between 'genuine refugees' and abusers of the asylum system.[137] Bhutan has steadfastly refused to recognize the refugee character of Bhutanese refugees in Nepal, instead describing them as illegal economic migrants who forfeited their citizenship when they voluntarily left Bhutan.[138] This has serious implications for their

---

[129] Kiley, S., 'Tanzania closes border to 100,000 Rwanda refugees', *The Times*, 1 Apr. 1995.

[130] See above, nn. 93, 94 and accompanying texts.

[131] Ms Tesfaye (Ethiopia): UN doc. A/AC.96/SR.529, para. 49 (1998).

[132] Mr Mbaya (Democratic Republic of Congo): UN doc. A/AC.96/SR.519, para. 84 (1997).

[133] Durieux and McAdam argue that denying the character of a flow may be counter-productive, since it may frustrate attempts at enlisting international solidarity, although the influxes from Indo-China, Bosnia, and Kosovo show that this is not always the case: Durieux, J.-F. & McAdam, J., '*Non-Refoulement* through Time: The Case for a Derogation Clause to the Refugee Convention in Mass Influx Emergencies', 16 *IJRL* 4, 7 (2004).

[134] Mr Khatib (United Republic of Tanzania): UN doc. A/AC.96/SR.563, para. 30 (2002).

[135] U Saw Tun (Observer for Myanmar): UN doc. A/AC.96/SR.556, para. 21 (2001).

[136] U Zaw Tun (Observer for Myanmar): UN doc. A/AC.96/SR.547, para. 31 (2000).

[137] U Saw Tun (Observer for Myanmar): UN doc. A/AC.96/SR.556, para. 21 (2001).

[138] Mr Lohani (Observer for Nepal): UN doc. A/AC.96/SR.508, para. 30 (1996); Mr Thinley (Observer for Bhutan): UN doc. A/A.96/SR.510, paras. 96–97 (1996); see also Mr Kesang (Observer

repatriation. Nepal noted the improbability that 'almost one sixth of the population of a country should voluntarily choose within a short period of time to renounce the safety and security of home and society in exchange for an uncertain future in a refugee camp in a foreign country'.[139]

Perhaps the most significant questioning of the principle of *non-refoulement* remains that which occurred in the Sub-Committee of the Whole on International Protection in 1989, when the US representative attempted to establish some of the groundwork for its domestic litigation strategy in support of Haitian interdiction. Despite earlier US declarations of support for the principle of 'first asylum',[140] the US delegate sought to distinguish between legally binding obligations and non-binding 'generally-accepted moral and political principles of refugee protection'.[141] The United States, he said, did not believe that countries had a legal obligation 'to admit persons seeking asylum':

As a matter of practice, the United States authorities did not return persons who were likely to be persecuted in their countries of origin . . . That was the practice, and . . . the policy of the United States, and not a principle of international law with which it conformed . . . It did not consider that the *non-refoulement* obligation under article 33 of the Convention included an obligation to admit an asylum seeker. The obligation . . . pertained only to persons already in the country and not to those who arrived at the frontier or who were travelling with the intention of entering the country but had not yet arrived at their destination. Furthermore, there was nothing to suggest that an obligation to admit asylum seekers had ripened into a rule of customary international law.[142]

The intervention, which attracted no support or comment from other States, was clearly drafted with the Haitian interdiction programme in mind; equally clearly, it failed to notice that *non-refoulement* is not so much about *admission* to a State, as about not returning refugees to where their lives or freedom may be endangered. It was also inconsistent with US support for the principle of first asylum, declared earlier in the same session, and even repeated in the same intervention.[143]

for Bhutan): UN doc. A/AC.96/SR.548, para. 7 (2000). For an academic analysis of the Bhutanese refugee situation, see Tang Lay Lee, 'Refugees from Bhutan: Nationality, Statelessness and the Right to Return', 10 *IJRL* 118 (1998); Saul, B., 'Cultural Nationalism, Self-Determination and Human Rights in Bhutan' 12 *IJRL* 321 (2000). For a long time, Côte d'Ivoire officially rejected the notion of 'refugees' and termed them 'brothers in distress': Mr N'Goran (Observer for Côte d'Ivoire): UN doc. A/A.96/SR.511, para. 47 (1996). Similarly, Nigeria refused to recognize Nigerian Ogoni refugees in Benin as such: Mrs Oko (Nigeria): UN doc. A/AC.96/SR.513, para. 18 (1996). Vietnam denied that certain of its nationals in China were 'refugees': Mr Le Lon Minh (Observer for Vietnam): UN doc. A/AC.96/SR.522, para. 76 (1997); Myanmar describes the majority of its nationals in Thailand as 'economic migrants looking for better job opportunities and higher wages': U Denzil Abel (Observer for Myanmar): UN doc. A/AC.96/SR.530, para. 37 (1998); U Zaw Tun (Observer for Myanmar): UN doc. A/AC.96/SR.547, para. 31 (2000).

[139] Mr Lohani (Observer for Nepal): UN doc. A/AC.96/SR.508, para. 30 (1996).

[140] See above, n. 84 and text. The concern of the United States to defend the principle of first asylum was motivated in particular by practices in South East Asia, where Indo-Chinese boat people were not infrequently denied access to coastal States, placed back on board ships returning to their country of origin, or towed out to sea, often with resulting loss of life.

[141] Mr Kelley (USA): UN doc. A/AC.96/SR.442, paras. 78–9 (1989).

[142] Ibid., paras. 80, 82.   [143] Ibid., para. 81.

Ultimately, however, this strategic departure from the accepted meaning of *non-refoulement* came too late to alter the obligations of the United States under international law.[144] Similarly, Australia's response to the Tampa crisis in 2001 attracted no support from other States, and consequently had no effect on the established scope of the principle of *non-refoulement* under international law.[145]

In 1996, the International Council of Voluntary Agencies objected strongly to a statement apparently made by the United States that *non-refoulement* was only a 'humanitarian principle'.[146] The Council observed that it was 'regrettable that the importance of the legal obligation which prohibited the refoulement of a refugee was being minimized'.[147] Perhaps as a result of the condemnation, in 1997 the United States affirmed its commitment to the principle of *non-refoulement*: 'The first principle and priority for both UNHCR and the international community should be to make every effort to work together with countries of asylum to ensure that respect for the principle of non-refoulement, which the United States was prepared to support, both in public and in private, in the strongest possible terms.'[148]

In the past decade, no State in the Executive Committee has sought to justify *refoulement*, and States have repeatedly reiterated their commitment to and respect for the principle of *non-refoulement*.[149] By 1997, Denmark regarded the principle as applying to States that were not yet party to the Convention or Protocol.[150]

---

[144] See further below, s. 3.3.1.   [145] For discussion of the *Tampa* incident, see s. 4.3 below.

[146] The meeting records, which are not a verbatim account of proceedings, do not indicate such a clear statement having been made, but note instead the US' reference to States' 'legal and moral responsibility to protect persons in danger'. It may be that in discussion, the United States emphasized the *moral* nature of the responsibility rather than its binding legal nature.

[147] Mr van Bernuth (International Council of Voluntary Agencies): UN doc. A/AC.96/SR.513, para. 2 (1996).   [148] Ms Oakley (United States): UN doc. A/AC.96/SR.516, para. 53 (1997).

[149] Mr Vergne Saboia (Brazil): UN doc. A/AC.96/SR.508, para. 34 (1996); Mr Abalo (Observer for Benin): UN doc. A/A.96/SR.511, para. 26 (1996); Ms Meng (China): UN doc. A/AC.96/SR.518, para. 51 (1997); Mr Uluçevik (Turkey): UN doc. A/AC.96/SR.518, para. 71 (1997); Mr van Wulfften Palthe (Netherlands): UN doc. A/AC.96/SR.526, para. 4 (1998); Ms Haaland Matlary (Norway): UN doc. A/AC.96/SR.526, para. 31 (1998); Mr Höynck (Germany): UN doc. A/AC.96/SR.526, para. 56 (1998); Mr Manning (United Kingdom): UN doc. A/AC.96/SR.527, para. 9 (1998); Ms Fahlén (Sweden): UN doc. A/AC.96/SR.527, para. 34 (1998); Mr Thlomeland (South Africa): UN doc. A/AC.96/SR.530, para. 56 (1998); Mr Irumba (Observer for Uganda): UN doc. A/AC.96/SR.532, para. 11 (1998); Mr Ruddock (Australia): UN doc. A/AC.96/SR.545, para. 10 (2000); Ms Klingvall (Sweden): UN doc. A/AC.96/SR.545, para. 19 (2000); Ms Negru (Observer for the Republic of Moldova): UN doc. A/AC.96/SR.547, para. 47 (2000); Mr Noirfalisse (Belgium): UN doc. A/AC.96/SR.552, para. 50 (2001); Mr Duque (Brazil): UN doc. A/AC.96/SR.555, para. 16 (2001); Mr Castrillon (Observer for Ecuador): UN doc. A/AC.96/SR.555, para. 52 (2001); U Saw Tun (Observer for Myanmar): UN doc. A/AC.96/SR.556, para. 21 (2001); Mr Prasad (India): UN doc. A/AC.96/SR.558, para. 3 (2001); Mr Chiaradia (Argentina): UN doc. A/AC.96/SR.562, para. 62 (2002); Mr Puri (India): UN doc. A/AC.96/SR.563, para. 61 (2002); Mr Rodríguez Cedeño (Venezuela): UN doc. A/AC.96/SR.563, para. 70 (2002); Mr Macedo (Mexico): UN doc. A/AC.96/SR.564, para. 46 (2002); Mr Gabriels (Nigeria): UN doc. A/AC.96/SR.566, para. 15 (2002); Ms Raoul (Observer for the Congo): UN doc. A/AC.96/R.581, para. 97 (2004).

[150] Mr McNamara (UNHCR, Department of International Protection): UN doc. A/AC.96/SR.522, para. 65 (1997).

Belgium echoed this view in 2001,[151] and Thailand—a non-signatory State—expressed its understanding that 'in line with the principle of *non-refoulement*, asylum countries were under an obligation to allow all refugees and displaced persons to enter their territory notwithstanding their limited resources and underdeveloped infrastructure'.[152]

Although States continued to express strong rhetorical support for the principle of *non-refoulement*, UNHCR observed their increasing reluctance to openly condemn other governments for violations of the principle. From late March 1999, the Former Yugoslavian Republic of Macedonia periodically closed its borders to large numbers of refugees seeking to leave Kosovo,[153] in some cases using violence to prevent border crossings.[154] These acts of *refoulement* were protested by the United Kingdom and the Netherlands as breaches of international law, and initially also by UNHCR, although UNHCR framed its opposition in terms of a failure to admit asylum seekers to the territory rather than expressly invoking the principle of *non-refoulement*.[155] At the 1999 Executive Committee meetings, Canada objected to border closures generally, but refrained from mentioning Macedonia.[156]

During the 1990s, some of the most serious instances of large-scale *refoulement* occurred in the Great Lakes of Africa, yet very few States publicly protested against them at the annual Executive Committee meetings. One of the strongest protests came from the Irish delegation in 1997, which was 'deeply concerned' by the violation of the principle of *non-refoulement* by the Democratic Republic of Congo. The delegation acknowledged the 'pain and complexity' of the Great Lakes context, but argued that 'the international community could not fail to speak out when Governments violated their obligations under international law if it was not

---

[151] Mr Noirfalisse (Belgium): UN doc. A/AC.96/SR.552, para. 50 (2001).

[152] Mr Futrakul (Thailand): UN doc. A/AC.96/SR.554, para. 60 (2001).

[153] Within five days of the NATO bombings, 130,000 Albanians had fled Kosovo; nine weeks later, 860,000 people had fled: see Suhrke, A., Barutciski, M., Sandison, P. & Garlock, R., *The Kosovo Refugee Crisis: An Independent Evaluation of UNHCR's Emergency Preparedness and Response* (UNHCR, Geneva, Feb. 2000) para. 31. For a critique of that report, see European Council on Refugees and Exiles (ECRE), 'The Kosovo Refugee Crisis: ECRE's Observations on the Independent Evaluation of UNHCR's Emergency Preparedness and Response' <http://www.ecre.org/statements/koseval.shtml>. More generally, see Independent International Commission on Kosovo, *Kosovo Report: Conflict, International Response, Lessons Learned* (2000).

[154] See Amnesty International, *Former Yugoslav Republic of Macedonia: The Protection of Kosovo Albanian Refugees* (1999) (AI Index EUR 65/03/99).

[155] Coleman, '*Non-Refoulement* Revised', above n. 96, 38, citing Suhrke, Barutciski, Sandison, & Garlock, *The Kosovo Refugee Crisis*, above n. 153. Coleman's references do not match the publicly available version of this report; see paras. 447–50. See also House of Commons Select Committee on International Development, *Kosovo: The Humanitarian Crisis* (3rd Report, 1999), HC 422, para. 79.

[156] Mr Dorais (Canada): UN doc. A/AC.96/SR.535, para. 42 (1999). Amnesty International suggested that '[t]he rush of the international community to evacuate refugees as soon as possible tacitly accept[ed]' this Macedonian position': Amnesty International, *Former Yugoslav Republic of Macedonia: The Protection of Kosovo Albanian Refugees* (1999) (AI Index EUR 65/03/99), s. 5.5.

to erode the fundamental human rights and humanitarian principles which were the bedrock of policy'.[157]

The Director of UNHCR's Department of International Protection acknowledged that the lack of formal protests to *refoulement* in the Great Lakes may have stemmed from the politicized context of that particular refugee situation, but also 'perhaps because the domestic refugee policies of many States fell short of international standards'.[158] Although, as a matter of customary international law, States' failure to protest against breaches of international law may indicate acquiescence,[159] the institutional role of UNHCR complicates this traditional model. Given the political sensitivity of many refugee flows, States may be more inclined to give tacit support to UNHCR's condemnation of breaches of *non-refoulement*, and certainly no State has protested against its actions in this regard. Given UNHCR's responsibility to provide protection and to oversee the application of refugee law, it can be assumed to act on behalf of the international community. Where States fail to protest openly at breaches of the principle of *non-refoulement*, they should not necessarily be viewed as acquiescing in such breach, particularly where UNHCR does so protest.

This view is supported by the positions in fact adopted by States. For example, the Norwegian delegation's deep concern at 'UNHCR reports of violations of the principle of protection in various regions'[160] reflects a general reticence by States formally to to label other governments' acts as *refoulement*. Similarly, Sweden expressed great concern at 'reports of continuing deportations of Afghan refugees [by Iran] to areas where their safety could not be guaranteed',[161] and Ireland described the systematic expulsion of whole populations from East Timor and Kosovo as a violation of human rights and humanitarian law.[162] In 2001, the Swiss representative at the Executive Committee meetings stated that Afghanistan's international borders should not be closed.[163]

Even though States have not always protested specific cases of *refoulement*, they have consistently maintained a position of respect for and commitment to the principle of *non-refoulement*. No State claims that *refoulement* is permissible under international law, but instead will go to great lengths to characterize instances of return as standard immigration control, as exclusion, or as not involving refugees. For example, there are few recorded protests to the instances of *refoulement* by Croatia in 1992, and most of those on record were by non-governmental organizations

---

Ms Anderson (Ireland): UN doc. A/AC.96/SR.518, para. 4 (1997).

Mr McNamara (UNHCR): UN doc. A/AC.96/SR.522, para. 57 (1997).

Brownlie, I., *Principles of Public International Law*, (6th edn., 2003), 8, 11–12; International Law Association, 'Statement of Principles Applicable to the Formation of General Customary International Law', *Report of the 69th Conference*, (2000), 734ff; see also International Law Association, Res. No. 16/2000, *Report of the 69th Conference*, (2000), 39.

Ms Haaland Matlary (Norway): UN doc. A/AC.96/SR.526, para. 31 (1998).

Ms Andersson (Sweden): UN doc. A/AC.96/SR.536, para. 1 (1999).

Ms Anderson (Ireland): UN doc. A/AC.96/SR.537, para. 24 (1999).

Mr Maurer (Switzerland): UN doc. A/AC.96/SR.554, para. 12 (2001).

rather than States.[164] UNHCR was hesitant to criticize Croatia, perhaps because it hosted large numbers of refugees during the crisis, and also because UNHCR sought to focus on practical solutions rather than principle, referring to the 'refusal of admission', rather than to *refoulement*.[165]

2.5.2 *State practice: some aspects*[166]

Despite States' continued support for the principle of *non-refoulement* as a corner-stone of the international protection regime, State practice does not always conform with international law. There have been frequent violations of the principle,[167] well documented by human rights organizations such as the US Committee for Refugees and Immigrants, Amnesty International and Human Rights Watch.

UNHCR has repeatedly stressed that failures in protection stem not from the international protection regime itself, but rather from 'the persistent failure of States to respect treaty obligations'.[168] The problem is one of implementation, not standards.[169] In this regard, the US delegate to the Executive Committee stated that when protection principles are not upheld by governments, 'the response should not be to lower them, but jointly to seek ways of bringing practice into line with them'.[170]

In 1997, the International Council of Voluntary Agencies noted breaches of the *non-refoulement* principle by Congo (in respect of Rwandan asylum seekers); Thailand and Bangladesh (in respect of asylum seekers from Myanmar); and Panama (in respect of Colombian asylum seekers).[171] In the same year, the High Commissioner emphasized that the expulsion of Rwandan refugees from the Goma area and violations of other human rights and humanitarian principles 'did not imply a need to revise basic principles', but that the foundational principle of *non-refoulement* and the right of refugees to asylum 'must be implemented in constructive, realistic and creative ways that took account of the legitimate concerns of States'.[172]

In the former Yugoslavia, refugees were often summarily removed,[173] but one of the most serious refugee crises of the 1990s occurred in the Great Lakes region of Africa. The Rwandan genocide in 1994 led to a mass influx of refugees into

---

[164] See Coleman, '*Non-Refoulement* Revised', above n. 96, 31–3. Coleman notes that none of the major UN conferences at the time commented on Croatia's border closures and forced returns.

[165] Ibid., 50.

[166] This section, which should be read in conjunction with s. 2.5.1, focuses on State practice since 1997; for earlier practice, see the 2nd edition of this work.

[167] See generally US Committee for Refugees and Immigrants, *World Refugee Survey* (all years).

[168] Mr McNamara (UNHCR): UN doc. A/AC.96/SR.522, para. 57 (1997).

[169] Ibid., para. 61.

[170] Ms Oakley (United States): UN doc. A/AC.96/SR.522, para. 85 (1997).

[171] Ms Makundi (International Council of Voluntary Agencies): UN doc. A/AC.96/SR.522, para. 30 (1997).

[172] Mrs Ogata (High Commissioner): UN doc. A/AC.96/SR.516, paras. 27–8 (1997).

[173] UNHCR, 'Note on International Protection', UN doc. A/AC.96/882 (2 Jul. 1997), para. 8.

Tanzania and Zaire, with significant security problems due to former soldiers and those guilty of genocide infiltrating refugee camps.[174] In its 1998 Note on International Protection, UNHCR reflected on a number of serious instances of large-scale *refoulement* in the Great Lakes region which took place, despite protests by States and UNHCR. In one instance, 4,400 refugees were expelled over a three-month period; in another, 2,000 were removed.[175] Significantly, however, the Tanzanian authorities maintained their support for the importance of the principle of *non-refoulement*, arguing that those expelled 'were not refugees', but illegal aliens or former refugees whose status has ceased.[176] At other times, they sought to excuse removals on the basis that local officials misunderstood national policy.[177] This persistent 're-characterization' supports the argument that violating States are *not* seeking to develop a counter-norm of customary international law to challenge the fundamental principle of *non-refoulement*.[178]

Since early 2003, conflict and human rights abuses in western Sudan have caused mass displacement.[179] In April 2005, two-and-a-half million people were affected by the conflict, and close to two million of them were internally displaced.[180]

UNHCR commended Chad's full respect for the principle of *non-refoulement* during a mass influx in 2004, but also noted serious cases of rejection at the frontier and forced removals by some other States. For example, in early 2004 UNHCR requested States in the Americas to stop forcibly returning people who had fled an outbreak of violence in their country of origin and provide them with temporary protection.[181] In 2005, UNHCR expressed grave concerns about the fate of asylum seekers from Africa and the Middle East arriving in southern Europe, who faced deportation to unsafe destinations and a real risk of persecution.[182] In particular, it was deeply concerned about the fate of asylum seekers arriving on the Italian island of Lampedusa, given reports of mass repatriations to Libya in October 2004 without individual claims for protection being considered or access to UNHCR being provided. The Italian government defended its actions, arguing that it was confronted with a 'humanitarian crisis'. It denied that it had engaged in 'expulsion', instead describing the returns as 'a refusal of entry at the border, which is in accordance with international law'.[183] Furthermore, it

---

[174] Chairman: UN doc. A/AC.96/SR.516, para. 15 (1997).

[175] UNHCR, 'Note on International Protection', UN doc. A/AC.96/898 (3 Jul. 1998), para. 13.

[176] US Committee for Refugees and Immigrants, *World Refugee Survey*, Tanzania (1998).

[177] US Committee for Refugees and Immigrants, *World Refugee Survey*, Tanzania (2000).

[178] Cf. Hathaway, J. C., *The Rights of Refugees under International Law*, (2005), 364, and further discussion below.

[179] See *Report of the International Commission of Inquiry on Darfur to the United Nations Secretary-General*, (25 Jan. 2005).

[180] UNHCR, 'Note on International Protection', UN doc. A/AC.96/1008 (4 Jul. 2005), para. 4.

[181] UNHCR, 'Note on International Protection', UN doc. A/AC.96/989 (7 Jul. 2004), para. 11.

[182] UNHCR, 'Note on International Protection', UN doc A/AC.96/1008 (4 Jul. 2005), para. 28.

[183] Comments of R. Buttiglione (5 Oct. 2004) and Minister of the Interior, G. Pisanu, cited in Migration Policy Group, 'Migration News Sheet', (Nov. 2004), 12.

stated that such removals were necessary to cope with threats of terrorism, and particular vigilance was required with respect to 'clandestine immigrants coming from the Horn of Africa, where al-Qaeda is well established, and those from the sub-Saharan zone where Islamic extremism is undergoing rapid growth'.[184] The Libyan Minister of the Interior confirmed that over 1,000 Egyptians had been expelled from Italy via Libya to Egypt, funded by the Italian government.[185] The International Council of Voluntary Agencies further condemned Italy's deportation of asylum seekers to the Libyan Arab Jamahiriya. It expressed grave concern at European plans to 'effectively cordon off the Mediterranean to asylum seekers and migrants and to keep them in processing centres in North Africa',[186] arguing that this would undermine the international protection regime and violate principles of responsibility-sharing.

Border closures,[187] deporting refugees for breaching conditions,[188] summary removals, and an absence of effective procedures to screen asylum seekers can also result in *refoulement*. In July 2005, Cambodia forcibly deported 100 Montagnard refugees to Vietnam. The United States raised objections with the governments of Cambodia and Vietnam, expressing disappointment 'that these individuals were repatriated before an internationally staffed monitoring program was in place in the Central Highlands of Vietnam and before other solutions could be considered for these individuals'.[189] In 2004, South Africa deported around 50,000 undocumented Zimbabweans without proper asylum screening, with NGOs accusing the government of setting unfairly high thresholds for asylum seekers coming from Zimbabwe. Tanzania similarly deported 90 Burundians in October 2004 without asylum screening.[190] In 2003, Malaysia forcibly returned more than 600 Indonesian Acehnese, including many who had been recognized as refugees by UNHCR.[191] Since 1986, China has had a treaty arrangement with North Korea by which it agrees to return 'defectors'. Although for a number of years China informally tolerated the presence of North Koreans, in 1999 it began returning large numbers of them, claiming that they were not refugees but 'food migrants'.[192]

---

[184] Comments of Minister of the Interior, G. Pisanu, ibid.

[185] Comments of Libyan Minister of the Interior, N. Al-Mabruk, ibid., 13.

[186] Mr Schenkenberg van Mierop (International Council of Voluntary Agencies): UN doc. A/AC.96/SR.585, para. 10 (2004).

[187] In 2004, Jordan declared its border closed to new refugees. Although immigration officers were stationed at 114 airports and borders in the Russian Federation, not one person was granted asylum in 2004 and no appeals were permitted: US Committee for Refugees and Immigrants, *World Refugee Survey* (2005). In 2003, Tanzania closed certain border crossing points, denying access to new asylum seekers, and Iran summarily deported people arriving at the border: US Committee for Refugees and Immigrants, *World Refugee Survey* (2004).

[188] Tanzania deported refugees found outside camp areas: US Committee for Refugees and Immigrants, *World Refugee Survey* (2005).

[189] Statement by White House Deputy Spokesman Adam Ereli (20 Jul. 2005), cited in International Commission of Jurists Media Release (8 Sept. 2005).

[190] US Committee for Refugees and Immigrants, *World Refugee Survey* (2005).

[191] Ibid., (2004).　　　[192] Ibid., (2003).

By 2004, China had removed at least 5,000 North Koreans, and was reported as permitting North Korean security forces periodically to enter China to abduct refugees.[193] In a US Senate Sub-Committee hearing, the US Committee for Refugees and Immigrants argued that 'China is attempting to simply define the North Koreans out of the [1951] Convention'.[194]

In light of cases such as these, UNHCR has welcomed the initiative by some States to engage in joint monitoring and screening agreements in unsettled border areas as alternatives to summary deportations,[195] and formal readmission agreements as an alternative to summary removals.[196]

UNHCR has reiterated that even in large-scale influxes of asylum seekers, there must be proper procedures for assessing status.[197] This requires political commitment by the receiving State as well as international cooperation with transit countries, and countries of origin, as envisaged by the EU Hague Programme's proposed 'regional protection programmes'.[198] UNHCR has noted that '[v]ery many countries, including many which have seen significant increases in the arrivals of refugees and asylum-seekers and others with large, longstanding refugee populations continue to respect the principle [of *non-refoulement*].[199] Indeed, despite serious concerns about the economic, environmental, and, at times social impact of mass refugee influxes on the local community, many States continued an open-door asylum policy by accepting large numbers of refugees on to their territory.[200] States which did not appear to respect the principle of *non-refoulement*, either by denying entry to or forcibly returning people arriving in large influxes, sought to excuse their behaviour by invoking their lack of resources, threats to national security, and fears of political destabilization.[201] While such concerns may be bona fide, the international protection regime provides the basis for a response grounded in responsibility sharing and the rule of law, rather than *refoulement*.

3. The scope of the principle of *non-refoulement*

3.1 PERSONAL SCOPE

The principle of *non-refoulement*, as it appears in article 33 of the 1951 Convention, applies clearly and categorically to refugees within the meaning of article 1. It also applies to *asylum seekers*, at least during an initial period and in appropriate circumstances, for otherwise there would be no effective protection. Those with a

---

[193] Ibid., (2005).   [194] Ibid., (2003).

[195] UNHCR 'Note on International Protection', UN doc. A/AC.96/951 (2001), para. 19.

[196] Ibid., para. 21.

[197] UNHCR, 'Note on International Protection', UN doc A/AC.96/1008 (4 Jul. 2005), para. 28.

[198] Ibid., para. 29.

[199] UNHCR, 'Note on International Protection', UN doc. A/AC.96/951, para. 16.

[200] For example, Iran, Iraq, Nepal, Côte d'Ivoire, Thailand, and Kenya.

[201] UNHCR, 'Note on International Protection', UN doc. A/AC.96/951, para. 18; Türk, V., 'Forced Migration and Security', 15 *IJRL* 113, 115 (2003).

presumptive or prima facie claim to refugee status are therefore entitled to protection, as the UNHCR Executive Committee has stressed, for example, in Conclusion No. 6 (1977), reaffirming 'the fundamental importance of the principle of *non-refoulement*... irrespective of whether or not individuals have been formally recognized as refugees'.[202] This has also been affirmed by the General Assembly.[203]

Equally irrelevant is the legal or migration status of the asylum seeker. It does not matter *how* the asylum seeker comes within the territory or jurisdiction of the State; what counts is what results from the actions of State agents once he or she does. If the asylum seeker is forcibly repatriated to a country in which he or she has a well-founded fear of persecution or faces a substantial risk of torture, then that is *refoulement* contrary to international law.

The status or personal circumstances of the asylum seeker, however, may control the options open to the receiving State. In the case of a stowaway asylum seeker, for example, the port of call State may require the ship's master to keep him or her on board and travel on to the next port of call; or it may call upon the flag State to assume responsibility where the next port of call is unacceptable; or it may allow temporary disembarkation pending resettlement elsewhere. Thus, by itself, a categorical refusal of disembarkation can only be equated with *refoulement* if it actually results in the return of refugees to persecution. Similar considerations apply also to rescue-at-sea cases seeking disembarkation, and even to boats of asylum seekers arriving directly. From a practical perspective, however, a refusal to take account of their claims to be refugees would not suffice to avoid liability for breach of the principle of *non-refoulement*.[204]

3.1.1 *The question of risk*

The legal, and to some extent logical, relationship between article 33(1) and article 1 of the 1951 Convention/1967 Protocol is evident in the correlation established in State practice, where entitlement to the protection of *non-refoulement* is conditioned simply upon satisfying the well-founded fear criterion. So far as the drafters of the 1951 Convention were aware of a divergence between the words defining refugee status and those requiring *non-refoulement*, they gave little thought to the consequences. Mr Rochefort, the French representative, suggested that article 1 referred to examination at the frontier of those wishing to enter a contracting State, whereas article 33 was concerned with provisions applicable at a later stage. The co-existence of these two possibilities was perfectly feasible, though he detected a distinct and somewhat uncomfortable inconsistency between article 33(1) and article 1.[205] This related not to the presence of conflicting standards of proof, however, or to issues of extraterritorial application, but to

[202] See also Executive Committee Conclusion No. 79 (1996), No. 81 (1997) and No. 82 (1997).
[203] UNGA res. 52/103 (12 Dec. 1997), para. 5.   [204] See further below, s. 4.
[205] United Nations Conference of Plenipotentiaries, *Summary Records*: UN doc. A/CONF.2/SR.35, 23 (1951).

the class and extent of those, principally criminals, who were to be excluded from refugee status and/or denied the benefit of *non-refoulement*.

The intimate link between articles 1 and 33 was nevertheless recognized;[206] in both, the status of 'refugee' was to be governed by the criterion of well-founded fear, and withdrawal of status or *refoulement* would always be exceptional and restricted.[207] The *travaux préparatoires* do not explain the different wording chosen for the formulations respectively of refugee status and *non-refoulement*; but neither do they give any indication that a different standard of proof was intended to be applied in one case, rather than in the other. In practice, the same standard is accepted at both national and international levels, reflecting the sufficiency of serious risk, rather than any more onerous standard of proof, such as the clear probability of persecution.[208]

At the international level, no distinction is recognized between refugee status and entitlement to *non-refoulement*. In only one instance were articles 1 and 33, as a coherent structure of protection, severed by a judicial ruling on literal meaning; and on that occasion, the executive branch of government took steps by regulation to bridge the gap between the refugee eligible for the discretionary grant of asylum and the refugee with a right to the benefit of *non-refoulement*.[209] The relation of refugee status and *non-refoulement* was described more coherently by the UK House of Lords in 1987, in *R. v. Secretary of State for the Home Department, ex p. Sivakumaran*:

It is... plain, as indeed was reinforced in argument... with reference to the travaux préparatoires, that the *non-refoulement* provision in article 33 was intended to apply to all persons determined to be refugees under article 1 of the Convention.[210]

Non-refoulement extends in principle, therefore, to every individual who has a well-founded fear of persecution, or where there are substantial grounds for believing that he or she would be in danger of torture, inhuman or degrading treatment or punishment if returned to a particular country.

3.2 EXCEPTIONS TO THE PRINCIPLE OF *NON-REFOULEMENT*

The Convention refugee definition is not an absolute guarantee of protection, and *non-refoulement* in article 33 is not an absolute principle.[211] 'National security'

---

[206] UN doc. A/CONF.2/SR.35, 22 (1951).   [207] UN doc. A/CONF.2/SR.16, 4, (1951).

[208] Support for the principle of serious risk as the determinant for refugee status and consequently also for *non-refoulement*, can be found in numerous national decisions; see above, Ch. 3, s. 3.

[209] See the US Supreme Court decisions in *INS* v. *Stevic*, 467 US 407 (1984) and *INS* v. *Cardoza-Fonseca* 480 US 421 (1987); for comment, see 2 *IJRL* 461–7 (1990). The remedy was provided by the *Final Rule on Asylum and Withholding of Deportation Procedures*, issued by the US Department of Justice Immigration and Naturalization Service in July 1990.

[210] [1989] 1 AC 958, 1001 (Lord Goff). UNHCR submitted an intervenor brief.

[211] For discussion of the absolute prohibition on return to torture or cruel, inhuman or degrading treatment or punishment, see Ch. 6.

and 'public order', for example, have long been recognized as potential justifications for derogation.[212] Article 33(2) expressly provides that the benefit of *non-
refoulement* may not be claimed by a refugee, 'whom there are reasonable grounds
for regarding as a danger to the security of the country . . . or who, having been
convicted by a final judgment of a particularly serious crime, constitutes a danger
to the community of that country'.[213] The exceptions to *non-refoulement* are thus
framed in terms of the individual, and whether he or she may be considered a
security risk is necessarily left very much to the judgement of the State authorities.[214] This, at least, was the intention of the British representative at the 1951
Conference, who proposed the inclusion of article 33(2), and such an approach to
security cases is supported both by article 32(2) of the Convention and by immigration law and practice generally.[215]

The inherent nature of *national* security, considered within a community of
'sovereign' States, means that the concept remains undefined in international law,
although its area of operation can be inferred, to some extent, from the right of
every State freely to choose its political, economic, social, and cultural system, to its
prima facie exclusive competence in the 'reserved domain of domestic jurisdiction',

---

[212] See, for example, art. 3, 1933 Convention relating to the International Status of Refugees: 159
LNTS 199; art. 5(2), 1938 Convention concerning the Status of Refugees coming from Germany:
192 *LNTS* 59. At the first session of the *Ad hoc* Committee, the British delegate suggested that *non-
refoulement* should not apply when national security was involved: UN doc. E/AC.32/SR.20, paras.
10–12. In the context of 'public order', the French representative had suggested limiting 'protected
opinions' to those not contrary to the purposes and principles of the United Nations: ibid., paras. 8,
19. Several States thought this a too drastic qualification: Belgium, Israel and the United States: ibid.,
paras. 13, 15, 16, and generally, while others remained concerned to protect public order, even if the
concept were somewhat ambiguous: cf. Venezuela: ibid., paras. 38–43. The concept of public order
was discussed further at the second session; see UN doc. E/AC.32/SR.40, 10–30 (1950); *Report* of
the *Ad hoc* Committee: UN doc. E/AC.32/8, para. 29.

[213] Although 'security' is mentioned in arts. 9, 28, 32, and 33 of the Convention, these provisions
do not give any indication of the content of the concept. By contrast to the exclusion clauses, a
refugee removed under art. 33(2) is not considered undeserving of protection, but rather has forfeited
the right to claim on-going protection from the host State by reason of his or her conduct. On the distinction, see, for example, *Pushpanathan* v. *Canada* [1998] 1 SCR 982, para. 58; *T* v. *Secretary of State
for the Home Dept.* [1996] 2 All ER 865; *Attorney-General* v. *Zaoui (No. 2)* [2005] 1 NZLR 690 (CA),
para. 166; *Moses Allueke*, 188981, France, Conseil d'Etat, 3 nov. 1999. The 'particularly serious
crime' in art. 33(2) must have been committed *after* the individual's admission as a refugee, otherwise
there would be an overlap with article 1F (on which, see above Ch. 4). See also Lauterpacht &
Bethlehem, '*Non-refoulement*: Opinion', above, n. 23, para. 149; Hathaway, *Rights of Refugees*,
(2005), 315; but cf. EU Qualification Directive, art. 14(4), (5), which purports to extend Member
States' discretionary competence ('Member States may . . .') to 'revoke, end or refuse to renew the status granted to a refugee' on the basis of art. 33(2) criteria, or not to grant status where a decision has
not yet been taken. As noted above in Ch. 4, art.14(6) of the Qualification Directive lays down a minimal 'status' for those to whom art. 33(2) CSR5I applies.

[214] The reference to 'reasonable grounds' was interpreted by one representative at the 1951
Conference as allowing States to determine whether there were sufficient grounds for regarding the
refugee as a danger and whether the danger likely to be encountered by the refugee on *refoulement* was
outweighed by the threat to the community: UN doc. A/CONF.2/SR.16, 8 (1951).

[215] See Goodwin-Gill, *Movement of Persons*, above, n. 2, 241–2, 247–50. Hathaway takes a different approach to this issue: *Rights of Refugees*, (2005), above n. 20, 354–5.

and to its right to use force in self-defence. Grahl-Madsen has suggested the following approach to 'security':

If a person is engaged in activities aiming at facilitating the conquest of the country where he is staying or a part of the country, by another State, he is threatening the security of the former country. The same applies if he works for the overthrow of the Government of his country of residence by force or other illegal means (e.g., falsification of election results, coercion of voters, etc), or if he engages in activities which are directed against a foreign Government, which as a result threaten the Government of the country of residence with repercussions of a serious nature. Espionage, sabotage of military installations and terrorist activities are among acts which customarily are labelled as threats to national security. Generally speaking, the notion of 'national security' or 'the security of the country' is invoked against acts of a rather serious nature endangering directly or indirectly the constitution (Government), the territorial integrity, the independence or the external peace of the country concerned.[216]

In general, neither 'national security' nor 'danger to national security' are defined in legislation dealing with refugees and asylum, although there are some recent exceptions, for example where legislation links 'security' to terrorism and locates both issues in the procedures for determining refugee status and granting asylum.[217] Also, in some States, legislation specifically on national security mechanisms and agencies may indicate typical issues of concern to State authorities charged with protecting security; this in turn may give an indication of the sorts of activities which States have in mind, and allow a sense of 'danger to security' to be inferred.[218]

Article 33(2) expressly refers to a danger to the security or community of the host State. Lauterpacht and Bethlehem correctly argue that it would be inappropriate for a State to remove an individual pursuant to that provision on the grounds that he or she constituted a threat to *another* State or the international community generally.[219] Hathaway invokes to the contrary what he terms the modern approach to national security, which permits *refoulement* 'where a refugee's presence or actions give rise to an objectively reasonable, real possibility of directly or indirectly inflicted substantial harm to the host State's most basic

---

[216] Grahl-Madsen, A., *Commentary on the Refugee Convention 1951*, 236; this work, drafted in 1962–63, was published by UNHCR, Geneva, in 1997.

[217] See, for example, Migration Act 1958 (Cth) ss. 500, 502 (Australia); Immigration and Refugee Protection Act 2001 ss. 3, 34, 115 (Canada); *Ordonnance relative aux conditions d'entrée et de séjour des étrangers en France*, as amended in 2003 (Loi n° 2003–1119 2003-11-26 art. 37, J.O. 27 nov. 2003), arts. 25 bis, 28; *Loi du 25 juillet 1952 relative au droit d'asile* (as amended to the loi n° 2003–1776 du 10 décembre 2003), art. 8 (France); *Zuwanderungsgesetz*, arts. 25, 60(8) (Germany); 1998 *Loi d'asile* s. 5 (Switzerland); EU Qualification Directive, recital 28: 'The notion of national security and public order also covers cases in which a third country national belongs to an association which supports international terrorism or supports such an association.'

[218] For attempts to define 'national security' in domestic law, see Security Intelligence Organisation Act 1979 (Cth), s. 4 (Australia); Canadian Security Intelligence Service Act 1985, s. 2 (Canada), see also *Suresh v. (Minister of Citizenship and Immigration* [2002] 1 SCR 3); Security Service Act 1989, s. 1 (UK); Terrorism Act 2000, s. 1 (UK); *Loi fédérale instituant des mesures visant au maintien de la sûreté intérieure*, arts. 2–3 (RS 120: Switzerland); EU Qualification Directive, recital 28.

[219] Lauterpacht & Bethlehem, '*Non-refoulement*: Opinion', above n. 23, para. 165.

interests, including the risk of an armed attack on its territory or its citizens, or the destruction of its democratic institutions'.[220] In *Suresh*, the Supreme Court of Canada found that a risk to national security 'may be grounded in distant events that indirectly have a real possibility of harming Canadian security',[221] and, clearly influenced by the attacks of 11 September 2001 on the United States, noted that 'the security of one country is often dependent on the security of other nations'.[222] This would not necessarily require targets to be geographically located in the host State, but could extend to terrorist acts abroad which have an impact on that State's interests.[223]

Lauterpacht and Bethlehem note that States' margin of appreciation in security cases is limited by two requirements. First, the State must demonstrate 'reasonable grounds' for believing that the particular refugee is a danger to that country's security by adducing evidence of a future risk.[224] Secondly, given the serious individual consequences of *refoulement*, the threshold for establishing an exception to *non-refoulement* ought to be very high. Accordingly, only a very serious danger to national security should justify *refoulement*.[225] They draw support for their conclusion from article 1F, noting that 'since the threshold of prospective danger in Article 33(2) is higher than that in Article 1F, it would hardly be consistent with the scheme of the Convention more generally to read the term "danger" in Article 33(2) as referring to anything less than very serious danger.'[226]

It is unclear to what extent, if at all, one convicted of a particularly serious crime must *also* be shown to constitute a danger to the community. The jurisprudence is relatively sparse and the notion of a 'particularly serious crime' is not a term of art,[227] but principles of natural justice and due process of law require something more than mere mechanical application of the exception.

---

[220] Hathaway, *Rights of Refugees* (2005), above, n. 70, 346.

[221] *Suresh*, above n. 218 para. 88. Note the US view: *A-H-*, 23 *I&N Dec* 774 (AG 2005): ' "danger to the security of the United States" means any nontrivial risk to the Nation's defense, foreign relations, or economic interests'.

[222] *Suresh*, above n. 218, para. 90. See also *Secretary of State for the Home Department. v. Rehman* [2003] 1 AC 153, [2001] UKHL 47.

[223] See *Suresh*, above n. 218, para. 91; Hathaway, *Rights of Refugee*, (2005), 346; *DJ*, 23 *I&N Dec* 572 (A.G. 2003).

[224] Lauterpacht & Bethlehem, '*Non-refoulement*: Opinion', para. 168. See, for example, *A-H-*, 23 *I&N Dec* 774 (AG 2005): ' "reasonable grounds for regarding" an alien as a danger to the national security [means] there is information that would permit a reasonable person to believe that the alien may pose such a danger'.

[225] Lauterpacht & Bethlehem, '*Non-refoulement*: Opinion', para. 169.

[226] Ibid., para. 170; UNHCR, 'Guidelines on International Protection: Application of the Exclusion Clauses: Article 1F of the 1951 Convention relating to the Status of Refugees', UN doc. HCR/GIP/03/05 (4 Sept. 2003), paras. 10, 44; House of Lords/House of Commons Joint Committee on Human Rights, 'The Nationality, Immigration and Asylum Act 2002 (Specification of Particularly Serious Crimes) Order 2004' (22nd Report of Session 2003–04), paras. 19–26.

[227] With respect to the analogous terms of art. 1F(b), see above Ch.4, s. 4.2; UNHCR, *Handbook*, paras. 155–6 Hathaway states that the conviction must also 'sustain the conclusion that the offender "constitutes a danger to the community"': Hathaway, J. C., *The Law of Refugee Status* (1991), 226; *Rights of Refugees*, (2005), 351.

Lauterpacht and Bethlehem appear to adopt the approach of the Australian courts,[228] which regard the critical factor as the danger the individual poses, rather than a painstaking classification of the crime.[229] In *A* v. *Minister for Immigration and Multicultural Affairs*, Burchett and Lee J. J. expressed the view that the 'principal statement of exclusion' in article 33(2) is that the individual constitutes a danger to the community or to national security, not that he or she has been convicted of a particularly serious crime.[230] Furthermore, since article 33(2) qualifies 'a principle concerned with some of the most precious of human rights, including life itself', it would be illogical if the mere fact of conviction could outweigh the danger posed by the individual to the host State.[231] Thus, a crime will not necessarily 'be characterised as particularly serious or not particularly serious merely by reference to the nature of the crime',[232] but will depend on the circumstances in which it was committed.

In the same case, Katz J. queried whether this approach was definitive, noting Finkelstein J.'s acknowledgment in *Betkoshabeh* v. *MIMA* that some crimes could be 'particularly serious' per se. Drawing on the 'conclusive presumption' (or non-rebuttable presumption) approach traditionally taken in US legislation,[233] he argued that a decision under article 33(2) could be made in one of two ways: once the decision-maker has concluded that the individual has committed a 'particularly serious crime', he or she must go on to 'consider separately the question of whether [that person] constitute[s] a danger to the Australian community or whether, alternatively, satisfaction as to his crime's having been a particularly

---

[228] Note that legislation now defines 'particularly serious crime': Migration Act 1958 (Cth), s. 91U.

[229] Lauterpacht & Bethlehem, '*Non-refoulement*: Opinion', para. 187; *A* v. *Minister for Immigration and Multicultural Affairs* [1999] FCA 227, paras. 3–5; *Betkoshabeh* v. *MIMA* (1998) 157 ALR 95, 100, reversed on a different point in (1999) 55 ALD 609.

[230] *A* v. *Minister for Immigration and Multicultural Affairs* [1999] FCA 227, para. 4.

[231] Ibid., para. 5. See above on context and proportionality, Ch. 4, s. 4.2.2.

[232] *Betkoshabeh* v. *MIMA* (1998) 157 ALR 95, 100. Finkelstein J. accepted that there might be crimes which are particularly serious per se, but implied that they would be rare. For examples of whether crimes are 'particularly serious', see, among others, *Toboso-Alfonso*, 20 *I&N Dec* 819 (BIA 1990)—burglary and possession of cocaine not 'particularly serious'; *Ipina* v. *INS* 868 F.2d 511 (1st Cir. 1989)—possession of cocaine with intent to distribute makes applicant ineligible for asylum; *L-S-J-*, 21 *I&N Dec* 973 (BIA 1997)—robbery with a deadly weapon (handgun) is a 'particularly serious crime' and renders applicant ineligible for asylum or withholding of deportation; *L-S-*, 22 *I&N Dec* 645 (BIA 1999)—three-and-a-half months' imprisonment for bringing an illegal alien into the United States not a 'particularly serious crime', based on nature and underlying circumstances of conviction; *Y-L-, A-G-, R-S-R-*, 23 *I&N Dec* 270 (AG 2002)—aggravated felonies involving unlawful trafficking in controlled substances presumptively constitute 'particularly serious crimes', and only the most extenuating, extraordinary and compelling circumstances would permit departure from this interpretation; *O.V.*, Federal Council *(Bundesrat)*, Switzerland, 23 Aug. 1989; 4 *Asyl* 1—applicant responsible for killing but acquitted by reason of insanity; notwithstanding absence of conviction 'by a final judgment', not entitled to *non-refoulement* because underlying purpose is to protect community from dangerous refugees. The New Zealand Supreme Court rightly pointed out in *Attorney-General* v. *Zaoui* [2005] NZSC 38 that some of the above references mistakenly appeared in the 2nd edn. of this work as examples of 'balancing', rather than of 'particularly serious crimes'.

[233] INA, s 238; 8 USC § 1228(c): 'An alien convicted of an aggravated felony shall be conclusively presumed to be deportable from the United States'.

serious one [gives] rise to a conclusive presumption that he constitute[s] a danger to the Australian community'.[234] The majority rejected this, stating:

> The logic of the syntax of the provision moves in the opposite direction. The principal statement of exclusion is 'who constitutes a danger to the community'. The phrase 'having been convicted . . . of a particularly serious crime' adds an additional element, but it is not expressed as if that additional element swallowed up the principal statement . . . The whole provision is concerned with perils represented by the refugee, either because of a threat to the security of the country, or because of a danger to its community.[235]

Along with a number of other jurisdictions,[236] Australia has now legislated contrary to this reasoning, by prescribing crimes which are to be regarded as 'particularly serious' for the purposes of article 33(2) of the 1951 Convention.[237] An approach in terms of the penalty imposed alone will likely be arbitrary.[238] In our view, and as a matter of international law, the interpretation and application of this concept in the context of an exception to *non-refoulement* ought necessarily to involve an assessment of all the circumstances,[239] including the nature of the offence, the

[234] *A* v. *Minister for Immigration and Multicultural Affairs* [1999] FCA 227, para. 42.

[235] Ibid., para. 3 (Burchett and Lee JJ.).

[236] Australia: Migration Act 1958 (Cth), s. 91U; Canada: Immigration and Refugee Protection Act 2001, s. 36. US law now defines the term to encompass 'aggravated felonies', the range of which is very broad and much wider than the exception to *non-refoulement* under the Convention: 8 USC §1101(a)(43)—a list comprising some twenty sub-headings and numerous sub-sub-headings. See *Y-L-, A-G-, R-S-R-,* 23 *I&N Dec.* 270 (AG, 2002) holding that: 'We find that the crime of trafficking of drugs is inherently a particularly serious crime.' The Attorney-General found it unnecessary to inquire into the nature and circumstances of the conviction. Section 241(b)(3)(B)(iv) of the INA, 8 USC §1231(b)(3)(B)(iv) provides for 'withholding' of removal and is intended to implement art. 33(2) CSR51. See, however, the Attorney-General's administrative ruling in *A-H-* 23 *I&N Dec.* 774 (AG 2005), adopting a subjective interpretation of this provision, according to which '[a]ny level of danger to national security is deemed unacceptable; it need not be "serious", "significant", or "grave" danger' (at 788).

[237] Migration Act 1958 (Cth), s. 91U. In Australia, this is not intended to oust the subsequent assessment of whether the individual is a danger to the community. The Department of Immigration's own guidelines on interpreting the 1951 Convention state: 'The legislation does not define the second limb of the test, whether a person is "a danger to the community". This assessment will continue to be undertaken on a case-by-case basis': DIMA, *Interpreting the Refugees Convention,* (2002), 55.

[238] On legislative classification of 'serious crimes' and the use of presumptions, see above, Ch. 4, s. 4.2.2.

[239] Lauterpacht & Bethlehem, '*Non-refoulement*: Opinion', above n. 23, paras. 177–9; UNHCR, *Handbook*, para. 156; UNHCR, 'Advisory Opinion regarding the Scope of the National Security Exception in Article 33(2)', 6 Jan. 2006: <http://www.unhcr.org>; Grahl-Madsen, *Commentary on the Refugee Convention* (1997), art. 33. In *Pushpanathan*, [1998] 1 SCR 982, para. 73, the court noted that domestic legislation provided for weighing the seriousness of the danger posed to Canadian society against the danger of persecution on *refoulement*. However, where a decision on the weighting of the applicant's conduct is made by a 'broad discretion', especially by a Minister, that decision should be respected unless it is patently unreasonable: *Suresh*, [2002] 1 SCR 3, paras. 32, 34, 37; *Secretary of State for the Home Dept* v. *Rehman* [2003] 1 AC 153, [2001] UKHL 47, para. 62 (Lord Hoffmann). In such cases, it is up to the Minister, and not the court, to weigh relevant factors: *Suresh*, para. 34. 'The court's task, if called upon to review the Minister's decision, is to determine whether the Minister has exercised her decision-making power within the constraints imposed by Parliament's legislation and the Constitution. If the Minister has considered the appropriate factors in conformity

background to its commission, the behaviour of the individual, and the actual terms of any sentence imposed. As in the case of article 1F(b),[240] *a priori* determinations of seriousness by way of legislative labelling or other measures substituting executive determinations for judicial (and judicious) assessments are inconsistent with the *international* standard which is required to be applied, and with the humanitarian intent of the Convention. After all, what is at issue here is action by the State in manifest disregard of what is recognized as serious danger (persecution) to the life or liberty of a refugee. It is the nature of presumptions that they disregard context and circumstances, and therefore also the principle of individual assessment. This approach has not always been understood by national tribunals, and recent legislation in some States has tended expressly to override this dimension.[241]

For example, section 55 of the UK's Immigration, Nationality and Asylum Act 2006[242] permits the Secretary of State to certify 'that the appellant is not entitled

with these constraints, the court must uphold her decision. It cannot set it aside even if it would have weighed the factors differently and arrived at a different conclusion.': ibid., para. 38; see also *Sogi* v. *Minister of Citizenship and Immigration* [2005] 1 FC 171. The balancing approach adopted in *Suresh* with respect to *refoulement* to torture is not consistent with international law, which proscribes removal to torture absolutely: see further below Ch. 6.

[240] See above, Ch. 2, s. 4.2.

[241] See, for example, UK Immigration, Nationality and Asylum Act 2006, s. 55; Anti-terrorism, Crime and Security Act 2001, s. 34; Nationality, Immigration and Asylum Act 2002, s. 72(8). Some commentators also appear to endorse the 'effective *refoulement*' approach, although the conclusory manner of presentation can often fail expressly to disclose a range of necessarily preceding assessments in which individual circumstances and proportionality can and ought to have been considered; cf. Hathaway, *Rights of Refugees*, (2005), 353, on art. 33(2): '*If* it is shown either that a refugee *is* a danger to national security, or that a refugee who *is* a serious criminal *poses a danger* to the safety of the community of that country, there is *therefore* no additional proportionality requirement to be met: by definition, no purely individuated risk of persecution can offset a real threat to such critical security interests of the receiving State' (emphasis supplied). The balancing approach was rejected by the NZ Supreme Court in *Attorney-General* v. *Zaoui* [2005] NZSC 38, para. 42, reversing the decision of the Court of Appeal on this point: see *Attorney-General* v. *Zaoui (No. 2)* [2005] NZLR 690, para. 157 (Glazebrook J.). The UNHCR *Handbook* does not deal with art. 33(2), although it argues for a balancing approach when dealing with exclusion under Article 1F: paras. 153–4. A 'balancing test' has been used in Belgium (see CPRR, W1916 of 9 Aug. 1995; CPRR, W4403 of 9 Mar. 1998; CPRR, W4589 of 23 Apr. 1998) and in Canada (at least with respect to crimes): *Pushpanathana* [1998] 1 SCR 982, para. 73: 'Article 33(2) as implemented in the Act by ss. 53 and 19 provides for weighing of the seriousness of the danger posed to Canadian society against the danger of persecution upon *refoulement*. This approach reflects the intention of the signatory states to create a humanitarian balance between the individual in fear of persecution on the one hand, and the legitimate concern of states to sanction criminal activity on the other.' Note also *Secretary of State for the Home Department* v. *Rehman* [2003] 1 AC 153, [2001] UKHL 47, para. 16 (Lord Slynn): 'Whether there is such a real possibility [of risk to national security] is a matter which has to be weighed up by the Secretary of State and balanced against the possible injustice to that individual if a deportation order is made'; and para. 56 (Lord Hoffmann): 'But the question in the present case is not whether a given event happened but the extent of future risk. This depends upon an evaluation of the evidence of the appellant's conduct against a broad range of facts with which they may interact. The question of whether the risk to national security is sufficient to justify the appellant's deportation cannot be answered by taking each allegation seriatim and deciding whether it has been established to some standard of proof. It is a question of evaluation and judgment, in which it is necessary to take into account not only the degree of probability of prejudice to national security but also the importance of the security interest at stake and the serious consequences of deportation for the deportee.'

[242] Replacing s. 33, Anti-terrorism, Crime and Security Act 2001.

to the protection of Article 33(1) of the Refugee Convention', either because article 1(F) applies or because article 33(2) applies on grounds of national security, in each case whether or not the individual concerned would otherwise be entitled to protection. The question remains whether the legislature's attempt to oust the 'proportionality test' in the United Kingdom will have any significant effect,[243] particularly in light of the judgment in *A* v. *Secretary of State for the Home Department*,[244] and the fact that the United Kingdom is bound by the specific provisions of the European Convention on Human Rights and by the doctrine of proportionality.

Lauterpacht and Bethlehem suggest that proportionality in the article 33(2) context necessitates consideration of factors such as:

(a) the seriousness of the danger posed to the security of the country;
(b) the likelihood of that danger being realised and its imminence;
(c) whether the danger to the security of the country would be eliminated or significantly alleviated by the removal of the individual concerned;
(d) the nature and seriousness of the risk to the individual from *refoulement*;
(e) whether other avenues consistent with the prohibition of *refoulement* are available and could be followed, whether in the country of refuge or by the removal of the individual concerned to a safe third country.[245]

From a due process perspective, whether a refugee is a danger to the community or a danger to the security of the country is a matter to be determined on the basis of the evidence relating to that individual, considered against an understanding of the concept of security.[246] 'Seriousness', 'security', and 'danger' are not self-applying concepts and their application in a particular case requires, as a matter of due process, that the individual should know and be able to meet the case against him or her, and have the opportunity to show why, in the circumstances, applying the exception would be disproportionate.[247]

The International Court of Justice has made clear that, while the essential interests of the State may include its own and its population's security, the threat occasioned by a grave and imminent peril must be objectively established and not merely apprehended. The response of the State will be excluded, however, if other lawful means are available, even if more costly and less convenient. Moreover, as the Court has emphasized elsewhere, the concept of necessity implies and permits only what is strictly necessary for the purpose.[248]

---

[243] Lord Rooker, *Hansard*, HL 629, col. 1253 (11 Dec. 2001).

[244] [2005] 2 AC 68, [2004] UKHL 56, esp. paras. 30, 121, 132, 236.

[245] Lauterpacht & Bethlehem, '*Non-refoulement*: Opinion', above n. 23, para. 178.

[246] For a 'democratic conception of security', see Lustgarten, L. & Leigh, I., *In from the Cold: National Security and Parliamentary Democracy*, (1994), 32, and generally.

[247] This does not exclude the use of 'security' procedures, provided that they in turn conform with the State's obligations with regard to due process and procedural guarantees; see above, Ch. 4, s. 4.5.

[248] In *Military and Paramilitary Activities in and against Nicaragua*, ICJ *Reports*, (1986), 3 and the *Case Concerning Oil Platforms*, ICJ *Reports* (2003), the International Court of Justice considered the lawfulness of measures taken, *inter alia*, to protect the 'essential security interests' of one of the

In contrast to the 1951 Convention, the 1969 OAU Convention declares the principle of *non-refoulement* without exception. No formal concession is made to overriding considerations of national security, although in cases of difficulty 'in continuing to grant asylum' appeal may be made directly to other member States and through the OAU. Provision is then made for temporary residence pending resettlement, although its grant is not mandatory.[249] The absence of any formal exception is the more remarkable in view of the dimensions of the refugee problems which have faced individual African States.

Article 3 of the Declaration on Territorial Asylum, adopted by the General Assembly only two years before the OAU Convention, not only acknowledges the national security exception, but also appears to authorize further exceptions 'in order to safeguard the population, as in the case of a mass influx of persons'.[250] The latter idea reappeared at the 1977 Conference on Territorial Asylum when Turkey, in a prescient move, proposed an amendment whereby *non-refoulement* might not be claimed 'in exceptional cases, by a great number of persons whose massive influx may constitute a serious problem to the security of a Contracting State'.[251] However, a mass influx alone does not justify *refoulement*; it must additionally jeopardize the safety or security of the local population, which is itself likely to be offset by an international response to the situation.[252] To argue that an exception to the principle of *non-refoulement* exists in situations of mass influx[253] is to overstate the case. Turkey's decision to close its border to Kurdish refugees in 1991, may not, in the circumstances, have breached *non-refoulement* (understood as a general principle of international law that includes the non-rejection at the frontier), yet it certainly consolidated the idea of an exception.[254] In the instant

parties. It held that the measures taken, 'must not merely be such as *tend* to protect' those interests (emphasis added), but must be necessary for that purpose; and 'whether a given measure is "necessary" is not purely a question for the subjective judgement of the party . . . and may thus be assessed by the Court': *Oil Platforms*, para. 43. See also *Gabčíkovo-Nagymoros Project Case*, ICJ *Reports*, (1997), 40–1, paras. 51–2.

[249] Art. II.

[250] For criticism of the terms, see Weis, P., 'The United Nations Declaration on Territorial Asylum' 7 *Can. YIL* 92, 113, 142–3 (1969). Weis nevertheless applauds rejection of the 'public order' exception, which he sees as too wide and susceptible of different connotations in civil and common law countries. For an examination of the *ordre public* concept in the context of entry and expulsion generally, see Goodwin-Gill, *Movement of Persons*, 168–9, 229–37, 298–9.

[251] UN doc. A/CONF.78/C.1/L.28/Rev.1, adopted in the Committee of the Whole by 24 votes to 20, with 40 abstentions, in a vote which requires to be understood in context with premature efforts to secure the agreement of States on a 'right to asylum'.

[252] On this point, see UNHCR, 'The Principle of *Non-Refoulement* as a Norm of Customary International Law: Response to the Questions Posed to UNHCR by the Federal Constitutional Court of the Federal Republic of Germany in Cases 2 BvR 1938/93, 2 BvR 1953/93, 2 BvR 1954/93, 31 Jan. 1994, para. 37. See Ch. 6 below.

[253] This is the position of Hathaway, *Rights of Refugees*, (2005), 355–63 and Coleman, '*Non-refoulement* revised', above n. 96. For the opposite view: Lauterpacht & Bethlehem, '*Non-refoulement*: Opinion', above, n. 23, para. 103.

[254] Turkey maintains the geographical limitation to its obligations under the 1951 Convention, and is thus not bound by treaty towards non-European refugees arriving on its territory or at its borders.

case, the international response was part of the problem, so far as the creation of a safe zone for Kurds in Iraq arguably removed the (legal) basis for departure in search of asylum. The uniqueness of the circumstances, however, might suggest that they have little precedential value, and that the principle of *non-refoulement* has emerged relatively unscathed, although proposals by EU States for reception processing centres in third countries may represent an attempt to mimic this practice.[255] Nevertheless, the prospect of a massive influx of refugees and asylum seekers exposes the limits of the State's obligation otherwise not to return or refuse admission to refugees.

Finally, has the broadened principle of *non-refoulement* under human rights law, which proscribes removal to persecution as well as to torture or cruel, inhuman or degrading treatment or punishment, rendered article 33(2) redundant?[256] A person who fears 'persecution' necessarily also fears at least inhuman or degrading treatment or punishment, if not torture.[257] The Joint Committee on Human Rights was aware of this in 2004 when it considered the UK's classification of a wide range of crimes as 'particularly serious' for the purposes of article 33(2). It thought it 'likely that an individual who is treated as being within the scope of Article 33(2)...would nevertheless still be protected against return by the operation of Article 3 ECHR'.[258] As such, the effect of applying article 33(2) was not necessarily *refoulement* but:

the deprivation of an opportunity to establish refugee status, and the various concomitant advantages which come with such status. In short, it operates like an exclusion clause, preventing a person who would otherwise qualify for refugee status from being recognised as such because of their having committed certain specified offences.[259]

---

[255] The creation of security zones in the former Yugoslavia in the 1990s was more *ad hoc*, although pursued under the auspices of a 'right to remain', that is, 'the basic right of the individual not to be forced into exile': UN High Commissioner for Refugees (Mrs Ogata) 'Statement to the Commission on Human Rights' (Geneva, 3 Mar. 1993); see also *Report on Human Rights in Former Yugoslavia*, UN doc. E/CN.4/1992/S-1/10 (1992), para. 25(b). Simply preventing refugee movements, especially where the emphasis is on halting flight rather than removing causes, is an untenable solution and may lead to further human rights violations. For comment on the efficacy of international protection measures, see Mooney, E. D., 'Presence, *ergo*, protection? UNPROFOR, UNHCR and the ICRC in Croatia and Bosnia and Herzegovina', 7 *IJRL* 407 (1995); Thorburn, J., 'Transcending Boundaries: Temporary Protection and Burden-Sharing in Europe', ibid., 459; Landgren, K., 'Safety Zones and International Protection: A Dark Grey Area', ibid., 436; Higgins, R., 'The United Nations and Former Yugoslavia', 69 *International Affairs* 3 (1993); Grant, S., 'Protection Mechanisms and the Yugoslav Crisis', *Interights Bulletin*, 8:1 (1994). On so-called 'preventive protection', see the 2nd edn. of this book, 282–91. On the EU proposals, see Ch. 7, s. 6.7.

[256] See, generally, Ch. 6; on the scope of *non-refoulement* under customary international law, see Ch. 6, s. 7.

[257] Some States impose different legal tests for the two concepts, which may in turn influence an applicant's ability to characterize his or her claim as one or the other. For example, in Canadian law, applicants fearing a risk of torture or cruel and unusual treatment or punishment must show that that risk is 'more likely than not'; whereas applicants fearing persecution need only show that there is a 'reasonable chance' of persecution: *Li v. Canada (Minister for Citizenship and Immigration)* [2005] 3 FCR 239 (FCA).

[258] Joint Committee on Human Rights, *Particularly Serious Crimes*, above, n. 226, para. 30.

[259] Ibid., para. 31.

The Committee's comments suggest that article 33(2) was being used primarily as a mechanism for denying asylum to asylum seekers who had not been excluded, but who had committed a crime in the United Kingdom and whose status remained to be finally determined.[260]

If article 33(2) is applied to a refugee, but his or her removal is precluded by virtue of the widened operation of *non-refoulement* under human rights law, what effect does that have on the refugee's legal status? The logic behind the distinction between article 1F and article 33(2) is that a refugee touched by article 33(2) *retains* his or her status as a Convention refugee,[261] whereas a person who is excluded by article 1F never was, nor can be, a Convention refugee.

3.3 TIME AND PLACE, WAYS AND MEANS

The recognition of refugee status under international law is essentially declaratory in nature.[262] The duty to protect refugees arises as soon as the individuals or group concerned satisfy the criteria for refugee status set out in the definition (flight from the State territory for relevant reasons) and come within the territory or jurisdiction of another State, regardless of whether refugee status has been formally determined. Under general principles of international law, State responsibility may arise directly from the acts and omissions of its government officials and agents, or indirectly where the domestic legal and administrative systems fail to enforce or guarantee the observance of international standards.[263] The fact that the harm caused by State action may be inflicted outside the territory of the actor, or in an area identified by municipal law as an international zone, in no way diminishes the responsibility of the State.[264]

3.3.1 Extraterritorial application

A State's obligations under international law extend beyond its physical territory. The United Nations Human Rights Committee has held that a State party may be

---

[260] The Qualification Directive seems to contemplate this possibility: art. 14(5).

[261] This is implicit in the decision of the Conseil d'Etat in CE, 21 mai 1997, 148.997, *M. P.*, ruling that, while art. 33(2) permits *refoulement* in certain circumstances, it does not imply that the benefit of refugee status can be withdrawn. See also Lambert, H., 'The EU Asylum Qualification Directive, Its Impact on the Jurisprudence of the United Kingdom and International Law', 55 *ICLQ* 161, 178 (2006), who states that while art. 33(2) may deprive an individual of the benefit of *non-refoulement*, 'it does not provide that such a person may not benefit from the provisions of the Refugee Convention at large. Article 33(2) is not an exclusion clause.' Art. 14(4) of the Qualification Directive provides that Member States may revoke, end, or refuse to renew refugee status where art. 33(2) applies, *but* pursuant to art. 14(6), such refugees remain entitled to the Convention rights contained in arts. 3 (non-discrimination), 4 (religion), 16 (access to courts), 22 (public education), 31 (refugees unlawfully in the country), 32 (expulsion), and 33 (*non-refoulement*). By contrast, art. 19, on revocation of subsidiary protection, is silent on the question of resultant rights. See further, McAdam, J., *Complementary Protection in International Refugee Law*, (2007), Ch. 2.

[262] See UNHCR, *Handbook*, para. 28.

[263] Brownlie, I., *System of the Law of Nations: State Responsibility, Part I*, (1983), 150–1.

[264] Ibid., at 135–7, 159–66.

accountable under article 2 ICCPR66 for violation of protected rights committed by its agents in the territory of another State, whether or not that State acquiesced. Although the text of article 2 suggests that a State's obligations under the Convenant extend only to individuals 'within its territory *and* subject to its jurisdiction' (emphasis added), the Human Rights Committee's interpretation seeks to accord with the treaty's general object and purpose. The Committee regards it as 'unconscionable' to interpret article 2 as territorially-anchored, since this would lead to a double standard whereby a State party could 'perpetrate violations of the Covenant on the territory of another State, which violations it could not perpetrate on its own territory'.[265] Thus, the phrase is interpreted as referring not to the place where the violation occurred, but rather to the relationship between the individual and the State concerned.[266]

Similarly, the European Court of Human Rights, and previously also the European Commission on Human Rights,[267] have affirmed that the concept of 'jurisdiction' in article 1 ECHR50 extends beyond Member States' national territory when 'acts of their authorities, whether performed within or outside national boundaries ... produce ... effects outside their own territory'.[268] Extraterritorial jurisdiction is thus effected when a State exercises authority or control over a territory or individuals.[269] In *Banković v. Belgium*, however, the Court stressed the exceptional nature of this principle.[270] In its view, it was limited to cases such as those in which the State assumes effective control of a territory, either by military occupation or the consent, invitation or acquiescence of the government of that territory, and exercises all or some of the public powers which that government

---

[265] *Lopez Burgos* v. *Uruguay*, Comm. No. R.12/52, UN doc. A/36/40 (1981), para. 12.3; *Celiberti de Casariego* v. *Uruguay*, Comm. No. R.13/56, UN doc. A/36/40 (1981), para. 10.3.

[266] *Lopez Burgos* v. *Uruguay*, above note, para. 12; *de Casariego* v. *Uruguay*, above note, para. 10. See also Human Rights Committee, General Comment No. 31 (2004), para. 10; 'Concluding Observations of the Human Rights Committee: Israel', UN doc. CCPR/C/79/Add.93 (18 Aug. 1998), para. 10; 'Concluding Observations of the Human Rights Committee: United States of America', UN doc. CCPR/C/79/Add.50 (6 Apr. 1995), para. 284; Inter-American Human Rights Commission, *Coard* v. *United States*, Case No. 10.951, Rep. No. 109/99 (29 Sept. 1999), para. 37: 'Given that individual rights inhere simply by virtue of a person's humanity, each American State is obliged to uphold the protected rights of any person subject to its jurisdiction'; Inter-American Human Rights Commission, *Haitian Refugee Cases*, Case No. 10.675, Inter-Am. C.H.R. 334, OEA/Ser.L/V/II.85, doc. 9 rev (1994)—ruling on the issue of admissibility that US interdiction policies appeared to violate, among others, the American Declaration of Human Rights and the American Convention on Human Rights. For additional cases, see Nowak, M., *UN Covenant on Civil and Political Rights: CCPR Commentary* (1993), Article 2, Section IV, paras. 27–30; and for further analysis of the extraterritorial application of the ICCPR, see Noll, G., 'Seeking Asylum at Embassies: A Right to Entry under International Law?', 17 *IJRL* 542, 557–64 (2005).

[267] *Cyprus* v. *Turkey*, Report of the Commission (10 Jul. 1976), (1982) 4 EHRR 482.

[268] *Loizidou* v. *Turkey* (1995) 20 EHRR 90, para. 62. In the Canadian context, see *United States* v. *Burns* [2001] 1 SCR 283, para. 60; *Canada* v. *Schmidt* [1987] 1 SCR 500, 522; *Suresh* v. *Minister of Citizenship and Immigration* [2002] 1 SCR 3, para. 54.

[269] Wilde terms these the '*spatial* basis for jurisdiction' and the '*personal* basis for jurisdiction' respectively: Wilde, R., 'The "Legal Space" or "*Espace Juridique*" of the European Convention on Human Rights: Is it Relevant to Extraterritorial State Action?', 2 *European Human Rights Law Review* 115, 116 (2005). [270] *Banković* v. *Belgium* (2001) 11 BHRC 435, para. 67.

would normally exercise,[271] and to cases 'involving the activities of its diplomatic or consular agents abroad and on board craft and vessels registered in, or flying the flag of, that state',[272] an aspect of particular relevance to asylum claims. Furthermore, the Court noted that the European Convention applies 'in an essentially regional context and notably in the legal space (*espace juridique*) of the Contracting States', and that it 'was not designed to be applied throughout the world, even in respect of the conduct of Contracting States'.[273] However, this apparent limitation on the extraterritorial application of ECHR50 is not reflected in the case law of the Court, including post-*Banković* decisions, which has extended the concept of 'jurisdiction' to other types of conduct occurring *outside* the territorial boundaries of contracting States.[274] This jurisprudence seems to support Wilde's thesis that the *Banković* dictum has been wrongly relied upon as a statement of principle about spatial application, instead of as an explanation of the original historical design of the European Convention.[275]

Unlike other provisions in the 1951 Convention which condition the rights and benefits accorded to refugees on degrees of presence and lawful residence, article 33(1) contains no such restriction. On the contrary, it prohibits the return of refugees '*in any manner whatsoever*' to the frontiers of territories where they may be persecuted, including by way of extradition, expulsion, deportation, or rejection at the frontier. The principle applies regardless of whether the relevant action occurs 'beyond the national territory of the State in question, at border posts or other points of entry, in international zones, at transit points, etc'.[276]

In domestic litigation arising out of the Haitian interdiction programme, the US Government argued that the prohibition against *non-refoulement* applies only

---

[271] Ibid., para. 71.

[272] *Banković*, above n. 270, para. 73. See also R. (*European Roma Rights Centre*) v. *Immigration Office at Prague Airport* [2005] 2 AC 1, paras. 21ff; R. (*on the Application of 'B'*) v. *Secretary of State for Foreign and Commonwealth Affairs* [2005] QB 643, [2004] EWCA Civ 1344, para. 66. 'Authorised agents of a State . . . bring other persons or property within the jurisdiction of that State to the extent that they exercise authority over such persons or property. In so far as they affect such persons or property by their acts or omissions, the responsibility of the State is engaged': M v. *Denmark* (1992) 73 D.R 193, para. 196.   [273] *Banković*, above n. 270, para. 80; Wilde, above n. 269,, 116.

[274] *Öcalan* v. *Turkey* (2000) 30 EHRR CD 231 (Admissibility); *Öcalan* v. *Turkey* (2003) 37 EHRR 10 (Merits); *Öcalan* v. *Turkey* (Grand Chamber) (12 May 2005), applying to Turkish activities in Kenya; *Issa* v. *Turkey* Application No. 31821/96 (Admissibility) (30 May 2000); *Issa* v. *Turkey* Application No. 31821/96 (Merits) (16 Nov. 2004), applying to Turkish activities in Iraq. See also *B's case*, above note. On reconciling these cases with *Banković*, above n. 270, see Wilde, R., 'Legal "Black Hole"? Extraterritorial State Action and International Treaty Law on Civil and Political Rights', 26 *Michigan Journal of International Law* 739, 795–7 (2005).

[275] Wilde, above n. 269 on the UK's obligations specifically, see Wilde, R., 'The Extraterritorial Application of the Human Rights Act' in Holder, J. & O'Cinneide, C., eds., *Current Legal Problems 2005* (2005). The question of extraterritorial application of human rights treaties is crucial to determining what States may and may not do in relation to policies intended to prevent the arrival or admission of asylum seekers; see further below, Ch. 7.

[276] Lauterpacht & Bethlehem, '*Non-refoulement*: Opinion', above n. 23, para. 67. They also observe that if an individual has taken refuge in a diplomatic mission within his or her own country, then the protecting State is subject to the prohibition on *refoulement*: para. 114.

to refugees within State territory. Beginning with a September 1981 Presidential Proclamation and Executive Order, the US Coast Guard regularly 'interdicted' Haitians and returned them to their country of origin, initially with a form of screening and guarantees for the non-return of those found to be refugees. The US Government informed the Haitian Government that it would not return any individual whom it determined to qualify for refugee status, and President Reagan's Executive Order likewise confirmed, 'that no person who is a refugee will be returned without his consent'. US officials made similar statements on other occasions in different fora.

Following the September 1991 military coup against the democratically elected Government of Haiti and President Jean Bertrand Aristide, repatriations were first suspended but then resumed after some six weeks. In May 1992, President Bush decided to continue interdiction and repatriation, but without offering the possibility of screening-in for those who might qualify as refugees.[277] The US Government encouraged in-country processing instead, considering it to be a 'viable substitute' for the right to leave one's home and seek protection from persecution.[278] President Clinton elected to maintain the interdiction practice, which continued until May 1994 when full refugee status determination interviews on board ships were announced.[279] Local court challenges were commenced, but in its 1993 decision in *Sale, Acting Commissioner, INS* v. *Haitian Centers Council,* the US Supreme Court ruled that neither domestic law nor article 33 of the 1951 Convention limited the power of the President to order the Coast Guard to repatriate undocumented aliens, including refugees, on the high seas.[280]

The Supreme Court decision, by an 8–1 majority, held first that domestic law provisions applied only in immigration proceedings for exclusion or deportation. As such proceedings do not operate outside the United States, neither the President nor the Coast Guard were under any statutory limitation in dealing with those found on the high seas while in flight from persecution, such as Haitians. The international law dimensions to the interdiction practice, not surprisingly, received little substantive attention. Although the Court made passing reference to the *travaux préparatoires* of the 1951 Convention, its essentially *policy* decision to deny a remedy to individuals beyond territorial jurisdiction relied mostly on the language of 'Congressional intent' at the time of enactment.[281]

[277] See Executive Order No. 12,807: 57 *Fed. Reg.* 23133 (also known as the 'Kennebunkport Order', reversed by President Clinton in 1994).
[278] See Miranda, C. O., 'Haiti and the United States during the 1980s and 1990s: Refugees, Immigration, and Foreign Policy', 32 *San Diego Law Review* 680, 720–1 (1995).
[279] 16 *Refugee Reports*, (28 Feb. 1995), 11.
[280] 509 US 155 (1993); see also *Cubtan-American Bar Ass'n Inc.* v. *Christopher*, 43 F. 3d 1412 (11th Cir., 1995) in which the Court ruled that refugees in safe haven camps outside the US do not enjoy constitutional due process and are not protected from forced return by art. 33 CSR51 or the Immigration and Nationality Act. See Frelick, B., '"Abundantly Clear": Refoulement', 19 *Georgetown Immigration Law Journal* 245 (2005).
[281] For further views, see the dissenting judgment of Blackmun J. and Goodwin-Gill's 'Comment' in 6 *IJRL* 71, 103 (1994).

The judgment of the Supreme Court attempted to confer domestic 'legality' on a practice of returning individuals to their country of origin, irrespective of their claims to have a well-founded fear of persecution. That decision could not and did not alter the State's international obligations,[282] as was recognized by the Inter-American Commission of Human Rights, which found the United States in breach of article 33(1) of the Convention.[283] The Commission also held that the practice breached the asylum seekers' right to life, liberty, and security of their persons, and the right to asylum protected by article XXVII of the American Declaration of the Rights and Duties of Man.[284]

The principle of *non-refoulement* can thus be seen to have crystallized into a rule of customary international law, the core element of which is the prohibition of *return in any manner whatsoever* of refugees to countries where they may face persecution. The scope and application of the rule are determined by this essential purpose, thus regulating State action *wherever* it takes place, whether internally, at the border, or through its agents outside territorial jurisdiction. This development is amply confirmed in instruments subsequent to the 1951 Convention, including declarations in different fora and treaties such as the 1984 UN Convention against Torture, by the will of States expressed in successive resolutions in the UN General Assembly or the Executive Committee of the UNHCR Programme, in the laws and practice of States, and especially in unilateral declarations by the US Government.

During the first ten years of the Haitian interdiction programme, senior US officials publicly and repeatedly affirmed the principle of *non-refoulement*, not only in the broad general sense,[285] but also in the specific context of Haitian operations. Moreover, the relevant Executive Order stated quite clearly that '[t]he Attorney General shall . . . take whatever steps are necessary to ensure . . . the strict observance of our international obligations concerning those who genuinely flee persecution in their homeland'.[286] In his 16 February 1982 letter to the UNHCR Chief of Mission in Washington, D.C., US Attorney General William French Smith extended unqualified recognition to international obligations.[287]

---

[282] Cf. UNHCR, Brief *amicus curiae*, 6 *IJRL* 85 (1994).

[283] *Haitian Center for Human Rights* v. *United States*, Case 10.675, Report No. 51/96, Inter-Am. CHR Doc. OEA/Ser.L/V/II.95 Doc. 7 rev. (13 Mar. 1997), paras. 156–8. See also Human Rights Committee, 'Concluding Observations of the Human Rights Committee: United States of America', UN doc. CCPR/C/79/Add.50 (6 Apr. 1995), para. 284.

[284] *Haitian Center for Human Rights* v. *United States*, above note, paras. 171, 163 respectively.

[285] See above nn. 84, 89, 56 and accompanying text.

[286] Executive Order 12324, 29 Sept. 1981, s. 3.

[287] ' . . . the Administration is firmly committed to the full observance of our international obligations and traditions regarding refugees, including . . . the principle of non-refoulement . . . If there were an indication of a colorable claim of asylum, the individual would be brought to the United States where a formal application for asylum would be filed . . . these procedures will insure that nobody with a well-founded fear of persecution is mistakenly returned to Haiti.' The relevant correspondence and statements are cited in UNHCR's *amicus curiae* brief: 6 *IJRL* 85 (1994). See also (1994) Memorandum to all INS employees assigned to duties related to interdiction at sea, revised

These substantial undertakings by US government officials were applied in practice for at least ten years, until the President decided to return even Haitians who might have a 'colorable claim' to be refugees. The combination of declarations in the sense of an international obligation with practice confirming that obligation is conclusive evidence of the applicability of the principle of *non-refoulement* to the extraterritorial activities of US agents. This conclusion is further strengthened by the fact that even though the US authorities considered that the vast majority of Haitians were leaving for economic reasons, they were still prepared, against interest, to take steps to ensure that no refugees among them were returned contrary to international obligations.

In its judgment in the *Nuclear Tests* Cases, the International Court of Justice observed that:

... declarations made by way of unilateral acts, concerning legal or factual situations, may have the effect of creating legal obligations ... [N]othing in the nature of a *quid quo pro* nor any subsequent acceptance of the declaration, nor even any reply or reaction from other States, is required for the declaration to take effect, since such a requirement would be inconsistent with the strictly unilateral nature of the juridical act by which the pronouncement of the State was made ... [288]

The Court further emphasized the central value of good faith in this context:

Just as the very rule of *pacta sunt servanda* in the law of treaties is based on good faith, so also is the binding character of an international obligation assumed by unilateral declaration. Thus interested States may take cognizance of unilateral declarations and place confidence in them, and are entitled to require that the obligation thus created be respected. [289]

UNHCR has been entrusted by the United Nations General Assembly with the international protection of refugees, and States in turn have formally undertaken to co-operate with UNHCR, 'in the exercise of its functions, and shall in particular facilitate its duty of supervising the application of the provisions' of the 1951 Convention/1967 Protocol. [290] UNHCR's legal interests are equivalent to those of States in the circumstances described by the International Court of Justice; it was entitled to take notice of and place confidence in the declarations of the United States.

---

26 Aug. 1982 under signature of the INS Associate Commissioner Examinations: 'The only function INS officers are responsible for is to ensure that the United States is in compliance with its obligations regarding actions towards refugees, including the necessity to be keenly attuned ... to any evidence which may reflect an individual's well-founded fear of persecution.' The list of authorities expressly cited for this memorandum included not only the Presidential Proclamation and Executive Order of 29 Sept. 1981, but also art. 33 of the 1951 Convention. INS Acting Commissioner Doris M. Meissner's letter of 29 Dec. 1981 to the UNHCR Chief of Mission: 'These *procedures* fully comply with our responsibilities under the UN Convention and Protocol' (emphasis supplied). Similar statements are cited by Blackmun, J., dissenting in *Sale v. Haitian Centers Council, Inc.*: 6 *IJRL* 71 (1994).

[288] *Nuclear Tests* case (Australia v. France), ICJ *Rep.*, (1974), 457, para. 46.
[289] Ibid., para. 49.   [290] Art. 35, 1951 Convention; art. II, 1967 Protocol.

In fact, UNHCR appears to have done just this. At no time did the Office challenge the exercise of jurisdiction on the high seas. Rather, it focused its interventions on the *adequacy* of the on-board procedures, to sift out effectively those Haitians who might have a 'colorable claim' to asylum.[291] The declaration of intent to abide by article 33, substantiated by ten years of practice in which all interdicted Haitians were screened, sufficiently confirms the 'extraterritorial' obligations of the United States, which are implicit in the words of the Convention.

Two final points remain for consideration. The first is that individuals must not be removed to 'the frontiers of territories' in which they face a risk of persecution or other serious harm. As Lauterpacht and Bethlehem rightly point out, the term 'territories' implies that return is prohibited to *any* territory in which the risk is material, irrespective of whether that territory is the individual's country of origin.[292] They argue further that the use of 'territories', rather than 'States' or 'countries', suggests that the legal status of the place is immaterial.[293] Accordingly, in their view if an individual has taken refuge in a diplomatic mission within his or her own country, or is protected there by the armed forces of another State, then the protecting State is subject to the prohibition on *refoulement* and cannot release the individual back into the jurisdiction of the country of origin.[294] Whether this can be reconciled with the requirement in article 1A(2) that a refugee is a person *outside* his or her country of origin is doubtful, since it requires interpreting 'outside' in a legal, jurisdictional sense, rather than a physical, territorial sense, an interpretation which is neither supported by State practice nor *opinio juris*.[295]

[291] For example, in its *amicus curiae* brief in *Haitian Refugee Center, Inc.* v. *Gracey*, UNHCR argued that, 'Given the applicability of the principle of *non-refoulement* to the broad field of State action or omission, the secondary principle of effectiveness of obligations itself obliges a State to establish procedures adequate and sufficient to ensure fulfilment of the primary duty... [W]here... a State of its own volition, elects to intercept asylum-seekers on the high seas and outside their own or any State's territory, particularly high standards must apply and be scrupulously implemented.' Motion for Leave to file Brief *Amicus Curiae* and Brief *Amicus Curiae* of the United Nations High Commissioner for Refugees in support of Haitian Refugee Center, Inc., *et al*, 8 Jul. 1985, Section III, 19–24.
[292] Art. 15(b) of the Qualification Directive only requires subsidiary protection status to be granted when an individual fears removal to torture or inhuman or degrading treatment or punishment *in his or her country of origin*. Although Member States remain bound by their international law obligations not to remove individuals to *any* territory where there is a risk of such harm, the nature of the domestic legal status—if any—that such persons are granted is uncertain.
[293] The original text read 'to the frontiers of their country of origin, or to territories'. Presumably because the term 'territories' also encompassed the 'country of origin', the UK delegation proposed the simpler formulation 'to the frontiers of territories', noting that 'the amendment would not alter the purport' of the paragraph: *Ad Hoc* Committee on Statelessness and Related Problems (1st Session), 'Summary Record of the 20th Meeting' (1 Feb. 1950) UN doc. E/AC.32/SR.20 (Sir Leslie Brass, United Kingdom), para. 7.
[294] Lauterpacht & Bethlehem, '*Non-refoulement*: Opinion', above n. 23 para. 114.
[295] *R. (European Roma Rights Centre)* v. *Immigration Officer at Prague Airport* [2005] 2 AC 1. That diplomatic asylum has a legal basis in the notion of extraterritoriality—a predominant view in the 19th century—has more recently been discredited and described as a 'fiction': see discussion in *Question of Diplomatic Asylum: Report of the Secretary-General* (Sept. 1975) UN doc. A/10150, paras. 301–2.

However, principles of international human rights law which prevent States from exposing individuals within their territory *or* jurisdiction to particular forms of serious harm may prevent the diplomatic mission from removing the individual.[296]

The notion of diplomatic asylum creates a conflict between the territorial jurisdiction of the State in which the embassy is physically located and the extraterritorial jurisdiction of the sending state—'an exception to the rule that the local jurisdiction covers persons, events and things, whether foreign or national, within the territory of the acting State'.[297] Whether diplomatic asylum forms part of general international law is disputed for this reason.[298] In *B's* case, two Afghan boys escaped from mandatory detention in Australia and made their way to the British consulate in Melbourne. There, they claimed asylum, and submitted that consular officials would breach article 3 ECHR50 if they returned them to the Australian authorities, since they would be returned to 'inhuman and degrading' immigration detention. Because the boys had escaped custody, the British High Court characterized them as fugitives,[299] stating:

The basic principle is that the authorities of the receiving State can require surrender of a fugitive in respect of whom they wish to exercise the authority that arises from their territorial jurisdiction; see Article 55 of the 1963 Vienna Convention. Where such a request is made the Convention cannot normally require the diplomatic authorities of the sending State to permit the fugitive to remain within the diplomatic premises in defiance of the receiving State. Should it be clear, however, that the receiving State intends to subject the fugitive to treatment so harsh as to constitute a crime against humanity, international law must surely permit the officials of the sending state to do all that is reasonably possible, including allowing the fugitive to take refuge in the diplomatic premises, in order to protect him against such treatment. In such circumstances the Convention may well impose a duty on a Contracting State to afford diplomatic asylum.[300]

---

[296] See Noll, G., 'Seeking Asylum at Embassies: A Right to Entry under International Law', 17 *LJRL* 542 (2005) (hereafter , Noll, 'Seeking Asylum at Embassies'). In our view, the shortcoming of the 1951 Convention is not the term *'refoulement'*, as Noll suggests at 555, but the requirement that the individual be outside his or her country of origin. Human rights forms of *non-refoulement* remain relevant (see below Ch. 6), but need to be reconciled with traditional perceptions, such as that expressed by the International Court of Justice in the *Asylum* case: 'In the case of diplomatic asylum, the refugee is within the territory of the State where the offence was committed. A decision to grant diplomatic asylum involves a derogation from the sovereignty of that State. It withdraws the offender from the jurisdiction of the territorial State and constitutes an intervention in matters which are exclusively within the competence of the State. Such a derogation from territorial sovereignty cannot be recognized unless its legal basis is established in each particular case.' *Asylum Case* [1950] ICJ *Rep.* 266, 274; cf. *R. (B)* v. *Secretary of State for Foreign and Commonwealth Affairs* [2005] QB 643, [2004] EWCA Civ. 1344.   [297] O'Connell, D.P., *International Law*, (1970), 734.

[298] See Jennings, R. & Watts, A., eds., *Oppenheim's International Law*, (9th edn., 1992), vol. 1, para. 495; *Question of Diplomatic Asylum*, above n. 295, para. 311; cf. paras. 312–21.

[299] 'Fugitive' implies a criminal, and yet the Australian High Court has stated that immigration detention is not 'punitive' but 'administrative': *Al-Kateb* v. *Godwin* [2004] HCA 37, (2004) 208 ALR 124.

[300] *B's case*, [2005] QB 643, [2004] EWCA Cir 1344, above n. 296, para. 88. See also Jennings & Watts , above, n. 298, para. 495.

The judgment went on to suggest that the treatment to which the individual may be exposed need not reach the severity of a crime against humanity, but that protection against inhuman or degrading treatment or punishment will only be forthcoming if 'the perceived threat to the *physical safety* of the applicants ... [is] *so immediate and severe*' that to return them would violate the host State's duties under international law.[301]

Is the position different if an asylum seeker, outside the territory of his or her country, seeks asylum in a diplomatic mission in a third State? In such cases, the principle of *non-refoulement* applies, since the asylum seeker is *outside* the country of origin. Nevertheless, unless the removal (or denial of an entry visa) directly exposes the individual to a risk of *refoulement*, article 33(2) will not be breached. Noll argues that article 33(1) does not create an implied right to an entry visa for persons seeking protection at embassies in third States, because the term '*refouler*' 'suggest[s] a direct sovereign relationship between the removing agent and the territory from which removal takes place',[302] and simply denying an entry visa cannot trigger it. This implies that removal in such circumstances can never result in *refoulement*, even if the State in which the embassy is situated takes measures to remove the individual to a State in which he or she faces persecution or serious harm.[303] Noll regards the act of *refoulement* as anchored to sovereign territorial connection and control,[304] maintaining that there must be 'a sufficient causal link between its actions or omissions and the infliction of harm'.[305]

It is well established that the principle of *non-refoulement* includes protection from return to territories where the individual, although not directly at risk of persecution, torture, or cruel, inhuman or degrading treatment or punishment, faces a danger of being expelled to other territories where such a risk exists.[306] How, then, is an act of removal by one State, which leads to an individual's *refoulement* by another, to be characterized as a matter of international law? Although this is commonly referred to as 'indirect' or 'chain' *refoulement*, such terminology is essentially descriptive and confuses the legal basis for liability, since the first State's act is not one of *refoulement* per se. As a matter of State responsibility, however, liability for breaches of international law can be both joint and several. While a State that *actually* returns a refugee to persecution or other serious harm remains primarily responsible for that act, the first State, through its act of expulsion, may be

---

[301] *B's case*, [2005] QB 643, [2004] EWCA Cir 1344, above n. 296, para. 93 (emphasis added).
[302] Noll, 'Seeking Asylum at Embassies', above n. 296, 555.   [303] Ibid., 553–6.
[304] Ibid., 555.
[305] Ibid., 568. On the other hand, Noll argues that States' obligations under the ECHR50 and CRC89 may, in exceptional circumstances, require an entry visa (but not necessarily 'protection') to be granted.
[306] Committee against Torture, General Comment No. 1 (1997), para. 2; *Korban* v. *Sweden* Comm. No. 88/1997 (16 Nov. 1998) UN doc. CAT/C/21/D/88/1997; Human Rights Committee, General Comment No. 31 (2004), para. 12; *R.* v. *Secretary of State for the Home Dept, ex p. Adan* [2001] 2 AC 477 (HL); *TI* v. *UK* [2000] INLR 211.

jointly liable for it.[307] Phrases such as 'indirect' or 'chain' *refoulement* are therefore misleading, since they divert attention from the basis of liability and the nature of the act attributable to the first State.[308] Removal by the first State may also breach other applicable human rights provisions where the process of refusal and return amounts to cruel, inhuman or degrading treatment.[309] It has also been suggested that the right to respect for private life under article 8 ECHR50 may include 'a positive duty on a state to regularize an immigrant's status with no prospect of removal within a reasonable timescale, where the result of limbo status is destitution through an inability to access the labour market together with a denial of access to the mainstream benefits regime'.[310]

3.3.2 'International zones'

Whereas State activities beyond territorial jurisdiction are sometimes said to be outside the scope of the *non-refoulement* obligation, in other circumstances international obligations are claimed to have limited effect even within the State. Any argument for the non-application of international obligations in State territory (for example, in transit or international zones, whether in the matter of refugees, asylum seekers, stowaways, or any other subject) faces substantial objections, however. It is a fundamental principle of international law that every State enjoys prima facie exclusive authority over its territory and persons within it, and with that authority or jurisdiction goes responsibility.[311] Thus, a State could hardly argue that it is not bound by international duties of protection with respect to diplomatic personnel, merely by reason of the fact of their location within an 'international' or transit area of an airport. The European Court of Human Rights stated in *Amuur* v. *France* that '[d]espite its name, the international zone does not have extraterritorial status'.[312] At the very least, a failure to examine

---

[307] UNGA res. 56/83, 'Responsibility of States for Internationally Wrongful Acts', (12 Dec. 2001), Annex, art. 47; *TI* v. *UK*, above n. 306; *Prince Hans-Adam II of Liechtenstein* v. *Germany* Application No. 42527/98, 12 Jul. 2001, para. 48; *Banković*, above n. 270. See also art. 16 of the Articles on State Responsibility, discussed in Legomsky, S. H., 'Secondary Refugee Movements and the Return of Asylum Seekers to Third Countries: The Meaning of Effective Protection', 15 *IJRL* 567, 620–1, 642ff (2003) (the 'complicity principle').

[308] Crawford, J. & Hyndman, P., 'Three Heresies in the Application of the Refugee Convention', 1 *IJRL* 155, 171 (1989): 'It is . . . clear that more than one State may share joint responsibility for decisions which result in the *refoulement* of a refugee . . . It follows that a State may not rely on the obligation of another State party to the Convention, even where there are good grounds for saying that the latter State is indeed under a particular obligation with respect to the refugee, if that reliance is likely to result in a violation of Article 33.'

[309] On the earlier practice of 'shuttlecocking' migrants, see Goodwin-Gill, G. S., *International Law and the Movement of Persons between States*, (1978), 287–8.

[310] Blake, N. & Husain, R., *Immigration, Asylum and Human Rights*, (2003), para. 4.64.

[311] See *Amuur* v. *France* (1996) 22 EHRR 533, in which France was held to have violated art. 5 ECHR50 by detaining asylum seekers in the transit zone of Paris-Orly airport.

[312] Ibid., para. 52.

an asylum request made in an international zone would constitute rejection at the frontier.[313]

Many States, of course, do choose to accord lesser rights in their municipal law to those awaiting formal admission, than to those who have entered. The United States is a typical example, where *physical* presence is not necessarily synonymous with *legal* presence for the purpose of determining constitutional guarantees. Other States make similar distinctions, for example, in the case of stowaways or illegal entrants, who are often deemed not to have entered the country. The purpose of such provisions is usually to facilitate summary or discretionary treatment, but from the perspective of international law, what counts is not the status or non-status conferred by municipal law, but the treatment in fact accorded. For international law purposes, *presence within State territory* is a juridically relevant fact sufficient in most cases to establish the necessary link with the authorities whose actions may be imputable to the State in circumstances giving rise to State responsibility. These flow from the fact of control over territory and include, with respect to human rights, the obligation of the State to ensure and to protect the human rights of everyone within its territory or subject to its jurisdiction.[314] Municipal courts, too, have rarely doubted their authority to extend their jurisdiction and protection into so-called international zones.[315]

---

[313] UNHCR, 'The Principle of Non-Refoulement as a Norm of Customary International Law: Response to the Questions Posed to UNHCR by the Federal Constitutional Court of the Federal Republic of Germany in Cases 2 BvR 1938/93, 2 BvR 1953/93, 2 BvR 1954/93, (31 Jan. 1994), para. 33.

[314] See art. 2(1) ICCPR66; art. 1 ECHR50; art. 1 ACHR69. Although ICCPR66 employs the phrase, '*and* subject to its jurisdiction', the Human Rights Committee has interpreted it to mean, 'or'; see above, n. 265 and text. The judgment of the Supreme Court of Canada in *Singh* is premised on the fact that those seeking Charter protection were physically present, and 'by virtue of that presence, amenable to Canadian law': *Singh* v. *Minister of Employment and Immigration* [1985] 1 SCR 177. Cf. habeas corpus jurisprudence: *Re Harding* (1929) 63 OLR 518 (Ontario Appeal Division); *Barnard* v. *Ford* [1892] AC 326; Cf. Habeas Corpus Act 1679, s. 10; Habeas Corpus Act 1816, s. 5; Habeas Corpus Act 1862; *The Sitka* (1855), 7 *Opinions of the Attorney General*, 122; *Calvin's Case* (1609) 7 Co. Rep. 1; cited by Sharpe, R. J., *The Law of Habeas Corpus*, (1976), 182. See also *Ramirez* v. *Weinberger* 745 F. 2d 1500 (DC Cir., 1984), where the court considered that US Constitutional guarantees of due process could be invoked by citizens whose property overseas is affected by US governmental action: 'Where . . . the court . . . has personal jurisdiction over the defendants, the extraterritorial nature of the property involved in the litigation is no bar to equitable relief.' So far as the power to expel and deport implicitly authorizes such extra-territorial constraint as is necessary to effect execution: *Attorney-General for Canada* v. *Cain* [1906] AC 542, 546–7, then the legality of such constraint remains reviewable so long as it continues: Cf. *R.* v. *Secretary of State, ex p. Greenberg* [1947] 2 All ER 550. Note also s. 6, UK Consular Relations Act 1968, which provides that a crew member on board a ship flying the flag of a designated State who is detained for a disciplinary offence shall not be deemed to be unlawfully detained unless (a) his detention is unlawful under the laws of that State or the conditions of detention are inhumane or unjustifiable severe; *or* (b) there is reasonable cause to believe that his life or liberty will be endangered for reasons of race, nationality, political opinion or religion, in any country to which the ship is likely to go. The British Court of Appeal held that acts of British consular and diplomatic officials in Australia fell 'within the jurisdiction' of the United Kingdom, and that the Human Rights Act 1998 was thus applicable to their actions in that country: *B's* case [2005] QB 643, above n. 296, para. 79.

[315] See Hamerslag, R. J., 'The Schiphol Refugee Centre Case', 1 *IJRL* 395 (1989); decisions of the French Constitutional Council (25 Feb. 1992) and Paris Tribunal de Grande (25 Mar. 1992)

In examining the legality and implications of such zones, the point of departure is the State's sovereign and prima facie exclusive authority or jurisdiction over all its territory, and the concomitant international legal responsibilities flowing from the fact of control and the activities of its agents. This authority or jurisdiction, with its basis in customary international law, is amply confirmed by international treaties, such as the 1944 Chicago Convention and the 1982 Convention on the Law of the Sea. No State, by treaty or practice, appears to have abandoned the territory comprised by its ports of entry; the extent of national control exercised therein sufficiently contradicts any assertion of their purely *international* character.

While obligations relating to *non-refoulement* and the protection of human rights come into play by reason of the juridically relevant facts of presence within State territory and jurisdiction, the State retains choice of means with regard to implementation. To apply different procedures and standards in such zones will not necessarily result in breach; the underlying practical issue is one of monitoring and compliance, but experience unfortunately confirms that errors of *refoulement* are more likely when procedural shortcuts are taken in zones of restricted guarantees and limited access.[316]

Australia's 'Pacific Strategy',[317] which delimits Australia's migration zone to deny legal presence—and thus the ability to make an asylum claim—to those who are in fact present in Australian territory, has been carefully constructed so as to fall within the letter, if not the spirit, of international law. Following the *Tampa* incident in 2001, the Australian Parliament passed a series of laws 'excising' various islands and coastal ports from the migration zone, requiring that asylum seekers who land at such places to be sent to offshore processing centres elsewhere in the region (Nauru, and Manus Island in Papua New Guinea) to have their asylum claims determined by UNHCR or Australian officials.[318] Such persons are termed

---

discussed in *Amuur* v. *France* (1996) 22 EHRR 533, paras. 21–2. Earlier cases dealt, for example, with habeas corpus and false imprisonment. See *Küchenmeister* v. *Home Office* [1958] 1 QB 496, in which a non-citizen in transit at London Airport succeeded in an action for false imprisonment, when immigration officers prevented him from joining his connecting flight after he had been refused permission to enter.

316 Cf. loi no. 92–625, 6 juill. 1992, sur la zone d'attente des ports et des aéroports: *JO*, 9 juill. 1992, 9185; Julien-Laferrière, F., 'Droit d'asile et politique d'asile en France', *Asyl*, 1993/4, 75–80—detention after four days can be continued only by decision of the president of the *tribunal de grande instance*, and entry can only be refused if the application is manifestly unfounded. See Recommendation 1163 (1991) of the Parliamentary Assembly on the Arrival of Asylum-Seekers at European Airports; Recommendation No. R (94) 5 of the Committee of Ministers on Guidelines to Inspire Practices of the Member States of the Council of Europe concerning the Arrival of Asylum-Seekers at European Airports; Recommendation 1475 (2000) of the Parliamentary Assembly on the Arrival of Asylum Seekers at European Airports.

317 For a detailed explanation of the history and operation of the Pacific Strategy (formerly the Pacific Solution), see Crock, M., Saul, B., & Dastyari, A., *Future Seekers II: Refugees and Irregular Migration in Australia* (2006), Ch. 7. See also Border Protection (Validation and Enforcement Powers) Act 2001 (Cth); Border Security Legislation Amendment Act 2002 (Cth).

318 Migration Amendment (Excision from Migration Zone) Act 2001 (Cth); Migration Amendment (Excision from Migration Zone) (Consequential Provisions) Act 2001 (Cth); Migration Amendment Regulations 2005 (No. 6) (Cth), excising territories previously disallowed in the proposed Migration

'offshore entry persons'[319] and are prohibited from instituting legal proceedings in Australian courts relating to their offshore entry, their status as unlawful non-citizens, the lawfulness of their detention, or anything relating to their removal to a third country under section 198A of the Migration Act.[320] It is estimated that around 4,891 places have been excised from Australia's migration zone.[321] In May 2006, the Australian government introduced draft legislation that sought, in effect, to excise the whole of the Australian mainland for migration purposes. It proposed to transfer all 'designated unauthorized arrivals' (people who arrived in Australia by boat without a visa) to offshore processing centres on Nauru, and pre-clude them from the prospect of resettlement in Australia. Following a highly crit-ical report by the (government-led) Senate Legal and Constitutional Affairs Committee, the government was unable to secure sufficient support and the Bill was withdrawn.[322]

By contrast to the varying interception measures applied by the United States, where physical presence on US soil affects an individual's ability to apply for asy-lum, excision of Australian territory means that any asylum seeker who reaches an excised offshore place is not permitted to apply for asylum within Australia. The countries with which Australia has processing agreements have been declared by the Minister for Immigration to provide access to effective asylum procedures, and protection for asylum seekers and refugees that meets relevant human rights standards[323] which in Australia's view satisfies its international legal obligations. Indeed, Australia has not sought to argue that excision relieves it of its inter-national obligations,[324] and such an argument would necessarily fail.[325] Rather, a key purpose of excision is to limit the operational scope of the Migration Act, and

---

Amendment Regulations 2003 (No. 8) on 24 Nov. 2003. The camps themselves are run by the International Organization for Migration.

[319] Migration Act 1958 (Cth), s. 5.

[320] Ibid., s. 494AA. This section does not exclude claims brought under the original jurisdiction of the High Court of Australia (Australian Constitution, s. 75).

[321] Response from the Department of Immigration, Multicultural and Indigenous Affairs to a question from the Committee: Senate Legal and Constitutional References Committee, *Migration Zone Exclusion: An Examination of the Migration Legislation Amendment (Further Border Protection Measures) Bill 2002 and Related Matters* (2002), 13, para. 2.34. This figure related to proposals which had earlier failed in the Senate, and the places in question were ultimately excised by Migration Amendment Regulations 2005 (No. 6) (Cth).

[322] Migration Amendment (Designated Unauthorised Arrivals) Bill 2006. See the Senate Legal and Constitutional Legislation Committee, *Provisions of the Migration Amendment (Designated Unauthorised Arrivals) Bill* (June 2006), which recommended against the adoption of the Bill. For discussion of the international law implications of the Bill, see, in particular, McAdam, J., Submission No. 64 to Senate Legal and Constitutional Legislation Committee Inquiry into the Provisions of the Migration Amendment (Designated Unauthorised Arrivals) Bill 2006 (May 2006).

[323] Migration Act 1958 (Cth), s. 198A(3).

[324] In introducing the Migration Amendment (Excision from Migration Zone) Bill 2001 (Cth) into the House of Representatives, the then Minister for Immigration stated: 'Australia will continue to honour our international protection obligations': Second Reading Speech (Mr Ruddock), Cth of Australia, House of Representatives, *Official Hansard* No. 14, 2001 (18 Sept. 2001), 30871.

[325] See discussion of *Amuur* v. *France* above, n. 311 and accompanying text.

to reduce the procedural entitlements of asylum seekers,[326] and thereby deterring them from seeking asylum in Australia. However, the excision of territory, as a means of denying access to asylum procedures, may also constitute a breach of Australia's duty to apply its 1951 Convention obligations in good faith, as well as other human rights instruments and customary international law,[327] and not to frustrate or defeat that treaty's object and purpose.[328]

3.3.3 Non-refoulement *and extradition*

The 1951 Convention says nothing about the extradition of refugees. In principle, *non-refoulement* should also apply in this context, for other provisions of the Convention already recognize the interests of the State of refuge in not committing itself to the reception of serious criminals. Furthermore, article 33(1) prohibits removal 'in any manner whatsoever'. In 1951, however, a number of States were of the view that article 33 did not prejudice extradition.[329] One suspected of a serious non-political crime would in any event be excluded from the benefits of refugee status,[330] but one suspected or guilty of a non-serious non-political crime would remain liable to extradition, even to the State in which he or she had a well-founded fear of persecution. Any conflict of treaty obligations might be further dependent upon which obligation was contracted first, although there is an absolute prohibition on removing an individual to a State in which he or she is at risk of torture.[331] Some States also proscribe extradition to capital punishment, or to cruel, inhuman or degrading treatment or punishment.[332]

[326] Crock, Saul, & Dastyari, *Future Seekers II*, above n. 326, 118.

[327] See Lukashuk, I.I., 'The Principle *pacta sunt servanda* and the Nature of Obligation under International Law', 83 *AJIL* 513, 515 (1989). See also the drafting records of the Vienna Convention on the Law of Treaties: Yearbook of the International Law Commission, 1964, vol. I (Summary Records of the 16th Session), 727th Meeting, (20 May 1964), 52ff; Yearbook of the International Law Commission, 1964, vol. II (Documents of the 16th Session) 7; Yearbook of the International Law Commission, 1965, vol. II (Documents of the First Part of the 17th Session), 788th Meeting, (21 May 1965), 87, 88.

[328] Arts. 26, 31, 1969 Vienna Convention on the Law of Treaties.

[329] See UN doc. A/CONF.2/SR.24, 10 (United Kingdom); ibid., SR.35, 21 (France). At the abortive 1977 United Nations Conference on Territorial Asylum, one article proposed would have protected refugees against extradition to a country in which they might face persecution. The German Democratic Republic and the USSR, however, both prepared amendments reiterating the paramountcy of States' extradition obligations. These conflicting approaches were not resolved at the Conference, and have been overtaken by consolidating State practice.   [330] See above, Ch. 3.

[331] See below, Ch. 6. See also *Soering* v. *United Kingdom* (1989) 11 EHRR 489, para. 88.

[332] On capital punishment, see, for example, art. 11, 1957 European Convention on Extradition; *Einhorn* v. *France*, Application No. 71555/01 (16 Oct. 2001), para. 33 (admissibility decision of the European Court of Human Rights). On cruel, inhuman or degrading treatment or punishment, see art. 3 ECHR50; Council Framework Decision of 13 June 2002 on the European Arrest Warrant and the Surrender Procedures between Member States, preambular para. 13: 'No person should be removed, expelled or extradited to a State where there is a serious risk that he or she would be subjected to the death penalty, torture or other inhuman or degrading treatment or punishment.' For examples of more general prohibitions, see art. 19(1), 1997 International Convention for the Suppression of Terrorist Bombings; art. 21, 1999 International Convention for the Suppression of the Financing of Terrorism; art. 15(1), 2002 Inter-American Convention against Terrorism. See generally Kapferer, S., 'The Interface between Extradition and Asylum', UNHCR Legal and Protection Policy Research

This issue today requires analysis of State practice since 1951, in light of the object and purpose of the Convention and the principle of *non-refoulement*. If States had reservations about the relationship between extradition and article 33 in 1951, these have been displaced by subsequent regional, bilateral, and multi-lateral State practice. The 1981 Inter-American Convention on Extradition pre-cludes extradition '[w]hen, from the circumstances of the case, it can be inferred that persecution for reasons of race, religion or nationality is involved, or that the position of the person sought may be prejudiced for any of these reasons'.[333] Similarly, the 1957 European Convention on Extradition, for example, prohibits extradition, 'if the requested Party has substantial grounds for believing that a request for extradition for an ordinary criminal offence has been made for the pur-pose of prosecuting or punishing a person on account of his race, religion, nation-ality or political opinion, *or that that person's position may be prejudiced for any of those reasons*'.[334] The Committee of Experts of the Council of Europe expanded this article expressly to include the basic elements of the refugee definition, although it declined to write in 'membership of a particular social group' on the ground that it might be interpreted too freely. That apart, every indication is that the Committee intended to close the gap between the political offender and the refugee. It further proposed that the transit of those extradited be excluded through any territory where the life or freedom of the person claimed could be threatened for any of the stated reasons, and this was included in article 21.[335]

Article 3 of the European Convention on Extradition now serves as a model for bilateral treaties and municipal laws.[336] It clearly influenced the Scheme for the Rendition of Fugitive Offenders adopted in 1966 by the Meeting of Commonwealth Law Ministers,[337] and implemented in many Commonwealth countries since then,[338] and is likewise reflected in a number of other multilateral agreements.[339]

Series, PPLA/2003/05 (Nov. 2003); Dugard, J. & van den Wyngaert, C., 'Reconciling Extradition with Human Rights', 92 *AJIL* 187 (1998).

[333] Art. 4(5).   [334] Art. 3(2), emphasis supplied; *ETS*, No. 24; see below, Annexe 2, No. 10.

[335] See generally *Supplementary Report of the Committee of Experts on Extradition to the Committee of Ministers*, Council of Europe doc. CM(57)52.

[336] See, for example, art. 19, 1979 Austrian Extradition Law (*Auslieferungs- und Rechtshilfegesetz: BGBl Nr.* 529/1979), which provides for non-extradition where the proceedings in the requesting State are likely to offend arts. 3 and 6 ECHR50; where the likely punishment is likely to offend art. 3 ECHR50; or where the requested person may face persecution or other serious consequences on grounds akin to those in art. 1 CSR51. Art. 3 of the 1976 Austria–Hungary Extradition Treaty (*BGBl Nr.* 340/1976) likewise provides for non-extradition (a) in respect of political offences; (b) when the person sought enjoys asylum in the requested State; and (c) when it is not in accord with other inter-national obligations of the requested State. Art 4 of the 1980 Austria–Poland Extradition Treaty (*BGBl Nr.* 146/1976) is to similar effect. For detailed examples of other municipal laws, see Kapferer, above, n. 332, para. 226.   [337] Cmn. 3008.

[338] For example UK Fugitive Offenders Act 1967, s. 4; Barbados Extradition Act 1979, s. 7; Kenya Extradition (Commonwealth) Countries Act 1968, s. 6; Papua New Guinea Extradition Act 1975, s. 8; Sierra Leone Extradition Act 1974, s. 15; Singapore Extradition Act 1968, ss. 8, 21; Zambia Extradition Act 1968, s. 31.

[339] Cf. art. 4, 1981 Inter-American Convention on Extradition, calling for non-extradition, 'when, from the circumstances of the case, it can be inferred that persecution for reasons of race, religion or nationality is invoked, or that the position of the person sought may be prejudiced for any of these

The inclusion of the principle *aut dedere aut judicare* in instruments aimed at suppressing certain crimes with an international dimension[340] is further acknowledgment that even the serious criminal may deserve protection against persecution or prejudice, while not escaping trial or punishment. Where non-extradition in such cases is prescribed as an *obligation*, the discretion of the State is significantly confined. *Non-refoulement* becomes obligatory[341] in respect of a class of alleged serious offenders, and no less should be required for the non-serious criminal who would otherwise fall within the exception.[342]

The extradition of refugees was examined in 1980 by the Executive Committee, which reaffirmed the fundamental character of the principle of *non-refoulement*, and recognized that 'refugees should be protected in regard to extradition *to a country where they have well-founded reasons to fear persecution on the grounds enumerated in Article 1(A)(2)* of the 1951 Convention'.[343] Anxious to ensure not only the protection of refugees, but also the prosecution and punishment of serious offences, the Executive Committee stressed 'that protection in

reasons'. See also art. 5, 1977 European Convention on the Suppression of Terrorism, in which non-extradition is optional ('Nothing in this Convention shall be interpreted as imposing an obligation to extradite if...'); art. 9, 1979 International Convention against the Taking of Hostages: UNGA res. 34/146, (17 Dec. 1979), which employs the 'extradition shall not be granted' formula, includes ethnic origin within the list of relevant grounds, and adds one further likely cause of prejudice: 'the reason that communication with [the person requested] by the appropriate authorities of the State entitled to exercise rights of protection cannot be effected'. Where extradition is not granted, art. 8 provides that the State in which the alleged offender is found 'shall... be obliged, without exception whatsoever and whether or not the offence was committed in its territory' to submit the case for prosecution.

[340] See, for example, art. 16, 1963 Tokyo Convention on Offences and Certain Other Acts Committed on Board Aircraft; art. 7(1) CAT84; art. 14, 1985. Inter-American Convention to Prevent and Punish Torture, OAS TS 67; art. VI, 1994; Inter-American Convention on Forced Disappearance of Persons 33 ILM 1429 (1994); art. 9(2), 1989 International Convention against the Recruitment, Use, Financing and Training of Mercenaries, 29 ILM 91 (1990); art. 10(4), 1984; Convention on the Safety of United Nations and Associated Personnel, 2051 *UNTS* 363; art. 7, 1957 European Convention on Extradition, *ETS* No 24; art. IV, 1987 South Asian Association for Regional Cooperation Regional Convention on Suppression of Terrorism; art. 6(h), 1998 Arab Convention on the Suppression of Terrorism; art. 6(8), 1999 Convention of the Organization of the Islamic Conference on Combating International Terrorism; art. 8(4), 1999 OAU Convention on the Prevention and Combating of Terrorism; art. 7, 1970 Convention for the Suppression of Unlawful Seizure of Aircraft, 860 *UNTS* 105; art. 7, 1971 Convention for the Suppression of Unlawful Acts against the Safety of Civil Aviation, 947 *UNTS* 177; art. 7, 1973 Convention on the Prevention and Punishment of Crimes against Internationally Protected Persons, including Diplomatic Agents, 1035 *UNTS* 167; art. 8(1), 1979 International Convention against the Taking of Hostages, 1316 *UNTS* 205; art. 10, 1980 Convention on the Physical Protection of Nuclear Material, 1456 *UNTS* 101.

[341] Given that the 'obligation' only arises where the State 'has substantial grounds' (that is, it has a discretion), it must be considered imperfect. That *non-refoulement* is obligatory does not entail either a duty to grant asylum or a duty not to expel; see further below, and Ch. 7.

[342] Australian legislation requires the Attorney-General to consider in extradition cases whether removal would breach art. 33 CSR51 or art. 3 CAT84, whereas asylum seekers' claims are assessed only against the former: Extradition Act 1998 (Cth), s. 22(3)(b).

[343] See Executive Committee Conclusion No. 17 (1980) (emphasis supplied); *Report* of the Sub-Committee of the Whole on International Protection: UN doc. A/AC.96/586, para. 16. The Sub-Committee's recommendations regarding the refugee, recognized in one State, whose extradition is then sought from another State in which he or she is temporarily visiting (UN doc. A/AC.96/586, para. 16, conclusions 8 and 9) were not adopted by the Executive Committee.

regard to extradition applies to persons who fulfil the criteria of the refugee definition and who are not excluded by virtue of Article 1(F)(b)' of the Convention.[344]

Judicial decisions from different jurisdictions support this approach. In the United Kingdom, a serious risk of prejudice has been considered sufficient to justify protection in extradition and refugee cases, certainly since the decision of the House of Lords in *Fernandez* v. *Government of Singapore*.[345] Courts in other States have also consolidated the basic principle of protection against extradition in favour of the refugee. In *Bereciartua-Echarri*, for example, the French *Conseil d'Etat* ruled in 1988 that the appellant could not be extradited so long as he retained the status of refugee, save in the serious cases contemplated by article 33(2) of the Convention. This was part of the general principles of refugee law, and to permit extradition would render the concept of protection ineffective.[346] In a 1990 decision, the *Schweizerisches Bundesgericht* (Swiss Federal Court) also ruled that a refugee could not be returned to his or her country of origin. Most States, said the Court, consider that article 33 is a legal bar to extradition; the article's purpose is to guarantee refugees against the loss of protection in the asylum State, and it would be unjust if a refugee who could not lawfully be expelled to the country of origin, could nevertheless be extradited.[347] Similarly, the Slovenian Constitutional Court held in 2000 that a decision granting asylum prevents any forcible removal of the individual concerned, including extradition.[348] Following this rationale, the Swiss *Bundesgericht* ruled that an extradition order would be given suspensive effect until refugee status had been finally determined, so as to avoid a conflict between Switzerland's extradition obligations and its duties

[344] As the Argentine delegate reiterated at the Executive Committee in 1989, 'While extradition was a legitimate practice in combating crime, it was inadmissible in international law in the case of a refugee': UN doc. A/AC.96/SR.442, para. 46. Later in the same session, the US delegate appeared to qualify his country's position: 'Concerning the extradition of refugees, the United States Government reserved its position on the application of the 1951 Convention and the 1967 Protocol to persons against whom extradition proceedings had been initiated until the courts hearing their cases had taken a formal position on them': ibid, para. 84. Given the ambiguity and general lack of clarity, one cannot be certain whether, in the context of extradition proceedings (which involve both a judicial process and an executive decision), the United States will or will not take refugee status into account. If it chooses to ignore status in the case of one who is not excluded or otherwise within the exceptions to *non-refoulement*, then violation of international obligations will result.

[345] [1971] 1 WLR 987.

[346] *Bereciartua-Echarri*, No. 85.234, *Recueil Lebon*, (1 Apr. 1988); Iogna-Prat, M., 'L'Affaire Bereciartua-Echarri,' 1 *IJRL* 403 (1989).

[347] *Schweizerisches Bundesgericht*, Ref. 1A.127/1990/tg, 18 Dec. 1990; abstracted as Case Abstract No. *IJRL/0152:* 5 *IJRL* 271 (1993). In its 1980 paper on extradition submitted to the Sub-Committee (UN doc. EC/SCP/14, 27 Aug. 1980), UNHCR stressed that the principle of speciality offered no defence against excessive punishment or prejudicial treatment. The court agreed, and remarked that it was no alternative to protection by non-extradition. The court further took into account art. 3 of the European Convention on Extradition, which it characterized as the concrete expression of *non-refoulement* in extradition law, additionally capable of protecting persons who had committed serious non-political crimes, and so might be denied protection under the 1951 Convention.

[348] Decision No. Up-78/00 of 29 June 2000, cited in Kapferer, 'The Interface between Extradition and Asylum', above, n. 332, para. 227.

under the 1951 Convention.[349] Extradition is also barred if there is a risk that the requesting State may expose the individual to *refoulement* by surrendering him or her to a third State.[350] In the French, Swiss, and Slovenian cases it was implicitly accepted that extradition might proceed, once or if asylum or refugee status were revoked in accordance with the Convention.

In the *Altun* case, the European Commission considered that even though extradition for a political offence did not necessarily raise an issue under article 3 ECHR50, the facts might nevertheless oblige it 'to determine whether ... there is a certain risk of prosecution for political reasons which could lead to an unjustified or disproportionate sentence being passed on the applicant and as a result inhuman treatment'. The Commission took account of the applicant's political past, the political background to the extradition request, and occurrences of torture in Turkey. It was unable to rule out 'with sufficient certainty that the criminal proceedings ... had been falsely inspired', or dismiss the fact that the applicant 'is not someone who may be considered protected from all danger'.[351]

State practice reflects an acceptance of 'conditional' extradition, based on guarantees by the receiving State that the transfer will not constitute *refoulement*. An assurance by the receiving State not to impose the death penalty, for example, even where that would be permissible under domestic law, is regarded by many States as sufficient to enable extradition within the framework of their human rights obligations. However, this practice has been criticized as incompatible with the absolute nature of States' *non-refoulement* obligations under article 3 ECHR50, article 3 CAT84, and article 7 ICCPR66, which cannot be 'contracted out of' by guarantees.[352] Some commentators suggest that guarantees may be appropriate to ensure that the individual will not be exposed to capital punishment or an unfair trial, but will generally be insufficient to relieve the State of its *non-refoulement* obligations with respect to torture or cruel, inhuman or degrading treatment or punishment, especially if there is a pattern of abuse in the receiving State.[353] The UN Commission on Human Rights Special Rapporteur on Torture and Other Cruel, Inhuman or Degrading Treatment or Punishment, Manfred Nowak, has

---

[349] *Schweizerisches Bundesgericht*, (11 Sept. 1996), BGE 122 II 373, 380–1.

[350] *Schweizerisches Asylrekurskommission*, EMARK 2001/4; *Conseil d'Etat*, (10 Apr. 1991), *Kilic*, as cited in Kapferer, 'The Interface between Extradition and Asylum', above n. 332, para. 229.

[351] *Altun* v. *Federal Republic of Germany* (10308/83), 36 *D & R* 201. See also *Kirkwood* v. *United Kingdom* (1984) 6 EHRR 373; Van den Wyngaert, C., 'Applying the European Convention on Human Rights to Extradition: Opening Pandora's Box?', 39 *ICLQ* 757 (1990).

[352] European Council on Refugees and Exiles, 'Comments on the Commission Working Document on the Relationship between Safeguarding Internal Security and Complying with International Protection Obligations and Instruments' (London, May 2002) <www.ecre.org/statements/security.shtml> (4 Feb. 2004), para. 2.3.2; see also *Kindler* v. *Canada*, Comm. No. 470/1991 (30 Jul. 1993): UN doc. CCPR/C/48/D/470/1991, para. 6.7.

[353] Kapferer, above, n. 332, para. 241; see also paras. 134–7. For political vis-à-vis legal considerations, see *Youssef* v. *Home Office* [2004] EWHC 1884 (QB); Goodwin-Gill, G. S. & Husain, R., 'Diplomatic Assurances and Deportation', paper given at the JUSTICE/Sweet & Maxwell Conference on Counter-Terrorism and Human Rights, 28 Jun. 2005.

expressed concern that States are using diplomatic assurances and memoranda of understanding to circumvent the absolute prohibition on torture under international law, noting that bilateral agreements are contrary to CAT84 and undermine the monitoring system provided by the UN treaty bodies. Furthermore, the fact that such agreements are sought 'is already an indicator of the systematic practice of torture in the requested States', yet they seek only to ensure that particular individuals are not tortured, rather than condemning the system of torture.[354]

In conclusion, State practice, and the greater body of opinion representing those most active in the protection of refugees and the development of refugee law, regards the principle of *non-refoulement* as likewise protecting the refugee from extradition.[355]

3.3.4 Non-refoulement *and expulsion*[356]

While States may be bound by the principle of *non-refoulement*, they as yet retain discretion as regards both the grant of 'durable asylum' and the conditions under which it may be enjoyed or terminated. States parties to the 1951 Convention/ 1967 Protocol, however, have acknowledged that the expulsion of refugees raises special problems, and under article 32 they undertake not to 'expel a refugee lawfully in their territory save on grounds of national security or public order'. Decisions to expel are further required to be in accordance with due process of law and, 'except where compelling reasons of national security otherwise require', refugees shall be accorded the right of appeal.[357] Moreover, refugees under order

---

[354] UN News Service, 'Bilateral Deportation Agreements Undermine International Human Rights Law—UN Expert', (26 Oct. 2005).

[355] See Recommendation No. R(80)9 of the Committee of Ministers of the Council of Europe to the effect that governments should not allow extradition to States not party to ECHR50 where there are substantial grounds to believe that art. 3(2) of the European Convention on Extradition would otherwise be applicable.

[356] Generally on States' power of expulsion, see Goodwin-Gill, *Movement of Persons*, above, n. 2, 201–310; and on expulsion to a particular State, 218–28. See also Hathaway, *Rights of Refugees*, (2005) 412, 657–95 (including references to asylum seekers generally and not just to 'refugees lawfully in the territory', as provided in art. 32 CSR51).

[357] See also art. 13 ICCPR66; Clark, T., 'Human Rights and Expulsion: Giving Content to the Concept of Asylum', 4 *IJRL* 189 (1992); Tiberghien, F., 'L'expulsion des réfugiés: Problèmes legislatifs et jurisprudentiels', *Doc. réf.*, no. 73, 5/14 mars 1989, Suppl., CJ, 1–8. The importance of procedural safeguards is perhaps best illustrated by cases in which they have been denied. In *Agiza* v. *Sweden*, the Committee against Torture found that Sweden had violated art. 3 CAT84 by expelling a suspected terrorist to Egypt, where he was tortured. The Committee explained that normally, individuals could appeal to the Swedish Migration Board and the Aliens Appeals Board for review of a decision to expel, and that these procedures satisfied art. 3 requirements of an effective, independent, and impartial review. 'In the present case, however, due to the presence of national security concerns, these tribunals relinquished the complainant's case to the Government, which took the first and at once final decision to expel him. The Committee emphasizes that there was no possibility for review of any kind of this decision. The Committee recalls that the Convention's protections are absolute, even in the context of national security concerns, and that such considerations emphasise the importance of appropriate review mechanisms. While national security concerns might justify some adjustments to be made to the particular process of review, the mechanism chosen must continue to

of expulsion are to be allowed a reasonable period within which to seek legal admission into another country, though States retain discretion to apply 'such internal measures as they may deem necessary'.

The restricted grounds of expulsion have been adopted in the laws of many States,[358] and have been taken into account in a number of judicial decisions.[359] The benefit is limited to refugees who enjoy what might loosely be called 'resident status' in the State in question, and one admitted temporarily remains liable to removal in the same way as any other alien.[360] The permitted power of expulsion, however, does not include the power to return the individual to the country in which his or her life or freedom may be threatened, unless the further exacting provisions which regulate exceptions to the principle of *non-refoulement* are also met.[361] Expulsion to torture is prohibited in all circumstances.[362] In 2005, the Executive Committee again expressed deep concern that 'refugee protection is seriously jeopardized by expulsion of refugees leading to refoulement', and called on States 'to refrain from taking such measures and in particular from returning or expelling refugees contrary to the principle of non-refoulement'.[363] Article 32 thus supplements, but is limited by, article 33.

---

satisfy art. 3's requirements of effective, independent and impartial review. In the present case, therefore, on the strength of the information before it, the Committee concludes that the absence of any avenue of judicial or independent administrative review of the Government's decision to expel the complainant does not meet the procedural obligation to provide for effective, independent and impartial review required by art. 3 of the Convention.': *Agiza* v. *Sweden*, UN doc. CAT/C/34/D/233/2003 (24 May 2005), para. 13.8.

[358] See, for example, the German *Aufenthaltsgesetz* §56(1) (since 1 Jan. 2005): 'Ein Ausländer, der . . . 5. als Asylberechtigter anerkannt ist, im Bundesgebiet die Rechtstellung eines ausländischen Flüchtlings genießt oder einen von einer Behörde der Bundesrepublik Deutschland ausgestellten Reiseausweis nach dem Abkommen über die Rechtstellung für Flüchtlinge vom 28. Juli 1951 . . . besitzt, genießt besonderen Ausweisungsschutz. Er wird nur aus schwerwiegenden Gründen der öffentlichen Sicherheit und Ordnung ausgewiesen.'; Asylum Law 1998 (*loi sur l'asile*) of Switzerland, art. 65: 'Le réfugié ne peut être expulsé que s'il compromet la sûreté intérieure ou extérieure de la Suisse ou s'il a porté gravement atteinte à l'ordre public. L'article 5 est réservé.'

[359] See, for example, *Yugoslav Refugee (Germany)* case: 26 *ILR* 496; *Homeless Alien (Germany)* case: 26 *ILR* 503; *Refugee (Germany)* case: 28 *ILR* 297; *Expulsion of an Alien (Austria)* case: 28 *ILR* 310; *R* v. *Immigration Appeal Tribunal, ex p. Musisi* [1984] Imm AR 175; *Bugdaycay* v. *Secretary of State for the Home Department* [1987] 1 AC 514 (HL); *Barrera* v. *Canada* (1992) 99 DLR (4th) 264; see generally *NAGV and NAGW of 2002* v. *Minister for Immigration and Multicultural and Indigenous Affairs* [2005] HCA 6, 213 ALR 668. See also Henckaerts, J.-M., *Mass Expulsion in Modern International Law and Practice*, (1995), 99–107.   [360] Robinson, *Commentary*, 157.

[361] In the *Refugee (Germany)* case (above note) the Federal Administrative Court held that a refugee unlawfully in the country could be expelled, provided he or she was not returned to the country in which life or freedom would be threatened. An almost identical conclusion was reached in a 1974 US decision, *Chim Ming* v. *Marks* 505 F.2d 1170 (2nd Cir.). In the *Expulsion of an Alien (Austria)* case (above note), the Austrian Supreme Court observed when upholding an expulsion order that it merely required a person to leave the State, but did not render him or her liable to be returned to a specific foreign country.

[362] See Ch. 6; *Agiza* v. *Sweden* UN doc. CAT/C/34/D/233/2003 (24 May 2005).

[363] Executive Committee General Conclusion on International Protection No. 102 (2005), para. (j), recalling its earlier Conclusion Nos. 6 (1977) and 7 (1977).

Article 32 may yet have both advantages and disadvantages for the refugee. Thus, one expelled for the serious reasons stated in article 32(1) is likely to face major difficulties in securing admission into any other country.[364] Return to the country of origin being ruled out, the refugee may be exposed to prosecution and detention for failure to depart. As only the State of nationality is obliged to admit the refugee,[365] the expelling country may find itself frustrated in its attempts at removal. For these reasons, in 1977, the Executive Committee recommended that expulsion should be employed only in very exceptional cases. Where execution of the order was impracticable, it further recommended that States consider giving refugee delinquents the same treatment as national delinquents, and that the refugee be detained only if absolutely necessary for reasons of national security or public order.[366]

3.3.5 Non-refoulement *and illegal entry*

In view of the normative quality of *non-refoulement* in international law, the precise legal status of refugees under the immigration or aliens law of the State of refuge is irrelevant, although a State seeking to avoid responsibility will often classify them as prohibited or illegal immigrants. Refugees who flee will frequently have no time for immigration formalities, and are in any case likely to be ineligible for visas sought through official migration channels. Allowance for this is contained in article 31 of the Convention, which of all articles comes closest to dealing with the controversial question of admission. This is not formally required; instead, penalties on account of illegal entry or presence shall not be imposed on refugees 'coming directly from a territory where their life or freedom was threatened... provided they present themselves without delay... and show good cause for their illegal entry or presence'.[367] Refugees are not required to have come directly from their country of origin, but other countries or territories passed through should also have constituted actual or potential threats to life or freedom. Indeed, the drafters of the provision expressly noted that someone who had spent a fortnight or so elsewhere before reaching the country in which he or she claimed asylum should not be precluded from the protection of article 31,[368] and this was

---

[364] See *Ad hoc* Committee on Statelessness and Related Problems, 'Memorandum by the Secretary-General', UN doc. E/AC.32/2, (3 Jan. 1950), 46.

[365] See Goodwin-Gill, *Movement of Persons*, above, n. 2, 20–1, 44–6. 136–7.

[366] Executive Committee Conclusion No. 7 (1977).

[367] For a comprehensive discussion of art. 31, including an analysis of national laws and State practice, see Goodwin-Gill, G. S, 'Article 31 of the 1951 Convention relating to the Status of Refugees: Non-Penalization, Detention, and Protection' in Feller, E., Türk, V., Nicholson, F., eds., *Refugee Protection in International Law: UNHCR's Global Consultations on International Protection*, (2003), 187 (hereafter, Goodwin-Gill, 'Article 31').

[368] Conference of Plenipotentiaries on the Status of Refugees and Stateless Persons, 'Summary Record of the 14th Meeting', Geneva, (10 Jul. 1951), UN doc. A/CONF.2/SR.14 (22 Nov. 1951), (Mr Herment, Belgium), 12. See Hathaway, *Rights of Refugees*, (2005), above, n. 70, 396 for comparative judicial decisions on this issue.

again endorsed by an Expert Roundtable in 2001.[369] The protection applies not only to persons ultimately accorded refugee status, but also to persons claiming asylum in good faith, including those travelling on false documents.[370] What remains unclear is whether the refugee is entitled to invoke article 31 when continued flight has been dictated more by the refusal of other countries to grant asylum, or by the operation of exclusionary provisions such as those on safe third country, safe country of origin or time limits. Whether these constitute 'good cause' for illegal entry would seem to rest with the State authorities, subject to the controlling impact of *non-refoulement*.[371] However, having a well-founded fear of persecution is generally recognized in itself as constituting 'good cause'.[372] Furthermore, in *Adimi*, Simon Brown L.J. found that refugees have 'some element of choice' as to where they claim asylum:

[A]ny merely short term stopover en route to such intended sanctuary cannot forfeit the protection of the Article, and . . . the main touchstones by which exclusion from protection should be judged are the length of stay in the intermediate country, the reasons for delaying there (even a substantial delay in an unsafe third country would be reasonable were the time spent trying to acquire the means of travelling on), and whether or not the refugee sought or found there protection *de jure* or *de facto* from the persecution they were fleeing.[373]

International law does not impose a duty on the asylum seeker to lodge a protection claim at any *particular* stage of flight. On the other hand, domestic law may preclude asylum seekers from lodging an asylum claim if they have transited through other 'safe' countries.[374] Furthermore, States may legislatively stipulate the meaning of 'without delay' by requiring that asylum seekers lodge an asylum claim within a prescribed period, or else lose entitlements to particular benefits.[375]

---

[369] Expert Roundtable, 'Summary Conclusions: Article 31 of the 1951 Convention' (Geneva, 8–9 Nov. 2001), paras. 10(b)–(d), in Feller, Türk & Nicholson, *Refugee Protection in International Law*, above, n. 367.   [370] *R. v. Uxbridge Magistrates' Court, ex p. Adimi* [2001] QB 667.

[371] See further below Ch. 7. Hathaway, *Law of Refugee Status*, (1991), 46–50.

[372] Goodwin-Gill, 'Article 31', above, n. 367, 196; Expert Roundtable, 'Summary Conclusions', above, note, para. 10(e).

[373] *Adimi*, [2001] QB 667, 678. This is supported by Executive Committee Conclusion No. 15 (1979), para. (h).

[374] In Australia, secondary movement can be used as a bar to asylum. Reg. 200.212.(1) of the Migration Regulations 1994 (Cth) provides that individuals who have resided for a continuous period of at least seven days in a country in which they could have sought and obtained effective protection are ineligible for a permanent protection visa, although under sub-s. (2), the Minister may waive this requirement. In practice, it is typically waived: Refugee and Immigration Legal Centre, 'Discussion Paper: Recent Developments and Future Directions', (Aug. 2005), <http://www.rile.org.au/repsubs.htm>. See Hathaway, *Rights of Refugees*, (2005), 372–3 for other examples.

[375] In the UK, see *R. (Limbuela) v. Secretary of State for the Home Department* [2006] 1 AC 396, [2005] UKHL 66. Whereas s. 95 of the Immigration and Asylum Act 1999 authorized the Secretary of State to provide support to asylum seekers who appeared to be destitute, s. 55 of the Nationality, Immigration and Asylum Act 2002 revoked that authority where the Secretary of State considered that the asylum claim had not been made as soon as reasonably practicable after the asylum seeker's arrival in the UK. In 'late' cases, support could only be provided when the Secretary of State considered it necessary to avoid a breach of the individual's rights under ECHR50: s. 55(5). The court held that the Secretary of State had a positive obligation to provide support, 'when it appears on a fair and

The term 'penalties' is not defined in article 31, prompting the question whether it encompasses only criminal sanctions, or whether it also extends to administrative penalties (such as administrative detention). Following the Human Rights Committee's reasoning that the term 'penalty' in article 15(1) ICCPR66 must be interpreted in light of that provision's object and purpose,[376] article 31 warrants a broad interpretation reflective of its aim to proscribe sanctions on account of illegal entry or presence. An overly formal or restrictive approach is inappropriate, since it may circumvent the fundamental protection intended.[377] Thus, measures such as arbitrary detention[378] or procedural bars on applying for asylum may constitute 'penalties'.[379] This is supported by Executive Committee Conclusion No. 22 (1981), which states that asylum seekers should 'not be penalized or exposed to any unfavourable treatment solely on the ground that their presence in the country is considered unlawful'.[380] In Conclusion No. 97 (2003), the Executive Committee made clear that intercepted asylum seekers 'should not become liable to criminal prosecution under the *Protocol against the Smuggling of Migrants by Land, Sea and Air* for the fact of having been the object of conduct set forth in article 6 of the Protocol; nor should any intercepted person incur any penalty for illegal entry or presence in a State in cases where the terms of Article 31 of the 1951 Convention are met'.[381]

Though administrative detention is technically permissible under article 31(2), it will be equivalent to a penal sanction whenever basic safeguards are lacking (with respect to conditions, duration, review, and so on). In this context, the distinction between administrative and criminal sanctions becomes irrelevant, and the key issue is whether the measures taken are reasonable and necessary, arbitrary or discriminatory, or a breach of human rights law.[382]

objective assessment of all relevant facts and circumstances that an individual applicant faces an imminent prospect of serious suffering caused or materially aggravated by denial of shelter, food or the most basic necessities of life': para. 5 (Lord Bingham). In Australia, asylum seekers who arrive on a visa of some kind are denied work rights and Medicare support if they do not lodge their asylum claim within 45 days of arrival: Migration Regulations 1994, (Cth) reg. 2.20.

[376] *Van Duzen* v. *Canada*, Comm. No. 50/1979, UN doc. CCPR/C/15/D/50/1979 (7 Apr. 1982), para. 10.2; see also Opsahl, T. & de Zayas, A., 'The Uncertain Scope of Article 15(1) of the International Covenant on Civil and Political Rights', (1983) *Canadian Human Rights Yearbook* 237.

[377] See, for example, Decision of the Social Security Commissioner in Case No. CIS 4439/98 (25 Nov. 1999), para. 16, where Commissioner Rowland found that *treatment* less favourable than that accorded to others, imposed on account of illegal entry, constitutes a penalty under art. 31, unless it is objectively justifiable on administrative grounds.

[378] See Expert Roundtable, 'Summary Conclusions', above, n. 369, para. 11(a). 'For the purposes of Article 31(2), there is no distinction between restrictions on movement ordered or applied *administratively*, and those ordered or applied *judicially*. The power of the State to impose a restriction must be related to a recognized object or purpose, and there must be a reasonable relationship of proportionality between the end and the means. Restrictions on movement must not be imposed unlawfully and arbitrarily (emphasis added). Cf. the majority's view in *Al-Kateb* v. *Goodwin* [2004] HCA 37.

[379] Note Executive Committee Conclusion No. 15 (1979), para. (i): 'While asylum-seekers may be required to submit their asylum request within a certain time limit, failure to do so, or the non-fulfilment of other formal requirements, should not lead to an asylum request being excluded from consideration.'

[380] Para. B.2(a).   [381] Para. (a)(vi).   [382] See further Ch. 9, s. 1.1 on detention.

To impose penalties in the absence of *individual* assessment of the asylum seeker's claim not only breaches article 31(1), but is also likely to violate the State's obligation to ensure and protect the human rights of everyone within its territory or subject to its jurisdiction.[383] A conviction may only be executed once it has been determined that the individual is not a Convention refugee; this has not always been respected in State practice.[384]

At the 1951 Conference, several representatives considered that the undertaking not to impose penalties did not exclude the possibility of resort to expulsion.[385] Article 31 does not require that refugees be permitted to remain, and paragraph 2 emphasizes this point indirectly, by providing:

The Contracting States shall not apply to the movements of such refugees restrictions other than those which are necessary and . . . [they] shall only be applied *until their status in the country is regularized or they obtain admission into another country*. The Contracting States shall allow such refugees a reasonable period and all the necessary facilities to obtain admission into another country (emphasis added).

Given that the principle of *non-refoulement* remains applicable, the freedom of the State finally to refuse regularization of status can well be circumscribed in practice. Article 31, on its face, nevertheless appears to allow the State to continue to keep the unsettled refugee under a regime of restricted movement, for example, in prison, camp, or settlement, or subject to other restrictions, such as denial of access to employment, social security, or equivalent support. For many States, however, their human rights obligations will further limit their freedom of action, and require that refugees not be rendered destitute or otherwise subject to inhuman or degrading treatment.[386]

4. Measures not amounting to *refoulement*

The core of meaning of *non-refoulement* requires States not to return refugees in any manner whatsoever to territories in which they face the possibility of persecution. But States may deny admission in ways not obviously amounting to breach of the principle. For example, stowaways and refugees rescued at sea may be refused entry; refugee boats may be towed back out to sea and advised to sail on; and

---

[383] Art. 2(1) ICCPR66; art. 1 ECHR50; art. 1 ACHR69.

[384] On State practice, see Goodwin-Gill, 'Article 31', above n. 367, 197–214; Dunstan, R., 'United Kingdom: Breaches of Article 31 of the 1951 Refugee Convention', 10 *IJRL* 205 (1998); cf. Immigration and Asylum Act 1999, s. 31; Hathaway, *Rights of Refugees*, (2005), 372–3.

[385] UN doc. A/CONF.2/SR.13, 12–14 (1951) (Canada, United Kingdom). Cf. art. 5, 1954 Caracas Convention on Territorial Asylum; see below, Annexe 2, No. 3.

[386] See further below, Ch. 6, s. 6.3, on the implications of *non-refoulement* through time; and Ch. 9, s.1.1 on detention. See also UNHCR, *Safeguards for Asylum Seekers and Refugees in the Context of Irregular Migration into and within Europe: A Survey of the Law and Practice of 31 European States* (Jun. 2001); Lawyers Committee for Human Rights, *Review of States' Procedures and Practices relating to Detention of Asylum Seekers* (Sept. 2002).

asylum applicants may be sent back to transit or 'safe third' countries. State authorities may also induce expulsion through various forms of threat and coercion.[387]

4.1 STOWAWAYS

Without breaching the principle of *non-refoulement*, the State where a stowaway asylum seeker arrives may require the ship's master to keep the stowaway on board and travel on to the next port of call; or it may call upon the flag State to assume responsibility where the next port of call is unacceptable; or it may allow temporary disembarkation pending resettlement elsewhere. In the absence of rules regulating the appropriate State to consider the asylum claim, the situation is comparable to that of refugees in orbit, while practical solutions are made more difficult to obtain by the tendency of States' immigration laws to deal summarily with stowaways.[388]

On several occasions during the Indo-China exodus, port of call States sought to make stowaways' disembarkation conditional on guarantees of resettlement from flag States, by analogy with the then developing practice for rescue-at-sea cases in South East Asia.[389]

The issue of stowaway asylum seekers was first briefly examined by an Executive Committee working group during a rescue-at-sea meeting in Geneva in July 1982. While it was agreed that the principle of *non-refoulement* should be maintained, there were widely diverging views on how problems should be solved, and the recommendations on stowaways were not adopted.[390] Although there was more success in 1988, the debate was not all plain sailing. Executive Committee

---

[387] In *Orantes-Hernandez* v. *Meese* 685 F. Supp. 1488 (C.D.Cal. 1988), aff'd sub nom. *Orantes-Hernandez* v. *Thornburgh* 919 F. 3d 549 (9th Cir., 1990), the court found that substantial numbers of Salvadoran asylum seekers were signing 'voluntary departure' forms under coercion, including threats of detention, deportation, relocation to a remote place, and communication of personal details to their government. See also Amnesty International British Section, *Playing Human Pinball*, (1995), 59–61 (coercion to effect 'voluntary departure' to 'safe third country').

[388] See, for example, the United States Immigration and Nationality Act 1952, 18 USC § 2199.

[389] As a port of call State, Australia had only limited success in arguing for this proviso with respect to flag States Greece, Italy, and Denmark. Most stowaways in the period 1979–82 were ultimately allowed to disembark and to lodge claims for refugee status; a few were resettled with relatives in third States. None of the States involved had ratified the 1957 International Convention relating to Stowaways, which still awaits entry into force. Art. 5(2) provides that in considering application of the Convention, 'the Master and the appropriate authorities of the port of disembarkation will take into account the reasons which may be put forward by the stowaway for not being disembarked at or returned to' various ports or States. Art. 5(3) declares that, 'The provisions of [the] Convention shall not in any way affect the power or obligation [*sic*] of a Contracting State to grant political asylum.' Art. 3 provides that where a stowaway is otherwise unreturnable to any other State, he may be returned to 'the Contracting State whose flag was flown by the ship in which he was found', unless subject to 'a previous individual order of deportation or prohibition from entry'. For text, see *Conférence diplomatique de droit maritime, 10ème session, Bruxelles*, 491–503, (1958). Both the United Kingdom and the Netherlands opposed these aspects of the Convention on the ground that they made too many inroads on national immigration control: ibid., 200, 436–7, 441–3, and 632–3.

[390] *Report* of the Working Group on problems related to the rescue of asylum-seekers in distress at sea: UN doc. EC/SCP/21, (1982), paras. 22ff.

Conclusion No. 53 (1988) emphasized that like other asylum seekers, stowaway asylum seekers 'must be protected against forcible return to their country of origin'. Without prejudice to any flag State responsibilities, it also recommended that they 'should, whenever possible, be allowed to disembark at the first port of call', with the opportunity to have their refugee claim determined, 'provided that this does not necessarily imply a durable solution in the country of the port of disembarkation'.[391]

State practice has not so far given rise to a rule on the treatment of stowaway asylum seekers, although attempts have been made to promote shared responsibilities for stowaways generally.[392] Guidelines promulgated by the International Maritime Organization (IMO) and reflected in the Convention on the Facilitation of Maritime Traffic, probably encapsulate the prevailing view of States, which recognizes that 'stowaways arriving at or entering a country without the required documents are, in general, illegal entrants', and '[d]ecisions on dealing with such situations are the prerogative of the countries where such arrival or entry occurs.'[393] In reality, however, the discretion of the coastal State may be limited by the particular facts of the case. If the flag State refuses to accept any responsibility for resettlement and if the ship's next port of call is in a country in which the stowaway asylum seeker's life or freedom may be threatened, then the practical effect of refusing disembarkation is *refoulement*. The nominal authority of the flag State to require diversion to a safe port, which would in any case be controversial where a charter party was involved, can hardly be considered a practical alternative, or 'last opportunity', to avoid *refoulement*. The paramount consideration remains the refugee status of those on board; a refusal to take account of their claims, either on the specious basis that they have not 'entered' State territory or on the (disputed) ground that they are the responsibility of the flag or any other State, would not suffice to avoid liability for breach of the principle of *non-refoulement*.[394]

---

[391] *Report* of the 39th Session: UN doc. A/AC.96/721 (13 Oct. 1988), para. 25. Greece proposed deletion of the words 'whenever possible', and the phrase beginning, 'provided that this does not necessarily imply . . .': ibid., para. 36.2. See also UNHCR, *Note on Stowaway Asylum-Seekers*: UN doc. EC/SCP/51 (22 Jul. 1988); Report of the Sub-Committee of the Whole on International Protection: UN doc. A/AC.96/717 (3 Oct. 1988), paras. 36–42; Venezuela: UN doc. A/AC.96/SR.431, para. 7; Australia: ibid., para. 9 (1988).

[392] Given that the 1957 Convention has not yet entered into force, the main instrument on the treatment of stowaways is the IMO, *Guidelines on the Allocation of Responsibilities to Seek the Successful Resolution of Stowaway Cases* (Res. A.871 (20), adopted 1997), the provisions of which are reflected in 2002 amendments to the 1965 Convention on Facilitation of International Maritime Traffic (amendments adopted 10 Jan. 2002, entered into force 1 May 2003). Regional agreements on responsibility for determining asylum claims (such as the Dublin Regulation) may also be relevant: see, for example, dispute between Italy and Malta discussed in Migration Policy Group, 'Migration News Sheet', (Nov. 2004), 13. The IMO compiles State reports of stowaway incidents, for example, IMO, 'Reports on Stowaway Incidents', Jan. to Mar. 2005, FAL.2/Circ.88 (31 Mar. 2005).

[393] IMO, *Guidelines on the Allocation of Responsibilities to Seek the Successful Resolution of Stowaway Cases* (Res. A.871 (20), adopted 1997), para. 4.1.

[394] Cf. *Yiu Sing Chun v. Sava* 708 F.2d 869 (2nd Cir., 1983), holding that under the 1980 United States Refugee Act, alien stowaways are entitled to an evidentiary hearing on their asylum applications. Such proceeding is now provided in the asylum regulations: 8 *CFR* §253.1(f).

4.2 ARRIVAL OF ASYLUM SEEKERS BY BOAT

The arrival of asylum seekers by boat puts at issue not only the interpretation of *non-refoulement*, but also the extent of freedom of navigation and of coastal States' right of police and control. In South East Asia during the Indo-China exodus, States several times prevented boats from landing, and towed back to the high seas many which had penetrated the territorial sea and internal waters.

The United States and Australia actively pursue interception policies, using coast guard or navy boats forcibly to prevent the arrival of boats carrying migrants.[395] As already noted, in 1981, the United States announced a policy of 'interdiction' on the high seas of boats which were believed to be bringing illegal aliens to that country. In September 2001, Australia established a naval interception programme called 'Operation Relex',[396] and began excising territory from its domestic 'migration zone' in order juridically to deny the fact of 'entry' to asylum seekers arriving by boat. As part of 'Operation Relex', two boats that entered Australian waters in October 2001 were intercepted, detained, and returned to Indonesian waters without any assurances by Indonesia to respect the principle of *non-refoulement*. Domestic attempts such as these to regulate access to territory cannot, however, circumvent States' obligations under international law.

From time to time, European States have also engaged in interception at sea.[397] Certain coastal States have refused to allow boats from North Africa to disembark, while others have been returned without allowing the asylum seekers on board to have a substantive hearing of their claims.[398] Italy has coordinated interception programmes in the Mediterranean. In November 2005, the 35 EuroMed States, comprising the 25 EU Member States and 10 Mediterranean partner governments, met for the first time in a decade to discuss cooperation on population movements across the Mediterranean Sea. UNHCR called on the EuroMed States to strengthen their commitment to the principles of refugee protection, in light of rising death tolls at sea and events involving asylum seekers leaving Morocco and Spain's North African enclaves.[399]

The high seas,[400] of course, are not subject to the exercise of sovereignty by any State, and ships are liable to the exclusive jurisdiction of the flag State, save in

---

[395] For detail of the Australian and US interception programmes, see van Selm, J. & Cooper, B., *The New 'Boat People': Ensuring Safety and Determining Status* (2006).

[396] 'Operation Relex II' remains in operation as at Sept. 2006: Australian Department of Defence <http://www.defence.gov.au/globalops.cfm>.

[397] For examples, see Selm & Cooper, above, n. 395. Italy has engaged in numerous attempts to turn around smuggling vessels from Albania (cf. *Xhavara* v. *Italy and Albania*, App. No. 39473/98 (11 Jan. 2001) (inadmissible)), or divert boats from North Africa, but has not boarded boats like the US Coast Guard. In Oct. 2004, a new naval operation called 'Neptune 3' began patrolling the Mediterranean with Italian and Maltese vessels and planes: Migration Policy Group, 'Migration News Sheet' (Nov. 2004), 13.   [398] UNHCR Global Report 2004, 'Western Europe', 452–3.

[399] UN News Service, 'UN Refugee Agency Calls on Mediterranean Countries to Recognize Refugee Rights' (25 Nov. 2005).

[400] Art. 1, 1958 Geneva Convention on the High Seas; art. 86, 1982 UN Convention on the Law of the Sea (UNCLOS82).

exceptional cases provided for by treaty or under general international law. The freedom of the high seas, however, is generally expressed as a freedom common to States,[401] while the boats of asylum seekers, like their passengers, will most usually be denied flag State protection. Similarly, the right of innocent passage for the purpose of traversing the territorial sea or entering internal waters is framed with normal circumstances in mind. A coastal State may argue, first, that boats of asylum seekers are to be assimilated to ships without nationality[402] and are subject to boarding and other measures on the high seas.[403] The better view is that this does not extend to a right to tow a boat to another part of the sea.[404] Additionally, the State may argue that existing exceptions to the principle of freedom of navigation, applying within the territorial sea and the contiguous zone,[405] justify such preventive measures as the coastal State deems necessary to avoid landings on its shores.

Under general international law, ships on the high seas may be boarded only in very limited circumstances, namely, suspicion of piracy or slave trading, where the ship has no nationality or has the same nationality as the warship purporting to exercise authority, or where the ship is engaged in unauthorized broadcasting.[406] Somewhat different considerations arise where, under a bilateral agreement, a flag State agrees to permit the authorities of another State to intercept its vessels. Precedents have existed for many years in regard to smuggling, slaving, and fisheries conservation. Under the Haitian interdiction programme, the US Coast Guard was instructed to stop and board specified vessels, including those of US nationality, or no nationality, or possessing the nationality of a State which had agreed to such measures. Those on board were to be examined and returned to their country of origin, 'when there is reason to believe that an offence is being committed against the United States immigration laws...'.[407] Australia's border

---

[401] Art. 2, 1958 Geneva Convention; art. 87 UNCLOS82.

[402] Art. 6, 1958 Geneva Convention; arts. 91, 92 UNCLOS82.

[403] Under the Protocol against the Smuggling of Migrants by Land, Sea and Air, supplementing the UN Convention against Transnational Organized Crime, UNGA res. 55/25. Annex III (adopted 15 Nov. 2000, entered into force 28 Jan. 2004), art. 8, States may board vessels without a flag State. However, States must simultaneously respect their *non-refoulement* obligations.

[404] Contrast the views of Churchill, R. & Lowe, A. V., *The Law of the Sea* (3rd edn, 1999), 214 with McDougal, M.S., & Burke, W. T., *The Public Order of the Oceans* (1962), 1084–5.

[405] See arts. 14–20, 24, 1958 Geneva Convention on the Territorial Sea and the Contiguous Zone; arts. 17–26, 33 UNCLOS82.

[406] Art. 22, 1958 Geneva Convention on the High Seas; art. 110 UNCLOS82. Because of doubts as to the obligation, if any, to submit to visit and search, O'Connell suggests that 'the only safe course to assume is that a right of boarding exists only under the law of the flag': O'Connell, D. P., *The International Law of the Sea*, vol. II, (Shearer, I., ed., 1984), (hereafter O'Connell, *Law of the Sea*, Vol. II, (1984)), 801–2. Cf. *Molvan v. Attorney-General for Palestine* [1948] AC 351, which is some authority for the view that even the 'freedom of the open sea' may be qualified by place or circumstance. In that case, the Privy Council found that no breach of international law resulted when a ship carrying illegal immigrants bound for Palestine was intercepted on the high seas by a British destroyer, and escorted into port where the vessel was forfeited. The Board nevertheless considered relevant the fact that the ship in question flew no flag, and could not therefore claim the protection of any State.

[407] Executive Order no. 12324, *Interdiction of Illegal Aliens*, s. 2(c)(3), which continued: '... or appropriate laws of a foreign country [with which an agreement exists]; provided, however, that no person who is a refugee will be returned without his consent'.

protection legislation permits the authorities to chase and board a foreign ship, including by force if necessary.[408] In Latin America, the Regional Conference on Migration has discussed programmes for returning boats intercepted on the high seas to their countries of origin with the assistance of the IMO.[409]

The lack of nationality perhaps most closely approximates the situation of asylum seekers, but even if their boats are without the effective protection of the country of origin, it is doubtful whether they can be assimilated to ships without nationality. No boat is ever entirely without the protection of the law. Obligations with regard to the rescue of those in distress at sea will circumscribe a State's freedom of action in certain cases. In others, elementary considerations of humanity[410] require that account be taken of the rights to life, liberty, and security of the person, and to freedom from torture, cruel, inhuman and degrading treatment or punishment; with respect to many such rights no derogation is permitted, even in time of public emergency threatening the life of the nation.

In the absence of an armed attack, the use of force against asylum seekers cannot be justified on the ground of self-defence.[411] Notions of necessity[412] or self-preservation,[413] as well as exceptions relating to the 'peace, good order or security' of the coastal State,[414] are subject to the limitations just set out. While a State necessarily enjoys a margin of appreciation in determining whether an influx of asylum seekers constitutes a threat, the lawfulness of measures taken to meet it will depend on there being some relationship of proportionality between the means and the end. International procedures for assistance and for finding solutions to refugee problems exist, and it is highly doubtful whether the use of such force as is reasonably likely to result in injury or death can ever be justified.[415]

4.2.1 Internal waters and the territorial sea

Internal waters, lying behind the baselines used to delimit territorial waters, are completely within the jurisdiction of the State. The territorial sea also is an area

---

[408] See generally Migration Act 1958 (Cth), ss. 245A–245H. Section 245C provides that outside the territorial sea of a foreign country, the Commander of a Commonwealth ship or aircraft chasing a ship may use 'any reasonable means consistent with international law to enable boarding of the chased ship', including 'where necessary and after firing a gun as a signal, firing at or into the chased ship to disable it or compel it to be brought to for boarding'.

[409] Executive Committee Standing Committee (18th Meeting), 'Interception of Asylum-Seekers and Refugees: The International Framework and Recommendations for a Comprehensive Approach', UN doc. EC/50/SC/CRP.17, (9 June 2000), para. 7.

[410] *Corfu Channel* case, ICJ *Rep.*, 1949, 4, at 22; Brownlie, I., *Principles of Public International Law*, (6th edn., 2003), 26–7 (hereafter, Brownlie, *Principles*).

[411] Brownlie, I., *International Law and the Use of Force by States*, (1963), 264 ff., 278–9. Schwarzenberger, G. & Brown, L., *A Manual of International Law*, (6th edn.), 150. On the distinction between self-defence and self-help, see Bowett, D., *Self-Defence in International Law*, (1958), 11–12, but see Migration Act 1958 (Cth), s. 245C.   [412] Brownlie, *Principles*, 448.

[413] Cf. Johnson, D. H. N. 'Refugees, Departees and Illegal Migrants' 9 *Sydney LR* 11 (1979–82), at 30–1; Bowett, *Self-Defence*, 22.

[414] See arts. 14, 19, and 24, 1958 Geneva Convention on the Territorial Sea and the Contiguous Zone; arts. 17–20, 27, 33 UNCLOS82. As Brownlie points out, coastal States' powers are essentially powers of police and control: *Principles*, 189–90.

[415] Cf. Johnson, below, n. 433 and accompanying text.

over which the coastal State exercises full sovereignty and in which, subject to the requirements of innocent passage, all the laws of the coastal State may be made applicable. The sovereignty here exercised is no different in kind from that over State territory.

Under international law, States are entitled to regulate innocent passage through the territorial sea,[416] for example, to prevent the infringement of immigration provisions. Non-compliance with such regulations may make passage non-innocent. Articles 19(2)(g) and 25 of the 1982 UN Law of the Sea Convention (UNCLOS) are probably declaratory of customary international law. Article 19(2)(g) provides:

Passage of a foreign ship shall be considered to be prejudicial to the peace, good order or security of the coastal State if in the territorial sea it engages in any of the following activities:

...

(g) the loading or unloading of any commodity, currency or person contrary to the customs, fiscal, immigration or sanitary laws and regulations of the coastal State ...

It is important to note that passage must be 'prejudicial to', not merely create a disturbance, and the relevant prejudicial activities listed in article 19(2)(g) are exhaustive.[417] Article 25 of UNCLOS82, and article 16 of the 1958 Geneva Convention on the Territorial Sea and the Contiguous Zone before it, provides expressly that, 'The coastal State may take the necessary steps in its territorial sea to prevent passage which is not innocent.' This does not necessarily authorize States to remove a vessel engaged in non-innocent passage from the territorial sea, since States are only permitted to take such steps as are *necessary* to prevent that passage.[418]

Although the territorial limits of a State run to the boundaries of its territorial sea, it does not follow that entry within the latter constitutes entry within the State, where 'entry' is the juridical fact necessary and sufficient to trigger the application of a particular system of international rules, such as those relating to landings in distress or immunity for illegal entry.[419] States generally apply their

---

[416] 'Regulation' does not necessarily imply the exercise of control; in principle, the law of the flag State governs the internal affairs of a ship, while neither civil nor criminal jurisdiction should be exercised, absent any actions prejudicial to the peace, good order, or security of the coastal State: art. 16, 1958 Geneva Convention on the Territorial Sea and the Contiguous Zone; cf. art. 21 UNCLOS82. Moreover, the power to suspend innocent passage temporarily in certain areas is qualified by the requirement that this be essential for the protection of security: art. 16(3), 1958 Geneva Convention; art. 25(3) UNCLOS82, and it is arguably not intended to be used against specific vessels, or for unrelated reasons.

[417] Pallis, M., 'Obligations of States towards Asylum Seekers at Sea: Interactions and Conflicts between Legal Regimes', 14 *IJRL* 329, 356 (2002), although see also Churchill & Lowe, above, n. 404, 85–6 who see the exhaustiveness of provisions to be open to question.

[418] Pallis, above, n. 357.

[419] O'Connell, D. P., *The International Law of the Sea*, vol. I, (Shearer, I., ed., 1982), 80–1, (hereafter, O'Connell, *Law of the Sea*, Vol I, (1982)), observes that art. 1 of the 1958 Geneva Convention on the Territorial Sea and the Contiguous Zone 'allows for the maximum implications that may be drawn from the concept of sovereignty, but it does not impose those implications on the coastal State;

immigration laws not within territorial waters, but within internal waters, even though it may be argued that 'entry' occurs at the moment when the outer limit of the territorial sea is crossed. Under article 31 of the 1951 Convention, refugees who cross into territorial waters and who otherwise satisfy the requirements of that provision could be said to have entered illegally and to be entitled to exemption from penalties. Entry within territorial waters may be an 'entry' for certain purposes,[420] but it is incorrect to generalize from these particulars. The notion of distress, or *force majeure*, reflects not so much a right of entry, as a limited immunity for having so entered in fairly well-defined circumstances.[421] The meaning of 'distress' is not defined, but may be linked to the preservation of human life,[422] or may result from 'the weather or from other causes affecting the management of the vessel'.[423] A vessel in distress may enter the territorial waters of another State and avoid sanctions for violation of domestic immigration or customs laws.[424] However, if the emergency is responded to at sea, as the Australian authorities sought to do in the case of the *Tampa*, then this will negate the need to enter another State's port.[425] Similarly, article 31 of the 1951 Convention, within its restricted area of application, operates as a defence to prosecution and penalty, but neither *force majeure* nor article 31 come into operation unless and until a measure of enforcement action is taken.

The coastal State may elect to exercise jurisdiction, and prosecute and punish, or simply prohibit and prevent the passage in question.[426] The fact that a vessel may be carrying refugees or asylum seekers who intend to request the protection of the coastal State arguably removes that vessel from the category of innocent passage, even though the status of the passengers may entitle them to claim immunity from penalties under article 31 of the 1951 Convention. Even if the refugee character of

---

it leaves them to be drawn in municipal law'. He notes further that ratification '... does not necessarily and automatically have the effect of altering the natural boundary. If that boundary encompasses the territorial sea, the Convention endorsed this by securing the recognition of the maximum implications on the part of all other States. If that boundary does not already encompass it, ratification by itself would not seem to affect the situation ...'

[420] *The Ship 'May'* v. *R.* [1931] SCR 374.

[421] O'Connell, *Law of the Sea*, vol. II, (1984), 853–8, at 856, citing authority for the proposition that if a ship incurs trouble while engaged in an illegal enterprise against the State in whose waters it takes refuge, it cannot claim immunity from the local jurisdiction, even if entry was indeed occasioned by distress. See also art. 18(2) UNCLOS82, on the meaning of 'passage': 'passage includes stopping and anchoring, but only in so far as the same are incidental to ordinary navigation or are rendered necessary by *force majeure* or distress or for the purpose of rendering assistance to persons, ships or aircraft in danger or distress'.   [422] Churchill & Lowe, above, n. 404, 63.

[423] *1929 US* v. *Mexico (Kate A. Hoff claim)*, (1951) 4 UNRIAA 444, 447.

[424] Røsæg, E., 'Refugees as Rescuees: The Tampa Problem', *Scandinavian Institute of Maritime Law Yearbook* 2002, 43, 57, citing Churchill & Lowe, above, n. 404, 63; Brown, E. D., *The International Law of the Sea*, vol. 1 (1994), 39; *Anklagemyndigheden* v. *Poulsen*, Case C-286/90, [1992] ECR I-6019 (in relation to fishery rules).

[425] Fonteyne, J.-P., 'Asylum-Seekers Afloat in Uncertainty', *Canberra Times*, 30 Aug. 2001; White, M., 'The Tampa and the Law', The Nautical Institute, London, (2001), 5–7. See below, s. 4.3.

[426] Arts. 19, 25 UNCLOS82; McDougal & Burke, *The Public Order of the Oceans*, (1962), 187–92, 272.

those on board were compatible with innocent passage, this would not alone entail a right of entry into any port, although other rules of international law may affect or control the discretionary decision as to what is to be done with respect to any particular vessel. International law nevertheless allows States to take all reasonable measures in the territorial sea to prevent the entry into port of a vessel carrying illegal immigrants, and to require such vessel to leave the territorial sea.

4.2.2 *The contiguous zone*

In the law of the sea, the term 'contiguous zone' describes the area of seas between twelve and twenty-four miles from the baselines employed to delimit the boundaries of the territorial sea.[427] In this zone, or equivalent areas, international law has long limited the range of permissible enforcement measures.[428]

Article 24 of the 1958 Geneva Convention on the Territorial Sea and the Contiguous Zone acknowledges a power of control, 'to prevent infringement within its territory or territorial sea'. O'Connell observes, however:

It is also arguable that necessary power to control does not include the right to arrest, because at this stage (i.e. that of a ship coming into the contiguous zone) the ship cannot have committed an offence. Enforced direction into port may not be arrest, in a technical sense, but it is tantamount to it and therefore is in principle excluded. The necessary examination should take place at sea, while the ship to be examined is in the zone.[429]

He further suggests that 'additional powers of seizure for the purpose of punishment' would come into operation where illegal immigrants have been landed, but this would be because the infringement of protected interests has already occurred in national territory.

The contiguous zone exists for the protection of the coastal State's customs, fiscal, sanitation, and immigration interests. Even before the crystallization of State competence in the 1958 Geneva Convention on the Territorial Sea and the Contiguous Zone, it was widely recognized that jurisdiction might be exercised beyond the 'exact boundaries' of a State's territory, for law enforcement purposes, or in order to preserve national safety.[430] The question is, whether 'the interest sought to be protected warrants the authority asserted for the time projected in the area specified'.[431] By comparison with those which run in the territorial sea,

---

[427] Art. 24, 1958 Geneva Convention on the Territorial Sea and the Contiguous Zone, now extended by art. 33 UNCLOS82.

[428] In *Croft* v. *Dunphy* [1933] AC 156, 164–5, for example, the Privy Council, upholding Canadian Customs Act provisions on 'hovering', took account of the fact that they did not apply to foreign vessels in the area of extended jurisdiction.   [429] O'Connell, *Law of the Sea*, vol. I, (1982), 1058.

[430] See McNair, *International Law Opinions*, vol. 2, (1956), 186 (enforcement of revenue laws in respect to vessels not yet within maritime jurisdiction); Jessup, P., *The Law of Territorial Waters and Maritime Jurisdiction*, (1927), 75–6, 242ff. O'Connell, *Law of the Sea*, vol. II, (1984), 1045–7, identifies Canada as the first State in modern times to assert a revenue jurisdiction independent of the territorial sea.

[431] McDougal & Burke, *The Public Order of the Oceans*, (1962), 584, 585ff. See also O'Connell, *Law of the Sea*, vol. II, (1984), 1057–61, noting the 'anticipatory' nature of contiguous zone powers.

the special jurisdictional rights which a State can exercise in the adjacent area of the contiguous zone do not clearly include the interception of vessels believed to be carrying asylum seekers.[432] One authority argues that 'such force and only such force may be used as will prevent the attempted incursion of illegal immigrants from becoming a danger to the preservation of the State'.[433] Although the basic principle of control is undisputed, this proposition begs the question, what is permissible in less extreme cases. The degree of force which might be used would need to be determined in light of all the circumstances, in the same way that the initial exercise of discretion would need to take into account the safety of passengers, the status of those on board, and the likely consequences of interdiction.[434]

If there are reasonable and probable grounds to believe that a vessel's intended purpose is to enter the territorial sea in breach of the immigration law, the coastal State may have the right to stop and board the vessel. Australian law authorizes naval vessels to fire warning shots into the ocean to encourage vessels to turn back, and if these are not heeded, to dispatch armed boarding parties to assume control of the vessel.[435] However, action taken under those powers, including inspection and redirection, might be objected to by flag States.[436] In the absence of the flag State, the Office of the United Nations High Commissioner for Refugees might be expected to make representations.[437]

In summary, the exercise and enforcement of jurisdiction over ships in the contiguous zone may violate international law where it is inconsistent with the purposes for which the contiguous zone exists and the limited authority allowed to coastal States; or because the exercise of enforcement powers (surveillance, identification, interception, and arrest) exceed what is permissible under that

---

[432] The powers allowed in the contiguous zone are only those permitted by international law: O'Connell, *Law of the Sea*, vol. I, (1982) 1058–9; also Morin, J.-Y., 'La zone de pêche exclusive du Canada', 2 *Can. YBIL* 77, 86 (1964),: 'la notion de zone contigue... est très stricte et ne comporte aucune extension de la compétence de l'Etat côtier sur les eaux situées au delà de sa mer territoriale ...'. He identifies the contiguous zone as forming part of the high seas, and as defined, 'précisement par l'absence de toute souveraineté étatique. Il n'est pas douteux que, dans la pratique, certains Etats voient dans la zone contigue le prolongement de leur mer territoriale et prétendent y exercer les mêmes compétences douanières ou fiscales, mais nous convenons... que ces Etats sont en opposition avec le droit international tel qu'établi par les conventions sur le droit de la mer.'

[433] Johnson, D. H. N., 'Refugees, Departees and Illegal Migrants', 9 *Sydney LR* (1979–82), 11, 32.

[434] Some attention would always need to be given to a vessel's next likely port of call, if all information available indicated that refugees, rather than migrants, were on board.

[435] Migration Act 1958 (Cth), ss. 245C, 245F (see generally Div. 12A).

[436] Obviously, all will turn on whether the flag State, if any, decides to object. The US interdiction programme was based upon the Haitian government's agreement thereto. The US–Great Britain Treaty of 1924 (concluded in the context of prohibition) included express agreement by the British to raise no objections to the boarding of private vessels flying the British flag and outside US territorial waters. Enquiries might be undertaken to determine whether the vessel was endeavouring to violate US laws, and vessels might be seized on reasonable cause: Jessup, *Territorial Waters*, above n. 430, 289–93.

[437] Such representations were indeed made when the use of force (such as towing out to sea at high speed) resulted in sinking and loss of life of asylum seekers arriving directly from Vietnam in Singapore and Malaysia in 1979.

law.[438] Furthermore, if forcing a ship from the contiguous zone to the high seas would leave refugees with no option but to return to their country of origin, or to a third State that would return them, this constitutes *refoulement*.

4.2.3 The consequences of enforcement action

The simple denial of entry of ships to territorial waters cannot be equated with breach of the principle of *non-refoulement*, which requires that State action have the effect or result of returning refugees to territories where their lives or freedom would be threatened. In its comments in 1950 on the draft convention, the *Ad hoc* Committee observed:

... the obligation not to return a refugee to a country where he was persecuted did not imply an obligation to admit him to the country where he seeks refuge. The return of a refugee-ship, for example, to the high seas could not be construed as a violation of this obligation.[439]

Denial of entry to internal or territorial waters must therefore be distinguished from programmes of interdiction of boats which are accompanied by the actual, physical return of passengers to their country of origin. Even in the latter situation, the principle of *non-refoulement* would come into play only in the presence of certain objective conditions indicating the possibility of danger befalling those returned.[440] It does not follow that States enjoy complete freedom of action over arriving boats, even if they come in substantial numbers and without nationality. The range of permissible measures is limited by obligations relating to rescue at sea and arising from elementary considerations of humanity, while action which would directly effect the return of refugees is prohibited by the principle of *non-refoulement*. Whether on the high seas or in waters subject to the jurisdiction of any State, refugees may also be protected by UNHCR in the exercise of its functional protection role.[441]

4.3 RESCUE-AT-SEA

Asylum seekers have been escaping by sea for years, only the most recent examples being Cubans, Haitians, Indo-Chinese, and Albanians. Historically, international

---

[438] See O'Connell on practical intervention and enforcement problems, which flow from international law restrictions on the use of force, and on the overall requirements of the necessary vessels: *Law of the Sea*, vol. II, (1984), 1064 and n. 25. See also at 1071ff. on the degree of force which may be used.

[439] See UN doc. E/AC.32/L.32/Add.1 (10 Feb. 1950), comment on draft article 28 (expulsion to country of persecution).

[440] Goodwin-Gill, G. S, '*Non-Refoulement* and the New Asylum Seekers', 26 *Virg. JIL* 897, 902 (1986).

[441] Ibid. On interception and non-arrival policies, see Ch. 7. In the absence of protest by States, the entitlement to invoke the responsibility of a State acting in violation of its obligations under the 1951 Convention falls to UNHCR, which States parties acknowledge as having the duty to supervise its application: art. 35 CSR51.

law has been unclear about State responsibility for persons rescued at sea. There were several options open to the State where those rescued arrived: it could refuse disembarkation absolutely and require ships' masters to remove them from the jurisdiction, or it could make disembarkation conditional upon satisfactory guarantees as to resettlement, care, and maintenance, to be provided by flag or other States, or by international organizations. Recent amendments to international maritime treaties for the first time impose an obligation on States to cooperate and coordinate the disembarkation of those rescued at sea,[442] although it remains to be seen how this will operate in practice.[443] Since asylum seekers' claims can only be finally determined after disembarkation, it is important that they are taken to a place of safety without delay. However, a categorical refusal of disembarkation cannot be equated with breach of the principle of *non-refoulement*, even though it may result in serious consequences for asylum seekers.[444]

The duty to rescue those in distress at sea is firmly established in both treaty[445] and general international law.[446] Article 98 of UNCLOS82, for example, requires ship captains to 'render assistance to any person found at sea in danger of being lost', and 'to proceed with all possible speed to the rescue of persons in distress', insofar as this is reasonable and will not seriously endanger the ship, its crew or its passengers.[447] The importance of this duty is reflected in the municipal law of States such as the United Kingdom and Germany, which impose criminal liability on ship masters who fail to render assistance to persons in distress at sea.[448] A number of international treaties require States to maintain effective search and

---

[442] See below, 283–4.

[443] The IMO cites as an 'excellent example of this inter-agency co-operation' the rescue in June 2006 of twenty-two people of various nationalities from the passenger ship, the *Noordam*, in the Aegean Sea between the Greek island of Samos and the coast of Turkey. However, it remains to be seen whether the same cooperation will be forthcoming with respect to asylum seekers. See <http://www.imo.org/Newsroom/mainframe.asp?topic_id51396>.

[444] The IMO Guidelines on the Treatment of Persons Rescued at Sea, partially incorporated through amendments to the SAR and SOLAS Conventions (below, n. 283–4) suggest that a ship's master should take protection needs into account. Unless he or she is acting in an official State capacity, the master, as a non-State actor, is not directly bound by international law, but is subject to national implementation measures.

[445] See, for example, art. 11, 1910 Brussels International Convention with respect to Assistance and Salvage at Sea: 1 *Bevans* 780 (1968); art. 45 (1), 1929 International Convention on the Safety of Life at Sea: 136 *LNTS* 82; ch. V, Reg. 10a, 1960 International Convention on the Safety of Life at Sea; art. 12, 1958 Convention on the High Seas; 1979 International Convention on Maritime Search and Rescue ('SAR Convention'), especially the 2004 amendments (in force 1 Jul. 2006); art. 98 UNCLOS82. The duty is so fundamental that it applies to rescue of the enemy: art. 16, 1958 Geneva Convention (X) for the Adaptation to Maritime Warfare of the Principles of the Geneva Convention.

[446] See the view of the International Law Commission with respect to its proposed draft of art. 12 of the 1958 Convention on the High Seas: 'Report of the International Law Commission to the General Assembly' (1956) II *YB ILC* 253, 281; see UN doc. A/3159 (1956). On the duty to rescue as customary international law, see Pallis, above, n. 417, 333–4, and generally, see Røsæg, above, n. 424.

[447] Røsæg notes, however, that this rule is frequently breached by shipmasters: above, n. 424, 49–50.

[448] This is not required under UNCLOS82; see UNHCR, 'Background Note on the Protection of Asylum-Seekers and Refugees Rescued at Sea' (18 Mar. 2002), para. 5; cf. Norwegian Maritime Code, s. 135(3).

rescue facilities,[449] to provide assistance 'regardless of the nationality or status of such a person',[450] and to deliver those rescued to 'a place of safety', commonly regarded as the nearest port of call.[451]

However, article 19(2)(g) of UNCLOS82 provides *inter alia* that a foreign ship's right to innocent passage will be violated if it loads or unloads any person contrary to the coastal State's immigration laws, and article 25 of UNCLOS82 and article 16 of the 1958 Geneva Convention on the High Seas before it expressly provide that '[t]he coast State may take the necessary steps in its territorial sea to prevent passage which is not innocent'.[452] Accordingly, there are gaps in international maritime and refugee law which States with conflicting interests may seek to exploit. Neither branch of law resolves the question of whether entering a State's territorial waters constitutes entry to State territory, or how to deal with the rescue of those who do not in fact enjoy the protection of their country of origin and are unable or unwilling to return home.[453]

The Executive Committee sought to address these lacunae during the Indo-China exodus, when, given the expense and delay which often resulted from attempting to disembark those rescued at sea, many in distress were simply ignored by ships' masters and left to their fate.[454] In a series of international conclusions promoting disembarkation and admission pending a durable solution,[455]

---

[449] Art. 98(2) UNCLOS82; SOLAS, reg. V-7(1) (formerly reg. V-15(a)); art. 2.1.1, Annex, 1979 Search and Rescue Convention.

[450] Art. 2.1.10, Annex, 1979 Search and Rescue Convention.

[451] Art. 1.1.3.2, Annex, 1979 Search and Rescue Convention; see further below.

[452] See above, s. 4.2.1.

[453] See generally, Grant, B., *The Boat People*, (1980), 68–72; Grahl-Madsen, *Status of Refugees*, vol. 2, 271–2; Pugash, J. Z., 'The Dilemma of the Sea Refugee: Rescue without Refuge', 18 *Harv. ILJ* 577 (1977); Pallis, M., 'Obligations of States towards Asylum Seekers at Sea: Interactions and Conflicts Between Legal Regimes', 14 *IJRL* 329 (2002); Executive Committee Standing Committee (18th Meeting), 'Interception of Asylum-Seekers and Refugees: The International Framework and Recommendations for a Comprehensive Approach', UN doc. EC/50/SC/CRP.17 (9 Jun. 2000). Art. 11 of the 1951 Convention requires contracting States to give 'sympathetic consideration' to the establishment within their territory of 'refugees regularly serving as crew members' on ships flying their flag. At the 1951 Conference, it was stated that this provision was intended to benefit genuine seamen, not those escaping by sea: UN doc. A/CONF.2/SR.12, 5 (1951). Likewise, the 1957 Agreement relating to Refugee Seamen (updated by the 1973 Protocol thereto) offers little solace to the asylum seeker at sea. Art. 1 defines a 'refugee seaman' as a refugee within the meaning of the Convention and Protocol, who 'is serving as a seafarer in any capacity on a mercantile ship, or habitually earns his living as a seafarer on such ship'. The objective is to determine the links which a refugee seaman may have with contracting States, with a view to establishing entitlement to residence and/or the issue of travel documents. The qualifying links are such as generally to exclude the seafaring asylum seeker; for example, 600 days service under the flag of a contracting State, previous lawful residence in a contracting State, or travel documents previously issued by a contracting State: arts. 2, 3. 'Sympathetic consideration' is to be given to extending the agreement's benefits to those not otherwise a qualifying: art. 5.

[454] See the 2nd edn. of this work for discussion of the legal developments during this period.

[455] *Report* of the 29th Session of the Executive Committee: UN doc. A/AC.96/559, para. 38.E. See Executive Committee Conclusions No. 2 (1976), No. 14 (1979), No. 15 (1979), No. 20 (1980), No. 21 (1981), No. 23 (1981), No. 25 (1982), No. 26 (1982), No. 29 (1983), No. 31 (1983), No. 33 (1984), No. 34 (1984), No. 36 (1985), No. 38 (1985), No. 41 (1986), No. 46 (1987), No. 47 (1987), No. 97 (2003).

the Executive Committee stressed the 'humanitarian obligation of all coastal States to allow vessels in distress to seek haven',[456] and noted that those rescued at sea 'should normally be disembarked at the next port of call'.[457] The Executive Committee emphasized that 'refugee problems are the concern of the international community and their resolution is dependent on the will and capacity of States to respond in concert and wholeheartedly, in a spirit of true humanitarianism and international solidarity'.[458] It recognized that the duty to rescue refugees required a division of responsibilities between flag, coastal, and resettlement States.[459]

The principle of flag State responsibility cannot be said to have established itself as 'international custom, as evidence of a general practice accepted as law'. International responses to the *Tampa* incident, discussed below, reaffirm this position. The special circumstances which affected the finding of solutions to the Indo-Chinese refugee problem dictated the emergence of a particular usage, limited also in time and place. In other situations, such as the *Tampa* crisis, it may be appropriate to emphasize the responsibility of the first port of call, given the inescapable but internationally relevant fact of the refugee's presence within the territory of the State. This is the approach favoured by UNHCR, which regards the 'coastal State in the immediate vicinity of the rescue' as the State which will generally be responsible for admitting the rescued asylum seekers and providing access to asylum determination procedures.[460] At a 2002 Expert Roundtable on rescue-at-sea, the meeting noted that coastal States have a 'responsibility to facilitate rescue through ensuring that the necessary enabling arrangements are in place', while flag States are responsible for ensuring that ships' masters come to the assistance of people in distress at sea.[461] UNHCR notes, however, that the flag State may retain responsibility where it is clear that those rescued intended to seek asylum from that State; if the numbers of those rescued are very small and it is reasonable for them to remain on the vessel until it reaches the flag State's territory; or if the flag State interdicts the asylum seekers.[462] There is also some practice in support of flagship responsibility for asylum seekers rescued close to their own territory.[463] As with stowaways, effective solutions ought in principle to be attainable

---

[456] Executive Committee Conclusion No. 15, para. (c).

[457] Executive Committee Conclusion No. 23, para. 3.

[458] Executive Committee Conclusion No. 52, Preamble; see also Conclusions Nos. 14, 15, 23.

[459] Executive Committee Conclusion No. 23.

[460] UNHCR, 'Background Note on the Protection of Asylum-Seekers and Refugees Rescued at Sea', (18 Mar. 2002), paras. 25–6, 30–1. See also Executive Committee Conclusion No. 14 (1979), para. c; Executive Committee Conclusion No. 15 (1979), para. (c); Executive Committee Conclusion No. 23 (1981), para. 3.

[461] UNHCR, 'Rescue-at-Sea: Specific Aspects relating to the Protection of Asylum-Seekers and Refugees', Expert Roundtable, Lisbon, (25–26 Mar. 2002) Summary of Discussions, (11 Apr. 2002), para. 13.

[462] UNHCR, 'Background Note on the Protection of Asylum-Seekers and Refugees Rescued at Sea', (18 Mar. 2002), paras. 25–26.

[463] Schaffer, R. P., 'The Singular Plight of Sea-Borne Refugees', 8 *Aust. YB Int'l Law* 213 (1978–80); Pugash, J. Z., 'The Dilemma of the Sea Refugee: Rescue without Refuge,' 18 *Harv. ILJ*

through a weighing of competing interests, taking account not only of the prospects, if any, of local integration, but also of notions of international solidarity and burden-sharing,[464] as well as the extent to which refusal of disembarkation may lead in fact to *refoulement*, or to other serious harm for the asylum seekers.

The most recent impetus for developments in standard-setting and clarification of legal principles concerning rescue-at-sea and disembarkation was the *Tampa* incident, which highlighted the exploitable gaps in international maritime and refugee law concerning State responsibility for rescue and landing. In August 2001, in response to an Australian-coordinated search and rescue operation, the Norwegian *MV Tampa* rescued 433 asylum seekers from a sinking Indonesian flagged vessel 75 nautical miles off the Australian coast. When the *Tampa* began heading towards the Australian port of Christmas Island, the Australian authorities asked the captain to change course towards Indonesia, warning that if the ship entered Australia's territorial sea with the intention of disembarking the rescued asylum seekers, he would be subject to prosecution under the Migration Act 1958 (Cth) for people smuggling.[465]

Norway's view, based on article 98 of UNCLOS82, customary international law, and generally accepted humanitarian standards (such as those reflected in Executive Committee Conclusions during the Indo-Chinese crisis, in which Australia had taken an active role), was that Australia had an obligation to allow the rescued asylum seekers to be disembarked at the nearest port, Christmas Island. Australia's legal position was not entirely clear, although it appeared to hold Indonesia responsible as the State of embarkation.[466] Australia defended its stance on the

577 (1977), cited in Crock, M., 'In the Wake of the *Tampa*: Conflicting Visions of International Refugee Law in the Management of Refugee Flows', 12 *Pacific Rim and Policy Journal* 49, 59 (2003).

[464] At the 1981 Executive Committee meeting, one speaker suggested that arrangements relating to rescue and resettlement 'already reflected the principle of burden-sharing between maritime and coastal States and should therefore be maintained': UN doc. A/AC.96/601, para. 52. See also UNHCR, 'Rescue-at-Sea', above n. 460, paras. 13, 15.

[465] For the facts, see Rothwell, D., 'The Law of the Sea and the M/V *Tampa* Incident: Reconciling Maritime Principles with Coastal State Sovereignty', 13 *Public Law Review* 118, 118 (2002). The international community's lack of support for the Australian response was perhaps best reflected in UNHCR's award of the 2002 Nansen Medal to the captain and crew of the *Tampa*. Note also the common practice of shifting responsibility on to the ship's captain or owners, rather than the flag State, which mirrors the imposition of carrier sanctions on airlines which transport passengers who lack the requisite documentation to enter the destination country. This has led in some cases to crew forcing stowaways overboard: BBC News, 'Ship Captain Held over Stowaways,' (29 May 2004): <http://news.bbc.co.uk/2/hi/europe/3760731.stm>. Three Ukrainian sailors were charged with murder in a South African court after it was alleged that they had forced seven Tanzanian stowaways to jump overboard to avoid having to pay for their repatriation: BBC News, 'Stowaways "Forced to Jump Ship"' (6 Jan. 2006): <http://news.bbc.co.uk/go/pr/fr/-/2/hi/africa/4584276.stm>. On the costs of delay and deviation of route: Røsæg, above, n. 424, 46–7.

[466] Australia asserted that the usual practice in maritime emergencies is for the rescuing vessel to continue on its planned route as closely as possible, and the appropriate port for disembarkation was accordingly Merak in Indonesia: Interview with Robert Illingworth, Deputy Secretary, Refugee Policy Branch, Dept. of Immigration, Multicultural and Indigenous Affairs, Sydney, 2 Apr. 2002, cited in Crock, 'In the Wake of the *Tampa*', above, n. 463, 55. See also Mathew, P., 'Australian Refugee Protection in the Wake of the Tampa', 96 *AJIL* 661, 671–2 (2002); *Ruddock* v. *Vadarlis* [2001] FCA 1329.

basis of national security and its sovereign right to determine who entered its territory and in what manner.[467] Although the doctrine of State sovereignty accords coastal States significant discretion in determining how to respond to the imminent arrival of refugee boats or rescued asylum seekers, it is clear that Australia (even if not exclusively) had protection responsibilities towards those rescued by the *Tampa*, arising from the undeniable refugee character of the individuals concerned, the Australian military's assertion of effective control over them through the search and rescue operation, and the fact that asylum requests were lodged in Australian waters.[468] Certainly, Australia had no right to impose protection responsibilities unilaterally on Norway or Indonesia. Neither international treaty law nor State practice arising from the Indo-Chinese exodus supports the imposition of an obligation on the flag State to engage in refugee status determination procedures, with the exception of naval vessels and other ships of State.

The *Tampa* incident provoked a number of attempts at the international level to clarify the principles relating to rescue-at-sea and disembarkation. In November 2001, the International Maritime Assembly adopted a resolution recommending a comprehensive review of safety measures and procedures for the treatment of rescued persons.[469] In March 2002, UNHCR convened an expert roundtable on rescue-at-sea, attended by thirty-three representatives from government, the shipping industry, international organizations, NGOs, and academia. It was organized partly in response to numerous representations to UNHCR from the shipping industry seeking assistance 'in bolstering the time-honoured tradition of rescue of persons in distress at sea against what were presented as very serious incursions',[470] and also to clarify State responsibilities on rescue. Representatives broadly agreed that rescue-at-sea is a predominantly humanitarian issue, and that 'rescue and alleviation of distress the first and absolute imperative, regardless of who the people are and how they came to be where they are'.[471] They noted that the ship's captain 'has the right to expect the assistance of coastal States with facilitation and completion of the rescue, which occurs only when the persons are landed somewhere or otherwise delivered to a safe place'.[472] Furthermore, it was observed that a non-State vessel is not an appropriate location for the screening and categorization of asylum seekers, nor should such a vessel be used as a 'floating detention centre'.[473]

---

[467] One year later, the Australian Immigration Minister described the arrivals as 'unauthorized refugees brought to Australia by people smugglers': Mr Ruddock (Australia): UN doc. A/AC.96/ SR.562, para. 13 (2002).

[468] On the issues of *force majeure* and necessity, due to impending deaths on board, see above n. 428 and accompanying text.

[469] Review of Safety Measures and Procedures for the Treatment of Persons Rescued at Sea, 22nd session, Agenda item 8, IMO Assembly res. A.920(22) (Nov. 2001).

[470] UNHCR, 'Note on International Protection', 53rd session, UN doc. A/AC.96/965 (11 Sept. 2002) para. 21.

[471] UNHCR, 'Rescue-at-Sea', above n. 461, para. 2.   [472] Ibid., para. 6.

[473] Ibid., para. 7.

Though acknowledging the gaps in international maritime and refugee law on the appropriate place for disembarkation and the States responsible for follow-up action and solutions, the experts observed that international law more generally provides a framework and 'indicators' for how such issues might be resolved.[474] Human rights principles were identified as 'an important point of first reference', since they apply to all persons irrespective of their nationality or status and stipulate certain standards and needs that must be respected at all times.[475]

UNHCR observed in its 2002 Note on International Protection that certain 'highly publicized incidents' in the past year, including that of the *Tampa*, highlighted the 'problem of access to territory and procedures for those arriving by sea'. The refusal by some States to disembark rescued persons or even to come to their rescue in the first place was described as a 'serious problem', while other States were commended for their commitment to the 'accepted maritime practice of permitting sometimes larger numbers of people, rescued for instance in the Mediterranean, to disembark on their territory'.[476] In the *Agenda for Protection*, UNHCR set out its aim 'to seek to reach common understandings [with States and other stakeholders] on responsibilities in the context of rescue at sea of asylum-seekers and refugees, including with regard to rescue itself, the disembarkation of those rescued and the solutions to be pursued'.[477] In furtherance of this goal, an inter-agency review group was established under the auspices of the IMO.[478] Its first meeting was held in July 2002 with representatives of the UN Division for Ocean Affairs and the Law of the Sea, UNHCR, the UN Office for Drug Control and Crime Prevention, and Office of the UN High Commissioner for Human Rights, the International Organization for Migration, and the IMO Secretariat. It agreed to review the safety of Life at Sea (SOLAS) and Search and Rescue (SAR) Conventions regarding the treatment of persons rescued at sea.

In May 2004, in response to post-*Tampa* discussions,[479] the SAR and SOLAS Conventions were amended to impose—for the first time—an obligation on States to 'cooperate and coordinate' to ensure that ships' masters are allowed to disembark rescued persons to a place of safety,[480] irrespective of the nationality or

---

[474] Ibid., para. 9.   [475] Ibid., para. 10.

[476] UNHCR, 'Note on International Protection', UN GAOR, 53rd session, para. 20, UN doc. A/AC.96/965 (2002).   [477] *Agenda for Protection*, (3rd edn., Oct. 2003), 47.

[478] The IMO's Secretary-General recommended in Nov. 2001 that a UN inter-agency group undertake a review of existing legislation concerning the delivery of persons rescued at sea to a place of safety, irrespective of their nationality, status, and the circumstances in which they were found: Review of Safety Measures and Procedures for the Treatment of Persons Rescued at Sea, 22nd session, Agenda item 8, IMO Assembly res. A.920(22) (Nov. 2001).

[479] IMO Assembly resolution A.920(22) on 'Review of Safety Measures and Procedures for the Treatment of Persons Rescued at Sea' (2001).

[480] Amendments adopted May 2004, in force 1 Jul. 2006. The amendments were based on the already applicable IMO, *Guidelines on the Treatment of Persons Rescued at Sea*, MSC.167 (78). Chapter 5 of SOLAS incorporates a definition of search and rescue service, and there is a new regulation on shipmasters' discretion, which make it clear that he or she has the sole discretion to make decisions necessary for the safety of life at sea. Chapter 2 of the SAR Convention defines 'persons in

status of those rescued,[481] and with minimal disruption to the ship's planned itinerary (implying that disembarkation should occur at the nearest coastal State—UNHCR's favoured approach). The amendments make clear that a ship's master has the sole discretion to make decisions which, in his or her professional judgement, are necessary for the safety of life at sea, including matters pertaining to rescue, treatment and care of those rescued, and where they should be landed. Section 2 of the 1965 Convention on Facilitation of Maritime Traffic has consequently also been amended to require public authorities to facilitate the arrival and departure of ships engaged in rescuing distressed persons at sea in order to provide a place of safety for such persons.[482]

While this helpfully clarifies States' responsibilities, the broader international protection regime, comprising refugee law, human rights law, and more generally applicable rules informed by the principle of good faith, in any case provide a normative and institutional framework for solutions. Furthermore, the very nature of the international protection regime is premised on States *not* acting unilaterally and in their own self-interest. UNHCR has repeatedly described the *Tampa* incident as a break or crack in the 'time-honoured tradition of rescue at sea', characterizing it as an aberration in State practice rather than indicative of a new rule.[483] No other State has formally supported the Australian position, and in 2003, the Executive Committee adopted a Conclusion on protection safeguards in interception measures, recalling the duty of States and ships' masters 'to ensure the safety of life and to come to the aid of those in distress or in danger of being lost at sea'.[484] The Australian approach is therefore inconsistent with the general international consensus on rescue-at-sea. While the gaps in international law provide room for competing interpretations based on conflicting State interests, the Australian view is at odds with State practice generally. The *Tampa* incident has, ironically, inspired a reaffirmation of the rescue-at-sea principles developed during the Indo-China exodus, and a buttressing of soft law on the issue by the international community.

distress'; Chapter 4 contains amendments relating to rescue coordination centres initiating the process of identifying the most appropriate places for disembarkation.

[481] Amendments to SOLAS, Ch. 5; see also amendments to SAR, Ch. 2. This obligation pertains to the flag State, as well as nearby States that receive those rescued.

[482] Amendments adopted 7 Jul. 2005, in force 1 Nov. 2006.

[483] Statement by Ms Erika Feller, Director, Dept. of International Protection, UNHCR, to the 24th Meeting of the Standing Committee (Geneva, 25 Jun. 2002). UNHCR has, however, noted that the tradition is at risk—and not for the first time—in the Adriatic, the Indian Ocean, the Mediterranean, and elsewhere.

[484] Executive Committee Conclusion No. 97 (2003). Compare the *Clementine Maersk* incident in June 2005, when a Danish ship rescued 27 asylum seekers in the Mediterranean and disembarked them at the next port of call, in the UK. The UK authorities conducted initial asylum interviews on board and then allowed the asylum seekers to disembark. This 'demonstrates that international maritime law, custom, and moral imperatives can successfully harmonize in potentially treacherous rescue situations, and that international organizations, commercial shippers, insurance companies and states acting together can find a relatively tranquil solution': van Selm & Cooper, above, n. 395, 27. See also Kessler, P., 'UNHCR Thanks Danish Ship for Rescuing Asylum Seekers Stranded at Sea', (8 Jun. 2005); <http://www.unhcr.org/cgi-bin/texis/vtx/news/opendoc.htm?tbl5NEWS&id542a70b5a4>.

6

Protection under Human Rights and General International Law

1. The meaning of 'complementary protection'

The principle of *non-refoulement* is wider than its expression in article 33 of the 1951 Refugee Convention. While States have always recognized, to varying degrees, the protection needs of people falling outside the 'refugee' definition in article 1A(2) of the Convention, it is only in the last decade that they have consciously sought to articulate such protection as a matter of international law, based on States' voluntarily assumed human rights obligations, rather than as a matter left to the discretion and humanitarian goodwill of national governments.[1] The term 'complementary protection' describes States' protection obligations arising from international legal instruments and custom that complement—or supplement—the 1951 Refugee Convention. It is, in effect, a shorthand term for the widened scope of *non-refoulement* under international law.[2]

The obligation not to return an individual to serious harm may be express or implied. Article 3 of the Convention against Torture, for example, expressly prohibits States from removing an individual in any manner whatsoever where there are substantial grounds for believing that doing so would expose him or her to a danger

---

[1] States' international obligations towards this extended class of refugees, both under treaty and customary law, pre-date the formalization and naming of the concept of 'complementary protection'. Most western countries, including the Member States of the European Union, Canada, and the United States, have a system of complementary protection in place. For discussion of these regimes, see sections 3 and 4 below. Australia and New Zealand do not, but the New Zealand government has acknowledged that it must not remove individuals to a risk of torture or cruel, inhuman or degrading treatment or punishment (*A-G v. Zaoui* [2005] NZSC 38, para.76), and is considering codifying a 'broader protection status' based on human rights law: NZ Department of Labour, 'Immigration Act Review: Discussion Paper' (Apr. 2006) section 14. In Australia, Senator Andrew Bartlett of the Australian Democrats (a minority party) introduced a Bill on complementary protection into Federal Parliament on 13 Sept. 2006, but it is unlikely to receive sufficient support to become law: Migration Legislation Amendment (Complementary Protection Visas) Bill 2006.

[2] Cf. Mandal, whose study on complementary protection focuses on the gap between UNHCR's expanded mandate and State practice, and accordingly concentrates on 'those aspects of national complementary protection regimes which appear to benefit persons who fall within UNHCR's mandate': Mandal, R., 'Protection Mechanisms outside of the 1951 Convention ("Complementary Protection")', UNHCR Legal and Protection Policy Research Series, PPLA/2005/02 (Jun. 2005), para. 13.

of being subjected to torture.[3] By contrast, the prohibition on torture or inhuman or degrading treatment or punishment contained in article 3 ECHR50 and article 7 ICCPR66[4] has been interpreted by the European Court of Human Rights and the UN Human Rights Committee respectively as precluding the removal of individuals who face a real risk of being exposed to those forms of harm.[5] A general principle of refuge, based on humanitarian law and human rights law, has also emerged in State practice, protecting those who flee civil war or generalized violence.[6]

'Complementary protection' is thus a legal concept that must be distinguished from protection granted solely on compassionate grounds, such as age, health, or family connections unrelated to an international protection need,[7] or for practical reasons, such as the inability to obtain travel documents.[8] Even though this type of protection is humanitarian in nature, it is not based on an international protection obligation and therefore does not come within the legal boundaries of 'complementary protection'.[9]

2. The history of complementary protection

Although the expression 'complementary protection' arose in the 1990s,[10] the practice which it describes has a long history.[11] Indeed, rudimentary examples of

---

[3] 1984 Convention against Torture and Other Cruel, Inhuman or Degrading Treatment or Punishment (in force 26 Jun. 1987): 1465 *UNTS* 85 (hereafter, CAT84).

[4] Art. 7 of the International Covenant on Civil and Political Rights (in force 23 Mar. 1976): 999 *UNTS* 171 (hereafter, ICCPR66) also prohibits 'cruel' treatment or punishment.

[5] ICCPR66: Human Rights Committee, 'General Comment 20: Article 7', (1992), para. 9; European Convention on Human Rights (ECHR50): see for example, *Soering* v. *UK* (1989) 11 EHRR 439; *Chahal* v. *UK* (1996) 23 EHRR 413.

[6] See Perluss, D. & Hartman, J. F., 'Temporary Refuge: Emergence of a Customary Norm', 26 *Virginia JIL* 551 (1986); Goodwin-Gill, G. S., '*Non-Refoulement* and the New Asylum Seekers', 26 *Virginia JIL* 897 (1986); cf. Hailbronner, K., '*Non-Refoulement* and "Humanitarian" Refugees: Customary International Law or Wishful Legal Thinking?', 26 *Virginia JIL* 857 (1986). The principle of refuge applies at least with respect to mass influxes, but in some cases also with respect to individuals: see, for example, EU Qualification Directive, art. 15(b); text below, Annexe 2, No. 19. On the principle of international cooperation in situations of mass influx, see Eggli, A.V., *Mass Refugee Influx and the Limits of Public International Law*, (2002) (hereafter, Eggli, *Mass Refugee Influx*).

[7] Sometimes health or family reasons may also be tied to an international protection need, such as under arts. 3 or 8 ECHR50, and there remains some scope to test the extent to which compassionate reasons may in fact have a legal basis. However, generally they describe reasons for stay not linked to any legal ground. See, for example, Executive Committee Conclusion No. 103 (LVI), 'The Provision of International Protection including through Complementary Forms of Protection' (2005), para. (j).

[8] Executive Committee, Standing Committee, 18th Meeting, 'Complementary Forms of Protection: Their Nature and Relationship to the International Refugee Protection Regime', UN doc. EC/50/SC/CRP.18 (9 Jun. 2000), paras. 4–5. During the drafting of the 1951 Convention, France had proposed that refugee status should extend to a person 'unable to obtain from [his or her] country [of origin] permission to return': *Ad hoc* Committee on Refugees and Stateless Persons, 'France: Proposal for a Draft Convention Preamble', UN doc. E/AC.32/L.3, (17 Jan. 1950).

[9] See also Executive Committee Conclusion No. 103 (above n. 7), para. j.

[10] UNHCR, 'Note on International Protection', UN doc. A/AC.96/799 (25 Jul. 1992), para. 5.

[11] See McAdam, J., *Complementary Protection in International Refugee Law*, (2007), Ch. 1 (hereafter, McAdam, *Complementary Protection*).

complementary protection can be traced back to the period of the League of Nations,[12] when States realized that not all those in need of international protection could be neatly encompassed by formal legal 'refugee' definitions (which at that time were based on national categories).[13] France, for example, extended the legal status set out in the 1933 Convention relating to the International Status of Refugees (which applied to Russian, Armenian, Assyrian, Assyro-Chaldean, assimilated refugees (of Syrian or Kurdish origin), and Turkish refugees[14]) to Spanish refugees fleeing the Civil War,[15] while the United Kingdom treated as refugees 'many thousands of persons who still enjoyed the protection of the Reich, and had extended its asylum to them, either for the purpose of enabling them to make a new home in the United Kingdom, or of staying there temporarily till plans for their settlement in some other country had been completed'.[16] An important feature of this practice was that the content of the protection granted was identical, regardless of whether the protected individual was a 'refugee' in accordance with the international legal definition of the period. The 'complementary' aspect of protection was simply the basis on which it was extended.[17] According to Ivor Jackson, States tended to follow this pattern until the 1980s, when more restrictive policies began to take effect and 'status' became a key political tool for differentiating between 'genuine' Convention refugees and others.[18] It is ironic, although perhaps not

---

[12] For history: Simpson, J. H., *The Refugee Problem: Report of a Survey*, (1939); Holborn, L. W., 'The Legal Status of Political Refugees, 1920–1938', 32 *AJIL* 680 (1938); Marrus, M. R., *The Unwanted: European Refugees from the First World War through the Cold War*, (2nd edn., 2002); Weis, P., 'The International Protection of Refugees', 48 *AJIL* 193 (1954); Hathaway, J. C., 'The Evolution of Refugee Status in International Law: 1920–1950', 33 *ICLQ* 348 (1984); Skran, C. M., *Refugees in Inter-War Europe: The Emergence of a Regime*, (1995).

[13] Note the remarks of the Swiss delegation that, as late as 1938, Switzerland received daily refugees who had lost their nationality due to events of the First World War, but who remained unprotected by any international refugee instrument: International Conference on German Refugees, 'Provisional Minutes: Fourth Meeting', Geneva, (8 Feb. 1938): CONF.CSRA/PV4 (10 Feb. 1938), 8.

[14] Convention relating to the International Status of Refugees of 28 Oct. 1933, 159 *LNTS* 199.

[15] Spanish refugees were defined as 'les personnes possédant ou ayant possédé la nationalité espagnole, ne possédant pas une autre nationalité et à l'égard desquelles il est établi, qu'en droit ou en fait, elles ne jouissent pas de la protection du gouvernement espagnol': Décret No. 45–766 du 15 mars 1945 accordant aux réfugiés espagnols le bénéfice de diverses dispositions (*Journal Officiel* de la République Française, 21 avril 1945) *Gazette du Palais* (1945) art. 2.

[16] International Conference on German Refugees (above n. 13), 8. The British *Kindertransport*, a quasi-protection, quasi-humanitarian assistance scheme enabled Jewish children forced to flee Germany to stay in Britain. It was reminiscent of a First World War programme that admitted several thousand Belgian children to Britain, and the admission in May 1937 of 3,800 Basque children as refugees of the Spanish Civil War: Sherman, A. J., *Island Refuge—Britain and Refugees from the Third Reich 1933–1939*, (2nd edn, 1994), 183–7; Göpfert, R., *Der jüdische Kindertransport von Deutschland nach England 1938/39: Geschichte und Erinnerung*, (1999).

[17] This pattern is followed by the 1969 OAU Convention, the 'regional complement' to the 1951 Convention, and in the domestic law of Canada (Immigration and Refugee Protection Act, s. 97) and the Netherlands (Aliens Act 2000, s. 27).

[18] Jackson, I. C., *The Refugee Concept in Group Situations*, (1999); see also Council of Europe, Parliamentary Assembly Recommendation 1327 (1997) on the Protection and Reinforcement of the Human Rights of Refugees and Asylum-Seekers in Europe, paras. 2–3.

coincidental, that just as States were extending UNHCR's mandate to refugees in large-scale influxes and displaced persons in refugee-like situations,[19] they started to contract their own domestic asylum policies.[20]

As noted in Chapter 1, there is a disjuncture between UNHCR's functional responsibilities and States' obligations under the 1951 Convention.[21] Whereas UNHCR's mandate has been successively extended by UNGA resolutions, the 1951 Convention text has only been amended once, by the 1967 Protocol, to remove the temporal and geographical limitations of the refugee definition in article 1A(2). In the regional refugee instruments of Africa[22] and Latin America,[23] the 'refugee' concept is defined more broadly than its international counterpart, encompassing (respectively) flight from 'external aggression, occupation, foreign domination or events seriously disturbing public order in either part or the whole of his country of origin or nationality',[24] and 'generalized violence, foreign aggression, internal conflicts, massive violation of human rights or other circumstances which have seriously disturbed public order'.[25]

---

[19] See, for example, UNGA resolutions 1499 (XV), 5 Dec. 1960; 1673 (XVI), 18 Dec. 1961; 1959 (XVIII) 12 Dec. 1963; 2294 (XXII), 11 Dec. 1967; 3143 (XXVIII), 14 Dec. 1973.

[20] This was affirmed by the 1977 Conference on Territorial Asylum: see Melander, G., 'The Two Refugee Definitions', Raoul Wallenberg Institute of Human Rights and Humanitarian Law, *Report No. 4* (Lund 1987), 11; Grahl-Madsen, A., *Territorial Asylum*, (1980), 61ff.

[21] See also UNHCR, 'Protection of Persons of Concern to UNHCR Who Fall Outside the 1951 Convention: A Discussion Note' (2 Apr. 1992), UN doc. EC/1992/SCP.CRP.5, para. 1; Jackson, *Refugee Concept in Group Situations,* above n. 18.

[22] The 1969 OAU Convention has been widely ratified. For States parties, see below Annexe 3, No. 2. See also Okoth-Obbo, G., 'Thirty Years On: A Legal Review of the 1969 OAU Convention Governing the Specific Aspects of Refugee Problems in Africa', 20 *RSQ* 79 (2001); Hyndman, J. & Nylund, B. V., 'UNHCR and the Status of Prima Facie Refugees in Kenya', 10 *IJRL* 21 (1998); Rutinwa, B., 'Prima Facie Status and Refugee Protection', UNHCR *New Issues in Refugee Research,* Working Paper No. 69 (Oct. 2002); Oloka-Onyango, J., 'Human Rights, the OAU Convention and the Refugee Crisis in Africa', 3 *IJRL* 453 (1991); Oloka-Onyango, J., 'The Place and Role of the OAU Bureau for Refugees in the African Refugee Crisis', 6 *IJRL* 34 (1994); generally see 21 (1–2) *RSQ* (2002); OAU/UNHCR Commemorative Symposium on Refugees and the Problems of Forced Population Displacements in Africa, Addis Ababa, (8–10 Sept. 1994), 7 *IJRL, Special Issue—Summer 1995.*

[23] Latin America is covered by a complex network of treaties and asylum practices: see 1889 Montevideo Treaty on International Penal Law; 1928 Havana Convention on Asylum; 1933 Montevideo Convention on Political Asylum; 1940 Montevideo Treaty on International Penal Law (revising that of 1889); 1954 Caracas Convention on Territorial Asylum (Annexe 2, No. 3); 1954 Caracas Convention on Diplomatic Asylum (Annexe 2, No. 4). See also Cuellar, R., García-Sayán, D., Montaño, J., Diegues, M. & Valladares Lanza, L., 'Refugee and Related Developments in Latin America: The Challenges Ahead', 3 *IJRL* 482 (1991); D'Alotto, A. & Garretón, R., 'Developments in Latin America: Some Further Thoughts', ibid., 499; Gros Espiell, H., Picado, S. & Valladares Lanza, L., 'Principles and Criteria for the Protection of and Assistance to Central American Refugees, Returnees and Displaced Persons in Central America', 2 *IJRL* 83 (1990); UNHCR, 'The Refugee Situation in Latin America: Protection and Solutions Based on the Pragmatic Approach of the Cartagena Declaration of Refugees of 1984', 18 *IJRL* 252 (2006); Fischel de Andrade, J. H., 'Regional Policy Approaches and Harmonization: A Latin American Prespective', 10 *IJRL* 389 (1998); Jubilut, L. L., 'Refugee Law and Protection in Brazil: A Model in South America?', 19 *JRS* 22 (2006).

[24] Art. I(2), OUA69.   [25] Art. III(3), 1984 Cartagena Declaration.

Although western States have typically eschewed the incorporation of additional categories into the Convention refugee concept,[26] they have nonetheless recognized that certain people, beyond those encompassed by article 1A(2), must not be returned to serious forms of harm. Typically, State practice has been characterized by highly varied, *ad hoc* responses at the national level, premised largely on executive discretion,[27] rather than a unified international approach. Differing approaches are evident in the UNHCR Executive Committee, with some States concerned to emphasize protection needs,[28] and others to stress their sovereign discretion,[29] denying any *obligation* to grant extra-Convention refugees asylum or provide any particular durable solution.[30] Yet, State practice has consistently revealed a dominant trend of offering some form of protection to 'persons whose life or freedom would be at risk as a result of armed conflict or generalized violence if they were returned involuntarily to their countries of origin'.[31] States have consistently recognized a right of refuge in cases of grave and urgent necessity (even if at times they have resisted formally classifying such people as *refugees* when outside the terms of the 1951 Convention/1967 Protocol). Crucially, no State has formally denied that such a right exists.[32]

In the mid-1980s, Perluss and Hartman, subsequently supported by Goodwin-Gill, demonstrated the development of a customary norm of 'temporary refuge', which prohibited States from forcibly repatriating foreigners who had fled generalized violence and other threats caused by internal armed conflict within their own State, until the violence ceased and the home State could assure the security and protection of its nationals.[33] Goodwin-Gill, at the time a legal adviser in UNHCR,

---

[26] Note, however, that expanded categories have been incorporated into the definition in some countries; for example, in Sweden, Ch. 4, s. 1 of the Aliens Act (in force 31 Mar. 2006) provides that a refugee includes someone who is persecuted 'on grounds of gender, sexual orientation or other membership of a particular social group'. See also Ch. 3, s. 4.2.4.

[27] Storey, H. *et al.*, 'Complementary Protection: Should There Be a Common Approach to Providing Protection to Persons Who Are Not Covered by the 1951 Geneva Convention?' (Joint ILPA/IARLJ Symposium, 6 Dec. 1999) (copy with authors), 3.

[28] See, for example, UN doc. A/AC.96/SR.374 (1985), paras. 57–60 (Tunisia and France); UN doc. A/AC.96/SR.507 (1996), para. 60 (US); UN doc. A/AC.96/SR.508 (1996), para. 5 (Sweden); UN doc. A/AC.96/SR.511 (1996), para. 6 (Egypt); UN doc. A/AC.96/SR.527 (1998), para. 9 (UK), para. 40 (Belgium), para. 44 (France).

[29] UNHCR, 'Note on International Protection', UN doc. A/AC.96/830 (7 Sept. 1994), para. 40; UN doc. A/AC.96/SR.518 (1997), para. 12 (Italy); UN doc. A/AC.96/SR.430 (1988), para. 42 (Switzerland); Summary Records, 36th Session, UN doc. A/AC.96/SR.391 (1985), para. 72 (The Netherlands); UN doc. A/AC.96/SR.418 (1987), para. 71 (Germany).

[30] A cogent account and analysis of State practice is given in Perluss and Hartman, above n. 6; see also Meron, T., *Human Rights and Humanitarian Norms as Customary Law*, (1989); Goodwin-Gill, above n. 6.   [31] UNHCR, 'Note on International Protection', (1994), above n. 29, para. 39.

[32] Coles, G. J. L., *The Question of a General Approach to the Problem of Refugees from Situations of Armed Conflict and Serious Internal Disturbance*, (1989), 21.

[33] Perluss and Hartman, above n. 6, 554, examples at 571ff. See also Goodwin-Gill, above n. 6, 902, noting that while customary international law had incorporated the core meaning of art. 33, it had also 'extend[ed] the principle of *non-refoulement* to include displaced persons who do not enjoy the protection of the government of their country of origin'; Fitzpatrick, J., 'Temporary Protection of Refugees: Elements of a Formalized Regime', 94 *AJIL* 279 (2000), 282–7. Note the dissenting views of Hailbronner, above n. 6.

originally framed this argument in terms of an enlarged concept of *non-refoulement*, a position that reflected the UNHCR's own views that *non-refoulement* demanded that 'no person shall be subjected to such measures as rejection at the frontier, or, if he has already entered the territory, expulsion or compulsory return to any country where he may have reason to fear persecution *or serious danger resulting from unsettled conditions or civil strife*'.[34] Indeed, UNHCR went further, describing such protection as being based on a customary norm of *jus cogens*.[35] A decade later, the second edition of this work argued that 'the impact on State competence of the broader developments relating to human rights and displacement would have been better served by characterizing State responsibilities in terms of a general principle of *refuge*'.[36] A decade further still, this practice has come to be encompassed by the concept of 'complementary protection', and, for persons fleeing in large numbers, by the European and international notion[37] of 'temporary protection'.[38]

Though the norm of temporary refuge was elucidated in the context of large-scale influx, and provides the legal foundation for subsequent formalized temporary protection regimes, there is nothing intrinsic that prevents its application to *individuals* fleeing generalized violence. Accordingly, complementary protection is its 'individual' counterpart, extending protection to single or small group arrivals on the same humanitarian basis. As noted above, this was recognized by the High Commissioner in 1985.[39]

As early as 1961, the European Commission on Human Rights had recognized that article 3 ECHR50, which prohibits torture and inhuman or degrading treatment or punishment, could encompass the principle of *non-refoulement*.[40] This principle was adopted by a Council of Europe Parliamentary Assembly recommendation in 1965, which stated that: 'by prohibiting inhuman treatment, [article 3] binds contracting parties not to return refugees to a country where their life or freedom would be threatened'.[41] From the mid-1970s, the Council of Europe had sought to unify European State practice relating to '*de facto* refugees'—'persons not recognised as refugees within the meaning of Article 1 of the [Refugee] Convention' and who were 'unable or unwilling for political, racial, religious or other valid

---

[34] Report of UNHCR to ECOSOC (1985) UN doc. E/1985/62, para. 22 (emphasis added).
[35] Ibid., paras. 22–3.   [36] *The Refugee in International Law*, 2nd edn., 136.
[37] This is to distinguish 'temporary protection' as applied in mass influx situations from domestic regimes, such as 'Temporary Protection Visas' in Australia, which apply to Convention refugees who have arrived in Australia 'unlawfully', that is, without a visa of any kind; and 'Temporary Protected Status' in the United States, which is similar, but not identical to, the international/European concept.
[38] Fitzpatrick, J., 'Human Rights and Forced Displacement: Converging Standards' in Bayefsky, A. F. & Fitzpatrick, J., eds., *Human Rights and Forced Displacement*, (2000), 8. See s. 6 below.
[39] See above, n. 34 and accompanying text.
[40] *X v. Belgium*, Application No. 984/61 (29 May 1961), 6 CD 39–40; *X v. Federal Republic of Germany* (1963) 6 *Yearbook* 462, 480, cited in Alleweldt, R., 'Protection Against Expulsion under Article 3 of the European Convention on Human Rights', 4 *EJIL* 360, 351 n. 5 (1993). The European Court did not affirm the principle until *Soering v. UK* (1989) 11 EHRR 439; see also *Chahal v. UK* (1996) 23 EHRR 413.
[41] Council of Europe Parliamentary Assembly Recommendation 434 (1965) concerning the Granting of the Right of Asylum to European Refugees.

reasons to return to their countries of origin'[42]—through a series of non-binding recommendations.[43] Although States were encouraged not to expel *de facto* refugees or restrict their political activities,[44] the instruments did not specify what legal status they should be granted. This, according to Weis, was their main disability.[45] He favoured the extension of article 1A(2) to encompass additional categories of protected persons, although he realized that, politically, this was unlikely.[46]

Internationally, progress was even slower. Complementary protection, as an issue requiring deliberate and principled consideration, did not emerge on the international agenda until the late 1980s, and tended for a long time to be raised in the context of mass influx.[47] The UNHCR-convened San Remo Round Table of 1989 was the first international forum to consider the protection of refugees in non-international armed conflicts as a legal responsibility, rather than just a moral obligation. It noted the importance of 'supplementing the traditional principles of law and doctrine with complementary new principles',[48] focusing in particular on human rights law as a primary source for refugee protection at all stages of the

---

[42] Council of Europe Parliamentary Assembly Recommendation 773 (1976) on the Situation of *de facto* Refugees, para. 1. This definition was one considered by the Report of the Group of Governmental Experts on International Co-operation to Avert New Flows of Refugees, Annex to 'International Co-operation to Avert New Flows of Refugees: Note by the Secretary-General', UN doc. A/41/324 (13 May 1986), 24.

[43] For further detail, see McAdam, *Complementary Protection*; Recommendation 773 (above n. 42); Council of Europe Parliamentary Assembly Recommendation 817 (1977) on Certain Aspects of the Right to Asylum; Council of Europe Parliamentary Assembly Recommendation 1016 (1985) on Living and Working Conditions of Refugees and Asylum Seekers; Council of Europe Committee of Ministers Recommendation No. R (84) 1 on the Protection of Persons Satisfying the Criteria in the Geneva Convention Who Are Not Formally Recognised as Refugees; Council of Europe Parliamentary Assembly Recommendation 1088 (1988) on the Right to Territorial Asylum; Communication from the Commission to the Council and the European Parliament on the Right of Asylum SEC 91 1857 final (11 Oct. 1991); Council of Europe Parliamentary Assembly Recommendation 1236 (1994) on the Right of Asylum; Council of Europe Parliamentary Assembly Recommendation 1237 (1994) on the Situation of Asylum-Seekers Whose Asylum Applications Have Been Rejected; Council Resolution of 14 Oct. 1996 laying down the Priorities for Cooperation in the Field of Justice and Home Affairs for the period from 1 July 1996 to 30 June 1998 (96/C 319/01); Council of Europe Parliamentary Assembly Recommendation 1327 (1997) on the Protection and Reinforcement of the Human Rights of Refugees and Asylum-Seekers in Europe; Council of Europe Committee of Ministers Recommendation R (98) 13 on the Right of Rejected Asylum Seekers to an Effective Remedy against Decisions on Expulsion in the Context of Article 3 of the European Convention on Human Rights; Council of Europe Parliamentary Assembly Recommendation 1440 (2000) on Restrictions on Asylum in the Member States of the Council of Europe and the EU; Council of Europe Committee of Ministers Recommendation R (2001) 18 on Subsidiary Protection; Council of Europe Parliamentary Assembly Recommendation 1525 (2001) on the United Nations High Commissioner for Refugees and the Fiftieth Anniversary of the Geneva Convention.

[44] Recommendation 773, above n. 42, para. 5(II).

[45] For national examples, see Weis, P., 'Convention Refugees and De Facto Refugees', in Melander, G. and Nobel, P., eds., *African Refugees and the Law*, (1978), 20.   [46] Ibid., 22.

[47] The modern notions of 'complementary protection' and 'temporary protection' both arose from the principle of temporary refuge.

[48] 'Report of the Round Table on Solutions to the Problem of Refugees and the Protection of Refugees', San Remo Italy, (12–14 Jul. 1989), para. 8. Annex to UNHCR, 'Solution to the Refugee Problem and the Protection of Refugees' (SCIP) (23 Aug. 1989) UN doc. EC/SCP/55, The experts, governmental and non-governmental, attended in a personal capacity.

refugee process.[49] In particular, the Round Table articulated the importance of conferring a legal status on beneficiaries of a wider protection practice, noting that it was unjust 'to deprive a human being of a community for many years, especially where the person lived under a continuing threat of expulsion'.[50] Two years later, a Working Group, convened at the behest of the Executive Committee,[51] identified seven categories of people with an international protection need, based on States' responsibilities under relevant international instruments, and UNHCR's mandate (as extended by various UNGA resolutions).[52] It was considered 'illogical' that people might be protected in certain regions of the world—namely, in Africa and Latin America where extended refugee definitions applied—but not in other parts.[53] The topic was considered

pertinent not only because of the large number of people affected, but also because of the complications that can arise when States must deal with such persons in an ad hoc manner that may not be understood or supported by public opinion. In addition, there is a growing gap between the responsibilities which States have been prepared to assume and those which they have asked UNHCR to perform.[54]

Of concern was not only who should benefit from extra-Convention protection, but also what the content of that protection should be.[55] In this respect, the Working Group considered the OAU Convention and Cartagena Declaration to be appropriate models, synthesizing institutional and State mandates.[56] These instruments not only contain a broadened refugee definition, but—significantly— extend the legal status set out in the 1951 Convention to those additional categories of people. This is important because it supports the notion that the Refugee Convention already provides an appropriate legal status for additional groups of refugees,[57] and that complementary protection does not have to signify subsidiary rights.

---

[49] Ibid. para. 33, Conclusion, para. 13.   [50] Ibid.
[51] Executive Committee Conclusion No. 56 (XL) 'Durable Solutions and Refugee Protection', (1989), para. (c).
[52] Executive Committee, 'Report of the Working Group on Solutions and Protection to the 42nd Session of the Executive Committee of the High Commissioner's Programme', (12 Aug. 1991), UN doc. EC/SCP/64, para. 8. See also Report of the Group of Governmental Experts on International Cooperation to Avert New Flows of Refugees, Annex to 'International Cooperation to Avert New Flows of Refugees: Note by the Secretary General', UN doc. A/41/324, (13 May 1986).
[53] Executive Committee 'Report of the Working Group', above note, para. 12.
[54] UNHCR, 'Report of the 13–14 April Meeting of the Sub-Committee of the Whole on International Protection': UN doc. EC/SCP/71 (7 Jul. 1992), para. 32.   [55] Ibid., para. 33.
[56] Executive Committee, 'Report of the Working Group', above n. 52, Recommendations, para. 55(b); see also UNHCR, 'Note on International Protection', above n. 29, para. 35; UNHCR, 'Note on International Protection', UN doc. A/AC.96/930 (7 Jul. 2000) paras. 40–1.
[57] Executive Committee 'Report of the Working Group' above n. 52, para. 11; see Annex to UNHCR, 'Report of the Round Table', above n. 48, Conclusion, para. 12; McAdam, *Complementary Protection*, Chs. 1, 6.

That extended protection was based on international law, not merely moral or humanitarian principles, was emphasized by the UN High Commissioner's 1991 'Note on International Protection':

Within the framework of this existing body of international law, three sets of principles have tended to develop separately, although in parallel, where they could perhaps have been linked more closely at an earlier stage. These are the law of refugee protection, human rights law generally and humanitarian law. Together, these three domains of law—which, in reality, are closely interrelated and often overlap—should ideally permit an individual to assert a claim, not only against his or her own country or, in certain situations, another country, but on the international community as whole—a claim to its direct involvement on humanitarian grounds. In other words, where Governments fail to recognize individual claims, or where there is no effective Government to which an individual in the first instance might turn, there is a pressing need for that person to be able to assert a claim more broadly. The international community seems already to be moving in this direction as a result of recent events and there might be value in examining how the legal foundations of this development could be strengthened.[58]

Given that part of the impetus behind these discussions was to narrow the gap between UNHCR's institutional mandate and States' protection obligations, a 1992 UNHCR discussion Note identified five categories of people within UNHCR's mandate: (a) those who fall under the Statute/1951 Convention definition and thus are entitled to benefit from the full range of UNHCR's functions; (b) those who belong to a broader category but have been recognized by States as being entitled to both the protection and assistance of UNHCR; (c) those to whom the High Commissioner extends his 'good offices', mainly but not exclusively to facilitate humanitarian assistance; (d) returning refugees, for whom the High Commissioner may provide reintegration assistance and a certain protection; and (e) non-refugee stateless persons whom UNHCR has a limited mandate to assist.[59] For the purposes of devising an expanded protection regime, the Note stated that those in category (b) were of most interest, and typically included persons covered by the definitions in the OAU Convention and the Cartagena Declaration. However, this Note marked a shift in thinking about the resultant status for such people. Whereas the regional instruments are complementary to the 1951 Convention, and people in the broader refugee class are entitled to the same legal status as Convention refugees, this Note for the first time acquiesced in the idea that protection extended on a complementary basis might be temporary in nature, observing that '[f]or the very large majority of persons of concern in the present context, return at some point will be the only available solution'.[60] The Note itself does not reveal the background discussions on this point. It may have been simply a pragmatic response designed to deal with large influxes of people, or

---

[58] UNHCR, 'Note on International Protection', UN d oc. A/AC.96/777, (9 Sept. 1991), para. 56; see also UNHCR, 'Note on International Protection', (1992), above n. 10 para. 1.

[59] UNHCR, 'Protection of Persons of Concern', (1992), above n. 21, para. 11.

[60] Ibid., para. 7.

based on the assumption that return would be possible at the end of a civil war. However, the acceptance of this point seems to have occurred without any comprehensive analysis of whether it was legally justifiable or necessary.[61] Furthermore, for the first time, and again without explanation, a separate complementary protection status, different from Convention status, was contemplated. It was based primarily on the standards set out in the 1981 Executive Committee Conclusion No. 22 on Protection of Asylum-Seekers in Situations of Large-Scale Influx.[62] Yet, at the same time, the Note concluded that:

There is nothing in the Convention definition which would exclude its application to persons caught up in civil war or other situations of generalized violence. Refugees are refugees when they flee or remain outside a country for reasons pertinent to refugee status, whether these reasons arise in civil war type situations, in international armed conflict or in peace time. Possibilities for identifying these persons should, therefore, not be precluded, but rather specifically provided for.[63]

By this time, there was a general consensus that a uniform international response to people not covered by article 1A(2) but in need of international protection was required in order to avoid differential treatment, uncertainty, and unequal burden-sharing.[64] However, agreement as to how this should be done was more tenuous. The possibility of drafting a Protocol to the Convention was discouraged on the basis that it would open up 'fundamental principles and precepts in the Convention itself' for renegotiation.[65] Instead, it was suggested that States should first bring their national laws into line with international and regional standards, and subsequently, a universal international regime could be developed. A 1994 Note canvassed four options: a new Convention; a declaration of guiding principles; regional harmonization; or concerted approaches in specific situations. UNHCR considered that a new international instrument—'an OAU refugee Convention writ large'[66]—would be the most attractive option, but conceded that States did not seem disposed to incur further legal obligations in relation to asylum.[67] For this reason, it was suggested that a set of guiding principles would be the most realistic means of obtaining a formal commitment by States to protect refugees from armed conflict (for which there was broad international consensus),[68] with harmonized regional approaches cited as 'perhaps the most promising option for strengthening protection'.[69]

---

[61] This aspect is discussed later in the context of the Qualification Directive. For 'cessation' of status under the 1951 Convention, see above, Ch. 4, ss. 1, 2.

[62] UNHCR, 'Protection of Persons of Concern to UNHCR who fall outside the 1951 Convention: A Discussion Note', UN doc. EC/1992/SCP/CRP.5, 2 Apr. 1992, paras. 20–1.

[63] Ibid., para. 21.

[64] Ibid., para. 3; cf. Executive Committee, 'Report of the Working Group', above n. 52, para. 25.

[65] Executive Committee, 'Report of the Working Group', above n. 52, para. 25; UNHCR 'Protection of Persons of Concern', above n. 62, para. 7.

[66] UNHCR, 'Note on International Protection', UN doc. A/AC.96/830 (7 Sept. 1994), para. 52.

[67] Ibid., para. 53.   [68] Ibid., para. 54.   [69] Ibid., para. 55.

Even though the European Court on Human Rights had confirmed in 1989 that States' obligations under article 3 ECHR50 prohibited *refoulement* to torture or inhuman or degrading treatment or punishment[70]—a view echoed by the Human Rights Committee in 1992 with respect to article 7 ICCPR66,[71] and the Committee against Torture in 1994 with respect to article 3 CAT84[72]—it was not until 1994 that the Executive Committee explicitly acknowledged that many States 'are parties to other international instruments that could be invoked in certain circumstances against the return of some non-Convention refugees to a place where their lives, freedom or other fundamental rights would [be] in jeopardy'.[73] In the same year, the Parliamentary Assembly of the Council of Europe stated that States' international protection obligations were 'based on the 1951 Geneva Convention *and* the Convention for the Protection of Human Rights and Fundamental Freedoms—remembering that *the latter also implies obligations* vis-à-vis *persons who are not necessarily refugees in the sense of the 1951 Geneva Convention*'.[74]

The identification of specific treaty obligations as extending the principle of *non-refoulement* beyond article 33 of the 1951 Convention marked the turning point in the modern development of complementary protection as tool based on international *law*, rather than a purely *ad hoc* domestic discretion. It was this that also came to differentiate 'complementary' and 'temporary' protection regimes, with the former operating in relation to identifiable 'individual' rights violations, and the latter covering broader humanitarian disturbances (based partly on humanitarian law, but perhaps more appropriately conceived as the customary law principle of temporary refuge). The logical flaw in the distinction is, of course, that so far as a State's actions may expose an individual to risk of violation of fundamental human rights, its responsibility should be duty-driven, rather than strictly correlative to any individual 'right'.[75] Furthermore, once a protection obligation has been identified, protection should be forthcoming regardless of whether an individual arrives alone or as part of a larger group. Indeed, although the discussion in the early 1990s about extra-Convention protection duties

[70] This affirmed the view expressed by the European Commission in 1961 in *X* v. *Belgium* and other cases, cited in Alleweldt, R., 'Protection against Expulsion under Article 3 of the European Convention on Human Rights', 4 *EJIL* 360 (1993).
[71] ICCPR66: Human Rights Committee, General Comment 20 (Forty-fourth session, 1992): Article 7: Replaces General Comment No. 7 (1992), para. 9.
[72] *Mutombo* v. *Switzerland*, Comm. No. 13/1993 (17 Apr. 1994): UN doc. CAT/C/12/D/13/1993. [73] Ibid., para. 40.
[74] Parliamentary Assembly Recommendation 1236 (1994) on the Right of Asylum, para. 8(iii) (emphasis added); see also Parliamentary Assembly Recommendation 1309 (1996) on the Training of Officials Receiving Asylum-Seekers at Border Points, para. 7(ii)(a), referring to the 'basics of asylum law' as including ECHR50.
[75] See also Kälin, W., *Grundriss des Asylverfahrens*, (1990), 211: 'In seinem *weiteren, menschenrechtlichen Sinn* schützt [das Prinzip des non-refoulements] vor Aushändigung an einen Staat, welcher aus irgend welchen Motiven den betroffenen Ausländer Folter oder bestimmten anderen schwerwiegenden Menschenrechtsverletzungen aussetzen würde.'

seemed to centre on mass influx situations, the records do not reveal any suggestion that this widened responsibility was *only* applicable to flight *en masse*.[76] For
this reason, those earlier deliberations comprise part of the development of the
modern notion of complementary protection.

3. Complementary protection at the international level[77]

Despite three decades of discussions at the European and international levels to
create a harmonized, legal approach to complementary protection, and the development of an extensive jurisprudence throughout the 1990s by the European
Court of Human Rights under article 3 ECHR50, the Human Rights Committee
under article 7 ICCPR66, and the Committee against Torture under article 3
CAT84, it was only in 2004 that a binding supranational legal instrument was
adopted by the EU Member States, and in late 2005 that a non-binding Executive
Committee Conclusion was agreed at the international level.

The 2005 Executive Committee Conclusion is an important soft-law instrument that calls for States to uphold their international obligations under the 1951
Convention, the statelessness treaties, human rights law, and humanitarian law;
acknowledges complementary protection as 'a positive way of responding prag-
matically to certain international protection needs';[78] and encourages States to use
'complementary forms of protection for individuals in need of international protection who do not meet the refugee definition under the 1951 Convention or the
1967 Protocol'.[79] It affirms that complementary protection should be applied 'in
a manner that strengthens, rather than undermines, the existing international
refugee protection regime',[80] and emphasizes the importance of applying and
developing international protection in a manner that avoids the creation or continuation of protection gaps.[81] However, the Conclusion's weakness is its failure to
call expressly for the equal treatment of Convention refugees and beneficiaries of
complementary protection.[82]

The clearest (and least controversial) treaty-based sources of complementary
protection under international human rights law are article 3 CAT84, which prohibits removal to State-sanctioned 'torture'; article 7 ICCPR66, which precludes
removal to 'torture or cruel, inhuman or degrading treatment or punishment';
and, for the Member States of the Council of Europe, article 3 ECHR50, which

---

[76] It is both legally and morally illogical to distinguish between a protection need arising by virtue
of flight as part of a large group, and individual or smaller group flight. Nevertheless, as the EU
Directives demonstrate, States do differentiate between the two.

[77] See also the discussion of *non-refoulement* under international treaty law in Ch. 5.

[78] Executive Committee Conclusion No. 103 (2005), para. (h).   [79] Ibid., para. (i).

[80] Ibid., para. (k).   [81] Ibid., para. (s).

[82] NGO delegations sought to have a statement to this effect included: Draft Conclusion on the
Provision of International Protection including through Complementary Forms of Protection',
NGO version, (12 Jul. 2005), para. 11; copy with authors. See s. 5 below.

prohibits removal to 'torture or inhuman or degrading treatment or punishment'. The prohibition on return to torture is a feature common to all domestic complementary protection regimes,[83] and of those regimes all but the United States extend this to non-removal to inhuman or degrading treatment or punishment as well.[84] A number of States also prohibit removal to the death penalty, in accordance with (variously) their obligations under the Protocols to ECHR50, article 37 CRC89, and the Second Optional Protocol to ICCPR66.[85]

At the international level, an individual facing removal contrary to the above-mentioned treaty provisions may be able to take his or her case directly to one of the treaty-monitoring Committees.[86] However, while those bodies may find that a State's *non-refoulement* obligations would be violated if the individual in question were removed, there is no guarantee that the State will follow its views. Decisions of the European Court of Human Rights are binding on the parties to the claim, but the Court (like the international Committees) does not specify what legal status should attach to the applicant if he or she is non-removable.[87] The following sections describe the nature and scope of the various treaty obligations and the way they have been interpreted by the relevant Committee or the Court. This helps to give content to the obligations to which States have subscribed by ratifying

[83] EU Qualification Directive, art. 15(b); USA: 8 CFR §208.16(4); Canada: Immigration and Refugee Protection Act s. 97(1)(a); Denmark: Aliens Act, s. 7(2).

[84] EU Qualification Directive, art. 15(b); Denmark: Aliens Act, s. 7(2); Canada: Immigration and Refugee Protection Act, s. 97(1)(b) (note that although the Act prohibits return to 'cruel and unusual treatment or punishment', this phrase has substantially the same meaning as 'inhuman or degrading treatment or punishment': *US* v. *Burns* [2001] 1 SCR 283, 2001 SCC 7. Proposed legislation in New Zealand is based on arts. 6 and 7 ICCPR66: NZ Department of Labour, 'Immigration Act Review: Discussion paper' (Apr. 2006), section 14. Australian Guidelines (which are not binding and only apply to the exercise of ministerial discretion): 'Guidelines on Ministerial Powers under Sections 345, 351, 391, 417, 454 and 501J of the *Migration Act* 1958 (MSI 386)', cited in Senate Select Committee on Ministerial Discretion in Migration Matters, *Inquiry into Ministerial Discretion in Migration Matters* (Cth of Austrtalia 2004), Annex 5. Note also the proposed Migration Legislation Amendment (Complementry Protection Visas) Bill 2006 (discussed above n. 1).

[85] EU Qualification Directive, art. 15(a); Canada: Immigration and Refugee Protection Act, s. 97(1)(b) ('risk to their life'). The NZ proposal refers to art. 6 ICCPR66, even though art. 6(2) expressly recognizes the use of the death penalty by some States, albeit for 'the most serious crimes' and 'pursuant to a final judgment rendered by a competent court'. See the UN Human Rights Committee's 'General Comment 6: The Right to Life', (30 Apr. 1982), paras. 6–7, which indicate that States are obliged to limit the use of the death penalty and that its abolition is desirable. Although the Second Optional Protocol to ICCPR66 requires States to abolish the death penalty within their jurisdiction, some interpret that as also prohibiting them from sending someone to face the death penalty elsewhere. See *Judge* v. *Canada*, Comm. No. 829/1998, UN doc. CCPR/C/78/D/829/1998, (5 Aug. 2003), para.10.6.

[86] The international treaty-monitoring bodies should, technically, operate as a fallback mechanism, since States have an obligation pursuant to their treaty obligations to implement rights at a domestic level and thereby codify non-return beyond the scope of art. 33 CSR51. In States which have not incorporated their international obligations into national law, such as Australia, the international Committees may provide the only opportunity for asylum seekers to have their claims considered against the relevant treaty provisions.

[87] See, for example, *Vijayanathan* v. *France* (1993) 15 EHRR 62; *Ahmed* v. *Austria* (1997) 24 EHRR 278 and discussion in Andrysek, O., 'Gaps in International Protection and the Potential for Redress through Individual Complaints Procedures', 9 *IJRL* 392 (1997).

particular treaties, and illustrates the criteria which should, at minimum, constitute grounds for complementary protection in national law.

3.1 HUMAN RIGHTS TREATIES: SOME PROCEDURAL CONSIDERATIONS

The ability for individuals to make a complaint to an international treaty-monitoring body is not automatic on a State's ratification of the treaty. For example, an individual may only take a claim to the Committee against Torture where the relevant State party (against whom the individual wishes to claim) has made an optional declaration under article 22 CAT84 recognizing the Committee's competence to receive and assess individual communications. Similarly, the Human Rights Committee may only consider complaints relating to ICCPR66 where the relevant State party has signed the First Optional Protocol. By contrast, all States parties to ECHR50 are automatically subject to the jurisdiction of the European Court of Human Rights.

Under CAT84, ICCPR66, and ECHR50, matters must first be declared admissible before they can be heard on the merits.[88] First, the applicant must have exhausted all domestic remedies,[89] unless they will be 'unreasonably prolonged'[90] or 'unlikely to bring effective relief'.[91] Revised rule 107(f) of the CAT Rules of Procedure requires that 'the time elapsed since the exhaustion of domestic remedies is not so unreasonably prolonged as to render consideration of the claims unduly difficult by the Committee or the State party'. The European Convention on Human Rights imposes a time limit by stipulating that the Court will only deal with the matter within six months from the date on which the final decision was taken.[92]

Secondly, both CAT84 and ECHR50 require that the claim has not already been examined under another international procedure.[93] By contrast, the Optional Protocol to ICCPR66 rules complaints inadmissible only when they are pending before another international body.[94] This means that the Human Rights Committee may examine a matter after it has already been considered by the Committee against Torture or the Court,[95] but most States parties to ECHR50 have entered reservations to article 5 of the Optional Protocol so that it operates like article 22(5)(a) CAT84 to eliminate this duplication.

[88] See art. 22 CAT84, and the Committee against Torture Rules of Procedure (adopted by the Committee at its 1st and 2nd sessions and amended at its 13th, 15th, and 28th sessions): UN doc. CAT/C/3/Rev.4 (9 Aug. 2002); art. 35 ECHR50, and ECHR50 Rules of Court (Nov. 2003); art. 41 ICCPR66, and Rules of Procedure of the Human Rights Committee, in Compilation of Rules of Procedure adopted by Human Rights Treaty Bodies UN doc. HRI/GEN/3.Rev.1 (28 Apr. 2003), 25.
[89] Art. 35(1) ECHR50; art. 41(1)(c) ICCPR66; arts. 2, 5(2)(b) ICCPR66 Optional Protocol.
[90] Art. 22(5)(b) CAT84; art. 41(1)(c) ICCPR66; art. 5(2)(b) ICCPR66 Optional Protocol.
[91] Art. 22(5)(b) CAT84; see also CAT Rules, above n. 88, revised rule 107(e).
[92] Art. 35(1) ECHR50.   [93] Art. 22(5)(a) CAT84; art. 35(2)(b) ECHR50.
[94] Art. 5(2)(a) ICCPR66 Optional Protocol.
[95] ICCPR66 Optional Protocol, UNGA res. 2200A (XXI), 16 Dec. 1966: 999 *UNTS* 302; text in Brownlie, I. & Goodwin-Gill, G. S., eds., *Basic Documents on Human Rights*, (5th edn., 2006), 358 (hereafter, Brownlie & Goodwin-Gill, *Basic Documents on Human Rights*).

Finally, communications will be declared inadmissible if they are anonymous,[96] incompatible with the treaty's provisions,[97] or considered by the Committee or the Court to be an abuse of process[98] or manifestly unfounded.[99]

Additionally, an applicant to the Court must be able to demonstrate that he or she is a 'victim of a violation' under article 34 ECHR50.[100] *Vijayanathan* v. *France* involved a direction to two Sri Lankans to leave French territory, after their request to be granted refugee status had been rejected.[101] The French government objected that the applicants were not 'victims', and the Court agreed. No expulsion order had been made against them, and the direction to leave French territory was not enforceable in itself,[102] even though the 'direction' amounted to an order to leave France within one month or be liable to the penalty of imprisonment and a fine.[103] The Court gave particular credence, however, to evidence of the practice of the French authorities with respect to asylum claims by Sri Lankans, including their use of information sources, case-by-case assessments, and the low incidence of actual expulsions.[104] As in *Vilvarajah* v. *United Kingdom*,[105] what counted for the Court was the authorities' knowledge and experience, and little weight was accorded to the applicants' request for a review of the merits.

Whereas decisions by the Court are binding on the parties to the claim,[106] and have a significant impact on EU and European domestic law,[107] those of the

---

[96] Art. 22(2) CAT84; art. 35(2)(a) ECHR50; art. 3 ICCPR66 Optional Protocol.

[97] Art. 22(2) CAT84; art. 35(3) ECHR50; art. 3 ICCPR66 Optional Protocol.

[98] Art. 22(2) CAT84; art. 35(3) ECHR50; art. 3 ICCPR66 Optional Protocol.

[99] CAT Rules, above n. 88, revised rule 107(b); art. 35(3) ECHR50.

[100] 'The Court may receive applications from any person, non-governmental organization or group of individuals claiming to be the victim of a violation by one of the High Contracting Parties of the rights set forth in the Convention or the protocols thereto. The High Contracting Parties undertake not to hinder in any way the effective exercise of this right.'

[101] *Vijayanathan and Pusparajah* v. *France* (1993) 15 EHRR 62.

[102] If an expulsion order were made, it could be appealed with suspensive effect: art. 22, ordonnance du 2 nov. 1945, as amended.

[103] At that time, it was a minimum one month, maximum one year; minimum 2,000 francs, maximum 20,000 francs, possibly followed by prohibition on residence and expulsion per art. 19, ordonnance du 2 nov. 1945, as amended; Judgment of the Court, paras. 10, 15. The Court did not consider whether the deliberate perpetuation of such a situation of insecurity and illegality by the State might itself be a violation of art. 3.

[104] Judgment of the Court, paras. 34–8, 44. See also *X* v. *Switzerland*, Application No. 14912/89, (1 Oct. 1990); Achermann, A., 'Neuansetzung einer Ausreisefrist für "Tolerierte"—Bemerkungen zum Entscheid der Europäischen Menschenrechtskommission i.S. X. c. Schweiz vom 1.10.1990, Beschwerde Nr. 14912/89', *Asyl*, 1991/2, 19–20. In the decision reviewed, the European Commission found the application manifestly ill-founded, as the government had given assurances of non-removal and/or if removal was contemplated, that the claimant would be 'granted sufficient opportunity to challenge the expulsion, if possible before the Swiss authorities, and in any event before the European Commission'. In the circumstances, there was no serious reason to believe a violation of arts. 2 or 3 was likely, and the applicant could not claim to be a victim of an alleged violation.   [105] (1991) 14 EHRR 248.

[106] Art. 46(1) ECHR50.

[107] See Einarsen, T., 'The European Convention on Human Rights and the Notion of an Implied Right to Asylum', 2 *IJRL* 361, 385 (1990): 'A single decision ... can have implications for the scope of

Committee against Torture and the Human Rights Committee are not. Instead, the Committees rely on their legal, moral, and political force to persuade States to follow their recommendations.[108] The Committee against Torture may request a State party found to be in violation of CAT84 to inform it of subsequent action taken to conform with the Committee's decision, and both the Torture and the Human Rights Committees may appoint a rapporteur to follow up on decisions.[109]

Importantly, all three bodies may request States to adopt interim measures to prevent an applicant's removal prior to a final determination of his or her claim. Although this is a non-binding mechanism under CAT84 and ICCPR66,[110] the European Court of Human Rights recently clarified its position by ruling that interim measures are binding on States.[111] In *Mamatkulov* v. *Turkey*, the Court stated that:

> by virtue of Article 34 of the Convention Contracting States undertake to refrain from any act or omission that may hinder the effective exercise of an individual applicant's right of application. A failure by a Contracting State to comply with interim measures is to be regarded as preventing the Court from effectively examining the applicant's complaint and as hindering the effective exercise of his or her right and, accordingly, as a violation of Article 34 of the Convention.[112]

A number of commentators describe the Court as a far more effective mechanism than the Committee against Torture and the Human Rights Committee.[113] By

---

discretion concerning national asylum law and policies among the several States of the Council of Europe.'

[108] Report of Committee against Torture, UN GAOR, 53rd Session, Supp. No. 44, Annex IX, 52–3, UN doc. A/53/44 1998. This is generally effective; but see *Elmi* v. *Australia*, Comm. No. 120/1998 (14 May 1999), UN doc. CAT/C/22/D/120/1998 and commentary in Senate Legal and Constitutional References Committee, *A Sanctuary under Review: An Examination of Australia's Refugee and Humanitarian Determination Processes* (2000), paras. 7.68–7.70, which shows how the lack of enforcement of the Committee's decisions, combined with the absence of a resultant legal status from a Committee finding of an international protection need, can lead to unpredictability in the nature of protection which the individual may receive.

[109] See Rule 114, CAT Rules; Rules 101, 103, HRC Rules; above n. 88.

[110] See Mowbray, A., 'A New Strasbourg Approach to the Legal Consequences of Interim Measures', 5 *Human Rights Law Review* 377 (2005). Note the Committee against Torture's remarks in *Chipana* v. *Venezuela*, Comm. No. 110/1998 (10 Nov. 1998), UN doc. CAT/C/21/D/110/1998, para. 8: 'The Committee considers that the State party, in ratifying the Convention and voluntarily accepting the Committee's competence under article 22, undertook to cooperate with it in good faith in applying the procedure. Compliance with the provisional measures called for by the Committee in cases it considers reasonable is essential in order to protect the person in question from irreparable harm, which could, moreover, nullify the end result of the proceedings before the Committee.'

[111] ECHR50 Rules, above n. 88, rule 39. The Court noted that art. 34 ECHR50 may be breached if States do not comply with interim measures: *Mamatkulov* v. *Turkey* Application. Nos. 46827/99 and 46951/99 (4 Feb. 2005), paras. 123–9.　[112] *Mamatkulov* v. *Turkey*, above note, para. 128.

[113] Lambert, H., 'Protection against *Refoulement* from Europe: Human Rights Law Comes to the Rescue', 48 *ICLQ* 515 (1999), at 517–8, 543; Andrysek, 'Gaps in International Protection'above n. 87, 393; Heffernan, L., 'A Comparative View of Individual Petition Procedures under the

contrast to the Court, the international bodies are newer, have a less-developed jurisprudence, meet only twice a year, are 'considerably overburdened and under-resourced',[114] and—most significantly—their non-binding decisions require voluntary State compliance to be effective.[115] Other disadvantages cited by Lambert include their more restrictive use of evidence,[116] inconsistent reasoning, and—with respect to the Human Rights Committee—a jurisprudence that reveals little more than 'a restrictive application of the principles developed by the Strasbourg organs'.[117]

3.2 THE 1984 CONVENTION AGAINST TORTURE (CAT84)

Although it was not conceived as an alternative protection mechanism, article 3 CAT84 has spawned an extensive jurisprudence, both at the international and domestic levels. The Committee against Torture has consistently affirmed that article 3 protects individuals from removal to 'another State where there are substantial grounds for believing that [they] would be in danger of being subjected to torture',[118] irrespective of their conduct.[119] It is a non-derogable provision, and—unlike the 1951 Convention—permits no exceptions to the principle of *non-refoulement*.[120]

European Convention on Human Rights and the International Covenant on Civil and Political Rights', 19 *HRQ* 78 (1997).

[114] Gorlick, B., 'The Convention and the Committee against Torture: A Complementary Protection Regime for Refugees', 11 *IJRL* 479, 490 (1999); Towle, R., 'Human Rights Standards: A Paradigm for Refugee Protection?', in Bayefsky, A. F. & Fitzpatrick, J., eds., *Human Rights and Forced Displacement*, (2000), 381.

[115] See O'Flaherty, M., *Human Rights and the UN: Practice before the Treaty Bodies*, (2nd edn., 2002), 47, n. 68.

[116] Art. 5(1) ICCPR66 Optional Protocol, including requirement for written evidence.

[117] Lambert, 'Protection from *Refoulement*', above n. 113, 532, n. 85; see McGoldrick, D., *The Human Rights Committee: Its Role in the Development of the International Covenant on Civil and Political Rights*, (1991), 368–71.

[118] Art. 3 CAT84. Article 16 CAT84 provides that States parties 'shall undertake to prevent in any territory under its jurisdiction other acts of cruel, inhuman or degrading treatment or punishment which do not amount to torture'. The Torture Committee has observed that article 3 'does not encompass situations of ill-treatment envisaged by article 16': *BS v. Canada*, Comm. No. 166/2000 (14 Nov. 2001), UN doc. CAT/C/27/D/166/2000, para. 7.4.

[119] *Tapia Paez v. Sweden*, Comm. No. 39/1996 (28 Apr. 1997) UN doc. CAT/C/18/D/39/1996, para. 14.5: 'The nature of the activities in which the person concerned engaged cannot be a material consideration when making a determination under article 3 of the Convention'; *Aemei v. Switzerland*, Comm. No. 34/1995 (9 May 1997), UN doc. CAT/C/18/D/34/1995, para. 9.8.

[120] The approach of the Supreme Court in *Suresh v. Canada* [2002] 1 SCR 3, which balances the right against compelling national security concerns, is contrary to international law and has been criticized by the Human Rigths Committee: 'Consideration of Reports: Concluding Observations on Canada', UN doc. CCPR/C/79/Add.105 (7 Apr. 1999), para. 13; cf. the approach of the European Court of Human Rights in *Selmouni v. France* (1999) 29 EHRR 403, para. 95.

The application of article 3 is necessarily limited to acts which meet the definition of 'torture' in article 1 CAT84. 'Torture' encompasses those acts

by which severe pain or suffering, whether physical or mental, is intentionally inflicted on a person for such purposes as obtaining from him or a third person information or a confession, punishing him for an act he or a third person has committed or is suspected of having committed, or intimidating or coercing him or a third person, or for any reason based on discrimination of any kind, when such pain or suffering is inflicted by or at the instigation of or with the consent or acquiescence of a public official or other person acting in an official capacity. It does not include pain or suffering arising only from, inherent in or incidental to lawful sanctions.

The meaning of 'torture', and accordingly the *non-refoulement* obligation under article 3, is therefore circumscribed by three requirements. First, only return to torture is prohibited. This immediately distinguishes the scope of CAT84 from ICCPR66, ECHR50, and ACHR69,[121] which provide protection from cruel, inhuman or degrading treatment or punishment as well.[122] Secondly, 'torture' encompasses only acts that are carried out or acquiesced in by the State.[123] By contrast, neither ICCPR66, ECHR50,[124] nor the 1951 Convention[125] contains this public requirement.[126] Under those instruments, where the risk of harm emanates from non-State actors, the key question is whether the authorities in

---

[121] Claims alleging a violation of art. 5(2) ACHR69 may be considered by the Inter-American Commission on Human Rights. Its decisions are not binding.

[122] Furthermore, the meaning of 'torture' under those instruments is not limited to the definition in art. 1 CAT84; art. 3 ECHR50 does not include 'cruel'.

[123] The rationale behind restricting the definition to acts of an official kind was the assumption that criminal acts carried out by private individuals would be prosecuted under domestic criminal law: Burgers, J. H. & Danelius, H., *The United Nations Convention against Torture: A Handbook on the Convention against Torture and Other Cruel, Inhuman or Degrading Treatment or Punishment*, (1988), 119–20. Cautioning against this rationale: Fitzpatrick, J., 'Harmonized Subsidiary Protection in the European Union—A View from the United States' in Bouteillet-Paquet, D., ed., *Subsidiary Protection of Refugees in the European Union: Complementing the Geneva Convention?* (2002), 126.

[124] ICCPR66: General Comment 20 of the Human Rights Committee specifically states that a claim under article 7 ICCPR66 can relate to acts committed by persons acting in an official capacity, in a non-official capacity or in a purely private capacity: 'General Comment 20', above n. 5, para. 2; Clapham, A., *Human Rights in the Private Sphere*, (1993), 108–11 Clapham., A., *Human Rights Obligations of Non-State Actors* (2006). ECHR50: *Ahmed* v. *Austria* (1997) 24 EHRR 278, para. 44 (absence of State authority immaterial); *HLR* v. *France* (1997) 26 EHRR 29, para. 40; *D* v. *UK* (1997) 24 EHRR 423, para. 49; *Altun* v. *Federal Republic of Germany* (1984) 36 D & R 209, para. 5; Einarsen, T., 'The European Convention on Human Rights and the Notion of an Implied Right to *De Facto* Asylum' 2 *IJRL* 361, 369–70 (1990); Ovey, C. & White, R. C. A., *Jacobs and White: European Convention on Human Rights*, (4th edn., 2006), 31–2.

[125] This is the interpretation favoured by UNHCR: UNHCR *Handbook*, para. 65. See also the Qualification Directive.

[126] As was noted by the Special Rapporteur on Torture in 1986, a State which does not intervene against quasi-public groups, such as tribes, that commit human rights abuses may be considered to have 'consented' or 'acquiesced' in their acts: 'Torture and Other Cruel, Inhuman or Degrading Treatment or Punishment: Report of the Special Rapporteur' UN doc. E/CN.4/1986/15 (1986), para. 38.

the receiving State can obviate it by providing appropriate protection.[127] Thirdly, pain or suffering arising out of 'lawful sanctions' is exempted from the definition of 'torture'. It is not clear from the text of the treaty whether 'lawful sanctions' refers to an international or domestic standard of 'lawfulness'. In *PQL* v. *Canada*, the Committee against Torture deferred to the domestic law of China, stating that 'imprisonment and the normal conditions of detention do not as such constitute torture as defined by the Convention and interpreted by the Committee'.[128] Deference to local standards has been criticized as potentially encouraging States to make acts of torture 'lawful sanctions', instead of outlawing them altogether.[129] However, where 'lawful sanctions' go beyond treatment that might be considered inherent in detention or imprisonment, it could be argued that such treatment is inconsistent with the international law prohibition on cruel, inhuman or degrading treatment or punishment,[130] or is disproportionate to 'the sovereign's right to survival or to its general obligations regarding the public welfare'.[131] This argument is strengthened by the requirement in article 4(1) CAT84 that States parties ensure that all acts of torture are offences under their domestic criminal law,[132] and the obligation in article 16 to prevent acts of cruel, inhuman or degrading treatment or punishment that do not amount to torture.

As a complementary protection mechanism, article 3 CAT84 may provide relief for those who are unable to demonstrate a link between torture (as a form of persecution[133]) and one of the five 1951 Convention grounds; those overlooked as refugees due to narrow domestic interpretations of the Convention definition;[134] and those

---

[127] *HLR.* v. *France* (1997) 26 EHRR 29, para. 40.

[128] Comm. No. 57/1996 (17 Nov. 1997), UN doc. CAT/C/19/D/57/1996, para. 5.4.

[129] See Burgers & Danelius, above n. 123, 121.

[130] For example, under art. 7 ICCPR66, art. 3 ECHR50, art. 5 ACHR69, art. 5 UDHR48; Burgers & Danelius, above n. 123, 122.

[131] von Sternberg, M. R., *The Grounds of Refugee Protection in the Context of International Human Rights and Humanitarian Law: Canadian and United States Case Law Compared*, (2002), 125.

[132] Under US law, the infliction of torture cannot be excused by virtue of its being a consequence of the imposition of ostensibly 'lawful sanctions' which themselves 'defeat the object and purpose of the Convention Against Torture': 8 CFR §208.18(a)(3), as referred to in *J-E-* 23 *I&N Dec.* 291 (BIA 2002).

[133] In our view, 'torture' will always constitute 'persecution' (although it may not necessarily be related to one of the five Convention grounds). UNHCR adopts a less absolute view, stating that in *most* cases, torture will amount to persecution: UNHCR 'Note on International Protection' (25 May 1998): UN doc. EC/48/SC/CRP.27, para. 6. By contrast, not all forms of persecution amount to torture. In submissions to the Human Rights Committee, Australia argued that 'persecution' is 'a much broader concept than that encompassed by article 7 ICCPR (torture or cruel, inhuman or degrading treatment) and refugee recognition should not lead the Committee to the conclusion that it is a necessary and foreseeable consequence of the author's return to Iran that he would be subjected to article 7 violations': *C* v. *Australia*, Comm. No. 900/1999 (13 Nov. 2002), UN doc. CCPR/C/76/D/900/1999, para. 4.13.

[134] UNHCR has consistently stressed that persons who ought to fall within the definition should be recognized as Convention refugees, so that complementary protection does not become a substitute status. See also Gorlick, above, n. 115.

expressly excluded from the Convention.[135] Return to 'another State' is precluded, which refers both 'to the State to which the individual concerned is being expelled, returned or extradited, as well as to any State to which the author may subsequently be expelled, returned or extradited'.[136] A State will not be considered safe merely by virtue of its having ratified CAT84; rather, the focus will be on actual treatment and conditions in that State.[137] For example, where a systematic practice of torture exists, the Committee may recommend against return.[138] Conversely, return to a State that is not party to CAT84 'would *de jure* bring the person to be expelled outside the protection of the Convention and its remedies of control'.[139] For example, in *Mutombo* v. *Switzerland*, the Committee noted that the applicant would not only be at risk of torture if returned to Zaire, but he would also lose the legal possibility of applying again to the Committee for protection, given that Zaire was not a party to CAT84.[140]

The standard of proof for article 3 is that there are 'substantial grounds' for believing that a person would be in danger of being subjected to torture if sent to another State. The Committee against Torture has consistently noted that 'substantial grounds' means a 'foreseeable, real and personal risk' of torture,[141] which goes 'beyond mere theory or suspicion' or 'a mere possibility of torture'.[142]

---

[135] Some States have sought to obviate its non-derogability by seeking diplomatic assurances from other countries that individuals returned there will not be tortured. However, such assurances do not relieve States from their international legal obligations; see Report by Gil-Robles, A., Council of Europe Commissioner for Human Rights, on his visit to Sweden (21–23 Apr. 2004), Council of Europe doc. CommDH (2004) 13 (8 Jul. 2004); *Agiza* v. *Sweden*, Comm. No. 233/2003 (20 May 2005): UN doc. CAT/C/34/D/233/2003, para. 13.4; Human Rights Watch, 'Still at Risk: Diplomatic Assurances No Safeguard against Torture', (Apr. 2005).

[136] Report of the Committee against Torture, UN GAOR 53rd Session Supp. No. 44 Annex IX, 52–3, UN doc. A/53/44 (1998); *Korban* v. *Sweden*, Comm. No. 88/1997 (16 Nov. 1998) UN doc. CAT/C/21/D/88/1997.   [137] *Korban* v. *Sweden*, above note.

[138] *Alan* v. *Switzerland*, Comm. No. 21/1995 (8 May 1996) UN doc. CAT/C/16/D/21/1995, para. 11.5.   [139] *Eggli*, *Mass Refugee Influx*, above n. 6, 203.

[140] *Mutombo* v. *Switzerland*, Comm. No. 13/1993 (17 Apr. 1994), UN doc. CAT/C/12/D/13/1993, para. 9.6; see also *Khan* v. *Canada*, Comm. No. 15/1994 (15 Nov. 1994), UN doc. CAT/C/13/D/15/1994, para. 12.5.

[141] See, for example, *EA* v. *Switzerland*, Comm. No. 28/1995 (10 Nov. 1997), UN doc. CAT/C/19/D/28/1995, para. 11.5; *X, Y and Z* v. *Sweden*, Comm. No. 61/1996 (6 May 1998), UN doc. CAT/C/20/D/61/1996, para. 11.5; *IAO* v. *Sweden*, Comm. No. 65/1997 (6 May 1998), UN doc. CAT/C/20/D/65/1997, para. 14.5; *KN* v. *Switzerland*, Comm. No. 94/1997 (19 May 1998), UN doc. CAT/C/20/D/94/1997, para. 10.5; *ALN* v *Switzerland*, Comm. No. 90/1997 (19 May 1998), UN doc. CAT/C/20/D/90/1997, para. 8.7; *JUA* v. *Switzerland*, Comm. No. 100/1997 (10 Nov. 1998), UN doc. CAT/C/21/D/100/1997, para. 6.6; *SMR and MMR* v. *Sweden*, Comm. No. 103/1998 (5 May 1999), UN doc. CAT/C/22/D/103/1998, para. 9.7; *MBB* v. *Sweden*, Comm. No. 104/1998 (5 May 1999), UN doc. CAT/C/22/D/104/1998, para. 6.8; *KT* v. *Switzerland*, Comm. No. 118/1998 (19 Nov. 1999), UN doc. CAT/C/23/D/118/1998, para. 6.5; *NM* v. *Switzerland*, Comm. No. 116/1998 (9 May 2000), UN doc. CAT/C/24/D/116/1998, para. 6.7; *SC* v. *Denmark*, Comm. No. 143/1999 (10 May 2000), UN doc. CAT/C/24/D/143/1999, para. 6.6; *HAD* v. *Switzerland*, Comm. No. 126/1999 (10 May 2000), UN doc. CAT/C/24/D/126/1999, para. 4.10; *US* v. *Finland*, Comm. No. 197/2002 (1 May 2003), UN doc. CAT/C/30/D/197/2002, para. 7.8; *MSH* v. *Sweden*, Comm. No. 235/2003 (14 Dec. 2005), UN doc. CAT/C/35/D/235/2003, para. 6.4; *Zare* v. *Sweden*, Comm. No. 256/2004 (17 May 2006), UN doc. CAT/C/36/D/256/2004, para. 9.3.

[142] *EA*, above note, para. 11.3.

The threat does not have to be 'highly probable'[143] or 'highly likely to occur'.[144] The applicant's activities in the country of origin, as well as in the country from which his or her removal is contemplated, are relevant in assessing whether 'substantial grounds' exist.[145] Other 'relevant considerations' under article 3(2) include the general human rights situation in the State to which the applicant fears return.[146] The existence of a pattern of 'gross, flagrant or mass violations of human rights' does not automatically give rise to the application of the *non-refoulement* principle; the applicant must show that he or she would be individually at risk of torture if removed.[147]

In domestic law, States have adopted different standards of proof for CAT84-based claims. For example, in the United States and Canada, the standard is 'more likely than not'.[148] This is a higher threshold than is demanded for refugee claims, where a 'well-founded fear of persecution' is interpreted in the United States as meaning a 'reasonable possibility' of persecution,[149] and in Canada as a 'reasonable chance' or 'serious possibility' of persecution.[150] Nevertheless, precisely what criteria the Committee against Torture employs in determining a 'substantial risk' of torture is difficult to ascertain. Its brief and formulaic decisions give little assistance in determining how, and against what standards of authority and corroboration, evidence is tested.

3.3 THE 1966 INTERNATIONAL COVENANT ON CIVIL AND POLITICAL RIGHTS (ICCPR66)

Article 7 ICCPR66 provides: 'No one shall be subjected to torture or to cruel, inhuman or degrading treatment or punishment.' Although this non-derogable[151]

---

[143] Report of the Committee against Torture, above n. 136, Annex IX.

[144] *EA*, above n. 141, para. 11.3.

[145] *Aemei* v. *Switzerland*, Comm. No. 34/1995 (9 May 1997), UN doc. CAT/C/18/D/34/1995, para. 9.5, above n. 121, para. 9.5.   [146] Art. 3(2) CAT84.

[147] See *Alan*, above n. 138, para. 11.2; *Tapia*, above n. 119, para. 14.2; *EA*, above n. 143, para. 11.2; *X, Y and Z*, above n. 141, para. 11.1; *IAO*, above n. 141, para. 14.2; *KN*, above n. 141, para. 10.2; *ALN*, above n. 141. para. 8.2; *Chipana* v. *Venezuela*, Comm. No. 110/1998, 10 Nov. 1998: UN doc. CAT/C/21/D/110/1998, para. 6.3; *JUA*, above n. 143, para. 6.3; *TA* v. *Sweden*, Comm. No. 226/2003, 27 May 2005: UN doc. CAT/C/34/D/226/2003, para. 7.2. For an example of an individual being unable to demonstrate the personalized nature of risk in Sudan, see *Elmansoub* v. *Switzerland*, Comm. No. 278/2005, (17 May 2006): UN doc. CAT/C/36/D/278/2005, para. 6.5.

[148] See *Li* v. *Canada (Minister for Citizenship and Immigration)* [2005] 3 FCR 239 (FCA), paras. 27–9, in relation to claims brought under ss. 97(1)(a) (torture) and 97(1)(b) (risk to life or of cruel and unusual treatment or punishment) of the Immigration and Refugee Protection Act 2001. This is contrary to the position espoused by the Immigration and Refugee Board when the Act came into force in June 2002, which suggested that s. 97 claims should benefit from the same legal test as s. 96 claims: Immigration and Refugee Board (Legal Services), 'Consolidated Grounds in the *Immigration and Refugee Protection Act*: Persons in Need of Protection: *Risk to Life or Risk of Cruel and Unusual Treatment or Punishment*' (15 May 2002), 37–8.

[149] Compare 8 CFR §208.16(c)(2) and §208.13(b)(2).

[150] *Adjei* v. *Canada (Minister of Employment and Immigration)* [1989] 2 FC 680, 57 DLR (4th) 153 (CA).

[151] ICCPR66 art. 4(2); Human Rights Committee, 'General Comment 20', (10 Mar. 1992), above n. 5, para. 3.

provision does not specifically proscribe *refoulement* to such ill-treatment, the Human Rights Committee has interpreted it as precluding the removal of people to places where they would face a 'real risk'—namely, 'a necessary and foreseeable consequence'—of a violation of rights under ICCPR66.[152] A 'real risk' is determined by considering 'the intent of the country to which the person concerned is to be deported, as well as from the pattern of conduct shown by the country in similar cases.'[153]

Compared to the Committee against Torture, the Human Rights Committee's *non-refoulement* jurisprudence is less comprehensive. This may be explained in part by the fact that individuals complaining against a European State are more likely to seek protection under article 3 ECHR50, which gives rise to binding judgments by the European Court of Human Rights rather than a non-enforceable 'view' by the Human Rights Committee.[154]

The scope of article 7 ICCPR66 is wider than article 3 CAT84, encompassing not only torture, but also cruel, inhuman or degrading treatment or punishment, whether inflicted physically or mentally. Unlike under CAT84, there is no requirement that any of these forms of ill-treatment be carried out by or with the acquiescence of the State.[155] Whereas the European Court of Human Rights has sought to give meaning to the different categories of harm, the Human Rights Committee considers it unnecessary 'to draw up a list of prohibited acts or to establish sharp distinctions between the different kinds of punishment or treatment; the distinctions depend on the nature, purpose and severity of the treatment applied'.[156] For this reason, it typically refers generically to 'severe treatment' or 'ill-treatment',[157] but has noted that 'for punishment to be degrading, the

---

[152] *GT* v. *Australia*, Comm. No. 706/1996 (4 Nov. 1997), UN doc. CCPR/C/61/0/706/1996, para. 8.1. See also Human Rights Committee 'General Comment No. 20' (10 Mar. 1992), para. 9: 'In the view of the Committee, States parties must not expose individuals to the danger of torture or cruel, inhuman or degrading treatment or punishment upon return to another country by way of their extradition, expulsion or refoulement. States parties should indicate in their reports what measures they have adopted to that end.'   [153] *GT* v. *Australia*, above note, para. 8.4.

[154] See generally Lambert, above n. 113. Although art. 2(3)(a) ICCPR66 obliges States parties to provide victims of a violation with an effective remedy, this is not enforceable: Human Rights Commmittee 'General Comment No. 20', 10 Mar. 1992, para. 14; see *C* v. *Australia*, Comm. No. 900/1999, UN doc. CCPR/C/76/D/1999, 13 Nov. 2002, para. 10.

[155] *Kindler* v. *Canada*, Comm. No. 470/1991, (30 Jul. 1993): UN doc. CCPR/C/48/D/470/ 1991, para. 6.2; see also *ARJ* v. *Australia*, Comm. No. 692/1996 CCPR/C/60/D/692/1996, (11 Aug. 1997), para. 6.8; *G. T* v. *Australia*, above n. 152, para. 8.1; Human Rights Committee 'General Comment 20', (10 Mar. 1992), para. 2.

[156] 'General Comment 20' (10 Mar. 1992), para. 4. For examples of conduct amounting to 'torture', 'cruel or inhuman treatment', and 'degrading treatment', see cases cited in *C* v. *Australia*, above n. 154, notes 28–30.

[157] Nowak, M., *UN Covenant on Civil and Political Rights: CCPR Commentary*, (1993), 135. Note that the International Criminal Tribunal for Former Yugoslavia (ICTY) has suggested that 'torture' under art. 7 ICCPR66 could potentially be wider than under art. 3 CAT84: *Prosecutor* v. *Kunarac*, Appeals Chamber, Case No. IT-96-23 & IT-96-23/1-A, (12 Jun. 2002), paras. 142–52.

humiliation or debasement involved must exceed a particular level and must, in any event, entail other elements beyond the mere fact of deprivation of liberty'.[158]

In *Kindler* v. *Canada*,[159] the Human Rights Committee held that an individual's deportation to face the death penalty, by a State that had itself abolished the death penalty, could not per se establish a violation of article 6 ICCPR66. This finding was based on the language of article 6(2), which recognizes that some States retain the discretion to impose the death penalty for the most serious crimes.[160] However, a decade later, in *Judge* v. *Canada*,[161] the Committee revised its position. It observed that since *Kindler*, 'there has been a broadening international consensus in favour of abolition of the death penalty, and in states which have retained the death penalty, a broadening consensus not to carry it out',[162] and noted that 'the Covenant should be interpreted as a living instrument and the rights protected under it should be applied in context and in the light of present-day conditions'.[163] Furthermore, the meaning of ICCPR66 rights should be interpreted at the time of the Committee's examination of the claim, not the time at which the alleged violation occurred.[164]

Thus, in *Judge* v. *Canada*, the Human Rights Committee found that States parties that have abolished the death penalty have an obligation under article 6(1) to protect the right to life in all circumstances, and 'may not remove, either by deportation or extradition, individuals from their jurisdiction if it may be reasonably anticipated that they will be sentenced to death, without ensuring that the death sentence would not be carried out'.[165] Paragraphs 2 to 6, which acknowledge that some States retain the death penalty as a form of punishment and set limits on its scope, are applicable only to those States parties that have not abolished the death penalty.[166] Accordingly, the Committee found that even though Canada had not yet ratified the Second Optional Protocol to ICCPR66 on the abolition of the death penalty,[167] it would violate article 6 if it deported an individual to a State

---

[158] *Vuolanne* v. *Finland*, Comm. No. 265/1987 (7 Apr. 1989), UN doc. CCPR/C/35/D/265/1987, para. 9.2.

[159] Comm. No. 470/1991, UN doc. CCPR/C/48/D/470/1991 (30 Jul. 1993).

[160] Art. 6(2) ICCPR66: 'In countries which have not abolished the death penalty, sentence of death may be imposed only for the most serious crimes in accordance with the law in force at the time of the commission of the crime and not contrary to the provisions of the present Covenant and to the Convention on the Prevention and Punishment of the Crime of Genocide. This penalty can only be carried out pursuant to a final judgement rendered by a competent court.'

[161] Comm. No. 829/1998, UN doc. CCPR/C/78/D/829/1998 (5 Aug. 2003).

[162] *Judge*, above note, para. 10.3. See also *ARJ* v. *Australia*, Comm. No. 692/1996, UN doc. CCPR/C/60/D/692/1996 (11 Aug. 1997), para. 6.13; *G.T.* v. *Australia*, Comm., above, n.152.

[163] *Judge*, above n. 161, para. 10.3. The Committee also considered significant the fact that Canada had itself recognized the need to amend its domestic law to protect individuals from return to face the death penalty; see *United States* v. *Burns* [2001] 1 SCR 283; Immigration and Refugee Protection Act, s. 97(1)(b).   [164] *Judge*, above n. 161, para. 10.7.

[165] *Judge*, above n. 161, para. 10.4.

[166] *Judge*, above n. 161, para. 10.4, referring to art. 6(2).

[167] UNGA res. 44/128, 15 Dec. 1989.

where he or she faced the death penalty, without first seeking assurances that that penalty would not be imposed: 'The Committee recognizes that Canada did not itself impose the death penalty on the author. But by deporting him to a country where he was under sentence of death, Canada established the crucial link in the causal chain that would make possible the execution of the author.'[168]

3.3.1 What rights are protected?

Although the bulk of claims relating to non-removal have been brought under articles 6 and 7 ICCPR66, the Human Rights Committee seems to have tacitly accepted that removing an individual to face a real risk of violation of *any* ICCPR66 right could constitute *refoulement*.[169] In *ARJ* v. *Australia*, the Committee stated that '[i]f a State party deports a person within its territory and subject to its jurisdiction in such circumstances that as a result, there is a real risk that his or her rights under the Covenant will be violated in another jurisdiction, that State party itself may be in violation of the Covenant'.[170] In that case, the Committee entertained claims brought under articles 6, 7, and 14, ICCPR66, although there was insufficient evidence to sustain a finding that removal should be precluded on any of those grounds. Certainly, there was no suggestion that those grounds could not give rise to a protection obligation. Similarly, the Committee has not dismissed out of hand the suggestion that removal leading to separation from one's family could constitute 'cruel, inhuman or degrading treatment' under article 7, although it has not yet so ruled in any particular case.[171]

The majority of article 7 *non-refoulement* cases before the Committee have failed on the evidence or for admissibility reasons (such as non-exhaustion of domestic remedies).[172] However, in *C* v. *Australia*, the Committee found that Australia would breach article 7 were it to deport a Convention refugee to his country of origin, without first demonstrating that the circumstances which led to the grant of refugee status had ceased.[173] Additionally, the Committee accepted medical evidence that the applicant was suffering from a severe psychiatric illness

---

[168] *Judge*, above n. 163, para. 10.6.
[169] 'General Comment 15: The Position of Aliens under the Covenant', (11 Apr. 1986), para. 5: States' *non-refoulement* obligations may be triggered 'when considerations of non-discrimination, prohibition of inhuman treatment and respect for family life arise'; see also 'General Comment 18: Non-Discrimination' (10 Nov. 1989).   [170] *ARJ*, above n. *, para. 6.9.
[171] *Canepa* v. *Canada*, Comm. No. 558/1993, UN doc. CCPR/C/59/D/558/1993, (3 Apr. 1997), para. 11.2.
[172] See also *Byahuranga* v. *Denmark*, Comm. No. 1222/2003, UN doc. CCPR/C/82/D/1222/2003 (1 Nov. 2004).
[173] *C* v. *Australia*, Comm. No. 900/1999, UN doc. CCPR/C/76/D/900/1999, 13 Nov. 2002, para. 8.5. Australia accepted that it had 'a limited obligation not to expose the author to violations of his rights under the Covenant by returning him to Iran', but sought to argue that this duty extended only to 'the most fundamental rights relating to the physical and moral integrity of the person', namely the threat of execution (art. 6) and torture (art. 7), based on the Committee's jurisprudence on non-removal: para. 4.11.

caused by his prolonged incarceration in immigration detention in Australia,[174] and held:

> In circumstances where the State party has recognized a protection obligation towards the author, the Committee considers that deportation of the author to a country where it is unlikely that he would receive the treatment necessary for the illness caused, in whole or in part, because of the State party's violation of the author's rights would amount to a violation of article 7 of the Covenant.[175]

The Committee has also recognized the importance of procedural rights in safeguarding the protection afforded by article 7. In *Ahani* v. *Canada*,[176] the applicant feared that he would be subjected to torture if removed to Iran. The Human Rights Committee had twice requested Canada to refrain from removing him until it had had the opportunity to examine the merits of his claim. However, following a decision by the Supreme Court of Canada that the applicant had not made out a prima facie case that he would be at substantial risk of torture if removed, and thus did not trigger the protection requirements of section 7 of the Canadian Charter of Rights and Freedoms,[177] Canada deported him to Iran.

The Committee observed that 'torture is, alongside the imposition of the death penalty, the most grave and irreparable of possible consequences to an individual of measures taken by the State party'.[178] It emphasized that where 'one of the highest values protected by the Covenant, namely the right to be free from torture, is at stake, the closest scrutiny should be applied to the fairness of the procedure applied to determine whether an individual is at a substantial risk of torture'.[179] The Committee determined that Canada had not provided the applicant with sufficient procedural protection to determine properly whether a substantial risk of torture existed, and stated that 'as with the right to life, the right to be free from torture requires not only that the State party not only refrain from torture but *take steps of due diligence* to avoid a threat to an individual of torture from third parties.'[180]

The Committee considered that an effective remedy, in accordance with article 2(3) ICCPR66, would be to compensate the applicant if he was in fact tortured following his deportation, and to take steps to ensure that the applicant 'is not, in the future, subjected to torture as a result of the events of his presence in, and removal from, the State party'. In particular, it noted Canada's obligation to avoid similar violations in the future by complying with the Committee's requests for interim measures of protection.[181]

---

[174] Ibid., paras. 3.1, 8.4. The Australian courts and tribunal had accepted this medical evidence.
[175] Ibid., para. 8.5.
[176] *Ahani* v. *Canada*, Comm. No. 1051/2002, UN doc. CCPR/C/80/D/1051/2002 (29 Mar. 2004).   [177] See *Ahani* v. *Canada*, [2002] 1 SCR72, 2002 SCC 2.
[178] *Ahani* v. *Canada*, above n. 176. para. 8.1.   [179] Ibid., para. 10.6.
[180] Ibid., para. 10.7 (emphasis added).   [181] Ibid., para. 12.

3.4 THE 1950 EUROPEAN CONVENTION ON HUMAN RIGHTS (ECHR50)

At first glance, the European Convention on Human Rights appears to offer substantial protection possibilities to refugees and asylum seekers.[182] Article 3, for example, prohibits torture and inhuman or degrading treatment, article 13 requires a remedy for every victim of a violation of protected rights, while even article 8 may be of indirect value, through the protection accorded to the family and the manner in which it has been applied to 'second generation migrants'[183] and the protection of 'private life'.[184] The jurisprudence of the European Court (and, previously also the European Commission of Human Rights) has considerable precedential value,[185] with a series of rulings in immigration and removal cases that seem to impose significant limitations on sovereign powers.[186] Although a decade ago, the second edition of this work expressed scepticism about the impact of the Court's jurisprudence on international protection, noting in particular its deference to States' margin of appreciation, the case law has since had a considerable impact on the development of the scope of *non-refoulement* beyond article 33 of the 1951 Convention. Notably, it has consistently reinforced the absolute and non-negotiable nature of article 3 ECHR50, and has been particularly influential on the domestic and supranational law of the EU Member States.[187]

Yet, though Member States recognize that they have a fundamental duty pursuant to article 3 ECHR50 not to return individuals to torture or inhuman or degrading treatment or punishment, the hurdle remains to convince a decision-maker (a) that the treatment feared is of a type encompassed by article 3, and (b) that there are substantial grounds for believing that the individual will be exposed

---

[182] On the uses of the European Convention, see for example, Lambert, H., 'The European Convention on Human Rights and the Protection of Refugees: Limits and Opportunities', 24 *RSQ* 39 (2005); Mole, N., 'Asylum and the European Convention on Human Rights', Council of Europe H/Inf (2002) 9; Lambert, H., 'Protection against *Refoulement* from Europe: Human Rights Law Comes to the Rescue', 48 *ICLQ* 515 (1999); Lambert, H., 'The European Court of Human Rights and the Right of Refugees and Other Persons in Need of Protection to Family Reunion', 11 *IJRL* 427 (1999); Alleweldt, R., 'Protection against Expulsion under Article 3 of the European Convention on Human Rights', 4 *EJIL* 360 (1993); Heffernan, L., 'A Comparative View of Individual Petition Procedures under the European Convention on Human Rights and the International Covenant on Civil and Political Rights', 19 *HRQ* 78 (1997); Einarsen, T., 'The European Convention on Human Rights and the Notion of an Implied Right to *de facto* Asylum', 2 *IJRL* 361 (1990).
[183] On the extent of the family relationship, see for example, *Berrehab* v. *The Netherlands* (1988) 11 EHRR 322; *Keegan* v. *Ireland* (1994) 18 EHRR 342; on expulsion of second generation migrants, see *Djeroud* v. *France* (1991) 14 EHRR 68; *Lamguindaz* v. *United Kingdom* (1993) 17 EHRR 213; *Beldjoudi* v. *France* (1992) 14 EHRR 801.
[184] See s. 3.4.3.2 below.   [185] Einarsen, above n. 182.
[186] The first time the European Commission recognized that art. 3 prevented *refoulement* to such treatment was in 1961: *X* v. *Belgium*, and *X* v. *Federal Republic of Germany*, cited in Alleweldt, above n. 182, 361 fn 5.
[187] Art. 3 ECHR50 is replicated in art. 15(b) of the EU Qualification Directive, which gives rise to subsidiary protection. Note, though, that the art.15(b) precludes return only where the feared harm occurs in the applicant's 'country of origin'. See s. 4 below.

to it if removed. It is with respect to the *meaning* of these types of harm that the European Court and national courts have sought to circumscribe carefully article 3's protection capacity,[188] seemingly reflecting the rationale expressed by the United Kingdom government in *Vilvarajah* that:

The consequences of finding a breach of Article 3 in the present case would be that all other persons in similar situations facing random risks on account of civil turmoil in the State in which they lived, would be entitled not to be removed, thereby permitting the entry of a potentially very class of people with the attendant serious social and economic consequences.[189]

3.4.1 Article 3

The most developed *non-refoulement* jurisprudence of the Court is in relation to article 3 ECHR50.[190] The seminal cases of *Soering*,[191] in which the Court held that extraditing a person to a territory where he or she faced a real risk of harm may breach article 3 ECHR50, and *Chahal*, in which that principle was expressly applied to expulsion as well,[192] both emphasized the absolute nature of article 3, and the fact that it applies irrespective of an applicant's conduct.[193] In that respect, it has a broader application than articles 32 and 33 of the 1951 Convention,[194] and may provide protection from *refoulement* to people expressly excluded from refugee status.[195] Blake and Husain have remarked that a 'text that at first blush failed to afford any rights to those seeking protection from persecution, has thus now extended protection in some areas beyond that provided by the Refugee Convention itself'.[196]

The absolute and non-derogable nature of article 3 was the subject of a challenge before the European Court of Human Rights in 2005. In *Ramzy* v. *The Netherlands*,[197] Lithuania, Portugal, Slovakia, and the UK intervened to challenge the on-going application of the *Chahal* doctrine, arguing that in some cases—given 'the increased and major threat posed by international terrorism'[198]—an individual's

---

[188] See, for example, *R. (Limbuela)* v. *Secretary of State for the Home Department*, [2006] 1 AC 396, [2005] UKHL 66.

[189] *Vilvarajah*, v. *UK* (1991) 14 EHRR 248, above n. *, para. 105. At the same time, though, the courts have recognized the potential scope of other ECHR50 rights to give rise to a protection obligation: see, for example, *Ullah* v. *Secretary of State for the Home Department* [2004] UKHL 26, in which the House of Lords recognized that, in principle, any ECHR50 right could give rise to the principle of *non-refoulement*.

[190] On the relationship to art. 1, see Ch. 5, s. 3.3.1; although often described in terms of 'extraterritoriality', the issue of application here is rather about the foreseeable consequences of a removal decision which exposes an individual to a 'real risk'.

[191] *Soering* v. *UK* (1989) 11 EHRR 439.   [192] *Chahal* v. *UK* (1996) 23 EHRR 413.

[193] *Soering*, above n. 191, para. 88.

[194] *Chahal*, above n. 192, para. 80; *Ahmed* v. *Austria* (1997) 24 EHRR 278 (criminal posing threat to national security).   [195] *Ahmed* v. *Austria*, above note.

[196] Blake, N. & Husain, R., *Immigration, Asylum and Human Rights*, (2003), para. 2.4.

[197] *Ramzy* v. *The Netherlands*, Application No. 25424/05.

[198] 'Observations of the Governments of Lithuania, Portugal, Slovakia and the United Kingdom intervening in Application No. 25424/05: Ramzy v The Netherlands' (22 Nov. 2005), para. 2.

(suspected) criminal activity should preclude him or her from benefiting from the principle of *non-refoulement* under article 3.[199] Reiterating the UK's earlier (unsuccessful) argument in *Chahal*,[200] they suggested that the absolute nature of article 3 should give way to a weighing up of 'the fundamental rights of the citizens of Contracting States who are threatened by terrorism' against the risk of ill-treatment to the individual whose removal is contemplated.[201]

The fact that the Court has 'consistently and repeatedly re-affirmed and re-asserted' the absolute nature of article 3, a view that has been adopted and strengthened by developments in European, national, and international law,[202] makes it doubtful that the arguments of the intervening governments will succeed. Were they to do so, however, the obligations of the States parties under international law would in any event remain unchanged: they would continue to be prevented by article 7 ICCCPR66, article 3 CAT84, and customary international law from returning people to such forms of harm.[203]

By contrast to the Human Rights Committee's relatively broad brush approach,[204] the meaning of the various terms of article 3 ECHR50 has been the subject of considerable scrutiny by the Court.[205] They are generally considered as describing

[199] Ibid. The UK has concluded memoranda of understanding with a number of countries to enable the 'secure return' of individuals without breaching article 3 ECHR50: House of Lords/House of Commons Joint Committee on Human Rights, *Counter-Terrorism Policy and Human Rights: Terrorism Bill and Related Matters* (3rd. Report of Session 2005–06), vol. 2, HL Paper 75-II, HC 561-II Ev 2 (Home Secretary, Mr Clarke). See further Goodwin-Gill, G. S. & Husain, R., 'Diplomatic Assurances and Deportation', JUSTICE/Sweet & Maxwell Conference on Counter-Terrorism and Human Rights, London, (28 Jun. 2005).

[200] *Chahal* v. *United Kingdom*, above n. 192, para. 76. Intervenors for the other side noted that the minority opinion in *Chahal* has never been followed by the Court: 'Mohammed Ramzy v The Netherlands: Third Party Intervention Submissions by Liberty & Justice', (22 Nov. 2005), para. 11 (copy with authors).

[201] 'Observations', above n. 198, para. 3. Note the comments of the Home Secretary, John Reid, that among the people who 'just don't get' the seriousness of the threat posed by terrorism to national security are 'European judges who passed the "Chahal judgement" that prohibited the home secretary from weighing the security of millions of British people if a suspected terrorist remained in the UK against the risk he faced if deported back to his own country': Travis, A., 'Anti-Terror Critics Just Don't Get It, Says Reid', *The Guardian*, 9 Aug. 2006, 6. Cf. *Suresh* v. *Minister for Citizenship and Immigration* [2002] 1 SCR 3, para. 78, and see above, Ch. 5, s. 3.2.

[202] See generally '*Ramzy* v. *The Netherlands*: Written Comments by Amnesty International Ltd, the Association for the Prevention of Torture, Human Rights Watch, Interights, the International Commission of Jurists, Open Society Justice Initiative and Redress, pursuant to Article 36 § 2 of the European Convention on Human Rights and Rule 44 § 2 of the Rules of the European Court of Human Rights' (22 Nov. 2005); Liberty submission, above n. 200; 'Ramzy and The Netherlands: Written Submissions on behalf of the AIRE Centre under Rules 44(2) of the Rules of Court' (with interveners Goodwin-Gill, G. S., Gil-Bazo, M-T., and ECRE) (2005) (copy with authors).

[203] This assessment is supported by House of Lords/House of Commons Joint Committee on Human Rights, *The UN Convention against Torture (UNCAT)*, (19th Report of Session 2005–06) vol. 1, HL Paper 185-I, HC 701-I (May 2006), para. 27.   [204] See above, n. 11.

[205] See discussion in McAdam, J., *Complementary Protection in International Refugee Law*, (2007), 140–3. See generally Alleweldt, above n. 182. The court does not consider the question of whether and how, if certain ECHR50 provisions give rise to a right not to be removed, they should apply to persons seeking admission from outside the territory of an ECHR50 Member State. For comparative

a hierarchy of ill-treatment, with torture the most extreme form. 'Inhuman treatment' encompasses 'at least such treatment as deliberately causes severe suffering, mental or physical, which, in the particular situation, is unjustifiable... Treatment or punishment of an individual may be said to be degrading if it grossly humiliates him before others or drives him to act against his will or conscience.'[206] 'Degrading treatment' is that which 'humiliates or debases an individual, showing a lack of respect for, or diminishing, his or her human dignity, or arouses feelings of fear, anguish or inferiority capable of breaking an individual's moral and physical resistance'.[207] By contrast, 'inhuman punishment' and 'degrading punishment' describe acts of inhuman and degrading treatment respectively that are imposed as a reprimand or penalty.[208] However, both the Court and the House of Lords have suggested that 'the increasingly high standard being required in the area of the protection of human rights'[209] may mean that treatment which was once characterized as 'inhuman or degrading' might now be regarded as 'torture'.

An applicant seeking to rely on article 3 ECHR50 to prevent his or her removal must demonstrate that there are substantial grounds for believing that he or she would face a real ('foreseeable'[210]) risk of being subjected to torture or inhuman or degrading treatment or punishment if removed.[211] While a mere possibility of harm is insufficient to meet this test, it is not necessary to show definitively that ill-treatment will occur. The ill-treatment must qualitatively attain a 'minimum

---

studies, see Lambert, above n. 182; Heffernan, above n. 182; Mole, above n. 182; Noll, G., 'Seeking Asylum at Embassies: A Right to Entry under International Law?', 17 *IJRL* 542 (2005).

[206] *Greek* case (1969) 12 *Yearbook* 1, 186. For an analysis of the distinction between 'torture', 'inhuman treatment' and 'degrading treatment', see Röhl, K., 'Fleeing Violence and Poverty: Non-refoulement Obligations under the European Convention of Human Rights', UNHCR, *New Issues in Refugee Research*, Working Paper No. 111, (Jan. 2005), 13–16.

[207] *Pretty* v. *UK* (2002) 35 EHRR 1, para. 52; see also *Ireland* v. *UK* (1979–80) 2 EHRR 25, para. 167. These matters also form part of the individual's right to respect for private life (as an aspect of bodily and physical integrity) under art. 8(1) (see Blake & Hussain, *Immigration, Asylum and Human Rights*, n. 196, para. 2.102), but whereas degrading treatment under art. 3 can never be justified, art. 8(2) permits the State to balance the individual's right with legitimate interests of the wider community, including social and economic considerations. There has not yet been a case in which the threat of degrading treatment alone has given rise to a protection obligation. Some scholars argue that, where a minimum level of severity exists, the concept may also encompass insufficient provision of basic services necessary for a dignified existence, such as access to health, shelter, social security, and the education and protection of children: Blake & Husain, above n. 196, para. 2.97; Schachter, O., 'Human Dignity as a Normative Concept', 77 *AJIL* 848, 851 (1983).

[208] Alleweldt, above n. 182, 364.

[209] *Selmouni* v. *France* (1999) 29 EHRR 403, para. 101, approved by the House of Lords in *A* v. *Secretary of State for the Home Department* [2005] 2 AC 68, [2004] UKHL 56, para. 53, which noted that the conduct complained of in *Ireland* v. *UK*, above n. 207, might now be viewed as 'torture'.

[210] *Soering*, above n. 191, para. 100.

[211] See Lauterpacht, E. & Bethlehem, D., 'The Scope and Content of the principle of *Non-Refoulement*: Opinion', in Feller, E., Türk, V., & Nicholson, F., eds., *Refugee Protection in International Law*, (2003) 87, paras. 246, 249, 252 (hereafter, Lauterpacht & Bethlehem, '*Non-Refoulement*: Opinion'). However, art. 3 also applies to the manner in which an expulsion is carried out: see Mole, above n. 182, 9, 40–1.

level of severity',[212] the assessment of which is relative and 'depends on all the circumstances of the case, such as the nature and context of the treatment or punishment, the manner and method of its execution, its duration, its physical or mental effects and, in some instances, the sex, age and state of health of the victim'.[213] Even a small risk may be significant and 'real' where the foreseeable consequences are very serious.[214] Analysis of the case law suggests that the more the ill-treatment is caused by underlying social and political disorder, such as civil war or terrorism, the higher the minimum level of severity will be assessed.[215]

3.4.2 Socio-economic rights

There is very little authority supporting a right to remain on socio-economic grounds, whether due to a severe paucity of resources in the country of origin generally or a lack of medical care there. Neither ICCPR66 nor ECHR50 contains a specific article expressly guaranteeing these rights,[216] and the 1966 International Covenant on Economic, Social and Cultural Rights (ICESCR66) is not readily enforceable either domestically or at the international level, in part due to the process of progressive realization.[217]

Accordingly, article 3 ECHR50 provides the strongest provision for articulating a claim based on these grounds, if the conditions to which the individual would be returned may be characterized as 'inhuman' or 'degrading'.[218] While a common

---

[212] *Greek case*, above n. 206, para. 11; *Ireland*, above n. 207, para. 162; *Soering*, above n. 190, para. 100.

[213] *Soering*, above n. 191, para. 100, 104. See also *Ireland*, above n. 207 paras. 162, 167, 174.

[214] Einarsen, above n. 182, 372; see also, for example, *Soering*, above n. 191.

[215] Fabbricotti, A., 'The Concept of Inhuman or Degrading Treatment in International Law and Its Application in Asylum Cases', 10 *IJRL* 637, 646 (1998); see Oraá, J., *Human Rights in States of Emergency in International Law*, (1992), 96.

[216] The ECHR50 is weak on the protection of socio-economic rights: see the First Protocol: ETS No. 9, arts.1, 2. In *Holub* v. *Secretary of State for the Home Department* [2001] 1 WLR 1359, the UK Court of Appeal held that the right to education under art. 2 First Protocol ECHR50 is a limited social right that does not comprise a right to remain when the State, exercising effective immigration control, refuses such leave. It invoked Strasbourg jurisprudence as indicating clearly that 'rights which are not absolute, such as the right to education, are not engaged where a state is exercising legitimate immigration control' (para. 21). Although the Court has not considered the matter in a protection case, it has entertained an argument based on ECHR50 and CRC89 that the forced relocation of children may lead to a denial of access to education (in cases involving the moving on of gypsies), although that case was unsuccessful on the facts: *Coster* v. *UK* (2001) 33 EHRR 479; *Lee* v. *UK* (2001) 33 EHRR 677; *Smith (Jane)* v. *UK* (2001) 33 EHRR 712.

[217] Art. 2(1) ICESCR66; Cholewinski, R., 'Enforced Destitution of Asylum Seekers in the United Kingdom: The Denial of Fundamental Human Rights', 10 *IJRL* 462 (1998); Hathaway, J. C ., *The Rights of Refugees under International Law*, (2005), 122–3 (hereafter, Hathaway, *Rights of Refugees*, (2005)). See also Taran, P. A., 'Human Rights of Migrants: Challenges of the New Decade', 38 *International Migration* 7, 29 (2000); cf. Hathaway, J. C., 'Is Refugee Status Really Elitist? An Answer to the Ethical Challenge', in Carlier J.-Y. & Vanheule, D., eds., *Europe and Refugees: A Challenge?* (1997).

[218] The key case is *D* v. *UK* (1997) 24 EHRR 423; for a recent interpretation, see *N* v. *Secretary of State for the Home Department* [2005] UKHL 31. Note also Cassese, A., 'Can the Notion of Inhuman and Degrading Treatment Be Applied to Socio-Economic Conditions?' 2 *EJIL* 141 (1991); Röhl, K., 'Fleeing Violence and Poverty: Non-refoulement Obligations under the European Convention of Human Rights', (2005), above n. 206.

sense approach would suggest that this augurs well for persons seeking protection for such reasons, the European Court has taken a very strict view, requiring applicants to demonstrate exceptional grounds—beyond the simple fact of lack of medical care or housing or employment—before the requisite threshold will be met. The focus is on the *particular* risk faced by the individual applicant.[219]

In this respect, the Court has indicated that receiving States are not required to meet the same standards of treatment as States parties to ECHR50.[220] States may therefore return people to countries that do not provide an equivalent level of rights to ECHR50,[221] provided that there will not be a flagrant breach—complete denial or nullification[222]—of the right in question on return.[223] Clearly, the policy reason behind this approach is a fear of 'opening the floodgates' to vast numbers of people in the developing world living in poverty, or suffering from unemployment or poor medical care,[224] and the associated costs of caring for such persons.[225] It is therefore

---

[219] See *D* v. *UK*, above note; see also *Vilvarajah*, v. *UK* (1991) 14 EHRR 248, para. 111; *SCC* v. *Sweden*, Application No. 46553/99 (15 Feb. 2000); *Henao* v. *The Netherlands*, Application No. 13669/03 (24 Jun. 2003); *Ndangoya* v. *Sweden*, Application No. 17868/03 (22 Jun. 2004); *Amegnigan* v. *The Netherlands*, Application No. 25629/04 (25 Nov. 2004). In *N* v. *Secretary of State for the Home Department* [2004] 2 AC 296 at para. 36, Lord Hope stated: 'it was the fact that he [the applicant in *D* v. *UK*] was already terminally ill while still present in the territory of the expelling state that made his case exceptional'.

[220] *Bensaid* v. *United Kingdom* (2001) 33 EHRR 205, para. 38. In *Salkic*, the Court reiterated that art. 3 will not be breached simply because the level of health care (including mental health care) in the receiving State is not of an equivalent standard to that available in the Member State: *Salkic* v. *Sweden* Application No. 7702/04 (29 Jun. 2004); see also *Amegnigan* v. *The Netherlands*, above note. In *Januzi* v. *Secretary of State for the Home Department* [2006] UKHL 5, the House of Lords held that an internal flight alternative can exist, even if the general standards of living in the 'safe' part of the country are not as high as in the State where asylum was sought. The position would be different, however, 'if the lack of respect for human rights posed threats to his life or exposed him to the risk of inhuman or degrading treatment or punishment': para. 19 (Lord Bingham), see also para. 45 (Lord Nicholls).

[221] Piotrowicz, R. & van Eck, C., 'Subsidiary Protection and Primary Rights', 53 *ICLQ* 107, 129 (2004); *Devaseelan* v. *Secretary of State for the Home Department* [2003] Imm AR 1, para. 107; Tomuschat, C., 'A Right to Asylum in Europe', 13 *Human Rights Law Journal* 257, 260 (1992); *Drozd and Janousek* v. *France and Spain* (1992) 14 EHRR 745; para. 110; *Amegnigan* v. *The Netherlands*, above n. 219.

[222] *Devaseelan* v. *Secretary of State for the Home Department*, above n. 221, aff'd in *Ullah* v. *Secretary of State for the Home Department* [2004] UKHL 26, para. 24 (Lord Bingham), para. 69 (Lord Carswell).

[223] Although the breach will normally result from the receiving State's inability or unwillingness to accord the right in question, in *D* v. *UK*, above n. 219, the ill-treatment was not an intentional State act but stemmed from generally poor living conditions. See also Sepúlveda, M., *The Nature of the Obligations under the International Covenant on Economic, Social and Cultural Rights*, (2003).

[224] See, for example, *HLR* v. *France* (1997) 20 EHRR 29, para. 42; see also the views of Torture Committee in *AD* v. *The Netherlands*, Comm. No. 96/1997 (24 Jan. 2000), UN doc. CAT/C/23/D/96/1997, para. 7.2.

[225] On this point, see *N*, above n. 219, para. 93 (Lord Brown): it would permit 'the patient to remain in the host state to enjoy decades of healthy life at the expense of that state—an expense both in terms of the cost of continuing treatment (the medication itself being said by the Intervener to cost some £7,000 per annum) and any associated welfare benefits, and [have implications] . . . in terms of immigration control and the likely impact of such a ruling upon other foreign AIDS sufferers aspiring to these benefits'.

unlikely that resource-related article 3 claims will develop into a meaningful protection alternative. The Court's general position is that:

aliens who are subject to expulsion cannot in principle claim any entitlement to remain in the territory of a Contracting State in order to continue to benefit from medical, social or other forms of assistance provided by the expelling State. In exceptional circumstances, however, an implementation of a decision to remove an alien may, owing to compelling humanitarian considerations, result in a violation of Article 3.[226]

As Lord Hope stated in *N* v. *Secretary of State for the Home Department*, if article 3 ECHR50 were not carefully circumscribed in medical cases, the effect would be to afford

all those in the appellant's condition a right of asylum in this country until such time as the standard of medical facilities available in their home countries for the treatment of HIV/AIDS had reached that which is available in Europe. It would risk drawing into the United Kingdom large numbers of people already suffering from HIV in the hope that they too could remain here indefinitely so that they could take the benefit of the medical resources that are available in this country. This would result in a very great and no doubt unquantifiable commitment of resources which it is, to say the least, highly questionable the states parties to the Convention would ever have agreed to.[227]

3.4.3 Other protected rights

Does the principle of non-return extend beyond article 3 cases to prevent removal to situations where an individual faces a real risk of a breach of other provisions of the Convention? The House of Lords considered this question in 2004 in *Ullah*, finding that, in the right factual circumstances, where the alleged ill-treatment does not 'meet the minimum requirements of article 3 of the Convention,' *any* ECHR50 provision could give rise to a *non-refoulement* obligation.[228] The European Court of Human Rights has itself stated that the removal of a person from a State party to ECHR50 may give rise to a protection issue under articles 2 (the right to life) or 3, and exceptionally under articles 5 or 6.[229]

While the Court has, in principle, recognized the potential of other ECHR50 rights to prevent the removal of asylum seekers, no asylum case has yet been successful on these grounds.[230] This can be explained in part because other rights are

[226] See, for example, *SCC* v. *Sweden*, Application No. 46553/99 (15 Feb. 2000); *Henao*, above n. 219. *Ndangoya* v. *Sweden*, Application No. 17868/03 (22 Jun. 2004), broadening the statement in *D* v. *UK*, above n. 217, para. 54.   [227] *N*, above n. 219, para. 53 (Lord Hope).

[228] *Ullah* v. *Secretary of State for the Home Department* [2004] UKHL 26, paras. 24–5 (Lord Bingham), 49–50 (Lord Steyn), 67 (Lord Carswell); see also *Secretary of State for the Home Department* v. *Kacaj* [2002] Imm AR 213, para. 39; *Drozd and Janousek* v. *France and Spain* (1992) 14 EHRR 745, 795 (Judge Matscher).

[229] *Soering* v. *UK* (1989) 11 EHRR 439, para. 91; *Cruz Varas* v. *Sweden* (1991) 14 EHRR 1, paras. 69–70; *Vilvarajah* v. *UK* (1991) 14 EHRR 248, para. 103. For further discussion of these provisions, see McAdam, *Complementary Protection*, above n. 11, 143ff.

[230] Some provisions have been successful in other non-removal contexts. For a comprehensive discussion of the potential of particular ECHR50 rights to be successfully invoked by asylum seekers, see McAdam, above note; also Piotrowicz, & van Eck, above n. 221.

typically invoked along with article 3, and should the Court find a breach of article 3, which gives rise unequivocally to the benefit of *non-refoulement*, then it will not go on to consider the protection capacity of the other provisions.[231]

For example, although the Court's jurisprudence suggests that article 2 may prevent removal where there are general risks to life, no protection claim has yet succeeded solely on this ground,[232] having either failed on the facts[233] or been decided under article 3 instead.[234] The death penalty is excluded from the ambit of article 2,[235] but the prohibition on the death penalty in Protocols 6 and 13 to ECHR50 has been interpreted by the EU Member States as prohibiting removal to face such a penalty.[236] In the right factual circumstances, article 2 might preclude the deportation of an individual to face forced sterilization, but this has not yet been determined conclusively.[237]

Additionally, whereas article 3 is absolute, many of the other relevant ECHR50 provisions (for example, articles 8 to 11) permit a weighing up of the individual applicant's interests against the public interest. Although immigration control is not, of itself, an interest which the State may expressly invoke, it provides 'the medium through which other legitimate aims are promoted',[238] such as national security, public safety, public health or morals, rights and freedoms of others, the country's economic well-being, and the prevention of disorder or crime.[239] Thus, if a violation of articles 8 to 11 is alleged, the balancing test means that the State has a right to interfere with the right contained in that provision where to do so has a legitimate motive, is prescribed by law, and is necessary rather than merely desirable (the

[231] *Chahal* v. *UK* (1996) 23 EHRR 413; *D* v. *UK*, above n. 218. This is also the approach adopted in *Ullah* v. *Secretary of State for the Home Department* [2004] UKHL 26, para. 1.

[232] *Tatete* v. *Switzerland*, Application No. 41874/98 (6 Jul. 2000) (settlement reached); *D* v. *UK*, above n. 218, (decided on art. 3); *Mamatkulov* v. *Turkey*, Application Nos. 46827/99;46951/99 (6 Feb. 2003, see also admissibility decision 31 Aug. 1999); *Ullah*, above note, para. 40 (Lord Steyn). See also *Secretary of State for the Home Department* v. *Kacaj* [2002] Imm AR 213; *Osman* v. *UK* (1998) 29 EHRR 245.

[233] *Gonzalez* v. *Spain*, Application No. 43544/98 (29 Jun. 1999); also *D* v. *UK*, above n. 218.

[234] See, for example, *D* v. *UK*. Note the remarks of the European Commission in *Dehwari* v. *The Netherlands* (2000) 29 EHRR CD 74, para. 62, that it would be incongruous if art. 3 could be relied on but art. 2 could not, '[g]iven the special importance attached to the right to life by modern human rights instruments'.

[235] Art. 2(1) ECHR50 reads: 'Everyone's right to life shall be protected by law. No one shall be deprived of his life intentionally save in the execution of a sentence of a court following his conviction of a crime for which this penalty is provided by law.'

[236] See Qualification Directive, art. 15(a), below Annexe 2, No. 19; Protocol No. 6 to ECHR50 (in force 1 Mar. 1985) *ETS* No. 114; Protocol No. 13 to ECHR50 (in force 1 Jul. 2003).

[237] Application No. 1287/61, cited in Ovey & White, above n. 124, 253.

[238] Blake & Husain, *Immigration, Asylum and Human Rights*, above n. 196 para. 4.72.

[239] See arts. 8–11; the list of grounds for interference are exhaustive: art.18; *Abdulaziz*, (1985) 7 EHRR 471, para. 65; *Vilvarajah* v. *UK* (1991) 14 EHRR 248, para. 102; *Chahal*, above n. 231, para. 73; *D* v. *UK* (1997) 24 EHRR 423, para. 46; *Bensaid* v. *UK* (2001) 33 EHRR 205, para. 32; *Boultif* v. *Switzerland* (2001) 33 EHRR 50, para. 46. Discussion: Blake & Husain, *Immigration, Asylum and Human Rights*, above n. 196, para 4.72; Ovey & White, above n. 124, 226ff. 'Proportionality is a long-established principle of international law: Brownlie, I., *Principles of Public International Law*, (6th edn., 2003) 550–2; *Saadi* v. *Secretary of State for the Home Department* [2002] UKHL 41, [2002] 1 WLR 3131, para. 31.

proportionality concept).[240] In the view of the UK Immigration Appeal Tribunal, 'it will be virtually impossible for an applicant to establish that control on immigration was disproportionate to any breach'.[241] Commentators on the European Convention similarly suggest that it is relatively simple for a State to characterize its actions as falling within a prescribed exception,[242] provided that the restrictions they place on rights are necessary and proportionate, and represent the minimum interference necessary to secure the desired aim.[243]

3.4.3.1 Article 8: family life

Article 8(1) ECHR50 protects the right to respect for private and family life, home, and correspondence.[244] It is, however, a qualified right, which means that it may be balanced against certain 'legitimate' State aims (relating to economic, health, and security factors) that are considered to be in the public interest.

In article 8 matters, the Court first considers whether an effective family life exists between the members of the family concerned. This is a question of fact, and relevant questions include whether there is financial[245] or other[246] dependency, or cohabitation (although the latter is not necessarily determinative[247]). While only husband–wife and dependent parent–child relationships have been expressly recognized as sufficiently close in cases involving non-citizens,[248] the

---

[240] Blake & Husain, *Immigration, Asylum and Human Rights*, above n. 196, para. 4.2. Note that art.18 ECHR50 prevents any further qualifications. The ICCPR66 regime is broadly similar (see arts. 18(3), 19(3), 22(2)); it contains a balancing clause with respect to freedom of movement but not in respect of family and private life (arts. 12(3), 17). The Human Rights Committee has stated that the right to family unity will sometimes outweigh States' discretion relating to border control (suggesting that even though ICCPR66 contains no balancing clause with respect to family reunion, it will be balanced against legitimate State interests): HRC, 'General Comment 19: Protection of the Family, the Right to Marriage and Equality of the Spouses' (27 Jul. 1990), para. 5.

[241] *Secretary of State for the Home Department* v. *Kacaj* [2002] Imm AR 213, para. 26; note also *Rutili* v. *Ministre de l'Intérieur* [1975] ECR 1219 (ECJ), which provides authority to suggest that interference with a right solely as a deterrence mechanism is not a legitimate aim (although this was not a case in the asylum field).   [242] Cf. Ovey & White, above n. 124, 226.

[243] Ibid., 7–8.

[244] See generally Feldman, D., 'The Developing Scope of Article 8 of the European Convention on Human Rights', [1997] *European HR L. Rev.* 265; Warbrick, C., 'The Structure of Article 8', [1998] *European HR L. Rev.* 32; Liddy, J., 'The Concept of Family Life under the ECHR', [1998] *European HR L. Rev.* 15; Kilkelly, U., *The Child and the European Convention on Human Rights*, (1999); Rogers, N., 'Immigration and the European Convention on Human Rights: Are New Principles Emerging?' [2003] 1 *European HR L. Rev.* 53. Note, however, the use of art. 8 in *Razgar* v. *Secretary of State for the Home Department* [2004] UKHL 27, where it was successfully invoked to prevent the applicant's return to Germany under the Dublin Regulation. It is unlikely that the facts of that case would have been sufficient to preclude removal to the country of origin under art. 8. Under international law, art. 10(1) CRC89 provides the strongest entitlement to family reunification where minor children are concerned.   [245] See, for example, Qualification Directive, art. 23(5).

[246] Council Directive 2003/86/EC of 22 September 2003 on the Right to Family Reunification [2003] O.J. L251/12, art. 4(2)(b): health grounds; for text of the Directive, see below, Annexe 2, No. 18.

[247] *Berrehab* v. *The Netherlands* (1988) 11 EHRR 322 para. 21 (where children lived with only one parent, leading Rogers to observe 'an apparent advantage to being divorced or separated'): Rogers above n. 244, 58; *Abdulaziz* v. *UK* (1985) 7 EHRR 471, paras. 61–3.

[248] *East African Asians* v. *UK* (1973) 3 EHRR 76; *X and Y* v. *UK* (1972) 39 CD 104; *Abdulaziz*, above note; *Berrehab*, above note. In *Sisojeva*, however, the break up of a family with *adult* children

Court has accepted that other relationships may qualify in certain circumstances.[249] Article 12 may be useful where applicants cannot yet demonstrate an existing family life but intend to establish one,[250] such as an engaged couple.

If the 'family life' test is met, then the Court determines whether it has been unlawfully interfered with. How this is carried out depends substantially on whether the application concerns an individual's *admission* for family reunion purposes, or the disruption of family unity due to an individual's proposed *removal*. Lambert has characterized this distinction as artificial in practice, since '[a]ny refusal to admit a family member, particularly a child, to the territory of a member State, indeed, suggests a strong expectation that the person lawfully residing in the territory will have to return to his or her country of origin'.[251]

In admission cases, the weighing up of individual–State interests occurs at the point of determining whether there is an interference with the right to a family life. The Court will not even consider article 8(2) if a family life may be established in another country, based on the premise that a State has the right to control the entry of non-nationals into its territory.[252] For this reason also, considerable deference is given to the State's discretion to deny entry.[253]

By contrast, there is a greater burden on the State in removal cases, since the balancing process occurs at the later point of deciding whether removal is 'necessary'.[254] In cases involving long-term residents and second-generation migrants, the Court has typically found in the individual's favour.[255] Its interference in such cases is explicable as the defence of a relatively known and manageable population, whose acquired residence claims already have some basis in general international law through the doctrine of effective nationality. The Court has noted

was considered as an interference with 'private' life, since the age of the children precluded the Court finding the continued existence of a 'family life': *Sisojeva v. Latvia* [2005] ECHR 405 paras. 103, 105; see below, n. 255.

[249] See, for example, *Marckx v. Belgium* (1979) 2 EHRR 330, para. 45 (between grandparents and grandchildren); *Boyle v. UK* (1995) 19 EHRR 179 (between an uncle and nephew); *Nsona v. The Netherlands*, Application No. 23366/94 (29 Nov. 1996), para. 144 (an orphaned child and aunt). Where the uncle and nephew or niece have not been residing together, the relationship has been found not to be close enough: *X v. Federal Republic of Germany* (1968) 11 *Yearbook* 494, 518. Same-sex relationships are considered to fall outside the scope of 'family life' but are recognized as part of 'private life': *X and Y v. UK* Application No. 9369/81 (3 May 1983); *Norris v. Ireland* (1988) 13 EHRR 186; *Dudgeon v. UK* (1981) 4 EHRR 149.

[250] *Abdulaziz v. UK* (1985) 7 EHRR 471; Storey, H., 'The Right to Family Life and Immigration Case Law at Strasbourg', 39 *ICLQ* 328, 341 (1990).

[251] Lambert, H., 'The European Court of Human Rights and the Right of Refugees and Other Persons in Need of Protection to Family Reunion', 11 *IJRL* 427, 442 (1999).

[252] *Abdulaziz*, above n. 250, para. 67. See discussion on admission cases in McAdam, *Complementary Protection*, 156–7, noting especially arts. 9, 10 CRC89 in relation to family reunification.

[253] See, for example, *Gül v. Switzerland* (1996) 22 EHRR 93.

[254] This is because expulsion will lead to the separation of families already within the European State, and thus interference is relatively straightforward to prove.

[255] *Berrehab*, above n. 247; *Moustaquim v. Belgium* (1991) 13 EHRR 802; *Sen v. The Netherlands*, Application No. 31465/96 (21 Dec. 2001); *Sisojeva v. Latvia* [2005] ECHR 405 (struck out by judgment of the Grand Chamber, Application No. 60654100, 15 Jan. 2007). See also *Boultif v. Switzerland* (2001) 33 EHRR 50, para. 48.

that States' decisions in the immigration sphere may interfere with article 8(1) 'in particular where the persons concerned possess strong personal or family ties in the host country which are liable to be seriously affected by an expulsion order'.[256] The provision has less potency for asylum seekers, however, since they can rarely demonstrate sufficiently strong social links or disruption of family life that would, on balance, secure a right to remain.[257] In such cases, the Court might consider it reasonable for the whole family to move to the State to which the family member is to be expelled.[258] The position may, however, be different for asylum seekers who have been in the State for a number of years awaiting a final decision.

In determining whether the proposed interference with the right to a family life is justified, the Court considers (a) whether it is in accordance with the law;[259] (b) whether it pursues a legitimate aim under article 8(2); and (c) whether it is in all circumstances necessary in a democratic society[260]—namely, whether it responds to an important social need and is proportionate.[261]

It is the last of these three elements that requires the Court to weigh up the severity of the interference on the individual vis-à-vis the public interest. The Court accords the State a wide margin of appreciation in determining what is 'proportionate'. Relevant matters include the length of the individual's residence in the State (although this factor no longer outweighs the existence of serious offences committed by the applicant);[262] the strength of family and other social ties;[263] immigration controls;[264] whether the applicant or family members were born in the State party;[265] the nature of links with the country of origin;[266] whether the applicant remains a national of the country of origin or desires to become a national of the State party;[267] and finally, if removal is due to an offence

---

[256] *Sisojeva* First section, above note, para. 101. On non-removal where a marriage would otherwise be destroyed: *Moustaquim*, above note, para. 36; *Beldjoudi* v. *France* (1992) 14 EHRR 801.

[257] See Lambert, above n. 251, 447–50; *Berrehab* above n. 247; *Moustaquim*, above n. 255; *Beldjoudi*, above note; *Boughanemi* v. *France* (1996) 22 EHRR 228; *Mthokozisi* v. *Secretary of State for the Home Department* [2004] EWHC 2964 (Admin). In *Amrollahi* v. *Denmark*, Application No. 56811/00 (11 Jul. 2002), the successful applicant was a recognized refugee with a permanent residence permit.

[258] See Lambert, above note 251, 448; *Amrollahi*, above n. 255, para. 35. In *Boultif*, above n. 255, the Court recognized that in cases where family members are likely to experience linguistic difficulties or lack of social ties if forced to relocate, and issues such as criminality do not arise, then the interference will generally be disproportionate: see Rogers, above n. 244, 62.

[259] *Sunday Times* v. *UK* (1979–80) 2 EHRR 245; *Barthold* v. *Germany* (1985) 7 EHRR 383.

[260] This analysis applies to arts. 8–11 ECHR50.

[261] *Silver* v. *UK* (1983) 5 EHRR 347, para. 97; *Abdulaziz*, above n. 250, para. 67; *Berrehab*, above n. 247, paras. 28–9; *Moustaquim*, above n. 255, para. 43; *Beldjoudi*, above n. 256, para. 74.

[262] For list of factors, see Lambert, above n. 251, 446–7.

[263] *Berrehab*, above n. 247; *Beldjoudi* above n. 256; *Mehemi* v. *France* (2000) 30 EHRR 739; note also the reasoning in *Fadele* v. *UK*, Application No. 13078/87 (12 Feb. 1990) (Commission).

[264] *Cruz* v. *Varas*, above n. 229; *Boughanemi* v. *France* (1996) 22 EHRR 228.

[265] *Beldjoudi*, above n. 256; *Mehemi*, above n. 263.

[266] *El Boujaidi*, v. *France* (2000) 30 EHRR 223; cf. *Mehemi*, above n. 263.

[267] *Boughanemi*, above n. 257; cf. *Beldjoudi*, above n. 256.

committed by the applicant, an assessment of its gravity, the age and mental health of the offender, and whether the offending behaviour persists.[268]

3.4.3.2 Article 8: private life

The term 'private life' has not been exhaustively defined, but includes 'physical and moral integrity of the person'[269] and mental health, since '[t]he preservation of mental stability is...an indispensable precondition to effective enjoyment of the right to respect for private life'.[270] In *Bensaid*, the Court acknowledged that ill-treatment falling below the article 3 threshold could nonetheless breach the right to a private life under article 8 'where there are sufficiently adverse effects on physical and moral integrity'.[271] The English Court of Appeal similarly accepted in principle that the expulsion of a homosexual to a State in which he or she might be subjected to a flagrant violation of article 8 rights could breach ECHR50.[272] Given that the protection of private life remains subject to the balancing test under article 8(2), and the Court is generally reluctant to intervene in domestic immigration policy, only very serious personal considerations will outweigh a State's decision to remove an asylum seeker on this ground.[273] Non-citizens who are integrated in the European host State have a greater likelihood of success. [274]

3.4.3.3 Article 13; remedies

For a long time, article 13 proved to be something of a non-starter. It requires that '[e]veryone whose rights and freedoms...are violated shall have an effective remedy before a national authority'. On the one hand, this has been construed to mean that an actual breach of the Convention is not an essential pre-condition to the availability of a remedy, but that neither must a remedy be made available for 'any supposed grievance', only for that which is 'an arguable one in terms of the

---

[268] *Moustaquim*, above n. 255; cf. *Chorfi* v. *Belgium* sub nom *C* v. *Belgium*, Application No. 21794/93 (7 Aug. 1996). See general list in *Amrollahi*, above n. 257; para. 35, in which expulsion of a refugee was found to be a breach of art. 8.

[269] *Stubbings* v. *UK* (1997) 23 EHRR 213 [59]. At times, it may be also simply be used as a substitute for 'family life': see *Sisojeva* above n. 258. In a non-protection context, the Court has held that the concept extends to 'relationships of a professional or business nature': *Chorfi*, above note, para. 25; see also *Niemetz* v. *Germany* (1993) 16 EHRR 97, para. 29.

[270] *Bensaid*, above n. 220, para. 47.

[271] Ibid., para. 46, referring to *Costello-Roberts* v. *UK* (1995) 19 EHRR 112, para. 36 (corporal punishment).

[272] *Z* v. *Secretary of State for the Home Department* [2002] Imm AR 560. Art. 8 ECHR50 is a ground for discretionary leave to remain in the United Kingdom.

[273] On deference to the original decision-maker, see Blake & Husain *Immigration, Asylum and Human Rights*, above n. 196, paras. 5.209–5.220.

[274] See, for example, *Beldjoudi*, above n. 256; *Sisojeva*, above n. 255; dissent in *Boughanemi*, above n. 257; (Judge Martens); *Nasri* v. *France* (1995) 21 EHRR 458; (Judges Wildhaber and Morenilla), as cited in Rogers, above n. 244, 55.

Convention'.[275] On the other hand, the Court has also repeatedly stated that there is no obligation to incorporate the Convention into domestic law, and that article 13 'does not go so far as to guarantee a remedy allowing a Contracting State's laws as such to be challenged before a national authority on the ground of being contrary to the Convention'.[276] This effectively debars claimants in States that have not specifically incorporated the Convention, or where it is not otherwise a part of domestic law, from seeking a local remedy for its breach.

Article 13 has been construed especially narrowly in proceedings involving non-nationals, refugees, and asylum seekers. In *Vilvarajah* it was argued that judicial review is not an effective remedy when what is at issue is the merits of a decision, in this case, the reasonableness of claimants' fear of persecution.[277] The Court maintained its acceptance of judicial review as explained in the *Soering* case, on the ground that the reviewing court was nonetheless able to review 'reasonableness' and strike down decisions 'tainted with illegality, irrationality or procedural impropriety'.[278] It was left to the Irish judge, Judge Walsh, to point out that the comparison with *Soering* was inappropriate, for there the facts were not in dispute; a remedy that excludes the competence to make a decision on the merits, he said, cannot meet the requirements of article 13.[279] The Court, however, attached particular importance to the knowledge and experience of the UK authorities in dealing with asylum claims such as those before it, concluding that 'substantial grounds' had not been established to show a breach of article 3.[280]

---

[275] *Boyle and Rice* (1988) 10 EHRR 425, para. 52; *Plattform 'Ärzte für das Leben'* (1988) 13 EHRR 204; *Powell and Rayner* v. *UK* (1990) 12 EHRR 355; see also Pettiti and Walsh, diss., in *Brannigan and McBride* v. *UK* (1993) 17 EHRR 539.

[276] *Sunday Times* v. *UK (No. 2)* (1991) 14 EHRR 153, para. 61; *Observer and Guardian* v. *UK* (1991), 14 EHRR 153, para. 76; *James and Others* v. *UK* (1996) 8 EHRR 123, paras. 84–5; *Case of the Holy Monasteries* v. *Greece* (1995), 20 EHRR 1, para. 90.

[277] *Vilvarajah* v. *UK* (1991) 14 EHRR 248.

[278] Ibid., para. 123. The Court was impressed by the fact that applicants had actually succeeded with judicial review in a number of cases; ibid., paras. 89–93. *Soering* v. *UK* (1989) 11 EHRR 439; Lillich, R. B. 'Notes and Comments: The *Soering* Case', 85 *AJIL* 128 (1991); Van den Wyngaert, C., 'Applying the European Convention on Human Rights to Extradition: Opening Pandora's Box?' 39 *ICLQ* 757 (1990).

[279] See also Walsh diss. in *Brannigan and McBride* v. *UK* (1993) EHRR 539: 'The application of Article 13 does not depend upon a violation being proved ... (Habeas corpus) depends upon showing a breach of national laws. It is not available for a claim that the detention is illegal by reason only of a breach of the Convention.' For an instance of judicial review in positive terms, see Ward, I., 'The Story of M: A Cautionary Tale from the United Kingdom', 6 *IJRL* 194 (1994).

[280] Cf. Hampson, F. J., 'The Concept of an "Arguable Claim" under Article 13 of the European Convention on Human Rights', 39 *ICLQ* 891 (1990). Note also that in the context of art. 6(1) (determination of civil rights and obligations or any criminal charge), the Court has ruled that decisions of administrative authorities that do not themselves satisfy the requirements of that article should be subject to subsequent control by a 'judicial body that has full jurisdiction': *Albert and Le Compte* v. *Belgium* (1983) 5 EHRR 533, para. 29; also *Ortenberg* v. *Austria* (1994) 19 EHRR 524, paras. 29–3; *Beaumartin* v. *France* (1994) 19 EHRR 485, in which the Court held, again with respect to art. 6(1), that, 'Only an institution that has full jurisdiction and satisfies a number of requirements, such as independence of the executive and also of the parties, merits the designation "tribunal",' within the meaning of art. 6(1). The Conseil d'Etat, which referred questions of treaty

However, in *Jabari* v. *Turkey*, the Court found that article 13 would be breached where there was no domestic mechanism available to the applicant to obtain a suspension of the decision to remove her from Turkey.[281] In that case, the Court found that the applicant would be subjected to a real risk of ill-treatment under article 3 if she were removed to Iran. Since she had made her asylum application out of time, she had not been given an opportunity to explain to the authorities why she feared deportation to Iran, nor the possibility to appeal against the rejection of her asylum claim. The Court emphasized that article 13 'guarantees the availability at national level of a remedy to enforce the substance of the Convention rights and freedoms', and accordingly requires 'the provision of a domestic remedy allowing the competent national authority both to deal with the substance of the relevant Convention complaint and to grant appropriate relief'.[282] It held that:

given the irreversible nature of the harm that might occur if the risk of torture or ill-treatment alleged materialised and the importance which it [the Court] attaches to Article 3, the notion of an effective remedy under Article 13 requires independent and rigorous scrutiny of a claim that there exist substantial grounds for fearing a real risk of treatment contrary to Article 3 and the possibility of suspending the implementation of the measure impugned. Since the Ankara Administrative Court failed in the circumstances to provide any of these safeguards, the Court is led to conclude that the judicial review proceedings relied on by the Government did not satisfy the requirements of Article 13.[283]

3.5 THE 1989 CONVENTION ON THE RIGHTS OF THE CHILD (CRC89)

The Convention on the Rights of the Child is the most widely ratified human rights treaty, having been ratified by all States except the United States and Somalia.[284] Article 3, which is binding and cannot be the subject of a reservation, provides:

In all actions concerning children, whether undertaken by public or private social welfare institutions, courts of law, administrative authorities or legislative bodies, the best interests of the child shall be a primary consideration.

interpretation to the executive for (binding) decision, did not meet these requirements. *Hadjianastassiou* v. *Greece* (1992) 16 EHRR 219—national courts must indicate with sufficient clarity the grounds on which they base their decision, which makes it possible for the accused to exercise usefully available rights of appeal.

[281] *Jabari* v. *Turkey* [2000] ECHR 369, para. 44.

[282] Ibid., para. 48. It has made these comments in earlier cases also: see, for example, *Soering* v. *UK* (1989) 11 EHRR 439, para. 120; *Chahal*, above n. 231, para. 145; *Vilvarajah*, above n. 277, para. 122. The Court noted that in some cases, the 'aggregate of remedies provided by national law' may satisfy article 13: *Jabari*, above note, para. 48, referring to *Chahal*, para. 145.

[283] *Jabari* v. *Turkey* above n. 281, para. 50.

[284] Both Somalia and the United States have signed it. Nearly nine-tenths of the 193 States which have ratified CRC89 did so within five years of its adoption by the General Assembly.

Though the requirement that children's best interests shall be a primary consideration in all actions concerning them should necessarily affect States' application of article 1A(2) of the 1951 Refugee Convention, by imposing an additional layer of consideration in cases involving children, it may also constitute a complementary ground of protection in its own right.[285] In particular, it may provide a ground of protection for children fleeing generalized violence. Goodwin-Gill and Hurwitz argue that wherever children are involved, 'a duty to protect may arise, absent any well-founded fear of persecution or possibility of serious harm'.[286] The Committee on the Rights of the Child has emphasized that the principle 'must be respected during all stages of the displacement cycle'.[287] In our view, article 3 CRC89 ought to be taken into account in all asylum claims concerning children, whether as primary applicants or as members of a family. While the courts have recognized that it may be relevant in cases where the deportation of a child's parent is proposed (that is, where the family is already in the host State),[288] we suggest that it should also be considered at the beginning of the asylum process, such that, in appropriate cases, the child's best interests may themselves give rise to a protection need. For example, in Sweden, the Aliens Act requires the best interests of the child to be considered in all cases concerning children,[289] including consideration of the child's health and development. The authorities must take this principle into account on reception, during investigation of the asylum claim, in assessing whether there are humanitarian reasons for granting a residence permit, in questions concerning family reunion, and where entry is refused. Although a child, like an adult, must be able to establish the probability of falling within one of the international protection categories in the Aliens Act (chapter 4, sections 2 to 3), 'children's mental reactions to excesses have been deemed to strengthen the credibility and weight of the reasons pleaded by the parent as grounds for asylum'.[290]

---

[285] See McAdam, *Complementary Protection*, above n. 11, Ch. 5.

[286] Goodwin-Gill, G. S. & Hurwitz, A., 'Memorandum' in Minutes of Evidence Taken before the EU Committee (Sub-Committee E) (10 Apr. 2002) para.10, in House of Lords Select Committee on the EU, *Defining Refugee Status and Those in Need of International Protection*, (2002), Oral Evidence Section, 2.

[287] Committee on the Rights of the Child, 'General Comment No. 6 (2005): 'Treatment of Unaccompanied and Separated Children Outside Their Country of Origin', UN doc. CRC/GC/2005/6, para. 19. The EU Qualification Directive stipulates that 'the best interest [sic] of the child shall be a primary consideration' when Member States are implementing the provisions relating to international protection, and the 2005 Executive Committee Conclusion on complementary protection encourages States to give 'due regard to the best interest [sic] of the child and family unity principles' in providing protection. However, both instruments invoke the best interests standard in relation to treatment *after* protection has already been accorded, rather than as a protection ground in its own right: Qualification Directive, art. 5, recital 12; Executive Committee Conclusion No. 103, (2005), para. (n).

[288] *Minister of State for Immigration and Ethnic Affairs* v. *Teoh* (1995) 183 CLR 273 (HCA); *Baker* v. *Canada* [1999] 2 SCR 817; *Beharry* v. *Reno* 183 F. Supp 2d 584 (EDNY 2002).

[289] Aliens Act, ch. 1 s. 1(2), which entered into force on 31 Mar. 2006.

[290] UN95/10540, cited in Schiratzki, J., 'The Best Interests of the Child in the Swedish Aliens Act', 14 *Int'l J. of Law, Policy and the Family* 206, 212 (2000).

Indeed, the *travaux préparatoires* of the Aliens Act state that the best interests of the child can allow residence permits to be granted on humanitarian grounds for less compelling reasons when children are affected than otherwise,[291] and the case law supports this approach.[292] Thus, children may be permitted to stay even when they cannot demonstrate the level of harm normally required to be shown, for example when they are physically or mentally ill,[293] disabled or have come from States involved in armed conflict.

4. The 2004 European Union Qualification Directive

The importance of delineating the precise scope and content of complementary protection was highlighted during the first phase of the Common European Asylum System, as EU Member States sought to agree on a harmonized EC law for the qualification and status of 'beneficiaries of subsidiary protection'. Existing national *ad hoc* schemes for '*de facto* refugees' meant that dramatically different levels of protection were available depending on the State where protection claim was lodged.[294] Despite numerous calls from the 1970s onwards for a common European approach,[295] it was not until 2001 that an EU Directive was formally proposed.[296] The Qualification Directive—the first supranational complementary protection regime—was adopted on 29 April 2004, and was to be transposed into the national law of each participating Member State by 10 October 2006.[297]

Article 2(e) defines as a 'person eligible for subsidiary protection':

a third country national or a stateless person who does not qualify as a refugee but in respect of whom substantial grounds have been shown for believing that the person concerned, if returned to his or her country of origin, or in the case of a stateless person, to his or her country of former habitual residence, would face a real risk of suffering serious harm as defined in Article 15, and to whom Article 17(1) and (2) do not apply, and is unable, or, owing to such risk, unwilling to avail himself or herself of the protection of that country.

---

[291] Gov. Bill Prop, 1996/97: 25 at 249, cited in Schiratzki, above note, 218.

[292] See cases discussed in Schiratzki, above n. 290.

[293] Aliens Appeals Board 970130, 970314, cited in ibid., 218.

[294] See generally, Bouteillet-Paquet, above n. 123.   [295] See above s. 2.

[296] Council Directive 2004/83/EC of 29 April 2004 on Minimum Standards for the Qualification and Status of Third Country Nationals or Stateless Persons as Refugees or as Persons Who Otherwise Need International Protection and the Content of the Protection Granted [2004] O.J. L304/12 (Qualification Directive). For text, see below, Annexe 2, No. 19.

[297] Denmark has opted out, in accordance with arts. 1 and 2 of the Protocol on the Position of Denmark annexed to the Treaty on European Union [2002] O. J. C325/5, and the Treaty establishing the European Community [2002] O. J. C325/33: Directive, recital 40. For the Danish position, see Kjær, K. U., 'The Abolition of the Danish *de facto* Concept', 15 *IJRL* 254 (2003). By 9 Oct. 2006, the European Commission had received six (out of twenty-four) instruments of transposition: European Commission, 'Entry into Force of European Rules on the Qualification and Status of Persons in Need of International Protection', MEMO/06/369, (10 Oct. 2006), 1.

'Serious harm', which is not part of international law and was devised for the purposes of the Directive, is defined in article 15 as meaning:

(a) death penalty or execution; or
(b) torture or inhuman or degrading treatment or punishment of an applicant in the country of origin; or
(c) serious and individual threat to a civilian's life or person by reason of indiscriminate violence in situations of international or internal armed conflict.[298]

Paragraph (a) was based on Protocol 6 to ECHR50, prohibiting the imposition of the death penalty in peace time,[299] and was subsequently strengthened by the entry into force of Protocol 13, which prohibits the death penalty in all circumstances.[300] Furthermore, all Member States except France are parties to the Second Optional Protocol to ICCPR66, which contains a similar requirement.[301] It is also consistent with the jurisprudence of the European Court of Human Rights.[302]

Paragraph (b) implements article 3 ECHR50, but imposes an additional limitation by requiring that the feared ill-treatment occur 'in the country of origin'. This caveat was inserted part way through the drafting process, and seems to be intended to prevent claims based on a lack of resources—in particular, a lack of medical treatment—in the country to which return is contemplated.[303] Furthermore, it would also obviate a claim by an asylum seeker that he or she would face torture in a third country to which return may be contemplated. However, in such cases, the individual may remain protected by the Member State's wider obligation under ECHR50 and ICCPR66. Accordingly, while the individual would not be eligible for subsidiary protection status, he or she would be protected from *refoulement*. Significantly, however, such protection would not guarantee a legal status but would simply classify the person as non-removable.[304]

Paragraph (c) reflects the consistent, albeit varied, European State practice of granting some form of complementary protection to persons fleeing the

---

[298] Earlier drafts contained another category of 'serious harm': a 'violation of a human right, sufficiently severe to engage the Member State's international obligations'. For discussion of this, see McAdam J., 'The European Union Qualification Directive: The Creation of a Subsidiary Protection Regime', 17 *IJRL* 461, 490–3 (2005).

[299] Protocol No. 6 to ECHR50: *ETS* No. 114; text in Brownlie & Goodwin-Gill, *Basic Documents on Human Rights*, 626.

[300] Protocol No. 13 to ECHR50: *ETS* No. 187; text in Brownlie & Goodwin-Gill, *Basic Documents on Human Rights*, 635.

[301] Second Optional Protocol to the International Covenant on Civil and Political Rights, Aiming at the Abolition of the Death Penalty (adopted by UNGA res. 44/128, 15 Dec. 1989); text in Brownlie & Goodwin-Gill, *Basic Documents on Human Rights*, 379.

[302] See, for example, *Soering* v. *UK* (1989) 11 EHRR 439, para. 88.

[303] Presidency Note to Strategic Committee on Immigration, Frontiers and Asylum, 25 Sept. 2002, Doc 12148/02 ASILE 43 (20 Sept. 2002), 6.

[304] In *Bonger* v. *The Netherlands*, Application No. 10154/04 (15 Sept. 2005) (inadmissible), 14, the European Court of Human Rights stated that 'neither Article 3 nor any other provision of the Convention and its Protocols guarantees, as such, a right to a residence permit'. On the implications of the 'in the country of origin' limitation, see Battjes, H., *European Asylum Law and International Law*, (2006).

indiscriminate effects of armed conflict or generalized violence without a specific link to Convention grounds.[305] It replicates in part Member States' obligations under the 2001 EU Temporary Protection Directive[306] and the Council of Europe's Recommendation on Subsidiary Protection,[307] as well as EU Member States' repeated support for UNHCR's mandate activities for victims of indiscriminate violence (linked to regional agreements such as the OAU Convention and the Cartagena Declaration).

Article 15(c) underwent substantial drafting changes. It was first proposed as encompassing anyone fearing:

a threat to his or her life, safety or freedom as a result of indiscriminate violence arising in situations of armed conflict, or as a result of systematic or generalised violations of their human rights . . .[308]

but was narrowed considerably by requiring applicants to demonstrate that they were at risk of a 'serious and individual' threat, and precluding claims based on threats resulting from systematic or generalized human rights violations. The meaning of an 'individual' risk is explained in part by recital 26, which states:

Risks to which a population of a country or a section of the population is generally exposed do normally not create in themselves an individual threat which would qualify as serious harm.[309]

Thus, despite the apparently wide reference to 'indiscriminate violence in situations of international or internal armed conflict' in article 15(c), asylum seekers will only fall within the terms of that provision if they can show that they will be personally at risk in a situation of indiscriminate violence,[310] even though this is somewhat counter-intuitive to the very notion of violence that is random and

---

[305] See ELENA, 'Complementary/Subsidiary Forms of Protection in the EU States—An Overview', (Apr. 1999). UNHCR's mandate extends to such persons: see, for example, UNGA res. 1671 (XVI),18 Dec. 1961; UNGA res. 1673 (XVI), 18 Dec. 1961; UNGA res. 3143 (XXVIII), 14 Dec. 1973. The UK also includes 'unlawful killing' in its definition of 'humanitarian protection' (its name for 'subsidiary protection'): Immigration Rules, Rule 339C; the Refugee or Person in Need of International Protection (Qualification) Regulations 2006, SI 2006/2525.

[306] Council Directive 2001/55/EC of 20 Jul. 2001 on Minimum Standards for Giving Temporary Protection in the Event of a Mass Influx of Displaced Persons and on Measures Promoting a Balance of Efforts between Member States in Receiving Such Persons and Bearing the Consequences thereof [2001] OJ L212/12; for text, see below, Annexe 2, No. 14.

[307] Council of Europe's Recommendation (2001) 18 of the Committee of Ministers on Subsidiary Protection, (27 Nov. 2001).

[308] Commission of the European Communities Proposal for a Council Directive on Minimum Standards for the Qualification and Status of Third Country Nationals and Stateless Persons as Refugees or as Persons Who Otherwise Need International Protection COM (2001) 510 final (12 Sept. 2001), art. 15(c).   [309] Qualification Directive, Recital 26.

[310] Indeed, given this restriction, it may be that many of the types of harm contemplated by para. (c) would already fall within paras. (a) or (b).

haphazard.[311] Whether or not the provision requires individuals actually to be singled out is unclear. To demand this would establish a higher threshold than is required for either Convention-based protection or protection under the EU Temporary Protection Directive. For article 15(c) to provide meaningful protection, it would seem that States will have to be relatively generous in determining the 'individual' aspect of the risk.[312]

Given the limitations on protection claims by individuals fleeing civil war, the more generous eligibility criteria under article 2(c) of the 2001 Temporary Protection Directive for those fleeing conflict *en masse* may seem aberrant. Under that provision, temporary protection is extended to those:

who have had to leave their country or region of origin, or have been evacuated... and are unable to return in safe and durable conditions because of the situation prevailing in that country, who may fall within the scope of Article 1A of the Geneva Convention or other international or national instruments giving international protection, in particular:

(i) persons who have fled areas of armed conflict or endemic violence;
(ii) persons at serious risk of, or who have been the victims of, systematic or generalised violations of their human rights.[313]

There is tacit recognition in the Temporary Protection Directive that this threshold is more easily satisfied than article 15(c) of the Qualification Directive. Pursuant to article 17 of the Temporary Protection Directive, individuals who arrive as part of a mass influx must be able to lodge an asylum claim for Convention or subsidiary protection. If that asylum claim is unsuccessful, the individual must continue to benefit from temporary protection until it expires.[314] In other words, temporary protection will attach even where the threshold of article 15(c) of the Qualification Directive cannot be met.

---

[311] See, for example, the UK Secretary of State's refusal of asylum on the basis of such violence, as recorded in *Vilvarajah* v. *UK* (1991) 14 EHRR 248 para. 13: 'But it is noted that the incidents you have related were random and part of the army's general activities directed at discovering and dealing with Tamil extremists and that they do not constitute evidence of persecution'; see also paras. 25, 40, 52, 62.

[312] See, for example, French jurisprudence on this provision: CRR, Sections réunies, (17 fév. 2006) 419.162, *Mlle K*—subsidiary protection granted on the basis of art. 15(c) due to a situation of generalized violence and internal armed conflict in Iraq, and the fact she was a single Assyro-Chaldean Christian woman without financial means; CRR, Sections réunies, (17 fév. 2006) 497,089, *M.A.*— subsidiary protection granted on the basis of art. 15(c) due to a situation of generalized violence and internal armed conflict in Iraq, and the fact that he had been an official in the former regime and was a member of a particular political party. Belgium has not transposed the individual requirement: 'les menaces graves contre la vie ou la personne d'un civil en raison d'une violence aveugle en cas de de conflict armé interne ou international': *Loi modifiant la loi du 15 décembre 1980 sur l'accès au territoire, le séjour, l'établissement et l'éloignement des étrangers* (15 Sep. 2006), art. 26, inserting new art. 48/4(2)(c) into the Aliens Act 1980. Lithuanian law does not contain the individual requirement either, providing that subsidiary protection may be granted to a person with a well-founded fear that 'his life, health, safety or freedom is under threat as result of endemic violence which spreads in an armed conflict or which has placed him at serious risk of systemic violation of his human rights': Law on the Legal Status of Aliens (29 April 2004) No IX-2206 (Official Gazette No. 73-2539, 3 April 2004), art. 87.

[313] Temporary Protection Directive, above n. 306, art. 2(c).   [314] Ibid., art. 19(2).

However, the 'catch' is that temporary protection is not self-executing: article 2(c) cannot take effect unless and until the Council of the EU decides, following a proposal by the Commission, that a mass influx exists.[315] Thus, this in-built trigger mechanism means that the application of the Temporary Protection Directive can be carefully controlled, whereas the Qualification Directive may be 'activated' by any person within the jurisdiction to whom article 15 applies. During the drafting of the Qualification Directive, the French delegation expressed (somewhat exaggerated) fears that if article 15(c) did not require an applicant to demonstrate individual harm, entire populations could flee and obtain subsidiary protection in the EU on the grounds of generalized violence.[316] A clear majority of Member States supported the 'individual' requirement on the grounds that this would avoid 'an undesired opening of the scope of this subparagraph'.[317] This 'individual' limitation is based on political concerns about numbers rather than any legal distinction between people fleeing individually and *en masse*.

The Qualification Directive was intended to unify *existing* Member State practice. It has not, therefore, created a new system of protection per se,[318] but has simply distilled State practice by drawing on the 'best' elements of the Member States' national systems.[319] It attains its significance as a supranational instrument that recognizes some of the Member States' *non-refoulement* obligations under international and regional law, and which, additionally and importantly, formalizes a legal status for certain beneficiaries of that protection.[320] However, it is not a flawless model. Though it partially closes a protection gap by *regulating* the eligibility and status of people in need of protection, instead of leaving these matters to State discretion, it creates additional gaps by omitting certain known categories of people with an international protection need,[321] expressly excluding others,[322] and unjustifiably entrenching a protection hierarchy, spearheaded by Convention

---

[315] Qualification Directive, art. 5(1).   [316] 12199/02 ASILE 45 (25 Sept. 2002).

[317] 12382/02 ASILE 47 (30 Sept. 2002), para. 4.

[318] Council of the EU Outcome of Proceedings of CIREA Meeting with Representatives of the Courts and Other Review Bodies Dealing with Asylum on 28 Nov. 2001, 'Summary of Discussions' doc. 5585/02 CIREA 7 (Brussels, 22 Mar. 2002) 4.

[319] 'Explanatory Memorandum' in Commission of the European Communities Proposal for a Council Directive on Minimum Standards for the Qualification and Status of Third Country Nationals and Stateless Persons as Refugees or as Persons Who Otherwise Need International Protection COM (2001) 510 final (12 Sept. 2001) 5. This was drafted before the 1 May 2004 enlargement of the EU and hence relied on the State practice of the then 15 Member States at that time.   [320] McAdam, *Complementary Protection*, 90ff.

[321] For example, the Directive applies only to people who are 'third country nationals'. As noted above in Ch. 3, s. 31, this contravenes art. 42 CSR51, which prohibits States from limiting the personal scope of art. 1 or making reservations to art. 3, and precludes EU citizens from accessing subsidiary protection. However, since the Member States remain bound by their obligations under international law, the effect of the 'third country nationals' limitation is to deny the status set out in the Qualification Directive to people who may remain protected by the principle of *non-refoulement* under the 1951 Convention or human rights law. On the relationship between EC Directives and international obligations, see Costello, C., 'The *Bosphorus* Ruling of the European Court of Human Rights: Fundamental Rights and Blurred Boundaries in Europe', 6 *Human Rights Law Review* 87 (2006).

[322] See discussion of Qualification Directive exclusion clauses above Ch.4, s. 4.4.

refugee status and followed by a lesser 'subsidiary protection' status. The Qualification Directive must therefore be viewed in context: as a pragmatic response to the political realities of the EU and the need for an instrument of compromise. 'Subsidiary protection' is a regional manifestation of the broader international legal concept of 'complementary protection'.

5. Status and exclusion from status

As noted at the beginning of this chapter, the majority of western countries have a domestic system of codified complementary protection in place.[323] These systems enable individuals to apply for protection on specified grounds that go beyond article 1A(2) of the 1951 Convention, and implement—at least in part—States' international treaty and customary law *non-refoulement* obligations. Importantly, beneficiaries of such extended protection are accorded a domestic legal status.

Given the increased codification of complementary protection in national law over the past decade,[324] State practice now confirms that beneficiaries of complementary protection should generally be accorded some form of domestic legal status,[325] although its nature, duration, and application vary considerably among States. While the treaties examined above all give rise to *non-refoulement* in certain contexts, they are silent on the resultant status of beneficiaries. The courts and treaty-monitoring bodies have not been particularly instructive on this point, either. Beyond recognizing that a protection need arises, they have not gone on to consider the status that should be afforded to the beneficiary.[326]

By contrast to the period from the 1950s to the 1980s, when States commonly extended protection to people fleeing generalized violence,[327] since the 1990s

---

[323] See above, n. 1.

[324] CAT84 was ratified by the United States in 1994 but not implemented by Congress until 1998. At that time, the Department of Justice and the Department of State were mandated to draft regulations making CAT84 relief available in immigration and extradition claims: Foreign Affairs Reform and Restructuring Act, Pub. L. No. 105-277, 112 Stat. 2681, §2242 (1998). Protection against removal on CAT84 grounds is now contained in 8 CFR §208.16(4).

[325] The 2005 Executive Committee Conclusion No. 103 on complementary protection does not address the issue of status, but calls on States to provide beneficiaries with 'the highest degree of stability and certainty ensuring [their] human rights and fundamental freedoms . . . without discrimination' para. (n).

[326] See, for example, *Vijayanathan*, above n. 304; *Ahmed*, above n. 87; *Bonger* v. *The Netherlands*, above n. 87; *TI* v. *UK* [2000] INLR 211; Lambert, H., 'The European Convention on Human Rights and the Protection of Refugees: Limits and Opportunities', 24 *RSQ* 39, 50 (2005). Note, however, comments in *Pančenko* v. *Latvia*, Application No. 40772/98 (28 Oct. 1999); *BB* v. *France*, Application No. 30930/96 (9 Mar. 1998); *HLR* v. *France* (1997) 26 EHRR 29; and with respect to long-term migrants, *Sisojeva* v. *Latvia* [2005] ECHR 405, para. 107; *Nasri* v. *France* (1995) EHRR 458, (Judge Morenilla), paras. 3–4. On the position of family members of a person at risk of inhuman or degrading punishment, see *Bader* v. *Sweden*, Application No. 13284/04 (8 Nov. 2005) and *D* v. *Turkey*, Application No. 24245/03 (22 Jun. 2006).

[327] See s. 6 below on the development of 'temporary protection'.

States have increasingly sought to isolate and articulate the international treaty obligations on which their complementary duty to protect rests. This has been accompanied, however, by a narrowing down of the status of those who benefit from it. This has two key implications: to consolidate the obligation to protect, but to differentiate between Convention refugees and 'others'. Historically, States did not draw a distinction between *de jure* and *de facto* refugees in this way. For example, in 1956, the Council of Europe requested all Member States 'to accord to all [Hungarian refugees] who are able to work the facilities available under the system established by the Statute relating to refugees and provided for under the Geneva Convention of 1951',[328] even though they did not come within the terms of article 1A(2) of that instrument. A memo from UNHCR the following year revealed that:

On the whole... no Government has, as far as we know, raised any objection to the application of the Convention to Hungarian refugees who otherwise fulfill the conditions of Article 1 of the Convention and it can, therefore, be assumed that the interpretation of the dateline of 1 January 1951 contained in Document A/AC.79/49 Annex IV is accepted by Governments parties to the Convention.[329]

Similarly, the regional OAU Convention and the Cartagena Declaration envisage the extension of Convention status to those who come within the wider scope of their 'refugee' definitions.[330]

Under international law, there are cogent reasons why a legal status equivalent to that accorded by the Refugee Convention ought to apply to all persons protected by the extended principle of *non-refoulement*.[331] McAdam argues that the 1951 Convention is a form of *lex specialis* (specialist law) for all people in need of international protection, which provides an appropriate legal status regardless of the source of the State's protection obligation.

Refugee protection is a sub-set of human rights law, and since the Convention is a specialist human rights instrument, the conceptualization of protection that it embodies has

---

[328] Resolution adopted by the Committee on Population and Refugees (Vienna, 15 Oct. 1956) COE doc. 587, adopted with certain amendments by Permanent Commission (Paris, 19 Nov. 1956) acting for Consultative Assembly between sessions, in Interoffice Memorandum to Mr M. Pagès, Director from P. Weis, 'Eligibility of Refugees from Hungary' (9 Jan. 1957) 22/1/HUNG, para. 3, in UNHCR Archives Fonds 11 Sub-fonds 1, 6/1/HUN.

[329] Memo from P. Weis to Mr J. Mersch, UNHCR Branch Office in Luxembourg 'Application of 1951 Convention to Hungarian Refugees' (28 May 1957) Ref.G.XV.7/1/8, 6/1/HUN, para. 3, in UNHCR Archives Fonds 11 Sub-fonds 1, 6/1/HUN.

[330] Art. VIII(2) OAU69. There is nothing in the Cartagena Declaration that suggests a different status should be accorded to its wider conception of 'refugees', and indeed that instrument refers to the OAU Convention as a precedent: Conclusions III(3), III(8). See also Fitzpatrick, J., 'Temporary Protection of Refugees: Elements of a Formalized Regime', 94 *AJIL* 270, 293 (2000).

[331] For further analysis, see McAdam, *Complementary Protection*, Ch. 6; see also McAdam, J., 'Complementary Protection and Beyond: How States deal with Human Rights Protection', UNHCR, *New Issues in Refugee Research*, Working Paper No. 118 (Geneva, Aug. 2005).

necessarily been extended by developments in human rights law. By contrast to the universal human rights instruments, which are based on a more abstract and wide-ranging human rights ideal, the Convention is unique in creating a legal status for its beneficiaries, the components of which are non-derogable and tailored to the precarious legal position of non-citizens whose own country of origin is unable or unwilling to protect them. The rights contained in the Refugee Convention are not innately superior to those in the universal human rights instruments, being largely based on and extended by the latter; they are simply applied differently. States tend to regard Convention rights as a *status* required by international law (whether through a grant of permanent residence or otherwise) once a person has been formally recognized as a 'refugee'. Conversely, the strong theoretical claims of universal human rights law do not always sit comfortably with the realities of State practice, where 'rights' may be elusive, hampered by poor implementation and a lack of access to domestic enforcement mechanisms.[332]

UNHCR and others similarly argue that there is no legal justification for treating beneficiaries of complementary protection differently from Convention refugees, noting that rights and entitlements should be based on the need for protection rather than the grounds on which protection was granted.[333] The House of Lords Select Committee on the EU stated that to distinguish between Convention refugees and beneficiaries of complementary protection in this way would be 'an apparently unjustified discrimination'.[334]

Yet, of the codified complementary protection systems in place, only Canada and the Netherlands—an exception to European practice under the Qualification Directive[335]—provide beneficiaries of complementary protection with a status equivalent to that of Convention refugees. For example, the nature of complementary protection in the EU is apparent from its name—'subsidiary protection'—a secondary status. Under the Qualification Directive, beneficiaries of subsidiary protection receive less extensive entitlements with respect to family unity;[336] access to and length of residence permits;[337] eligibility for travel documents;[338]

---

[332] McAdam, *Complementary Protection*, 6.

[333] UNHCR's Observations on the European Commission's Proposals for a Council Directive on Minimum Standards for the Qualification of Third Country Nationals and Stateless Persons as Refugees or as Persons who Otherwise Need International Protection', 14109/01 ASILE54 (16 Nov. 2001), para. 46; UNHCR, 'Note on Key Issues of Concern to UNHCR on the Draft Qualification Directive', Mar. 2004, 2; UNHCR, 'Towards a Common European Asylum System', in de Sousa, C.D.U. & de Bruycker, P., eds., *The Emergence of a European Asylum Policy*, (2004), 249–50. See also Amnesty International Irish Section, 'The Case for Complementary Protection', (Jan. 2003): <http://www.amnesty.ie/act/refug/protection.shtml>; Refugee Council (UK), 'Refugee Council's Response to the Home Office Consultation on Changes to the Policy of Issuing of Certificates of Identity', (Feb. 2003): <http://www.refugeecouncil.org.uk/downloads>.

[334] House of Lords, Select Committee on the EU, *Defining Refugee Status*, above n. 286, para. 111. It noted that giving both groups an equivalent status would also obviate appeals to upgrade status.

[335] The Netherlands has implemented a uniform residence permit which provides all beneficiaries of international protection with the same rights and benefits: Aliens Act 2000 s. 27.

[336] Qualification Directive, art. 23.   [337] Ibid., art. 24.   [338] Ibid., art. 25.

access to employment;[339] social welfare entitlements;[340] health care entitlements;[341] access to integration facilities;[342] and rights of accompanying family
members.[343] Analysis of the Qualification Directive drafting records reveals that
the creation of a two-tier system was politically motivated, rather than based on
any solid legal foundation.[344]

No existing national or supranational regime, however expansive, 'covers the
field' of complementary protection. Indeed, each one represents a selective
domestic implementation of the State's international obligations. This is most
pertinently illustrated by the existence of exclusion clauses,[345] based on article 1F
of the 1951 Convention.[346] In the EU, they are even broader, encompassing
people who have committed any 'serious crime',[347] and those who constitute 'a
danger to the community or to the security of the Member State in which he or
she is present'.[348] Under international law, non-return to torture or cruel, inhuman or degrading treatment or punishment is absolute, no matter how reprehen-
sible or dangerous an individual's conduct.[349]

While exclusion clauses in domestic complementary protection regimes may
deny a legal status to certain categories of 'undesirable' people, they do not absolve
States of their wider *non-refoulement* obligations under international law. In other

[339] Ibid., art. 26.   [340] Ibid., art. 28.   [341] Ibid., art. 29.   [342] Ibid., art. 33.
[343] Ibid., art. 23(5).
[344] See discussion in McAdam, *Complementary Protection*, 90–3. Germany would only agree to
the Directive if social and economic rights were reduced further for beneficiaries of subsidiary protection: British Refugee Council, 'International Protection Project Update', (Sept. 2002), 2.
[345] See, for example, Qualification Directive, art. 17; Canadian Immigration and Refugee
Protection Act, s. 98. US law also excludes certain 'undesirable' people from 'withholding of removal'
(the standard status granted to people who fear removal pursuant to art. 3 CAT84), but gives them
'deferral of removal' status (amounting to little more than toleration of their presence). Under
s. 241(b)(3)(B) of the Immigration and Nationality Act, an applicant is ineligible for 'withholding of
removal' if the Attorney General decides that: '(i) the alien ordered, incited, assisted, or otherwise participated in the persecution of an individual because of the individual's race, religion, nationality,
membership in a particular social group, or political opinion; (ii) the alien, having been convicted by
a final judgment of a particularly serious crime, is a danger to the community of the United States;
(iii) there are serious reasons to believe that the alien committed a serious nonpolitical crime outside
the United States before the alien arrived in the United States; or (iv) there are reasonable grounds to
believe that the alien is a danger to the security of the United States.' Under 8 CFR §208.16(d)(2),
with respect to the above, 'an alien who has been convicted of a particularly serious crime shall be considered to constitute a danger to the community'.
[346] The Canadian Immigration and Refugee Protection Act 2001, s. 98 provides: 'A person referred
to in section E or F of Article 1 of the Refugee Convention is not a Convention refugee or a person in
need of protection.' For the status of refugees to whom art. 33(2) CSR51 applies, see above Ch. 4, s. 4.
[347] Qualification Directive, art. 17(1)(b). This is different from art. 1F(b) CSR51, which only
excludes those who have committed a serious non-political crime.
[348] Qualification Directive, art. 17(1)(d). Note also art. 17(3): 'Member States may exclude a
third country national or a stateless person from being eligible for subsidiary protection, if he or she
prior to his or her admission to the Member State has committed one or more crimes, outside the
scope of paragraph 1, which would be punishable by imprisonment, had they been committed in the
Member State concerned, and if he or she left his or her country of origin solely in order to avoid
sanctions resulting from these crimes.'   [349] *Chahal* v. *UK* (1998) 23 EHRR 413.

words, domestic complementary protection regimes cannot oust States' international protection responsibilities—they simply leave them unregulated at the
domestic level. The result is that people protected by the principle of *non-
refoulement* under international law, but expressly excluded from national versions
of 'complementary protection', are left in a legal limbo. As Gil-Bazo has explained
in the context of the EU Qualification Directive, there is now 'a category of persons
protected by EC law, *in addition* to those that shall remain protected by the national
legal orders of Member States *in fulfilment of their international obligations*'.[350]

The status of the 'domestically excluded' is particularly precarious,[351] in part
because international law does not provide a clear remedy. Human rights law
obviously applies, but in practice this may not mean much at all. For example, many
States undertake human rights obligations at the formal level, but do not ensure that
the rights subscribed to can actually be claimed.[352] Without undertaking special
measures to ensure that such provisions are translated into national law, certain benefits may be inaccessible.[353] Even where individuals are not expressly barred from
the enjoyment of a right, 'they are in practice often deprived of it inasmuch as it is
dependent on the fulfilment of certain formalities, such as production of documents, intervention of consular or other authorities, with which . . . they are not in a
position to comply'.[354] While human rights law requires States to respect the rights
it sets out in relation to *all* persons within its jurisdiction or territory, the quality of
each right may vary depending on the individual's legal position vis-à-vis the State.
Thus, while the *standard* of compliance with human rights law is international, the
State retains discretion in its choice of *implementation*—whether and how to incorporate treaty provisions into domestic law.[355] At a minimum, international law
requires that no person shall be subjected to treatment in the host State which itself
amounts to inhuman or degrading treatment.[356] General human rights law assists in
filling in the content of treatment to which all people are entitled.[357]

---

[350] Gil-Bazo, M.-T., 'Refugee Status, Subsidiary Protection and the Right to be Granted Asylum under EC Law', UNHCR, *New Issues in Refugee Research*, (Nov. 2006), 11.

[351] This is compounded by the Directive's suggestion that any person not covered by its terms is necessarily a compassionate or humanitarian case: Gilbert, G., 'Is Europe Living Up to Its Obligations to Refugees?' 15 *EJIL* 963, 980 (2004).

[352] Goodwin-Gill, G. S. & Kumin, J., 'Refugees in Limbo and Canada's International Obligations', Caledon Institute of Social Policy, (Sept. 2000), 4. See also UNHCR, 'Note on Inter-national Protection' UN doc. A/AC.96/898, (3 Jul. 1998), para.45.

[353] Goodwin-Gill & Kumin, above note, 5. As Hathaway notes, 'more than half a century after inauguration of the United Nations system of international human rights law, we must concede that there are only minimal legal tools for the imposition of genuine and truly universal state accountabil-ity . . . Instead of a universal and comprehensive system of human rights law, the present reality is instead a patchwork of standards of varying reach, implemented through mechanisms that range from the purely facilitative to the modestly coercive': Hathaway, *Rights of Refugees*, (2005) 6.

[354] United Nations, '*A Study of Statelessness*' UN doc. E/1112, E/1112.Add.1, New York, (Aug. 1949); Andrysek, O., 'Gaps in International Protection and the Potential for Redress through Individual Complaints Procedures', 9 *IJRL* 392, 411 (1997).

[355] See further McAdam, *Complementary Protection*, Ch. 6.

[356] On destitution, see *R. (Limbuela) v. Secretary of State for the Home Department* [2006] 1 AC 396.

[357] See McAdam, *Complementary Protection*, Ch. 6, who considers this in detail.

In sum, complementary protection is not an optional extra to protection under article 1A(2) of the Refugee Convention, but simply another arm of the international protection regime.

6. *Non-refoulement* in cases of mass influx and the development of 'temporary protection'

6.1 MASS INFLUX AND *NON-REFOULEMENT*

'Mass influx' is a common catchphrase of asylum discourse, but is not mentioned in the 1951 Convention, the 1967 Protocol, or the 1969 OAU Convention. The term is defined in the EU Temporary Protection Directive as the arrival of 'a large number of displaced persons, who come from a specific country or geographical area'.[358] As UNHCR has noted, mass influx cannot be defined in absolute numerical terms because its very existence depends on the resources of the receiving State: if a State can process the flow of refugees through conventional individual status determination procedures, then a special mass influx response is not required.[359] An Executive Committee Conclusion on mass influx and international cooperation noted that mass influx situations may include the following characteristics:

(i) considerable numbers of people arriving over an international border; (ii) a rapid rate of arrival; (iii) inadequate absorption or response capacity in host States, particularly during the emergency; (iv) individual asylum procedures, where they exist, which are unable to deal with the assessment of such large numbers.[360]

A mass influx emergency therefore exists only when the combination of the flow's size and suddenness makes individual refugee status determination procedurally impractical, placing strains on the host State's institutions and resources.

As a matter of international law, *refoulement* is not justifiable no matter how debilitating a sudden influx of refugees might be on a State's resources, economy, or political situation.[361] Nothing in article 33 of the 1951 Convention suggests its

---

[358] Temporary Protection Directive, art. 2(d).

[359] UNHCR, 'UNHCR Commentary on the Draft European Union Directive on Temporary Protection in the Event of a Mass Influx', 3 (2000): <http://www.ecre.org/eu_developments/>

[360] Executive Committee Conclusion No. 100 (LV) (2004), para. (a).

[361] This is the case under human rights law also: see, for example, Report of the Human Rights Committee, vol. 1 1997–98, GAOR, 53rd Session, Supp. No. 40 (A/53/40), 'United Republic of Tanzania', para. 401. See also Global Consultations on International Protection, 'Report of the First Meeting in the Third Track', UN doc. EC/GC/01/8/Rev.1 (28 Jun. 2001), para. 5; Lauterpacht & Bethlehem, '*Non-refoulement*: Opinion', para. 104; Durieux, J.-F. & McAdam, J., '*Non-Refoulement* through Time: The Case for a Derogation Clause to the Refugee Convention in Mass Influx Emergencies', 16 *IJRL* 4, 9, 13 (2004); Eggli, *Mass Refugee Influx*, above n. 6, Ch. 5; Durieux, J.-F. & Hurwitz, A., 'How Many Is Too Many? African and European Legal Responses to Mass Influxes and Refugees', 47 *German Yearbook of International Law* 105 (2004); but note UN Declaration on Territorial Asylum, UNGA res. 2312 (XXII), 14 Dec. 1967, para. 3(2).

inapplicability to mass influx situations, and Lauterpacht and Bethlehem argue that, given the Convention's humanitarian object and purpose, 'the principle must apply unless its application is clearly excluded'.³⁶² However, it appears that respect for the peremptory norm of *non-refoulement* in mass influx situations comes at a price: the trade-off for accepting the obligation to admit large numbers is 'a *de facto* suspension of all but the most immediate and compelling protections provided by the Convention'.³⁶³ The OAU Convention, the Cartagena Declaration, Executive Committee Conclusions, the EU Temporary Protection Directive,³⁶⁴ and UNHCR's views,³⁶⁵ all affirm the applicability of *non-refoulement* to mass influx situations.³⁶⁶

6.1.1 Some aspects of State practice

The views of States, and to some extent their practice, indicate an uncertain dimension to the principle of *non-refoulement*, particularly in cases of mass influx that may constitute a threat to the security of the receiving State.³⁶⁷ Reservations with respect to the security aspects of mass influxes have not died away since they were formally recognized in the 1967 UN Declaration on Territorial Asylum, and continue to surface in the discourse of many 'frontline' States, such as Turkey, Thailand, Zaire, Tanzania, and Macedonia. Clearly, from 1979 onwards, resettlement guarantees and substantial financial contributions were a major factor in preserving the so-called principle of first asylum. In October 1979, for example, Thailand announced the reversal of a policy which had earlier led to the forcible return of some 40,000 Kampucheans; henceforth, all asylum seekers were to allowed to enter.³⁶⁸ Likewise, the unnerving prospect

³⁶² Lauterpacht & Bethlehem, '*Non-refoulement:* Opinion', para. 104.
³⁶³ Durieux & McAdam, above n. 361, 13; See also above, Ch. 5.
³⁶⁴ Temporary Protection Directive, arts. 3(2), 6(2).
³⁶⁵ UNHCR, 'Protection of Refugees in Mass Influx Situations: Overall Protection Framework', UN doc. EC/GC/01/4 (19 Feb. 2001), paras. 6, 13; Executive Committee Conclusion No. 19 (XXXI) (1980) on Temporary Refuge, para. (a); Executive Conclusion No. 74 (1994), para. (r).
³⁶⁶ Executive Committee Conclusion No. 22 (1981); Executive Committee Conclusion No. 74 (1994), para. (r); Executive Committee Conclusion No. 100 (2004), para. (i).
³⁶⁷ The practical necessity for UNHCR to involve other States in the provision of material and political support for countries of first asylum has clear implications for the manner in which UNHCR can seek to uphold the basic principle. See Coleman, N., '*Non-Refoulement* Revised: Renewed Review of the Status of *Non-Refoulement* as Customary International Law', 5 *EJML* 23 (2003). However, there is insufficient State practice to conclude, as Coleman does, that a new customary international norm of *non-refoulement* has emerged excepting States from this obligation in situations of mass influx. Instruments such as the EU Temporary Protection Directive seem to negate this proposition. Eggli queries whether a mass influx emergency could ever constitute a 'public emergency which threatens the life of the nation', such that it would permit the declaration of a state of emergency and the suspension of fundamental human rights. She notes that for such a condition to be met, the emergency would have to threaten the nation as a whole; measures taken would have to be strictly required by the exigencies of the situation and proportionate to the dangers posed by the emergency, both as a matter of degree and duration: Eggli, *Mass Refugee Influx*, above **n. 6**, Ch. 5. Durieux & McAdam, above n. 361, 20, support this view.
³⁶⁸ See *Report* of the Secretary-General: UN doc. A/34/627 (1949), para. 48; Annex 1, para. 8.

of a repeat operation on behalf of Kurdish refugees imminently leaving northern Iraq for Turkey was a factor in the decision to establish a security zone, thereby removing or attenuating the factor of risk that would otherwise have triggered the principle of *non-refoulement*, if not its application in the particular circumstances.[369] In 1999, in response to threatened border closures by the Former Yugoslavian Republic of Macedonia, UNHCR took the unprecedented move of coordinating an international Humanitarian Evacuation Programme (and later a Humanitarian Transfer Programme) for thousands of refugees fleeing Kosovo. This novel strategy in international protection, and a shift in UNHCR's traditional practice of keeping refugees within the region of displacement, saw the temporary hosting of 92,000 refugees by 29 States.[370] UNHCR described it as an example of solidarity and burden-sharing, evidencing 'an exemplary political will to avert a risk of destabilisation created by the presence of large numbers of refugees in precarious circumstances'.[371] Others criticized it as 'an acceptance and therefore implicit condoning of Macedonian policy to reject refugees at the border until their transfer had been arranged'.[372] Some years earlier in the Executive Committee, the Netherlands delegation had expressed the general view that UNHCR's '[i]nsistence on the protection of refugees' rights should come before the understandable urge to provide relief'.[373] While it may be argued that UNHCR must be attuned to the political realities of a given situation and should not insist on abstract legal norms at the expense of compromise protection responses, it is also important that UNHCR retain its independence and assert its mandate to promote international law, properly characterizing acts of *refoulement* instead of reverting to the language of admission. In the case of the former Yugoslavia, UNHCR ultimately favoured practical solutions and compromise to secure protection over legal principle.[374]

---

[369] Both art. II(4), 1969 OAU Convention and paras. 3 and 4 of Council of Europe Resolution 67 (14) acknowledge that States may have difficulty in fulfilling their obligations without international co-operation. Cf. Fonteyne, J.-P., 'Burden-Sharing: An Analysis of the Nature and Function of International Solidarity in Cases of Mass Influx of Refugees', 8 *Aust. YB Int'l Law* 162 (1983).

[370] Mr Schatzer (IOM): UN doc. A/AC.96/SR.540 (1999).

[371] UNHCR, 'Annual Theme: Strengthening Partnership to Ensure Protection, Also in relation to Security', UN doc. A/AC.96/923 (14 Sept. 1999), para. 18.

[372] Coleman, above n. 367, 39, referring also to Amnesty International's 1999 report on the protection of Kosovo refugees in Macedonia (AI Index EUR 65/03/99), 11; Suhrke, A., Barutciski, M., Sandison, P. & Garlock, R., *The Kosovo Refugee Crisis: An Independent Evaluation of UNHCR's Emergency Preparedness and Response*, UNHCR, EPAU/2000/001, Feb. 2000, Part 6 (the page numbers cited in Coleman, do not match those in the Report published by UNHCR). Coleman (55) argues that European States' imposition of visa requirements on persons seeking to flee formed 'at least a major barrier to entry of this mass influx', and that the airlift operation for Kosovar refugees 'condoned mass rejection at the frontier, and formed a participation in a practice contrary to the previous protection-before-burden-sharing tradition'.

[373] Mr van Wulfften Palthe (Netherlands): UN doc. A/AC.96/SR.526, para. 8 (1998).

[374] A US diplomat who led negotiations about refugee admissions during the Kosovo crisis stated: 'UNHCR was impossibly dogmatic on the Blace question. I told them, you can't solve that problem by citing chapter and verse from the Convention': Suhrke, Barutciski, Sandison & Garlock,

Tanzania has been one of the strongest proponents of the 'contingency' of *non-refoulement* in mass influx situations, premising its capacity to provide international protection on financial assistance by other States. In 1996, the Tanzanian delegate to the Executive Committee stated that mass refugee influxes 'had caused tremendous destruction to the surrounding environment, increased the insecurity of the Tanzanian people and had been a political as well as social burden on the Government'.[375] It noted the 'heavy responsibilities' which international law placed on asylum countries,[376] and warned that it could not continue supporting refugees without financial support from the international community.[377] A year later, the same representative stated that: 'While Tanzania would continue to accept genuine refugees and to endeavour to fulfil its international obligations in that regard, the burden of asylum could endanger national security, exacerbate tensions between States and cause extensive damage to the environment and infrastructures.'[378] Again in 2002, the Tanzanian representative maintained that 'host States must ensure that refugees and asylum-seekers were accorded due international protection, but that did not mean that the security concerns of the host country should be overlooked'.[379] The United States described the Great Lakes crisis, to which the Tanzanian remarks related, as severely testing and at times overturning the norms of refugee protection and voluntary repatriation.[380] The Swiss delegation regarded the situation as 'wholly foreign to the circumstances envisaged by those who had drafted the 1951 Convention', and accordingly UNHCR's decisions had to be 'evaluated in that context rather than according to the criteria for an ideal refugee operation'.[381]

Other States have also voiced difficulties in providing for refugees without financial aid. Pakistan explained that without international solidarity, 'the fragile

The Kosovo Refugee Crisis, above n. 372, Part 6, cited in Coleman, above n. 367, 39. Suhrke, Barutciski, Sandison, & Garlock also report that some UNHCR staff recognized that its agreement to evacuation programmes could be characterized as submission to host government demands: ibid., Part 6, although the official line was that evacuation was an appropriate burden sharing mechanism: Briefing to the Security Council, by Mrs Sadako Ogata, United Nations High Commissioner for Refugees, (5 May 1999), 2.

[375] Mr Mwambulukutu (United Republic of Tanzania): UN doc. A/AC.96/SR.510, para. 14 (1996). For other accounts of the damage caused by refugees: Mr Sembereka (Malawi): UN doc. A/AC.96/SR.510, para. 25 (1996); Mr Momanyi (Observer for Kenya): UN doc. A/AC.96/SR.511, para. 11 (1996); Mr Aleem (Sudan): UN doc. A/AC.96/SR.511, para. 33 (1996); Mr N'Goran (Observer for Côte d'Ivoire): UN doc. A/AC.96/SR.511, para. 48 (1996); Mr Miguil (Observer for Djibouti): UN doc. A/AC.96/SR.511, para. 52 (1996).

[376] Mr Mwambulukutu (United Republic of Tanzania): UN doc. A/AC.96/SR.510, para. 16 (1996).   [377] Ibid., para. 18.

[378] Mr Mwambulukutu (United Republic of Tanzania): UN doc. A/AC.96/SR.520, para. 77 (1997).

[379] Mr Seif Khatib (United Republic of Tanzania): UN doc. A/AC.96/SR.567, para. 60 (2002).

[380] Ms Oakley (United States): UN doc. A/AC.96/SR.516, para. 48 (1997).

[381] Mr Gyger (Switzerland): UN doc. A/AC.96/SR.518, para. 17 (1997). Cf. views of Ireland (Ms Anderson), ibid., paras. 4–5: 'While acknowledging the pain and complexity of the recent history of the Great Lakes region, the international community could not fail to speak out when Governments violated their obligations under international law if it was not to erode the fundamental human rights and humanitarian principles which were the bedrock of policy.'

economies of the South would be unable to fulfil their humanitarian obliga-tions'.[382] In 2000, it closed its borders, citing a lack of support by the international community for the two million Afghan refugees it had already admitted.[383] Tunisia stated that 'it was unrealistic to believe that certain countries of the South could escape their economic marginalization when they had had to cope with mass influxes of refugees'.[384] Côte d'Ivoire also noted its difficulties in ensuring refugee protection 'at a time when food aid was suffering drastic reduc-tions and income-generating projects were not producing the desired results'.[385] Zimbabwe asserted that '[d]eveloping countries were prepared to grant asylum provided that the burden on their economies was not too great and assistance was forthcoming from UNHCR, which in turn was funded by member States'.[386]

Industrialized States have countered claims of contingency by insisting that 'there should be no mitigation of the absolute responsibility of States to observe the international principles of behaviour towards refugees, [but] there must also be a greater commitment to preventive approaches and increased readiness to help receiving countries cope'.[387] The EU has emphasized that responsibility-sharing 'must not be a prerequisite for respecting the fundamental principles of refugee and human rights law, including asylum, non-refoulement and family unity',[388] and the Council of Europe has affirmed that States' obligation to respect the prin-ciple of *non-refoulement* 'is not dependent on burden-sharing arrangements between states'.[389] While, as a matter of law, international protection is not *con-tingent* on burden-sharing, there is some acknowledgment that practical responses to alleviate the pressure on countries of first asylum may be necessary to ensure that the principle is not violated. The Humanitarian Evacuation Programme in Kosovo is one such example.

Despite concerns about providing protection to large numbers of refugees, most States faced with a mass influx will respect the principle of *non-refoulement*, if nothing else.[390] Although such States voice a desire for burden-sharing, in practice, their response to large numbers of refugees has not been made contingent on it. The element of contingency tends to relate to what *other* rights are granted apart from *non-refoulement*, and these may depend on the level of international assistance offered. It is therefore important to distinguish carefully between situations of mass influx and other situations where a failure to apply the principle has led to protest.

---

[382] Mr Khan (Pakistan): UN doc. A/AC.96/SR.527, para. 12 (1998).
[383] See references in Hathaway, *Rights of Refugees*, (2005), 281–2.
[384] Mr Morjane (Tunisia): UN doc. A/AC.96/SR.527, para. 32 (1998).
[385] Mr N'Goran (Observer for Côte d'Ivoire): UN doc. A/AC.96/SR.511, para. 50 (1996).
[386] Mr Mukaro (Zimbabwe): UN doc. A/AC.96/SR.530, para. 61 (1998).
[387] Ms Anderson (Ireland): UN doc. A/AC.96/SR.518, para. 5 (1997).
[388] Mr Kreid (Austria, on behalf of the EU): UN doc. A/AC.96/SR.525, para. 45 (1998); see also Ms Haaland Matlary (Norway): UN doc. A/AC.96/SR.526, para. 34 (1998); Ms Anderson (Ireland): UN doc. A/AC.96/SR.528, para. 1 (1998); Mr Brylle (Denmark): UN doc. A/AC.96/SR.528, para. 54 (1998).
[389] Council of Europe Committee of Ministers, 'Recommendation No. R (2000) 9 on Temporary Protection', (3 May 2000) preambular para. 8.   [390] See Ch. 7.

6.2 TEMPORARY PROTECTION[391]

The term 'temporary protection' gained prominence during the 1990s in relation to the crisis in the former Yugoslavia,[392] but the practice it describes is simply another link in the historical chain of protecting people fleeing generalized violence and civil war.[393] The contemporary international law understanding of 'temporary protection' is based predominantly on European practice, and describes the exceptional, emergency, time-bound response of granting protection to a mass influx of asylum seekers fleeing armed conflict, endemic violence, or a serious risk of systematic or generalized violations of human rights.[394] UNHCR argues that temporary protection should be premised on the receiving State's normal asylum procedures being overwhelmed by the large number of people seeking protection, such that individual status determination procedures under the 1951 Convention are necessarily suspended until processing may resume in the usual way.[395] By contrast, although EU law recognizes that the inability of national asylum systems to absorb a mass influx of asylum seekers is a common feature of mass influx, it is not a prerequisite for temporary protection in that region.[396] Importantly, both regard

---

[391] See also s. 4 above.

[392] For an overview, see Fitzpatrick, J., 'Temporary Protection of Refugees: Elements of a Formalized Regime', 94 *AJIL* 279 (2000); Eggli, *Mass Refugee Influx*, above n. 361; 139–43; Kerber, K., 'Temporary Protection: An Assessment of the Harmonisation Policies of European Union Member States', 9 *IJRL* (1997); Marx, R., Temporary Protection—Refugees from Former Yugoslavia: International Protection or Solution Orientated Approach?', ECRE, Jun. 1994; Kjaerum, M., 'Temporary Protection in Europe in the 1990s', 6 *IJRL* 444 (1994); Luca, D., 'Questioning Temporary Protection, together with a Selected Bibliography on Temporary Refuge/Temporary Protection', 6 *IJRL* 535 (1994); Thorburn, J., 'Transcending Boundaries: Temporary Protection and Burden-Sharing in Europe', 7 *IJRL* 459 (1995).

[393] On the principle of temporary refuge, see s. 2 above. Fitzpatrick observed that, in the absence of a harmonized temporary protection regime, States reinvented the system of protection each time a mass influx occurred, tailoring its application and scope to domestic and international pressures, rather than according to a formal and predictable legal regime: Fitzpatrick, 'Temporary Protection', above note, 281.

[394] Temporary Protection Directive, arts. 2(a), (c), (d). Curiously, even though the inherent nature of temporary protection is that it is granted in the absence of individual status determination, the Directive provides that certain people may be excluded: art. 28. Note that some States have created temporary visa regimes, which differ markedly in terms of their purpose, beneficiaries, and entitlement (for example, Australia's Temporary Protection Visa (TPV) and the United States' Temporary Protected Status (TPS)). These do not fall within the international law concept of temporary protection. TPS, for example, may be granted to eligible nationals of *designated* countries. It has never been used as an admissions programme: Fitzpatrick, J., 'Temporary Protection', above n. 392, referring to 8 USC §1254a(c)(5); see also at 285. The Secretary of Homeland Security may 'designate' a country in which there has been an environmental disaster or other circumstances preventing the safe return of nationals: INA §244, 8 USC §1254. To date, TPS has only been granted to persons already in the United States on the date of designation, and has not been used to facilitate the admission of persons outside the United States.

[395] UNHCR Global Consultations, 'Protection of Refugees in Mass Influx Situations: Overall Protection Framework', UN doc. EC/GC/01/4 (2001), para. 14.

[396] Art. 2(a) of the Temporary Protection Directive states that temporary protection may apply '*in particular* if there is...a risk that the asylum system will be unable to process this influx without

temporary protection as being premised on (eventual) return.[397] In this respect, the international/European concept differs from the South East Asian model of temporary refuge, commonly employed during the 1970s and 1980s, which was initially premised on third country resettlement, and only later joined by voluntary or involuntary repatriation in the aftermath of the Comprehensive Plan of Action.[398] The international/European version of temporary protection is further distinguished by being linked to admission to State territory, rather than to camps, whereas temporary refuge was contingent on guarantees by others that the State providing refuge would not pay the costs, and would not bear any residual burden.[399] Temporary protection may also be contrasted to the African practice of granting *prima facie* refugee status to members of a mass influx.[400]

6.2.1 Status

In theory, temporary protection is not an attempt to displace or renegotiate the 1951 Convention's rules and standards, but rather is a pragmatic response intended to clarify the application of the principle of *non-refoulement* in certain circumstances, and to prioritize the granting of particular rights to persons arriving *en masse*.[401] Under the Temporary Protection Directive, beneficiaries receive a status

adverse effects for its efficient operation' (emphasis added). This reflects a compromise position, based on the reluctance of Germany, France, Italy, Austria, and the United Kingdom to accept overwhelmed procedures as a prerequisite for temporary protection: Council Docs. 6128/01 ASILE 15 (16 Feb. 2001), 3; 6709/01 ASILE 22 (5 Mar. 2001), 3, as cited in Durieux & Hurwitz, above n. 361, 145. This, of course, provides States with greater discretion in determining the existence of a mass influx.

[397] Temporary Protection Directive, art. 4(1). However, the Directive does permit individuals who have arrived as part of a mass influx to lodge a claim for Convention or subsidiary protection status. Art. 17(1) provides: 'Persons enjoying temporary protection must be able to lodge an application for asylum at any time.' This is at odds with the idea in art. 2(a) that a key reason for instituting temporary protection is 'a risk that the asylum system will be unable to process this influx without adverse effects for its efficient operation'. This reinforces Fitzpatrick's concern that States may resort to temporary protection as an alternative to refugee status determination and thereby dilute entitlements. Fitzpatrick, 'Temporary Protection', above n. 392. If the asylum claim is unsuccessful, the individual must continue to enjoy temporary protection until that status expires: art. 19(2). See also discussion at s. 4 above.

[398] See further the 2nd. edition of this work, Ch. 5.

[399] In effect, temporary refuge for Indo-Chinese refugees was bought and paid for by (mostly) western countries, on terms which kept the majority of asylum seekers away from their frontiers while leaving them able also to pick and choose among candidates for permanent settlement.

[400] See Durieux & McAdam, above n. 361; Durieux & Hurwitz, above n. 361. This chapter discusses the current international law notion of temporary protection, which is premised on the European model. For the South East Asian practice of temporary refuge, see the 2nd. edition of this work, Ch. 5.

[401] See the Proposal for a Council Directive on Minimum Standards for Giving Temporary Protection in the Event of a Mass Influx of Displaced Persons and on Measures Promoting a Balance of Efforts between Member States in Receiving Such Persons and Bearing the Consequences thereof', COM (2000) 303 final (24 May 2000), O.J. 2000 C311, para. 1.4, which clarifies that temporary protection is not a third form of protection (in addition to subsidiary protection and Convention-based protection), but 'a component of the system, and more specifically a tool enabling the system to operate smoothly and not collapse under a mass influx. It is accordingly a tool in the service of a common European asylum system and of the full operation of the Geneva Convention.' At the international level, Executive Committee Conclusion No. 22 (1981) sets out basic standards of

that is a 'middle ground' between that of an asylum seeker and a Convention refugee.[402] They are entitled to housing, social welfare, some medical care, and access to education.[403] Access to the labour market is conditional on the Member States' right to 'give priority to EU citizens and citizens of States bound by the Agreement on the European Economic Area and also to legally resident third-country nationals who receive unemployment benefit'.[404] The definition of 'family' is broader than under the Qualification Directive,[405] and family members described in paragraph (a) (spouse and minor children) have an automatic right to reunification, while those in paragraph (b) (other close relatives) may be reunited, depending on 'the extreme hardship they would face if the reunification did not take place'.[406]

Crucially, temporary protection under the Directive is carefully circumscribed by a trigger mechanism. The Directive does not take effect unless the Council of the EU designates a particular flow as constituting a 'mass influx'.[407] This, perhaps, explains the relatively generous entitlements for beneficiaries, since access to such rights can be carefully controlled.

To date, the Temporary Protection Directive has not been activated. If and when it is, it will be important that it is utilized carefully and in a principled manner, lest it become a poor substitute for Convention protection. Even though article 17(1) permits beneficiaries of temporary protection to lodge an asylum claim at any time, there is no obligation on Member States to adjudicate an asylum claim within a particular period. Furthermore, under article 19(1), Member States may withdraw the higher temporary protection status while an asylum claim is under consideration, which itself may act as a disincentive to apply for protection on an individual basis.[408] Indeed, when ethnic cleansing in Bosnia forced masses of displaced persons to western Europe, temporary protection—and its focus on return as the most appropriate solution—provided the rationale for 'a more limited range of rights and benefits . . . in the initial stage than would customarily be accorded to refugees granted asylum under the Convention and the 1967 Protocol'.[409]

---

treatment for asylum seekers arriving *en masse*. Its value must, however, be qualified by the fact that it was drafted in the specific context of the mass exodus from Indo-China from the mid-1970s, a region in which the majority of States were not party to the 1951 Convention.

[402] Durieux & Hurwitz, above n. 361, 149.

[403] Temporary Protection Directive, arts. 8–16.   [404] Ibid., art. 12.

[405] Ibid., art. 15(1): '(a) the spouse of the sponsor or his/her unmarried partner in a stable relationship, where the legislation or practice of the Member State concerned treats unmarried couples in a way comparable to married couples under its law relating to aliens; the minor unmarried children of the sponsor or of his/her spouse, without distinction as to whether they were born in or out of wedlock or adopted; (b) other close relatives who lived together as part of the family unit at the time of the events leading to the mass influx, and who were wholly or mainly dependent on the sponsor at the time.' Cf. Qualification Directive, art. 2(h).

[406] Temporary Protection Directive, arts. 15(2), (3).

[407] Ibid., art. 5. Durieux & Hurwitz suggest this may be the Directive's 'fundamental weakness': above n. 361, 148.   [408] Ibid., 153.

[409] UNHCR, 'Note on International Protection', UN doc. A/AC.96/830, 7 Sept. 1994, para. 46.

Fitzpatrick argued that it would have been feasible at the time of the arrivals to process the claims in the usual way instead of allowing the situation to drag on.[410]

There is thus a tension between the use of temporary protection as a rapid humanitarian response mechanism, on the one hand, and, on the other, as a means of tightly controlling the beginning and end points of protection, while simultaneously diluting entitlements. Whereas eligibility for temporary protection is typically much broader than under the 1951 Convention, the rights accorded to beneficiaries may be more limited. Temporary protection may thus be employed as 'part of a strategy to de-legalize refugee protection and to relocate it in the realm of politics and humanitarian assistance'.[411]

6.3 *NON-REFOULEMENT* THROUGH TIME?

However labelled, the concept of temporary refuge/temporary protection as the practical consequence of *non-refoulement* through time provides, first, the necessary theoretical nexus between the admission of refugees and the attainment of a lasting solution. It establishes, *a priori*, no hierarchy in the field of solutions, but allows a pragmatic, flexible, yet principled approach to the idiosyncrasies of each situation. So, for example, it does not rule out the eventual local integration or third country resettlement of all or a proportion of a mass influx in the State of first refuge, acting in concert with others and pursuant to principles of international solidarity and equitable burden-sharing.[412] Secondly, the concept provides a platform upon which to build principles of protection for refugees pending a durable solution, whereby minimum rights and standards of treatment may be secured.

Without underestimating the necessity to ensure that regimes for the reception and treatment of refugees and asylum seekers conform with the requirements of international law, words such as 'refuge' and 'protection' may offer some advantages over any comparable use of the word 'asylum' in situations of mass influx. Asylum is undefined; it can be used broadly to signify protection of refugees, or it can be used in the narrow sense of a durable or permanent solution, involving residence and lasting protection against the exercise of jurisdiction by the State of origin. A receiving State called upon to grant 'asylum' to large numbers may well demur; admission is more likely to be facilitated by reference to the norm of *non-refoulement* and to its manifestation as refuge or protection in the dynamic sense, through time, pending arrangements for whatever solution is appropriate to the particular problem. The peremptory character of *non-refoulement* makes it independent of principles of solidarity and burden-sharing, but these cannot be

---

[410] Fitzpatrick 'Temporary Protection', above n. 392, 289.   [411] Ibid., 281.

[412] These principles may find expression not just in offers of resettlement, but also in financial and material assistance, moral and political support.

ignored in a society of interdependent States.[413] In situations of large-scale influx, protection cannot cease with the fact of admission; on the contrary, it must move towards solutions in full knowledge of the political and practical consequences which result from a State abiding by *non-refoulement*.

The political and legal reality of mass influx is that States generally have not undertaken, and foreseeably will not undertake, an obligation to grant asylum in the sense of a lasting solution.[414] The peremptory norm of *non-refoulement* secures admission and, in the individual case, may raise the presumption or at least a reasonable expectation that a local durable solution will be forthcoming. In the case of large-scale movements, however, no such presumption is raised. In attaining its present universal and peremptory character, *non-refoulement* has separated itself from asylum in the sense of a lasting solution. *Non-refoulement* through time is nonetheless the core element both promoting admission and protection, and simultaneously emphasizing the responsibility of nations at large to find the solutions. Thus, in admitting large numbers of persons in need of protection and in scrupulously observing *non-refoulement*, the State of first admission can be seen as acting on behalf of the international community.

The concept of temporary refuge/temporary protection in the context of large movements, thus stands paradoxically as both the link and the line between the peremptory, normative aspects of *non-refoulement* and the continuing discretionary aspect of a State's right in the matter of asylum as a permanent or lasting solution, and in the treatment to be accorded to those in fact admitted. As Fitzpatrick observed:

For refugee agencies such as the United Nations High Commissioner for Refugees, TP serves as a short-term strategy to secure the immediate physical safety of refugees and a way station to more durable protection. But where TP is offered as a diluted substitute protection for Convention refugees, it represents a threat to the 1951 refugee regime.... States, especially those under pressure from domestic constituencies preoccupied with migration, hope that TP will help them save costs on status determination, reduce social and economic benefits to asylum seekers, resist full integration of those who are granted asylum, and prioritize their rapid repatriation . . . Yet states also remain skeptical about formalizing temporary protection, since international TP obligations might expand the numbers of

---

[413] Note, however, that in the debate on international solidarity in 1988, the Sub-Committee left for further discussion in plenary the following proposed operative paragraph, in which the Executive Committee would have underlined, 'that, while international solidarity is important for the satisfactory resolution of refugee problems, *the absence of solidarity cannot serve as the pretext for failing to respect basic humanitarian principles*': *Report* of the Sub-Committee of the Whole on International Protection: UN doc. A/AC.96/717, (3 Oct. 1988), para. 35, (emphasis added). As finally adopted, para. 4 of Executive Committee Conclusion No. 52 (1988) merely recalled that, 'the respect for fundamental humanitarian principles is an obligation for all members of the international community, it being understood that the principle of international solidarity is of utmost importance to the satisfactory implementation of these principles'.

[414] Hailbronner attributes refusal to accept a treaty-based asylum obligation to fear of 'restriction of political decision-making through the concept of an individual right': Hailbronner, '*Non-Refoulement* and "humanitarian Refugees",' above n. 6, 347.

forced migrants eligible for legal protection against repatriation and pledges of international solidarity may create unpredictable and politically costly future burdens.[415]

It would appear, therefore, that the real argument against full applicability of the Convention regime to refugees in mass influx situations is a legal-political one.[416]

7. *Non-refoulement* as a principle of customary international law

While there is little difficulty in showing the extent of *treaty* obligations of *non-refoulement*, establishing the status of the principle in general or customary international law is more complex. In 1954, twenty-seven States participating in the UN Conference on the Status of Stateless Persons unanimously expressed the view that the *non-refoulement* provision of the 1951 Convention was 'an expression of the generally accepted principle' of non-return; for that reason, it was considered unnecessary to include an equivalent article for stateless persons.[417] That assessment was premature, but, as shown above,[418] the principle of *non-refoulement* has since been reiterated and refined, included in a range of regional refugee, human rights, and extradition treaties, repeatedly endorsed in a variety of international fora, and its violation protested by UNHCR and States.

Both article 33 of the 1951 Convention and article 3 of the 1984 Convention against Torture are of a 'fundamentally norm-creating character such as could be regarded as forming the basis of a general rule of law', as that phrase was used by the International Court of Justice in the *North Sea Continental Shelf* cases.[419] The prohibition on *refoulement* to torture or cruel, inhuman or degrading treatment or punishment is absolute.[420] That *refoulement* may be permitted under the 1951 Convention in exceptional circumstances does not deny this premise, but rather indicates the boundaries of discretion.[421] So far as both provisions are formally

---

[415] Fitzpatrick, 'Temporary protection', above n. 392, 280.

[416] See, for example, 'Protracted Refugee Situations: Impact and Challenges', speech by the Assistant High Commissioner for Refugees, Mr Kemal Morjane, Copenhagen (23 Oct. 2002), 1: 'Camps and idle populations do not simply appear as a natural consequence of forced displacement—they are established in response to political realities and constraints' which stem from a lack of political will to resolve conflicts and to find durable solutions for refugees'.

[417] Final Act, UN Conference on the Status of Stateless Persons: 360 *UNTS* 117.

[418] See above, Ch. 5.   [419] ICJ *Rep.*, (1969), 3, 42.

[420] In *N* v. *Secretary of State for the Home Department* [2005] UKHL 31, para. 48, Lord Hope described this as one of the basic principles of the European Court's jurisprudence on art. 3 (although it is being challenged in *Ramzy*), see abov n. 197 and accompanying text.

[421] In 1984, the Cartagena Declaration included a reference to the actual or imminent *jus cogens* status of the principle of *non-refoulement*; see Conclusions and Recommendations, III, 5; below Annexe 2 No. 7. In 1985, the High Commissioner observed in his report to the General Assembly that the principle of non-return had crystallized to the status of a peremptory norm of international law, unrestricted by geographical or territorial limitations: *Report* of the United Nations High Commissioner for Refugees: UN E/1985/62 (1985), paras. 22–3. A peremptory norm is one

addressed to the contracting parties, the universality of the principle of *non-refoulement* has nevertheless been a constant emphasis of other instruments, including declarations, recommendations, and resolutions at both international and regional levels. The proof of international customary law requires consistency and generality of practice, but no particular duration; universality and complete uniformity are not required, but the practice must be accepted as law. In many cases, this *opinio juris* may be inferred from the evidence of a general practice, or a consensus in the literature.[422]

The evidence relating to the meaning and scope of *non-refoulement* in its treaty sense amply supports the conclusion that today the principle forms part of general international law. There is substantial, if not conclusive, authority that the principle is binding on all States, independently of specific assent. State practice before 1951 is, at the least, equivocal as to whether, in that year, article 33 of the Convention reflected or crystallized a rule of customary international law.[423] State practice since then, however, is persuasive evidence of the concretization of a customary rule, even in the absence of any formal judicial pronouncement.[424] In this context, special regard should also be paid to the practice of international organizations, such as the UN General Assembly and the UNHCR. General Assembly resolutions dealing with the annual report of the High Commissioner—and consistently endorsing the principle of *non-refoulement*—tend to be adopted by consensus. While consensus decision-making denotes the absence of formal dissent,[425] it still allows States the opportunity to express opposing views in debate and in summary records.[426] No formal or informal opposition to the principle of *non-refoulement* is to be found, and

'accepted and recognized by the international community of States as a whole as a norm from which no derogation is permitted and which can be modified only by a subsequent norm of general international law having the same character': art. 53, 1969 Vienna Convention on the Law of Treaties. Although a sound case can be made for the customary international law status of the principle of *non-refoulement*, its claim to be part of *jus cogens* is far less certain, and it may be that little is likely to be achieved by insisting on its status as such. See, however, Allain, J., 'The *Jus Cogens* Nature of *Non-Refoulement*', 13 *IJRL* 533 (2001).

[422] See Brownlie, I., *Principles of Public International Law*, (6th edn., 2003), 8–10.

[423] This conclusion represents a modification of views first set out in Goodwin-Gill, *Movement of Persons*, 141. See also Lauterpacht & Bethlehem, '*Non-refoulement*:. Opinion'.

[424] See *United States Diplomatic and Consular Staff in Tehran*, ICJ *Rep.*, (1980), 3, at 41 (para. 88), in which the Court hints at the 'legal difficulties, in internal and international law' which might have resulted from the United States acceding to Iran's request for the extradition of the former Shah.

[425] The Special Committee on the Rationalization of the Procedures and Organization of the General Assembly concluded that 'the adoption of decisions and resolutions by consensus is desirable when it contributes to the effective and lasting settlement of differences, thus strengthening the authority of the United Nations'. The Committee emphasized, however, 'that the right of every Member State to set forth its views in full must not be prejudiced by this procedure': *Report* of the Special Committee, *GAOR*, 26th Sess., Supp. no. 26 (A/8426), (1971), paras. 28–9; Rules of Procedure of the General Assembly, A/520/Rev.12 (1974), annexe V, para. 104. See D'Amato, A., 'On Consensus', 8 *Can. YIL* 104 (1970); Buzan, B., 'Negotiating by Consensus: Developments in Techniques at the United Nations Conference on the Law of the Sea', 75 *AJIL* 324 (1981).

[426] On 16 Dec. 1981, the General Assembly adopted without a vote res. 36/148 on International Co-operation to Avert New Flows of Refugees, on the recommendations of the Special Political Committee (*Report:* UN doc. A/36/790). In the course of debate in the Committee, a number of

where objection has been made on occasion to the protection and assistance activities of UNHCR, it has been founded on a challenge to the status as refugees of the individuals involved. UNHCR has recounted numerous instances when it has made representations to States not party to the 1951 Convention or 1967 Protocol, relying on the principle of *non-refoulement* as part of customary international law. States' responses have 'almost invariably' reflected an acceptance of the principle's normative character, and have frequently 'sought to explain a case of actual or intended refoulement by providing additional clarifications and/or by claiming that the person in question was not to be considered a refugee'.[427] Moreover, while a number of commentators have disagreed as to the legal inferences to be drawn from the practice of States, none has been able to dispute the factual record.[428]

Lauterpacht and Bethlehem's recent comprehensive study on the scope and content of the principle of *non-refoulement* further supports these conclusions, and proposes an even wider formulation of the principle based on the proscription of return to torture or cruel, inhuman or degrading treatment or punishment under human rights law. They assert that *non-refoulement* has crystallized as a norm of customary international law in the following terms:

(a) No person shall be rejected, returned, or expelled in any manner whatsoever where this would compel him or her to remain in or return to a territory where substantial grounds can be shown for believing that he or she would face a real risk of being subjected to torture or cruel, inhuman or degrading treatment or punishment. This principle allows of no limitation or exception.

(b) In circumstances which do not come within the scope of paragraph 1, no person seeking asylum may be rejected, returned, or expelled in any manner whatever where this would compel him or her to remain in or to return to a territory where he or she may face a

---

delegates made statements in explanation which included substantial reservations regarding the draft resolution; other delegates expressly stated that they would have abstained, had the draft been put to the vote: UN doc. A/SPC/36/SR.45, paras. 49ff.

[427] UNHCR 'The Principle of *Non-Refoulement* as a Norm of Customary International Law: Response to the Questions Posed to UNHCR by the Federal Constitutional Court of the Federal Republic of Germany in Cases 2 BvR 1938/93, 2 BvR 1953/93, 2 BvR 1954/93 (31 Jan. 1994), para. 5. For examples, see above, Ch. 5, s. 2.5.

[428] For a detailed and cogent account of State practice, see Perluss, D. & Hartman, J., 'Temporary Refuge: Emergence of a Customary International Norm', 26 *Virg. JIL* 551 (1986). Contemporary criticism of the argument failed to address either the facts or the legal issues; for example, see Martin, D. A., 'Effects of International Law on Migration Policy and Practice', 23 *Int. Mig. Rev.* 547 (1989), who asserts (at 567) that Perluss & Hartmann (and Goodwin-Gill, G. S., '*Non-refoulement* and the new asylum seekers', 26 *Virg. JIL* 897 (1986)) 'essentially' propound the idea, 'hardly credible to the average citizen or to politicians and government officials', that international law forbids return if there is danger in the homeland. Both Perluss & Hartman, and Goodwin-Gill, in fact are somewhat more subtle. Martin further asserts (ibid., n. 62) that Hailbronner (above n. 6) 'offered a detailed examination of the evidence used', to conclude that practice does not support a norm of customary international law. In fact, Hailbronner scarcely comments at all on the extensive examples offered by Perluss & and Hartman, concentrating mostly on *municipal* law, limiting himself to disagreeing with their conclusions while dealing principally with an interesting, but peripheral issue, namely, the extent to which art. 3 ECHR50 had been (untill then) of little use to refugees. See also Hathaway, *Rights of Refugees*, (2005), 363ff.

threat of persecution or a threat to life, physical integrity, or liberty. Save as provided in paragraph 3, this principle allows of no limitation or exception.

(c) Overriding reasons of national security or public safety will permit a State to derogate from the principle expressed in paragraph 2 in circumstances in which the threat of persecution does not equate to and would not be regarded as being on a par with a danger of torture or cruel, inhuman or degrading treatment or punishment and would not come within the scope of other non-derogable customary principles of human rights. The application of these exceptions is conditional on the strict compliance with principles of due process of law and the requirement that all reasonable steps must first be taken to secure the admission of the individual concerned to a safe third country.[429]

While there is ample support in treaty law and jurisprudence for the widened scope of *non-refoulement* on the basis of torture, whether non-return to cruel, inhuman or degrading treatment or punishment has also become part of customary international law is more contentious. Lauterpacht and Bethlehem base their conclusions on the customary law scope of *non-refoulement* on the fact that over 150 States are party to at least one binding international instrument proscribing torture *and* cruel, inhuman or degrading treatment or punishment,[430] and because (somewhat circularly) 'the evidence points overwhelmingly to a broad formulation of the prohibition as including torture or cruel, inhuman or degrading treatment or punishment'—that is, a single prohibition.[431] The Human Rights Committee, for example, tends not to distinguish between the different

---

[429] Lauterpacht & Bethlehem, '*Non-refoulement:* Opinion', para. 253.

[430] In addition to being found in art. 3 CAT84, art. 7 ICCPR66 and art. 3 ECHR50 it is also contained in art. 5, UDHR48; art. 5(2) ACHR69; art. 4, EU Charter of Fundamental Rights; art. 2, 1948 Convention on the Prevention and Punishment of the Crime of Genocide, UNGA res. 260A (III), 9 Dec. 1948 (implicit in 'genocide'); art. 2, International Convention on the Suppression and Punishment of the Crime of Apartheid, 1015 *UNTS* 244; arts, 1, 2, Declaration on the Protection of All Persons from Being Subjected to Torture and Other Cruel, Inhuman or Degrading Treatment or Punishment, UNGA res. 3452 (XXX), 9 Dec. 1975; art. 5, 1981 African Charter on Human and Peoples' Rights, the 1985 Inter-American Convention to Prevent and Punish Torture; the 1987 European Convention for the Prevention of Torture and Inhuman or Degrading Treatment or Punishment, *ETS* No. 126, as amended; art. 37 CRC89; art. 10, 1990 International Convention on the Protection of the Rights of All Migrant Workers and Members of Their Families, UNGA res. 45/158, 18 Dec. 1990; art. 1, 1992 Declaration on the Protection of All Persons from Enforced Disappearances, UNGA res. 47/133, 18 Dec. 1992. For texts of the above instruments, see Brownlie & Goodwin-Gill, *Basic Documents on Human Rights.* See also the 1949 Geneva Conventions and 1977 Additional Protocols: GCI, arts. 3, 50; GCII, art. 51; GCIII, art. 130; GCIV, art.147; AP I, art. 75; APII, art. 4; texts in Roberts, A. & Guelff, R., *Documents on the Laws of War,* (3rd edn., 2000); and see further arts. 8(2)(a)(ii), 55(1)(b), Rome Statute of the International Criminal Court; art. 2, Statute of the International Criminal Tribunal for Former Yugoslavia; art. 2, Statute of the International Criminal Tribunal for Rwanda. The ICTY's pronouncements on the customary international law prohibition on torture are instructive; see, for example, *Prosecutor* v. *Furundzija* Case IT-95-17/1-T10 Trial Ct Judgment (10 Dec. 1998). See also Lauterpacht & Bethlehem, '*Non-refoulement:* Opinion', paras. 222–9.

[431] Lauterpacht & Bethlehem, '*Non-refoulement:* Opinion', para. 223, and generally paras. 222–9; Human Rights Committee, 'General Comment 24: Issues relating to Reservations Made upon Ratification or Accession to the Covenant or the Optional Protocols thereto, or in relation to Declarations under Article 41 of the Covenant', (4 Nov. 1994), para. 8; UNGA res. 39/118, 'Human

categories of treatment, instead regarding them as elements in a hierarchy of 'severe treatment' or 'ill-treatment',[432] with torture the most severe manifestation.[433] The UN Declaration on the Protection of All Persons from Being Subjected to Torture and Other Cruel, Inhuman or Degrading Treatment or Punishment identifies cruel, inhuman or degrading treatment or punishment as a form of treatment not sufficiently severe to amount to 'torture'.[434] Case law has given further meaning to the terms.[435] In the *Greek* case, the European Commission held that 'inhuman treatment' covers 'at least such treatment as deliberately causes severe suffering, mental or physical, which, in the particular situation, is unjustifiable'.[436] In *Pretty* v. *United Kingdom*, the European Court developed existing Strasbourg jurisprudence to describe 'degrading treatment' as occurring '[w]here treatment humiliates or debases an individual, showing a lack of respect for, or diminishing, his or her human dignity, or arouses feelings of fear, anguish or inferiority capable of breaking an individual's moral and physical resistance, it may be characterised as degrading and also fall within the prohibition of Article 3'.[437] If certain levels of severity are met, 'degrading treatment' might also encompass the denial or insufficient provision of basic services necessary to preserve dignity, including access to health, shelter, social security, and education for children.[438] Inhuman or degrading 'punishment' refers to ill-treatment imposed

---

Rights in the Administration of Justice', 14 Dec. 1984, para. 1. That art. 3 ECHR50 prevents removal to inhuman and degrading treatment or punishment is clearly accepted by States: see 'Observations of the Governments of Lithuania, Portugal, Slovakia and the United Kingdom intervening in Application No. 25424/05 Ramzy v. The Netherlands', para. 19. Note that in defining the critical elements of 'effective protection', the Lisbon Expert Roundtable included 'respect for fundamental human rights . . . in accordance with applicable international standards, including . . . no real risk that the person would be subjected to torture or to cruel, inhuman or degrading treatment or punishment': Lisbon Expert Roundtable, 'Summary Conclusions on the Concept of "Effective Protection" in the Context of Secondary Movements of Refugees and Asylum-Seekers', (9–10 Dec. 2002), para. 15(b).

[432] Nowak, M., *UN Covenant on Civil and Political Rights: CCPR Commentary* (1993) 135.

[433] *Ireland* v. *UK* (1979–80) 2 EHRR 25, para. 167, reflecting Declaration on the Protection of All Persons from Being Subjected to Torture; Anker, D. E., *Law of Asylum in the United States*, (3rd rev'd edn., 1999), 465, 482, 485; Suntinger, W., 'The Principle of *Non-Refoulement*: Looking Rather to Geneva than to Strasbourg?', 49 *Austrian J. Public Int'l L.* 203, 212 (1995).

[434] Art. 1(2) thus defines torture as 'an aggravated and deliberate form of cruel, inhuman or degrading treatment or punishment'; *Ireland* v. *UK* (1979–80) 2 EHRR 25, para. 167.

[435] On 'inhuman treatment', see *Greek* case (1969) 12 *Yearbook* 1, 186; on 'degrading treatment', see *East African Asians* (1973) 3 EHRR 76, para. 189.

[436] *Greek* case (1969) 12 *Yearbook* 1, 186.

[437] *Pretty* v. *UK* (2002) 35 EHRR 1, para. 52. See also *East African Asians* (1973) 3 EHRR 76, paras. 189, 195; *Ireland* v. *UK* (1979–80) 2 EHRR 25, para. 167; *Tyrer* v. *UK* (1979–80) 2 EHRR 1, para. 32. See also discussion in *R. (Limbuela)* v. *Secretary of State for the Home Department* [2005] UKHL 66, paras. 7 (Lord Bingham), 46, 54–5 (Lord Hope), 78 (Baroness Hale). In no case so far has the threat of degrading treatment alone given rise to a protection obligation: Pellonpää, M., 'ECHR Case-Law on Refugees and Asylum Seekers and Protection under the 1951 Convention: Similarities and Differences', Paper presented at the 4th Conference of the International Association of Refugee Law Judges, 'The Changing Nature of Persecution Conference', Bern, 2000, 146.

[438] Blake & Husain, *Immigration, Asylum and Human Rights*, above n. 196, para. 2.97; Schachter, O., 'Human Dignity as a Normative Concept', 77 *AJIL* 848, 851 (1983). This accords with the

as a reprimand or penalty, including where it is wholly disproportionate to the offence committed.

One difficulty with asserting a wider customary norm of *non-refoulement* relating to severe treatment is finding sufficient evidence of State practice. Certainly there are international and regional norms preventing return in those circumstances, but also some notable gaps.[439] Can it be said that all States respect a norm of general law preventing them from removing individuals who face a substantial risk of cruel, inhuman or degrading treatment or punishment? At first blush, this seems insupportable. There is ample evidence of States expelling individuals to considerable hardship and insecurity. The key lies, however, in the *legal* meaning of 'cruel, inhuman or degrading treatment or punishment', as established by international and regional jurisprudence. The European Court of Human Rights has adopted a narrow approach to these terms under article 3 ECHR50, such that ill-treatment on account of underlying social or political disorder,[440] or a severe paucity of resources,[441] will only satisfy the requisite level of severity in the most exceptional circumstances.[442] Article 3 does not preclude return to territories

---

approach in *R. (Limbuela)* v. *Secretary of State for the Home Department* [2005] UKHL 66; see also *Selçuk* v. *Turkey*, Application No. 23184/94, 23185/94, 24 Apr. 1998, para. 78; *Hajrizi Dzemajl* v. *Yugoslavia* Comm. No. 161/2000, CAT/C/29/D/161/2000, 21 Nov. 2002, para. 9.2. See generally McCourt, K. & Lambert, M., *Interpretation of the Definition of Torture or Cruel, Inhuman or Degrading Treatment or Punishment in the Light of European and International Case Law* (OMCT Europe, 30 Oct. 2004), Ch 2: <http://www.omct.org/>.

[439] Australia is exceptional in this respect. Australian law does not contain a prohibition on removal to torture, inhuman or degrading treatment or punishment. Asylum seekers may only claim protection on the basis of art. 1A(2) CSR51: Migration Act s. 36. By contrast, under the Extradition Act, the Minister must consider whether extraditing an individual would constitute removal to torture: Extradition Act 1988 (Cth), s. 22(3)(b).

[440] The mere existence of generalized violence is insufficient to satisfy art. 3: *HLR* v. *France* (1997) 26 EHRR 29, para. 42. See also *AD* v. *The Netherlands,* Comm. No. 96/1997 (24 Jan. 2000), CAT/C/23/D/96/1997, para. 7.2.

[441] *D* v. *UK* (1997) 24 EHRR 423, para. 54; *Henao* v. *The Netherlands*, Application No. 13669/03 (24 Jun. 2003). In *Larioshina* v. *Russian Federation*, Application No. 56869/00 (23 Apr. 2002), the European Court of Human Rights stated that in principle, a complaint against a wholly insufficient pension could raise an issue under art. 3 ECHR50. In *Moldovan* v. *Romania*, the European Court declared admissible a case in which Roma claimed that following the wilful destruction of their homes, their living conditions amounted to inhuman or degrading treatment: Application No. 64320/01 (3 Jun. 2003). In *Ayder* v. *Turkey*, the European Court found that the conditions in which the applicants' houses were burnt, and their resulting forced relocation, constituted inhuman and degrading treatment: Application No. 23656/94 (8 Jan. 2004).

[442] The only cases in which the Court has indicated that an individual should be permitted to remain on health grounds are *D* v. *UK* (above note) and *BB* v. *France*, Application No. 30930/96 (9 Mar. 1998); see also *Tatete* v. *Switzerland*, Application No. 41874/98 (18 Nov. 1998) on admissibility; cf. *Karara* v. *Finland*, Application No. 40900/98 (29 May 1998); *SCC* v. *Sweden*, Application No. 46553/99 (15 Feb. 2000); *Bensaid* v. *United Kingdom* (2001) 33 EHRR 205; *Henao* v. *The Netherlands*, Application No. 13669/03 (24 Jun. 2003); *Ndangoya* v. *Sweden*, Application No. 17868/03 (22 Jun. 2004); *Amegnigan* v. *The Netherlands*, Application No. 25629/04 (25 Nov. 2004). See also *N* v. *Secretary of State for the Home Department* [2005] UKHL 31; [2005] 2 AC 296.

which cannot guarantee the same level of rights as the European Convention, unless there will be a flagrant breach of the right in question on return.[443] The concept of inhuman and degrading treatment is thus carefully circumscribed.

The OAU Convention and the Cartagena Declaration both extend States' protection responsibilities beyond article 1A(2) of the 1951 Convention to encompass flight from 'external aggression, occupation, foreign domination or events seriously disturbing public order in either part or the whole of his country of origin or nationality',[444] and 'generalized violence, foreign aggression, internal conflicts, massive violation of human rights or other circumstances which have seriously disturbed public order'.[445] On the basis of their treaty obligations, most western States proscribe *refoulement* to torture or cruel, inhuman or degrading treatment or punishment,[446] while the United States proscribes *refoulement* to torture. Viewed in this light, the State practice of Australia appears as an aberration in otherwise consistent State practice. *Non-refoulement* under customary international law encompasses non-return to persecution *as well as* to cruel, inhuman or degrading treatment or punishment.

At the other extreme is the position taken by Hathaway. In his view, there is insufficient evidence to establish the principle of *non-refoulement*, however narrowly defined, as part of customary international law.[447] In other words, he does not accept that the prohibition on *refoulement* in article 33 of the 1951 Convention has crystallized as a customary norm. Attempting to counter evidence that no State has expelled refugees by arguing that *refoulement* is permissible in contemporary international law, he claims that 'the absence of an assertion that acts of *refoulement* are justified by legal norms is clearly not the same thing as the existence of state

---

[443] *Drozd and Janousek* v. *France and Spain* (1992) 14 EHRR 745, para.110; *Devaseelan* v. *Secretary of State for the Home Department* [2003] Imm AR 1, para. 108; *Salkic* v. *Sweden* Application No. 7702/04 (29 Jun. 2004); Piotrowicz, R. & van Eck, C., 'Subsidiary Protection and Primary Rights', 53 ICLQ 107, 129 (2004); Tomuschat C., 'A Right to Asylum in Europe', 13 *Human Rights Law Journal* 257, 260 (1992). In *Januzi* v. *Secretary of State for the Home Department* [2006] UKHL 5, the House of Lords held that a person may be removed where an internal flight alternative exists, even if the general standards of living in that part of the country are not as high as in the State where asylum was sought. The position would be different, however, 'if the lack of respect for human rights posed threats to his life or exposed him to the risk of inhuman or degrading treatment or punishment': para. 19 (Lord Bingham), see also para. 45 (Lord Nicholls). Other States have held that the treatment in the country of origin must reach a certain standard if the internal flight alternative is to be triggered: *Butler* v. *Attorney-General* [1999] NZAR 205, para. 50; *Refugee Appeal No. 71684/99* [2000] INLR 165, paras. 60–1; see also the Australian approach in *Randhawa* v. *Minister for Immigration, Local Government and Ethnic Affairs* (1994) 52 FCR 437, 442 (Black CJ), 450–51 (Beaumont J); *Perampalam* v. *Minister for Immigration and Multicultural Affairs* [1999] FCA 165, (1999) 84 FCR 274, 288; *Al-Amidi* v. *Minister for Immigration and Multicultural Affairs* [2000] FCA 1081, (2000) 177 ALR 506, 510.   [444] Art. I(2) OAU69.

[445] Cartagena Declaration, art. III(3).

[446] Canada prohibits *refoulement* to torture or to where there is a personal risk to life or a risk of cruel and unusual treatment or punishment: Immigration and Refugee Protection Act 2001, s. 97(1); art. 3 ECHR50 has been interpreted and applied so as to prohibit removal to torture or inhuman or degrading treatment or punishment.   [447] Hathaway, *Rights of Refugees* (2005), 363.

practice which affirms a duty not to send refugees back'.[448] The problem with this
position is that it ignores the lengths to which States have gone to characterize
returns as something 'other' than *refoulement*. An examination of State reports
to the Human Rights Committee and the Committee against Torture over the
past decade reveals that no State has ever described its removals, deportations,
expulsions—or refusals to admit—as *refoulement*. China, for example, has sought
to characterize Montagnard Vietnamese refugees as 'illegal immigrants' in order to
justify their deportation.[449] Similarly, during the Indo-Chinese exodus, a number
of the States which Hathaway describes as having 'routinely refused to be formally
bound to avoid *refoulement*'[450] went to great lengths to deny the refugee character
of the flows. A State that did not consider itself bound by the customary principle
of *non-refoulement* would have no reason to do this, since it would not regard the
refoulement of refugees as a breach of international law.[451]

Curiously, Hathaway's position has shifted over the past 15 years. In his first
monograph, although he was sceptical of an expanded refugee concept in customary international law, he recognized that there was some 'international legal consensus on an expanded conceptualization of refugee status based upon custom',
albeit at a relatively low level of commitment.[452] While he thought that Goodwin-
Gill's idea of a right to protection from *refoulement* overstated 'the extant scope of
customary law in regard to non-Convention refugees',[453] he nonetheless con-
tended that Hailbronner, who regarded a customary norm of temporary protection
as 'wishful legal thinking',[454] had overlooked 'the consensus at the global, regional,
and national levels in favour of *addressing in some way* the claims of those persons in
one's territory or at one's borders who fear harm in their country of origin as a result
of serious disturbances of public order'.[455] Drawing on UNHCR practice, international consensus at the Conference on Territorial Asylum, regional refugee
instruments, and 'relatively consistent state practice', he argued that there was

[448] Ibid., 364, 375. States, of course, do sometimes breach the principle and the General
Assembly has repeatedly expressed concern about violations of *non-refoulement*: UNGA res. 35/41
(25 Nov. 1980), preambular para. 7; UNGA res. 37/195 (18 Dec. 1982), para. 3; UNGA res. 42/109
(7 Dec. 1987), para. 2; UNGA res. 43/117 (8 Dec. 1988), para. 3; UNGA res. 51/75 (12 Dec. 1996),
para. 6; UNGA res. 52/132 (12 Dec. 1997), preambular para. 12; UNGA res. 57/183 (6 Feb. 2003),
para. 15; UNGA res. 58/149 (24 Feb. 2004), para. 16. On inconsistent practice which does not
'count' in the absence of a claim of right and generally, see *Nicaragua (Merits) Case*, ICJ *Rep.* (1986),
14, 108–9, paras. 206–8; Mendelson, M., 'The Formation of Customary International Law', 272
Hague *Recueil* 155, 275–7 (1998).
[449] See further above, Ch. 5, s. 2.5.1.
[450] Hathaway, *Rights of Refugees*, (2005), 364.
[451] See Schachter, O., *International Law in Theory and Practice*, (1991), 337–40, who argues that
on-going censure of certain conduct provides a sufficient pattern for the purposes of establishing customary international law; cf. Simma, B. & Alston, P., 'The Sources of Human Rights Law: Custom,
Jus Cogens, and General Principles', 12 *Aust. YBIL* 82 (1988–89).
[452] Hathaway, J. C., *The Law of Refugee Status*, (1991), 25.   [453] Ibid.
[454] Hailbronner, K., '*Non-Refoulement* and "Humanitarian" Refugees: Custormary International
Law or Wishful Legal Thinking?', 26 *Virginia JIL* 857 (1986); and see below, n. 466.
[455] Hathaway, *Law of Refugee Status*, 26.

general agreement that people 'who have been victimized by serious disturbances of public order in their country of origin' should be afforded '*some opportunity for special consideration*', and that '[n]o aspect of international practice has questioned the duty to examine their need for protection.'[456] He concluded:

> The level of commitment is lower than that suggested by Goodwin-Gill, but an intermediate category of refugee protection does now exist. The customary norm rooted in international usage is a right to be considered for temporary admission, whether by formal procedure or administrative discretion, *on the basis of a need for protection*. That is, customary international law precludes the making of decisions to reject or expel persons who come from nations in which there are serious disturbances of public order without explicit attention being paid to their humanitarian needs. This duty may be met through the granting of formal status as is contemplated by the three regional refugee accords, through the discretionary programs of 'B' status, special measures, or extended voluntary departure that exists in Western developed states, or by seeking the assistance of other states of the international community to share the burden of actual or impending refugee flows.[457]

In his 2005 monograph, Hathaway takes a very conservative approach to customary international law. Accordingly, his refusal there to regard *non-refoulement* as a principle of customary international law is unremarkable when one considers that the only human rights norm he believes has attained the status of customary international law is freedom from systemic racial discrimination.[458] Though noting that 'senior publicists' argue that freedom from genocide; slavery; extrajudicial execution or enforced disappearance; torture, cruel, inhuman, or degrading treatment or punishment; prolonged arbitrary detention; and serious unfairness in criminal prosecution are all part of customary international law, Hathaway rejects these because he can identify examples of State practice where these norms are violated.[459]

This reflects a misunderstanding of a basic tenet of customary international law. The International Court of Justice has affirmed that State practice does not have to be entirely consistent for a norm of customary international law to be established. Instead, State conduct that is inconsistent with a particular customary principle should generally be treated as a breach of that principle, not as an indication of a new rule. 'If a State acts in a way *prima facie* incompatible with a recognized rule, but defends its conduct by appealing to exceptions or justifications contained within the rule itself, then whether or not the State's conduct is in fact justifiable on that basis, the significance of that attitude is to confirm rather than to weaken the rule.'[460]

Furthermore, Hathaway relies mistakenly on the House of Lords decision in the *Roma Rights* case to support his position.[461] In that case, UK immigration officers

[456] Ibid.   [457] Ibid.   [458] Hathaway, *Rights of Refugees*, (2005), 36.
[459] Ibid., 36–9.   [460] *Nicaragua case*, ICJ *Rep.* (1986), para. 186.
[461] *R. (European Roma Rights Centre)* v. *Immigration Officer at Prague Airport (United Nations High Commissioner for Refugees intervening)* [2005] 2 AC 1, discussed in more detail in Ch. 7.

stationed at Prague airport had prevented Czech citizens of Roma origin from leaving the Czech Republic to seek asylum in the UK. One argument advanced by the appellants and UNHCR (as intervener) was that the UK had created a 'virtual frontier' in the Czech Republic, and that denying asylum seekers the opportunity to board planes was tantamount to rejection at the frontier pursuant to article 33 of the 1951 Convention. Hathaway argues that the House of Lords 'was insistent that despite the obvious benefit to at-risk persons of expanding the scope of the duty of *non-refoulement* beyond what Art. 33 requires, there simply was not sufficient evidence of relatively consistent state practice to substantiate a relevant customary norm'.[462] However, this ignores both the specific context and the precise ruling that was made. In the previous paragraph, the House of Lords *accepted* that the principle of *non-refoulement* forms part of customary international law, and that it encompasses non-rejection at the frontier.[463] In the instant case, though, the appellants could not take advantage of that norm because they had not yet left their country of origin and could not be said to be at the frontier of the United Kingdom, 'save in a highly metaphorical sense'.[464] The court then went on to determine whether there is 'a rule of customary international law which provides that if a national of country A, wishing to travel to country B to claim asylum, applies in country A to officials of country B, he may not be denied leave to enter country B without appropriate enquiry into the merits of his asylum claim'.[465] It was solely in response to *that* more limited question that the House of Lords rejected the existence of a rule of customary international law. This is a wholly different question from whether or not the principle of *non-refoulement* more generally forms part of customary international law—a proposition which the House of Lords accepted.

Thus, though a minority of commentators continue to deny the existence of *non-refoulement* as a principle of customary international law,[466] the general consensus is that it has now attained that status. It encompasses *non-refoulement* to persecution, based on article 33 of the 1951 Convention, and also to torture or cruel, inhuman or degrading treatment or punishment.

---

[462] Hathaway, *Rights of Refugees*, (2005), 366, citing para. 28 (sc. para. 27) of the judgment of the House of Lords in the *Roma Rights* case, above note.

[463] *Roma Rights* case, above n. 461, para. 26 (Lord Bingham).

[464] Ibid.   [465] Ibid.

[466] Hailbronner appears still to maintain his 1986 position (above n. 6) on the customary international law dimensions to *non-refoulement*; see Hailbronner, K., 'Principles of International Law regarding the Concept of Subsidiary Protection', in Bouteillet-Paquet, D., *Subsidiary Protection of Refugees in the European Union: Complementing the Geneva Convention?* (2000), 3, 13.

7

The Concept of Asylum

1. Introduction

The meaning of the word 'asylum' tends to be assumed by those who use it, but its content is rarely explained. The Universal Declaration of Human Rights refers to 'asylum from persecution', the UN General Assembly urges the grant of asylum and observance of the principle of asylum, and States' constitutions and laws offer the promise of asylum, yet nowhere is this act of States defined. The word itself and the phrase 'right of asylum' have lost much of their pristine simplicity.[1] With the growth of nation States and the corresponding development of notions of territorial jurisdiction and supremacy, the institution of asylum underwent a radical change. It came to imply not only a place of refuge, but also the right to give protection, not so much to the ordinary criminal, as to the one class previously excluded, namely, exiles and refugees...[2] The anomalous position of exiles had already been noted by the jurist Wolff who, writing in 1764, observed that 'exiles do not cease to be men... [By] nature the right belongs to them to dwell in any place in the world which is subject to some other nation.'[3] But this was a 'right' which even Wolff tempered with recognition of the fact of sovereignty. Compassion ought to be shown to those in flight, but admission might be refused for good reasons.[4] The interest of the State in admission or non-admission continued to

[1] See generally Reale, E., 'Le droit d'asile', Hague *Recueil* (1938-I), 473; Koziebrodski, L.B., *Le droit d'asile* (1962); Reville, A. '*L'abjuratio regni*: histoire d'une institution anglaise', *Revue historique*, (1892), 1; Trenholme, N. M., 'The Right of Sanctuary in England', 1 *Univ. Missouri Studies*, No. 5 (1903); Kimminich, O., *Der internationale Rechtsstatus des Flüchtlings*, (1962) 65–98; Sinha, S. P., *Asylum and International Law*, (1971); Grahl-Madsen, A., 'The European Tradition of Asylum and the Development of Refugee Law' in Macalister-Smith, P. Alfredsson, G., eds., *The Land Beyond: Collected Essays on Refugee Law and Policy by Atle Grahl-Madsen*, (2001); Grahl-Madsen, A., *The Status of Refugees in International Law*, vol. 2, (1972); Garcia-Mora, M. R., *International Law and Asylum as a Human Right*, (1956); Bau, I., *This Ground is Holy*, (1985), 124–71. For some alternative perspectives, see the articles by Gorman, R., 'Poets, Playwrights, and the Politics of Exile and Asylum in Ancient Greece and Rome', 6 *IJRL* 402 (1994); and 'Revenge and Reconciliation: Shakespearean Models of Exile and Banishment', 2 *IJRL* 211 (1990); and for an encyclopedia of comparative and historical perspective, see Gibney, M. J. Hansen, R., eds., *Immigration and Asylum: from 1900 to the Present*, 3 vols., (2005).
[2] Reale, Hague *Recueil* (1938-I), 499–550, 544–54, locates the beginning of this development in the mid-eighteenth century, with its hardening into an institution after the events in Europe of 1848–49.
[3] *Jus Gentium Methodo Scientifica Pertractatum*, (1764), s. 147.
[4] Ibid. s. 148; see also Vattel, E., *The Law of Nations*, Chitty, J., ed., I, Ch. XIX, §§229–30; Grotius, *De Jure Belli et Pacis*, (1646), iii. 20. xli.

predominate.[5] Moore, in 1908, noted that the right to grant asylum 'is to be exercised by the government in the light of its own interests, and of its obligations as a representative of social order'.[6] Hackworth similarly observed the freedom of each sovereign State to deal with refugees 'as its domestic policy or its international obligations may seem to dictate'.[7] In 1949, Morgenstern settled the competence of States to grant asylum upon 'the undisputed rule of international law' that every State has exclusive control over the individuals in its territory, including all matters relating to exclusion, admission, expulsion, and protection against the exercise of jurisdiction by other States.[8]

This element, protection granted to a foreign national against the exercise of jurisdiction by another State, lies at the heart of the traditional institution of asylum,[9] but today it also connotes protection against harm, specifically violations of fundamental human rights, and is implicitly linked to the goal of *solution*. Protection must nevertheless be distinguished in its international law and municipal law aspects. In international law, protection is founded either in an exercise of territorial jurisdiction or on treaty or some regional or local custom. The latter bases are particularly relevant to the institution of 'diplomatic asylum', understood in the sense of protection against *local* jurisdiction granted in embassies and consulates and on warships.[10] Although the notion of extraterritoriality has been relied on in support of the practice,[11] regional treaty and custom appear to be its surer foundations.[12] In the *Asylum* case in 1950 the International Court of Justice described the practice as involving,

a derogation from the sovereignty of [the local] State. It withdraws the offender from the jurisdiction of the territorial State and constitutes an intervention in matters which are

---

[5] Generally on States' powers over entry and exclusion, see Goodwin-Gill, G. S., *International Law and the Movement of Persons between States*, (1978); also, Hailbronner, K., 'The Right to Asylum and the Future of Asylum Procedures in the European Community', 2 *IJRL* 341 (1990).

[6] Moore, *Digest*, ii, 757.

[7] Hackworth, *Digest*, ii, 622.

[8] 'The Right of Asylum', 26 *BYIL* 327 (1949). See also Koziebrodski, *Droit d'asile*, above n.1, 24, 79–81; Simpson, J. H., *The Refugee Problem*, (1939), 230: 'Asylum is a privilege conferred by the State. It is not a condition inherent in the individual'; Arboleda, E. & Hoy, I., 'The Convention Refugee Definition in the West: Disharmony of Interpretation and Application', 5 *IJRL* 66 (1993).

[9] Cf. the definition adopted by the Institute of International Law at its 1950 Bath Session: 'Asylum is the protection which a State grants on its territory or in some other place under the control of its organs to a person who comes to seek it': 1 *Annuaire*, (1950), 167, art. 1.

[10] Note also the recognition given after the 1973 coup in Chile to UNHCR 'safe havens', that is, refuges for foreign refugees granted asylum under the Allende government; see UN doc. A/AC.96/ 508, 5 (1974). Cited also by the Chilean representative to the UNHCR Executive Committee in 1992: UN doc. A/AC.96/SR.477, para. 51. See Ch. 5, 250–3.

[11] See, for example, *R. (on the application of 'B')* v. *Secretary of State for Foreign and Commonwealth Affairs* [2004] EWCA Civ 1344, [2005] QB 643: actions of consular officials abroad may be subject to ECHR50 (though extraterritoriality not expressly mentioned); Noll, G., 'Seeking Asylum at Embassies: A Right to Entry under International Law?', 17 *IJRL* 542 (2005); Cole, C.V., 'Is There Safe Refuge in Canadian Missions Abroad?' 9 *IJRL* 654 (1997).

[12] Many States do not accept the institution of diplomatic asylum, or do so only in very limited cases. Despite some support, a Uruguayan proposal to extend the right of asylum in the Universal

exclusively within the competence of that State . . . In the case of extradition, the refugee is within the territory of the State of refuge. A decision with regard to extradition implies only the normal exercise of territorial sovereignty. The refugee is outside the territory of the State where the offence was committed, and a decision to grant him asylum in no way derogates from the sovereignty of that State.[13]

The generality of these last dicta can be misleading unless the normative effect of extradition treaties is taken into account, as well as more recent developments which limit or qualify the 'normal exercise' of sovereignty.[14] From the point of view of international law, therefore, the grant of protection in its territory derives from the State's sovereign competence, a statement of the obvious. The content of that grant of protection—whether it embraces permanent or temporary residence, freedom of movement and integration or confinement in camps, freedom to work and attain self-sufficiency or dependence on national and international charity—is less easy to determine. What cannot be ignored, however, is the close relationship between the issue of refugee status and the principle of *non-refoulement*, on the one hand, and the concept of asylum, on the other hand. These three elements are, as it were, all links in the chain between the refugee's flight and his or her attainment of a durable solution.

Certain legal consequences flow from the existence of a class of refugees known to and defined by general international law and, in particular, from the principle

Declaration of Human Rights to diplomatic asylum in embassies and legations, based on State practice in Latin America, was rejected: UN doc. A/C.3/268, reproduced in UN doc. A/C.3/285/Rev.1 in UNGAOR Part 1 (3rd Session, 1948) 'Annexes', 25. The Pakistani representative regarded this concept of extraterritoriality as having 'dangerous implications': UNGAOR Part 1 (3rd Session, 1948) 'Summary Records of Meetings', 121st Meeting (3 Nov. 1948), 337 (Mr Shahi, Pakistan). See also debate in the International Law Commission in 1949: *Yearbook of the ILC*, paras. 49, 87–8; debate on the draft Declaration on the Right of Asylum in 1966: UN doc. A/6570, para. 11; Moore, *Digest*, ii, 755ff.; Hackworth, *Digest*, ii, 623ff.; Whiteman, *Digest*, vi, 445ff.; McNair, 'Extradition and Exterritorial Asylum', 28 *BYIL* 172 (1951); 7 *BDIL*, 905–23. In 1974, on an Australian initiative, the General Assembly requested the Secretary-General to prepare and circulate a report on the practice of diplomatic asylum and invited Member States to make known their views: UNGA res. 3321 (XXIX), 14 Dec. 1974. The report (UN doc. A/10139) confirmed the regional nature of the practice; of twenty-five States which made known their views, only seven favoured drawing up an international convention on the matter. Further consideration of the subject was postponed indefinitely: UNGA res. 3497(XXX), 15 Dec. 1975. Cf. Riveles, S., 'Diplomatic Asylum as a Human Right: The Case of the Durban Six', 11 *HRQ* 139 (1989); Noll, 'Seeking Asylum at Embassies', above n. 11.

[13] ICJ *Rep.*, (1950), 266, at 274. In this and the *Haya de la Torre* case, ICJ *Rep.*, (1951), 71, the Court was concerned, among others, with interpretation of the 1928 Havana Convention on Asylum, in force between Colombia and Peru, which embodied the right to grant asylum in embassies to political offenders in urgent cases. Colombia's claim that it was entitled to qualify the offence in question as political and also to determine the urgency of the case was rejected by the Court, as was its further claim that the territorial State was bound to allow the asylee to leave. Nevertheless, the Court agreed that the offence was political, but disagreed on the issue of urgency. The resulting stalemate, in which Columbia was not bound to hand over the fugitive, notwithstanding the improper grant of asylum, and Peru was not bound to allow safe passage, was not covered by the Convention or by any regional custom; the parties were urged to reach a friendly settlement.

[14] On which, see above Ch. 4, s. 4.2.1.1.

of *non-refoulement*. In regard to asylum, however, it will be seen that the argument for obligation fails, both on account of the vagueness of the institution and of the continuing reluctance of States formally to accept such obligation and to accord a right of asylum enforceable at the insistence of the individual. Nevertheless, while individuals may not be able to claim a 'right to asylum', States have a duty under international law not to obstruct the individual's right to *seek* asylum. This calls into question the legality of non-arrival and non-admission policies increasingly employed by States as tools of migration control.

2. Asylum in international conventions, other instruments, and acts

The refusal of States to accept an obligation to grant asylum, in the sense of admission to residence and lasting protection against the jurisdiction of another State, is amply evidenced by the history of international conventions and other instruments. Measures taken between the two world wars related, initially, to arrangements for the issue of identity and travel documents which would facilitate the resettlement of refugees, but no obligations to resettle were assumed. The 1933 Convention, which proposed non-rejection of refugees at the frontier, was ratified by only a few States, while it, too, made no provision in respect of permanent asylum. Likewise, those States which subscribed to the constitution of the International Refugee Organization, though urged to cooperate in its function of resettling refugees, accepted no obligations to that end. Little progress was marked by the statement in article 14(1) UDHR48 that 'everyone has the right to seek and to enjoy . . . asylum from persecution'. Lauterpacht rightly noted that States had no intention to assume even a moral obligation in the matter,[15] although the drafting debates do reveal a tension between States that regarded asylum as their sovereign prerogative, and those which saw it as a duty of the international community.[16] The original text proposed by the Commission on Human Rights had indeed provided that '[e]veryone has the right to seek *and be granted*, in other countries, asylum from persecution'.[17] At the suggestion of the United Kingdom,

[15] Lauterpacht, H., *International Law and Human Rights*, (1950), 421; see further below, text to n. 33. As Kimminich succinctly puts it: 'Das Recht, Asyl zu suchen, bedeutet nichts anderes als das Recht, sich auf die Flucht zu begeben': *Internationale Rechtsstatus des Flüchtlings*, 81.
[16] France's suggestion that the United Nations itself should be empowered to secure asylum was also opposed: UN doc. A/C.3/244; UNGAOR Part 1 (3rd Session, 1948), 'Summary Records of Meetings', 121st Meeting (3 Nov. 1948), 328 (Mr Cassin, France), supported by Bolivia, 329, Mexico, 333 (note that 'opposite' should read 'apposite'); Belgium, 334; Pakistan, 338; opposed by the United Kingdom, 330; The Netherlands, 331; United States, 334; Philippines, 335; Lebanon, 336; Australia, 338; USSR, 342; some support in principle: India, 335; Brazil, 340. See also the Uruguayan proposal and Pakistan comment, above n. 12.
[17] UN doc. A/C.3/285/Rev.1, in UNGAOR Part 1 (3rd Session, 1948), 'Annexes', 24 (emphasis added).

the text was altered to remove the obligation on States to accord asylum to individuals seeking it, replacing the words 'and be granted' with the vaguer and far more innocuous 'and to enjoy'.[18]

Thus amended, the text, while limiting the obligation of the State, would indicate that there was a right of asylum to which persecuted persons could have recourse, that the exercise of that right could not be penalized, and that States which offered asylum to refugees would not be compelled to extradite them.[19]

A number of States explained their support for the amended text on the ground that it imposed no legal obligation on them actually to grant asylum.[20] Contemporary opinion thus held that to grant asylum to refugees within its territory was the sovereign right of every State, while the corresponding duty was respect for that asylum by all other States.

While the UK delegation expressed its sympathy towards the plight of persecuted persons, 'no foreigner could claim the right of entry into any State unless that right were granted by treaty'.[21] It defined the right of asylum as the right of States, not individuals, noting that this was also its understanding of the expression 'to enjoy asylum' contained in its draft.[22] However, once a State had given an individual permission to enter, 'the right to enjoy fully the asylum granted him by that State could not be disputed'.[23] If article 14 were to include a right to be granted asylum, as the original text had proposed, 'its application might actually lead to persecution by encouraging States to take action against an undesirable minority and then to invite it to make use of the right of asylum'.[24] The Australian delegation similarly objected to 'formulas implying obligation', regarding the

---

[18] UN doc. A/C.3/253, reproduced in UN doc. A/C.3/285/Rev.1, UNGAOR Part 1 (3rd Session, 1948), 'Annexes', 24.

[19] UNGAOR Part 1 (3rd Session, 1948), 'Summary Records of Meetings', 121st Meeting (3 Nov. 1948), 330–1 (Mrs Corbet, UK). Interestingly, while the United Kingdom was very supportive of the Universal Declaration, it was keen to avoid language that might be interpreted as imposing obligations on States. It proposed 'to make minor changes in the articles concerning the right to asylum, the right of equal pay, and the right to work. Article 21 concerning the right to work they now feel may be interpreted to mean that Governments are required to find work for everyone': Letter from R. A. D. Ford to Escott Reid, (13 Sept. 1948), NAC RG 25, vol. 3699, File 5475-DG-2-40, cited in Schabas, W. A., 'Canada and the Adoption of the Universal Declaration of Human Rights,' 43 *McGill Law Journal* 403, 417 (1998).

[20] UNGAOR Part 1 (3rd Session, 1948), 'Summary Records of Meetings', 122nd Meeting (4 November 1948), 345 (Mr Saint-Lot, Haiti), 345 (Miss Zuloaga, Venezuela), 346 (Mr Contoumas, Greece).

[21] UNGAOR Part 1 (3rd Session, 1948) 'Summary Records of Meetings', 121st Meeting (3 Nov. 1948), 330 (UK). Similarly, the Saudi Arabian delegate (Mr Baroody) stated that while every persecuted person should be able to enjoy the right of asylum, '[t]hat did not mean . . . that everyone had the right to obtain asylum in the country of his choice . . . Such a principle would be a flagrant violation of the sovereignty of the State concerned': 331. See also the remarks of the Venezuelan delegate (Mr Plaza), 332; Indian delegate (Mr Habib), 335.

[22] UNGAOR Part 1 (3rd Session, 1948) 'Summary Records of Meetings', 121st Meeting (3 Nov. 1948), 330 (Mrs Corbet, UK).

[23] Ibid., 335 (Mr Habib, India); 340 (Mrs Corbet, UK); see also support by the Australian delegation, 338.　　　　　　　　　[24] Ibid., 331 (Mrs Corbet, UK).

Universal Declaration as a statement of human rights that should not refer to any corresponding State duties. In its view, each State must be free to decide the form in which the right of asylum should be applied.[25]

By contrast, the French representative viewed asylum as an issue where national interests should yield to those of the international community. Mr Cassin disagreed with the UK 'restrictive conception' of the term 'to enjoy', arguing that for the right to have any meaning, a persecuted individual 'would need to receive asylum, not merely the right of asylum'.[26] Although ultimately voting for the amended text 'because it was essential for the declaration to contain an article dealing with the right of asylum', Mr Cassin argued that '[i]t had been a mistake ... to recognize the individual's right to seek asylum while neither imposing upon States the obligation to grant it nor invoking the support of the United Nations'.[27] The USSR's delegate similarly regarded the right to seek asylum as having little value without provisions for implementing it.[28] The Lebanese representative understood the expression 'and to enjoy ... asylum' as meaning that 'the individual should be guaranteed the right of being granted asylum, and not merely the right of enjoying asylum in the country which had received him, once that right had been acquired'.[29] The inclusion of a right in the Universal Declaration should not be dependent on States' ability to comply with it.[30] Brazil described the right of asylum as 'recognized and accepted by the chief civilizations of the world', and an essential component of any human rights declaration.[31] Pakistan appears to have supported a very wide concept of asylum, available to any individual whose human rights, as set out in the Universal Declaration, were violated. In its view, article 14 was a corollary to the breach of other human rights: 'If everyone had the right of freedom of thought and expression, a person could obviously preserve his intellectual and moral integrity only by seeking refuge abroad, should his own country deny him the enjoyment of those essential liberties.'[32]

Lauterpacht was highly critical of the final text of article 14. In his view, it simply restated States' existing right under international law to grant refuge to individuals. Its inclusion in a declaration of human rights, posited as though it were a right pertaining to individuals, was 'artificial to the point of flippancy',[33] since it lacked any correlative duty on States to give effect to that right and thus any assurance that the

[25] Ibid., 338 (Mr Watt, Australia).
[26] UNGAOR Part 1 (3rd Session, 1948) 'Summary Records of Meetings', 122nd Meeting (4 Nov. 1948), 342 (Mr Cassin, France).   [27] Ibid., 347 (Mr Cassin, France).
[28] Ibid., 343 (Mr Pavlov, USSR).
[29] UNGAOR Part 1 (3rd Session, 1948), 'Summary Records of Meetings', 121st Meeting (3 Nov. 1948), 336 (Mr Azkoul, Lebanon).   [30] Ibid., 335 (Mr Azkoul, Lebanon).
[31] Ibid., 340 (Mr de Athayde, Brazil).   [32] Ibid., 337 (Mr Shahi, Pakistan).
[33] Lauterpacht, above, n. 15, 422. Lauterpacht drafted his own International Bill of Rights, which he submitted to the Brussels Conference of the International Law Association in 1948. In a revised draft, he proposed in art. 10 that: 'Within the limits of public security and economic capacity of the State, there shall be full and effective recognition of the right of asylum for political offenders and for fugitives from persecution.' Ibid., 345–6. See also Lauterpacht, H., 'The Universal Declaration of Human Rights', 25 *BYIL* 354 (1948).

right to seek asylum would result in protection. In fact, the correlative duty, if any, is that which obliges other States to respect the grant of asylum, as it must respect any other lawful exercise of territorial jurisdiction.

Recognizing the Declaration's shortcomings, the Commission on Human Rights resolved in 1947 'to examine at an early opportunity the question of the inclusion of the right of asylum of refugees from persecution in the International Bill of Human Rights or in a special Convention for the purpose'.[34] Debate about the desirability of such a right thus re-opened as the Commission on Human Rights began drafting the human rights covenants in the 1950s. Supporters argued that the right was 'one of the fundamental rights of the human being' and the 'natural corollary' of other human rights in international law.[35] A joint proposal by Chile, Uruguay, and Yugoslavia deemed that the right should be granted to 'any person accused of political offences, and in particular to any person accused or persecuted on account of his participation in the struggle for national independence or political freedom or on account of his activities for the achievement of the purposes and principles proclaimed in the Charter of the United Nations and in the Universal Declaration of Human Rights'.[36] An alternative USSR proposal accorded the right to 'all persons persecuted for their activities in defence of democratic interests, for their scientific work or for their participation in the struggle for national liberation',[37] while a French amendment to both proposals provided simply that '[e]veryone has the right to seek asylum from persecution', stressing the importance of international cooperation in safeguarding that right.[38] The French and USSR proposed that asylum be denied to those who had committed acts contrary to the purposes and principles of the United Nations, while the joint proposal excluded those who had committed acts that were inconsistent with the principles of the UN Charter or the Universal Declaration of Human Rights. The French amendment also excluded persons wanted for prosecution for non-political crimes, while the USSR excluded persons wanted for war crimes or other criminal offences.

Other States noted the desirability of granting asylum, but regarded the formulation of the right in the three proposals as insufficiently precise.[39] Accordingly, they were ultimately rejected on the grounds that:

there was no fundamental right of the individual to be granted asylum but only a right of the State to extend its protection to him; that it was at once impracticable and undesirable

---

[34] UN doc. E/600, para. 48, as cited in Weis, P., 'Human Rights and Refugees', 1 *Israel Yearbook on Human Rights* 35, 38 (1971).

[35] It was said to be 'the complement of the right of peoples to self-determination and of the right to life; and its guarantee against extradition in certain instances was a proper concomitant of the right against arbitrary expulsion': UN Commission on Human Rights, *Report of the 8th Session* (1952), UN doc. E/2256, para. 202.   [36] UN doc. E/CN.4/L.190/Rev.2 (2 Jun. 1952).

[37] UN doc. E/CN.4/L.184 (28 May 1952).

[38] 'The High Contracting Parties shall strive to take steps, individually and in concert with the other High Contracting Parties and with the United Nations, to ensure the effective granting of this right.': UN doc. E/CN.4/L.191 (2 Jun. 1952).

[39] UN Commission on Human Rights, *Report of the 8th Session* (1952), UN doc. E/2256, para. 203.

to impose on States the obligation in advance of opening their territory to an unascertainable number of persons who might qualify for asylum under any one of the heads that had been proposed; and that experience in the drafting of the Universal Declaration of Human Rights and of the Final Act of the Conference of Plenipotentiaries on Refugees and Stateless Persons had shown that States were unwilling to surrender their prerogative of deciding in each instance which aliens they would admit to their territory.[40]

This approach was substantially reiterated in the UN General Assembly resolution establishing UNHCR, which simply urged States to cooperate with the High Commissioner by, among other matters, admitting refugees.[41] Draft conventions submitted by France and the UN Secretariat in the course of debate on the 1951 Convention both contained an article on admission of refugees,[42] but the Conference of Plenipotentiaries preferred to leave asylum and admission to be covered by exhortatory statements in the Final Act.[43]

Nevertheless, efforts continued in other fora. In 1957, France proposed a declaration on the right of asylum to the UN Economic and Social Council,[44] and in 1959, the General Assembly called on the International Law Commission to work on its codification.[45] The subject was included in the ILC's future work programme

[40] Ibid. France's amendment was rejected by 9 votes to 3 with 6 abstentions; the USSR's proposal was rejected by 10 votes to 5 with 3 abstentions; and the joint proposal was rejected by 10 votes to 4 with 4 abstentions: ibid., para. 204. This was despite interventions by the UN High Commissioner for Refugees and UNHCR's Chief Legal Adviser: Holborn, L.W., *Refugees: A Problem of Our Time: The Work of the United Nations High Commissioner for Refugees, 1951–1972*, vol. 1, (1975), 228.

[41] UNGA res. 428(V), 14 Dec. 1950; see also UNGA res. 430(V) of the same date, urgently appealing to States to assist the IRO in its resettlement efforts.

[42] *Ad Hoc* Committee on Statelessness and Related Problems, Memorandum by the Secretary-General: UN doc. E/AC.32/2, (3 Jan. 1950), 22, preliminary draft convention, art. 3: '1. In pursuance of Article 14 of the Universal Declaration..., the High Contracting Parties shall give favourable consideration to the position of refugees seeking asylum from persecution or the threat of persecution...2. [They] shall to the fullest possible extent relieve the burden assumed by initial reception countries which have afforded asylum...They shall do so, *inter alia*, by agreeing to receive a certain number of refugees in their territory.' The Committee decided that the convention should not deal with the right of asylum; see comments by the US delegate, Louis Henkin, in the first session of the *Ad hoc* Committee: UN doc. E/AC.32/SR.20 (10 Feb. 1950), paras. 15, 44, 54–6; also UN doc. E/AC.32/SR.21, paras. 12, 16, 26. See Weis, P., 'Legal Aspects of the Convention of 28 July 1951 relating to the Status of Refugees', 30 *BYIL* 478, 481 (1953). Generally for the preparatory works, see Takkenberg, A. & Tahbaz, C., *The Collected travaux préparatoires of the 1951 Convention relating to the Status of Refugees*, 3 vols., (1988); UNHCR, *RefWorld*, DVD-Rom, (15th edn., 2006).

[43] For discussion in the 1951 Conference on asylum as a right and not a duty of the State, see Colombia: A/CONF.2/SR.13, 12; United Kingdom, ibid., 14. Cf. France, 'the right of asylum was implicit in the Convention, even if it was not explicitly proclaimed therein, for the very existence of refugees depended on it': ibid., 13. ECOSOC's instructions to the *Ad Hoc* Committee on Statelessness and Related Problems were to draft a binding legal instrument implementing art. 14 and 15 UDHR48: *Ad Hoc* Committee on Statelessness and Related Problems, First Session, 'Summary Record of the 1st Meeting', (New York, 16 Jan. 1950), UN doc E/AC.32/SR.1 (23 Jan. 1950), para. 4 (Secretariat).

[44] ECOSOC, *Official Records*, 22nd Sess., Supp., paras. 109–12. Other States objected, citing issues of sovereignty and domestic jurisdiction; see UN doc. E/CN.4/781, 3 (Czechoslovakia); ibid., 10–11 (United Kingdom).

[45] UNGA res. 1400(XIV), 21 Sept. 1959. The International Law Commission (ILC) had been tentatively involved with the issue some ten years previously, in debate on an article proposed for

in 1962,[46] but in the absence of progress generally it fell to the Commission on Human Rights and to the Third and Sixth Committees to take up the cause, culminating in the Declaration on Territorial Asylum, adopted unanimously by the General Assembly in 1967.[47]

The Declaration on Territorial Asylum recommends that States should base their asylum practice upon the principles declared, but it stresses throughout the sovereign competence aspect of territorial asylum and reaffirms the position of each State as sole judge of the grounds upon which it will extend such protection.[48] Article 2, however, acknowledges that the plight of refugees remains of concern to the international community, and that where a State finds difficulty in granting or continuing to grant asylum, other States 'shall consider', in a spirit of international solidarity, measures to lighten the burden. Article 3 declares the principle of *non-refoulement* and, should a State contemplate making an exception, it 'shall consider' the possibility of according those affected the opportunity, 'by way of provisional asylum or otherwise', of going to another State.

Discussions in the UN Sixth Committee shortly before the Declaration's adoption had revealed some expectation that it would be the precursor to a universal convention.[49] The first draft of such a convention on asylum was in fact proposed, not by the International Law Commission (as General Assembly resolutions might have anticipated), but by a group of experts meeting in 1971 and 1972 under the auspices of the Carnegie Endowment for International Peace, in consultation with UNHCR. Article 1 of their text proposed that contracting States 'acting in an international and humanitarian spirit, *shall use [their] best endeavours to grant asylum* in [their] territory, which … includes permission to remain in that territory'.[50] The draft was discussed in the Third Committee later in 1972, where it was decided that the High Commissioner should consult governments, with a

---

inclusion in a draft declaration on the rights and duties of States: *Yearbook of the ILC*, (1949), 125, paras. 49ff. The proposed article, providing that '[e]very State has the right to accord asylum to persons of any nationality who request it in consequence of persecutions for offences which the State according asylum deems to have a political character', was ultimately not adopted, because it was considered too complex an issue to be dealt with in a single article: UN doc. A/CN.4/SR.20 (1949). During debate, it was said that '[t]he duty corresponding to the right of asylum was not that of granting asylum whenever it was requested, but that of respect for the asylum granted on the part of the State of which the refugee was a national. That State should in no case consider the granting of asylum as an unfriendly act against it.': International Law Commission, First Session, 'Summary Record of the 16th Meeting' (5 May 1949) UN doc. A/CN.4/SR.16, 16 (Mr Yepes).

[46] UN doc. A/CN.4/245. In 1972, the International Law Association adopted texts for draft conventions on diplomatic and territorial asylum: ILA, *Report of the 55th Session*, (1972), 109–207.

[47] UNGA res. 2312(XXII), 14 Dec. 1967. For text, see below, Annexe 1, No. 6. For a detailed account of the background, see Weis, P., 'The United Nations Declaration on Territorial Asylum', 7 *Can. YIL* 92 (1969). The 1967 Protocol relating to the Status of Refugees was limited to updating the refugee definition and does not deal with the question of asylum.   [48] Art. 1(1), (2).

[49] See UN docs. A/C.6/SR. 983–9; A/6912, *Report* of the Sixth Committee, paras. 64–5; also the Preamble to the 1967 Declaration, adopted by UNGA res. 2312(XXII), 14 Dec. 1967.

[50] UN doc. A/8712 appx., annexe 1. This and other drafts are collected in Grahl-Madsen, A., *Territorial Asylum*, (1980), annexes KK and following.

view to the eventual convening of an international conference.[51] When governments were canvassed, many appeared to favour a convention,[52] and the General Assembly decided that the text should be reviewed.[53]

The UN Group of Experts' revision indicated continuing adherence to the discretionary aspect of asylum practice.[54] Article 1 proposed that 'Each Contracting State, *acting in the exercise of its sovereign rights, shall use its best endeavours* in a humanitarian spirit to grant asylum in its territory...'[55] The same 'best endeavours' formula was again introduced in article 3 where, following a statement of the principle of *non-refoulement* on behalf of those 'in the territory of a contracting State', it would have operated to reduce the level of obligation in relation to rejection at the frontier from that previously adopted in both the 1967 Declaration and the 1969 OAU Convention.[56] Acting on the Group of Experts' report, the General Assembly requested the Secretary-General, in consultation with the High Commissioner, to convene a conference on territorial asylum in early 1977.[57]

Dissatisfaction with much of the proposed texts inspired a working group of non-governmental organizations to suggest an alternative version,[58] the asylum provisions of which were largely supported by consensus at a Nansen Symposium held in 1976.[59] In both cases, the proposals favoured an obligation to grant asylum, subject to certain exceptions; confirmation of the notion of non-rejection at the frontier within the principle of *non-refoulement*; and general recognition of the principle of provisional admission as a minimum requirement.

The 1977 United Nations Conference on Territorial Asylum was an abject failure, with close voting on major issues apparently heralding emerging divisions between States and on matters of principle.[60] One article only, that on asylum, was considered by the drafting committee, which reduced the 'best endeavours' formula of the Group of Experts draft to that of 'shall endeavour... to grant

[51] UN docs. A/C.3/SR.1956 and 1957, paras. 25, 32.

[52] UN doc. A/9612/Add.3, annexe (1974). Of ninety-one States which made known their views, seventy-six favoured elaboration of a convention on territorial asylum. See also UN doc. A/C.3/SR.2098–2101; and SR.2103, paras. 44–60. (1974).

[53] UNGA res. 3272(XXIX), 9 Jan. 1975.

[54] UN doc. A/10177 and Corr. 1 (1975); Grahl-Madsen, *Territorial Asylum*, above n. 50, annexe RR; also UN doc. A/C.3/SR.2161-4.

[55] Cf. the draft prepared by the International Law Association at its 55th Conference in 1972, under which States would 'undertake to grant refuge in their territories to all those who are seeking asylum...', save where danger to the security of the country or to the safety and welfare of the community was apprehended (art. 1(b)). Art. 3, however, proposed that 'A grant of asylum does not imply any right of permanent immigration'. ILA, *Report of 55th Session*, (1972); text also in Grahl-Madsen, *Territorial Asylum*, annexe LL.

[56] Art. 4 did provide for provisional admission pending consideration of a request for asylum, but meeting the qualifications still gave no entitlement to the grant of asylum.

[57] UNGA res. 3456(XXX), 9 Dec. 1975.

[58] Text in Grahl-Madsen, *Territorial Asylum*, annexe TT.

[59] 'Towards an Asylum Convention', Report of the Nansen Symposium (1977); text of draft convention proposed by Grahl-Madsen and Melander also in Grahl-Madsen, *Territorial Asylum*, annexe UU.

[60] See generally, Grahl-Madsen, *Territorial Asylum*; Weis, P., 'The Draft Convention on Territorial Asylum', 50 *BYIL* 176 (1979); Weis, 'Human Rights and Refugees', above n. 34.

asylum'.[61] On the other hand, non-rejection at the frontier was endorsed overall within the principle of *non-refoulement*, though the latter generally would have been qualified by States' preoccupation with numbers and security. Recognizing that little of substance had been achieved, the Conference at its final session recommended that the General Assembly consider reconvening it at a suitable time.[62] Later that year, however, the Third Committee declined to submit any formal proposal to that effect, and it was thought more appropriate that the High Commissioner continue consultations with governments.[63]

Since 1977, there has been no further progress towards reconvening the Conference; on the contrary, refugee problems, including aspects of asylum, status, *non-refoulement*, and solutions have responded more to regional initiatives, such as the comprehensive programmes implemented for Central America (CIRE-FCA), Indo-China (CPA),[64] and more recently the Common European Asylum System (CEAS).[65] Though there has been no progress towards a universal instrument on asylum, various soft law resolutions and declarations have consistently affirmed its importance. In 1993, the Vienna Declaration on Human Rights and Programme of Action reaffirmed the right to seek and enjoy asylum.[66] The Sub-Commission on Human Rights in 2000 adopted a resolution on the right to seek and enjoy asylum, which expressed deep concern that:

restrictive policies and practices of many States may lead to difficulties for people to gain effective access to protection in the territory of asylum States while escaping persecution and serious human rights violations in their own countries, [and noted] that such policies and practices, including certain incidents of the detention of asylum-seekers, may be incompatible with the principles of applicable refugee and human rights law.[67]

This was reaffirmed in subsequent resolutions.[68] UNHCR's Executive Committee has repeatedly stressed the importance of the right to seek asylum,[69] and has also gone some way to defining its content.[70]

[61] For full text of the articles considered by the Committee of the Whole and by the Drafting Committee, see 'Report of the United Nations Conference on Territorial Asylum', UN doc. A/CONF.78/12, (21 Apr. 1977).

[62] See *Report* of the Conference, above note, para. 25; also *Report* of the UNHCR to ECOSOC: UN doc. E/5987, paras. 10–16 (June 1977). [63] UN doc. A/C.3732/SR.49, paras. 16–19 (Nov. 1977).

[64] Generally see UNHCR, *The State of the World's Refugees*, (1993), 26–9, 117–20; 'Focus on the Comprehensive Plan of Action', 5 *IJRL* 507 (1993).

[65] The various measures adopted since the entry into force of the Treaty of Amsterdam and the Tampere Conclusions in 1999 are discussed throughout this work.

[66] Vienna Declaration and Programme of Action, UN World Conference on Human Rights (1993) UN doc. A/CONF.157/23 (12 Jul. 1993), para. 23.

[67] Sub-Commission on Human Rights Resolution 2000/20 on 'The Right to Seek and Enjoy Asylum', (18 Aug. 2000).

[68] Sub-Commission on Human Rights, Resolution 2001/16 on 'International Protection for Refugees and Displaced Persons', (16 Aug. 2001); Sub-Commission on Human Rights, Resolution 2002/23 on 'International Protection for Refugees', (14 Aug. 2002).

[69] Executive Committee Conclusion No. 52 (1988), No. 71 (1993), No. 75 (1994), No. 77 (1995), No. 82 (1997) No. 85 (1998), No. 94 (2002), No. 97 (2003), No. 101 (2004), No. 103 (2005).

[70] See Executive Committee Conclusion No. 82 on Safeguarding Asylum (1997), para. (d), stressing the importance of the principle of *non-refoulement*, irrespective of whether persons have been

3. Asylum in regional agreements

On a regional level, some progress can be discerned. The European Convention on Human Rights (ECHR50) has facilitated an overall improvement in the situation of individuals at large, whether citizens, non-nationals, or refugees.[71] Under treaty arrangements generally, the obligation to provide a remedy to victims of human rights violations is usually predicated on two conditions: (a) recognition of the specific right violated as a protected right within the system in question; and (b) the existence of a sufficient link between the actual or putative victim and the State from which a remedy is sought. Article 3 ECHR50, which prohibits torture and inhuman or degrading treatment or punishment, has significantly limited States' freedom to remove individuals who may be at risk of such ill-treatment in the territories to which return is contemplated. The UK House of Lords suggested in a 2004 judgment that protection against *refoulement* could, in the right factual circumstances, inhere in *any* ECHR50 right, not just article 3.[72] Nevertheless, neither article 3 nor any other ECHR50 provision accords a right to enter a State,[73] or a right to asylum. This has been clearly recognized in the jurisprudence of the European Court of Human Rights and the Commission, even as they marked out the boundaries beyond which exclusion or expulsion might infringe that provision.[74]

formally granted refugee status; access to fair and effective procedures for determining status and protection needs; the need to admit refugees to State territories; the need to grant UNHCR rapid, unimpeded, and safe access to persons of concern; scrupulous application of the exclusion clauses; the duty to treat refugees and asylum seekers in accordance with international human rights and refugee law standards; States' responsibility to ensure the civil nature of asylum by separating refugees from armed elements; and the obligation of refugees and asylum seekers to abide by the laws of host States. The 2001 Declaration of States Parties calls on States to 'take measures to strengthen asylum and render protection more effective', and to 'continue their efforts aimed at ensuring the integrity of the asylum institution': Declaration of States Parties to the 1951 Convention and/or its 1967 Protocol relating to the Status of Refugees (13 Dec. 2001), UN doc. HCR/MMSP/2001/09 (16 Jan. 2002), paras. 6 and 7 respectively; text below, Annexe 1, No. 10.

[71] See further Ch. 6.

[72] *Ullah* v. *Secretary of State for the Home Dept* [2004] 2 AC 323, [2004] UKHL 26, paras. 24–25 (Lord Bingham), 49–50 (Lord Steyn), 67 (Lord Carswell). See also *Secretary of State for the Home Department* v. *Kacaj* [2002] Imm AR 213, para. 39; *Drozd and Janousek* v. *France and Spain* (1992) 14 EHRR 745, 795 (Judge Matscher).

[73] In relation to art. 8, see, for example, Liddy, J., 'The Concept of Family Life under the ECHR', [1998] *European HR L. Rev.* 15; Kilkelly, U., *The Child and the European Convention on Human Rights*, (1999), Ch. 7; Lambert, H., 'The European Court of Human Rights and the Right of Refugees and Other Persons in Need of Protection to Family Reunion', 11 *IJRL* 427 (1999).

[74] See *Becker* v. *Denmark* Application No. 7011/75, (3 Oct.1975), 4 *D & R* 215, in which the European Commission took the view that it was not within the government's power to give guarantees as to what would happen to children whom it proposed to repatriate to South Vietnam, and that it was neither reasonable nor feasible to require guarantees. In *TI* v. *United Kingdom* [2000] INLR 211, the Court considered it 'irrelevant' that any permission for the applicant to remain in the UK would only be for three months and would be subject to review. Lambert has characterized the European Court's approach as one of 'redress', concerned with State compliance with judgments

The 1957 European Convention on Extradition, on the other hand, formulates the principle of non-extradition for political offences in the form of an obligation ('extradition shall not be granted') and applies the same principle where the request is made for the purpose of prosecuting or punishing a person on account of race, religion, nationality, or political opinion, or where a person's position may be prejudiced for any of these reasons.[75] In 1965, the Council of Europe Parliamentary Assembly noted the desirability of elaborating an international instrument giving legal recognition to States' practice in granting asylum,[76] and in 1967 the Committee of Ministers recommended that member governments 'should act in a particularly liberal and humanitarian spirit in relation to persons who seek asylum in their territory', though it recognized 'the necessity of safeguarding national security and of protecting the community from serious danger'.[77] Observance of the principle of *non-refoulement* was called for and, where exceptions were contemplated, the individual should 'as far as possible and under such conditions as [were considered] appropriate' be accorded the opportunity of going to another State.

Article 18 of the 2000 Charter of Fundamental Rights of the European Union, and article II-78 of the European Constitution (yet to enter into force), provide: 'The right to asylum shall be guaranteed with due respect for the rules of the Geneva Convention of 28 July 1951 and the Protocol of 31 January 1967 relating to the status of refugees and in accordance with' the Treaty establishing the European Community and the European Constitution respectively.

While a reference to the 'right *to* asylum'[78] at first glance appears expansive, the Charter seeks only to consolidate existing fundamental EU rights rather than elaborate or amend them.[79] The Preamble of the Charter refers to a 'reaffirmation' of rights stemming from international and domestic law, and to the Charter's role

rather than their impact on individual claimants: Lambert, H. 'The European Convention on Human Rights and the Protection of Refugees: Limits and Opportunities', 24 *RSQ* 39, 50 (2005). But see Noll, 'Seeking Asylum at Embassies', above n. 11, on the limited role of ECHR50 in providing a right to entry where visa applications are made at diplomatic missions abroad.

[75] *ETS* No. 24, art. 3(2).

[76] Council of Europe Parliamentary Assembly Recommendation 434 (1965).

[77] Res. (67) 14 of 29 June 1967 on Asylum to Persons in Danger of Persecution, Preamble and para. 1. See also the earlier Recommendations 234 of 22 January 1960 and 293 of 26 September 1961 of the Consultative Assembly of the Council of Europe, proposing that the Committee of Experts be instructed to include an article on asylum in a protocol to ECHR50; this was rejected by the Committee of Experts, which favoured either a separate convention or a resolution. See also Parliamentary Assembly of the Council of Europe, Recommendation 1236 on the Right of Asylum (12 April 1994), para. 6. The principles of the 1967 resolution were reaffirmed in the Declaration on Territorial Asylum adopted by the Committee on Ministers on 18 Nov. 1977. For texts, see the Online Resource Centre: <http://www.oup.com/uk/refugeelaw>.

[78] The French, Spanish, and Italian versions refer to a right *of* asylum ('droit d'asile'; 'derecho de asils' 'diritto di asilo'). Thank you to María-Teresa Gil-Bazo for drawing this to our attention.

[79] See art. 51(2): 'This Charter does not establish any new power or task for the Community or the Union, or modify powers and tasks defined by the Treaties.' Art. 52(3) provides that the Charter respects ECHR50, its Protocols, and the case law of the European Court of Human Rights.

in making existing rights more 'visible', suggesting a 'replicative approach'.[80] The right is limited to a procedural right to apply for asylum, rather than an substantive right to obtain it. Nonetheless, the right is framed as one pertaining to the individual.[81] Ultimately, it stems from the right to *seek* asylum in article 14 UDHR48, which implies a right to have a claim considered on its merits, in combination with the principle of *non-refoulement*, which necessarily requires States to examine asylum claims if they are to satisfy themselves that they will not violate the principle by removing a particular individual.[82]

Developments in other regions are mixed. Within Latin America, the 1954 Caracas Convention on Territorial Asylum reaffirmed the territorial State's sovereign right to grant asylum, the duty of other States to respect such asylum, and the exemption from any obligations to surrender or expel persons 'sought for political offenses' or 'persecuted for political reasons or offenses'.[83] As regards diplomatic asylum,[84] another Caracas Convention of the same year stressed that while 'every State has the right to grant asylum . . . it is not obligated to do so or state its reasons for refusing it'; and that it rests with 'the State granting asylum to determine the nature of the offense or the motives for the persecution'.[85] The Convention provides further that 'the State granting asylum is not bound to settle him in its territory, but it may not return him to his country of origin, unless this is the express wish of the asylee'.[86] These conventions are not especially relevant to today's refugee problems, however.

The 1969 OAU Convention, by contrast, besides broadening the refugee definition, also strengthens the institution of asylum. Member States of the OAU, proclaims article II, 'shall use their best endeavours . . . to receive refugees and to secure the settlement' of those unable or unwilling to be repatriated. The principle of *non-refoulement* is declared without exception, although once again a call is made to lighten the burden on countries of first refuge.[87] A further provision, dealing with the refugee who has not received the right to reside in any country, merely acknowledges that he or she 'may' be granted temporary residence pending resettlement. On asylum at large, the OAU Convention affirms that its grant is a

---

[80] Noll, 'Seeking Asylum at Embassies', above, n. 11, 547.

[81] In the European Constitution, the term 'asylum' seems to imply Convention status, in contrast to subsidiary protection status and temporary protection status: 'The Union shall develop a common policy on asylum, subsidiary protection and temporary protection with a view to offering appropriate status to any third-country national requiring international protection and ensuring compliance with the principle of non-refoulement' (art. III-266(1)), and 'a uniform status of subsidiary protection for nationals of third countries who, without obtaining European asylum, are in need of international protection' (art. III-266(2)(b)). Note also the combined effects of arts. 13, 21, and 24(1) of the EU Qualification Directive; below, Ch. 9, s. 3.1.

[82] Vedsted-Hansen, J., 'Non-Admission Policies and the Right to Protection: Refugees' Choice versus States' Exclusion?', in Nicholson, F. & Twomey, P., eds., *Refugee Rights and Realities: Evolving International Concepts and Regimes*, (1999) 274–5.   [83] Arts. 1–4; see below, Annexe 2, No. 3.

[84] That is, asylum granted 'in legations, war vessels, and military camps or aircraft, to persons being sought for political offenses': art. 1, 1954 Caracas Convention on Diplomatic Asylum; see below, Annexe 2, No. 4.   [85] Ibid., arts. 2, 4.

[86] Ibid., art. 17.   [87] Art. II(4) OAU69; see below, Annexe 2, No. 1. The OAU has been succeeded by the African Union (AU).

peaceful and humanitarian act, and thus not to be regarded as unfriendly. It also emphasizes the duty of refugees to abide by the laws of the country in which they find themselves and to refrain from subversive activities against any Member State.

Despite the encouraging tone of the OAU Convention, neither this instrument nor any other permits the conclusion that States have accepted an international obligation to grant asylum to refugees, in the sense of admission to residence and lasting protection against persecution and/or the exercise of jurisdiction by another State.[88] Nonetheless, State practice is replete with examples of asylum given; the humanitarian practice exists, but the sense of obligation is missing.

The practice of international organizations tends to support this view, while simultaneously revealing an awareness of the need for pragmatic, flexible responses. In the years after the Second World War, for example, many thousands of refugees had the benefit, at least, of asylum in the refugee camps of Europe.[89] Their principal need was for resettlement, and the General Assembly repeatedly called upon immigration countries to allow refugees access to their programmes.[90] On other occasions, the General Assembly reiterated that permanent solutions should be sought in voluntary repatriation and assimilation within new national communities, either locally in countries of first refuge or in countries of immigration.[91] The initial burden may fall in fact upon the receiving country,[92] but solutions are the responsibility of the international community at large.[93]

4. Obstructing asylum: trends in State practice

4.1 ACCESS

The question of *access* to protection and assistance has acquired critical dimensions over the last two decades, touching directly on issues of territorial sovereignty,

---

[88] UNGA resolutions simply affirm the right to seek asylum, and do not explain the meaning of the concept: UNGA res. 50/152 (21 Dec. 1995) para. 4; 51/75 (12 Dec. 1996), para. 3; 52/103 (9 Feb. 1998), para. 5; 53/125 (12 Feb. 1999), para. 5; 54/146 (17 Dec. 1999), para. 6; 55/74 (4 Dec. 2000), para. 6.

[89] See generally, Vernant, J., *The Refugee in the Post-War World*, (1953); Holborn, L., *The International Refugee Organization*, (1956).

[90] See, for example, UNGA res. 430(V), 14 Dec. 1950, urgently appealing to all States to assist the IRO with resettlement; UNGA res. 538(VI), 2 Feb. 1952, appealing specially to States interested in migration.

[91] UNGA res. 1166(XII), 26 Nov. 1957, para. 2, reaffirming the basic approach set out in para. 1 of the UNHCR Statute; also UNGA res. 1285(XIII), 5 Dec. 1958, on special efforts to be made in the context of World Refugee Year.

[92] UNGA res. 832(IX), 21 Oct. 1954, '*Considering* that, while the ultimate responsibility for ... refugees ... falls in fact upon the countries of residence, certain of these countries have to face particularly heavy burdens as a result of their geographical situation, and some complementary aid has been shown to be necessary ...'

[93] UNGA res. 1167(XII), 26 Nov. 1957, recognizing the heavy burden placed on the government of Hong Kong by the massive influx of Chinese refugees, and noting that the problem is such 'as to be of concern to the international community'.

control, and the reserved domain of domestic jurisdiction. Denial of access is the objective for many States anxious to avoid the requirement to abide by certain peremptory obligations, such as *non-refoulement*. Refugees and asylum seekers are directly 'interdicted' while outside territorial jurisdiction, and their movements are increasingly controlled indirectly, through the application of restrictive visa policies and/or carrier sanctions. Those who arrive in the territory of the State may be denied access to a procedure for the determination of asylum or refugee status, or to courts and tribunals generally for the protection of their rights, or to the sources of information that ought to be the essential foundation for informed decision-making. Even where refugees secure admission, they may be denied access to relief or basic services, such as health care and education. Access has another dimension in situations of conflict, when internally displaced populations requiring humanitarian assistance become hostages to fortune, with international efforts to relieve their suffering linked to political or military advantages sought by one or other side.

One of the difficulties with evaluating these various deflection techniques through the lens of international refugee law is the 1951 Convention's silence on admission procedures. Though human rights law provides a general standards framework, States retain considerable discretion to construct sophisticated interception and non-arrival policies within the letter, if not the spirit, of the law. However, while it is true that no international instrument imposes an express duty on States to grant asylum to persons fleeing persecution, the right to seek asylum, when read in conjunction with the right to freedom of movement and the totality of rights protected by the UDHR48 and ICCPR66, implies an obligation on States to respect the individual's right to leave his or her country in search of protection. Thus, States that impose barriers on individuals seeking to leave their own country,[94] or that seek to deflect or obstruct access to asylum procedures, may breach this obligation and, more generally, demonstrate a lack of good faith in implementing their treaty obligations.[95]

The question of access to countries and therefore also to procedures for the determination of refugee status and the grant of asylum falls between competing responsibilities, only some of which are clearly regulated by rules of international law. For example, State agents who intercept refugees on the high seas and return them directly to a country in which they are persecuted violate the principle of *non-refoulement*. On the other hand, State agents who, by refusing a visa to individuals with a well-founded fear of persecution, prevent or obstruct their flight to safety, do not breach the prohibition on *returning* refugees to persecution.[96]

---

[94] See, for example, the UK pre-clearance procedures in *R. (European Roma Rights Centre)* v. *Immigration Officer at Prague Airport (UNHCR Intervening)* [2005] 2 AC 1, [2004] UKHL 55 (hereafter '*Roma Rights* case').

[95] On good faith in international law, see above, Ch. 5. In relation to good faith and the right to seek asylum: Lauterpacht, H., *International Law and Human Rights* (1950) 346.

[96] See *Roma Rights* case, above, n. 94; although see discussion below, with respect to the protection afforded by ECHR50 and CRC89: Noll, 'Seeking Asylum at Embassies', above n. 11.

Nonetheless, the Human Rights Committee has expressed concern at States' imposition of carrier sanctions and 'other pre-frontier arrangements' that affect the right of the individual to leave any country, raising the question of their compatibility with article 12(2) ICCPR66.[97] At the same time, though, it has acknowledged that article 12 'does not guarantee an unrestricted right to travel from one country to another', and does not confer a right for a person to enter a country other than his or her own.[98] In the *Roma Rights* case, the House of Lords held that State practice did not support the proposition that a State's *non-refoulement* obligations extend to general deterrence measures, especially those whose impact is felt *within* the country of origin or transit, noting in particular the widespread practice of visa regimes enforced by carrier sanctions.[99]

The 'right to seek asylum' is certainly restricted, and State practice to date has not recognized directly correlative duties obliging States to adjust visa or immigration policies accordingly. On the contrary, States have repeatedly insisted on their right to apply visa and related controls, including sanctions against transportation companies which bring undocumented or insufficiently documented passengers to their ports and airports. Thus, while some have argued that the Universal Declaration on Human Rights, in whole or part, has acquired the status of customary international law,[100] there remains insufficient State practice or *opinio juris* to support a concomitant duty on the State to grant asylum to those seeking it.[101]

4.2 INTERCEPTION

There is no internationally accepted definition of 'interception', but the term describes measures applied by States outside their national boundaries which prevent, interrupt, or stop the movement of people without the necessary immigration documentation from crossing their borders by land, sea, or air.[102] Interception encompasses both physical or 'active' interception, such as the interdiction of boats, as well as administrative or 'passive' measures, such as stationing immigration and

---

[97] 'Concluding Observations of the Human Rights Committee: Austria', UN doc. CCPR/C/79/Add.103, (19 Nov. 1998), para. 11. The Human Rights Committee has also requested States to 'include information in their reports on measures that impose sanctions on international carriers which bring to their territory persons without required documents, where those measures affect the right to leave another country': General Comment No. 27 (1999), para. 10.

[98] *Lichtensztejn v. Uruguay*, Comm. No. 77/1980, UN doc. A/38/40 (31 Mar. 1983), para. 8.3; *Montero v. Uruguay*, Comm. No. 106/1981, UN doc. A/38/40 (31 Mar. 1983) 186 at para. 9.4; *Nuñez v. Uruguay*, Comm No. 108/1981, UN doc. A/38/40 (22 July 1983), paras. 9.2 and 9.3. See above, Ch. 5, s. 3.3.1, on extraterritoriality; Hathaway, J. C., *The Rights of Refugees under International Law* (2005), 314 (hereafter, *Rights of Refugees*, (2005)).

[99] *Roma Rights* case, above n. 44, para. 28.

[100] See discussion in Schachter, O., *International Law in Theory and Practice*, (1991), 336–41.

[101] Noll, G., *Negotiating Asylum* (2000), 357–62 argues that neither the UDHR48 generally, nor art. 14 specifically, amount to binding international law.

[102] Executive Committee Standing Committee (18th Meeting), 'Interception of Asylum-Seekers and Refugees: The International Framework and Recommendations for a Comprehensive Approach', UN doc. EC/50/SC/CRP.17, (9 Jun. 2000), para. 10. On interception at sea, see Ch. 5, s. 4.2.

airline liaison officers in departure and transit countries to identify passengers with false or inadequate documentation and to prevent them from leaving for the destination State.[103] A 2003 Executive Committee Conclusion adopted a narrower definition focusing solely on active means of interception—preventing embarkation, preventing further onward travel, and asserting control of vessels— but noted that it was specifically for the purposes of that Conclusion and without prejudice to international law.[104]

Interception policies are not new, but have increasingly become a standard migration tool for western States.[105] In the past two decades in particular, States have taken advantage of the absence of a concrete obligation to provide asylum both to deter asylum seekers from leaving their countries to search for protection, and to deflect those already on the move; restrictive measures have become routine.[106] While they are in part a response to people smuggling and trafficking networks, they are frequently exploited under the rubric of national security, and reflect a wider practice among States to curtail 'irregular' migration. Though the trend towards increasingly restrictive asylum policies pre-dates 11 September 2001, security concerns following the terrorist attacks on the United States and elsewhere have reshaped asylum regimes in a number of countries. Detention grounds have been expanded, exclusion clauses have been applied more broadly than international law stipulates, and stronger links have been forged between immigration, intelligence services, and criminal law enforcement.[107]

Existing principles of international refugee law, human rights law, criminal law, the law of the sea, and the law of State responsibility nevertheless provide a framework for the regulation of interception.[108] Key among these is the principle of *non-refoulement* which as the Sub-Commission on the Promotion and Protection

---

[103] Ibid., para. 13; see further below, s. 4.3.2.

[104] Executive Committee Conclusion No. 97 (2003).

[105] For example, the 2003 Pre-ExCom Consultations with NGOs revealed interception practices in Australia, Canada, the United States and the European Union: *Report on Pre-ExCom Consultations with Non-Governmental Organisations* (Geneva, 24–26 Sep. 2003), Annex IX, (2 Oct. 2003).

[106] Since 1999, the European Union has spent millions of Euros on increasing and strengthening border patrols and maritime surveillance, including the use of satellites to detect people crossing borders, and biometric and fingerprinting equipment to track their movement once they arrive in the European Union: European Council on Refugees and Exiles (ECRE), 'Broken Promises—Forgotten Principles: An ECRE Evaluation of the Development of EU Minimum Standards for Refugee Protection, Tampere 1999—Brussels 2004' (June 2004), 15. See Council Regulation (EC) No. 2725/ 2000 of 11 December 2000, concerning the Establishment of 'Eurodac' for the Comparison of Fingerprints for the Effective Application of the Dublin Convention, [2000] O.J. L316/1; Council Regulation (EC) No. 407/2002 of 28 February. 2002 laying down Certain Rules to Implement Regulation (EC) No. 2725/2000 concerning the Establishment of 'Eurodac' for the Comparison of Fingerprints for the Effective Application of the Dublin Convention, [2002] O.J. L62/1.

[107] Türk, V., 'Forced Migration and Security', 15 *IJRL* 113, 115, (2003). Cf. references to asylum in the following Security Council resolutions on terrorism, adopted after 11 Sept. 2001: SC Res. 1373, 28 Sept. 2001; SC Res. 1624, 14 Sept. 2005. See also, however, Executive Committee Conclusion No. 94 (2002), on the civilian and humanitarian character of asylum.

[108] Executive Committee Standing Committee (18th Meeting), 'Interception of Asylum-Seekers and Refugees' above, n. 102, para. 20.

of Human Rights has observed, not only applies without geographical limitation, but also prohibits the indirect return of a refugee to where he or she may be persecuted.[109] National and regional courts have also supported this approach.[110]

Since the primary purpose of interception is migration control, it focuses on preventing unauthorized arrivals without inquiring into the reasons for movement. Interception measures typically lack sufficient safeguards for distinguishing those in need of international protection from other migrants, and in practice operate as barriers to the right to seek asylum. Executive Committee Conclusion No. 97 (2003) attempts to reconcile States' interests in interception, as a migration control tool, with the international protection needs of asylum seekers. It contains eight guiding principles to ensure 'adequate treatment' of intercepted persons: the State primarily responsible for protection needs is that where interception occurs; intercepted persons are to be treated humanely in accordance with human rights law; States must take into account the fundamental differences between asylum seekers and other migrants; asylum seekers must be given access to international protection mechanisms and, where needed, durable solutions, and States must respect the principle of *non-refoulement*; States must take into account the special needs of women, children, and vulnerable persons; those intercepted should not be liable to criminal prosecution or punished for illegal entry; those not in need of international protection should be swiftly returned; and those acting for the State in implementing interception measures should have specialized human rights and refugee protection training.

NGOs have criticized this Conclusion for placing the primary responsibility for intercepted persons on the State within whose territory or territorial waters the interception occurs, rather than on the State engaging in the act of interception. Since the law of State responsibility requires States to observe their international obligations extraterritorially,[111] they should be held accountable for the results of their actions wherever they occur: 'Particularly when interception occurs in the territory of a State that is not party to the Convention or that lacks fair and effective asylum procedures, the intercepting State must accept responsibility for the protection of the person.'[112] Others have noted that the Conclusion fails to refer to the principle of non-discrimination, which imposes limits on interception measures targeting particular groups.[113] Moreover, States remain liable under international human rights law if the methods they employ to deflect or deter

---

[109] Sub-Commission on the Promotion and Protection of Human Rights Res. 2000/20, 'The Right to Seek and Enjoy Asylum', preambular para. 11.

[110] *R. v. Secretary of State for the Home Department, ex p. Adan* [2001] 2 AC 477; *TI v. UK* [2000] INLR 211.

[111] *Report on Pre-ExCom Consultations*, above n. 105, Annex IX, (2 Oct. 2003).

[112] Ibid. NGOs called for UNHCR to elaborate *Guidelines on Safeguards for Interception Measures*, as stated in the *Agenda for Protection* (Goal 2, Objective 1). See further Ch. 5, ss. 3.3.1, 4.2.

[113] Brouwer, A. & Kumin, J., 'Interception and Asylum: When Migration Control and Human Rights Collide', 21 *Refuge* 6, 18 (2003).

asylum seekers constitute torture or cruel, inhuman or degrading treatment or punishment under CAT84, ICCPR66, or ECHR50.

4.3 NON-ARRIVAL POLICIES

States employ a variety of 'non-arrival' policies to prevent asylum seekers from ever reaching their territory. While passive measures, such as visa regimes, carrier sanctions, and pre-entry clearance procedures, are typically distinguished from active acts of interception, the effect of both is to deny access to territory and thereby hamper the refugee's ability to lodge an asylum claim.

4.3.1 Visa regimes

Visa regimes are a standard feature of most immigration systems, can be a permissible tool for immigration control, but are not always lawful. For example, a visa policy that maintains a system of racial discrimination clearly violates international law, while visa regimes which seek to obstruct access to protection undermine the institution of asylum and international human rights and refugee law principles.[114]

In some circumstances, visa controls may indeed reflect a reasonable, non-abusive policy and programme of restriction. This may be the case where other protection opportunities exist, such as an 'internal flight alternative' or internationally guaranteed safety zone, where the quality of the protection conforms with regional and international human rights standards.[115] In the absence of such alternatives, the possibility for abuse of rights arises.

Visa regimes are frequently exploited by States as a means of curbing unwanted migrants. They typically do not apply in a uniform manner to all foreign nationals, but 'reflect a state's political, economic, or historical ties'.[116] As a means of halting arrivals of asylum seekers, a number of States have introduced visa requirements in direct response to increased refugee claims from nationals of particular countries, sometimes with considerable success.[117] The imposition of visa

---

[114] Sianni, A., 'Interception Practices in Europe and Their Implications', 21 *Refuge* 25, 26 (2003). See, for example, Council Regulation (EC) No. 539/2001of 15 March 2001, Listing the Third Countries Whose Nationals Must Be in Possession of Visas When Crossing the External Borders and Those Whose Nationals are Exempt from that Requirements [2001] O. J. L81/1; also, No. 453/2003 (6 Mar. 2003), [2003] O. J. L69/10. A large number of refugee-producing countries are included. Australia requires all foreign nationals to have visas: Migration Act 1958 (Cth), s. 42.

[115] Although note comments by the House of Lords in *Januzi* v. *Secretary of State for the Home Department* [2006] UKHL 5; see also above, Ch. 5, s. 5.6.1

[116] Brouwer & Kumin, 'Interception and Asylum', above n. 113, 8.

[117] For example, during the exodus of refugees from Bosnia-Herzegovina in 1992, Finland and the Benelux States introduced visa requirements for Bosnians: Argent, T., 'Croatia's Crucible: Providing Asylum for Refugees from Bosnia and Hercegovina', (United States Committee for Refugees, Issues Paper, Oct. 1992) 17; see also Amnesty International, 'Recommended Actions relating to Bosnia-Hercegovina: Gross Abuses of Basic Human Rights' (AI Index EUR 48/26/92) 4–5.

requirements on nationals of refugee-producing countries has been described as 'the most explicit blocking mechanism for asylum flows',[118] since it hinders the individual's ability to seek asylum and may force asylum seekers into illegal migration channels, such as trafficking and smuggling networks. Furthermore, the imposition of visa requirements by one State may have a domino effect, as other States fear that without visa regimes they may become target countries for asylum seekers. During the Bosnian crisis in 1992, the visa regimes applied by many European States meant that countries that might otherwise have only been used as transit countries, such as Croatia and Slovenia, had to accommodate large numbers of refugees who were effectively 'locked in'.[119]

For many refugees, obtaining necessary passports from persecutory State authorities is too dangerous, while in countries where national institutions have broken down, consular authorities may be non-existent.[120] Flight is commonly very sudden, and there may not be time to obtain the requisite travel documents. Furthermore, visas are not generally issued for protection reasons,[121] and even a standard tourist visa may not be granted if it is suspected that the individual will seek asylum on arrival in the destination State. The visa regimes of the European Union and North America effectively close off whole parts of the world to asylum seekers.[122]

If external movement is premised on the acquisition of a visa, and visas for asylum are not forthcoming, then all legal means of seeking asylum are denied. Individuals are either forced into trying to obtain a visa on false premises simply to gain entry into a State in which a protection claim may be lodged, or into moving illegally.[123] Though States may lawfully control their borders, 'such control policies—if

Brouwer & Kumin cite Citizenship and Immigration Canada statistics pertaining to the introduction of visas for Hungarians and Zimbabweans in Dec. 2001, which had a dramatic effect on the reduction of asylum claims. In the case of Hungarians, numbers fell from 4,163 in 2001 to almost zero in 2002: 'Interception and Asylum', above n. 113, 6, note 16.

[118] See, for example, Morrison, J., & Crosland, B., 'The Trafficking and Smuggling of Refugees: The End Game in European Asylum Policy', UNHCR, *New Issues in Refugee Research*, Working Paper No. 39, (2001), 28.

[119] Coleman, N., '*Non-Refoulement* Revised: Renewed Review of the Status of the Principle of *Non-Refoulement* as Customary International Law', 5 *EJML* 23, 30 (2003).

[120] Council of Europe and UNHCR, 'Proceedings: Roundtable Process on Carriers' Liabilty: Second Expert Meeting on Carriers' Liability, Topic B: Respect of the Humanitarian Dimension', (Brussels, 24 Jun. 2002) 3, cited in Brouwer & Kumin, above, n. 113, fn 17.

[121] For discussion of protected entry procedures, see below, s.4.3.1. Resettlement countries may issue visas for persons already recognized as refugees or others in need of international protection: see, for example, the variety of offshore humanitarian visas issued by Australia: Migration Regulations 1994 (Cth), Sch. 1, 1402.

[122] Council Regulations 539/2001 and above n.114; Agreement between the Government of Canada and the Government of the United States of America for Cooperation in the Examination of Refugee Status Claims from Nationals of Third Countries (5 Dec. 2002).

[123] Although the impact of such measures can be offset by resettlement programmes (even from countries of origin), in practice States tend to give priority to limiting the opportunities for spontaneous movement.

pursued in isolation—can be counterproductive'.[124] It is estimated that 90 per cent of asylum seekers rely on illegal methods to enter the European Union.[125]

Partly in response to this scenario, some EU States have explored extraterritorial processing schemes called 'protected entry procedures'.[126] These schemes enable individuals to approach the diplomatic missions of States abroad and apply for asylum or another form of international protection, and for States to grant an entry permit if the claim warrants it. Discussions among EU Member States revealed insufficient support for the establishment of a formalized, self-standing EU policy on protected entry procedures, but the Commission noted that in certain circumstances, and with respect for individual Member States' discretion, a protected entry mechanism could be facilitated at the EU level as an 'emergency strand' of wider resettlement programmes to safeguard immediate and urgent protection needs.[127] UNHCR welcomed the proposal as one which could 'strengthen protection and may well complement anti-trafficking and anti-smuggling programmes by enabling refugees to find safety without having to rely on smugglers and traffickers'.[128] It acknowledged that protected entry procedures might be useful where resettlement would be 'too slow or otherwise inappropriate for particularly deserving or urgent cases', although noted that both the substantive and procedural aspects of the Commission's proposal required further clarification.[129] While protected entry procedures are important for individual asylum seekers,

[124] ECRE, 'The ECRE Tampere Dossier', (Jun. 2000), 12.

[125] ECRE, 'Broken Promises', above, n. *, 17.

[126] For example, Austria, Denmark, France, the Netherlands, Spain, and the United Kingdom in 2002, based on the legacy of protective passports during the 1940s: Noll, G., Fagerlund, J. & Liebaut, F., 'Study on the Feasibility of Processing Asylum Claims outside the EU against the Background of the Common European Asylum System and the Goal of a Common Asylum Procedure', (2003).

[127] Communication from the Commission to the Council and the European Parliament on the Managed Entry in the EU of Persons in Need of International Protection and the Enhancement of the Protection Capacity of the Regions of Origin: 'Improving Access to Durable Solutions', COM(2004) 410 final, (4 Jun. 2004), para. 35. ECRE supported this approach: 'Comments of the European Council on Refugees and Exiles on the Communication from the Commission to the Council and the European Parliament, on the Managed Entry in the EU of Persons in Need of International Protection and the Enhancement of the Protection Capacity of the Regions of Origin: "Improving Access to Durable Solutions", COM(2004) 410 final', (Sept. 2004), 5.

[128] UNHCR, 'Note on International Protection', UN doc. A/AC.96/989 (7 Jul. 2004), para. 31. See also UNHCR, 'Convention Plus Issues Paper' on 'Addressing Irregular Secondary Movements of Refugees and Asylum-Seekers', FORUM/CG/SM/03 (11 Mar. 2004), para. 16. In 2006, Human Rights Watch encouraged EU Member States to '[i]mmediately implement "protected entry procedures" through embassies in Tripoli and resettle refugees [from Libya] identified by UNHCR as being in need of resettlement', noting that this should be done 'only as a supplement' rather than as an alternative to allowing asylum seekers arriving spontaneously access to EU territory and asylum procedures: *Stemming the Flow: Abuses against Migrants, Asylum Seekers and Refugees*, (Sept. 2006) HRW Index No. E1805, Section XI.

[129] UNHCR, 'Observations on the European Commission Communication "On the Managed Entry in the EU of Persons in Need of International Protection and Enhancement of the Protection Capacity of the Regions of Origin: Improving Access to Durable Solutions" (COM(2004) 410 final, 4 June 2004)', (30 Aug. 2004), para. 11.

they do not address the global extent of refugee flows and are not an appropriate mechanism for addressing migration management concerns.[130]

4.3.2 *Pre-entry clearance and carrier sanctions*

Many States, including the United Kingdom, the United States, Canada, Australia, and several European States have immigration officials posted abroad to advise airlines and other States about fraudulent travel documents.[131] Between 1996 and 2002, Canadian officers reportedly intercepted over 40,000 persons attempting to travel to Canada with inappropriate documents.[132] In conjunction with carrier sanctions imposed on airlines, shipping and other transport companies,[133] these practices are designed to prevent passengers who do not possess valid visas or passports from leaving for a third State; they focus on verifying documents, not on the motivations for travel.[134]

A further problem with carrier sanctions and pre-arrival screening is that many of the officers checking documents do not have sufficient training to identify those with protection needs,[135] and there are rarely mechanisms in place for referring people without adequate documentation to a protection screening process. The priorities for private, commercial carriers are more likely to be the validity of documents and the avoidance of fines, than the assessment of protection needs.[136]

---

[130] See House of Lords European Union Committee, *Handling EU Asylum Claims: New Approaches Examined* (HL Paper 74, 11th Report of Session 2003–04), para. 89. This process can be differentiated from proposals to establish transit processing centres (by the United Kingdom, Denmark, the Netherlands, and Germany), which, according to Noll, 'rest on an altogether different paradigm, and raise different legal issues.': Noll 'Seeking Asylum at Embassies', above, n. 11, 545; also, Noll, G., 'Visions of the Exceptional: Legal and Theoretical Issues Raised by Transit Processing Centres and Protection Zones', 5 *EJML* 303 (2003).

[131] Council Regulation (EC) No 377/2004 of 19 February 2004 on the Creation of an Immigration Liaison Officers Network [2004] O.J. L 64/1.

[132] Brouwer & Kumin, above n. 113, 10, referring to Citizenship and Immigration Canada, 'Fact Sheet: 11 Sept. 11, 2001, A Year Later'.

[133] See, for example, Council Directive 2001/51/EC of 28 June 2001 supplementing the Provisions of Article 26 of the Convention implementing the Schengen Agreement of 14 June 1985 [2001] O.J. L 187/45.

[134] Such schemes have been described as an arbitrary form of burden-sharing which cannot be properly monitored by UNHCR and others due to the circumstances and locations in which interceptions occur: UNHCR Global Consultations on International Protection, 'NGO Background Paper on the Refugee and Migration Interface', (28–29 Jun. 2001), in 22 *RSQ* 373, 380 (2003). The IOM, which supports and is active in interception, does not have a protection mandate and is not primarily concerned with the protection entitlements of intercepted persons. For evaluation of a March 2003 proposal by Spain to require carriers to report passenger data to Member States' immigration authorities before travel, and information about passengers who had not used their return tickets, see House of Lords European Union Committee, *Fighting Illegal Immigration: Should Carriers Carry the Burden?* (5th Report of Session 2003–04, HL Paper 29, 2004).

[135] Executive Committee Standing Committee (18th Meeting), 'Interception of Asylum-Seekers and Refugees', above n. 102, paras. 17–18. See also UNHCR, 'Note on International Protection', UN doc. A/AC.96/898, (3 Jul. 1998), para. 16.

[136] The EU waives fines where an undocumented passenger subsequently applies for asylum: Council Directive 2001/51/EC, above n. 133, Preamble. However, it does not ensure *non-refoulement* or provide access to remedies for asylum seekers who have been refused permission to travel at

The House of Lords considered the legality of particular pre-entry screening measures in 2004. Since mid-2001, the United Kingdom had intermittently stationed immigration officials at Prague Airport to 'pre-clear' passengers before they boarded flights to the United Kingdom. The objective was to 'stem the flow of asylum seekers from the Czech Republic' by denying leave to enter 'to those who stated that they were intending to claim asylum in the UK and those who the officers concluded were intending to do so'.[137] The case was not strictly about asylum since it concerned the lawfulness of procedures applied to potential asylum seekers who had not yet left their country of origin. However, the appellants and UNHCR (as intervener) challenged the procedures on the grounds that they were incompatible with the UK's obligations under the 1951 Convention/1967 Protocol and customary international law, and secondly, that they involved discrimination on the ground of race, contrary to international and domestic law. The case was brought by six Czech nationals of Roma ethnic origin, who had been denied leave to enter the United Kingdom (and thus to depart the Czech Republic for that destination), and by the European Roma Rights Centre, a non-governmental organization that seeks to protect the rights of Roma in Europe.

The House of Lords held that while the 1951 Convention should be given 'a generous and purposive interpretation, bearing in mind its humanitarian objects and purpose clearly stated in the preamble . . . the court's task remains one of interpreting the written document to which the contracting states have committed themselves'.[138] Though States have an obligation to interpret international treaties in good faith, in accordance with the principle of *pacta sunt servanda*,[139] 'there is no want of good faith if a state interprets a treaty as meaning what it says and declines to do anything significantly greater than or different from what it agreed to do'.[140] The court held that article 33 only applied to asylum seekers either already in or at the frontier of a State, and in the instant case, the individuals concerned had neither 'left the Czech Republic nor presented themselves, save in a highly metaphorical sense, at the frontier of the United Kingdom'.[141] Accordingly, their argument was inconsistent with the text of the Convention, 'since it puts those expressly excluded from the protection of the Convention in the same position as those expressly included'.[142] Importantly, though, the court recognized that there is 'general acceptance' that the principle of *non-refoulement* has evolved to encompass non-rejection at the frontier.[143] The relevance of this finding is that

their point of departure or are forced to return to a country where they may face violations of their rights: ECRE, 'Broken Promises', above n. 106, 16.

[137] *Roma Rights* case, [2005] 2 AC 1, para. 4.

[138] Ibid., para. 18 (Lord Bingham); para. 48 (Lord Hope); para. 72 (Baroness Hale); para. 106 (Lord Carswell).

[139] Vienna Convention on the Law of Treaties, art. 26. For UNHCR's Written Submissions, see 17 *IJRL* 427 (2005).

[140] *Roma Rights* case [2005] 2 AC 1, para. 19; see also paras. 63–4 (Lord Hope).

[141] Ibid., para. 26 (Lord Bingham); see also para. 43 (Lord Steyn).   [142] Ibid., para. 20.

[143] Ibid., para. 26. For background discussion, see paras. 22ff.

it implies a right of at least temporary admission for asylum seekers to have their protection needs assessed.[144]

In the instant case, however, the court was not prepared to accept that the United Kingdom had created a 'virtual frontier' at Prague Airport, or that refusals in Prague to grant leave to enter the United Kingdom therefore constituted rejection at the frontier in violation of the principle of *non-refoulement*.[145] Lord Bingham distinguished the present case from that of *Sale* v. *Haitian Centers Council* on the ground that the Haitian asylum seekers were already outside their country of origin and (in contrast to the appellants in the instant case) were not free to travel to any other country.[146] The customary international law principle of *non-refoulement*, encompassing non-rejection at the frontier, was therefore found not to apply only because the persons concerned had not yet reached the frontier of the United Kingdom.

The appeal was successful, however, on the ground that the pre-clearance procedure was discriminatory, since it treated Roma seeking to travel to the United Kingdom less favourably on racial grounds than others.[147] Lord Steyn summarized the key features of the operation:

It was designed as a response to an influx of Czech Roma into the United Kingdom. The immigration oficers knew that the reason why they were stationed in Prague was to stop asylum seekers travelling to the United Kingdom. They also knew that almost all Czech asylum seekers were Roma, because the Roma are a disadvantaged racial minority in the Czech Republic. Thus there was from the outset a high risk that individuals recognised as Roma would be targeted by specially intrusive and sceptical questioning. There was a striking difference in treatment of Roma and non Roma at the hands of immigration officers operating at Prague Airport. The statistics show that almost 90% of Roma were refused leave to enter and only 0.2% of non Roma were refused leave to enter. Roma were 400 times more likely than non Roma to be refused permission.[148]

Accordingly, the court found that the practice was 'not only unlawful in domestic law but also contrary to our obligations under customary international law and under international treaties to which the United Kingdom is a party',[149] however,

---

[144] See further above, Ch. 5.

[145] Interestingly, a representative of the Air Transport Association of Canada described the threat of carrier sanctions, effectively requiring airline personnel to pre-screen passengers, as transporting the border to the embarkation point: Canadian Council for Refugees, 'Interdiction and Refugee Protection: Bridging the Gap', (International Workshop, Ottawa, 29 May 2003), 16. Others have described visa regimes and carrier sanctions as having 'pushed back' the border to countries of origin: see House of Lords Select Committee on the European Union, *Proposals for a European Border Guard* (Session 2002–03, 29th Report), para. 13.

[146] *Roma Rights* case [2005] 2 AC 1, para. 21, referring to *Sale* v. *Haitian Centers Council* 509 US 155 (1993).

[147] *Roma Rights* case [2005] 2 AC 1, paras. 104–05; paras. 10, 31 (Lord Bingham); paras. 38, 47 (Lord Steyn); para. 48 (Lord Hope); paras. 106, 114 (Lord Carswell).

[148] Ibid., para. 34 (Lord Steyn); see also paras. 85, 92, 93 (Baroness Hale).

[149] Ibid., para. 98 (Baroness Hale); paras. 38, 47 (Lord Steyn); see also UNHCR's submissions on the prohibition of discrimination on the grounds of race: 'Written Case', 17 *IJRL* 427, 440–45 (2005).

it did not constitute discrimination under article 3 of the 1951 Convention because that provision applied only to recognized refugees and not to asylum seekers whose status had not yet been determined.[150]

International human rights law may thus offer some of the strongest arguments against States' implementation of deterrence measures, although admittedly the norm of non-discrimination in international law carries a particular weight not shared by all human rights principles. Apart from discrimination cases, however, human rights law offers a basis upon which to challenge both the procedural and substantive operation of deterrence schemes, and provides the content of those other obligations in international law with which the actions of States must be compatible.[151]

5. International law responses

In the *Roma Rights* case, the House of Lords held that State practice did not support the proposition that a State's *non-refoulement* obligations extend to general deterrence measures, noting in particular the widespread practice of visa regimes enforced by carrier sanctions,[152] whose effect was likened to the pre-clearance procedures imposed on the appellants. Since 'it could not plausibly be argued that a visa regime would have been contrary to the practice of the nations ... [t]hat conclusion must in my opinion apply also to the pre-clearance procedure which the appellants challenge'.[153]

However, where the *effect* of such regimes is to obstruct the flight of persons at risk of persecution or other serious harm, then other international legal obligations may be triggered which render deterrence measures unlawful.[154]

5.1 THE RIGHT TO LEAVE ANY COUNTRY

The right to leave any country, including one's own, is a feature of most international human rights instruments.[155] It immediately precedes the right to seek asylum in UDHR48, and is expressed as a binding State duty in article 12

---

[150] The United States applies different standards of screening to boats intercepted in the Carribean, depending on the nationality of those on board. For details of the different procedures, see Frelick, B., 'The United States: Maritime Interdiction' in Canadian Council for Refugees 'Interdiction and Refugee Protection: Bridging the Gap', above n, 145, 4–5; van Selm, J. & Cooper, B., *The New 'Boat People': Ensuring Safety and Determining Status*, (2005). Differential treatment raises serious questions about access to protection and solutions (see Brouwer & Kumin, above, n. 113, 8), and may contravene the non-discrimination principle under international human rights treaties and customary international law.
[151] Goodwin-Gill, G. S., 'State Responsibility and the "Good Faith" Obligation in International Law', in Fitzmaurice, M. & Sarooshi, D., *Issues of State Responsibility before International Judicial Institutions*, (2004), 75, 96–100.   [152] *Roma Rights* case, above, n. 94, para. 28.
[153] Ibid., above, n. 94, para. 28.   [154] See discussion of 'good faith', below, at s. 5.4.
[155] Art. 13(1) UDHR48; art. 12 ICCPR66; art. 2 ECHR50 Protocol 4; art. 22 ACHR69; art. 12(2) ACHPR81; art. 21 ArabCHR. The right also appears in other contexts: see, for example, art. 5

ICCPR66.[156] Although it operates without limitation in article 13(2) UDHR48, it has never been considered an absolute right. Thus, ICCPR66 restricts the right to leave where 'necessary to protect national security, public order (*ordre public*), public health or morals or the rights and freedoms of others', provided this is consistent with the other ICCPR66 rights and stipulated by law. The ECHR50 and ACHR69 provide that restrictions must also be 'necessary in a democratic society'. Such exceptions were incorporated to prevent people leaving purely to escape legal proceedings, paying fines, taxes, or maintenance allowances, or to avoid obligations such as national service.[157] State practice reveals additional limitations on the right to leave, including visa requirements. The European Court of Human Rights has stated that the right to leave any country under article 2 of Protocol 4 ECHR50, 'implies a right to leave for such a country of the person's choice *to which he may be admitted*'.[158] This restriction is not found in the text of Protocol 4, but has been interpolated from the gap between the individual's right to leave and the absence of a correlative duty on a third State to admit.

The Human Rights Committee has expressed concerns that domestic legal and bureaucratic obstacles may seriously impinge on the right to leave a country, emphasizing that any restrictions under article 12(3) must be based on clear legal grounds, be *necessary* to protect the prescribed purposes, conform with the principle of proportionality, and be the least intrusive measure to achieve the desired result.[159] As a matter of general policy, immigration controls that prevent an

ICERD65; art. 2, 1973 Convention on the Suppression and Punishment of the Crime of Apartheid; art. 4(1), 1977 European Convention on the Status of Migrant Workers; art. 10(2) CRC89; art. 5(2), 1985 UN Declaration on the Rights of Non-Nationals; art. 8, 1990 Convention on the Protection of the Rights of All Migrant Workers and Members of Their Families. See also Declaration on the Right to Leave and the Right to Return, adopted by the Uppsala Colloquium, (1972); Strasbourg Declaration on the Right to Leave and Return, adopted by the Meeting of Experts in Strasbourg, (1986).

[156] Botswana has made a reservation to art. 12(3) to 'the extent that the provisions are compatible with Section 14 of the Constitution of the Republic of Botswana relating to the imposition of restrictions reasonably required in certain exceptional instances'. Denmark, Ireland, and the Netherlands have formally objected to this, arguing that it raises doubts about Botswana's commitment to fulfil its commitments under the ICCPR and is incompatible with the treaty's object and purpose.

[157] UN doc. A/2929 (1955). For further examples of restrictions, see Human Rights Committee, 'Initial Report: Tajikistan', UN doc. CCPR/C/TJK/2001/4, (11 Apr. 2005), para. 159; 'Third Periodic Report: Netherlands', UN doc. CCPR/C/NET/99/3, (25 Aug. 2000), paras. 84, 609; 'Third Periodic Report: Netherlands (Addendum)', UN doc. CCPR/C/NET/99/3/Add.1, (21 May 2001), para. 48; 'Fourth Periodic Report: Yugoslavia', UN doc. CCPR/C/YUG/99/4, (28 Jun. 1999), para. 220 (where the right to leave may be denied to prevent the spread of contagious diseases, pursuant to art. 30 of the Yugoslavian Constitution); 'Initial Report: Israel (Addendum), UN doc. CCPR/C/81/Add.13, (2 Jun. 1998), para. 378.

[158] *Peltonen* v. *Finland*, Application No. 19583/92 (20 Feb. 1995) (inadmissible); *KS* v. *Finland*, Application No. 21228/93 (24 May 1995) (inadmissible); *Napijalo* v. *Croatia*, Application No. 66485/01 (13 Nov. 2003), para. 68. Hannum, H., *The Right to Leave and Return in International Law and Practice*, (1987).

[159] Human Rights Committee, General Comment No. 27 (1999), paras. 14, 16, 17. See further Boutkevitch, V., 'Working Paper on the Right to Freedom of Movement and Related Issues', UN doc. E/CN.4/Sub.2/1997/22, (19 July. 1997), 20.

individual's right to leave a country will not satisfy those requirements. As one commentator has observed, the yardstick must be that the exercise of the right to leave is the rule, and limitations the exception.[160] Furthermore, any restrictive measures must comply with other principles of human rights law, including non-discrimination. This is why, in the *Roma Rights* case, the discriminatory application of pre-entry clearance was deemed unlawful by the House of Lords.

The broader enunciation of the right to leave any country in article 13 UDHR48 lacks a mechanism for international implementation. As expressed, it is a right engaging the responsibility of individual States, rather than the international community as a whole. The right to leave is not a right which other States need to 'complete' through a duty to admit; rather, it is simply a right which each State must guarantee to those within its own territories, as a matter of constitutional principle. However, where a State refuses to let an individual depart because he or she does not possess the necessary documentation to enter a third State, then the right loses its binary State–individual focus and necessarily acquires an international dimension. In the context of asylum, this has important consequences with respect to the host State's ability to prevent entry, and the receiving State's obligations to asylum seekers.

The right to leave, the right to seek and to enjoy asylum, and the principle of *non-refoulement* share a delicate but significant relationship. The right to leave suggests a dual obligation on the State: a negative obligation not to prevent departure, and a positive obligation to issue travel documents (at least with respect to nationals).[161] It is, however, an incomplete right, since there is no corresponding duty on other States to guarantee entry to persons other than their own nationals or those with 'special ties to or claims in relation to a given country'.[162] While the principle of *non-refoulement* circumscribes State action in this regard, it still cannot be fully equated with a legal right of entry.[163]

---

[160] Hofmann, R., *Die Ausreisefreiheit nach Völkerrecht und staatlichem Recht*, (1988), 315, as referred to in Hailbronner, K., 'Comments On: The Right to Leave, the Right to Return and the Question of a Right to Remain', in Gowlland-Debbas, V., ed., *The Problem of Refugees in the Light of Contemporary International Law Issues*, (1996), 112. See also, CSCE, 'Document of the Copenhagen Meeting of the Second Conference on the Human Dimension', (1990), s. 9.5: restrictions on the right to leave 'will have the character of very rare exceptions'. Text in Brownlie, I. & Goodwin-Gill, G. S., *Basic Documents on Human Rights*, (5th edn., 2006), 849.

[161] Chétail, V., 'Freedom of Movement and Transnational Migrations: A Human Rights Perspective', in Aleinikoff, T. A. & Chétail, V., eds., *Migration and International Legal Norms*, (2003), 55.

[162] Human Rights Committee, General Comment No. 27, para. 20. In the view of the Committee, art. 12 ICCPR66 'permits a broader interpretation that might embrace other categories of long-term residents, including but not limited to stateless persons arbitrarily deprived of the right to acquire the nationality of the country of such residence'. The right to return to one's State is expressly limited to nationals in ECHR50, ACHR69, and Arab CHR 2004. Elsewhere, it is generally argued that the right extends to nationals and permanent residents: see Chétail, above n. 161 for additional references.

[163] It depends, of course, on how one chooses to characterize the operation of the principle. Generally, States will allow asylum seekers to enter their territory in fact while their protection needs are assessed, even though they may not be admitted as a matter of law. It is the principle of *non-refoulement* that ultimately means that those with a protection need cannot be removed, and so in a

The right of asylum is important for protection purposes because 'a person who *leaves* the state of his nationality and applies to the authorities of another state for asylum, whether at the frontier of the second state or from within it, should not be rejected or returned to the first state without appropriate enquiry into the persecution of which he claims to have a well-founded fear'.[164] Given the protection orientation and objectives of refugee and human rights law, the limited notion of the right to leave to seek asylum from persecution may be the only aspect of the right to leave one's country in international law to impose any duty on other States. In this sense, the nearest correlative duty may be not to frustrate the exercise of that right in such a way as to leave individuals exposed to persecution or other violations of their human rights; and that correspondingly intentional policies and practices of containment *without protection* constitute an abuse of rights.[165]

This is where the international dimension of the right, alluded to above, is triggered. In situations where individuals or groups in one State are exposed to persecution or serious human rights violations, then, in accordance with international law, States are also obliged to respect the right to leave to seek and enjoy asylum, and ought not to exercise their own rights to control the movement of people in such a way as to frustrate attempts to find effective protection. This argument is supported by the principle of non-rejection at the frontier and prohibitions on removal under human rights law, which limit States' freedom to remove individuals from their territory. Yet, in *Xhavara* v. *Italy and Albania*,[166] the European Court of Human Rights held that Italian interception measures did not breach the right to freedom of movement under article 2(2) of Protocol 4 ECHR50, for they were aimed at preventing entry to Italy, rather than preventing departure from Albania.

Under international law, the right of asylum is broader than a mere procedural right to lodge an application for protection within or at the frontier of another territory, although that is a necessary component.[167] While it falls short of imposing

circuitous sense, it is this principle that secures 'entry'. Austria amended its Aliens Act in 2002 to provide that *refusal of entry*, expulsion, or deportation are unlawful if they would lead to a violation of art. 2 or 3 ECHR50 or of Protocol 6. Edwards argues that the right to leave any country and the right to seek asylum 'are two sides of the same coin in the refugee context', and that 'it would make a nonsense of the 1951 Convention' if it were not intended to permit an asylum seeker to enter a State 'at least for the purposes of refugee status determination, especially where an individual has reached a country's territory, such as its territorial seas or a waiting zone in an international airport': Edwards, A., 'Human Rights, Refugees, and the Right "to Enjoy" Asylum', 17 *IJRL* 293, 302 (2005).

[164] *Roma Rights* case, [2005] 2 AC 1, para. 26 (Lord Bingham) (emphasis added).

[165] To paraphrase a former ILC Rapporteur on State Responsibility, a 'primary' rule of international law forbids the 'abusive' exercise of rights of control over the movement of persons, which rights will be violated if certain limits are exceeded in the course of their exercise, or if they are exercised with the (sole) intention of harming others. Cf. Ago, R., *Second Report on State Responsibility*, UN doc. A/CN.4/233: Yearbook of the ILC, 1970-II, 191, 193.

[166] Application No. 39473/98 (11 Jan. 2001) (inadmissible).

[167] The drafting debates appear to accept that any individual in search of asylum would have an opportunity to request it; see, for example, UNGAOR Part 1 (3rd Session, 1948), 'Summary Records of Meetings', 121st Meeting (3 Nov. 1948), 330–31 (Mrs Corbet, UK). The European Parliament

an obligation on States to grant asylum to anyone seeking it, the operation of principles of international refugee and human rights law, in particular the principle of *non-refoulement*, requires States to consider asylum claims and provide protection to persons with a demonstrated international protection need. To have any meaning, the right to seek asylum implies not only a right to access asylum procedures, but also to be able to leave one's country in search of protection.

5.2 ARTICLE 31 OF THE 1951 CONVENTION

Article 31 of the 1951 Convention recognizes that the circumstances compelling flight may lead refugees to seek entry to States without possessing proper documentation, and in view of this stipulates that States must not penalize refugees for irregular entry. Read in conjunction with article 33 on *non-refoulement*, and the right to leave a country and seek asylum, article 31 provides support for a limited right of (at least) temporary admission for asylum seekers to access fair and effective refugee status procedures.[168]

Article 31 reveals that international law does not require asylum seekers to enter States in a regular manner, provided that they can show 'good cause' for entering without the requisite documentation.[169] This fundamental aspect of the 1951 Convention underscores the right of people in distress to seek protection, even if their actions constitute a breach of the domestic laws of a country of asylum. Irregular or no documentation does not reveal anything about the credibility of a protection claim. Article 31 recognizes that the circumstances compelling flight commonly force refugees to travel without passports, visas, or other documentation, while restrictive immigration policies mean that most refugees are likely to be ineligible for visas through official migration channels. The Protocol against the Smuggling of Migrants by Land, Air and Sea, and the Protocol to Prevent, Suppress and Punish Trafficking in Persons, which supplement the UN Convention against Transnational Organized Crime, each includes a savings clause noting that nothing in those instruments affects the applicability of the principle of *non-refoulement*.[170]

Yet, the asylum seeker exercising his or her right under international law to seek asylum frequently becomes the 'unlawful non-citizen' under domestic law.[171]

---

describes the right of asylum as a procedural right to apply for asylum, rather than a substantive right to obtain asylum, but in our view it is not *only* a procedural right: <http://www.europarl.eu.int/comparl/libe/elsj/charter/art18/default_en.htm>.

[168] This protection applies to asylum seekers travelling on false documents: *R. v. Uxbridge Magistrates' Court;, ex p. Adimi* [2001] QB 667, [1999] Imm AR 560.

[169] For discussion of 'good cause', see above, Ch. 5, s. 3.3.5; Hathaway, J. C., *The Law of Refugee Status*, (1991), 46–50.

[170] Protocol against the Smuggling of Migrants by Land, Air and Sea, art. 14(1); Protocol to Prevent, Suppress and Punish Trafficking in Persons, art. 19(1).

[171] See, for example, Migration Act 1958 (Cth), s. 14.

He or she suffers the 'imputation of double criminality',[172] having entered in an irregular manner, often with the assistance of people smugglers, and being aligned with 'crime' by officials and the media, leading to assumptions about the (il)legitimacy of their claims.[173] For example, the Australian government sought to justify the non-admission of some 400 asylum seekers arriving by boat in 2001 as an approach that 'saved lives—by deterring people from undertaking dangerous journeys from places of protection—and saved space—for the unseen, unheard refugees who could not afford people smugglers'.[174] Despite the fact that all were subsequently recognized as Convention refugees, the Australian focus on the lack of visas was used to tarnish their authenticity and responsibility as refugees, and to imply that their flight had slowed the resettlement of others still abroad.[175]

5.3 STATE RESPONSIBILITY FOR EXTRATERRITORIAL ACTS

The extraterritorial application of the principle of *non-refoulement* under the 1951 Convention was examined in Chapter 5. There it was argued that a State's obligations under international law extend beyond its physical territory; accordingly, removing refugees 'in any manner whatsoever' to territories where they may be persecuted, whether removal occurs within or outside State territory, will breach article 33(1).

However, the principle of *non-refoulement* under the 1951 Convention can only be triggered once an asylum seeker is outside his or her country of origin or habitual residence. The House of Lords rejected the idea of a 'virtual frontier', created by the imposition of entry controls at foreign border posts from which potential refugees may seek to depart, on the basis that the Convention text makes clear that a refugee is someone already outside his or her home State.[176] Unlike the 1951 Convention, however, human rights treaties precluding *refoulement* do not require the refugee to be outside his or her country before a potential receiving State's obligations are engaged. Thus, if an airline liaison officer[177] employed by a

---

[172] See generally, Harding, J., *The Uninvited: Migrant Journeys to the Rich World*, (2000).

[173] See further UNHCR, *Addressing Security Concerns without Undermining Refugee Protection: UNHCR's Perspective*, (2001).

[174] Mr Ruddock (Australia): UN doc. A/AC.96/SR.562, para. 14 (2002) (in relation to the *Tampa* incident).

[175] Australia's refugee programme is designed to have this effect. There are annual onshore and offshore refugee quotas. If numbers arriving onshore exceed the annual designated quota, then the offshore quota is reduced accordingly.

[176] *R. (European Roma Rights Centre)* v. *Immigration Officer at Prague Airport* (*UNHCR Intervening*) [2005] 2 AC 1, [2004] UKHL 55.

[177] Whether the actions of airline employees refusing embarkation to passengers lacking the requisite immigration documents for fear of incurring carrier sanctions imposed by potential receiving States can be attributed to those States, and whether those actions in turn constitute violations of specific international obligations, will be much more difficult to establish. The conduct in question and the underlying laws and policies may be better considered as evincing a lack of good faith to implement treaty obligations.

receiving State refuses embarkation to an individual fearing inhuman treatment in the country he or she seeks to leave, this could potentially constitute a breach of that receiving State's obligations under article 7 ICCPR66 or article 3 ECHR50, in addition to obstructing the right to leave and seek asylum.[178]

The problem, of course, is that pre-entry clearance does not generally contain procedures for identifying those with international protection needs. The imposition of fines on airline carriers that allow the embarkation of passengers without the appropriate travel documentation has effectively shifted migration control away from State authorities to private, commercial entities. As a matter of international law, States cannot contract out or 'privatize' their legal obligations: they may contract out performance, but not responsibility. While the imposition of carrier sanctions on airlines and transport companies shifts immigration screening on to private corporations, this does not absolve States of responsibility if asylum seekers are denied the right to leave a country and/or subjected to *refoulement*.[179] The law of State responsibility attributes the conduct of private entities 'empowered by the law of that State to exercise elements of the governmental authority' to the State itself.[180] Similarly, the conduct of an individual or group of persons is 'considered as an act of a State under international law if the person or group of persons is in fact acting on the instructions of, or under the direction or control of, that State in carrying out the conduct'.[181] In the refugee context, Lauterpacht and Bethlehem also note that the principle of *non-refoulement* applies 'to the conduct of State officials or those acting on behalf of the State *wherever this occurs*', including extraterritorially.[182]

---

[178] There is no principled reason for applying a higher threshold than States would apply if the individual had already reached their territory; indeed, given that they are still present in the territory in which ill-treatment is feared, one could argue that the risk of such treatment is even more immediate. Note the particular reasoning in *R. (B) v. Secretary of State for Foreign and Commonwealth Affairs* [2005] QB 643, where the asylum seekers had fled immigration detention in Australia and so were regarded as 'fugitives', to whom extradition law principles should apply. Accordingly, the court regarded a request by Australian authorities for the asylum seekers' return as mandatory, unless refusing to do so would be 'clearly necessary in order to protect them from the immediate likelihood of experiencing serious injury': para. 89. But see *R. (Al-Skeini) v. Secretary of State for Defence* [2006] 3 WLR 508, [2005] EWCA Civ. 1609, paras. 113–128, on the notion of 'effective control' as a basis for human rights responsibilities.

[179] Sometimes carrier sanctions legislation will provide that it is to operate without prejudice to the State's international obligations; see, for example, Council Directive 2001/51/EC, above n. 133; Immigration and Refugee Protection Act, s. 148 (Canada).

[180] See art. 5, 'Conduct of persons or entities exercising elements of governmental authority', in the ILC's 'Articles on the Responsibility of States for Internationally Wrongful Acts', UNGA res. 56/83, 12 Dec. 2001, Annex. The ILC's commentary to art. 5 specifically mentions as an example of attribution the situation where, 'Private or State-owned airlines may have delegated to them certain powers in relation to immigration control or quarantine.' See Crawford, J., *The International Law Commission's Articles on State Responsibility: Introduction, Text and Commentaries*, (2002), 100.

[181] Art. 8, 'Conduct directed or controlled by a State'; see also the cases cited in the Commentary thereto: Crawford, above note, 110, fn 161.

[182] Lauterpacht, E. & Bethlehem, D., 'The Scope and Content of the Principle of *Non-Refoulement*: Opinion' in Feller, E., Türk, V. & Nicholson, F., eds., *Refugee Protection in International Law: UNHCR's Global Consultations on International Protection*, (2003), para. 67.

As UNHCR has observed, while States may have a legitimate interest in curtailing irregular migration through interception measures, they must also respect their international obligations and implement transparent systems for identifying individuals in need of international protection.[183] At a minimum, the combined operation of the right to leave, the right to seek and to enjoy asylum, and the principle of *non-refoulement* requires States to grant asylum seekers access to an asylum determination procedure.[184]

5.4 GOOD FAITH

A basic principle of international law is that States have a responsibility to implement their treaty obligations in good faith.[185] This duty is breached if a combination of acts or omissions has the overall effect of rendering the fulfilment of treaty obligations obsolete, or defeat the object and purpose of a treaty. A lack of good faith is distinct from (although may also encompass) a violation of an express term of a treaty. The duty requires parties to a treaty 'not only to observe the letter of the law, but also to abstain from acts which would inevitably affect their ability to perform the treaty'.[186] Thus, a State lacks good faith 'when it seeks to avoid or to "divert" the obligation which it has accepted, or to do indirectly what it is not permitted to do directly'.[187] The test for good faith is an objective one; it looks to the practical effect of State action, not its intent or motivations.[188]

In the context of the right to seek asylum, measures which have the effect of blocking access to procedures or to territory may not only breach express

---

[183] Executive Committee Standing Committee, 18th Meeting, 'Interception of Asylum-Seekers and Refugees: The International Framework and Recommendations for a Comprehensive Approach', UN doc. EC/50/SC/CRP.17, (9 Jun. 2000) paras. 17–18. See also UNHCR, 'Note on International Protection', UN doc. A/AC.96/898 (3 Jul. 1998), para. 16.

[184] As explained below (Ch. 10) refugee status determination is implicitly required by the principle of *non-refoulement*, while the nature of the refugee definition itself supposes case-by-case determination of claims. The right of an asylum seeker to a hearing was expressly recognized by the Inter-American Commission of Human Rights in *Haitian Center for Human Rights* v. *United States*, Case 10/675, Rep. No. 51/96, (13 Mar. 1997), Inter-Am.C.H.R., OEA/Ser.L/V/II.95 Doc. 7 rev. at 550 (1997), para. 155. See also Pallis, M., 'Obligations of the States towards Asylum Seekers at Sea: Interactions and Conflicts between Legal Regimes' 14 *IJRL* 329, 346–7 (2002).

[185] 1969 Vienna Convention on the Law of Treaties, 1155 *UNTS* 331, arts. 26, 31; Declaration on Principles of International Law concerning Friendly Relations and Cooperation among States in accordance with the Charter of the United Nations, UNGA res 2625 (XXV) (24 Oct. 1970), para. 3. See Goodwin-Gill, G. S., 'State Responsibility and the "Good Faith" Obligation in International Law', in Fitzmaurice, M. & Sarooshi, D., eds., *Issues of State Responsibility before International Judicial Institutions* (2004), esp. 85–8. See also UNHCR's submissions in the *Roma Rights* case: UNHCR, 'Written Case', 17 *IJRL* 427 (2005), paras. 24–38. The House of Lords rejected the issue of good faith on the basis that the 1951 Convention did not apply, as the individuals concerned had not yet left their country of origin: *Roma Rights* case, [2005] 2 AC 1, para. 64 (Lord Hope).

[186] *Yearbook of the International Law Commission*, 1964, vol. I (Summary Records of the 16th Session), 727th Meeting (20 May 1964), 70.

[187] UNHCR, 'Written Case', above, n. 185, para. 32.

[188] Brownlie, I., *Principles of Public International Law*, (6th edn., 2003), 425–30, 444; Crawford, *Articles on State Responsibility*, above, n. 180, 84.

obligations under international human rights and refugee law, but may also violate the principle of good faith.[189] Although States do not have a duty to facilitate travel to their territories by asylum seekers, the options available to States wishing to frustrate the movement of asylum seekers are limited by specific rules of international law and by States' obligations to fulfil their international commitments in good faith. Even though immigration control per se may be a legitimate exercise of State sovereignty, it must nevertheless be pursued within the boundaries of international law.

Thus, any State imposing extraterritorial interception or pre-entry clearance measures with regard to those having an international protection need ought, as a matter of law, to consider the facts relating to conditions in the country of origin, especially with respect to human rights, persecution, and discrimination. It ought further to consider the impact of its proposed regime on the rights and obligations of other States and the rights and interests of individuals, especially where these are protected by treaty or general international law; ensure that its actions are compatible with its international obligations; act in accordance with the rules of general international law; and exercise its rights reasonably—proportionately to a lawful purpose—and with due regard to alternatives. Non-arrival policies, which effectively prevent the occurrence of events which would otherwise trigger breaches of international law, are therefore problematic. Removing the necessity for flight, as in the creation of a 'security zone' or 'safe haven' in northern Iraq in 1991, is vastly different from *preventing* flight for those who are in need of international protection. Through pre-entry clearance at Prague airport, the United Kingdom obstructed access for asylum seekers, such that there was no lawful way for an asylum seeker to travel to the United Kingdom.[190] The deliberate implementation of such measures, the express purpose of which is to prevent the State's international obligations from ever being triggered, opens up the perennial question of abuse of rights in international law, and the operation of the principle of good faith.

Although the House of Lords ultimately rejected the good faith argument in the *Roma Rights* case, it did so on the basis of the principle's relation to the 1951 Convention alone, rather than other aspects of human rights law.[191] Lord Hope

---

[189] For example, in the *Roma Rights* case, the Czech Republic was obliged to allows its citizens to leave its territory by virtue of art. 2 Protocol 4 ECHR50, and the UK had accepted a duty to protect freedom of movement and non-discrimination in the application of the law: arts. 12, 26 ICCPR66 (although the UK has entered a reservation to art. 12, reserving its right to 'continue to apply such immigration legislation governing entry into, stay in and departure from the United Kingdom as they may deem necessary from time to time').

[190] Under the Immigration Rules, asylum is not listed as a 'recognized purpose' for seeking entry to the United Kingdom. The United Kingdom regarded its Convention obligations as limited to not taking enforcement action against an asylum seeker already in the country, which would result in *refoulement*: Home Office, Statement of Immigration Rules, paras. 327–52.

[191] The court regarded it more as 'an underlying principle of an explanatory and legitimating rather than an active or creative nature': *Roma Rights* case, [2005] 2 AC 1, para. 60, see also para. 62.

observed that the 1951 Convention, in terms, 'does not require the state to abstain from controlling the movements of people outside its borders who wish to travel to it in order to claim asylum'.[192] He reasoned:

The conclusion must be that steps which are taken to control the movements of such people who have not yet reached the state's frontier are not incompatible with the acceptance of the obligations which arise when refugees have arrived in its territory. To argue that such steps are incompatible with the principle of good faith as they defeat the object and purpose of the treaty is to argue for the enlargement of the obligations which are to be found in the Convention.[193]

The good faith argument had been put to the court in much broader terms. It had been argued that the actions of the United Kingdom and the Czech Republic demonstrated a lack of good faith in relation both to the 1951 Convention, and to ICCPR66, the 1966 International Convention for the Elimination of All Forms of Racial Discrimination (ICERD66), and ECHR50.[194] The court did not refer to these in its judgment, but dealt only with the issue of good faith in relation to *particular* non-arrival measures. Nevertheless, in certain contexts, such as physical interdiction, the principle of good faith may still serve to underline the illegality of State action, by delimiting the lawful *extent* of deterrence measures, given the possibility for *refoulement* or chain *refoulement*.

In its Advisory Opinion on *Reservations to the Genocide Convention*, the International Court of Justice stated that in the area of human rights law, of which refugee law is an integral part, treaties have 'a purely humanitarian and civilizing purpose'. In such treaties:

the contracting States do not have any interests of their own; they merely have, one and all, a common interest, namely, the accomplishment of those high purposes which are the *raison d'être* of the convention. Consequently, in ... convention[s] of this type one cannot speak of individual advantages or disadvantages to States, or of the maintenance of a perfect contractual balance between rights and duties.[195]

While there is no provision in the 1951 Convention that expressly mandates States to process asylum seekers within their borders, a combination of provisions (no penalties for illegal entry, non-discrimination, *non-refoulement*, access to courts, and the status which Contracting States owe to refugees) reinforces the object and purpose of the 1951 Convention as assuring to refugees 'the widest possible exercise of ... fundamental rights and freedoms'.[196] States are responsible for refugees in their territory, as well as those whom they subject to enforcement action beyond their territorial jurisdiction. This responsibility entails ensuring that refugees are not returned in any manner to territories in which they face—or

[192] Ibid., para. 64.   [193] Ibid.
[194] See UNHCR, 'Written Case', 17 *IJRL* 427 (2005), paras 24–38.
[195] *Reservations to the Genocide Convention* (Advisory Opinion) (1951) ICJ *Reports* 15, 23.
[196] Preamble, 1951 Convention.

risk return to—persecution, torture, or other cruel, inhuman or degrading treatment or punishment; *and,* if sent elsewhere, that they have access to protection and durable solutions.

Furthermore, for States to seek to avoid their obligations by contracting them out to other States frustrates the goals of the multilateral treaty regime and is incompatible with the 1951 Convention's object and purpose.

The principle of good faith requires States to consider the use of reasonable alternatives proportionate to its policy objectives in international affairs, which are least likely to violate its international obligations.[197] The broader international protection regime, comprising refugee law, human rights law, and more generally applicable rules informed by the principle of good faith, provides a normative and institutional framework for solutions. The very nature of the international protection regime is premised on States *not* acting unilaterally and in their own self-interest. Indeed, a State that sends out a message of unilateral disregard of the principles of international cooperation will inevitably lead to a disinclination on the part of other States to contribute to solutions.

6. Non-admission policies: the 'safe' country and the concept of 'effective protection'

6.1 JURISDICTIONAL ISSUES: IDENTIFYING THE STATE RESPONSIBLE FOR DETERMINING A CLAIM

The principle of access to a fair and efficient procedure for the determination of claims to asylum and refugee status has long been a cardinal principle in UNHCR's protection policy, and has been endorsed with equal consistency by the UN General Assembly.[198] In practice, however, various devices may be employed to keep asylum seekers from the procedural door. In addition to the interception measures described above, the notion of the 'safe country' (whether of origin or asylum) creates a further buffer zone between the countries from which asylum seekers have fled and the States in which they hope to find protection.

Debate over the right of access to procedures and the related question of responsibility to determine claims continues in various fora. The UNHCR Executive

[197] Goodwin-Gill, 'State Responsibility and the "Good Faith" Obligation', above n. 185', 98.
[198] See for example, the 1988 statement by UN High Commissioner for Refugees Jean-Pierre Hocké: 'UNHCR's concern was that fair and efficient asylum procedures guaranteeing full access by those in search of asylum should be the undisputed basis for all future developments': UN doc. A/AC.96/SR.425, para. 66; full text annexed to *Report* of the 39th Session: UN doc. A/AC.96/721 (1988). Also, UNGA res. 48/116, 20 Dec. 1993, para. 4; 49/169, (23 Dec. 1994)—the latter calling for access to procedures, 'or, as appropriate, to other mechanisms to ensure that persons in need of international protection are identified and granted ... protection, while not diminishing the protection afforded to refugees under the terms of the 1951 Convention, the 1967 Protocol and relevant regional instruments': para. 5.

Committee in 1985, for example, examined the question of so-called irregular movements of refugees and asylum seekers, defined to include those who move, without first obtaining authorization, from countries in which they have already found protection in order to seek asylum or permanent resettlement elsewhere.[199] Executive Committee Conclusion No. 58, finally adopted in 1989, recognized that there might be compelling reasons for such onward movement, and emphasized that return should only be contemplated where the refugee was protected against *refoulement*, allowed to remain in the country in question, and treated in accordance with basic human rights standards pending a durable solution.

Since then, both the Executive Committee and the UN General Assembly have repeatedly endorsed the general principle of access to refugee procedures,[200] and the specific need for agreement on responsibility.[201] An increasing trend has been for States to emphasize that *non-refoulement* does not stand in the way of returns to 'safe third countries'.[202] Generally, however, States have accepted that 'the fundamental criterion when considering resort to the notion (of safe third country), [is] protection against *refoulement*'.[203]

The fact of an asylum seeker's presence in or transit through a State does raise certain issues of jurisdiction. However, at first glance, and from the perspective of customary international law, these appear more permissive than mandatory, in the sense that such a State *may* determine whether an asylum seeker is a refugee, but is not *obliged* so to determine unless minded to return the individual to a country in which his or her life or freedom may be threatened. Possible exceptions, such as arise in the case of obligations to extradite or to prosecute, are almost exclusively based on formal agreements.

---

[199] UNHCR, 'Irregular Movements of Asylum Seekers and Refugees': UN doc. EC/SCP/40/ Rev.1 (1985); *Report* of the Sub-Committee of the Whole on International Protection: UN doc. A/AC.96/671 (Oct. 1985); *Report* of the 36th Session of the Executive Committee: UN doc. A/AC.96/673, (Oct. 1985), paras. 77–82. Adoption of the Conclusions was delayed until 1989, owing to German reservations.

[200] See, for example, UNGA res. 49/169, 23 Dec. 1995, para. 5, reiterating 'the importance of ensuring access, for all persons seeking international protection, to fair and efficient procedures for the determination of refugee status...' See further below, Ch. 10, s. 2.1, n.120, for changes in the language of the resolutions.

[201] See, for example, Executive Committee General Conclusion on International Protection No. 71 (1993), *Report* of the 44th Session: UN doc. A/AC.96/821 (1993), para. 19(k), (l), recognizing 'the advisability of concluding agreements among States directly concerned... to provide for the protection of refugees through the adoption of common criteria and related arrangements to determine which State shall be responsible for considering an application for asylum... and for granting the protection required,' and emphasizing 'that such procedures, measures and agreements must include safeguards adequate to ensure... that persons in need of international protection are identified and that refugees are not subject to *refoulement*'; Executive Committee Conclusion No. 85 (1998), para. (p); Executive Committee Conclusion No. 90 (2001), para. (k); Executive Committee Conclusion No. 93 (2002), para. (c).

[202] Mr Wrench (United Kingdom): UN doc. A/AC.96/SR.430, para. 53, (1988). This interpretation was reiterated the following year; see UN doc. A/AC.96/SR.442, para. 51 (1989).

[203] *Report* of the Sub-Committee of the Whole on International Protection: UN doc. A/AC.96/781 (9 Oct. 1991), para. 34. The notion of 'internal flight alternative' raises similar questions relating to the availability of protection, though in a quite different context. See above, Ch. 3, s. 5.6.1.

6.2 THE 'SAFE COUNTRY' MECHANISM

Under international law, States are responsible for examining asylum claims made in their territory or jurisdiction. However, at a procedural level, a number of States deny access to national protection determination processes if an asylum seeker could have obtained effective protection elsewhere.[204] The concept of the 'safe country' is a procedural mechanism for shuttling asylum seekers to other States said to have primary responsibility for them, thereby avoiding the necessity to make a decision on the merits because another country is deemed or imagined to be secure.[205] This technique encourages the use of accelerated procedures,[206] and typically reduces or excludes rights of appeal.[207] While there is no *necessary* connection between having had a previous opportunity to apply for asylum/refugee status and thereafter being able to access the full range of refugee entitlements, this approach has been largely followed in practice, particularly among European States. States justify this practice by arguing that an individual genuinely fleeing persecution would seek asylum in the first non-persecuting State, and that any 'secondary' movement is therefore for migration, rather than protection purposes. This argument is flawed for a number of reasons. First, the blanket designation of States as 'safe' neglects to take into account the individual circumstances of the asylum seeker, which may in fact make the country unsafe for him or her, for example, by reason of membership of a minority group.[208] As the House of Lords noted in this context, '[g]eneral rules cannot cater for every situation';[209] a country may be safe for some groups of asylum seekers but not for others. Secondly, international law does not impose a duty on an asylum seeker to seek protection in the first State in which effective protection might be available. Thirdly, international law would appear to recognize a right to at least limited choice about where asylum is sought, especially where family members already reside in another State.[210]

---

[204] Although this more typically forms part of western State practice, it does sometimes occur elsewhere. For instance, Kenya denied entry to Sudanese refugees coming from Uganda in 2004 on the grounds that they were coming from a safe country: US Committee for Refugees and Immigrants, *World Refugee Survey* (2005). For historical background, see the 2nd edition of this work, 333–44.

[205] For a detailed examination of the human rights implications of such policies, see Goodwin-Gill, G. S., 'The Individual Refugee, the 1951 Convention and the Treaty of Amsterdam', in Guild, E. & Harlow, C., eds., *Implementing Amsterdam: Immigration and Asylum Rights in EC Law*, (2001).

[206] Accelerated procedures were initially introduced as a means of dealing quickly with 'manifestly unfounded' claims, but in some States, such as the Netherlands, they are also employed for matters deemed not to require 'time-consuming investigation'. Accelerated procedures necessarily truncate examination of the merits of the claim, and, on the assumption that claims are unfounded, may contain an inherent bias towards rejection. The Executive Committee regards accelerated procedures as inappropriate unless the claim is 'clearly fraudulent' or not related to the criteria in the 1951 Convention: Executive Committee Conclusion No. 30 (1983).

[207] UNHCR, 'Asylum Processes (Fair and Efficient Asylum Procedures)' UN doc. EC/GC/01/12 (31 May 2001), para. 12.   [208] Ibid., paras. 12–18 for discussion of best practice.

[209] House of Lords, above n. 130, *Handling EU Asylum Claims:* para. 66.

[210] For example, Executive Committee Conclusion No. 15 (1979). Hathaway & Neve suggest that asylum seekers have a right to choose where to seek protection, but do not substantiate this as a

6.3 'EFFECTIVE PROTECTION'

While the 'safe country'[211] concept arises in a number of different contexts—safe country of origin, safe first country of asylum, and safe third country—each raises the same fundamental concern: whether 'effective protection' is available.[212] From an international law perspective, the principal issue is the *safety* of the State to which return of the asylum seeker is contemplated. Other relevant considerations include the procedural safeguards in place in the third State, and the connection between the receiving State and the asylum seeker.

In order for States to observe their *non-refoulement* and human rights obligations, a precondition to exercising the safe third country mechanism is that the third State can provide the individual with 'effective protection'. A refugee enjoys fundamental human rights common to citizens and foreign nationals; where these are generally assured, where due process of law is acknowledged, and where measures of appeal and judicial review permit examination of the merits and the legality of administrative decisions, then the refugee also may be sufficiently protected.[213] The term 'effective protection' is frequently invoked by States but lacks

---

matter of law: Hathaway, J. C. & Neve, R. A., 'Fundamental Justice and the Deflection of Refugees from Canada', 34 *Osgoode Hall Law Journal* 213 (1996). See further in favour of such a right, Hathaway, *Law of Refugee Status*, above n. 169, 46, 47; Hathaway, *Rights of Refugees*, (2005), 324. Hathaway notes the dilution of the Executive Committee's earlier position that an asylum seeker's intentions with respect to where he or she wishes to claim asylum should be taken into account as far as possible (Executive Committee Conclusion No. 15 (1979), para. (h)(iii)), to a point where UNHCR now encourages States to consider concluding readmission agreements (see, for example, UNHCR, 'Asylum Processes', above, n. 207, para. 18). However, this may reflect a practical response to unilateral decisions to return individuals to third States, rather than a shift in principle. Against the existence of such a right; see Melander, G., *Refugees in Orbit*, (1978), 2; Lambert, H., *Seeking Asylum: Comparative Law and Practice in Selected European Countries*, (1995), 91, 98. Vedsted-Hansen argues that 'there is neither a strict "direct flight" requirement, nor any legally protected right of individual choice.' He argues that focusing on whether there is an individual right to choose an asylum country may be the wrong approach, since the 'combined focus on refugee law and standards of human rights law represents a considerable challenge to contemporary developments in the European refugee protection system', which mitigate what the State may do: Vedsted-Hansen, J., 'Non-admission Policies and the Right to Protection: Refugees' Choice versus States' Exclusion?', in Nicholson, F. & Twomey, P., eds., *Refugee Rights and Realities: Evolving International Concepts and Regimes*, (1999), 287.

[211] Though noting the conceptual and theoretical distinctions between the three practices, we use the term 'safe country' to encompass the underlying basis of all three mechanisms. Similarly, Legomsky analyses the first country of asylum and safe third country concepts together because 'in actual practice the two strategies occupy two points on the same continuum.': Legomsky, S. H., 'Secondary Refugee Movements and the Return of Asylum Seekers to Third Countries: The Meaning of Effective Protection', 15 *IJRL* 567 (2003).

[212] UNHCR, 'Asylum Processes', above n. 207, para. 10. See also Executive Committee Conclusion No. 85 (1998); Executive Committee Conclusion No. 87 (1999). Conclusion No. 85 provides that the host country must treat the asylum seeker in accordance with accepted international standards, ensure protection against *refoulement*, and provide the asylum seeker with the possibility to seek and enjoy asylum.

[213] For a fuller discussion of what 'effective protection' should encompass, see Phuong, C., 'The Concept of "Effective Protection" in the Context of Irregular Secondary Movements and Protection in Regions of Origin', *Global Migration Perspectives*, No. 26 (Apr. 2005). See also Lisbon Expert Roundtable, 'Summary Conclusions on the Concept of "Effective Protection" in the Context of

a clear and uniform definition. UNHCR's approach focuses on the legal limitations on the transfer of asylum seekers to third States.[214] While the legal framework in a particular State is important in determining whether or not it is 'safe', even more significant is what it does in practice. The simple ratification of human rights and refugee instruments does not equate to compliance with their standards.[215] Respect for the principle of *non-refoulement* is a necessary element of effective protection, but is not of itself conclusive.[216]

UNHCR has indicated that '[u]nder certain circumstances and with appropriate guarantees in the individual case, the transfer of responsibility for assessing an asylum claim to another country may be an appropriate measure',[217] but cautions strongly against returns where there is no individual assessment of risk, but simply a list of countries deemed to be safe. 'A country may be "safe" for asylum-seekers of a certain origin and "unsafe" for others of a different origin, also depending on the individual's background and profile.'[218] Removal will constitute unlawful deportation—and may result in *refoulement* by the third State, for which the first State may be jointly liable[219]—unless it can be ascertained that each individual will be readmitted to the third country, will enjoy effective protection against *refoulement*, will have the possibility to seek and enjoy asylum, and will be treated in accordance with accepted international standards.[220]

In 2004, UNHCR's Director of International Protection clarified that protection could only be considered adequate,

if the risk of persecution, refoulement or torture was non-existent; if there was no actual risk to a person's life; if a genuinely accessible and durable solution was in prospect; if a person was not exposed to arbitrary expulsion and deprivation of liberty, and had an adequate and dignified means of subsistence; if family unity and integrity was preserved; and if specific protection needs (such as those arising from age or gender) were recognized and respected.[221]

She noted that States should not use the 'safe country' concept to shirk their international legal responsibilities towards asylum seekers or refugees, observing that

Secondary Movements of Refugees and Asylum-Seekers', Lisbon Expert Roundtable, (9–10 Dec. 2002); Legomsky, S. H., 'Secondary Refugee Movements and the Return of Asylum Seekers to Third Countries: The Meaning of Effective Protection', 15 *IJRL* 567 (2003); van Selm, J., *Access to Procedures: 'Safe Third Countries', 'Safe Countries of Origin' and 'Time Limits'* (UNHCR and Carnegie Endowment for International Peace, Background Paper for Third Track of Global Consultations, 2001).

[214] Statement by Ms Erika Feller, Director, Department of International Protection, at the 55th session of the Executive Committee of the High Commissioner's Programme, Geneva, (7 Oct. 2004).

[215] See Executive Committee Conclusion No. 58 (1989).

[216] See Executive Committee Conclusion No. 15 (1979).

[217] UNHCR, 'Note on International Protection', UN doc. A/AC.96/975 (2 Jul. 2003), para. 12; Lisbon Expert Roundtable 'Summary Conclusions', above, n. 213, para. 12.

[218] UNHCR, 'Note on International Protection' UN doc. A/AC.96/914 (7 Jul. 1999), para. 20; and House of Lords, *Handling EU Asylum Claims*, above, n. 130.

[219] See above, Ch. 5, s. 252–3.

[220] UNHCR, 'Note on International Protection', UN doc. A/AC.96/914 (7 July 1999), para. 19.

[221] Ms Feller (UNHCR): UN doc. A/AC.96/SR.585, para. 28 (2004). UNHCR has documented cases of *refoulement* as the result of applying the 'safe third country' mechanism: UNHCR, 'Note on International Protection', UN doc. A/AC.96/898 (3 Jul. 1998), para. 14.

the 1951 Convention 'was more concerned to ensure a certain standard of protection rather than to ensure that protection was available in a particular country'.[222] The Human Rights Committee has expressed similar concerns about the 'safe third country' principle. In its view effective protection in accordance with articles 6 and 7 ICCPR66 requires that refugee claims be assessed on an individual basis, and the application of 'safe third country' mechanisms may prevent this.[223]

As part of UNHCR's Global Consultations in 2001, the Lisbon Expert Roundtable found that protection is only 'effective' in a third State if the asylum seeker does not fear persecution there, is not at risk of being sent to another State in which effective protection would not be forthcoming, has access to means of subsistence sufficient to maintain an adequate standard of living, and has his or her fundamental human rights respected in accordance with international standards. Furthermore, the third State must have expressly agreed to admit the individual as an asylum seeker or refugee, comply with international refugee and human rights law in practice (not just in theory),[224] grant access to fair and efficient determination procedures which include protection grounds that would be recognized in the State in which asylum was originally sought,[225] take into account any special vulnerabilities of the individual, and maintain the privacy interests of the individual and his or her family.[226] NGOs have suggested that the concept of 'effective protection' must encompass at least physical and material security, access to humanitarian assistance, access to secondary education and livelihood opportunities, timely access to durable solutions, a functioning judicial system, the rule of law, and respect for refugees' rights, including protection from *refoulement* and respect for their fundamental (including socio-economic) rights.[227]

At present, the most that can be said is that international law permits the return of refugees and asylum seekers to another State if there is substantial evidence of admissibility, such as possession of a Convention travel document or other proof of entitlement to enter. With respect to the 'safe country' notion, there must be substantive and procedural human rights guarantees.[228] Compliance with the principle of *non-refoulement* under article 33 of the 1951 Convention and human

[222] Ibid.

[223] *Report of the Human Rights Committee*, vol. 1, (2002–03) UNGAOR (58th Session) Supp. No. 40 (A/58/40), 'Estonia', para. 79(13).

[224] In particular, the third State must be a party to the 1951 Convention and/or 1967 Protocol and comply with those instruments, or at least demonstrate that it has developed a practice akin to what those instruments require: Lisbon Expert Roundtable, 'Summary Conclusions', above n. 213, para. 15(e).

[225] This is particularly important in light of the EU's recognition of subsidiary protection grounds.

[226] Lisbon Expert Roundtable, 'Summary Conclusions', above n. 213, para. 15. See also Legomsky's seven elements of 'effective protection': Legomsky, 'Secondary Refugee Movements', above n. 211, 629–64.

[227] *Report on Pre-ExCom Consultations*, above n. 105, Annex IX, (2 Oct. 2003).

[228] Executive Committee Conclusion No. 85 (1998); Executive Committee Conclusion No. 87 (1999).

rights law more broadly is a key factor. *Non-refoulement* is most likely to be observed if there is access to a fair and effective procedure for the determination of claims to refugee status, in accordance with prevailing international standards. However, formal effectiveness may be prejudiced by restrictions on access, for example, because of time limits, geographical limitations on the extent of obligations, policy reasons affecting particular groups, or legal reasons affecting certain classes, such as illegal entrants. In any case, actual return is likely to satisfy a best practice standard only if the receiving State is able to provide certain effective guarantees, including (a) willingness to readmit asylum seekers; (b) acceptance of responsibility to determine claims to refugee status, notwithstanding departure from the country in question or the circumstances of initial entry; (c) the treatment of applicants during the determination process in accordance with generally accepted standards;[229] and (d) some provision with respect to subsistence and human dignity issues, such as social assistance or access to the labour market in the interim, family unity, education of children, and so forth. Besides the question of fulfilment of obligations deriving from the 1951 Convention/1967 Protocol, a country's human rights record will also be relevant. This may include both procedural and substantive standards, including questions of remedies, non-discriminatory or equivalent treatment with local nationals, and protection of fundamental human rights.

6.4 THE 2005 EUROPEAN UNION PROCEDURES DIRECTIVE

The Procedures Directive,[230] adopted as part of the first phase of the Common European Asylum System established under the Amsterdam Treaty,[231] establishes

---

[229] Ideally, such standards will deal with detention or other restrictions on liberty, the length of proceedings, the availability of interpreters, legal advice, access to UNHCR, etc.

[230] Council Directive 2005/85/EC of 1 December 2005 on Minimum Standards on Procedures in Member States for Granting and Withdrawing Refugee Status, [2005] O.J. L 236/13; for text, see below, Annexe 2, No. 20. Whether or not the Directive applies to subsidiary protection is left to the individual Member States' discretion. It is only mandated for subsidiary protection where Member States have a procedure in which asylum applications are automatically treated as applications for refugee status *and* other forms of international protection: art. 3(3). See critiques by Costello, C., 'The Asylum Procedures Directive and the Proliferation of Safe Country Practices', 7 *EJML* 35 (2005); Immigration Law Practitioners' Association (prepared by C. Costello), 'Analysis and Critique of Council Directive on Minimum Standards on Procedures in Member States for Granting and Withdrawing Refugee Status (30 April 2004)', (Jul. 2004).

[231] Entry into force 1 May 1999. The Schengen *acquis*, consisting of the Schengen Agreement, the Schengen Convention, the Accession Protocols and Agreements to the 1985 Agreement and the 1990 Implementation Convention, and decisions and declarations adopted by the Schengen Executive Committee, is annexed to and forms an integral part of the Treaty of Amsterdam. It is binding in international law. For details of the Schengen instruments, see Noll, *Negotiating Asylum*, above, n. 101, 123–6, Ch. 4, s. 1.2.2. The binding legislative tools of art 251 TEC (directives, decisions, and regulations) and the jurisdiction of the European Court of Justice are now engaged. All asylum provisions are contained in a new Title IV: 'Visas, asylum, immigration and other policies related to freedom of movement of persons'.

a harmonized approach by the EU Member States to the minimum procedural standards for granting and withdrawing refugee status.[232] It is the first supranational instrument containing rules on the application of safe third country, safe country of origin, and country of first asylum notions, and will have a major impact on access to asylum determination procedures in the EU. Although the Preamble acknowledges that designating a country as a safe country of origin 'cannot establish an absolute guarantee of safety for nationals',[233] the instrument lacks sufficient safeguards to ensure that return will safeguard the principle of *nonrefoulement* in all cases.[234]

Under the Directive, the concept of admissibility is 'restricted to determining whether the Member State in question should consider the substance of the application, or whether the applicant should be sent to a third country'.[235] An asylum application is deemed inadmissible if, *inter alia*, the asylum seeker can be transferred to another Member State in accordance with the Dublin Regulation;[236] another Member State has already granted refugee status;[237] the asylum seeker has already obtained protection in another, non-Member State ('first country of asylum'[238]); or the asylum seeker has transited through, or otherwise has access to, a 'safe third country' in which protection could be requested.[239] Similarly, where an asylum seeker is considered to come from a safe country of origin, the asylum claim may be presumed to be manifestly unfounded and subject to an accelerated

---

[232] Harmonization is to take place in two stages. The work programme for the first stage was set out in the 1999 Tampere Conclusions, and required the first legislative instruments to be agreed by 1 May 2004. The second phase is set out in the 2004 Hague Programme, and is to be completed by 2010. Cf. *R.* v. *Secretary of State for the Home Department, ex p. Adan* [2001] 2 AC 477, in which the House of Lords determined that France and Germany could not be considered as safe countries because they did not regard non-State agents as agents of persecution under the 1951 Convention, and this could lead to *refoulement*. The harmonized laws are designed to overcome the possibility for such future findings within the EU.   [233] Preamble, 21.

[234] Indeed, the Directive was so criticized during its drafting that NGOs took the unprecedented move of calling for its abandonment. See ECRE, Press Releases, 'Refugee NGOs in more than 30 European Countries Reject Draft Directive on Asylum Procedures', (30 Sep. 2003); 'Refugee and Human Rights Organisations across Europe Call on EU to Scrap Key Asylum Proposal', (29 Mar. 2004); 'Refugee and Human Rights Organisations across Europe Express Their Deep Concern at the Expected Agreement on Asylum Measures in Breach of International Law', (28 Apr. 2004).

[235] Commission of the European Communities, Proposal for a Council Directive on Minimum Standards on Procedures in Member States for Granting and Withdrawing Refugee Status, COM(2000) 578 final, (20 Sep. 2000), 18.

[236] Procedures Directive, art. 25(1). See Council Regulation (EC) No. 343/2003 of 18 Feb. 2003 establishing the Criteria and Mechanisms for Determining the Member State Responsible for Examining an Asylum Application Lodged in One of the Member States by a Third-Country National [2003] O.J. L 50/1 (25 Feb. 2003). This is inconsistent with *TI* v. *UK* [2000] INLR 211, which held that a State will breach art. 3 ECHR50 if it removes an individual to a State from which he or she risks removal to another State, in which he or she would be at risk of torture or inhuman or degrading treatment or punishment. In *R. (Yogathas)* v. *Secretary of State for the Home Department* [2003] 1 AC 920, [2002] UKHL 36, para. 61, the principle expressed in *TI* was extended to art. 33 CSR51. See below 400ff for further discussion of the Dublin Regulation.   [237] Procedures Directive, art. 25(2)(a).

[238] Procedures Directive, art. 25(2)(b), preambular para. 22.

[239] Procedures Directive, art. 25(2)(c). Under art. 28(2), the claim may also be considered manifestly unfounded (see also art. 23(4)(c)(ii)).

procedure.[240] By implication, article 7(2) of the Qualification Directive suggests that an asylum seeker's country of origin will generally be safe where the State (or parties or organizations controlling all or part of it) 'take[s] reasonable steps to prevent the persecution or suffering of serious harm, *inter alia*, by operating an effective legal system for the detection, prosecution and punishment of acts constituting persecution or serious harm, and the applicant has access to such protection'.[241] The test that has typically been used by the European Court of Human Rights for determining whether a country is sufficiently safe for an individual's return is whether it has created effective criminal law measures, provides policing and criminal justice systems to enforce them, and whether it takes 'reasonable operational measures where there is a "real and immediate" risk to the life of a particular individual from the criminal acts of another person'.[242] Lambert argues that this test is arguably higher than that in the Qualification Directive, since it rests on a State's duty to protect its nationals and aims at reducing harm to less than a 'real risk'.[243]

A 'first country of asylum' is defined in article 26 of the Procedures Directive as one in which an applicant was recognized as a refugee and can still avail him- or herself of that protection, or where he or she can otherwise enjoy 'sufficient protection', including the benefit of the principle of *non-refoulement*, if readmitted.[244] According to Legomsky, '[t]he longer, the more meaningful, the more formal, and the more secure the person's stay in the third country, the more likely it is that the country will be described as a "first country of asylum" rather than a "safe third country"'.[245] There is no duty on Member States to allow challenges to the application of this concept, despite the fact that Member States are not required to obtain conclusive evidence that an individual has already been granted protection in a particular State which remains accessible and valid.[246] While a claimant

---

[240] See, for example, Procedures Directive, arts. 23(4)(c)(i), 31(2). For meaning of 'safe country of origin': art. 31.

[241] See above, Ch. 1, s. 4. Lambert observes that this is similar to the House of Lords' approach in *Horvath* v. *Secretary of State for the Home Dept.* [2001] 1 AC 489, to the effect that the State must have a criminal law in force making violent attacks by persecutors punishable by sentences commensurate with the crime's gravity; the victim must be entitled to the protection of the law; and there must be a reasonable willingness by law enforcement agencies to prosecute and punish (see, in particular, Lord Clyde at 510–11, adopting the approach of Stuart-Smith L.J. in the Court of Appeal, [2000] INLR 15, para. 22). In the United Kingdom, this test has been extended beyond the 1951 Convention to ECHR50 cases, even though Lambert regards it as falling short of the European Court's requirements: Cf. *R. (Bagdanavicius)* v. *Secretary of State for the Home Department* [2005] 2 AC 668, [2005] UKHL 38, para. 30 (Lord Brown, for the court): 'a broadly similar approach is adopted under both Conventions to the requirement for the person concerned to demonstrate in addition to the risk of harm a failure in the receiving state to provide a reasonable level of protection'. See Lambert, H., 'The EU Asylum Qualification Directive, Its Impact on the Jurisprudence of the United Kingdom and International Law' 55 *ICLQ* 161, 181 (2006).

[242] Mowbray, A., *Cases and Materials on the European Convention on Human Rights*, (2001), 62; Mowbray, A., 'Duties of Investigation under the European Convention on Human Rights', 51 *ICLQ* 437(2002), cited in Lambert (2006), above, n. 241, 181.   [243] Lambert, above n. 241, 181.

[244] Procedures Directive, art. 26.

[245] Legomsky, 'Secondary Refugee Movements', above n. 211, 571.

[246] Vedsted-Hansen, 'Non-Admission Policies' above, n. 82, 284. This view is acknowledged in Executive Committee Conclusion No. 15 (1979), paras. (h)(iv) and (k); Executive Committee Conclusion No. 58 (1989), paras. (f) and (g).

may appeal a decision on inadmissibility,[247] this will not necessarily have suspensive effect, thus rendering the right to appeal nugatory. Furthermore, if the third State refuses to admit the asylum seeker, then Member States must ensure that access to an asylum determination procedure is granted.[248] The Procedures Directive overlooks the fact that secondary movement from a first country of asylum may be lawful where an individual no longer enjoys effective protection, is not given a proper legal status, or does not have access to effective remedies.

The 'safe third country' concept is defined in article 27. It may be applied where a Member State is satisfied that an asylum seeker will be treated according to the following principles in the third State: the asylum seeker's life and liberty will not be threatened on account of race, religion, nationality, membership of a particular social group, or political opinion; the principle of *non-refoulement*, in accordance with the 1951 Convention and with respect to torture and cruel, inhuman or degrading treatment, will be respected; and the asylum seeker may request refugee status and obtain protection in accordance with the 1951 Convention if found to be a refugee.[249] In contrast to the 'first country of asylum' procedure under article 26, Member States must ensure that an asylum seeker has access to a determination procedure if the third country to which return is contemplated refuses to readmit him or her.[250] Under national law, Member States must establish rules requiring a reasonable connection between the asylum seeker and the third country. While the Explanatory Memorandum states that the meaning of 'connection' is to be based on Executive Committee Conclusion No. 15 (1979), which identifies such matters as family links or previous stay,[251] the fact that this is left to the discretion of individual States means that practice may be highly variable.

Although it appears that article 27 requires Member States to conduct an individual case-by-case assessment of the safety of a particular country for a particular applicant, this is misleading. Member States may adopt their own national methodology for determining how the concept applies, and this specifically permits 'national designation of countries considered to be generally safe'.[252] Costello argues that this gives Member States 'an option to ignore the individual circumstances and privilege the generalised determination of safety'.[253] The Explanatory Memorandum further suggests that a Member State is *only* required to examine individual claims if 'there has so far been no precedent with respect to the safety of this country *for an applicant of his nationality*'.[254] If the Member State has 'already successfully designated the third country as a safe third country ... or has issued a policy statement to that end, for instance by putting the country on its list of safe third countries, there is no need to carry out this investigation'.[255] This

---

[247] Procedures Directive, art. 39(1)(a)(i).   [248] Procedures Directive, art. 27(4).

[249] Procedures Directive, art. 27(1). The Directive does not stipulate what status must be accorded to a person found to have a protection need based on a complementary protection ground.

[250] Procedures Directive, art. 27(4).

[251] Explanatory Memorandum, COM/2000/0578 final, 20.

[252] Procedures Directive, art. 27(2)(b).   [253] Costello (ILPA), above, n. 230, 24.

[254] Explanatory Memorandum, above n. 231, 19 (emphasis added).   [255] Ibid.

is subject only to the requirement that Member States must, in accordance with international law, at least permit the asylum seeker 'to challenge the application of the safe third country concept on the grounds that he/she would be subjected to torture, cruel, inhuman or degrading treatment or punishment'.[256] While the importance of this rebuttable presumption should not be understated, an individual's safety in a third State entails more than simply protection from ill-treatment.[257]

This raises serious questions about the integrity of the principle of *non-refoulement*. A country that may be 'generally safe' may not be safe for a particular individual or minority group. Furthermore, circumstances can change quickly, and a State designated as generally safe may not remain so. Since asylum seekers considered to have access to a safe third country may be subject to accelerated procedures,[258] gathering sufficient evidence to challenge the assumption may prove difficult in the shortened timeframe. Accelerated procedures are not subject to the already minimal level of procedural protections contained in the Procedures Directive. Finally, even though decisions made under article 27 may be appealed, appeals do not necessarily have suspensive effect.[259]

An even more restrictive approach applies to asylum seekers who illegally enter an EU Member State from 'European safe third countries'. This has been described as the 'super safe' third country concept, because it assumes the inherent safety—without recourse to individual examination—of any State which has ratified and observes the 1951 Convention and ECHR50 (including with respect to effective remedies), has an asylum procedure prescribed by law, and has been designated as a safe third country by the Council.[260] Under article 36, Member States have the discretion to refuse to consider an application made by an asylum seeker arriving from such a country,[261] and there is no opportunity for the asylum seeker to rebut the presumption of safety. It has been rightly argued that this could lead to cases of refugees in orbit or chain *refoulement*.[262] Member States may provide for exceptions on humanitarian or political grounds, or for reasons of public international law.[263] If the safe country refuses to readmit the asylum seeker, then the host Member State must ensure access to a determination procedure.[264]

The Dublin Regulation,[265] which superseded the Dublin and Schengen Conventions in 2003, establishes the criteria and mechanisms for determining

---

[256] Procedures Directive, art. 27(2).

[257] For discussion of 'effective protection', and the idea of '*non-refoulement* through time', see above, Ch 5, 207–8.   [258] Procedures Directive, art. 23(4)(c)(ii).

[259] Procedures Directive, art. 39(1)(a)(i).

[260] Procedures Directive, art. 36(2). For a critique of certain countries listed there, see Costello (ILPA), above n. 230, 30.   [261] Procedures Directive, art. 36(1).

[262] ECRE, 'Broken Promises', above n. 106, 11.   [263] Procedures Directive, art. 36(4).

[264] Procedures Directive, art. 36(6).

[265] Council Regulation (EC) No. 343/2003 of 18 February 2003 establishing the Criteria and Mechanisms for Determining the Member State Responsible for Examining an Asylum Application Lodged in One of the Member States by a Third-Country National' [2003] O.J. L 50/1; for text, see

which Member State has responsibility for examining an asylum application. Its expressed aim is to identify a *single* responsible State and to require it to determine the asylum claim, thereby reducing the likelihood of multiple, successive applications by asylum seekers, and eliminating asylum seekers 'in orbit'. States retain the discretion to examine an asylum claim lodged by an applicant who could be removed pursuant to the Dublin Regulation,[266] or to send an asylum seeker to a safe third country other than a Member State.[267] The Regulation is premised on the harmonized application of asylum law in the EU, which has been significantly strengthened by the shift of asylum and migration matters from the third to the first pillar under the Treaty of Amsterdam[268] and the adoption of binding asylum Directives.[269] Its operation is facilitated by mechanisms such as the Eurodac Regulation, which collates and compares fingerprints of asylum applicants and illegal migrants in order to assist in establishing the Member State responsible for examining a particular application.[270] Responsibility under the Dublin Regulation is determined according to a hierarchy of criteria, including the presence of family members (strictly defined),[271] the possession of a valid residence document or visa,[272] and the first Member State entered irregularly.[273]

A review of the Regulation's operation by ECRE three years after its adoption revealed 'intrinsic flaws' and 'a failure by states to properly implement it'.[274] Contrary to the Regulation, many applicants were being denied both access to an asylum procedure in the responsible State,[275] and an effective opportunity to

Annexe 2, No. 17. Commission Regulation (EC) No. 1560/2003 of 2 September 2003 laying down Detailed Rules for the Application of Council Regulation (EC) No. 343/2003 establishing the Criteria and Mechanisms for Determining the Member State Responsible for Examining an Asylum Application Lodged in One of the Member States by a Third-Country National, [2003] O.J. L222. Note, however, that the Dublin Convention remains in force between Denmark and the Member States bound by the Dublin Regulation.

[266] Dublin Regulation, art. 3(2).

[267] Dublin Regulation, art. 3(3). Note that all EU Member States are considered as safe third countries: Dublin Regulation, Preamble, para. 2.

[268] Entry into force 1 May 1999. For details of the Schengen instruments, see Noll, *Negotiating Asylum*, above n. 101, 123–6, Ch. 4, s. 1.2.2.

[269] See Treaty establishing the European Community [2002] O.J. C 325/33, arts. 61–3; Tampere Conclusions; 2004 Hague Programme.

[270] Council Regulation (EC) No. 2725/2000, above, n. 106; Council Regulation (EC) No. 407/2002, above, n. 106. See also Council Regulation (EC) 539/2001, above, n. 114.

[271] Dublin Regulation, arts. 6–8. For definition of 'family members', see art. 2(i).

[272] Dublin Regulation, art. 9.

[273] Dublin Regulation, art. 10. Though curtailing the individual asylum seeker's choice to seek asylum in a particular country, safe third country measures ironically represent a considerable restriction on the principle of State sovereignty. In the EU context, they oblige Member States to admit asylum seekers in certain circumstances and to provide asylum to those found to have an international protection need: Vedsted-Hansen, 'Non-Admission Policies', above n. 82, 273–4.

[274] ECRE, 'Summary Report on the Application of the Dublin II Regulation in Europe' (AD2/3/2006/EXT/MH, Mar. 2006), 3.

[275] See especially Greek practice: ibid., 5–6. There have been successful challenges in Austria, Finland, France, Italy, the Netherlands, Norway, and Sweden based on the claim that Greece is not a safe third country.

appeal against transfer. While the Dublin Regulation and its predecessor conventions may in theory have curbed the problem of the 'refugee in orbit', shuttled from State to State within the EU, the wider application of the safe country concept under the Procedures Directive may in fact precipitate this. Indeed, the absence of a duty on Member States to ensure that asylum seekers will be guaranteed access to an effective asylum procedure on return, means that asylum seekers may be moved on to other States, and may be *refouled* or left 'in orbit'. Removing an asylum seeker to another State for status determination does not absolve the removing State of its responsibilities under international law, and it may also be liable if that individual is subsequently *refouled* to persecution or other ill-treatment.[276]

In addition to designating third countries as safe, the Procedures Directive contains elaborate rules for determining when an asylum seeker's *country of origin* is sufficiently safe for return. The effect is to deny substantive consideration of protection claims made by nationals of particular States on the basis of a generic classification of those States as safe. Article 29 provides that the European Council, following consultation with the European Parliament, must adopt (and may subsequently amend) a minimum common list of 'safe countries of origin'.[277] Member States are required to regard such countries as 'safe', and may independently add to these, but not subtract from them, through national lists.[278] Costello warns that this raises serious 'competence concerns', since the EU is only permitted to establish 'minimum standards' in this area, yet precludes Member States from adopting higher standards on this point.[279] States which, before the adoption of the Directive, had legislation in place deeming certain countries to be safe may retain it. However, they must be satisfied that persons in those third countries are generally not subjected to persecution or to torture or inhuman or degrading treatment or punishment.[280]

The criteria for determining a safe country of origin are set out in Annex II of the Procedures Directive. A country of origin is deemed 'safe' if:

on the basis of the legal situation, the application of the law within a democratic system and the general political circumstances, it can be shown that there is generally and consistently no persecution as defined in Article 9 of Directive 2004/83/EC, no torture or inhuman or degrading treatment or punishment and no threat by reason of indiscriminate violence in situations of international or internal armed conflict.

---

[276] See *Adan* [2001] 2 AC 477; above, Ch. 5, s. 5.3.3.

[277] Procedures Directive, art. 29.

[278] Procedures Directive, art. 30(1). Before the introduction of the Directive, only a small number of EU States utilized safe country lists: Costello (ILPA), above n. 230, 25. The requirement not to subtract from the EU-wide list is subject only to art. 29(4)–(5), which temporarily suspends a particular Member State's requirement to treat a country as 'safe' if it submits a request to have it removed, or, in the case of a request by Council, temporarily suspends the requirement for all Member States.

[279] Costello (ILPA), above n. 230, 25.   [280] Procedures Directive, art. 30(2)–(5).

In assessing this, consideration must be given to the extent to which protection is provided against persecution or mistreatment by the country's laws and regulations, and the manner in which they are applied; whether the rights and freedoms provided for in ICCPR66, CAT84, and ECHR50 are observed (especially those which are non-derogable); whether the principle of *non-refoulement* under the 1951 Convention is respected; and whether there is a system of effective remedies against violations of such rights and freedoms. As Costello notes, the EU's 'politicised decision-making process may often lead to foreign policy concerns tainting the objectivity of the assessment'.[281]

Article 31 provides that a designated country of origin is 'safe' if an asylum seeker is a national (or stateless and a prior habitual resident) of that 'safe' State, and has not submitted serious grounds for considering the country not to be safe, based on his or her particular circumstances.[282] Furthermore, there is no right of appeal with respect to safe country of origin decisions, in contrast to decision on inadmissibility[283] or 'safe third country' under article 36.[284] However, appeals do not necessarily have suspensive effect[285] and asylum seekers only have a right to remain pending initial determination.[286] The individual may therefore be *refouled* before the case is heard, effectively rendering the appeal right 'illusory'. This raises questions of compatibility with the right to an effective remedy under article 13 ECHR50. The European Court of Human Rights has held that provided a complaint is arguable,[287] article 13 requires a remedy that is 'effective' in practice as well as in law.[288] In *Jabari* v. *Turkey*, the Court stated:

given the irreversible nature of the harm that might occur if the risk of torture or ill-treatment alleged materialised and the importance which it attaches to Article 3, the notion of an effective remedy under Article 13 requires independent and rigorous scrutiny of a claim that there exist substantial grounds for fearing a real risk of treatment contrary to Article 3 and the possibility of suspending the implementation of the measure impugned.[289]

6.5 'SAFE COUNTRY' NOTIONS ELSEWHERE

Although it originated in Europe,[290] the safe third country mechanism is now much more widespread, but also highly varied in its application. Australia developed a comprehensive jurisprudence on the notion of 'effective protection' in a

---

281 Costello (ILPA), above, n. 230, 26.   282 Procedures Directive, art. 31(1).
283 Procedures Directive, art. 39(1)(a)(i).   284 Procedures Directive, art. 39(1)(a)(iii).
285 Procedures Directive, art. 39(3).   286 Procedures Directive, art. 7.
287 *Chahal* v. *United Kingdom* (1996) 23 EHRR 413, para. 147; *Čonka* v. *Belgium* [2002] ECHR 14, para. 76.   288 *Čonka* v. *Belgium*, above n. 287, para. 75.
289 *Jabari* v. *Turkey* [2000] ECHR 369, para. 50; see also *Čonka* v. *Belgium* above n. 287, para. 79.
290 van Selm, above n. 213, para. 5.

long line of decisions beginning with *Thiyagarajah*,[291] which were ultimately overturned by the High Court in 2005.[292] In *Thiyagarajah*, the Full Federal Court established that Australia did not owe protection obligations to any person whom it could remove to any other State in which effective protection would be provided. This interpretation was based on section 36(2) of the Migration Act 1958 (Cth), requiring asylum seekers to show that there was no other country in which they could obtain effective protection, even if they were refugees within the meaning of the 1951 Convention and even if protection in that other country encompassed little more than tolerated presence.[293] In *NAGV*, the High Court rejected this interpretation, holding that Australia owes protection obligations to any person in Australia who satisfies the definition of a refugee, not just to those who cannot be removed to a 'safe third country'. The Minister argued that the first appellant's right of return to Israel meant that Australia did not owe him or his wife 'protection obligations' under section 36(2). However, the court held that if Parliament had intended to provide for the removal of any person who could claim protection in a third country, it should have done so in plain terms. Amendments to the Migration Act adopted in December 1999 achieved this.[294]

Kirby J., who agreed with the majority but gave separate reasons, was strongly critical of the approach that would prevent protection visas from being granted to Convention refugees who may be entitled by law, regardless of on what basis, to another State's protection.[295] 'It would be an absurd result if the generosity of other States' refugee laws meant that Australia was thereby relieved of international obligations that it voluntarily accepted with other nations. Such a result should not be reached by implication.'[296] However, although the revised legislation cited above contains exceptions for people who would be persecuted (or subjected to 'chain *refoulement*') on the basis of article 1A(2) of the 1951 Convention,[297] there is no requirement to consider ill-treatment on the basis of torture or cruel, inhuman or degrading treatment or punishment even *temporary* protection in a third State is seen as sufficient for removing a person.

In addition to limiting the concept of 'protection obligations', Australian legislation also deals with the meaning of 'safe third countries', in section 91D of the Migration Act. Such countries are prescribed under the regulations (thus, there is a safe list), as are the requisite 'connections' that individuals must have for a country

---

[291] *Minister for Immigration and Multicultural Affairs* v. *Thiyagarajah* (1997) 80 FCR 543.

[292] *NAGV and NAGW of 2002* v. *Minister for Immigration and Multicultural and Indigenous Affairs* [2005] HCA 6, (2005) 213 ALR 668.

[293] See *Patto* v. *Minister for Immigration and Multicultural Affairs* [2000] FCA 1554.

[294] S. 36(3) provides: 'Australia is taken not to have protection obligations to a non-citizen who has not taken all possible steps to avail himself or herself of a right to enter and reside in, whether temporarily or permanently and however that right arose or is expressed, any country apart from Australia, including countries of which the non-citizen is a national.' This provision did not apply in *NAGV*, since the appellants had applied for a protection visa prior to its enactment.

[295] *NAGV*, above n. 292, paras. 91–3, 97.   [296] Ibid, para. 91.

[297] Migration Act 1958 (Cth), ss. 36(4) and (5).

to be considered safe.[298] These include factors such as presence in the third country at a particular time, and a right to enter and reside in that country, but real or practical connections are not, of themselves, considered relevant. For a country to be deemed safe, the Minister must provide Parliament with information about the country's compliance with 'relevant international law concerning the protection of persons seeking asylum'; whether the country meets 'relevant human rights standards for the persons in relation to whom the country is prescribed as a safe third country'; and that country's willingness to (a) accept returned asylum seekers, (b) allow them to remain there while their protection claims are determined, and (c) if found to be refugees, remain there until a durable solution can be found. This falls short of requiring a guarantee for readmission. Additionally, section 91M provides that any non-citizen who 'can avail himself or herself of protection from a third country', either because of nationality or some other right to re-enter and reside there, 'should seek protection from the third country instead of applying in Australia for a protection visa, or, in some cases, any other visa.' Section 91N(3) authorizes the Minister (after receiving any advice that UNHCR may provide) to designate a country as one which:

(i) provides access, for persons seeking asylum, to effective procedures for assessing their need for protection; and
(ii) provides protection to persons to whom that country has protection obligations; and
(iii) meets relevant human rights standards for persons to whom that country has protection obligations.

If an asylum seeker has ever resided in a designated country for a continuous period of at least seven days, and has a right to re-enter and (temporarily) reside in that country, then he or she is barred from applying for a protection visa in Australia.[299] Although the Minister has a discretion to waive this provision if he or she considers that the individual concerned may not be able to avail him- or herself of protection in that designated country, it is a non-compellable, personal discretion which need only be invoked if the Minister considers it in the public interest to do so.[300] Of principal concern, from the perspective of international law, is the absence of any *requirement* for *individual* assessment once it is determined that an individual is eligible for return to a designated safe country.

By contrast, the safe third country notion has not been applied at all in New Zealand. Although section 129L(1)(d) of the Immigration Act 1987 empowers

---

[298] Migration Regulations 1994, reg. 2.12A. On the Australian regime generally, see Taylor, S., 'Protection Elsewhere/Nowhere', 18 *IJRL* 283 (2006); Hadaway, A., 'Safe Third Countries in Australian Refugee Law: *NAGV* v. *Minister of Immigration and Multicultural Affairs*', 27 *Sydney LR* 727 (2005).

[299] Migration Act 1958 (Cth), s. 91P(2). If the non-citizen has not yet been immigration cleared, he or she is not allowed to apply for *any* visa, including a protection visa: s. 91P(2). Under s. 91N(1), a person who has two nationalities is also covered by these provisions.

[300] Migration Act 1958 (Cth), s. 91Q. Subsection 7 provides: 'The Minister does not have a duty to consider whether to exercise the power under subsection (1) in respect of any non-citizen, whether he or she is requested to do so by the non-citizen or by any other person, or in any other circumstances.'

decision makers to determine whether, 'in the light of any relevant international arrangement or agreement, a person who may have lodged a claim for refugee status in another country, or had the opportunity to lodge such a claim, may have a claim for refugee status accepted for consideration in New Zealand', it has never been used. The Refugee Status Appeals Authority has disapproved of the 'direct flight' requirement imposed by some States.[301] A 2006 discussion paper, relating to review of the Immigration Act 1987, recommends against the EU approach of establishing safe country lists, on the ground that such provisions signal a shift away from individual determination, are not advocated by UNHCR, and can lead to *refoulement* if individual circumstances are not considered.[302]

The United States enacted a safe third country provision in 1996, which is premised on the United States entering into agreements with third States, rather than drawing up a list of safe countries.[303] A 'safe third country' is defined as one in which the asylum seeker's life or freedom would not be threatened for a 1951 Convention reason, and he or she 'would have access to a full and fair procedure for determining a claim to asylum or equivalent temporary protection'.

Under Canadian law, section 101(1)(e) of the Immigration and Refugee Protection Act provides that a protection claim may be declared ineligible if an applicant has come 'directly or indirectly' from a State designated by regulation. Regulation 159.3 designates the United States as such a country, noting that it 'complies with Article 33 of the Refugee Convention and Article 3 of the Convention Against Torture'.

Pursuant to these provisions, the United States and Canada entered into a bilateral safe third country agreement which took effect on 29 December 2004,[304] under which asylum seekers may be returned to the first North American country they entered.[305] In comparison with the Canadian protection system, asylum processes in the United States are restrictive, and it has been argued that the United States cannot always be considered a safe third country for asylum seekers.[306] The agreement has

---

[301] RSAA, *Re SA*, Refugee Appeal No. 1/92, (30 Apr. 1992). Thank you to Rodger Haines, QC, for drawing our attention to this case. See also the extensive discussion there of the origin and development of the 'safe country' principle.

[302] NZ Department of Labour, 'Immigration Act Review: Discussion Paper', (Apr. 2006), para. 1212.

[303] 8 USC §1158(a)(2)(A). See, for example, Agreement between the Government of Canada and the Government of the United States of America for Cooperation in the Examination of Refugee Status Claims from Nationals of Third Countries, 5 Dec. 2002.

[304] On earlier attempts to reach agreement, based on an October 1995 'Memorandum of Agreement', see the 2nd edition of this work, 336.

[305] Exceptions include asylum seekers with a family member in the receiving State who has an eligible refugee application pending or lawful immigration status (other than visitor status); unaccompanied minors; persons not required to obtain a visa; or persons with a valid visa (other than a transit visa) to enter the receiving State: see Agreement between the Government of Canada and the Government of the United States of America above n. 303 art. 4(2).

[306] See, for example, the account in 'Bordering on Failure: The US–Canada Safe Third Country Agreement Fifteen Months after Implementation' (Harvard Law School, Mar. 2006), 11–15. For the principal grounds of challenge to the Agreement, see Canadian Council for Refugees, 'Closing the

reduced the numbers of asylum seekers able to claim asylum in Canada by up to fifty per cent at the land border.[307] It has thereby restricted access to protection in a State which applies broader criteria, imposes a lower standard of proof, and has more extensive procedural guarantees.[308]

In December 2005, the Canadian Council for Refugees, Amnesty International, and the Canadian Council of Churches, in conjunction with an asylum seeker, launched a challenge to the Safe Third Country Agreement in the Federal Court of Canada, claiming it is unconstitutional and in contravention of international law. The groups will ask the Federal Court to overturn the designation of the United States as a safe third country, on the basis that it does not respect its obligations under the 1951 Convention and the Convention against Torture, and that Canada's removal of asylum seekers to the United States violates its own international obligations and the rights of asylum seekers under the Canadian Charter.[309]

6.6 READMISSION AGREEMENTS

Apart from the responsibility-determining context of the Dublin Regulation and US–Canada agreement, State practice has been mostly unilateral, in the sense that one or other State has declined to consider an asylum application or extend protection, after determining, generally without consultation, that another State was responsible. Alternatively, asylum seekers have been dealt with under general bilateral agreements on the readmission of nationals and non-nationals, but without the issue of responsibility for asylum determination being considered.

Having a 'safe third country' rule in national legislation is one thing; being able effectively to implement it, quite another, and in places, a marked chasm separates rhetoric and reality, whether it relates to other States' compliance with obligations towards refugees and asylum seekers, or to the effectiveness of removal policies. Readmission agreements have become increasingly common. These are typically bilateral arrangements between States, which oblige States to readmit their own nationals and sometimes also non-citizens who have transited through the country.[310] They are primarily border control mechanisms which focus on *all* irregular

---

Front Door on Refugees: Report on the First Year of the Safe Third Country Agreement', (Dec. 2005), Appendix III.

[307] Canadian Council for Refugees, 'Closing the Front Door', above, n. 306, 3.

[308] See 'Bordering on Failure', above, n. 306, 11–15. The recognition rate for Haitian asylum seekers in the United States in 2004 was 34.7 per cent (by the US Immigration and Nationality Service) and 18.3 per cent (US Executive Office of Immigration Review) as compared to 61.1 per cent in Canada: UNHCR, *2004 Global Refugee Trends: Overview of Refugee Populations, New Arrivals, Durable Solutions, Asylum-Seekers, Stateless and Other Persons of Concern to UNHCR* (17 Jun. 205), Table 8. Particular concerns have been expressed about differing rates for Colombians: Canadian Council for Refugees, 'Closing the Front Door', above n. 306, 8–9.

[309] Canadian Council for Refugees, Media Release, 'Safe Third Country Agreement Shown to Violate Refugee Rights', (29 Mar. 2006).

[310] The Dublin Regulation and the US–Canada agreement go beyond a standard readmission agreement, since they also determine the State responsible for examining the asylum claim.

entrants, not just asylum seekers. Accordingly, they often make no specific provision for asylum seekers and refugees, and do not necessarily require the receiving State to assess the asylum claim, let alone provide protection. They are simply an agreement to readmit an individual, and without more, may lead to breaches of the principle of *non-refoulement*.[311] Both practice and principle suggest that inter-State agreements on responsibility, return, and procedural and substantive guarantees, including *non-refoulement*, are essential if the protection of refugees is to be effective.[312]

6.7 EXTRATERRITORIAL PROCESSING

The concept of 'effective protection' arises in another context: extraterritorial processing. This concept, examplified by the Australian Pacific Strategy, has been described by UNHCR as an example of 'a general narrowing of access to asylum procedures across the region'.[313] The rationale behind extraterritorial processing may be seen as twofold: first, to keep asylum seekers geographically distant from potential asylum States, and secondly (and relatedly) as an attempt to distance States from their legal obligations to them.[314] Although transferring asylum seekers 'offshore' cannot divest the receiving State of its international obligations, it

---

[311] In principle, UNHCR prefers readmission agreements to safe third country decisions, since they are not subject to unilateral decision-making and guarantee readmission; see, for example, 'UNHCR's Observations on the European Commission's Proposal for a Council Directive on Minimum Standards on Procedures for Granting and Withdrawing Refugee Status (COM(2000) 578 final, 20 September 2000)', Jul. 2001, para. 38; UNHCR Position on Readmission Agreements, 'Protection Elsewhere' and Asylum Policy (1 Aug. 1994), Pt. 5, cited in Legomsky, 'Secondary Refugee Movements', above n. 211, 630–1.

[312] See Amnesty International British Section, *Playing Human Pinball: Home Office Practice in 'Safe Third Country' Asylum Cases*, Jun. 1995. This comprehensive and compelling report by Richard Dunstan tracks sixty cases over a nine-month period, to show that the policy on safe third country denials had achieved nothing, with the Home Office rescinding its original decision in the majority of cases and agreeing to consider the claims on their merits.

[313] UNHCR, *Report of the United Nations High Commissioner for Refugees*, UN doc. E/2002/14, (28 May 2002), para. 75. In May 2006, Australia proposed extending this practice by sending all asylum seekers arriving by boat to other countries (such as Nauru) for processing. 'Designated unauthorised arrivals', as they were to be known, would have been subjected to different procedures and standards of treatment from onshore claimants, including no independent merits review or any guarantee of future resettlement in Australia for those found to be refugees. See Migration Act (Designated Unauthorised Arrivals) Bill 2006 (Cth); Senate Legal and Constitutional Legislation Committee, *Provisions of the Migration Amendment (Designated Unauthorised Arrivals) Bill* (June 2006); McAdam, J., Submission No. 64 to Senate Legal and Constitutional Legislation Committee Inquiry into the Provisions of the Migration Amendment (Designated Unauthorised Arrivals) Bill 2006 (May 2006).

[314] While States have a firm legal duty to respect ECHR50 in relation to those within their territory and jurisdiction, the precise scope and *locus* of the latter remains contested after *Banković* v. *Belgium* (2001) 11 BHRC 435, leaving the legal status of offshore processing unclear. See discussion in Ch. 5, 245ff. The UK Court of Appeal in *R. (Al-Skeini)* v. *Secretary of State for Defence* [2006] 3 WLR 508, [2005] EWCA Civ. 1609 applied *Banković* narrowly (paras. 70ff); conversely, in *R. (B)* v. *Secretary of State for Commonwealth Affairs* [2005]QB 643, the Court of Appeal was prepared to accept the extraterritorial application of ECHR50 (para. 66). The House of Lords expressed some

sends a strong message to asylum seekers that they are not welcome, and may result in refugee warehousing, the practice by which refugees are kept 'in protracted situations of restricted mobility, enforced idleness, and dependency—their lives on indefinite hold—in violation of their basic rights under the 1951 UN Refugee Convention'.[315]

In March 2003, the United Kingdom proposed the creation of an extraterritorial regime, intended as a radical new approach to asylum processing rather than merely a complement to existing procedures.[316] The aim was to develop a system of legal migration to Europe, including through resettlement (not a traditional element of EU asylum policy).[317] It proposed the establishment of regional protection areas for asylum seekers close to major refugee-producing countries, as well as transit processing centres, located in transit countries or on the external borders of the EU, to which asylum seekers arriving in the EU could be returned for processing. These centres would effectively act as camps from which refugees could be resettled or locally integrated.[318]

Aligning itself with UNHCR's 'Convention Plus' Initiative, the UK proposal sought to 'deal more successfully with irregular migrants within their regions of origin' through four strategies: working to prevent the events that precipitate population movement; working to ensure better protection in the regions from which asylum seekers come; developing a quota-based resettlement system; and raising awareness and acceptance of State responsibility to accept returnees. Included in this proposal was the possibility of moving asylum seekers already in

doubt regarding this conclusion (see *Rome a Rights* case [2005] 2 AC 1, para. 21), but has not formally interpreted *Banković*: The case law of the European Court of Human Rights is inconsistent with a strict reading of *Banković*: see *Öcalan* v. *Turkey* (2000) 30 EHRR CD 231 (Admissibility); *Öcalan* v. *Turkey* (2003) 37 EHRR 10 (Merits); *Öcalan* v. *Turkey* (Grand Chamber) (12 May 2005), applying to Turkish activities in Kenya; *Issa* v. *Turkey*, Application. No. 31821/96 (30 May 2000) (Admissibility); *Issa* v. *Turkey*, Application No. 31821/96 (Merits) (16 Nov. 2004), applying to Turkish activities in Iraq.

[315] Smith, M., 'Warehousing Refugees: A Denial of Rights, A Waste of Humanity', in US Committee for Refugees, *World Refugee Survey* 2004, 38; see also Chen, G., 'A Global Campaign to End Refugee Warehousing', ibid. 21.

[316] Secretary of State for the Home Department, 'Statement on Zones of Protection' (27 Mar. 2003), Stat010/2003, to which is appended the UK's proposal 'New International Approaches to Asylum Processing and Protection', contained in House of Lords European Union Committee, *Handling EU Asylum Claims: New Approaches Examined* (HL Paper 74, 11th Report of Session 2003–04), Appendix 5.

[317] While a number of States have traditionally resettled recognized refugees residing in camps abroad, the UK and UNHCR proposals are considerably different. 'They are not concerned with the resettlement of those already recognised as refugees. They involve the use by one State of another's territory, in order to determine claims to asylum which either have already been lodged on its own territory, or might have been lodged there if the claimant had not been intercepted en route': House of Lords European Union Committee, *Handling EU Asylum Claims,* above n. 130 para. 73.

[318] Communication from the European Commission to the Council and the European Parliament, 'Towards more Accessible, Equitable and Managed Asylum Systems' (3 Jun. 2003) COM (2003) 315 final. See further Noll, 'Visions of the Exceptional', above n. 130.

Europe back to regional processing centres for status determination or even temporary protection, provided that the domestic courts of EU Member States were
satisfied with the level of protection provided there. With respect to temporary
protection, the centres were envisaged as holding blocks for persons found not to be
Convention refugees, but who could not yet be returned to their countries of origin
due to prevailing conditions of unrest or violence. In effect, it would act as a replacement for forms of complementary or humanitarian protection in Member State
territory, without the necessary assurances and legal protection guaranteed there.

The other aspect of the proposal was to establish transit processing centres in
third States (presumably transit countries), to which asylum seekers reaching the
EU could be returned to have their protection claims assessed. It was to be managed by the IOM in accordance with UNHCR-approved screening procedures.
Persons identified as having a protection need would subseqently be resettled in
the EU in accordance with burden-sharing policies, or granted temporary asylum
there. The aim of this approach was to 'act as a deterrent to abuse of the asylum
system, whilst preserving the right to protection for those who are genuinely entitled to it'.[319] While the proposal recognized the application of the 1951
Convention and the ECHR50 to such procedures, it did not elaborate how these
would be engaged or applied.

The Commission examined the proposal and, while it shared the UK government's concerns about the deficiencies of the current asylum system, it did not
endorse the mechanisms proposed to address them.[320] At the Thessaloniki
European Council in June 2003, a number of States expressed significant opposition to the UK proposal for transit processing centres, and in 2003 the government confirmed that it was no longer pursuing this option.[321] The European
Council then invited the Commission to have a thorough look at ways to ensure
'orderly and managed entry' to the EU of those in need of protection, at how to
enhance regional protection capacity, and at the legal implications.[322] UNHCR
proposed a similar EU-based asylum procedure, with pre-screening and registration being undertaken at the EU rather than national level, and the eventual
establishment of an EU Asylum Agency.[323]

---

[319] 'New International Approaches to Asylum Processing and Protection', House of Lords,
Handling EU Asylum Claims, above n. 130, Appendix 5, 56.
[320] Communication 'Towards more Accessible, Equitable and Managed Asylum Systems', above
n. 130, 6–7.
[321] House of Lords, *Handling EU Asylum Claims*, above n. 130, para. 57.
[322] Thessaloniki European Council Conclusions (19–20 June 2003), para. 26.
[323] UNHCR Working Paper, 'UNHCR's Three-Pronged Proposal', (Jun. 2003); UNHCR
Working Paper, 'A Revised "EU Prong" Proposal', (22 Dec. 2003), especially in relation to cases that
could be processed in reception centres. This proposal has also been subject to criticism, particularly
because it would seem to shift responsibility from Member States to the EU; see, for example, House
of Lords, *Handling EU Asylum Claims*, above, n. 130, paras. 80–8.

Though initially met with widespread rejection,[324] extraterritorial controls have recurred in various guises since 2003.[325] While there is still insufficient support for an EU-wide processing model, a number of States have developed pilot schemes, such as Italy's removal of asylum seekers arriving on Lampedusa to transit centres in Libya since 2004. Such procedures may breach the 1951 Convention and the ECHR50, especially where receiving States (such as Libya) are not party to those instruments. Although the 1951 Convention does not prescribe admission or determination procedures, the Executive Committee has continually stressed that States have an obligation to admit asylum seekers, at least temporarily, to provide access to fair and effective asylum procedures.[326] In order to comply with the principle of *non-refoulement*, this obligation requires States not to remove individuals to other territories for processing unless it can be determined that, for the individual concerned, the particular country is 'safe'.[327] Certainly, States cannot extract themselves from their international legal obligations by removing asylum seekers to third States. The House of Lords Select Committee on the EU objected strongly to the establishment of extraterritorial asylum processing as an alternative to national determination procedures. It noted the importance of ensuring 'effective protection' in any extraterritorial processing system,[328] and that the application of the 'safe third country' concept must be individually scrutinized in each case, rather than systematically applied where certain objective conditions are met.[329] Amnesty International viewed the proposals as an attempt by States to circumvent their international legal obligations, by 'denying access to territory

[324] For an excellent account of the proposals, see Noll, 'Visions of the Exceptional', above, n. 130. See also House of Lords, *Handling EU Asylum Claims*, above n. 130; Office of the United Nations High Commissioner for Refugees, *The State of the World's Refugees: Human Displacement in the New Millennium* (2006), 38–9.

[325] Noll 'Visions of the Exceptional', above n. 130. Note also UNHCR's three-pronged proposals, above n. 323, which rejects *external* processing centres, but proposes regional solutions, improved domestic asylum procedures, and the processing of certain cases at reception centres *within* the borders of the EU.

[326] Executive Committee Conclusion No. 22 (1981), Pt 2A, para. 2; Executive Committee Conclusion No. 82 (1997), para. d(iii); Executive Committee Conclusion No. 85 (1998) para. q; see also Office of the UNHCR, UNGA Res. A/RES/51/75, 82nd Plenary Meeting, paras. 3–4 (1996). See also UNHCR, 'Rescue-at-Sea: Specific Aspects relating to the Protection of Asylum-Seekers and Refugees', Expert Roundtable, Lisbon, (25–26 Mar. 2002), (Summary of Discussions, 11 Apr. 2002), para. 14.

[327] See, for example, UNHCR, *Handbook*, para. 192(vii). For further discussion of the international legal implications, see MacDonald, I. & Finch, N., 'In the Matter of the Proposal by the United Kingdom to Establish Transit Processing Centres in Third Countries and the Compatibility of this Proposal with the United Kingdom's Obligations under the 1951 Refugee Convention and the European Convention on Human Rights: Opinion', London, (22 Jun. 2003): <http://www.justice.org.uk.>

[328] House of Lords, *Handling EU Asylum Claims*, above n. 130, para. 61. On the meaning of 'effective protection', see above, s. 6.3.

[329] House of Lords, *Handling EU Asylum Claims*, above n. 130, para. 68; see also House of Lords European Union Committee, *Minimum Standards in Asylum Procedures* (HL Paper 59, 11th Report of Session 2000–01), paras. 122–3.

and shifting the asylum-seekers to processing zones outside the EU, where responsibility, enforceability and accountability for refugee protection would be weak and unclear'.[330]

7. Standards of treatment for asylum seekers and refugees

The 1951 Convention does not expressly enumerate the rights of asylum seekers who have not yet been recognized as refugees. Certain rights, however, must inevitably attach until status is determined for the system of protection envisaged by the Convention to operate effectively. Thus, asylum seekers must benefit from *non-refoulement* under article 33 until it has been finally determined that they are not refugees or otherwise in need of international protection. UNHCR has described the gradations of treatment in the Convention as 'a useful yardstick in the context of defining reception standards for asylum-seekers. At a minimum, the 1951 Convention provisions that are not linked to lawful stay or residence would apply to asylum-seekers in so far as they relate to humane treatment and respect for basic rights'.[331]

Additionally, international and regional human rights instruments and norms elaborate standards of treatment for all people within a State's territory or jurisdiction, and emphasize the principle of non-discrimination.[332] While human rights entitlements may in some respects be more extensive than the treatment for refugees envisaged by the Convention, they are frequently difficult to access.[333]

At a minimum, procedures should conform with standards set down by various Executive Committee Conclusions. For example, Conclusion No. 93 (2002) requires, *inter alia*, that asylum seekers have access to assistance for basic support needs, such as food, clothing, accommodation, medical care, and respect for privacy; that reception arrangements are sensitive to gender and age, in particular the educational, psychological, recreational, and other special needs of children, and the specific needs of victims of sexual abuse and exploitation, trauma and torture; and that family groups be housed together. Executive Committee Conclusion No. 8

---

[330] Amnesty International, 'UK/EU/UNHCR: Unlawful and Unworkable—Amnesty International's Views on Proposals for Extra-Territorial Processing of Asylum Claims', (2003), AI Index IOR 61/004/2003.

[331] UNHCR, 'Reception of Asylum-Seekers, including Standards of Treatment, in the Context of Individual Asylum Systems', Global Consultations on International Protection, UN doc. EC/GC/01/17 (4 Sept. 2001), para. 3, referring to arts. 3, 4, 5, 7, 8, 12, 16, 20, 22, 31, and 33 of the 1951 Convention.   [332] For example, art. 2 ICCPR66; art. 14 ECHR50.

[333] See Ch. 6. Both Hathaway and Edwards have independently argued that refugee status comprises Convention status *plus* human rights law entitlements: Hathaway, *Rights of Refugees*, (2005), 8; Edwards, A., 'Human Rights, Refugees, and the Right "To Enjoy" Asylum', 17 *IJRL* 293 (2005). Grahl-Madsen, earlier had observed that the 'catalog of rights and benefits due to refugees' had been extended through various Council of Europe and ILO agreements: Grahl-Madsen, A., 'The European Tradition of Asylum and the Development of Refugee Law', (1966), in Macalister-Smith, P. & Alfredson, G., *The Law Beyond*, (2001), 34, 41.

(1977) stipulates, *inter alia*, that recognized refugees be issued with documentation certifying that status and that persons not recognized as refugees have a reasonable time to appeal. Numerous Conclusions emphasize that UNHCR should be given access to asylum seekers, and asylum seekers should be entitled to have access to UNHCR.[334] Above all, treatment must not be inhuman or degrading.[335]

In the EU, the Reception Conditions Directive lists minimum entitlements owed by Member States to individuals seeking protection as Convention refugees.[336] By contrast to the aspirational tone of international and regional human rights instruments, the Directive is very restrictive and reflects the idea that rights are a privilege, rather than matters of duty on the part of the State. Under that instrument, asylum seekers do not have to be granted complete freedom of movement in the Member State, and may be assigned an 'area' in which they are permitted to move.[337] A place of residence may be assigned for reasons of public interest, public order, or for processing and effective monitoring,[338] and individuals may be confined to a particular place for legal reasons or public order,[339] although States must make provision for the possibility for temporary leave from the assigned place.[340] Although the practice has often been used by European (and other) States, assigned residence potentially contravenes articles 26 and 31(2) of the 1951 Convention, which permit States to curtail asylum seekers' movement only until their identities are established and basic security concerns have been investigated (regularization of status).[341] Where States provide housing, they must respect family unity as much as possible.[342] Housing may be an accommodation centre, provided it guarantees an adequate standard of living, protects family life, and permits communication with relatives, lawyers, and NGOs.[343]

Under the Directive, access to employment may be restricted for up to at least a year,[344] and even once granted, priority may be given to citizens of the EU, States parties to the EEA Agreement, and legally resident third-country nationals.[345]

[334] Executive Committee Conclusions No. 33 (1984), No. 44 (1986), No. 48 (1987), No. 75 (1994), No. 82 (1997), No. 93 (2002), No. 101 (2004).

[335] Art. 7 ICCPR66; arts. 3, 16 CAT84.

[336] The extension of these conditions to persons seeking subsidiary protection is optional, and will not apply for example in the UK: Asylum Seekers (Reception Conditions) Regulations 2005; 'Implementation of Council Directive 2003/9/EC of 27 January 2003 laying down Minimum Standards for the Reception of Asylum Seekers: Responses to the Home Office Consultation', (14 Jan. 2004), paras. 36–7, noting criticisms of that approach. See also House of Lords Select Committee on the EU, *Minimum Standards of Reception Conditions for Asylum Seekers* (8th Report, 27 Nov. 2001), para. 81; Executive Committee Conclusion No. 82 (1997); Rogers, N., 'Minimum Standards for Reception', 4 *EJML* 215 (2002); Guild, E., 'Seeking Asylum: Storm Clouds between International Commitments and EU Legislative Measures', 29 *European Law Review* 198 (2004).

[337] States must ensure that this restriction does not interfere with private life or ability to access the rights in the Directive: art. 7(4); see art. 12 ICCPR66.

[338] Reception Conditions Directive, art. 7(2).

[339] Reception Conditions Directive, art. 7(3).

[340] Reception Conditions Directive, art. 7(5).

[341] Cf. Hathaway, J. C., 'What's in a Label?', 5 *EJIL* 1, 11 (2003).

[342] Reception Conditions Directive, art. 8.

[343] Reception Conditions Directive, art. 14.   [344] Reception Conditions Directive, art. 11.

[345] Reception Conditions Directive, art. 11(4).

Access to vocational training may be provided,[346] but health care may be restricted to emergency medical treatment and essential treatment of illness.[347] Member States must ensure 'a standard of living adequate for the health of applicants and capable of ensuring their subsistence',[348] in particular for persons in detention or with special needs, but may limit access to all or part of the reception conditions and health care entitlements to those asylum seekers who cannot support themselves.[349] Furthermore, article 16(2) allows States to deny benefits in cases where an asylum seeker did not lodge the asylum claim as soon as practicable after arrival in the Member State. In some cases, this may lead to breaches of article 3 ECHR50.[350]

8. Conclusion

The plight of the refugee in search of asylum has been a dominant theme on the international agenda since the late 1970s, as is evident from repeated appeals by the Executive Committee, the General Assembly, intergovernmental organizations and other concerned bodies.[351] At one level, State practice nevertheless permits only one conclusion: the individual still has no right to be granted asylum. The right itself is in the form of a discretionary power—the State has discretion whether to exercise its right, as to whom it will favour, and, consistently with its obligations generally under international law, as to the form and content of the asylum to be granted. Save in so far as treaty or other rules confine its discretion, for example, by requiring the extradition of war criminals, the State remains free to grant asylum to refugees as defined by international law or to any other person or group it deems fit. It is likewise free to prescribe the conditions under which asylum is to be enjoyed. It may thus accord the refugee the right to permanent or temporary residence, it may permit or decline the right to work, or confine refugees to camps, dependent on international assistance pending some future solution, such as repatriation or resettlement. Refugees may also be subject to measures falling short of *refoulement*, which nevertheless prevent them from effectively making a claim to status or asylum, or in securing admission to a particular country.

---

[346] Reception Conditions Directive, art. 12.
[347] Reception Conditions Directive, art. 15(1). Art. 15(2) provides: 'Member States shall provide necessary medical or other assistance to applicants who have special needs.'   [348] Art. 13(2).
[349] Reception Conditions Directive, art. 13(3).
[350] See *R. (Limbuela)* v. *Secretary of State for the Home Department* [2006] 1 AC 396, [2005] UKHL 66, discussed above in Ch.5, 265, n. 375.
[351] See, for example, the annual reports of the UNHCR Executive Committee, the yearly resolutions of the UN General Assembly on UNHCR and related issues, and reviews by NGOs, such as the *World Refugee Survey* published each year by the US Committee for Refugees and Immigrants.

After 1951, many States in fact adopted the refugee definition as the criterion for the grant of asylum and, until the peremptory effect of human rights obligations made itself clear, as the sole criterion for the grant of the specific, limited, but fundamental protection of *non-refoulement*. Likewise, in the practice of many States party to the 1951 Convention/1967 Protocol, the recognized refugee, the person with a well-founded fear of persecution, is not only effectively entitled to asylum in the sense of residence, but is also protected against return to the country in which he or she runs the risk of persecution or other relevant harm.

There is nevertheless a certain discontinuity in the protection regime established by the 1951 Convention/1967 Protocol and general international law, and between the status of refugee and a solution to the problem of the refugee. Refugees benefit from *non-refoulement* and refugee status is often, but not necessarily, the sufficient condition for the grant of permanent or durable asylum. But there is no *necessary* connection between *non-refoulement* and admission or asylum. In international law, as well as in national practice, the discretion to grant asylum and the obligation to abide by *non-refoulement* remain divided, even as they are linked by the common definitional standards of well-founded fear or risk of torture or other relevant harm.

The ideal of asylum as an obligation on States to accord lasting solutions, with or without a correlative right of the individual, continues to be resisted. Asylum remains an institution which operates between subjects of international law. Moreover, in an era of mass exodus, of actual or perceived threats to national security, States are still not prepared to accept an obligation without determinable content or dimension. Experience shows that efforts to secure agreement on such a divisive issue are more likely to produce equivocation, qualification, and exception, that can tend only to dilute the rules and principles already established in State practice.[352] But asylum as lasting solution, though a preferred sense, represents one aspect only. State practice is not solely concerned with permanent protection, and the concept of asylum at large cannot be analysed adequately apart from the concept of refuge and the normative principle of *non-refoulement*. States *are* obliged to protect refugees, and consequently they are obliged to abide by *non-refoulement* through time. That time is not and cannot be determined by any

---

[352] This is not to say the individual's right to asylum may not have some future; merely that progress is more likely to be achieved through the development of regional instruments and the promotion of effective municipal laws, particularly to ensure the integrity of the principle of *non-refoulement*. Note, however, the 1991 decision of the *Conseil constitutionnel* of France on the right of asylum and the Schengen Convention. Referring to the Preamble of the 1946 Constitution ('Tout homme persécuté en raison de son action en faveur de la liberté a droit d'asile sur les territoires de la République'), the court decided that the Schengen Convention might be ratified without infringing this right, because it expressly reserved to States the entitlement to consider an asylum claim *even though it was properly the responsibility of another State party*: Conseil constitutionnel, Décision no. 91-294 DC, 25 juillet 1991, paras. 30–1; Oliver, P., 'The French Constitution and the Treaty of Maastricht', 43 *ICLQ* 1 (1994).

principle of international law, but likewise the duty to accord *non-refoulement* through time cannot be separated in practice from that other complex duty which recognizes the responsibility of the community of States in finding durable solutions.[353]

So far as a State's actions may expose an individual to the risk of violation of his or her human rights, its responsibility is duty-driven, rather than strictly correlative to any individual right. The duty not to return refugees to persecution or to a situation of danger to life or limb is owed to the international community of States which, for many purposes, is represented by UNHCR. The international community is likewise entitled to require of individual States, not only that they accord to refugees the benefit of *non-refoulement* through time, but also the opportunity of finding a lasting solution to their plight. The degree of protection required is that commensurate with the occasion, and given the present level of development of international law, certain exceptions in favour of the State remain. The area continues to be governed by discretion, rather than duty, but analysis reveals that discretion is not only confined by principle, but also structured in the light of other legally relevant considerations, including international solidarity, burden-sharing, and the right of functional protection enjoyed by UNHCR.

Freedom to grant or to refuse permanent asylum remains, but save in exceptional and now almost notional circumstances, States do not enjoy the right to return refugees to persecution or relevant situations of danger. Protection against the immediate eventuality is the responsibility of the country of first refuge. So far as a State is required to grant that protection, the minimum content of which is *non-refoulement* through time, it is required also to treat the refugee in accordance with such standards as will permit an appropriate solution, whether voluntary repatriation, local integration, or resettlement in another country. There was some support in the past for the overall primary responsibility in fact falling on the first country of refuge,[354] but experience in South East Asia, Central America, Western Asia, Africa, and Europe, where so many States declined to allow refugees to regularize their status or otherwise to remain within their borders, has served to emphasize the international dimension to burden-sharing.

Although the trend towards increasingly restrictive asylum policies pre-dates 11 September 2001, security concerns following the terrorist attacks on the United States have reshaped asylum regimes in a number of States. Detention grounds have been expanded, exclusion clauses have been applied more extensively than international law permits, and stronger links have been forged between immigration, intelligence, and criminal law enforcement agencies.[355] Security Council resolutions passed post-11 September 2001 on terrorism have expressly noted that 'the protections afforded by the Refugees Convention and its Protocol shall

---

[353] See above, Ch. 5.
[354] Cf. UNGA resolutions 832(LX), 21 Oct. 1954, and 1166(XII), 26 Nov. 1957.
[355] Türk, V., 'Forced Migration and Security', 15 *IJRL* 113, 115 (2003).

not extend to any person with respect to whom there are serious reasons for considering that he has been guilty of acts contrary to the purposes and principles of the United Nations'.³⁵⁶ Tighter migration controls, coupled with the high political profile of illegal migration, transfer the focus away from the border to 'elsewhere'—boats of asylum seekers, airports, people smugglers, and so on—such that the border 'in its conventional territorial configuration is thus eroded relatively—and not just absolutely—as a site of control'.³⁵⁷

---

³⁵⁶ For example, SC res. 1624, 14 Sept. 2005; SC res. 1373 28 Sept. 2001, para. 3(f), where the Security Council called upon States to: 'Take appropriate measures in conformity with the relevant provisions of national and international law, including international standards of human rights, before granting refugee status, for the purpose of ensuring that the asylum-seeker has not planned, facilitated or participated in the commission of terrorist acts.' See also SC res. 1624, 14 Sept. 2005, preambular paras. 2, 7; operative para. 4.

³⁵⁷ Crowley, J., 'Differential Free Movement and the Sociology of the "Internal Border"', in Guild, E. & Harlow, C., eds., *Implementing Amsterdam: Immigration and Asylum Rights in EC Law* (2001), 21. See also Lahav, G., 'Immigration and the State: The Devolution and Privatisation of Immigration Control in the EU', 24 *Journal of Ethnic and Migration Studies* 675 (1998).

PART 3
PROTECTION

8

International Protection

The lack or denial of protection is a principal feature of refugee character, and it is for international law, in turn, to substitute its own protection for that which the country of origin cannot or will not provide. *Non-refoulement* is the foundation-stone of international protection, and in this and the following two chapters the content of that protection is examined in more detail, with attention specifically to international institutions, treaties, solutions, and the incorporation of international standards in municipal law.

1. International institutions

The first intergovernmental arrangements on behalf of refugees were contemporaneous with the establishment of various institutions charged with their implementation.[1] In 1921, Gustave Ador, President of the International Committee of the Red Cross, addressed the Council of the League of Nations on behalf of an estimated 800,000 Russians scattered throughout Europe, without protection or status.[2] So it was that in June 1921 the Council decided to appoint a High Commissioner for Russian Refugees, naming Dr Fridtjof Nansen to the post some two months later.[3] The tasks of the High Commissioner included defining the legal status of refugees; organizing their repatriation or 'allocation' to potential resettlement countries and, together with private organizations, providing relief.[4]

---

[1] On the inter-war years generally, see Simpson, J. H., *The Refugee Problem*, (1939); Reale, E., 'Le problème des passeports', 50 Hague *Recueil*, (1934-IV), 89; *A Study of Statelessness*, (1949): UN doc. E/1112 and Add. 1, 34–8; Sjöberg, T., *The Powers and the Persecuted: The Refugee Problem and the Intergovernmental Committee on Refugees*, (1991), Ch. 1.

[2] (1921) 2(2) *LNOJ* 227. They included some 50,000 former prisoners of war unwilling to return, civilians who had fled the Bolshevik revolution, as well as members of the various defeated armies which had opposed the revolutionaries during the first years. The *de facto* unprotected status of many was further compounded by two decrees of October and December 1921, under which Soviet citizenship was forfeited by certain groups residing abroad; see generally Fisher Williams, J., 'Denationalization', 8 *BYIL* 45 (1927).

[3] See generally Reynolds, E. E., *Nansen* (1932, rev. edn. 1949).

[4] Annexe 224, Minutes of the 13th Session of the Council of the League of Nations, Geneva, 17–28 June 1921; cited by Weis, P., 'The International Protection of Refugees', 48 *AJIL* 193, 207–8 (1954). During the 1920s, large-scale relief operations were undertaken by private organizations for the multitudes displaced by the First World War and its aftermath: Marrus, M., *The Unwanted—European*

In this period, the League also acted for many other groups; they included Armenians, whose exodus from Turkey to various neighbouring countries had begun in 1915, and began again in 1921;[5] Assyrians and Assyro-Chaldeans; and a group of one hundred and fifty persons of Turkish origin who, under the terms of the Protocol of Lausanne of 24 July 1923, were expressly barred from returning to their country of origin.[6] Also beginning in the 1920s came the flight from fascism, first from Italy, then from Spain, and finally from Germany and its conquered or incorporated territories in the 1930s.

A 1928 arrangement[7] recommended that the services normally rendered to nationals abroad by consular authorities should be discharged on behalf of refugees by representatives of the High Commissioner. Unless within the exclusive competence of national authorities, such services were to include: certifying the identity and position of refugees; certifying their family position and civil status, so far as that was based on documents issued or action taken in the refugees' country of origin; testifying to the regularity, validity, and conformity with the previous law of their country of origin of documents issued in that country; certifying the signature of refugees and copies and translations of documents drawn up in their own language; testifying before the authorities of the country to the good character and conduct of individual refugees, their previous record, professional qualifications, and university or academic standing; and recommending individual refugees to the competent authorities with a view to obtaining visas, residence permits, admission to schools, libraries, and so forth.[8] In order to give legal effect to these recommendations two States, France and Belgium, concluded an agreement authorizing the High Commissioner's representatives to issue the documents in question.[9]

Refugees in the Twentieth Century, (1985), 82–6. In the same period, considerable international attention and assistance focused also on spontaneous, coerced and agreed population exchanges in the Balkans; on the exchanges between Greece and Turkey and Greece and Bulgaria: Marrus, *The Unwanted*, 96–109; Meindersma, C., 'Population Exchanges: International Law and State Practice— Part I', 9 *IJRL* 335 (1997); 'Part 2', 9 *IJRL* 613 (1997).

[5] Marrus, *The Unwanted*, 74–81, 119–21. Arrangement relating to the Issue of Identity Certificates to Russian and Armenian Refugees of 12 May 1926: 84 *LNTS* No. 2006.

[6] Arrangement concerning the Extension to other Categories of Refugees of certain Measures taken in favour of Russian and Armenian Refugees of 30 June 1928: 89 *LNTS* No. 2006.

[7] Arrangement relating to the legal status of Russian and Armenian refugees, 30 June 1928: 89 *LNTS* No. 2005. It came into force between ten States.

[8] Ibid., Res. (1). Other resolutions made recommendations, among others, in respect of choice of law in matters of marriage and divorce; that refugees not be denied certain rights and privileges on the basis of lack of reciprocity; that they be exempt from the *cautio judicatum solvi* (security for costs in legal proceedings); that they be accorded national treatment in matters of taxation.

[9] Agreement concerning the functions of the representatives of the League of Nations High Commissioner for Refugees: 93 *LNTS* No. 2126. In France, this function was taken over by the International Refugee Organization (IRO) (agreement cited by Weis, P., 'Legal Aspects of the Convention of 28 Jul. 1951 relating to the Status of Refugees', 30 *BYIL* 478, 484 (1953)), and subsequently by the *Office français de protection des réfugiés et apatrides* (OFPRA): *loi no. 52–893* du 25 juillet 1952, art. 4, *décret no. 53–377* du 2 mai 1953, art. 5. See now, *décret no. 2004–814* du 14 août 2004; *loi du 10 décembre 2003* (loi 2003-1176, 10 décembre 2003, en vigueur le 1er janvier 2004).

In the period 1923–9, certain 'technical services' principally relating to assistance, were entrusted to the International Labour Organization, leaving the High Commissioner responsible for the political and legal protection of refugees. With Nansen's death in 1930, the Assembly of the League of Nations established the Nansen Office to undertake humanitarian activities on behalf of refugees, and entrusted protection to the Secretary-General. A succession of other bodies followed: first, the High Commissioner's Office for Refugees Coming from Germany was established in 1933;[10] then, in 1938, came the High Commissioner's office for all refugees, charged with providing political and legal protection, superintending the entry into force of the relevant conventions, co-ordinating humanitarian assistance, and assisting governments and private organizations in their efforts to promote emigration and permanent settlement.[11] The same year, following the thirty-two nation Evian Conference convened on the initiative of the United States to deal with 'the question of involuntary emigration', the Intergovernmental Committee on Refugees (IGCR) was created.[12] At this time of a continuing outflow from Germany and Austria, the answer was thought to lie in coordinating involuntary emigration with existing immigration laws and practices, in collaboration with the country of origin.

From October 1939, the IGCR was essentially non-functional, although it was substantially reorganized and its mandate extended following an Anglo-American meeting in Bermuda in April 1943.[13] In November of that year, the Allies also set up the United Nations Relief and Rehabilitation Administration (UNRRA); as the name and time imply, its role was to provide relief to the millions displaced by the Second World War and, in particular, to assist those wishing to repatriate.[14]

[10] This office was initially set up outside the League, owing to German Government opposition. Two years later, the High Commissioner, James G. McDonald, resigned, observing in a letter of 27 Dec. 1935 to the Secretary-General of the League, that private and international organizations could only mitigate an increasingly grave and complex situation. Given the condition of the world economy, resettlement opportunities were few and the problem had to be tackled at source. An annexe to his letter called attention to human rights in Germany, to that country's international obligations towards minorities, and the violation of the rights and territorial sovereignty of other States that was involved by forced migration, denationalization, and withdrawal of protection: see Marrus, *The Unwanted*, 161–6; Jennings, R.Y., 'Some International Law Aspects of the Refugee Question', 20 *BYIL* 98 (1939).

[11] League of Nations, *O.J.* Special Supp., no. 189, (1938) 86; see also Provisional Arrangement concerning the Status of Refugees coming from Germany of 4 Jul. 1936: 171 *LNTS* No. 3952.

[12] The functions of the Committee were defined in a resolution adopted on 14 Jul. 1938; text in *A Study of Statelessness*, (above, n.1), 116–18. For a full account, see Sjöberg, T., *The Powers and the Persecuted: The Refugee Problem and the Intergovernmental Committee on Refugees (IGCR), 1938–1947*, (1991). And for later developments, Salomon, K., *Refugees in the Cold War: Toward a New International Refugee Regime in the Early Postwar Era*, (1991).

[13] Sjöberg, *The Powers and the Persecuted*, Ch. 4. Issues discussed included a British proposal to provide temporary asylum to refugees 'as near as possible to the areas in which the people find themselves at the present time and from which they may be returned to their homelands with the greatest expediency on the termination of hostilities': ibid., 135.

[14] See generally Woodbridge, G., *UNRRA: The History of the United Nations Relief and Rehabilitation Administration*, 3 vols., (1950); Salomon, K., *Refugees in the Cold War*, (1991), 46–54, 57–61 and generally; Salomon, K., 'UNRRA and the IRO as Predecessors of UNHCR', in Rystad, G.,

UNRRA was conceived as a temporary institution, and its only concern with refugees arose from its relief responsibilities. Notwithstanding some remarkable success in overseeing the return movements of the displaced,[15] by June 1947 nearly 650,000 still remained without solutions, most of them east Europeans and many of them refugees from the events of the post-war. In 1946, however, the United Nations had recognized the fundamental principle that no refugees with valid objections to returning to their countries of origin should be compelled to do so.[16] Following the recommendation of ECOSOC, it also created the International Refugee Organization (IRO)[17] and defined those within its mandate.[18] While there was general agreement on the necessity to assist the victims of nazi, fascist and similar regimes, many countries remained adamantly opposed to providing international protection to so-called political dissidents. These same countries argued that the number of 'non-repatriables' would be considerably reduced if hostile propaganda ceased in the camps, and if the activities of war criminals and the like were curbed. This opposition extended to a refusal to contribute to the financing of large-scale resettlement operations.[19]

The IRO operated until 28 February 1952,[20] its functions defined in its Constitution to include: repatriation; identification; registration and classification; care and assistance; legal and political protection; and transport, resettlement, and re-establishment of persons of concern to the Organization.[21] Throughout its life, the IRO and particularly its resettlement work, were sharply attacked in the United Nations, both directly and indirectly.[22] Direct attacks concentrated on the IRO's 'complicity' in resettlement activities designed to meet labour demands and to provide shelter for expatriate organizations hatching plots and threatening

---

ed., *The Uprooted: Forced Migration as an International Problem in the Post-War Era*, (1990), 157; Hathaway, J., 'The Evolution of Refugee Status in International Law: 1920–1950', 33 *ICLQ* 348 (1984).

[15] By the beginning of 1946, an estimated three-quarters of the displaced in Europe had been sent home: Marrus, *The Unwanted*, 320.   [16] UNGA res. 8(I), 12 Feb. 1946.

[17] The IRO Constitution was adopted by thirty votes to five, with eighteen abstentions: UNGA res. 62(I), 15 Dec. 1946. A Preparatory Commission (PCIRO) was set up to ensure continuity between UNRRA and the IGCR (both of which were wound up on 30 June 1947) and the IRO, pending sufficient ratifications to bring the latter's Constitution into force. This became effective 20 Aug. 1948.

[18] See generally UNGAOR, 1st Sess., 2nd Part, Supplement No. 2, *Report* of ECOSOC to the General Assembly, 53–62; UN doc. A/265, *Report* of the Third Committee, Summary Records, 1420–54; UN doc. A/275, Budget of the IRO. The budget was based on an estimated total of 844,525 European refugees and displaced persons at 1 Jan. 1947. For background (and highly political) debate in the Third Committee, see UNGAOR, Third Committee, 1st Sess., 1st Part, Summary Records: UN doc. A/C.3/SR.4, SR.5, SR.6, SR.7 and SR.8.

[19] Under art. 10, IRO Constitution, as amended by the Fifth Committee, contributions to large-scale resettlement operations were to be made on a voluntary basis: UN doc. A/275, para. 7 and Annex I.   [20] See generally Holborn, L., *The International Refugee Organization*, (1956).

[21] Art. 2, Constitution of the IRO.

[22] See UNGAOR, 2nd Sess., (1947), Plenary, Summary Records, 1025–31; Annex 12, 257–66. Also, UNGAOR, 4th Sess., (1949), Third Committee, Summary Records, 72–89; Plenary, Summary Records, 212–25.

world peace.[23] The responses were generally muted, relying more on statements of principle—the freedom to return or not to return—and only rarely charging east European countries with direct responsibility for the exodus.[24] IRO operations continued in a period of heightening east-west tension. It remained funded by only eighteen of the fifty-four governments then members of the United Nations, and it is hardly surprising, either that its policies should be caught up in the politics of the day, or that there may not have been some truth behind the 'immigration bureau' charge.

Many tens of thousands of refugees and displaced persons were resettled under IRO auspices.[25] The self-interest of States was at work, and refugee resettlement policies also served broader political interests.[26] And yet at the same time, there was a vast humanitarian problem then facing individual States and the international community. Refugee situations can and do lead to instability; if left unresolved, they may breed refugee discontent, leading to political tensions at the local, regional, or universal level. Solutions had to be found; given the relations then prevailing between east and west, given the west's popular endorsement of human rights and freedom of choice, and given population pressures in much of Europe, third country resettlement was the single most attractive option available to those States committed to resolving the problem.

The IRO existed to deal with the aftermath of the Second World War and the immediate consequences of political change. Even during its lifetime, however, the General Assembly acknowledged the need for a successor organization, and in the days of the IRO's demise, the major questions debated were *definitional*—just who should benefit from international action; and *functional*—what should be done for refugees, who should do it, and who should pay. Eastern European countries continued to voice their suspicions, but there was also a significant change in the policy of the United States, the major donor. The IRO had been expensive, and increasingly the US authorities came to rely on their own refugee schemes (such as the escapee programme), on bilateral and regional arrangements, and on the Intergovernmental Committee for European Migration, set up in 1951 outside the United Nations system.[27] While these developments were yet to come, the General Assembly decided in 1949 to establish a High Commissioner's Office for Refugees.[28]

[23] See, for example, UNGAOR, 3rd Sess., 2nd Part, Third Committee, Summary Records, 434 (Poland); 446 (Yugoslavia); 451 (Ukrainian SSR); also, UNGAOR, 3rd Sess., 2nd Part, Plenary, Summary Records, 504–18.

[24] See UNGAOR, 4th Sess., Third Committee, Summary Records, 82–3 for an exception, the UK representative referring to instances of forced migration and deportation in the USSR.

[25] Holborn, L., *Refugees: A Problem of our Time*, (1975), 31.

[26] See Loescher, G. & Scanlan, J., *Calculated Kindness*, (1986), 15–24.

[27] See further below, s. 1.4.1.

[28] UNGA res. 319(IV), 3 Dec. 1949. For completeness sake, mention should also be made of the United Nations Relief and Works Agency for Palestine Refugees in the Near East (UNRWA), established by UNGA res. 302(IV), 8 Dec. 1949, and on which see further below at s. 1.2; and the United Nations Korean Reconstruction Agency established by UNGA res. 401A and B(V), 1 Dec. 1950,

1.1 THE OFFICE OF THE UNITED NATIONS HIGH COMMISSIONER FOR REFUGEES (UNHCR)[29]

At its 1950 session, the General Assembly formally adopted the Statute of UNHCR as an annexe to resolution 428(V),[30] in which it also called upon governments to cooperate with the Office. The functions of UNHCR encompass 'providing international protection' and 'seeking permanent solutions' to the problem of refugees by way of voluntary repatriation or assimilation in new national communities.[31] The Statute expressly provides that 'the work of the High Commissioner shall be of an entirely non-political character; it shall be humanitarian and social and shall relate, as a rule, to groups and categories of refugees'.[32] Of the two functions, the provision of international protection is of primary importance, for without protection, such as intervention to secure admission and *non-refoulement* of refugees, there can be no possibility of finding lasting solutions.[33]

Besides defining refugees, the UNHCR Statute prescribes the relationship of the High Commissioner with the General Assembly and the Economic and Social Council (ECOSOC), makes provision for organization and finance, and identifies ways in which the High Commissioner is to provide for protection.[34] These develop the functions engaged in by predecessor organizations and include: (1) promoting the conclusion of international conventions for the protection of refugees, supervising their application and proposing amendments thereto; (2) promoting through special agreements with governments the execution of any measures calculated to improve the situation of refugees and to reduce the number requiring protection; and (3) promoting the admission of refugees.[35]

which was principally concerned with relief and economic reconstruction, and concluded its activities in 1958.

[29] For a comprehensive review of UNHCR's performance since it was established, see Loescher, G., *The UNHCR and World Politics: A Perilous Path*, (2001); for a critique of the international protection regime and proposals for its evolution, see Helton, A. C., *The Price of Indifference: Refugees and Humanitarian Action in the New Century*, (2002).

[30] For full text of resolution and Statute, see below Annexe 1, No. 3. Adopted by thirty-six votes to five, with eleven abstentions. The United Kingdom abstained, principally because of concerns over the refugee definition in the Statute, including the fact that, in a remarkably prescient observation, the High Commissioner was likely to have difficulty in practice in determining the persons whom he was competent to protect: UNGAOR, 5th Sess., Plenary, Summary records, 669–80, paras. 66–8, 14 Dec. 1950. [31] Statute, para. 1.

[32] Ibid., para. 2. The 'non-political' qualification was introduced on the proposal of Yugoslavia. Para. 3, however, obliges the High Commissioner to follow policy directives of the General Assembly and the Economic and Social Council; see UNGA res. 60/129, 16 Dec. 2005, para. 13.

[33] The protection of refugees has its origins in a human rights context, and the General Assembly has reaffirmed international protection as a principal function of UNHCR since at least 1974: UNGA res. 3272(XXIX), 10 Dec. 1974. Recent resolutions also emphasize that 'the protection of refugees is primarily the responsibility of States, whose full and effective cooperation, action and political resolve are required to enable the Office to fulfil its functions': UNGA res. 60/129, 16 Dec. 2005, para. 7. [34] Statute, para. 8.

[35] Besides the declared functions, UNHCR's indirect or promotional activities encompass the application of national laws and regulations benefitting refugees, the development and adoption of

Notwithstanding the statutory injunction that the work of the Office shall relate, as a rule, to groups and categories of refugees, a major part of UNHCR's protection work has long been concerned with individual cases, as was that of its predecessor organizations. No State has objected to UNHCR taking up individual cases as such,[36] although States may, and do, question whether an individual is indeed a refugee.[37] Nevertheless, the individual dimension to the protection function is a natural corollary to the declared task of supervising the application of international conventions. Such instruments define refugees in essentially individualistic terms and provide rights on behalf of refugees which can only be understood in the sense of the particular. The acquiescence of States in the individual protection function of UNHCR, however, significantly delineates both the competence of the Office and the status of the individual refugee in international law.

Today, most States clearly want the United Nations to assume responsibilities for a broad category of persons obliged to flee their countries for a variety of reasons.[38] The General Assembly has endorsed UNHCR activities for humanitarian reasons, but also essentially because the lack of protection creates a vacuum.[39]

appropriate national laws, regulations, and procedures, promotion of accession to international instruments, the development of new legal instruments, and overall the development of doctrine; see Lewis, C., 'UNHCR's Contribution to the Development of International Refugee Law: Its Foundations and Evolution', 17 *IJRL* 67–90 (2005); Türk, V., 'The Role of UNHCR in the Development of International Refugee Law', in Nicholson, F. & Twomey, P., *Refugee Rights and Realities*, (1999), 153. The Executive Committee has also approved the dissemination and promotion of refugee law, training and information; see, for example, *Report* of the 31st Session (1980): UN doc. A/AC.96/588, para. 48(1) (k).

[36] Sadruddin Aga Khan, 'Legal problems relating to refugees and displaced persons', Hague *Recueil* (1976-I) 331–2; Schnyder, F., 'Les aspects juridiques actuels du problème des réfugiés', Hague *Recueil* (1965-I) 319, 416.

[37] See above, Ch. 2, s. 3.2.

[38] In 1980, for example, the UNHCR Executive Committee 'emphasized . . . the leading responsibility of (UNHCR) in emergency situations which involve refugees in the sense of its Statute or of General Assembly resolution 1388(XIV) and its subsequent resolutions': *Report* of the 31st Session (1980): UN doc. A/AC.96/588, paras. 29.A(c), 29.B(c)(e)(f)). Those 'subsequent resolutions' in turn tracked the UNHCR's good offices work in securing contributions for assistance to refugees not within the competence of the UN, its development to include protection and assistance activities, and eventual recognition of a general responsibility to seek solutions to the problems of refugees and displaced persons of concern to UNHCR, wherever they occur; see UNGA resolutions 1499(XV), 5 Dec. 1960; 1673(XVI), 18 Dec. 1961; 1959(XVIII), 12 Dec. 1963; 2294(XXII), 11 Dec. 1967; 3143(XXVIII), 14 Dec. 1973; 34/60, 29 Nov. 1979. Beginning in the early 1990s, UNHCR has engaged in a number of operations outside its general mandate to protect refugees, including the provision of humanitarian assistance in an active conflict zone (Bosnia & Herzegovina), and it has frequently been pressed to take on a more active assistance and protection role with internally displaced persons, for example, in Kosovo and Darfur. See further below, Ch. 9, s. 2.

[39] During debate on the Statute, one representative suggested that the lack of protection should be the sole criterion for determining UNHCR's competence: UNGAOR, 5th Session, Third Committee, Summary Records, 324th Meeting, 22 Nov. 1950, para. 40f (United Kingdom); see also ibid., 325th Meeting, 24 Nov. 1950, para. 36 (Chile—protection should be extended to anyone who, for reasons beyond their control, could no longer live in the country of their birth); 329th Meeting, 29 Nov. 1950, paras. 3, 8f (Turkey—those needing protection included fugitives from war or persecution, or for political reasons). While in 1950 the debate was premised on the assumption that those needing protection would have left their country of origin, UNHCR has been increasingly called on

This in turn may be due to the legal consequences of statelessness;[40] or it may be a matter of fact, where an individual is unable or unwilling to avail himself or herself of the protection of the government of their country, either because of a well-founded fear of persecution, or because of some man-made disaster, such as violence resulting from a variety of sources.[41]

The underlying rationale for international protection is thus that humanitarian necessity which derives from valid reasons involving elements of coercion and compulsion. The refugee in flight from persecution and the refugee in flight from the violence of a 'man-made disaster' are alike the responsibility of the United Nations, even as the present system of duty and cooperation falls short of demanding durable solutions from sovereign States. General Assembly resolutions can extend the functional responsibilities of UNHCR, its subsidiary organ, but they do not thereby directly impose obligations on States.

1.1.1 Relation of UNHCR to the General Assembly and its standing in general international law

UNHCR was established by the General Assembly as a subsidiary organ under article 22 of the UN Charter,[42] and the parent body has continued its role in expanding or approving extensions of the mandate of the Office.[43] The relationship of the two organizations is laid down in the Statute, which declares that UNHCR acts, not at the direction of the UN Secretary-General, but 'under the

to provide protection and humanitarian assistance to persons displaced within their own countries. See below, Ch. 9, s. 2 and above, Ch. 2, s. 3.3.

[40] In resolutions 3274(XXIX), 10 Dec. 1974, and 31/36, 30 Nov. 1976, the General Assembly entrusted UNHCR with responsibilities under arts. 11 and 20 of the 1961 Convention on the Reduction of Statelessness (examination of claims and assistance in their presentation to the appropriate authorities). See also Executive Committee Conclusion No. 78 (1995), *Report* of the 46th Session, UN doc. A/AC.96/860, para. 20; UNHCR, 'UNHCR's Activities in the Field of Statelessness: Progress Report', UN doc. EC/51/SC/CRP.13, 30 May 2001, in 13 *IJRL* 702 (2001); Executive Committee Conclusion No. 106 (2006), 'Identification, Prevention and Reduction of Statelessness and Protection of Stateless Persons'.

[41] Man-made disasters have never been precisely defined, but General Assembly resolutions have indicated typical instances; see, for example, on refugees from Algeria: UNGA resolutions 1286(XIII), 5 Dec. 1958; 1389(XIV), 20 Nov. 1959; 1500(XV), 5 Dec. 1960 and 1672(XVI), 18 Dec. 1961. See also UNGA resolutions 1671(XVI), 18 Dec. 1961 (Angolan refugees in the Congo); 2790(XXVI), 6 Dec. 1971 (East Pakistan refugees in India); 3271(XXIX), 10 Dec. 1974 (voluntary repatriation of refugees from territories emerging from colonial rule). 'Man-made disasters' are now 'human-made', according to the 1998 Guiding Principles on Internal Displacement.

[42] 'The General Assembly may establish such subsidiary organs as it deems necessary for the performance of its functions.' UNHCR was originally set up for three years; its mandate is now subject to renewal every five years and was recently renewed in 2002 for a further five years from 1 Jan. 2004: UNGA res. 57/186, 18 Dec. 2002. See further, Sarooshi, D., 'The Legal Framework Governing United Nations Subsidiary Organs', 67 *BYIL* 413 (1997); Sarooshi, D., *International Organizations and their Exercise of Sovereign Powers*, (2005).

[43] From the beginning, the General Assembly acknowledged that refugees were an international responsibility, and that it would be necessary and desirable to modify and extend the competence of UNHCR to new groups of refugees and to new fields of activity: see UNGA res. 319(IV), 3 Dec. 1949, Annex, para. 3.

authority of the General Assembly',[44] that it shall 'follow policy directives given by [that body] or the Economic and Social Council',[45] and that it 'shall engage in such additional activities, including repatriation and resettlement, as the General Assembly may determine'.[46]

The High Commissioner is further required to report annually to the General Assembly, through the Economic and Social Council, and the report is to be considered as a separate agenda item.[47] Finally, the Statute calls upon the High Commissioner, particularly where difficulties arise, to request the opinion of the advisory committee on refugees, if it is created.[48] Such a committee was first established in 1951,[49] and was replaced four years later by the UN Refugee Fund Executive Committee,[50] whose functions included supervision of material assistance programmes financed by the fund. The General Assembly called for its replacement in turn by the Executive Committee of the High Commissioner's Programme, which was set up by the Economic and Social Council in 1958.[51] Originally comprising twenty-four States, it has been progressively enlarged to its present (2007) membership of seventy.[52] The Committee's original terms of reference included advising the High Commissioner, on request, in the exercise of the Office's statutory functions; and advising on the appropriateness of providing international assistance through the Office in order to solve any specific refugee problems. In 1975, the Executive Committee set up a Sub-Committee of the Whole on International Protection,[53] which regularly reviewed situations of concern, and whose conclusions, when adopted in Plenary, constituted some of the 'soft law' background to refugee protection, particularly between 1977 and

---

[44] Statute, para. 3. The High Commissioner is elected by the General Assembly, on the nomination of the Secretary-General: ibid. para. 13. This (compromise) solution was adopted precisely in order to shelter the High Commissioner from the highly political work of the UN Secretariat, and to ensure that UNHCR enjoyed the necessary independence, authority and impartiality to carry out its humanitarian work. On background and one Secretary-General's attempt to pre-empt established consultative procedures, see 'Sadako Ogata elected as UN High Commissioner for Refugees', 3 *IJRL* 120 (1991).   [45] Statute, para. 4.

[46] Ibid., para. 9. Since 1972, at least, such additional activities have also included assistance and *de facto* protection to repatriating refugees and internally displaced persons, or assistance to local populations affected by a refugee influx. To these specific or implied mandate responsibilities must now also be added the special humanitarian tasks entrusted to UNHCR, for example, in former Yugoslavia, including assistance and, within difficult limits, protection of populations at risk in their own land.

[47] Ibid., para. 11. As a corollary, the same paragraph entitles the High Commissioner to present his or her views before the General Assembly and ECOSOC and their subsidiary bodies. Since 1969, the practice has been to transmit the report without debate to the General Assembly, unless one or more ECOSOC members or the High Commissioner request otherwise: Decision on Item 9, ECOSOC, *OR*, Resumed 47th Session: UN doc. E/4735/Add.1.

[48] Statute, para. 1. By para. 4 ECOSOC was empowered to establish such a committee.
[49] ECOSOC res. 393B(XIII), 10 Sept. 1951.
[50] ECOSOC res. 565(XIX), 31 Mar. 1955, further to UNGA res. 832(IX), 21 Oct. 1954.
[51] UNGA res. 1166(XII), 26 Nov. 1957, and ECOSOC res. 672(XXV), 30 Apr. 1958.
[52] For membership, see below, Annexe 3.
[53] *Report* of the 26th Session (1975): UN doc. A/AC.96/521, para. 69(h).

1994.[54] At its 1995 session, the Executive Committee reorganized its meetings around one annual plenary session and a number of inter-sessional meetings of a new Standing Committee of the Whole, which replaced the Sub-Committees with a general competence over protection, programme and financial issues.[55] Notwithstanding the apparently limited role anticipated by the Executive Committee's initial terms of reference, it has come to exercise considerably more influence on the day-to-day management of UNHCR, as well as in the development of policy.[56]

Each of the above elements involves the participation of States, at varying levels, in the principal international institutions concerned with the protection of refugees. The practice of such organizations is therefore relevant in assessing both the standing of UNHCR and the legal status of the rules benefitting refugees in general international law. UNHCR is not only a forum in which the views of States may be represented; it is also, as a subject of international law, an actor in the relevant field whose actions count in the process of law formation.[57] Specific authority to involve itself in the protection of refugees has been accorded to the Office by States parties to the 1951 Convention and/or the 1967 Protocol relating to the Status of Refugees. Article 35 of the Convention, for example, provides: 'The contracting States undertake to cooperate with the Office of the United Nations High Commissioner for Refugees... in the exercise of its functions, and shall in particular facilitate its duty of supervising the application of the provisions of this Convention'.[58] The 1969 OAU Convention requires member States to cooperate similarly, while declaring itself to be the 'effective regional complement in Africa' of the 1951 Convention.[59] UNHCR, however, is not itself a party to those instruments, and its standing must be located in more general principles and in relevant practice, including its formal participation in the drafting and implementation of comprehensive approaches to refugee problems, such as CIREFCA and the CPA.

Clearly, by derivation and intention, UNHCR does enjoy international personality. As a subsidiary organ of the General Assembly, its 'personality' (its capacity to

[54] For text of selected conclusions, see the Online Resource Centre: <http://www.oup.com/uk/refugeelaw> and for a full collection, see <http://www.unhcr.org> and UNHCR, *Refworld*, 15th edn., 2006; also Sztucki, J., 'The Conclusions on the International Protection of Refugees adopted by the Executive Committee of the UNHCR Programme', 1 *IJRL* 285 (1989).

[55] See *Report* of the 46th Session: UN doc. A/AC.96/860 (23 Oct. 1995), para. 32.

[56] Cf. Morris, N., 'Refugees: Facing Crisis in the 1990s—A Personal View from within UNHCR', 2 *IJRL, Special Issue—September 1990*, 38.

[57] Cf. Sarooshi, *International Organizations*, above n.42; Alvarez, J. E., *International Organizations as Law-makers*, (2005).

[58] Art. II of the 1967 Protocol is to similar effect. See Kälin, W., 'Supervising the 1951 Convention Relating to the Status of Refugees: Article 35 and beyond', in Feller, Türk, & Nicholson, *Refugee Protection in International Law*, 613; Summary Conclusions on supervisory responsibility, ibid., 667

[59] Art. VIII; Cartagena Declaration on Refugees, Conclusion and Recommendations, II; below, Annexe 2, No. 7.

possess international rights and duties) can be traced to the United Nations at large.[60] Moreover, its Statute shows that the Office was intended by the General Assembly to act on the international plane.[61] Its standing in regard to protection has been further reinforced by successive General Assembly resolutions urging all States to support the High Commissioner's activities, for example, by granting asylum, observing the principle of *non-refoulement* and acceding to the relevant international treaties. While it is trite knowledge that General Assembly resolutions are not legally binding, 'it is another thing', as Judge Lauterpacht noted in the *Voting Procedure* case, 'to give currency to the view that they have no force at all, whether legal or other, and that therefore they cannot be regarded as forming in any sense part of a legal system of supervision'.[62] On this occasion, the 'legal system of supervision' was the mandate in respect of South West Africa. In his separate opinion, Judge Lauterpacht noted that, while the mandatory had the right not to accept a recommendation of the supervising body, it was nevertheless bound to give it due consideration in good faith, which in turn entailed giving reasons for non-acceptance.

Admittedly, General Assembly resolutions with regard to refugees and to UNHCR do not have the same degree of particularity as a recommendation relating to the administration of a mandate. Nevertheless, against the background of the UN Charter and general international law, UNHCR, with its principal function of providing 'international protection' to refugees, can be seen to occupy the central role in an analogous legal system of supervision. Indeed, though discretions continue to favour States in certain of their dealings with refugees, the peremptory character of the principle of *non-refoulement* puts it in a higher class than the 'intangible and almost nominal' obligation to consider in good faith a recommendation of a supervisory body, such as Judge Lauterpacht discerned in the *Voting Procedure* case.[63] The entitlement of UNHCR to exercise protection on the basis of a universal jurisdiction receives additional support from the decision of the International Court of Justice in the *Reparations* case. There, the Court read into the rights and duties of the United Nations Organization, as a 'necessary intendment', the capacity to exercise a measure of functional protection on behalf of its agents.[64] UNHCR, by comparison, is *expressly* ascribed the function of providing international protection to refugees; State practice reflects 'recognition or

[60] See generally, *Reparations* case, ICJ *Rep.*, (1949), 174 at 178–9.

[61] For example, the Statute refers to the High Commissioner supervising the application of international conventions, promoting certain measures through special agreements with governments, and consulting governments on the need to appoint local representatives: paras. 8(a), (b), 16.

[62] See generally, *South West Africa, Voting Procedure*, Advisory Opinion, ICJ *Rep.*, (1955), 67, at 120–2—separate opinion of Judge Lauterpacht, noting that General Assembly resolutions are 'one of the principal instrumentalities of the formation of the collective will and judgment of the community of nations represented by the United Nations'.

[63] *Voting Procedure* case, ICJ *Rep.*, (1955), 67, at 119. See also Judge Lauterpacht's remarks generally in regard to good faith in the exercise of discretion: ibid., 120.

[64] *Reparations* case, ICJ *Rep.*, (1949), 174, at 184.

acquiescence in the assumption of such jurisdiction'[65] universally, and without regard to any requirement of treaty ratification. The 'effective discharge'[66] of this function evidently requires capacity to assert claims on behalf of individuals and groups falling within the competence of the Office.

Given States' obligations with regard to refugees, to whom are they owed? The individual is still not considered to be a subject of international law, capable of enforcing his or her rights on the international plane,[67] while the problems faced by refugees (such as interdiction on the high seas, or violations of human rights), are not such as would prompt exercise of the right of diplomatic protection on the part of the State of nationality. In the case of States parties to the 1951 Convention and the 1967 Protocol, the existence of obligations *inter se* is established, and this has certain theoretical advantages for the refugee with a willing protecting State behind him or her. Refugees recognized under the Convention/Protocol are entitled to exercise certain rights in every Contracting State, and each Party owes the duty of implementation to every other State party. Article 16, for example, provides that 'A refugee shall have free access to the courts of law on the territory of all Contracting States', and this benefit applies to *all* refugees and to *all* Contracting States, irrespective of the place of residence of the refugees. A failure to allow a recognized refugee to access the courts represents therefore a very simple example of breach of obligation.

The legal effects of participating in a multilateral treaty can be set out in a simple and straightforward manner. First, each State party undertakes an obligation towards every other State party to implement the treaty in good faith.[68] Secondly, the responsibility of each State party is engaged at the *bilateral* level, in that each State party has undertaken toward every other State party, not only a general obligation to implement the treaty in good faith, but also a series of specific obligations in the form of the particular articles of the treaty. In the present case, therefore, the State is not only obliged to ensure that recognized refugees generally have access to its courts, but it is also specifically obligated towards such other State party with regard to the refugees recognized by the latter, and who are within its territory or jurisdiction.

---

[65] Cf. Schwarzenberger & Brown, *A Manual of International Law*, (6th edn., 1976), 115, commenting on the movement of an implied consensual right or exercise of functional protection from its basis in consent to its acquisition of 'an increasingly absolute validity'.

[66] *Reparations* case, ICJ *Rep.*, (1949), 174, at 180.

[67] In Schwarzenberger & Brown, *Manual*, at 64, the traditional view was stated thus: 'Whether [the individual] is entitled to benefit from customary or consensual rules of international law depends on his own link—primarily through nationality—with a subject of international law which, on the international level, is alone competent to assert his rights against another subject of international law.' Later, the authors noted that, 'By means of conventions, attempts have been made to alleviate the position of refugees and stateless persons. Otherwise, they are objects of international law for whom no subject of international law is internationally responsible—a notable twentieth-century contribution to the category of *res nullius*': 114–15. This was questionable, even in 1976. See now Jennings, R.Y. & Watts, A., eds., *Oppenheim's International Law*, (9th edn., 1992), vol.1, paras. 150, 411, 511–15.

[68] See art. 26, 1969 Vienna Convention on the Law of Treaties: 'Every treaty in force is binding upon the parties to it and must be performed by them in good faith.'

Thus, the State whose recognized refugees are denied Convention rights in another State party is entitled to invoke that State's responsibility. The recognizing State has incurred injury, first, at the direct inter-State level, through the violation of the article in question;[69] it does not need to rely on obligations *erga omnes partes*, for here an action or omission attributable to the State under international law clearly constitutes a breach of an international obligation of that State.[70] Moreover, the breach of obligation in the present case would fall within the categories described in article 42 of the International Law Commission's Articles on State responsibility, for the obligation is both owed to the State individually, and, so far as it is also owed to all the States party to the Convention, the obligation breached 'specifically affects' that State by way of injury to one of 'its' recognized refugees.[71] The ILC has further observed that:

[A]lthough a multilateral treaty will characteristically establish a framework of rules applicable to all the States parties, in certain cases its performance in a given situation involves a relationship of a bilateral character between the two parties. Multilateral treaties of this kind have often been referred to as giving rise to 'bundles of bilateral relations'.[72]

Arguably, the obligations laid down in the 1951 Convention are also of this nature. A violation of its terms may affect all States parties, but not necessarily in the same way. The State whose subjective right has been violated is the injured State competent to claim; in the present context, it is the State which, through the denial of access to the courts to its 'own' refugees, is directly or individually affected, rather than the other States parties to the Convention/Protocol, which are not directly or not individually affected, but nonetheless potentially competent to claim if able to bring themselves within the terms of article 48.

Although theoretically of benefit to the refugee recognized in one State and denied Convention rights in another, the practical difficulty of persuading the

---

[69] Kälin has argued that the obligations to implement the provisions of the 1951 Convention/1967 Protocol are, 'obligations *erga omnes partes*, that is, obligations towards the other States parties as a whole. This is clearly evidenced by Article 38 of the 1951 Convention and Article IV of the 1967 Protocol, entitling each State Party to the Convention or the Protocol to refer a dispute with another State "relating to its interpretation or application" to the International Court of Justice even if it has not suffered material damage.' Kälin, W., 'Supervising the 1951 Convention Relating to the Status of Refugees', in Feller, Türk, & Nicholson, *Refugee Protection in International Law*, 613, 632; see also at 636.

[70] See art. 2, International Law Commission, Articles on the Responsibility States for Internationally Wrongful Acts; text annexed to UNGA res. 56/83, 'Responsibility of States for internationally wrongful acts', 12 Dec. 2001.

[71] Ibid., art. 42. See also Crawford, J., *The International Law Commission's Articles on State Responsibility*, (2002), Introduction, 38–42; ILC Commentary, ibid., 254–60.

[72] Crawford, above note, 'Commentary', para. 8, ibid., at 258; see also para. 11, ibid., at 259 on injury arising from violations of collective obligations. This situation is therefore distinct from that described in art. 48 of the ILC 'Articles', dealing with the category of obligations '*erga omnes partes*', that is, obligations owed, for example, to all the States party to a specific legal regime, such as a regional human rights convention. The phrase '*erga omnes*' commonly describes obligations with a broader reach, to the international community of States as a whole. Overlap is likely between the two, especially in the human rights field. See Sicilianos, L.-A., 'The Classification of Obligations and the Multilateral Dimension of the Relations of International Responsibility', 13 *EJIL* 1125, 1136 (2002).

former to 'exercise protection' remains to be overcome. At the national level also, the claims of recognized refugees (like those of citizens) may face both procedural and substantive obstacles in the face of judicial caution in confronting executive discretion, particularly on issues touching foreign affairs.[73] Both the Convention and the Protocol expressly provide for the settlement of disputes relating to their interpretation or application, and for reference to the International Court of Justice at the request of any of the parties to the dispute, should other means of settlement fail.[74] No litigation has resulted, however, despite the precedents that would appear to support States in the legal defence of matters other than those which affect directly their material interests.[75]

Under article 24 of the European Convention on Human Rights, by contrast, any contracting State may refer to the European Commission an alleged breach of the Convention by another party. The instrument itself thus provides for a 'European public order', a regime in which all States parties have a sufficient interest in the observance of the European Convention's provisions to allow for the assertion of claims. While there are similarities in the objectives of the European Convention and the refugee conventions—both call for certain standards of treatment to be accorded to certain groups of persons—the refugee conventions lack effective investigation, adjudication, and enforcement procedures; they can hardly be considered to offer the same opportunity for judicial or quasi-judicial solutions. Nonetheless, in view of the importance of the rights involved, all States have an interest in their protection;[76] and UNHCR, by express agreement of some States and by the acquiescence of others, is the qualified representative of the 'international public order' in such matters. A cogent theory of responsibility remains to be developed to cover this situation, however, and the legal consequences that may flow from a breach of the international obligations in question are still unclear.

International claims can take the form of protest, a call for an inquiry, negotiation, or a request for submission to arbitration or to the International Court of Justice. Both the nature of breaches of obligation affecting refugees and the nature of the protecting organization rule out certain types of claims, such as arbitration,[77]

---

[73] See *R. (on the application of Al Rawi) v. Secretary of State for Foreign and Commonwealth Affairs* [2006] EWCA Civ. 1279; *R. (on the application of Abassi) v. Secretary of State for Foreign and Commonwealth Affairs* [2002] EWCA Civ 1598.

[74] 1951 Convention, art. 38; 1967 Protocol, art. IV. Under the Protocol, but not under the Convention, States are entitled to make reservations to the article on settlement of disputes, and many have; see below, Ch. 10, s. 1.

[75] See *South West Africa* cases, preliminary objections, ICJ *Rep.*, (1962), 319, at 424–33 (separate opinion of Judge Jessup). But cf. *South West Africa* cases, second phase, ICJ *Rep.*, (1966), 6 at 32–3, 47 (holding that individual States do not have a legal right to require the performance of South Africa's mandate over South West Africa).

[76] *Barcelona Traction* case, ICJ *Rep.*, (1970), 3 at 32; also 1967 Declaration on Territorial Asylum, art. 2(1). An inter-State procedure also exists under other regional arrangements, such as the 1969 American Convention on Human Rights (arts. 45, 62), the 1981 African Charter on Human and Peoples' Rights (art. 47), and the 1966 International Covenant on Civil and Political Rights, art. 41; the last-mentioned has not so far been used.   [77] But see Ch. 9.

while strictly legal considerations might exclude, for example, recourse to the International Court of Justice.[78] The possibility of interim measures ordered by the Court under article 41 of the Statute should not be discounted, however.[79] In *United States Diplomatic and Consular Staff in Tehran (Request for the Indication of Provisional Measures)*,[80] the Court noted that the object of its power to indicate such measures is to preserve the respective rights of the parties pending the decision of the Court, and presupposes that irreparable prejudice should not be caused to rights which are the subject of dispute in judicial proceedings. The rights of the United States to which the Court referred included the rights of its nationals to life, liberty, protection, and security. It held that continuation of the situation exposed those individuals to privation, hardship, anguish, and even danger to health and life and thus to a serious possibility of irreparable harm. The Government of the Islamic Republic of Iran was ordered, among others, to ensure the immediate release of those held.[81] In its judgment on the merits, the Court noted that, 'Wrongfully to deprive human beings of their freedom and to subject them to physical constraint in conditions of hardship is in itself manifestly incompatible with the principles of the Charter of the United Nations, as well as with the fundamental principles enunciated in the Universal Declaration of Human Rights.'[82]

The potential for further development of a limited protection competence is also implicit in the Court's rulings on the requests by Bosnia and Herzegovina for interim measures to prevent genocide, and in its finding that a human rights instrument, the 1948 Genocide Convention, was a sufficient basis for the exercise of jurisdiction, so far as the subject-matter of the dispute related to the 'interpretation, application or fulfilment' of that treaty.[83] As Merrills points out, however, the function of interim measures is to protect the *rights* of both sides pending a decision on the merits, and many of those for which the applicant sought protection were outside the scope of the Convention.[84]

In most other cases, the simple existence of obligations owed at large may provide sufficient justification, not just for 'expressions of international concern',[85] but also for formal protest on the part of UNHCR. The significance of this

---

[78] For example, only the General Assembly or the Security Council may request advisory opinions; 'other organs' of the UN and specialized agencies may be authorized by the General Assembly to request such opinions, 'on legal questions arising within the scope of their activities': art. 96, UN Charter; art. 65, Charter of the ICJ. But see also *Legal Consequences of the Construction of a Wall in the Occupied Palestinian Territory*, Advisory Opinion, ICJ *Rep.*, (2004), No. 131.

[79] Art. 41 provides: 'The Court shall have the power to indicate, if it considers that circumstances so require, any provisional measures which ought to be taken to preserve the rights of either party.' See Merrills, J. G., 'Interim Measures of Protection in the Recent Jurisprudence of the International Court of Justice', 44 *ICLQ* 90 (1995). 			[80] ICJ *Rep.*, 1979, 7.

[81] Ibid., paras. 36, 37, 42, 91. 				[82] ICJ *Rep.*, 1980, 3 at 42 (para. 91).

[83] See *Genocide Convention* Case, ICJ *Rep.*, (1993), 16; *The Wall* case, above n. 78.

[84] Merrills, above n. 79, 103. Thus, the Court rejected claims relating to the territorial integrity of the applicant, as genocide concerns 'the intended destruction of "a national, ethnic, racial or religious group" and not the disappearance of a State as a subject of international law': ICJ *Rep.*, (1993), 345, para. 42; Merrills, ibid., 105. 				[85] See Goodwin-Gill, *Movement of Persons*, 23.

development for the individual's standing in general international law should not be underestimated.

1.2 THE UNITED NATIONS RELIEF AND WORKS AGENCY FOR PALESTINIAN REFUGEES IN THE NEAR EAST (UNRWA)

On 29 November 1947, the United Nations General Assembly voted in favour of a plan to partition Palestine into two separate States, one Arab and one Jewish;[86] fighting between the two communities commenced almost at once. The British mandate terminated on 14 May 1948, and the next day the Jewish community proclaimed the State of Israel. The first Arab-Israel war followed, with many thousands of Palestinian Arabs fleeing into neighbouring countries. When a formal armistice was finally declared just over a year later, the emergent Israeli State had control over most of the territory of the former Mandate Palestine with the exception of the areas known as the West Bank and the Gaza Strip, which were respectively under the control of Jordan and Egypt. An estimated 750,000 Palestinians fled and/or were forced to leave their homes or were expelled and were living in refugee camps in the Gaza Strip, the West Bank, Jordan, Lebanon, and Syria.[87]

On 11 December 1948, the General Assembly established a Conciliation Commission for Palestine (UNCCP), charged with taking steps to achieve a final settlement.[88] A year later, in December 1949, the United Nations Relief and Works Agency for Palestine Refugees in the Near East (UNRWA) was set up as a subsidiary organ of the General Assembly, to assist those who had left Palestine as a result of the conflict;[89] that assistance is mainly in the fields of relief, health and education. As already described above in Chapter 4 with regard to the interpretation of article 1D of the Convention, none of the General Assembly resolutions providing for relief to Palestine refugees, or establishing agencies for the provision of such relief, defines those who are to benefit. UNRWA has therefore developed and modified its working definitions over the years, which have been communicated to the General Assembly and never opposed. So far as registration with UNRWA determined the provision of relief, funding constraints have led to limitations on eligibility and to the exclusion from UNRWA rolls of numbers of Palestinians who became refugees as a result of the 1948 conflict. Rules issued in 1993 defined a 'Palestine refugee' for UNRWA purposes as 'any person whose normal place of residence was Palestine during the period 1 June 1946 to 15 May 1948 and who lost both home and means of livelihood as a result of the 1948 conflict'.

---

[86] UNGA res. 181(II) A, 29 Nov. 1947, adopted with thirty-three votes in favour, thirteen against (including Lebanon, Saudi Arabia, Syria, and Yemen) and ten abstentions.
[87] See generally, Morris, B., *The Birth of the Palestinian Refugee Problem, 1947–1949* (1987); Schraum, A., *The Iron Wall*, (2000); Minority Rights Group, *The Palestinians*, (1984).
[88] UNGA res. 194(III), 11 Dec. 1948.
[89] The Agency succeeded the Special Fund for Relief of Palestine Refugees, set up by UNGA res. 212(III), 19 Nov. 1948.

Provision is also made for registration entitlement to descend, though through the male line only, and for a Palestinian not presently receiving relief to apply for it.[90]

This definition has been extended to the children of such refugees, and following the 1967 War, the General Assembly approved the provision of humanitarian assistance by UNRWA, 'on an emergency basis and as a temporary measure, to other persons in the area who are at present displaced and are in serious need of immediate assistance as a result of the recent hostilities'. Notwithstanding the 'temporary' and 'emergency' aspects of this measure, it has been endorsed in later General Assembly resolutions and extended further to those displaced by 'subsequent hostilities'.[91] UNRWA assistance has always been limited as to locality, being restricted to Lebanon, Syria, Jordan, the Gaza Strip and, after the 1967 displacements, Egypt; and limited also as to refugees registered and actually residing in those host countries. Registration, which initially facilitated ration distribution, acquired greater significance in the countries of refuge, where it was increasingly equated with acceptance as a refugee and *prima facie* entitlement to remain.[92]

As has been noted above, Palestinian refugees were excluded from the competence of UNHCR, and later also from the 1951 Convention relating to the Status of Refugees. Political reasons were partly responsible, as was the necessity to delimit formally the mandates of UNHCR, the United Nations Relief and Works Agency (UNRWA), and the United Nations Conciliation Commission for Palestine (UNCCP).[93] At the time, both protection and assistance for Palestinian refugees fell within institutional arrangements that included UNCCP and UNRWA. Solutions, repatriation or compensation, were also expected to eventuate; the General Assembly, for example, intended UNCCP to take on, 'in so far as it considers necessary in existing circumstances, the functions given to the United Nations Mediator on Palestine by resolution 186(S-2) ... '[94] Those functions had in turn been defined to include the use of:

... good offices with the local and community authorities in Palestine to (i) Arrange for the operation of common services necessary to the safety and well-being of the population of Palestine; ... (iii) Promote a peaceful adjustment of the future situation of Palestine.[95]

[90] UNRWA, 'Consolidated Registration Instructions', 1 Jan. 1993, para. 2.13;
[91] UNGA resolution 2252 (ES-V), 4 Jul. 1967 (confirmed by UNGA res. 2341 B(XXII), 19 Dec. 1967); and UNGA res. 56/54, 10 Dec. 2001.
[92] In Lebanon, UNRWA-registered Palestinian refugees are entitled to residence permits; those not registered have no right to reside in the country, and neither do the children of unregistered Palestinian parents: McDowall, D., *Lebanon: A Conflict of Minorities*, (1986), 8; Buehrig, E., *The UN and the Palestinian Refugees—A Study in Non-Territorial Administration*, (1971), 43. See also Cervenak, C. M., 'Promoting Inequality: Gender-Based Discrimination in UNRWA's Approach to Palestine Refugee Status', 16 *HRQ* 300 (1994).
[93] Statute, para. 7(1); Convention, art. 1D; see above, Ch. 4, s. 3.2. See, however, recent statements by UNHCR regarding its responsibilities towards Palestinians outside UNRWA's area of operations: *Report* of the 29th Meeting of the Standing Committee, UN doc. A/AC.96/988, 7 Jul. 2004, para. 30; *Report* of the 20th Meeting of the Standing Committee, UN doc. A/AC.96/945, 2 Jul. 2001, para. 22.   [94] UNGA res. 194(III), 11 Dec. 1948.
[95] Ibid., para. 11: 'the refugees wishing to return to their homes and live at peace with their neighbours should be permitted to do so at the earliest practicable date, and ... compensation should be

The UN Conciliation Commission was instructed to 'facilitate the repatriation, resettlement and economic and social rehabilitation of the refugees and the payment of compensation', and by resolution 394(V) of 14 December 1950, to 'continue consultations with the parties concerned regarding measures for the protection of the rights, property and interests of the refugees'. But already the effectiveness of UNCCP, contingent upon the cooperation and political will of the States concerned, was in doubt; the summary of debate in the General Assembly is brief but eloquent testimony to the fundamental differences between the parties, upon whom depended a solution to the refugee problem. To one side, the objective of a peaceful settlement required direct negotiations; to the other, direct negotiations were contingent on full recognition of the rights of the Arabs to Palestine and to their own homes.[96] With the passing of the years, the General Assembly's repeated requests to the Conciliation Commission to continue its efforts became increasingly formal, almost ritualistic. The prospects for repatriation, resettlement, rehabilitation, and compensation waned, UNCCP became irrelevant to the protection needs of Palestinian refugees, and UN institutional mechanisms were unable to bridge the gap.

UNRWA's role continued as the provider of international assistance to Palestinian refugees, save that with the beginnings of the *intifada* movement in 1989, it came in practice also to exercise a significant, if limited, protection role on behalf of Palestinians against the occupying forces.[97] The perception of the Palestinian refugee problem as 'temporary', however, accounts in part for the fact that the nationality status of many individual Palestinians remains unresolved.[98]

1.3 THE UNITED NATIONS OFFICE FOR THE COORDINATION OF HUMANITARIAN AFFAIRS (OCHA)

1.3.1 *Strengthening coordination*

Following the 1986 Report of the Group of Government Experts, some initial steps were taken to improve the UN's capacity to respond to forcible displacement, in particular, by the establishment of the Office for Research and Collection of Information (ORCI) in an attempt to provide the UN system with some form

---

paid for the property of those choosing not to return and for loss of or damage to property which, under principles of international law or in equity, should be made good by the Governments or authorities responsible'. Lawand, K., 'The Right to Return of Palestinians in International Law', 8 *IJRL* 532 (1996).

[96] Cf. UNGAOR, 5th Sess., Plenary, Summary Records, 325th Meeting, 14 Dec. 1950, paras. 170–211. In his 1948 report to the General Assembly, the Mediator for Palestine, Count Bernadotte, referred to the misgivings of the Provisional Government in Israel regarding the return of Palestinian refugees; these derived from security, as well as from economic and political conditions. At that time, the Mediator doubted whether the security fears were in fact well-founded.

[97] See Takkenberg, L., 'The Protection of Palestine Refugees in the Territories Occupied by Israel', 3 *IJRL* 414 (1991).

[98] To the policies of States of refuge must be added the aspirations of the Palestinian people to self-determination and statehood. See further below, s. 3.

of early warning of impending mass movements.[99] Dissatisfaction with the effect-iveness of these first measures led to the proposal for the designation by the United Nations Secretary-General of 'a high level official . . . as emergency relief co-ordinator'.

On 19 December 1991, the General Assembly adopted resolution 46/182 on strengthening the coordination of United Nations humanitarian emergency assistance.[100] Annexed to that resolution was a set of guidelines, principles and proposals, which included the standards of humanity, neutrality, and impartiality as the essential basis for the provision of humanitarian assistance;[101] but also respect for 'the sovereignty, territorial integrity and national unity of States', and recognition of the responsibility of each State, 'first and foremost to take care of the victims of natural disasters and other emergencies occurring on its territory'.[102] States with populations in need of humanitarian assistance are called upon to facilitate the work of appropriate intergovernmental and non-governmental organ-izations, while neighbouring States are urged to participate closely with affected countries. The nexus between disaster prevention and preparedness, and eco-nomic growth and sustainable development, is also acknowledged.[103]

The senior position of Emergency Relief Coordinator (ERC), created by reso-lution 46/182, brought together the functions previously carried out by various representatives of the Secretary-General for major and complex emergencies, and the responsibilities for natural disasters which had been entrusted to the UN Disaster Relief Coordinator (UNDRO).[104] In 1998 the Department of Humani-tarian Affairs was reorganized into the Office for the Coordination of Humani-tarian Affairs (OCHA), with an expanded mandate over the coordination of the

[99] See Ramcharan, B. G., 'Early Warning at the United Nations: The First Experiment', 1 *IJRL* 379 (1989); Beyer, G. A., 'Human Rights Monitoring and the Failure of Early Warning: A Practitioner's View', 2 *IJRL* 56 (1990)—the relevant recommendations of the Group of Governmental Experts and an extract from the United Nations *Organization Manual* describing the functions and organization of ORCI appear at 75–81; Beyer, G. A., 'Monitoring Root Causes of Refugee Flows and Early Warning: The Need for Substance', 2 *IJRL Special Issue—September 1990* 71; Rusu, S., 'The Role of the Collector in Early Warning', 2 *IJRL Special Issue—September 1990* 65; Ruiz, H. A., 'Early Warning Is Not Enough: The Failure to Prevent Starvation in Ethiopia, 1990', 2 *IJRL Special Issue—September 1990* 83; Dimitrichev, T. F., 'Conceptual Approaches to Early Warning: Mechanisms and Methods—A View from the United Nations', 3 *IJRL* 264 (1991); Drüke, L., *Preventive Action for Refugee Producing Situations*, (1990).

[100] See UN doc. A/46/L.55, 17 Dec. 1991 (Sweden); *Report* of the Secretary-General on the review of the capacity, experience and coordination arrangements in the United Nations system for humani-tarian assistance: UN doc. A/46/568.

[101] These principles in the provision of humanitarian assistance derive directly from ICRC doc-trine. See also *Report* of the Third Committee, Draft resolution I, Promotion of international cooper-ation in the humanitarian field: UN doc. A/45/751 (21 Nov. 1990).

[102] UNGA res. 46/182, 19 Dec. 1991, Annex, paras. 2–4.

[103] Ibid., para. 10; see also paras. 13–17 (Prevention); 18–20 (Preparedness, including early warn-ing); 35(h) (Coordinator to promote transition from relief to rehabilitation and reconstruction); 40–2 (Continuum from relief to rehabilitation and development).

[104] UNGA res. 46/182 also created the Inter-Agency Standing Committee (IASC), the Consolidated Appeals Process (CAP) and the Central Emergency Revolving Fund (CERF), in order further to improve coordination.

UN's humanitarian response programmes. Coordination is promoted through the Inter-Agency Standing Committee, chaired by the ERC, and the participants include UN agencies, the Red Cross Movement and NGOs.[105]

The role of OCHA and the Emergency Relief Coordinator is, in principle, wide enough to allow the promotion of significantly higher levels of inter-State and inter-organization cooperation than have been seen so far.[106] The Coordinator is responsible not only for processing requests from States for emergency assistance, but also overseeing all emergencies through 'the systematic pooling and analysis of early-warning information'.[107] While expected to organize needs assessment missions 'in consultation with the Government of the affected country', the Coordinator is also authorized to facilitate the provision of emergency assistance 'by obtaining the consent of all the parties',[108] for example, in a situation of internal conflict, or where no effective governmental authority exists. In addition, the Coordinator acts as a central focal point on UN emergency relief operations,[109] and is expected to work closely not only with agencies in the UN system, but also with the ICRC, the International Federation of Red Cross and Red Crescent Societies, IOM, and 'relevant non-governmental organizations'.

During the 1990s, however, inter-agency coordination was also pursued through other mechanisms, in particular, the lead agency model, though with mixed results.[110] A new approach, 'clusters', was introduced in 2005, following the Secretary-General's report on strengthening the co-ordination of the UN's emergency humanitarian assistance.[111] This identified 'significant capacity gaps' in, among others, shelter and camp management and protection. It recognized that the protection of civilians is primarily the responsibility of States, but also that 'the humanitarian system must work to fill protection gaps . . .',[112] and that 'Partnerships within the system may be necessary to overcome those gaps in assistance—such as protection and camp management in situations involving internally displaced persons—that do not enjoy leadership from any one agency.'[113]

---

[105] See *Report* of the Secretary-General, 'Strengthening of the coordination of emergency humanitarian assistance of the United Nations', UN doc. A/60/87, 23 Jun. 2005; UNGA res. 60/124, 15 Dec. 2005. On the work of OCHA, see <http://ochaonline.un.org>.

[106] UNGA res. 46/182, 19 Dec. 1991, Annex, paras. 33–9 (leadership of the Secretary-General, role and responsibilities of the Coordinator, establishment of Inter-Agency Standing Committee, and country-level co-ordination).

[107] Ibid., para. 20: 'Early-warning information should be made available in an unrestricted and timely manner to all interested Governments and concerned authorities, in particular of affected or disaster-prone countries. The capacity of disaster-prone countries to receive, use and disseminate this information should be strengthened . . .' Also, para. 35(g), identifying among the Coordinator's responsibilities, 'providing consolidated information, including early warning on emergencies, to all interested Governments and concerned authorities . . .'.   [108] Ibid., para. 35(d).

[109] UN res. 46/182, Annex, para. 36. See *Report* of the Secretary-General, above n. 105.

[110] See Pugh, M. & Cunliffe, S. A., 'The Lead Agency Concept in Humanitarian Assistance: The Case of the UNHCR', *Security Dialogue*, vol. 28(1): 17–30 (1997).

[111] *Report* of the Secretary-General, above n. 105.

[112] Ibid., para. 28.   [113] Ibid., para. 37; see also paras. 53–8.

It went on to recommend that humanitarian response capacity be strengthened by broadening the capacity base, making more efficient use of available resources, strengthening financial mechanisms, and preserving the 'humanitarian space' in integrated missions.[114]

A 'humanitarian response review' commissioned by the UN Emergency Relief Coordinator was published two months later, in August 2005.[115] It looked at complex (man-made) emergencies and natural disasters, at preparedness and response capacities, and at protection in relation to the latter. It found 'a conspicuous lack of recognition of a generally accepted definition of the meaning and requirements of protection'.[116] The *Review* took a broad view of protection, which it saw as covering, 'a wide range of activities, including physical presence, bilateral negotiations, multilateral diplomacy, training, education, data collection, dissemination, and advocacy and gaining access to victims...'. The concept of protection generally was only vaguely understood, however, and capacity to respond here was severely lacking, notwithstanding the fact that protection was 'a cross-cutting issue in all response sectors', requiring special and urgent attention.[117]

Although a number of coordination elements were in place, the *Review* noted the feeling that the time for a more inclusive mechanism had arrived. The 'lead agency' approach applied by UNHCR in the 1990s had not gained much support,[118] but might do so now if there were 'appropriate and transparent terms of reference, including strong obligations for consultation and accountability (including financial accountability) towards partner organizations'.[119]

1.3.2 The complementary role of UN agencies

In dealing with the crises of forcible displacement, many United Nations agencies become involved. For example, the original mandate of UNICEF, the United

---

[114] Ibid., paras. 78–82.

[115] See OCHA, *Humanitarian Response Review*, an independent report commissioned by the United Nations Emergency Relief Coordinator and Under-Secretary-General for Humanitarian Affairs, Office for the Coordination of Humanitarian Affairs, New York, Geneva, Aug. 2005. The report was prepared by Costanza Adinolfi, David S. Bassiouni, Halvor Fossum Lauritzsen, and Howard Roy Williams. [116] Ibid., s. 4.2, at 30–1.

[117] Ibid., 31.

[118] On which see, among others, Pugh M. & Cunliffe, S. A., 'The Lead Agency Concept in Humanitarian Assistance: The Case of the UNHCR', *Security Dialogue*, 1997, vol. 28(1), 17–30; Lautze, S., Jones, B. & Duffield, M., 'Strategic Humanitarian Co-ordination in the Great Lakes Region, 1996–1997: An Independent Assessment', Policy, Information and Advocacy Division, Office for the Co-ordination of Humanitarian Affairs, United Nations, New York, March 1998; Mooney, E. D., 'Presence, *ergo* Protection? UNPROFOR, UNHCR and the ICRC in Croatia and Bosnia and Herzegovina', 7 *IJRL* 407 (1995); Mendiluce, J. M., 'War and disaster in the former Yugoslavia: The limits of humanitarian action,' in *World Refugee Survey—1994*, 16.

[119] Above n. 115, Ch. III, s. 2.2, p. 47. For constructive criticism of early experience with the cluster approach (but also an appreciation of its potential for coordination and information sharing), see Action Aid, 'The Evolving UN Cluster Approach in the Aftermath of the Pakistan Earthquake: an NGO perspective', 24 Apr. 2006. See also, Goodwin-Gill, G. S., 'International Protection and Assistance for Refugees and the Displaced: Institutional Challenges and United Nations Reform', Refugee Studies Centre, Oxford, May 2006: <http://refugeelaw.qeh.ox.ac.uk>.

Nations Children's Fund established in 1946, was to provide assistance to children in countries which were the victims of aggression; now it provides both emergency and long-term assistance to mothers and children in need throughout the world. UNICEF's work with children frequently extends into refugee situations, providing assistance to unaccompanied children, for example, or establishing safe water supplies and therapeutic feeding.[120]

The FAO (Food and Agriculture Organization) also has long been involved in disaster assistance, and the UN's capacity to respond was strengthened in the 1960s with the creation of World Food Programme (WFP),[121] responsible for disposing of surplus food and channelling aid to meet food needs and emergencies inherent in chronic malnutrition.[122] WFP has its own staff in many countries, and the UNDP (United Nations Development Programme) Resident Representative also acts on its behalf.

Article 2(d) of the Constitution of WHO (World Health Organization) empowers it to furnish appropriate technical assistance and, in emergencies, necessary aid upon the request or acceptance of Governments. WHO is strongly represented throughout the world, with Programme Coordinators or National Programme Coordinators working in almost every country. Obviously, mass displacements across borders can contribute to the incidence and spread of disease, particularly where large numbers are crowded into makeshift camps with poor sanitation. In emergencies, WHO can provide advice and the services of specialists, as well as urgently needed medicaments from its Geneva and regional stocks.[123]

1.4 OTHER INTERNATIONAL AND INTERGOVERNMENTAL ORGANIZATIONS AND AGENCIES

1.4.1 *International Organization for Migration (IOM)*

Founded outside the United Nations as the Intergovernmental Committee for European Migration in 1951, the International Organization for Migration now brings together some one hundred and eighteen States. It is premised on the idea of freedom of movement, and the preamble of the revised Constitution, adopted in 1989, recognizes that migration assistance at an international level is often required 'to ensure the orderly flow of migration movements throughout the world and to facilitate ... settlement and ... integration'.[124]

---

[120] See <http://www.unicef.org>.

[121] UNGA res. 1714 (XVI), 19 Dec. 1961; see further, <http://www.fao.org> and <http://www.wfp.org>.

[122] The WFP definition of emergency includes 'urgent situations in which there is clear evidence that an event has occurred which causes human suffering or loss of livestock and which the Government concerned has not the means to remedy; and it is a demonstrably abnormal event which produced dislocation in the life of the community on an exceptional scale'.

[123] See also, <http://www.who.int>.

[124] Perruchoud, R., 'From the Intergovernmental Committee for European Migration to the International Organization for Migration', 1 *IJRL* 501 (1989). For the revised Constitution, see

In the organization's first years of operation, it focused on displaced persons and refugees in, and orderly migration from, Europe. Since them, IOM's objectives and functions have become world-wide and include orderly and planned migration for employment purposes; the movement of qualified human resources, including family members; the organized transfer of refugees, displaced persons, and other persons compelled to leave their country of origin; technical assistance and advisory services on migration policies, legislation, administration, and programmes; and the provision of a forum in which States and organizations concerned can exchange views and experiences, and promote cooperation and coordination on migration issues.[125] IOM is also involved in migration information, both in its own right and in cooperation with UNHCR.

IOM's working concept of displaced persons includes refugees within the sense of the OAU Convention or the Cartagena Declaration, as well as those in flight from man-made disasters. It also assists asylum seekers in various countries, who have either been accepted under the immigration programmes of third States, or have elected to return home voluntarily. In 1972, it helped many stateless persons and former citizens of Uganda, then facing expulsion. In September 1990, in a United Nations inter-agency context, IOM assumed responsibility for the repatriation of third country nationals displaced or expelled in the aftermath of the Iraqi invasion of Kuwait. In September 1991, working with UNHCR and within the context of the Comprehensive Plan of Action for Indo-Chinese refugees, IOM signed a memorandum of understanding with the Socialist Republic of Vietnam, with respect to the return of Vietnamese citizens from countries of refuge in South East Asia. In Europe, IOM operates programmes of limited assistance to asylum seekers whose claims have been definitively rejected, or who have withdrawn their applications. The focus is on pre-departure assistance, re-installation and, occasionally, also on counselling and re-insertion in the labour market.[126]

Lately, its range of activities have included evacuation from Lebanon, repatriation to Timor-Leste, involvement in emergency relief and rehabilitation for victims of disasters, assistance to internally displaced persons in Darfur and, more controversially, administration of off-shore processing centres in Nauru and Papua New Guinea on behalf of Australia and as part of the latter's 'Pacific strategy'.

below Annexe 1, No. 9. The Constitution recognizes a number of key organizational and developmental principles: the relationship between migration and economic, social and cultural conditions in developing countries; and close cooperation and coordination on migration and refugee matters, among States, international organizations, governmental and non-governmental. See further, <http://www.iom.int>.

[125] See Perruchoud, R., 'Persons falling under the Mandate of the International Organization for Migration, to Whom the Organization may Provide Migration Services', 4 *IJRL* 205, 211f (1992). The breadth of IOM's mandate means that it can often provide appropriate services to individuals whose status is unclear, or who are not the responsibility of any other organization, such as rejected asylum seekers or internally displaced persons.

[126] These activities are complementary to many other IOM programmes, for example, with respect to migration generally or in the field of return of talent.

1.4.2 *International Committee of the Red Cross (ICRC)*

In many respects, the International Committee of the Red Cross (ICRC) has comparable protection responsibilities to UNHCR, but under the system consolidated by the 1949 Geneva Conventions and the 1977 Additional Protocols. Article 8, common to the first three Geneva Conventions, and article 9 of the Fourth Convention, each provide for their respective provisions to 'be applied with the cooperation and under the scrutiny of the Protecting Powers whose duty it is to safeguard the interests of the Parties to the conflict'. Each Convention likewise recognises the 'humanitarian activities which the International Committee of the Red Cross or any other impartial humanitarian organization may . . . undertake for the protection of . . .' persons within their scope, and for their relief.[127] In addition, the Conventions provide for the appointment of substitutes for the Protecting Powers, such as 'an organization which offers all guarantees of impartiality and efficacy'.[128]

Humanitarian objectives and the role of the ICRC are stressed throughout each of the four Geneva Conventions, in common article 3, and in their respective provisions on protected persons and the meaning of protection.[129] In addition to its activities under the Conventions, the ICRC is recognized as retaining its right of initiative,[130] the freedom to engage in 'toute initiative humanitaire, . . . toute action que les conventions n'auraient pas prévues mais qui serait nécessaire pour la protection des victimes'.[131]

1.4.3 *Regional organizations*

The protection of refugees may also be promoted, directly and indirectly, by regional organizations, including, for example, the African Union (formerly the Organization of African Unity),[132] the Organization of American States, and the Council of Europe. These have generated, among others, instruments such as the 1969 AU/OAU Convention on the Specific Aspects of Refugee Problems in Africa,[133] the 1969 American Convention on Human Rights, the 1950 European

[127] See art. 9 of the First (wounded and sick, medical personnel, and chaplains), Second (including shipwrecked persons), and Third (prisoners of war) Conventions; and art. 10 of the Fourth Convention (civilian persons).

[128] Art. 10 of the First, Second and Third Conventions; art. 11 of the Fourth Convention. The Conventions further provide for Protecting Powers to 'lend their good offices' with a view to settling disputes: art. 11 of the First, Second and Third Conventions; art. 12 of the Fourth Convention. Compare generally art. 5, 1977 Protocol I, and see Veuthey, M., *Guérilla et droit humanitaire*, (1983), 329–32.

[129] See, in particular, common art. 3, 1949 Geneva Conventions; art. 81, 1977 Additional Protocol I; Veuthey, above note, 332–4. With respect to the ICRC's functions on behalf of interned enemy civilians or other protected persons; see arts. 41, 78, 132–4, Fourth Geneva Convention (1949); art. 75, Additional Protocol 1; arts. 4–6, Additional Protocol 2.

[130] Art. 9 of the first three Conventions; art. 10 of the Fourth Convention.

[131] Veuthey, above 128, 332–3.

[132] See Bakwesegha, C. J., 'The Role of the Organization of African Unity in Conflict Prevention, Management and Resolution', 7 *IJRL Special Issue—Summer 1995* 207; Oloka-Onyango, J., 'The Place and Role of the OAU Bureau for Refugees in the African Refugee Crisis', 6 *IJRL* 34 (1994).

[133] For text, see below, Annexe 2, No. 1.

Convention on Human Rights, the 1959 European Agreement on the Abolition of Visas for Refugees, the 1967 European Agreement on Consular Functions, together with the Protocol concerning the Protection of Refugees, and the 1980 European Agreement on Transfer of Responsibility for Refugees. As noted throughout this work, since the adoption of the Treaty of Amsterdam in 1997, the European Union has also pursued the goal of harmonizing asylum practice among the Member States.

The necessity for inter-agency and inter-State cooperation in migration and refugee continues to be a priority in different forums, such as the Organization (formerly the Conference) on Security and Co-operation in Europe.[134] Although the OSCE process may fall short of the high normative character of an international treaty, cooperation has been a central element in each meeting, the focus of which is increasingly detailed.[135] At the CSCE Vienna Meeting in 1986–87, participating States covered a range of relevant issues, among them the freedom to leave any country, including one's own, and to return there, and the entitlement of refugees to repatriate.[136]

The final document of the CSCE Copenhagen Conference on the Human Dimension in June 1990 also endorsed basic human rights, including freedom of movement and a comprehensive right to effective remedies.[137] Even as they stressed the desirability of freer movement, participating States also declared that 'they will consult and, where appropriate, co-operate in dealing with problems that might emerge as a result of the increased movement of persons'.[138] In November 1990, CSCE States adopted the Charter of Paris for a New Europe, with guidelines for strengthening democratic institutions, fostering 'the rich contribution of national minorities', combatting all forms of ethnic hatred and discrimination, 'as well as persecution on religious and ideological grounds'.[139] Notwithstanding the formal, non-obligatory nature of much of the OSCE process,

[134] The 1992 appointment of a CSCE High Commissioner for National Minorities is perhaps the most evident illustration of regional concern and intention to act.

[135] Principle IX of the Declaration on Principles guiding Relations between Participating States, Helsinki Final Act, 1 Aug. 1975, declared: 'The participating States will develop their co-operation with one another and with all States in all fields in accordance with the purposes and principles of the United Nations...' CSCE and OSCE texts can be found in Brownlie & Goodwin-Gill, *Basic Documents on Human Rights*, 817ff.

[136] Conference on Security and Co-operation in Europe (CSCE): Concluding Document from the Vienna Meeting (4 Nov. 1986—17 Jan. 1987). The Concluding Document specifically identified (a) general principles, including human rights, freedom of movement and repatriation of refugees; (b) cooperation on, among other areas, migrant workers; (c) cooperation in humanitarian and other fields, including human contacts and the freedom to leave and to return; and (d) the human dimension—human rights, human contacts and other humanitarian issues.

[137] The participating States reaffirmed 'that the protection and promotion of the rights of migrant workers have their human dimension'. They are the concern of all, and as such should be addressed within the CSCE process: CSCE: Document of the Copenhagen Meeting of the Conference on the Human Dimension: 29 Jun. 1990. See arts. (9.5), (11), (22).

[138] Ibid., art. (20). Significantly, at the Moscow Meeting, it was accepted that a participating State may request a CSCE mission 'to address or contribute to the resolution of questions in its territory relating to the human dimension of the CSCE'.

[139] CSCE: Charter of Paris for a New Europe, 21 Nov. 1990.

the repeated endorsement of basic principles by participating States is important evidence of a consolidating norm of cooperation, sufficiently broad to include the relations of States between themselves and practical inter-agency cooperation.

1.4.4 Non-governmental organizations (NGOs)

Protection concerns reveal a commonality of interest; *effective* protection demands a purposeful degree of cooperation, by no means limited to States or international organizations. For example, in 1980, the Economic and Social Council recognized the 'essential role played by inter-governmental organizations, the International Committee of the Red Cross and other non-governmental organizations' in meeting humanitarian needs in emergency situations.[140] Many hundreds of national and international NGOs are involved in assisting and protecting refugees and asylum seekers around the world. Among the widely known are *Médecins sans Frontières*, which specializes in bringing medical care and health services to refugees in emergency camps and settlements; the *US Committee for Refugees*, which regularly carries out field visits and publishes situational and issues papers focusing on areas of concern; the *European Council on Refugees and Exiles*, a forum established in 1973 for co-operation which now brings together more than seventy western European NGOs concerned with refugees and the right of asylum; the various *Refugee Councils* in the Netherlands, the United Kingdom and other European countries, which provide legal or other counselling, or seek to influence national policy on refugees and asylum seekers; as well as *human rights organizations* whose reporting, monitoring and lobbying activities include refugees and the persecuted as a natural extension to their mandate.

For example, there is a clear complementarity between protection of refugees and *Amnesty International*'s statutory concern with 'prisoners of conscience', that is, men and women 'imprisoned, detained or otherwise physically restricted by reason of their political, religious or other conscientiously held beliefs or by reason of their ethnic origin, sex, colour or language, provided that they have not used or advocated violence'.[141]

2. The protection of refugees in international law

Day-to-day protection activities are necessarily dictated by the needs of refugees and asylum seekers, but a summary reading of both the UNHCR Statute and the

---

[140] ECOSOC res. 1980/43, 23 Jul. 1980. Amnesty International, the Anti-Slavery Society, the Minority Rights Group and the International Commission of Jurists are typical of those NGOs whose activities can be called 'protection'. The international role of NGOs in the human rights field has been confirmed and developed, among others, through the mechanism of consultative status with ECOSOC (under art. 71 of the UN Charter) and thereby also with bodies such as the former Commission on Human Rights (now replaced by the Human Rights Council).

[141] Art. 1(a), Statute of Amnesty International, as amended by the 12th International Council, Louvain, Belgium, 6–9 Sept. 1979: *1980 Report*, appx. 1, 383. See further, <http://www.amnesty.org>.

1951 Convention gives a general picture. There are, first, both direct and indirect aspects to the protection function, with the latter comprising UNHCR's promotion activities already mentioned. Direct protection activities, including intervention on behalf of individuals or groups, involve protection of the refugee's basic human rights, for example, non-discrimination, liberty, and security of the person.[142] UNHCR is also concerned specifically with the following: (1) the prevention of the return of refugees to a country or territory in which their life or liberty may be endangered;[143] (2) access to a procedure for the determination of refugee status; (3) the grant of asylum; (4) the prevention of expulsion; (5) release from detention; (6) the issue of identity and travel documents; (7) the facilitation of voluntary repatriation; (8) the facilitation of family reunion; (9) the assurance of access to educational institutions; (10) the assurance of the right to work and the benefit of other economic and social rights; (11) treatment generally in accordance with international standards, not excluding access to and by UNHCR, the provision of physical and medical assistance, and personal security; and (12) the facilitation of naturalization. Of these, the first four, together with the general function, are traditionally considered to be of prime importance, with the principle of *non-refoulement* standing as the essential starting-point in the search for permanent solutions. However, the measures to which refugees have been subject, and the conditions under which they must frequently live, have given added weight to claims for personal security, family reunion, assistance, and international efforts to achieve solutions.

As a matter of international law, the precise standard of treatment to be accorded to refugees will vary, depending on whether the State in which they find themselves has ratified the Convention and Protocol or any other relevant treaty. It may further depend on whether the refugee falls within the narrow or broad sense of the term, is lawfully or unlawfully in the territory of the State, or has been formally recognized as a refugee.

[142] In many ways, UNHCR acts much as does a national consul, although formal recognition of this role was a divisive issue at the 1963 United Nations Conference on Consular Relations and no article thereon was agreed; see UN doc. A/CONF.25/L.6, setting out UNHCR's position. The 1967 European Convention on Consular Functions has gone some way to protect refugees *against* the exercise of consular functions by consuls who are nationals of the refugees' country of origin: *ETS* No. 61, art. 47. Art. 2(2) of the Protocol to the same convention, moreover, expressly recognizes a protection role for the consuls of a refugee's State of habitual residence, 'in consultation, whenever possible, with the Office of the United Nations High Commissioner for Refugees'. For a view of the 'collective vision' of UNHCR lawyers and their role, see Kennedy, D., 'International Refugee Protection', 8 *HRQ* 1 (1986).

[143] This in turn may cover a wide range of activities. During the height of the conflict in El Salvador in the 1980s, UNHCR 'roving protection officers' patrolled the border on the Honduras side, leading asylum seekers to refugee camps, and often interceding directly with Honduran military to prevent forced return. In other situations, protection may mean maintaining a watching brief at airports and in transit areas, to try to prevent summary removals, or interceding with legal arguments to ensure that claims generally receive substantive determination. On the agency's retreat from positions of principle during the 1990s, see Goodwin-Gill, G. S., 'Refugee Identity and Protection's Fading Prospect', in Nicholson, F. & Twomey, P., *Refugee Rights and Realities*, (1999), 220.

2.1 GENERAL INTERNATIONAL LAW

With regard to basic human rights, the lawfulness or otherwise of presence is as irrelevant as the distinction between national and alien,[144] while certain provisions of the 1966 Covenants on human rights are indicative of standards going beyond a purely treaty-based regime. Article 2(2) ICCPR66, for example, obliges the State to respect and to ensure the rights declared to 'all individuals within its territory and subject to its jurisdiction'. The same article elaborates a principle of non-discrimination in broad terms, including national or social origin, birth or other status, within the list of prohibited grounds of distinction. Article 4(1), it is true, permits derogation in certain circumstances,[145] and contains a narrower statement of the principle of non-discrimination that would allow States to distinguish between nationals and aliens. Nevertheless, any measures in derogation must be consistent with States' other obligations under international law,[146] and no derogation is allowed from those provisions which guarantee the right to life, or which forbid torture or inhuman treatment, slavery, servitude, or conviction or punishment under retroactive laws. The right to recognition as a person before the law and the right to freedom of conscience, thought, and religion are also declared in absolute terms.[147]

The Covenant has been widely ratified,[148] while certain rights and standards also possess a positive foundation in general international law. In one oft quoted dictum, the International Court of Justice observed that 'the principles and rules concerning the basic human rights of the human person, including protection from slavery and racial discrimination',[149] figure within the class of obligations owed by States *erga omnes*, that is to the international community of States as a whole. Although this concept is not without its difficulties, the rights in question frequently appear in conventions among those from which no derogation is permitted, even in exceptional circumstances. Other rights of a similar fundamental character ought likewise to benefit everyone, and they would include the right to life; the right to be protected against torture or cruel or inhuman treatment or punishment; the right not to be subject to retroactive criminal penalties and the

[144] Applicable standards, with particular regard to immigration, are analysed in more detail in Goodwin-Gill, *Movement of Persons*, Chs. IV and V.

[145] Derogation is permitted in 'time of public emergency which threatens the life of the nation and the existence of which is officially proclaimed'.

[146] Thus, in view of the peremptory character of the rule of non-discrimination on the ground of race, measures taken against a particular class of foreign nationals determinable solely by reference to such characteristics would not be justified. See also, Committee on the Elimination of Racial Discrimination, 'General Recommendation 30: Discrimination against Non-Citizens', UN doc. CERD/C/64/Misc.11/rev.3; *R. (European Roma Rights Centre)* v. *Immigration Officer at Prague Airport* [2005] 2 AC 1.

[147] Art. 4(2). Cf. annexe III, Elles, *International Provisions protecting the Human Rights of Non-Citizens*: UN doc. E/CN.4/Sub.2/392/Rev.1, (1980), 57.

[148] At 31 Jan. 2007, 160 States were parties to ICCPR66.

[149] *Barcelona Traction* case, ICJ *Rep.*, 1970, 3, at 32.

right to recognition as a person before the law.[150] Such rights clearly allow for no distinction between national and alien, whether the latter be a migrant, visitor, refugee, or asylum seeker, and whether lawfully or unlawfully in the State.[151] The obligations of respect and protection are incumbent on States, irrespective of ratification of treaties, and refugees ought in principle to benefit, whether admitted on a temporary, indefinite, or a permanent basis. In practice, however, this objective may remain elusive, particularly where the State of refuge is unable or unwilling to take the necessary measures. Refugees have thus fallen victim to external, armed aggression; to attacks by pirates resulting in murder, rape, abduction, and robbery; to abandonment when in distress at sea; to threats to life and security by para-military 'death squads'; to forced conscription, even as children; to arbitrary detention and torture; and to rape and other sexual violence.[152] The exercise of protection on such occasions is a difficult and delicate task, whether attempted by UNHCR or by concerned States, and the problem is further exacerbated where the injury takes place in an area formally beyond the jurisdiction of any State. While international solidarity may manifest itself in calls for action, practical results can be far harder to obtain.

Once refugees have secured admission, however, the goal of attaining a lasting solution to their plight would seem to entail certain further standards of treatment geared to that objective. In 1981, a Group of Experts considered the implications of the concept of temporary refuge, and proposed a list of some sixteen 'basic human standards' which, in its view, should govern the treatment of those temporarily admitted; these were duly endorsed by the Executive Committee and the General Assembly later that year.[153] The objective, the initiative for which drew especially on generally negative practices in South East Asia, was rather the promotion of certain practically attainable standards, than the formulation of rules. The Executive Committee thus reiterated the need to observe fundamental rights,

---

[150] See Goodwin-Gill, *Movement of Persons*, 72–3, 85–7; and with respect to persecution, see above Ch. 3, s. 5.

[151] Cf. ILO Migrant Workers (Supplementary Provisions) Convention 1975 (no. 143). Art. 1 affirms that 'Each Member for which this Convention is in force undertakes to respect the basic human rights of all migrant workers'. The ILO Committee of Experts proposed for inclusion within this category of rights, the right to life, to protection against torture, cruel, inhuman or degrading treatment or punishment, liberty and security of the person, protection against arbitrary arrest and detention, and the right to a fair trial: *Migrant Workers*, report of the Committee of Experts, International Labour Conference, 66th Session, 1980, 68–9. Art. 9(1) of this same convention requires further that illegal migrant workers, whose position cannot be regularized, should receive 'equal treatment' for themselves and their families in respect of rights arising out of past employment in matters of pay, social security, etc. See also Goodwin-Gill, G. S., 'International Law and Human Rights: Trends concerning International Migrants and Refugees', 23 *Int. Mig. Rev.* 526 (1989); 'Migration: International Law and Human Rights', in Ghosh, B., ed., *Managing Migration*, (2000), 160.

[152] Summary reports on the risks and injuries faced by refugees are included in UNHCR's annual 'Notes' on International Protection, submitted each year to the Executive Committee, and in UNHCR's reports to the Economic and Social Council.

[153] Executive Committee Conclusion No. 22 (1981), *Report* of the 32nd Session, UN doc. A/AC.96/601, para. 57(2); also UNGA res. 36/125, 14 Dec. 1981.

including the principle of non-discrimination. It also recommended that asylum seekers be located by reference to their safety and well-being, as well as the security of the State of refuge;[154] that they be provided with the basic necessities of life; that the principle of family unity be respected and that assistance with tracing of relatives be given; that minors and unaccompanied children be adequately protected; that the sending and receiving of mail, and receipt of material assistance from friends be allowed; that, where possible, appropriate arrangements be made for the registration of births, deaths, and marriages; that asylum seekers be permitted to transfer to the country in which a lasting solution is found, any assets brought into the country of temporary refuge; and that all necessary facilities be granted to enable the attainment of a satisfactory durable solution, including voluntary repatriation.

These recommendations are not of a normative character, although a rules base can certainly be found for many of them among basic human rights principles.[155] They were formulated primarily with a view to reaching solutions which, in the case of refugees from Indo-China, meant first asylum followed by third country resettlement. Nevertheless, they are regularly invoked as a statement of the minimum standards applicable, particularly in the first phases of a refugee movement.[156]

2.2 TREATIES AND MUNICIPAL LAW

Basic human rights derive their force from customary international law, and indicate the content of the *general* obligations which control and structure the treatment by States of nationals and aliens. For States which have ratified treaties specifically benefitting refugees, the particular standards required ought to be easier to determine. This, however, raises the problem of the obligation, if any, requiring ratifying States to incorporate or otherwise implement the provisions of the treaties in question in their municipal law. The 1951 Convention contains no provision requiring legislative incorporation or any other formal implementing step; indeed, article 36, which obliges States to provide information on national legislation, refers only to such laws and regulations as States 'may' adopt to ensure application of the Convention. Similarly, nothing is said with regard to the establishment of procedures for the determination of refugee status, or otherwise for ascertaining and identifying those who are to benefit from the substantive provisions of the Convention.

Although it offers little assistance in the solution of specific problems, the *general* duty of a party to a treaty to ensure that its domestic law is in conformity with

---

[154] With respect to military attacks on refugee camps and settlements, see Ch. 9, s. 1.3.
[155] The Executive Committee was somewhat more peremptory, however, in its statement on cooperation with UNHCR: Executive Committee Conclusion No. 22 (1981), Ch. III.
[156] On 'temporary protection', see above, Ch. 6, s. 6.

its international obligations is beyond contradiction.[157] The governing principles, however, do not include an obligation as such to incorporate the provisions of treaties into domestic law.[158] The International Law Commission's final articles on State responsibility abandon the distinction previously drawn between obligations of conduct, obligations of result, and obligations to prevent a particular occurrence. Many commentators have observed that, while these distinctions may serve a useful analytical purpose and in determining when a breach has occurred (provided always that they are used correctly . . .), they do not have either specific or direct consequences for responsibility.[159] Dupuy and others pointed out that in the typology originally developed by the former Rapporteur on State responsibility, Roberto Ago, the conduct/result distinction was back to front; in civil law, an obligation of *conduct* is 'une obligation de s'efforcer', that is, to endeavour or to strive to realize a certain goal or to prevent a certain occurrence.[160] An obligation of *result*, by contrast, is precisely that—an obligation, to borrow Crawford's words, which involves,

in some measure a guarantee of the outcome, whereas obligations of conduct are in the nature of best efforts obligations to do all in one's power to achieve a result, but without ultimate commitment.[161]

In the one case, the fact that the result is not achieved is both necessary and sufficient to generate responsibility; in the other, 'what counts is the violation of the best effort obligation, not the end result generally achieved'.[162] In each case, it is the primary rule which determines the relevant standard of performance:

Some obligations of conduct or means may only be breached if the ultimate event occurs (i.e. damage to the protected interest); others may be breached by a failure to act even without eventual damage. International law neither has, nor needs to have, a presumption or rule either way. It depends on the context, and on all the factors relevant to the interpretation of treaties or the articulation of custom.[163]

---

[157] McNair, *The Law of Treaties*, (1961), 78–9; see also Brownlie, I., *Principles of Public International Law*, (6th edn., 2003), 34–5; Brownlie, I., *System of the Law of Nations: State Responsibility (Part I)*, (1983), 241–76; *Treatment of Polish Nationals in Danzig*, PCIJ ser. A/B no. 44 at 24; *Greco-Bulgarian Communities*, PCIJ, ser. B, no. 17, 32; *Free Zones*, PCIJ ser. A, no. 24, 12; ser. A/B, no. 46, 167; art. 27, 1969 Vienna Convention on the Law of Treaties; *Advisory Opinion, Applicability of the Obligation to Arbitrate under Section 21 of the United Nations Headquarters Agreement of 26 June 1947*, ICJ *Rep.*, (1988), 12.

[158] The International Court has stressed that failure to enact legislation necessary to ensure fulfilment of international obligations will not relieve a State of responsibility; see *Exchange of Greek and Turkish Populations*, PCIJ ser. B, no. 10, 20.

[159] Crawford, J., *The International Law Commission's Articles on State Responsibility*, (2002), art. 12, Commentary, para. 11, 129–30.

[160] P-M-. Dupuy, 'Reviewing the difficulties of codification: On Ago's classification of obligations of means and obligations of result in relation to State responsibility', 10 *EJIL* 371–86 (1999), 375; thus, the doctor's duty is to treat the patient to the standard required of doctors, but not specifically to cure.

[161] Crawford, J., 'Second Report on State Responsibility', UN doc. A/CN.4/498, 17 Mar. 1999, para. 57, cited by Dupuy, above note, 378. [162] Dupuy, above n. 160, 379.

[163] Crawford, *ILC Articles*, Introduction, 22.

At the level of analysis, the result/conduct distinction can nevertheless play a helpful role, not least in the human rights field, where *process* (and the adequacy, effectiveness and ultimately legality thereof) is also relevant. Conduct and result overlap; torture, ill treatment, arbitrary deprivation of life and *refoulement*, are all examples of forbidden conduct; but due process and accountability mechanisms are necessary, linked, though still separate bases for determining whether 'protection' is available or effective.

The particular nature of treaties generally and those for the protection of individuals and of human rights obligations illustrates the variety of what is required to avoid responsibility.[164] So, for example, article 22(1) of the 1961 Vienna Convention on Diplomatic Relations declares a clear obligation of result: 'The premises of the mission shall be inviolable. The agents of the receiving State may not enter them, except with the consent of the head of the mission.'[165] In this case, the internationally required result is that of omission by the organs of the receiving State; in other cases, positive action may be required. Thus, States parties to the 1966 International Convention on the Elimination of All Forms of Racial Discrimination agree, among others, 'to amend, rescind or nullify any laws or regulations which have the effect of creating or perpetuating racial discrimination wherever it exists'.[166] Similarly, the specific *enactment* of legislation may be required, as by article 20 of the 1966 International Covenant on Civil and Political Rights: 'Any propaganda for war shall be prohibited by law'.[167] In all such cases, the international obligation requires a specifically determined result, and ascertaining if the obligation has been fulfilled simply turns on whether the State's act or omission is or is not in fact in conformity with the internationally required result, the sufficient injury being the breach of legal duty.[168]

Other international obligations, by their nature or the manner in which they are framed, may concede the State's full freedom in its choice of means for implementation. Article 22(2) of the 1961 Vienna Convention on Diplomatic Relations declares the receiving State's 'special duty to take all appropriate steps to protect the premises of the mission', but defines those steps no further. Article 10 of the ILO Migrant Workers (Supplementary Provisions) Convention 1975 (No. 143) obliges 'Each Member for which the Convention is in force...to declare and pursue a national policy designed to promote and to guarantee, *by*

---

[164] See also the discussion in Crawford, 'Second Report on State Responsibility', above n. 161, paras. 69–76.

[165] 500 UNTS 95; Brownlie, I., *Basic Documents in International Law*, (5th edn., 2002), 162.

[166] Art. 2(1)(c): 660 *UNTS* 195.

[167] Text annexed to UNGA res. 2200(XXI), 16 Dec. 1966. Some States have made reservations to this article, on the basis of its inconsistency with the freedom of expression recognized in art. 19. See *Multilateral Treaties deposited with the Secretary-General: Status as at 31 December 2005:* UN doc. ST/LEG/SER.E/24/ (2006), recording reservations by Australia, Belgium, Denmark, Finland, Iceland, Ireland, Luxembourg, Malta, Netherlands, New Zealand, Norway, Sweden, Switzerland (withdrawn, 1995), United Kingdom, and the United States.

[168] *United States Diplomatic and Consular Staff in Tehran*, (*USA* v. *Iran*), ICJ *Rep.*, (1980), 3 at 30–1.

methods appropriate to national conditions and practice, equality of opportunity and treatment...'[169] Such 'obligations of conduct' are especially common in standard-setting treaties (for example, treaties of establishment guaranteeing most-favoured-nation treatment) and in human rights instruments. On occasion, full freedom of choice can be implied from the terms of the treaty itself, while in other cases a preference for the adoption of legislative measures will be indicated. Nevertheless, though legislation may be considered appropriate, even essential, it is evidently only one way by which the international obligation can be fulfilled. It is not so much the law which counts, as that compliance be assured. As the International Law Commission noted in 1977: '... so long as the State has not failed to achieve *in concreto* the result required by an international obligation, the fact that it has not taken a certain measure which would have seemed especially suitable for that purpose—in particular, that it has not enacted a law—cannot be held against it as a breach of that obligation'.[170]

In two human rights treaties concluded in the 1960s, States are called upon to enact such 'legislative or other measures as may be necessary'[171] to give effect to rights; and to 'prohibit and bring to an end' certain conduct, 'by all appropriate means, including legislation as required by circumstances'.[172] Words such as 'necessary' and 'appropriate' indicate that the State enjoys discretion in its choice of implementing measures, but the standard of compliance remains an international one. The question is that of effective or efficient implementation of the treaty provisions, *in fact*, and in the light of the principle of effectiveness of obligations.[173] Just as taking the theoretically most appropriate measures of implementation is not conclusive as to the fulfilment of an international obligation, so failing to take such measures is not conclusive as to breach.[174] The same holds good with regard

---

[169] See also art. 24, ILO Constitution, whereby every Member State 'binds itself effectively to observe within its jurisdiction any Convention to which it is a party'; 1949 Geneva Conventions, common art. 1: 'The High Contracting Parties undertake to respect and to ensure respect for the present Convention in all circumstances.'

[170] The ILC invoked particularly clear statements of the principle submitted by Poland and Switzerland to the Preparatory Committee of the 1930 Hague Conference for the Codification of International Law; cited in *Yearbook of the ILC* (1977), ii, 23.

[171] Art. 2(2) ICCPR66; See also, OAS Additional Protocol to the American Convention on Human Rights in the area of Economic, Social and Cultural (Protocol of San Salvador, 14 Nov. 1988), art. 2: 'If the exercise of the rights set forth in this Protocol is not already guaranteed by legislative or other provisions, the States Parties undertake to adopt, in accordance with their constitutional processes and the provisions of this Protocol, such legislative or other measures as may be necessary for making those rights a reality', 28 *ILM* 156 (1989).   [172] Art. 2(1)(d) ICERD66.

[173] See generally, Lauterpacht, H., *The Development of International Law by the International Court*, (1958) 257, 282; art. 31(1), 1969 Vienna Convention on the Law of Treaties; McNair, *The Law of Treaties*, (1961) 540–1.

[174] See *Tolls on the Panama Canal* (1911–12): Hackworth, *Digest*, vi, 59 (views of the United States); *German Interests in Polish Upper Silesia* (Merits), PCIJ (1926) Ser. A, no. 7, 19. The Permanent Court's reference in the *German Settlers in Poland* case to the necessity for '... equality in fact... as well as ostensible legal equality in the sense of absence of discrimination in the words of the law': PCIJ (1923) Ser. B, no. 6, 24, is founded on an equivalent principle. See further *Yearbook of the ILC* (1977), ii, 23–7.

to a State's adoption of a potentially obstructive measure, so long as such measure does not itself create a specific situation incompatible with the required result; what counts is what in fact results, not enactment and promulgation, but application and enforcement.[175]

The test of implementation of international obligations might suggest simply comparing what is required with what is achieved. In practice, however, major problems of interpretation and appreciation arise in view of, amongst others, the relative imprecision of the terminology employed in standard-setting conventions; the variety of legal systems and practices of States; the role of discretion, first, in the State's initial choice of means, and secondly, in its privilege on occasion to require resort to such remedial measures as it may provide. In a standard setting context, local remedies are especially important;[176] their availability and effectiveness will often determine the question of fulfilment or breach of obligation, the 'generation' of international responsibility and the implementation of this responsibility.

The difficulties attaching to the general issue of incorporation are illustrated by two occasions on which the UK performance in the light of its international obligations was called in question, and notwithstanding the passage of time, the central issues remain relevant. In 1979, the United Kingdom was examined by the Human Rights Committee with regard to its report on the implementation of the International Covenant on Civil and Political Rights. The UK representative disagreed with the view that States were obliged to adopt positive measures;[177] what mattered was the treatment that people received and the way in which the law worked in practice.[178] This position was maintained when incorporation

---

[175] *Ireland* v. *United Kingdom* (1978) 2 EHRR 25, paras. 236ff. Art. 1 ECHR50 provides: 'The High Contracting Parties shall secure to everyone within their jurisdiction the rights and freedoms defined . . .' Cf. *Abdulaziz, Cabales and Balkandali* v. *United Kingdom*, (1985) 7 EHRR 471, where the European Court found, among others, a violation of art. 13 (requiring an effective remedy for everyone whose rights and freedoms are violated), in a case in which discrimination on the ground of sex was the result of norms incompatible in this respect with the European Convention. Since the Convention was not then incorporated into UK law, there could be no 'effective remedy' (paras. 92, 93); see also the reservations expressed by Judge Bernhardt on this point in a concurring opinion.

[176] The local remedies rule is firmly based in general international law, and also figures in human rights instruments; see, for example, art. 26, ECHR50; arts. 11(3), 14(7)(a) ICERD66; art. 41(1)(c) ICCPR66 and art. 5(2)(b), Optional Protocol thereto.

[177] One expert noted that the United Kingdom had no written constitution and that the Covenant was not part of its internal legal order; if there were no laws, he wondered how the Committee could determine the degree of compliance with the Covenant: Mr Movchan, expert from the Soviet Union: UN doc. CCPR/C/SR.147, paras. 8, 9; a more lively account appears in United Nations press releases HR/1792–4, 25–6 Apr. 1979. At the time, the Soviet Union figured among those States which, despite the apparently express requirement of art. V of the Genocide Convention, had not found it necessary to enact specific legislation: Ruhashyankiko, *Study of the Question of the Prevention and Punishment of the Crime of Genocide*, (1978): UN doc. E/CN.4/Sub. 2/416, para. 501. Another expert believed that art. 2(2) required the adoption of specific measures and that it was not sufficient to state that existing laws were consonant with the Covenant: Mr Sadi, expert from Jordan: UN doc. CCPR/C/SR.147, para. 13.

[178] Mr Richard (United Kingdom): UN doc. CCPR/C/SR.147, para. 18 and SR.149, para. 18; also Mr Cairncross (United Kingdom): ibid., SR.147, para. 32.

and effective implementation of the 1951 Convention relating to the Status of Refugees were discussed in the House of Commons in May 1979,[179] continuing a debate begun the previous year in the House of Lords.[180] The Minister for State noted that nothing in the Convention required incorporation, and that it imposed no obligation and offered no guidance in the matter of procedures for the determination of refugee status.[181] While accepting that the Executive Committee's 1977 recommendations[182] might comprehend 'the basic requirements for the effective implementation of the Convention', he nevertheless felt that the UK's existing procedure was sufficient.

The arguments regarding legislative implementation and establishment of a procedure, while formally correct in the light of obligations actually assumed, fail to go to the heart of the matter, which is effectiveness of implementation. That incompatibilities with the Convention had developed was impliedly admitted in the announcement of certain changes in practice.[183] UK law, like that of many countries, was of general application, making no special provision for refugees. It therefore needed to be supplemented by a judicious use of administrative discretion, both to avoid the application of the general law and to secure appropriate benefits.[184] Since then, the United Kingdom has witnessed a plethora of immigration and asylum legislation, to the point that the courts have been driven to conclude that the 1951 Convention has been effectively incorporated into domestic law.[185]

The effective implementation of the 1951 Convention must therefore first take into account the fact that States parties have undertaken particularly important obligations governing (a) the legal definition of the term 'refugee'; (b) the application of the Convention to refugees without discrimination; (c) the issue of travel documents to refugees; (d) the treatment of refugees entering illegally; (e) the expulsion of refugees; and (f) the *non-refoulement* of refugees. These topics all fall,

---

[179] 967 HC Deb. cols. 1363–81 (25 May 1979).

[180] 392 HL Deb. cols. 799–819 (22 May 1978). The debate arose out of a UNHCR note to the British government proposing various reforms, in particular, that 'all those provisions of the 1951 Convention and the 1967 Protocol which are not provided for in the existing law', should be specifically incorporated; and that there should be established 'a formal procedure for the determination of refugee status by an independent body' in accordance with UNHCR Executive Committee recommendations: ibid., cols. 815–6 (Lord Wells-Pestell).

[181] 967 HC Deb. col. 1376 (Mr Raison). A similar argument was stated the previous year in the Executive Committee by the UK representative, Mr Gould, who noted that 'the States Parties to the 1951 Convention and the 1967 Protocol were under a duty to comply with those instruments and it was entirely for them to decide whether the provisions of those texts should for that purpose be incorporated in their national law': UN doc. A/AC.96/SR.302, para. 17, commenting on UN doc. A/AC.96/555, para. 6; also UN doc. A/AC.96/553, paras. 517–18.

[182] Executive Committee Conclusion No. 8 (1977).   [183] 967 HC Deb. cols. 1379–80.

[184] That the situation of refugees and asylum seekers in the United Kingdom continued to be unsatisfactory may be inferred from the enactment of the Asylum and Immigration Appeal Act 1993, and from a comparison of its provisions and the latest relevant immigration rules with those prevailing formerly.

[185] For recent judicial views, see the *Roma Rights* case [2005] 2 AC 1, paras. 7, 40–3, 50; see generally, Stevens, D., *UK Asylum Law and Policy: Historical and Contemporary Perspectives*, (2004).

somewhat loosely, within the field of immigration or aliens law; such law itself is most usually of general application, so that if special measures are not taken to single out the refugee, he or she is likely to be denied the rights and benefits due under the Convention and Protocol.[186] Secondly, the Convention defines a status to which it attaches consequences, but says nothing about procedures for identifying those who are to benefit. While the choice of means may be left to States, some such procedure would seem essential for the effective implementation and fulfilment of Convention obligations. It should be available to deal with claims to refugee status, whether made in the context of applications for asylum either at the border or after admission, for a travel document, for a social security benefit, or in an appeal against expulsion.[187]

Specific *legislative* action in the above matters may well be sufficient to remove the refugee from the ambit of the general law; it might therefore be considered a necessary condition for effective implementation. The establishment of a procedure for the determination of refugee status, given the object and purpose of the instruments in question, may likewise be considered a further necessary condition. Whether in any given case such measures, either together or alone, are sufficient conditions for effective implementation remains to be judged in the light of the actual workings of the municipal system as a whole.

2.2.1 The principle of good faith

Closely allied to every State's obligation to ensure that its domestic law conforms to its international obligations stands the principle of good faith already referred to in specific protection contexts.[188] In the words of the International Court of Justice in the *Nuclear Tests* case, good faith is 'One of the basic principles governing the creation and performance of legal obligations, *whatever their source . . .* '.[189] Article 2(2) of the United Nations Charter places the principle in the forefront of those which are to govern the conduct of Members.[190] While it has an ethical

---

[186] Similar considerations may apply to other human rights instruments that have an impact on State powers to expel or refuse admission to non-nationals, such as art. 3 CAT84; or art. 7 ICCPR66. States are beginning to appreciate the necessity to ensure that such issues are accommodated in appropriate decision-making procedures; see, for example, the Canadian *Immigration and Refugee Protection Act 2001*.

[187] The State again benefits from choice of means, but the standard of effective implementation itself will be affected by the practice of other States and, so far as they reflect consensus, the recommendations of bodies such as the UNHCR Executive Committee.   [188] See above, Ch. 7, s. 5.4.

[189] *Nuclear Tests (Australia v. France) Case*, ICJ *Rep.*, (1974), 253, 268, para. 46; see also *Case Concerning Border and Transborder Armed Actions*, ICJ *Rep.*, (1988), 105, para. 94; *Cameroon v. Nigeria*, Preliminary Objections, Judgment, ICJ *Rep.*, (1998), para. 38. For background, see O'Connor, J. F., *Good Faith in International Law*, (1991). O'Connor notes: 'The elaboration of the concept of *bona fides* in Roman law as involving a *legal* obligation to do what a decent, fair and conscientious man would do in particular circumstances contributed very largely to the association of good faith, in a wider ethical sense, with *pacta sunt servanda*. In relation to keeping promises and agreements, good faith acquired the meaning of not only the obligation to observe literally the undertakings given, but also the advertence to the real intentions of the parties or to the "spirit" of the agreement.' Ibid., 39.

[190] See Simma, B., *The United Nations Charter: A Commentary*, (2nd edn., 2004), 91–101. See also, 1970 Declaration on Principles of International Law Concerning Friendly Relations and

content,[191] its essentially legal character in international law has also been recognized. In the *Norwegian Loans* case, Judge Lauterpacht observed that, 'Unquestionably, the obligation to act in accordance with good faith, being a general principle of law, is also part of international law.'[192] Fitzmaurice, a former Special Rapporteur on the Law of Treaties and Judge of the International Court of Justice, defined the principle as follows:

The essence of the doctrine is that although a State may have a strict right to act in a particular way, it must not exercise this right in such a manner as to constitute an abuse of it; it must exercise its rights in good faith and with a sense of responsibility; it must have bona fide reasons for what it does, and not act arbitrarily and capriciously.[193]

Lack of good faith in the implementation of a treaty must be distinguished from a violation of the treaty itself. A State lacks good faith in the application of a treaty, not only when it openly refuses to implement its undertakings, but more precisely, when it seeks to avoid or to 'divert' the obligation which it has accepted, or to do indirectly what it is not permitted to do directly.[194] In the *Free Zones* case, France was under treaty obligations to maintain certain frontier zones with Switzerland free from customs barriers. The Permanent Court of International Justice, while recognizing that France had the sovereign and undoubted right to establish a police cordon at the political frontier for the control of traffic and even for the imposition of fiscal taxes other than customs duties, held that, 'A reservation must be made as regards the case of abuses of a right, since it is certain that France must not evade the obligation to maintain the zones by erecting a customs barrier under the guise of a control cordon.'[195] Similarly, in the *North Atlantic Coast Fisheries* case (Great Britain–United States), it was recognized that Great Britain had the right and duty, as the local sovereign, to legislate in regulation of fisheries. However, ' ... treaty obligations are to be executed in perfect good faith, therefore

Co-operation among States in accordance with the Charter of the United Nations, adopted by consensus in UNGA res. 2625 (XXV), 24 Oct. 1970, para. 3.

[191] Virally, M., 'Review Essay: Good Faith in Public International Law', 77 *AJIL* 130–4, 133 (1983). See also Rosenne, S., *Developments in the Law of Treaties 1945–1986*, (1989), 135–6: 'Its normative content is to be distinguished from the role of good faith against the broader background of international relations ... Without denying ... that good faith, as a concept, is *also* one of public and of private morality, the view that it is *only* a moral or a metaphysical concept is one that cannot be entertained ...'

[192] *Certain Norwegian Loans*, ICJ Rep., (1957), 53. See also, Lauterpacht, H., *The Development of International Law by the International Court of Justice*, (1958), 163; Rosenne, S., *Developments in the Law of Treaties, 1945–1986*, (1989), 139–40.

[193] Fitzmaurice, G., 'The Law and Procedure of the International Court of Justice, 1951–54: General Principles and Sources of Law', 27 *BYIL* 1, 12–13 (1950).

[194] Lord McNair, *The Law of Treaties*, (1961), 540, 550: 'A State may take certain action or be responsible for certain inaction, which, though not in form a breach of a treaty, is such that its effect will be equivalent to a breach of treaty; in such cases, a tribunal demands good faith and seeks for the reality rather than the appearance.' Among various examples, he suggests that, 'the making of regulations by one party which in substance destroyed or frustrated the right of the other party would be a breach of good faith and of the treaty'.

[195] *Free Zones* case, (Merits), (1930), PCIJ Ser. A/B, 46, 167.

excluding the right to legislate *at will* concerning the subject-matter of the treaty, and limiting the exercise of sovereignty of the State bound by a treaty with respect to that subject-matter to such acts as are consistent with the treaty'.[196]

The question is, to what extent, if at all, does the principle of good faith directly oblige a State to a particular course of conduct.[197] The doctrine of abuse of rights is not commonly accepted today as a source of obligation in itself, but notions of reasonableness and proportionality do play a comparable role, particularly in the field of human rights. Moreover, the principle of good faith invites particular attention to the *effects* of State action, rather than to the (subjective) intent or motivation, if any, of the State itself.

In relation to the implementation of treaty obligations, the good faith dimension may be relatively clear; for example, only if the appropriate legislative and administrative steps are taken, will refugees be identified and guaranteed protection against *refoulement*. What remains less clear is the legality of State action *outside* the scope of a particular treaty, for example, in relation to control measures applied beyond territorial jurisdiction, with a view to preventing those in search of refuge from reaching the State and claiming asylum. This is an area with much grey in it, but also one the parameters of which are nonetheless laid down in many 'peripheral' rules dealing, among others, with the use of force, racial discrimination, and, it is submitted, reasonableness and proportionality.[198]

3. Palestinian refugees: nationality, statelessness, and protection

Palestine was a British mandate during the time of the League of Nations, up until 15 May 1948. Under Ottoman rule, the inhabitants of Palestine were considered Turkish nationals; under the mandates system, the local inhabitants were not to be considered as nationals of the administering powers, although they might benefit from the exercise of diplomatic protection.[199] Palestinian citizenship was regulated by UK statutory instrument,[200] and included acquisition by birth, but a

---

[196] UNRIAA, vol. XI, 167, 188 (1910), emphasis in original. See also, *Rights of US Nationals in Morocco*, ICJ *Rep.*, 1952, 212.

[197] In *R. (European Roma Rights Centre)* v. *Immigration Officer at Prague Airport* [2005] 2 AC 1, for example, the Court was of the view that the principle of good faith could not 'create' an international obligation; the extent to which good faith nevertheless has a normative impact on discretion or State action in otherwise unregulated areas remains open. Cf. Byers, M., 'Abuse of Rights: An Old Principle, A New Principle, A new Age', 47 *McGill, L. J.* 389 (2001–02).

[198] See the *Roma Rights* case, above note; and further, Goodwin-Gill, G. S., 'State Responsibility and the "Good Faith" Obligation in International Law', in Fitzmaurice, M. & Sarooshi, D., eds., *Issues of State Responsibility before International Judicial Institutions*, (2004), 75.

[199] See League Council resolution, 22 Apr. 1923: O.J., 1923, 604, quoted in Weis, P., *Nationality and Statelessness in International Law*, (2nd edn., 1979), 20. Administering powers did not acquire sovereignty over the territories in question; see per Judge McNair, *South West Africa Case*, ICJ *Rep.*, (1950), 128, 150.

[200] Mandate citizenship was regulated by the Palestinian Citizenship Order 1925–41, S.R. & O., 1925, No. 25.

Palestinian citizen was not a British subject,[201] and Palestinian citizens were treated in Great Britain as British Protected Persons.[202] Palestinian citizens were eligible for a British passport issued by the government of Palestine, which referred to the national status of its holder as 'Palestinian citizen under Article One or Three of the Palestinian Citizenship Order, 1925–41'.[203]

As a result of the Arab–Islamic conflict which began in 1948, Palestinian refugees were not only barred from returning to their homes, but were also effectively and retroactively deprived of their citizenship. Palestinian citizenship, as a product of the mandatory's authority, terminated with the mandate and with the proclamation of the State of Israel, even though there is some authority in international law for the continuance of certain internal laws upon the cession or abandonment of territory.[204] Israel had no nationality legislation until 1952.

Nationality falls, *prima facie*, within the reserved domain of domestic jurisdiction; that is, international law recognizes that each State determines who are its citizens, and how such citizenship shall be obtained or transmitted.[205] International law is not indifferent to those claimed or disclaimed, but the amount of positive guidance is limited, and much depends upon the context. For international law purposes, States do not enjoy the freedom to denationalize their nationals in order to expel them as 'non-citizens';[206] however, if the effects of such denationalization are internal only, for example, the denial of civic rights, international law traditionally has had little to say on the matter.[207] There is likewise no obligation in international law to naturalize a resident non-citizen, even though such non-citizen may over time and for certain international law purposes acquire the effective nationality of the State of residence.[208]

The existence of a State implies a body of nationals, and a population within a relatively well-defined territory is an accepted criterion of statehood. In early decisions, however, Israeli courts held that with the termination of the Palestine mandate, former Palestine citizens had lost their citizenship without acquiring any

---

[201] See *R. v. Ketter* [1940] 1 KB 787, where it was held that the appellant, a native of Palestine born when that territory was under Turkish sovereignty, but holding a passport marked 'British Passport— Palestine', had not become a British subject by virtue of art. 30 of the Treaty of Lausanne of 24 Jul. 1923 (UKTS, No. 16/1923), or under the terms of the Mandate agreement of 24 Jul. 1922, since Palestine was not transferred to and, consequently, was not annexed by Great Britain by either Treaty or Mandate. [202] Weis, *Nationality and Statelessness*, above n. 199, 18–20, 22.

[203] See Takkenberg, L., *The Status of Palestinian Refugees in International Law*, (1998), 180, n. 35, citing a copy of a passport on file.

[204] Cf. debates in the United Kingdom on the Palestine Act, cited in O'Connell, D. P., *State Succession in Municipal Law and International Law*, vol. 1, (1967), 128–9.

[205] *Nationality Decrees* case, PCIJ, (1923), Ser. B, no. 4, 23–4; Schwarzenberger, G., *International Law*, (3rd edn., 1957), vol. I, 354; O'Connell, *International Law*, (2nd edn., 1970), 670; Weis, P., *Nationality and Statelessness in International Law*, (2nd edn., 1979), 239; Jennings & Watts, *Oppenheim's International Law*, (9th edn., 1992), vol. 1, paras. 378–82.

[206] Cf. O'Connell, *State Succession*, above n. 204, 498–9.

[207] Cf. *Kahane (Successor)* v. *Parisi and Austrian State*, 5 *Ann. Dig.* (1929–30), No. 131, in which the tribunal regarded Romanian Jews as Romanian nationals; even though Romania withheld citizenship, it did not consider them to be stateless persons. With developments in related human rights, international law is unlikely to remain silent today. [208] Cf. *Nottebohm Case*, ICJ *Rep.*, (1955), 4.

other.[209] This view was rejected in one case only, where the fact of residence and the international law governing succession of States were invoked.[210] For the purposes of Israeli municipal law, however, the issue was resolved by the Supreme Court in *Hussein* v. *Governor of Acre Prison*, and by the 1952 Nationality Law.

In *Hussein*'s case, the Court agreed that Palestinian citizenship had come to an end, and that former Palestine citizens had not become Israeli citizens.[211] The Nationality Law confirmed the repeal of the Palestine Citizenship Orders 1925–42, retroactively to the day of the establishment of the State of Israel. It declared itself the exclusive law on citizenship, which was available by way of return,[212] residence, birth, and naturalization.[213] Former Palestinian citizens of Arab origin might be incorporated in the body of Israeli citizens, provided they met certain conditions: they must have been registered under the Register of Inhabitants Ordinance on 1 March 1952; have been inhabitants of Israel on the day of entry into force of the Nationality Law (14 July 1952); and have been in Israel, or an area which became Israel, from the day of establishment of the State to the day of entry into force of the law, or have entered legally during that period.[214] These strict requirements meant that the majority of those displaced by the conflict in 1948 were effectively denied Israeli citizenship. If international law raised a presumption of entitlement to local citizenship for residents at the moment of establishment of the State,[215] subsequent developments have made any such claims redundant.[216]

---

[209] *Oseri* v. *Oseri* (1953) 8 PM 76; 17 ILR 111 (1950); this decision of the Tel Aviv District Court, ostensibly based on the fact of termination of Palestinian citizenship, is likely also to have been inspired by a desire not to recognize Palestinian Arabs as citizens of Israel.

[210] See *A.B.* v. *M.B.* 17 ILR 110 (1950); Zeltner J. said: 'So long as no law has been enacted providing otherwise, my view is that every individual who, on the date of the establishment of the State of Israel, was resident in the territory which today constitutes the State of Israel, is also a national of Israel.'

[211] (1952) 6 PD 897, 901; 17 ILR 111 (1950); *Nakara* v. *Minister of the Interior* (1953) 7 PD 955; 20 ILR 49. See also, Kattan, V., 'The Nationality of Denationalized Palestinians', 74 *Nordic Journal of International Law* 67–102 (2005).   [212] Under the Law of Return, 5710–1950.

[213] Nationality Law, 5712–1952, s. 1.

[214] Section 3. There were some authorized returns for the purposes of family reunion.

[215] Cf. Goodwin-Gill, G. S., *International Law and the Movement of Persons between States*, (1978), 4–11. Succession of States commonly links citizenship to residence, with frequent recognition of the right of option; see examples cited ibid., 7, n. 4.

[216] Under s. 30(a) of the Prevention of Infiltration (Offences and Jurisdiction) Law 1954, the Minister of Defence is empowered to order the deportation of an infiltrator, defined by s. 1 as a person who has entered Israel knowingly and unlawfully, and who, at any time between 29 Nov. 1947 (the date of the UN decision to partition Palestine) and his entry was a national, resident or visitor in the Arab countries hostile to Israel, or a former Palestine citizen or resident who had left his ordinary place of residence in an area which became part of Israel. By contrast, the Jordanian Nationality Law of 4 Feb. 1954 (following a 1949 amendment of the 1928 Trans-Jordan Nationality Law) conferred citizenship on all inhabitants of the West Bank and on residents who had been Palestinian citizens before 15 May 1948, were ordinarily resident in Jordan, and not Jewish. See generally, *Laws Concerning Nationality*, UN Leg. Ser., 1954, 1959; also US Department of State, *Country Reports on Human Rights Practices for 1987*, (1988), 1205, for the view that Jordanian citizens of Palestinian origin enjoy an 'unrestricted right to live, work, and own property'.

In fact, many of the Palestinians who fled, at least initially during the conflict of 1947–49, were citizens of Palestine under British mandate and, as 'British protected persons', entitled to the protection of the Crown. With the termination of the British mandate on 14/15 May 1948, their nationality status may have become uncertain from a *municipal law* perspective, although from an international law perspective, their 'link' to the territory remained.[217] Palestinian refugees were admitted to neighbouring countries on what was expected to be a temporary basis; local citizenship, for the most part, was not available, other than in Jordan. In these circumstances, many Palestinians, not being recognized as a citizen or national of any State, were clearly stateless.[218] The formal legal situation remains problematic, notwithstanding the recognition accorded by some States to the entity 'Palestine', and notwithstanding the United Nations' recognition of the Palestine Liberation Organization as the legitimate representative of the Palestinian people.[219] The status of Palestinians will therefore continue to raise difficulties, so far as they may individually seek protection as stateless persons or as refugees under article 1D of the Convention.[220] Palestinians who, for any reason, are not included in the peace settlement (for example, if they do not or are not able to return to Palestinian territory, and/or to obtain protection from the Palestinian authorities), will likely come within the terms of article 1D of the Convention. If required to leave their countries of habitual residence in the future, then their situation not having been 'definitively settled in accordance with the relevant resolutions adopted by the General Assembly', they will be entitled to international protection as refugees or, in the alternative, as stateless persons.

---

[217] UN General Assembly res. 194 (III) recognizes this principle; moreover, the 'international status' of Palestinians as mandate citizens arguably entails a right of representation and protection in favour of countries of refuge, on behalf of the international community and on the basis of UN General Assembly and Security Council resolutions. In the absence of any such protection function, the attainment of the compensation and related goals established internationally would be unlikely and the relevant resolutions rendered ineffective.

[218] A stateless person is defined as 'a person who is not considered as a national by any State under the operation of its law': art. 1, 1954 UN Convention relating to the Status of Stateless Persons: 360 *UNTS* 117. Cf. 1961 UN Convention on the Reduction of Statelessness: UN doc. A/CONF.9/15, Final Act, recommending that 'persons who are stateless *de facto* should as far as possible be treated as stateless *de jure* to enable them to acquire an effective nationality'. See also United Nations, *A Study of Statelessness*, (1949), 8–9 and generally.

[219] Pending further developments in the peace process, the status of Palestine as a State in the sense of international law (having a permanent population, a defined territory, government and the capacity to enter into relations with other States, including full membership of international organizations), remains undetermined; see art. 1, 1933 Montevideo Convention on Rights and Duties of States: 165 *LNTS* 19; 28 *AJIL* Supp., (1934), 75.

[220] See above, Ch. 4, s. 3.2; also, New Zealand, RSAA, *Refugee Appeal No. 73873*, 28 Apr. 2006; for an account of problems even in establishing statelessness, see the 2nd edition of this work, 244–6.

9

Protection and Solutions

1. General protection issues

1.1 DETENTION

That States have the competence to detain non-nationals pending removal or pending decisions on their entry is confirmed in judicial decisions and the practice of States.[1] From the international law perspective, therefore, the issue is not whether the power is recognized, but whether its exercise or duration are limited in the case of refugees and asylum seekers by operation of law or principle.

The 1951 Convention explicitly acknowledges that States retain the power to restrict the freedom of movement of refugees, for example, in exceptional circumstances, in the interests of national security, or if necessary after illegal entry.[2] Article 31's non-penalization provision[3] is of limited application, and the 1951 Conference of Plenipotentiaries discussed the possibility of detention 'for a few days' to verify identity.[4] Article 31(2) seems to imply that thereafter States may only impose restrictions on movement which are 'necessary', for example, on security grounds or in the special circumstances of a mass influx, although restrictions are generally to be applied only until status is regularized or admission obtained into another country.

---

[1] See, for example, *Attorney General for Canada* v. *Cain* [1906] AC 542; *Shaughnessy* v. *US ex rel. Mezei* 345 U.S. 206 (1953); art. 5 ECHR50; Note, 'The indefinite detention of excluded aliens: statutory and constitutional justifications and limitations', 82 *Mich. L. Rev.* 61 (1983). The legality of indefinite detention continues to be contested, however; see *Al-Kateb* v. *Godwin* (2004) 78 ALJR 1099, in which a majority of the High Court of Australia held that indefinite detention of an 'unlawful non-citizen' was permitted by statute, which was not subject to any 'purposive limitation', an intention not to affect fundamental rights, or a 'reasonable period' requirement. Other jurisdictions have held that detention is permissible only so long as removal is a reasonable prospect; see also, Legomsky, S. H., 'The Detention of Aliens: Theories, Rules, and Discretion', 30 *Inter-American Law Review* 531 (1999).

[2] Art. 9 CSR51 permits a State to take 'provisional measures' against a particular person, 'pending a determination that that person is in fact a refugee and that the continuance of such measures is necessary in the interests of national security'. The Convention does not limit the period of detention, require review of its legality or its necessity, or otherwise confine the discretion of the State. For reservations to arts. 9 and 26, see below Ch. 10, s. 1.2. For background, see Goodwin-Gill, G. S., 'International Law and the detention of refugees and asylum-seekers', 20 *Int. Mig. Rev.* 193, 205–9 (1986); Goodwin-Gill, G. S., 'The detention of non-nationals, with particular reference to refugees and asylum-seekers', 9 *In Defense of the Alien* (1986), 138, 141–6.   [3] See above, Ch. 5, s. 3.3.5; Ch. 7, s. 5.2.

[4] See generally UN docs. A/CONF.2/SR.13, 13–15; SR.14, 4, 10–11; SR.35, 11–13, 15–16, 19.

Apart from the few days for investigation, it may be argued that the drafters of the 1951 Convention intended that further detention would need to be justified as necessary under article 31(2), or exceptional under article 9.[5] This receives some support from article 32 on the expulsion of lawfully resident refugees, which limits the grounds and calls for certain procedural guarantees. In addition, a refugee under order of expulsion is to be allowed a reasonable period within which to seek legal entry into another country, although States do retain discretion to apply 'such internal measures as they may deem necessary'.[6] In short, a number of limitations on the detention of refugees can be inferred from the provisions of the 1951 Convention, and references to 'necessary' measures of detention imply an objective standard, subject to independent review.[7]

If the 1951 Convention and 1967 Protocol offer only limited protection against detention, human rights law goes further. Although State practice recognizes the power to detain in the immigration context, human rights treaties affirm that no one shall be subject to *arbitrary* arrest or detention.[8] The first line of protection thus requires that all detention must be in accordance with and authorized by law; the second, that detention should be reviewed as to its legality and necessity, according to the standard of what is reasonable and necessary in a democratic society.[9] Arbitrary embraces not only what is illegal, but also what is unjust.[10] The *conditions* of detention may also put in question a State's compliance with generally

---

[5] On art. 9, see Ch. 10, s. 1.2.   [6] On art. 32, see below Ch. 10, s.1.2.5.

[7] See Samuels, H., 'The Detention of Vietnamese Asylum Seekers in Hong Kong: *Re Pham Van Hgo and 110 Others*', 41 *ICLQ* 422 (1992), for an interesting summary of the detention of 111 Vietnamese whose ship was damaged, and who wanted repairs and then to sail on to Japan. Instead they were detained, successfully challenged the legality of their detention, were re-arrested, and eventually released, and determined to be refugees and allowed to remain pending resettlement.

[8] See, for example, art. 9 ICCPR66; art. 5 ECHR50; art. 2 Protocol 4, European Convention; art. 7 ACHR69; art. 6 ACHPR81; also art. 5 1985 United Nations Declaration on the Human Rights of Individuals who are not Nationals of the Country in which They Live: UNGA res. 40/l44, 13 Dec. 1985, Annex. In *Gisbert* v. *US Attorney General* 988 F.2d 1437 (5th Cir., 1993), however, the court held that customary international law prohibitions against prolonged arbitrary detention cannot supersede US statute, the Attorney General's actions and judicial decisions.

[9] Emergency powers and the inherent limitations to many human rights are nevertheless a problem for refugees and asylum seekers, given the generality and vagueness of the wording of exceptions (public emergency, life of the nation, national security, *ordre public*, necessary in a democratic society), but also by experience with State practice in the face of actual or perceived threats. See generally Higgins, R., 'Derogations under Human Rights Treaties', 48 *BYIL* 281 (1976–77). Judicial decisions like *Fernandez-Roque* v. *Smith* 567 F. Supp. 1115 (1981) are relatively rare, particularly now, in the security climate of the new century. In that case, the District Court for the Northern District of Georgia considered that the government's power to detain non-nationals was conditional on there being clear and convincing evidence that those affected were likely to abscond, or posed a risk to national security, or a significant and serious threat to persons or property. Reversing this decision, 734 F.2d 576 (11th Cir., 1984), the Court of Appeals concluded that the applicants lacked a sufficient constitutional liberty interest, and did not address the international law arguments. Cf. *Barrera-Echavarria* v. *Rison* 21 F.3d 314 (9th Cir., 1994): eight years imprisonment of an excluded alien who had arrived from Cuba with the Mariel boatlift because US government considered him a danger to society violated his Fifth Amendment rights because such extended detention was 'excessive in relation to its regulatory goal'.

[10] This interpretation was adopted in the work of the Commission on Human Rights on the right of everyone to be free from arbitrary arrest, detention and exile; see UN doc. E/CN.4/826/Rev.1,

accepted standards of treatment, including the prohibition on cruel, inhuman, or degrading treatment;[11] the special protection due to the family and to children;[12] and the general recognition given to basic procedural rights and guarantees.[13]

The detention of refugees and asylum seekers was considered by the Executive Committee at its 37th session in 1986, where the debate in the Sub-Committee of the Whole on International Protection was long, often heated, and divided between those anxious to ensure that detention remained an exception and those who sought the widest powers in controlling movement and entry.[14] The Working Group's conclusions were duly adopted,[15] and although not as progressive as some had hoped for, and by no means as committed to detention as exception which had been UNHCR's goal, the Conclusions nevertheless accept the principle that 'detention should normally be avoided'. However, the Executive Committee expressly recognized that:

if necessary, detention may be resorted to only on grounds prescribed by law to verify identity; to determine the elements on which the claim to refugee status or asylum is based; to deal with cases where refugees or asylum seekers have destroyed their travel and/or identity documents or have used fraudulent documents in order to mislead the authorities of the State in which they intend to claim asylum; or to protect national security or public order.[16]

It also noted that 'fair and expeditious procedures' for determining refugee status are an important protection against prolonged detention; and that 'detention

---

paras. 23–30. Also, Hassan, P., 'The word "arbitrary" as used in the Universal Declaration of Human Rights: "Illegal or Unjust"?' 10 *Harv. Int'l L.J.* 225 (1969); Lillich, R., 'Civil Rights', in Meron, T., ed., *Human Rights in International Law*, (1984), 15, 12lf.

[11] In *S* v. *Department of Immigration and Multicultural Affairs* (2005) 216 ALR 252, [2005] FCA 549, the Federal Court of Australia held that the Commonwealth of Australia (but not the Department) owed a duty of care to detainees, which required that a level of medical care was available which was reasonably designed to meet detainees' needs; the failure to provide psychiatric care following protest and hunger strike was a breach of that duty. See also Fazel, M. & Silove, D., 'Detention of refugees', *British Medical Journal*, 2006, vol. 332, 251–2, 4 Feb. 2006, noting that damage to mental health was one reason why Australia abandoned its policy of mandatory detention, and 'that models of community accommodation for asylum seekers lead to better mental health outcomes and that humane but rigorous forms of monitoring can still be instituted in these settings'.

[12] Tribunal civil (Réf.)-Bruxelles, 25 nov. 1993, No. 56.865, *D.D. & D.N. c/ Etat belge, Min. de l'Interieur et Min. de la santé publique, de l'Environnment et de l'Intégration sociale*, in which the court found the detention of an asylum seeker and her new-born baby to be inhuman and degrading, contrary to arts. 3 and 8 ECHR50: *RDDE*, No. 76, nov–dec. 1993, 604. For a particularly strong indictment of detention and its effects on children, see McCallin, M., 'Living in Detention: A review of the psychological well-being of Vietnamese children in the Hong Kong detention centres', (1992).

[13] Cf. *United States Diplomatic and Consular Staff in Tehran*, where the International Court of Justice observed that, 'Wrongfully to deprive human beings of their freedom and to subject them to physical constraint in conditions of hardship is in itself manifestly incompatible with the principles of the Charter of the United Nations, as well as with the fundamental principles enunciated in the Universal Declaration of Human Rights': ICJ *Rep.*, (1980), 42, para. 9l.

[14] For an account of the debate, see the 2nd edn. of this work, 249–51.

[15] Executive Committee Conclusion No. 44 (1986), *Report* of the 37th Session (1986): UN doc. A/AC.96/688, para. 128.

[16] Executive Committee Conclusion No. 44 (1986), above note, para. (b).

measures taken in respect of refugees and asylum seekers should be subject to judicial or administrative review'.[17]

Further study of the issue took place in the context of UNHCR's Global Consultations on International Protection, and with particular reference to article 31 of the Convention.[18] The conclusions adopted following a meeting on the topic recalled that the Executive Committee had several times acknowledged that refugees often have justifiable reasons for illegal entry, but that the implementation of article 31 requires positive steps, including identification of refugees at the earliest possibility. It was again emphasized that only such restrictions be applied to refugees entering illegally as are strictly necessary *in the individual case.* Moreover, article 31 benefits not only those who come directly from their country of origin, but also those who have briefly transited other countries, or are unable to find effective protection in the first country or countries of refuge. With regard to article 31(2), the exceptional nature of detention was stressed, and appropriate standards set out for the application of restrictions under this provision.[19]

1.1.1 Detention and mass influx

In the case of a mass influx, the principles contained in article 31 remain applicable; State practice, however, reflects a general tendency to use closed or restricted camps as an interim solution, pending repatriation or third country resettlement.[20] One commentator in 1951 considered that article 26 on freedom of movement would not be violated in 'special situations where refugees have to be accommodated in special camps or in special areas even if this does not apply to aliens generally'.[21] Such measures are now the usual response in situations of large-scale influx, justified by reference to national security, community welfare, and even 'humane deterrence'. Both case-by-case determination of refugee status and case-by-case review of confinement may indeed be unrealistic, and there *may* also exist good reasons—racial, cultural, religious, economic—why alternatives to detention cannot be used in any particular context; but the conditional nature of these statements should not be overlooked.

The Executive Committee's 1981 conclusions on the protection of asylum seekers in situations of mass influx make basic provision for the conditions of

[17] See further, UNHCR, 'Guidelines on Applicable Criteria and Standards relating to the Detention of Asylum Seekers', Geneva, Feb. 1999.

[18] Goodwin-Gill, G. S., 'Article 31 of the 1951 Convention relating to the Status of Refugees: Non-penalization, detention, and protection', in Feller, E., Türk, V. & Nicholson, F., eds., *Refugee Protection in International Law,* (2003), 185; Summary Conclusions on Article 31, ibid., 253.

[19] Summary Conclusions on Article 31, above note, 253, 256–7.

[20] Just as there are a number of notable exceptions, including the use of settlements with a self-sufficiency component in Africa, Central America and Pakistan, and special temporary legal regimes for refugees from conflict, so also 'interim' settlements may endure for many years, leading to justifiable concern about 'warehousing'; see US Committee for Refugees and Immigrants: <http://www.refugees.org>.

[21] Robinson, N., *The 1951 Convention relating to the Status of Refugees: A Commentary,* (1953), 133, n. 207.

detention.[22] Other international standards, as applicable to individuals as to large groups, include the prohibition on forced or compulsory labour. At the 1951 Conference the practice of labour contract and group settlement schemes was defended, under which refugees who were admitted were required to remain in a particular job for a particular time.[23] Today, however, objections would likely be based on a variety of treaty provisions.[24]

1.2 REFUGEE RIGHTS IN CAMPS AND SETTLEMENTS

As a matter of international law, the primary responsibility to ensure and protect the rights of refugees falls on the State where the refugees are present.[25] The standard of treatment due is to be determined by reference to the State's treaty commitments, including any reservations, and to its obligations in general international law. In practice, however, the rights actually enjoyed may be largely contingent not only on the conditions under which refugees are admitted, but also on the level of international assistance provided by States through UNHCR, other international organizations, and NGOs. In addition, the factual situation may be affected by perceptions as to the final outcome of the refugee movement in question, and whether refugees are expected to be able to return relatively quickly or will be resettled in third States. In the interim, the entitlement of refugees effectively to claim rights which are due in theory is often substantially qualified, and may be equally uncertain in camps or settlements administered by United Nations agencies such as UNHCR, or 'protected' by peacekeeping forces acting under UN or regional organization authority.

The question, and the difficulty, of invoking responsibility in such cases is self-evident. The State may be primarily responsible in its capacity as territorial sovereign, but its capacity to act with regard to a large refugee community settled in part of its territory, even if only temporarily, may be undermined by lack of resources; in consequence, it may have delegated responsibility for day-to-day management to UNHCR and simply not be present in the settlements. This raises a number of critical legal questions, to which ready answers are not yet available. Recent investigative research has nevertheless set the agenda and usefully thrown light on the issues, particularly so far as they may engage the legal responsibility of international organizations where refugee rights are violated.[26]

As shown above,[27] UNHCR enjoys international personality derivative from that of the United Nations itself, but implicit also in its Statute and in its activities

---

[22] See above, Ch. 6, s. 2.1.   [23] UN doc. E/AC.32/SR.11, 6.
[24] See art. 2, 1930 ILO Convention (No. 29) concerning Forced Labour; art. 1, 1957 ILO Convention (No. 105) concerning the Abolition of Forced Labour. In 1984 the ILO Committee of Experts noted that German legislation allowed for asylum seekers to be required to perform 'socially useful work' if they wished to maintain welfare entitlements. It called on the government to bring law and practice into conformity with ILO Convention No. 29, above.
[25] This elementary point of principle also figures now in General Assembly resolutions; see, for example, UNGA res. 60/129, 16 Dec. 2005, para. 7.   [26] See below, nn. 28, 31.
[27] See above, Ch. 8, s. 1.

on the international plane. In principle, therefore, it is capable of having human rights obligations, even as States nevertheless retain their own liability.[28] As Clapham explains:

... international organizations are capable of violating international obligations with regard to human rights; and where those organizations remain unaccountable for such violations, states retain their own international obligations to ensure respect for human rights. The acts and omissions of international organizations may thus give rise to both international human rights violations by the organization and, in some circumstances, also for the relevant states. This is so where the 'international organization aids or assists, or directs or controls, a State in the commission of a wrongful act'.[29]

Clapham also shows how general principles of liability have long been accepted in the practice of the UN, particularly in the resolution of claims of a private law character arising in the course of peacekeeping operations. Nevertheless, the UN is 'not a State and does not possess the juridical and administrative powers necessary to independently discharge many of the obligations provided for under international humanitarian law'.[30] Operations involving UN forces are often the subject of detailed agreements with States, but the situation may well be less clear where a UN agency assumes certain governmental functions over a certain population in a certain territory.

The legal responsibility of UNHCR in camp management situations has been highlighted in recent analyses by Wilde, drawing strongly and by analogy on the long history of 'international territorial administration'.[31] Whereas earlier criticisms of institutional accountability mechanisms focused on general issues of mandate performance,[32] the recent approach is very much rights-based and centred on the individual refugee as rights-holder. So far as such analysis draws on direct experience in camps and settlements, it is also anchored in the manifest need of the refugee to have access to an effective remedy, whether the alleged violator of rights is from within the refugee community, an NGO, or an international organization.

As Wilde and others have shown, there is no reason in principle why human rights cannot be integrated into any UN or international administration of territory.

---

[28] Clapham, A., *Human Rights Obligations of Non-State Actors*, (2006), 109, citing the European Court of Human Rights in *Waite and Kennedy* v. *Germany* (2000) 30 EHRR 261, para. 67. See also *Report of the International Law Commission*, 58th Session, 2006, UN doc. A/61/10, 284–6.

[29] Clapham, above note, 109–10.   [30] Ibid., 119, quoting UN official Ralph Zacklin.

[31] See Wilde, R., '*Quis custodiet ipsos custodes?*: Why and How UNHCR Governance of "Development" Refugee Camps should be Subject to International Human Rights Law', 1 *Yale Human Rights and Development Law Journal* 107 (1998); 'From Danzig to East Timor and Beyond: The Role of International Territorial Administration', 95 *AJIL* 583 (2001); 'The Complex Role of the Legal Adviser when International Organizations administer Territory', *Proceedings of the 95th Annual Meeting of the American Society of International Law*, (2001), 251; also, 'Representing International Territorial Administration: A Critique of some Approaches', 15 *EJIL* 71 (2004). See further Stahn, C., 'International Territorial Administration in the former Yugoslavia: Orgins, Development and Challenges Ahead', 61 *Zeitschrift für ausländisches Recht und Völkerrecht* 107 (2001).

[32] For example, with regard to UNHCR's engagement in extra-mandate activities that compromised the right to seek asylum, or where UNHCR appeared to 'promote' the return of refugees to unsafe conditions.

Indeed, this was partially achieved in Kosovo,[33] for example, although qualified by certain remaining immunities for military and police officials.[34] Likewise, the current work of the International Law Commission (ILC) on the responsibility of international organizations draws closely on the articles already agreed on the responsibility of States, and takes the premise of responsibility as a given.[35] By 2006, the ILC had provisionally adopted a number of articles, the second of which provides that for the purposes of the draft, 'the term "international organization" refers to an organization established by treaty or other instrument governed by international law and possessing its own international legal personality'. Article 4 sets out the principle of attribution in familiar terms, to provide that the 'conduct of an organ or agent of an international organization in the performance of functions of that organ or agent shall be considered as an act of that organization under international law whatever position the organ or agent holds in respect of that organization'.[36] Conduct will continue to be so attributed, even though it 'exceeds the authority of that organ or agent or contravenes instructions'.[37] The draft articles provide also for responsibility in connection with the act of a State (or another international organization), for example, where the international organization aids or assists the State in committing an internationally wrongful act, if it 'does so with knowledge of the circumstances of the internationally wrongful act', and 'the act would be internationally wrongful if committed by that organization'.[38] As noted above in general terms, the draft articles also acknowledge the principle that a *State* may be responsible for acts of an international organization, for example, where it has accepted responsibility, or has led the injured party to rely on its responsibility.[39]

The Special Rapporteur's Fourth Report considers circumstances precluding wrongfulness, such as *force majeure*.[40] One example mentioned is that of a failure by States to pay their contributions, with the consequence that the international organization is unable to meet its obligations generally, or in relation to its mandate.[41] On the other hand, 'nothing precludes the wrongfulness of any act of an international organization which is not in conformity with an obligation arising under a peremptory norm of general international law'.[42] With crimes against humanity and torture (and return to torture also) now recognized as among the

---

[33] See s. 2, UNMIK Regulation No. 1999/1, as amended by Regulation No. 2000/59, on observance of internationally recognized standards. The Media Appeals Board of Kosovo expressly took into account both ICCPR66 and ECHR50, as well as the relevent jurisprudence.

[34] Clapham, *Human Rights Obligations of Non-State Actors*, 130–1.

[35] On State responsibility, see UNGA res. 56/82, 12 Dec. 2001, Annex.

[36] See *Report of the International Law Commission*, 58th Session, 2006, UN doc. A/61/10, 246–92; text of draft art. 4 at 253.   [37] Ibid., 254.

[38] Draft art. 12: ibid., 256; 'Third Report on responsibility of international organizations', Giorgio Gaja, Special Rapporteur, UN doc. A/CN.4/553, 13 May 2005, paras. 25–44. See also draft art. 25 on aid or assistance by a State in the commission of an internationally wrongful act by an international organization: *Report of the ILC*, 279–80.   [39] Draft arts. 25–9; *Report of the ILC*, 279–91.

[40] 'Fourth Report on responsibility of international organizations', Giorgio Gaja, Special Rapporteur, UN doc. A/CN.4/564, 28 Feb. 2006, paras. 26–32.   [41] Ibid., para. 31.

[42] Draft art. 23, ibid., paras. 47–9, *Report of the ILC*, 275–6.

body of such norms, any room for manoeuvre or excuses for conduct which might be justified on grounds precluding wrongfulness are now clearly constrained for an organization such as UNHCR.

Nevertheless, though welcome as developments towards more accountable international organizations, the draft articles remain written at a highly theoretical level. It is difficult to see exactly how they will work down to the grass roots, and ensure, among others, that the refugee as rights-holder is assured an effective remedy against any violation. Wilde identifies the issue of responsibility as arising most acutely in the context of so-called 'development refugee camps', that is, refugee settlements located in developing States which do not have the capacity to fulfil their protection responsibilities without the assistance of international organizations.[43] He argues that in such circumstances UNHCR acts much as a *de facto* sovereign, and in an operational context largely divorced from treaty or general rules.[44] Taking UNHCR's sufficient legal personality as a starting point, he considers that human rights law is not only compatible with its mandate, but 'actually an essential component of the refugees' actual needs'. First and foremost, this means truly representative systems of consultation, which may be particularly hard to put in place in a first, emergency phase, at least in a formal sense. As Farmer shows, drawing on experience in Guinea, it is difficult to secure local protection whenever refugees do not have a clearly defined and provable status.[45] She, too, sees 'rights-based refuge' as not yet having succeeded in incorporating basic accountability mechanisms and access to justice, as the violence and violations facing refugee women clearly show.[46] Although the Guinean government, UNHCR and NGOs together exercise 'State-like' functions, yet they do not do enough and do not coordinate their efforts. For example, UNHCR did not provide adequate ration and identification cards; the government had taken steps to incorporate women's rights, but many women refugees in particular did not know what had been done or how to access justice; and NGO field offices seemed far less aware of the rights-based approach than were head offices. In each case, 'all fail to guard the human rights of women refugees in similar ways: lack of enforcement of laws and policy designed to protect women, limited access to justice, and ineffective accountability mechanisms'.[47] Host States cannot alone be responsible for the human rights of refugees, however, and what is needed is a 'multi-layered accountability system', with an obligation to promote durable solutions.[48] In her view, the

---

[43] Wilde, '*Quis custodiet ipsos custodes?*', above n. 31, 109–10.   [44] Ibid., 111, 113.

[45] Farmer, A., 'Refugee Responses, State-Like Behavior, and Accountability for Human Rights Violations: A Case Study of Sexual Violence in Guinea's Refugee Camps', 9 *Yale Human Rights and Development Law Journal* 44 (2006).   [46] Ibid., 46.

[47] Ibid., 72. Farmer also sees a *de facto* State quality in the refugee camps: ibid., 72–81, drawing not so much on 'international territorial administration', as on Fukuyama's criteria for determining the strength of a State or State-like institution: Fukuyama, F., *State Building: Governance and World Order in the 21st Century*, (2004).

[48] Farmer, above n. 45, 119. The desirability of adopting such an approach as a matter of policy is probably clear, even as one may have reservations about translating UNHCR's institutional responsibilities (cf. UNHCR Statute, para.1) into the language of obligation.

law to apply is that which would apply to the host State, so far as UNHCR had adopted the State's role towards refugees.[49] It is at the point of implementation and effectiveness, however, that the thesis begins to show its fault lines. It takes little account of the continuing authority of the territorial State, which was nowhere more evident perhaps than in the 1996 'returns' of Rwandans from Tanzania.[50] In addition, the language of international human rights instruments is not capable of applying automatically to international organizations; not surprisingly, many obligations are framed expressly with the State in mind, with all its powers of police and enforcement. Refugee camps are also commonly in evolution, from emergency reception, shelter, and assistance locations, through to more settled communities of greater or less permanence. Even for the State, in situations which may reasonably be classified as 'emergency' at one or other stage, exactly what human rights are due is not always clear.

This presents its own challenges and functional issues. The *general* obligation of a present and administering international organization to ensure and protect human rights is clear; what is now needed is a more finely tuned approach geared closely to UNHCR, and in the form of an oversight body.[51] At the practical level, where refugee lives are lived, more must be done to build capacity and strengthen access to *domestic* courts.[52] Refugees need a forum in which to bring complaints, while UNHCR operations in turn require separate and independent auditing. Equally, both UNHCR and refugees could benefit from strengthening the capacity of the former to protect the latter, even through the use of local institutions, especially when host States seek to limit rights in situations of mass influx.

In many respects the analogy with international territorial administration or State-like activity is helpful in understanding just how deeply UNHCR and other actors are embedded in refugees' daily lives, particularly in camps and settlements. It is clear, too, that the camp environment can foster human rights violations and administration otherwise than in accordance with the rule of law. As Farmer puts it, 'state-like functioning and . . . rights-based rhetoric should be accompanied by refugee-driven accountability mechanisms'.[53] The basis of obligation, however, can be more simply stated, and resides firstly in the fact, and secondly in the degree, of control;[54] in the nature of things, legal responsibility is also unlikely to reside exclusively in the hands of just one party. Moreover, certain functions, such as those of the police and courts, or of discipline of punishment, are inappropriate

---

[49] Ibid. For (extensive) suggestions as to the applicable law, see ibid., 120.

[50] See above, Ch. 5, s. 2.5.2. By contrast with the instances of international territorial administration detailed in Wilde's later writings, the territorial State is capable at any moment of resuming control of refugee camps and settlements. Moreover, it is able to, and does, determine the conditions of UNHCR access in a context which may well find the agency anxious to secure presence, if not regardless, then at the price of certain rights.   [51] Farmer, abvoe n. 45, 82, 83.

[52] In principle, this approach has the theoretical advantage of underlining the overall responsibility of the territorial State while also strengthening the link between international human rights law and national implementation. It also reduces the separation between refugees and host communities which can lead to a loss of accountability.   [53] Farmer, above n. 45, 84.

[54] Cf. *R. (Al-Skeini)* v. *Secretary of State for Defence* [2006] 3 WLR 508, [2005] EWCA Civ 1609.

for international organizations or NGOs, and not necessarily best left in refugees' own hands, again for want of representative capacity and overall accountability. Ensuring responsibility to international human rights standards and holding both organizations and individuals to account is necessarily a multifaceted exercise. Experience nevertheless suggests as a minimum that basic human rights, as well as refuge rights, should be referenced in every UNHCR–State agreement or memorandum of understanding. Depending on the circumstances, consideration should also be given to local justice mechanisms as means of redress, with appropriate international support to strengthen capacity where necessary. Agreements between UNHCR and NGOs or between States and NGOs will likewise need to recall the basic principles of accountability and to indicate how complaints are handled and redress is sought.

Where UNHCR itself is allegedly responsible for programmes, policies, or actions which result in violations of refugees' rights, it may not be appropriate in all circumstances to have recourse to legal process, save as a last resort. Depending on the nature of the grievance in question, the general emphasis may be on efficient and effective remedies, perhaps through a permanent 'Refugee and Human Rights Commissioner' or ombudsperson. Again, however, the process must be known and accessible, the office holder must be clearly independent and impartial, and ideally should also be able to engage in inquiry and investigation on his or her own initiative.

1.3 PERSONAL SECURITY AND RELATED MEASURES

Efforts to provide protection or bring humanitarian assistance to threatened populations in conflict-stricken areas have frequently exposed relief workers to personal danger, and many have been killed or wounded in the course of their duties. Refugees and the internally displaced have also been the object of attacks, and used as political pawns by opposing sides, as shields for military operations or as sources of supplies and combatants. Recent practice suggests the emergence of a principle of *humanitarian access*, on the one hand, and a rule protecting relief workers, on the other. International law also prohibits military and armed attacks on refugee camps and settlements, at least so far as they maintain their civilian and humanitarian character.

1.3.1 *Refugees and asylum seekers*

Neither UNHCR nor any other international agency has any secure place of asylum and no formal way to protect the personal security of refugees and asylum seekers, which in principle remains largely the responsibility of governments. Refugees and asylum seekers are often exposed to danger during flight, however, particularly in areas of military activity, and on occasion, UNHCR protection officers have been there to guide new arrivals to places of safety.[55] UNHCR has also successfully called for the establishment of safe havens, particularly for

[55] UNHCR's border presence in Thailand and Honduras in the 1980s, in particular, ensured that many found refuge.

refugees awaiting enforced departure from their country of asylum.[56] In 1980, the Executive Committee called on UNHCR and others to intensify efforts to protect refugees in danger from pirate attacks at sea;[57] by then many had been killed or assaulted, and many women and girls raped or abducted. Bilateral and multilateral actions involving UNHCR, States and NGOs eventually produced an anti-piracy programme and a decline in the percentage of boats attacked.[58] Programmes for victims of violence (including rape, torture, and other forms of persecution) are thus a natural and practical extension of the protection function, oriented also towards re-integration of the individual and thereby towards a durable solution.[59]

In addition, refugee camps, settlements, and centres need to be places of safety, located in light of the security of the refugees, while remaining accessible. This means taking account of the possibility of armed attacks, whether from within State territory or outside.[60] Internal policing may also be required, as well as external protection against harassment or forced recruitment. The UNHCR Executive Committee first looked at the question of military attacks in 1982, following a number of raids in southern Africa. The debate turned out to be protracted, and controversial, with varying emphasis placed upon the necessity to maintain the civilian and humanitarian character of such camps; conclusions on the subject were not agreed until five years later,[61] but many of the lessons seem not to have been learned, including by UNHCR.[62]

---

[56] With respect to foreign refugees in Chile after the 1973 coup, see UN doc. A/AC.96/508, (1974), 5; *Report* to the General Assembly, 29 GAOR, Supp. 12A, 28: UN doc. A/9612/Add.1 (1974).

[57] Executive Committee Conclusion No. 20 (1981).

[58] 'Note on International Protection': UN doc. A/AC.96/660, 23 Jul. 1985, para. 23; see also above, Ch. 6, s. 2.1.

[59] See UNHCR, 'Note on Refugee Women and International Protection': UN doc. EC/SCP/39, 8 Jul. 1985; *Report* of the Sub-Committee: UN doc. A/AC.96/671, paras. 8–19; *Report* of the Executive Committee, 37th Session: UN doc. A/AC.96/673, para. 115(4), (1985).

[60] See Mtango, E-E., 'Military and Armed Attacks on Refugee Camps', in Loescher, G. & Monahan, L., eds., *Refugees and International Relations*, (1989), 87.

[61] For background, see UNHCR, 'Military Attacks on Refugee Camps and Settlements in Southern Africa and Elsewhere': UN doc. EC/SCP/23 (Oct. 1982); *Report* of the Sub-Committee: UN doc. A/AC.96/613 (1982), paras. 12–21; *Report* of the 33rd Session (1982): UN doc. A/AC.96/614, paras. 42(i), 63, 70(3); *Report* of the Sub-Committee: UN doc. A/AC.96/629 (1983), paras. 13–16; *Report* of the 34th Session (1983): UN doc. A/AC.96/631, paras. 93–5, 97(4); *Report* by Ambassador Felix Schnyder, 'Military Attacks on Refugee Camps and Settlements in Southern Africa and Elsewhere': UN doc. EC/SCP/26 (Mar. 1983); also UN doc. EC/SCP/31 (Aug. 1983); UN doc. EC/SCP/27 (Jun. 1983); 'Draft Principles on Military Attacks': UN doc. EC/SCP/32 (Sept. 1983); UN doc. EC/SCP/34 and Add.1 (July 1984); *Report* of the Sub-Committee: UN doc. A/AC.96/649 (1984) and Add.1, paras. 6–13; UN doc. EC/SCP/38; *Report* of the Sub-Committee: UN doc. A/AC.96/671 (9 Oct. 1985), paras. 20–6; *Report* of the 37th Session (1986): UN doc. A/AC.96/688 and Corr.1, para. 129; 'Note' on Military and Armed Attacks on Refugee Camps and Settlements: UN doc. EC/SCP/47, 10 Aug. 1987; *Report* of the Sub-Committee: UN doc. A/AC.96/700, 5 Oct. 1987, paras. 21–30; *Report* of the 38th Session: UN doc. A/AC.96/702, 22 Oct. 1987, para. 206: Executive Committee Conclusion No. 48 (1987) on Military and Armed Attacks on Refugee Camps and Settlements. In its 1988 'Note on International Protection': UN doc. A/AC.96/713, paras. 24–36, UNHCR noted that the effect of the 1987 Conclusion was yet to be to be felt, provided statistics of attacks in one African country (para. 28), and suggested various remediable measures, such as relocation (paras. 31–4).

[62] See Goodwin-Gill, G. S., 'Refugee identity and protection's fading prospect', in Nicholson, F. & Twomey, P., *Refugee Rights and Realities*, (1999), 220.

1.3.2 *Women refugees*[63]

During refugee movements, women and girls risk further violations of their human rights, and have repeatedly been targeted as victims of rape and abduction.[64] Their passage to safety may have to be bought at the price of sexual favours, and even within the relative security of a refugee camp or settlement and bearing additional responsibilities as heads of households, they face discrimination in food distribution, access to health, welfare and education services—doubly disadvantaged as refugees and as women. These facts were common knowledge for years, but apart from the particular attention given to piracy attacks in the South China Sea, the protection of women refugees did not appear on the agenda of the UNHCR Executive Committee until 1985. At that time, the primary question was not so much the physical security or systemic discrimination which women face in flight and in refuge, but whether women might constitute a particular social group, membership of which could give rise in appropriate circumstances to a well-founded fear of persecution.[65]

From 1988 onwards, however, women have featured regularly, with particular reference to questions of safety, discrimination, and sexual exploitation.[66] In 1990, under pressure from a number of governments, UNHCR first raised the possibility of developing a *policy* on refugee women,[67] while also looking at their specific needs in the refugee determination context, and in that of physical safety.[68] With respect to the latter, UNHCR noted that special measures were needed in camps and settlements in order to protect women from abuse, especially women heads of household and single women.[69] Action was required to ensure the provision of food, water, and relief supplies, to meet health and reproductive health needs, to provide education and to promote skills training and economic activities. Women also face problems in making their voices heard on important decisions, such as voluntary repatriation.[70]

---

[63] UNHCR, 'Selected Bibliography on Refugee Women, 1990—June 2005', update to the Select Bibliography Section of the Special Issue on Refugee Women, 21 *Refugee Survey Quarterly* (2002); Forbes Martin, S., *Refugee Women*, (2nd edn., 2003). [64] See above on piracy, Ch. 6, s. 2.1.

[65] See 'Refugee Women and International Protection': UN doc. EC/SCP/39 (1985); *Report* of the Sub-Committee: UN doc. A/AC.96/671 (9 Oct. 1985), paras. 8–19; Executive Committee Conclusion No. 39 (1985), *Report* of the 36th Session, UN doc. A/AC.96/673, para. 115(4); also, Bhabha, J., 'Demography and Rights: Women, Children and Access to Asylum', 16 *IJRL* 227 (2004). On gender as a basis for persecution and the social group question, see further above, Ch. 3, s. 4.2.4.4.

[66] See UNHCR, *Note on International Protection:* UN doc. A/AC.96/713, (15 Aug. 1988), para. 36; *Note on International Protection:* UN doc. A/AC.96/728 (2 Aug. 1989), paras. 30–6; Also, Johnsson, A. B., 'The International Protection of Women Refugees', 1 *IJRL* 221 (1989); Kelley, N., 'Report on the International Consultation on Refugee Women, held in Geneva, 15–19 November 1988', 1 *IJRL* 233 (1989). [67] *UNHCR Policy on Refugee Women:* UN doc. A/AC.96/754 (20 Aug. 1990).

[68] 'Note on Refugee Women and International Protection': UN doc. EC/SCP/59 (28 Aug. 1990).

[69] Such measures should include not only counselling and assistance to victims of sexual violence and prosecution and punishment of offenders, but also basic preventive steps, such as adequate lighting in camps, or planting thorn bushes around women's areas.

[70] Ibid., paras. 29–56; *Report* of the Sub-Committee: UN doc. A/AC.96/758 (2 Oct. 1990); Executive Committee Conclusion No. 64 (1990), *Report* of the 41st Session, UN doc. A/AC.96/760, para. 23.

Guidelines on the protection of refugee women were drafted in 1991 for the use of UNHCR personnel,[71] but the following year the US representative remarked in the Executive Committee that protection of women and children was still not of sufficient concern to many UNHCR field offices.[72] In 1993, UNHCR produced a comprehensive note on certain aspects of sexual violence against women,[73] which in turn led to an equally wide-ranging conclusion.[74] Also in 1993, the UN General Assembly adopted the Declaration on the Elimination of Violence against Women,[75] recognizing that this is an issue of international concern and that all States have an obligation to work towards its eradication. It interprets such violence widely in article 1, as 'any act of gender-based violence that results in, or is likely to result in, physical, sexual or psychological harm or suffering to women, including threats of such acts, coercion or arbitrary deprivation of liberty, whether occurring in public or private life'. Moreover, such violence is seen not so much in terms of individual behaviour, as a 'manifestation of historically unequal power relationships between men and women', which may occur in the family, in the general community, or be perpetrated or condoned by the State. It recognizes that some groups, such as refugee women, women belonging to minority groups, indigenous women, and women in situations of armed conflict, are especially vulnerable.[76] That implementation continues to present challenges, however, is clear, both generally and in particular contexts, such as camps and settlements.[77]

[71] See 'Information Note on UNHCR's Guidelines on the Protection of Refugee Women': UN doc. EC/SCP/67 (22 Jul. 1991), Annexe; 'Progress Report on Implementation of the UNHCR Guidelines on the Protection of Refugee Women': UN doc. EC/SCP/74 (22 Jul. 1992); 'Progress Report on Implementation of the UNHCR Policy on Refugee Women': UN doc. EC/SC.2/55 (26 Aug. 1992); *Report* of the Sub-Committee: UN doc. A/AC.96/802 (6 Oct. 1992), paras. 35–46.

[72] UN doc. A/AC.96/SR.472 (1992), para. 71 (USA): 'The number of women who were still victims of rape was the best example of the failure of traditional protection measures.'

[73] 'Note on Certain Aspects of Sexual Violence against Women': UN doc. A/AC.96/822 (12 Oct. 1993). Originally issued as a 'conference room paper', it was re-issued as a session document at the express request of the Executive Committee: *Report* of the 44th Session: UN doc. A/AC.96/821, para. 21(m).

[74] Executive Committee Conclusion No. 73 (1993) on Refugee Protection and Sexual Violence. Guidelines on preventing and responding to sexual violence have also been drafted: 'Report of the Working Group on Refugee Women and Refugee Children': UN doc. EC/SCP/85 (5 Jul. 1994), para. 42. As part of overall policy, it was proposed that UNHCR sign 'gender clauses' with implementing partners, such as NGOs, requiring them to provide equal and appropriate benefits to refugee women, and to employ female staff members in relevant functions: ibid., para. 56. Extracts from the guidelines were published in 7 *IJRL* (1995). See also, Verdirime, G., 'Testing the Effectiveness of International Norms: UN Humanitarian Assistance and Sexual Apartheid in Afghanistan', 23 *HRQ* 733 (2001).

[75] UNGA res. 48/104, 20 Dec. 1993; Charlesworth, H., 'The Declaration on the Elimination of All Forms of Violence against Women', *ASIL Insight*, No. 3, (1994).

[76] See also UNHCR, Guidelines on International Protection: 'The application of Article 1A(2) of the 1951 Convention/1967 Protocol relating to the Status of Refugees to victims of trafficking and persons at risk of being trafficked', HCR/GIP/06/07, 7 Apr. 2006.

[77] See UNHCR, 'Report on the High Commissioner's Five Commitments to Refugee Women', Standing Committee, 33rd meeting, doc. EC/55/SC/CRP.17, 13 Jun. 2005; UNHCR, 'Operational

1.3.3 Child refugees

The need for special care and protection for *all* children was first recognized internationally in the 1924 League of Nations declaration on the rights of the child.[78] Though followed by a series of similar and related declarations,[79] another sixty-five years were to pass before the international community acknowledged both the very special status of children, and the value of States entering into a treaty on their behalf. The 1989 UN Convention on the Rights of the Child, now ratified by 193 States, is a critical milestone in legal protection generally. In fact, however, neither the 1951 Convention nor the Convention on the Rights of the Child, so far as they address the situation of children as refugees, provide an entirely satisfactory legal basis. The 1951 Convention does little more than recommend measures to ensure family unity and protection, and provide for access at least to primary education. Article 22 of the Convention on the Rights of the Child (CRC89) endorses the entitlement of refugee children to 'appropriate protection and humanitarian assistance', but essentially by cross-referencing the body of the Convention and other international instruments, while emphasizing cooperation in tracing and family reunion.[80] On the other hand, and unlike many other human rights treaties, the Convention has no general derogation clause for times of emergency. Consequently, it may ensure that in some circumstances children are better protected than adults.[81] States parties to CRC89 undertake to 'respect and ensure the rights' proclaimed to 'each child within their jurisdiction'. A child who takes refuge in the territory of a State party benefits as much from its provisions as child nationals of that country.

The idea of the child as someone entitled to *special protection* derives in part from the specific context of the 1949 Geneva Conventions and international humanitarian law—the laws of war. States are obliged, for example, to allow the free passage of assistance intended for children under 15 and expectant mothers, or required to

Protection in Camps and Settlements: A reference guide of good practices in the protection of refugees and other persons of concern', (2006), 14 (age, gender, and diversity mainstreaming), 79 (sexual- and gender-based violence—prevention and response); UNHCR, 'Policy on Refugee Women and Guidelines on Their Protection: An Assessment of Ten Years of Implementation.' An independent assessment by the Women's Commission for Refugee Women and Children, May 2002; UNHCR, Global Consultations on International Protection, doc. EC/GC/02/8, Refugee Women, 25 Apr. 2002.

[78] Generally, see Ressler, E., Boothby, N. & Steinbock, D., *Unaccompanied Children: Care and Protection in Wars, Natural Disasters and Refugee Movements*, (1988).

[79] See, for example, the 1959 UN Declaration on the Rights of the Child and the 1974 UN Declaration on the Protection of Women and Children in Emergencies and Armed Conflicts.

[80] See UNHCR, 'Family Protection Issues', UN doc. EC/49/SC/CRP.14, 4 Jun. 1999, in 11 *IJRL* 583 (1999).

[81] See Cohn, I., 'The Convention on the Rights of the Child: What it Means for Children in War,' 3 *IJRL* 291 (1991); under CRC89, there is thus no possibility to derogate from arts. 37 or 40 (torture, arbitrary detention, administration of justice guarantees); McCallin, M., 'The Convention on the Rights of the Child: An Instrument to Address the Psychosocial Needs of Refugee Children', 2 *IJRL Special Issue—September 1990*, 82; Cohen, C. P., 'The Rights of the Child: Implications for Change in the Care and Protection of Refugee Children' 3 *IJRL* 675 (1991).

facilitate the good functioning of institutions for the care of children in occupied territory.[82] The 1977 Additional Protocols go further, expressly confirming the special protection due to children. Article 77 of *Additional Protocol I*,[83] declares in its opening paragraph that:

Children shall be the object of special respect and shall be protected against any form of indecent assault. The Parties to the conflict shall provide them with the care and aid they require, whether because of their age or for any other reason.

Both the Geneva Conventions and the Additional Protocols repeatedly link the protection of the child to the maintenance of *family life*.[84] Even in cases of internment, families should be kept together, and every effort made to promote the reunion of families separated by reason of armed conflict. The general intent is to preserve family life and, by inference, the natural process of child development. Similar objectives are clear in the human rights context, where States have recognized that the family should receive 'protection by society and the State'; and that 'special measures of protection and assistance should be taken on behalf of all children and young persons'.[85] Together with the principle of the best interests of the child as a primary consideration,[86] these principles put in question any solution for child refugees that might either 'officially' remove the child from the actual or potential family environment, or have the effect of leaving the child without care and support, for example, on return to the country of origin when family have not been found and interim arrangements in the country of refuge are no longer viable.[87]

UNHCR brought the situation of refugee children before the Executive Committee in 1987, stating its intention to include within its protection and assistance activities, 'refugees, asylum seekers and displaced persons of concern to UNHCR, up to the age of 18, unless under applicable national law, the age of majority is less'.[88] In a comprehensive conclusion adopted the same year, the Executive Committee condemned the violence often facing refugee children, reiterated the 'widely-recognized principle that children must be among the first to receive protection and assistance', and recognized that the situation of refugee children 'often gives rise to special protection and assistance problems as well as to problems in

---

[82] A complete account of the provisions intended to benefit children during armed conflict is beyond the scope of the present analysis. Some twenty-five articles in the Geneva Conventions and the Additional Protocols deal with the special protection of children.

[83] See also art. 4, *Additional Protocol II*, confirming the obligation to provide children with the requisite care and aid, and referring expressly to education, family reunion, limitations on recruitment, and temporary evacuation.

[84] See Singer, S., 'The protection of children during armed conflict situations', *International Review of the Red Cross*, May–June 1986, 133.

[85] Art. 23(1) ICCPR66; and art. 10(3) ICESR66, respectively.

[86] Art. 3(1) CRC89; see also art. 4, 1990 African Charter on the Rights and Welfare of the Child.

[87] For the work of the Committee on the Rights of the Child, see <http://www.ohchr.org/english/bodies/crc/>.

[88] UNHCR, 'Note on Refugee Children': UN doc. E/SCP/46, 9 Jul. 1987, para. 8.

the area of durable solutions'.[89] In 1988, UNHCR issued the first edition of its *Guidelines on Refugee Children*, confirming its policy not only to intervene with governments to ensure that they defend the safety and liberty of refugee children, but also 'to assume direct responsibility in many situations for protecting the safety and liberty of refugee children'. Revised in 1994, these *Guidelines* recognize the centrality of CRC89 as 'a normative frame of reference' for UNHCR's action, laying down legally required standards and legally established goals.[90] The sections on particularly vulnerable children and solutions reflect that content.[91]

The *Guidelines* emphasize that all work with children must be founded on detail and verification, and that action should begin as soon as possible to trace relatives and to promote family reunion.[92] Children can become separated for many reasons, including abduction, when they are sent out of the country of origin by parents who remain behind, or when parents return home. Military recruitment of minors,[93] detention or internment of parents, and the actions of aid workers have also led to children being separated from their families.[94]

Where tracing is successful, family reunion can still be delayed, for example, because of immigration restrictions.[95] Several States have made reservations to CRC89 provisions on family reunion, despite the importance otherwise given to the family as the basic unit of society. Restrictions on family reunion possibilities also result from the conditions attached to certain types of status, such as temporary

---

[89] Executive Committee Conclusion No. 47; see also Executive Committee Conclusion No. 59. The Executive Committee has adopted conclusions on refugee children every year since 1991, although none as comprehensive as that adopted in 1987. See also 'UNHCR Policy on Refugee Children': UN doc. EC/SCP/82 (6 Aug. 1993); 'Programming for the Benefit of Refugee Children': UN doc. EC/SC.2/CRP.15 (25 Aug. 1993); *Report* of the Working Group on Refugee Women and Refugee Children: UN doc. EC/SCP/85 (5 Jul. 1994).

[90] UNHCR, *Refugee Children: Guidelines on Protection and Care*, (1994), 19. Also, 'UNHCR Policy on Refugee Children': UN doc. EC/SCP/82 (6 Aug. 1993)—identifying the primary goals as ensuring the protection and healthy development of refugee children and durable solutions appropriate to immediate and long-term developmental needs (para. 25); 'Report of the Working Group on Refugee Women and Refugee Children': UN doc. EC/SCP/85 (5 Jul. 1994).

[91] UNHCR, *Guidelines*, 121–49; see also, UNHCR, 'Report on the High Commissioner's Five Global Priority Issues for Refugee Children', Standing Committee, 36th meeting, doc. EC/57/SC/CRP.16, 6 Jun. 2006; 'Meeting the rights and protection needs of refugee children'—An independent evaluation of the impact of UNHCR's activities, Valid International, Oxford, UK, HCR doc. EPAU/2002/02, May 2002.

[92] Ibid., 128–9. Close cross-border cooperation is also essential, but may be difficult to arrange in highly politicized or conflict situations. Computerized tracing systems are beginning to be developed, and other agencies, such as the International Committee of the Red Cross (ICRC), have considerable long-term experience in tracing family members separated as a result of conflict; coordination with such agencies is essential in order to enhance the prospects of finding separated family members. See ICRC, *Inter-Agency Guiding Principles on Unaccompanied and Separated Children*, (Jan. 2004); UNGA res. 56/136, 'Assistance to unaccompanied refugee minors', 16 Dec. 2001; UNHCR, 'Guidelines on Policies and Procedures in dealing with Unaccompanied Children Seeking Asylum', Feb. 1997. [93] See Cohn, I. & Goodwin-Gill, G. S., *Child Soldiers*, (1994), 77–8, 152–3.

[94] UNHCR, *Guidelines*, above n. 90, 122.

[95] Jastram, K. & Newland, K., 'Family Unity & Final Act, 1951 UN Conference', in Feller, E., Türk, V. & Nicholson, F., *Refugee Protection in International Law*, (2003), 555.

protection which, although they facilitate the grant of refuge, may be so circumscribed as to frustrate fundamental rights relating to the family, and seriously undermine the best interests of the child.[96]

The situation of refugee children differs substantially from that of children still living in their country of birth. They may be orphaned, with relatives in different countries, and they may be living with an unrelated family which would like to adopt them.[97] Reaching the most appropriate solution, however, becomes more difficult when there is no national decision-making body competent to make or confirm arrangements for a child's future. For example, UNHCR recognizes that while family reunion is the primary aim for unaccompanied refugee children, adoption can be considered, where reunion either would not be in the best interests of the child, or is not likely to be realized within a reasonable time, normally at least two years.[98]

Although UNHCR considers that the authorities of the country of asylum have the necessary legal responsibility to take adoption decisions, in practice such States do not always accept that refugee children on their territory are 'habitually resident' within the meaning of the Hague Convention in respect of Intercountry Adoption.[99] The situation is further complicated by the fact that in a 'normal' inter-country adoption, the State of origin also bears a substantial responsibility to decide whether the child should benefit.[100]

These jurisdictional and practical concerns in the area of adoption seem equally valid with respect to international child abduction. The 1980 Hague Convention[101] is again premised on the relatively 'normal' situation of interference by one party with another's custody rights. It aims 'to protect children internationally from the harmful effects of their wrongful removal or retention and to establish

---

[96] Recognizing this basic premise, the UNHCR/UNICEF guidelines on evacuation of children from conflict areas emphasize that the first priority is to enable families to meet the needs of children in their care; and the second, if evacuation is considered necessary, 'that children be evacuated as part of a family unit, children being kept with their primary care givers': UNICEF & UNHCR, *Evacuation of Children from Conflict Areas: Considerations and Guidelines*, Geneva, 1992, 23. Where evacuation without parents occurs, records must be kept and the operation closely monitored with a view to bringing about family reunion as soon as possible.

[97] *Evacuation of Children*, above note, 22.

[98] UNHCR, *Guidelines*, 130–1. Adoption is also not to be carried out if it against the expressed wishes of the child or the parent; or if 'voluntary repatriation in conditions of safety and dignity appears feasible in the near future and options in the child's country of origin would provide better for the psychological and cultural needs of the child than adoption in the country of asylum or a third country': ibid., 131. See also McLeod, M., 'Legal Protection of Refugee Children separated from their Parents: Selected Issues', 27 *International. Migration*. 295 (1989).

[99] Cf. *Convention on the Civil Aspects of International Child Abduction*, Explanatory Report by Elisa Pérez-Vera, (1980), paras. 66–7.

[100] See, for example, the extensive scope of art. 4, *1993 Convention on Protection of Children and Co-operation in respect of Intercountry Adoption*; also, UNGA res. 41/85, 3 Dec. 1986, 'Declaration on Social and Legal Principles relating to the Protection and Welfare of Children, with Special Reference to Foster Placement and Adoption Nationally and Internationally'.

[101] *Convention on the Civil Aspects of International Child Abduction*, adopted by the Fourteenth Session of the Hague Conference on Private International Law, 25 Oct. 1980: <http://hcch.net>.

procedures to ensure their prompt return to the State of their habitual residence'. Children *are* abducted in the course of refugee movements; some are taken forcibly into a country of asylum, others are abducted from refugee camps and settlements, for example, to work or take part in military operations, and still others are targeted for 'illegal' adoption. Although some cases of abduction will involve removal in the sense of the 1980 Hague Convention, the greatest need is for comparable procedures to protect children against other, more common abductions.

The absence of rules, the lack of national and international bodies with jurisdictional competence and authority to act prejudices refugee children at both ends of the spectrum. On the one hand, they commonly fall outside the protective umbrella of the procedures and institutions established by the State under the relevant conventions; on the other hand, they can be denied timely access to the one durable solution that may be appropriate in their case, adoption, solely by reason of the inability or unwillingness of national authorities to act on their behalf.

In October 1994, the Special Commission on the Implementation of the 1993 Convention on adoption cooperation approved a recommendation which goes some way towards meeting needs and filling gaps. Referring to the situations of refugee children and children who are internationally displaced as a result of disturbances in their countries, the Special Commission proposed a number of principles to be considered in applying the Convention.[102] First, States should not discriminate against refugee and displaced children in determining whether they are habitually resident. Moreover, the 'State of origin' should be considered to be 'the State where the child is residing after being displaced'.[103] The competent authorities in any such State should take particular care in the case of proposed inter-country adoptions. They should ensure that 'all reasonable measures' have been taken to trace family and bring about reunion, and that repatriation for reunion purposes is not feasible or desirable, because the child cannot receive appropriate care or benefit from 'satisfactory protection'.[104] They should also obtain the necessary consents and, 'so far as is possible under the circumstances', ensure that all relevant information regarding the child has been collected.[105] In this regard, the authorities must also take particular care 'not to harm the well-being of persons still within the child's country'.[106]

If implemented, in practice, these recommendations may remedy some of the problems. Nonetheless, the variety of issues and difficulties standing between refugee and internationally displaced children and a solution to their problems strongly suggests that a supplementary legal instrument may be called for, in order

[102] Hague Conference on Private International Law, Special Commission on the Implementation of the Convention of 29 May 1993, 17–21 Oct. 1994, Work. Doc. No. 39 (21 Oct. 1994).
[103] Ibid., para. 1.
[104] With respect to tracing and repatriation, cooperation with other national and international bodies, particularly UNHCR, is recommended. Para. 4 further proposes that 'the States shall facilitate the fulfilment, in respect to children referred to in this Recommendation, of the protection mandate of the United Nations High Commissioner for Refugees'. [105] Ibid., para. 2.
[106] Ibid., para. 3.

to protect against abduction and unlawful adoption. Two related objectives may help delineate the nature of the solution and the agency for its implementation. First, such agency should be able to initiate and facilitate communication and assistance between the refugee child's country of origin and the country of asylum or potential 'receiving State', as appropriate, with a view to achieving a solution that is in the best interests of the child; and secondly, if no such links can be established, for any reason, it should be the international substitute for the Central Authority, if any, 'normally' competent for the child, and assume the role and responsibilities of such Authority as set out in the relevant conventions, adjusted to the particular situation of displacement. Whether that agency should be UNHCR, which already enjoys competence to provide international protection to refugees, and is recognized as entitled to act on their behalf in dealings with governments, is another matter. In the circumstances, an agency having child welfare and child rights experience may be better placed to assume these particular responsibilities.

1.3.4 Relief workers

In recent emergencies, relief workers have been the object of kidnappings, threats, aerial bombardment, and fighting between different factions.[107] The Security Council has repeatedly demanded that all parties take the necessary steps to ensure the safety of UN personnel, among others, in former Yugoslavia,[108] Cambodia,[109] Somalia,[110] and Mozambique.[111]

In 1992, the UN General Assembly also expressed its concern, and the following year urged support for initiatives 'concerning the safety of United Nations and associated personnel, in particular the consideration of new measures to enhance (their) safety'.[112] The resolutions in question refer specifically to 'international *and local staff* undertaking humanitarian work', which has obvious implications for jurisdiction and responsibility. The UNHCR Executive Committee also has endorsed the necessity of safety for relief workers.[113]

---

[107] See UN Commission on Human Rights, *Report on the Situation of Human Rights in the Sudan:* UN doc. E/CN.4/1994/48, paras. 34, 116.

[108] On behalf of UNPROFOR and international humanitarian agencies, see SC resolutions 758, 8 Jun. 1992, para. 7; 761, 29 Jun. 1992, para. 8; 770, 13 Aug. 1992, para. 6—'UN and other personnel engaged in the delivery of humanitarian assistance'; 859, 24 Aug. 1993, para. 4.

[109] SC res. 810, 8 Mar. 1993, para. 18.   [110] SC res. 897, 4 Feb. 1994, para. 8.

[111] SC res. 912, 21 Apr. 1994, preamble—expressing concern for the safety and security 'of personnel of non-governmental organizations who are assisting in implementing the peace process and in distributing humanitarian relief'. See also SC res. 966, 8 Dec. 1994, on Angola, para. 10.

[112] UNGA res. 47/105, 16 Dec. 1992, para. 20—UNHCR staff and other relief workers; see also UNGA resolutions 48/116, 20 Dec. 1993, para. 22; 49/169, 23 Dec. 1994, para. 17.

[113] See UNHCR, Executive Committee Conclusion No. 72 (1993); Executive Committee Conclusion on the Security of UNHCR Staff (1994), *Report* of the 45th Session (1994): UN doc. A/AC.96/839, para. 28; Conclusion on the Situation of Refugees, Returnees and Displaced Persons in Africa (1994): ibid., para. 29(m). On a related issue, see Wiseberg, L. S., 'Protecting Human Rights Activists and NGOs: What More can be Done?' 13 *HRQ* 525 (1991).

In 1993, the General Assembly established an *ad hoc* committee to draw up an international convention on 'the safety and security of United Nations and associated personnel'.[114] A year later the Sixth Committee (Legal) duly submitted a 29-article draft,[115] and in December 1994, the General Assembly adopted the Convention and opened it for signature.[116]

The Convention defines United Nations personnel as persons engaged or deployed by the Secretary-General as members of a military, police or civilian component of a United Nations operation, as well as officials and experts on missions of the United Nations and its specialized agencies. It extends to associated personnel, that is, persons assigned by a government or an intergovernmental organization, under agreement to carry out activities directly connected with a United Nations operation. Also included are those engaged by the Secretary-General or a specialized agency, or deployed by a humanitarian non-governmental organization or agency under agreement with the Secretary-General or with a specialized agency. However, the convention will *not* apply to a UN operation authorized by the Security Council as an enforcement action under Chapter VII of the Charter, in which personnel are engaged as combatants against organized armed forces and to which the law of international armed conflict applies.

The Convention obliges States parties to establish jurisdiction over those who commit crimes against personnel involved in United Nations operations; defines the duties of States to ensure the safety and security of personnel and to release or return personnel captured or detained; and calls on host States and the United Nations to conclude agreements on the status of United Nations operations and personnel.

2. Internally displaced persons (IDPs)

From an international law perspective, primary responsibility for the protection of and assistance to internally displaced persons rests with the territorial State, in virtue of its sovereignty and the principle of non-intervention. In practice, internal displacement often occurs as a result of civil conflict, in situations where the authority of the central government is itself in dispute, and its capacity or willingness to provide protection and assistance are equally in doubt.

---

[114] UNGA res. 48/37, 9 Dec. 1993, on the question of responsibility for attacks on United Nations and associated personnel and measures to ensure that those responsible for such attacks are brought to justice.

[115] UN doc. A/C.6/49/L.9. The Sixth Committee approved the draft resolution without a vote, although a number of States expressed reservations with respect to the consent of the receiving State, definitions, transit, extradition, and jurisdiction over nationals abroad.

[116] UNGA res. 49/59, 9 Dec. 1994—Convention on the Safety of United Nations and Associated Personnel; text also in 7 *IJRL* 526 (1995); Roberts, A. & Guelff, R., *Documents on the Laws of War*, (3rd edn., 2000), 623.

Internally displaced persons are by no means a new item on the international agenda. In the late 1940s, for example, Greece suggested that international help also be extended to those displaced internally by civil war. They might not need 'legal protection', but their material needs exceeded the resources of a country such as itself, ravaged by domestic conflict and foreign occupation.[117] Both Pakistan and India emphasized that the United Nations should take a universal approach, not excluding refugees merely by reason of the fact that they possessed the nationality of the country in which they now found themselves. The Pakistani representative noted that statelessness, or lack of legal protection, might be a problem, but it was perhaps the least of misfortunes for those dying of disease and starvation.[118] Eleanor Roosevelt, for the United States, on the other hand, stressed that the United Nations' responsibility should be to provide for a specific category of refugees, namely, those who required *legal* protection. Refugees within their own countries, who still enjoyed the protection of their governments, did not come within the scope of the discussion, though they might be in great need of material assistance.[119]

UNHCR's relief and rehabilitation programmes for refugees and returnees have included those 'displaced within the country' since at least 1972, when ECOSOC and the General Assembly endorsed operations in the Sudan.[120] The same year the General Assembly kept the mandate door open by asking the High Commissioner to continue to participate, at the Secretary-General's request, in 'those humanitarian endeavours of the United Nations for which his Office has particular expertise and experience'.[121] Resolutions in later years contained frequent references to 'displaced persons', though generally without qualification as internal or external. So far as the context remained assistance activities to refugees, returnees and displaced persons,[122] it is reasonable to infer an expectation that such programmes might usefully benefit the internally displaced; this is also in line with the then growing recognition of the necessity to link assistance for refugees and returnees to the general question of development.

[117] See UNGAOR, 4th Sess., Third Committee, Summary Records, 110 (1949).

[118] Ibid., 116 (Pakistan), 123 (India), 128 (Pakistan), 144 (India, stating that it was not convinced of the need for an international organization whose sole responsibility would be to provide legal protection, when its own refugees were dying of starvation), 146 (Pakistan).

[119] Ibid., 132. With what seems irony in retrospect, Mrs Roosevelt also commented on the need to preserve the essentially deliberative character of the United Nations, in face of the increasing tendency to drive the organization into the field of international relief: ibid., 135. See also UNGAOR, 4th Sess., Plenary, 2 Dec. 1949, 473.

[120] See ECOSOC res. 1705(LIII), 27 Jul. 1972, referring to Sudan and to 'the assistance required for voluntary repatriation, rehabilitation and resettlement of the refugees returning from abroad, as well as of persons displaced within the country'; also UNGA res. 2958(XXVII), 12 Dec. 1972.

[121] UNGA res. 2956(XXVII), 12 Dec. 1972. Para. 9 of the UNHCR Statute requires the High Commissioner to 'follow policy directives' from the General Assembly and ECOSOC and to 'engage in such additional activities ... as the General Assembly may determine within the limits of the resources placed at his disposal'.

[122] See, for example, UNGA resolutions 3454(XXX), 9 Dec. 1975; 31/35, 30 Nov. 1976; 34/60, 29 Nov. 1979; 35/41, 25 Nov. 1980; 40/118, 13 Dec. 1985.

In the period 1988–91, the General Assembly, under pressure from major donors, began to emphasize the necessity for better *co-ordination* of relief programmes for the internally displaced,[123] a task initially entrusted to UNDP Resident Representatives.[124] In 1990, ECOSOC requested a system-wide review to assess the experience and capacity of UN organizations involved in assistance to all refugees, displaced persons, and returnees,[125] which was duly followed by the Commission on Human Rights focusing on the need of internally displaced persons (IDPs) for relief assistance *and* protection.[126] The Commission requested the Secretary-General to appoint a representative on IDPs, a role entrusted to Francis Deng in July 1992 (and assumed by Walter Kälin in 2004). The Representative presented the first of several reports the following year,[127] and identified his goal as the development of 'a doctrine of protection specifically tailored to the needs of the internally displaced'.[128]

In 1996, the Representative presented his final report,[129] identifying a number of gaps relating to the applicability and application of existing international legal norms to the special circumstances of IDPs. In addition to normative gaps, where the law simply did not cover particular protection needs of IDPs,[130] there were 'consensus gaps', relating to a lack of agreement about how general norms in humanitarian or human rights law might be applied to the specific needs of the internally displaced,[131] and 'applicability gaps', concerning the non-applicability of legal principles to particular displacement contexts. For example, displacement occurring in a situation of generalized violence rather than armed conflict would

---

[123] UNGA res. 43/116, 8 Dec. 1988. Cf. Plender, R., 'The Legal Basis of International Jurisdiction to Act with Regard to the Internally Displaced', 6 *IJRL* 345 (1994).

[124] UNGA resolutions 44/136, 15 Dec. 1989; 45/137, 14 Dec. 1990.

[125] ECOSOC res. 1990/78, 27 Jul. 1990, para. 1.

[126] CHR res. 1992/73, 5 Mar. 1992; UN doc. E/CN.4/1992/L.11/Add.6; CHR res. 1991/25, 5 Mar. 1991. See also *Analytical Report* of the Secretary-General on Internally Displaced Persons: UN doc. E/CN.4/1992/23, 14 Feb. 1992.

[127] 'Comprehensive Study on the Human Rights Issues relating to Internally Displaced Persons': UN doc. E/CN.4/1993/35; Internally Displaced Persons. *Report* of the Representative of the Secretary-General: UN doc. E/CN.4/1994/44; See the series of addenda, 'Profiles in Displacement': Sri Lanka: UN doc. E/CN.4/1994/44/Add.1 (25 Jan. 1994); Colombia: UN doc. E/CN.4/1995/50/Add.1 (3 Oct. 1994); Burundi: UN doc. E/CN.4/1995/50/Add.2 (28 Nov. 1994); published in 14 *RSQ*, Nos. 1 & 2, (1995); also, Deng, F. M., 'The International Protection of the Internally Displaced', 7 *IJRL Special Issue—Summer 1995* 74.

[128] UN doc. E/CN.4/1994/44, para. 28; text in 6 *IJRL* 291 (1994); also UN doc. E/CN.4/1995/50; text in 14 *RSQ*, Nos. 1 & 2, 192 (1995). For suggestions on the standards issue, see Petrasek, D., 'New Standards for the Protection of Internally Displaced Persons: A Proposal for a Comprehensive Approach', 14 *RSQ*, Nos. 1 & 2, 285 (1995).

[129] 'Internally Displaced Persons: Compilation and Analysis of Legal Norms': UN doc. E/CN.4/1996/52/Add.2, 5 Dec. 1995, transformed into a field handbook: UNHCR, *International Legal Standards applicable to the Protection of Internally Displaced Persons: A Reference Manual for UNHCR Staff*, Geneva, 1996; 'Compilation and Analysis of Legal Norms, Part II: Legal Aspects relating to the Protection against Arbitrary Displacement': UN doc. E/CN.4/1998/53/Add.1, 11 Feb. 1998.

[130] 'Internally Displaced Persons: Compilation and Analysis of Legal Norms', UN doc. E/CN.4/1996/52/Add.2, 5 Dec. 1995, para. 416.

[131] Ibid., para. 415. Cohen, R. & Deng, F. M., *Masses in Flight: The Global Crisis of Internal Displacement*, (1998), 123.

mean that humanitarian law, which might otherwise provide protection, would
not be triggered. Even in cases where humanitarian law clearly applied, there
remained questions about whether the protection attaching to special categories of
persons would also encompass the internally displaced.[132] Furthermore, humanitarian and human rights law can only formally bind States, not non-State actors.[133]

In direct response to the report, the 1998 Guiding Principles on Internal
Displacement sought to address these lacunae by identifying 'the rights and guarantees relevant to protection of the internally displaced in all phases of displacement'. They provide guidance to States as well as 'authorities, groups and persons
irrespective of their legal status'[134] and apply to all internal displacement contexts.
The Guiding Principles do not purport to create a new legal category of forced
migrant *per se*, but rather seek to elucidate, clarify and refine existing protection
norms under international law. For this reason, they provide only a 'descriptive
identification',[135] rather than a formal legal definition, of 'internally displaced
persons': 'persons or groups of persons who have been forced or obliged to flee or
to leave their homes or places of habitual residence, in particular as a result of or in
order to avoid the effects of armed conflict, situations of generalized violence, violations of human rights or natural or human-made disasters, and who have not
crossed an internationally recognized State border'.[136]

The Guiding Principles are not binding, but 'reflect and are consistent with
international human rights and humanitarian law and analogous refugee law'.[137]
While States and other actors cannot be held liable for their violation, except to

---

[132] The ICRC maintains that in situations of armed conflict, international humanitarian law
'remains fully adequate to address most problems of internal displacement': International
Committee of the Red Cross 'Internally Displaced Persons: The Mandate and Role of the
International Committee of the Red Cross', 838 *International Review of the Red Cross* 491 (2000).
[133] For analysis, see Phuong, C., *The International Protection of Internally Displaced Persons*,
(2004), 48–52.
[134] Guiding Principles, principle 2(1). For text, see Brownlie, I. & Goodwin-Gill, G. S., *Basic
Documents on Human Rights*, (5th edn., 2005), 220.
[135] Kälin, W., 'The Guiding Principles on Internal Displacement: Introduction', 10 *IJRL* 557,
560 (1998).
[136] Guiding Principles, para. 2. This definition responds to criticisms to the Representative's provisional definition, which required flight 'in large numbers'—a matter which is irrelevant to a definition premised on displacement and need. See 'Comprehensive Study on the Human Rights Issues
relating to Internally Displaced Persons': UN doc. E/CN.4/1993/35; also the similar definition proposed by the International Law Association: ILA Declaration of International Law Principles on
Internally Displaced Persons (29 July 2000), art. 1, and commentary in ILA Committee on Internally Displaced Persons, 'Report and Draft Declaration for Consideration at the 2000 Conference',
(2000), 5–8. Phuong argues that the ILA Declaration is much more abstract than the Guiding
Principles and offers little guidance on how it should be applied in practice: Phuong, *The International Protection of Internally Displaced Persons*, 67. The International Committee of the Red Cross
has criticized the Guiding Principles definition for operational purposes, 'as it covers a group that is so
wide and whose needs are so varied that it exceeds the capacities and expertise of any single organization'. It notes that some organizations narrow down the definition in practice: International Committee of the Red Cross, 'Internally Displaced Persons: The Mandate and Role of the International
Committee of the Red Cross', 838 *International Review of the Red Cross* 491 (2000).
[137] 'Introductory Note by the Representative of the Secretary-General on Internally Displaced
Persons Mr Francis M. Deng', OCHA *Guiding Principles on Internal Displacement*, (2nd edn., 2004).

the extent that they reiterate binding treaty or customary international law obligations, they are perhaps more comprehensive and wide-ranging than a binding instrument might have been.[138] Though the drafters took care to ensure that all principles had a solid foundation in existing international law, they also endeavoured 'to progressively develop certain general principles of human rights law where the existing treaties and conventions may contain some gaps'.[139] According to Phuong, the distinction is at times blurred, and certain provisions do amount to new law.[140] An example is the Guiding Principles' acknowledgement of IDPs' 'right to be protected against forcible return to or resettlement in any place where their life, safety, liberty and/or health would be at risk'.[141] Though persons who have crossed an international border are protected by the principle of *non-refoulement* in refugee and human rights law, there is no comparable right in general international law for those who have been forcibly displaced within their own State. However, the proscription of torture, inhuman, or degrading treatment or punishment in human rights law implies a right not to be removed to such treatment, wherever it occurs. Furthermore, other human rights, such as freedom of movement, may also be invoked in support of a principle of non-return.

The Guiding Principles are a welcome standard-setting step, but they are not self-applying and will not alone resolve the problems of mandates and coordination which have frequently hindered international responses to IDPs.[142]

UNHCR, whose growing involvement with IDPs had led it to publish internal guidelines in April 1993,[143] subsequently adopted the Guiding Principles as a normative means of addressing the issue, describing them as 'a useful set of standards against which to measure the protection objectives and promote dialogue with state and non-state actors of violence'.[144] Yet, UNHCR's involvement with

---

[138] Phuong, *The International Protection of Internally Displaced Persons*, 66. On shortcomings of the Guiding Principles, see ILA Committee on Internally Displaced Persons, 'Report and Draft Declaration for Consideration at the 2000 Conference', (2000), para. 3.

[139] Kälin, W., 'The Guiding Principles on Internal Displacement: Introduction', 10 *IJRL* 557, 561 (1998). Phuong notes that where a specific need of internally displaced persons was identified, but could not be linked to an existing authoritative legal provision, it was omitted: Phuong, *The International Protection of Internally Displaced Persons*, 60. [140] Phuong, above note, 60.

[141] Guiding Principles, principle 15(d). See generally Phuong, above n. 139, 61–5. Cf. ILA Declaration of International Law Principles on Internally Displaced Persons, 29 Jul. 2000, art. 5(2), which states only that '[i]nternally displaced persons shall not be detained or placed in an area which exposes them to the dangers of armed conflict and/or internal strife'.

[142] See, for example, Hovil, L. & Okello, M. P., 'Only Peace Can Restore the Confidence of the Displaced': Update on the Implementation of the Recommendations made by the UN Secretary-General's Representative on Internally Displaced Persons following his Visit to Uganda, Internal Displacement Monitoring Centre, Norwegian Refugee Council and Refugee Law Project, 2nd edn., Oct. 2006: <http://www.refugeelawproject.org/papers/reports/RLP.IDMC2.pdf>.

[143] UNHCR, 'UNHCR's Role with Internally Displaced Persons', IOM/33/93–FOM/33/93, 28 Apr. 1993. Prior to this, IDPs were considered in a desultory way by the UNHCR Executive Committee Working Group on Solutions and Protection: UN doc. EC/SCP/64, 12 Aug. 1991, paras. 43–9, 54(k), 55(l), but no substantive observations or recommendations emerged.

[144] UNHCR, 'Internally Displaced Persons: The Role of the High Commissioner for Refugees': UN doc. E/50/SC/INF.2, 20 Jun. 2000, 6.

IDPs is not uncontroversial.[145] Recognizing its lack of general legal competence for IDPs,[146] in 1993 it set out to explore the rationale for its engagement. Taking its lead from paragraph 14 of UN General Assembly resolution 47/105, it identified these as a *specific request* from the Secretary-General or other competent authority, and the *consent of the State* concerned.[147] At this time, it (appropriately) did not invoke article 9 of the UNHCR Statute, which states that '[t]he High Commissioner shall engage in additional activities, including repatriation and resettlement, as the General Assembly may determine, within the limits of the resources placed at his disposal', as a rationale for intervention. UNHCR's subsequent references to this provision as providing a legal basis for IDP activities are therefore incorrect, since its context is refugee-specific and it does not provide a blank cheque for protection activities generally.[148]

The Executive Committee endorsed this somewhat cautious approach, stressing also that UNHCR's involvement should focus only on situations that 'call for the Office's particular expertise', and pay 'due regard to the complementary mandates and specific expertise of other relevant organizations as well as the availability of sufficient resources'.[149] An Executive Committee Conclusion in

[145] Goodwin-Gill, G. S., 'UNHCR and Internal Displacement: Stepping into a Legal and Political Minefield', *World Refugee Survey 2000*, (2000), 26–31.

[146] UNHCR, 'UNHCR's Role with Internally Displaced Persons', IOM/33/93–FOM/33/93, 28 Apr. 1993; UNHCR, 'Internally Displaced Persons: The Role of the High Commissioner for Refugees': UN doc. E/50/SC/INF.2, 20 Jun. 2000, 5–6.

[147] Interestingly, the 1993 UNHCR guidelines acknowledge the possible role of other relevant entities, presumably authorities in fact, if not in law. UNGA res. 46/182, 19 Dec. 1991, on the Strengthening of the Coordination of Humanitarian Emergency Assistance, also stressed consent and respect for sovereignty, territorial integrity, and national unity: ibid., Annex, para. 3, but did not exclude the possibility of negotiating the provision of emergency assistance 'by obtaining the consent of *all parties concerned*': ibid., para. 35(d). One commentator has noted with respect to the discussions leading to Additional Protocol II of the 1949 Geneva Conventions that 'States strongly opposed any reference to offers of relief, even emanating from neutral third parties, which might constitute an interference in their internal affairs', and that Additional Protocol II consequently contains minimal provisions on relief (art. 18(2)): Macalister-Smith, P., *International Humanitarian Assistance: Disaster Relief Actions in International Law and Organization*, (1985), 31, cited in Plender, R., 'The Legal Basis of International Jurisdiction to Act with Regard to the Internally Displaced', 6 *IJRL* 345 (1994).

[148] See UNHCR, 'Internally Displaced Persons: The Role of the High Commissioner for Refugees': UN doc. E/50/SC/INF.2, 20 Jun. 2000, 9.

[149] UNHCR Executive Committee, General Conclusion on International Protection: *Report* of the 44th Session (1993): UN doc. A/AC.96/821, para. (s). The UN General Assembly affirmed this approach in subsequent resolutions: UNGA res. 48/116, 20 Dec. 1993, para. 12; UNGA res. 49/169, 23 Dec. 1994, para. 10; UNGA res. 50/152, 21 Dec. 1995, para. 10; UNGA res. 51/75, 12 Dec. 1996, para. 13; UNGA res. 53/125, 9 Dec. 1998, para. 16. Cf. the view of the Netherlands, favouring the assignment of 'general competence to UNHCR to provide protection to internally displaced persons and local populations under siege in refugee-like and potential refugee-generating situations': UN doc. A/AC.96/SR.482 (1993), para. 31. See also UNGA res. 48/135, 20 Dec. 1993, in which the General Assembly welcomed, 'the decision by the Executive Committee . . . to extend, on a case-by-case basis and under specific circumstances, protection and assistance to the internally displaced . . .' On developments in 2005, see Goodwin-Gill, G. S., 'International Protection and Assistance for Refugees and the Displaced: Institutional Challenges and United Nations Reform', Refugee Studies Centre, Oxford: <http://refugeelaw.qeh.ox.ac.uk>.

1994[150] emphasized that 'activities on behalf of internally displaced persons must not undermine the institution of asylum, including the right to seek and enjoy in other countries asylum from persecution'. It also laid great stress on the necessity for inter-agency cooperation.[151] Neither UNHCR nor States suggested that UNHCR should be granted a general competence for IDPs.

UNHCR's 1993 guidelines represent an attempt to refine the criteria for its engagement with IDPs, rather than an excursus on how it should protect them. Its revised guidelines of 2000 are perhaps even more pertinent in this regard, stipulating additional preconditions for intervention, namely, that UNHCR must have access to the population, adequate security for its staff, adequate resources, and 'clear lines of responsibility and accountability with the ability to intervene directly with all parties concerned, particularly on protection matters'.[152] These reflect operational rather than legal concerns, and are characteristic of UNHCR's functional (rather than protection-based) approach to IDPs. The political nature of UNHCR involvement in IDP situations is underscored by its discretion to decline to become involved in a particular displacement situation, on the basis of that situation's likely impact on UNHCR's non-political and humanitarian mandate, its impact on refugee protection and the institution of asylum, whether UNHCR's involvement can improve protection and find solutions (giving preference to operations where there are political efforts to resolve displacement), and the relevance of UNHCR's expertise and experience.[153]

Besides the UN agencies regularly working with the internally displaced, such as UNICEF, WHO and WFP, other organizations likely to be involved in assistance and related activities include IOM and the ICRC. The IOM constitution authorizes the provision of migration services to the displaced, and internal displacement is approached largely as an aspect of internal migration. The ICRC has a clear legal interest, deriving from the fact that most IDPs move as a consequence of armed conflict, and its mandate is to ensure the application of international

---

[150] For background, see UNHCR, 'Note on the Protection Aspects of UNHCR Activities on behalf of Internally Displaced Persons': UN doc. EC/1994/SCP/CRP.2, 4 May 1994; text in 6 *IJRL* 485 (1994). Also, *Report* of the 18–19 May 1994 Meeting of the Sub-Committee of the Whole on International Protection: UN doc. EC/SCP/89 (29 Sept. 1994), paras. 6–36. Cf. Petrasek, D., 'New Standards for the Protection of Internally Displaced Persons: A Proposal for a Comprehensive Approach', 14 *RSQ*, Nos. 1 & 2, 285 (1995); Norwegian Refugee Council & Refugee Policy Group, 'Roundtable Discussion on United Nations Human Rights Protection for Internally Displaced Persons', Nyon, Switzerland, Feb. 1993; Refugee Policy Group, 'Human Rights Protection for Internally Displaced Persons', Report of an International Conference, 24–25 June 1991.

[151] Executive Committee Conclusion No. 75 (1994), *Report* of the 45th Session, UN doc. A/AC.96/839, para. 20(r), (s)—referring to the leadership of the Emergency Relief Coordinator.

[152] UNHCR, 'Internally Displaced Persons: The Role of the High Commissioner for Refugees', UN doc. E/50/SC/INF.2, 20 Jun. 2000, 8.

[153] Ibid., 7–8. For an overview of UNHCR's involvement in IDP situations worldwide to May 2000: UNHCR, 'Internally Displaced Persons: The Role of the High Commissioner for Refugees': UN doc. E/50/SC/INF.2, 20 Jun. 2000, 12–23. For example, UNHCR declined requests for intervention in Cambodia and Zaire in 1992: Loescher, G., *The UNHCR and Global Politics: A Perilous Path*, (2001), 294.

humanitarian law. The ICRC's paramount consideration in any operation remains the interest of the victims, rather than attention to categories, or to ulterior objectives, such as the avoidance of transfrontier flight.[154]

Increasing international attention to the problems of IDPs,[155] their functional needs and institutional requirements, will likely continue to confront the traditional requirement of consent as a pre-condition to the provision of relief. The classical model of the sovereign State is hardly redundant after Iraq,[156] and although it may repay re-evaluation in light of the implications of membership in the United Nations, a number of States remain concerned at the extension of the UN's sphere of interest.[157] Nevertheless, it is increasingly difficult for States to resist criticism of internal policies and practices that result in displacement.[158] International 'findings' on these issues could conceivably become part of a process leading to the provision of international relief, even including protection, that is *not* contingent on request or consent, and not limited to the relatively rare instances in which State authority has effectively disappeared.

At this point, definitions will have a role to play, either in an operational sense, as triggers to action; or jurisdictionally, by delimiting the competence of different organizations. It is here, perhaps, that the criterion of size ('large numbers') may be an appropriate pre-condition to launching international assistance, while not having crossed a frontier may determine which agency should assume overall responsibility, for example, the Office for the Coordination of Humanitarian Affairs or UNHCR.[159]

---

[154] For a brief but clear statement of ICRC's role with IDPs, see International Committee of the Red Cross, 'Internally Displaced Persons: The Mandate and Role of the International Committee of the Red Cross', 838 *International Review of the Red Cross* 491 (2000); also Krill, F., 'The ICRC's Policy on Refugees and Internally Displaced Civilians', 843 *International Review of the Red Cross* 607 (2001).

[155] Cf. Council of Europe, Recommendation Rec(2006)6 of the Committee of Ministers to Member States on internally displaced persons, 5 Apr. 2006, with particular reference to the Guidelines and their authority.

[156] In April 1991, three States—Cuba, Yemen, and Zimbabwe—voted against SC res. 688, the sole and somewhat ambiguous 'authority' for humanitarian operations in northern Iraq.

[157] In the Commission on Human Rights in 1992, India, Bangladesh and a number of other Third World countries all expressed deep reservations on the proposal for an independent expert to study human rights issues related to the internally displaced. In Sept. 1992, China, India and Zimbabwe also abstained on SC resolutions 770 and 776 where, amongst other things, the Security Council endorsed military protection of humanitarian assistance and convoys of released detainees in former Yugoslavia. In 2000, a number of developing States expressed concern at the increasing prominence being given to internal displacement, and thirty States abstained from voting in favour of para. 20 of UNGA res. 55/74 (2 Dec. 2000), which stressed 'the continuing relevance of the Guiding Principles': see Goodwin-Gill, G. S., 'Paragraph 20 of General Assembly resolution 55/74', 13 *IJRL* 225 (2001); Phuong , C., *The International Protection of Internally Displaced Persons*, 71–2. State resistance appears to be moderating; see Goodwin-Gill, 'Institutional Challenges', above n. 149.

[158] See, for example, UNGA resolutions 47/142, 18 Dec. 1992, 48/147, 20 Dec. 1993, and 49/198, 23 Dec. 1994, expressing alarm at 'the large number of internally displaced persons and victims of discrimination in the Sudan, including members of minorities who have been forcibly displaced in violation of their human rights and who are in need of relief assistance and of protection'.

[159] See among others, Borgen, J. *et al.*, 'Institutional Arrangements for Internally Displaced Persons: The Ground Level Experience,' Norwegian Refugee Council, 1 *Report* (1995).

3. Solutions

A refugee movement necessarily has an international dimension, but neither general international law nor treaty obliges any State to accord durable solutions. Indeed, some consider such a development undesirable, as tending to relieve the country of origin of its responsibility to establish the conditions permitting return, while also 'institutionalizing' exile at the expense of human rights.[160] The 1986 General Assembly initiative on cooperation to avert new flows of refugees both reaffirmed 'the right of refugees to return to their homes in their homelands', but also the right of those not wishing to return to receive adequate compensation.[161] The former continues to hold primary position in the hierarchy of solutions, but the right of refugees to compensation has still a fairly weak normative base in international law and, like the putative duty to provide solutions, possibly little to recommend it. The subject of damages for the expulsion of foreign nationals remains controversial,[162] and there are few precedents concerning refugees.[163] Although the principle of compensating the victims of violations of human rights has much to commend it, introducing a financial substitute for State and community obligations risks lending respectability to ethnic, religious, and ideological cleansing.[164]

The fact that, apart from the duty of the State to readmit its nationals, solutions fall generally outside the area of legal obligation, justifies close attention to the policies and positions of States, particularly as revealed in statements in the UNHCR Executive Committee and in their practice. UNHCR's primary responsibility is to provide international protection to refugees and to seek 'permanent solutions for the problem of refugees by assisting Governments and, subject to the approval of the Governments concerned, private organizations to facilitate the voluntary repatriation of... refugees, or their assimilation within new national

---

[160] See views expressed by Australia in 1981 on the German Federal Republic's initiative regarding international cooperation to avert new flows of refugees: *Report* of Secretary-General: UN doc. A/36/582, 23 Oct. 1981, 5. Similar sentiments were expressed by other countries, including Belgium (at 9), Egypt (at 15), Qatar (at 36), with varying emphasis depending on each State's perception of the initiative. Cf. Executive Committee Conclusions No. 67 (1991), para. (g)—resettlement 'only as a last resort'; and No. 68 (1992), para. (s)—voluntary repatriation as 'the preferred solution'. For later discussion of some of the issues, see Anker, D., Fitzpatrick, J. & Shacknove, A., 'Crisis and Cure: A Reply to Hathaway/Neve and Schuck', 11 *Harvard Human Rights Journal* 295 (1998).

[161] UNGA res. 35/124, 11 Dec. 1980; 36/148, 16 Dec. 1981. On 'return' in the Palestinian context, see above Ch. 3, s. 3.2; Ch. 6, s. 1.2.

[162] Goodwin-Gill, *Movement of Persons*, 278–80.

[163] The indemnification of the victims of Nazi persecution by the Federal Republic of Germany is one of the few relevant precedents, as is the payment by the Government of Uganda, through UNHCR, of compensation to 'Asians of undetermined nationality' expelled in 1972; Goodwin-Gill, *Movement of Persons*, 216, n. 1.

[164] But see Lee, L.T., 'The declaration of principles of international law on compensation to refugees: its significance and implications', 6 *JRS* 65 (1993); also Lee, L.T., 'The right to compensation: Refugees and countries of asylum', 80 *AJIL* 532 (1986).

communities'.[165] It is to provide for protection by, among others, 'assisting...
efforts to promote voluntary repatriation or assimilation', and by 'promoting the
admission of refugees, not excluding those in the most destitute categories'.
Finally, the High Commissioner is authorized to 'engage in such additional activities, including repatriation and resettlement' as the General Assembly may determine.[166] The latter reference to 'activities' supposes an operational dimension to
UNHCR which, since the 1960s and early 1970s, has also provided assistance and
de facto protection to repatriating refugees and internally displaced persons, and
assistance to local populations affected by a refugee influx.[167]

Notwithstanding the weight of rule and principle, UNHCR's capacity to
obtain protection and asylum for refugees is often closely linked to, if not contingent on, its success in promoting solutions.[168] Evidently also, the absence or failure to provide solutions will have a destabilizing effect on populations, likely
leading to further displacement, or to what some States have characterized as
irregular movements.[169] The temporary nature of the refugees' predicament has
also frequently been acknowledged, particularly in the case of those fleeing internal
disorder resulting from independence struggles.[170]

3.1 LOCAL INTEGRATION

Although there is some authority for the proposition that a recognized refugee has
an expectation of 'asylum', in the sense of admission to residence,[171] the practice

[165] Statute, para. 1. UNGA res. 428(V), adopting the Statute, also calls upon governments to assist 'the High Commissioner in his efforts *to promote... voluntary repatriation'*. See generally, Luca, D., 'La notion de "solution" au problème des réfugiés', *Revue de droit international*, janv.–mars 1987, 1; Fonteyne, J.-P., 'Burden-Sharing: An Analysis of the Nature and Function of International Solidarity in Cases of Mass Influx of Refugees', 8 *Aust. YB Int'l Law* 162 (1983). [166] Statute, para. 9.

[167] To these specific or implied mandate responsibilities may now also be added the special humanitarian tasks entrusted to UNHCR, for example, in former Yugoslavia, including assistance and, within difficult limits, protection of populations at risk in their own land; however, these do not, strictly speaking, fall within the *mandate* of UNHCR, which remains refugee-specific.

[168] Cf. Executive Committee General Conclusions on International Protection (1990), *Report* of the 41st Session: UN doc. A/AC.96/760, para. 20(e); and No. 50 (1988), *Report* of the 39th Session: UN doc. A/AC.96/721, para. 22(e), noting the 'close nexus between international protection and solutions'.

[169] See Executive Committee Conclusion No. 58 (1989), *Report* of the 40th Session, UN doc. A/AC.96/737, para. 25(b), noting that irregular movements are largely due to 'the absence of educa-tional and employment possibilities and the non-availability of long-term durable solutions by way of voluntary repatriation, local integration and resettlement'.

[170] See, for example, UNGA res. 1500(XV), 5 Dec. 1960, and 1672(XVI), 18 Dec. 1961, regard-ing refugees from Algeria in Tunisia and Morocco; 1671(XVI), 18 Dec. 1961, regarding refugees from Angola; 2040(XX), 7 Dec. 1965, regarding African refugees generally; UNGA res. 2790(XXVI), 6 Dec. 1971, refugees from East Pakistan during the war of secession; Executive Committee Conclusion No. 18 (1980), para. (a).

[171] Among the most significant provisions of the EU Qualification Directive are art. 13, which pro-vides that 'Member States shall grant refugee status to a third country national or a stateless person, who qualifies as a refugee'; art. 21, which confirms that 'Member States shall respect the principle of *non-refoulement* in accordance with their international obligations'; and art. 24(1): 'As soon as possible

of States also provides evidence of resistance to local integration, particularly in situations of mass influx. The UNHCR Executive Committee adopted a Conclusion on Local Integration in 2005, but took the opportunity to reiterate the traditional hierarchy of solutions, when it reaffirmed that:

...that voluntary repatriation, local integration and resettlement are the traditional durable solutions, and that all remain viable and important responses to refugee situations; reiterat[ed] that voluntary repatriation, in safety and dignity, where and when feasible, remains the most preferred solution in the majority of refugee situations; [and noted] that a combination of solutions, taking into account the specific circumstances of each refugee situation, can help achieve lasting solutions...[172]

The Executive Committee also emphasized that there is no obligation to accord a solution by way of local integration, even for States party to the relevant refugee instruments. Local integration 'is a sovereign decision and an option to be exercised by States guided by their treaty obligations and human rights principles, and that the provisions of this Conclusion are for the guidance of States and UNHCR when local integration is to be considered...'.

It is difficult to reconcile the absoluteness of this statement with the obligations which many States have expressly accepted, for example, in articles 2–34 of the 1951 Convention and articles II and III of the 1969 AU/OAU Convention. Neither instrument, of course, contains obligations in regard to specific solutions; the AU/OAU Convention comes nearest, so far as States undertake to 'use their best endeavours consistent with their respective legislations to receive refugees and to secure the settlement of...refugees', and to accord temporary residence where the refugee 'has not received the right to reside in any country'.[173] The fact is, however, that the continuing gap between *non-refoulement* and a solution lies very much at the heart of the problems facing the 6.2 million refugees in 38 'protected situations' worldwide, who find themselves without any immediate or even medium-term prospect of an end to their plight.[174]

In its 2005 resolution on UNHCR, the General Assembly also endorsed the approach to local integration in terms of 'a sovereign decision', even as it acknowledged that allowing local integration contributes to burden- and responsibility-sharing.[175]

---

after their status has been granted, Member States shall issue to beneficiaries of refugee status a residence permit...'. Effectively, a refugee recognized in the EU now has a 'right of asylum'.

[172] Executive Committee Conclusion No. 104 (2005), on Local Integration, *Report* of the 56th Session, UN doc. A/AC.96/1021. [173] Art. II(1), (5).

[174] See US Committee for Refugees and Immigrants, 'Anti-Warehousing Campaign': <http://www.uscr.org>.

[175] UNGA res. 60/129, 16 Dec. 2005, paras. 15, 16; Mangala Munuma, J., 'Le partage de la charge des réfugiés quand l'urgence s'impose', *Revue du droit des étrangers*, 2001, n° 113, 183; Noll, G., 'Prisoners' Dilemma in Fortress Europe: On the Prospects for Equitable Burden-Sharing in the European Union', 40 *German Yearbook of International Law* 405 (1997).

3.2 VOLUNTARY REPATRIATION

The UNHCR Statute calls upon the High Commissioner to facilitate and to promote voluntary repatriation. One of the unresolved theoretical paradoxes of
UNHCR's institutional responsibilities is the extent to which its duty to provide
international protection pervades the field of cessation of refugee status and voluntary return. Formal categories frequently provide inadequate descriptions of
refugee realities, and in practice it is often difficult to be certain whether circumstances have changed to such a degree as to warrant formal termination of refugee
status, even supposing that it was ever formally recognized. The assessment of
change involves subjective elements of appreciation, in a continuum where the
fact of repatriation may be the sufficient *and* necessary condition, bringing the situation or status of refugee to an end. Moreover, in the uncertain and fluid dynamics
which characterize mass exodus, this fact of return can itself be an element in the
change of circumstances, contributing to the re-emergence or consolidation of
stability and to national reconciliation.[176]

Voluntary repatriation has institutional and human rights dimensions. Both
the facilitation and the promotion of voluntary repatriation fall within the
province of UNHCR,[177] while the right to return to one's own country locates
such efforts squarely in a human rights context.[178] To ignore this dimension and

---

[176] Goodwin-Gill, G. S. 'Voluntary Repatriation: Legal and Policy Issues', in Loescher, G. &
Monahan, L., *Refugees and International Relations*, (1989), 255; Hofmann, R., 'Voluntary
Repatriation and UNHCR', 44 *ZaöRV* 327 (1984). Barutciski, M., 'Involuntary Repatriation when
Refugee Protection is no longer necessary: Moving forward after the 48th Session of the Executive
Committee', 10 *IJRL* 236 (1998); Hathaway, J. C., 'The Meaning of Voluntary Repatriation', 9 *IJRL*
551 (1997); and, for a strong critique of the notion of 'safe return', see Chimni, B. S., 'The Meaning
of Words and the Role of the UNHCR in Voluntary Repatriation', 5 *IJRL* 442 (1993). Chimni, B. S.,
'Perspectives on Voluntary Repatriation: A Critical Note', 3 *IJRL* 541 (1991); See also Cuny, F. C.,
Stein, B. N. & Reed, P., eds., *Repatriation during Conflict in Africa and Asia*, (1992); Stein, B. N.,
Cuny, F. C. & Reed, P., eds., *Refugee Repatriation during Conflict*, (1995); Larkin, M. A., Cuny, F. C., &
Stein, B. N., *Repatriation under Conflict in Central America*, (1991); Bhatia, M., 'Repatriation under
a Peace Process: Mandated Return in the Western Sahara', 15 *IJRL* 786 (2003).

[177] Statute, paras. 1, 8(c); UNGA res. 428(V), para. 2(d); Executive Committee Conclusion No.
65 (1991), *Report* of the 42nd Session, UN doc. A/AC.96/783, para. 21(j).

[178] See arts. 9, 13(2) UDHR48; art. 5 ICERD65; art. 12 ICCPR66; Executive Committee
General Conclusion on International Protection, *Report* of the 45th Session (1994): UN doc.
A/AC.96/839; para. 19(v); UNGA res. 49/169, 23 Dec. 1994, para. 9. Stavropoulou, M., 'Bosnia and
Herzegovina and the Right to Return in International Law', in O'Flaherty, M. & Gisvold, G., eds.,
Post-War Protection of Human Rights in Bosnia and Herzegovina, (1998), 123. Source countries are
sometimes less than enthusiastic about the return of those who have fled, however. When it sought
UNHCR assistance with repatriation in 1975, the Provisional Revolutionary Government of South
Vietnam emphasized that authorization for return fell within the government's sovereign rights, and
that each case would need to be examined: UN doc. A/AC.96/521, para. 105 (Observer for the
Democratic Republic of Vietnam). In 1974, the Chilean government legislated to prohibit the return
of Chileans on various grounds, such as national security, and a 1978 amnesty left generally unchanged
the legal situation of Chilean exiles wishing to repatriate: UN doc. A/33/331, para. 433; also
E/CN.4/1310, paras. 129–38 (Study of Reported Violations of Human Rights in Chile, Feb. 1979).

the legal implications arising from the concept of nationality would be to condone exile at the expense of human rights. Voluntary repatriation also involves a dimension of *responsibility*, namely, the responsibility of the international community to find solutions without 'institutionalizing' exile to such a degree that it disregards the interests of individuals and communities.[179]

A particular legal context for protection in repatriation is offered by article V of 1969 OAU Convention,[180] which stresses its essentially voluntary character, the importance of country of origin and country of refuge collaboration, of amnesties and non-penalization, as well as assistance to those returning. Because repatriation may itself cause serious practical difficulties, the General Assembly has authorized UNHCR involvement in rehabilitation and reintegration programmes,[181] and a fund for durable solutions was at one time proposed, to assist developing countries to meet some of the costs.[182]

A potentially active UNHCR role is anticipated in Executive Committee conclusions adopted in 1980 and 1985, the first of which, closely modelled on the OAU Convention, looks towards *facilitation*, rather than the promotion of return movement.[183] These conclusions recognize that voluntary repatriation is generally the most appropriate solution, while stressing the necessity for arrangements to establish voluntariness, in both individual and large-scale movements. Visits to the country of origin by refugees or refugee representatives for the purpose of informing themselves of the situation are seen as useful,[184] and formal guarantees for the safety of returnees are also called for, together with mechanisms to ensure the dissemination of relevant information.[185] The Executive Committee considered that 'UNHCR could appropriately be called upon—with the agreement of the parties concerned—to monitor the situation of returning refugees . . . '.

[179] On 'international co-operation' as a principle of international law, see below s. 4.

[180] For text see below, Annexe 2, No. 1.

[181] See UNGA res. 2956(XXVII), 12 Dec. 1972; 3143(XXVIII), 14 Dec. 1973; 3271(XXIX), 10 Dec. 1974; 3454(XXX), 9 Dec. 1975; 31/35, 30 Nov. 1976; 33/26, 29 Nov. 1978; 34/60, 29 Nov. 1979; and 35/41, 25 Nov. 1980.

[182] See UN doc. A/AC.96/569 and summary of debate in the Executive Committee: A/AC.96/SR.312, paras. 48–9 (30th Session, 1979); A/AC.96/SR.322, paras. 66–73; SR.323, paras. 14–36 (31st Session, 1980). Some States feared that UNHCR might, through the fund, become involved in developmental activities better left to other international agencies; see A/AC.96/SR.305, para. 16 and SR.319, para. 25 (statements by the Netherlands representative in 1979 and 1980).

[183] See Executive Committee Conclusion No. 18 (1980); UNHCR, Note on Voluntary Repatriation: UN doc. EC/SCP/13, 27 Aug. 1980; *Report* of the Sub-Committee: UN doc. A/AC.96/586, 8 Oct. 1980, paras. 17–29.

[184] Cf. Executive Committee General Conclusion on International Protection (1994), *Report* of the 45th Session: UN doc. A/AC.96/839, para. 19(v).

[185] *Report* of the Sub-Committee: UN doc. A/AC.96/586, paras. 23–4. The 1979 Arusha Conference on the Situation of Refugees in Africa recommended that appeals for repatriation and related guarantees be made known by every possible means: UN doc. A/AC.96/INF.158, paras. 3, 4. The importance of adequate information was also recognized in the 1946 IRO Constitution: see Annex I: Definitions, Part I, Section C, para. 1.

The Executive Committee looked at voluntary repatriation again in 1985[186] and 2004.[187] The right of the individual to return was accepted as a fundamental premise, but linked to the principle of the free, voluntary and individual nature of all repatriation movements. UNHCR's mandate was considered broad enough to enable it to take initiatives, including those which might promote favourable conditions. Some, indeed, considered that UNHCR had a responsibility to begin the dialogue, although others cautioned against its becoming entangled in political issues. UNHCR involvement with returnees was recognised as a legitimate concern, particularly where return takes place under amnesty or similar guarantee, although legal difficulties might arise with the government of the country of origin.[188]

3.2.1 *Facilitating and promoting*

The duty to provide international protection justifies a cautious distinction between *facilitation* and *promotion*.[189] The former presupposes an informed and voluntary decision by an individual, while the latter anticipates varying degrees of encouragement by outside bodies. For UNHCR, the principal consideration in a promotion context must be the interest of the refugee, and the protection of his or her rights, security, and welfare.[190] The individual's right to return stands together with other acquired rights; it does not just become a duty to leave, and a danger in agency-sponsored repatriation operations is that protection ultimately may be compromised. Some critics have challenged UNHCR's role and activities, so far as they appear to support State-inspired policies of 'containment', or promote 'preventive protection' oriented more to reducing admissions and costs, than to ensuring the interests of refugees. The promotion of (voluntary) repatriation by governments is seen as suspect, particularly when presented in the context of 'safe return', rather than on the basis of the voluntary choice of the individual.

---

[186] See Executive Committee Conclusion No. 40 (1985); UNHCR, Voluntary Repatriation: UN doc. EC/SCP/41, 1 Aug. 1985; *Report* of the Sub-Committee: UN doc. A/AC.96/671, 9 Oct. 1985; *Report* of the Executive Committee: UN doc. A/AC.96/673, 22 Oct. 1985, paras. 100–6; and for the summary records of debate: UN docs. A/AC.96/SR.385–400.

[187] Executive Committee Conclusion No. 101 (2004), on 'Legal Safety Issues in the Context of Voluntary Repatriation of Refugees'.

[188] In brief, Executive Committee Conclusion No. 40 (1985), also stresses the voluntary and individual character of repatriation and the necessity for it to be carried out in conditions of safety, preferably to the refugee's former place of residence, emphasizes the inseparability of causes and solutions, the primary responsibility of States to create conditions conducive to return, and that the UNHCR mandate is broad enough to allow it to promote dialogue, act as intermediary, facilitate communication, and actively pursue return in appropriate circumstances.

[189] Cf. Executive Committee General Conclusion on International Protection: *Report* of the 45th Session (1994): UN doc. A/AC.96/839, para. 19(y), underscoring UNHCR's role in 'promoting, facilitating and coordinating voluntary repatriation . . . , including ensuring that international protection continues to be extended to those in need until such time as they can return in safety and dignity . . .'.

[190] Ibid., para. 19(ii), endorsing the High Commissioner's efforts with respect to reducing or eliminating the threat of landmines.

UNHCR's protection responsibilities require it to obtain the best available information regarding conditions in the country of origin, and an accurate analysis of the extent to which the causes of flows have modified or ceased. Such information must in turn be shared with refugees and governmental and non-governmental agencies involved, including repatriation commissions and implementing partners. UNHCR's duty to provide international protection clearly obliges the Office to refrain from *promotion* where circumstances have not changed, or where instability and insecurity continue;[191] similarly, UNHCR ought to oversee the application of guarantees or assurances that are integral to the process of return (by being there, by close contact with returnees and implementing agencies, and by activating regional political and human rights mechanisms); and also to contribute morally and materially to successful re-integration in the national community.[192]

Country of origin and country of asylum may themselves co-operate to facilitate the return of refugees, either with or without UNHCR involvement. For example, although overtaken by persistent conflict, a 1988 agreement between Afghanistan and Pakistan recognized that all refugees should have the opportunity to return in freedom, free choice of domicile and freedom of movement, the right to work and to participate in civic affairs, and the same rights and privileges as other citizens. Pakistan, in turn, agreed to facilitate 'voluntary orderly and peaceful repatriation', and mixed commissions were also to be established.[193]

Although it can provoke logistical demands often difficult to meet, recognizing the primacy of the refugee's own decision generally makes good sense, even to the extent of *facilitating* repatriation in circumstances which, objectively considered, may be far from ideal.[194] It often does not matter what UNHCR, NGOs, or even

---

[191] The issue of coercion and pressure to return calls for close monitoring, and was central to the controversy which surrounded the second phase of repatriation from Djibouti to Ethiopia in 1986 and 1987; see Goodwin-Gill, 'Voluntary Repatriation', 255, 277–80. See also with respect to Bangladesh and Myanmar, Médecins sans Frontières/Artsen zonder Grenzen, 'Awareness Survey: Rohingya Refugee Camps, Cox's Bazar District, Bangladesh, 15 March 1995', The Netherlands, 1995; and for States' comments: UN doc. A/AC.96/SR.473 (1992), para. 32 (Australia); SR.476, paras. 45–51 (Bangladesh); SR.477, paras. 12–15 (Myanmar).

[192] Cf. Executive Committee General Conclusion on International Protection: *Report* of the 42nd Session (1991): UN doc. A/AC.96/783, para. 21(j), urging States, among others, to allow their citizens to return 'in safety and dignity to their homes without harassment, arbitrary detention or physical threats . . .'. For recent criticism of UNHCR's (lack of) action in a repatriation operation, see Human Rights Watch, 'No Sanctuary: Ongoing Threats to Indigenous Montagnards in Vietnam's Central Highlands', Vol. 18, No. 3 (C), Jun. 2006.

[193] See Bilateral Agreement between the Republic of Afghanistan and the Islamic Republic of Pakistan on the Voluntary Return of Refugees: 27 *ILM* 585 (1988); also Afghanistan-Pakistan–Union of Soviet Socialist Republics–United States: Accords on the Peaceful Resolution of the Situation in Afghanistan, Geneva, 14 Apr. 1988: ibid., 577. Cf. US Committee for Refugees, 'Left out in the Cold: The perilous homecoming of Afghan refugees', Dec. 1992. For other examples of agreements touching on the repatriation of refugees, see India–Sri Lanka: Agreement to Establish Peace and Normalcy in Sri Lanka, Colombo, 29 July 1987: 26 *ILM* 1175 (1987); South Africa-UNHCR, Memorandum of Understanding on the Voluntary Repatriation and Reintegration of South African Returnees: 31 *ILM* 522 (1992); UNHCR, *RefWorld*, DVD/CD-ROM, 15th edn., 2006.

[194] See Executive Committee Conclusion No. 40 (1985), para. (h), recognizing the importance of 'spontaneous return'.

States want; if refugees themselves choose to return, so they will, even to situations that outsiders consider highly insecure and undesirable. The virtue of voluntariness lies in the fact that it is an inherent safeguard against *forced* return, while being one manifestation of the 'right to return', to be exercised within a human rights framework, and whether or not Convention refugees in the strict sense are involved. Put another way, voluntariness (the choice of the individual) is justified because in the absence of formal cessation, the refugee is the best judge of when and whether to go back; because it allows for the particular experiences of the individual, such as severe persecution and trauma, to receive due weight; and finally because there is a value in individual choice. The voluntary character of repatriation is the necessary correlative to the subjective fear which gave rise to flight; willingness to return negatives that fear, but it requires equal verification.[195]

Voluntary repatriation will continue as the preferred solution to refugee problems, both as a matter of principle (it reflects the right of the citizen to return), and on the ground of self-interest (most States of refuge prefer to limit their obligations to refugees). The success of voluntary repatriation will depend on political factors, however, including the clearly expressed wish of the country of origin that the refugees should return, and on the personal choice of the refugees themselves. Independence, successful secession, an amnesty or other change of circumstances may indicate that the basis for a claim to refugee status has been removed, and the State of refuge must decide whether this is a sufficient or necessary reason for requiring the individual to quit national territory. This may be justified, for example, where the period of refuge has been relatively short, or where sheer numbers alone have meant that only temporary protection could be accorded. In other cases, however, the former refugee should benefit from standards generally applicable to resident aliens, including respect for any 'acquired right of residence' deriving from lengthy stay, integration, and local connections, establishment of business, marriage, and so forth.[196]

3.2.2 Safe return

From having been a description of the preferred consequence or effect of repatriation, the notion of 'safe return' has come to occupy an interim position between the refugee deciding voluntarily to go back home and any other non-national who, having no claim to international protection, faces deportation or is otherwise required to leave. In 1994, the Executive Committee linked temporary protection (admission to safety, respect for basic human rights, protection against

---

[195] See Goodwin-Gill, G. S., 'Voluntary Repatriation: Legal and Policy Issues', in Loescher, G. & Monahan, L., *Refugees in International Relations*, (1989), 255, where these ideas are developed more fully, with illustrations from a number of repatriation programmes. From a practical perspective, establishing the views of large numbers of refugees can pose problems of logistics and principle, touching issues of information and representative (or not) decision-making.
[196] See further below, Ch. 10, s. 5.2.

refoulement) to 'safe return when conditions permit'.[197] This reflects States' acceptance of an intermediate category in need of protection, but raises questions as to
both the obligation to protect and the modalities governing termination of protection. The former has been considered above, while the latter remains controlled
by international law only at its outermost boundary. In particular, although the
State remains bound by such provisions as prohibit torture or cruel and inhuman
treatment, no rule of international law appears formally to require that a State
proposing to implement returns take into account and act on assessments of
both 'legal' safety and safety in fact, including basic issues like absence of conflict,
de-mining, and a working police and justice system.[198]

Increasingly, 'safe return' has become part of the policy thinking of governments, but the central issue in the distinction between voluntary repatriation and
safe return is, Who decides?[199] International law provides no clear answers to situations involving large movements of people in flight from complex situations of
risk. If the conditions that caused flight have fundamentally changed, the 'refugee'
is no longer a 'refugee' and, all things being equal, can be required to return home
like any other foreign national. That a 'refugee' may voluntarily repatriate seems
to imply a decision to return while the conditions for a well-founded fear of persecution continue to exist. State proponents of 'safe return' effectively substitute
'objective' (change of) circumstances for the refugee's subjective assessment,
thereby crossing the refugee/non-refugee line.

So far as safe return *may* have a role to play in the construction of policy, its
minimum conditions include a transparent process based on credible information, which involves States, UNHCR as the agent of the interest of the international community,[200] and a representative element from among the refugees or
displaced themselves. These or equivalent means seem most likely to ensure that
the element of risk is properly appreciated, so reducing the chance of States acting
in breach of their protection obligations.

3.3 RESETTLEMENT

Resettlement is about refugees moving from a transit or country of first asylum to
another, or third, State. Resettlement policy aims to achieve a variety of objectives,
the first and perhaps most fundamental being to provide a durable solution for

[197] Executive Committee General Conclusion on International Protection (1994): *Report* of the
45th Session: UN doc. A/AC.96/839, paras. 19(r), (u).
[198] Cf. the potential (but out of context) implications for 'safe return' arguments of the House of
Lords' reasoning on 'internal flight' and refugee status in *Jamzi*, v. *Secretary of State for the Home
Department* [2006] 2 WLR 397, [2006] UKHL 5.
[199] Durieux, J.-F. & Hurwitz, A., 'How Many is Too Many? African and European Legal Responses
to Mass Influxes of Refugees', 47 *German Yearbook of International Law* 105, 154–5 (2005).
[200] Executive Committee General Conclusion on International Protection (1994), above n. 197,
para. 19(u) calls on UNHCR, amongst other matters, to provide guidance on the implementation of
temporary protection, 'including advice . . . on safe return once the need for international protection
has ceased'.

refugees unable to return home or to remain in their country of immediate refuge.[201] A further goal is to relieve the strain on receiving countries, sometimes in a quantitative way, at others in a political way, by assisting them in relations with countries of origin. Resettlement also provides significant potential for the development of a resource base for the return of professional and skilled personnel at some future time when repatriation may become viable; returns to El Salvador and Chile illustrate this process. Finally, resettlement contributes to international solidarity and to maintaining the fundamental principles of protection.[202]

Successive refugee crises in Indo-China, Latin America, and Europe, have underlined the necessity for States on occasion to go beyond financial assistance and to offer resettlement opportunities. This 'least preferred option'[203] may be dictated by a variety of factors, including political, economic, and ethnic pressures on the State of first admission, and concern for the security of the refugees themselves. States, however, have very different perceptions as to the desirability of various solutions. Broadly, these demonstrate (a) an emphasis on regional responsibility and local integration; or (b) an emphasis on global responsibility and a broadening of the resettlement burden; or (c) a resistance to local integration, with a corresponding emphasis on extra-regional resettlement. Certain States have also at times expressly accepted responsibility, as countries of first admission, to accept for local integration a proportion of asylum seekers, provided that other States lighten the burden by offering appropriate resettlement opportunities.[204]

Not surprisingly, the self-same reasons which may be advanced against resettlement by certain States (for example, their physical, demographic, and socio-economic limitations, together with the potential for culture shock and problems of adjustment for resettled refugees), are also relied on by other States unwilling to accept refugees for local integration.[205] Economic and social problems caused by large numbers of refugees, in both developing and developed countries,[206]

---

[201] Executive Committee Conclusion No. 22 (1981), IV, para. (3),(4).

[202] For a particularly coherent account of resettlement policy from the perspective of UNHCR, see Troeller, G. G., 'UNHCR Resettlement as an Instrument of International Protection', 3 *IJRL* 564 (1991); also, Bach, R. L., 'Third Country Resettlement', in Loescher, G. & Monahan, L., eds., *Refugees and International Relations*, (1989), 313; Salomon, K., *Refugees in the Cold War: Toward a New International Refugee Regime in the Early Postwar Era*, (1991), Ch. 5.

[203] 'Least preferred' by whom?

[204] This view has been expressed by Australia and adopted in regard to refugees disembarked on its shores after rescue at sea; see above, Ch. 4, s.4.2.

[205] See, for example, the views expressed by the Netherlands: UN doc. A/AC.96/SR.295, para. 2 and by UNHCR: ibid., SR.299, para. 13 (1978). On problems of adjustment faced by resettled refugees, see Chan, K. B. & Indra, D. M., eds., *Uprooting, Loss and Adaptation: The Resettlement of Indo-Chinese Refugees in Canada*, (1987); Beach, H. & Ragvald, L., *A New Wave on the Northern Shore: The Indochinese Refugees in Sweden*, (1982); Fifth Seminar on Adaptation and Integration of Permanent Immigrants (Geneva, 6–10 Apr. 1981), 19 *Int. Mig.* 1 (1981); Rutledge, P. J., *The Vietnamese Experience in America* (1992).

[206] See statements by Austria: UN doc. A/AC.96/SR.296, para. 1 (1978); SR.300, para. 29 (1979) and SR.325, paras. 46–7 (1980); and by Italy: ibid., SR.307, para. 48 (1979). On occasion, a commitment to resettlement has also been linked to attempts to 'cap' the numbers of spontaneous asylum seekers; see proposals by Denmark: UN doc. A/AC.96/SR.432 (1988), paras. 7–16.

as well as political and security factors, can likewise militate against local acceptance.[207]

At the individual level, however, resettlement can still mean the difference between life and death. Refugees may be denied basic human rights in the country of first refuge; their lives and freedom may be threatened by local elements motivated by racial, religious, or political reasons, or by attacks and assassinations directed from outside. The authorities in turn may be unable or unwilling to offer effective protection. In such circumstances, resettlement becomes not the solution of last resort, but the principal objective. Similar considerations apply to other categories such as children, the disabled, or rescue at sea cases, for whom the exercise of protection without prospect of solution is otherwise quite meaningless. UNHCR, States and the Executive Committee have also recognized that the special protection needs of women refugees may call for resettlement opportunities.

In a background paper entitled 'Resettlement as an Instrument of Protection', submitted to the Sub-Committee of the Whole on International Protection in 1991,[208] UNHCR emphasized the 'last resort' character of resettlement, to be pursued when it is the 'only available measure to guarantee protection and/or offer a refugee a future commensurate with fundamental human rights'. Besides security concerns, resettlement could also contribute to 'humanitarian protection', for women at risk,[209] torture victims, the physically or mentally handicapped, and certain medical and family reunion cases.[210] However, while over 1.2 million had been resettled out of South East Asia, particularly to protect 'first asylum', future resettlement, in UNHCR's view, would be more protection-oriented and involve

---

[207] These factors have been stressed repeatedly by first refuge countries; see statements by Djibouti: UN doc. A/AC.96/SR.307, para. 63 (1979) and SR.319, para. 54 (1980); Malaysia: ibid., SR.306, para. 81 (1979) and Indonesia: ibid., SR.308, para. 42 (1979). The settlement problems of refugees may be further exacerbated by the break-up of families; see Executive Committee Conclusion No. 24 (1981), para. 7 on tracing and family reunion. Family unity and the right to respect for family life and to protection of the family are recognized in most human rights instruments; see art. 16(3) UDHR48; arts. 17 and 23 ICCPR66; art. 8 ECHR50; see also Recommendation B, Final Act of the 1951 Convention. The Indo-China refugee problem highlighted the need to take account of traditional extended family relationships; incorporating recognition of such relationships in resettlement programmes can in turn cause problems, however, as where other migrant groups perceive themselves disadvantaged by comparison.

[208] 'Resettlement as an Instrument of Protection: Traditional Problems in achieving this Durable Solution and New Directions in the 1990s': UN doc. EC/SCP/65 (9 Jul. 1991); Troeller, above n. 202.

[209] Cf. Executive Committee Conclusion on Refugee Women (1988), *Report* of the 39th Session: UN doc. A/AC.96/721, para. 26, recognizing that refugee women face particular hazards, especially threats to physical safety and sexual exploitation, and calling for support for special resettlement programmes. See also Executive Committee Conclusion on Refugee Women (1989), *Report* of the 40th Session: UN doc. A/AC.96/737, para. 26(c); Executive Committee Conclusion No. 64 (1990), para. (a)(xi); and above, s. 1.3.2.

[210] UN doc. EC/SCP/65 (9 Jul. 1991), paras. 2, 3, 4. The 'vulnerable' categories potentially eligible for 'humanitarian protection' through resettlement were first defined in guidelines issued in 1990, with a sixth category of 'long-stayers'. Some States expressed concern at the narrow scope of 'vulnerable groups', and suggested additional categories, such as the elderly and children traumatized by war: *Report* of the Sub-Committee of the Whole on International Protection: UN doc. A/AC.96/781 (9 Oct. 1991), paras. 19–26, at 22.

smaller numbers.[211] Such down-grading of an important if specialized pillar of the solutions structure doubtless satisfied some of UNHCR's constituency at the time, but did little for refugees or international protection at large. Since then, UNHCR has raised the status of its resettlement division within the Department of International Protection, and the international commitment to resettlement has begun to recover.[212] A small number of countries provide places on a regular basis, and see resettlement as an important and effective means of making concrete the rhetoric of solidarity and cooperation.[213]

3.4 ASSISTANCE AND DEVELOPMENT

A distinction has sometimes been drawn between UNHCR's protection and assistance functions, particularly in light of the additional humanitarian activities periodically entrusted to it. In practice, however, protection and assistance activities have tended to mingle, as programmes were extended beyond local integration, employment, and self-sufficiency projects, to cover returnees and the internally displaced. There is no necessary, hard, and fast division between the humanitarian role of meeting material needs, and a legal interest in security and welfare, and at times a clear rights element may be present, for example in the provision of adequate food.[214]

By 1989, *refugee aid and development*[215] had become well established in the relief and assistance vocabulary, as a way of linking refugees and host communities. Integration programmes and large-scale repatriations almost always involve some sort of contribution to development: from roads, water supplies, and schools, to employment, the provision of seeds, farming equipment, and livestock. For agencies such as UNHCR, the question is to determine how far its responsibility extends, and to ascertain respective agency competence for promoting conditions conducive to voluntary repatriation, including support for sustainable

---

[211] UN doc. EC/SCP/65 (9 Jul. 1991), paras. 13, 14 (obstacles to resettlement); 15–19 (future resettlement). Basic statistics illustrate changing times: in the late 1970s/early 1980s, some 200,000 resettlement places were available annually, principally for those in camps in South East Asia; by the mid-1990s, places had fallen to around 50,000, notwithstanding a significant global increase in total refugee numbers.

[212] For explanations, criteria and practical information, see UNHCR, Department of International Protection, *Resettlement Handbook*, Geneva, 2004. See also UNHCR, 'New Directions for Resettlement Policy', UN doc. EC/51/SC/INF.2, 14 June 2001, in 13 *IJRL* 690 (2001); Troeller, G., 'UNHCR Resettlement: Evolution and Future Direction', 14 *IJRL* 85 (2002).

[213] See UNGA res. 60/129, 16 Dec. 2005, para. 11, welcoming progress in increasing the numbers of refugees resettled and following up on the Executive Committee General Conclusion on International Protection No. 102 (2005). The United States' annual intake of refugees was seriously reduced in the aftermath of the events of 11 Sept. 2001, and has only just begun to recover at the time of writing.

[214] See arts. 2, 11 ICESCR66, and the emphasis on international cooperation. See generally Alston, P. & Tomaševski, K., eds., *The Right to Food*, (1984).

[215] The terminology has now changed to 'DAR'—Development Assistance for Refugees; see UNHCR *Agenda for Protection*, Goal 5.

development, control of arms supplies and demining, and actually organizing and accompanying transport.

The inter-connectedness of assistance, protection and solutions is evident in international action with respect to the situations in Indo-China and Central America. The 1979 United Nations Conference on Indo-Chinese Refugees produced a package of undertakings with respect to material support and resettlement in favour of so-called first asylum countries in South East Asia.[216] Ten years later, the second international conference adopted a Declaration and Comprehensive Plan of Action (CPA) and 'noted with satisfaction' that durable solutions had been found for so many Indo-Chinese, 'as a result of combined efforts on the part of Governments and international organizations concerned'.[217] The Conference nevertheless accepted that a complex problem required a 'comprehensive set of mutually re-enforcing humanitarian undertakings'.[218]

A similar level of cooperation was endorsed by States represented at the May 1989 International Conference which adopted the Declaration and Concerted Plan of Action in Favour of Central American Refugees, Returnees and Displaced Persons.[219] This in turn recognized that solutions to the problems of refugees and displaced persons in the region were intimately linked to the peace process, to development and to economic cooperation. CIREFCA grew out of a political commitment to improve regional stability, and sought to incorporate solutions for the uprooted into a more comprehensive durable plan.

Although a protection component can be identified in the resolution of the problems of displacement in Indo-China and Central America, the contribution of each to the legal situation is far less clear, whether considered from an institutional or an individual perspective. While the principle of international cooperation between States may have been strengthened, the continuing place of protection within the operational mandate of an organization such as UNHCR, which is called on more and more to provide assistance, poses a range of institutional challenges that have yet to be resolved.

---

[216] See *Report* of the Secretary-General on the Meeting on Refugees and Displaced Persons in South East Asia, Geneva, 20–21 July 1979, and subsequent developments: UN doc. A/34/637.

[217] Draft Declaration and Comprehensive Plan of Action, approved by the Preparatory Meeting for the International Conference on 8 March 1989: 'Note by the Secretary-General': UN doc. A/CONF.148/2, 26 Apr. 1989, were adopted without amendment and by consensus at the June 1989 conference.

[218] Generally on the CPA, see Bronée, S. A., 'The History of the Comprehensive Plan of Action', 5 *IJRL* 534 (1993); Bari, S., 'Refugee Status Determination under the Comprehensive Plan of Action (CPA)' 4 *IJRL* 487 (1992); Helton, A. C., 'Refugee Determination under the Comprehensive Plan of Action; Overview and Assessment', 5 *IJRL* 544 (1993); Mushkat, R., 'Implementation of the CPA in Hong Kong: Compatibility with International Standards?', 5 *IJRL* 559 (1993).

[219] The process and plan of action came to be known as CIREFCA, after the Spanish acronym for the international conference. See also UNHCR, 'Consolidating Peace in Central America through an Inter-Agency Approach to Longer-Term Needs of the Uprooted. Report on the Conclusion of the CIREFCA Process': UN doc. A/AC.96/831, 31 Aug. 1994; Espiell, H.G., Picado, S. & Lanza, L. V., 'Principles and Criteria for the Protection of and Assistance to Central American Refugees, Returnees and Displaced Persons in Central America', 2 *IJRL* 83 (1990).

4. International cooperation

The general principle of cooperation with respect to persons moving across borders flows from the obligations assumed by Member States under the Charter of the United Nations, and as members of the international community.[220] Commenting on the typhus epidemic in Poland after the First World War and the resulting need for collective measures, Schwarzenberger observed that, 'No compulsion exists for a State to join in any such cooperative effort. It is its own self-interest which prompts it to do so.'[221] Although today the institutions of international cooperation are more comprehensive, more universal, and more firmly established, the underlying truth remains, emphasizing the degree to which cooperation in practice still depends upon the formal consent of States.

The *Declaration on Principles of International Law concerning Friendly Relations and Cooperation among States in accordance with the Charter of the United Nations* outlines the basic approach:

States have the duty to cooperate with one another, irrespective of the differences in their political, economic and social systems, in the various spheres of international relations, in order to maintain international peace and security and to promote international economic stability and progress, the general welfare of nations and international cooperation free from discrimination based on such differences.[222]

The principle of cooperation in the present context reflects recognition of the inherently *international* dimension to the movements of persons across borders.

Increasing numbers of refugees notwithstanding, the 1984 United Nations International Conference on Population found 'broad agreement' that through international cooperation within the framework of the United Nations an attempt should be made to avert the causes of new flows of refugees, with due regard to the principle of non-intervention in the internal affairs of sovereign States. There was nevertheless a 'need for *continuing international cooperation in finding durable solutions*... and for the provision of *support and assistance to first countries of asylum*'.[223]

The Comprehensive Plan of Action on the problems in South East Asia contemplated measures to deter clandestine departures from the country of origin,

---

[220] UN Charter, arts. 1, 13.1(b), 55, 56.

[221] Schwarzenberger, G., *Power Politics*, (2nd rev. edn., 1954), 228.

[222] See UNGA res. 2625(XXV), 24 Oct. 1970, Annex, Principle (d): The duty of States to cooperate with one another in accordance with the Charter. The resolution, which 'approves the Declaration', was adopted without vote.

[223] 1984 United Nations International Conference on Population, Recommendation 47: UNHCR, *Note* on the United Nations International Conference on Population: UN doc. A/AC.96/INF.170, 3 Sept. 1984 (emphasis supplied).

including mass media activities and regular consultation between the countries concerned; encouragement of regular departure (emigration/immigration) programmes; provisions for reception and temporary refuge for new arrivals; region-wide refugee status determination procedures; resettlement undertakings for long-stayers and for new arrivals found to be refugees; and repatriation of non-refugees. To ensure continued coordination and adaptation, a Steering Committee was established, consisting of 'representatives of all Governments making specific commitments' under the CPA.[224]

The undertakings given on such occasions, considered together with the actions thereafter introduced at national and regional level, are thus necessarily elements in the evolution of rules with respect to international cooperation in the relief and resolution of the problems of refugees and the displaced.

One of the most striking instances of a formal obligation to assist featured in article 254 of the 1989 Lomé IV Convention, concluded between the European Community and African, Caribbean and Pacific (ACP) countries.[225] Article 60 of its successor instrument, the 2000 Cotonou Agreement,[226] declares that financing may include support to 'humanitarian and emergency assistance including assistance to refugees and displaced persons', but article 72 expressly provides:

1. Humanitarian and emergency assistance *shall* be accorded to the population in ACP States faced with serious economic and social difficulties of an exceptional nature resulting from natural disasters, man-made crises such as wars and other conflicts or extraordinary circumstances having comparable effects. The humanitarian and emergency assistance shall be maintained for as long as necessary to deal with the emergency needs resulting from these situations...

3. Humanitarian and emergency assistance shall aim to...

(d) address the needs arising from the displacement of people (refugees, displaced persons and returnees) following natural or man-made disasters so as to meet, for as long as necessary, all the needs of refugees and displaced persons (wherever they may be) and facilitate action for their voluntary repatriation and re-integration in their country of origin...

Examples such as this show States' recognition of the need to cooperate, in particular, to ensure that movements across borders do not place an undue or disproportionate burden on receiving States. However, article 13 of the 2000 Cotonou Agreement pursues another, and by no means unrelated theme, declaring that migration, 'shall be the subject of an in-depth dialogue within the framework of

---

[224] Cf. Statement of the Fourth Steering Committee: Reaffirmation of the Comprehensive Plan of Action: 3 *IJRL* 367 (1991). A similar level of cooperation was endorsed by States party to the CIREFCA process; see above n. 501.   [225] For text, see 28 *ILM* 1382 (1989).

[226] The Cotonou Agreement is described as a 'Partnership Agreement' between the members of the African, Caribbean and Pacific Group of States, on the one part, and the European Community and its Member States, on the other part. It was signed in Cotonou, Benin, on 23 Jun. 2000, and came into force on 1 Apr. 2003.

the ACP-EU Partnership', and that the parties, 'reaffirm their existing obligations and commitments in international law to ensure respect for human rights and to eliminate all forms of discrimination based particularly on origin, sex, race, language and religion'. Paragraphs (2) and (3), however, emphasize that the primary focus of this article is on those legally residing or legally employed. While paragraph (4) puts 'normalising migratory flows' into a development context, paragraph (5) targets illegal immigration, prevention, return and readmission.[227] In practice, as a number of non-governmental organizations have pointed out, the 'dialogue' seems to have led in particular to the penalization of *emigration*, contrary to article 13(1) of the Universal Declaration of Human Rights.[228]

The connection today is probably inescapable. However, so far as the Cotonou Agreement also focuses on the situation of refugees and externally displaced persons, it may provide support for the principles recognized in the Preamble to the 1951 Convention relating to the Status of Refugees, if often imperfectly realized:

> *Considering* that the grant of asylum may place unduly heavy burdens on certain countries, and that a satisfactory solution of a problem of which the United Nations has recognized the international scope and nature cannot therefore be achieved without international co-operation,
> *Expressing* the wish that all States, recognizing the social and humanitarian nature of the problem of refugees, will do everything within their power to prevent this problem from becoming a cause of tension between States ...

A significant level of practical cooperation nevertheless exists, even if material contributions and political or moral support for the displaced waver and formal obligations are elusive.[229] Certainly, the principles of cooperation and international solidarity have been consistently endorsed within the Executive Committee of the UNHCR Programme. In 1988, for example, it reaffirmed that 'refugee problems are the concern of the international community and their resolution is dependent on the will and capacity of States to respond in concert and wholeheartedly, in a spirit of true humanitarianism and international solidarity'.[230] The General Assembly also regularly endorses a combination of principles and (recommendations for) practical action, and comprehensive responses to the

---

[227] Nevertheless, the Parties undertake 'to ensure that the rights and dignity of individuals are respected' in any procedure for the return of illegal immigrants, and that any relevant bilateral agreements should be concluded, 'with due regard for the relevant rules of international law': ibid., art. 13(5)(c).

[228] See Rodier, C., '«Emigration illégale»: une notion à bannir', *Libération*, 13 juin 2006; available at <http://www.migreurop.org/article922.html>; see also, Statewatch, 'The fallacies of the EU-Africa dialogue on immigration: EU-African ministerial conference on immigration, 10–11 July 2006': <http://www.statewatch.org/news/2006/jul/06rabat.htm>.

[229] Cf. Morris, N., 'Refugees: Facing Crisis in the 1990s—A Personal View from within UNHCR', 2 *IJRL Special Issue—September 1990*, 38; also, Guest, I., 'The United Nations, the UNHCR, and Refugee Protection—A Non-Specialist Analysis', 3 *IJRL* 585 (1991).

[230] Executive Committee Conclusion No. 52 (1988) on International Solidarity and Refugee Protection.

problems of persons moving across borders clearly depend upon significant measures of international cooperation for their success.[231]

National self-interest may prevail when States are confronted with population displacements on their borders, but national goals will often be best achieved through cooperation with others. Arguably, an emerging principle requires States to cooperate, in accordance with the principles of international solidarity and burden sharing, and to promote solutions, for example, by dealing with causes; and by providing local integration or resettlement for people in distress who, owing to a well-founded fear of being persecuted for reasons of race, religion, national or ethnic origin, social group or political opinion, are unable or unwilling to return to their own country. Arguably, however, and by contrast with article 72(1) and (2) on emergency assistance, article 72(4) of the Cotonou Agreement proposes a less categoric obligation with respect to refugee-related matters, in terms resonating more closely with the continuing dominance of discretion: 'Similar assistance, as set out above, *may* be granted to ACP States taking in refugees or returnees to meet acute needs not covered by emergency assistance' (emphasis supplied).

Although the formal statements of obligation may vary, a clear intention to provide assistance is apparent. Exactly how effective these provisions are in mobilizing European Union assistance is another matter, however, and requires further evaluation.

---

[231] On proposals for a 'New International Humanitarian Order', see letter of 28 Oct. 1981 from the Permanent Representative of Jordan to the United Nations: UN doc. A/36/245; UNGA res. 36/136, 14 Dec. 1981; 37/201, 18 Dec. 1982; 38/125, 16 Dec. 1983; 42/120 and 42/121, 7 Dec. 1987; 43/129, 8 Dec. 1988; *Report* of the Third Committee, Draft Resolution II: UN doc. A/45/751 (21 Nov. 1990); *Report* of the Secretary-General, Development and International Economic Co-operation, New international humanitarian order: moral aspects of development: UN doc. A/40/591 (11 Sept. 1985); *Report* of the Secretary-General submitted pursuant to General Assembly resolution 38/125: UN doc. A/40/348 (9 Oct. 1985); UNGAOR, 3rd Ctte., 6 Dec. 1985: UN doc. A/C.3/40/SR.69; *Report* of the Third Committee, Draft Resolution III, Promotion of international cooperation in the humanitarian field; also Draft Resolution I, Humanitarian assistance to victims of natural disasters and similar emergency situations: UN doc. A/45/751 (21 Nov. 1990).

10

Treaty Standards and their Implementation in National Law

The main treaties governing the status and treatment of refugees have attracted wide, if not universal acceptance, although they do not in fact either comprehend every refugee known to the world, or, in many cases, offer any but the most basic guarantees. Nevertheless, both the 1951 Convention and the 1967 Protocol are widely accepted; for those found to qualify, the benefits for which they call are often improved upon in actual practice, and supplemented substantially by the provisions of regional and related instruments. The Convention and the Protocol represent a point of departure in considering the appropriate standard of treatment of refugees, often exceeded, but still at base proclaiming the fundamental principles of protection, without which no refugee can hope to attain a satisfactory and lasting solution to his or her plight. The present chapter briefly examines the provisions of these and related agreements, with a view to determining the appropriate convention standards of treatment applicable to refugees and asylum seekers, whether lawfully or unlawfully in the territory of contracting States.[1]

1. The 1951 Convention and the 1967 Protocol relating to the Status of Refugees

The importance of the 1951 Convention as a statement of the minimum rights of refugees has been stressed repeatedly in the preceding chapters. Time has shown its provisions to be inadequate to deal with certain aspects of today's refugee problems,[2] but its principal objective was always the regulation of issues of legal status

---

[1] As of 31 January 2007, 147 States had ratified the 1951 Convention and/or the 1967 Protocol. For full texts, see Annexe 1, Nos. 4 & 5; and for States parties, Annexe 3, No. 1.

[2] This assessment, made in the first edition of this work (1983), may be even more justified today, though perhaps for different reasons. Whereas a primary concern in the past was the necessity to ensure protection for a broader category of refugees, a number of States currently perceive the Convention as an obstacle to efficient 'migration management', or as diverting resources from countries of first refuge to fund refugee determination for the few who make their way to the developed world, or as a potential security threat. Cf. Jackson, I. C., 'The 1951 Convention relating to Status of Refugees: A Universal Basis for Protection', 3 *IJRL* 403 (1991).

and treatment, rather than the grand design of universally acceptable solutions. It should not be forgotten that the Convention has its origin in the cold war climate of the late 1940s and early 1950s, when concern centred on refugees in Europe. Similarly, the very European flavour of many of the provisions can be readily understood when it is realized that of the twenty-six States which participated in drafting and adopting the Convention, seventeen were from Europe and four more of a Western European/North American disposition.[3] What is remarkable is that the 1951 Convention still attracts both ratifications and support among States from all regions.

By resolution 429(V) of 14 December 1950, the United Nations General Assembly decided to convene a Conference of Plenipotentiaries to draft and sign a convention on refugees and stateless persons; it duly met in July 1951, but was able only to complete its work with regard to the former.[4] The Conference took as its basis for discussion a draft prepared by the *Ad hoc* Committee on Refugees and Stateless Persons, adopted at its second session in Geneva in August 1950,[5] save that the Preamble was that adopted by the Economic and Social Council,[6] while article 1 was as recommended by the General Assembly and annexed to resolution 429(V). The Conference also unanimously adopted five recommendations covering travel documents, family unity, non-governmental organizations, asylum, and application of the Convention beyond its contractual scope.

As noted in Chapter 2, article 1 limited the definition of refugees by reference not only to a well-founded fear of persecution, but also to a dateline (those resulting from 'events occurring before 1 January 1951'), and offered States the option of further restricting their obligations to refugees resulting from events occurring *in Europe* before the critical date. It was the object of the 1967 Protocol to remove that stipulative date, but the geographical option remains.[7] For the sake of

---

[3] Criticism of the western/European focus of the 1951 Convention generally fails to note that the invitation to participate in the Conference of Plenipotentiaries was extended to *all* United Nations Member States. As one participant noted at the time, the non-appearance of so many non-European States contributed in no small degree to the initial orientation of art. 1; see UN doc. A/CONF.2/ SR.3, p. 12 (Mr Rochefort).

[4] The proposed Protocol formed the basis of the 1954 Convention relating to the Status of Stateless Persons: 360 *UNTS* 117, finalized after a further conference. For background and review, see Batchelor, C. A., 'Stateless Persons: Some Gaps in International Protection', 7 *IJRL* 232 (1995).

[5] UN doc. E/1850. This draft, that adopted by the *Ad Hoc* Committee at its first session (UN doc. E/1618), and the draft prepared by the UN Secretariat (UN doc. E/AC.32/2) are included in UNHCR, *RefWorld*, DVD/CD-ROM, 15th edn., (2006); and in Takkenberg, A. & Tahbaz, C. C., *The Collected travaux préparatoires of the 1951 Convention relating to the Status of Refugees*, 3 vols., (1988). See also Robinson, N., *Convention relating to the Status of Refugees: A Commentary*, (1953), 181–9, 190–214.   [6] ECOSOC res. 319 B II (XI), 11 Aug. 1950.

[7] At 31 January 2007, four States maintained the geographical limitation: Congo, Madagascar, Monaco, and Turkey. See *Multilateral Treaties deposited with the Secretary-General*, regularly updated in the series UN doc. ST/LEG/SER.E. The information below relating to reservations and declarations is based on the web version at <http://untreaty.un.org/>. and on the March 2006 UNHCR publications, 'Declarations and Reservations to the 1951 Convention relating to the Status of Refugees' and 'Declarations and Reservations to the 1967 Protocol relating to the Status of Refugees' (hereafter UNHCR, 'Declarations—Convention' and UNHCR, 'Declarations—Protocol'), available at <http://www.unhcr.org>.

convenience the 1967 Protocol has been referred to as 'amending' the 1951 Convention; in fact, it does no such thing. The Protocol is an independent instrument, not a revision within the meaning of article 45 of the Convention.[8] States parties to the Protocol, which can be ratified or acceded to by a State without becoming a party to the Convention,[9] simply agree to apply articles 2 to 34 of the Convention to refugees defined in article 1 thereof, as if the dateline were omitted.[10] While reservations are generally permitted under both instruments,[11] the integrity of certain articles is absolutely protected, including articles 1 (definition); 3 (non-discrimination), 4 (religion), 16(1) (access to courts), and 33 (*non-refoulement*).[12] A number of existing reservations are also of doubtful validity. Guatemala, for example, has purported to accede to the Convention and Protocol, 'with the reservation that it will not apply provisions of those instruments in respect of which the Convention allows reservations if those provisions contravene constitutional precepts in Guatemala or norms of public order under domestic law'. Belgium, France, Germany, Italy, Luxembourg, and the Netherlands have objected to the lack of clarity, considering it impossible for other States parties to determine the scope of a reservation expressed in such broad terms and which refers for the most part to domestic law.[13]

[8] See generally Weis, P., 'The 1967 Protocol relating to the Status of Refugees and some Questions of the Law of Treaties', 42 *BYIL* 39 (1967).

[9] Cape Verde, Swaziland, the United States of America and Venezuela have acceded only to the Protocol, while Madagascar, Monaco, and St Kitts and Nevis are party only to the Convention. There are some advantages in ratifying only the Protocol, for example, with respect to dispute settlement; see n. 12 below. Swaziland's accession to the Protocol alone in Jan. 1969 appears to have been inspired in part by a desire to 'accede' as a Member of the UN, rather than to become a party to the Convention by way of 'succession': UNHCR, 'Declarations—Convention', 4. The United Kingdom had extended the territorial application of the 1951 Convention to Swaziland in 1960, but not the 1967 Protocol, which the United Kingdom ratified in 1968.

[10] Art. I of the Protocol. Note also art. I(3), on the geographical limitation.

[11] See generally Blay, S. K. N. & Tsamenyi, B. M., 'Reservations and Declarations under the 1951 Convention and the 1967 Protocol relating to the Status of Refugees', 2 *IJRL* 527 (1990).

[12] Under the Convention, reservations are further prohibited with respect to arts. 36–46, which include a provision entitling any party to a dispute to refer the matter to the International Court of Justice (art. 38). The corresponding provision of the Protocol (art. IV) may be the subject of reservation, and such has been made by Botswana, China, Congo, El Salvador, Ghana, Jamaica, Rwanda, Tanzania, St Vincent and the Grenadines, and Venezuela. It is also not clear from art. VII of the Protocol whether reservations may be made to art. II (cooperation with the United Nations); they are clearly permissible under the corresponding Convention provision (art. 35), although none has been made; cf. Peru's declaration on ratification of the Protocol.

[13] Malta's reservations on accession excluded entirely application of arts. 7(2), 14, 23, 27, and 28, and qualified arts. 7(3), (4)(5), 8, 9, 11, 17, 18, 31, 32, and 34 as applicable 'to Malta compatibly with its own special problems, its peculiar position and characteristics': ibid. Most of these reservations were withdrawn in 2002, and those remaining (regarding arts. 23, 11 and 34) were withdrawn in 2004: UNHCR, 'Declarations—Convention, 32–3. Cf. Objections by Finland, Germany, Ireland, Norway, Portugal, and Sweden to reservations lodged by Bangladesh, Djibouti, Indonesia, Jordan, Kuwait, Qatar, and Tunisia, with respect to the 1989 Convention on the Rights of the Child: *Multilateral Treaties deposited with the Secretary-General*, above n. 7.

1.1 REQUIRED STANDARDS OF TREATMENT

As was the case with some of the inter-war arrangements,[14] the objective of the 1951 Convention and the 1967 Protocol is both to establish certain fundamental rights, such as *non-refoulement*, and to prescribe certain standards of treatment. The refugee may be stateless and therefore, as a matter of law, unable to secure the benefits accorded to nationals of his or her country of origin. Alternatively, even if nationality is retained, the refugee's unprotected status can make obtaining such benefits a practical impossibility. The Convention consequently proposes, as a minimum standard, that refugees should receive at least that treatment which is accorded to aliens generally.[15] Most-favoured-nation treatment[16] is called for in respect of the right of association (article 15),[17] and the right to engage in wage-earning employment (article 17(1)). The latter is of major importance to the refugee in search of an effective solution, but it is also the provision which has attracted most reservations.[18] Many States have thus emphasized that the reference to most-favoured-nation shall not be interpreted as entitling refugees to the benefit of special or regional customs, or economic or political agreements.[19] Other States have expressly rejected most-favoured-nation treatment, limiting their obligation to accord only that standard applicable to aliens generally,[20] while some view article 17 merely as a recommendation,[21] or agree to apply it 'so far as the law allows'.[22]

National treatment, finally, is to be granted in respect of a wide variety of matters, including the freedom to practise religion and as regards the religious education of children (article 4); the protection of artistic rights and industrial property (article 14); access to courts, legal assistance, and exemption from the requirement

---

[14] Art. 37 lists the agreements replaced, as between the parties, by the Convention.

[15] Art. 7(1). The Republic of Korea does not accept the provision on exemption from legislative reciprocity; Honduras understands art. 7 to mean 'that it shall accord to refugees such facilities and treatment as it shall deem appropriate at its discretion, taking into account the economic, social, democratic and security needs of the country'. Note also arts. 5, 6, 13, 18, 19, 21, 22(2); see further below on art. 26.

[16] Goodwin-Gill, G. S., *International Law and the Movement of Persons between States*, (1978), 186 and note, and sources cited.

[17] Cf. reservation by Ecuador, limiting acceptance of art. 15, 'so far as those provisions are in conflict with the constitutional and statutory provisions... prohibiting aliens, and consequently refugees, from being members of political bodies'.

[18] See UNHCR, 'Declarations—Convention', *passim*.

[19] See reservations by Angola, Belgium, Brazil, Burundi, Cape Verde, Denmark, Finland, Guatemala, Iran, Lativia, Luxembourg, Madagascar, Netherlands, Norway, Peru, Portugal, Spain, Sweden, Uganda, and Venezuela. Also Kiss, A., 'La convention européenne et la clause de la nation la plus favorisée', *Ann. Fr.* 478–89 (1957).

[20] Bahamas, Honduras, Ireland, Liechtenstein, Malawi, Moldova, Monaco, Mozambique, Switzerland, Zambia, and Zimbabwe.

[21] Austria, Burundi, Ethiopia, Latvia, Moldova (art. 17(2)), and Sierra Leone; Papua New Guinea does not accept any obligation with respect to art. 17(1).

[22] Jamaica; see also reservations by Malta, Mexico, Sweden, the United Kingdom, and Zambia.

to give security for costs in court proceedings (*cautio judicatum solvi*) (article 16);[23] rationing (article 20); elementary education (article 22(1)),[24] public relief (article 23);[25] labour legislation and social security (article 24(1));[26] and fiscal charges (article 29).

1.2 STANDARDS APPLICABLE TO REFUGEES AS REFUGEES

Although the stipulative provisions of article 1 are excluded from reservation, three States have made declarations which may affect claims to refugee status. The Netherlands, for example, declared on ratification that Ambionese transported to that country after 17 December 1949 (the date of Indonesia's accession to independence) were not considered eligible for refugee status. Turkey, on the other hand, stated on signature that it considered the Convention should apply also to 'Bulgarian refugees of Turkish extraction ... who, being unable to enter Turkey, might seek refuge on the territory of another Contracting State'.[27] Somalia, somewhat portentously, declared that its accession to the Convention was not to be construed so as to prejudice or adversely affect 'the national status or political aspiration of displaced people from Somali territories under alien domination'.[28] Such evidently political statements, not amounting to reservations, appear to have had little if any substantive effect on the application of the Convention generally or on the interpretation of the refugee definition. Of interest, however, is Portugal's 1999 extension of the Protocol to Macau, subsequently confirmed by

---

[23] China has excluded application of this entire article; Timor-Leste has made a reservation to art. 16(2).

[24] Ethiopia, Malawi, Monaco, Mozambique, and Zambia consider this provision a recommendation only; Swaziland, Papua New Guinea, and Timor-Leste accept no obligation.

[25] Estonia, Iran, Timor-Leste, Monaco, and Zimbabwe consider this a recommendation only, and it was not accepted by Malta until 2004; for Canada's interpretation of the phrase 'lawfully staying' in both arts. 23 and 24, see further below, n. 105.

[26] Reservations have been made to this article by Canada, Estonia, Finland (art. 24(3)), Honduras, Iran, Jamaica, Latvia, Liechtenstein, Malawi, Moldova, Monaco, New Zealand, Sweden, Switzerland, Timor-Leste, the United Kingdom, and the United States. Turkey has declared that refugees shall not enjoy greater rights than Turkish citizens in Turkey. Poland does not accept art. 24(2).

[27] In 1989, 320,000 Bulgarians of Turkish ethnic origin did indeed cross into Turkey; see above, Ch. 4, s. 2.5.1. On ratification, Turkey also expressed its understanding that the terms 're-availment' and 're-acquisition' in art. 1C implied not only a request by the individual concerned, but also the consent of the State in question.

[28] Ethiopia in 1979 objected to this declaration, stating 'that it does not recognize it as valid on the ground that there are no Somali territories under alien domination'. In Oct. 1983, Argentina submitted to the Secretary-General a 'formal objection' to the United Kingdom's extension, in 1956, of the 1951 Convention to the Falkland/Malvinas Islands. The United Kingdom declared that the objection was without effect: UNHCR, 'Declarations—Convention', 34. Georgia, which ratified in 1999, stated that, 'before the full restoration of the territorial integrity of Georgia, this Convention is applicable only to the territory where the jurisdiction of Georgia is exercised': UNHCR, 'Declarations—Convention', 9.

communications from the Governments of Portugal and China. On resuming sovereignty over Macau, China advised that the Convention would also apply to Macau Special Administrative Region, subject to China's reservation.[29]

Of greater importance is the varying degree to which States have been prepared to accept and to apply benefits and standards of treatment established by the Convention on behalf of refugees as refugees. Article 8, for example, makes a half-hearted attempt to exempt refugees from the application of exceptional measures which might otherwise affect them by reason only of their nationality. Several States have made reservations, of which some exclude entirely any obligation, some regard the article as a recommendation only, while others expressly retain the right to take measures based on nationality in the interests of national security.[30] Article 9, indeed, expressly preserves the right of States to take 'provisional measures' on the grounds of national security against a particular person, 'pending a determination by the Contracting State that that person is in fact a refugee and that the continuance of such measures is necessary . . . in the interests of national security'. Nevertheless, this has not prevented certain States from seeking further to entrench their powers by way of reservation.[31] Similar concern is evident in States' responses to article 26, which prescribes such freedom of movement for refugees as is accorded to aliens generally in the same circumstances. Seventeen States have made and maintain reservations, some half of which expressly retain the right to designate places of residence, either generally, or on grounds of national security, public order (*ordre public*), or the public interest.[32] Burundi, reflecting concerns shared by many African countries and reiterated in the 1969 OAU Convention,[33] declares that it accepts article 26 provided refugees (a) do not choose their place of residence in a region bordering on their country of origin; and (b) refrain in any event, when exercising their right to move freely, from any activity or incursion of a subversive nature with respect to the country of which they are nationals.[34]

---

[29] UNHCR, 'Declarations—Convention', 27; UNHCR, 'Declarations—Protocol', 6–7. The United Kingdom did not extend either the Convention or the Protocol to Hong Kong, and it has not been so extended to the Hong Kong Special Administrative Region.

[30] Reservations by Ethiopia, Fiji, Finland, Israel, Jamaica, Latvia, Madagascar, Malta, Spain, Sweden, Uganda, and the United Kingdom.

[31] Reservations by Angola, Ethiopia, Fiji, Finland, Jamaica, Madagascar, Malta, Uganda, and the United Kingdom.

[32] Reservations by Angola, Burundi, Honduras, Latvia, Malawi, Mexico, Moldova, Mozambique, Netherlands, Rwanda, Spain, Sudan, Zambia, and Zimbabwe. Botswana has made an 'open' reservation, Iran considers art. 26 to be a recommendation only, while Papua New Guinea accepts no obligation. At the 1951 Conference, it was said that art. 26 was not infringed where, under a labour contract or group-settlement scheme, refugees who were admitted were required to remain in a particular job for a particular time: UN doc. E/AC.32/SR.11, 6. Robinson further considered that art. 26 would not be breached in the case of 'special situations where refugees have to be accommodated in special camps or in special areas even if this does not apply to aliens generally': *Commentary*, 133, n. 207.

[33] Arts. II(6) and III.

[34] Corliss, S., 'Asylum State Responsibility for the Hostile Acts of Foreign Exiles', 2 *IJRL* 181 (1990).

The principal articles still to be considered fall loosely into two groups: first, those under which States parties agree to provide certain facilities to refugees; and secondly, those by which States have undertaken to recognize and protect certain 'rights' on behalf of refugees. The first group includes the provision of administrative assistance (article 25);[35] the issue of identity papers (article 27);[36] the issue of travel documents (article 28);[37] the grant of permission to transfer assets (article 30); and the facilitation of naturalization (article 34).[38] Within the second group are included the following specific 'rights':[39] recognition of the law of personal status (article 12);[40] exemption from penalties in respect of illegal entry or presence (article 31);[41] limitations on the liability to expulsion (article 32);[42] and the benefit of *non-refoulement* (article 33).

1.2.1 Administrative assistance: article 25

The drafters of the 1951 Convention knew that refugees often arrive in countries of prospective asylum without identity documents. Their recognition of the refugee's need for an identity, as inherent in his or her dignity and integrity, was reflected in the Convention, in particularly articles 25, 27, and 28. Read together, these three articles form a single system of protection of the refugee's entitlement to identity and documentation.

[35] Some common law countries, where affidavits and statutory declarations may take the place of official documents, have made reservations; see, for example, those of Fiji, Ireland, Jamaica, Uganda, and the United Kingdom. Estonia, and Sweden have also limited their obligations; Finland withdrew its reservation in 2004; see below, s. 1.2.1.

[36] See Executive Committee Conclusion No. 35 (1984), recommending that States provide such documents and also issue provisional documentation to asylum seekers; see also UNHCR, 'Identity Documents for Refugees': UN doc. EC/SCP/33 (July 1984); *Report* of the Sub-Committee of the Whole on International Protection: UN doc. A/AC.96/649 & Add.1, paras. 22–30—incidentally observing that registration and documentation in situations of large-scale influx should be without prejudice to subsequent case-by-case determination: paras. 29–30. See further below, s. 1.2.2.

[37] In 2004, Finland withdrew the reservation under which it did not accept an obligation to issue travel documents, but agreed to recognize those issued by other contracting States. Israel agrees to issue CTDs subject to the limitations provided for in its passport law, while Zambia does not consider itself bound to issue a travel document with a return clause, where another State has accepted a refugee from Zambia. Estonia limited its obligation for five years from ratification in 1997. See further below, s. 1.2.3.

[38] Honduras, Malawi, Mozambique and Swaziland accept no obligation to accord more favourable facilities than those ordinarily available to aliens; Papua New Guinea and Latvia accept no obligation.

[39] Art. 10, which protects certain types of residence otherwise affected by the events of the Second World War, is not considered further. For art. 11, in respect of refugee seamen, see above, Ch. 279, n. 453.

[40] The general rule is that personal status shall be governed by the law of a refugee's country of domicile or residence. Sweden maintains that status is governed by the law of nationality; Botswana and Israel do not accept art. 12, while Spain reserves its position with regard to para. 1.

[41] Honduras has reserved the right, equally with respect to arts. 26 and 31, to designate, change or limit the place of residence or restrict the freedom of movement of refugees. Papua New Guinea accepts no obligation under art. 31, Botswana has made entered a reservation, and Mexico also, but with respect to art. 31(2). See further below, s. 1.2.4.

[42] Not accepted by Papua New Guinea and Botswana. Mexico reserves by reference to Art. 33 of its Constitution, but without prejudice to *non-refoulement*. See further below, s. 1.2.5.

The origins of article 25 can be found in the earliest efforts of the League of Nations to address the problems of refugees. The League's 1926 Arrangement regarding Russian and Armenian Refugees, for example, was specifically organized around the objective of certifying the identity and 'position' of refugees.[43]

Article 25 of the 1951 Convention continues this practice and provides that States 'shall arrange' that certain administrative assistance shall be afforded to refugees in certain circumstances. Moreover, contracting States 'shall deliver or cause to be delivered' certain documents, such documents 'shall stand in the stead' of international documents, and 'shall be given credence in the absence of proof to the contrary'. The article concludes by requiring that fees for service 'shall be moderate'.

When the *Ad hoc* Committee which drafted the 1951 Convention discussed the proposed article on administrative assistance, Paul Weis, representing the International Refugee Organization, pointed out that it should not pose a particular problem in common law countries. Because of the practice of accepting affidavit evidence, he said, 'no new legislation or administrative procedures were required to protect refugees'.[44] Some common law countries, including the United Kingdom, have in fact made reservations to this article,[45] but the *travaux préparatoires* show clearly that the United Kingdom's only concern, both during the *Ad hoc* Committee sessions in 1950 and at the 1951 Conference, was that it should not have to enact implementing legislation in a field amply and sufficiently covered by the common law through the simple instrumentality of the sworn affidavit.[46]

The Report of the *Ad hoc* Committee further clarified the object and purpose of the draft article on administrative assistance:

> Refugees do not enjoy the protection and assistance of the authorities of their country of origin. Consequently, even if the government of the country of asylum grants the refugee a status which ensures him treatment equivalent to or better than that enjoyed by aliens, he may not in some countries be in a position to enjoy the rights granted him. Often he will require the assistance of an authority which will perform for him the services performed by national authorities in the case of persons with a nationality.

In its comment on paragraph 2 of the draft article, the *Ad hoc* Committee noted that it required the authorities to deliver to refugees the documents and certifications which are normally delivered to aliens who possess a nationality, either by

---

[43] Arrangement relating to the Issue of Identity Certificates to Russian and Armenian Refugees, 12 May 1926: 84 *LNTS* No. 2006. See also Arrangement relating to the Legal Status of Russian and Armenian Refugees, 30 June 1928: 89 *LNTS* No. 2005.

[44] *Ad hoc* Committee on Statelessness and Related Problems, UN doc. E/AC.32/SR.19, 8 Feb. 1950, Meeting of 1 Feb. 1950, 4, 6; Weis went on to be come UNHCR's first legal adviser. See also Mr Hoare (United Kingdom), Conference of Plenipotentiaries on the Status of Refugees and Stateless Persons, UN doc. A/CONF.2/SR.11, 22 Nov. 1951, 15.

[45] See, for example, the reservations of Estonia, Fiji, Ireland, Jamaica, Uganda, Sweden, and the United Kingdom.

[46] *Ad hoc* Committee on Statelessness and Related Problems, Summary Record of the 19th Meeting, UN doc. E/AC.32/SR.19, 8 Feb. 1950, 2–6.

the judicial or administrative authorities of their country of nationality or by its consular activities. A footnote provides an indication of the types of documents involved, such as those certifying the identity and the position of the refugees, their family position and civil status, the regularity, validity and conformity with the previous law of their country of origin of documents issued in that country, certifying the signature of refugees and copies and translations of documents drawn up in their own language, the refugee's previous record, professional qualifications, university degrees, diplomas, etc.[47]

At the 1951 Conference, the UK representative said that he had taken no part in the discussion,

... for the reason that common law applied in the United Kingdom, and that, as a consequence, the documents referred to ... would not be required to enable refugees to exercise rights in that country. Affidavits would be sufficient. The United Kingdom delegation might have to enter a reservation on article 20 in order to make its position clear, especially since paragraph 2, as at present drafted, would make it mandatory on the United Kingdom authorities to supply the documents which would under Continental systems of law be issued by national authorities. Such an obligation would be unacceptable to the United Kingdom Government. But he wished to emphasize that he was in no way opposed to the general tenor of the article. ... [48]

The UK's reservation to article 25 declares that it cannot undertake to give effect to the obligations contained in paragraphs 1 and 2 and can only undertake to apply the provisions of paragraph 3 so far as the law allows. Its own comment on this reservation provides:

No arrangements exist in the United Kingdom for the administrative assistance for which provision is made in article 25 nor have any such arrangements been found necessary in the case of refugees. Any need for the documents or certifications mentioned in paragraph 2 of that article would be met by affidavits.[49]

The drafters were nevertheless concerned that without specific assistance, refugees might not be able to enjoy the rights accorded them in the Convention. As the representative for Belgium said, this provision could not be left to discretion.[50] The *Ad hoc* Committee recognized that documentation issued to refugees must be credible and authoritative, and suggested that Contracting States should 'give documents issued ... *the same validity* as if the documents had been issued by the

---

[47] Report of the *Ad hoc* Committee on Statelessness and Related Problems, UN doc. E/1618 and Corr.1, 17 Feb. 1950, Comment on draft Article 20.

[48] 1951 Conference, Summary Record of the 11th Meeting, UN doc. A/CONF.2/SR.11, 22 Nov. 1951, 8; see also the comments of the representative for Belgium and the High Commissioner, 6–8.

[49] UNHCR, 'Declarations and Reservations to the 1951 Convention relating to the Status of Refugees', Geneva, 1 Mar. 2006, 21–2.

[50] Mr Herment (Belgium), 1951 Conference, UN doc. A/CONF.2/SR.11, 22 Nov. 1951, 11–16, at 12, 14.

competent authority of the country of nationality...'.[51] This was amended by the 1951 Conference to 'credence in the absence of proof to the contrary', an understandably lesser standard of validity than that of 'original' documents. Such 'lesser validity' is inherent in the circumstances—'documents' issued under article 25 are clearly not originals—but the standard also reflects the experience with affidavit evidence familiar to common law countries, and the legal principle that evidence given under oath should be presumed to be true.[52] The standard of 'credence' also serves to protect the interests of Contracting States, which remain free to annul or modify any benefit granted on the strength of such document, on the basis of later contrary evidence.

1.2.2 Identity documents: article 27

Article 27 lays down an unequivocal obligation on Contracting States to 'issue identity papers to any refugee in their territory who does not possess a valid travel document'. The duty is subject to no exceptions, and the *travaux préparatoires* make it clear that every refugee was intended to benefit.[53] Moreover, while article 27 is within the category of provisions to which States may make reservations,[54] no State Party has done so.

The question of identity papers for refugees was considered at both sessions of the *Ad hoc* Committee, in February and August 1950. The Secretariat invoked the precedent of article 2 of the 1933 Convention relating to the International Status of Refugees: 'Each of the Contracting States undertakes to issue Nansen certificates, valid for not less than one year, to refugees residing regularly in its territory',[55] and noted that, 'It is a general principle to issue identity papers, under various designations, which serve both as identity cards and as residence permits.'[56]

Although the Belgian representative had some reservations about issuing documents to those who were unlawfully on State territory, both the US representative, Mr Henkin, and the IRO representative, Mr Weis, confirmed that 'every refugee

---

[51] Report of the *Ad hoc* Committee on Statelessness and Related Problems: UN doc. E/1618 and Corr.1, 17 Feb. 1950, Comments to (then) draft Article 20.

[52] Thus, when an applicant swears to the truth of certain allegations, this creates a presumption that those allegations are true unless there is reason to doubt their truthfulness: *Villaroel* v. *Minister for Employment and Immigration* (1979) 61 NR 50; *Maldonado* v. *Minister for Employment and Immigration* (1980) 2 FC 302, 305, cited with approval in *Sathanandan* v. *Canada (Minister of Employment and Immigration)* (1991) 15 Imm. L.R. (2d) 310 (Federal Court of Appeal), *Fajardo* v. *Canada* (1993) 21 Imm L.R. (2d) 113, and *Siad* v. *Canada* [1997] 1 FC 698.

[53] *Ad hoc* Committee on Refugees and Stateless Persons, UN doc. E/AC.32/SR.38, 26 Sept. 1950, 23–5.

[54] Art. 42(1) of the 1951 Convention permits reservations to articles of the Convention other than Art. 1, 3, 4, 16(1), 33, 36–46 inclusive.

[55] Art. 2, 1933 Convention relating to the International Status of Refugees, 159 *LNTS* No. 3663.

[56] *Ad hoc* Committee, Draft Report, UN doc. E/AC.32/L.38, 15 Feb. 1950.

should be provided with some sort of document certifying his identity',[57] and this was accepted.[58]

1.2.3 The Convention Travel Document: article 28

Article 28 of the 1951 Convention maintains the practice of issuing travel documents to refugees, initiated under the League of Nations, and provides in paragraph 2 for documents issued under earlier arrangements to continue to be recognized.[59] The operative part of article 28 is succinct: 'The Contracting States shall issue to refugees lawfully staying in their territory travel documents for the purpose of travel outside their territory unless compelling reasons of national security or public order otherwise require. . . . ' The criterion of entitlement, 'lawfully staying', is examined more fully below, but the words of this provision may well place the refugee in a better position with regard to the issue of travel documentation than the citizen of the State in which he or she resides.[60] A Schedule to the Convention prescribes the form of the travel document and makes provision, among other matters, for renewal, recognition, and return to the State of issue. Article 28(1) also empowers States, in their discretion, to issue travel documents to refugees not linked to them by the nexus of lawful stay, who may be present temporarily or even illegally.

Where the applicant for a travel document is indeed a refugee within the Convention and/or the Protocol, and meets the requirement of lawful stay, article 28 permits few exceptions to the obligation to issue. The reference to 'compelling' reasons of national security and public order as justifying an exception clearly indicates that restrictive interpretation is called for. It was thus emphasized at the 1951 Conference that the refugee is not required to justify his or her proposed

[57] *Ad hoc* Committee, Summary Records, UN docs. E/AC.32/SR.15, paras. 57–129 (the first session debate dealt almost exclusively with issues of residence and security); E/AC.32/SR.38, 23–5 (a Canadian comment in the debate suggests some confusion between identity documents and travel or re-entry documents: 23); E/AC.32/SR.41, 20 (the draft article was adopted with the substitution in the French text of the heading of the phrase 'Pièce d'identité' for 'Carte de légitimation'); E/AC.32/SR.42, 11–35 (primarily discussing the meaning of the French phrase, 'résidant régulièrement'). Mr Weis also noted that, 'A man without papers was a pariah subject to arrest for that reason alone': UN doc. E/AC.32/SR.38, 26 Sept. 1950, 24. It was nevertheless recognized that the issue of identity papers was without prejudice to the right of the government to expel a person illegally present.

[58] See also, UNHCR, 'Identity Documents for Refugees': UN doc. EC/SCP/33, 20 Jul. 1984, paras. 3, 4–8, 10, 12; Executive Committee Conclusion No. 35 (1984): *Report* of the 35th Session: UN doc. A/AC.96/651, para. 87(3); Goodwin-Gill, G. S. & Kumin, J., 'Refugees in Limbo and Canada's International Obligations', (2000).

[59] See also Recommendation A of the Final Act.

[60] Generally on passports and the right to travel, see Goodwin-Gill, *Movement of Persons*, Ch. II. Robinson notes that at the 1951 Conference, the representative of Venezuela, despite the wording of art. 28(1), held to the view that the issue of travel documents to refugees would not be considered mandatory in the absence of a similar obligation benefitting nationals: *Commentary*, 135, n. 212. Cf. Turkey's 'general' declaration that 'no provisions of [the] Convention may be interpreted as granting to refugees greater rights than those accorded to Turkish citizens in Turkey'. See also, EU Qualification Directive, art. 25.

travel;[61] on the other hand, paragraph 14 of the Schedule to the Convention (which declares that the Schedule's provisions in no way affect laws and regulations governing admission, transit, residence, establishment, and departure), might be interpreted as permitting a somewhat broader range of restrictions. In this context, 'public order' (*ordre public*) still remains a relatively fluid concept, and certain States have not excluded the possibility of applying to the issue of Convention travel documents the same restrictions as they would apply with regard to national passports.[62]

A more serious obstacle in practice to the issue of Convention travel documents can result from the absence within a State's administration of any procedure for consideration and determination of applications for refugee status. Even where such procedures do exist, they may be limited to consideration of refugee status in the context of asylum, that is, at the point at which questions of admission, residence, and expulsion arise. The refugee admitted under a resettlement programme, or allowed to remain otherwise than by reference to his or her refugee status (for example, as a student or business person, or by reason of marriage to a local citizen) may be unable, quite simply, to invoke such status and thereby to secure treatment in accordance with the Convention. The standard of reasonably efficient and efficacious implementation suggests that some sort of procedure is required, if States are to meet their obligations under provisions such as article 28.

The Schedule prescribes the format of the Convention travel document,[63] and further regulates its issue and renewal, extension, recognition by other States, and guarantee of the holder's returnability to the issuing country.[64] Geographical validity for the largest possible number of countries is called for, and the document is to be valid for one or two years, at the discretion of the issuing State.[65] Renewal shall be by the State of issue, so long as the holder has not established lawful residence in another country,[66] and diplomatic and consular offices abroad are to be empowered to effect limited extensions of validity.[67] Contracting States undertake to recognize Convention travel documents issued by other parties (even, it may be supposed, if they do not accept that the holder is a refugee) and to accept them for visa purposes.[68] Paragraph 13(1) of the Schedule makes clear the obligation of the issuing State to readmit the holder of one of its travel documents, 'at any time during the period of its validity'.[69] The right of the refugee to return

---

[61] UN docs. E/AC.32/SR.16, 13–15; SR.42, 5–7; A/CONF.2/SR.12, 4–13; SR.17, 4–11.

[62] See the reservation by Israel: UNHCR, 'Declarations—Convention', 11.

[63] See generally UNHCR, 'Note on Travel Documents for Refugees': UN doc. EC/SCP/10 (1978).

[64] On 'returnability' as an essential incident to travel documentation, see Goodwin-Gill, *Movement of Persons*, 44–6.   [65] Schedule, paras. 4, 5.

[66] Ibid., paras. 6(1), 11, 12.   [67] Schedule, para. 6(2); see also para. 6(3).

[68] Schedule, paras. 7, 8, 9. The obligation to recognize CTDs, of course, does not oblige States to admit their holders.

[69] The return clause only gradually became an integral part of the refugee travel document; see Goodwin-Gill, *Movement of Persons*, 42–4. Some States, on a bilateral basis, have agreed to re-admission even after expiration of validity; see, for example, arts. 2 and 4, 1974 Austria–France Agreement on the Residence of Refugees (collected with other related instruments in Council of Europe

to the country which had issued him or her with a travel document was extensively discussed in the *Ad hoc* Committee. It was agreed that without a right of return, a travel document was practically worthless. The IRO representative, Mr Weis, noted that agreement on the 'return clause' was important because 'not only did it provide for rights for refugees of the greatest value but it also created relations between States'.[70] Although there were some differences among participating States regarding the formalities attaching to departure and return, the basic question of return was not disputed. The representative of Denmark, for example, considered that a travel document was implicitly understood to confer on the holder the right of re-entry; what he was concerned to ensure was that issuing States, 'should assume an *unconditional* commitment to re-admit holders of their own travel documents'.[71] The representative of France reiterated that without a return clause a travel document was completely meaningless, while the UK representative, Mr Hoare, was of the view that:

The basic principle underlying the provisions of paragraph 13 was that States issuing travel documents to refugees resident within their territory would bind themselves to allow such refugees re-entry during the period of validity of the document. He was anxious that the principle should not be tampered with.[72]

Paragraph 13(3) nevertheless empowers States 'in exceptional cases, or in cases where the refugee's stay is authorized for a specific period . . .' to limit the return clause to not less than three months. Article 28 already acknowledges States' discretionary competence to issue travel documents to refugees not otherwise 'lawfully staying' in their territory. The Schedule confirms that discretion, by allowing States to avoid any long-term responsibility towards refugees whom they wish simply to assist with resettlement in a third State.[73] In practice, however, it is clear that excessive limitation of the return clause can result in serious problems for refugees, who may find themselves unable to return to the country of issue of their travel document and yet without any entitlement to residence elsewhere.[74]

doc. EXP/AT.Re(77) 3, 21–3). A similar provision is included in art. 4, 1980 European Agreement on Transfer of Responsibility for Refugees: *ETS* no. 107.

[70] *Ad hoc* Committee on Statelessness and Related Problems, Summary Records, 39th Meeting, UN doc. E/AC.32/SR.39, 27 Sept. 1950, 6–10; 41st Meeting, UN doc. E/AC.32/SR.41, 28 Sept. 1950, 12–13; 42nd Meeting, UN doc. E/AC.32/SR.42, 28 Sept. 1950, 3–6.

[71] 1951 Conference, Summary Record of the 18th Meeting, UN doc. A/CONF.2/SR.18. 23 November 1951, 5, 8 (emphasis supplied).

[72] Ibid., 7. In *Al Rawi*, which concerned a claim for protection by, among others, two British-recognized refugees detained in Guantanamo, the Court of Appeal failed to consider both the international and the domestic legal implications of the fact that each held a valid CTD with a ten-year return clause: *R. (Al Rawi) v. Secretary of State for Foreign and Commonwealth Affairs (UNHCR Intervening)* [2006] EWCA Civ 1279.

[73] Robinson, *Commentary*, 145; see also the general discussion in *Report* of the Executive Committee, 29th Session, (1978): UN doc. A/AC.96/558, paras. 35–7.

[74] See UNHCR, 'Note on Asylum': UN doc. EC/SCP/12, paras. 19–23 (1979); *Report* of the Executive Committee, 30th Session, (1979): UN doc. A/AC.96/572, paras. 60, 72(2)(m), (n). In 1978, the Observer for Botswana, in urging other countries to offer resettlement opportunities,

With the aim of resolving some at least of those issues, a number of States have concluded agreements regulating 'transfer of responsibility' for refugees who change their lawful residence from one country to another. Paragraph 6 of the Schedule predicates responsibility for renewal and extension of CTDs on the fact that 'the holder has not established lawful residence in another territory and resides lawfully in the territory' of the renewing authority. Paragraph 11, in turn, predicates transfer of responsibility for the issue of a CTD on the fact that the refugee 'has lawfully taken up residence in the territory of another Contracting State'. Given the divergence in national immigration laws and concepts, these terms are clearly capable of many different interpretations. Inter-State agreements have therefore attempted to provide objective criteria for ascertaining the moment of transfer. Article 2(1) of the 1980 European Agreement, for example, declares:

> Responsibility shall be considered to be transferred on the expiry of a period of two years of actual and continuous stay in the second State with the agreement of its authorities or earlier if the second State has permitted the refugee to remain in its territory either on a permanent basis or for a period exceeding the validity of the travel document.

The same article provides a method of calculation of the relevant period, and permits disregard of stay allowed solely for study, training, or medical care, and of periods of imprisonment.[75]

Finally, paragraph 15 of the Schedule to the Convention declares that neither the issue of a CTD nor entries on it shall affect the status of the holder, particularly as to nationality, and paragraph 16 affirms that the CTD holder is not entitled to diplomatic protection by the issuing State, and that that State acquires no right to exercise such protection.[76] However, a recognized refugee possesses an 'international status', and recognition entitles him or her to exercise certain rights in other Contracting States. If such rights are violated, it remains open to the State

---

noted that it was unfair that Botswana should be asked to readmit those who had gone abroad for education, solely because it had been the country of first refuge: UN doc. A/AC.96/SR.302, para. 14. Zambia has reserved the right not to issue a travel document with a return clause, 'where a country of second asylum has accepted or indicated its willingness to accept a refugee from Zambia'.

[75] Art. 2(2). Temporary absences not exceeding three months on any one occasion or six months in all are not deemed to interrupt stay.

[76] Cf. Grahl-Madsen, A., 'Protection of Refugees by their Country of Origin', 11 *Yale J.I.L.* 362 (1986), arguing for a rule under which the State of origin of refugees, 'by breaking its ties with a refugee', loses any right to exercise protection until such time as the refugee willingly returns. Para. 16 appears to have been included in the Schedule simply because it had appeared in the 1946 London Agreement on the Adoption of a Travel Document for Refugees. The *Ad hoc* Committee debated its deletion, but participants also mentioned both the possibility of exceptions to the general rule (for example, where the country of 'transit' accepted the exercise of protection by the country of issue), and the need for such protection. The US representative, Mr Henkin, suggested that the Committee, 'might quite well examine the question of the right of protection from the viewpoint, not of stateless persons, but of refugees, stateless or not, who did not enjoy any diplomatic protection'. *Ad hoc* Committee on Statelessness and Related Problems, Summary Records, 18th Meeting, UN doc. E/AC.32/SR.18, 8 Feb. 1950, 8–9. This has also recently been proposed by the ILC's Special Rapporteur on Diplomatic Protection, John Dugard; see 'First Report on Diplomatic Protection', UN doc. A/CN.4/506, 7 Mar. 2000, paras. 175–84.

which has recognized the refugee to take up the breach of treaty in the normal way, irrespective of the limits imposed by the rules of diplomatic protection.[77] In practice, diplomatic assistance falling short of full protection is often accorded by issuing States, while the fact of possession of a CTD would constitute *prima facie* evidence at least of the holder's entitlement to protection by UNHCR.

1.2.4 *Treatment of refugees entering illegally: article 31*

Article 31 has already been analysed in its relation to the principle of *non-refoulement* and asylum, and separately with respect to detention.[78] Although not comprehensive, this provision serves as a point of departure in determining the minimum standard of treatment to be accorded to those whose situation remains unregularized in the country of first refuge. It applies first to refugees who, 'coming directly from a territory where their life or freedom was threatened in the sense of article 1, enter or are present . . . without authorization, provided they present themselves without delay to the authorities and show good cause for their illegal entry or presence'. A proposal to exempt illegally entering refugees from penalties was first included in the draft convention prepared by the 1950 *Ad hoc* Committee on Statelessness and Related Problems in February 1950.[79] As was commented at the time, 'A refugee whose departure from his country of origin is usually a flight, is rarely in a position to comply with the requirements for legal entry (possession of national passport and visa) into the country of refuge.'[80] When the Committee reconvened in August that year, no changes were made in the text, although the Committee noted 'that in some countries freedom from penalties on account of illegal entry is also extended to those who give assistance to such refugees for honourable reasons'.[81] The Committee's draft text was then considered by the 1951 Conference of Plenipotentiaries.

The record of negotiations confirms the 'ordinary meaning' of article 31(1), which applies to refugees who enter or are present without authorization, whether

---

[77] See the *LaGrand* Case (Germany v United States of America), ICJ *Rep.*, (2001), 104. In this case, Germany was able to invoke two separate causes of action; the first was based on breach by the US of its treaty obligations to Germany, and the second on the injury done to two German nationals. The Court accepted that these were separate and independent claims. Cf. Reiterer, M., *The Protection of Refugees by Their State of Asylum*, (1984), 63–4: 'As paragraph 16 clearly refers to the "*issue*" of the document, it can in no way negate the right of protection originating from *another* legal relationship, such as a State's interest in seeing the grant of asylum respected or its interest in seeing another Contracting Party comply in good faith with the provisions of the 1951 Convention.'

[78] See above, Ch. 5, s. 3.3.5; Ch. 7, s. 5.2.

[79] Belgium and the United States: Proposed Text for Article 24 of the Draft Convention relating to the Status of Refugees: UN doc. E/AC.32/L.25, 2 Feb. 1950; Decisions of the Committee on Statelessness and Related Problems taken at the meetings of 2 Feb. 1950: UN doc. E/AC.32.L.26, 2 Feb. 1950.

[80] Draft Report of the *Ad hoc* Committee on Statelessness and Related Problems. Proposed Draft Convention relating to the Status of Refugees: UN doc. E/AC.32.L.38, 15 Feb. 1950, Annex I (draft Article 26); Annex II (comments. 57).

[81] Draft Report of the *Ad hoc* Committee on Refugees and Stateless Persons: UN doc. E/AC.32.L.43, 24 August 1950, 9.

they have come directly from their country of origin, or from any other territory in which their life or freedom was threatened, provided they show good cause for such entry or presence. So far as the references to refugees who 'come directly' and show 'good cause' may be ambiguous, the *travaux préparatoires* illustrate that these terms were intended specifically to address one particular concern of the French delegation. Because the draft article 'trespassed' on the delicate 'sovereign' areas of admission and asylum, France was concerned that it should not allow those who had already '*found asylum*... to move freely from one country to another without having to comply with frontier formalities'.[82] The French delegate gave the example of 'a refugee who, having found asylum in France, tried to make his way unlawfully into Belgium. It was obviously impossible for the Belgian Government to acquiesce in that illegal entry, since the life and liberty of the refugee would be in no way in danger at the time.'[83] The essential question between France and other participating States was whether the requirement that the refugee should show 'good cause' for entering or being present illegally was adequate, (as the UK representative argued), or whether more explicit wording was required, as suggested by the French delegate.[84]

Other countries, however, recognized that refugees might well have good cause for leaving any first country of refuge. The United Nations High Commissioner for Refugees, Dr van Heuven Goedhart, recalled his own wartime experiences and expressed concern about 'necessary transit' and the difficulties facing a refugee arriving in an ungenerous country.[85] The UK representative, Mr Hoare, said that fleeing persecution was itself good cause for illegal entry, but there could be other good causes. The French suggested that their proposed amendment be changed so as to exclude refugees, 'having been unable to find even temporary asylum in a country other than the one in which... life or freedom would be threatened'. This was opposed by the British representative on practical grounds (it would impose on the refugee the impossible burden of proving a negative); and by the Belgian representative on language and drafting grounds (it would exclude from the benefit of the provision any refugee who had managed to find a few days' asylum in any country through which he had passed).[86] Although the French continued to have concerns about the wording, the present text was finally settled.

---

[82] 1951 Conference, Summary Records: UN doc. A/CONF.2/SR.13, (Mr Colemar, France).

[83] Ibid.

[84] '[I]t was often difficult to define the reasons which could be regarded as constituting good cause for the illegal entry into, or presence in, the territory of a State of refuge. But it was precisely on account of that difficulty that it was necessary to make the working of paragraph 1 more explicit... To admit without any reservation that a refugee who had settled temporarily in a receiving country was free to enter another, would be to grant him a right of immigration which might be exercised for reasons of mere personal convenience': 1951 Conference, Summary Records: UN doc. A/CONF.2/SR.14, 8, 10 (Mr Colemar, France).

[85] 1951 Conference, Summary Records: UN doc. A/CONF.2/SR.14, 4–5; see above Ch. 4, s. 3.1.

[86] 1951 Conference, Summary Records: UN doc. A/CONF.2/SR.14, 7, 10–11.

The UNHCR Executive Committee has considered 'illegal' or 'irregular' movements of refugees and asylum seekers on at least two occasions. Each time, while expressing concern in regard to such movements, participating States have acknowledged that refugees may have justifiable reasons for such action, including fear of persecution or danger to safety or freedom, and that they may have to use fraudulent documentation to leave.[87] Whether other circumstances amount to 'good cause' will depend very much on the facts.[88]

Such refugees who come within article 31 are not to be subjected to 'penalties', which appears to comprehend prosecution, fine, and imprisonment, but not administrative detention.[89] Article 31(2) makes it clear that States may impose 'necessary' restrictions on movement, which would include those prompted by security considerations or special circumstances like a large influx.[90] Such measures also come within article 9, and are an exception to the freedom of movement called for by article 26. Article 31(2) nevertheless calls for restrictions to be applied only until status in the country of refuge is regularized,[91] or admission obtained into another country; moreover, contracting States are to allow refugees a reasonable period and all necessary facilities to obtain such admission. Those facilities clearly include access to the representatives of other States and of UNHCR. The United Kingdom considered that provisional detention was not ruled out if necessary to investigate the circumstances of entry. The Conference President likewise distinguished between detention to investigate and penalties for illegal entry, the latter being prohibited where entry was justified.[92]

---

[87] See Executive Committee Conclusion No. 15 (XXX)—1979, Refugees without an Asylum Country', *Report* of the 30th Session: UN doc. A/AC.96/572, para. 72(2)(k); Executive Committee Conclusion No. 58 (XL)—1989, 'The Problem of Refugees and Asylum Seekers who Move in an Irregular Manner from a Country in which They had already found Protection': *Report* of the 40th Session of the Executive Committee: UN doc. A/AC.96/737, 23.

[88] UNHCR *Handbook*, paras. 190, 198—the circumstances which lead asylum seekers to flee their country may also make them apprehensive about approaching persons in authority.

[89] See discussion at the 1951 Conference: UN docs. A/CONF.2/SR.13, 13–15; SR.14, 4, 10–11; SR.35, 10–20; also art. 5, 1954 Caracas Convention on Territorial Asylum; below, Annexe 2, No. 3. Cf. Campiche, M.-P., 'Entrée illégale et séjour irrégulier des réfugiés et requérants d'asile: La pratique des cantons', *Asyl*, 1994/3, 51–7, showing different sanctions practice and different interpretations prevailing among the 'frontier' cantons with respect to both Swiss law and art. 31; also, Dunstan, R., 'United Kingdom: Breaches of Article 31 of the 1951 Refugee Convention', 10 *IJRL* 205 (1998). Following the judgment in *R.* v. *Uxbridge Magistrates' Court, ex p. Adimi* [2001] QB 657, on which see above, Ch. 5, s. 3.3.5, the United Kingdom included defences to offences related to false documentation in s.31, Immigration and Asylum Act 1999. In *R.* v. *Makuwa* [2006] 1 WLR 2755, [2006] EWCA Crim 175, the court, quashing a conviction, held that where the defendant adduced sufficient evidence in support of a claim to refugee status, the prosecution had the burden of proving to the usual standard that he or she was not a refugee. See also s. 2, Asylum and Immigration (Treatment of Claimants) Act 2004.   [90] Robinson, *Commentary*, 154.

[91] Cf. art. 9: 'pending a determination ... that [the] person is in fact a refugee ...' Vietnamese detained after arriving in Hong Kong after 2 Jul, 1982 were to be given 'all reasonable facilities' to obtain authorization to enter another State, or to leave Hong Kong, with or without such authorization: Immigration Amendment Ordinance 1982 (no. 42/82) s. 7 (adding new s. 13D).

[92] UN doc. A/CONF.2/SR.35, 10–20. In the *Ad hoc* Committee in 1950, the Swiss delegate proposed that immunity from penalty also be accorded to those who assisted refugees to enter illegally. States were more concerned about smuggling organizations, however, and the problem of identifying

1.2.5 Expulsion of refugees: article 32

Article 32, which limits the circumstances in which refugees 'lawfully in their territory' may be expelled by contracting States, has also been analysed above in the context of *non-refoulement*.[93] The meaning of 'lawfully' in article 32 is examined further below, and for the present it suffices to recall that this provision limits expulsion to grounds of national security or public order;[94] that it requires a decision to be reached in accordance with due process of law; that some form of appeal should be generally permitted; and that the refugee should be allowed a reasonable period in which to seek admission into another country. As with most Convention provisions, and subject always to conformity with its other obligations under international law, the State clearly enjoys choice of means with regard to its implementation of article 32. Thus, it may be sufficient to adopt internal, *ad hoc* administrative procedures regulating the exercise of the discretion to set removal machinery in motion, so that formal incorporation of the limitations on expulsion is not necessary. Moreover, some uncertainty surrounds the precise implications of the reference to decisions in accordance with due process of law. The French version of the text (*'une décision rendue conformément à la procédure prévue par la loi'*) suggests that formal compliance with the law is all that is required.[95] However, the concept of due process today includes, as minimum requirements, (a) knowledge of the case against one, (b) an opportunity to submit evidence to rebut that case, (c) reasoned negative decisions, and (d) the right to appeal against an adverse decision before an impartial tribunal independent of the initial decision-making body. It is a moot point to what extent these higher standards of procedural due process are now required by general international law.[96]

those acting in good faith; turning down the idea, the US representative suggested that its spirit be reflected in the summary records: UN doc. E/AC.32/SR.40, 4–9. Cf. *Doc. réf.*, 208: 16 jan./1 fév. 1993, 2, reporting the conviction of M & Mme Colak for 'aide à l'entrée, à la circulation ou au séjour irrégulier d'étrangers en France'. They travelled to the border between Hungary and Croatia and helped twelve relatives to get out and then into France. The family members were caught, reconducted to the border with Germany, but later allowed to return to France with visas and to apply for asylum. The couple were sentenced to 15 months suspended and fined 2000 francs.

[93] See above, Ch. 5, s. 3.3.4.

[94] In 1991, France expelled a recognized Moroccan refugee, Abdelmoumen Diouri, resident since 1974, to Gabon, under the 'urgence absolue' procedure, on the grounds of his 'contacts' with groups and foreign powers prejudicial to public security and national interests. He returned to France after the *tribunal administratif de Paris*, following the advice of the *commissaire du gouvernement* found that 'les conditions de l'urgence absolue n'étaient pas réunies, pas plus que la nécéssité impérieuse pour la sûreté de l'Etat et la sécurité publique'. The *Conseil d'Etat* rejected the Minister's appeal in Oct. 1991, the *commissaire du gouvernement* accepting that while M. Diouri could present a public security threat, those conditions did not exist at the time of his expulsion: Conseil d'Etat, Assemblée, 11 Oct. 1991, 128.128, *Diouri*.

[95] This appears to be Ireland's interpretation, as stated on ratification. Cf. Uganda's reservation to art. 32: 'Without recourse to legal process the Government . . . shall, in the public interest, have the unfettered right to expel any refugee . . . and may at any time apply such internal measures as the Government may deem necessary in the circumstances; so however that any action taken by the Government . . . in this regard shall not operate to the prejudice of the provisions of art. 33 . . . '

[96] Cf. Goodwin-Gill, *Movement of Persons*, 227–8, 238–40, 308–9.

1.2.6 Non-refoulement: *article 33*

The scope of the principle of *non-refoulement*, both as a treaty rule and as a rule of general international law, has been fully analysed in Chapters 5–7.

1.3 THE CRITERIA OF ENTITLEMENT TO TREATMENT IN ACCORDANCE WITH THE CONVENTION

Some provisions of the Convention are limited to refugees 'lawfully staying' in contracting States, some apply to those 'lawfully in' such States, while others apply to refugees *tout court*, whether lawfully or unlawfully present.[97] Regrettably, there is little consistency in the language of the Convention, be it English or French, but three general categories may be distinguished: simple presence, lawful presence, and lawful residence; for some purposes also reference may be required to the concept of habitual residence.

1.3.1 Simple presence

Some benefits extend to refugees, by virtue of their status alone as refugees, without in any way being dependent upon their legal situation. Article 33, for example, refers simply to refugees, as does article 3.[98] Articles 2, 4, and 27 are predicated on the fact of presence ('the country in which he finds himself'; 'refugees within their territories'; 'any refugee in their territory'/'*du pays où il se trouve*'; '*réfugiés sur leur territoire*'; '*tout réfugié se trouvant sur leur territoire*'), while article 31 is specifically applicable to cases of illegal entry or presence ('in their territory without authorization'/'*se trouve sur leur territoire sans autorisation*').

1.3.2 Lawful presence

Lawful presence is to be distinguished from lawful residence; it implies admission in accordance with the applicable immigration law, for a temporary purpose, for example, as a student, visitor, or recipient of medical attention. Owing to the different approaches adopted within national systems, the distinction is often difficult to maintain in practice. For the purposes of the Convention, articles 18, 26, and 32 apply to refugees whose presence is lawful ('lawfully in'/'*qui se trouvent régulièrement*').[99]

The extension of article 32 benefits to refugees who are merely lawfully present in contracting States, even if only on a temporary basis, may be disputed in the light of the practice of some States,[100] and in principle there appears to be no

---

[97] Cf. Hathaway, J. C., 'What's in a Label?' 5 *European Journal of Migration and Law* 1, 11 (2003).
[98] See also art. 16(1).
[99] Cf. art. 11, which refers to refugees 'regularly serving as crew members/*régulièrement employés comme membres de l'équipage*'.
[100] See, for example, *Kan Kim Lin v. Rinaldi* 361 F.Supp. 177, 186 (1973); aff'd., 493 F.2d (1974), the Court, referring to the *travaux préparatoires* on art. 32, observed that the term 'lawfully in their

reason why the temporarily present refugee should not be subject to the same regime of deportation as applies to aliens generally. It may be assumed that he or she will still enjoy the right of return to the State which issued a travel document and the benefit of article 33 will apply in any event. It may be argued that the grounds of public order/*ordre public* include breach of any aspect of a country's immigration or aliens law,[101] in which case little substantive protection is offered to distinguish the refugee lawfully present from the refugee lawfully resident. On balance, article 32 may interpreted as a substantial limitation upon the State's power of expulsion, but with its benefits confined to lawfully resident refugees, that is, those in the State on a more or less indefinite basis. However, there is very little recorded practice specifically addressing the legal issues raised by measures to expel refugees, as opposed to those whose applications for refugee status have been rejected.

1.3.3 Lawful residence

Finally, many articles apply only to refugees lawfully resident in the contracting State, that is, those who are, as it were, enjoying asylum in the sense of residence and lasting protection. Again the terminology varies. Article 25 refers to States 'in whose territory (the refugee) is residing'/'*sur le territoire duquel il réside*'. Articles 14 and 16(2) invoke the country of the refugee's 'habitual residence'/'*résidence habituelle*', while articles 15, 17(1), 19, 21, 23, 24, and 28 employ, in English, the somewhat imprecise term 'lawfully staying'.[102] The corresponding phrase in the French text is '*résident régulièrement*' (or some variation thereof); it is evident from the *travaux préparatoires* concerning article 28, for example, that the English phrase was selected for its approximation to the French term, particularly as the concept of residence in common law systems is often replete with contradiction. The terminology adopted in the Convention, however, is not free from difficulty. It was noted at the second session of the *Ad hoc* Committee in 1950 that a resident in France may be a privileged, ordinary, or temporary resident.[103] The cases of those present only for a short period of time might cause problems, but in the view of the French representative, '. . . an examination of the various articles in which the words "résident régulièrement" appeared would show that they all implied a settling down and consequently a certain length of residence'.[104] In order to obtain the benefit of the articles cited above, the refugee must show something

territory' would 'exclude a refugee who, while lawfully admitted, has overstayed the period for which he was admitted or was authorized to stay or who had violated any other condition attached to his admission or stay'. In *Chim Ming* v. *Marks* 505 F.2d 1170 (1974), the Court of Appeals considered that the 'only rational interpretation' of the phrase was 'one consistent with the definition of unlawfulness in article 31 as involving the status of being in a nation "without authorization". Since a nation's immigration laws provide authorization, one unlawfully in the country is in violation of those laws.'

[101] See cases cited in Goodwin-Gill, *Movement of Persons*, 298, n. 1, and generally, 295–9.
[102] See also the terminology of residence used in paras. 6 and 11 of the Schedule.
[103] UN doc. E/AC.32/SR.42, 11–20.   [104] Ibid., 12.

more than mere lawful presence.[105] Generalizations are difficult in the face of different systems of immigration control, but evidence of permanent, indefinite, unrestricted or other residence status, recognition as a refugee, issue of a travel document, or grant of a re-entry visa, will raise a strong presumption that the refugee should be considered as lawfully staying in the territory of a contracting State. It would then fall to that State to rebut the presumption by showing, for example, that the refugee was admitted for a limited time and purpose, or that he or she is in fact the responsibility of another State.[106]

1.3.4 Habitual residence

The phrase 'former habitual residence' appears in article 1A(2) of the 1951 Convention to identify the country with respect to which a stateless person might establish his or her status as a refugee, on the basis of a well-founded fear of persecution. In this context, the drafters gave little attention to the precise meaning of the phrase, the *Ad hoc* Committee observing simply that the expression did not refer to a locality, but to 'the country in which (the refugee) had resided and where he had suffered or fears he would suffer persecution if he returned'.[107] Habitual residence for a stateless person would necessarily seem to imply some degree of security, of status, of entitlement to remain and to return, which were in part the objectives of inter-government arrangements of the inter-war period.[108] Where the term 'habitual residence' is used in other articles of the 1951 Convention, it signifies more than a stay of short duration, but was apparently not intended necessarily to imply permanent residence or domicile.[109]

'Domicile', indeed, is a term of art fraught with problems in common law and other jurisdictions, and is distinguished from residence in article 12 of the Convention:

1. The personal status of a refugee shall be governed by the law of the country of his domicile or, if he has no domicile, by the law of the country of his residence.

[105] In its reservation to arts. 23 and 24, Canada states that it interprets 'lawfully staying' as referring only to refugees admitted for permanent residence; refugees admitted for temporary residence are to be accorded the same treatment with respect to those articles as is accorded to visitors generally. With the later development of due process and constitutional protection, this may now be a distinction without a difference.

[106] The Protocol to the 1962 Switzerland–Federal Republic of Germany agreement on transfer of responsibility, for example, while discounting periods of stay for educational, medical, or convalescence purposes, deems authorization of establishment to arise, '*lorsque le réfugié a obtenu une autorisation de séjour illimitée ou lorsqu'il peut justifier d'une résidence régulière de trois ans...*'. Agreements such as this one deal with transfer of responsibility *between States*, and no such period of elapsed residence is required for the refugee seeking to invoke the benefit of Convention articles vis-à-vis his or her country of asylum.

[107] UN doc. E/1618, 39. UNHCR, *Handbook* (1979), paras. 101, 104–5. *Minister for Immigration and Multicultural Affairs* v. *Savvin* (2000) 98 FCR 168, [2000] FCA 478; *Al-Anezi* v. *Minister for Immigration and Multicultural Affairs* (1999) 92 FCR 283, [1999] FCR 355.

[108] See United Nations, *A Study of Statelessness*, (1949), Introduction and Part I.

[109] Art. 14 provides that the same protection of artistic rights and industrial property is to be accorded to refugees in their country of habitual residence, as is accorded to nationals. See debate in the Conference of Plenipotentiaries: UN doc. A/CONF.2/SR.7, 20; SR.8, 6; SR.23, 26.

State practice differs on the law that should govern issues of personal status (legal capacity, capacity to marry, family rights, succession, and so forth); some have opted for the law of the individual's domicile, and others for the law of the individual's State of nationality. Article 12 is intended to address the problems that may arise for refugees, but it is not always easy to determine when one domicile has been abandoned, and another acquired;[110] hence, the use of the residuary concept of residence.[111]

'Habitual residence' and even 'residence' alone involve elements of fact and intention. For example, whether those admitted for permanent residence to Canada do in fact establish such residence in Canada does not necessarily follow, as citizenship courts have confirmed. On the one hand, residency is now conceded to have an 'extended meaning' (that is, it is flexible enough to accommodate periods of absence).[112] On the other hand, the grant of the special status of citizenship requires more than a place of abode and an intent to return;[113] it requires that the individual 'centralize his or her mode of living' in Canada, and this in turn may depend upon additional factors, such as family ties, only temporary links overseas, and continuing connections with Canada (bank accounts, investments, and the like).[114]

In determining the country of former habitual residence, the exact purpose for which the determination is required must first be identified. Both the 1951 Convention and municipal law rely on different conceptions of residence for different purposes, as the above sections show. Similarly, in municipal law, certain benefits, such as social security or relief from deportation,[115] may require a qualifying

---

[110] Domicile involves both subjective and objective factors. See *Trottier* v. *Dame Lionel Rajotte* [1940] SCR 203, in which the Supreme Court of Canada stated that the principles governing change of domicile of origin or birth are that a domicile of origin cannot be lost until a new domicile has been acquired. This involves two factors: the acquisition of residence in fact in a new place, and the intention of permanently settling there. Leaving a country with the intention of never returning is not enough, in the absence of a permanent residence established in another country, 'general and indefinite in its future contemplation'.

[111] See *Ad hoc* Committee on Statelessness and Related Problems: UN doc. E/AC.7/SR.8, paras. 14, 19; SR.9, para. 2.

[112] *Re Citizenship Act and in re Antonios E. Papadogiorgakis* [1978] 2 FC 208. This case, it has been said, 'imposed on the courts an enquiry covering both intention and fact, neither of these elements being considered determinative by itself': per Joyal J. in *Canada (Secretary of State)* v. *Nakhjavani* [1987] FCJ No. 721.

[113] In *Canada (Secretary of State)* v. *Nakhjavani* [1987] FCJ No. 721, the court found that the respondents, stateless persons holding Canadian certificates of identity, maintained a pied-à-terre in Canada, but resided principally in Haifa, Israel, by reason of the husband's religious and administrative duties on behalf of the Baha'i Faith. Their brief visits to Canada did not qualify them for citizenship.

[114] See *Re Chan* [1988] FCJ No. 323, a successful appeal against refusal of citizenship. The applicant had completed undergraduate and graduate training in Canada, and had left for Hong Kong only after experiencing difficulties in finding a job in Canada commensurate with his qualifications. He kept rooms in his parents' house, made frequent return trips, maintained strong family ties and other social relations, took only temporary, furnished accommodation overseas, kept bank accounts and filed income tax returns. He was held to meet the residency requirements of the Citizenship Act.

[115] For example, under the United Kingdom Commonwealth Immigrants Act 1962, no recommendation for deportation was to be made against a Commonwealth citizen who satisfied the court that he or she was 'ordinarily resident' in the UK, and had been continuously so resident for at least

period of residence, while entitlements such as citizenship generally require evidence of greater commitment to the community.

The identification of the country of former habitual residence can serve either of two purposes: (1) to clarify which State, if any, is properly to be considered as the putative State of persecution in a claim to refugee status by a stateless person; or (2) to establish which State is 'responsible' for the individual concerned, in the sense of having an obligation to readmit him or her, and/or to deal with any claim to refugee status or to treatment under the 1951 Convention.

2. Protection in national law: the refugee status determination procedure

Whether a State takes steps to protect refugees within its jurisdiction and, if so, which steps, are matters very much in the realm of sovereign discretion. For States parties to the Convention and Protocol, however, the outer limits of that discretion are confined by the principle of effectiveness of obligations, and the measures it adopts will be judged by the international standard of reasonable efficacy and efficient implementation. Legislative incorporation may not itself be expressly called for, but effective implementation requires, at least, some form of procedure whereby refugees can be identified, and some measure of protection against laws of general application governing admission, residence, and removal.[116] State practice understandably reveals widely divergent methods of implementation, from which it is difficult to extract any easy formula for determining adequacy and sufficiency. The effectiveness of formal measures depends not only upon the overall efficacy of a State's internal administrative and judicial system, but also upon the particular problems with which that system is faced. Procedures designed for the individual asylum seeker may fail to absorb, let alone survive, a mass influx; the needs of the latter, moreover, will often differ radically, requiring less sophisticated, often purely material solutions, at least in the short term.

A potentially useful distinction is that between refugee status, on the one hand, and the legal consequences which flow from that status, on the other hand; the latter may include an entitlement to residence formally recognized by municipal law or simply eligibility for consideration under a discretionary power only distantly

---

five years prior to the date of conviction of a relevant criminal offence. The Immigration Act 1971 maintained the like immunity. In France, under the former system, 'privileged residents' enjoyed similar benefits, as did the class of *Aufenthaltsberechtigter* in the German Federal Republic—those resident for five years who have adapted themselves economically and socially to local life.

[116] As Legomsky rightly notes, 'an unfair procedure necessarily produces an unjustifiably high risk of violating the individual's substantive rights. Thus, a fair refugee status determination is one essential component of the... prohibition on *refoulement*...': Legomsky, S. H., 'Second Refugee Movements and the Return of Asylum Seekers to Third Countries: The Meaning of Effective Protection', 15 *IJRL* 567, 654 (2003).

confined by international law. In practice, that distinction is often difficult to maintain, particularly where status is itself the criterion for residence and where normal residence requirements—relating, for example, to character or potential for assimilation—may filter back to influence the decision whether someone is a refugee. Similarly, the mere fact that a State treats refugees separately from others will not be conclusive evidence of effective protection. A refugee enjoys fundamental human rights common to citizens and foreign nationals; where these are generally assured, where due process of law is acknowledged, and where measures of appeal and judicial review permit examination of the merits and the legality of administrative decisions, then the refugee also may be sufficiently protected.

States' differing approaches to the problem of definition have already been mentioned.[117] The criteria of the 1951 Convention are commonly adopted, with additional provision now increasingly made also for others in need of complementary or subsidiary protection. The practice in extradition laws of recognizing the 'political offender' as someone worthy of exceptional treatment has also been noted. Similar jurisdictions may employ similar concepts of political offence, but the act of characterization was for long dominated by municipal law considerations. Although it is not concerned with political offences as such,[118] international law is directly concerned with the treatment anticipated for the returned offender. State practice demonstrates, if not universal agreement, then a broad consensus that liability to persecution or prejudice should serve as the underlying rationale, the international standard precluding return.

2.1 GENERAL STANDARDS FOR THE DETERMINATION
OF REFUGEE STATUS

The basic refugee definition, both in international law and in the form adopted by municipal systems, is highly individualistic. It supposes a dispassionate case-by-case examination of subjective and objective elements, which may well prove impractical in the face of large numbers, although they too require the benefit of certain minimum standards.[119] For asylum seekers generally, the very existence of procedures for the determination of status can guarantee both *non-refoulement* and treatment in accordance with the relevant international instruments. At its session on protection 30 years ago in 1977, the Executive Committee expressed the hope that all States parties to the Convention and Protocol would establish such procedures and also give favourable consideration to UNHCR participation.[120] As

---

[117] See above, Ch. 2, s. 6.   [118] See above, Ch. 3, s. 5.5.2.

[119] See Report of the 1979 Arusha Conference, recommendations on the term 'refugee' and determination of refugee status: UN doc. A/AC.96/INF/158, at 9 (1979).

[120] For many years, the annual General Assembly resolution on UNHCR called for asylum seekers to have access to 'fair and efficient procedures'. The last such references appear to have been in 1995 and 1996: UNGA resolutions 50/152, 21 Dec. 1995, para. 5; 51/175, 12 Dec. 1996. The next year's resolution emphasized the right to seek asylum, which should not be jeopardized: UNGA res. 52/103, 12 Dec. 1997, para. 5; and this formula was joined in 1998 by the General Assembly's call for full application of the 1951 Convention/1967 Protocol: UNGA res. 53/125, 9 Dec. 1998, paras. 3,

described below, the Committee further recommended basic procedural requirements, designed at such a level of generality as to be capable of adoption by most
States.[121]

Formal procedures for the determination of refugee status clearly go far towards
securing the effective internal implementation and application of the 1951 Convention and the 1967 Protocol. In adopting the UNHCR Statute in 1950, the
General Assembly urged Governments to cooperate with the High Commissioner
not only by becoming parties to international conventions, but also by taking the
necessary steps of implementation. In succeeding years the General Assembly has
repeated this call, inviting States in particular to improve the legal status of refugees
residing in their territory. One of UNHCR's principal objectives has long been the
establishment of fair and expeditious procedures for the determination of refugee
status, preferably guaranteeing 'full access' by those in search of asylum, and with
the opportunity for independent review of negative decisions.[122]

Although neither the Convention nor the Protocol formally require procedures
as a necessary condition for full implementation, their object and purpose of protection and assurance of fundamental rights and freedoms for refugees without
discrimination, argue strongly for the adoption of such effective internal measures. At its 1977 session, the Executive Committee elaborated this approach, not
only urging Governments to establish formal procedures,[123] but also recommending the following basic procedural requirements:

1. The competent official (for example, immigration officer or border police officer) to whom applicants address themselves at the border or in the territory of
   a contracting State, should have clear instructions for dealing with cases which
   might come within the purview of the relevant international instruments. The

---

5. This double call continued for just two years: UNGA resolutions 54/146, 17 Dec. 1999, paras. 3,
6; 55/74, 4 Dec. 2000, paras. 4, 6, but in 2001 all references to the right to seek asylum were dropped,
while the call for full or full and effective application of the Convention/Protocol has continued:
UNGA resolutions 56/137, 19 Dec. 2001, para. 3; 57/187, 18 Dec. 2002, para. 4; 58/151, 22 Dec.
2003, para. 3; 59/170, 20 Dec. 2004, para. 3; 60/129, 16 Dec. 2005, para. 3; 61/137, 19 Dec. 2006,
para. 3. In the latest resolutions, 'full respect for the principle of *non-refoulement*' and 'humane treatment of asylum seekers' have also begun to appear. However, there is no reason to suppose that fair
and efficient procedures are any less essential to the fulfilment of international obligations and the
effective identification and protection of refugees.

[121] For an early account of State procedures, see Avery, C., 'Refugee Status Decision-making: The
Systems of Ten Countries', 19 *Stanford Journal of International Law*, 235 (1983). National procedures
seem to be in a perpetual State of evolution (or regression); for references to contemporary analysis,
see the second edition of this work, 325–6, n. 5.

[122] For earlier statements on the Office's position and policy regarding procedures, see UNHCR,
'Note on International Protection': UN doc. A/AC.96/694 (3 Aug. 1987), paras. 13, 25–8; UN High
Commissioner Jean-Pierre Hocké: UN doc. A/AC.96/SR.425 (1988), para. 66; and the following
'Notes' on International Protection: UN doc. A/AC.96/750 (27 Aug. 1990), para. 15; UN doc.
A/AC.96/777 (9 Sept. 1991), paras. 25–6; UN doc. A/AC.96/815 (31 Aug. 1993), para. 19.

[123] *Report* of the 28th Session (1977): UN doc. A/AC.96/549, para. 36. Compare Council of
Europe Recommendation no. R(81) 16 on the harmonization of national procedures relating to
asylum, adopted by the Committee of Ministers on 5 Nov. 1981.

official should be required to act in accordance with the principle of *non-refoulement* and to refer such cases to a higher authority.

2. Applicants should receive the necessary guidance as to the procedure to be followed.

3. There should be a clearly identified authority—wherever possible a single central authority—with responsibility for examining requests for refugee status and taking a decision in the first instance.

4. Applicants should be given the necessary facilities, including the services of competent interpreters for submitting their case to the authorities concerned. Applicants should also be given the opportunity, of which they should be duly informed, to contact a representative of UNHCR.

5. Applicants recognized as refugees should be informed accordingly and issued with documentation certifying refugee status.

6. Applicants not recognized should be given a reasonable time to appeal for a formal reconsideration of the decision, either to the same or a different authority, whether administrative or judicial, according to the prevailing system.

7. Applicants should be permitted to remain in the country pending decisions on the initial request by the competent authority referred to in paragraph (3) above, unless it has been established by that authority that the request is clearly abusive. They should also be permitted to remain in the country while an appeal to a higher administrative authority or to the courts is pending.[124]

In recent years, UNHCR has regularly expressed its concern to the Executive Committee regarding restrictive trends, particularly with regard to access, 'admissibility', and accelerated procedures.[125] It has also sought to influence harmonization efforts, for example, with regard to the European Union, and expressed serious concerns about aspects of the Directive on Minimum Standards for Procedures. In its view, the 'safe third country' concept should be limited and should include an effective opportunity to rebut a presumption of safety; accelerated procedures should be limited to clearly well-founded or clearly abusive or manifestly unfounded cases; the same minimum procedural guarantees should apply for all asylum examinations; the right to an effective remedy should include suspensive effect; and the 'safe country of origin' concept should be applied narrowly.[126]

---

[124] Executive Committee Conclusion No. 8 (1977). Although these conclusions were followed up in 1982, States were not generally prepared to accept stricter procedural requirements. Instead, they expressed concern about the need to safeguard procedures in the face of manifestly unfounded and abusive applications; there were also different perceptions of UNHCR's role in the determination of refugee status, and something less than wholehearted endorsement; see *Report* of the Sub-Committee of the Whole on International Protection: UN doc. A/AC.96/613, paras. 37–8; also *Report* of the 33rd Session (1982): UN doc. A/AC.96/614, paras. 65–6, 70(4). See further below, s. 2.2.

[125] See, in particular, UNHCR's 'Notes' on International Protection for 1999 (UN doc. A/AC.96/914, 7 Jul. 1999), 2002 (UN doc. A/AC.96/965, 11 Sept. 2002), and 2005 (UN doc. A/AC.96/1008, 4 Jul. 2005)

[126] See Summary of UNHCR's Provisional Observations on the Proposal for a Council Directive on Minimum Standards on Procedures in Member States for Granting and Withdrawing Refugee

2.2 THE ROLE OF UNHCR IN NATIONAL PROCEDURES

Participation by UNHCR in the determination of refugee status derives sensibly from its supervisory role and from the obligations of States parties to cooperate with the Office, and it allows UNHCR to monitor closely matters of status and of the entry and removal of asylum seekers. The procedures themselves will differ, necessarily, in the light of States' own administrative and judicial framework; so too will the nature and degree of involvement of UNHCR. The fundamental issue, however, remains the same—identifying those who should benefit from recognition of their refugee status, and ensuring, so far as is practical, consistent and generous interpretations of essentially international criteria.

In a few countries, UNHCR participates directly in the decision-making process; in others, the local office may attend hearings in an observer capacity, while in yet others the exact role may be determined *ad hoc*, for example, by intervening at appellate level, or by submitting *amicus curiae* briefs.[127] Generally, UNHCR's procedural responsibilities may be summarized as contributing to the effective identification of refugees in need of protection. This may entail: (1) offering an assessment of the applicant's credibility in the light of the claim and of conditions known to exist in his or her country of origin;[128] (2) providing information on the treatment of similar cases or similar legal points in other jurisdictions;[129] (3) representing the international community's interest by providing authoritative interpretations of fundamental concepts, such as 'well-founded fear', and persecution; and (4) promoting an application of the Convention and Protocol that best concords with their humanitarian objectives.

Status, Mar. 2005. See also above, Ch. 7, s. 6.4; Costello, C., 'The Asylum Procedures Directive and the Proliferation of Safe Country Practices: Deterrence, Deflection and the Dismantling of International Protection', 7 *European Journal of Migration and Law* (2005).

[127] Summary information provided to UNHCR by governments in 1989 revealed some five levels of participation, from no formal role, through observer on an advisory committee or similar, voting member of an appeals body, joint decision-maker, to being informed of cases and being asked for views from time to time; see UNHCR, 'Note on Procedures for the Determination of Refugee Status under International Instruments': UN doc. A/AC.96/INF.152/Rev.8 (12 Sept. 1989).

[128] UNHCR's duty to provide international protection to refugees also requires that it provide information known to it regarding conditions in an asylum seeker's country of origin, at least if such information is critical for the determination of refugee status. Because of the political sensitivities involved, and also because UNHCR is not always equipped to collect, assess and analyse relevant information, increasing reliance is placed on information in the public domain, to which appropriate standards of verification and corroboration can be applied in an objective manner.

[129] This task has been facilitated by the development of UNHCR's composite collection of legal and other databases, *RefWorld*, published on DVD/CD-ROM and now in its 15th edn. (2006). On the other hand, UNHCR's protection responsibilities to both refugees and States were seriously compromised (ostensibly to save money) by the progressive destruction of its Centre for Documentation on Refugees (later, the Centre for Documentation and Research) from the mid-1990s onwards. This entailed, first, the abandonment of its Country of Origin Information Project, followed by the physical closure of its premises and the dispersal of its substantial holdings of original material, research, doctrine, and jurisprudence. The 'Refugee Status and Protection Information Section', located in the Department of International Protection, seeks to maintain *RefWorld*, though with considerably limited resources.

2.3 DUE PROCESS IN THE DETERMINATION OF REFUGEE STATUS

International law has little to say with respect to the procedural aspects of due process, particularly as the responsibility of the State for the fulfilment of its obligations turns essentially on what results in fact. The UNHCR Executive Committee recommendations offer a very basic agenda, comprising guidance to applicants, the provision of competent interpreters, a reasonable time to 'appeal for formal reconsideration' of a negative decision, 'either to the same or a different authority, whether administrative or judicial, according to the prevailing system'. They are not binding, but indicate a practically necessary minimum if refugees are to be identified and accorded protection in accordance with international obligations.

Reaching decisions quickly and removing those who are found not to require international protection are perceived by many States as essential to reduce instances of abuse and to render the asylum process more manageable. In practice, few have succeeded in marrying an efficient and expeditious national process (and national legal traditions) to the fulfilment of international obligations.

Procedural rights nevertheless remain very much within the area of 'choice of means' among States parties to the Convention and Protocol; national procedures vary considerably, drawing mostly on local legal culture and due process traditions. Those in the United States, for example, have a constitutional right to a full and fair hearing,[130] while applicants for admission are entitled to such due process as may be accorded by statute. Notice of the 'right to apply for asylum' is often limited, for example, to those in custody or otherwise subject to immigration processing.[131] In Canada, oral hearings are accorded at each level,[132] and the claimant is entitled to be assisted by an interpreter.[133] In the United States, there is no right

---

[130] *Wong Yang Sung* v. *McGrath* 339 US 33 (1950).

[131] See, for example, *Orantes-Hernandez* v. *Meese* 685 F. Supp. 1488, (DC CD Calif.), aff'd 919 F.2d 549 (9th Cir. 1990), where the Court, among others, ordered the INS to advise class members (citizens of El Salvador in INS custody) of their rights to be represented by an attorney, to request a deportation hearing, and to apply for asylum; a copy of a list of free legal services was also to be supplied; see now 8 §208.5(a), requiring the Service to provide the appropriate application forms and, if available, a list of persons or private agencies able to assist in the preparation of the application, but only when such alien 'expresses fear of persecution or harm upon return to his country of origin or to agents thereof'.

[132] The judgment in *Singh* v. *Minister of Employment and Immigration* [1985] SCR 177 was translated into the refugee determination procedure by the next following Immigration Act, and is continued by the *Immigration and Refugee Protection Act 2001*; see now Refugee Protection Division Rules, SOR/2002-228, 14.

[133] The right to an interpreter has been upheld by the Federal Court of Appeal. In *Owusu* v. *Minister of Employment and Immigration* [1989] FCJ No. 33, the Court noted that the right only comes into play when the need for an interpreter is demonstrated in the circumstances of a particular case. In *Ming* v. *Minister of Employment and Immigration* [1990] FCJ No. 173, the Court observed that the applicant was entitled to a *competent* interpreter, citing Wilson J. in *Sociétés Acadiens du Nouveau-Brunswick Inc.* v. *Association of Parents for Fairness in Education* [1986] 1 SCR 549, 622: 'the ability to understand and be understood is a minimal requirement of due process'. See also Conseil d'Etat, 29 juin 1990, No. 35.346 (IIIe ch), *Nwokolo c/ Etat belge*—if an interpreter has

to the interpretation of the entire proceedings, but only of questions directed to the claimant and responses thereto.[134] In other jurisdictions, the availability of interpretation may depend upon the 'nature' of the proceedings, being limited sometimes to criminal cases, or of the 'civil' character of the right in question.[135]

Jurisdictional differences also govern the right to counsel, with the United States recognizing the right but at no expense to the government,[136] while the Canadian system provides that every claimant has, and shall be informed of, the right to counsel, in certain circumstances at government expense.[137]

An important related issue, both for claimants and for States, is that of confidentiality of proceedings. Again, the interest of the asylum seeker, including the necessity to protect friends and family in the country of origin, will often run counter to legal traditions of public hearings and open courts.[138] Many jurisdictions provide for confidentiality in matrimonial cases, however, and in proceedings involving juveniles or sexual assault. Where the principle of open court has constitutional status, a balance between the advantages of confidentiality and the public interest may yet be achieved. This might be done, for example, by legislating a presumption in favour of *in camera* proceedings, save that where a member of the public seeks to attend, the claimant would have the onus of showing that

not been or appears not to have been used, this is a violation of ECHR50 and CSR51 rights, so far as the claimant has not had the chance properly to defend his or her rights: *RDDE*, No. 60, sept.–oct. 1990, 245; Conseil d'Etat, 19 fev. 1992, No. 38.798 (IIIe ch.), *Manou c/ Etat belge*—where another refugee claimant was used as interpreter, but had little knowledge of the applicant's language, the court quashed the decision to refuse suspension of removal: *RDDE*, No. 69, mai–juin–juillet–août, 1992, 191.

[134] But see *El Rescate Legal Services* v. *Executive Office for Immigration Review* 727 F. Supp. 557 (CD Calif., 1989). For concerns as to the adequacy of interpretation, see Anker, D., 'Determining Asylum Claims in the United States—Summary Report of an Empirical Study of the Adjudication of Asylum Claims before the Immigration Court', 2 *IJRL* 252, 257 (1990).

[135] With regard to France, see Conseil d'Etat, 2/6 SSR, 7 nov. 1990, 93.993, *Serwaah*, to the effect that the right to an interpreter laid down in art. 6(3) ECHR50 applies only in penal proceedings; Conseil d'Etat, 2ème et 7ème sous-sections réunies, 12 juin 2006, 282275, rejecting challenge to the legality of 'holding centres' without available interpreters lodged by NGOs (GISTI and CIMADE).

[136] 8 CFR §208.9(g). There is no *Sixth Amendment* right to counsel, as at a criminal trial, and the right is essentially a *statutory* right, strengthened by *Fifth Amendment* due process requirements. Counsel may be present, but have a very limited role at the first instance proceeding before an Asylum Officer: ibid. For information, see US Citizenship and Immigration Services: <http://www.uscis.gov>. In *Ukrainian-American Bar Association* v. *Shultz* 695 F.Supp. 33 (DDC 1988), plaintiffs obtained an order, based the First Amendment right to communicate effectively, requiring INS to furnish each person seeking asylum from a Soviet or East Bloc country with written information describing the Association's offer to provide free legal services and how to contact.

[137] The right to counsel is protected by the Canadian *Charter of Rights and Freedoms* and by s. 167, *Immigration and Refugee Protection Act 2001*; costs are generally met through legal aid schemes. It is widely recognized that good representation in asylum proceedings leads to better decision-making; see Schoenholtz, A. I. & Jacobs, J., 'The State of Asylum Representation: Ideas for Change', 16 *Georgetown Immigration Law Journal* 739 (2002).

[138] In Canada, for example, hearings before the Refugee Protection Division (RPD) of the Immigration and Refugee Board are held *in camera*, and randomly selected initials are used in, and identifying information removed from, decisions selected for publication. Once claimants seek review in the Federal Court, however, they are identified by name.

the life, liberty, or security of any person might be endangered if the hearing were held in open court.[139]

Most jurisdictions require decision-makers to base their determinations on evidence adduced at the hearing which is found to be credible and trustworthy in the circumstances, and to take account of all the evidence. The claimant in turn is generally entitled to present evidence, to challenge that submitted against his or her case,[140] and sometimes also to cross-examine witnesses.[141] Finally, the claimant must be advised of the decision which, if negative, should be accompanied by written reasons.

Reasons for decisions are an essential pre-requisite for fundamental justice, allowing the applicant for refugee status to know why his or her claim has been refused and to make a meaningful appeal or application for review. The reasons alone will be practically meaningless, however, unless accompanied by a statement of the relevant facts.[142] The reasons requirement provides justification for the decision, showing that the decision-maker has identified the material facts in the applicant's claim; identified relevant country of origin evidence and assessed its weight; assessed the credibility of the applicant; identified and interpreted the relevant rule or rules of law; applied the law to the facts in a reasoned way (to show, for example, whether what the claimant fears is persecution, or whether the group to which he or she belongs is a 'social group', or whether he or she has what amounts to a well-founded fear); and determined whether the claimant is a refugee.

2.3.1 Appeal or review

The Executive Committee employed somewhat ambiguous language with respect to appeal or review from initial decisions on asylum or refugee status, merely recommending that claimants have 'a reasonable time to *appeal for a formal reconsideration* of the decision', and leaving open both the identity and composition of the re-examining body,[143] and the administrative or judicial nature of the process.

---

[139] See McAllister, D. M., 'Refugees and Public Access to Immigration Hearings in Canada: A Clash of Constitutional Values', 2 *IJRL* 562 (1990); *Pacific Press* v. *Minister of Employment and Immigration* [1991] FCJ No. 331 (Federal Court of Appeal); also Wilson J. in *Edmonton Journal* v. *Alberta* [1989] SCJ No. 124 (Supreme Court of Canada).

[140] Conseil d'Etat, 2/6 SSR, 18 nov. 1987, 78.981, *Bokwa Kimbolo*; the CRR rapporteur having failed to share relevant documents with the claimant, 'le caractère contradictoire de la procédure n'a pas été respecté...'.

[141] The availability of 'cross-examination' depends very much on the nature of the procedure, whether adversarial (as generally in the United States and the United Kingdom), or investigatory (as in Canada). Martin has doubted whether rebuttal evidence, cross-examination and confrontation provide 'the best way to resolve controversies involving disputes over adjudicative facts' (citing Davis, K. C., *Administrative Law Treatise*, (2nd. edn., 1980), ss.15.3 at 144): Martin, D. A., 'Reforming Asylum Adjudication: On Navigating the Coast of Bohemia', 138 *University of Pennsylvania Law Review* 1247, 1346 (1990).

[142] See per Estey, J., in *Northwestern Utilities Ltd.* v. *City of Edmonton* [1979] 1 SCR 684, 705; *MEI* v. *Miah* [1995] FCJ No. 381—no need to give reasons for positive decisions, but if given, must be adequate.

[143] Cf. Conseil d'Etat, 2/6 SSR, 7 nov. 1990, 93.993, *Serwaah*, in which the court ruled that as the *Commission des recours de réfugiés* does not determine questions of civil obligation, its composition

Many States have responded to the 'crisis of numbers' in refugee procedures by abolishing appeals, or levels of appeal, or by confining review to legal issues. It is difficult and perhaps unwise to generalize across systems, but experience nevertheless suggests that while the initial decision-maker may be best placed to judge certain issues, such as the personal credibility of the claimant,[144] restricting later review to a narrow category of legal issues may not be the most effective way to address the problem and ensure that international obligations are satisfied.

There is nevertheless a long tradition of deference to first level finders of fact, particularly by 'specialist tribunals'. This is typified in a New Zealand case, in which the High Court stressed that it will only interfere with a credibility finding by a specialist tribunal such as the Refugee Status Appeals Authority in clear cases of unreasonableness or serious and material errors of fact.[145] Thus in the case of *O & L* v. *RSAA*, the High Court emphasized that:

The plaintiffs' rights were strictly circumscribed by well-settled rules relating to judicial review which is very much a process-based remedy. The High Court has no jurisdiction to revisit the facts or the substance of the decisions (except in very limited circumstances). . . . [146]

In Ireland, on the other hand, the High Court has stressed that credibility assessment must not only concord with established legal principles, but also with 'the principles of constitutional justice'.[147] This suggests a possibly wider view of the traditional error of law doctrine, and a greater readiness to review the materiality of error.[148] In the United Kingdom, the jurisprudence has tended to fall somewhere along the spectrum between deference and review, but since the enactment of and entry into force of the Nationality, Immigration and Asylum Act 2002, the Asylum and Immigration Tribunal's jurisdiction has been limited to points of law, as has the jurisdiction of the reviewing court.[149] Facts and inferences from facts

---

(including a member of the council of OFPRA, the initial decision-maker), does not violate art. 6 ECHR50.

[144] Courts generally are reluctant to overturn first instance credibility findings, where supported by evidence in the record. See Legomsky, S. H., 'Political Asylum and the Theory of Judicial Review', 73 *Minnesota L.R.* 1205 (1989); Blum, C. P., 'The Ninth Circuit and the Protection of Asylum Seekers since the Passage of the Refugee Act of 1980', 23 *San Diego L.R.* 327, 364ff (1986).

[145] See *Sakran* v. *Minister of Immigration* CIV 2003-409-001876, where the New Zealand Court also inclined to find an over-emphasis on the credibility of the applicant: <http://www.refugee.org.nz>.

[146] *O & L* v. *RSAA* CIV-2003-404-5724/5725, High Court, Auckland, (2004): <http://www.refugee. org.nz>.

[147] *T. (A. M.)* v. *Refugee Appeals Tribunal and Minister for Justice, Equality & Law Reform* [2004] IEHC 606.

[148] See *Imafu* v. *Minister for Justice Equality & Law Reform & Ors* [2005] IEHC 416; *Ashu* v. *The Refugee Appeals Tribunal & Anor* [2005] IEHC 469; *R.K.S.* v. *Refugee Appeals Tribunal and Minister for Justice, Equality and Law Reform* [2004] IEHC 436. Although in principle control may be exercised on the basis of error of fact, as well as law, in practice initial decision-makers rarely rely on an immaterial fact or completely misinterpret the facts presented. Part of the problem is also due to continuing attachment to individual case-by-case determination, even for manifestly well-founded claims.

[149] Ss. 101, 103.

are different creatures, however, and it is not clear that an equal amount of deference is required in each case; as the Irish High Court recently said, in *R.K.S.* v. *Refugee Appeals Tribunal* (2004):

One's experience of life hones the instincts, and there comes a point where we can feel that the truth can, if it exists, be smelt. But reliance on what one firmly believes is a correct instinct or gut feeling that the truth is not being told is an insufficient tool for use by an administrative body such as the Refugee Appeals Tribunal. Conclusions must be based on correct findings of fact.

International law generally favours a second, effective look at asylum claims, if only from the perspective of the effectiveness of obligations.[150] At both national and international levels, some sort of appeal, going both to facts and to legality, would appear to offer the best chance of correcting error and ensuring consistency.

3. The 2005 European Union Procedures Directive[151]

Several aspects of the Procedures Directive have been examined above, with particular reference to the provisions on 'safe country', their implications for review and appeal, and the likely impact of implementation on the international obligations of the State.[152] Many of the provisions have been criticized by UNHCR and NGOs, while a Parliamentary challenge was also pending at the time of writing.[153] This section presents a brief overview of the remaining principal articles of the Directive and considers their relation to internationally required results, such as a status for refugees, *non-refoulement*, and protection of human rights. The focus therefore is on the principle of effectiveness of obligations, although as yet without benefit of practice.[154] The Directive also only provides for 'minimum standards',[155] and the width of discretion conceded in choice of means will ensure that

---

[150] See Tribunal civil (Réf.)-Bruxelles, 8 oct. 1993, *X c/ Etat belge*, to the effect that the right to an effective remedy in the case of breach of fundamental rights constitutes an essential element of the rule of law: *RDDE*, No. 75, sept.–oct. 1993, 454.   [151] For text, see below, Annexe 2, No. 20.

[152] See arts. 27, 29–31, 36 of the Procedures Directive, and above, Ch. 7, s. 6.4.

[153] See Case C-133/06 *European Parliament* v. *Council of the EU*, Application O.J. C108, 6 May 2006; UNHCR, 'Provisional Comments on the proposal for a Council Directive on Minimum Standards on Procedures in Member States for Granting and Withdrawing Refugee Status (Council Document 14203/04, ASILE 64)', 10 Feb. 2005; ECRE, 'Information Note on the Council Directive 2005/85/EC of 11 December 2005 April 2004 on Minimum Standards on Procedures in Member States for Granting and Withdrawing Refugee Status', Oct. 2006, noting 'that the recommendations issued during the drafting process ... by UNHCR, NGOs and the other civil organizations, as well as the opinion of the European Parliament, have not been taken account'. The Parliament alone proposed some 102 amendments.

[154] The transposition date for the Procedures Directive is 1 Dec. 2007 (art. 15 on legal assistance and representation: 1 Dec. 2008).

[155] See art. 4, which is not without its problems so far as it appears in principle to *prohibit* the introduction of higher standards if they are 'incompatible' with the Directive, but necessary to ensure compliance with international obligations.

refugee status determination in Europe remains a patchwork of not necessarily consistent or compatible procedures.

Although the Preamble makes several references to Member States' international obligations and to the fundamental rights recognized 'in particular' by the EU Charter, what exactly is intended is unclear.[156] One might have expected the Directive to be framed in terms precisely of those obligations, particularly where they have been clarified in judgments of the European Court of Human Rights. In *Jabari* v. *Turkey*, for example, the Court expressly stated that, given the irreversible nature of article 3 harm, 'an effective remedy under Article 13 requires *independent and rigorous scrutiny* of a claim that there exist substantial grounds for fearing a real risk of treatment contrary to Article 3 and *the possiblility of suspending the implementation of the measure impugned*'.[157]

In *Čonka* v. *Belgium*, the Court again emphasized:

... that Article 13 of the Convention guarantees the availability at national level of a remedy to enforce the substance of the Convention rights and freedoms in whatever form they may happen to be secured in the domestic legal order. The effect of Article 13 is thus to require the provision of a domestic remedy to deal with the substance of an 'arguable complaint' under the Convention and to grant appropriate relief. The scope of the Contracting States' obligations under Article 13 varies depending on the nature of the applicant's complaint; however, the remedy required by Article 13 must be 'effective' in practice as well as in law. The 'effectiveness' of a 'remedy' within the meaning of Article 13 does not depend on the certainty of a favourable outcome for the applicant. Nor does the 'authority' referred to in that provision necessarily have to be a judicial authority; but if it is not, its powers and the guarantees which it affords are relevant in determining whether the remedy before it is effective...

... the requirements of Article 13, and of the other provisions of the Convention, take the form of a guarantee and not of a mere statement of intent or a practical arrangement. That is one of the consequences of the rule of law, one of the fundamental principles of a democratic society, which is inherent in all the Articles of the Convention. ... [158]

As has already been pointed out above, the determination of refugee status and thus an *effective* procedure to that end are implicit in the 1951 Convention and essential to its implementation in good faith; a first reading of the Procedures Directive, however, suggests that there are many areas of potential incompatibility with these principles, as and when it is translated into practice.

---

[156] For example, para. (9) recalls that Member States are bound by international instruments prohibiting discrimination, but other obligations are not mentioned.

[157] *Jabari* v. *Turkey* [2000] 9 BHRC 1, para. 50 (emphasis supplied); see also paras. 39, 40, emphasizing the need for 'rigorous scrutiny' and finding 'no meaningful assessment' on the facts before it. See also *TI* v. *United Kingdom* [2000] INLR 211, Application No. 43844/98, 3 Mar. 2000, where the Court considered that even removal to another party to ECHR50, for example, under the Dublin or similar arrangement, does not affect the responsibility of the State to ensure that the individual concerned is not subject to treatment contrary to art. 3 ECHR50.

[158] *Čonka* v. *Belgium* [2002] 34 EHRR 1298, paras. 75, 83.

3.1 ORGANIZATION OF THE PROCEDURES DIRECTIVE

The Directive is organized into five substantive chapters, a thirty-four paragraph preamble and chapter of final provisions, and three annexes (the 'determining authority) in Ireland, the designation of safe countries of origin, and the definition of asylum applicant in Spain).

The Preamble is a mix of history, principles and aspirations: a 'minimum framework' for procedures (5, 7); decisions on the facts by qualified personnel (10); prompt decision-making (11); effective access to procedures and procedural guarantees, subject to certain exceptions (13); endorsement of existing border procedures and the possibility of further exceptions (16); confirmation of the 'safe country of origin' approach, including a minimum common list (17–21); substantive examination of all applicants, except when the Directive provides otherwise, for example, in the case of protection elsewhere (22–25); procedural guarantees in the case of withdrawal of refugee status, but not necessarily in all cases (26); and an effective remedy, at least in principle (27). Among its final paragraphs, the Preamble notes that the Directive does not affect Member State powers and responsibilities in relation to law and order, internal security, and the 'Dublin Regulation', and that implementation is to be reviewed at two-yearly intervals (28, 29, 30).[159]

Chapter I's 'General Provisions' reiterate the focus on asylum applications from 'third country nationals' and stateless persons, following the Qualification Directive.[160] A 'determining authority' is defined as any 'quasi-judicial or administrative body in a Member State responsible for examining applications for asylum and competent to take decisions in the first instance',[161] so missing out on an opportunity to require a higher level authority, either independent or autonomous, as a first step towards raising standards region-wide. Member States are required to designate such authority,[162] but they may also replace that authority by another for the purposes of decision-making related to the Dublin Regulation, safe third country cases, and various other purposes.[163] Article 3 provides that the Directive applies to 'all applications for asylum made in the territory . . . at the border or in the transit zones', and to withdrawal of status; but it does not apply to 'requests for diplomatic asylum submitted to representations of Member States'. If States adopt a single procedure for both Convention and subsidiary protection, then the Directive applies as well.

Chapter II, 'Basic Principles and Guarantees', is the most extensive part of the Directive and deals, as the title indicates, with the essentials of refugee determination (articles 6–22). It contains a number of good points; for example, article 6

---

[159] It also notes that Ireland and the UK have opted in, and Denmark, out.
[160] See above, Ch. 3, s. 3.1.   [161] Art. 2(e).   [162] Art. 4(1).
[163] These may include national security, preliminary examination of subsequent applications, and the processing of border claims: arts. 4(2), 32, 35, 36.

deals with the modalities of access to the procedure, recognizing the right of every adult of legal capacity to apply, but leaving it to Member States to determine when a minor may make an application.[164] Article 7 recognizes the right also of every applicant to remain pending the determination of his or her claim at first instance but, like so much in the Directive, there are exceptions potentially damaging to the integrity of the protection system, for example, in the case of 'subsequent applications' or where it is proposed to extradite the individual or surrender him or her to an international criminal jurisdiction.

Article 8 lays down some useful ground rules: no application shall be rejected or excluded simply because it was not made as soon as possible; applications must be 'examined and decisions taken individually, objectively and impartially'; 'precise and up-to-date' country of origin information is to be obtained;[165] and decision-makers must be qualified. Articles 9 and 10 continue, requiring decisions to be in writing, reasons in fact and law to be given for rejections, advice on the modalities for challenge,[166] and information about the procedure to be followed, not in a language the claimant understands, but one which he or she 'may reasonably be supposed to understand'.[167] The services of an interpreter are also to be provided 'whenever necessary', the opportunity to communicate with UNHCR or 'any other organisation working on behalf of UNHCR' is 'not [to] be denied', and notice of decisions is to be given 'in reasonable time'.[168] Article 11 sets out the 'obligations' of the asylum applicant, such as attending the authorities, supplying relevant documents, and so forth.

Given the Directive's earlier endorsement of 'effective' access to procedures, the opportunity to cooperate and communicate and to present the relevant facts, it is all the more surprising that article 12 offers so many exceptions to what ought, as experience shows, to be the central pillar of the determination process, namely, the personal interview. While an imminent positive decision is unobjectionable, the same cannot be said where the competent authority has already had a 'meeting' with the claimant,[169] has already come to an 'unfounded' decision,[170] or an interview is 'not reasonably practicable'. As personal credibility is now perceived as crucial in many national systems, it makes little practical sense to do away precisely with the opportunity to clarify possible misunderstandings, inconsistencies,

---

[164] See also art. 12 (Member States can determine whether a minor should have a personal interview); art. 17 (guarantees for 'unaccompanied minors' and recognition of the 'best interests' principle).

[165] Nothing is said, however, about the standards attaching to such information, or whether it should be available also to applicants and their representatives.

[166] Although with the possibility of exceptions in minor, but questionable circumstances: art. 9(2).

[167] Art. 10(1)(a).

[168] Art. 10(1)(b), (c), (d); these guarantees apply also to appeal procedures under Ch. V.

[169] In relation to such 'meeting', however, see art. 13(5).

[170] 'Unfounded' is to be understood by reference to art. 23(4)(a)—little relevant evidence; art. 23(4)(c)—safe country of origin or safe third country cases; art. 23(4)(g)—inconsistent, contradictory, unlikely or insufficient representations; and art. 23(4)(h)—application made to delay or frustrate removal.

or other errors.[171] Similarly, article 15 on legal assistance and representation states the basic right in terms of an entitlement to consult a lawyer at the applicant's own cost, and limits 'free' legal advice and representation to appeals. Such a limitation and others in the same article and in article 16, go against the results of research across several jurisdictions, which show that better quality decisions, negative and positive, result when advice and representation are available as early as possible.[172]

On the positive side, however, article 21 provides that Member States shall allow UNHCR (and any organization working in the State on its behalf) to have access to asylum seekers (including those in detention or transit zones), to have access to information on individual applications and the course of the procedure, and to make known its views on individual applications.

Chapter III deals with procedures at first instance (articles 23–36), much of it dedicated to a range of some sixteen circumstances in which the Member State 'may' provide for prioritisation or acceleration—so-called 'unfounded' claims, including safe country cases, cases where there is insufficient information as to identity, or where the applicant's claim is clearly unconvincing because of 'inconsistent, contradictory, improbable or insufficient representations'.[173] Similarly, although the general support for an appropriate procedure in the case of withdrawal of refugee status is welcome, article 38 provides that Member States 'may decide that ... refugee status shall lapse by law', presumably without the necessity for a procedure and a decision, in certain cases of cessation, namely, re-availment of protection, re-acquisition of nationality, acquisition of a new nationality and protection, or re-establishment in the country of origin. As shown above,[174] these are issues that frequently involve matters of fact and appreciation, which cannot be settled by some sort of 'legislative lapsing'. What is missing overall is any controlling provision which would ensure that decisions in such cases nevertheless meet the necessary legal standards of protection and ensure that the State's international obligations are satisfied.[175] This requirement, moreover, is not entirely satisfied by Chapter V, 'Appeals Procedures', comprising a single article 39. Although entitled, 'The right to an effective remedy', it is ultimately equivocal on the issue of suspensive effect,[176] making no attempt to present a set of rationally justifiable circumstances in which it might, indeed, be appropriate not to allow an applicant for refugee status to remain pending the outcome of an appeal.

---

[171] Cf. art. 13(3), which provides that 'Member States *shall* take appropriate steps to ensure that personal interviews are conducted under conditions which allow applicants to present the grounds for their applications in a comprehensive manner ...'.

[172] See, among others, ECRE, 'The Way Forward. Europe's Role in the Global Refugee System—Towards Fair and Efficient Asylum Systems in Europe', Sept. 2005, 38–9.

[173] Art. 23(4). Art. 25 adds a further category of 'inadmissible applications'.

[174] See above, Ch. 4, s. 1. As noted (140, n. 28), this point was not understood by the High Court of Australia in *MIMIA* v. *QAAH* [2006] HCA 53, although local law may have left the Court with little opportunity to take into account and apply the relevant international legal standards.

[175] Other provisions of this Chapter are dealt with above; see Ch. 7, s. 6, particularly with regard to the safe country concept.   [176] See above, text to n. 157.

At this, stage, it is not possible to determine how States will seek to implement the Directive at the national level. Experience suggests, however, that if practice develops with an eye on every exception, breaches of international obligations will be difficult to avoid.

4. Process in refugee status determination: getting to 'Yes'; getting to 'No'

The 1951 Convention/1967 Protocol do not require a refugee to have fled by reason of persecution, or that persecution should actually have occurred. The focus is more on the future, but there are inherent weaknesses in a system of protection founded, as international law would seem to require, upon essays in prediction. Although subjective fear or at least apprehension may be relevant, the key issues are nevertheless factual, and the key question is whether there are sufficient facts to permit the finding that, if returned to his or her country of origin, the claimant would face a serious risk of harm. The credibility of the applicant and the weight of the evidence are thus of critical importance.

The UNHCR *Handbook on Procedures and Criteria for Determining Refugee Status*, prepared at the request of States members of the UNHCR Executive Committee, deals in large measure with some of the practical problems of determining refugee status, from the standard of proof to guidelines for the conduct of hearings. It acknowledges the general legal principle that the burden of proof lies on the person submitting a claim, but recalls that an applicant for refugee status is normally in a particularly vulnerable situation which may occasion serious difficulties in presenting the case.[177] Although an applicant must generally prove the *facts* on which he or she relies on a balance of probabilities, the legal test for the *risk* of persecution is not set so high.[178] In practice also, many of the facts relating to conditions in the country of origin will be common knowledge, or will be capable of proof on the basis of authoritative documentary information. In such circumstances, what counts is the personal situation of the applicant, who will often be unable to support his or her statements with 'hard evidence'. Ideally, these factors will influence both the procedure and evidentiary requirements, leading to a hearing in which the claimant is best able to present his or her story, and to decision-making premised on appropriate standards of proof.[179]

The minimum outline for refugee status procedures is relatively straightforward, as are the guidelines for examiners and decision-makers. The basic issues

---

[177] UNHCR, *Handbook*, paras. 190, 196. Particular care will be needed in cases involving torture; see Dignam, Q., 'The Burden of Proof: Torture and Testimony in the Determination of Refugee Status in Australia', 4 *IJRL* 343 (1992); Rhys Jones, D. & Smith, S. V., 'Medical Evidence in Asylum and Human Rights Appeals', 16 *IJRL* 381 (2004).

[178] On evidence and the standard of proof, see UNHCR, *Handbook*, paras. 37–43; and for more detailed analysis, see above Ch. 3, s. 3.

[179] On evidence and the benefit of the doubt, see UNHCR, *Handbook*, paras. 197–9; 203–5.

involve establishing the narrative of flight, including the reasons, clarifying country of origin conditions, and reaching an assessment of the whole in light of the essentially future orientation of the refugee definition. Asylum applicants have a responsibility to tell the truth and present their case fully, but counsel and examiners too have a duty and a role to play in the process of presentation. This is not a rule of law, but a general notion flowing from the nature of the proceedings, where the ultimate objective, recognizing and protecting refugees, may otherwise get lost in the process.

Experience shows that the refugee status determination process is often unstructured. As the Irish High Court acknowledged in the case cited above, decision-makers commonly rely on instinct and a feel for credibility, but with inadequate attention to the problems of assessment, identification of material facts, the weight of the evidence, and standards of proof.[180] Even where decisions are felt to be correct, lack of confidence can result from systematically basing oneself on subjective assessments and failing to articulate clearly the various steps which lead to particular conclusions and the reasons which justify each stage. Such lack of confidence can increasingly undermine the capacity to deal effectively with the caseload, whatever the strengths or weaknesses of individual applications, and no matter how many unstructured decisions are in fact right.

Considered in its simplest form, the process of determining refugee status involves no more than the application of a legal formula to a particular set of facts. In practice, there are many inherent problems. Decision-makers, for example, must be able to elicit relevant information from the narrative which is the applicant's story; to assess the credibility of applicants, witnesses and experts, and to justify decisions on credibility; to weigh the evidence rationally; to determine and state what are the material facts; to apply the law to the facts; to take decisions and to justify those decisions by reference to reasons and principle. This in turn requires a degree of competence, even skill, in the arts of questioning, interviewing, and examination, and a capacity to bring out the relevant elements from an individual narrative. It requires skill also in the use of interpreters, as well as confidence in the use of country of origin and jurisprudential information, discrimination in the selection of such sources, and in their evaluation and assessment.

In addition, a sound knowledge of the legal and procedural framework is called for, including its national and international aspects, and a sensitivity to other influential factors in the process, for example, the subjective element of fear, both as a dimension of the refugee definition and of the proceedings themselves; cultural factors which influence the narration of events, including practices of truth

---

[180] *R.K.S.* v. *Refugee Appeals Tribunal and Minister for Justice, Equality and Law Reform*, [2004] 1 EHC 436. Cf. *Minister for Immigration and Multicultural Affairs* v. *Singh* (2000) 98 FCR 469, [2000] FCA 845—a fact is 'material' if the decision in the practical circumstances of the particular case turns upon whether that fact did or did not exist, and specifically matters that are objectively material to whether a person is in truth a refugee.

and concealment, and the attribution of family and other relationships of greater and lesser dependence; and the relationship of group fear to individual cases.

4.1 THE INTERVIEW, EXAMINATION, OR HEARING

The object of the interview, examination or hearing is to encourage and obtain a narrative, and an understanding of the applicant's reasons for leaving, or refusing to return to, his or her country of origin. The process itself, whether conducted directly or through counsel, is one of communication, and communication operates on many levels, including the content or the information transmitted, and the context, which explains what the message is about. Context includes not only the words used and the manner of their presentation, but also the reactive aspects which flow from environment, questioning and expectations. For the message sent is not necessarily the message received, either because examiner and applicant move in different contexts and are misreading each other's responses; or because of an absence of shared symbols, such as language and culture; or because of the emotion attendant on the process (the intimidating aspect of proceedings, the trauma of recalling torture, sexual abuse, ill-treatment, or other suffering).

In a process of case-by-case determination, the hearing must nevertheless be used to elucidate the applicant's reasons for flight and unwillingness to return, in the light of what is known about conditions in the country of origin, as gathered from what the applicant says, from other information provided, and from the decision-maker's own knowledge. The facts given must in turn be interpreted in light of the applicable legal criteria—the *well-foundedness* of the fear, whether what is feared is *persecution* and whether the persecution feared is *attributable* to any of the *reasons* specified in the 1951 Convention.

Often what is important in a person's narrative are *events*, and in particular, their *impact* on the claimant as an individual. Events may be *proximate and personal*, in the sense that the applicant has actually experienced, for example, torture, brutality, discrimination, or imprisonment; or they may be more *distant*, though no less relevant, such as the related experience of others which the applicant (and the observer) perceives to bear upon his or her own case.[181] If there are patterns of persecution of those who share similar characteristics, that may suffice to raise a strong presumption of a reasonable possibility or serious risk of persecution. A credible information base, in turn, will help to show whether such patterns do in fact exist.

---

[181] The United States Asylum Regulations, 8 CFR §208.13(b)(2)(C)(iii), provide: 'In evaluating whether the applicant has sustained the burden of proving that he or she has a well-founded fear of persecution, the asylum officer or immigration judge shall not require the applicant to provide evidence that there is a reasonable possibility that he or she would be singled out individually for persecution if: (A) The applicant establishes that there is a pattern or practice in his or her country of nationality or, if stateless, in his or her country of last habitual residence, of persecution of a group of persons similarly situated to the applicant on account of race, religion, nationality, membership in a particular social group, or political opinion; and (B) The applicant establishes his or her own inclusion in, and identification with, such group of persons such that his or her fear of persecution upon return is reasonable.'

Having identified the events which are central to the applicant's story, the decision-maker must evaluate the *apprehensions*, the *fears* founded upon them. Are they *reasonable* in the circumstances; are they *well-founded*, in the the sense of revealing a serious risk of persecution.

In articulating decisions on individual cases, a framework of rights and interests, reasons, restrictions, and likelihood can be helpful. First, what are the *rights or interests* of the applicant that are claimed to be at risk? Where do they stand in the hierarchy of importance? Secondly, upon what *grounds*, for what *reasons*, are those rights or interests the object of attention? Next, what is the nature of the *restriction or measure* which it is feared may affect, repress, deny, or injure the rights and interests in issue? Are questions of proportionality involved? Are there any competing State or community interests?

Finally, although this fact is integral to the whole process, how *likely* is it that the applicant may be the victim of measures which otherwise must be considered as persecution within the meaning of the Convention? Is there a reasonable, or serious, possibility of such measures eventuating? Is the risk one which, on balance, can be discounted? Or is the nature of the interest such that even an otherwise remote possibility cannot be disregarded, particularly in light of the overall objective of the process, which is to provide protection, to ensure that dignity and integrity and fundamental human rights are assured.

The question of the likelihood of persecution is in practice inseparable from the personal circumstances of the individual considered in light of the general situation prevailing in the country of origin. Likelihood may vary over time and space, depending, for example, on fluctuations in conflicts, or on the physical proximity of individuals to localities in which law and order do not prevail.

4.2 USES AND ABUSES OF COUNTRY AND OTHER INFORMATION

The hearing rarely provides enough information, and although nowadays there are few limits to the sources that might be consulted, extensive searches often raise rather than answer questions. Credible and trustworthy information is nevertheless increasingly recognized as the essential foundation for good decisions. States and decision-makers have long maintained document collections of newspaper items, foreign broadcast reports, governmental and non-governmental human rights assessments, analyses from embassies in countries of origin, and so forth.[182]

The inherent difficulties of coherently assessing the authority of such disparate sources and the necessity to inform decision-makers spread across five regions led the Canadian Immigration and Refugee Board to establish, from the beginning, a Documentation Centre with the objective of becoming 'the principal resource in Canada for the provision of credible and trustworthy evidence relevant to the

---

[182] See also, Barnes, J., 'Expert Evidence—The Judicial Perception in Asylum and Human Rights Appeals', 16 *IJRL* 349 (2004); Good, A., 'Expert Evidence in Asylum and Human Rights' Appeals— An Expert's View', 16 *IJRL* 358 (2004).

process of refugee determination, including country of origin information and information on jurisprudential questions'.[183] The Centre undertook to disseminate such information to the major actors in the refugee determination process, to provide 'objective, reliable and cogent analysis and evaluations', to acquire, disseminate and exchange information, and to establish the necessary databases.

As part of its commitment to producing and disseminating authoritative information, the IRB Documentation Centre (now the Research Directorate) based itself exclusively on material in the public domain, and guidelines published in 1990 stressed that every factual statement or report, in principle, should be corroborated by three different sources.[184] The important principles of public domain information and corroboration have also been incorporated in the collection and dissemination practices of other centres, including UNHCR's Centre for Documentation on Refugees (CDR), until it was abolished.[185] Many other countries now have such documentation and research centres for refugee determination purposes.[186]

There can be no doubting the value of accurate, in-depth, up-to-date, and trustworthy information in the refugee determination context. For example, refugees may have fled a country as a result of counter-insurgency operations. The fuller picture will show the historical origins of the conflict, such as resistance to dispossession of historical land rights; the protagonists (such as the military, representing a dominant non-indigenous elite); the policies (such as institutionalized or systemic discrimination against particular ethnic, linguistic, religious, or economic groups or classes); and the tactics (such as the abduction, torture and arbitrary killing of group representatives). A complete picture will never be available, but a comprehensive approach will contribute significantly to identifying refugee-related reasons for flight. Knowing past patterns and present conditions enables one to make reasonably accurate predictions about the future; about the way certain elements are likely to react and interact; and therefore about the degree of security awaiting those returned or returning to their country of origin.

---

[183] Immigration and Refugee Board Documentation Centre (IRBDC), Mandate, Ottawa, 1989; the terminology of 'credible and trustworthy information' was taken from the Immigration Act, as amended. See generally, Rusu, S., 'The Development of Canada's Immigration and Refugee Board Documentation Centre', 1 *IJRL* 319 (1989); Houle, F., 'The Credibility and Authoritativeness of Documentary Information in Determining Refugee Status: The Canadian Experience', 6 *IJRL* 6 (1994). On standards for human rights reporting and assessment, see Barsh, R. L., 'Measuring Human Rights: Problems of Methodology and Purpose', 15 *HRQ* 87 (1993); Donnelly, J. & Howard, R. E., 'Assessing Nations Human Rights Performance: A Theoretical Framework', 10 *HRQ* 214 (1988).

[184] For a summary of the research methodology, see <http://www.irb-cisr.gc.ca/en/research/about_e.htm#meth/>. For a critique of evidence assessment, see Houle, F., 'Le fonctionnement du régime de preuve libre dans un système non-expert: le traitement symptomatique des preuves par la Section de la protection des réfugiés', (2004) *Revue juridique Thémis* 263.

[185] As noted above, some of CDR's functions have been continued by the Status Determination and Protection Information Section of the Department of International Protection Services. These include publication of *RefWorld* on DVD/CD-ROM (15th edn., 2006). A revised *RefWorld* website was to be launched in 2006.

[186] See Morgan, B., Gelsthorpe, V., Crawley, H. & Jones, G. A., *Country of Origin Information: A User and Content evaluation*, Home Office Research Study No. 271, London, 2003.

Documentary evidence, particularly electronically accessible country reports, has a seductive air, often seeming sufficient to decide the case. But like any other material, documentary evidence must still be assessed and put in context, whether it relates personally to the claimant, or to conditions in the country of origin. Information of the latter kind often gives only a general impression, more or less detailed, of what is going on. Like the refugee determination process itself, it has the artificial quality of freezing time, in a way which can lead to single events acquiring greater significance than is their due.[187] Situations remain fluid, however. Recognizing that, and drawing the right sorts of inference from evidence acknowledged as credible and trustworthy, are nevertheless the hallmarks of sound decisions.

Although the Canadian system has many positive features, it has not been free of criticism, particularly in relation to its overall approach to the evidence. The Refugee Protection Division is not bound by any legal or technical rules of evidence, and may receive and base a decision on evidence which is adduced in the proceedings and considered credible or trustworthy in the circumstances. Nevertheless, problems of jurisprudential culture are said to persist. According to Houle, the common law transmits what might be called a latent presumption of bad faith, that is, disbelief, in the personal testimony of the claimant; and a latent presumption of objectivity, authority, or weight, with regard to documents in the public domain. The result, she says, is that too often a simple contrast of the contradictions between personal testimony and documentary information is used, without more, to justify a negative finding on credibility.[188] Indeed, the IRB Guidelines expressly state that:

The Board is entitled to rely on documentary evidence in preference to the testimony provided by a claimant, even if it finds the claimant trustworthy and credible. However, RPD members must provide clear and sufficient reasons for accepting documentary evidence over the evidence of the claimant, especially when it is uncontradicted.[189]

In one case, however, the judge warned that:

The danger in preferring documentary evidence over [a claimant's] direct evidence, is that documentary evidence is usually general in nature. [A claimant's] recitation of what occurred to him, or her, is particular and personal. Thus, without some clear explanation as to why the general is preferred over the particular one may doubt a conclusion that is based on a preference for the former over the latter.[190]

In Houle's view, decision-makers need to attend more carefully to determining what *weight* to attribute to documentary information, in addition to assessing its credibility and trustworthiness.

---

[187] See, for example, Norway's view in 1987, namely, that since the conclusion of the peace agreement with India, 'there was no further basis for receiving asylum seekers from Sri Lanka': UN doc. A/AC.96/SR.415 (1987) para. 52.   [188] See Houle, above n. 184.

[189] IRB, Refugee Protection Division, 'Assessment of Credibility in Claims for Refugee Protection', Jan. 2004, s. 2.4.7: <http://www.irb-cisr.gc.ca/en/references/legal>.

[190] *Kandasamy* v. *Minister of Citizenship and Immigration* (1997) 138 FTR 126 (Reed J.).

4.3 ASSESSING CREDIBILITY AND DRAWING INFERENCES FROM THE EVIDENCE

Refugee claims made by people from different backgrounds raise a variety of issues.[191] The cross-cultural dimension is obvious on some levels, but the decision-maker's understanding of credibility is almost always affected by the fact that he or she is dealing with knowledge at greater or lesser remove. Simply considered, there are just two issues: First, could the applicant's story have happened, or could his or her apprehensions come to pass, on their own terms, given what we know from available country of origin information? Secondly, is the applicant personally believable? If the story is consistent with what is what is known about the country of origin, then the basis for the right inferences has been laid.[192]

Occasionally, the legislature may attempt to determine what shall and what shall not be considered credible, or at least to influence the weight which decision-makers are required to give to certain events. For example, section 8 of the UK Asylum and Immigration (Treatment of Claimants) Act 2004 emphasizes elements which damage credibility, namely, conduct which conceals, misleads, or obstructs. It presumes to establish presumptions as to the negative quality of individual behaviour—the failure to produce a valid passport, or the destruction, alteration or disposal, without reasonable explanation, of a passport, ticket or other documentation connected with travel, or the failure to answer questions, again without reasonable explanation.

Other countries have not found legislation necessary, or have adopted a mixture of law and guidelines. At the institutional level, the Canadian Immigration and Refugee Board has published extensive guidelines for the use of Board Members in assessing credibility. These identify the central issues as: considering all the evidence; making clear findings on credibility and providing adequate reasons; basing decisions on significant and relevant evidence and aspects of the claim, and dealing with contradictions, inconsistencies, omissions, and materiality; relying on trustworthy evidence to make adverse findings of credibility; and allowing the claimant to clarify contradictions or inconsistencies in the testimony.

In October 2006, Guidance on the Assessment of Credibility was published, for use by the Australian Migration Review Tribunal and the Refugee Review Tribunal. It emphasizes the assessment of credibility as a finding of *fact*, the need again to consider all the evidence, and for credibility findings to be clear and rational and based on the evidence. It also recognizes that a 'not credible' finding in some respects is not necessarily inconsistent with the existence of a well-founded

---

[191] For a detailed study of the issues and some of the challenges involved, see Barsky, R. F., *Arguing and Justifying: Assessing the Convention Refugees' Choice of Moment, Motive and Host Country*, (2000); also, Noll, G., ed., *Proof, Evidentiary Assessment and Credibility in Asylum Procedures*, (2005); Cohen, J., 'Questions of Credibility: Omissions, Discrepancies and Errors of Recall in the Testimony of Asylum Seekers', 13 *IJRL* 293 (2001).

[192] This approach was approved by the Irish High Court in *Ashu* v. *Refugee Appeals Tribunal* [2005] IEHC 469; see also *T. (A. M.)* v. *Refugee Appeals Tribunal and Minister for Justice, Equality & Law Reform* [2004] IEHC 606.

fear of persecution in other respects; and stresses the responsibility of the decision-maker to *inquire*, to raise issues with the claimant, to test for internal consistency and consistency with external sources or information, and to allow an opportunity to respond. 'Delay' may be a relevant consideration in the assessment of credibility, and go to the genuineness or depth of the claimant's fear. On the other hand, it counsels caution in the assessment of personal demeanour.

In the case of documents, however, Canada has legislated. In addition to providing acceptable documentation establishing identity,[193] section 100(4) of the Immigration and Refugee Protection Act provides in part that, 'the claimant must produce all documents and information as required by the rules'; and Rule 7 of the Refugee Protection Division Rules states that:

> The claimant must provide acceptable documents establishing identity *and other elements of the claim.* A claimant who does not provide acceptable documents must explain why they were not provided and what steps were taken to obtain them.[194]

As now is the case under the UK Asylum and Immigration (Treatment of Claimants) Act 2004, the lack of acceptable documents without reasonable explanation is thus a relevant and significant factor in determining the credibility of the applicant. The Canadian Guidelines are nonetheless sensitive to context, stressing that what is 'reasonable' will depend on the circumstances of the case, and in some circumstances it may well be *unreasonable* to expect a claimant to obtain documents from his or her country of origin.[195]

Inconsistencies must be assessed as material or immaterial. *Material* inconsistencies go to the heart of the claim, and concern, for example, the key experiences that are the cause of flight and fear. Being crucial to acceptance of the story, applicants ought in principle to be invited to explain contradictions and clarify confusions.

Inconsistency may be *immaterial* if it relates to incidentals, such as travel details, or distant dates of lesser significance. A statement from which different inferences can be drawn, however, is not an inconsistency, and generally a negative inference as to credibility ought only to be based on inconsistencies that are material or substantial; a series of minor inconsistencies and contradictions may nevertheless combine together to cast doubt on the truthfulness of the claimant. In practice, negative inferences will often be drawn from the claimant's destruction of documents, withholding of information, failure to provide evidence of identity, and persistent vagueness in response, particularly where the claimant is also unable or unwilling to provide a reasonable explanation.

---

[193] S. 106 of the Immigration and Refugee Protection Act provides: 'The Refugee Protection Division must take into account, with respect to the credibility of a claimant, whether the claimant possesses acceptable documentation establishing identity, and if not, whether they have provided a reasonable explanation for the lack of documentation or have taken reasonable steps to obtain the documentation.'

[194] IRB Refugee Protection Division Rules, Rule 7 (emphasis supplied): <http://www.irb-cisr. gc.ca/en/references/policy>.

[195] *Owusu-Ansah* v. *Canada (Minister of Employment and Immigration)* (1989), 8 Imm.L.R. (2d) 106 (FC).

Holes or inconsistencies that appear in the fabric of the narrative can be dealt with through question and answer, provided some care is used in the choice of questions. Research shows that errors in testimony increase dramatically in response to specific questions (25%–33% more errors), by comparison with spontaneous testimony given in the form of a free report, which nevertheless can be more time-consuming. Such free reports also tend to be sketchy and incomplete, however, and can be most effectively filled out by using 'open', rather than 'closed' questions. The open question solicits views, opinions, thoughts and feelings, founded on personal experience; the closed question invites the monosyllabic answer, yes or no; a simple statement of fact; a closed answer.[196]

The process of narration is also a process of communication, and all behaviour, even silence or inactivity, may convey its own message. But, as already noted, the message sent is not necessarily the message received. Although witness behaviour, such as the manner of expression, politeness, firmness of speech, nervousness or openness, is sometimes considered a good guide to credibility, cultural differences can often invalidate this approach. Similarly, to work successfully, cross-examination requires a fairly sophisticated understanding of a language common to all the parties, but is quite unsuited to the questioning of one not fluent, or where question and answer must pass through the medium of an interpreter.[197]

Indeed, the use of interpreters in a manner which will best elicit the narrative of the claimant is something of an art.[198] Translation is *not* a mechanical process, but a two-way, sometimes three-way street, that places particular responsibilities on every participant in the refugee determination process. The interpreter is both link and obstacle; *link*, because he or she facilitates an oral dialogue; and *obstacle*, because the questioner's intentions may be misunderstood, either because of a failure to communicate clearly and coherently, or because both parties do not possess a common basis of understanding and values. What the applicant says comes across *filtered* and then has to pass by the decision-maker's own baggage of preconceptions. Accepted universals, like time, family, common sense, are upset by other people's world views.[199]

---

[196] For example, ask not, 'When did you leave your country?' but, 'Why did you leave,...and when was this?' Not, 'Were you ever mistreated?' but, 'Please describe any difficulties you had...' Not, 'Do you like your government?' but, 'How you feel about your government?' Not, 'Are you willing to return?' but, 'How do you feel about returning, and what do you think might happen?'

[197] On the limits of cross-examination, see Eggleston, Sir Richard, 'What is Wrong with the Adversary System?' 49 *Australian Law Journal* 428 (1975); also, 'Is Your Cross-Examination Really Necessary?' *Proceedings of the Medico-Legal Society of Victoria*, vol. IX, 84 (1961). On problems in establishing facts in civil trials, see Cannon, A. J., 'Effective fact finding', *Civil Justice Quarterly* 2006 25(Jul), 327–48.

[198] See Kälin, W., 'Troubled Communication: Cross-Cultural Misunderstandings in the Asylum Hearing', 20 *Int. Mig. Rev.* 230 (1986); also, in another not unrelated context, Mirdal, G. M., 'The Interpreter in Cross-Cultural Therapy', 26 *International Migration* 327 (1988).

[199] Alvarez, L. & Loucky, J., 'Inquiry and Advocacy: Attorney-Expert Collaboration in the Political Asylum Process', 11 *NAPA Bulletin* 43 (1992) (American Anthropological Association); with reference to claims involving Maya from Huehuetenango, Guatemala, the authors examine practical problems in using expert testimony in asylum proceedings, including the role of the anthropologist in countering

Refugee claims are not like other cases; they rarely present hard facts, let alone positive proof or corroboration. More often than not, the decision-maker must settle for inferences instead, that is, conclusions drawn from the generally inadequate material available. In the absence of hard evidence, the possibility of persecution must be inferred from the personal circumstances of the applicant, and from the general situation prevailing in the country of origin. The credibility of testimony is thus both an essential pre-condition to the drawing of inferences relating to refugee status; and a matter of inference in itself. Inference in this context does not mean the strict logical consequences of known premises, or the process of reaching results by deduction or induction from something known or assumed. Rather, it is the practical business of arriving at a conclusion which, although not logically derivable from the assumed or known, *nonetheless possesses some degree of probability relative to those premises.*

Conjecture must be distinguished from inference, though the line is often difficult to draw:

A conjecture may be plausible but it is of no legal value, for its essence is that of a mere guess. An inference in the legal sense, on the other hand, is a deduction from the evidence, and if it is a reasonable deduction it may have the validity of legal proof. The attribution of an occurrence to a cause is . . . always a matter of inference.[200]

Thus, an inference as to the facts (what happened), or as to the credibility of the claimant (is he or she to be believed) must be based on the evidence and be reasonably open to the decision-maker.

5. The status of refugees and the termination of refugee status in national law

A fully comprehensive survey of the status and rights of refugees in national law is beyond the scope of this work, which is primarily concerned with international law. The following is therefore intended merely to sketch out some of the areas requiring attention if an effective national and international system of protection is to be maintained.

A first distinction exists between those States which have and those which have not ratified the relevant international instruments. For certain States parties, the very act of ratification may cause the treaty to have internal effect, so that it can be relied upon at law by the refugee who seeks to establish status or to secure a

---

political interference, cultural insensitivity, lack of impartiality, and lack of information. Also, Akram, S. M., 'Orientalism Revisited in Asylum and Refugee Claims', 12 *IJRL* 7 (2000).

[200] *Minister for Employment and Immigration* v. *Satiacum* [1989] FCJ No. 505; (1989) 99 NR 171, Federal Court of Appeal of Canada, citing Lord MacMillan in *Jones* v. *Great Western Railway Co.* (1930) 47 TLR 39 at 45.

particular advantage or standard of treatment.[201] Even in such countries, how-ever, specific measures of incorporation may be appropriate, particularly in pro-cedural matters. In other States, including many with a common law tradition, specific legislation is essential if the concept of refugee status is to have any legal content, and if standards of treatment are to be legally enforceable, rather than dependent upon executive discretion.

The divorce between refugee status, on the one hand, and asylum in the sense of a lasting solution, on the other hand, has been analysed above; States are bound by one consequence of refugee status, *non-refoulement*, but retain discretion in the grant of asylum.[202] Between the obligation and the liberty, refugees may yet find themselves in a limbo of varying degrees of legal and administrative security. Many States in practice allow or tolerate the presence of asylum seekers pending the conclusion of procedures for the determination of status.[203] Other countries permit residence pending decision, although departure to a third country can be required. Temporary residence, again under varying conditions, is also granted to asylum seekers pending resettlement elsewhere. Legislation introduced in Hong Kong in 1981 went so far as to *define* a Vietnamese refugee as a person who '(a) was previously resident in Vietnam; and (b) is permitted to remain in Hong Kong as a refugee pending his resettlement elsewhere'.[204] The law provided for sanctions to encourage onward movement by making it a condition of stay that an offer of resettlement elsewhere should not be refused 'without reasonable excuse'.[205]

In many countries, formal recognition of refugee status is the practical precur-sor to the grant of asylum in the sense of lawful residence.[206] On occasion, asylum follows as a matter of legal right or of administrative practice. In other cases, how-ever, it is clear that even recognized refugees are, openly or tacitly, expected to move on to other countries. Where asylum in the sense of residence does follow, then the precise standards of treatment to be accorded will again depend upon the standing of the relevant international treaties in the local law and upon the provi-sions of any incorporating legislation. Protection against extradition, expulsion and *refoulement* may be secured by law indirectly (for example, where deportation appeals tribunals are empowered to take all relevant factors into account); or

---

[201] See, for example, art. 65 of the Constitution of the Netherlands, under which self-executing treaties have the force of law as from their publication, taking precedence over existing statutes and those which follow. See also arts. 25 and 59, Constitution of the Federal Republic of Germany; arts. 53 and 55, 1958 Constitution of France.   [202] For the EU exception, see below, n. 206.

[203] See, for example, Conseil d'Etat, Assemblée, 13 déc. 1991, 120.560, *Dakoury*, confirming the asylum seeker's right to remain until the asylum application has been determined.

[204] Immigration Amendment Ordinance 1981 (no. 35/81) s. 2; Mushkat, R., 'Hong Kong as a country of temporary refuge: an interim analysis', 12 *Hong Kong LJ* 157 (1982).

[205] Ibid. s. 3 (adding new s. 13A(3) to the principal ordinance). Further amendments in 1982, intended to discourage further arrivals, prescribed wide powers of detention and removal of Vietnamese arriving after 2 July of that year: Immigration Amendment Ordinance 1982 (no. 42/82), s. 7.

[206] See also arts. 13, 21, 24(1) of the EU Qualification Directive.

directly, by express restrictions upon the permissible grounds of expulsion and choice of destination.

5.1 REFUGEE STATUS AND THE 'OPPOSABILITY' OF DECISIONS

The existence of an international legal definition of refugees raises the question of the opposability of determinations of refugee status by UNHCR and individual States parties to the 1951 Convention. UNHCR is charged with protection of refugees and is alone competent to decide who comes within its jurisdiction under the Statute or any relevant General Assembly resolution. Given States' acquiescence in UNHCR's protection function, its determinations of status are in principle binding on States, at least so far as meeting its mandate responsibilities is concerned. The very definition of refugees, however, incorporates areas of appreciation, so that in practice UNHCR's position on individuals and groups may be challenged. Nevertheless, as noted in another context,[207] UNHCR's opinions must be considered by objecting States in good faith and a refusal to accept its determinations requires substantial justification.[208]

The 'international character' of refugee status was expressly recognized in Executive Committee Conclusion No. 12 (1978) on the extraterritorial effect of determinations.[209] The Executive Committee 'considered that one of the essential aspects of refugee status, as defined by the 1951 Convention and the 1967 Protocol, is its international character,' and noted that States parties to the Convention and Protocol undertake to recognize and accept for visa purposes CTDs issued by other States.[210] It noted further, 'that several provisions of the 1951 Convention enable a refugee residing in one Contracting State to exercise certain rights—as a refugee—in another Contracting State and that the exercise of such rights is not subject to a new determination of ... refugee status'.[211] Moreover, it recognized that:

refugee status as determined in one Contracting State should only be called into question by another Contracting State when it appears that the person manifestly does not fulfil the requirements of the Convention, e.g. if facts become known indicating that the statements initially made were fraudulent or showing that the person concerned falls within the terms of a cessation or exclusion provision of the 1951 Convention. ... [212]

---

[207] See above, Ch. 8, s. 1.1.1.

[208] UNHCR's decisions on refugee status, although possessing an international character, do not have the same binding character as, say, the 'housekeeping' or technical resolutions of international organizations, which may directly create obligations for member States.

[209] See UN doc. EC/SCP/9.   [210] 1951 Convention, Schedule, para. 7.

[211] UNHCR's background note cited arts. 12, 14, and 16 among those, the exercise of which is not necessarily related to the refugee's 'lawfully staying' in the territory of a Contracting State: 'Note on the Extraterritorial Effect of the Determination of Refugee Status under the 1951 Convention and the 1967 Protocol relating to the Status of Refugees': UN doc. EC/SCP/9, 24 August 1978, para. 18.

[212] Executive Committee Conclusion No. 12 (1978), *Report* of the 29th Session, UN doc. A/AC.96/559, para. 68.2. It was also accepted that a decision by one State *not* to recognize refugee status does not preclude another State from examining a new request by the person concerned.

Apart from providing for the exercise of certain rights, neither the Convention nor the Protocol makes any express provision for extraterritorial effect as such. The undertaking to 'recognize the validity' of travel documents issued under article 28 is arguably limited to their validity for visa, identity, and returnability purposes. However, just as a passport is generally accepted as *prima facie* proof of nationality,[213] so as a matter of comity if not obligation, ought the CTD to be accepted as evidence that the holder possesses the international legal status of refugee. State practice either for or against the Executive Committee's recommendations is sparse, and the occasions on which one State will challenge another's determinations are likely to be rare. A refugee who has offended the law can generally be deported to the State which issued the travel document. A more acute problem arises, however, where the extradition is sought of a refugee recognized in one State but physically present in another. Where the requesting State is the country of origin, the protecting or asylum State may justifiably object to the potential *refoulement* of 'its' refugee. In such a case the refusal to accept the latter's determination of status, followed by extradition of the refugee, constitutes a putative wrong to the protecting State.[214]

5.2 THE PRINCIPLE OF ACQUIRED RIGHTS

The justification for refugee status may come to an end in a variety of circumstances. The question then arises whether that State, in the exercise of its discretion generally over the conditions of residence of foreign nationals, is entitled to require the former refugee to leave its territory. As a matter of law, and at first glance, this aspect of sovereign competence cannot be doubted. In practice, however, it has been common to find that, once asylum is granted, the issue of refugee status is reviewed only if, by their own actions, refugees render themselves liable to deportation (for example, by engaging in criminal activity). Where refugee status ceases in other cases, then the individual becomes subject to the ordinary law governing the residence of foreign nationals. The corollary is that he or she is entitled to the same standards of treatment, including the right not to be arbitrarily expelled. This right, it has been argued elsewhere, entails not only that decisions on expulsion be in accordance with law, but that the foreign national's 'legitimate expectations' be taken into account, including such 'acquired rights' as may derive from long residence and establishment, business, marriage, and local integration.[215]

[213] Goodwin-Gill, *Movement of Persons*, 45–9.
[214] Cf. *R. (on the application of Al Rawi) v. Secretary of State for Foreign Affairs* [2006] EWCA Civ. 1279, discussed above, 518–20.
[215] Goodwin-Gill, *Movement of Persons* 178–9, 230, 255–61, 294.

6. Afterword

Notwithstanding sixty or more years of relatively sophisticated international law and practice, there are still significant lacunae in the international regime of refugee protection and solutions. Among them are the general failure to appreciate the full implications of the international legal status which refugees, in principle, enjoy; and the equal failure still to recognize that the international scope and nature of the refugee phenomenon requires full and effective cooperation between States in good faith, if lasting solutions are to be found for refugees and the future necessity for flight avoided.

These conclusions, among others, are simply stated, but it is probably clear from the preceding chapters that the protection of refugees reflects a perpetual tension between international legal principles, on the one hand, and the legal and policy means chosen for their implementation at the national level, on the other hand. The rules are clear and States continue to express support for the regime of international protection and the role of UNHCR, but domestic concerns and perceptions appear increasingly to lead to laws and policies intended to reflect minimum commitment and maximum room for manoeuvre. There is indeed a strong body of international law favouring the refugee and protecting the human rights of all who move between States, but one must beware of imagining it as an idealized and complete system. The law will need to prove its value in the years to come, not only in continuing to ensure refuge for those in need of protection, but also in navigating the pressures of globalization and the competing and competitive interests of States. In particular, the legal component of the international refugee regime will have to be flexible enough to encompass States' security concerns, but without compromising principle; and sufficiently adaptable to accommodate both the lawful needs of those in flight, and the now perhaps inescapable desire of many States for order in migration. Clearly, the tension will continue, and the art and aim will be to ensure that what has been achieved so far is not lost.

Annexes

TABLE OF CONTENTS
Annexe 1
Basic Instruments

Annexe 2
Selected Regional Instruments

Annexe 3
States Parties to the 1951 Convention, the 1967 Protocol, and the 1969 OAU Convention; Delegations participating in the 1984 Cartagena Declaration; and Members of the Executive Committee of the High Commissioner's Programme (at 31 January 2007)

1. 1946 Constitution of the International Refugee Organization—Extracts

Entry into force: 20 August 1948

Text: 18 *UNTS* 3

Preamble

The Governments accepting this Constitution, recognizing:

that genuine refugees and displaced persons constitute an urgent problem which is international in scope and character;

that as regards displaced persons, the main task to be performed is to encourage and assist in every way possible their early return to their country of origin;

that genuine refugees and displaced persons should be assisted by international action, either to return to their countries of nationality or former habitual residence, or to find new homes elsewhere, under the conditions provided for in this Constitution; or in the case of Spanish Republicans, to establish themselves temporarily in order to enable them to return to Spain when the present Falangist regime is succeeded by a democratic regime;

that resettlement and reestablishment of refugees and displaced persons be contemplated only in cases indicated clearly in the Constitution;

that genuine refugees and displaced persons, until such time as their repatriation or resettlement and reestablishment is effectively completed, should be protected in their rights and legitimate interests, should receive care and assistance and, as far as possible, should be put to useful employment in order to avoid the evil and anti-social consequences of continued idleness; and that the expenses of repatriation to the extent practicable should be charged to Germany and Japan for persons displaced by those Powers from countries occupied by them:

Have agreed, for the accomplishment of the foregoing purposes in the shortest possible time, to establish and do hereby establish, a non-permanent organization to be called the International Refugee Organization, a specialized agency to be brought into relationship with the United Nations . . .

ANNEX 1: DEFINITIONS

General Principles

1. The following general principles constitute an integral part of the definitions as laid down in Parts I and II of this Annex.

(a) The main object of the Organization will be to bring about a rapid and positive solution of the problem of bona fide refugees and displaced persons, which shall be just and equitable to all concerned.

(b) The main task concerning displaced persons is to encourage and assist in every way possible their early return to the countries of origin, having regard to the principles laid down in paragraph (c) (ii) of the resolution adopted by the General Assembly of the United Nations on 12 February 1946 regarding the problem of refugees (Annex III).

(c) As laid down in the resolution adopted by the Economic and Social Council on 16 February 1946, no international assistance should be given to traitors, quislings and war criminals, and nothing should be done to prevent in any way their surrender and punishment.

(d) It should be the concern of the Organization to ensure that its assistance is not exploited in order to encourage subversive or hostile activities directed against the Government of any of the United Nations.

(e) It should be the concern of the Organization to ensure that its assistance is not exploited by persons in the case of whom it is clear that they are unwilling to return to their countries of origin because they prefer idleness to facing the hardships of helping in the reconstruction of their countries, or by persons who intend to settle in other countries for purely economic reasons, thus qualifying as emigrants.

(f) On the other hand it should equally be the concern of the Organization to ensure that no bona fide and deserving refugee or displaced person is deprived of such assistance as it may be in a position to offer.

(g) The Organization should endeavour to carry out its functions in such a way as to avoid disturbing friendly relations between nations. In the pursuit of this objective, the Organization should exercise special care in cases in which the re-establishment or resettlement of refugees or displaced persons might be contemplated, either in countries contiguous to their respective countries of origin or in non-self-governing countries. The Organization should give due weight, among other factors, to any evidence of genuine apprehension and concern felt in regard to such plans, in the former case, by the country of origin of the persons involved, or, in the latter case, by the indigenous population of the non-self-governing country in question.

2. To ensure the impartial and equitable application of the above principles and of the terms of the definition which follows, some special system of semi-judicial machinery should be created, with appropriate constitution, procedure and terms of reference.

Part I: Refugees and Displaced Persons within the Meaning
of the Resolution adopted by the Economic and Social Council of the United Nations on
16 February 1946

Section A—Definition of Refugees

1. Subject to the provisions of sections C and D and of Part II of this Annex, the term 'refugee' applies to a person who has left, or who is outside of, his country of nationality or of former habitual residence, and who, whether or not he had retained his nationality, belongs to one of the following categories:

(a) victims of the Nazi or fascist regimes or of regimes which took part on their side in the second world war, or of the quisling or similar regimes which assisted them against the United Nations, whether enjoying international status as refugees or not;

(b) Spanish Republicans and other victims of the Falangist regime in Spain, whether enjoying international status as refugees or not;

(c) persons who were considered refugees before the outbreak of the second world war, for reasons of race, religion, nationality or political opinion.

2. Subject to the provisions of sections C and D and of Part II of this Annex regarding the exclusion of certain categories of persons, including war criminals, quislings and traitors, from the benefits of the Organization, the term 'refugee' also applies to a person, other than a displaced person as defined in section B of this Annex, who is outside of his country of nationality or former habitual residence, and who, as a result of events subsequent to the outbreak of the Second World War, is unable or unwilling to avail himself of the protection of the Government of his country of nationality or former nationality.

3. Subject to the provisions of Section D and of Part II of this Annex, the term 'refugee' also applies to persons who, having resided in Germany or Austria, and being of Jewish origin or foreigners or stateless persons, were victims of Nazi persecution and were detained in, or were obliged to flee from, and were subsequently returned to, one of those countries as a result of enemy action, or of war circumstances, and have not yet been firmly resettled therein.

4. The term 'refugee' also applies to unaccompanied children who are war orphans or whose parents have disappeared, and who are outside their countries of origin. Such children, 16 years of age or under, shall be given all possible priority assistance, including, normally, assistance in repatriation in the case of those whose nationality can be determined.

Section B—Definition of Displaced Persons

The term 'displaced person' applies to a person who, as a result of the actions of the authorities of the regimes mentioned in Part I, section A, paragraph 1 (a) of this Annex has been deported from, or has been obliged to leave his country of nationality or of former habitual residence, such as persons who were compelled to undertake forced labour or who were deported for racial, religious or political reasons. Displaced persons will only fall within the mandate of the Organization subject to the provisions of sections C and D of Part I and to the provisions of Part II of this Annex. If the reasons for their displacement have ceased to exist, they should be repatriated as soon as possible in accordance with article 2, paragraph 1 (a) of this Constitution, and subject to the provision of paragraph (c), sub-paragraphs (ii) and (iii) of the General Assembly resolution of 12 February 1946 regarding the problem of refugees . . . [1]

---

[1] In the resolution referred to, UNGA res. 8(I) on the question of refugees, the General Assembly decided to refer the problem to the Economic and Social Council for thorough examination, recommending that it establish a special committee to this end, and that it take the following principles into consideration (para. (c)): '(i) this problem is international in scope and nature; (ii) no refugees or displaced persons who have finally and definitely, in complete freedom, and after receiving full knowledge of the facts, including adequate information from the governments of their countries of origin, expressed valid objection to returning to their country of origin . . . shall be compelled to return to their country of origin. The future of such refugees or displaced persons shall become the concern of whatever international body may be recognized or established . . . (iii) the main task concerning displaced persons is to encourage and assist in every way possible their early return to their countries of origin. Such assistance may take the form of promoting the conclusion of bilateral arrangements for mutual assistance in the repatriation of such persons having regard to the principles laid down in paragraph (c)(ii) . . .'. Paragraph (d) provided that 'no action taken as a result of this resolution shall be of such a character as to interfere with the surrender and punishment of war criminals, quislings and traitors . . .'.

Section C—Conditions under which 'Refugees' and 'Displaced Persons' will become the Concern of the Organization

1. In the case of all the above categories except those mentioned in section A, paragraphs 1 (b) and 3 of this Annex, persons will become the concern of the Organization in the sense of the resolution adopted by the Economic and Social Council on 16 February 1946 if they can be repatriated, and the help of the Organization is required in order to provide for their repatriation, or if they have definitely, in complete freedom and after receiving full knowledge of the facts, including adequate information from the Governments of their countries of nationality or former habitual residence, expressed valid objections to returning to those countries.

(a) The following shall be considered as valid objections:

    (i) persecution, or fear, based on reasonable grounds of persecution because of race, religion, nationality or political opinions, provided these opinions are not in conflict with the principles of the United Nations, as laid down in the Preamble of the Charter of the United Nations;

    (ii) objections of a political nature judged by the Organization to be 'valid', as contemplated in paragraph 8 (a)[2] of the report of the Third Committee of the General Assembly as adopted by the Assembly on 12 February 1946.

    (iii) in the case of persons falling within the category mentioned in section A, paragraphs 1 (a) and 1 (c) compelling family reasons arising out of previous persecution, or, compelling reasons of infirmity or illness.

(b) The following shall normally be considered 'adequate information': information regarding conditions in the countries of nationality of the refugees and displaced persons concerned, communicated to them directly by representatives of the Governments of these countries, who shall be given every facility for visiting camps and assembly centres of refugees and displaced persons in order to place such information before them.

2. In the case of all refugees falling within the terms of Section A paragraph 1 (b) of this Annex, persons will become the concern of the Organization in the sense of the resolution adopted by the Economic and Social Council of the United Nations on 16 February 1946, so long as the Falangist regime in Spain continues. Should that regime be replaced by a democratic regime they will have to produce valid objections against returning to Spain corresponding to those indicated in paragraph 1 (a) of this section.

Section D—Circumstances in which Refugees and Displaced Persons will cease to be the Concern of the Organization

Refugees or displaced persons will cease to be the concern of the Organization:

(a) when they have returned to the countries of their nationality in United Nations territory, unless their former habitual residence to which they wish to return is outside their country of nationality; or

---

[2] Paragraph 8 (a). 'In answering the representative of Belgium, the Chairman stated that it was implied that the international body would judge what were, or what were not, "valid objections"; and that such objections clearly might be of a "political nature".'

(b) when they have acquired a new nationality; or

(c) when they have, in the determination of the Organization become otherwise firmly established; or

(d) when they have unreasonably refused to accept the proposals of the Organization for their resettlement or repatriation; or

(e) when they are making no substantial effort towards earning their living when it is possible for them to do so, or when they are exploiting the assistance of the Organization.

Part II: Persons who will not be the Concern of the Organization

1. War criminals, quislings and traitors.

2. Any other persons who can be shown:

(a) to have assisted the enemy in persecuting civil populations of countries, Members of the United Nations; or

(b) to have voluntarily assisted the enemy forces since the outbreak of the Second World War in their operations against the United Nations.[3]

3. Ordinary criminals who are extraditable by treaty.

4. Persons of German ethnic origin, whether German nationals or members of German minorities in other countries, who:

(a) have been or may be transferred to Germany from other countries;

(b) have been, during the Second World War, evacuated from Germany to other countries;

(c) have fled from, or into, Germany, or from their places of residence into countries other than Germany in order to avoid falling into the hands of Allied armies.

5. Persons who are in receipt of financial support and protection from their country of nationality, unless their country of nationality requests international assistance for them.

6. Persons who, since the end of hostilities in the Second World War:

(a) have participated in any organization having as one of its purposes the overthrow by armed force of the Government of their country of origin, being a Member of the United Nations; or the overthrow by armed force of the Government of any other Member of the United Nations, or have participated in any terrorist organization;

(b) have become leaders of movements hostile to the Government of their country of origin being a Member of the United Nations or sponsors of movements encouraging refugees not to return to their country of origin;

(c) at the time of application for assistance, are in the military or civil service of a foreign State.

---

[3] Mere continuance of normal and peaceful duties, not performed with the specific purpose of aiding the enemy against the Allies or against the civil population of territory in enemy occupation, shall not be considered to constitute 'voluntary assistance'. Nor shall acts of general humanity, such as care of wounded or dying, be so considered except in cases where help of this nature given to enemy nationals could equally well have been given to Allied nationals and was purposely withheld from them.

2. 1948 Universal Declaration of Human Rights—Extracts

Adopted by the United Nations General Assembly on 10 December 1948

Text: UNGA resolution 217 A(III)

Article 13

1. Everyone has the right to freedom of movement and residence within the borders of each State.

2. Everyone has the right to leave any country, including his own, and to return to his country.

Article 14

1. Everyone has the right to seek and to enjoy in other countries asylum from persecution.

2. This right may not be invoked in the case of prosecutions genuinely arising from non-political crimes or from acts contrary to the purposes and principles of the United Nations.

Article 15

1. Everyone has the right to a nationality.

2. No one shall be arbitrarily deprived of his nationality nor denied the right to change his nationality.

3. 1950 Statute of the Office of the United Nations High Commissioner for Refugees

GENERAL ASSEMBLY RESOLUTION 428 (V) OF 14 DECEMBER 1950

The General Assembly,
In view of its resolution 319 A (IV) of 3 December 1949,

1. Adopts the Annex to the present resolution, being the Statute of the Office of the United Nations High Commissioner for Refugees;

2. Calls upon Governments to co-operate with the United Nations High Commissioner for Refugees in the performance of his functions concerning refugees falling under the competence of his office, especially by:

(a) Becoming parties to international conventions providing for the protection of refugees, and taking the necessary steps of implementation under such conventions;

(b) Entering into special agreements with the High Commissioner for the execution of measures calculated to improve the situation of refugees and to reduce the number requiring protection;

(c) Admitting refugees to their territories, not excluding those in the most destitute categories;

(d) Assisting the High Commissioner in his efforts to promote the voluntary repatriation of refugees;

(e) Promoting the assimilation of refugees, especially by facilitating their naturalization;

(f) Providing refugees with travel and other documents such as would normally be provided to other aliens by their national authorities, especially documents which would facilitate their resettlement;

(g) Permitting refugees to transfer their assets and especially those necessary for their resettlement;

(h) Providing the High Commissioner with information concerning the number and condition of refugees, and laws and regulations concerning them;

3. Requests the Secretary-General to transmit the present resolution, together with the Annex attached thereto, also to States non-members of the United Nations, with a view to obtaining their co-operation in its implementation.

ANNEX: STATUTE OF THE OFFICE OF THE UNITED NATIONS HIGH COMMISSIONER FOR REFUGEES

Chapter I—General Provisions

1. The United Nations High Commissioner for Refugees, acting under the authority of the General Assembly, shall assume the function of providing international protection, under the auspices of the United Nations, to refugees who fall within the scope of the present Statute and of seeking permanent solutions for the problem of refugees by assisting Governments and, subject to the approval of the Governments concerned, private organizations to facilitate the voluntary repatriation of such refugees, or their assimilation within new national communities.

In the exercise of his functions, more particularly when difficulties arise, and for instance with regard to any controversy concerning the international status of these persons, the High Commissioner shall request the opinion of the advisory committee on refugees if it is created.

2. The work of the High Commissioner shall be of an entirely non-political character; it shall be humanitarian and social and shall relate, as a rule, to groups and categories of refugees.

3. The High Commissioner shall follow policy directives given him by the General Assembly or the Economic and Social Council.

4. The Economic and Social Council may decide, after hearing the views of the High Commissioner on the subject, to establish an advisory committee on refugees, which shall consist of representatives of States Members and States non-members of the United Nations, to be selected by the Council on the basis of their demonstrated interest in and devotion to the solution of the refugee problem.

5. The General Assembly shall review, not later than at its eighth regular session, the arrangements for the Office of the High Commissioner with a view to determining whether the Office should be continued beyond 31 December 1953.

Chapter II—Functions of the High Commissioner

6. The competence of the High Commissioner shall extend to:

A. (i) Any person who has been considered a refugee under the Arrangements of 12 May 1926 and of 30 June 1928 or under the Conventions of 28 October 1933 and 10 February 1938, the Protocol of 14 September 1939 or the constitution of the International Refugee Organization.

(ii) Any person who, as a result of events occurring before 1 January 1951 and owing to well-founded fear of being persecuted for reasons of race, religion, nationality or political opinion, is outside the country of his nationality and is unable or, owing to such fear or for reasons other than personal convenience, is unwilling to avail himself of the protection of that country; or who, not having a nationality and being outside the country of his former habitual residence, is unable or, owing to such fear or for reasons other than personal convenience, is unwilling to return to it.

Decisions as to eligibility taken by the International Refugee Organization during the period of its activities shall not prevent the status of refugee being accorded to persons who fulfil the conditions of the present paragraph;

The competence of the High Commissioner shall cease to apply to any person defined in section A above if:

(a) He has voluntarily re-availed himself of the protection of the country of his nationality; or

(b) Having lost his nationality, he has voluntarily re-acquired it; or

(c) He has acquired a new nationality, and enjoys the protection of the country of his new nationality; or

(d) He has voluntarily re-established himself in the country which he left or outside which he remained owing to fear of persecution; or

(e) He can no longer, because the circumstances in connection with which he has been recognized as a refugee have ceased to exist, claim grounds other than those of personal convenience for continuing to refuse to avail himself of the protection of the country of his nationality. Reasons of a purely economic character may not be invoked; or

(f) Being a person who has no nationality, he can no longer, because the circumstances in connection with which he has been recognized as a refugee have ceased to exist and he is able to return to the country of his former habitual residence, claim grounds other than those of personal convenience for continuing to refuse to return to that country;

B. Any other person who is outside the country of his nationality, or if he has no nationality, the country of his former habitual residence, because he has or had well-founded fear of persecution by reason of his race, religion, nationality or political opinion and is unable or, because of such fear, is unwilling to avail himself of the protection of the government of the country of his nationality, or, if he has no nationality, to return to the country of his former habitual residence.

7. Provided that the competence of the High Commissioner as defined in paragraph 6 above shall not extend to a person:

(a) Who is a national of more than one country unless he satisfies the provisions of the preceding paragraph in relation to each of the countries of which he is a national; or

(b) Who is recognized by the competent authorities of the country in which he has taken residence as having the rights and obligations which are attached to the possession of the nationality of that country; or

(c) Who continues to receive from other organs or agencies of the United Nations protection or assistance; or

(d) In respect of whom there are serious reasons for considering that he has committed a crime covered by the provisions of treaties of extradition or a crime mentioned in article VI of the London Charter of the International Military Tribunal or by the provisions of article 14, paragraph 2, of the Universal Declaration of Human Rights.

8. The High Commissioner shall provide for the protection of refugees falling under the competence of his Office by:

(a) Promoting the conclusion and ratification of international conventions for the protection of refugees, supervising their application and proposing amendments thereto;

(b) Promoting through special agreements with Governments the execution of any measures calculated to improve the situation of refugees and to reduce the number requiring protection;

(c) Assisting governmental and private efforts to promote voluntary repatriation or assimilation within new national communities;

(d) Promoting the admission of refugees, not excluding those in the most destitute categories, to the territories of States;

(e) Endeavouring to obtain permission for refugees to transfer their assets and especially those necessary for their resettlement;

(f) Obtaining from Governments information concerning the number and conditions of refugees in their territories and the laws and regulations concerning them;

(g) Keeping in close touch with the Governments and inter-governmental organizations concerned;

(h) Establishing contact in such manner as he may think best with private organizations dealing with refugee questions;

(i) Facilitating the co-ordination of the efforts of private organizations concerned with the welfare of refugees.

9. The High Commissioner shall engage in such additional activities, including repatriation and resettlement, as the General Assembly may determine, within the limits of the resources placed at his disposal.

10. The High Commissioner shall administer any funds, public or private, which he receives for assistance to refugees, and shall distribute them among the private and, as appropriate, public agencies which he deems best qualified to administer such assistance. The High Commissioner may reject any offers which he does not consider appropriate or which cannot be utilized. The High Commissioner shall not appeal to Governments for funds or make a general appeal, without the prior approval of the General Assembly. The High Commissioner shall include in his annual report a statement of his activities in this field.

11. The High Commissioner shall be entitled to present his views before the General Assembly, the Economic and Social Council and their subsidiary bodies.

The High Commissioner shall report annually to the General Assembly through the Economic and Social Council; his report shall be considered as a separate item on the agenda of the General Assembly.

12. The High Commissioner may invite the co-operation of the various specialized agencies.

Chapter III—Organization and Finances

13. The High Commissioner shall be elected by the General Assembly on the nomination of the Secretary-General. The terms of appointment of the High Commissioner shall be proposed by the Secretary-General and approved by the General Assembly. The High Commissioner shall be elected for a term of three years, from 1 January 1951.

14. The High Commissioner shall appoint, for the same term, a Deputy High Commissioner of a nationality other than his own.

15. (a) Within the limits of the budgetary appropriations provided, the staff of the Office of the High Commissioner shall be appointed by the High Commissioner and shall be responsible to him in the exercise of their functions.

(b) Such staff shall be chosen from persons devoted to the purposes of the Office of the High Commissioner.

(c) Their conditions of employment shall be those provided under the staff regulations adopted by the General Assembly and the rules promulgated thereunder by the Secretary-General.

(d) Provision may also be made to permit the employment of personnel without compensation.

16. The High Commissioner shall consult the Government of the countries of residence of refugees as to the need for appointing representatives therein. In any country recognizing such need, there may be appointed a representative approved by the Government of that country. Subject to the foregoing, the same representative may serve in more than one country.

17. The High Commissioner and the Secretary-General shall make appropriate arrangements for liaison and consultation on matters of mutual interest.

18. The Secretary-General shall provide the High Commissioner with all necessary facilities within budgetary limitations.

19. The Office of the High Commissioner shall be located in Geneva, Switzerland.

20. The Office of the High Commissioner shall be financed under the budget of the United Nations. Unless the General Assembly subsequently decides otherwise, no expenditure other than administrative expenditures relating to the functioning of the Office of the High Commissioner shall be borne on the budget of the United Nations and all other expenditures relating to the activities of the High Commissioner shall be financed by voluntary contributions.

21. The administration of the Office of the High Commissioner shall be subject to the Financial Regulations of the United Nations and to the financial rules promulgated thereunder by the Secretary-General.

22. Transactions relating to the High Commissioner's funds shall be subject to audit by the United Nations Board of Auditors, provided that the Board may accept audited accounts from the agencies to which funds have been allocated. Administrative arrangements for the custody of such funds and their allocation shall be agreed between the High Commissioner and the Secretary-General in accordance with the Financial Regulations of the United Nations and rules promulgated thereunder by the Secretary-General.

4. 1951 Convention relating to the Status of Refugees

Text: 189 *UNTS* 150

Entry into force: 22 April 1954

FINAL ACT OF THE UNITED NATIONS CONFERENCE OF PLENIPOTENTIARIES ON THE STATUS OF REFUGEES AND STATELESS PERSONS

I

The General Assembly of the United Nations, by Resolution 429(V) of 14 December 1950, decided to convene in Geneva a Conference of Plenipotentiaries to complete the drafting of, and to sign, a Convention relating to the Status of Refugees and a Protocol relating to the Status of Stateless Persons.

The Conference met at the European Office of the United Nations in Geneva from 2 to 25 July 1951.

The Governments of the following twenty-six States were represented by delegates who all submitted satisfactory credentials or other communications of appointment authorizing them to participate in the Conference:

Australia	Italy
Austria	Luxembourg
Belgium	Monaco
Brazil	Netherlands
Canada	Norway
Colombia	Sweden
Denmark	Switzerland (the Swiss delegation also
Egypt	represented Liechtenstein)
France	Turkey
Federal Republic of Germany	United Kingdom of Great Britain
Greece	and Northern Ireland
Holy See	United States of America
Iraq	Venezuela
Israel	Yugoslavia

The Governments of the following two States were represented by observers:

Cuba
Iran

Pursuant to the request of the General Assembly, the United Nations High Commissioner for Refugees participated, without the right to vote, in the deliberations of the Conference.

The International Labour Organization and the International Refugee Organization were represented at the Conference without the right to vote.

The Conference invited a representative of the Council of Europe to be represented at the Conference without the right to vote.

Representatives of... Non-Governmental Organizations in Consultative relationship with the Economic and Social Council were also present as observers...

[List of Non-Governmental Organizations omitted]

Representatives of Non-Governmental Organizations which have been granted consultative status by the Economic and Social Council as well as those entered by the Secretary-General on the Register referred to in Resolution 288 B(X) of the Economic and Social Council, paragraph 17, had under the rules of procedure adopted by the Conference the right to submit written or oral statements to the Conference.

The Conference elected Mr Knud Larsen, of Denmark, as President, and Mr A. Herment, of Belgium, and Mr Talat Miras, of Turkey, as Vice-Presidents.

At its second meeting, the Conference, acting on a proposal of the representative of Egypt, unanimously decided to address an invitation to the Holy See to designate a plenipotentiary representative to participate in its work. A representative of the Holy See took his place at the Conference on 10 July 1951.

The Conference adopted as its agenda the Provisional Agenda drawn up by the Secretary-General (A/CONF.2/2/Rev.l). It also adopted the Provisional Rules of Procedure drawn up by the Secretary-General, with the addition of a provision which authorized a representative of the Council of Europe to be present at the Conference without the right to vote and to submit proposals (A/CONF.2/3/Rev.l).

In accordance with the Rules of Procedure of the Conference, the President and Vice-Presidents examined the credentials of representatives and on 17 July 1951 reported to the Conference the results of such examination, the Conference adopting the report.

The Conference used as the basis of its discussions the draft Convention relating to the Status of Refugees and the draft Protocol relating to the Status of Stateless Persons prepared by the *ad hoc* Committee on Refugees and Stateless Persons at its second session held in Geneva from 14 to 25 August 1950, with the exception of the preamble and article 1 (Definition of the term 'refugee') of the draft Convention. The text of the preamble before the Conference was that which was adopted by the Economic and Social Council on 11 August 1950 in Resolution 319 B II(XI). The text of article 1 before the Conference was that recommended by the General Assembly on 14 December 1950 and contained in the Annex to Resolution 429(V). The latter was a modification of the text as it had been adopted by the Economic and Social Council in Resolution 319 B II(XI).[4]

The Conference adopted the Convention relating to the Status of Refugees in two readings. Prior to its second reading it established a Style Committee composed of the President and the representatives of Belgium, France, Israel, Italy, the United Kingdom of Great Britain and Northern Ireland and the United States of America, together with the High Commissioner for Refugees, which elected as its Chairman Mr G. Warren, of the United States of America. The Style Committee re-drafted the text which had been

---

[4] The texts referred to in the paragraph above are contained in document A/CONF.2/1.

adopted by the Conference on first reading, particularly from the point of view of language and of concordance between the English and French texts.

The Convention was adopted on 25 July by 24 votes to none with no abstentions and opened for signature at the European Office of the United Nations from 28 July to 31 August 1951. It will be re-opened for signature at the permanent headquarters of the United Nations in New York from 17 September 1951 to 31 December 1952.

The English and French texts of the Convention, which are equally authentic, are appended to this Final Act.

II

The Conference decided, by 17 votes to 3 with 3 abstentions, that the titles of the chapters and of the articles of the Convention are included for practical purposes and do not constitute an element of interpretation.

III

With respect to the draft Protocol relating to the Status of Stateless Persons, the Conference adopted the following resolution:

'*The Conference,*

'*Having considered* the draft Protocol relating to the Status of Stateless Persons,

'*Considering* that the subject still requires more detailed study,

'*Decides* not to take a decision on the subject at the present Conference and refers the draft Protocol back to the appropriate organs of the United Nations for further study.'

IV

The Conference adopted unanimously the following recommendations:

A

'*The Conference,*

'*Considering* that the issue and recognition of travel documents is necessary to facilitate the movement of refugees, and in particular their resettlement,

'*Urges* Governments which are parties to the Inter-Governmental Agreement on Refugee Travel Documents signed in London on 15 October 1946, or which recognize travel documents issued in accordance with the Agreement, to continue to issue or to recognize such travel documents, and to extend the issue of such documents to refugees as defined in article 1 of the Convention relating to the Status of Refugees or to recognize the travel documents so issued to such persons, until they shall have undertaken obligations under article 28 of the said Convention.'

B

'*The Conference,*

'*Considering* that the unity of the family, the natural and fundamental group unit of society, is an essential right of the refugee, and that such unity is constantly threatened, and

'*Noting* with satisfaction that, according to the official commentary of the *ad hoc* Committee on Statelessness and Related Problems (E/1618, p. 40), the rights granted to a refugee are extended to members of his family,

'*Recommends* Governments to take the necessary measures for the protection of the refugee's family especially with a view to:

'(1) Ensuring that the unity of the refugee's family is maintained particularly in cases where the head of the family has fulfilled the necessary conditions for admission to a particular country,

'(2) The protection of refugees who are minors, in particular unaccompanied children and girls, with special reference to guardianship and adoption.'

C

'*The Conference,*

'*Considering* that, in the moral, legal and material spheres, refugees need the help of suitable welfare services, especially that of appropriate non-governmental organizations,

'*Recommends* Governments and inter-governmental bodies to facilitate, encourage and sustain the efforts of properly qualified organizations.'

D

'*The Conference,*

'*Considering* that many persons still leave their country of origin for reasons of persecution and are entitled to special protection on account of their position,

'*Recommends* that Governments continue to receive refugees in their territories and that they act in concert in a true spirit of international co-operation in order that these refugees may find asylum and the possibility of resettlement.'

E

'*The Conference,*

'*Expresses* the hope that the Convention relating to the Status of Refugees will have value as an example exceeding its contractual scope and that all nations will be guided by it in granting so far as possible to persons in their territory as refugees and who would not be covered by the terms of the Convention, the treatment for which it provides.'

In Witness Whereof the President, Vice Presidents and the Executive Secretary of the Conference have signed this Final Act.

Done at Geneva this twenty-eighth day of July one thousand nine hundred and fifty-one in a single copy in the English and French languages, each text being equally authentic. Translations of this Final Act into Chinese, Russian and Spanish will be prepared by the Secretary-General of the United Nations, who will, on request, send copies thereof to each of the Governments invited to attend the Conference.

The President of the Conference: Knud Larsen
The Vice Presidents of the Conference: A. Herment. Talat Miras
The Executive Secretary of the Conference: John P. Humphrey

CONVENTION RELATING TO THE STATUS OF REFUGEES

Preamble

The High Contracting Parties,

Considering that the Charter of the United Nations and the Universal Declaration of Human Rights approved on 10 December 1948 by the General Assembly have affirmed the principle that human beings shall enjoy fundamental rights and freedoms without discrimination,

Considering that the United Nations has, on various occasions, manifested its profound concern for refugees and endeavoured to assure refugees the widest possible exercise of these fundamental rights and freedoms,

Considering that it is desirable to revise and consolidate previous international agreements relating to the status of refugees and to extend the scope of and protection accorded by such instruments by means of a new agreement,

Considering that the grant of asylum may place unduly heavy burdens on certain countries, and that a satisfactory solution of a problem of which the United Nations has recognized the international scope and nature cannot therefore be achieved without international co-operation,

Expressing the wish that all States, recognizing the social and humanitarian nature of the problem of refugees will do everything within their power to prevent this problem from becoming a cause of tension between States,

Noting that the United Nations High Commissioner for Refugees is charged with the task of supervising international conventions providing for the protection of refugees, and recognizing that the effective co-ordination of measures taken to deal with this problem will depend upon the co-operation of States with the High Commissioner,

Have agreed as follows:

Chapter I—General Provisions

Article 1
Definition of the term 'Refugee'

A. For the purposes of the present Convention, the term 'refugee' shall apply to any person who:

(1) Has been considered a refugee under the Arrangements of 12 May 1926 and 30 June 1928 or under the Conventions of 28 October 1933 and 10 February 1938, the Protocol of 14 September 1939 or the Constitution of the International Refugee Organization;

Decisions of non-eligibility taken by the International Refugee Organization during the period of its activities shall not prevent the status of refugee being accorded to persons who fulfil the conditions of paragraph 2 of this section;

(2) As a result of events occurring before 1 January 1951 and owing to well-founded fear of being persecuted for reasons of race, religion, nationality, membership of a particular social group or political opinion, is outside the country of his nationality and is unable or, owing to such fear, is unwilling to avail himself of the protection of that country; or who, not having a nationality and being outside the country of his former habitual residence as a result of such events, is unable or, owing to such fear, is unwilling to return to it.

In the case of a person who has more than one nationality, the term 'the country of his nationality' shall mean each of the countries of which he is a national, and a person shall not be deemed to be lacking the protection of the country of his nationality if, without any valid reason based on well-founded fear, he has not availed himself of the protection of one of the countries of which he is a national.

B. (1) For the purposes of this Convention, the words 'events occurring before 1 January 1951' in Article 1, Section A, shall be understood to mean either

(a) 'events occurring in Europe before 1 January 1951'; or

(b) 'events occurring in Europe or elsewhere before 1 January 1951', and each Contracting State shall make a declaration at the time of signature, ratification or accession, specifying which of these meanings it applies for the purpose of its obligations under this Convention.

(2) Any Contracting State which has adopted alternative (a) may at any time extend its obligations by adopting alternative (b) by means of a notification addressed to the Secretary-General of the United Nations.

C. This Convention shall cease to apply to any person falling under the terms of Section A if:

(1) He has voluntarily re-availed himself of the protection of the country of his nationality; or

(2) Having lost his nationality, he has voluntarily re-acquired it, or

(3) He has acquired a new nationality, and enjoys the protection of the country of his new nationality; or

(4) He has voluntarily re-established himself in the country which he left or outside which he remained owing to fear of persecution; or

(5) He can no longer, because the circumstances in connection with which he has been recognized as a refugee have ceased to exist, continue to refuse to avail himself of the protection of the country of his nationality;

Provided that this paragraph shall not apply to a refugee falling under Section A(1) of this Article who is able to invoke compelling reasons arising out of previous persecution for refusing to avail himself of the protection of the country of nationality;

(6) Being a person who has no nationality he is, because of the circumstances in connection with which he has been recognized as a refugee have ceased to exist, able to return to the country of his former habitual residence;

Provided that this paragraph shall not apply to a refugee falling under section A(1) of this Article who is able to invoke compelling reasons arising out of previous persecution for refusing to return to the country of his former habitual residence.

D. This Convention shall not apply to persons who are at present receiving from organs or agencies of the United Nations other than the United Nations High Commissioner for Refugees protection or assistance.

When such protection or assistance has ceased for any reason, without the position of such persons being definitively settled in accordance with the relevant resolutions adopted by the General Assembly of the United Nations, these persons shall *ipso facto* be entitled to the benefits of this Convention.

E. This Convention shall not apply to a person who is recognized by the competent authorities of the country in which he has taken residence as having the rights and obligations which are attached to the possession of the nationality of that country.

F. The provisions of this Convention shall not apply to any person with respect to whom there are serious reasons for considering that:

(a) he has committed a crime against peace, a war crime, or a crime against humanity, as defined in the international instruments drawn up to make provision in respect of such crimes;

(b) he has committed a serious non-political crime outside the country of refuge prior to his admission to that country as a refugee;

(c) he has been guilty of acts contrary to the purposes and principles of the United Nations.

Article 2
General obligations

Every refugee has duties to the country in which he finds himself, which require in particular that he conform to its laws and regulations as well as to measures taken for the maintenance of public order.

Article 3
Non-discrimination

The Contracting States shall apply the provisions of this Convention to refugees without discrimination as to race, religion or country of origin.

Article 4
Religion

The Contracting States shall accord to refugees within their territories treatment at least as favourable as that accorded to their nationals with respect to freedom to practise their religion and freedom as regards the religious education of their children.

Article 5
Rights granted apart from this Convention

Nothing in this Convention shall be deemed to impair any rights and benefits granted by a Contracting State to refugees apart from this Convention.

Article 6
The term 'in the same circumstances'

For the purposes of this Convention, the term 'in the same circumstances' implies that any requirements (including requirements as to length and conditions of sojourn or residence) which the particular individual would have to fulfil for the enjoyment of the right in question, if he were not a refugee, must be fulfilled by him, with the exception of requirements which by their nature a refugee is incapable of fulfilling.

Article 7
Exemption from reciprocity

1. Except where this Convention contains more favourable provisions, a Contracting State shall accord to refugees the same treatment as is accorded to aliens generally.

2. After a period of three years' residence, all refugees shall enjoy exemption from legislative reciprocity in the territory of the Contracting States.

3. Each Contracting State shall continue to accord to refugees the rights and benefits to which they were already entitled, in the absence of reciprocity, at the date of entry into force of this Convention for that State.

4. The Contracting States shall consider favourably the possibility of according to refugees, in the absence of reciprocity, rights and benefits beyond those to which they are entitled according to paragraphs 2 and 3, and to extending exemption from reciprocity to refugees who do not fulfil the conditions provided for in paragraphs 2 and 3.

5. The provisions of paragraphs 2 and 3 apply both to the rights and benefits referred to in Articles 13, 18, 19, 21 and 22 of this Convention and to rights and benefits for which this Convention does not provide.

Article 8
Exemption from exceptional measures

With regard to exceptional measures which may be taken against the person, property or interests of nationals of a foreign State, the Contracting States shall not apply such measures to a refugee who is formally a national of the said State solely on account of such nationality. Contracting States which, under their legislation, are prevented from applying the general principle expressed in this Article, shall, in appropriate cases, grant exemptions in favour of such refugees.

Article 9
Provisional measures

Nothing in this Convention shall prevent a Contracting State, in time of war or other grave and exceptional circumstances, from taking provisionally measures which it considers to be essential to the national security in the case of a particular person, pending a determination by the Contracting State that that person is in fact a refugee and that the continuance of such measures is necessary in his case in the interests of national security.

Article 10
Continuity of residence

1. Where a refugee has been forcibly displaced during the Second World War and removed to the territory of a Contracting State, and is resident there, the period of such enforced sojourn shall be considered to have been lawful residence within that territory.

2. Where a refugee has been forcibly displaced during the Second World War from the territory of a Contracting State and has, prior to the date of entry into force of this Convention, returned there for the purpose of taking up residence, the period of residence before and after such enforced displacement shall be regarded as one uninterrupted period for any purposes for which uninterrupted residence is required.

Article 11
Refugee seamen

In the case of refugees regularly serving as crew members on board a ship flying the flag of a Contracting State, that State shall give sympathetic consideration to their establishment on its territory and the issue of travel documents to them or their temporary admission to its territory particularly with a view to facilitating their establishment in another country.

Chapter II—Juridical Status
Article 12
Personal status

1. The personal status of a refugee shall be governed by the law of the country of his domicile or, if he has no domicile, by the law of the country of his residence.

2. Rights previously acquired by a refugee and dependent on personal status, more particularly rights attaching to marriage, shall be respected by a Contracting State, subject to compliance, if this be necessary, with the formalities required by the law of that State, provided that the right in question is one which would have been recognized by the law of that State had he not become a refugee.

Article 13
Movable and immovable property

The Contracting States shall accord to a refugee treatment as favourable as possible and, in any event, not less favourable than that accorded to aliens generally in the same circumstances, as regards the acquisition of movable and immovable property and other rights pertaining thereto, and to leases and other contracts relating to movable and immovable property.

Article 14
Artistic rights and industrial property

In respect of the protection of industrial property, such as inventions, designs or models, trade marks, trade names, and of rights in literary, artistic, and scientific works, a refugee shall be accorded in the country in which he has his habitual residence the same protection as is accorded to nationals of that country. In the territory of any other Contracting State, he shall be accorded the same protection as is accorded in that territory to nationals of the country in which he has his habitual residence.

Article 15
Right of association

As regards non-political and non-profit making associations and trade unions the Contracting States shall accord to refugees lawfully staying in their territory the most favourable treatment accorded to nationals of a foreign country, in the same circumstances.

Article 16
Access to courts

1. A refugee shall have free access to the courts of law on the territory of all Contracting States.

2. A refugee shall enjoy in the Contracting State in which he has his habitual residence the same treatment as a national in matters pertaining to access to the Courts, including legal assistance and exemption from *cautio judicatum solvi.*

3. A refugee shall be accorded in the matters referred to in paragraph 2 in countries other than that in which he has his habitual residence the treatment granted to a national of the country of his habitual residence.

Chapter III—Gainful Employment

Article 17
Wage-earning employment

1. The Contracting State shall accord to refugees lawfully staying in their territory the most favourable treatment accorded to nationals of a foreign country in the same circumstances, as regards the right to engage in wage-earning employment.

2. In any case, restrictive measures imposed on aliens or the employment of aliens for the protection of the national labour market shall not be applied to a refugee who was already exempt from them at the date of entry into force of this Convention for the Contracting State concerned, or who fulfils one of the following conditions:

(a) He has completed three years' residence in the country;

(b) He has a spouse possessing the nationality of the country of residence. A refugee may not invoke the benefits of this provision if he has abandoned his spouse;

(c) He has one or more children possessing the nationality of the country of residence.

3. The Contracting States shall give sympathetic consideration to assimilating the rights of all refugees with regard to wage-earning employment to those of nationals, and in particular of those refugees who have entered their territory pursuant to programmes of labour recruitment or under immigration schemes.

Article 18
Self-employment

The Contracting States shall accord to a refugee lawfully in their territory treatment as favourable as possible and, in any event, not less favourable that that accorded to aliens generally in the same circumstances, as regards the right to engage on his own account in agriculture, industry, handicrafts and commerce and to establish commercial and industrial companies.

Article 19
Liberal professions

1. Each Contracting State shall accord to refugees lawfully staying in their territory who hold diplomas recognized by the competent authorities of that State, and who are desirous of practising a liberal profession, treatment as favourable as possible and, in any event, not less favourable than that accorded to aliens generally in the same circumstances.

2. The Contracting States shall use their best endeavours consistently with their laws and constitutions to secure the settlement of such refugees in the territories, other than the metropolitan territory, for whose international relations they are responsible.

Chapter IV—Welfare

Article 20
Rationing

Where a rationing system exists, which applies to the population at large and regulates the general distribution of products in short supply, refugees shall be accorded the same treatment as nationals.

Article 21
Housing

As regards housing, the Contracting States, in so far as the matter is regulated by laws or regulations or is subject to the control of public authorities, shall accord to refugees lawfully staying in their territory treatment as favourable as possible and, in any event, not less favourable than that accorded to aliens generally in the same circumstances.

Article 22
Public education

1. The Contracting States shall accord to refugees the same treatment as is accorded to nationals with respect to elementary education.

2. The Contracting States shall accord to refugees treatment as favourable as possible, and, in any event, not less favourable than that accorded to aliens generally in the same circumstances, with respect to education other than elementary education and, in particular, as regards access to studies, the recognition of foreign school certificates, diplomas and degrees, the remission of fees and charges and the award of scholarships.

Article 23
Public relief

The Contracting States shall accord to refugees lawfully staying in their territory the same treatment with respect to public relief and assistance as is accorded to their nationals.

Article 24
Labour legislation and social security

1. The Contracting States shall accord to refugees lawfully staying in their territory the same treatment as is accorded to nationals in respect of the following matters:

(a) In so far as such matters are governed by laws or regulations or are subject to the control of administrative authorities: remuneration, including family allowances where these form part of remuneration, hours of work, overtime arrangements, holidays with pay, restrictions on home work, minimum age of employment, apprenticeship and training, women's work and the work of young persons, and the enjoyment of the benefits of collective bargaining;

(b) Social security (legal provisions in respect of employment injury, occupational diseases, maternity, sickness, disability, old age, death, unemployment, family responsibilities and any other contingency which, according to national laws or regulations, is covered by a social security scheme), subject to the following limitations:

(i) There may be appropriate arrangements for the maintenance of acquired rights and rights in course of acquisition;

(ii) National laws or regulations of the country of residence may prescribe special arrangements concerning benefits or portions of benefits which are payable wholly out of public funds, and concerning allowances paid to persons who do not fulfil the contribution conditions prescribed for the award of a normal pension.

2. The right to compensation for the death of a refugee resulting from employment injury or from occupational disease shall not be affected by the fact that the residence of the beneficiary is outside the territory of the Contracting State.

3. The Contracting States shall extend to refugees the benefits of agreements concluded between them, or which may be concluded between them in the future, concerning the maintenance of acquired rights and rights in the process of acquisition in regard to social security, subject only to the conditions which apply to nationals of the States signatory to the agreements in question.

4. The Contracting States will give sympathetic consideration to extending to refugees so far as possible the benefits of similar agreements which may at any time be in force between such Contracting States and non-contracting States.

Chapter V—Administrative measures

Article 25
Administrative assistance

1. When the exercise of a right by a refugee would normally require the assistance of authorities of a foreign country to whom he cannot have recourse, the Contracting States in whose territory he is residing shall arrange that such assistance be afforded to him by their own authorities or by an international authority.

2. The authority or authorities mentioned in paragraph 1 shall deliver or cause to be delivered under their supervision to refugees such documents or certifications as would normally be delivered to aliens by or through their national authorities.

3. Documents or certifications so delivered shall stand in the stead of the official instruments delivered to aliens by or through their national authorities, and shall be given credence in the absence of proof to the contrary.

4. Subject to such exceptional treatment as may be granted to indigent persons, fees may be charged for the services mentioned herein, but such fees shall be moderate and commensurate with those charged to nationals for similar services.

5. The provisions of this Article shall be without prejudice to Articles 27 and 28.

Article 26
Freedom of movement

Each Contracting State shall accord to refugees lawfully in its territory the right to choose their place of residence and to move freely within its territory, subject to any regulations applicable to aliens generally in the same circumstances.

Article 27
Identity papers

The Contracting States shall issue identity papers to any refugee in their territory who does not possess a valid travel document.

Article 28
Travel documents

1. The Contracting States shall issue to refugees lawfully staying in their territory travel documents for the purpose of travel outside their territory unless compelling reasons of national security or public order otherwise require, and the provisions of the Schedule to this Convention shall apply with respect to such documents. The Contracting States may issue such a travel document to any other refugee in their territory; they shall in particular give sympathetic consideration to the issue of such a travel document to refugees in their territory who are unable to obtain a travel document from the country of their lawful residence.

2. Travel documents issued to refugees under previous international agreements by parties thereto shall be recognized and treated by the Contracting States in the same way as if they had been issued pursuant to this article.

Article 29
Fiscal charges

1. The Contracting States shall not impose upon refugee duties, charges or taxes, of any description whatsoever, other or higher than those which are or may be levied on their nationals in similar situations.

2. Nothing in the above paragraph shall prevent the application to refugees of the laws and regulations concerning charges in respect of the issue to aliens of administrative documents including identity papers.

Article 30
Transfer of assets

1. A Contracting State shall, in conformity with its laws and regulations, permit refugees to transfer assets which they have brought into its territory, to another country where they have been admitted for the purposes of resettlement.

2. A Contracting State shall give sympathetic consideration to the application of refugees for permission to transfer assets wherever they may be and which are necessary for their resettlement in another country to which they have been admitted.

Article 31
Refugees unlawfully in the country of refuge

1. The Contracting States shall not impose penalties, on account of their illegal entry or presence, on refugees who, coming directly from a territory where their life or freedom was threatened in the sense of Article 1, enter or are present in their territory without

authorization, provided they present themselves without delay to the authorities and show good cause for their illegal entry or presence.

2. The Contracting States shall not apply to the movements of such refugees restrictions other than those which are necessary and such restrictions shall only be applied until their status in the country is regularized or they obtain admission into another country. The Contracting States shall allow such refugees a reasonable period and all the necessary facilities to obtain admission into another country.

Article 32
Expulsion

1. The Contracting States shall not expel a refugee lawfully in their territory save on grounds of national security or public order.

2. The expulsion of such a refugee shall be only in pursuance of a decision reached in accordance with due process of law. Except where compelling reasons of national security otherwise require, the refugee shall be allowed to submit evidence to clear himself, and to appeal to and be represented for the purpose before competent authority or a person or persons specially designated by the competent authority.

3. The Contracting States shall allow such a refugee a reasonable period within which to seek legal admission into another country. The Contracting States reserve the right to apply during that period such internal measures as they may deem necessary.

Article 33
Prohibition of expulsion or return ('refoulement')

1. No Contracting State shall expel or return ('refouler') a refugee in any manner whatsoever to the frontiers of territories where his life or freedom would be threatened on account of his race, religion, nationality, membership of a particular social group or political opinion.

2. The benefit of the present provision may not, however, be claimed by a refugee whom there are reasonable grounds for regarding as a danger to the security of the country in which he is, or who, having been convicted by a final judgment of a particularly serious crime, constitutes a danger to the community of that country.

Article 34
Naturalization

The Contracting States shall as far as possible facilitate the assimilation and naturalization of refugees. They shall in particular make every effort to expedite naturalization proceedings and to reduce as far as possible the charges and costs of such proceedings.

Chapter VI—Executory and transitory provisions

Article 35
Co-operation of the national authorities with the United Nations

1. The Contracting States undertake to co-operate with the Office of the United Nations High Commissioner for Refugees, or any other agency of the United Nations which may

succeed it, in the exercise of its functions, and shall in particular facilitate its duty of supervising the application of the provisions of this Convention.

2. In order to enable the Office of the High Commissioner or any other agency of the United Nations which may succeed it, to make reports to the competent organs of the United Nations, the Contracting States undertake to provide them in the appropriate form with information and statistical data requested concerning:

(a) the condition of refugees,

(b) the implementation of this Convention, and

(c) laws, regulations and decrees which are, or may hereafter be, in force relating to refugees.

Article 36
Information on national legislation

The Contracting States shall communicate to the Secretary-General of the United Nations the laws and regulations which they may adopt to ensure the application of this Convention.

Article 37
Relation to previous Conventions

Without prejudice to Article 28, paragraph 2, of this Convention, this Convention replaces, as between parties to it, the Arrangements of 5 July 1922, 31 May 1924, 12 May 1926, 30 June 1928 and 30 July 1935, the Conventions of 28 October 1933 and 10 February 1938, the Protocol of 14 September 1939 and the Agreement of 15 October 1946.

Chapter VII—Final clauses
Article 38
Settlement of disputes

Any dispute between parties to this Convention relating to its interpretation or application, which cannot be settled by other means, shall be referred to the International Court of Justice at the request of any one of the parties to the dispute.

Article 39
Signature, ratification and accession

1. This Convention shall be opened for signature at Geneva on 28 July 1951 and shall hereafter be deposited with the Secretary-General of the United Nations. It shall be open for signature at the European Office of the United Nations from 28 July to 31 August 1951 and shall be re-opened for signature at the Headquarters of the United Nations from 17 September 1951 to 31 December 1952.

2. This Convention shall be open for signature on behalf of all States Members of the United Nations, and also on behalf of any other State invited to attend the Conference of Plenipotentiaries on the Status of Refugees and Stateless Persons or to which an invitation

to sign will have been addressed by the General Assembly. It shall be ratified and the instruments of ratification shall be deposited with the Secretary-General of the United Nations.

3. This Convention shall be open from 28 July 1951 for accession by the States referred to in paragraph 2 of this Article. Accession shall be effected by the deposit of an instrument of accession with the Secretary-General of the United Nations.

Article 40
Territorial application clause

1. Any State may, at the time of signature, ratification or accession, declare that this Convention shall extend to all or any of the territories for the international relations of which it is responsible. Such a declaration shall take effect when the Convention enters into force for the State concerned.

2. At any time thereafter any such extension shall be made by notification addressed to the Secretary-General of the United Nations and shall take effect as from the ninetieth day after the day of receipt by the Secretary-General of the United Nations of this notification, or as from the date of entry into force of the Convention for the State concerned, whichever is the later.

3. With respect to those territories to which this Convention is not extended at the time of signature, ratification or accession, each State concerned shall consider the possibility of taking the necessary steps in order to extend the application of this Convention to such territories, subject, where necessary for constitutional reasons, to the consent of the governments of such territories.

Article 41
Federal clause

In the case of a Federal or non-unitary State, the following provisions shall apply:

(a) With respect to those Articles of this Convention that come within the legislative jurisdiction of the federal legislative authority, the obligations of the Federal Government shall to this extent be the same as those of Parties which are not Federal States,

(b) With respect to those Articles of this Convention that come within the legislative jurisdiction of constituent States, provinces or cantons which are not, under the constitutional system of the federation, bound to take legislative action, the Federal Government shall bring such Articles with a favourable recommendation to the notice of the appropriate authorities of States, provinces or cantons at the earliest possible moment.

(c) A Federal State Party to this Convention shall, at the request of any other Contracting State transmitted through the Secretary-General of the United Nations, supply a statement of the law and practice of the Federation and its constituent units in regard to any particular provision of the Convention showing the extent to which effect has been given to that provision by legislative or other action.

Article 42
Reservations

1. At the time of signature, ratification or accession, any State may make reservations to articles of the Convention other than to Articles 1, 3, 4, 16(1), 33, 36–46 inclusive.

2. Any State making a reservation in accordance with paragraph 1 of this article may at any time withdraw the reservation by a communication to that effect addressed to the Secretary-General of the United Nations.

Article 43
Entry into force

1. This Convention shall come into force on the ninetieth day following the day of deposit of the sixth instrument of ratification or accession.

2. For each State ratifying or acceding to the Convention after the deposit of the sixth instrument of ratification or accession, the Convention shall enter into force on the ninetieth day following the date of deposit by such State of its instrument of ratification or accession.

Article 44
Denunciation

1. Any Contracting State may denounce this Convention at any time by a notification addressed to the Secretary-General of the United Nations.

2. Such denunciation shall take effect for the Contracting State concerned one year from the date upon which it is received by the Secretary-General of the United Nations.

3. Any State which has made a declaration or notification under Article 40 may, at any time thereafter, by a notification to the Secretary-General of the United Nations, declare that the Convention shall cease to extend to such territory one year after the date of receipt of the notification by the Secretary-General.

Article 45
Revision

1. Any Contracting State may request revision of this Convention at any time by a notification addressed to the Secretary-General of the United Nations.

2. The General Assembly of the United Nations shall recommend the steps, if any, to be taken in respect of such request.

Article 46
Notifications by the Secretary-General of the United Nations

The Secretary-General of the United Nations shall inform all Members of the United Nations and non-member States referred to in Article 39:

(a) of declarations and notifications in accordance with Section B of Article 1;

(b) of signatures, ratifications and accessions in accordance with Article 39;

(c) of declarations and notifications in accordance with Article 40;

(d) of reservations and withdrawals in accordance with Article 42;

(e) of the date on which this Convention will come into force in accordance with Article 43;

(f) of denunciations and notifications in accordance with Article 44;

(g) of requests for revision in accordance with Article 45.

IN FAITH WHEREOF the undersigned, duly authorized, have signed this Convention on behalf of their respective Governments,

DONE at GENEVA, this twenty-eighth day of July, one thousand nine hundred and fifty-one, in a single copy, of which the English and French texts are equally authentic and which shall remain deposited in the archives of the United Nations, and certified true copies of which shall be delivered to all Members of the United Nations and to the non-member States referred to in Article 39.

Schedule[5]

Paragraph 1

1. The travel document referred to in Article 28 of this Convention shall be similar to the specimen annexed hereto.

2. The document shall be made out in at least two languages, one of which shall be English or French.

Paragraph 2

Subject to the regulations obtaining in the country of issue, children may be included in the travel document of a parent or, in exceptional circumstances, of another adult refugee.

Paragraph 3

The fees charged for issue of the document shall not exceed the lowest scale of charges for national passports.

Paragraph 4

Save in special or exceptional cases, the document shall be made valid for the largest possible number of countries.

Paragraph 5

The document shall have a validity of either one or two years, at the discretion of the issuing authority.

Paragraph 6

1. The renewal or extension of the validity of the document is a matter for the authority which issued it, so long as the holder has not established lawful residence in another territory and resides lawfully in the territory of the said authority. The issue of a new document is, under the same conditions, a matter for the authority which issued the former document.

2. Diplomatic or consular authorities, specially authorized for the purpose, shall be empowered to extend, for a period not exceeding six months, the validity of travel documents issued by their Governments.

---

[5] The Annex with details of the Specimen Travel Document is omitted.

3. The Contracting States shall give sympathetic consideration to renewing or extending the validity of travel documents or issuing new documents to refugees no longer lawfully resident in their territory who are unable to obtain a travel document from the country of their lawful residence.

Paragraph 7

The Contracting States shall recognize the validity of the documents issued in accordance with the provisions of Article 28 of this Convention.

Paragraph 8

The competent authorities of the country to which the refugee desires to proceed shall, if they are prepared to admit him and if a visa is required, affix a visa on the document of which he is the holder.

Paragraph 9

1. The Contracting States undertake to issue transit visas to refugees who have obtained visas for a territory of final destination.

2. The issue of such visas may be refused on grounds which would justify refusal of a visa to any alien.

Paragraph 10

The fees for the issue of exit, entry or transit visas shall not exceed the lowest scale of charges for visas on foreign passports.

Paragraph 11

When a refugee has lawfully taken up residence in the territory of another Contracting State, the responsibility for the issue of a new document, under the terms and conditions of Article 28, shall be that of the competent authority of that territory, to which the refugee shall be entitled to apply.

Paragraph 12

The authority issuing a new document shall withdraw the old document and shall return it to the country of issue, if it is stated in the document that it should be so returned; otherwise it shall withdraw and cancel the document.

Paragraph 13

1. Each Contracting State undertakes that the holder of a travel document issued by it in accordance with Article 28 of this Convention shall be re-admitted to its territory at any time during the period of its validity.

2. Subject to the provisions of the preceding sub-paragraph, a Contracting State may require the holder of the document to comply with such formalities as may be prescribed in regard to exit from or return to its territory.

3. The Contracting States reserve the right, in exceptional cases, or in cases where the refugee's stay is authorized for a specific period, when issuing the document, to limit the period during which the refugee may return to a period of not less than three months.

Paragraph 14

Subject only to the terms of paragraph 13, the provisions of this Schedule in no way affect the laws and regulations governing the conditions of admission to, transit through, residence and establishment in, and departure from, the territories of the Contracting States.

Paragraph 15

Neither the issue of the document nor the entries made thereon determine or affect the status of the holder, particularly as regards nationality.

Paragraph 16

The issue of the document does not in any way entitle the holder to the protection of the diplomatic or consular authorities of the country of issue, and does not confer on these authorities a right of protection.

5. 1967 Protocol relating to the Status of Refugees

Entry into force: 4 October 1967

Text: 606 *UNTS* 267

Preamble

The States Parties to the present Protocol,
Considering that the Convention relating to the Status of Refugees done at Geneva on 28 July 1951 (hereinafter referred to as the Convention) covers only those persons who have become refugees as a result of events occurring before 1 January 1951,

Considering that new refugee situations have arisen since the Convention was adopted and that the refugees concerned may therefore not fall within the scope of the Convention,

Considering that it is desirable that equal status should be enjoyed by all refugees covered by the definition in the Convention irrespective of the dateline 1 January 1951,
Have agreed as follows:

Article I
General provision

1. The States Parties to the present Protocol undertake to apply Articles 2 to 34 inclusive of the Convention to refugees as hereinafter defined.

2. For the purpose of the present Protocol, the term 'refugee' shall, except as regards the application of paragraph 3 of this Article, mean any person within the definition of Article 1 of the Convention as if the words 'As a result of events occurring before 1 January 1951 and . . .' and the words ' . . . a result of such events', in Article 1 A(2) were omitted.

3. The present Protocol shall be applied by the States Parties hereto without any geographic limitation, save that existing declarations made by States already Parties to the Convention in accordance with Article 1 B(1)(a) of the Convention, shall, unless extended under Article 1 B(2) thereof, apply also under the present Protocol.

Article II
Co-operation of the national authorities with the United Nations

1. The States Parties to the present Protocol undertake to co-operate with the Office of the United Nations High Commissioner for Refugees, or any other agency of the United Nations which may succeed it, in the exercise of its functions, and shall in particular facilitate its duty of supervising the application of the provisions of the present Protocol.

2. In order to enable the Office of the High Commissioner, or any other agency of the United Nations which may succeed it, to make reports to the competent organs of the United Nations, the States Parties to the present Protocol undertake to provide them with the information and statistical data requested, in the appropriate form, concerning:

(a) The condition of refugees;

(b) The implementation of the present Protocol;

(c) Laws, regulations and decrees which are, or may hereafter be, in force relating to refugees.

Article III
Information on national legislation

The States Parties to the present Protocol shall communicate to the Secretary-General of the United Nations the laws and regulations which they may adopt to ensure the application of the present Protocol.

Article IV
Settlement of disputes

Any dispute between States Parties to the present Protocol which relates to its interpretation or application and which cannot be settled by other means shall be referred to the International Court of Justice at the request of any one of the parties to the dispute.

Article V
Accession

The present Protocol shall be open for accession on behalf of all States Parties to the Convention and of any other State Member of the United Nations or member of any of the specialized agencies or to which an invitation to accede may have been addressed by the General Assembly of the United Nations. Accession shall be effected by the deposit of an instrument of accession with the Secretary-General of the United Nations.

Article VI
Federal clause

In the case of a Federal or non-unitary State, the following provisions shall apply:

(a) With respect to those articles of the Convention to be applied in accordance with Article I, paragraph 1, of the present Protocol that come within the legislative jurisdiction of the federal legislative authority, the obligations of the Federal Government shall to this extent be the same as those of States Parties which are not Federal States.

(b) With respect to those articles of the Convention to be applied in accordance with Article I, paragraph 1, of the present Protocol that come within the legislative jurisdiction of constituent States, provinces or cantons which are not, under the constitutional system of the federation, bound to take legislative action, the Federal Government shall bring such articles with a favourable recommendation to the notice of the appropriate authorities of States, provinces or cantons at the earliest possible moment;

(c) A Federal State Party to the present Protocol shall, at the request of any other State Party hereto transmitted through the Secretary-General of the United Nations, supply a statement of the law and practice of the Federation and its constituent units in regard to any particular provision of the Convention to be applied in accordance with Article I, paragraph 1, of the present Protocol, showing the extent to which effect has been given to that provision by legislative or other action.

Article VII
Reservations and declarations

1. At the time of accession, any State may make reservations in respect of Article IV of the present Protocol and in respect of the application in accordance with Article I of the present Protocol of any provisions of the Convention other than those contained in Articles 1, 3, 4, 16 (1) and 33 thereof, provided that in the case of a State Party to the Convention reservations made under this Article shall not extend to refugees in respect of whom the Convention applies.

2. Reservations made by States Parties to the Convention in accordance with Article 42 thereof shall, unless withdrawn, be applicable in relation to their obligations under the present Protocol.

3. Any State making a reservation in accordance with paragraph 1 of this Article may at any time withdraw such reservation by a communication to that effect addressed to the Secretary-General of the United Nations.

4. Declarations made under Article 40, paragraphs 1 and 2, of the Convention by a State Party thereto which accedes to the present Protocol shall be deemed to apply in respect of the present Protocol, unless upon accession a notification to the contrary is addressed by the State Party concerned to the Secretary-General of the United Nations. The provisions of Article 40, paragraphs 2 and 3, and of Article 44, paragraph 3, of the Convention shall be deemed to apply *mutatis mutandis* to the present Protocol.

Article VIII
Entry into force

1. The present Protocol shall come into force on the day of deposit of the sixth instrument of accession.

2. For each State acceding to the Protocol after the deposit of the sixth instrument of accession, the Protocol shall come into force on the date of deposit by such State of its instrument of accession.

Article IX
Denunciation

1. Any State Party hereto may denounce this Protocol at any time by a notification addressed to the Secretary-General of the United Nations.

2. Such denunciation shall take effect for the State Party concerned one year from the date on which it is received by the Secretary-General of the United Nations.

Article X
Notifications by the Secretary-General of the United Nations

The Secretary-General of the United Nations shall inform the States referred to in Article V above of the date of entry into force, accessions, reservations and withdrawals of reservations to and denunciations of the present Protocol, and of declarations and notifications relating hereto.

Article XI
Deposit in the archives of the Secretariat of the United Nations

A copy of the present Protocol, of which the Chinese, English, French, Russian and Spanish texts are equally authentic, signed by the President of the General Assembly and by the Secretary-General of the United Nations, shall be deposited in the archives of the Secretariat of the United Nations. The Secretary-General will transmit certified copies thereof to all States Members of the United Nations and to the other States referred to in Article V above.

GENERAL ASSEMBLY RESOLUTION 2198 (XXI) OF 16 DECEMBER 1966

Protocol relating to the Status of Refugees

The General Assembly,

Considering that the Convention relating to the Status of Refugees, signed at Geneva on 28 July 1951, covers only those persons who have become refugees as a result of events occurring before 1 January 1951,

Considering that new refugee situations have arisen since the Convention was adopted and that the refugees concerned may therefore not fall within the scope of the Convention,

Considering that it is desirable that equal status should be enjoyed by all refugees covered by the definition in the Convention, irrespective of the date-line of 1 January 1951,

Taking note of the recommendation of the Executive Committee of the Programme of the United Nations High Commissioner for Refugees that the draft Protocol relating to the Status of Refugees should be submitted to the General Assembly after consideration by the Economic and Social Council, in order that the Secretary-General might be authorized to open the Protocol for accession by Governments within the shortest possible time,

Considering that the Economic and Social Council, in its resolution 1186 (XLI) of 18 November 1966, took note with approval of the draft Protocol contained in the addendum to the report of the United Nations High Commissioner for Refugees and concerning measures to extend the personal scope of the Convention and transmitted the addendum to the General Assembly,

1. *Takes note* of the Protocol relating to the Status of Refugees, the text of which is contained in the addendum to the report of the United Nations High Commissioner for Refugees;

2. *Requests* the Secretary-General to transmit the text of the Protocol to the States mentioned in article V thereof, with a view to enabling them to accede to the Protocol.[6]

6. 1967 United Nations Declaration on Territorial Asylum

Adopted by the General Assembly of the United Nations on 14 December 1967
Text: UNGA resolution 2312 (XXII)

The General Assembly,
   Recalling its resolutions 1839 (XVII) of 19 December 1962, 2100 (XX) of 20 December 1965 and 2203 (XXI) of 16 December 1966 concerning a declaration on the right of asylum,
   Considering the work of codification to be undertaken by the International Law Commission in accordance with General Assembly resolution 1400 (XIV) of 21 November 1959,
   Adopts the following Declaration:

DECLARATION ON TERRITORIAL ASYLUM

The General Assembly,
   Noting that the purposes proclaimed in the Charter of the United Nations are to maintain international peace and security, to develop friendly relations among all nations and to achieve international co-operation in solving international problems of an economic, social, cultural or humanitarian character and in promoting and encouraging respect for human rights and for fundamental freedoms for all without distinction as to race, sex, language or religion,
   Mindful of the Universal Declaration of Human Rights, which declares in article 14 that:
   '1. Everyone has the right to seek and to enjoy in other countries asylum from persecution.'
   '2. This right may not be invoked in the case of prosecutions genuinely arising from non-political crimes or from acts contrary to the purposes and principles of the United Nations.'

---

[6] The Protocol was signed by the President of the General Assembly and by the Secretary-General on 31 January 1967.

Recalling also article 13, paragraph 2, of the Universal Declaration of Human Rights, which states: 'Everyone has the right to leave any country, including his own, and to return to his country',

Recognizing that the grant of asylum by a State to persons entitled to invoke article 14 of the Universal Declaration of Human Rights is a peaceful and humanitarian act and that, as such, it cannot be regarded as unfriendly by any other State,

Recommends that, without prejudice to existing instruments dealing with asylum and the status of refugees and stateless persons, States should base themselves in their practices relating to territorial asylum on the following principles:

Article 1

1. Asylum granted by a State, in the exercise of its sovereignty, to persons entitled to invoke article 14 of the Universal Declaration of Human Rights, including persons struggling against colonialism, shall be respected by all other States.

2. The right to seek and to enjoy asylum may not be invoked by any person with respect to whom there are serious reasons for considering that he has committed a crime against peace, a war crime or a crime against humanity, as defined in the international instruments drawn up to make provision in respect of such crimes.

3. It shall rest with the State granting asylum to evaluate the grounds for the grant of asylum.

Article 2

1. The situation of persons referred to in article 1, paragraph 1, is, without prejudice to the sovereignty of States and the purposes and principles of the United Nations, of concern to the international community.

2. Where a State finds difficulty in granting or continuing to grant asylum, States individually or jointly or through the United Nations shall consider, in a spirit of international solidarity, appropriate measures to lighten the burden on that State.

Article 3

1. No person referred to in article 1, paragraph 1, shall be subjected to measures such as rejection at the frontier or, if he has already entered the territory in which he seeks asylum, expulsion or compulsory return to any State where he may be subjected to persecution.

2. Exception may be made to the foregoing principle only for overriding reasons of national security or in order to safeguard the population, as in the case of a mass influx of persons.

3. Should a State decide in any case that exception to the principle stated in paragraph 1 of this article would be justified, it shall consider the possibility of granting to the person concerned, under such conditions as it may deem appropriate, an opportunity, whether by way of provisional asylum or otherwise, of going to another State.

Article 4

States granting asylum shall not permit persons who have received asylum to engage in activities contrary to the purposes and principles of the United Nations.

7. 1984 United Nations Convention against Torture and Other Cruel, Inhuman or Degrading Treatment or Punishment—Extracts

Entry into force: 26 June 1987

Text: UNGA resolution 39/46, 10 December 1984; 1465 *UNTS* 85

Article 1

1. For the purposes of this Convention, the term 'torture' means any act by which severe pain or suffering, whether physical or mental, is intentionally inflicted on a person for such purposes as obtaining from him or a third person information or a confession, punishing him for an act he or a third person has committed or is suspected of having committed, or intimidating or coercing him or a third person, or for any reason based on discrimination of any kind, when such pain or suffering is inflicted by or at the instigation of or with the consent or acquiescence of a public official or other person acting in an official capacity. It does not include pain or suffering arising only from, inherent in or incidental to lawful sanctions.

2. This article is without prejudice to any international instrument or national legislation which does or may contain provisions of wider application.

Article 2

1. Each State Party shall take effective legislative, administrative, judicial or other measures to prevent acts of torture in any territory under its jurisdiction.

2. No exceptional circumstances whatsoever, whether a state of war or a threat of war, internal political instability or any other public emergency, may be invoked as a justification of torture.

3. An order from a superior officer or a public authority may not be invoked as a justification of torture.

Article 3

1. No State Party shall expel, return ('refouler') or extradite a person to another State where there are substantial grounds for believing that he would be in danger of being subjected to torture.

2. For the purpose of determining whether there are such grounds, the competent authorities shall take into account all relevant considerations including, where applicable, the existence in the State concerned of a consistent pattern of gross, flagrant or mass violations of human rights.

. . .

Article 11

Each State Party shall keep under systematic review interrogation rules, instructions, methods and practices as well as arrangements for the custody and treatment of persons subjected to any form of arrest, detention or imprisonment in any territory under its jurisdiction, with a view to preventing any cases of torture.

Article 12

Each State Party shall ensure that its competent authorities proceed to a prompt and impartial investigation, wherever there is reasonable ground to believe that an act of torture has been committed in any territory under its jurisdiction.

Article 13

Each State Party shall ensure that any individual who alleges he has been subjected to torture in any territory under its jurisdiction has the right to complain to, and to have his case promptly and impartially examined by, its competent authorities. Steps shall be taken to ensure that the complainant and witnesses are protected against all ill-treatment or intimidation as a consequence of his complaint or any evidence given.

Article 14

1. Each State Party shall ensure in its legal system that the victim of an act of torture obtains redress and has an enforceable right to fair and adequate compensation, including the means for as full rehabilitation as possible. In the event of the death of the victim as a result of an act of torture, his dependants shall be entitled to compensation.

2. Nothing in this article shall affect any right of the victim or other persons to compensation which may exist under national law.

Article 15

Each State Party shall ensure that any statement which is established to have been made as a result of torture shall not be invoked as evidence in any proceedings, except against a person accused of torture as evidence that the statement was made.

Article 16

1. Each State Party shall undertake to prevent in any territory under its jurisdiction other acts of cruel, inhuman or degrading treatment or punishment which do not amount to torture as defined in article 1, when such acts are committed by or at the instigation of or with the consent or acquiescence of a public official or other person acting in an official capacity. In particular, the obligations contained in articles 10, 11, 12 and 13 shall apply with the substitution for references to torture of references to other forms of cruel, inhuman or degrading treatment or punishment.

2. The provisions of this Convention are without prejudice to the provisions of any other international instrument or national law which prohibits cruel, inhuman or degrading treatment or punishment or which relates to extradition or expulsion.

. . .

8. 1989 United Nations Convention on the Rights of the Child—Extracts

Entry into force: 20 September 1990

Text: UNGA resolution 44/25, 20 November 1989; 1577 *UNTS* 3

Article 1

For the purposes of the present Convention, a child means every human being below the age of eighteen years unless, under the law applicable to the child, majority is attained earlier.

Article 2

1. States Parties shall respect and ensure the rights set forth in the present Convention to each child within their jurisdiction without discrimination of any kind, irrespective of the child's or his or her parent's or legal guardian's race, colour, sex, language, religion, political or other opinion, national, ethnic or social origin, property, disability, birth or other status.

2. States Parties shall take all appropriate measures to ensure that the child is protected against all forms of discrimination or punishment on the basis of the status, activities, expressed opinions, or beliefs of the child's parents, legal guardians, or family members.

Article 3

1. In all actions concerning children, whether undertaken by public or private social welfare institutions, courts of law, administrative authorities or legislative bodies, the best interests of the child shall be a primary consideration.

2. States Parties undertake to ensure the child such protection and care as is necessary for his or her well-being, taking into account the rights and duties of his or her parents, legal guardians, or other individuals legally responsible for him or her, and, to this end, shall take all appropriate legislative and administrative measures.

3. States Parties shall ensure that the institutions, services and facilities responsible for the care or protection of children shall conform with the standards established by competent authorities, particularly in the areas of safety, health, in the number and suitability of their staff, as well as competent supervision.

Article 4

States Parties shall undertake all appropriate legislative, administrative, and other measures for the implementation of the rights recognized in the present Convention. With regard to economic, social and cultural rights, States Parties shall undertake such measures to the maximum extent of their available resources and, where needed, within the framework of international co-operation.

...

Article 12

1. States Parties shall assure to the child who is capable of forming his or her own views the right to express those views freely in all matters affecting the child, the views of the child being given due weight in accordance with the age and maturity of the child.

2. For this purpose, the child shall in particular be provided the opportunity to be heard in any judicial and administrative proceedings affecting the child, either directly, or through a representative or an appropriate body, in a manner consistent with the procedural rules of national law.

...

Article 19

1. States Parties shall take all appropriate legislative, administrative, social and educational measures to protect the child from all forms of physical or mental violence, injury or abuse, neglect or negligent treatment, maltreatment or exploitation, including sexual abuse, while in the care of parent(s), legal guardian(s), or any other person who has the care of the child.

2. Such protective measures should, as appropriate, include effective procedures for the establishment of social programmes to provide necessary support for the child and for those who have the care of the child, as well as for other forms of prevention and for identification, reporting, referral, investigation, treatment and follow-up of instances of child maltreatment described heretofore, and, as appropriate, for judicial involvement.

Article 20

1. A child temporarily or permanently deprived of his or her family environment, or in whose own best interests cannot be allowed to remain in that environment, shall be entitled to special protection and assistance provided by the State.

2. States Parties shall in accordance with their national laws ensure alternative care for such a child.

3. Such care could include, *inter alia*, foster placement, *kafalah* of Islamic law, adoption or if necessary placement in suitable institutions for the care of children. When considering solutions, due regard shall be paid to the desirability of continuity in a child's upbringing and to the child's ethnic, religious, cultural and linguistic background.

Article 21

States Parties that recognize and/or permit the system of adoption shall ensure that the best interests of the child shall be the paramount consideration and they shall:

(a) Ensure that the adoption of a child is authorized only by competent authorities who determine, in accordance with applicable law and procedures and on the basis of all pertinent and reliable information, that the adoption is permissible in view of the child's status concerning parents, relatives and legal guardians and that, if required, the persons concerned have given their informal consent to the adoption on the basis of such counselling as may be necessary;

(b) Recognize that inter-country adoption may be considered as an alternative means of child's care, if the child cannot be placed in a foster or an adoptive family or cannot in any suitable manner be cared for in the child's country of origin;

(c) Ensure that the child concerned by inter-country adoption enjoys safeguards and standards equivalent to those existing in the case of national adoption;

(d) Take all appropriate measures to ensure that, in inter-country adoption, the placement does not result in improper financial gain for those involved in it;

(e) Promote, where appropriate, the objectives of the present article by concluding bilateral or multilateral arrangements or agreements, and endeavour, within this framework, to ensure that the placement of the child in another country is carried out by competent authorities or organs.

Article 22

1. States Parties shall take appropriate measures to ensure that a child who is seeking refugee status or who is considered a refugee in accordance with applicable international or domestic law and procedures shall, whether unaccompanied or accompanied by his or her parents or by any other person, receive appropriate protection and humanitarian assistance in the enjoyment of applicable rights set forth in the present Convention and in other international human rights or humanitarian instruments to which the said States are Parties.

2. For this purpose, States Parties shall provide, as they consider appropriate, co-operation in any efforts by the United Nations and other competent intergovernmental organizations or non-governmental organizations co-operating with the United Nations to protect and assist such a child and to trace the parents or other members of the family of any refugee child in order to obtain information necessary for reunification with his or her family. In cases where no parents or other members of the family can be found, the child shall be accorded the same protection as any other child permanently or temporarily deprived of his or her family environment for any reason, as set forth in the present Convention.

9. 1987 Constitution of the International Organization for Migration[7]

Preamble

The High Contracting Parties,

Recalling the Resolution adopted on 5 December 1951 by the Migration Conference in Brussels,

Recognizing that the provision of migration services at an international level is often required to ensure the orderly flow of migration movements throughout the world and to

---

[7] The present text incorporates into the Constitution of the Intergovernmental Committee for European Migration (former designation of the Organization; original Constitution of 19 October 1953 in force 30 November 1954) the amendments adopted on 20 May 1987, which in turn entered into force on 14 November 1989.

facilitate, under the most favourable conditions, the settlement and integration of the migrants into the economic and social structure of the country of reception,

that similar migration services may also be required for temporary migration, return migration and intra-regional migration,

that international migration also includes that of refugees, displaced persons and other individuals compelled to leave their homelands, and who are in need of international migration services,

that there is a need to promote the co-operation of States and international organizations with a view to facilitating the emigration of persons who desire to migrate to countries where they may achieve self-dependence through their employment and live with their families in dignity and self-respect,

that migration may stimulate the creation of new economic opportunities in receiving countries and that a relationship exists between migration and the economic, social and cultural conditions in developing countries,

that in the co-operation and other international activities for migration the needs of developing countries should be taken into account,

that there is a need to promote the co-operation of States and international organizations, governmental and non-governmental, for research and consultation on migration issues, not only in regard to the migration process but also the specific situation and needs of the migrant as an individual human being,

that the movement of migrants should, to the extent possible, be carried out with normal transport services but that, on occasion, there is a need for additional or other facilities,

that there should be close co-operation and co-ordination among States, international organizations, governmental and non-governmental, on migration and refugee matters,

that there is a need for the international financing of activities related to international migration,

Do hereby establish the International Organization for Migration, hereinafter called the Organization, and

Accept this Constitution.

Chapter I—Purposes and Functions

Article 1

1. The purposes and functions of the Organization shall be:

(a) to make arrangements for the organized transfer of migrants, for whom existing facilities are inadequate or who would not otherwise be able to move without special assistance, to countries offering opportunities for orderly migration;

(b) to concern itself with the organized transfer of refugees, displaced persons and other individuals in need of international migration services for whom arrangements may be made between the Organization and the States concerned, including those States undertaking to receive them;

(c) to provide, at the request of and in agreement with the States concerned, migration services such as recruitment, selection, processing, language training, orientation activities, medical examination, placement, activities facilitating reception and integration, advisory services on migration questions, and other assistance as is in accord with the aims of the Organization;

(d) to provide similar services as requested by States, or in co-operation with other interested international organizations, for voluntary return migration, including voluntary repatriation;

(e) to provide a forum to States as well as international and other organizations for the exchange of views and experiences, and the promotion of co-operation and co-ordination of efforts on international migration issues, including studies on such issues in order to develop practical solutions.

2. In carrying out its functions, the Organization shall co-operate closely with international organizations, governmental and non-governmental, concerned with migration, refugees and human resources in order, *inter alia*, to facilitate the co-ordination of international activities in these fields. Such co-operation shall be carried out in the mutual respect of the competences of the organizations concerned.

3. The Organization shall recognize the fact that control of standards of admission and the number of immigrants to be admitted are matters within the domestic jurisdiction of States, and, in carrying out its functions, shall conform to the laws, regulations and policies of the States concerned.

Chapter II—Membership

Article 2

The Members of the Organization shall be:

(a) the States being Members of the Organization which have accepted this Constitution according to Article 34, or to which the terms of Article 35 apply;

(b) other States with a demonstrated interest in the principle of free movement of persons which undertake to make a financial contribution at least to the administrative requirements of the Organization, the rate of which will be agreed to by the Council and by the State concerned, subject to a two-thirds majority vote of the Council and upon acceptance by the State of this Constitution.

Article 3

Any Member State may give notice of withdrawal from the Organization effective at the end of a financial year. Such notice must be in writing and must reach the Director General of the Organization at least four months before the end of the financial year. The financial obligations to the Organization of a Member State which has given notice of withdrawal shall include the entire financial year in which notice is given.

Article 4

1. If a Member State fails to meet its financial obligations to the Organization for two consecutive financial years, the Council may by a two-thirds majority vote suspend the voting rights and all or part of the services to which this Member State is entitled. The Council shall have the authority to restore such voting rights and services by a simple majority vote.

2. Any Member State may be suspended from membership by a two-thirds majority vote of the Council if it persistently violates the principles of this Constitution. The Council shall have the authority to restore such membership by a simple majority vote.

Chapter III—Organs

Article 5

There are established as the organs of the Organization:

(a) the Council;

(b) the Executive Committee;

(c) the Administration.

Chapter IV—Council

Article 6

The functions of the Council, in addition to those mentioned in other provisions of this Constitution, shall be:

(a) to determine the policies of the Organization;

(b) to review the reports and to approve and direct the activities of the Executive Committee;

(c) to review the reports and to approve and direct the activities of the Director General;

(d) to review and approve the programme, the Budget, the expenditure and the accounts of the Organization;

(e) to take any other appropriate action to further the purposes of the Organization.

Article 7

1. The Council shall be composed of representatives of the Member States.

2. Each Member State shall have one representative and such alternates and advisers as it may deem necessary.

3. Each Member State shall have one vote in the Council.

Article 8

The Council may admit, upon their application, non-member States and international organizations, governmental or non-governmental, concerned with migration, refugees or human resources as observers at its meetings under conditions which may be prescribed in its rules of procedure. No such observers shall have the right to vote.

Article 9

1. The Council shall meet in regular session once a year.

2. The Council shall meet in special session at the request of:

(a) one third of its members;

(b) the Executive Committee;

(c) the Director General or the Chairman of the Council in urgent circumstances.

3. The Council shall elect, at the beginning of each regular session, a Chairman and other officers for a one-year term.

Article 10

The Council may set up such sub-committees as may be required for the proper discharge of its functions.

Article 11

The Council shall adopt its own rules of procedure.

Chapter V—Executive Committee

Article 12

The functions of the Executive Committee shall be:

(a) to examine and review the policies, programmes and activities of the Organization, the annual reports of the Director General and any special reports;

(b) to examine any financial or budgetary questions falling within the competence of the Council;

(c) to consider any matter specifically referred to it by the Council, including the revision of the Budget, and to take such action as may be deemed necessary thereon;

(d) to advise the Director General on any matters which he may refer to it;

(e) to make, between sessions of the Council, any urgent decisions on matters falling within the competence of the Council, which shall be submitted for approval by that body at its next session;

(f) to present advice or proposals to the Council or the Director General on its own initiative;

(g) to transmit reports and/or recommendations to the Council on the matters dealt with.

Article 13

1. The Executive Committee shall be composed of the representatives of nine Member States. This number may be increased by a two-thirds majority vote of the Council, provided it shall not exceed one third of the total membership of the Organization.

2. These Member States shall be elected by the Council for two years and shall be eligible for re-election.

3. Each member of the Executive Committee shall have one representative and such alternates and advisers as it may deem necessary.

4. Each member of the Executive Committee shall have one vote.

Article 14

1. The Executive Committee shall meet at least once a year. It shall meet, as necessary, in order to perform its functions, at the request of:

(a) its Chairman;

(b) the Council;

(c) the Director General after consultation with the Chairman of the Council;

(d) a majority of its members.

2. The Executive Committee shall elect a Chairman and a Vice-Chairman from among its members for a one-year term.

Article 15

The Executive Committee may, subject to review by the Council, set up such sub-committees as may be required for the proper discharge of its functions.

Article 16

The Executive Committee shall adopt its own rules of procedure.

Chapter VI—Administration

Article 17

The Administration shall comprise a Director General, a Deputy Director General and such staff as the Council may determine.

Article 18

1. The Director General and the Deputy Director General shall be elected by a two-thirds majority vote of the Council and may be re-elected. Their term of office shall normally be five years but may, in exceptional cases, be less if a two-thirds majority of the Council so decides. They shall serve under contracts approved by the Council, which shall be signed on behalf of the Organization by the Chairman of the Council.

2. The Director General shall be responsible to the Council and the Executive Committee. The Director General shall discharge the administrative and executive functions of the Organization in accordance with this Constitution and the policies and decisions of the Council and the Executive Committee and the rules and regulations established by them. The Director General shall formulate proposals for appropriate action by the Council.

Article 19

The Director General shall appoint the staff of the Administration in accordance with the staff regulations adopted by the Council.

Article 20

1. In the performance of their duties, the Director General, the Deputy Director General and the staff shall neither seek nor receive instructions from any State or from any authority external to the Organization. They shall refrain from any action which might reflect adversely on their position as international officials.

2. Each Member State undertakes to respect the exclusively international character of the responsibilities of the Director General, the Deputy Director General and the staff and not to seek to influence them in the discharge of their responsibilities.

3. Efficiency, competence and integrity shall be the necessary considerations in the recruitment and employment of the staff which, except in special circumstances, shall be recruited among the nationals of the Member States of the Organization, taking into account the principle of equitable geographical distribution.

Article 21

The Director General shall be present, or be represented by the Deputy Director General or another designated official, at all sessions of the Council, the Executive Committee and any sub-committees. The Director General or the designated representative may participate in the discussions but shall have no vote.

Article 22

At the regular session of the Council following the end of each financial year, the Director General shall make to the Council, through the Executive Committee, a report on the work of the Organization, giving a full account of its activities during that year.

Chapter VII—Headquarters

Article 23

1. The Organization shall have its Headquarters in Geneva. The Council may, by a two-thirds majority vote, change its location.

2. The meetings of the Council and the Executive Committee shall be held in Geneva, unless two-thirds of the members of the Council or the Executive Committee respectively have agreed to meet elsewhere.

Chapter VIII—Finance

Article 24

The Director General shall submit to the Council, through the Executive Committee, an annual budget covering the administrative and operational requirements and the anticipated resources of the Organization, such supplementary estimates as may be required and the annual or special accounting statements of the Organization.

Article 25

1. The requirements of the Organization shall be financed:

(a) as to the Administrative part of the Budget, by cash contributions from Member States, which shall be due at the beginning of the financial year to which they relate and shall be paid promptly;

(b) as to the Operational part of the Budget, by contributions in cash, in kind or in services from Member States, other States, international organizations, governmental or non-governmental, other legal entities or individuals, which shall be paid as early as possible and in full prior to the expiration of the financial year to which they relate.

2. Member States shall contribute to the Administrative part of the Budget of the Organization at a rate agreed to by the Council and by the Member State concerned.

3. Contributions to the operational expenditure of the Organization shall be voluntary and any contributor to the Operational part of the Budget may stipulate with the Organization

terms and conditions, consistent with the purposes and functions of the Organization, under which its contributions may be used.

4. (a) All Headquarters administrative expenditure and all other administrative expenditure except that incurred in pursuance of the functions outlined in paragraph 1(c) and (d) of Article 1 shall be attributed to the Administrative part of the Budget;

(b) all operational expenditure and such administrative expenditure as is incurred in pursuance of the functions outlined in paragraph 1(c) and (d) of Article 1 shall be attributed to the Operational part of the Budget.

5. The Council shall ensure that the management is conducted in an efficient and economical manner.

Article 26

The financial regulations shall be established by the Council.

Chapter IX—Legal Status

Article 27

The Organization shall possess full juridical personality. It shall enjoy such legal capacity, as may be necessary for the exercise of its functions and the fulfilment of its purposes, and in particular the capacity, in accordance with the laws of the State: (a) to contract; (b) to acquire and dispose of immovable and movable property; (c) to receive and disburse private and public funds; (d) to institute legal proceedings.

Article 28

1. The Organization shall enjoy such privileges and immunities as are necessary for the exercise of its functions and the fulfilment of its purposes.

2. Representatives of Member States, the Director General, the Deputy Director General and the staff of the Administration shall likewise enjoy such privileges and immunities as are necessary for the independent exercise of their functions in connection with the Organization.

3. These privileges and immunities shall be defined in agreements between the Organization and the States concerned or through other measures taken by these States.

Chapter X—Miscellaneous Provisions

Article 29

1. Except as otherwise expressly provided in this Constitution or rules made by the Council or the Executive Committee, all decisions of the Council, the Executive Committee and all sub-committees shall be taken by a simple majority vote.

2. Majorities provided for in this Constitution or rules made by the Council or the Executive Committee shall refer to members present and voting.

3. No vote shall be valid unless a majority of the members of the Council, the Executive Committee or the sub-committee concerned are present.

Article 30

1. Texts of proposed amendments to this Constitution shall be communicated by the Director General to Governments of Member States at least three months in advance of their consideration by the Council.

2. Amendments shall come into force when adopted by two-thirds of the members of the Council and accepted by two-thirds of the Member States in accordance with their respective constitutional processes, provided, however, that amendments involving new obligations for Members shall come into force in respect of a particular Member only when that Member accepts such amendments.

Article 31

Any dispute concerning the interpretation or application of this Constitution which is not settled by negotiation or by a two-thirds majority vote of the Council shall be referred to the International Court of Justice in conformity with the Statute of the Court, unless the Member States concerned agree on another mode of settlement within a reasonable period of time.

Article 32

Subject to approval by two-thirds of the members of the Council, the Organization may take over from any other international organization or agency the purposes and activities of which lie within the purposes of the Organization such activities, resources and obligations as may be determined by international agreement or by mutually acceptable arrangements entered into between the competent authorities of the respective organizations.

Article 33

The Council may, by a three-quarters majority vote of its members, decide to dissolve the Organization.

Article 34[8]

This Constitution shall come into force, for those Governments Members of the Intergovernmental Committee for European Migration which have accepted it in accordance with their respective constitutional processes, on the day of the first meeting of that Committee after:

(a) at least two-thirds of the Members of the Committee, and

(b) a number of Members whose contributions represent at least 75 per cent of the Administrative part of the Budget, shall have communicated to the Director their acceptance of this Constitution.

Article 35

Those Governments Members of the Intergovernmental Committee for European Migration which have not by the date of coming into force of this Constitution communicated to the

---

[8] Articles 34 and 35 were implemented at the time of the entry into force of the Constitution on 30 November 1954.

Director their acceptance of this Constitution may remain Members of the Committee for a period of one year from that date if they contribute to the administrative requirements of the Committee in accordance with paragraph 2 of Article 25, and they shall retain during that period the right to accept the Constitution.

Article 36

The English, French and Spanish texts of this Constitution shall be regarded as equally authentic.

10. 2001 Declaration of States Parties to the 1951 Convention and/or its 1967 Protocol relating to the Status of Refugees[9]

Preamble

We, representatives of States Parties to the 1951 Convention relating to the Status of Refugees and/or its 1967 Protocol, assembled in the first meeting of States Parties in Geneva on 12 and 13 December 2001 at the invitation of the Government of Switzerland and the United Nations High Commissioner for Refugees (UNHCR),

1. Cognizant of the fact that the year 2001 marks the 50th anniversary of the 1951 Geneva Convention relating to the Status of Refugees,

2. Recognizing the enduring importance of the 1951 Convention, as the primary refugee protection instrument which, as amended by its 1967 Protocol, sets out rights, including human rights, and minimum standards of treatment that apply to persons falling within its scope,

3. Recognizing the importance of other human rights and regional refugee protection instruments, including the 1969 Organisation of African Unity (OAU) Convention governing the Specific Aspects of the Refugee Problem in Africa and the 1984 Cartagena Declaration, and recognizing also the importance of the common European asylum system developed since the 1999 Tampere European Council Conclusions, as well as the Programme of Action of the 1996 Regional Conference to Address the Problems of Refugees, Displaced Persons, Other Forms of Involuntary Displacement and Returnees in the Countries of the Commonwealth of Independent States and Relevant Neighbouring States,

4. Acknowledging the continuing relevance and resilience of this international regime of rights and principles, including at its core the principle of *non-refoulement*, whose applicability is embedded in customary international law,

5. Commending the positive and constructive role played by refugee-hosting countries and recognizing at the same time the heavy burden borne by some, particularly developing

---

[9] Adopted on 13 December 2001 in Geneva at the Ministerial Meeting of States Parties to the 1951 Convention and/or its 1967 Protocol relating to the Status of Refugees: UN doc. HCR/MMSP/2001/09, 16 January 2002.

countries and countries with economies in transition, as well as the protracted nature of many refugee situations and the absence of timely and safe solutions,

6. Taking note of complex features of the evolving environment in which refugee protection has to be provided, including the nature of armed conflict, ongoing violations of human rights and international humanitarian law, current patterns of displacement, mixed population flows, the high costs of hosting large numbers of refugees and asylum-seekers and of maintaining asylum systems, the growth of associated trafficking and smuggling of persons, the problems of safeguarding asylum systems against abuse and of excluding and returning those not entitled to or in need of international protection, as well as the lack of resolution of long-standing refugee situations,

7. Reaffirming that the 1951 Convention, as amended by the 1967 Protocol, has a central place in the international refugee protection regime, and believing also that this regime should be developed further, as appropriate, in a way that complements and strengthens the 1951 Convention and its Protocol,

8. Stressing that respect by States for their protection responsibilities towards refugees is strengthened by international solidarity involving all members of the international community and that the refugee protection regime is enhanced through committed international cooperation in a spirit of solidarity and effective responsibility and burden-sharing among all States,

Operative Paragraphs

1. Solemnly reaffirm our commitment to implement our obligations under the 1951 Convention and/or its 1967 Protocol fully and effectively in accordance with the object and purpose of these instruments;

2. Reaffirm our continued commitment, in recognition of the social and humanitarian nature of the problem of refugees, to upholding the values and principles embodied in these instruments, which are consistent with Article 14 of the Universal Declaration of Human Rights, and which require respect for the rights and freedoms of refugees, international cooperation to resolve their plight, and action to address the causes of refugee movements, as well as to prevent them, *inter alia*, through the promotion of peace, stability and dialogue, from becoming a source of tension between States;

3. Recognize the importance of promoting universal adherence to the 1951 Convention and/or its 1967 Protocol, while acknowledging that there are countries of asylum which have not yet acceded to these instruments and which do continue generously to host large numbers of refugees;

4. Encourage all States that have not yet done so to accede to the 1951 Convention and/or its 1967 Protocol, as far as possible without reservation;

5. Also encourage States Parties maintaining the geographical limitation or other reservations to consider withdrawing them;

6. Call upon all States, consistent with applicable international standards, to take or continue to take measures to strengthen asylum and render protection more effective including through the adoption and implementation of national refugee legislation and procedures for the determination of refugee status and for the treatment of asylum-seekers and refugees,

giving special attention to vulnerable groups and individuals with special needs, including women, children and the elderly;

7. Call upon States to continue their efforts aimed at ensuring the integrity of the asylum institution, *inter alia*, by means of carefully applying Articles 1F and 33 (2) of the 1951 Convention, in particular in light of new threats and challenges;

8. Reaffirm the fundamental importance of UNHCR as the multilateral institution with the mandate to provide international protection to refugees and to promote durable solutions, and recall our obligations as State Parties to cooperate with UNHCR in the exercise of its functions;

9. Urge all States to consider ways that may be required to strengthen the implementation of the 1951 Convention and/or 1967 Protocol and to ensure closer cooperation between States parties and UNHCR to facilitate UNHCR's duty of supervising the application of the provisions of these instruments;

10. Urge all States to respond promptly, predictably and adequately to funding appeals issued by UNHCR so as to ensure that the needs of persons under the mandate of the Office of the High Commissioner are fully met;

11. Recognize the valuable contributions made by many non-governmental organizations to the well-being of asylum-seekers and refugees in their reception, counselling and care, in finding durable solutions based on full respect of refugees, and in assisting States and UNHCR to maintain the integrity of the international refugee protection regime, notably through advocacy, as well as public awareness and information activities aimed at combating racism, racial discrimination, xenophobia and related intolerance, and gaining public support for refugees;

12. Commit ourselves to providing, within the framework of international solidarity and burden-sharing, better refugee protection through comprehensive strategies, notably regionally and internationally, in order to build capacity, in particular in developing countries and countries with economies in transition, especially those which are hosting large-scale influxes or protracted refugee situations, and to strengthening response mechanisms, so as to ensure that refugees have access to safer and better conditions of stay and timely solutions to their problems;

13. Recognize that prevention is the best way to avoid refugee situations and emphasize that the ultimate goal of international protection is to achieve a durable solution for refugees, consistent with the principle of *non-refoulement*, and commend States that continue to facilitate these solutions, notably voluntary repatriation and, where appropriate and feasible, local integration and resettlement, while recognizing that voluntary repatriation in conditions of safety and dignity remains the preferred solution for refugees;

14. Extend our gratitude to the Government and people of Switzerland for generously hosting the Ministerial Meeting of States Parties to the 1951 Convention and/or its 1967 Protocol relating to the Status of Refugees.

1. 1969 Convention on the Specific Aspects of Refugee Problems in Africa

Entry into force: 20 June 1974

Text: 1000 *UNTS* 46

Preamble

We, the Heads of State and Government assembled in the city of Addis Ababa, from 6–10 September 1969,

1. *Noting with concern* the constantly increasing numbers of refugees in Africa and desirous of finding ways and means of alleviating their misery and suffering as well as providing them with a better life and future,

2. *Recognizing* the need for an essentially humanitarian approach towards solving the problems of refugees,

3. *Aware,* however, that refugee problems are a source of friction among many Member States, and desirous of eliminating the source of such discord,

4. *Anxious* to make a distinction between a refugee who seeks a peaceful and normal life and a person fleeing his country for the sole purpose of fomenting subversion from outside,

5. *Determined* that the activities of such subversive elements should be discouraged, in accordance with the Declaration on the Problem of Subversion and Resolution on the Problem of Refugees adopted at Accra in 1965,

6. *Bearing in mind* that the Charter of the United Nations and the Universal Declaration of Human Rights have affirmed the principle that human beings shall enjoy fundamental rights and freedoms without discrimination,

7. *Recalling* Resolution 2312 (XXII) of 14 December 1967 of the United Nations General Assembly, relating to the Declaration on Territorial Asylum,

8. *Convinced* that all the problems of our continent must be solved in the spirit of the Charter of the Organization of African Unity and in the African context,

9. *Recognizing* that the United Nations Convention of 28 July 1951, as modified by the Protocol of 31 January 1967, constitutes the basic and universal instrument relating to the status of refugees and reflects the deep concern of States for refugees and their desire to establish common standards for their treatment,

10. *Recalling* Resolutions 26 and 104 of the OAU Assemblies of Heads of State and Government, calling upon Member States of the Organization who had not already done so to accede to the United Nations Convention of 1951 and to the Protocol of 1967 relating to the Status of Refugees, and meanwhile to apply their provisions to refugees in Africa,

11. *Convinced* that the efficiency of the measures recommended by the present Convention to solve the problem of refugees in Africa necessitates close and continuous collaboration between the Organization of African Unity and the Office of the United Nations High Commissioner for Refugees,

Have agreed as follows:

Article I
Definition of the term 'Refugee'

1. For the purposes of this Convention, the term 'refugee' shall mean every person who, owing to well-founded fear of being persecuted for reasons of race, religion, nationality, membership of a particular social group or political opinion, is outside the country of his nationality and is unable or, owing to such fear, is unwilling to avail himself of the protection of that country, or who, not having a nationality and being outside the country of his former habitual residence as a result of such events is unable or, owing to such fear, is unwilling to return to it.

2. The term 'refugee' shall also apply to every person who, owing to external aggression, occupation, foreign domination or events seriously disturbing public order in either part or the whole of his country of origin or nationality, is compelled to leave his place of habitual residence in order to seek refuge in another place outside his country of origin or nationality.

3. In the case of a person who has several nationalities, the term 'a country of which he is a national' shall mean each of the countries of which he is a national, and a person shall not be deemed to be lacking the protection of the country of which he is a national if, without any valid reason based on well-founded fear, he has not availed himself of the protection of one of the countries of which he is a national.

4. This Convention shall cease to apply to any refugee if:

(a) he has voluntarily re-availed himself of the protection of the country of his nationality, or,

(b) having lost his nationality, he has voluntarily reacquired it, or,

(c) he has acquired a new nationality, and enjoys the protection of the country of his new nationality, or,

(d) he has voluntarily re-established himself in the country which he left or outside which he remained owing to fear of persecution, or,

(e) he can no longer, because the circumstances in connection with which he was recognized as a refugee have ceased to exist, continue to refuse to avail himself of the protection of the country of his nationality, or,

(f) he has committed a serious non-political crime outside his country of refuge after his admission to that country as a refugee, or,

(g) he has seriously infringed the purposes and objectives of this Convention.

5. The provisions of this Convention shall not apply to any person with respect to whom the country of asylum has serious reasons for considering that:

(a) he has committed a crime against peace, a war crime, or a crime against humanity, as defined in the international instruments drawn up to make provision in respect of such crimes;

(b) he committed a serious non-political crime outside the country of refuge prior to his admission to that country as a refugee;

(c) he has been guilty of acts contrary to the purposes and principles of the Organization of African Unity;

(d) he has been guilty of acts contrary to the purposes and principles of the United Nations.

6. For the purposes of this Convention, the Contracting State of asylum shall determine whether an applicant is a refugee.

Article II
Asylum

1. Member States of the OAU shall use their best endeavours consistent with their respective legislations to receive refugees and to secure the settlement of those refugees who, for well-founded reasons, are unable or unwilling to return to their country of origin or nationality.

2. The grant of asylum to refugees is a peaceful and humanitarian act and shall not be regarded as an unfriendly act by any Member State.

3. No person shall be subjected by a Member State to measures such as rejection at the frontier, return or expulsion, which would compel him to return to or remain in a territory where his life, physical integrity or liberty would be threatened for the reasons set out in Article I, paragraphs 1 and 2.

4. Where a Member State finds difficulty in continuing to grant asylum to refugees, such Member State may appeal directly to other Member States and through the OAU, and such other Member States shall in the spirit of African solidarity and international co-operation take appropriate measures to lighten the burden of the Member State granting asylum.

5. Where a refugee has not received the right to reside in any country of asylum, he may be granted temporary residence in any country of asylum in which he first presented himself as a refugee pending arrangement for his resettlement in accordance with the preceding paragraph.

6. For reasons of security, countries of asylum shall, as far as possible, settle refugees at a reasonable distance from the frontier of their country of origin.

Article III
Prohibition of Subversive Activities

1. Every refugee has duties to the country in which he finds himself, which require in particular that he conforms with its laws and regulations as well as with measures taken for the maintenance of public order. He shall also abstain from any subversive activities against any Member State of the OAU.

2. Signatory States undertake to prohibit refugees residing in their respective territories from attacking any State Member of the OAU, by any activity likely to cause tension between Member States, and in particular by use of arms, through the press, or by radio.

Article IV
Non-Discrimination

Member States undertake to apply the provisions of this Convention to all refugees without discrimination as to race, religion, nationality, membership of a particular social group or political opinions.

Article V
Voluntary Repatriation

1. The essentially voluntary character of repatriation shall be respected in all cases and no refugee shall be repatriated against his will.

2. The country of asylum, in collaboration with the country of origin, shall make adequate arrangements for the safe return of refugees who request repatriation.

3. The country of origin, on receiving back refugees, shall facilitate their resettlement and grant them the full rights and privileges of nationals of the country, and subject them to the same obligations.

4. Refugees who voluntarily return to their country shall in no way be penalized for having left it for any of the reasons giving rise to refugee situations. Whenever necessary, an appeal shall be made through national information media and through the Administrative Secretary-General of the OAU, inviting refugees to return home and giving assurance that the new circumstances prevailing in their country of origin will enable them to return without risk and to take up a normal and peaceful life without fear of being disturbed or punished, and that the text of such appeal should be given to refugees and clearly explained to them by their country of asylum.

5. Refugees who freely decide to return to their homeland, as a result of such assurances or on their own initiative, shall be given every possible assistance by the country of asylum, the country of origin, voluntary agencies and international and intergovernmental organizations, to facilitate their return.

Article IV
Travel Documents

1. Subject to Article III, Member States shall issue to refugees lawfully staying in their territories travel documents in accordance with the United Nations Convention relating to the Status of Refugees and the Schedule and Annex thereto, for the purpose of travel outside their territory, unless compelling reasons of national security or public order otherwise require. Member States may issue such a travel document to any other refugee in their territory.

2. Where an African country of second asylum accepts a refugee from a country of first asylum, the country of first asylum may be dispensed from issuing a document with a return clause.

3. Travel documents issued to refugees under previous international agreements by States Parties thereto shall be recognized and treated by Member States in the same way as if they had been issued to refugees pursuant to this Article.

Article VII
Co-operation of the National Authorities with the Organization of African Unity

In order to enable the Administrative Secretary-General of the Organization of African Unity to make reports to the competent organs of the Organization of African Unity, Member States undertake to provide the Secretariat in the appropriate form with information and statistical data requested concerning:

(a) the condition of refugees;

(b) the implementation of this Convention, and

(c) laws, regulations and decrees which are, or may hereafter be, in force relating to refugees.

Article VIII
Co-operation with the Office of the United Nations High Commissioner for Refugees

1. Member States shall co-operate with the Office of the United Nations High Commissioner for Refugees.

2. The present Convention shall be the effective regional complement in Africa of the 1951 United Nations Convention on the Status of Refugees.

Article IX
Settlement of Disputes

Any dispute between States signatories to this Convention relating to its interpretation or application, which cannot be settled by other means, shall be referred to the Commission for Mediation, Conciliation and Arbitration of the Organization of African Unity, at the request of any one of the Parties to the dispute.

Article X
Signature and Ratification

1. This Convention is open for signature and accession by all Member States of the Organization of African Unity and shall be ratified by signatory States in accordance with their respective constitutional processes. The instruments of ratification shall be deposited with the Administrative Secretary-General of the Organization of African Unity.

2. The original instrument, done if possible in African languages, and in English and French, all texts being equally authentic, shall be deposited with the Administrative Secretary-General of the Organization of African Unity.

3. Any independent African State, Member of the Organization of African Unity, may at any time notify the Administrative Secretary-General of the Organization of African Unity of its accession to this Convention.

Article XI
Entry into force

This Convention shall come into force upon deposit of instruments of ratification by one-third of the Member States of the Organization of African Unity.

Article XII
Amendment

This Convention may be amended or revised if any Member State makes a written request to the Administrative Secretary-General to that effect, provided however that the proposed amendment shall not be submitted to the Assembly of Heads of State and Government for consideration until all Member States have been duly notified of it and a period of one year has elapsed. Such an amendment shall not be effective unless approved by at least two-thirds of the Member States Parties to the present Convention.

Article XIII
Denunciation

1. Any Member State Party to this Convention may denounce its provisions by a written notification to the Administrative Secretary-General.

2. At the end of one year from the date of such notification, if not withdrawn, the Convention shall cease to apply with respect to the denouncing State.

Article XIV

Upon entry into force of this Convention, the Administrative Secretary-General of the OAU shall register it with the Secretary-General of the United Nations, in accordance with Article 102 of the Charter of the United Nations.

Article XV
Notifications by the Administrative Secretary-General of the Organization of African Unity

The Administrative Secretary-General of the Organization of African Unity shall inform all Members of the Organization:

   (a) of signatures, ratifications and accessions in accordance with Article X;

   (b) of entry into force, in accordance with Article XI;

   (c) of requests for amendments submitted under the terms of Article XII;

   (d) of denunciations, in accordance with Article XIII.

. . .

2. 1981 African Charter on Human and Peoples' Rights—Extracts

Entry into force: 1 October 1986

Text: OAU doc. CAB/LEG/67/3 rev. 5; 1520
UNTS No. 26,363; 21 *ILM* 58 (1982)

Article 12

1. Every individual shall have the right to freedom of movement and residence within the borders of a State provided he abides by the law.

2. Every individual shall have the right to leave any country including his own, and to return to his country. This right may only be subject to restrictions, provided for by law for the protection of national security, law and order, public health or morality.

3. Every individual shall have the right, when persecuted, to seek and obtain asylum in other countries in accordance with the law of those countries and international conventions.

4. A non-national legally admitted in a territory of a State Party to the present Charter, may only be expelled from it by virtue of a decision taken in accordance with the law.

5. The mass expulsion of non-nationals shall be prohibited. Mass expulsion shall be that which is aimed at national, racial, ethnic or religious groups.

. . .

Article 23

1. All peoples shall have the right to national and international peace and security. The principles of solidarity and friendly relations implicitly affirmed by the Charter of the United Nations and reaffirmed by that of the Organization of African Unity shall govern relations between States.

2. For the purpose of strengthening peace, solidarity and friendly relations, States parties to the present Charter shall ensure that:

(a) any individual enjoying the right of asylum under Article 12 of the present Charter shall not engage in subversive activities against his country of origin or any other State party to the present Charter;

(b) their territories shall not be used as bases for subversive or terrorist activities against the people of any other State party to the present Charter.

. . .

3. 1954 Caracas Convention on Territorial Asylum

Entry into force: 29 December 1954

Text: OAS Official Records, OEA/Ser.X/1. Treaty Series 34

The Governments of the Member States of the Organization of American States, desirous of concluding a Convention regarding Territorial Asylum, have agreed to the following articles:

Article 1

Every State has the right, in the exercise of its sovereignty, to admit into its territory such persons as it deems advisable, without, through the exercise of this right, giving rise to complaint by any other State.

Article 2

The respect which, according to international law, is due to the jurisdictional right of each State over the inhabitants in its territory, is equally due, without any restriction whatsoever, to that which it has over persons who enter it proceeding from a State in which they are persecuted for their beliefs, opinions, or political affiliations, or for acts which may be considered as political offenses.

Any violation of sovereignty that consists of acts committed by a government or its agents in another State against the life or security of an individual, carried out on the territory of another State, may not be considered attenuated because the persecution began outside its boundaries or is due to political considerations or reasons of state.

Article 3

No State is under the obligation to surrender to another State, or to expel from its own territory, persons persecuted for political reasons or offenses.

Article 4

The right of extradition is not applicable in connection with persons who, in accordance with the qualifications of the solicited State, are sought for political offenses, or for common offenses committed for political ends, or when extradition is solicited for predominantly political motives.

Article 5

The fact that a person has entered into the territorial jurisdiction of a State surreptitiously or irregularly does not affect the provisions of this Convention.

Article 6

Without prejudice to the provisions of the following articles, no State is under the obligation to establish any distinction in its legislation, or in its regulations or administrative acts applicable to aliens, solely because of the fact that they are political asylees or refugees.

Article 7

Freedom of expression of thought, recognized by domestic law for all inhabitants of a State, may not be ground of complaint by a third State on the basis of opinions expressed publicly against it or its government by asylees or refugees, except when these concepts constitute systematic propaganda through which they incite to the use of force or violence against the government of the complaining State.

Article 8

No State has the right to request that another State restrict for the political asylees or refugees the freedom of assembly or association which the latter States's internal legislation grants to all aliens within its territory, unless such assembly or association has as its purpose fomenting the use of force or violence against the government of the soliciting State.

Article 9

At the request of the interested State, the State that has granted refuge or asylum shall take steps to keep watch over, or to intern at a reasonable distance from its border, those political refugees or asylees who are notorious leaders of a subversive movement, as well as those against whom there is evidence that they are disposed to join it.

Determination of the reasonable distance from the border, for the purpose of internment, shall depend upon the judgment of the authorities of the State of refuge.

All expenses incurred as a result of the internment of political asylees and refugees shall be chargeable to the State that makes the request.

Article 10

The political internees referred to in the preceding article shall advise the government of the host State whenever they wish to leave its territory. Departure therefrom will be granted, under the condition that they are not to go to the country from which they came and the interested government is to be notified.

Article 11

In all cases in which a complaint or request is permissible in accordance with this Convention, the admissibility of evidence presented by the demanding State shall depend on the judgment of the solicited State.

Article 12

This Convention remains open to the signature of the Member States of the Organization of American States, and shall be ratified by the signatory States in accordance with their respective constitutional procedures.

Article 13

The original instrument, whose texts in the English, French, Portuguese, and Spanish languages are equally authentic, shall be deposited in the Pan American Union, which shall send certified copies to the governments for the purpose of ratification. The instruments of ratification shall be deposited in the Pan American Union; this organization shall notify the signatory governments of said deposit.

Article 14

This Convention shall take effect among the States that ratify it in the order in which their respective ratifications are deposited.

Article 15

This Convention shall remain effective indefinitely, but may be denounced by any of the signatory States by giving advance notice of one year, at the end of which period it shall cease to have effect for the denouncing State, remaining, however, in force among the remaining signatory States. The denunciation shall be forwarded to the Pan American Union which shall notify the other signatory States thereof.

4. 1954 Caracas Convention on Diplomatic Asylum

Entry into force: 29 December 1954

Text: OAS Official Records, OEA/Ser.X/1. Treaty Series 34

The Governments of the Member States of the Organization of American States, desirous of concluding a Convention on Diplomatic Asylum, have agreed to the following articles:

Article 1

Asylum granted in legations, war vessels, and military camps or aircraft, to persons being sought for political reasons or for political offenses shall be respected by the territorial State in accordance with the provisions of this Convention. For the purposes of this Convention, a legation is any seat of a regular diplomatic mission, the residence of chiefs of mission, and the premises provided by them for the dwelling places of asylees when the number of the latter exceeds the normal capacity of the buildings. War vessels or military aircraft that may be temporarily in shipyards, arsenals, or shops for repair may not constitute a place of asylum.

Article 2

Every State has the right to grant asylum; but it is not obligated to do so or to state its reasons for refusing it.

Article 3

It is not lawful to grant asylum to persons who, at the time of requesting it, are under indictment or on trial for common offenses or have been convicted by competent regular courts and have not served the respective sentence, nor to deserters from land, sea, and air forces, save when the acts giving rise to the request for asylum, whatever the case may be, are clearly of a political nature.

Persons included in the foregoing paragraph who de facto enter a place that is suitable as an asylum shall be invited to leave or, as the case may be, shall be surrendered to the local authorities, who may not try them for political offenses committed prior to the time of the surrender.

Article 4

It shall rest with the State granting asylum to determine the nature of the offense or the motives for the persecution.

Article 5

Asylum may not be granted except in urgent cases and for the period of time strictly necessary for the asylee to depart from the country with the guarantees granted by the Government of the territorial State, to the end that his life, liberty, or personal integrity may not be endangered, or that the asylee's safety is ensured in some other way.

Article 6

Urgent cases are understood to be those, among others, in which the individual is being sought by persons or mobs over whom the authorities have lost control, or by the authorities themselves, and is in danger of being deprived of his life or liberty because of political persecution and cannot, without risk, ensure his safety in any other way.

Article 7

If a case of urgency is involved, it shall rest with the State granting asylum to determine the degree of urgency of the case.

Article 8

The diplomatic representative, commander of a warship, military camp, or military airship, shall, as soon as possible after asylum has been granted, report the fact to the Minister of Foreign Affairs of the territorial State, or to the local administrative authority if the case arose outside the Capital.

Article 9

The official furnishing asylum shall take into account the information furnished to him by the territorial government in forming his judgment as to the nature of the offense or the existence of related common crimes; but this decision to continue the asylum or to demand a safe-conduct for the asylee shall be respected.

Article 10

The fact that the Government of the territorial State is not recognized by the State granting asylum shall not prejudice the application of the present Convention, and no act carried out by virtue of this Convention shall imply recognition.

Article 11

The Government of the territorial State, may, at any time, demand that the asylee be withdrawn from the country, for which purpose the said State shall grant a safe-conduct and the guarantees stipulated in Article 5.

Article 12

Once asylum has been granted, the State granting asylum may request that the asylee be allowed to depart for foreign territory, and the territorial State is under obligation to grant immediately, except in case of force majeure, the necessary guarantees, referred to in Article 5, as well as the corresponding safe-conduct.

Article 13

In the cases referred to in the preceding articles the State granting asylum may require that the guarantees be given in writing, and may take into account, in determining the rapidity of the journey, the actual conditions of danger involved in the departure of the asylee.

The State granting asylum has the right to transfer the asylee out of the country. The territorial State may point out the preferable route for the departure of the asylee, but this does not imply determining the country of destination.

If the asylum is granted on board a warship or military airship, departure may be made therein, but complying with the previous requisite of obtaining the appropriate safe-conduct.

Article 14

The State granting asylum cannot be held responsible for the prolongation of asylum caused by the need for obtaining the information required to determine whether or not the said asylum is proper, or whether there are circumstances that might endanger the safety of the asylee during the journey to a foreign country.

Article 15

When, in order to transfer an asylee to another country it may be necessary to traverse the territory of a State that is a party to this Convention, transit shall be authorized by the latter, the only requisite being the presentation, through diplomatic channels, of a safe-conduct, duly countersigned and bearing a notation of his status as asylee by the diplomatic mission that granted asylum. En route, the asylee shall be considered under the protection of the State granting asylum.

Article 16

Asylees may not be landed at any point in the territorial State or at any place near thereto, except for exigencies of transportation.

Article 17

Once the departure of the asylee has been carried out, the State granting asylum is not bound to settle him in its territory; but it may not return him to his country of origin, unless this is the express wish of the asylee.

If the territorial State informs the official granting asylum of its intention to request the subsequent extradition of the asylee, this shall not prejudice the application of any provision of the present Convention. In that event, the asylee shall remain in the territory of the State granting asylum until such time as the formal request for extradition is received, in accordance with the juridical principles governing that institution in the State granting asylum. Preventive surveillance over the asylee may not exceed thirty days.

Payment of the expenses incurred by such transfer and of preventive control shall devolve upon the requesting State.

Article 18

The official furnishing asylum may not allow the asylee to perform acts contrary to the public peace or to interfere in the internal politics of the territorial State.

Article 19

If as a consequence of a rupture of diplomatic relations the diplomatic representative who granted asylum must leave the territorial State, he shall abandon it with the asylees.

If this is not possible for reasons independent of the wish of the asylee or the diplomatic representative, he must surrender them to the diplomatic mission of a third State, which is a party to this Convention, under the guarantees established in the Convention.

If this is also not possible, he shall surrender them to a State that is not a party to this Convention and that agrees to maintain the asylum. The territorial State is to respect the said asylum.

Article 20

Diplomatic asylum shall not be subject to reciprocity. Every person is under its protection, whatever his nationality.

Article 21

The present Convention shall be open for signature by the Member States of the Organization of American States and shall be ratified by the signatory States in accordance with their respective constitutional procedures.

Article 22

The original instrument, whose texts in the English, French, Spanish, and Portuguese languages are equally authentic, shall be deposited in the Pan American Union, which shall send certified copies to the governments for the purpose of ratification. The instruments of ratification shall be deposited in the Pan American Union, and the said organization shall notify the signatory governments of the said deposit.

Article 23

The present Convention shall enter into force among the States that ratify it in the order in which their respective ratifications are deposited.

Article 24

The present Convention shall remain in force indefinitely, but may be denounced by any of the signatory States by giving advance notice of one year, at the end of which period it shall cease to have effect for the denouncing State, remaining in force, however, among the remaining signatory States. The denunciation shall be transmitted to the Pan American Union, which shall inform the other signatory States thereof.

5. 1969 American Convention on Human Rights—Extracts

Entry into force: 18 July 1978

Text: OAS *Treaty Series* No. 36 (1969); OAS, Official Records: OEA/Ser.K/XVI/1.1. doc. 65, Rev. 1, Corr. 1 of 7 January 1970; 9 *ILM* 99

Article 20

1. Every person has the right to a nationality.

2. Every person has the right to the nationality of the State in whose territory he was born if he does not have the right to any other nationality.

3. No one shall be arbitrarily deprived of his nationality or of the right to change it.

...

Article 22
Freedom of Movement and Residence

1. Every person lawfully in the territory of a State Party has the right to move about in it and to reside in it subject to the provisions of the law.

2. Every person has the right to leave any country freely, including his own.

3. The exercise of the foregoing rights may be restricted only pursuant to a law to the extent necessary in a democratic society to prevent crime or to protect national security, public safety, public order, public morals, public health, or the rights or freedoms of others.

4. The exercise of the rights recognized in paragraph 1 may also be restricted by law in designated zones for reasons of public interest.

5. No one can be expelled from the territory of the State of which he is a national or be deprived of the right to enter it.

6. An alien lawfully in the territory of a State Party to this Convention may be expelled from it only pursuant to a decision reached in accordance with law.

7. Every person has the right to seek and be granted asylum in a foreign territory, in accordance with the legislation of the State and international conventions, in the event he is being pursued for political offenses or related common crimes.

8. In no case may an alien be deported or returned to a country, regardless of whether or not it is his country of origin, if in that country his right to life or personal freedom is in danger of being violated because of his race, nationality, religion, social status, or political opinions.

9. The collective expulsion of aliens is prohibited.

6. 1981 Inter-American Convention on Extradition—Extracts

Entry into force: 28 March 1982

Text: OAS *Treaty Series* No. 60 (1982): OEA/Ser.A/36

Article 4
Grounds for denying extradition

Extradition shall not be granted:

1. When the person sought has completed his punishment or has been granted amnesty, pardon or grace for the offense for which extradition is sought, or when he has been acquitted or the case against him for the same offense has been dismissed with prejudice.

2. When the prosecution or punishment is barred by the statute of limitations according to the laws of the requesting State or the requested State prior to the presentation of the request for extradition.

3. When the person sought has been tried or is to be tried before an extraordinary or ad hoc tribunal of the requesting State.

4. When, as determined by the requested State, the offense for which the person is sought is a political offense, an offense related thereto, or an ordinary criminal offense prosecuted for political reasons. The requested State may decide that the fact that the victim of the punishable act in question performed political functions does not in itself justify the designation of the offense as political.

5. When, from the circumstances of the case, it can be inferred that persecution for reasons of race, religion or nationality is involved, or that the position of the person sought may be prejudiced for any of these reasons.

6. With respect to offenses that in the requested State cannot be prosecuted unless a complaint or charge has been made by a party having a legitimate interest.

...

Article 6
Right of asylum

No provision of this Convention may be interpreted as a limitation on the right of asylum when its exercise is appropriate.

7. 1984 Cartagena Declaration on Refugees

Adopted at a Colloquium entitled 'Coloquio Sobre la Protección Internacional de los Refugiados en América Central, México y Panamá: Problemas Jurídicos y Humanitarios' held at Cartagena, Colombia from 19–22 November 1984

Text: OAS/Ser.L/V/II.66, doc. 10, rev. 1, pp. 190–3

Conclusions and Recommendations
I

Recalling the conclusions and recommendations adopted by the Colloquium held in Mexico in 1981 on Asylum and International Protection of Refugees in Latin America, which established important landmarks for the analysis and consideration of this matter;

Recognizing that the refugee situation in Central America has evolved in recent years to the point at which it deserves special attention;

Appreciating the generous efforts which have been made by countries receiving Central American refugees, notwithstanding the great difficulties they have had to face, particularly in the current economic crisis;

Emphasizing the admirable humanitarian and non-political task which UNHCR has been called upon to carry out in the Central American countries, Mexico and Panama in accordance with the provisions of the 1951 United Nations Convention and the 1967 Protocol, as well as those of resolution 428 (V) of the United Nations General Assembly, by which the mandate of the United Nations High Commissioner for Refugees is applicable to all States whether or not parties to the said Convention and/or Protocol;

Bearing in mind also the function performed by the Inter-American Commission on Human Rights with regard to the protection of the rights of refugees in the continent;

Strongly supporting the efforts of the Contadora Group to find an effective and lasting solution to the problem of Central American refugees, which constitute a significant step in the negotiation of effective agreements in favour of peace in the region;

Expressing its conviction that many of the legal and humanitarian problems relating to refugees which have arisen in the Central American region, Mexico and Panama can only be tackled in the light of the necessary co-ordination and harmonization of universal and regional systems and national efforts;

II

Having acknowledged with appreciation the commitments with regard to refugees included in the Contadora Act on Peace and Co-operation in Central America, the bases of which the Colloquium fully shares and which are reproduced below:

(a) 'To carry out, if they have not yet done so, the constitutional procedures for accession to the 1951 Convention and the 1967 Protocol relating to the Status of Refugees.'

(b) 'To adopt the terminology established in the Convention and Protocol referred to in the foregoing paragraph with a view to distinguishing refugees from other categories of migrants.'

(c) 'To establish the internal machinery necessary for the implementation, upon accession, of the provisions of the Convention and Protocol referred to above.'

(d) 'To ensure the establishment of machinery for consultation between the Central American countries and representatives of the Government offices responsible for dealing with the problem of refugees in each State.'

(e) 'To support the work performed by the United Nations High Commissioner for Refugees (UNHCR) in Central America and to establish direct co-ordination machinery to facilitate the fulfilment of his mandate.'

(f) 'To ensure that any repatriation of refugees is voluntary, and is declared to be so on an individual basis, and is carried out with the co-operation of UNHCR.'

(g) 'To ensure the establishment of tripartite commissions, composed of representatives of the State of origin, of the receiving State and of UNHCR with a view to facilitating the repatriation of refugees.'

(h) 'To reinforce programmes for protection of and assistance to refugees, particularly in the areas of health, education, labour and safety.'

(i) 'To ensure that programmes and projects are set up with a view to ensuring the self-sufficiency of refugees.'

(j) 'To train the officials responsible in each State for protection of and assistance to refugees, with the co-operation of UNHCR and other international agencies.'

(k) 'To request immediate assistance from the international community for Central American refugees, to be provided either directly, through bilateral or multilateral agreements, or through UNHCR and other organizations and agencies.'

(l) 'To identify, with the co-operation of UNHCR, other countries which might receive Central American refugees. In no case shall a refugee be transferred to a third country against his will.'

(m) 'To ensure that the Governments of the area make the necessary efforts to eradicate the causes of the refugee problem.'

(n) 'To ensure that, once agreement has been reached on the bases for voluntary and individual repatriation, with full guarantees for the refugees, the receiving countries permit official delegations of the country of origin, accompanied by representatives of UNHCR and the receiving country, to visit the refugee camps.'

(o) 'To ensure that the receiving countries facilitate, in co-ordination with UNHCR, the departure procedure for refugees in instances of voluntary and individual repatriation.'

(p) 'To institute appropriate measures in the receiving countries to prevent the participation of refugees in activities directed against the country of origin, while at all times respecting the human rights of the refugees.'

III

The Colloquium adopted the following conclusions:

1. To promote within the countries of the region the adoption of national laws and regulations facilitating the application of the Convention and the Protocol and, if necessary, establishing internal procedures and mechanisms for the protection of refugees. In addition, to ensure that the national laws and regulations adopted reflect the principles and criteria of the Convention and the Protocol, thus fostering the necessary process of systematic harmonization of national legislation on refugees.

2. To ensure that ratification of or accession to the 1951 Convention and the 1967 Protocol by States which have not yet taken these steps is unaccompanied by reservations limiting the scope of those instruments, and to invite countries having formulated such reservations to consider withdrawing them as soon as possible.

3. To reiterate that, in view of the experience gained from the massive flows of refugees in the Central American area, it is necessary to consider enlarging the concept of a refugee, bearing in mind, as far as appropriate and in the light of the situation prevailing in the region, the precedent of the OAU Convention (article I, paragraph 2) and the doctrine employed in the reports of the Inter-American Commission on Human Rights. Hence the definition or concept of a refugee to be recommended for use in the region is one which, in addition to containing the elements of the 1951 Convention and the 1967 Protocol, includes among refugees persons who have fled their country because their lives, safety or freedom have been threatened by generalized violence, foreign aggression, internal conflicts, massive violation of human rights or other circumstances which have seriously disturbed public order.

4. To confirm the peaceful, non-political and exclusively humanitarian nature of grant of asylum or recognition of the status of refugee and to underline the importance of the internationally accepted principle that nothing in either shall be interpreted as an unfriendly act towards the country of origin of refugees.

5. To reiterate the importance and meaning of the principle of *non-refoulement* (including the prohibition of rejection at the frontier) as a corner-stone of the international protection of

refugees. This principle is imperative in regard to refugees and in the present state of international law should be acknowledged and observed as a rule of *jus cogens*.

6. To reiterate to countries of asylum that refugee camps and settlements located in frontier areas should be set up inland at a reasonable distance from the frontier with a view to improving the protection afforded to refugees, safeguarding their human rights and implementing projects aimed at their self-sufficiency and integration into the host society.

7. To express its concern at the problem raised by military attacks on refugee camps and settlements which have occurred in different parts of the world and to propose to the Governments of the Central American countries, Mexico and Panama that they lend their support to the measures on this matter which have been proposed by the High Commissioner to the UNHCR Executive Committee.

8. To ensure that the countries of the region establish a minimum standard of treatment for refugees, on the basis of the provisions of the 1951 Convention and 1967 Protocol and of the American Convention on Human Rights, taking into consideration the conclusions of the UNHCR Executive Committee, particularly No. 22 on the Protection of Asylum Seekers in Situations of Large-Scale Influx.

9. To express its concern at the situation of displaced persons within their own countries. In this connection, the Colloquium calls on national authorities and the competent international organizations to offer protection and assistance to those persons and to help relieve the hardship which many of them face.

10. To call on States parties to the 1969 American Convention on Human Rights to apply this instrument in dealing with asilados and refugees who are in their territories.

11. To make a study, in countries in the area which have a large number of refugees, of the possibilities of integrating them into the productive life of the country by allocating to the creation or generation of employment the resources made available by the international community through UNHCR, thus making it possible for refugees to enjoy their economic, social and cultural rights.

12. To reiterate the voluntary and individual character of repatriation of refugees and the need for it to be carried out under conditions of absolute safety, preferably to the place of residence of the refugee in his country of origin.

13. To acknowledge that reunification of families constitutes a fundamental principle in regard to refugees and one which should be the basis for the regime of humanitarian treatment in the country of asylum, as well as for facilities granted in cases of voluntary repatriation.

14. To urge non-governmental, international and national organizations to continue their worthy task, co-ordinating their activities with UNHCR and the national authorities of the country of asylum, in accordance with the guidelines laid down by the authorities in question.

15. To promote greater use of the competent organizations of the inter-American system, in particular the Inter-American Commission on Human Rights, with a view to enhancing the international protection of asilados and refugees. Accordingly, for the performance of this task, the Colloquium considers that the close co-ordination and co-operation existing between the Commission and UNHCR should be strengthened.

16. To acknowledge the importance of the OAS/UNHCR Programme of Co-operation and the activities so far carried out and to propose that the next stage should focus on the problem raised by massive refugee flows in Central America, Mexico and Panama.

17. To ensure that in the countries of Central America and the Contadora Group the international norms and national legislation relating to the protection of refugees, and of human rights in general, are disseminated at all possible levels. In particular, the Colloquium believes it especially important that such dissemination should be undertaken with the valuable co-operation of the appropriate universities and centres of higher education.

IV

The Cartagena Colloquium therefore

Recommends:

— That the commitments with regard to refugees included in the Contadora Act should constitute norms for the 10 States participating in the Colloquium and be unfailingly and scrupulously observed in determining the conduct to be adopted in regard to refugees in the Central American area.
— That the conclusions reached by the Colloquium (III) should receive adequate attention in the search for solutions to the grave problems raised by the present massive flows of refugees in Central America, Mexico and Panama.
— That a volume should be published containing the working document and the proposals and reports, as well as the conclusions and recommendations of the Colloquium and other pertinent documents, and that the Colombian Government, UNHCR and the competent bodies of OAS should be requested to take the necessary steps to secure the widest possible circulation of the volume in question.
— That the present document should be proclaimed the 'Cartagena Declaration on Refugees'.
— That the United Nations High Commissioner for Refugees should be requested to transmit the contents of the present declaration officially to the heads of State of the Central American countries, of Belize and of the countries forming the Contadora Group.

Finally, the Colloquium expressed its deep appreciation to the Colombian authorities, and in particular to the President of the Republic, Mr Belisario Betancur, the Minister for Foreign Affairs, Mr Augusto Ramírez Ocampo, and the United Nations High Commissioner for Refugees, Mr Poul Hartling, who honoured the Colloquium with their presence, as well as to the University of Cartagena de Indias and the Regional Centre for Third World Studies for their initiative and for the realization of this important event. The Colloquium expressed its special recognition of the support and hospitality offered by the authorities of the Department of Bolivar and the City of Cartagena. It also thanked the people of Cartagena, rightly known as the 'Heroic City', for their warm welcome.

In conclusion, the Colloquium recorded its acknowledgement of the generous tradition of asylum and refuge practised by the Colombian people and authorities.

Cartagena de Indias, 22 November 1984

8. 1950 European Convention on Human Rights and Fundamental Freedoms—Extracts

Entry into force: 3 September 1953

Text: *ETS* No. 5

Article 1

The High Contracting Parties shall secure to everyone within their jurisdiction the rights and freedoms defined in Section 1 of this Convention.

...

Article 3

No one shall be subjected to torture or to inhumane or degrading treatment or punishment.

...

Article 13

Everyone whose rights and freedoms as set forth in this Convention are violated shall have an effective remedy before a national authority notwithstanding that the violation has been committed by persons acting in an official capacity.

Article 14

The enjoyment of the rights and freedoms set forth in this Convention shall be secured without discrimination on any ground such as sex, race, colour, language, religion, political or other opinion, national or social origin, association with a national minority, property, birth or other status.

Article 15

1. In time of war or other public emergency threatening the life of the nation any High Contracting Party may take measures derogating from its obligations under this Convention to the extent strictly required by the exigencies of the situation, provided that such measures are not inconsistent with its other obligations under international law.

2. No derogation from Article 2, except in respect of deaths resulting from lawful acts of war, or from Article 3, 4 (paragraph 1) and 7 shall be made under this provision.

3. Any High Contracting Party availing itself of this right of derogation shall keep the Secretary-General of the Council of Europe fully informed of the measures which it has taken and the reasons therefor. It shall also inform the Secretary-General of the Council of Europe when such measures have ceased to operate and the provisions of the Convention are again being fully executed.

9. 1963 Protocol No. 4 to the European Convention on the Protection of Human Rights and Fundamental Freedoms—Extracts

Entry into force: 2 May 1968

Text: *ETS* No. 46

Article 2

1. Everyone lawfully within the territory of a State shall, within that territory, have the right to liberty of movement and freedom to choose his residence.

2. Everyone shall be free to leave any country, including his own.

3. No restrictions shall be placed on the exercise of these rights other than such as are in accordance with law and are necessary in a democratic society in the interests of national security or public safety, for the maintenance of 'ordre public', for the prevention of crime, for the protection of health or morals, or for the protection of the rights and freedoms of others.

4. The rights set forth in paragraph 1 may also be subject, in particular areas, to restrictions imposed in accordance with law and justified by the public interests in a democratic society.

Article 3

1. No one shall be expelled, by means either of an individual or of a collective measure, from the territory of the State of which he is a national.

2. No one shall be deprived of the right to enter the territory of the State of which he is a national.

Article 4

Collective expulsion of aliens is prohibited.

10. 1957 European Convention on Extradition—Extracts

Entry into force: 18 April 1960

Text: *ETS* No. 24

Article 3
Political offences

1. Extradition shall not be granted if the offence in respect of which it is requested is regarded by the requested Party as a political offence or as an offence connected with a political offence.

2. The same rule shall apply if the requested Party has substantial grounds for believing that a request for extradition for an ordinary criminal offence has been made for the purpose of prosecuting or punishing a person on account of his race, religion, nationality or political opinion, or that that person's position may be prejudiced for any of these reasons.

3. The taking or attempted taking of the life of a Head of State or a member of his family shall not be deemed to be a political offence for the purposes of this Convention.

4. This Article shall not affect any obligations which the Contracting Parties may have undertaken or may undertake under any other international convention of a multilateral character.

...

Article 21

1. Transit through the territory of one of the Contracting Parties shall be granted on submission of a request . . . provided that the offence concerned is not considered by the Party requested to grant transit as an offence of a political or purely military character having regard to Articles 3 and 4 of the Convention.

11. 1975 Additional Protocol to the European Convention on Extradition—Extracts

Entry into force: 20 August 1979

Text: *ETS* No. 86

Article 1

For the application of Article 3 of the Convention, political offences shall not be considered to include the following:

(a) the crimes against humanity specified in the Convention on the Prevention and Punishment of the Crime of Genocide adopted on 9 December 1948 by the General Assembly of the United Nations;

(b) the violations specified in Article 50 of the 1949 Geneva Convention for the Amelioration of the Condition of the Wounded and Sick in Armed Forces in the Field, Article 51 of the 1949 Geneva Convention for the Amelioration of the Condition of Wounded, Sick and Shipwrecked Members of Armed Forces at Sea, Article 130 of the 1949 Geneva Convention relative to the Treatment of Prisoners of War and Article 147 of the 1949 Geneva Convention relative to the Protection of Civilian Persons in Time of War;

(c) any comparable violations of the laws of war having effect at the time when this Protocol enters into force and of customs of war existing at that time, which are not already provided for in the above-mentioned provisions of the Geneva Conventions.

12. 1977 European Convention on the Suppression of Terrorism—Extracts

Entry into force: 4 August 1970

Text: *ETS* No. 90

Article 1

For the purposes of extradition between Contracting States, none of the following offences shall be regarded as a political offence or as an offence connected with a political offence or as an offence inspired by political motives:

(a) an offence within the scope of the Convention for the Suppression of Unlawful Seizure of Aircraft, signed at The Hague on 16 December 1970;

(b) an offence within the scope of the Convention for the Suppression of Unlawful Acts against the Safety of Civil Aviation, signed at Montreal on 23 September 1971;

(c) a serious offence involving an attack against the life, physical integrity or liberty of internationally protected persons, including diplomatic agents;

(d) an offence involving kidnapping, the taking of a hostage or serious unlawful detention;

(e) an offence involving the use of a bomb, grenade, rocket, automatic firearm or letter or parcel bomb if this use endangers persons;

(f) an attempt to commit any of the foregoing offences or participation as an accomplice of a person who commits or attempts to commit such an offence.

Article 2

1. For the purposes of extradition between Contracting States, a Contracting State may decide not to regard as a political offence or as an offence connected with a political offence or as an offence inspired by political motives a serious offence involving an act of violence, other than one covered by Article 1, against the life, physical integrity or liberty of a person.

2. The same shall apply to a serious offence involving an act against property, other than one covered by Article 1, if the act created a collective danger for persons.

3. The same shall apply to an attempt to commit any of the foregoing offences or participation as an accomplice of a person who commits or attempts to commit such an offence.

Article 3

The provisions of all extradition treaties and arrangements applicable between Contracting States, including the European Convention on Extradition, are modified as between Contracting States to the extent that they are incompatible with this Convention.
...

Article 5

Nothing in this Convention shall be interpreted as imposing an obligation to extradite if the requested State has substantial grounds for believing that the request for extradition for an offence mentioned in Article 1 or 2 has been made for the purpose of prosecuting or punishing a person on account of his race, religion, nationality or political opinion, or that that person's position may be prejudiced for any of these reasons.

Article 6

1. Each Contracting State shall take such measures as may be necessary to establish its jurisdiction over an offence mentioned in Article 1 in the case where the suspected offender is present in its territory and it does not extradite him after receiving a request for extradition from a Contracting State whose jurisdiction is based on a rule of jurisdiction existing equally in the law of the requested State.

2. This Convention does not exclude any criminal jurisdiction exercised in accordance with national law.

Article 7

A Contracting State in whose territory a person suspected to have committed an offence mentioned in Article 1 is found and which has received a request for extradition under the conditions mentioned in Article 6, paragraph 1, shall, if it does not extradite that person, submit the case, without exception whatsoever and without undue delay, to its competent authorities for the purpose of prosecution. Those authorities shall take their decision in the same manner as in the case of any offence of a serious nature under the law of that State.

Article 8

1. Contracting States shall afford one another the widest measure of mutual assistance in criminal matters in connection with proceedings brought in respect of the offences mentioned in Article 1 or 2. The law of the requested State concerning mutual assistance in criminal matters shall apply in all cases. Nevertheless this assistance may not be refused on the sole ground that it concerns a political offence or an offence connected with a political offence or an offence inspired by political motives.

2. Nothing in this Convention shall be interpreted as imposing an obligation to afford mutual assistance if the requested State has substantial grounds for believing that the request for mutual assistance in respect of an offence mentioned in Article 1 or 2 has been made for the purpose of prosecuting or punishing a person on account of his race, religion, nationality or political opinion or that that person's position may be prejudiced for any of these reasons.

3. The provisions of all treaties and arrangements concerning mutual assistance in criminal matters applicable between Contracting States, including the European Convention on Mutual Assistance in Criminal Matters, are modified as between Contracting States to the extent that they are incompatible with this Convention.

13. 2000 European Union Charter of Fundamental Rights—Extracts[1]

Preamble

The peoples of Europe, in creating an ever closer union among them, are resolved to share a peaceful future based on common values.

---

[1] *Official Journal* of the European Communities C 364/1, 18.12.2000 (2000/C 364/01).

Conscious of its spiritual and moral heritage, the Union is founded on the indivisible, universal values of human dignity, freedom, equality and solidarity; it is based on the principles of democracy and the rule of law. It places the individual at the heart of its activities, by establishing the citizenship of the Union and by creating an area of freedom, security and justice.

The Union contributes to the preservation and to the development of these common values while respecting the diversity of the cultures and traditions of the peoples of Europe as well as the national identities of the Member States and the organisation of their public authorities at national, regional and local levels; it seeks to promote balanced and sustainable development and ensures free movement of persons, goods, services and capital, and the freedom of establishment.

To this end, it is necessary to strengthen the protection of fundamental rights in the light of changes in society, social progress and scientific and technological developments by making those rights more visible in a Charter.

This Charter reaffirms, with due regard for the powers and tasks of the Community and the Union and the principle of subsidiarity, the rights as they result, in particular, from the constitutional traditions and international obligations common to the Member States, the Treaty on European Union, the Community Treaties, the European Convention for the Protection of Human Rights and Fundamental Freedoms, the Social Charters adopted by the Community and by the Council of Europe and the case-law of the Court of Justice of the European Communities and of the European Court of Human Rights.

Enjoyment of these rights entails responsibilities and duties with regard to other persons, to the human community and to future generations.

The Union therefore recognises the rights, freedoms and principles set out hereafter.

...

Chapter II
Freedoms

Article 18—*Right to asylum*

The right to asylum shall be guaranteed with due respect for the rules of the Geneva Convention of 28 July 1951 and the Protocol of 31 January 1967 relating to the status of refugees and in accordance with the Treaty establishing the European Community.

Article 19—*Protection in the event of removal, expulsion or extradition*

1. Collective expulsions are prohibited.

2. No one may be removed, expelled or extradited to a State where there is a serious risk that he or she would be subjected to the death penalty, torture or other inhuman or degrading treatment or punishment.

...

Chapter VII
General Provisions

Article 51—*Scope*

1. The provisions of this Charter are addressed to the institutions and bodies of the Union with due regard for the principle of subsidiarity and to the Member States only when they

are implementing Union law. They shall therefore respect the rights, observe the principles and promote the application thereof in accordance with their respective powers.

2. This Charter does not establish any new power or task for the Community or the Union, or modify powers and tasks defined by the Treaties.

Article 52—Scope of guaranteed rights

1. Any limitation on the exercise of the rights and freedoms recognised by this Charter must be provided for by law and respect the essence of those rights and freedoms. Subject to the principle of proportionality, limitations may be made only if they are necessary and genuinely meet objectives of general interest recognised by the Union or the need to protect the rights and freedoms of others.

2. Rights recognised by this Charter which are based on the Community Treaties or the Treaty on European Union shall be exercised under the conditions and within the limits defined by those Treaties.

3. In so far as this Charter contains rights which correspond to rights guaranteed by the Convention for the Protection of Human Rights and Fundamental Freedoms, the meaning and scope of those rights shall be the same as those laid down by the said Convention. This provision shall not prevent Union law providing more extensive protection.

Article 53—Level of protection

Nothing in this Charter shall be interpreted as restricting or adversely affecting human rights and fundamental freedoms as recognised, in their respective fields of application, by Union law and international law and by international agreements to which the Union, the Community or all the Member States are party, including the European Convention for the Protection of Human Rights and Fundamental Freedoms, and by the Member States' constitutions.

Article 54—Prohibition of abuse of rights

Nothing in this Charter shall be interpreted as implying any right to engage in any activity or to perform any act aimed at the destruction of any of the rights and freedoms recognised in this Charter or at their limitation to a greater extent than is provided for herein.

14. 2001 European Union Council Directive on Temporary Protection[2]

The Council of the European Union,

Having regard to the Treaty establishing the European Community, and in particular point 2(a) and (b) of Article 63 thereof,

Having regard to the proposal from the Commission,

---

[2] EU Council Directive 2001/55/EC on minimum standards for giving temporary protection in the event of a mass influx of displaced persons and on measures promoting a balance of efforts between Member States in receiving such persons and bearing the consequences thereof: *Official Journal* of the European Communities, 7.8.2001, L 212/12 (footnotes omitted).

Having regard to the opinion of the European Parliament,
Having regard to the opinion of the Economic and Social Committee,
Having regard to the opinion of the Committee of the Regions,

Whereas:

(1) The preparation of a common policy on asylum, including common European arrangements for asylum, is a constituent part of the European Union's objective of establishing progressively an area of freedom, security and justice open to those who, forced by circumstances, legitimately seek protection in the European Union.

(2) Cases of mass influx of displaced persons who cannot return to their country of origin have become more substantial in Europe in recent years. In these cases it may be necessary to set up exceptional schemes to offer them immediate temporary protection.

(3) In the conclusions relating to persons displaced by the conflict in the former Yugoslavia adopted by the Ministers responsible for immigration at their meetings in London on 30 November and 1 December 1992 and Copenhagen on 1 and 2 June 1993, the Member States and the Community institutions expressed their concern at the situation of displaced persons.

(4) On 25 September 1995 the Council adopted a Resolution on burden-sharing with regard to the admission and residence of displaced persons on a temporary basis, and, on 4 March 1996, adopted Decision 96/198/JHA on an alert and emergency procedure for burden-sharing with regard to the admission and residence of displaced persons on a temporary basis.

(5) The Action Plan of the Council and the Commission of 3 December 1998 provides for the rapid adoption, in accordance with the Treaty of Amsterdam, of minimum standards for giving temporary protection to displaced persons from third countries who cannot return to their country of origin and of measures promoting a balance of effort between Member States in receiving and bearing the consequences of receiving displaced persons.

(6) On 27 May 1999 the Council adopted conclusions on displaced persons from Kosovo. These conclusions call on the Commission and the Member States to learn the lessons of their response to the Kosovo crisis in order to establish the measures in accordance with the Treaty.

(7) The European Council, at its special meeting in Tampere on 15 and 16 October 1999, acknowledged the need to reach agreement on the issue of temporary protection for displaced persons on the basis of solidarity between Member States.

(8) It is therefore necessary to establish minimum standards for giving temporary protection in the event of a mass influx of displaced persons and to take measures to promote a balance of efforts between the Member States in receiving and bearing the consequences of receiving such persons.

(9) Those standards and measures are linked and interdependent for reasons of effectiveness, coherence and solidarity and in order, in particular, to avert the risk of secondary movements. They should therefore be enacted in a single legal instrument.

(10) This temporary protection should be compatible with the Member States' international obligations as regards refugees. In particular, it must not prejudice the recognition of refugee status pursuant to the Geneva Convention of 28 July 1951 on the

status of refugees, as amended by the New York Protocol of 31 January 1967, ratified by all the Member States.

(11) The mandate of the United Nations High Commissioner for Refugees regarding refugees and other persons in need of international protection should be respected, and effect should be given to Declaration No 17, annexed to the Final Act to the Treaty of Amsterdam, on Article 63 of the Treaty establishing the European Community which provides that consultations are to be established with the United Nations High Commissioner for Refugees and other relevant international organisations on matters relating to asylum policy.

(12) It is in the very nature of minimum standards that Member States have the power to introduce or maintain more favourable provisions for persons enjoying temporary protection in the event of a mass influx of displaced persons.

(13) Given the exceptional character of the provisions established by this Directive in order to deal with a mass influx or imminent mass influx of displaced persons from third countries who are unable to return to their country of origin, the protection offered should be of limited duration.

(14) The existence of a mass influx of displaced persons should be established by a Council Decision, which should be binding in all Member States in relation to the displaced persons to whom the Decision applies. The conditions for the expiry of the Decision should also be established.

(15) The Member States' obligations as to the conditions of reception and residence of persons enjoying temporary protection in the event of a mass influx of displaced persons should be determined. These obligations should be fair and offer an adequate level of protection to those concerned.

(16) With respect to the treatment of persons enjoying temporary protection under this Directive, the Member States are bound by obligations under instruments of international law to which they are party and which prohibit discrimination.

(17) Member States should, in concert with the Commission, enforce adequate measures so that the processing of personal data respects the standard of protection of Directive 95/46/EC of the European Parliament and the Council of 24 October 1995 on the protection of individuals with regard to the processing of personal data and on the free movement of such data.

(18) Rules should be laid down to govern access to the asylum procedure in the context of temporary protection in the event of a mass influx of displaced persons, in conformity with the Member States' international obligations and with the Treaty.

(19) Provision should be made for principles and measures governing the return to the country of origin and the measures to be taken by Member States in respect of persons whose temporary protection has ended.

(20) Provision should be made for a solidarity mechanism intended to contribute to the attainment of a balance of effort between Member States in receiving and bearing the consequences of receiving displaced persons in the event of a mass influx. The mechanism should consist of two components. The first is financial and the second concerns the actual reception of persons in the Member States.

(21) The implementation of temporary protection should be accompanied by administrative cooperation between the Member States in liaison with the Commission.

(22) It is necessary to determine criteria for the exclusion of certain persons from temporary protection in the event of a mass influx of displaced persons.

(23) Since the objectives of the proposed action, namely to establish minimum standards for giving temporary protection in the event of a mass influx of displaced persons and measures promoting a balance of efforts between the Member States in receiving and bearing the consequences of receiving such persons, cannot be sufficiently attained by the Member States and can therefore, by reason of the scale or effects of the proposed action, be better achieved at Community level, the Community may adopt measures in accordance with the principle of subsidiarity as set out in Article 5 of the Treaty. In accordance with the principle of proportionality as set out in that Article, this Directive does not go beyond what is necessary in order to achieve those objectives.

(24) In accordance with Article 3 of the Protocol on the position of the United Kingdom and Ireland, annexed to the Treaty on European Union and to the Treaty establishing the European Community, the United Kingdom gave notice, by letter of 27 September 2000, of its wish to take part in the adoption and application of this Directive.

(25) Pursuant to Article 1 of the said Protocol, Ireland is not participating in the adoption of this Directive. Consequently and without prejudice to Article 4 of the aforementioned Protocol, the provisions of this Directive do not apply to Ireland.

(26) In accordance with Articles 1 and 2 of the Protocol on the position of Denmark, annexed to the Treaty on European Union and to the Treaty establishing the European Community, Denmark is not participating in the adoption of this Directive, and is therefore not bound by it nor subject to its application,

Has Adopted this Directive:

Chapter I
General Provisions

Article 1

The purpose of this Directive is to establish minimum standards for giving temporary protection in the event of a mass influx of displaced persons from third countries who are unable to return to their country of origin and to promote a balance of effort between Member States in receiving and bearing the consequences of receiving such persons.

Article 2

For the purposes of this Directive:

(a) 'temporary protection' means a procedure of exceptional character to provide, in the event of a mass influx or imminent mass influx of displaced persons from third countries who are unable to return to their country of origin, immediate and temporary protection to such persons, in particular if there is also a risk that the asylum system will be unable to process this influx without adverse effects for its efficient operation, in the interests of the persons concerned and other persons requesting protection;

(b) 'Geneva Convention' means the Convention of 28 July 1951 relating to the status of refugees, as amended by the New York Protocol of 31 January 1967;

(c) 'displaced persons' means third-country nationals or stateless persons who have had to leave their country or region of origin, or have been evacuated, in particular in response to an appeal by international organisations, and are unable to return in safe and durable conditions because of the situation prevailing in that country, who may fall within the scope of Article 1A of the Geneva Convention or other international or national instruments giving international protection, in particular:

   (i) persons who have fled areas of armed conflict or endemic violence;

   (ii) persons at serious risk of, or who have been the victims of, systematic or generalised violations of their human rights;

(d) 'mass influx' means arrival in the Community of a large number of displaced persons, who come from a specific country or geographical area, whether their arrival in the Community was spontaneous or aided, for example through an evacuation programme;

(e) 'refugees' means third-country nationals or stateless persons within the meaning of Article 1A of the Geneva Convention;

(f) 'unaccompanied minors' means third-country nationals or stateless persons below the age of eighteen, who arrive on the territory of the Member States unaccompanied by an adult responsible for them whether by law or custom, and for as long as they are not effectively taken into the care of such a person, or minors who are left unaccompanied after they have entered the territory of the Member States;

(g) 'residence permit' means any permit or authorisation issued by the authorities of a Member State and taking the form provided for in that State's legislation, allowing a third country national or a stateless person to reside on its territory;

(h) 'sponsor' means a third-country national enjoying temporary protection in a Member State in accordance with a decision taken under Article 5 and who wants to be joined by members of his or her family.

Article 3

1. Temporary protection shall not prejudice recognition of refugee status under the Geneva Convention.

2. Member States shall apply temporary protection with due respect for human rights and fundamental freedoms and their obligations regarding non-refoulement.

3. The establishment, implementation and termination of temporary protection shall be the subject of regular consultations with the Office of the United Nations High Commissioner for Refugees (UNHCR) and other relevant international organisations.

4. This Directive shall not apply to persons who have been accepted under temporary protection schemes prior to its entry into force.

5. This Directive shall not affect the prerogative of the Member States to adopt or retain more favourable conditions for persons covered by temporary protection.

Chapter II
Duration and Implementation of Temporary Protection

Article 4

1. Without prejudice to Article 6, the duration of temporary protection shall be one year. Unless terminated under the terms of Article 6(1)(b), it may be extended automatically by six monthly periods for a maximum of one year.

2. Where reasons for temporary protection persist, the Council may decide by qualified majority, on a proposal from the Commission, which shall also examine any request by a Member State that it submit a proposal to the Council, to extend that temporary protection by up to one year.

Article 5

1. The existence of a mass influx of displaced persons shall be established by a Council Decision adopted by a qualified majority on a proposal from the Commission, which shall also examine any request by a Member State that it submit a proposal to the Council.

2. The Commission proposal shall include at least:

(a) a description of the specific groups of persons to whom the temporary protection will apply;

(b) the date on which the temporary protection will take effect;

(c) an estimation of the scale of the movements of displaced persons.

3. The Council Decision shall have the effect of introducing temporary protection for the displaced persons to which it refers, in all the Member States, in accordance with the provisions of this Directive. The Decision shall include at least:

(a) a description of the specific groups of persons to whom the temporary protection applies;

(b) the date on which the temporary protection will take effect;

(c) information received from Member States on their reception capacity;

(d) information from the Commission, UNHCR and other relevant international organisations.

4. The Council Decision shall be based on:

(a) an examination of the situation and the scale of the movements of displaced persons;

(b) an assessment of the advisability of establishing temporary protection, taking into account the potential for emergency aid and action on the ground or the inadequacy of such measures;

(c) information received from the Member States, the Commission, UNHCR and other relevant international organisations.

5. The European Parliament shall be informed of the Council Decision.

Article 6

1. Temporary protection shall come to an end:

(a) when the maximum duration has been reached; or

(b) at any time, by Council Decision adopted by a qualified majority on a proposal from the Commission, which shall also examine any request by a Member State that it submit a proposal to the Council.

2. The Council Decision shall be based on the establishment of the fact that the situation in the country of origin is such as to permit the safe and durable return of those granted

temporary protection with due respect for human rights and fundamental freedoms and Member States' obligations regarding non-refoulement. The European Parliament shall be informed of the Council Decision.

Article 7

1. Member States may extend temporary protection as provided for in this Directive to additional categories of displaced persons over and above those to whom the Council Decision provided for in Article 5 applies, where they are displaced for the same reasons and from the same country or region of origin. They shall notify the Council and the Commission immediately.

2. The provisions of Articles 24, 25 and 26 shall not apply to the use of the possibility referred to in paragraph 1, with the exception of the structural support included in the European Refugee Fund set up by Decision 2000/596/EC, under the conditions laid down in that Decision.

Chapter III
Obligations of the Member States Towards Persons Enjoying Temporary Protection

Article 8

1. The Member States shall adopt the necessary measures to provide persons enjoying temporary protection with residence permits for the entire duration of the protection. Documents or other equivalent evidence shall be issued for that purpose.

2. Whatever the period of validity of the residence permits referred to in paragraph 1, the treatment granted by the Member States to persons enjoying temporary protection may not be less favourable than that set out in Articles 9 to 16.

3. The Member States shall, if necessary, provide persons to be admitted to their territory for the purposes of temporary protection with every facility for obtaining the necessary visas, including transit visas. Formalities must be reduced to a minimum because of the urgency of the situation. Visas should be free of charge or their cost reduced to a minimum.

Article 9

The Member States shall provide persons enjoying temporary protection with a document, in a language likely to be understood by them, in which the provisions relating to temporary protection and which are relevant to them are clearly set out.

Article 10

To enable the effective application of the Council Decision referred to in Article 5, Member States shall register the personal data referred to in Annex II, point (a), with respect to the persons enjoying temporary protection on their territory.

Article 11

A Member State shall take back a person enjoying temporary protection on its territory, if the said person remains on, or, seeks to enter without authorisation onto, the territory of another Member State during the period covered by the Council Decision referred to in

Article 5. Member States may, on the basis of a bilateral agreement, decide that this Article should not apply.

Article 12

The Member States shall authorise, for a period not exceeding that of temporary protection, persons enjoying temporary protection to engage in employed or self-employed activities, subject to rules applicable to the profession, as well as in activities such as educational opportunities for adults, vocational training and practical workplace experience. For reasons of labour market policies, Member States may give priority to EU citizens and citizens of States bound by the Agreement on the European Economic Area and also to legally resident third-country nationals who receive unemployment benefit. The general law in force in the Member States applicable to remuneration, access to social security systems relating to employed or self-employed activities and other conditions of employment shall apply.

Article 13

1. The Member States shall ensure that persons enjoying temporary protection have access to suitable accommodation or, if necessary, receive the means to obtain housing.

2. The Member States shall make provision for persons enjoying temporary protection to receive necessary assistance in terms of social welfare and means of subsistence, if they do not have sufficient resources, as well as for medical care. Without prejudice to paragraph 4, the assistance necessary for medical care shall include at least emergency care and essential treatment of illness.

3. Where persons enjoying temporary protection are engaged in employed or self-employed activities, account shall be taken, when fixing the proposed level of aid, of their ability to meet their own needs.

4. The Member States shall provide necessary medical or other assistance to persons enjoying temporary protection who have special needs, such as unaccompanied minors or persons who have undergone torture, rape or other serious forms of psychological, physical or sexual violence.

Article 14

1. The Member States shall grant to persons under 18 years of age enjoying temporary protection access to the education system under the same conditions as nationals of the host Member State. The Member States may stipulate that such access must be confined to the state education system.

2. The Member States may allow adults enjoying temporary protection access to the general education system.

Article 15

1. For the purpose of this Article, in cases where families already existed in the country of origin and were separated due to circumstances surrounding the mass influx, the following persons shall be considered to be part of a family:

(a) the spouse of the sponsor or his/her unmarried partner in a stable relationship, where the legislation or practice of the Member State concerned treats unmarried couples in a way comparable to married couples under its law relating to aliens; the minor unmarried children of the sponsor or of his/her spouse, without distinction as to whether they were born in or out of wedlock or adopted;

(b) other close relatives who lived together as part of the family unit at the time of the events leading to the mass influx, and who were wholly or mainly dependent on the sponsor at the time.

2. In cases where the separate family members enjoy temporary protection in different Member States, Member States shall reunite family members where they are satisfied that the family members fall under the description of paragraph 1(a), taking into account the wish of the said family members. Member States may reunite family members where they are satisfied that the family members fall under the description of paragraph 1(b), taking into account on a case by case basis the extreme hardship they would face if the reunification did not take place.

3. Where the sponsor enjoys temporary protection in one Member State and one or some family members are not yet in a Member State, the Member State where the sponsor enjoys temporary protection shall reunite family members, who are in need of protection, with the sponsor in the case of family members where it is satisfied that they fall under the description of paragraph 1(a). The Member State may reunite family members, who are in need of protection, with the sponsor in the case of family members where it is satisfied that they fall under the description of paragraph 1(b), taking into account on a case by case basis the extreme hardship which they would face if the reunification did not take place.

4. When applying this Article, the Member States shall take into consideration the best interests of the child.

5. The Member States concerned shall decide, taking account of Articles 25 and 26, in which Member State the reunification shall take place.

6. Reunited family members shall be granted residence permits under temporary protection. Documents or other equivalent evidence shall be issued for that purpose. Transfers of family members onto the territory of another Member State for the purposes of reunification under paragraph 2, shall result in the withdrawal of the residence permits issued, and the termination of the obligations towards the persons concerned relating to temporary protection, in the Member State of departure.

7. The practical implementation of this Article may involve cooperation with the international organisations concerned.

8. A Member State shall, at the request of another Member State, provide information, as set out in Annex II, on a person receiving temporary protection which is needed to process a matter under this Article.

Article 16

1. The Member States shall as soon as possible take measures to ensure the necessary representation of unaccompanied minors enjoying temporary protection by legal guardianship, or, where necessary, representation by an organisation which is responsible for the care and well-being of minors, or by any other appropriate representation.

2. During the period of temporary protection Member States shall provide for unaccompanied minors to be placed:

(a) with adult relatives;

(b) with a foster-family;

(c) in reception centres with special provisions for minors, or in other accommodation suitable for minors;

(d) with the person who looked after the child when fleeing.

The Member States shall take the necessary steps to enable the placement. Agreement by the adult person or persons concerned shall be established by the Member States. The views of the child shall be taken into account in accordance with the age and maturity of the child.

Chapter IV
Access to the Asylum Procedure in the Context of Temporary Protection

Article 17

1. Persons enjoying temporary protection must be able to lodge an application for asylum at any time.

2. The examination of any asylum application not processed before the end of the period of temporary protection shall be completed after the end of that period.

Article 18

The criteria and mechanisms for deciding which Member State is responsible for considering an asylum application shall apply. In particular, the Member State responsible for examining an asylum application submitted by a person enjoying temporary protection pursuant to this Directive, shall be the Member State which has accepted his transfer onto its territory.

Article 19

1. The Member States may provide that temporary protection may not be enjoyed concurrently with the status of asylum seeker while applications are under consideration.

2. Where, after an asylum application has been examined, refugee status or, where applicable, other kind of protection is not granted to a person eligible for or enjoying temporary protection, the Member States shall, without prejudice to Article 28, provide for that person to enjoy or to continue to enjoy temporary protection for the remainder of the period of protection.

Chapter V
Return and Measures after Temporary Protection Has Ended

Article 20

When the temporary protection ends, the general laws on protection and on aliens in the Member States shall apply, without prejudice to Articles 21, 22 and 23.

Article 21

1. The Member States shall take the measures necessary to make possible the voluntary return of persons enjoying temporary protection or whose temporary protection has ended.

The Member States shall ensure that the provisions governing voluntary return of persons enjoying temporary protection facilitate their return with respect for human dignity.

The Member State shall ensure that the decision of those persons to return is taken in full knowledge of the facts. The Member States may provide for exploratory visits.

2. For such time as the temporary protection has not ended, the Member States shall, on the basis of the circumstances prevailing in the country of origin, give favourable consideration to requests for return to the host Member State from persons who have enjoyed temporary protection and exercised their right to a voluntary return.

3. At the end of the temporary protection, the Member States may provide for the obligations laid down in Chapter III to be extended individually to persons who have been covered by temporary protection and are benefiting from a voluntary return programme. The extension shall have effect until the date of return.

Article 22

1. The Member States shall take the measures necessary to ensure that the enforced return of persons whose temporary protection has ended and who are not eligible for admission is conducted with due respect for human dignity.

2. In cases of enforced return, Member States shall consider any compelling humanitarian reasons which may make return impossible or unreasonable in specific cases.

Article 23

1. The Member States shall take the necessary measures concerning the conditions of residence of persons who have enjoyed temporary protection and who cannot, in view of their state of health, reasonably be expected to travel; where for example they would suffer serious negative effects if their treatment was interrupted. They shall not be expelled so long as that situation continues.

2. The Member States may allow families whose children are minors and attend school in a Member State to benefit from residence conditions allowing the children concerned to complete the current school period.

Chapter VI
Solidarity

Article 24

The measures provided for in this Directive shall benefit from the European Refugee Fund set up by Decision 2000/596/EC, under the terms laid down in that Decision.

Article 25

1. The Member States shall receive persons who are eligible for temporary protection in a spirit of Community solidarity. They shall indicate—in figures or in general terms—their capacity to receive such persons. This information shall be set out in the Council Decision referred to in Article 5. After that Decision has been adopted, the Member States may

indicate additional reception capacity by notifying the Council and the Commission. This information shall be passed on swiftly to UNHCR.

2. The Member States concerned, acting in cooperation with the competent international organisations, shall ensure that the eligible persons defined in the Council Decision referred to in Article 5, who have not yet arrived in the Community have expressed their will to be received onto their territory.

3. When the number of those who are eligible for temporary protection following a sudden and massive influx exceeds the reception capacity referred to in paragraph 1, the Council shall, as a matter of urgency, examine the situation and take appropriate action, including recommending additional support for Member States affected.

Article 26

1. For the duration of the temporary protection, the Member States shall cooperate with each other with regard to transferral of the residence of persons enjoying temporary protection from one Member State to another, subject to the consent of the persons concerned to such transferral.

2. A Member State shall communicate requests for transfers to the other Member States and notify the Commission and UNHCR. The Member States shall inform the requesting Member State of their capacity for receiving transferees.

3. A Member State shall, at the request of another Member State, provide information, as set out in Annex II, on a person enjoying temporary protection which is needed to process a matter under this Article.

4. Where a transfer is made from one Member State to another, the residence permit in the Member State of departure shall expire and the obligations towards the persons concerned relating to temporary protection in the Member State of departure shall come to an end. The new host Member State shall grant temporary protection to the persons concerned.

5. The Member States shall use the model pass set out in Annex I for transfers between Member States of persons enjoying temporary protection.

Chapter VII
Administrative Cooperation

Article 27

1. For the purposes of the administrative cooperation required to implement temporary protection, the Member States shall each appoint a national contact point, whose address they shall communicate to each other and to the Commission. The Member States shall, in liaison with the Commission, take all the appropriate measures to establish direct cooperation and an exchange of information between the competent authorities.

2. The Member States shall, regularly and as quickly as possible, communicate data concerning the number of persons enjoying temporary protection and full information on the national laws, regulations and administrative provisions relating to the implementation of temporary protection.

Chapter VIII
Special Provisions

Article 28

1. The Member States may exclude a person from temporary protection if:

(a) there are serious reasons for considering that:

(i) he or she has committed a crime against peace, a war crime, or a crime against humanity, as defined in the international instruments drawn up to make provision in respect of such crimes;

(ii) he or she has committed a serious non-political crime outside the Member State of reception prior to his or her admission to that Member State as a person enjoying temporary protection. The severity of the expected persecution is to be weighed against the nature of the criminal offence of which the person concerned is suspected. Particularly cruel actions, even if committed with an allegedly political objective, may be classified as serious non-political crimes. This applies both to the participants in the crime and to its instigators;

(iii) he or she has been guilty of acts contrary to the purposes and principles of the United Nations;

(b) there are reasonable grounds for regarding him or her as a danger to the security of the host Member State or, having been convicted by a final judgment of a particularly serious crime, he or she is a danger to the community of the host Member State.

2. The grounds for exclusion referred to in paragraph 1 shall be based solely on the personal conduct of the person concerned. Exclusion decisions or measures shall be based on the principle of proportionality.

Chapter IX
Final Provisions

Article 29

Persons who have been excluded from the benefit of temporary protection or family reunification by a Member State shall be entitled to mount a legal challenge in the Member State concerned.

Article 30

The Member States shall lay down the rules on penalties applicable to infringements of the national provisions adopted pursuant to this Directive and shall take all measures necessary to ensure that they are implemented. The penalties provided for must be effective, proportionate and dissuasive.

Article 31

1. Not later than two years after the date specified in Article 32, the Commission shall report to the European Parliament and the Council on the application of this Directive in the Member States and shall propose any amendments that are necessary. The Member

States shall send the Commission all the information that is appropriate for drawing up this report.

2. After presenting the report referred to at paragraph 1, the Commission shall report to the European Parliament and the Council on the application of this Directive in the Member States at least every five years.

Article 32

1. The Member States shall bring into force the laws, regulations and administrative provisions necessary to comply with this Directive by 31 December 2002 at the latest. They shall forthwith inform the Commission thereof.

2. When the Member States adopt these measures, they shall contain a reference to this Directive or shall be accompanied by such reference on the occasion of their official publication. The methods of making such a reference shall be laid down by the Member States.

Article 33

This Directive shall enter into force on the day of its publication in the *Official Journal of the European Communities*.

Article 34

This Directive is addressed to the Member States in accordance with the Treaty establishing the European Community.

Done at Brussels, 20 July 2001 . . .

Annex I

Model pass for the transfer of persons enjoying temporary protection (details omitted)

Annex II

The information referred to in Articles 10, 15 and 26 of the Directive includes to the extent necessary one or more of the following documents or data:

(a) personal data on the person concerned (name, nationality, date and place of birth, marital status, family relationship);

(b) identity documents and travel documents of the person concerned;

(c) documents concerning evidence of family ties (marriage certificate, birth certificate, certificate of adoption);

(d) other information essential to establish the person's identity or family relationship;

(e) residence permits, visas or residence permit refusal decisions issued to the person concerned by the Member State, and documents forming the basis of decisions;

(f) residence permit and visa applications lodged by the person concerned and pending in the Member State, and the stage reached in the processing of these.

The providing Member State shall notify any corrected information to the requesting Member State.

15. 2001 European Union Council Common Position on Combating Terrorism[3]

The Council of the European Union

Having regard to the Treaty on European Union, and in particular Articles 15 and 34 thereof,

Whereas:

(1) At its extraordinary meeting on 21 September 2001, the European Council declared that terrorism is a real challenge to the world and to Europe and that the fight against terrorism will be priority objective of the European Union.

(2) On 28 September 2001, the United Nations Security Council adopted resolution 1373(2001), reaffirming that terrorist acts constitute threat to peace and security and setting out measures aimed at combating terrorism and in particular the fight against the financing of terrorism and the provision of safe havens for terrorists.

(3) On 8 October 2001, the Council reaffirmed the determination of the EU and its Member States to play their full part, in coordinated manner, in the global coalition against terrorism, under the aegis of the United Nations. The Council also reiterated the Union's determination to attack the sources which fund terrorism, in close cooperation with the United States.

(4) On 19 October 2001, the European Council declared that it is determined to combat terrorism in every form throughout the world and that it will continue its efforts to strengthen the coalition of the international community to combat terrorism in every shape and form, for example by the increased cooperation between the operational services responsible for combating terrorism: Europol, Eurojust, the intelligence services, police forces and judicial authorities.

(5) Action has already been taken to implement some of the measures listed below.

(6) Under these extraordinary circumstances, action by the Community is needed in order to implement some of the measures listed below,

Has Adopted this Common Position:

Article 1

The wilful provision or collection, by any means, directly or indirectly, of funds by citizens or within the territory of each of the Member States of the European Union with the intention that the funds should be used, or in the knowledge that they are to be used, in order to carry out terrorist acts shall be criminalized.

Article 2

Funds and other financial assets or economic resources of:

— persons who commit, or attempt to commit, terrorist acts or participate in or facilitate the commission of terrorist acts;

---

[3] EU Council Common Position on Combating Terrorism, 2001/930/CFSP, of 27 December 2001: *Official Journal* of the European Communities 28.12.2001, L 344/90 (Acts adopted pursuant to Title V of the Treaty on European Union).

— entities owned or controlled, directly or indirectly, by such persons; and
— persons and entities acting on behalf of or under the direction of such persons and entities,

including funds derived or generated from property owned or controlled directly or indirectly by such persons and associated persons and entities, shall be frozen.

Article 3

Funds, financial assets or economic resources or financial or other related services shall not be made available, directly or indirectly, for the benefit of:

— persons who commit or attempt to commit or facilitate or participate in the commission of terrorist acts;
— entities owned or controlled, directly or indirectly, by such persons; and
— persons and entities acting on behalf of or under the direction of such persons.

Article 4

Measures shall be taken to suppress any form of support, active or passive, to entities or persons involved in terrorist acts, including measures aimed at suppressing the recruitment of members of terrorist groups and eliminating the supply of weapons to terrorists.

Article 5

Steps shall be taken to prevent the commission of terrorist acts, including by the provision of early warning among Member States or between Member States and third States by exchange of information.

Article 6

Safe haven shall be denied to those who finance, plan, support, or commit terrorist acts, or provide safe havens.

Article 7

Persons who finance, plan, facilitate or commit terrorist acts shall be prevented from using the territories of the Member States of the European Union for those purposes against Member States or third States or their citizens.

Article 8

Persons who participate in the financing, planning, preparation or perpetration of terrorist acts or in supporting terrorist acts shall be brought to justice; such terrorist acts shall be established as serious criminal offences in laws and regulations of Member States and the punishment shall duly reflect the seriousness of such terrorist acts.

Article 9

Member States shall afford one another, as well as third States, the greatest measure of assistance in connection with criminal investigations or criminal proceedings relating to the financing or support of terrorist acts in accordance with international and domestic law, including assistance in obtaining evidence in the possession of a Member State or third State which is necessary for the proceedings.

Article 10

The movement of terrorists or terrorist groups shall be prevented by effective border controls and controls on the issuing of identity papers and travel documents, and through measures for preventing counterfeiting, forgery or fraudulent use of identity papers and travel documents. The Council notes the Commission's intention to put forward proposals in this area, where appropriate.

Article 11

Steps shall be taken to intensify and accelerate the exchange of operational information, especially regarding actions or movements of terrorist persons or networks; forged or falsified travel documents; traffic in arms, explosives or sensitive materials; use of communication technologies by terrorist groups; and the threat posed by the possession of weapons of mass destruction by terrorist groups.

Article 12

Information shall be exchanged among Member States or between Member States and third States in accordance with international and national law, and cooperation shall be enhanced among Member States or between Member States and third States on administrative and judicial matters to prevent the commission of terrorist acts.

Article 13

Cooperation among Member States or between Member States and third States, particularly through bilateral and multilateral arrangements and agreements, to prevent and suppress terrorist attacks and take action against perpetrators of terrorist acts shall be enhanced.

Article 14

Member States shall become parties as soon as possible to the relevant international conventions and protocols relating to terrorism listed in the Annex.

Article 15

Member States shall increase cooperation and fully implement the relevant international conventions and protocols relating to terrorism and United Nations Security Council Resolutions 1269(1999) and 1368(2001).

Article 16

Appropriate measures shall be taken in accordance with the relevant provisions of national and international law, including international standards of human rights, before granting refugee status, for the purpose of ensuring that the asylum-seeker has not planned, facilitated or participated in the commission of terrorist acts. The Council notes the Commission's intention to put forward proposals in this area, where appropriate.

Article 17

Steps shall be taken in accordance with international law to ensure that refugee status is not abused by the perpetrators, organisers or facilitators of terrorist acts and that claims of political motivation are not recognised as grounds for refusing requests for the extradition of alleged terrorists. The Council notes the Commission's intention to put forward proposals in this area, where appropriate.

Article 18

This Common Position shall take effect on the date of its adoption.

Article 19

This Common Position shall be published in the Official Journal.

Done at Brussels, 27 December 2001 . . .

Annex
List of international conventions and protocols relating to terrorism referred to in Article 14

1. Convention on Offenses and Certain Other Offenses Committed on Board Aircraft—Tokyo 14.9.1963

2. Convention for the Unlawful Seizure of Aircraft—The Hague 16.12.1970

3. Convention for the Suppression of Unlawful Acts Against the Safety of Aircraft—Montreal 23.9.1971

4. Convention on the Prevention and Punishment of Crimes Against Internationally Protected Persons, Including Diplomatic Personnel—New York 14.12.1973

5. European Convention for the Suppression of Terrorism—Strasbourg 27.1.1977

6. Convention Against the Taking of Hostages—New York 17.12.1979

7. Convention on the Physical Protection of Nuclear Materials—Vienna 3.3.1980

8. Protocol for the Suppression of Unlawful Acts of Violence at Airports Serving International Aviation, complementary to the Convention for the Suppression of Unlawful Acts Against the Safety of Aircraft—Montreal 24.2.1988

9. Convention for the Suppression of unlawful Acts Against the Safety of Maritime Navigation—Rome 10.3.1988

10. Protocol for the Suppression of Unlawful Acts Against the Safety of Fixed Platforms on the Continental Shelf—Rome 10.3.1988

11. Convention on the Marking of Plastic Explosives for the Purpose of Detection—Montreal 1.3.1991

12. UN Convention for the Suppression of Terrorist Bombings—New York 15.12.1997

13. UN Convention for the Suppression of Financing of Terrorism—New York 9.12.1999

16. 2003 European Union Council Directive on the Reception of Asylum Seekers[4]

The Council of the European Union,

Having regard to the Treaty establishing the European Community, and in particular point (1)(b) of the first subparagraph of Article 63 thereof,

Having regard to the proposal from the Commission,

Having regard to the opinion of the European Parliament,

Having regard to the opinion of the Economic and Social Committee,

Having regard to the opinion of the Committee of the Regions,

Whereas:

(1) A common policy on asylum, including a Common European Asylum System, is a constituent part of the European Union's objective of progressively establishing an area of freedom, security and justice open to those who, forced by circumstances, legitimately seek protection in the Community.

(2) At its special meeting in Tampere on 15 and 16 October 1999, the European Council agreed to work towards establishing a Common European Asylum System, based on the full and inclusive application of the Geneva Convention relating to the Status of Refugees of 28 July 1951, as supplemented by the New York Protocol of 31 January 1967, thus maintaining the principle of non-refoulement.

(3) The Tampere Conclusions provide that a Common European Asylum System should include, in the short term, common minimum conditions of reception of asylum seekers.

(4) The establishment of minimum standards for the reception of asylum seekers is a further step towards a European asylum policy.

(5) This Directive respects the fundamental rights and observes the principles recognised in particular by the Charter of Fundamental Rights of the European Union. In particular, this Directive seeks to ensure full respect for human dignity and to promote the application of Articles 1 and 18 of the said Charter.

(6) With respect to the treatment of persons falling within the scope of this Directive, Member States are bound by obligations under instruments of international law to which they are party and which prohibit discrimination.

(7) Minimum standards for the reception of asylum seekers that will normally suffice to ensure them a dignified standard of living and comparable living conditions in all Member States should be laid down.

(8) The harmonisation of conditions for the reception of asylum seekers should help to limit the secondary movements of asylum seekers influenced by the variety of conditions for their reception.

---

[4] EU Council Directive 2003/9/EC of 27 January 2003 laying down minimum standards for the reception of asylum seekers: *Official Journal* of the European Union, 6.2.2003, L 31/18 (footnotes omitted).

(9) Reception of groups with special needs should be specifically designed to meet those needs.

(10) Reception of applicants who are in detention should be specifically designed to meet their needs in that situation.

(11) In order to ensure compliance with the minimum procedural guarantees consisting in the opportunity to contact organisations or groups of persons that provide legal assistance, information should be provided on such organisations and groups of persons.

(12) The possibility of abuse of the reception system should be restricted by laying down cases for the reduction or withdrawal of reception conditions for asylum seekers.

(13) The efficiency of national reception systems and cooperation among Member States in the field of reception of asylum seekers should be secured.

(14) Appropriate coordination should be encouraged between the competent authorities as regards the reception of asylum seekers, and harmonious relationships between local communities and accommodation centres should therefore be promoted.

(15) It is in the very nature of minimum standards that Member States have the power to introduce or maintain more favourable provisions for third-country nationals and stateless persons who ask for international protection from a Member State.

(16) In this spirit, Member States are also invited to apply the provisions of this Directive in connection with procedures for deciding on applications for forms of protection other than that emanating from the Geneva Convention for third country nationals and stateless persons.

(17) The implementation of this Directive should be evaluated at regular intervals.

(18) Since the objectives of the proposed action, namely to establish minimum standards on the reception of asylum seekers in Member States, cannot be sufficiently achieved by the Member States and can therefore, by reason of the scale and effects of the proposed action, be better achieved by the Community, the Community may adopt measures in accordance with the principles of subsidiarity as set out in Article 5 of the Treaty. In accordance with the principle of proportionality, as set out in that Article, this Directive does not go beyond what is necessary in order to achieve those objectives.

(19) In accordance with Article 3 of the Protocol on the position of the United Kingdom and Ireland, annexed to the Treaty on European Union and to the Treaty establishing the European Community, the United Kingdom gave notice, by letter of 18 August 2001, of its wish to take part in the adoption and application of this Directive.

(20) In accordance with Article 1 of the said Protocol, Ireland is not participating in the adoption of this Directive. Consequently, and without prejudice to Article 4 of the aforementioned Protocol, the provisions of this Directive do not apply to Ireland.

(21) In accordance with Articles 1 and 2 of the Protocol on the position of Denmark, annexed to the Treaty on European Union and to the Treaty establishing the European Community, Denmark is not participating in the adoption of this Directive and is therefore neither bound by it nor subject to its application,

Has Adopted this Directive:

Chapter I
Purpose, Definitions and Scope

Article 1—Purpose

The purpose of this Directive is to lay down minimum standards for the reception of asylum seekers in Member States.

Article 2—Definitions

For the purposes of this Directive:

(a) 'Geneva Convention' shall mean the Convention of 28 July 1951 relating to the status of refugees, as amended by the New York Protocol of 31 January 1967;

(b) 'application for asylum' shall mean the application made by a third-country national or a stateless person which can be understood as a request for international protection from a Member State, under the Geneva Convention. Any application for international protection is presumed to be an application for asylum unless a third-country national or a stateless person explicitly requests another kind of protection that can be applied for separately;

(c) 'applicant' or 'asylum seeker' shall mean a third country national or a stateless person who has made an application for asylum in respect of which a final decision has not yet been taken;

(d) 'family members' shall mean, in so far as the family already existed in the country of origin, the following members of the applicant's family who are present in the same Member State in relation to the application for asylum:

   (i) the spouse of the asylum seeker or his or her unmarried partner in a stable relationship, where the legislation or practice of the Member State concerned treats unmarried couples in a way comparable to married couples under its law relating to aliens;

   (ii) the minor children of the couple referred to in point (i) or of the applicant, on condition that they are unmarried and dependent and regardless of whether they were born in or out of wedlock or adopted as defined under the national law;

(e) 'refugee' shall mean a person who fulfils the requirements of Article 1(A) of the Geneva Convention;

(f) 'refugee status' shall mean the status granted by a Member State to a person who is a refugee and is admitted as such to the territory of that Member State;

(g) 'procedures' and 'appeals', shall mean the procedures and appeals established by Member States in their national law;

(h) 'unaccompanied minors' shall mean persons below the age of eighteen who arrive in the territory of the Member States unaccompanied by an adult responsible for them whether by law or by custom, and for as long as they are not effectively taken into the care of such a person; it shall include minors who are left unaccompanied after they have entered the territory of Member States;

(i) 'reception conditions' shall mean the full set of measures that Member States grant to asylum seekers in accordance with this Directive;

(j) 'material reception conditions' shall mean the reception conditions that include housing, food and clothing, provided in kind, or as financial allowances or in vouchers, and a daily expenses allowance;

(k) 'detention' shall mean confinement of an asylum seeker by a Member State within a particular place, where the applicant is deprived of his or her freedom of movement;

(l) 'accommodation centre' shall mean any place used for collective housing of asylum seekers.

Article 3—Scope

1. This Directive shall apply to all third country nationals and stateless persons who make an application for asylum at the border or in the territory of a Member State as long as they are allowed to remain on the territory as asylum seekers, as well as to family members, if they are covered by such application for asylum according to the national law.

2. This Directive shall not apply in cases of requests for diplomatic or territorial asylum submitted to representations of Member States.

3. This Directive shall not apply when the provisions of Council Directive 2001/55/EC of 20 July 2001 on minimum standards for giving temporary protection in the event of a mass influx of displaced persons and on measures promoting a balance of efforts between Member States in receiving such persons and bearing the consequences thereof are applied.

4. Member States may decide to apply this Directive in connection with procedures for deciding on applications for kinds of protection other than that emanating from the Geneva Convention for third-country nationals or stateless persons who are found not to be refugees.

Article 4—More favourable provisions

Member States may introduce or retain more favourable provisions in the field of reception conditions for asylum seekers and other close relatives of the applicant who are present in the same Member State when they are dependent on him or for humanitarian reasons insofar as these provisions are compatible with this Directive.

Chapter II
General Provisions on Reception Conditions

Article 5—Information

1. Member States shall inform asylum seekers, within a reasonable time not exceeding fifteen days after they have lodged their application for asylum with the competent authority, of at least any established benefits and of the obligations with which they must comply relating to reception conditions.

Member States shall ensure that applicants are provided with information on organisations or groups of persons that provide specific legal assistance and organisations that might be able to help or inform them concerning the available reception conditions, including health care.

2. Member States shall ensure that the information referred to in paragraph 1 is in writing and, as far as possible, in a language that the applicants may reasonably be supposed to understand. Where appropriate, this information may also be supplied orally.

Article 6—Documentation

1. Member States shall ensure that, within three days after an application is lodged with the competent authority, the applicant is provided with a document issued in his or her own name certifying his or her status as an asylum seeker or testifying that he or she is allowed to stay in the territory of the Member State while his or her application is pending or being examined.

   If the holder is not free to move within all or a part of the territory of the Member State, the document shall also certify this fact.

2. Member States may exclude application of this Article when the asylum seeker is in detention and during the examination of an application for asylum made at the border or within the context of a procedure to decide on the right of the applicant legally to enter the territory of a Member State. In specific cases, during the examination of an application for asylum, Member States may provide applicants with other evidence equivalent to the document referred to in paragraph 1.

3. The document referred to in paragraph 1 need not certify the identity of the asylum seeker.

4. Member States shall adopt the necessary measures to provide asylum seekers with the document referred to in paragraph 1, which must be valid for as long as they are authorised to remain in the territory of the Member State concerned or at the border thereof.

5. Member States may provide asylum seekers with a travel document when serious humanitarian reasons arise that require their presence in another State.

Article 7—Residence and freedom of movement

1. Asylum seekers may move freely within the territory of the host Member State or within an area assigned to them by that Member State. The assigned area shall not affect the unalienable sphere of private life and shall allow sufficient scope for guaranteeing access to all benefits under this Directive.

2. Member States may decide on the residence of the asylum seeker for reasons of public interest, public order or, when necessary, for the swift processing and effective monitoring of his or her application.

3. When it proves necessary, for example for legal reasons or reasons of public order, Member States may confine an applicant to a particular place in accordance with their national law.

4. Member States may make provision of the material reception conditions subject to actual residence by the applicants in a specific place, to be determined by the Member States. Such a decision, which may be of a general nature, shall be taken individually and established by national legislation.

5. Member States shall provide for the possibility of granting applicants temporary permission to leave the place of residence mentioned in paragraphs 2 and 4 and/or the assigned area mentioned in paragraph 1. Decisions shall be taken individually, objectively and impartially and reasons shall be given if they are negative.

The applicant shall not require permission to keep appointments with authorities and courts if his or her appearance is necessary.

6. Member States shall require applicants to inform the competent authorities of their current address and notify any change of address to such authorities as soon as possible.

Article 8—Families

Member States shall take appropriate measures to maintain as far as possible family unity as present within their territory, if applicants are provided with housing by the Member State concerned. Such measures shall be implemented with the asylum seeker's agreement.

Article 9—Medical screening

Member States may require medical screening for applicants on public health grounds.

Article 10—Schooling and education of minors

1. Member States shall grant to minor children of asylum seekers and to asylum seekers who are minors access to the education system under similar conditions as nationals of the host Member State for so long as an expulsion measure against them or their parents is not actually enforced. Such education may be provided in accommodation centres.

The Member State concerned may stipulate that such access must be confined to the State education system.

Minors shall be younger than the age of legal majority in the Member State in which the application for asylum was lodged or is being examined. Member States shall not withdraw secondary education for the sole reason that the minor has reached the age of majority.

2. Access to the education system shall not be postponed for more than three months from the date the application for asylum was lodged by the minor or the minor's parents. This period may be extended to one year where specific education is provided in order to facilitate access to the education system.

3. Where access to the education system as set out in paragraph 1 is not possible due to the specific situation of the minor, the Member State may offer other education arrangements.

Article 11—Employment

1. Member States shall determine a period of time, starting from the date on which an application for asylum was lodged, during which an applicant shall not have access to the labour market.

2. If a decision at first instance has not been taken within one year of the presentation of an application for asylum and this delay cannot be attributed to the applicant, Member States shall decide the conditions for granting access to the labour market for the applicant.

3. Access to the labour market shall not be withdrawn during appeals procedures, where an appeal against a negative decision in a regular procedure has suspensive effect, until such time as a negative decision on the appeal is notified.

4. For reasons of labour market policies, Member States may give priority to EU citizens and nationals of States parties to the Agreement on the European Economic Area and also to legally resident third-country nationals.

Article 12—Vocational training

Member States may allow asylum seekers access to vocational training irrespective of whether they have access to the labour market.

Access to vocational training relating to an employment contract shall depend on the extent to which the applicant has access to the labour market in accordance with Article 11.

Article 13—General rules on material reception conditions and health care

1. Member States shall ensure that material reception conditions are available to applicants when they make their application for asylum.

2. Member States shall make provisions on material reception conditions to ensure a standard of living adequate for the health of applicants and capable of ensuring their subsistence.

Member States shall ensure that that standard of living is met in the specific situation of persons who have special needs, in accordance with Article 17, as well as in relation to the situation of persons who are in detention.

3. Member States may make the provision of all or some of the material reception conditions and health care subject to the condition that applicants do not have sufficient means to have a standard of living adequate for their health and to enable their subsistence.

4. Member States may require applicants to cover or contribute to the cost of the material reception conditions and of the health care provided for in this Directive, pursuant to the provision of paragraph 3, if the applicants have sufficient resources, for example if they have been working for a reasonable period of time.

If it transpires that an applicant had sufficient means to cover material reception conditions and health care at the time when these basic needs were being covered, Member States may ask the asylum seeker for a refund.

5. Material reception conditions may be provided in kind, or in the form of financial allowances or vouchers or in a combination of these provisions.

Where Member States provide material reception conditions in the form of financial allowances or vouchers, the amount thereof shall be determined in accordance with the principles set out in this Article.

Article 14—Modalities for material reception conditions

1. Where housing is provided in kind, it should take one or a combination of the following forms:

(a) premises used for the purpose of housing applicants during the examination of an application for asylum lodged at the border;

(b) accommodation centres which guarantee an adequate standard of living;

(c) private houses, flats, hotels or other premises adapted for housing applicants.

2. Member States shall ensure that applicants provided with the housing referred to in paragraph 1(a), (b) and (c) are assured:

(a) protection of their family life;

(b) the possibility of communicating with relatives, legal advisers and representatives of the United Nations High Commissioner for Refugees (UNHCR) and non-governmental organisations (NGOs) recognised by Member States. Member States shall pay particular attention to the prevention of assault within the premises and accommodation centres referred to in paragraph 1(a) and (b).

3. Member States shall ensure, if appropriate, that minor children of applicants or applicants who are minors are lodged with their parents or with the adult family member responsible for them whether by law or by custom.

4. Member States shall ensure that transfers of applicants from one housing facility to another take place only when necessary. Member States shall provide for the possibility for applicants to inform their legal advisers of the transfer and of their new address.

5. Persons working in accommodation centres shall be adequately trained and shall be bound by the confidentiality principle as defined in the national law in relation to any information they obtain in the course of their work.

6. Member States may involve applicants in managing the material resources and non-material aspects of life in the centre through an advisory board or council representing residents.

7. Legal advisors or counsellors of asylum seekers and representatives of the United Nations High Commissioner for Refugees or non-governmental organisations designated by the latter and recognised by the Member State concerned shall be granted access to accommodation centres and other housing facilities in order to assist the said asylum seekers. Limits on such access may be imposed only on grounds relating to the security of the centres and facilities and of the asylum seekers.

8. Member States may exceptionally set modalities for material reception conditions different from those provided for in this Article, for a reasonable period which shall be as short as possible, when:

— an initial assessment of the specific needs of the applicant is required,
— material reception conditions, as provided for in this Article, are not available in a certain geographical area,
— housing capacities normally available are temporarily exhausted,
— the asylum seeker is in detention or confined to border posts.

These different conditions shall cover in any case basic needs.

Article 15—Health care

1. Member States shall ensure that applicants receive the necessary health care which shall include, at least, emergency care and essential treatment of illness.

2. Member States shall provide necessary medical or other assistance to applicants who have special needs.

Chapter III
Reduction or Withdrawal of Reception Conditions

Article 16—Reduction or withdrawal of reception conditions

1. Member States may reduce or withdraw reception conditions in the following cases:

(a) where an asylum seeker:

— abandons the place of residence determined by the competent authority without informing it or, if requested, without permission, or

— does not comply with reporting duties or with requests to provide information or to appear for personal interviews concerning the asylum procedure during a reasonable period laid down in national law, or

— has already lodged an application in the same Member State.

When the applicant is traced or voluntarily reports to the competent authority, a duly motivated decision, based on the reasons for the disappearance, shall be taken on the reinstallation of the grant of some or all of the reception conditions;

(b) where an applicant has concealed financial resources and has therefore unduly benefited from material reception conditions.

If it transpires that an applicant had sufficient means to cover material reception conditions and health care at the time when these basic needs were being covered, Member States may ask the asylum seeker for a refund.

2. Member States may refuse conditions in cases where an asylum seeker has failed to demonstrate that the asylum claim was made as soon as reasonably practicable after arrival in that Member State.

3. Member States may determine sanctions applicable to serious breaching of the rules of the accommodation centres as well as to seriously violent behaviour.

4. Decisions for reduction, withdrawal or refusal of reception conditions or sanctions referred to in paragraphs 1, 2 and 3 shall be taken individually, objectively and impartially and reasons shall be given. Decisions shall be based on the particular situation of the person concerned, especially with regard to persons covered by Article 17, taking into account the principle of proportionality. Member States shall under all circumstances ensure access to emergency health care.

5. Member States shall ensure that material reception conditions are not withdrawn or reduced before a negative decision is taken.

Chapter IV
Provisions for Persons with Special Needs

Article 17—General principle

1. Member States shall take into account the specific situation of vulnerable persons such as minors, unaccompanied minors, disabled people, elderly people, pregnant women, single parents with minor children and persons who have been subjected to torture, rape or other serious forms of psychological, physical or sexual violence, in the national legislation implementing the provisions of Chapter II relating to material reception conditions and health care.

2. Paragraph 1 shall apply only to persons found to have special needs after an individual evaluation of their situation.

Article 18—Minors

1. The best interests of the child shall be a primary consideration for Member States when implementing the provisions of this Directive that involve minors.

2. Member States shall ensure access to rehabilitation services for minors who have been victims of any form of abuse, neglect, exploitation, torture or cruel, inhuman and degrading treatment, or who have suffered from armed conflicts, and ensure that appropriate mental health care is developed and qualified counselling is provided when needed.

Article 19—Unaccompanied minors

1. Member States shall as soon as possible take measures to ensure the necessary representation of unaccompanied minors by legal guardianship or, where necessary, representation by an organisation which is responsible for the care and well-being of minors, or by any other appropriate representation. Regular assessments shall be made by the appropriate authorities.

2. Unaccompanied minors who make an application for asylum shall, from the moment they are admitted to the territory to the moment they are obliged to leave the host Member State in which the application for asylum was made or is being examined, be placed:

(a) with adult relatives;

(b) with a foster-family;

(c) in accommodation centres with special provisions for minors;

(d) in other accommodation suitable for minors.

Member States may place unaccompanied minors aged 16 or over in accommodation centres for adult asylum seekers.

As far as possible, siblings shall be kept together, taking into account the best interests of the minor concerned and, in particular, his or her age and degree of maturity. Changes of residence of unaccompanied minors shall be limited to a minimum.

3. Member States, protecting the unaccompanied minor's best interests, shall endeavour to trace the members of his or her family as soon as possible. In cases where there may be a threat to the life or integrity of the minor or his or her close relatives, particularly if they have remained in the country of origin, care must be taken to ensure that the collection, processing and circulation of information concerning those persons is undertaken on a confidential basis, so as to avoid jeopardising their safety.

4. Those working with unaccompanied minors shall have had or receive appropriate training concerning their needs, and shall be bound by the confidentiality principle as defined in the national law, in relation to any information they obtain in the course of their work.

Article 20—Victims of torture and violence

Member States shall ensure that, if necessary, persons who have been subjected to torture, rape or other serious acts of violence receive the necessary treatment of damages caused by the aforementioned acts.

Chapter V
Appeals

Article 21—Appeals

1. Member States shall ensure that negative decisions relating to the granting of benefits under this Directive or decisions taken under Article 7 which individually affect asylum seekers may be the subject of an appeal within the procedures laid down in the national law. At least in the last instance the possibility of an appeal or a review before a judicial body shall be granted.

2. Procedures for access to legal assistance in such cases shall be laid down in national law.

Chapter VI
Actions to Improve the Efficiency of the Reception System

Article 22—Cooperation

Member States shall regularly inform the Commission on the data concerning the number of persons, broken down by sex and age, covered by reception conditions and provide full information on the type, name and format of the documents provided for by Article 6.

Article 23—Guidance, monitoring and control system

Member States shall, with due respect to their constitutional structure, ensure that appropriate guidance, monitoring and control of the level of reception conditions are established.

Article 24—Staff and resources

1. Member States shall take appropriate measures to ensure that authorities and other organisations implementing this Directive have received the necessary basic training with respect to the needs of both male and female applicants.

2. Member States shall allocate the necessary resources in connection with the national provisions enacted to implement this Directive.

Chapter VII
Final Provisions

Article 25—Reports

By 6 August 2006, the Commission shall report to the European Parliament and the Council on the application of this Directive and shall propose any amendments that are necessary.

Member States shall send the Commission all the information that is appropriate for drawing up the report, including the statistical data provided for by Article 22 by 6 February 2006.

After presenting the report, the Commission shall report to the European Parliament and the Council on the application of this Directive at least every five years.

Article 26—Transposition

1. Member States shall bring into force the laws, regulations and administrative provisions necessary to comply with this Directive by 6 February 2005. They shall forthwith inform the Commission thereof.

When the Member States adopt these measures, they shall contain a reference to this Directive or shall be accompanied by such a reference on the occasion of their official publication. Member States shall determine how such a reference is to be made.

2. Member States shall communicate to the Commission the text of the provisions of national law which they adopt in the field relating to the enforcement of this Directive.

Article 27—Entry into force

This Directive shall enter into force on the day of its publication in the *Official Journal of the European Union*.

Article 28—Addressees

This Directive is addressed to the Member States in accordance with the Treaty establishing the European Union.

Done at Brussels, 27 January 2003 . . .

17. 2003 European Union Council Regulation on the Criteria and Mechanisms for Determining the Member State responsible for Examining an Asylum Application[5]

The Council of the European Union,

Having regard to the Treaty establishing the European Community, and in particular Article 63, first paragraph, point (1)(a),

Having regard to the proposal from the Commission,

Having regard to the opinion of the European Parliament,

Having regard to the opinion of the European Economic and Social Committee,

Whereas:

(1) A common policy on asylum, including a Common European Asylum System, is a constituent part of the European Union's objective of progressively establishing an area of freedom, security and justice open to those who, forced by circumstances, legitimately seek protection in the Community.

(2) The European Council, at its special meeting in Tampere on 15 and 16 October 1999, agreed to work towards establishing a Common European Asylum System, based on the full and inclusive application of the Geneva Convention relating to the Status of Refugees of 28 July 1951, as supplemented by the New York Protocol of 31 January 1967, thus

---

[5] EU Council Regulation (EC) No 343/2003 of 18 February 2003 establishing the criteria and mechanisms for determining the Member State responsible for examining an asylum application lodged in one of the Member States by a third-country national: *Official Journal* of the European Union L 50/1, 25.2.2003 (Acts whose publication is obligatory)—footnotes omitted.

ensuring that nobody is sent back to persecution, i.e. maintaining the principle of non-refoulement. In this respect, and without affecting the responsibility criteria laid down in this Regulation, Member States, all respecting the principle of non-refoulement, are considered as safe countries for third-country nationals.

(3) The Tampere conclusions also stated that this system should include, in the short term, a clear and workable method for determining the Member State responsible for the examination of an asylum application.

(4) Such a method should be based on objective, fair criteria both for the Member States and for the persons concerned. It should, in particular, make it possible to determine rapidly the Member State responsible, so as to guarantee effective access to the procedures for determining refugee status and not to compromise the objective of the rapid processing of asylum applications.

(5) As regards the introduction in successive phases of a common European asylum system that should lead, in the longer term, to a common procedure and a uniform status, valid throughout the Union, for those granted asylum, it is appropriate at this stage, while making the necessary improvements in the light of experience, to confirm the principles underlying the Convention determining the State responsible for examining applications for asylum lodged in one of the Member States of the European Communities, signed in Dublin on 15 June 1990 (hereinafter referred to as the Dublin Convention), whose implementation has stimulated the process of harmonising asylum policies.

(6) Family unity should be preserved in so far as this is compatible with the other objectives pursued by establishing criteria and mechanisms for determining the Member State responsible for examining an asylum application.

(7) The processing together of the asylum applications of the members of one family by a single Member State makes it possible to ensure that the applications are examined thoroughly and the decisions taken in respect of them are consistent. Member States should be able to derogate from the responsibility criteria, so as to make it possible to bring family members together where this is necessary on humanitarian grounds.

(8) The progressive creation of an area without internal frontiers in which free movement of persons is guaranteed in accordance with the Treaty establishing the European Community and the establishment of Community policies regarding the conditions of entry and stay of third country nationals, including common efforts towards the management of external borders, makes it necessary to strike a balance between responsibility criteria in a spirit of solidarity.

(9) The application of this Regulation can be facilitated, and its effectiveness increased, by bilateral arrangements between Member States for improving communications between competent departments, reducing time limits for procedures or simplifying the processing of requests to take charge or take back, or establishing procedures for the performance of transfers.

(10) Continuity between the system for determining the Member State responsible established by the Dublin Convention and the system established by this Regulation should be ensured. Similarly, consistency should be ensured between this Regulation and Council Regulation (EC) No 2725/2000 of 11 December 2000 concerning the establishment of 'Eurodac' for the comparison of fingerprints for the effective application of the Dublin Convention.

(11) The operation of the Eurodac system, as established by Regulation (EC) No 2725/2000 and in particular the implementation of Articles 4 and 8 contained therein should facilitate the implementation of this Regulation.

(12) With respect to the treatment of persons falling within the scope of this Regulation, Member States are bound by obligations under instruments of international law to which they are party.

(13) The measures necessary for the implementation of this Regulation should be adopted in accordance with Council Decision 1999/468/EC of 28 June 1999 laying down the procedures for the exercise of implementing powers conferred on the Commission.

(14) The application of the Regulation should be evaluated at regular intervals.

(15) The Regulation observes the fundamental rights and principles which are acknowledged in particular in the Charter of Fundamental Rights of the European Union. In particular, it seeks to ensure full observance of the right to asylum guaranteed by Article 18.

(16) Since the objective of the proposed measure, namely the establishment of criteria and mechanisms for determining the Member State responsible for examining an asylum application lodged in one of the Member States by a third-country national, cannot be sufficiently achieved by the Member States and, given the scale and effects, can therefore be better achieved at Community level, the Community may adopt measures in accordance with the principle of subsidiarity as set out in Article 5 of the Treaty. In accordance with the principle of proportionality, as set out in that Article, this Regulation does not go beyond what is necessary in order to achieve that objective.

(17) In accordance with Article 3 of the Protocol on the position of the United Kingdom and Ireland, annexed to the Treaty on European Union and to the Treaty establishing the European Community, the United Kingdom and Ireland gave notice, by letters of 30 October 2001, of their wish to take part in the adoption and application of this Regulation.

(18) In accordance with Articles 1 and 2 of the Protocol on the position of Denmark, annexed to the Treaty on European Union and to the Treaty establishing the European Community, Denmark does not take part in the adoption of this Regulation and is not bound by it nor subject to its application.

(19) The Dublin Convention remains in force and continues to apply between Denmark and the Member States that are bound by this Regulation until such time an agreement allowing Denmark's participation in the Regulation has been concluded,

Has Adopted this Regulation:

Chapter I
Subject-matter and Definitions

Article 1

This Regulation lays down the criteria and mechanisms for determining the Member State responsible for examining an application for asylum lodged in one of the Member States by a third-country national.

Article 2

For the purposes of this Regulation:

(a) 'third-country national' means anyone who is not a citizen of the Union within the meaning of Article 17(1) of the Treaty establishing the European Community;

(b) 'Geneva Convention' means the Convention of 28 July 1951 relating to the status of refugees, as amended by the New York Protocol of 31 January 1967;

(c) 'application for asylum' means the application made by a third-country national which can be understood as a request for international protection from a Member State, under the Geneva Convention. Any application for international protection is presumed to be an application for asylum, unless a third-country national explicitly requests another kind of protection that can be applied for separately;

(d) 'applicant' or 'asylum seeker' means a third country national who has made an application for asylum in respect of which a final decision has not yet been taken;

(e) 'examination of an asylum application' means any examination of, or decision or ruling concerning, an application for asylum by the competent authorities in accordance with national law except for procedures for determining the Member State responsible in accordance with this Regulation;

(f) 'withdrawal of the asylum application' means the actions by which the applicant for asylum terminates the procedures initiated by the submission of his application for asylum, in accordance with national law, either explicitly or tacitly;

(g) 'refugee' means any third-country national qualifying for the status defined by the Geneva Convention and authorised to reside as such on the territory of a Member State;

(h) 'unaccompanied minor' means unmarried persons below the age of eighteen who arrive in the territory of the Member States unaccompanied by an adult responsible for them whether by law or by custom, and for as long as they are not effectively taken into the care of such a person; it includes minors who are left unaccompanied after they have entered the territory of the Member States;

(i) 'family members' means insofar as the family already existed in the country of origin, the following members of the applicant's family who are present in the territory of the Member States:

    (i) the spouse of the asylum seeker or his or her unmarried partner in a stable relationship, where the legislation or practice of the Member State concerned treats unmarried couples in a way comparable to married couples under its law relating to aliens;

    (ii) the minor children of couples referred to in point (i) or of the applicant, on condition that they are unmarried and dependent and regardless of whether they were born in or out of wedlock or adopted as defined under the national law;

    (iii) the father, mother or guardian when the applicant or refugee is a minor and unmarried;

(j) 'residence document' means any authorisation issued by the authorities of a Member State authorising a third-country national to stay in its territory, including the documents substantiating the authorisation to remain in the territory under temporary protection arrangements or until the circumstances preventing a removal order from being carried out no longer apply, with the exception of visas and residence authorisations issued during the period required to determine the responsible Member State as established in this Regulation or during examination of an application for asylum or an application for a residence permit;

(k) 'visa' means the authorisation or decision of a Member State required for transit or entry for an intended stay in that Member State or in several Member States. The nature of the visa shall be determined in accordance with the following definitions:

  (i) 'long-stay visa' means the authorisation or decision of a Member State required for entry for an intended stay in that Member State of more than three months;

  (ii) 'short-stay visa' means the authorisation or decision of a Member State required for entry for an intended stay in that State or in several Member States for a period whose total duration does not exceed three months;

  (iii) 'transit visa' means the authorisation or decision of a Member State for entry for transit through the territory of that Member State or several Member States, except for transit at an airport;

  (iv) 'airport transit visa' means the authorisation or decision allowing a third-country national specifically subject to this requirement to pass through the transit zone of an airport, without gaining access to the national territory of the Member State concerned, during a stopover or a transfer between two sections of an international flight.

Chapter II
General Principles

Article 3

1. Member States shall examine the application of any third-country national who applies at the border or in their territory to any one of them for asylum. The application shall be examined by a single Member State, which shall be the one which the criteria set out in Chapter III indicate is responsible.

2. By way of derogation from paragraph 1, each Member State may examine an application for asylum lodged with it by a third-country national, even if such examination is not its responsibility under the criteria laid down in this Regulation. In such an event, that Member State shall become the Member State responsible within the meaning of this Regulation and shall assume the obligations associated with that responsibility. Where appropriate, it shall inform the Member State previously responsible, the Member State conducting a procedure for determining the Member State responsible or the Member State which has been requested to take charge of or take back the applicant.

3. Any Member State shall retain the right, pursuant to its national laws, to send an asylum seeker to a third country, in compliance with the provisions of the Geneva Convention.

4. The asylum seeker shall be informed in writing in a language that he or she may reasonably be expected to understand regarding the application of this Regulation, its time limits and its effects.

Article 4

1. The process of determining the Member State responsible under this Regulation shall start as soon as an application for asylum is first lodged with a Member State.

2. An application for asylum shall be deemed to have been lodged once a form submitted by the applicant for asylum or a report prepared by the authorities has reached the competent authorities of the Member State concerned. Where an application is not made in writing, the time elapsing between the statement of intention and the preparation of a report should be as short as possible.

3. For the purposes of this Regulation, the situation of a minor who is accompanying the asylum seeker and meets the definition of a family member set out in Article 2, point (i), shall be indissociable from that of his parent or guardian and shall be a matter for the Member State responsible for examining the application for asylum of that parent or guardian, even if the minor is not individually an asylum seeker. The same treatment shall be applied to children born after the asylum seeker arrives in the territory of the Member States, without the need to initiate a new procedure for taking charge of them.

4. Where an application for asylum is lodged with the competent authorities of a Member State by an applicant who is in the territory of another Member State, the determination of the Member State responsible shall be made by the Member State in whose territory the applicant is present. The latter Member State shall be informed without delay by the Member State which received the application and shall then, for the purposes of this Regulation, be regarded as the Member State with which the application for asylum was lodged.

The applicant shall be informed in writing of this transfer and of the date on which it took place.

5. An asylum seeker who is present in another Member State and there lodges an application for asylum after withdrawing his application during the process of determining the Member State responsible shall be taken back, under the conditions laid down in Article 20, by the Member State with which that application for asylum was lodged, with a view to completing the process of determining the Member State responsible for examining the application for asylum.

This obligation shall cease, if the asylum seeker has in the meantime left the territories of the Member States for a period of at least three months or has obtained a residence document from a Member State.

Chapter III
Hierarchy of Criteria

Article 5

1. The criteria for determining the Member State responsible shall be applied in the order in which they are set out in this Chapter.

2. The Member State responsible in accordance with the criteria shall be determined on the basis of the situation obtaining when the asylum seeker first lodged his application with a Member State.

Article 6

Where the applicant for asylum is an unaccompanied minor, the Member State responsible for examining the application shall be that where a member of his or her family is legally present, provided that this is in the best interest of the minor.

In the absence of a family member, the Member State responsible for examining the application shall be that where the minor has lodged his or her application for asylum.

Article 7

Where the asylum seeker has a family member, regardless of whether the family was previously formed in the country of origin, who has been allowed to reside as a refugee in a Member State, that Member State shall be responsible for examining the application for asylum, provided that the persons concerned so desire.

Article 8

If the asylum seeker has a family member in a Member State whose application has not yet been the subject of a first decision regarding the substance, that Member State shall be responsible for examining the application for asylum, provided that the persons concerned so desire.

Article 9

1. Where the asylum seeker is in possession of a valid residence document, the Member State which issued the document shall be responsible for examining the application for asylum.

2. Where the asylum seeker is in possession of a valid visa, the Member State which issued the visa shall be responsible for examining the application for asylum, unless the visa was issued when acting for or on the written authorisation of another Member State. In such a case, the latter Member State shall be responsible for examining the application for asylum. Where a Member State first consults the central authority of another Member State, in particular for security reasons, the latter's reply to the consultation shall not constitute written authorisation within the meaning of this provision.

3. Where the asylum seeker is in possession of more than one valid residence document or visa issued by different Member States, the responsibility for examining the application for asylum shall be assumed by the Member States in the following order:

(a) the Member State which issued the residence document conferring the right to the longest period of residency or, where the periods of validity are identical, the Member State which issued the residence document having the latest expiry date;

(b) the Member State which issued the visa having the latest expiry date where the various visas are of the same type;

(c) where visas are of different kinds, the Member State which issued the visa having the longest period of validity, or, where the periods of validity are identical, the Member State which issued the visa having the latest expiry date.

4. Where the asylum seeker is in possession only of one or more residence documents which have expired less than two years previously or one or more visas which have expired less than six months previously and which enabled him actually to enter the territory of a

Member State, paragraphs 1, 2 and 3 shall apply for such time as the applicant has not left the territories of the Member States.

Where the asylum seeker is in possession of one or more residence documents which have expired more than two years previously or one or more visas which have expired more than six months previously and enabled him actually to enter the territory of a Member State and where he has not left the territories of the Member States, the Member State in which the application is lodged shall be responsible.

5. The fact that the residence document or visa was issued on the basis of a false or assumed identity or on submission of forged, counterfeit or invalid documents shall not prevent responsibility being allocated to the Member State which issued it. However, the Member State issuing the residence document or visa shall not be responsible if it can establish that a fraud was committed after the document or visa had been issued.

Article 10

1. Where it is established, on the basis of proof or circumstantial evidence as described in the two lists mentioned in Article 18(3), including the data referred to in Chapter III of Regulation (EC) No 2725/2000, that an asylum seeker has irregularly crossed the border into a Member State by land, sea or air having come from a third country, the Member State thus entered shall be responsible for examining the application for asylum. This responsibility shall cease 12 months after the date on which the irregular border crossing took place.

2. When a Member State cannot or can no longer be held responsible in accordance with paragraph 1, and where it is established, on the basis of proof or circumstantial evidence as described in the two lists mentioned in Article 18(3), that the asylum seeker—who has entered the territories of the Member States irregularly or whose circumstances of entry cannot be established—at the time of lodging the application has been previously living for a continuous period of at least five months in a Member State, that Member State shall be responsible for examining the application for asylum.

If the applicant has been living for periods of time of at least five months in several Member States, the Member State where this has been most recently the case shall be responsible for examining the application.

Article 11

1. If a third-country national enters into the territory of a Member State in which the need for him or her to have a visa is waived, that Member State shall be responsible for examining his or her application for asylum.

2. The principle set out in paragraph 1 does not apply, if the third-country national lodges his or her application for asylum in another Member State, in which the need for him or her to have a visa for entry into the territory is also waived. In this case, the latter Member State shall be responsible for examining the application for asylum.

Article 12

Where the application for asylum is made in an international transit area of an airport of a Member State by a third-country national, that Member State shall be responsible for examining the application.

Article 13

Where no Member State responsible for examining the application for asylum can be designated on the basis of the criteria listed in this Regulation, the first Member State with which the application for asylum was lodged shall be responsible for examining it.

Article 14

Where several members of a family submit applications for asylum in the same Member State simultaneously, or on dates close enough for the procedures for determining the Member State responsible to be conducted together, and where the application of the criteria set out in this Regulation would lead to them being separated, the Member State responsible shall be determined on the basis of the following provisions:

(a) responsibility for examining the applications for asylum of all the members of the family shall lie with the Member State which the criteria indicate is responsible for taking charge of the largest number of family members;

(b) failing this, responsibility shall lie with the Member State which the criteria indicate is responsible for examining the application of the oldest of them.

Chapter IV
Humanitarian Clause

Article 15

1. Any Member State, even where it is not responsible under the criteria set out in this Regulation, may bring together family members, as well as other dependent relatives, on humanitarian grounds based in particular on family or cultural considerations. In this case that Member State shall, at the request of another Member State, examine the application for asylum of the person concerned. The persons concerned must consent.

2. In cases in which the person concerned is dependent on the assistance of the other on account of pregnancy or a newborn child, serious illness, severe handicap or old age, Member States shall normally keep or bring together the asylum seeker with another relative present in the territory of one of the Member States, provided that family ties existed in the country of origin.

3. If the asylum seeker is an unaccompanied minor who has a relative or relatives in another Member State who can take care of him or her, Member States shall if possible unite the minor with his or her relative or relatives, unless this is not in the best interests of the minor.

4. Where the Member State thus approached accedes to the request, responsibility for examining the application shall be transferred to it.

5. The conditions and procedures for implementing this Article including, where appropriate, conciliation mechanisms for settling differences between Member States concerning the need to unite the persons in question, or the place where this should be done, shall be adopted in accordance with the procedure referred to in Article 27(2).

Chapter V
Taking Charge and Taking Back

Article 16

1. The Member State responsible for examining an application for asylum under this Regulation shall be obliged to:

(a) take charge, under the conditions laid down in Articles 17 to 19, of an asylum seeker who has lodged an application in a different Member State;

(b) complete the examination of the application for asylum;

(c) take back, under the conditions laid down in Article 20, an applicant whose application is under examination and who is in the territory of another Member State without permission;

(d) take back, under the conditions laid down in Article 20, an applicant who has withdrawn the application under examination and made an application in another Member State;

(e) take back, under the conditions laid down in Article 20, a third-country national whose application it has rejected and who is in the territory of another Member State without permission.

2. Where a Member State issues a residence document to the applicant, the obligations specified in paragraph 1 shall be transferred to that Member State.

3. The obligations specified in paragraph 1 shall cease where the third-country national has left the territory of the Member States for at least three months, unless the third-country national is in possession of a valid residence document issued by the Member State responsible.

4. The obligations specified in paragraph 1(d) and (e) shall likewise cease once the Member State responsible for examining the application has adopted and actually implemented, following the withdrawal or rejection of the application, the provisions that are necessary before the third-country national can go to his country of origin or to another country to which he may lawfully travel.

Article 17

1. Where a Member State with which an application for asylum has been lodged considers that another Member State is responsible for examining the application, it may, as quickly as possible and in any case within three months of the date on which the application was lodged within the meaning of Article 4(2), call upon the other Member State to take charge of the applicant.

Where the request to take charge of an applicant is not made within the period of three months, responsibility for examining the application for asylum shall lie with the Member State in which the application was lodged.

2. The requesting Member State may ask for an urgent reply in cases where the application for asylum was lodged after leave to enter or remain was refused, after an arrest for an

unlawful stay or after the service or execution of a removal order and/or where the asylum seeker is held in detention.

The request shall state the reasons warranting an urgent reply and the period within which a reply is expected. This period shall be at least one week.

3. In both cases, the request that charge be taken by another Member State shall be made using a standard form and including proof or circumstantial evidence as described in the two lists mentioned in Article 18(3) and/or relevant elements from the asylum seeker's statement, enabling the authorities of the requested Member State to check whether it is responsible on the basis of the criteria laid down in this Regulation.

The rules on the preparation of and the procedures for transmitting requests shall be adopted in accordance with the procedure referred to in Article 27(2).

Article 18

1. The requested Member State shall make the necessary checks, and shall give a decision on the request to take charge of an applicant within two months of the date on which the request was received.

2. In the procedure for determining the Member State responsible for examining the application for asylum established in this Regulation, elements of proof and circumstantial evidence shall be used.

3. In accordance with the procedure referred to in Article 27(2) two lists shall be established and periodically reviewed, indicating the elements of proof and circumstantial evidence in accordance with the following criteria:

(a) Proof:

  (i) This refers to formal proof which determines responsibility pursuant to this Regulation, as long as it is not refuted by proof to the contrary.

  (ii) The Member States shall provide the Committee provided for in Article 27 with models of the different types of administrative documents, in accordance with the typology established in the list of formal proofs.

(b) Circumstantial evidence:

  (i) This refers to indicative elements which while being refutable may be sufficient, in certain cases, according to the evidentiary value attributed to them.

  (ii) Their evidentiary value, in relation to the responsibility for examining the application for asylum shall be assessed on a case-by-case basis.

4. The requirement of proof should not exceed what is necessary for the proper application of this Regulation.

5. If there is no formal proof, the requested Member State shall acknowledge its responsibility if the circumstantial evidence is coherent, verifiable and sufficiently detailed to establish responsibility.

6. Where the requesting Member State has pleaded urgency, in accordance with the provisions of Article 17(2), the requested Member State shall make every effort to conform to the time limit requested. In exceptional cases, where it can be demonstrated that the examination of a request for taking charge of an applicant is particularly complex, the requested Member State may give the reply after the time limit requested, but in any case within one

month. In such situations the requested Member State must communicate its decision to postpone a reply to the requesting Member State within the time limit originally requested.

7. Failure to act within the two-month period mentioned in paragraph 1 and the one-month period mentioned in paragraph 6 shall be tantamount to accepting the request, and entail the obligation to take charge of the person, including the provisions for proper arrangements for arrival.

Article 19

1. Where the requested Member State accepts that it should take charge of an applicant, the Member State in which the application for asylum was lodged shall notify the applicant of the decision not to examine the application, and of the obligation to transfer the applicant to the responsible Member State.

2. The decision referred to in paragraph 1 shall set out the grounds on which it is based. It shall contain details of the time limit for carrying out the transfer and shall, if necessary, contain information on the place and date at which the applicant should appear, if he is travelling to the Member State responsible by his own means. This decision may be subject to an appeal or a review. Appeal or review concerning this decision shall not suspend the implementation of the transfer unless the courts or competent bodies so decide on a case by case basis if national legislation allows for this.

3. The transfer of the applicant from the Member State in which the application for asylum was lodged to the Member State responsible shall be carried out in accordance with the national law of the first Member State, after consultation between the Member States concerned, as soon as practically possible, and at the latest within six months of acceptance of the request that charge be taken or of the decision on an appeal or review where there is a suspensive effect.

If necessary, the asylum seeker shall be supplied by the requesting Member State with a *laissez passer* of the design adopted in accordance with the procedure referred to in Article 27(2).

The Member State responsible shall inform the requesting Member State, as appropriate, of the safe arrival of the asylum seeker or of the fact that he did not appear within the set time limit.

4. Where the transfer does not take place within the six months' time limit, responsibility shall lie with the Member State in which the application for asylum was lodged. This time limit may be extended up to a maximum of one year if the transfer could not be carried out due to imprisonment of the asylum seeker or up to a maximum of eighteen months if the asylum seeker absconds.

5. Supplementary rules on carrying out transfers may be adopted in accordance with the procedure referred to in Article 27(2).

Article 20

1. An asylum seeker shall be taken back in accordance with Article 4(5) and Article 16(1)(c), (d) and (e) as follows:

(a) the request for the applicant to be taken back must contain information enabling the requested Member State to check that it is responsible;

(b) the Member State called upon to take back the applicant shall be obliged to make the necessary checks and reply to the request addressed to it as quickly as possible and under no circumstances exceeding a period of one month from the referral. When the request is based on data obtained from the Eurodac system, this time limit is reduced to two weeks;

(c) where the requested Member State does not communicate its decision within the one month period or the two weeks period mentioned in subparagraph (b), it shall be considered to have agreed to take back the asylum seeker;

(d) a Member State which agrees to take back an asylum seeker shall be obliged to readmit that person to its territory. The transfer shall be carried out in accordance with the national law of the requesting Member State, after consultation between the Member States concerned, as soon as practically possible, and at the latest within six months of acceptance of the request that charge be taken by another Member State or of the decision on an appeal or review where there is a suspensive effect;

(e) the requesting Member State shall notify the asylum seeker of the decision concerning his being taken back by the Member State responsible. The decision shall set out the grounds on which it is based. It shall contain details of the time limit on carrying out the transfer and shall, if necessary, contain information on the place and date at which the applicant should appear, if he is travelling to the Member State responsible by his own means. This decision may be subject to an appeal or a review. Appeal or review concerning this decision shall not suspend the implementation of the transfer except when the courts or competent bodies so decide in a case-by-case basis if the national legislation allows for this.

If necessary, the asylum seeker shall be supplied by the requesting Member State with a *laissez passer* of the design adopted in accordance with the procedure referred to in Article 27(2).

The Member State responsible shall inform the requesting Member State, as appropriate, of the safe arrival of the asylum seeker or of the fact that he did not appear within the set time limit.

2. Where the transfer does not take place within the six months' time limit, responsibility shall lie with the Member State in which the application for asylum was lodged. This time limit may be extended up to a maximum of one year if the transfer or the examination of the application could not be carried out due to imprisonment of the asylum seeker or up to a maximum of eighteen months if the asylum seeker absconds.

3. The rules of proof and evidence and their interpretation, and on the preparation of and the procedures for transmitting requests, shall be adopted in accordance with the procedure referred to in Article 27(2).

4. Supplementary rules on carrying out transfers may be adopted in accordance with the procedure referred to in Article 27(2).

Chapter VI
Administrative Cooperation

Article 21

1. Each Member State shall communicate to any Member State that so requests such personal data concerning the asylum seeker as is appropriate, relevant and non-excessive for:

(a) the determination of the Member State responsible for examining the application for asylum;

(b) examining the application for asylum;

(c) implementing any obligation arising under this Regulation.

2. The information referred to in paragraph 1 may only cover:

(a) personal details of the applicant, and, where appropriate, the members of his family (full name and where appropriate, former name; nicknames or pseudonyms; nationality, present and former; date and place of birth);

(b) identity and travel papers (references, validity, date of issue, issuing authority, place of issue, etc.);

(c) other information necessary for establishing the identity of the applicant, including fingerprints processed in accordance with Regulation (EC) No 2725/2000;

(d) places of residence and routes travelled;

(e) residence documents or visas issued by a Member State;

(f) the place where the application was lodged;

(g) the date any previous application for asylum was lodged, the date the present application was lodged, the stage reached in the proceedings and the decision taken, if any.

3. Furthermore, provided it is necessary for the examination of the application for asylum, the Member State responsible may request another Member State to let it know on what grounds the asylum seeker bases his application and, where applicable, the grounds for any decisions taken concerning the applicant. The Member State may refuse to respond to the request submitted to it, if the communication of such information is likely to harm the essential interests of the Member State or the protection of the liberties and fundamental rights of the person concerned or of others. In any event, communication of the information requested shall be subject to the written approval of the applicant for asylum.

4. Any request for information shall set out the grounds on which it is based and, where its purpose is to check whether there is a criterion that is likely to entail the responsibility of the requested Member State, shall state on what evidence, including relevant information from reliable sources on the ways and means asylum seekers enter the territories of the Member States, or on what specific and verifiable part of the applicant's statements it is based. It is understood that such relevant information from reliable sources is not in itself sufficient to determine the responsibility and the competence of a Member State under this Regulation, but it may contribute to the evaluation of other indications relating to the individual asylum seeker.

5. The requested Member State shall be obliged to reply within six weeks.

6. The exchange of information shall be effected at the request of a Member State and may only take place between authorities whose designation by each Member State has been communicated to the Commission, which shall inform the other Member States thereof.

7. The information exchanged may only be used for the purposes set out in paragraph 1. In each Member State such information may, depending on its type and the powers of the recipient authority, only be communicated to the authorities and courts and tribunals entrusted with:

(a) the determination of the Member State responsible for examining the application for asylum;

(b) examining the application for asylum;

(c) implementing any obligation arising under this Regulation.

8. The Member State which forwards the information shall ensure that it is accurate and up-to-date. If it transpires that that Member State has forwarded information which is inaccurate or which should not have been forwarded, the recipient Member States shall be informed thereof immediately. They shall be obliged to correct such information or to have it erased.

9. The asylum seeker shall have the right to be informed, on request, of any data that is processed concerning him.

If he finds that this information has been processed in breach of this Regulation or of Directive 95/46/EC of the European Parliament and the Council of 24 October 1995 on the protection of individuals with regard to the processing of personal data and on the free movement of such data, in particular because it is incomplete or inaccurate, he is entitled to have it corrected, erased or blocked.

The authority correcting, erasing or blocking the data shall inform, as appropriate, the Member State transmitting or receiving the information.

10. In each Member State concerned, a record shall be kept, in the individual file for the person concerned and/or in a register, of the transmission and receipt of information exchanged.

11. The data exchanged shall be kept for a period not exceeding that which is necessary for the purposes for which it is exchanged.

12. Where the data is not processed automatically or is not contained, or intended to be entered, in a file, each Member State should take appropriate measures to ensure compliance with this Article through effective checks.

Article 22

1. Member States shall notify the Commission of the authorities responsible for fulfilling the obligations arising under this Regulation and shall ensure that those authorities have the necessary resources for carrying out their tasks and in particular for replying within the prescribed time limits to requests for information, requests to take charge of and requests to take back asylum seekers.

2. Rules relating to the establishment of secure electronic transmission channels between the authorities mentioned in paragraph 1 for transmitting requests and ensuring that senders automatically receive an electronic proof of delivery shall be established in accordance with the procedure referred to in Article 27(2).

Article 23

1. Member States may, on a bilateral basis, establish administrative arrangements between themselves concerning the practical details of the implementation of this Regulation, in order to facilitate its application and increase its effectiveness. Such arrangements may relate to:

(a) exchanges of liaison officers;

(b) simplification of the procedures and shortening of the time limits relating to transmission and the examination of requests to take charge of or take back asylum seekers;

2. The arrangements referred to in paragraph 1 shall be communicated to the Commission. The Commission shall verify that the arrangements referred to in paragraph 1(b) do not infringe this Regulation.

Chapter VII
Transitional Provisions and Final Provisions
Article 24

1. This Regulation shall replace the Convention determining the State responsible for examining applications for asylum lodged in one of the Member States of the European Communities, signed in Dublin on 15 June 1990 (Dublin Convention).

2. However, to ensure continuity of the arrangements for determining the Member State responsible for an application for asylum, where an application has been lodged after the date mentioned in the second paragraph of Article 29, the events that are likely to entail the responsibility of a Member State under this Regulation shall be taken into consideration, even if they precede that date, with the exception of the events mentioned in Article 10(2).

3. Where, in Regulation (EC) No 2725/2000 reference is made to the Dublin Convention, such reference shall be taken to be a reference made to this Regulation.

Article 25

1. Any period of time prescribed in this Regulation shall be calculated as follows:

(a) where a period expressed in days, weeks or months is to be calculated from the moment at which an event occurs or an action takes place, the day during which that event occurs or that action takes place shall not be counted as falling within the period in question;

(b) a period expressed in weeks or months shall end with the expiry of whichever day in the last week or month is the same day of the week or falls on the same date as the day during which the event or action from which the period is to be calculated occurred or took place. If, in a period expressed in months, the day on which it should expire does not occur in the last month, the period shall end with the expiry of the last day of that month;

(c) time limits shall include Saturdays, Sundays and official holidays in any of the Member States concerned.

2. Requests and replies shall be sent using any method that provides proof of receipt.

Article 26

As far as the French Republic is concerned, this Regulation shall apply only to its European territory.

Article 27

1. The Commission shall be assisted by a committee.

2. Where reference is made to this paragraph, Articles 5 and 7 of Decision 1999/468/EC shall apply.

The period laid down in Article 5(6) of Decision 1999/468/EC shall be set at three months.

3. The Committee shall draw up its rules of procedure.

Article 28

At the latest three years after the date mentioned in the first paragraph of Article 29, the Commission shall report to the European Parliament and the Council on the application of this Regulation and, where appropriate, shall propose the necessary amendments. Member States shall forward to the Commission all information appropriate for the preparation of that report, at the latest six months before that time limit expires.

Having submitted that report, the Commission shall report to the European Parliament and the Council on the application of this Regulation at the same time as it submits reports on the implementation of the Eurodac system provided for by Article 24(5) of Regulation (EC) No 2725/2000.

Article 29

This Regulation shall enter into force on the 20th day following that of its publication in the *Official Journal of the European Union*.

It shall apply to asylum applications lodged as from the first day of the sixth month following its entry into force and, from that date, it will apply to any request to take charge of or take back asylum seekers, irrespective of the date on which the application was made. The Member State responsible for the examination of an asylum application submitted before that date shall be determined in accordance with the criteria set out in the Dublin Convention.

This Regulation shall be binding in its entirety and directly applicable in the Member States in conformity with the Treaty establishing the European Community.

Done at Brussels, 18 February 2003 . . .

18. 2003 European Union Council Directive on the Right to Family Reunification[6]

The Council of the European Union,

Having regard to the Treaty establishing the European Community, and in particular Article 63(3)(a) thereof,
Having regard to the proposal from the Commission,
Having regard to the opinion of the European Parliament,
Having regard to the opinion of the European Economic and Social Committee,
Having regard to the opinion of the Committee of the Regions,

Whereas:

(1) With a view to the progressive establishment of an area of freedom, security and justice, the Treaty establishing the European Community provides both for the

[6] EU Council Directive 2003/86/EC of 22 September 2003 on the right to family reunification: *Official Journal* of the European Union 3.10.2003, L 251/12 (footnotes omitted).

adoption of measures aimed at ensuring the free movement of persons, in conjunction with flanking measures relating to external border controls, asylum and immigration, and for the adoption of measures relating to asylum, immigration and safeguarding the rights of third country nationals.

(2) Measures concerning family reunification should be adopted in conformity with the obligation to protect the family and respect family life enshrined in many instruments of international law. This Directive respects the fundamental rights and observes the principles recognised in particular in Article 8 of the European Convention for the Protection of Human Rights and Fundamental Freedoms and in the Charter of Fundamental Rights of the European Union.

(3) The European Council, at its special meeting in Tampere on 15 and 16 October 1999, acknowledged the need for harmonisation of national legislation on the conditions for admission and residence of third country nationals. In this context, it has in particular stated that the European Union should ensure fair treatment of third country nationals residing lawfully on the territory of the Member States and that a more vigorous integration policy should aim at granting them rights and obligations comparable to those of citizens of the European Union. The European Council accordingly asked the Council rapidly to adopt the legal instruments on the basis of Commission proposals. The need for achieving the objectives defined at Tampere have been reaffirmed by the Laeken European Council on 14 and 15 December 2001.

(4) Family reunification is a necessary way of making family life possible. It helps to create sociocultural stability facilitating the integration of third country nationals in the Member State, which also serves to promote economic and social cohesion, a fundamental Community objective stated in the Treaty.

(5) Member States should give effect to the provisions of this Directive without discrimination on the basis of sex, race, colour, ethnic or social origin, genetic characteristics, language, religion or beliefs, political or other opinions, membership of a national minority, fortune, birth, disabilities, age or sexual orientation.

(6) To protect the family and establish or preserve family life, the material conditions for exercising the right to family reunification should be determined on the basis of common criteria.

(7) Member States should be able to apply this Directive also when the family enters together.

(8) Special attention should be paid to the situation of refugees on account of the reasons which obliged them to flee their country and prevent them from leading a normal family life there. More favourable conditions should therefore be laid down for the exercise of their right to family reunification.

(9) Family reunification should apply in any case to members of the nuclear family, that is to say the spouse and the minor children.

(10) It is for the Member States to decide whether they wish to authorise family reunification for relatives in the direct ascending line, adult unmarried children, unmarried or registered partners as well as, in the event of a polygamous marriage, minor children of a further spouse and the sponsor. Where a Member State authorises family reunification of these persons, this is without prejudice of the possibility, for Member States which do not recognise the existence of family ties in the cases covered by this provision,

of not granting to the said persons the treatment of family members with regard to the right to reside in another Member State, as defined by the relevant EC legislation.

(11) The right to family reunification should be exercised in proper compliance with the values and principles recognised by the Member States, in particular with respect to the rights of women and of children; such compliance justifies the possible taking of restrictive measures against applications for family reunification of polygamous households.

(12) The possibility of limiting the right to family reunification of children over the age of 12, whose primary residence is not with the sponsor, is intended to reflect the children's capacity for integration at early ages and shall ensure that they acquire the necessary education and language skills in school.

(13) A set of rules governing the procedure for examination of applications for family reunification and for entry and residence of family members should be laid down. Those procedures should be effective and manageable, taking account of the normal workload of the Member States' administrations, as well as transparent and fair, in order to offer appropriate legal certainty to those concerned.

(14) Family reunification may be refused on duly justified grounds. In particular, the person who wishes to be granted family reunification should not constitute a threat to public policy or public security. The notion of public policy may cover a conviction for committing a serious crime. In this context it has to be noted that the notion of public policy and public security covers also cases in which a third country national belongs to an association which supports terrorism, supports such an association or has extremist aspirations.

(15) The integration of family members should be promoted. For that purpose, they should be granted a status independent of that of the sponsor, in particular in cases of breakup of marriages and partnerships, and access to education, employment and vocational training on the same terms as the person with whom they are reunited, under the relevant conditions.

(16) Since the objectives of the proposed action, namely the establishment of a right to family reunification for third country nationals to be exercised in accordance with common rules, cannot be sufficiently achieved by the Member States and can therefore, by reason of the scale and effects of the action, be better achieved by the Community, the Community may adopt measures, in accordance with the principle of subsidiarity as set out in Article 5 of the Treaty. In accordance with the principle of proportionality as set out in that Article, this Directive does not go beyond what is necessary in order to achieve those objectives.

(17) In accordance with Articles 1 and 2 of the Protocol on the position of the United Kingdom and Ireland, annexed to the Treaty on European Union and to the Treaty establishing the European Community and without prejudice to Article 4 of the said Protocol these Member States are not participating in the adoption of this Directive and are not bound by or subject to its application.

(18) In accordance with Article 1 and 2 of the Protocol on the position of Denmark, annexed to the Treaty on European Union and the Treaty establishing the European Community, Denmark does not take part in the adoption of this Directive, and is not bound by it or subject to its application,

Has Adopted this Directive:

Chapter I
General provisions
Article 1

The purpose of this Directive is to determine the conditions for the exercise of the right to family reunification by third country nationals residing lawfully in the territory of the Member States.

Article 2

For the purposes of this Directive:

(a) 'third country national' means any person who is not a citizen of the Union within the meaning of Article 17(1) of the Treaty;

(b) 'refugee' means any third country national or stateless person enjoying refugee status within the meaning of the Geneva Convention relating to the status of refugees of 28 July 1951, as amended by the Protocol signed in New York on 31 January 1967;

(c) 'sponsor' means a third country national residing lawfully in a Member State and applying or whose family members apply for family reunification to be joined with him/her;

(d) 'family reunification' means the entry into and residence in a Member State by family members of a third country national residing lawfully in that Member State in order to preserve the family unit, whether the family relationship arose before or after the resident's entry;

(e) 'residence permit' means any authorisation issued by the authorities of a Member State allowing a third country national to stay legally in its territory, in accordance with the provisions of Article 1(2)(a) of Council Regulation (EC) No 1030/2002 of 13 June 2002 laying down a uniform format for residence permits for third country nationals;

(f) 'unaccompanied minor' means third country nationals or stateless persons below the age of eighteen, who arrive on the territory of the Member States unaccompanied by an adult responsible by law or custom, and for as long as they are not effectively taken into the care of such a person, or minors who are left unaccompanied after they entered the territory of the Member States.

Article 3

1. This Directive shall apply where the sponsor is holding a residence permit issued by a Member State for a period of validity of one year or more who has reasonable prospects of obtaining the right of permanent residence, if the members of his or her family are third country nationals of whatever status.

2. This Directive shall not apply where the sponsor is:

(a) applying for recognition of refugee status whose application has not yet given rise to a final decision;

(b) authorised to reside in a Member State on the basis of temporary protection or applying for authorisation to reside on that basis and awaiting a decision on his status;

(c) authorised to reside in a Member State on the basis of a subsidiary form of protection in accordance with international obligations, national legislation or the practice of the Member States or applying for authorisation to reside on that basis and awaiting a decision on his status.

3. This Directive shall not apply to members of the family of a Union citizen.

4. This Directive is without prejudice to more favourable provisions of:

(a) bilateral and multilateral agreements between the Community or the Community and its Member States, on the one hand, and third countries, on the other;

(b) the European Social Charter of 18 October 1961, the amended European Social Charter of 3 May 1987 and the European Convention on the legal status of migrant workers of 24 November 1977.

5. This Directive shall not affect the possibility for the Member States to adopt or maintain more favourable provisions.

Chapter II
Family Members

Article 4

1. The Member States shall authorise the entry and residence, pursuant to this Directive and subject to compliance with the conditions laid down in Chapter IV, as well as in Article 16, of the following family members:

(a) the sponsor's spouse;

(b) the minor children of the sponsor and of his/her spouse, including children adopted in accordance with a decision taken by the competent authority in the Member State concerned or a decision which is automatically enforceable due to international obligations of that Member State or must be recognised in accordance with international obligations;

(c) the minor children including adopted children of the sponsor where the sponsor has custody and the children are dependent on him or her. Member States may authorise the reunification of children of whom custody is shared, provided the other party sharing custody has given his or her agreement;

(d) the minor children including adopted children of the spouse where the spouse has custody and the children are dependent on him or her. Member States may authorise the reunification of children of whom custody is shared, provided the other party sharing custody has given his or her agreement.

The minor children referred to in this Article must be below the age of majority set by the law of the Member State concerned and must not be married.

By way of derogation, where a child is aged over 12 years and arrives independently from the rest of his/her family, the Member State may, before authorising entry and residence under this Directive, verify whether he or she meets a condition for integration provided for by its existing legislation on the date of implementation of this Directive.

2. The Member States may, by law or regulation, authorise the entry and residence, pursuant to this Directive and subject to compliance with the conditions laid down in Chapter IV, of the following family members:

(a) first-degree relatives in the direct ascending line of the sponsor or his or her spouse, where they are dependent on them and do not enjoy proper family support in the country of origin;

(b) the adult unmarried children of the sponsor or his or her spouse, where they are objectively unable to provide for their own needs on account of their state of health.

3. The Member States may, by law or regulation, authorise the entry and residence, pursuant to this Directive and subject to compliance with the conditions laid down in Chapter IV, of the unmarried partner, being a third country national, with whom the sponsor is in a duly attested stable long-term relationship, or of a third country national who is bound to the sponsor by a registered partnership in accordance with Article 5(2), and of the unmarried minor children, including adopted children, as well as the adult unmarried children who are objectively unable to provide for their own needs on account of their state of health, of such persons.

Member States may decide that registered partners are to be treated equally as spouses with respect to family reunification.

4. In the event of a polygamous marriage, where the sponsor already has a spouse living with him in the territory of a Member State, the Member State concerned shall not authorise the family reunification of a further spouse.

By way of derogation from paragraph 1(c), Member States may limit the family reunification of minor children of a further spouse and the sponsor.

5. In order to ensure better integration and to prevent forced marriages Member States may require the sponsor and his/her spouse to be of a minimum age, and at maximum 21 years, before the spouse is able to join him/her.

6. By way of derogation, Member States may request that the applications concerning family reunification of minor children have to be submitted before the age of 15, as provided for by its existing legislation on the date of the implementation of this Directive. If the application is submitted after the age of 15, the Member States which decide to apply this derogation shall authorise the entry and residence of such children on grounds other than family reunification.

Chapter III
Submission and Examination of the Application

Article 5

1. Member States shall determine whether, in order to exercise the right to family reunification, an application for entry and residence shall be submitted to the competent authorities of the Member State concerned either by the sponsor or by the family member or members.

2. The application shall be accompanied by documentary evidence of the family relationship and of compliance with the conditions laid down in Articles 4 and 6 and, where applicable, Articles 7 and 8, as well as certified copies of family member(s)' travel documents.

If appropriate, in order to obtain evidence that a family relationship exists, Member States may carry out interviews with the sponsor and his/her family members and conduct other investigations that are found to be necessary.

When examining an application concerning the unmarried partner of the sponsor, Member States shall consider, as evidence of the family relationship, factors such as a common child, previous cohabitation, registration of the partnership and any other reliable means of proof.

3. The application shall be submitted and examined when the family members are residing outside the territory of the Member State in which the sponsor resides.

By way of derogation, a Member State may, in appropriate circumstances, accept an application submitted when the family members are already in its territory.

4. The competent authorities of the Member State shall give the person, who has submitted the application, written notification of the decision as soon as possible and in any event no later than nine months from the date on which the application was lodged.

In exceptional circumstances linked to the complexity of the examination of the application, the time limit referred to in the first subparagraph may be extended.

Reasons shall be given for the decision rejecting the application. Any consequences of no decision being taken by the end of the period provided for in the first subparagraph shall be determined by the national legislation of the relevant Member State.

5. When examining an application, the Member States shall have due regard to the best interests of minor children.

Chapter IV
Requirements for the exercise of the right to family reunification

Article 6

1. The Member States may reject an application for entry and residence of family members on grounds of public policy, public security or public health.

2. Member States may withdraw or refuse to renew a family member's residence permit on grounds of public policy or public security or public health.

When taking the relevant decision, the Member State shall consider, besides Article 17, the severity or type of offence against public policy or public security committed by the family member, or the dangers that are emanating from such person.

3. Renewal of the residence permit may not be withheld and removal from the territory may not be ordered by the competent authority of the Member State concerned on the sole ground of illness or disability suffered after the issue of the residence permit.

Article 7

1. When the application for family reunification is submitted, the Member State concerned may require the person who has submitted the application to provide evidence that the sponsor has:

(a) accommodation regarded as normal for a comparable family in the same region and which meets the general health and safety standards in force in the Member State concerned;

(b) sickness insurance in respect of all risks normally covered for its own nationals in the Member State concerned for himself/herself and the members of his/her family;

(c) stable and regular resources which are sufficient to maintain himself/herself and the members of his/her family, without recourse to the social assistance system of the Member State concerned. Member States shall evaluate these resources by reference to their nature and regularity and may take into account the level of minimum national wages and pensions as well as the number of family members.

2. Member States may require third country nationals to comply with integration measures, in accordance with national law.

With regard to the refugees and/or family members of refugees referred to in Article 12 the integration measures referred to in the first subparagraph may only be applied once the persons concerned have been granted family reunification.

Article 8

Member States may require the sponsor to have stayed lawfully in their territory for a period not exceeding two years, before having his/her family members join him/her.

By way of derogation, where the legislation of a Member State relating to family reunification in force on the date of adoption of this Directive takes into account its reception capacity, the Member State may provide for a waiting period of no more than three years between submission of the application for family reunification and the issue of a residence permit to the family members.

Chapter V
Family reunification of refugees

Article 9

1. This Chapter shall apply to family reunification of refugees recognised by the Member States.

2. Member States may confine the application of this Chapter to refugees whose family relationships predate their entry.

3. This Chapter is without prejudice to any rules granting refugee status to family members.

Article 10

1. Article 4 shall apply to the definition of family members except that the third subparagraph of paragraph 1 thereof shall not apply to the children of refugees.

2. The Member States may authorise family reunification of other family members not referred to in Article 4, if they are dependent on the refugee.

3. If the refugee is an unaccompanied minor, the Member States:

(a) shall authorise the entry and residence for the purposes of family reunification of his/her first-degree relatives in the direct ascending line without applying the conditions laid down in Article 4(2)(a);

(b) may authorise the entry and residence for the purposes of family reunification of his/her legal guardian or any other member of the family, where the refugee has no relatives in the direct ascending line or such relatives cannot be traced.

Article 11

1. Article 5 shall apply to the submission and examination of the application, subject to paragraph 2 of this Article.

2. Where a refugee cannot provide official documentary evidence of the family relationship, the Member States shall take into account other evidence, to be assessed in accordance with national law, of the existence of such relationship. A decision rejecting an application may not be based solely on the fact that documentary evidence is lacking.

Article 12

1. By way of derogation from Article 7, the Member States shall not require the refugee and/or family member(s) to provide, in respect of applications concerning those family members referred to in Article 4(1), the evidence that the refugee fulfils the requirements set out in Article 7.

Without prejudice to international obligations, where family reunification is possible in a third country with which the sponsor and/or family member has special links, Member States may require provision of the evidence referred to in the first subparagraph.

Member States may require the refugee to meet the conditions referred to in Article 7(1) if the application for family reunification is not submitted within a period of three months after the granting of the refugee status.

2. By way of derogation from Article 8, the Member States shall not require the refugee to have resided in their territory for a certain period of time, before having his/her family members join him/her.

Chapter VI
Entry and residence of family members

Article 13

1. As soon as the application for family reunification has been accepted, the Member State concerned shall authorise the entry of the family member or members. In that regard, the Member State concerned shall grant such persons every facility for obtaining the requisite visas.

2. The Member State concerned shall grant the family members a first residence permit of at least one year's duration. This residence permit shall be renewable.

3. The duration of the residence permits granted to the family member(s) shall in principle not go beyond the date of expiry of the residence permit held by the sponsor.

Article 14

1. The sponsor's family members shall be entitled, in the same way as the sponsor, to:

(a) access to education;

(b) access to employment and self-employed activity;

(c) access to vocational guidance, initial and further training and retraining.

2. Member States may decide according to national law the conditions under which family members shall exercise an employed or self-employed activity. These conditions shall set a time limit which shall in no case exceed 12 months, during which Member States may examine the situation of their labour market before authorising family members to exercise an employed or self-employed activity.

3. Member States may restrict access to employment or self- employed activity by first-degree relatives in the direct ascending line or adult unmarried children to whom Article 4(2) applies.

Article 15

1. Not later than after five years of residence, and provided that the family member has not been granted a residence permit for reasons other than family reunification, the spouse or unmarried partner and a child who has reached majority shall be entitled, upon application, if required, to an autonomous residence permit, independent of that of the sponsor.

Member States may limit the granting of the residence permit referred to in the first subparagraph to the spouse or unmarried partner in cases of breakdown of the family relationship.

2. The Member States may issue an autonomous residence permit to adult children and to relatives in the direct ascending line to whom Article 4(2) applies.

3. In the event of widowhood, divorce, separation, or death of first-degree relatives in the direct ascending or descending line, an autonomous residence permit may be issued, upon application, if required, to persons who have entered by virtue of family reunification. Member States shall lay down provisions ensuring the granting of an autonomous residence permit in the event of particularly difficult circumstances.

4. The conditions relating to the granting and duration of the autonomous residence permit are established by national law.

Chapter VII
Penalties and redress

Article 16

1. Member States may reject an application for entry and residence for the purpose of family reunification, or, if appropriate, withdraw or refuse to renew a family member's residence permit, in the following circumstances:

(a) where the conditions laid down by this Directive are not or are no longer satisfied.

When renewing the residence permit, where the sponsor has not sufficient resources without recourse to the social assistance system of the Member State, as referred to in Article 7(1)(c), the Member State shall take into account the contributions of the family members to the household income;

(b) where the sponsor and his/her family member(s) do not or no longer live in a real marital or family relationship;

(c) where it is found that the sponsor or the unmarried partner is married or is in a stable long-term relationship with another person.

2. Member States may also reject an application for entry and residence for the purpose of family reunification, or withdraw or refuse to renew the family member's residence permits, where it is shown that:

(a) false or misleading information, false or falsified documents were used, fraud was otherwise committed or other unlawful means were used;

(b) the marriage, partnership or adoption was contracted for the sole purpose of enabling the person concerned to enter or reside in a Member State.

When making an assessment with respect to this point, Member States may have regard in particular to the fact that the marriage, partnership or adoption was contracted after the sponsor had been issued his/her residence permit.

3. The Member States may withdraw or refuse to renew the residence permit of a family member where the sponsor's residence comes to an end and the family member does not yet enjoy an autonomous right of residence under Article 15.

4. Member States may conduct specific checks and inspections where there is reason to suspect that there is fraud or a marriage, partnership or adoption of convenience as defined by paragraph 2. Specific checks may also be undertaken on the occasion of the renewal of family members' residence permit.

Article 17

Member States shall take due account of the nature and solidity of the person's family relationships and the duration of his residence in the Member State and of the existence of family, cultural and social ties with his/her country of origin where they reject an application, withdraw or refuse to renew a residence permit or decide to order the removal of the sponsor or members of his family.

Article 18

The Member States shall ensure that the sponsor and/or the members of his/her family have the right to mount a legal challenge where an application for family reunification is rejected or a residence permit is either not renewed or is withdrawn or removal is ordered.

The procedure and the competence according to which the right referred to in the first subparagraph is exercised shall be established by the Member States concerned.

Chapter VIII
Final provisions

Article 19

Periodically, and for the first time not later than 3 October 2007, the Commission shall report to the European Parliament and the Council on the application of this Directive in the Member States and shall propose such amendments as may appear necessary. These proposals for amendments shall be made by way of priority in relation to Articles 3, 4, 7, 8 and 13.

Article 20

Member States shall bring into force the laws, regulations and administrative provisions necessary to comply with this Directive by not later than 3 October 2005. They shall forthwith inform the Commission thereof.

When Member States adopt these measures, they shall contain a reference to this Directive or be accompanied by such a reference on the occasion of their official publication. The methods of making such reference shall be laid down by the Member States.

Article 21

This Directive shall enter into force on the day of its publication in the *Official Journal of the European Union*.

Article 22

This Directive is addressed to the Member States in accordance with the Treaty establishing the European Community.

Done at Brussels, 22 September 2003 . . .

19. 2004 European Union Council Directive on Qualification and Status as Refugees or Persons otherwise in need of International Protection[7]

The Council of the European Union,

Having regard to the Treaty establishing the European Community, and in particular points 1(c), 2(a) and 3(a) of Article 63 thereof,
Having regard to the proposal from the Commission,
Having regard to the opinion of the European Parliament,

---

[7] EU Council Directive 2004/83/EC of 29 April 2004 on minimum standards for the qualification and status of third country nationals or stateless persons as refugees or as persons who otherwise need international protection and the content of the protection granted *Official Journal* of the European Union 30.9.2004 L 304/12 (footnotes omitted).

Having regard to the opinion of the European Economic and Social Committee,
Having regard to the opinion of the Committee of the Regions,

Whereas:

(1) A common policy on asylum, including a Common European Asylum System, is a constituent part of the European Union's objective of progressively establishing an area of freedom, security and justice open to those who, forced by circumstances, legitimately seek protection in the Community.

(2) The European Council at its special meeting in Tampere on 15 and 16 October 1999 agreed to work towards establishing a Common European Asylum System, based on the full and inclusive application of the Geneva Convention relating to the Status of Refugees of 28 July 1951 (Geneva Convention), as supplemented by the New York Protocol of 31 January 1967 (Protocol), thus affirming the principle of non-refoulement and ensuring that nobody is sent back to persecution.

(3) The Geneva Convention and Protocol provide the cornerstone of the international legal regime for the protection of refugees.

(4) The Tampere conclusions provide that a Common European Asylum System should include, in the short term, the approximation of rules on the recognition of refugees and the content of refugee status.

(5) The Tampere conclusions also provide that rules regarding refugee status should be complemented by measures on subsidiary forms of protection, offering an appropriate status to any person in need of such protection.

(6) The main objective of this Directive is, on the one hand, to ensure that Member States apply common criteria for the identification of persons genuinely in need of international protection, and, on the other hand, to ensure that a minimum level of benefits is available for these persons in all Member States.

(7) The approximation of rules on the recognition and content of refugee and subsidiary protection status should help to limit the secondary movements of applicants for asylum between Member States, where such movement is purely caused by differences in legal frameworks.

(8) It is in the very nature of minimum standards that Member States should have the power to introduce or maintain more favourable provisions for third country nationals or stateless persons who request international protection from a Member State, where such a request is understood to be on the grounds that the person concerned is either a refugee within the meaning of Article 1(A) of the Geneva Convention, or a person who otherwise needs international protection.

(9) Those third country nationals or stateless persons, who are allowed to remain in the territories of the Member States for reasons not due to a need for international protection but on a discretionary basis on compassionate or humanitarian grounds, fall outside the scope of this Directive.

(10) This Directive respects the fundamental rights and observes the principles recognised in particular by the Charter of Fundamental Rights of the European Union. In particular this Directive seeks to ensure full respect for human dignity and the right to asylum of applicants for asylum and their accompanying family members.

(11) With respect to the treatment of persons falling within the scope of this Directive, Member States are bound by obligations under instruments of international law to which they are party and which prohibit discrimination.

(12) The 'best interests of the child' should be a primary consideration of Member States when implementing this Directive.

(13) This Directive is without prejudice to the Protocol on asylum for nationals of Member States of the European Union as annexed to the Treaty Establishing the European Community.

(14) The recognition of refugee status is a declaratory act.

(15) Consultations with the United Nations High Commissioner for Refugees may provide valuable guidance for Member States when determining refugee status according to Article 1 of the Geneva Convention.

(16) Minimum standards for the definition and content of refugee status should be laid down to guide the competent national bodies of Member States in the application of the Geneva Convention.

(17) It is necessary to introduce common criteria for recognising applicants for asylum as refugees within the meaning of Article 1 of the Geneva Convention.

(18) In particular, it is necessary to introduce common concepts of protection needs arising *sur place*; sources of harm and protection; internal protection; and persecution, including the reasons for persecution.

(19) Protection can be provided not only by the State but also by parties or organisations, including international organisations, meeting the conditions of this Directive, which control a region or a larger area within the territory of the State.

(20) It is necessary, when assessing applications from minors for international protection, that Member States should have regard to child-specific forms of persecution.

(21) It is equally necessary to introduce a common concept of the persecution ground 'membership of a particular social group'.

(22) Acts contrary to the purposes and principles of the United Nations are set out in the Preamble and Articles 1 and 2 of the Charter of the United Nations and are, amongst others, embodied in the United Nations Resolutions relating to measures combating terrorism, which declare that 'acts, methods and practices of terrorism are contrary to the purposes and principles of the United Nations' and that 'knowingly financing, planning and inciting terrorist acts are also contrary to the purposes and principles of the United Nations'.

(23) As referred to in Article 14, 'status' can also include refugee status.

(24) Minimum standards for the definition and content of subsidiary protection status should also be laid down. Subsidiary protection should be complementary and additional to the refugee protection enshrined in the Geneva Convention.

(25) It is necessary to introduce criteria on the basis of which applicants for international protection are to be recognised as eligible for subsidiary protection. Those criteria should be drawn from international obligations under human rights instruments and practices existing in Member States.

(26) Risks to which a population of a country or a section of the population is generally exposed do normally not create in themselves an individual threat which would qualify as serious harm.

(27) Family members, merely due to their relation to the refugee, will normally be vulnerable to acts of persecution in such a manner that could be the basis for refugee status.

(28) The notion of national security and public order also covers cases in which a third country national belongs to an association which supports international terrorism or supports such an association.

(29) While the benefits provided to family members of beneficiaries of subsidiary protection status do not necessarily have to be the same as those provided to the qualifying beneficiary, they need to be fair in comparison to those enjoyed by beneficiaries of subsidiary protection status.

(30) Within the limits set out by international obligations, Member States may lay down that the granting of benefits with regard to access to employment, social welfare, health care and access to integration facilities requires the prior issue of a residence permit.

(31) This Directive does not apply to financial benefits from the Member States which are granted to promote education and training.

(32) The practical difficulties encountered by beneficiaries of refugee or subsidiary protection status concerning the authentication of their foreign diplomas, certificates or other evidence of formal qualification should be taken into account.

(33) Especially to avoid social hardship, it is appropriate, for beneficiaries of refugee or subsidiary protection status, to provide without discrimination in the context of social assistance the adequate social welfare and means of subsistence.

(34) With regard to social assistance and health care, the modalities and detail of the provision of core benefits to beneficiaries of subsidiary protection status should be determined by national law. The possibility of limiting the benefits for beneficiaries of subsidiary protection status to core benefits is to be understood in the sense that this notion covers at least minimum income support, assistance in case of illness, pregnancy and parental assistance, in so far as they are granted to nationals according to the legislation of the Member State concerned.

(35) Access to health care, including both physical and mental health care, should be ensured to beneficiaries of refugee or subsidiary protection status.

(36) The implementation of this Directive should be evaluated at regular intervals, taking into consideration in particular the evolution of the international obligations of Member States regarding non-refoulement, the evolution of the labour markets in the Member States as well as the development of common basic principles for integration.

(37) Since the objectives of the proposed Directive, namely to establish minimum standards for the granting of international protection to third country nationals and stateless persons by Member States and the content of the protection granted, cannot be sufficiently achieved by the Member States and can therefore, by reason of the scale and effects of the Directive, be better achieved at Community level, the Community may adopt measures, in accordance with the principle of subsidiarity as set out in Article 5 of the Treaty. In accordance with the principle of proportionality,

as set out in that Article, this Directive does not go beyond what is necessary in order to achieve those objectives.

(38) In accordance with Article 3 of the Protocol on the position of the United Kingdom and Ireland, annexed to the Treaty on European Union and to the Treaty establishing the European Community, the United Kingdom has notified, by letter of 28 January 2002, its wish to take part in the adoption and application of this Directive.

(39) In accordance with Article 3 of the Protocol on the position of the United Kingdom and Ireland, annexed to the Treaty on European Union and to the Treaty establishing the European Community, Ireland has notified, by letter of 13 February 2002, its wish to take part in the adoption and application of this Directive.

(40) In accordance with Articles 1 and 2 of the Protocol on the position of Denmark, annexed to the Treaty on European Union and to the Treaty establishing the European Community, Denmark is not taking part in the adoption of this Directive and is not bound by it or subject to its application,

Has Adopted this Directive,

Chapter I
General Provisions

Article 1—Subject matter and scope

The purpose of this Directive is to lay down minimum standards for the qualification of third country nationals or stateless persons as refugees or as persons who otherwise need international protection and the content of the protection granted.

Article 2—Definitions

For the purposes of this Directive:

(a) 'international protection' means the refugee and subsidiary protection status as defined in (d) and (f);

(b) 'Geneva Convention' means the Convention relating to the status of refugees done at Geneva on 28 July 1951, as amended by the New York Protocol of 31 January 1967;

(c) 'refugee' means a third country national who, owing to a well-founded fear of being persecuted for reasons of race, religion, nationality, political opinion or membership of a particular social group, is outside the country of nationality and is unable or, owing to such fear, is unwilling to avail himself or herself of the protection of that country, or a stateless person, who, being outside of the country of former habitual residence for the same reasons as mentioned above, is unable or, owing to such fear, unwilling to return to it, and to whom Article 12 does not apply;

(d) 'refugee status' means the recognition by a Member State of a third country national or a stateless person as a refugee;

(e) 'person eligible for subsidiary protection' means a third country national or a stateless person who does not qualify as a refugee but in respect of whom substantial grounds have been shown for believing that the person concerned, if returned to his or her country of origin, or in the case of a stateless person, to his or her country of former habitual residence, would face a real risk of suffering serious harm as defined in Article

15, and to whom Article 17(1) and (2) do not apply, and is unable, or, owing to such risk, unwilling to avail himself or herself of the protection of that country;

(f) 'subsidiary protection status' means the recognition by a Member State of a third country national or a stateless person as a person eligible for subsidiary protection;

(g) 'application for international protection' means a request made by a third country national or a stateless person for protection from a Member State, who can be understood to seek refugee status or subsidiary protection status, and who does not explicitly request another kind of protection, outside the scope of this Directive, that can be applied for separately;

(h) 'family members' means, insofar as the family already existed in the country of origin, the following members of the family of the beneficiary of refugee or subsidiary protection status who are present in the same Member State in relation to the application for international protection:

— the spouse of the beneficiary of refugee or subsidiary protection status or his or her unmarried partner in a stable relationship, where the legislation or practice of the Member State concerned treats unmarried couples in a way comparable to married couples under its law relating to aliens,

— the minor children of the couple referred to in the first indent or of the beneficiary of refugee or subsidiary protection status, on condition that they are unmarried and dependent and regardless of whether they were born in or out of wedlock or adopted as defined under the national law;

(i) 'unaccompanied minors' means third-country nationals or stateless persons below the age of 18, who arrive on the territory of the Member States unaccompanied by an adult responsible for them whether by law or custom, and for as long as they are not effectively taken into the care of such a person; it includes minors who are left unaccompanied after they have entered the territory of the Member States;

(j) 'residence permit' means any permit or authorisation issued by the authorities of a Member State, in the form provided for under that State's legislation, allowing a third country national or stateless person to reside on its territory;

(k) 'country of origin' means the country or countries of nationality or, for stateless persons, of former habitual residence.

Article 3—More favourable standards

Member States may introduce or retain more favourable standards for determining who qualifies as a refugee or as a person eligible for subsidiary protection, and for determining the content of international protection, in so far as those standards are compatible with this Directive.

Chapter II
Assessment of Applications for International Protection

Article 4—Assessment of facts and circumstances

1. Member States may consider it the duty of the applicant to submit as soon as possible all elements needed to substantiate the application for international protection. In cooperation

with the applicant it is the duty of the Member State to assess the relevant elements of the application.

2. The elements referred to in of paragraph 1 consist of the applicant's statements and all documentation at the applicants disposal regarding the applicant's age, background, including that of relevant relatives, identity, nationality(ies), country(ies) and place(s) of previous residence, previous asylum applications, travel routes, identity and travel documents and the reasons for applying for international protection.

3. The assessment of an application for international protection is to be carried out on an individual basis and includes taking into account:

(a) all relevant facts as they relate to the country of origin at the time of taking a decision on the application; including laws and regulations of the country of origin and the manner in which they are applied;

(b) the relevant statements and documentation presented by the applicant including information on whether the applicant has been or may be subject to persecution or serious harm;

(c) the individual position and personal circumstances of the applicant, including factors such as background, gender and age, so as to assess whether, on the basis of the applicant's personal circumstances, the acts to which the applicant has been or could be exposed would amount to persecution or serious harm;

(d) whether the applicant's activities since leaving the country of origin were engaged in for the sole or main purpose of creating the necessary conditions for applying for international protection, so as to assess whether these activities will expose the applicant to persecution or serious harm if returned to that country;

(e) whether the applicant could reasonably be expected to avail himself of the protection of another country where he could assert citizenship.

4. The fact that an applicant has already been subject to persecution or serious harm or to direct threats of such persecution or such harm, is a serious indication of the applicant's well-founded fear of persecution or real risk of suffering serious harm, unless there are good reasons to consider that such persecution or serious harm will not be repeated.

5. Where Member States apply the principle according to which it is the duty of the applicant to substantiate the application for international protection and where aspects of the applicant's statements are not supported by documentary or other evidence, those aspects shall not need confirmation, when the following conditions are met:

(a) the applicant has made a genuine effort to substantiate his application;

(b) all relevant elements, at the applicant's disposal, have been submitted, and a satisfactory explanation regarding any lack of other relevant elements has been given;

(c) the applicant's statements are found to be coherent and plausible and do not run counter to available specific and general information relevant to the applicant's case;

(d) the applicant has applied for international protection at the earliest possible time, unless the applicant can demonstrate good reason for not having done so; and

(e) the general credibility of the applicant has been established.

Article 5—International protection needs arising sur place

1. A well-founded fear of being persecuted or a real risk of suffering serious harm may be based on events which have taken place since the applicant left the country of origin.

2. A well-founded fear of being persecuted or a real risk of suffering serious harm may be based on activities which have been engaged in by the applicant since he left the country of origin, in particular where it is established that the activities relied upon constitute the expression and continuation of convictions or orientations held in the country of origin.

3. Without prejudice to the Geneva Convention, Member States may determine that an applicant who files a subsequent application shall normally not be granted refugee status, if the risk of persecution is based on circumstances which the applicant has created by his own decision since leaving the country of origin.

Article 6—Actors of persecution or serious harm

Actors of persecution or serious harm include:

(a) the State;

(b) parties or organisations controlling the State or a substantial part of the territory of the State;

(c) non-State actors, if it can be demonstrated that the actors mentioned in (a) and (b), including international organisations, are unable or unwilling to provide protection against persecution or serious harm as defined in Article 7.

Article 7—Actors of protection

1. Protection can be provided by:

(a) the State; or

(b) parties or organisations, including international organisations, controlling the State or a substantial part of the territory of the State.

2. Protection is generally provided when the actors mentioned in paragraph 1 take reasonable steps to prevent the persecution or suffering of serious harm, *inter alia*, by operating an effective legal system for the detection, prosecution and punishment of acts constituting persecution or serious harm, and the applicant has access to such protection.

3. When assessing whether an international organisation controls a State or a substantial part of its territory and provides protection as described in paragraph 2, Member States shall take into account any guidance which may be provided in relevant Council acts.

Article 8—Internal protection

1. As part of the assessment of the application for international protection, Member States may determine that an applicant is not in need of international protection if in a part of the country of origin there is no well-founded fear of being persecuted or no real risk of suffering serious harm and the applicant can reasonably be expected to stay in that part of the country.

2. In examining whether a part of the country of origin is in accordance with paragraph 1, Member States shall at the time of taking the decision on the application have regard to the

general circumstances prevailing in that part of the country and to the personal circumstances of the applicant.

3. Paragraph 1 may apply notwithstanding technical obstacles to return to the country of origin.

Chapter III
Qualification for Being a Refugee

Article 9—Acts of persecution

1. Acts of persecution within the meaning of article 1 A of the Geneva Convention must:

(a) be sufficiently serious by their nature or repetition as to constitute a severe violation of basic human rights, in particular the rights from which derogation cannot be made under Article 15(2) of the European Convention for the Protection of Human Rights and Fundamental Freedoms; or

(b) be an accumulation of various measures, including violations of human rights which is sufficiently severe as to affect an individual in a similar manner as mentioned in (a).

2. Acts of persecution as qualified in paragraph 1, can, *inter alia*, take the form of:

(a) acts of physical or mental violence, including acts of sexual violence;

(b) legal, administrative, police, and/or judicial measures which are in themselves discriminatory or which are implemented in a discriminatory manner;

(c) prosecution or punishment, which is disproportionate or discriminatory;

(d) denial of judicial redress resulting in a disproportionate or discriminatory punishment;

(e) prosecution or punishment for refusal to perform military service in a conflict, where performing military service would include crimes or acts falling under the exclusion clauses as set out in Article 12(2);

(f) acts of a gender-specific or child-specific nature.

3. In accordance with Article 2(c), there must be a connection between the reasons mentioned in Article 10 and the acts of persecution as qualified in paragraph 1.

Article 10—Reasons for persecution

1. Member States shall take the following elements into account when assessing the reasons for persecution:

(a) the concept of race shall in particular include considerations of colour, descent, or membership of a particular ethnic group;

(b) the concept of religion shall in particular include the holding of theistic, non-theistic and atheistic beliefs, the participation in, or abstention from, formal worship in private or in public, either alone or in community with others, other religious acts or expressions of view, or forms of personal or communal conduct based on or mandated by any religious belief;

(c) the concept of nationality shall not be confined to citizenship or lack thereof but shall in particular include membership of a group determined by its cultural, ethnic, or linguistic identity, common geographical or political origins or its relationship with the population of another State;

(d) a group shall be considered to form a particular social group where in particular:

— members of that group share an innate characteristic, or a common background that cannot be changed, or share a characteristic or belief that is so fundamental to identity or conscience that a person should not be forced to renounce it, and

— that group has a distinct identity in the relevant country, because it is perceived as being different by the surrounding society;

depending on the circumstances in the country of origin, a particular social group might include a group based on a common characteristic of sexual orientation. Sexual orientation cannot be understood to include acts considered to be criminal in accordance with national law of the Member States: Gender related aspects might be considered, without by themselves alone creating a presumption for the applicability of this Article;

(e) the concept of political opinion shall in particular include the holding of an opinion, thought or belief on a matter related to the potential actors of persecution mentioned in Article 6 and to their policies or methods, whether or not that opinion, thought or belief has been acted upon by the applicant.

2. When assessing if an applicant has a well-founded fear of being persecuted it is immaterial whether the applicant actually possesses the racial, religious, national, social or political characteristic which attracts the persecution, provided that such a characteristic is attributed to the applicant by the actor of persecution.

Article 11—Cessation

1. A third country national or a stateless person shall cease to be a refugee, if he or she:

(a) has voluntarily re-availed himself or herself of the protection of the country of nationality; or

(b) having lost his or her nationality, has voluntarily reacquired it; or

(c) has acquired a new nationality, and enjoys the protection of the country of his or her new nationality; or

(d) has voluntarily re-established himself or herself in the country which he or she left or outside which he or she remained owing to fear of persecution; or

(e) can no longer, because the circumstances in connection with which he or she has been recognised as a refugee have ceased to exist, continue to refuse to avail himself or herself of the protection of the country of nationality;

(f) being a stateless person with no nationality, he or she is able, because the circumstances in connection with which he or she has been recognised as a refugee have ceased to exist, to return to the country of former habitual residence.

2. In considering points (e) and (f) of paragraph 1, Member States shall have regard to whether the change of circumstances is of such a significant and non-temporary nature that the refugee's fear of persecution can no longer be regarded as well-founded.

Article 12—Exclusion

1. A third country national or a stateless person is excluded from being a refugee, if:

(a) he or she falls within the scope of Article 1D of the Geneva Convention, relating to protection or assistance from organs or agencies of the United Nations other than the United Nations High Commissioner for Refugees. When such protection or assistance has ceased for any reason, without the position of such persons being definitely settled in accordance with the relevant resolutions adopted by the General Assembly of the United Nations, these persons shall ipso facto be entitled to the benefits of this Directive;

(b) he or she is recognised by the competent authorities of the country in which he or she has taken residence as having the rights and obligations which are attached to the possession of the nationality of that country; or rights and obligations equivalent to those.

2. A third country national or a stateless person is excluded from being a refugee where there are serious reasons for considering that:

(a) he or she has committed a crime against peace, a war crime, or a crime against humanity, as defined in the international instruments drawn up to make provision in respect of such crimes;

(b) he or she has committed a serious non-political crime outside the country of refuge prior to his or her admission as a refugee; which means the time of issuing a residence permit based on the granting of refugee status; particularly cruel actions, even if committed with an allegedly political objective, may be classified as serious non-political crimes;

(c) he or she has been guilty of acts contrary to the purposes and principles of the United Nations as set out in the Preamble and Articles 1 and 2 of the Charter of the United Nations.

3. Paragraph 2 applies to persons who instigate or otherwise participate in the commission of the crimes or acts mentioned therein.

Chapter IV
Refugee Status

Article 13—Granting of refugee status

Member States shall grant refugee status to a third country national or a stateless person, who qualifies as a refugee in accordance with Chapters II and III.

Article 14—Revocation of, ending of or refusal to renew refugee status

1. Concerning applications for international protection filed after the entry into force of this Directive, Member States shall revoke, end or refuse to renew the refugee status of a third country national or a stateless person granted by a governmental, administrative, judicial or quasi-judicial body, if he or she has ceased to be a refugee in accordance with Article 11.

2. Without prejudice to the duty of the refugee in accordance with Article 4(1) to disclose all relevant facts and provide all relevant documentation at his/her disposal, the Member

State, which has granted refugee status, shall on an individual basis demonstrate that the person concerned has ceased to be or has never been a refugee in accordance with paragraph 1 of this Article.

3. Member States shall revoke, end or refuse to renew the refugee status of a third country national or a stateless person, if, after he or she has been granted refugee status, it is established by the Member State concerned that:

(a) he or she should have been or is excluded from being a refugee in accordance with Article 12;

(b) his or her misrepresentation or omission of facts, including the use of false documents, were decisive for the granting of refugee status.

4. Member States may revoke, end or refuse to renew the status granted to a refugee by a governmental, administrative, judicial or quasi-judicial body, when:

(a) there are reasonable grounds for regarding him or her as a danger to the security of the Member State in which he or she is present;

(b) he or she, having been convicted by a final judgement of a particularly serious crime, constitutes a danger to the community of that Member State.

5. In situations described in paragraph 4, Member States may decide not to grant status to a refugee, where such a decision has not yet been taken.

6. Persons to whom paragraphs 4 or 5 apply are entitled to rights set out in or similar to those set out in Articles 3, 4, 16, 22, 31 and 32 and 33 of the Geneva Convention in so far as they are present in the Member State.

Chapter V
Qualification for Subsidiary Protection
Article 15—Serious harm

Serious harm consists of:

(a) death penalty or execution; or

(b) torture or inhuman or degrading treatment or punishment of an applicant in the country of origin; or

(c) serious and individual threat to a civilian's life or person by reason of indiscriminate violence in situations of international or internal armed conflict.

Article 16—Cessation

1. A third country national or a stateless person shall cease to be eligible for subsidiary protection when the circumstances which led to the granting of subsidiary protection status have ceased to exist or have changed to such a degree that protection is no longer required.

2. In applying paragraph 1, Member States shall have regard to whether the change of circumstances is of such a significant and non-temporary nature that the person eligible for subsidiary protection no longer faces a real risk of serious harm.

Article 17—Exclusion

1. A third country national or a stateless person is excluded from being eligible for subsidiary protection where there are serious reasons for considering that:

(a) he or she has committed a crime against peace, a war crime, or a crime against humanity, as defined in the international instruments drawn up to make provision in respect of such crimes;

(b) he or she has committed a serious crime;

(c) he or she has been guilty of acts contrary to the purposes and principles of the United Nations as set out in the Preamble and Articles 1 and 2 of the Charter of the United Nations;

(d) he or she constitutes a danger to the community or to the security of the Member State in which he or she is present.

2. Paragraph 1 applies to persons who instigate or otherwise participate in the commission of the crimes or acts mentioned therein.

3. Member States may exclude a third country national or a stateless person from being eligible for subsidiary protection, if he or she prior to his or her admission to the Member State has committed one or more crimes, outside the scope of paragraph 1, which would be punishable by imprisonment, had they been committed in the Member State concerned, and if he or she left his or her country of origin solely in order to avoid sanctions resulting from these crimes.

Chapter VI
Subsidiary Protection Status

Article 18—Granting of subsidiary protection status

Member States shall grant subsidiary protection status to a third country national or a stateless person eligible for subsidiary protection in accordance with Chapters II and V.

Article 19—Revocation of, ending of or refusal to renew subsidiary protection status

1. Concerning applications for international protection filed after the entry into force of this Directive, Member States shall revoke, end or refuse to renew the subsidiary protection status of a third country national or a stateless person granted by a governmental, administrative, judicial or quasi-judicial body, if he or she has ceased to be eligible for subsidiary protection in accordance with Article 16.

2. Member States may revoke, end or refuse to renew the subsidiary protection status of a third country national or a stateless person granted by a governmental, administrative, judicial or quasi-judicial body, if after having been granted subsidiary protection status, he or she should have been excluded from being eligible for subsidiary protection in accordance with Article 17(3).

3. Member States shall revoke, end or refuse to renew the subsidiary protection status of a third country national or a stateless person, if:

(a) he or she, after having been granted subsidiary protection status, should have been or is excluded from being eligible for subsidiary protection in accordance with Article 17(1) and (2);

(b) his or her misrepresentation or omission of facts, including the use of false documents, were decisive for the granting of subsidiary protection status.

4. Without prejudice to the duty of the third country national or stateless person in accordance with Article 4(1) to disclose all relevant facts and provide all relevant documentation at his/her disposal, the Member State, which has granted the subsidiary protection status, shall on an individual basis demonstrate that the person concerned has ceased to be or is not eligible for subsidiary protection in accordance with paragraphs 1, 2 and 3 of this Article.

Chapter VII
Content of International Protection

Article 20—General rules

1. This Chapter shall be without prejudice to the rights laid down in the Geneva Convention.

2. This Chapter shall apply both to refugees and persons eligible for subsidiary protection unless otherwise indicated.

3. When implementing this Chapter, Member States shall take into account the specific situation of vulnerable persons such as minors, unaccompanied minors, disabled people, elderly people, pregnant women, single parents with minor children and persons who have been subjected to torture, rape or other serious forms of psychological, physical or sexual violence.

4. Paragraph 3 shall apply only to persons found to have special needs after an individual evaluation of their situation.

5. The best interest of the child shall be a primary consideration for Member States when implementing the provisions of this Chapter that involve minors.

6. Within the limits set out by the Geneva Convention, Member States may reduce the benefits of this Chapter, granted to a refugee whose refugee status has been obtained on the basis of activities engaged in for the sole or main purpose of creating the necessary conditions for being recognised as a refugee.

7. Within the limits set out by international obligations of Member States, Member States may reduce the benefits of this Chapter, granted to a person eligible for subsidiary protection, whose subsidiary protection status has been obtained on the basis of activities engaged in for the sole or main purpose of creating the necessary conditions for being recognised as a person eligible for subsidiary protection.

Article 21—Protection from refoulement

1. Member States shall respect the principle of non-refoulement in accordance with their international obligations.

2. Where not prohibited by the international obligations mentioned in paragraph 1, Member States may refoule a refugee, whether formally recognised or not, when:

(a) there are reasonable grounds for considering him or her as a danger to the security of the Member State in which he or she is present; or

(b) he or she, having been convicted by a final judgement of a particularly serious crime, constitutes a danger to the community of that Member State.

3. Member States may revoke, end or refuse to renew or to grant the residence permit of (or to) a refugee to whom paragraph 2 applies.

Article 22—Information

Member States shall provide persons recognised as being in need of international protection, as soon as possible after the respective protection status has been granted, with access to information, in a language likely to be understood by them, on the rights and obligations relating to that status.

Article 23—Maintaining family unity

1. Member States shall ensure that family unity can be maintained.

2. Member States shall ensure that family members of the beneficiary of refugee or subsidiary protection status, who do not individually qualify for such status, are entitled to claim the benefits referred to in Articles 24 to 34, in accordance with national procedures and as far as it is compatible with the personal legal status of the family member.

In so far as the family members of beneficiaries of subsidiary protection status are concerned, Member States may define the conditions applicable to such benefits.

In these cases, Member States shall ensure that any benefits provided guarantee an adequate standard of living.

3. Paragraphs 1 and 2 are not applicable where the family member is or would be excluded from refugee or subsidiary protection status pursuant to Chapters III and V.

4. Notwithstanding paragraphs 1 and 2, Member States may refuse, reduce or withdraw the benefits referred therein for reasons of national security or public order.

5. Member States may decide that this Article also applies to other close relatives who lived together as part of the family at the time of leaving the country of origin, and who were wholly or mainly dependent on the beneficiary of refugee or subsidiary protection status at that time.

Article 24—Residence permits

1. As soon as possible after their status has been granted, Member States shall issue to beneficiaries of refugee status a residence permit which must be valid for at least three years and renewable unless compelling reasons of national security or public order otherwise require, and without prejudice to Article 21(3).

Without prejudice to Article 23(1), the residence permit to be issued to the family members of the beneficiaries of refugee status may be valid for less than three years and renewable.

2. As soon as possible after the status has been granted, Member States shall issue to beneficiaries of subsidiary protection status a residence permit which must be valid for at least one year and renewable, unless compelling reasons of national security or public order otherwise require.

Article 25—Travel document

1. Member States shall issue to beneficiaries of refugee status travel documents in the form set out in the Schedule to the Geneva Convention, for the purpose of travel outside their territory unless compelling reasons of national security or public order otherwise require.

2. Member States shall issue to beneficiaries of subsidiary protection status who are unable to obtain a national passport, documents which enable them to travel, at least when serious humanitarian reasons arise that require their presence in another State, unless compelling reasons of national security or public order otherwise require.

Article 26—Access to employment

1. Member States shall authorise beneficiaries of refugee status to engage in employed or self-employed activities subject to rules generally applicable to the profession and to the public service, immediately after the refugee status has been granted.

2. Member States shall ensure that activities such as employment-related education opportunities for adults, vocational training and practical workplace experience are offered to beneficiaries of refugee status, under equivalent conditions as nationals.

3. Member States shall authorise beneficiaries of subsidiary protection status to engage in employed or self-employed activities subject to rules generally applicable to the profession and to the public service immediately after the subsidiary protection status has been granted. The situation of the labour market in the Member States may be taken into account, including for possible prioritisation of access to employment for a limited period of time to be determined in accordance with national law. Member States shall ensure that the beneficiary of subsidiary protection status has access to a post for which the beneficiary has received an offer in accordance with national rules on prioritisation in the labour market.

4. Member States shall ensure that beneficiaries of subsidiary protection status have access to activities such as employment-related education opportunities for adults, vocational training and practical workplace experience, under conditions to be decided by the Member States.

5. The law in force in the Member States applicable to remuneration, access to social security systems relating to employed or self-employed activities and other conditions of employment shall apply.

Article 27—Access to education

1. Member States shall grant full access to the education system to all minors granted refugee or subsidiary protection status, under the same conditions as nationals.

2. Member States shall allow adults granted refugee or subsidiary protection status access to the general education system, further training or retraining, under the same conditions as third country nationals legally resident.

3. Member States shall ensure equal treatment between beneficiaries of refugee or subsidiary protection status and nationals in the context of the existing recognition procedures for foreign diplomas, certificates and other evidence of formal qualifications.

Article 28—Social welfare

1. Member States shall ensure that beneficiaries of refugee or subsidiary protection status receive, in the Member State that has granted such statuses, the necessary social assistance, as provided to nationals of that Member State.

2. By exception to the general rule laid down in paragraph 1, Member States may limit social assistance granted to beneficiaries of subsidiary protection status to core benefits which will then be provided at the same levels and under the same eligibility conditions as nationals.

Article 29—Health care

1. Member States shall ensure that beneficiaries of refugee or subsidiary protection status have access to health care under the same eligibility conditions as nationals of the Member State that has granted such statuses.

2. By exception to the general rule laid down in paragraph 1, Member States may limit health care granted to beneficiaries of subsidiary protection to core benefits which will then be provided at the same levels and under the same eligibility conditions as nationals.

3. Member States shall provide, under the same eligibility conditions as nationals of the Member State that has granted the status, adequate health care to beneficiaries of refugee or subsidiary protection status who have special needs, such as pregnant women, disabled people, persons who have undergone torture, rape or other serious forms of psychological, physical or sexual violence or minors who have been victims of any form of abuse, neglect, exploitation, torture, cruel, inhuman and degrading treatment or who have suffered from armed conflict.

Article 30—Unaccompanied minors

1. As soon as possible after the granting of refugee or subsidiary protection status Member States shall take the necessary measures, to ensure the representation of unaccompanied minors by legal guardianship or, where necessary, by an organisation responsible for the care and well-being of minors, or by any other appropriate representation including that based on legislation or Court order.

2. Member States shall ensure that the minor's needs are duly met in the implementation of this Directive by the appointed guardian or representative. The appropriate authorities shall make regular assessments.

3. Member States shall ensure that unaccompanied minors are placed either:

(a) with adult relatives; or

(b) with a foster family; or

(c) in centres specialised in accommodation for minors; or

(d) in other accommodation suitable for minors.

In this context, the views of the child shall be taken into account in accordance with his or her age and degree of maturity.

4. As far as possible, siblings shall be kept together, taking into account the best interests of the minor concerned and, in particular, his or her age and degree of maturity. Changes of residence of unaccompanied minors shall be limited to a minimum.

5. Member States, protecting the unaccompanied minor's best interests, shall endeavour to trace the members of the minor's family as soon as possible. In cases where there may be a threat to the life or integrity of the minor or his or her close relatives, particularly if they have remained in the country of origin, care must be taken to ensure that the collection, processing and circulation of information concerning those persons is undertaken on a confidential basis.

6. Those working with unaccompanied minors shall have had or receive appropriate training concerning their needs.

Article 31—Access to accommodation

The Member States shall ensure that beneficiaries of refugee or subsidiary protection status have access to accommodation under equivalent conditions as other third country nationals legally resident in their territories.

Article 32—Freedom of movement within the Member State

Member States shall allow freedom of movement within their territory to beneficiaries of refugee or subsidiary protection status, under the same conditions and restrictions as those provided for other third country nationals legally resident in their territories.

Article 33—Access to integration facilities

1. In order to facilitate the integration of refugees into society, Member States shall make provision for integration programmes which they consider to be appropriate or create pre-conditions which guarantee access to such programmes.

2. Where it is considered appropriate by Member States, beneficiaries of subsidiary protection status shall be granted access to integration programmes.

Article 34—Repatriation

Member States may provide assistance to beneficiaries of refugee or subsidiary protection status who wish to repatriate.

Chapter VIII
Administrative Cooperation

Article 35—Cooperation

Member States shall each appoint a national contact point, whose address they shall communicate to the Commission, which shall communicate it to the other Member States.

Member States shall, in liaison with the Commission, take all appropriate measures to establish direct cooperation and an exchange of information between the competent authorities.

Article 36—Staff

Member States shall ensure that authorities and other organisations implementing this Directive have received the necessary training and shall be bound by the confidentiality principle, as defined in the national law, in relation to any information they obtain in the course of their work.

Chapter IX
Final Provisions

Article 37—Reports

1. By 10 April 2008, the Commission shall report to the European Parliament and the Council on the application of this Directive and shall propose any amendments that are necessary. These proposals for amendments shall be made by way of priority in relation to Articles 15, 26 and 33. Member States shall send the Commission all the information that is appropriate for drawing up that report by 10 October 2007.

2. After presenting the report, the Commission shall report to the European Parliament and the Council on the application of this Directive at least every five years.

Article 38—Transposition

1. The Member States shall bring into force the laws, regulations and administrative provisions necessary to comply with this Directive before 10 October 2006. They shall forthwith inform the Commission thereof.

When the Member States adopt those measures, they shall contain a reference to this Directive or shall be accompanied by such a reference on the occasion of their official publication. The methods of making such reference shall be laid down by Member States.

2. Member States shall communicate to the Commission the text of the provisions of national law which they adopt in the field covered by this Directive.

Article 39—Entry into force

This Directive shall enter into force on the twentieth day following that of its publication in the *Official Journal of the European Union*.

Article 40—Addressees

This Directive is addressed to the Member States in accordance with the Treaty establishing the European Community.

Done at Luxembourg, 29 April 2004...

20. 2005 European Union Council Directive on Minimum Standards on Procedures for Granting and Withdrawing Refugee Status[8]

The Council of the European Union,

Having regard to the Treaty establishing the European Community, and in particular point (1)(d) of the first paragraph of Article 63 thereof,

---

[8] EU Council Directive 2005/85/EC of 1 December 2005 on minimum standards on procedures in Member States for granting and withdrawing refugee status: *Official Journal* of the European Union, 13.12.2005, L 326/13 (footnotes omitted).

Having regard to the proposal from the Commission,
Having regard to the opinion of the European Parliament,
Having regard to the opinion of the European Economic and Social Committee,

Whereas:

(1) A common policy on asylum, including a Common European Asylum System, is a constituent part of the European Union's objective of establishing progressively an area of freedom, security and justice open to those who, forced by circumstances, legitimately seek protection in the Community.

(2) The European Council, at its special meeting in Tampere on 15 and 16 October 1999, agreed to work towards establishing a Common European Asylum System, based on the full and inclusive application of the Geneva Convention of 28 July 1951 relating to the status of refugees, as amended by the New York Protocol of 31 January 1967 (Geneva Convention), thus affirming the principle of non-refoulement and ensuring that nobody is sent back to persecution.

(3) The Tampere Conclusions provide that a Common European Asylum System should include, in the short term, common standards for fair and efficient asylum procedures in the Member States and, in the longer term, Community rules leading to a common asylum procedure in the European Community.

(4) The minimum standards laid down in this Directive on procedures in Member States for granting or withdrawing refugee status are therefore a first measure on asylum procedures.

(5) The main objective of this Directive is to introduce a minimum framework in the Community on procedures for granting and withdrawing refugee status.

(6) The approximation of rules on the procedures for granting and withdrawing refugee status should help to limit the secondary movements of applicants for asylum between Member States, where such movement would be caused by differences in legal frameworks.

(7) It is in the very nature of minimum standards that Member States should have the power to introduce or maintain more favourable provisions for third country nationals or stateless persons who ask for international protection from a Member State, where such a request is understood to be on the grounds that the person concerned is a refugee within the meaning of Article 1(A) of the Geneva Convention.

(8) This Directive respects the fundamental rights and observes the principles recognised in particular by the Charter of Fundamental Rights of the European Union.

(9) With respect to the treatment of persons falling within the scope of this Directive, Member States are bound by obligations under instruments of international law to which they are party and which prohibit discrimination.

(10) It is essential that decisions on all applications for asylum be taken on the basis of the facts and, in the first instance, by authorities whose personnel has the appropriate knowledge or receives the necessary training in the field of asylum and refugee matters.

(11) It is in the interest of both Member States and applicants for asylum to decide as soon as possible on applications for asylum. The organisation of the processing of applications for asylum should be left to the discretion of Member States, so that they may,

in accordance with their national needs, prioritise or accelerate the processing of any application, taking into account the standards in this Directive.

(12) The notion of public order may cover a conviction for committing a serious crime.

(13) In the interests of a correct recognition of those persons in need of protection as refugees within the meaning of Article 1 of the Geneva Convention, every applicant should, subject to certain exceptions, have an effective access to procedures, the opportunity to cooperate and properly communicate with the competent authorities so as to present the relevant facts of his/her case and sufficient procedural guarantees to pursue his/her case throughout all stages of the procedure. Moreover, the procedure in which an application for asylum is examined should normally provide an applicant at least with the right to stay pending a decision by the determining authority, access to the services of an interpreter for submitting his/her case if interviewed by the authorities, the opportunity to communicate with a representative of the United Nations High Commissioner for Refugees (UNHCR) or with any organisation working on its behalf, the right to appropriate notification of a decision, a motivation of that decision in fact and in law, the opportunity to consult a legal adviser or other counsellor, and the right to be informed of his/her legal position at decisive moments in the course of the procedure, in a language he/she can reasonably be supposed to understand.

(14) In addition, specific procedural guarantees for unaccompanied minors should be laid down on account of their vulnerability. In this context, the best interests of the child should be a primary consideration of Member States.

(15) Where an applicant makes a subsequent application without presenting new evidence or arguments, it would be disproportionate to oblige Member States to carry out a new full examination procedure. In these cases, Member States should have a choice of procedure involving exceptions to the guarantees normally enjoyed by the applicant.

(16) Many asylum applications are made at the border or in a transit zone of a Member State prior to a decision on the entry of the applicant. Member States should be able to keep existing procedures adapted to the specific situation of these applicants at the border. Common rules should be defined on possible exceptions made in these circumstances to the guarantees normally enjoyed by applicants. Border procedures should mainly apply to those applicants who do not meet the conditions for entry into the territory of the Member States.

(17) A key consideration for the well-foundedness of an asylum application is the safety of the applicant in his/her country of origin. Where a third country can be regarded as a safe country of origin, Member States should be able to designate it as safe and presume its safety for a particular applicant, unless he/she presents serious counter-indications.

(18) Given the level of harmonisation achieved on the qualification of third country nationals and stateless persons as refugees, common criteria for designating third countries as safe countries of origin should be established.

(19) Where the Council has satisfied itself that those criteria are met in relation to a particular country of origin, and has consequently included it in the minimum common list of safe countries of origin to be adopted pursuant to this Directive, Member States should be obliged to consider applications of persons with the nationality of that country, or of stateless persons formerly habitually resident in that country, on

the basis of the rebuttable presumption of the safety of that country. In the light of the political importance of the designation of safe countries of origin, in particular in view of the implications of an assessment of the human rights situation in a country of origin and its implications for the policies of the European Union in the field of external relations, the Council should take any decisions on the establishment or amendment of the list, after consultation of the European Parliament.

(20) It results from the status of Bulgaria and Romania as candidate countries for accession to the European Union and the progress made by these countries towards membership that they should be regarded as constituting safe countries of origin for the purposes of this Directive until the date of their accession to the European Union.

(21) The designation of a third country as a safe country of origin for the purposes of this Directive cannot establish an absolute guarantee of safety for nationals of that country. By its very nature, the assessment underlying the designation can only take into account the general civil, legal and political circumstances in that country and whether actors of persecution, torture or inhuman or degrading treatment or punishment are subject to sanction in practice when found liable in the country concerned. For this reason, it is important that, where an applicant shows that there are serious reasons to consider the country not to be safe in his/her particular circumstances, the designation of the country as safe can no longer be considered relevant for him/her.

(22) Member States should examine all applications on the substance, i.e. assess whether the applicant in question qualifies as a refugee in accordance with Council Directive 2004/83/EC of 29 April 2004 on minimum standards for the qualification and status of third country nationals or stateless persons as refugees or as persons who otherwise need international protection and the content of the protection granted, except where the present Directive provides otherwise, in particular where it can be reasonably assumed that another country would do the examination or provide sufficient protection. In particular, Member States should not be obliged to assess the substance of an asylum application where a first country of asylum has granted the applicant refugee status or otherwise sufficient protection and the applicant will be readmitted to this country.

(23) Member States should also not be obliged to assess the substance of an asylum application where the applicant, due to a connection to a third country as defined by national law, can reasonably be expected to seek protection in that third country. Member States should only proceed on this basis where this particular applicant would be safe in the third country concerned. In order to avoid secondary movements of applicants, common principles for the consideration or designation by Member States of third countries as safe should be established.

(24) Furthermore, with respect to certain European third countries, which observe particularly high human rights and refugee protection standards, Member States should be allowed to not carry out, or not to carry out full examination of asylum applications regarding applicants who enter their territory from such European third countries. Given the potential consequences for the applicant of a restricted or omitted examination, this application of the safe third country concept should be restricted to cases involving third countries with respect to which the Council has satisfied itself that the high standards for the safety of the third country concerned, as set out in this

Directive, are fulfilled. The Council should take decisions in this matter after consultation of the European Parliament.

(25) It follows from the nature of the common standards concerning both safe third country concepts as set out in this Directive, that the practical effect of the concepts depends on whether the third country in question permits the applicant in question to enter its territory.

(26) With respect to the withdrawal of refugee status, Member States should ensure that persons benefiting from refugee status are duly informed of a possible reconsideration of their status and have the opportunity to submit their point of view before the authorities can take a motivated decision to withdraw their status. However, dispensing with these guarantees should be allowed where the reasons for the cessation of the refugee status is not related to a change of the conditions on which the recognition was based.

(27) It reflects a basic principle of Community law that the decisions taken on an application for asylum and on the withdrawal of refugee status are subject to an effective remedy before a court or tribunal within the meaning of Article 234 of the Treaty. The effectiveness of the remedy, also with regard to the examination of the relevant facts, depends on the administrative and judicial system of each Member State seen as a whole.

(28) In accordance with Article 64 of the Treaty, this Directive does not affect the exercise of the responsibilities incumbent upon Member States with regard to the maintenance of law and order and the safeguarding of internal security.

(29) This Directive does not deal with procedures governed by Council Regulation (EC) No 343/2003 of 18 February 2003 establishing the criteria and mechanisms for determining the Member State responsible for examining an asylum application lodged in one of the Member States by a third-country national.

(30) The implementation of this Directive should be evaluated at regular intervals not exceeding two years.

(31) Since the objective of this Directive, namely to establish minimum standards on procedures in Member States for granting and withdrawing refugee status cannot be sufficiently attained by the Member States and can therefore, by reason of the scale and effects of the action, be better achieved at Community level, the Community may adopt measures, in accordance with the principle of subsidiarity as set out in Article 5 of the Treaty. In accordance with the principle of proportionality, as set out in that Article, this Directive does not go beyond what is necessary in order to achieve this objective.

(32) In accordance with Article 3 of the Protocol on the position of the United Kingdom and Ireland, annexed to the Treaty on European Union and to the Treaty establishing the European Community, the United Kingdom has notified, by letter of 24 January 2001, its wish to take part in the adoption and application of this Directive.

(33) In accordance with Article 3 of the Protocol on the position of the United Kingdom and Ireland, annexed to the Treaty on European Union and to the Treaty establishing the European Community, Ireland has notified, by letter of 14 February 2001, its wish to take part in the adoption and application of this Directive.

(34) In accordance with Articles 1 and 2 of the Protocol on the position of Denmark, annexed to the Treaty on European Union and to the Treaty establishing the European Community, Denmark does not take part in the adoption of this Directive and is not bound by it or subject to its application,

Has Adopted this Directive:

Chapter I
General Provisions

Article 1—Purpose

The purpose of this Directive is to establish minimum standards on procedures in Member States for granting and withdrawing refugee status.

Article 2—Definitions

For the purposes of this Directive:

(a) 'Geneva Convention' means the Convention of 28 July 1951 relating to the status of refugees, as amended by the New York Protocol of 31 January 1967;

(b) 'application' or 'application for asylum' means an application made by a third country national or stateless person which can be understood as a request for international protection from a Member State under the Geneva Convention. Any application for international protection is presumed to be an application for asylum, unless the person concerned explicitly requests another kind of protection that can be applied for separately;

(c) 'applicant' or 'applicant for asylum' means a third country national or stateless person who has made an application for asylum in respect of which a final decision has not yet been taken;

(d) 'final decision' means a decision on whether the third country national or stateless person be granted refugee status by virtue of Directive 2004/83/EC and which is no longer subject to a remedy within the framework of Chapter V of this Directive irrespective of whether such remedy has the effect of allowing applicants to remain in the Member States concerned pending its outcome, subject to Annex III to this Directive;

(e) 'determining authority' means any quasi-judicial or administrative body in a Member State responsible for examining applications for asylum and competent to take decisions at first instance in such cases, subject to Annex I;

(f) 'refugee' means a third country national or a stateless person who fulfils the requirements of Article 1 of the Geneva Convention as set out in Directive 2004/83/EC;

(g) 'refugee status' means the recognition by a Member State of a third country national or stateless person as a refugee;

(h) 'unaccompanied minor' means a person below the age of 18 who arrives in the territory of the Member States unaccompanied by an adult responsible for him/her whether by law or by custom, and for as long as he/she is not effectively taken into the care of such a person; it includes a minor who is left unaccompanied after he/she has entered the territory of the Member States;

(i) 'representative' means a person acting on behalf of an organisation representing an unaccompanied minor as legal guardian, a person acting on behalf of a national organisation which is responsible for the care and well-being of minors, or any other appropriate representation appointed to ensure his/her best interests;

(j) 'withdrawal of refugee status' means the decision by a competent authority to revoke, end or refuse to renew the refugee status of a person in accordance with Directive 2004/83/EC;

(k) 'remain in the Member State' means to remain in the territory, including at the border or in transit zones, of the Member State in which the application for asylum has been made or is being examined.

Article 3—Scope

1. This Directive shall apply to all applications for asylum made in the territory, including at the border or in the transit zones of the Member States, and to the withdrawal of refugee status.

2. This Directive shall not apply in cases of requests for diplomatic or territorial asylum submitted to representations of Member States.

3. Where Member States employ or introduce a procedure in which asylum applications are examined both as applications on the basis of the Geneva Convention and as applications for other kinds of international protection given under the circumstances defined by Article 15 of Directive 2004/83/EC, they shall apply this Directive throughout their procedure.

4. Moreover, Member States may decide to apply this Directive in procedures for deciding on applications for any kind of international protection.

Article 4—Responsible authorities

1. Member States shall designate for all procedures a determining authority which will be responsible for an appropriate examination of the applications in accordance with this Directive, in particular Articles 8(2) and 9.

In accordance with Article 4(4) of Regulation (EC) No 343/2003, applications for asylum made in a Member State to the authorities of another Member State carrying out immigration controls there shall be dealt with by the Member State in whose territory the application is made.

2. However, Member States may provide that another authority is responsible for the purposes of:

(a) processing cases in which it is considered to transfer the applicant to another State according to the rules establishing criteria and mechanisms for determining which State is responsible for considering an application for asylum, until the transfer takes place or the requested State has refused to take charge of or take back the applicant;

(b) taking a decision on the application in the light of national security provisions, provided the determining authority is consulted prior to this decision as to whether the applicant qualifies as a refugee by virtue of Directive 2004/83/EC;

(c) conducting a preliminary examination pursuant to Article 32, provided this authority has access to the applicant's file regarding the previous application;

(d) processing cases in the framework of the procedures provided for in Article 35(1);

(e) refusing permission to enter in the framework of the procedure provided for in Article 35(2) to (5), subject to the conditions and as set out therein;

(f) establishing that an applicant is seeking to enter or has entered into the Member State from a safe third country pursuant to Article 36, subject to the conditions and as set out in that Article.

3. Where authorities are designated in accordance with paragraph 2, Member States shall ensure that the personnel of such authorities have the appropriate knowledge or receive the necessary training to fulfil their obligations when implementing this Directive.

Article 5—More favourable provisions

Member States may introduce or maintain more favourable standards on procedures for granting and withdrawing refugee status, insofar as those standards are compatible with this Directive.

Chapter II
Basic Principles and Guarantees

Article 6—Access to the procedure

1. Member States may require that applications for asylum be made in person and/or at a designated place.

2. Member States shall ensure that each adult having legal capacity has the right to make an application for asylum on his/her own behalf.

3. Member States may provide that an application may be made by an applicant on behalf of his/her dependants. In such cases Member States shall ensure that dependent adults consent to the lodging of the application on their behalf, failing which they shall have an opportunity to make an application on their own behalf.

Consent shall be requested at the time the application is lodged or, at the latest, when the personal interview with the dependant adult is conducted.

4. Member States may determine in national legislation:

(a) the cases in which a minor can make an application on his/her own behalf;

(b) the cases in which the application of an unaccompanied minor has to be lodged by a representative as provided for in Article 17(1)(a);

(c) the cases in which the lodging of an application for asylum is deemed to constitute also the lodging of an application for asylum for any unmarried minor.

5. Member States shall ensure that authorities likely to be addressed by someone who wishes to make an application for asylum are able to advise that person how and where he/she may make such an application and/or may require these authorities to forward the application to the competent authority.

Article 7—Right to remain in the Member State pending the examination of the application

1. Applicants shall be allowed to remain in the Member State, for the sole purpose of the procedure, until the determining authority has made a decision in accordance with the procedures at first instance set out in Chapter III. This right to remain shall not constitute an entitlement to a residence permit.

2. Member States can make an exception only where, in accordance with Articles 32 and 34, a subsequent application will not be further examined or where they will surrender or extradite, as appropriate, a person either to another Member State pursuant to obligations in accordance with a European arrest warrant or otherwise, or to a third country, or to international criminal courts or tribunals.

Article 8—Requirements for the examination of applications

1. Without prejudice to Article 23(4)(i), Member States shall ensure that applications for asylum are neither rejected nor excluded from examination on the sole ground that they have not been made as soon as possible.

2. Member States shall ensure that decisions by the determining authority on applications for asylum are taken after an appropriate examination. To that end, Member States shall ensure that:

(a) applications are examined and decisions are taken individually, objectively and impartially;

(b) precise and up-to-date information is obtained from various sources, such as the United Nations High Commissioner for Refugees (UNHCR), as to the general situation prevailing in the countries of origin of applicants for asylum and, where necessary, in countries through which they have transited, and that such information is made available to the personnel responsible for examining applications and taking decisions;

(c) the personnel examining applications and taking decisions have the knowledge with respect to relevant standards applicable in the field of asylum and refugee law.

3. The authorities referred to in Chapter V shall, through the determining authority or the applicant or otherwise, have access to the general information referred to in paragraph 2(b), necessary for the fulfilment of their task.

4. Member States may provide for rules concerning the translation of documents relevant for the examination of applications.

Article 9—Requirements for a decision by the determining authority

1. Member States shall ensure that decisions on applications for asylum are given in writing.

2. Member States shall also ensure that, where an application is rejected, the reasons in fact and in law are stated in the decision and information on how to challenge a negative decision is given in writing.

Member States need not state the reasons for not granting refugee status in a decision where the applicant is granted a status which offers the same rights and benefits under national and Community law as the refugee status by virtue of Directive 2004/83/EC. In these cases, Member States shall ensure that the reasons for not granting refugee status are stated in the applicant's file and that the applicant has, upon request, access to his/her file.

Moreover, Member States need not provide information on how to challenge a negative decision in writing in conjunction with a decision where the applicant has been provided with this information at an earlier stage either in writing or by electronic means accessible to the applicant.

3. For the purposes of Article 6(3), and whenever the application is based on the same grounds, Member States may take one single decision, covering all dependants.

Article 10—Guarantees for applicants for asylum

1. With respect to the procedures provided for in Chapter III, Member States shall ensure that all applicants for asylum enjoy the following guarantees:

(a) they shall be informed in a language which they may reasonably be supposed to understand of the procedure to be followed and of their rights and obligations during the procedure and the possible consequences of not complying with their obligations and not cooperating with the authorities. They shall be informed of the time-frame, as well as the means at their disposal for fulfilling the obligation to submit the elements as referred to in Article 4 of Directive 2004/83/EC. This information shall be given in time to enable them to exercise the rights guaranteed in this Directive and to comply with the obligations described in Article 11;

(b) they shall receive the services of an interpreter for submitting their case to the competent authorities whenever necessary. Member States shall consider it necessary to give these services at least when the determining authority calls upon the applicant to be interviewed as referred to in Articles 12 and 13 and appropriate communication cannot be ensured without such services. In this case and in other cases where the competent authorities call upon the applicant, these services shall be paid for out of public funds;

(c) they shall not be denied the opportunity to communicate with the UNHCR or with any other organisation working on behalf of the UNHCR in the territory of the Member State pursuant to an agreement with that Member State;

(d) they shall be given notice in reasonable time of the decision by the determining authority on their application for asylum. If a legal adviser or other counsellor is legally representing the applicant, Member States may choose to give notice of the decision to him/her instead of to the applicant for asylum;

(e) they shall be informed of the result of the decision by the determining authority in a language that they may reasonably be supposed to understand when they are not assisted or represented by a legal adviser or other counsellor and when free legal assistance is not available. The information provided shall include information on how to challenge a negative decision in accordance with the provisions of Article 9(2).

2. With respect to the procedures provided for in Chapter V, Member States shall ensure that all applicants for asylum enjoy equivalent guarantees to the ones referred to in paragraph 1(b), (c) and (d) of this Article.

Article 11—Obligations of the applicants for asylum

1. Member States may impose upon applicants for asylum obligations to cooperate with the competent authorities insofar as these obligations are necessary for the processing of the application.

2. In particular, Member States may provide that:

(a) applicants for asylum are required to report to the competent authorities or to appear before them in person, either without delay or at a specified time;

(b) applicants for asylum have to hand over documents in their possession relevant to the examination of the application, such as their passports;

(c) applicants for asylum are required to inform the competent authorities of their current place of residence or address and of any changes thereof as soon as possible. Member States may provide that the applicant shall have to accept any communication at the most recent place of residence or address which he/she indicated accordingly;

(d) the competent authorities may search the applicant and the items he/she carries with him/her;

(e) the competent authorities may take a photograph of the applicant; and

(f) the competent authorities may record the applicant's oral statements, provided he/she has previously been informed thereof.

Article 12—Personal interview

1. Before a decision is taken by the determining authority, the applicant for asylum shall be given the opportunity of a personal interview on his/her application for asylum with a person competent under national law to conduct such an interview.

Member States may also give the opportunity of a personal interview to each dependent adult referred to in Article 6(3).

Member States may determine in national legislation the cases in which a minor shall be given the opportunity of a personal interview.

2. The personal interview may be omitted where:

(a) the determining authority is able to take a positive decision on the basis of evidence available; or

(b) the competent authority has already had a meeting with the applicant for the purpose of assisting him/her with completing his/her application and submitting the essential information regarding the application, in terms of Article 4(2) of Directive 2004/83/EC; or

(c) the determining authority, on the basis of a complete examination of information provided by the applicant, considers the application to be unfounded in cases where the circumstances mentioned in Article 23(4)(a), (c), (g), (h) and (j) apply.

3. The personal interview may also be omitted where it is not reasonably practicable, in particular where the competent authority is of the opinion that the applicant is unfit or unable to be interviewed owing to enduring circumstances beyond his/her control. When in doubt, Member States may require a medical or psychological certificate.

Where the Member State does not provide the applicant with the opportunity for a personal interview pursuant to this paragraph, or where applicable, to the dependant, reasonable efforts shall be made to allow the applicant or the dependant to submit further information.

4. The absence of a personal interview in accordance with this Article shall not prevent the determining authority from taking a decision on an application for asylum.

5. The absence of a personal interview pursuant to paragraph 2(b) and (c) and paragraph 3 shall not adversely affect the decision of the determining authority.

6. Irrespective of Article 20(1), Member States, when deciding on the application for asylum, may take into account the fact that the applicant failed to appear for the personal interview, unless he/she had good reasons for the failure to appear.

Article 13—Requirements for a personal interview

1. A personal interview shall normally take place without the presence of family members unless the determining authority considers it necessary for an appropriate examination to have other family members present.

2. A personal interview shall take place under conditions which ensure appropriate confidentiality.

3. Member States shall take appropriate steps to ensure that personal interviews are conducted under conditions which allow applicants to present the grounds for their applications in a comprehensive manner. To that end, Member States shall:

(a) ensure that the person who conducts the interview is sufficiently competent to take account of the personal or general circumstances surrounding the application, including the applicant's cultural origin or vulnerability, insofar as it is possible to do so; and

(b) select an interpreter who is able to ensure appropriate communication between the applicant and the person who conducts the interview. The communication need not necessarily take place in the language preferred by the applicant for asylum if there is another language which he/she may reasonably be supposed to understand and in which he/she is able to communicate.

4. Member States may provide for rules concerning the presence of third parties at a personal interview.

5. This Article is also applicable to the meeting referred to in Article 12(2)(b).

Article 14—Status of the report of a personal interview in the procedure

1. Member States shall ensure that a written report is made of every personal interview, containing at least the essential information regarding the application, as presented by the applicant, in terms of Article 4(2) of Directive 2004/83/EC.

2. Member States shall ensure that applicants have timely access to the report of the personal interview. Where access is only granted after the decision of the determining authority, Member States shall ensure that access is possible as soon as necessary for allowing an appeal to be prepared and lodged in due time.

3. Member States may request the applicant's approval of the contents of the report of the personal interview.

Where an applicant refuses to approve the contents of the report, the reasons for this refusal shall be entered into the applicant's file.

The refusal of an applicant to approve the contents of the report shall not prevent the determining authority from taking a decision on his/her application.

4. This Article is also applicable to the meeting referred to in Article 12(2)(b).

Article 15—Right to legal assistance and representation

1. Member States shall allow applicants for asylum the opportunity, at their own cost, to consult in an effective manner a legal adviser or other counsellor, admitted or permitted as such under national law, on matters relating to their asylum applications.

2. In the event of a negative decision by a determining authority, Member States shall ensure that free legal assistance and/or representation be granted on request, subject to the provisions of paragraph 3.

3. Member States may provide in their national legislation that free legal assistance and/or representation is granted:

(a) only for procedures before a court or tribunal in accordance with Chapter V and not for any onward appeals or reviews provided for under national law, including a rehearing of an appeal following an onward appeal or review; and/or

(b) only to those who lack sufficient resources; and/or

(c) only to legal advisers or other counsellors specifically designated by national law to assist and/or represent applicants for asylum; and/or

(d) only if the appeal or review is likely to succeed.

Member States shall ensure that legal assistance and/or representation granted under point (d) is not arbitrarily restricted.

4. Rules concerning the modalities for filing and processing requests for legal assistance and/or representation may be provided by Member States.

5. Member States may also:

(a) impose monetary and/or time-limits on the provision of free legal assistance and/or representation, provided that such limits do not arbitrarily restrict access to legal assistance and/or representation;

(b) provide that, as regards fees and other costs, the treatment of applicants shall not be more favourable than the treatment generally accorded to their nationals in matters pertaining to legal assistance.

6. Member States may demand to be reimbursed wholly or partially for any expenses granted if and when the applicant's financial situation has improved considerably or if the decision to grant such benefits was taken on the basis of false information supplied by the applicant.

Article 16—Scope of legal assistance and representation

1. Member States shall ensure that a legal adviser or other counsellor admitted or permitted as such under national law, and who assists or represents an applicant for asylum under the terms of national law, shall enjoy access to such information in the applicant's file as is liable to be examined by the authorities referred to in Chapter V, insofar as the information is relevant to the examination of the application.

Member States may make an exception where disclosure of information or sources would jeopardise national security, the security of the organisations or person(s) providing the information or the security of the person(s) to whom the information relates or where the investigative interests relating to the examination of applications of asylum by the competent authorities of the Member States or the international relations of the Member States would be compromised. In these cases, access to the information or sources in question shall be available to the authorities referred to in Chapter V, except where such access is precluded in cases of national security.

2. Member States shall ensure that the legal adviser or other counsellor who assists or represents an applicant for asylum has access to closed areas, such as detention facilities and transit zones, for the purpose of consulting that applicant. Member States may only limit the possibility of visiting applicants in closed areas where such limitation is, by virtue of national legislation, objectively necessary for the security, public order or administrative management of the area, or in order to ensure an efficient examination of the application, provided that access by the legal adviser or other counsellor is not thereby severely limited or rendered impossible.

3. Member States may provide rules covering the presence of legal advisers or other counsellors at all interviews in the procedure, without prejudice to this Article or to Article 17(1)(b).

4. Member States may provide that the applicant is allowed to bring with him/her to the personal interview a legal adviser or other counsellor admitted or permitted as such under national law.

Member States may require the presence of the applicant at the personal interview, even if he/she is represented under the terms of national law by such a legal adviser or counsellor, and may require the applicant to respond in person to the questions asked.

The absence of a legal adviser or other counsellor shall not prevent the competent authority from conducting the personal interview with the applicant.

Article 17—Guarantees for unaccompanied minors

1. With respect to all procedures provided for in this Directive and without prejudice to the provisions of Articles 12 and 14, Member States shall:

(a) as soon as possible take measures to ensure that a representative represents and/or assists the unaccompanied minor with respect to the examination of the application. This representative can also be the representative referred to in Article 19 of Directive 2003/9/EC of 27 January 2003 laying down minimum standards for the reception of asylum seekers;

(b) ensure that the representative is given the opportunity to inform the unaccompanied minor about the meaning and possible consequences of the personal interview and, where appropriate, how to prepare himself/herself for the personal interview. Member States shall allow the representative to be present at that interview and to ask questions or make comments, within the framework set by the person who conducts the interview.

Member States may require the presence of the unaccompanied minor at the personal interview, even if the representative is present.

2. Member States may refrain from appointing a representative where the unaccompanied minor:

(a) will in all likelihood reach the age of maturity before a decision at first instance is taken; or

(b) can avail himself, free of charge, of a legal adviser or other counsellor, admitted as such under national law to fulfil the tasks assigned above to the representative; or

(c) is married or has been married.

3. Member States may, in accordance with the laws and regulations in force on 1 December 2005, also refrain from appointing a representative where the unaccompanied minor is 16 years old or older, unless he/she is unable to pursue his/her application without a representative.

4. Member States shall ensure that:

(a) if an unaccompanied minor has a personal interview on his/her application for asylum as referred to in Articles 12, 13 and 14, that interview is conducted by a person who has the necessary knowledge of the special needs of minors;

(b) an official with the necessary knowledge of the special needs of minors prepares the decision by the determining authority on the application of an unaccompanied minor.

5. Member States may use medical examinations to determine the age of unaccompanied minors within the framework of the examination of an application for asylum. In cases where medical examinations are used, Member States shall ensure that:

(a) unaccompanied minors are informed prior to the examination of their application for asylum, and in a language which they may reasonably be supposed to understand, of the possibility that their age may be determined by medical examination. This shall include information on the method of examination and the possible consequences of the result of the medical examination for the examination of the application for asylum, as well as the consequences of refusal on the part of the unaccompanied minor to undergo the medical examination;

(b) unaccompanied minors and/or their representatives consent to carry out an examination to determine the age of the minors concerned; and

(c) the decision to reject an application for asylum from an unaccompanied minor who refused to undergo this medical examination shall not be based solely on that refusal.

The fact that an unaccompanied minor has refused to undergo such a medical examination shall not prevent the determining authority from taking a decision on the application for asylum.

6. The best interests of the child shall be a primary consideration for Member States when implementing this Article.

Article 18—Detention

1. Member States shall not hold a person in detention for the sole reason that he/she is an applicant for asylum.

2. Where an applicant for asylum is held in detention, Member States shall ensure that there is a possibility of speedy judicial review.

Article 19—Procedure in case of withdrawal of the application

1. Insofar as Member States provide for the possibility of explicit withdrawal of the application under national law, when an applicant for asylum explicitly withdraws his/her

application for asylum, Member States shall ensure that the determining authority takes a decision to either discontinue the examination or reject the application.

2. Member States may also decide that the determining authority can decide to discontinue the examination without taking a decision. In this case, Member States shall ensure that the determining authority enters a notice in the applicant's file.

Article 20—Procedure in the case of implicit withdrawal or abandonment of the application

1. When there is reasonable cause to consider that an applicant for asylum has implicitly withdrawn or abandoned his/her application for asylum, Member States shall ensure that the determining authority takes a decision to either discontinue the examination or reject the application on the basis that the applicant has not established an entitlement to refugee status in accordance with Directive 2004/83/EC.

Member States may assume that the applicant has implicitly withdrawn or abandoned his/her application for asylum in particular when it is ascertained that:

(a) he/she has failed to respond to requests to provide information essential to his/her application in terms of Article 4 of Directive 2004/83/EC or has not appeared for a personal interview as provided for in Articles 12, 13 and 14, unless the applicant demonstrates within a reasonable time that his/her failure was due to circumstances beyond his control;

(b) he/she has absconded or left without authorisation the place where he/she lived or was held, without contacting the competent authority within a reasonable time, or he/she has not within a reasonable time complied with reporting duties or other obligations to communicate.

For the purposes of implementing these provisions, Member States may lay down time-limits or guidelines.

2. Member States shall ensure that the applicant who reports again to the competent authority after a decision to discontinue as referred to in paragraph 1 of this Article is taken, is entitled to request that his/her case be reopened, unless the request is examined in accordance with Articles 32 and 34.

Member States may provide for a time-limit after which the applicant's case can no longer be re-opened.

Member States shall ensure that such a person is not removed contrary to the principle of non-refoulement.

Member States may allow the determining authority to take up the examination at the stage where it was discontinued.

Article 21—The role of UNHCR

1. Member States shall allow the UNHCR:

(a) to have access to applicants for asylum, including those in detention and in airport or port transit zones;

(b) to have access to information on individual applications for asylum, on the course of the procedure and on the decisions taken, provided that the applicant for asylum agrees thereto;

(c) to present its views, in the exercise of its supervisory responsibilities under Article 35 of the Geneva Convention, to any competent authorities regarding individual applications for asylum at any stage of the procedure.

2. Paragraph 1 shall also apply to an organisation which is working in the territory of the Member State concerned on behalf of the UNHCR pursuant to an agreement with that Member State.

Article 22—Collection of information on individual cases

For the purposes of examining individual cases, Member States shall not:

(a) directly disclose information regarding individual applications for asylum, or the fact that an application has been made, to the alleged actor(s) of persecution of the applicant for asylum;

(b) obtain any information from the alleged actor(s) of persecution in a manner that would result in such actor(s) being directly informed of the fact that an application has been made by the applicant in question, and would jeopardise the physical integrity of the applicant and his/her dependants, or the liberty and security of his/her family members still living in the country of origin.

Chapter III
Procedures at First Instance

Section I

Article 23—Examination procedure

1. Member States shall process applications for asylum in an examination procedure in accordance with the basic principles and guarantees of Chapter II.

2. Member States shall ensure that such a procedure is concluded as soon as possible, without prejudice to an adequate and complete examination.

Member States shall ensure that, where a decision cannot be taken within six months, the applicant concerned shall either:

(a) be informed of the delay; or

(b) receive, upon his/her request, information on the time-frame within which the decision on his/her application is to be expected. Such information shall not constitute an obligation for the Member State towards the applicant concerned to take a decision within that time-frame.

3. Member States may prioritise or accelerate any examination in accordance with the basic principles and guarantees of Chapter II, including where the application is likely to be well-founded or where the applicant has special needs.

4. Member States may also provide that an examination procedure in accordance with the basic principles and guarantees of Chapter II be prioritised or accelerated if:

(a) the applicant, in submitting his/her application and presenting the facts, has only raised issues that are not relevant or of minimal relevance to the examination of whether he/she qualifies as a refugee by virtue of Directive 2004/83/EC; or

(b) the applicant clearly does not qualify as a refugee or for refugee status in a Member State under Directive 2004/83/EC; or

(c) the application for asylum is considered to be unfounded:

    (i) because the applicant is from a safe country of origin within the meaning of Articles 29, 30 and 31, or

    (ii) because the country which is not a Member State, is considered to be a safe third country for the applicant, without prejudice to Article 28(1); or

(d) the applicant has misled the authorities by presenting false information or documents or by withholding relevant information or documents with respect to his/her identity and/or nationality that could have had a negative impact on the decision; or

(e) the applicant has filed another application for asylum stating other personal data; or

(f) the applicant has not produced information establishing with a reasonable degree of certainty his/her identity or nationality, or it is likely that, in bad faith, he/she has destroyed or disposed of an identity or travel document that would have helped establish his/her identity or nationality; or

(g) the applicant has made inconsistent, contradictory, improbable or insufficient representations which make his/her claim clearly unconvincing in relation to his/her having been the object of persecution referred to in Directive 2004/83/EC; or

(h) the applicant has submitted a subsequent application which does not raise any relevant new elements with respect to his/her particular circumstances or to the situation in his/her country of origin; or

(i) the applicant has failed without reasonable cause to make his/her application earlier, having had opportunity to do so; or

(j) the applicant is making an application merely in order to delay or frustrate the enforcement of an earlier or imminent decision which would result in his/her removal; or

(k) the applicant has failed without good reason to comply with obligations referred to in Article 4(1) and (2) of Directive 2004/83/EC or in Articles 11(2)(a) and (b) and 20(1) of this Directive; or

(l) the applicant entered the territory of the Member State unlawfully or prolonged his/her stay unlawfully and, without good reason, has either not presented himself/herself to the authorities and/or filed an application for asylum as soon as possible, given the circumstances of his/her entry; or

(m) the applicant is a danger to the national security or public order of the Member State, or the applicant has been forcibly expelled for serious reasons of public security and public order under national law; or

(n) the applicant refuses to comply with an obligation to have his/her fingerprints taken in accordance with relevant Community and/or national legislation; or

(o) the application was made by an unmarried minor to whom Article 6(4)(c) applies, after the application of the parents or parent responsible for the minor has been rejected and no relevant new elements were raised with respect to his/her particular circumstances or to the situation in his/her country of origin.

Article 24—Specific procedures

1. Member States may provide for the following specific procedures derogating from the basic principles and guarantees of Chapter II:

(a) a preliminary examination for the purposes of processing cases considered within the framework set out in Section IV;

(b) procedures for the purposes of processing cases considered within the framework set out in Section V.

2. Member States may also provide a derogation in respect of Section VI.

Section II

Article 25—Inadmissible applications

1. In addition to cases in which an application is not examined in accordance with Regulation (EC) No 343/2003, Member States are not required to examine whether the applicant qualifies as a refugee in accordance with Directive 2004/83/EC where an application is considered inadmissible pursuant to this Article.

2. Member States may consider an application for asylum as inadmissible pursuant to this Article if:

(a) another Member State has granted refugee status;

(b) a country which is not a Member State is considered as a first country of asylum for the applicant, pursuant to Article 26;

(c) a country which is not a Member State is considered as a safe third country for the applicant, pursuant to Article 27;

(d) the applicant is allowed to remain in the Member State concerned on some other grounds and as result of this he/she has been granted a status equivalent to the rights and benefits of the refugee status by virtue of Directive 2004/83/EC;

(e) the applicant is allowed to remain in the territory of the Member State concerned on some other grounds which protect him/her against refoulement pending the outcome of a procedure for the determination of status pursuant to point (d);

(f) the applicant has lodged an identical application after a final decision;

(g) a dependant of the applicant lodges an application, after he/she has in accordance with Article 6(3) consented to have his/her case be part of an application made on his/her behalf, and there are no facts relating to the dependant's situation, which justify a separate application.

Article 26—The concept of first country of asylum

A country can be considered to be a first country of asylum for a particular applicant for asylum if:

(a) he/she has been recognised in that country as a refugee and he/she can still avail himself/herself of that protection; or

(b) he/she otherwise enjoys sufficient protection in that country, including benefiting from the principle of non-refoulement;

provided that he/she will be re-admitted to that country.

In applying the concept of first country of asylum to the particular circumstances of an applicant for asylum Member States may take into account Article 27(1).

Article 27—The safe third country concept

1. Member States may apply the safe third country concept only where the competent authorities are satisfied that a person seeking asylum will be treated in accordance with the following principles in the third country concerned:

(a) life and liberty are not threatened on account of race, religion, nationality, membership of a particular social group or political opinion;

(b) the principle of non-refoulement in accordance with the Geneva Convention is respected;

(c) the prohibition of removal, in violation of the right to freedom from torture and cruel, inhuman or degrading treatment as laid down in international law, is respected; and

(d) the possibility exists to request refugee status and, if found to be a refugee, to receive protection in accordance with the Geneva Convention.

2. The application of the safe third country concept shall be subject to rules laid down in national legislation, including:

(a) rules requiring a connection between the person seeking asylum and the third country concerned on the basis of which it would be reasonable for that person to go to that country;

(b) rules on the methodology by which the competent authorities satisfy themselves that the safe third country concept may be applied to a particular country or to a particular applicant. Such methodology shall include case-by-case consideration of the safety of the country for a particular applicant and/or national designation of countries considered to be generally safe;

(c) rules in accordance with international law, allowing an individual examination of whether the third country concerned is safe for a particular applicant which, as a minimum, shall permit the applicant to challenge the application of the safe third country concept on the grounds that he/she would be subjected to torture, cruel, inhuman or degrading treatment or punishment.

3. When implementing a decision solely based on this Article, Member States shall:

(a) inform the applicant accordingly; and

(b) provide him/her with a document informing the authorities of the third country, in the language of that country, that the application has not been examined in substance.

4. Where the third country does not permit the applicant for asylum to enter its territory, Member States shall ensure that access to a procedure is given in accordance with the basic principles and guarantees described in Chapter II.

5. Member States shall inform the Commission periodically of the countries to which this concept is applied in accordance with the provisions of this Article.

Section III

Article 28—Unfounded applications

1. Without prejudice to Articles 19 and 20, Member States may only consider an application for asylum as unfounded if the determining authority has established that the applicant does not qualify for refugee status pursuant to Directive 2004/83/EC.

2. In the cases mentioned in Article 23(4)(b) and in cases of unfounded applications for asylum in which any of the circumstances listed in Article 23(4)(a) and (c) to (o) apply, Member States may also consider an application as manifestly unfounded, where it is defined as such in the national legislation.

Article 29—Minimum common list of third countries regarded as safe countries of origin

1. The Council shall, acting by a qualified majority on a proposal from the Commission and after consultation of the European Parliament, adopt a minimum common list of third countries which shall be regarded by Member States as safe countries of origin in accordance with Annex II.

2. The Council may, acting by a qualified majority on a proposal from the Commission and after consultation of the European Parliament, amend the minimum common list by adding or removing third countries, in accordance with Annex II. The Commission shall examine any request made by the Council or by a Member State to submit a proposal to amend the minimum common list.

3. When making its proposal under paragraphs 1 or 2, the Commission shall make use of information from the Member States, its own information and, where necessary, information from UNHCR, the Council of Europe and other relevant international organisations.

4. Where the Council requests the Commission to submit a proposal for removing a third country from the minimum common list, the obligation of Member States pursuant to Article 31(2) shall be suspended with regard to this third country as of the day following the Council decision requesting such a submission.

5. Where a Member State requests the Commission to submit a proposal to the Council for removing a third country from the minimum common list, that Member State shall notify the Council in writing of the request made to the Commission. The obligation of this Member State pursuant to Article 31(2) shall be suspended with regard to the third country as of the day following the notification to the Council.

6. The European Parliament shall be informed of the suspensions under paragraphs 4 and 5.

7. The suspensions under paragraphs 4 and 5 shall end after three months, unless the Commission makes a proposal before the end of this period, to withdraw the third country from the minimum common list. The suspensions shall in any case end where the Council rejects a proposal by the Commission to withdraw the third country from the list.

8. Upon request by the Council, the Commission shall report to the European Parliament and the Council on whether the situation of a country on the minimum common list is still in conformity with Annex II. When presenting its report, the Commission may make such recommendations or proposals as it deems appropriate.

Article 30—National designation of third countries as safe countries of origin

1. Without prejudice to Article 29, Member States may retain or introduce legislation that allows, in accordance with Annex II, for the national designation of third countries other than those appearing on the minimum common list, as safe countries of origin for the purposes of examining applications for asylum. This may include designation of part of a country as safe where the conditions in Annex II are fulfilled in relation to that part.

2. By derogation from paragraph 1, Member States may retain legislation in force on 1 December 2005 that allows for the national designation of third countries, other than those appearing on the minimum common list, as safe countries of origin for the purposes of examining applications for asylum where they are satisfied that persons in the third countries concerned are generally neither subject to:

(a) persecution as defined in Article 9 of Directive 2004/83/EC; nor

(b) torture or inhuman or degrading treatment or punishment.

3. Member States may also retain legislation in force on 1 December 2005 that allows for the national designation of part of a country as safe, or a country or part of a country as safe for a specified group of persons in that country, where the conditions in paragraph 2 are fulfilled in relation to that part or group.

4. In assessing whether a country is a safe country of origin in accordance with paragraphs 2 and 3, Member States shall have regard to the legal situation, the application of the law and the general political circumstances in the third country concerned.

5. The assessment of whether a country is a safe country of origin in accordance with this Article shall be based on a range of sources of information, including in particular information from other Member States, the UNHCR, the Council of Europe and other relevant international organisations.

6. Member States shall notify to the Commission the countries that are designated as safe countries of origin in accordance with this Article.

Article 31—The safe country of origin concept

1. A third country designated as a safe country of origin in accordance with either Article 29 or 30 may, after an individual examination of the application, be considered as a safe country of origin for a particular applicant for asylum only if:

(a) he/she has the nationality of that country; or

(b) he/she is a stateless person and was formerly habitually resident in that country;

and he/she has not submitted any serious grounds for considering the country not to be a safe country of origin in his/her particular circumstances and in terms of his/her qualification as a refugee in accordance with Directive 2004/83/EC.

2. Member States shall, in accordance with paragraph 1, consider the application for asylum as unfounded where the third country is designated as safe pursuant to Article 29.

3. Member States shall lay down in national legislation further rules and modalities for the application of the safe country of origin concept.

Section IV

Article 32—Subsequent application

1. Where a person who has applied for asylum in a Member State makes further representations or a subsequent application in the same Member State, that Member State may examine these further representations or the elements of the subsequent application in the framework of the examination of the previous application or in the framework of the examination of the decision under review or appeal, insofar as the competent authorities can take into account and consider all the elements underlying the further representations or subsequent application within this framework.

2. Moreover, Member States may apply a specific procedure as referred to in paragraph 3, where a person makes a subsequent application for asylum:

(a) after his/her previous application has been withdrawn or abandoned by virtue of Articles 19 or 20;

(b) after a decision has been taken on the previous application. Member States may also decide to apply this procedure only after a final decision has been taken.

3. A subsequent application for asylum shall be subject first to a preliminary examination as to whether, after the withdrawal of the previous application or after the decision referred to in paragraph 2(b) of this Article on this application has been reached, new elements or findings relating to the examination of whether he/she qualifies as a refugee by virtue of Directive 2004/83/EC have arisen or have been presented by the applicant.

4. If, following the preliminary examination referred to in paragraph 3 of this Article, new elements or findings arise or are presented by the applicant which significantly add to the likelihood of the applicant qualifying as a refugee by virtue of Directive 2004/83/EC, the application shall be further examined in conformity with Chapter II.

5. Member States may, in accordance with national legislation, further examine a subsequent application where there are other reasons why a procedure has to be re-opened.

6. Member States may decide to further examine the application only if the applicant concerned was, through no fault of his/her own, incapable of asserting the situations set forth in paragraphs 3, 4 and 5 of this Article in the previous procedure, in particular by exercising his/her right to an effective remedy pursuant to Article 39.

7. The procedure referred to in this Article may also be applicable in the case of a dependant who lodges an application after he/she has, in accordance with Article 6(3), consented to have his/her case be part of an application made on his/her behalf. In this case the preliminary examination referred to in paragraph 3 of this Article will consist of examining whether there are facts relating to the dependant's situation which justify a separate application.

Article 33—Failure to appear

Member States may retain or adopt the procedure provided for in Article 32 in the case of an application for asylum filed at a later date by an applicant who, either intentionally or owing to gross negligence, fails to go to a reception centre or appear before the competent authorities at a specified time.

Article 34—Procedural rules

1. Member States shall ensure that applicants for asylum whose application is subject to a preliminary examination pursuant to Article 32 enjoy the guarantees provided for in Article 10(1).

2. Member States may lay down in national law rules on the preliminary examination pursuant to Article 32. Those rules may, *inter alia*:

(a) oblige the applicant concerned to indicate facts and substantiate evidence which justify a new procedure;

(b) require submission of the new information by the applicant concerned within a time-limit after he/she obtained such information;

(c) permit the preliminary examination to be conducted on the sole basis of written submissions without a personal interview.

The conditions shall not render impossible the access of applicants for asylum to a new procedure or result in the effective annulment or severe curtailment of such access.

3. Member States shall ensure that:

(a) the applicant is informed in an appropriate manner of the outcome of the preliminary examination and, in case the application will not be further examined, of the reasons for this and the possibilities for seeking an appeal or review of the decision;

(b) if one of the situations referred to in Article 32(2) applies, the determining authority shall further examine the subsequent application in conformity with the provisions of Chapter II as soon as possible.

Section V

Article 35—Border procedures

1. Member States may provide for procedures, in accordance with the basic principles and guarantees of Chapter II, in order to decide at the border or transit zones of the Member State on applications made at such locations.

2. However, when procedures as set out in paragraph 1 do not exist, Member States may maintain, subject to the provisions of this Article and in accordance with the laws or regulations in force on 1 December 2005, procedures derogating from the basic principles and guarantees described in Chapter II, in order to decide at the border or in transit zones as to whether applicants for asylum who have arrived and made an application for asylum at such locations, may enter their territory.

3. The procedures referred to in paragraph 2 shall ensure in particular that the persons concerned:

(a) are allowed to remain at the border or transit zones of the Member State, without prejudice to Article 7;

(b) are be immediately informed of their rights and obligations, as described in Article 10(1) (a);

(c) have access, if necessary, to the services of an interpreter, as described in Article 10(1)(b);

(d) are interviewed, before the competent authority takes a decision in such procedures, in relation to their application for asylum by persons with appropriate knowledge of the relevant standards applicable in the field of asylum and refugee law, as described in Articles 12, 13 and 14;

(e) can consult a legal adviser or counsellor admitted or permitted as such under national law, as described in Article 15(1); and

(f) have a representative appointed in the case of unaccompanied minors, as described in Article 17(1), unless Article 17(2) or (3) applies.

Moreover, in case permission to enter is refused by a competent authority, this competent authority shall state the reasons in fact and in law why the application for asylum is considered as unfounded or as inadmissible.

4. Member States shall ensure that a decision in the framework of the procedures provided for in paragraph 2 is taken within a reasonable time. When a decision has not been taken within four weeks, the applicant for asylum shall be granted entry to the territory of the Member State in order for his/her application to be processed in accordance with the other provisions of this Directive.

5. In the event of particular types of arrivals, or arrivals involving a large number of third country nationals or stateless persons lodging applications for asylum at the border or in a transit zone, which makes it practically impossible to apply there the provisions of paragraph 1 or the specific procedure set out in paragraphs 2 and 3, those procedures may also be applied where and for as long as these third country nationals or stateless persons are accommodated normally at locations in proximity to the border or transit zone.

Section VI

Article 36—The European safe third countries concept

1. Member States may provide that no, or no full, examination of the asylum application and of the safety of the applicant in his/her particular circumstances as described in Chapter II, shall take place in cases where a competent authority has established, on the basis of the facts, that the applicant for asylum is seeking to enter or has entered illegally into its territory from a safe third country according to paragraph 2.

2. A third country can only be considered as a safe third country for the purposes of paragraph 1 where:

(a) it has ratified and observes the provisions of the Geneva Convention without any geographical limitations;

(b) it has in place an asylum procedure prescribed by law;

(c) it has ratified the European Convention for the Protection of Human Rights and Fundamental Freedoms and observes its provisions, including the standards relating to effective remedies; and

(d) it has been so designated by the Council in accordance with paragraph 3.

3. The Council shall, acting by qualified majority on a proposal from the Commission and after consultation of the European Parliament, adopt or amend a common list of third countries that shall be regarded as safe third countries for the purposes of paragraph 1.

4. The Member States concerned shall lay down in national law the modalities for implementing the provisions of paragraph 1 and the consequences of decisions pursuant to those provisions in accordance with the principle of non-refoulement under the Geneva Convention, including providing for exceptions from the application of this Article for humanitarian or political reasons or for reasons of public international law.

5. When implementing a decision solely based on this Article, the Member States concerned shall:

(a) inform the applicant accordingly; and

(b) provide him/her with a document informing the authorities of the third country, in the language of that country, that the application has not been examined in substance.

6. Where the safe third country does not re-admit the applicant for asylum, Member States shall ensure that access to a procedure is given in accordance with the basic principles and guarantees described in Chapter II.

7. Member States which have designated third countries as safe countries in accordance with national legislation in force on 1 December 2005 and on the basis of the criteria in paragraph 2(a), (b) and (c), may apply paragraph 1 to these third countries until the Council has adopted the common list pursuant to paragraph 3.

Chapter IV
Procedures for the Withdrawal of Refugee Status

Article 37—Withdrawal of refugee status

Member States shall ensure that an examination to withdraw the refugee status of a particular person may commence when new elements or findings arise indicating that there are reasons to reconsider the validity of his/her refugee status.

Article 38—Procedural rules

1. Member States shall ensure that, where the competent authority is considering withdrawing the refugee status of a third country national or stateless person in accordance with Article 14 of Directive 2004/83/EC, the person concerned shall enjoy the following guarantees:

(a) to be informed in writing that the competent authority is reconsidering his or her qualification for refugee status and the reasons for such a reconsideration; and

(b) to be given the opportunity to submit, in a personal interview in accordance with Article 10(1)(b) and Articles 12, 13 and 14 or in a written statement, reasons as to why his/her refugee status should not be withdrawn.

In addition, Member States shall ensure that within the framework of such a procedure:

(c) the competent authority is able to obtain precise and up-to-date information from various sources, such as, where appropriate, from the UNHCR, as to the general situation prevailing in the countries of origin of the persons concerned; and

(d) where information on an individual case is collected for the purposes of reconsidering the refugee status, it is not obtained from the actor(s) of persecution in a manner that would result in such actor(s) being directly informed of the fact that the person concerned is a refugee whose status is under reconsideration, nor jeopardise the physical integrity of the person and his/her dependants, or the liberty and security of his/her family members still living in the country of origin.

2. Member States shall ensure that the decision of the competent authority to withdraw the refugee status is given in writing. The reasons in fact and in law shall be stated in the decision and information on how to challenge the decision shall be given in writing.

3. Once the competent authority has taken the decision to withdraw the refugee status, Article 15, paragraph 2, Article 16, paragraph 1 and Article 21 are equally applicable.

4. By derogation to paragraphs 1, 2 and 3 of this Article, Member States may decide that the refugee status shall lapse by law in case of cessation in accordance with Article 11(1)(a) to (d) of Directive 2004/83/EC or if the refugee has unequivocally renounced his/her recognition as a refugee.

Chapter V
Appeals Procedures

Article 39—The right to an effective remedy

1. Member States shall ensure that applicants for asylum have the right to an effective remedy before a court or tribunal, against the following:

(a) a decision taken on their application for asylum, including a decision:

   (i) to consider an application inadmissible pursuant to Article 25(2),

  (ii) taken at the border or in the transit zones of a Member State as described in Article 35(1),

 (iii) not to conduct an examination pursuant to Article 36;

(b) a refusal to re-open the examination of an application after its discontinuation pursuant to Articles 19 and 20;

(c) a decision not to further examine the subsequent application pursuant to Articles 32 and 34;

(d) a decision refusing entry within the framework of the procedures provided for under Article 35(2);

(e) a decision to withdraw of refugee status pursuant to Article 38.

2. Member States shall provide for time-limits and other necessary rules for the applicant to exercise his/her right to an effective remedy pursuant to paragraph 1.

3. Member States shall, where appropriate, provide for rules in accordance with their international obligations dealing with:

(a) the question of whether the remedy pursuant to paragraph 1 shall have the effect of allowing applicants to remain in the Member State concerned pending its outcome;

(b) the possibility of legal remedy or protective measures where the remedy pursuant to paragraph 1 does not have the effect of allowing applicants to remain in the Member State concerned pending its outcome. Member States may also provide for an ex officio remedy; and

(c) the grounds for challenging a decision under Article 25(2)(c) in accordance with the methodology applied under Article 27(2)(b) and (c).

4. Member States may lay down time-limits for the court or tribunal pursuant to paragraph 1 to examine the decision of the determining authority.

5. Where an applicant has been granted a status which offers the same rights and benefits under national and Community law as the refugee status by virtue of Directive 2004/83/EC, the applicant may be considered as having an effective remedy where a court or tribunal decides that the remedy pursuant to paragraph 1 is inadmissible or unlikely to succeed on the basis of insufficient interest on the part of the applicant in maintaining the proceedings.

6. Member States may also lay down in national legislation the conditions under which it can be assumed that an applicant has implicitly withdrawn or abandoned his/her remedy pursuant to paragraph 1, together with the rules on the procedure to be followed.

Chapter VI
General and Final Provisions

Article 40—Challenge by public authorities

This Directive does not affect the possibility for public authorities of challenging the administrative and/or judicial decisions as provided for in national legislation.

Article 41—Confidentiality

Member States shall ensure that authorities implementing this Directive are bound by the confidentiality principle as defined in national law, in relation to any information they obtain in the course of their work.

Article 42—Report

No later than 1 December 2009, the Commission shall report to the European Parliament and the Council on the application of this Directive in the Member States and shall propose any amendments that are necessary. Member States shall send the Commission all the information that is appropriate for drawing up this report. After presenting the report, the Commission shall report to the European Parliament and the Council on the application of this Directive in the Member States at least every two years.

Article 43—Transposition

Member States shall bring into force the laws, regulations and administrative provisions necessary to comply with this Directive by 1 December 2007. Concerning Article 15, Member States shall bring into force the laws, regulations and administrative provisions necessary to comply with this Directive by 1 December 2008. They shall forthwith inform the Commission thereof.

When Member States adopt those provisions, they shall contain a reference to this Directive or shall be accompanied by such a reference on the occasion of their official publication. The methods of making such reference shall be laid down by Member States.

Member States shall communicate to the Commission the text of the provisions of national law which they adopt in the field covered by this Directive.

Article 44—Transition

Member States shall apply the laws, regulations and administrative provisions set out in Article 43 to applications for asylum lodged after 1 December 2007 and to procedures for the withdrawal of refugee status started after 1 December 2007.

Article 45—Entry into force

This Directive shall enter into force on the 20th day following its publication in the *Official Journal of the European Union*.

Article 46—Addressees

This Directive is addressed to the Member States in conformity with the Treaty establishing the European Community.

Done at Brussels, 1 December 2005 . . .

Annex I
Definition of 'determining authority'

When implementing the provision of this Directive, Ireland may, insofar as the provisions of section 17(1) of the *Refugee Act* 1996 (as amended) continue to apply, consider that:

— 'determining authority' provided for in Article 2(e) of this Directive shall, insofar as the examination of whether an applicant should or, as the case may be, should not be declared to be a refugee is concerned, mean the *Office of the Refugee Applications Commissioner*; and

— 'decisions at first instance' provided for in Article 2(e) of this Directive shall include recommendations of the *Refugee Applications Commissioner* as to whether an applicant should or, as the case may be, should not be declared to be a refugee.

Ireland will notify the Commission of any amendments to the provisions of section 17(1) of the *Refugee Act* 1996 (as amended).

Annex II
Designation of safe countries of origin for the purposes of Articles 29 and 30(1)

A country is considered as a safe country of origin where, on the basis of the legal situation, the application of the law within a democratic system and the general political circumstances, it can be shown that there is generally and consistently no persecution as defined in Article 9 of Directive 2004/83/EC, no torture or inhuman or degrading treatment or punishment and no threat by reason of indiscriminate violence in situations of international or internal armed conflict.

In making this assessment, account shall be taken, *inter alia*, of the extent to which protection is provided against persecution or mistreatment by:

(a) the relevant laws and regulations of the country and the manner in which they are applied;

(b) observance of the rights and freedoms laid down in the European Convention for the Protection of Human Rights and Fundamental Freedoms and/or the International Covenant for Civil and Political Rights and/or the Convention against Torture, in particular the rights from which derogation cannot be made under Article 15(2) of the said European Convention;

(c) respect of the non-refoulement principle according to the Geneva Convention;

(d) provision for a system of effective remedies against violations of these rights and freedoms.

Annex III
Definition of 'applicant' or 'applicant for asylum'

When implementing the provisions of this Directive Spain may, insofar as the provisions of *'Ley 30/1992 de Régimen jurídico de las Administraciones Públicas y del Procedimiento Administrativo Común'* of 26 November 1992 and *'Ley 29/1998 reguladora de la Jurisdicción Contencioso-Administrativa'* of 13 July 1998 continue to apply, consider that, for the purposes of Chapter V, the definition of 'applicant' or 'applicant for asylum' in Article 2(c) of this Directive shall include *'recurrente'* as established in the abovementioned Acts.

A 'recurrente' shall be entitled to the same guarantees as an 'applicant' or an 'applicant for asylum' as set out in this Directive for the purposes of exercising his/her right to an effective remedy in Chapter V.

Spain will notify the Commission of any relevant amendments to the abovementioned Act.

ANNEXE 3

STATES PARTIES TO THE 1951 CONVENTION, THE 1967 PROTOCOL, AND THE 1969 OAU CONVENTION; DELEGATIONS PARTICIPATING IN THE 1984 CARTAGENA DECLARATION; AND MEMBERS OF THE EXECUTIVE COMMITTEE OF THE HIGH COMMISSIONER'S PROGRAMME (AT 31 JANUARY 2007)

1. States Parties to the 1951 Convention relating to the Status of Refugees and the 1967 Protocol

Date of entry into force: 22 April 1954 (Convention); 4 October 1967 (Protocol).
Total Number of States Parties to the 1951 Convention: 144
Total Number of States Parties to the 1967 Protocol: 144
States Parties to both the Convention and Protocol: 141
States Parties to one or both of these instruments: 147

States Parties to the 1951 Convention only: Madagascar, Monaco, Saint Kitts and Nevis
States Parties to the 1967 Protocol only: Cape Verde, Swaziland, USA and Venezuela
States Parties which maintain the geographical limitation: Congo, Madagascar, Monaco, Turkey.

Afghanistan	Burundi	Dominican Republic
Albania	Cambodia	Ecuador
Algeria	Cameroon	Egypt
Angola	Canada	El Salvador
Antigua and Barbuda	Cape Verde	Equatorial Guinea
Argentina	Central African Republic	Estonia
Armenia	Chad	Ethiopia
Australia	Chile	Fiji
Austria	China	Finland
Azerbaijan	Colombia	France
Bahamas	Congo	Gabon
Belarus	Congo, Democratic	Gambia
Belgium	Republic of	Georgia
Belize	Costa Rica	Germany
Benin	Côte d'Ivoire	Ghana
Bolivia	Croatia	Greece
Bosnia and Herzegovina	Cyprus	Guatemala
Botswana	Czech Republic	Guinea
Brazil	Denmark	Guinea-Bissau
Bulgaria	Djibouti	Haiti
Burkina Faso	Dominica	Holy See

Honduras
Hungary
Iceland
Iran, Islamic
 Republic of
Ireland
Israel
Italy
Jamaica
Japan
Kazakhstan
Kenya
Korea, Republic of
Kyrgyzstan
Latvia
Lesotho
Liberia
Liechtenstein
Lithuania
Luxembourg
Macedonia, Former
 Yugoslav Republic of
Madagascar
Malawi
Mali
Malta
Mauritania
Mexico
Moldova, Republic of
Monaco

Montenegro
Morocco
Mozambique
Namibia
Netherlands
New Zealand
Nicaragua
Niger
Nigeria
Norway
Panama
Papua New Guinea
Paraguay
Peru
Philippines
Poland
Portugal
Romania
Russian Federation
Rwanda
Saint Kitts and Nevis
Saint Vincent and the
 Grenadines
Samoa
Sao Tome and Principe
Senegal
Serbia
Seychelles
Sierra Leone
Slovakia

Slovenia
Solomon Islands
Somalia
South Africa
Spain
Sudan
Suriname
Swaziland
Sweden
Switzerland
Tajikistan
Tanzania, United
 Republic of
Timor-Leste
Togo
Trinidad and Tobago
Tunisia
Turkey
Turkmenistan
Tuvalu
Uganda
Ukraine
United Kingdom
United States of America
Uruguay
Venezuela
Yemen
Zambia
Zimbabwe

2. States Parties to the 1969 OAU Convention

Date of entry into force: 20 June 1974
Number of States Parties: 45*

Algeria
Angola
Benin
Botswana
Burundi
Burkina Faso
Cameroon
Cape Verde

Central African Republic
Chad
Congo
Congo, Democratic
 Republic of
Côte d'Ivoire
Comoros
Egypt

Equatorial Guinea
Ethiopia
Gabon
Gambia
Ghana
Guinea
Guinea Bissau
Kenya

Lesotho	Rwanda	Togo
Liberia	Senegal	Tunisia
Libya	Seychelles	Uganda
Malawi	Sierra Leone	Zambia
Mali	South Africa	Zimbabwe
Mauritania	Sudan	
Mozambique	Swaziland	
Niger	Tanzania, United	
Nigeria	Republic of	

* Morocco, formerly a party, withdrew from the OAU in 1984, following admission of the Sahrawi Arab Democratic Republic; it remains outside the African Union.

3. Government Delegations participating in the 1984 Cartagena Declaration

Adopted 22 November 1984
Number of Governments participating: 10

Belize	Guatemala	Panama
Colombia	Honduras	Venezuela
Costa Rica	Mexico	
El Salvador	Nicaragua	

4. States Members of the Executive Committee of the High Commissioner's Programme

Number of Member States: 70**

Algeria	Cyprus	Iran, Islamic Republic of
Argentina	Denmark	Ireland
Australia	Ecuador	Israel
Austria	Egypt	Italy
Bangladesh	Ethiopia	Japan
Belgium	Finland	Jordan
Brazil	France	Kenya
Canada	Germany	Korea, Republic of
Chile	Ghana	Lebanon
China	Greece	Lesotho
Colombia	Guinea	Madagascar
Congo, Democratic	Holy See	Mexico
Republic of	Hungary	Morocco
Côte d'Ivoire	India	Mozambique

Namibia	Russian Federation	Tunisia
Netherlands	Serbia	Turkey
New Zealand	Somalia	Uganda
Nicaragua	South Africa	United Kingdom
Nigeria	Spain	United States of
Norway	Sudan	America
Pakistan	Sweden	Venezuela
Philippines	Switzerland	Yemen
Poland	Tanzania, United	Zambia
Portugal	Republic of	
Romania	Thailand	

** By resolution 60/127, 16 December 2005, the General Assembly decided to increase the number of members from sixty-eight to seventy States; Jordan and Portugal were elected by the Economic and Social Council in May 2006. A further increase of two more States was approved by UNGA resolution 61/136, 19 December 2006, with the election to take place in 2007.

Select Bibliography

BOOKS AND MONOGRAPHS

Aitchison, C.U., *A Collection of Treaties, Engagements and Sanads Relating to India and Neighbouring Countries*, 4th edn., Calcutta: Superintendent Government Printing, India, 13 vols., 1909.

Aleinikoff, T. A. & Chetail, V., eds., *Migration and International Legal Norms*, The Hague: TMC Asser Press, 2003.

Alland, D. & Teitgen-Colly, C., *Traité du droit d'asile*, Paris: Presses Universitaires de France, 2002.

American Law Institute, *Restatement of the Law, Third, Foreign Relations Law of the United States*, 2 vols. St. Paul, Minnesota: American Law Institute Publishers, 1987.

Anker, D. A., *Law of Asylum in the United States*, Boston, Mass.: Refugee Law Center Inc., 3rd edn., 1999, and 'Law and Procedures Supplement 2002'.

BADIL, *Closing Protection Gaps: Handbook on Protection of Palestinian Refugees in States signatories to the 1951 Refugee Convention*, Bethlehem: BADIL, 2005.

Barker, R., *Conscience, Government and War*, London: Routledge & Kegan Paul, 1982.

Barsky, R. F., *Arguing and Justifying: Assessing the Convention Refugees' Choice of Moment, Motive and Host Country*, Aldershot: Ashgate, 2000.

Batiffol, H. & Lagarde, P., *Droit international privé*, Paris: Librairie générale de droit et de jurisprudence, 7th edn., 1983.

Battjes, H., *European Asylum Law and International Law*, Leiden: Martinus Nijhoff Publishers, 2006.

Bassiouni, M. C., *Crimes against Humanity in International Criminal Law*, Dordrecht: Martinus Nijhoff Publishers, 1992.

Bau, I., *This Ground is Holy*, Mahwah, New Jersey: Paulist Press, 1985.

Bayefsky, A. F. & Fitzpatrick, J., eds., *Human Rights and Forced Displacement*, The Hague: Martinus Nijhoff Publishers, 2000.

Beach, H. & Ragvald, L., *A New Wave on the Northern Shore: The Indochinese Refugees in Sweden*, Statents Invandrarverk: Arbetsmarknadsstyrelsen, Noorköping, 1982.

Bethell, N., *The Last Secret*, London: André Deutsch, 1974.

Bhabha, J. & Coll, G., *Asylum Law and Practice in Europe and North America*, Washington DC: Federal Publications Inc., 1992.

Blake, N. & Husain, R., *Immigration, Asylum and Human Rights*, Oxford: Oxford Univesity Press, 2003.

Borchard, E. M., *The Diplomatic Protection of Citizens Abroad*, New York: Banks Law Publishing Company, 1928.

Bouteillet-Paquet, D., ed., *Subsidiary Protection of Refugees in the European Union: Complementing the Geneva Convention?*, Brussels: Bruylant, 2002.

Bowett, D., *Self-Defence in International Law*, Manchester: Manchester University Press, 1958.

Brett, R. & McCallin, M., *Children: The Invisible Soldiers*, Sweden: Rädda Barnen, 2nd edn., 1998.

Brown, E. D., *The International Law of the Sea*, Aldershot: Dartmouth, 1994.

Brown, N. & Bell, J., *French Administrative Law*, Oxford: Oxford University Press, 5th edn., 1998.

Brownlie, I., *Principles of Public International Law*, Oxford: Clarendon Press, 6th edn., 2003.

Brownlie, I., *Basic Documents in International Law*, Oxford: Oxford University Press, 5th edn., 2002.

Brownlie, I., *The Rule of Law in International Affairs*, The Hague: Martinus Nijhoff Publishers, 1998.

Brownlie, I., *System of the Law of Nations: State Responsibility, Part I*, Oxford: Clarendon Press, 1983.

Brownlie, I. & Goodwin-Gill, G. S., eds., *Basic Documents on Human Rights*, Oxford: Oxford University Press, 5th edn., 2006.

Buehrig, E., *The UN and the Palestinian Refugees—A Study in Non-Territorial Administration*, Bloomington: Indiana University Press, 1971.

Burgers, J. H., & Danelius, H., *The United Nations Convention against Torture: A Handbook on the Convention against Torture and Other Cruel, Inhuman or Degrading Treatment or Punishment*, Dordrecht: Martinus Nijhoff Publishers, 1988.

Carlier J.-Y. & Vanheule, D., eds., *Europe and Refugees: A Challenge?* The Hague: Kluwer Law International, 1997.

Carlier, J.-Y., Vanheule, D., Hullmann, K., & Peña Galiano, C., eds., *Who is a Refugee? A Comparative Case Law Study*, The Hague: Kluwer Law International, 1997.

Castles, S., Crawley, H., & Loughna, S., *States of Conflict: Causes and Patterns of Forced Migration to the EU and Policy Responses*, London: Institute for Public Policy Research, 2003.

Chan, K. B. & Indra, D. M., eds., *Uprooting, Loss and Adaptation: The Resettlement of Indo-Chinese Refugees in Canada*, Ottawa: Canadian Public Health Association, 1987.

Chetail, V. & Gowlland-Debbas, V., eds., *Switzerland and the International Protection of Refugees*, The Hague: Kluwer Law International, 2002.

Churchill, R. & Lowe, A. V., *The Law of the Sea*, Manchester: Manchester University Press, 3rd edn., 1999.

Clapham, A., *Human Rights Obligations of Non-State Actors*, Oxford: Oxford University Press, 2006.

Clapham, A., *Human Rights in the Private Sphere*, Oxford: Oxford University Press, 1993.

Cohen, R. & Deng, F. M., *Masses in Flight: The Global Crisis of Internal Displacement*, Washington DC: Brookings Institution, 1998.

Coles, G. J. L., *The Question of a General Approach to the Problem of Refugees from Situations of Armed Conflict and Serious Internal Disturbance*, San Remo: International Institute of Humanitarian Law, 1989.

Cohn, I. & Goodwin-Gill, G. S., *Child Soldiers: The Role of Children in Armed Conflict*, Oxford: Clarendon Press, 1994.

Commission des recours des réfugiés, *Contentieux des réfugiés: Jurisprudence du Conseil d'Etat et de la Commission des recours des réfugiés*, Année 2005, Année 2004: <http://www.commission-refugies.fr/>.

Corlett, D., *Following them Home The Fate of the Returned Asylum Seekers*, Melbourne: Black Inc., 2005.

Corsellis, J. & Ferrar, M., *Slovenia 1945: Memories of Death and Survival*, London: I.B. Tauris, 2005.

Council of Europe, *Human Rights and the Fight against Terrorism—The Guidelines of the Council of Europe*, Strasbourg: Council of Europe Publishing, 2002, 2005.

Crawford, J., *The International Law Commission's Articles on State Responsibility: Introduction, Text and Commentaries*, Cambridge: Cambridge University Press, 2002.

Crawley, H., *Refugees and Gender: Law and Process*, Bristol: Jordan Publishing, 2001.

Crock, M., Saul, B., & Dastyari, A., *Future Seekers II: Refugees and Irregular Migration in Australia*, Sydney: Federation Press, 2006.

Cubie, D. & Ryan F., *Immigration, Refugee and Citizenship Law in Ireland: Cases and Materials*, Dublin: Thomson Round Hall, 2004.

Cuny, F. C., Stein, B. N., & Reed, P., eds., *Repatriation during Conflict in Africa and Asia*, Dallas: Center for the Study of Societies in Crisis, 1992.

de Sousa, C. D. U. & de Bruycker, P., eds., *The Emergence of a European Asylum Policy*, Brussels: Bruylant, 2004.

Drüke, L., *Preventive Action for Refugee Producing Situations*, Frankfurt-am-Main: Peter Lang, 1990.

Eggli, A. V., *Mass Refugee Influx and the Limits of Public International Law*, The Hague: Martinus Nijhoff Publishers, 2002.

Evans, C., *Freedom of Religion under the European Convention on Human Rights*, Oxford: Oxford University Press, 2001.

Fawcett, J., *The Application of the European Convention on Human Rights*, Oxford: Oxford University Press, 2nd edn., 1987.

Feller, E., Türk, V., & Nicholson, F., eds., *Refugee Protection in International Law: UNHCR's Global Consultations on International Protection*, Cambridge: Cambridge University Press, 2003.

Fitzmaurice, M. & Sarooshi, D., eds., *Issues of State Responsibility before International Judicial Institutions*, Oxford: Hart Publishing, 2004.

Foreign Language Press, *The Hoa in Vietnam*, Hanoi, 1978.

Garcia-Mora, M. R., *International Law and Asylum as a Human Right*, Washington DC: Public Affairs Press, 1956.

Germov, R. & Motta, F., *Refugee Law in Australia*, Melbourne: Oxford University Press, 2003.

Ghosh, B., ed., *Managing Migration: Time for a New International Regime?* Oxford: Oxford University Press, 2000.

Gibney, M. J., *The Ethics and Politics of Asylum: Liberal Democracy and the Response to Refugees*, Cambridge: Cambridge University Press, 2004.

Gibney, M. J. & Hansen, R., eds., *Immigration and Asylum Law and Policy: From 1900 to the Present*, Santa Barbara: ABC-CLIO Inc., 2005.

Goodwin-Gill, G. S., *International Law and the Movement of Persons between States*, Oxford: Clarendon Press, 1978.

Goodwin-Gill, G. S. & Talmon, S., eds., *The Reality of International Law: Essays in Honour of Ian Brownlie*, Oxford: Clarendon Press, 1999.

Göpfert, R., *Der jüdische Kindertransport von Deutschland nach England 1938/39: Geschichte und Erinnerung*, Frankfurt am Main: Campus Verlag, 1999.

Gowlland-Debbas, V., ed., *The Problem of Refugees in the Light of Contemporary International Law Issues*, The Hague: Martinus Nijhoff Publishers, 1996.

Grahl-Madsen, A., *Commentary on the Refugee Convention 1951* (1962–63), Geneva: UNHCR, 1997.

Grahl-Madsen, A., *Territorial Asylum*, Stockholm: Almqvist & Wiksell International, 1980.

Grahl-Madsen, A., *The Status of Refugees in International Law*, vols. 1 & 2, Leyden: Sijthoff, 1966, 1972.

Grant, B., *The Boat People*, Middlesex: Penguin Books, 1979.

Guild, E. & Harlow, C., eds., *Implementing Amsterdam: Immigration and Asylum Rights in EC Law*, Oxford: Hart Publishing, 2001.

Hambro, E., *The Problem of Chinese Refugees in Hong Kong*, Leyden: Sijthoff, 1955.

Hannum, H., *The Right to Leave and Return in International Law and Practice*, Dordrecht: Martinus Nijhoff Publishers, 1987.

Happold, M., *Child Soldiers in International Law*, Manchester: Manchester University Press, 2005.

Harding, J. *The Uninvited: Migrant Journeys to the Rich World*, London: Profile Books, 2000.

Hathaway, J. C., *The Rights of Refugees under International Law*, Cambridge: Cambridge University Press, 2005.

Hathaway, J. C., *The Law of Refugee Status*, Toronto: Butterworths, 1991.

Hayes, D., *Challenge of Conscience. The Story of the Conscientious Objectors of 1939–1949*, London: Allen & Unwin, 1949.

Helton, A. C., *The Price of Indifference: Refugees and Humanitarian Action in the New Century*, Oxford: Oxford University Press, 2002.

Henckaerts, J.-M., *Mass Expulsion in Modern International Law and Practice*, The Hague: Martinus Nijhoff Publishers, 1995.

Hofmann, R., *Die Ausreisefreiheit nach Völkerrecht und staatlichem Recht*, Berlin: Springer-Verlag, 1988.

Holborn, L. W., *Refugees: A Problem of Our Time: The Work of the United Nations High Commissioner for Refugees, 1951–1972*, 2 vols., Metuchen: Scarecrow Press, 1975.

Holborn, L. W., *The International Refugee Organization: A Specialized Agency of the United Nations. Its History and Work 1946–1952*, London: University Press, 1956.

Independent International Commission on Kosovo, *Kosovo Report: Conflict, International Response, Lessons Learned*, Oxford: Oxford University Press, 2000.

Jackson, I. C., *The Refugee Concept in Group Situations*, The Hague: Martinus Nijhoff Publishers, 1999.

Janis, M. & Evans, C., eds., *Religion and International Law*, Leiden: Martinus Nijhoff Publishers, 2004.

Jennings, R. & Watts, A., eds., *Oppenheim's International Law*, London: Longmans, 9th edn., 2 vols, 1992.

Jessup, P., *The Law of Territorial Waters and Maritime Jurisdiction*, New York: G.A. Jennings Co., Inc., 1927.

Kälin, W., *Guiding Principles on Internal Displacement: Annotations*, Washington: American Society of International Law and The Brookings Institution, 2000.

Kälin, W., *Grundriss des Asylverfahrens*, Basel: Helbing & Lichtenhahn, 1990.

Kälin, W., *Das Prinzip des Non-Refoulement*, Bern: Peter Lang, 1982.

Kilkelly, U., *The Child and the European Convention on Human Rights*, Dartmouth: Ashgate, 1999.

Kimminich, O., *Der internationale Rechtsstatus des Flüchtlings*, Köln: Carl Heymans Verlag, 1962.

Köfner, G. & Nicolaus, P., *Grundlagen des Asylrechts in der Bundesrepublik Deutschland*, Mainz, München: Kaiser, Grünewald, 1986.

Kourula, P., *Broadening the Edges: Refugee Definition and International Protection Revisited*, The Hague: Martinus Nijhoff Publishers, 1997.

Koziebrodski, L. B., *Le droit d'asile*, Leyden: Sijthoff, 1962.

La Protección Internacional de los Refugiados en América Central, México y Panamá: Problemas Jurídicos y Humanitarios, National University of Colombia, 1984.

Lambert, H., *Seeking Asylum: Comparative Law and Practice in Selected European Countries*, Dordrecht: Martinus Nijhoff Publishers, 1995.

Larkin, M. A., Cuny, F. C., & Stein, B. N., *Repatriation under Conflict in Central America*, Washington, D.C.: CIPRA and Intertect, 1991.

Lauterpacht, H., *The Development of International Law by the International Court*, London: Stevens, 1958.

Lauterpacht, H., *International Law and Human Rights*, London: Stevens, 1950.

Loescher, G., *The UNHCR and World Politics: A Perilous Path*, Oxford: Oxford University Press, 2001.

Loescher, G., *Beyond Charity: International Cooperation and the Global Refugee Crisis*, New York: Oxford University Press, 1993.

Loescher, G. & Monahan, L., eds., *Refugees and International Relations*, Oxford: Oxford University Press, 1989.

Loescher, G. & Scanlan, J., *Calculated Kindness*, New York: The Free Press, Macmillan, 1986.

Lustgarten, L. & Leigh, I., *In from the Cold: National Security and Parliamentary Democracy*, Oxford: Clarendon Press, 1994.

Macalister-Smith, P., *International Humanitarian Assistance: Disaster Relief Actions in International Law and Organization*, Dordrecht: Martinus Nijhoff Publishers, 1985.

Macalister-Smith, P. & Alfredsson, G., eds., *The Land Beyond: Collected Essays on Refugee Law and Policy by Atle Grahl-Madsen*, The Hague: Martinus Nijhoff Publishers, 2001.

Malanczuk, P., ed., *Akehurst's Modern Introduction to International Law*, London: Routledge, 7th rev. edn., 1997.

Marrus, M. *The Unwanted: European Refugees from the First World War through the Cold War*, 2nd edn., Philadelphia: Temple University Press, 2002.

Martin, D. A., ed., *The New Asylum Seekers*, Dordrecht: Martinus Nijhoff Publishers, 1988.

Martin, S. Forbes, *Refugee Women*, Lanham, Maryland: Lexington Books, 2nd edn., 2003.

Marx, R., *Kommentar zum Asylverfahrensgesetz*, Berlin: Luchterhand Verlag, 6. Auflag, 2005.

Marx, R., *Kommentar zum Ausländer- und Asylrecht*, Deutscher Anwalt Verlag, 2. Auflag., 2005.

McAdam, J., *Complementary Protection in International Refugee Law*, Oxford: Oxford University Press, 2007.

McCarthy, J., *Death and Exile: The Ethnic Cleansing of Ottoman Muslims, 1821–1922*, Princeton, N.J.: The Darwin Press, 1995.

McDougal, M. S. & Burke, W. T., *The Public Order of the Oceans*, New Haven: Yale University Press, 1962.

McGoldrick, D., *The Human Rights Committee: Its Role in the Development of the International Covenant on Civil and Political Rights*, Oxford: Clarendon Press, 1991.

McNair, Lord (Arnold Duncan McNair), *The Law of Treaties*, Oxford: Clarendon Press, 1961.

McNair, Lord (Arnold Duncan McNair), *International Law Opinions*, Cambridge: Cambridge University Press, 1956.

Melander, G., *Refugees in Orbit*, Geneva: International University Exchange Fund, 1978.

Melander, G. & Nobel, P., eds., *African Refugees and the Law*, Uppsala: Scandinavian Institute of African Studies, 1978.

Meron, T., *Human Rights and Humanitarian Norms as Customary Law*, Oxford: Clarendon Press, 1989.

Minority Rights Group, *The Baha'is of Iran*, London: Minority Rights Group, Report No. 51, 1985.

Minority Rights Group, *The Kurds*, London: Minority Rights Group, Report No. 23, rev. edn., 1981.

Minority Rights Group, *The Crimean Tatars, Volga Germans and Meskhetians*, London: Minority Rights Group, Report No. 6, rev. edn., 1980.

Minority Rights Group, *The Two Irelands—The Double Minority*, London: Minority Rights Group, Report No. 2, rev. edn., 1979.

Minority Rights Group, *The Palestinians*, London: Minority Rights Group, Report No. 24, rev. edn., 1979.

Minority Rights Group, *The Namibians of South West Africa*, London: Minority Rights Group, Report No. 19, rev. edn., 1978.

Minority Rights Group, *Problems of a Displaced Minority: The New Position of East Africa's Asians*, London: Minority Rights Group, Report No. 16, rev. edn., 1978.

Minority Rights Group., *Religious Minorities in the Soviet Union*, London: Minority Rights Group, Report no. 1, rev. edn., 1977.

Minority Rights Group, *What Future for the Amerindians of South America?* London: Minority Rights Group, Report No. 15, rev. edn., 1977.

Minority Rights Group, *Jehovah's Witnesses in Central Africa*, London: Minority Rights Group, Report No. 29. 1976.

Minority Rights Group, *Selective Genocide in Burundi*, London: Minority Rights Group, Report no. 20, 1974.

Minority Rights Group, *The Asian Minorities of East and Central Africa*, London: Minority Rights Group, Report No. 4, 1971.

Moore, J. B., *Digest of International Law*, Washington, D.C.: Government Printing Office, 8 vols., 1906.

Morgan, B., Gelsthorpe, V., Crawley, H., & Jones, G. A., *Country of Origin Information: A User and Content Evaluation*, Home Office Research Study No. 271, London, 2003.

Mowbray, A., *Cases and Materials on the European Convention on Human Rights*, Oxford: Oxford University Press, 2001.

Nash, A., *Human Rights and the Protection of Refugees under International Law*, Halifax, Nove Scotia: Institute for Research on Public Policy, Canadian Human Rights Foundation, 1988.

Nicholson, F. & Twomey, P., eds., *Refugee Rights and Realities: Evolving International Concepts and Regimes*, Cambridge: Cambridge University Press, 1999.

Noll, G., ed., *Proof, Evidentiary Assessment and Credibility in Asylum Procedures*, Leiden: Martinus Nijhoff Publishers, 2005.

Noll, G., *Negotiating Asylum: The EU Acquis, Extraterritorial Protection and the Common Market of Deflection*, The Hague: Martinus Nijhoff Publishers, 2000.

Nowak, M., *UN Covenant on Civil and Political Rights: CCPR Commentary* Arlington: NP Engel 1993.

O'Connell, D. P., *The International Law of the Sea*, 2 vols., Shearer, I., ed., Oxford: Clarendon Press, 1982, 1984.

O'Connell, D. P., *International Law*, London: Stevens, 2 vols., 2nd edn., 1970.

O'Connell, D. P., *State Succession in Municipal Law and International Law*, vol. 1, Cambridge: Cambridge University Press, 1967.

O'Connor, J. F., *Good Faith in International Law*, Aldershot: Dartmouth, 1991.

Oppenheim, L., *International Law*, Lauterpacht, H., ed., London: Longmans, Green, 2 vols., 8th edn., 1955.

Oraá, J., *Human Rights in States of Emergency in International Law*, Oxford: Clarendon Press, 1992.

Ovey, C. & White, R. C. A., *Jacobs and White: European Convention on Human Rights*, Oxford: Oxford University Press, 3rd edn., 2002.

Palley, C., *Constitutional Law and Minorities* London: Minority Rights Group, Report No. 36, 1978.

Parry C., ed., *British Digest of International Law*, London: Stevens, 1965.

Pentassuglia, G., *Minorities in International Law*, Strasbourg: ECMI Handbook Series, 2002.

Phuong, C., *The International Protection of Internally Displaced Persons*, Cambridge: Cambridge University Press, 2005.

Reiterer, M., *The Protection of Refugees by Their State of Asylum*, Vienna: Wilhelm Braumüller, 1984.

Ressler, E., Boothby, N. & Steinbock, D., *Unaccompanied Children: Care and Protection in Wars, Natural Disasters and Refugee Movements*, New York: Oxford University Press, 1988.

Reynolds, E. E., *Nansen* London: Penguin, 1932, rev. edn., 1949.

Roberts, A. & Guelff, R., *Documents on the Laws of War*, Oxford: Oxford University Press, 3rd edn., 2001.

Robinson, N., *The 1951 Convention relating to the Status of Refugees: A Commentary*, New York: Institute of Jewish Affairs, 1953.

Rosenne, S., *Developments in the Law of Treaties 1945–1986*, Cambridge: Cambridge University Press, 1989.

Ruthström-Ruin, C., *Beyond Europe: The Globalization of Refugee Aid*, Lund: Lund University Press, 1993.

Rystad, G., ed., *The Uprooted: Forced Migration as an International Problem in the Post-War Era*, Lund: Lund University Press, 1990.

Salomon, K., *Refugees in the Cold War: Toward a New International Refugee Regime in the Early Postwar Era*, Lund: Lund University Press, 1991.

Sarooshi, D., *International Organizations and their Exercise of Sovereign Powers*, Oxford: Oxford University Press, 2005.

Saul, B., *Defining Terrorism in International Law*, Oxford: Oxford University Press, 2006.

Schachter, O., *International Law in Theory and Practice*, Dordrecht: Martinus Nijhoff Publishers, 1991.

Schwarzenberger, G., *Power Politics*, London: Stevens, 2nd edn., 1951.

Schwarzenberger, G. & Brown, L., *A Manual of International Law*, Milton: Professional Books, 6th edn., 1976.

Sepúlveda, M., *The Nature of the Obligations under the International Covenant on Economic, Social and Cultural Rights*, Antwerp: Intersentia, 2003.

Shah, P. A., *Refugees, Race and the Legal Concept of Asylum in Britain*, London: Cavendish Publishing, 2000.

Sharpe, R. J., *The Law of Habeas Corpus*, Oxford: Clarendon Press, 2nd edn., 1989.

Shearer, I. A., *Extradition in International Law*, Manchester: Manchester University Press, 1971.

Sherman, A. J., *Island Refuge—Britain and Refugees from the Third Reich 1933–1939*, Ilford: Frank Cass, 2nd edn., 1994.

Simma, B., ed., *The United Nations Charter: A Commentary*, Oxford: Oxford University Press, 2nd edn., 2004.

Simpson, J. H., *The Refugee Problem: Report of a Survey*, London: Oxford University Press, 1939.

Sinha, S. P., *Asylum and International Law*, The Hague: Nijhoff, 1971.

Sjöberg, T., *The Powers and the Persecuted: The Refugee Problem and the Inter-Governmental Committee on Refugees*, Lund: Lund University Press, 1991.

Skran, C. M., *Refugees in Inter-War Europe: The Emergence of a Regime*, Oxford: Clarendon Press, 1995.

Stein, B. N., Cuny, F. C. & Reed, P., eds., *Refugee Repatriation during Conflict*, Dallas: Center for the Study of Societies in Crisis, 1995.

Stevens, D., *UK Asylum Law and Policy: Historical and Contemporary Perspectives*, London: Sweet & Maxwell, 2004.

Tajfel H., *The Social Psychology of Minorities*, London: Minority Rights Group, Report No. 38, 1978.

Takkenberg, L., *The Status of Palestinian Refugees in International Law*, Oxford: Clarendon Press, 1998.

Takkenberg, L. & Tahbaz, C. C., *The Collected Travaux Préparatoires of the 1951 Convention relating to the Status of Refugees*, 3 vols., Amsterdam: Dutch Refugee Council/European Legal Network on Asylum, 1988.

Tang, Lay Lee, *Statelessness, Human Rights and Gender*, Leiden: Martinus Nijhoff Publishers, 2005.

Tiberghien, F., *La protection des réfugiés en France*, Presses Universitaires d'Aix-Marseille: Economica, 2nd edn., 1988.

Tolstoy, N., *Victims of Yalta*, London: Hodder & Stoughton, 1977; London: Corgi, rev. edn., 1979.

UK Ministry of Defence, *The Manual of the Law of Armed Conflict*, Oxford: Oxford University Press, 2005.

UNHCR *RefWorld*, DVD/CD-ROM, Geneva: UNHCR, 15th edn., 2006.

UNHCR, *The State of the World's Refugees: Human Displacement in the New Millennium*, Oxford: Oxford University Press, 2006.

UNHCR, *An Agenda for Protection*, Geneva: UNHCR, 3rd edn., 2003.

UNHCR, *The State of the World's Refugees*, London: Penguin, 1993.

UNHCR, *Handbook on Procedures and Criteria for Determining Refugee Status*, Geneva: UNHCR, 1979, re-edited 1992.

UNHCR, *A Mandate to Protect and Assist Refugees*, Geneva: UNHCR, 1971.

van Selm, J. & Cooper, B., *The New 'Boat People': Ensuring Safety and Determining Status*, Washington D.C.: Migration Policy Institute, 2005.

Verdirame, G. & Harrell-Bond, B., *Rights in Exile: Janus-Faced Humanitarianism*, New York, Oxford: Berghahn Books, 2005.

Vernant, J., *The Refugee in the Post-War World*, New Haven, New Jersey: Yale Press, 1953.

Veuthey, M., *Guérilla et droit humanitaire*, Geneva: Comité International de la Croix Rouge, 1983.

Vierdag, E. W., *The Concept of Discrimination in International Law*, The Hague: Nijhoff, 1973.

Vincent, M. & Refslund Sorensen, B., eds., *Caught between Borders: Response Strategies of the Internally Displaced*, London: Pluto Press, 2001.

von Sternberg, M. R., *The Grounds of Refugee Protection in the Context of International Human Rights and Humanitarian Law: Canadian and United States Case Law Compared*, The Hague: Martinus Nijhoff Publishers, 2002.

Weis, P., *Nationality and Statelessness in International Law*, Leyden: Sijthoff, 2nd edn., 1979.

Whiteman, M., *Digest of International Law*, Washington, D.C.: Department of State, Government Printing Office, 15 vols., 1962–73.

Woodbridge, G., *UNRRA: The History of the United Nations Relief and Rehabilitation Administration*, New York: Columbia Universiity Press, 3 vols., 1950.

Ziegler, K. S., *Fluchtverursachung als völkerrechtliches Delikt*, Berlin: Dunker & Humbolt, 2002.

ARTICLES, CHAPTERS, REPORTS, AND OCCASIONAL PAPERS

Ablard, T. & Novak, A., 'L'évolution du droit d'asile en Allemagne jusqu'à la réforme de 1993', 7 *IJRL* 260 (1995).

Achermann, A. & Gattiker, M., 'Safe Third Countries: European Developments', 7 *IJRL* 19 (1995).

Adelman, H., 'Humanitarian Intervention: The Case of the Kurds', 4 *IJRL* 4 (1992).

Aga Khan, Sadruddin, 'Legal problems relating to Refugees and Displaced Persons', Hague *Recueil* (1976-I) 287.

Akhavan, P., 'Punishing War Crimes in the Former Yugoslavia: A Critical Juncture for the New World Order', 15 *HRQ* 262 (1993).

Akram, S. M., 'Orientalism Revisited in Asylum and Refugee Claims', 12 *IJRL* 7 (2000).

Akram, S. M. & Rempel, T., 'Temporary Protection as an Instrument for Implementing the Right of Return of Palestinian Refugees', 22 *Boston University International Law Journal* 1 (2004).

Aleinikoff, T. A., 'Protected Characteristics and Social Perceptions: An Analysis of the Meaning of "Membership of a Particular Social Group",' in Feller, Türk, & Nicholson, *Refugee Protection in International Law*, 263 (2003).

Alexander, M., 'Refugee Status Determination Conducted by UNHCR', 11 *IJRL* 251 (1999).

Allain, J., 'The *Jus Cogens* Nature of *Non-Refoulement*', 13 *IJRL* 533 (2001).

Alleweldt, R., 'Protection Against Expulsion under Article 3 of the European Convention on Human Rights', 4 *EJIL* 360 (1993).

Alvarez, L. & Loucky, J., 'Inquiry and Advocacy: Attorney-Expert Collaboration in the Political Asylum Process', 11 *NAPA Bulletin* 43 (1992) (American Anthropological Association).

Andrysek, O., 'Gaps in International Protection and the Potential for Redress through Individual Complaints Procedures', 9 *IJRL* 392 (1997).

Anker, D., 'Rape in the Community as a Basis for Asylum: The Treatment of Women Refugees' Claims to Protection in Canada and the United States', 2 *Bender's Immigration Bulletin*, No. 12 (15 June 1997), Part I—Canada, 476–84; No. 15 (1 August 1997), Part II—The United States, 608–22.

Anker, D., 'Determining Asylum Claims in the United States—Summary Report of an Empirical Study of the Adjudication of Asylum Claims before the Immigration Court', 2 *IJRL* 252 (1990).

Anker, D., Fitzpatrick, J., & Shacknove, A., 'Crisis and Cure: A Reply to Hathaway/Neve and Schuck', 11 *Harvard Human Rights Journal* 295 (1998).

Anker, D., Gilbert, L., & Kelly, N., 'Women whose governments are unable or unwilling to provide reasonable protection from domestic violence may qualify as refugees under United States asylum law', 11 *Georgetown Immigration Law Journal* 709 (1997).

Anker, D., Blum, C. P., & Johnson, K. R., '*INS v. Zacarias:* Is There Anyone Out There?' 4 *IJRL* 266 (1992).

Arboleda, E., 'The Cartagena Declaration of 1984 and Its Similarities to the 1969 OAU Convention—A Comparative Perspective,' 7 *IJRL Special Issue—Summer 1995*, 87 (1995).

Arboleda, E., 'Refugee Definition in Africa and Latin America: The Lessons of Pragmatism,' 3 *IJRL* 185 (1991).

Arboleda, E. & Hoy, I., 'The Convention Refugee Definition in the West: Disharmony of Interpretation and Application', 5 *IJRL* 66 (1993).

Australia, Senate Legal and Constitutional References Committee *A Sanctuary under Review: An Examination of Australia's Refugee and Humanitarian Determination Processes*, Canberra: Commonwealth of Australia, Jun. 2000.

Australia, Senate Select Committee on Ministerial Discretion in Migration Matters, *Inquiry into Ministerial Discretion in Migration Matters*, Canberra: Commonwealth of Australia, 2004.

Avery, C., 'Refugee Status Decision-Making: The Systems of Ten Countries', 19 *Stanford Journal of International Law* 235 (1983).

Bach, R. L., 'Third Country Resettlement', in Loescher & Monahan, eds., *Refugees and International Relations* 313 (1989).

Bagambiire, D., 'Terrorism and Convention Refugee Status in Canadian Immigration Law: The Social Group Category according to *Ward v. Canada*', 5 *IJRL* 183 (1993).

Bakwesegha, C. J., 'The Role of the Organization of African Unity in Conflict Prevention, Management and Resolution', 7 *IJRL Special Issue—Summer 1995* 207.

Barak, A., 'A Judge on Judging: the Role of a Supreme Court in a Democracy', 116 *Harvard Law Review LR* 16 (2002).

Bari, S., 'Refugee Status Determination under the Comprehensive Plan of Action (CPA)', 4 *IJRL* 487 (1992).

Barnes, J., 'Expert Evidence—The Judicial Perception in Asylum and Human Rights Appeals', 16 *IJRL* 349 (2004).

Barsh, R. L., 'Measuring Human Rights: Problems of Methodology and Purpose', 15 *HRQ* 87 (1993).

Barutciski, M., 'Involuntary Repatriation when Refugee Protection is No Longer Necessary: Moving forward after the 48th Session of the Executive Committee', 10 *IJRL* 236 (1998).

Batchelor, C. A., 'Statelessness and the Problem of Resolving Nationality Claims', 10 *IJRL* 156 (1998).

Batchelor, C. A., 'Stateless Persons: Some Gaps in International Protection', 7 *IJRL* 232 (1995).

Beck, R. J., 'Britain and the 1933 Refugee Convention: National or State Sovereignty?' 11 *IJRL* 597 (1999).

Beyer, G. A., 'Human Rights Monitoring and the Failure of Early Warning: A Practitioner's View', 2 *IJRL* 56 (1990).

Beyer, G. A., 'Monitoring Root Causes of Refugee Flows and Early Warning: The Need for Substance', 2 *IJRL Special Issue—September 1990* 71.

Bhabha, J., 'Demography and Rights: Women, Children and Access to Asylum', 16 *IJRL* 227 (2004).

Bhabha, J. & Young, W., 'Not Adults in Miniature: Unaccompanied Child Asylum Seekers and The New U.S. Guidelines', 11 *IJRL* 84 (1999).

Bhatia, M., 'Repatriation under a Peace Process: Mandated Return in the Western Sahara', 15 *IJRL* 786 (2003).

Blay, S. K. N. & Zimmermann, A., 'Recent Changes in German Refugee Law: A Critical Assessment', 88 *AJIL* 361 (1994).

Blay, S. K. N. & Tsamenyi, B. M., 'Reservations and Declarations under the 1951 Convention and the 1967 Protocol relating to the Status of Refugees', 2 *IJRL* 527 (1990).

Blum, C. P., 'The Ninth Circuit and the Protection of Asylum Seekers since the Passage of the Refugee Act of 1980', 23 *San Diego L.R.* 327 (1986).

Bodart, S., 'Les réfugiés apolitiques: guerre civile et persécution de groupe au regard de la Convention de Genève', 7 *IJRL* 39 (1995).

Bouteillet-Paquet, D., 'Subsidiary Protection: Progress or Set-Back of Asylum Law in Europe? A Critical Analysis of the Legislation of the Member States of the European Union' in Bouteillet-Paquet, D., ed., *Subsidiary Protection of Refugees in the European Union: Comlementing the Geneva Convention?* (2002).

Bribosia, E. & Weyembergh, A., 'Extradition et asile: vers un espace judiciaire européen?' (1997) *Rev. belge dr.int.* 69.

Bronée, S. A., 'The History of the Comprehensive Plan of Action', 5 *IJRL* 534 (1993).

Brouwer, A. & Kumin, J., 'Interception and Asylum: When Migration Control and Human Rights Collide', 21 *Refuge* 6 (2003).

Bruin, R. & Wouters, K., 'Terrorism and the Non-Derogability of *Non-Refoulement*'. 15 *IJRL* 5 (2003).

Buzan, B., 'Negotiating by Consensus: Developments in Techniques at the United Nations Conference on the Law of the Sea', 75 *AJIL* 324 (1981).

Campiche, M.-P., 'Entrée illégale et séjour irrégulier des réfugiés et requérants d'asile: La pratique des cantons', *Asyl*, 1994/3, 51.

Cannon, A. J., 'Effective fact finding', *Civil Justice Quarterly* 2006 25(Jul), 327.

Carlier, J.-Y., 'La demande d'asile introduite par un mineur non accompagné', *RDDE*, 19–20 mai 1994, 94.

Castel, J. R., 'Rape, Sexual Assault and the Meaning of Persecution', 4 *IJRL* 39 (1992).

Cervenak, C. M., 'Promoting Inequality: Gender-Based Discrimination in UNRWA's Approach to Palestine Refugee Status', 16 *HRQ* 300 (1994).

Charlesworth, H., 'The Declaration on the Elimination of All Forms of Violence against Women', *ASIL Insight*, No. 3 (1994).

Chetail, V., 'Freedom of Movement and Transnational Migrations: A Human Rights Perspective', in Aleinikoff, T. A. & Chetail, V., eds., *Migration and International Legal Norms*, 55.

Chimni, B. S., 'The Meaning of Words and the Role of the UNHCR in Voluntary Repatriation', 5 *IJRL* 442 (1993).

Chimni, B. S., 'Perspectives on Voluntary Repatriation: A Critical Note', 3 *IJRL* 541 (1991).

Cholewinski, R., 'Enforced Destitution of Asylum Seekers in the United Kingdom: The Denial of Fundamental Human Rights', 10 *IJRL* 462 (1998).

Cohen, C. P., 'The Rights of the Child: Implications for Change in the Care and Protection of Refugee Children', 3 *IJRL* 675 (1991).

Cohen, J., 'Questions of Credibility: Omissions, Discrepancies and Errors of Recall in the Testimony of Asylum Seekers', 13 *IJRL* 293 (2001).

Cohn, I., 'The Convention on the Rights of the Child: What it Means for Children in War,' 3 *IJRL* 291 (1991).

Cole, C. V., 'Is there Safe Refuge in Canadian Missions Abroad?' 9 *IJRL* 654 (1997).

Coleman, N., '*Non-Refoulement* Revised: Renewed Review of the Status of the Principle of *Non-Refoulement* as Customary International Law', 5 *European Journal of Migration and Law* 23 (2003).

Corey, J. M., 'INS v Doherty: The Politics of Extradition, Deportation and Asylum', 16 *Maryland J.Int'l. L & Trade* 83 (1992).

Corliss, S., 'Asylum State Responsibility for the Hostile Acts of Foreign Exiles', 2 *IJRL* 181 (1990).

Costello, C., 'The *Bosphorus* Ruling of the European Court of Human Rights: Fundamental Rights and Blurred Boundaries in Europe', 6 *Human Rights Law Review* 87 (2006).

Costello, C., 'The Asylum Procedures Directive and the Proliferation of Safe Country Practices: Deterrence, Deflection and the Dismantling of International Protection', 7 *European Journal of Migration and Law* 35 (2005).

Crawford, J. & Hyndman, P., 'Three Heresies in the Application of the Refugee Convention', 1 *IJRL* 152 (1989).

Crock, M., 'In the Wake of the *Tampa*: Conflicting Visions of International Refugee Law in the Management of Refugee Flows', 12 *Pacific Rim and Policy Journal* 49 (2003).

Crowley, J., 'Differential Free Movement and the Sociology of the "Internal Border"', in Guild, & Harlow, C., eds., *Implementing Amsterdam: Immigration and Asylum Rights in EC Law*, 21.

Cuellar, R., García-Sayán, D., Montaño, J., Diegues, M. & Valladares Lanza, L., 'Refugee and Related Developments in Latin America: The Challenges Ahead', 3 *IJRL* 482 (1991).

D'Alotto, A. & Garretón, R., 'Developments in Latin America: Some Further Thoughts', 3 *IJRL* 499 (1991).

Daley, K. & Kelley, N., 'Particular Social Group: A Human Rights Based Approach in Canadian Jurisprudence', 12 *IJRL* 148 (2000).

Dauvergne, C., 'Chinese Fleeing Sterilisation: Australia's Response against a Canadian Background', 10 *IJRL* 77 (1998).

Degni-Ségui, R., 'Rapports sur la situation des droits de l'homme au Rwanda du 28 juin 1994 et du 12 août 1994', 13 *RSQ*, Nos. 2 & 3, 116 (1994).

Deng, F. M., 'The International Protection of the Internally Displaced', 7 *IJRL Special Issue—Summer 1995*, 74.

Dignam, Q., 'The Burden of Proof: Torture and Testimony in the Determination of Refugee Status in Australia', 4 *IJRL* 343 (1992).

Dimitrichev, T. F., 'Conceptual Approaches to Early Warning: Mechanisms and Methods—A View from the United Nations', 3 *IJRL* 264 (1991).

Donnelly, J. & Howard, R. E., 'Assessing Nations Human Rights Performance: A Theoretical Framework', 10 *HRQ* 214 (1988).

Dugard, J. & van den Wyngaert, C., 'Reconciling Extradition with Human Rights', 92 *AJIL* 187 (1998).

Dunstan, R., 'United Kingdom: Breaches of Article 31 of the 1951 Refugee Convention', 10 *IJRL* 205 (1998).

Dupuy, P. M., 'Reviewing the Difficulties of Codification: On Ago's Classification of Obligations of Means and Obligations of Result in relation to State Responsibility', 10 *EJIL* 371 (1999).

Durieux, J.-F. & Hurwitz, A., 'How Many Is Too Many? African and European Legal Responses to Mass Influxes and Refugees', 47 *German Yearbook of International Law* 105 (2004).

Durieux, J.-F. & McAdam, J., '*Non-Refoulement* through Time: The Case for a Derogation Clause to the Refugee Convention in Mass Influx Emergencies', 16 *IJRL* 4 (2004).

Edwards, A., 'Human Rights, Refugees, and the Right "to Enjoy" Asylum', 17 *IJRL* 293 (2005).

Eggleston, Sir Richard, 'What is Wrong with the Adversary System?' 49 *Australian Law Journal* 428 (1975).

Eggleston, Sir Richard, 'Is Your Cross-Examination Really Necessary?' *Proceedings of the Medico-Legal Society of Victoria*, vol. IX, 84 (1961).

Einarsen, T., 'The European Convention on Human Rights and the Notion of an Implied Right to Asylum', 2 *IJRL* 361 (1990).

Epps, V., 'The Validity of the Political Offence Exception in Extradition Treaties in Anglo-American Jurisprudence', 20 *Harv. ILJ* 61 (1979).

Espiell, H. G., Picado, S. & Lanza, L. V., 'Principles and Criteria for the Protection of and Assistance to Central American Refugees, Returnees and Displaced Persons in Central America', 2 *IJRL* 83 (1990).

European Council on Refugees and Exiles (ECRE), 'The Kosovo Refugee Crisis: ECRE's Observations on the Independent Evaluation of UNHCR's Emergency Preparedness and Response': <http://www.ecre.org/statements/koseval.shtml>.

Fabbricotti, A., 'The Concept of Inhuman or Degrading Treatment in International Law and its Application in Asylum Cases', 10 *IJRL* 637 (1998).

Farmer, A., 'Refugee Responses, State-Like Behavior, and Accountability for Human Rights Violations: A Case Study of Sexual Violence in Guinea's Refugee Camps', 9 *Yale Human Rights & Development Law Journal* 44 (2006).

Fazel, M. & Silove, D., 'Detention of Refugees', *British Medical Journal*, 2006, vol. 332, 251–2, 4 Feb. 2006.

Federal Ministry of the Interior, 'Recent Developments in the German Law on Asylum and Aliens,' 6 *IJRL* 265 (1994).

Fischel de Andrade, J. H., 'Regional Policy Approaches and Harmonization: A Latin American Perspective', 10 *IJRL* 389 (1998).

Fisher Williams, J., 'Denationalization', 8 *BYIL* 45 (1927).

Fitzmaurice, G., 'The Law and Procedure of the International Court of Justice, 1951–54: General Principles and Sources of Law', 27 *BYIL* 1 (1950).

Fitzpatrick, J., 'Harmonized Subsidiary Protection in the European Union—A View from the United States' in Bouteillet-Paquet, D., ed., *Subsidiary Protection of Refugees in the European Union: Complementing the Geneva Convention?*, 126 (2002).

Fitzpatrick, J., 'Human Rights and Forced Displacement: Converging Standards' in Bayefsky & Fitzpatrick, eds., *Human Rights and Forced Displacement*, 8 (2000).

Fitzpatrick, J., 'Temporary Protection of Refugees: Elements of a Formalized Regime', 94 *AJIL* 279 (2000).

Fitzpatrick, J., 'The End of Protection: Legal Standards for Cessation of Refugee Status and Withdrawal of Temporary Protection', 13 *Georgetown Immigration Law Journal* 343 (1999).

Fitzpatrick, J., 'The International Dimension of U.S. Refugee Law', 15 *Berkeley Journal of International Law* 1 (1997).

Fitzpatrick, J., 'Revitalizing the 1951 Refugee Convention', 9 *Harvard Human Rights Journal* 229 (1996).

Fitzpatrick, J. & Bonoan, R., 'Cessation of Refugee Protection', in Feller, Türk, & Nicholson, *Refugee Protection in International Law*, 491 (2003).

Fong, Chooi, 'Some Legal Aspects of the Search for Admission into other States of Persons leaving the Indo-Chinese Peninsular in Small Boats', 52 *BYIL* 53 (1982).

Fonteyne, J.-P., 'Burden-Sharing: An Analysis of the Nature and Function of International Solidarity in Cases of Mass Influx of Refugees', 8 *Aust. YB Int'l Law* 162 (1983).

Fortin, A., 'The Meaning of "Protection" in the Refugee Definition', 12 *IJRL* 548 (2001).

Frelick, B., ' "Abundantly Clear": Refoulement', 19 *Georgetown Immigration Law Journal* 245 (2005).

Gallagher, M. S., 'Soldier Boy Bad: Child Soldiers, Culture and Bars to Asylum', 13 *IJRL* 310 (2001).

Garcia Marquez, G., 'The Vietnam Wars', *Rolling Stone*, May 1980.

Gibney, M., 'A "Well-founded Fear" of Persecution', 10 *HRQ* 109 (1988).

Gil-Bazo, M.-T., 'Refugee Status and Subsidiary Protection under EC Law. The EC Qualification Directive and the Right to be granted Asylum', in Baldaccini, A., Guild, E., & Toner, H., eds., *Whose Freedom, Security and Justice? EU Immigration and Asylum Law after 1999*, Oxford: Hart Publishing, 2007.

Gilbert, G., 'Is Europe Living Up to Its Obligations to Refugees?' 15 *EJIL* 963 (2004).

Gilbert, G., 'Current Issues in the Application of the Exclusion Clauses', in Feller, Türk, & Nicholson, *Refugee Protection in International Law*, 425 (2003).

Gold, M. E., 'Non-extradition for Political Offences: the Communist Perspective', 11 *Harv. ILJ* 191 (1970).

Good, A., 'Persecution for Reasons of Religion under the 1951 Refugee Convention: An Anthropological Approach', 2006 Elizabeth Colson Lecture, Refugee Studies Centre, Oxford.

Good, A., 'Expert Evidence in Asylum and Human Rights' Appeals—An Expert's View', 16 *IJRL* 358 (2004).

Goodwin-Gill, G. S., 'International Protection and Assistance for Refugees and the Displaced: Institutional Challenges and United Nations Reform', Refugee Studies Centre, University of Oxford, May 2006: <http://refugeelaw.geh.ox.ac.uk>.

Goodwin-Gill, G. S., 'State Responsibility and the "Good Faith" Obligation in International Law', in Fitzmaurice, M. & Sarooshi, D., eds., *Issues of State Responsibility before International Judicial Institutions*, Oxford: Hart Publishing, 2004, 120.

Goodwin-Gill, G. S., 'Article 31 of the 1951 Convention relating to the Status of Refugees: Non-penalization, Detention, and Protection', in Feller, Türk, & Nicholson, eds., *Refugee Protection in International Law*, 185 (2003).

Goodwin-Gill, G. S., 'Refugees and Responsibility in the Twenty-First Century: More Lessons from the South Pacific', 12 *Pacific Rim Law & Policy Journal* 23 (2003).

Goodwin-Gill, G. S., 'The Individual Refugee, the 1951 Convention and the Treaty of Amsterdam', in Guild, E. & Harlow, C., eds., *Implementing Amsterdam: Immigration and Asylum Rights in EC Law*, 141.

Goodwin-Gill, G. S., 'Note on paragraph 20 of General Assembly resolution 55/74', 13 *IJRL* 255 (2001).

Goodwin-Gill, G. S., 'Comment: Refugee Status and "Good Faith"', 12 *IJRL* 663 (2000).

Goodwin-Gill, G. S., 'UNHCR and Internal Displacement: Stepping into a Legal and Political Minefield', in US Committee for Refugees, *World Refugee Survey 2000*, Washington, D.C., (2000), 26–31.

Goodwin-Gill, G. S., 'Crimes in International Law: Obligations *Erga Omnes* and the Duty to Prosecute', in Goodwin-Gill, G. S. & Talmon, S., eds., *The Reality of International Law: Essays in Honour of Ian Brownlie*, 199 (1999).

Goodwin-Gill, G. S., 'Judicial Reasoning and "Social Group" after *Islam* and *Shah*', 11 *IJRL* 537 (1999).

Goodwin-Gill, G. S., 'Refugee Identity and Protection's Fading Prospect', in Nicholson & Twomey, eds., *Refugee Rights and Realities*, 220 (1999).

Goodwin-Gill, G. S., 'Different Types of Forced Migration Movements as an International and National Problem', in Rystad, G., ed., *The Uprooted: Forced Migration as an International Problem in the Post-War Era*, 15 (1990).

Goodwin-Gill, G. S. 'Voluntary Repatriation: Legal and Policy Issues', in Loescher & Monahan, eds., *Refugees and International Relations*, 255 (1989).

Goodwin-Gill, G. S., 'International Law and Human Rights: Trends concerning International Migrants and Refugees', 23 *Int. Mig. Rev.* 526 (1989).

Goodwin-Gill, G. S., 'The Language of Protection,' 1 *IJRL* 6 (1989).

Goodwin-Gill, G. S., 'Refugees: The Functions and Limits of the Existing Protection System,' in Nash, A., ed., *Human Rights and the Protection of Refugees under International Law*, 149 (1988).

Goodwin-Gill, G. S., 'International Law and the detention of refugees and asylum-seekers', 20 *Int. Mig. Rev.* 193 (1986).

Goodwin-Gill, G. S., '*Non-Refoulement* and the New Asylum Seekers', 26 *Virginia JIL* 897 (1986).

Goodwin-Gill, G. S. & Husain, R., 'Diplomatic Assurances and Deportation', JUSTICE/Sweet & Maxwell Conference on Counter-Terrorism and Human Rights, London, 28 Jun. 2005.

Goodwin-Gill, G. S. & Hurwitz, A., 'Memorandum' in Minutes of Evidence Taken before the EU Committee (Sub-Committee E) (10 Apr. 2002), in House of Lords Select Committee on the EU, 'Defining Refugee Status and Those in Need of International Protection', The Stationery Office, London, 2002, Oral Evidence Section, 2.

Goodwin-Gill, G. S. & Kumin, J., 'Refugees in Limbo and Canada's International Obligations', Toronto: Caledon Institute of Social Policy, Sept. 2000.

Gorlick, B., 'The Convention and the Committee against Torture: A Complementary Protection Regime for Refugees', 11 *IJRL* 479 (1999).

Gorman, R., 'Poets, Playwrights, and the Politics of Exile and Asylum in Ancient Greece and Rome', 6 *IJRL* 402 (1994).

Gorman, R., 'Revenge and Reconciliation: Shakespearean Models of Exile and Banishment', 2 *IJRL* 211 (1990).

Gottwald, M., 'Asylum Claims and Drug Offences: The Seriousness Threshold of Article 1F(b) of the 1951 Convention relating to the Status of Refugees and the UN Drug Conventions', 18 *IJRL* 81 (2006).

Grahl-Madsen, A., 'The European Tradition of Asylum and the Development of Refugee Law' in Macalister-Smith, & Alfredsson, *The Land Beyond: Collected Essays on Refugee Law and Policy by Atle Grahl-Madsen*, (2001), 34.

Grahl-Madsen, A., 'Protection of Refugees by their Country of Origin', 11 *Yale J.I.L.* 362 (1986).

Grant, S., 'Protection Mechanisms and the Yugoslav Crisis', *Interights Bulletin*, 8:1 (1994).

Grief, N., 'British Quakers, the Peace Tax and International Law', in Janis, M. W. & Evans, eds., *Religion and International Law*, (1999), 339.

Gros Espiell, H., Picado, S., & Valladares Lanza, L., 'Principles and Criteria for the Protection of and Assistance to Central American Refugees, Returnees and Displaced Persons in Central America', 2 *IJRL* 83 (1990).

Guedalla, V., 'Representing unaccompanied refugee children in the asylum process', *Childright*, Dec. 1994, No. 112.

Guest, I., 'The United Nations, the UNHCR, and Refugee Protection—A Non-Specialist Analysis', 3 *IJRL* 585 (1991).

Guild, E., 'Seeking Asylum: Storm Clouds between International Commitments and EU Legislative Measures', 29 *European Law Review* 198 (2004).

Hailbronner, K., 'Comments On: The Right to Leave, the Right to Return and the Question of a Right to Remain', in Gowlland-Debbas, ed., *The Problem of Refugees in the Light of Contemporary International Law Issues*, 112 (1996).

Hailbronner, K., 'Rechtsfragen der Aufnahme von "Gewaltflüchtlingen" in Westeuropa— am Beispiel Jugoslawien', *Schweizerische Zeitschrift für internationales und europäisches Recht* 517 (1993).

Hailbronner, K., 'The Right to Asylum and the Future of Asylum Procedures in the European Community', 2 *IJRL* 341 (1990).

Hailbronner, K., '*Non-Refoulement* and "Humanitarian" Refugees: Customary International Law or Wishful Legal Thinking?', 26 *Virginia JIL* 857 (1986); also published in Martin, D., *The New Asylum-Seekers* (1988).

Haines, R., 'Gender-related persecution', in Feller, Türk, & Nicholson, eds., *Refugee Protection in International Law*, 319 (2003).

Hamerslag, R. J., 'The Schiphol Refugee Centre Case,' 1 *IJRL* 395 (1989).

Hampson, F. J., 'The Concept of an "Arguable Claim" under Article 13 of the European Convention on Human Rights', 39 *ICLQ* 891 (1990).

Happold, M., 'Excluding Children from Refugee Status: Child Soldiers and Article 1F of the Refugee Convention', 17 *American University International Law Review* 1131 (2002).

Hassan, P., 'The word "arbitrary" as used in the Universal Declaration of Human Rights: "Illegal or Unjust"?' 10 *Harv. ILJ* 225 (1969).

Hathaway, J. C., 'What's in a Label?', 5 *EJIL* 1, (2003).

Hathaway, J. C., 'Is Refugee Status Really Elitist? An Answer to the Ethical Challenge', in Carlier & Vanheule, eds., *Europe and Refugees: A Challenge?* (1997).

Hathaway, J. C., 'The Meaning of Voluntary Repatriation', 9 *IJRL* 551 (1997).

Hathaway, J., 'A Reconsideration of the Underlying Premise of Refugee Law', 31 *Harv. ILJ* 129 (1990).

Hathaway, J. C., 'The Evolution of Refugee Status in International Law: 1920–1950', 33 *ICLQ* 348 (1984).

Hathaway, J. C. & Hicks, W. S., 'Is there a Subjective Element in the Refugee Convention's Requirement of "Well-Founded Fear"?', 26 *Michigan Journal of International Law* 505 (2005).

Hathaway, J. C. & Neve, R. A., 'Fundamental Justice and the Deflection of Refugees from Canada', 34 *Osgoode Hall Law Journal* 213 (1996).

Heffernan, L., 'A Comparative View of Individual Petition Procedures under the European Convention on Human Rights and the International Covenant on Civil and Political Rights', 19 *HRQ* 78 (1997).

Helton, A. C., 'Refugee Determination under the Comprehensive Plan of Action; Overview and Assessment', 5 *IJRL* 544 (1993).

Helton, A. C., 'Persecution on Account of Membership in a Social Group as a Basis for Refugee Status', 15 *Columbia Human Rights Law Review* 39 (1983).

Helton, A. C. & Münker, J., 'Religion and Persecution: Should the United States provide Refuge to German Scientologists?' 11 *IJRL* 310 (1999).

Heyman, M. G., 'Domestic Violence and Asylum: Toward a Working Model of Affirmative State Obligations', 17 *IJRL* 729 (2005).

Higgins, R., 'The United Nations and Former Yugoslavia', 69 *International Affairs* 3 (1993).

Higgins, R., 'Derogations under Human Rights Treaties', 48 *BYIL* 281 (1976–77).

Hofmann, R., 'Voluntary Repatriation and UNHCR', 44 *ZaöRV* 327 (1984).

Holborn, L. W., 'The Legal Status of Political Refugees, 1920–1938', 32 *AJIL* 680 (1938).

Houle, F., 'Le fonctionnement du régime de preuve libre dans un système non-expert: le traitement symptomatique des preuves par la Section de la protection des réfugiés', *Revue juridique Thémis* 263 (2004).

Houle, F., 'The Credibility and Authoritativeness of Documentary Information in Determining Refugee Status: The Canadian Experience', 6 *IJRL* 6 (1994).

Hurwitz, A., 'The 1990 Dublin Convention: A Comprehensive Assessment', 11 *IJRL* 646 (1999).

Hyndman, J., & Nylund, B. V., 'UNHCR and the Status of Prima Facie Refugees in Kenya', 10 *IJRL* 21 (1998).

International Committee of the Red Cross, 'Internally Displaced Persons: The Mandate and Role of the International Committee of the Red Cross', 838 *International Review of the Red Cross* 491 (2000).

Jackman, B., 'Well-Founded Fear of Persecution and Other Standards of Decision-Making: A North American Perspective', in Bhabha & Coll, *Asylum Law and Practice in Europe and North America* 44 (1992).

Jackson, I. C., 'The 1951 Convention relating to Status of Refugees: A Universal Basis for Protection', 3 *IJRL* 403 (1991).

Jaeger, G., 'Les Nations Unies et les réfugiés', *Revue belge de Droit international*, 1989/1, 18.

Jennings, R. Y., 'Some International Law Aspects of the Refugee Question', 20 *BYIL* 98, (1939).

Johnsson, A. B., 'The International Protection of Women Refugees', 1 *IJRL* 221 (1989).

Johnson, D. H. N., 'Refugees, Departees and Illegal Migrants', 9 *Sydney L.R.* 11 (1979–82).

Joly, D., 'The Porous Dam: European Harmonization on Asylum in the Nineties', 6 *IJRL* 159 (1994).

Julien-Laferrière, F., 'Droit d'asile et politique d'asile en France', *Asyl*, 1993/4, 75.

Kagan, M., 'The Beleaguered Gatekeeper: Protection Challenges posed by UNHCR Refugee Status Determination', 18 *IJRL* 1 (2006).

Kagan, M. & Johnson, W. P., 'Persecution in the Fog of War: The House of Lords' Decision in *Adan*', 23 *Michigan Journal of International Law* 247 (2002).

Kälin, W., 'Supervising the 1951 Convention Relating to the Status of Refugees: Article 35 and Beyond', in Feller, Türk, & Nicholson, *Refugee Protection in International Law* (2003), 613.

Kälin, W., 'Flight in times of war', *International Review of the Red Cross*, No. 843, 629 (2001).

Kälin, W., 'Non-State Agents of Persecution and the Inability of the State to Protect', 15 *Georgetown Immigration Law Journal* 415 (2001).

Kälin, W., 'The Guiding Principles on Internal Displacement: Introduction', 10 *IJRL* 557, (1998).

Kälin, W., 'The Legal Condition of Refugees in Switzerland,' 24 *Swiss Reports presented at the XIVth International Congress of Comparative Law* 57 (1994).

Kälin, W., 'Refugees and Civil Wars: Only a Matter of Interpretation?' 3 *IJRL* 435 (1991).

Kälin, W., Comment on Bundesverfassungsgericht (BRD) v. 10.7.1989—2 BvR 502/86 u.a. (EuGRZ 1989, S.444–455): *Asyl*, 1990/4, 13.

Kälin, W., 'Troubled Communication: Cross-Cultural Misunderstandings in the Asylum Hearing', 20 *Int. Mig. Rev.* 230 (1986).

Kattan, V., 'The Nationality of Denationalized Palestinians', 74 *Nordic Journal of International Law* 67 (2005).

Kelley, N., 'Internal Flight/Relocation/Protection Alternative: Is it Reasonable?' 14 *IJRL* 4 (2002).

Kelley, N., 'The Convention Refugee Definition and Gender-Based Persecution: A Decade's Progress', 13 *IJRL* 559 (2001).

Kelley, N., 'Report on the International Consultation on Refugee Women, held in Geneva, 15–19 November 1988', 1 *IJRL* 233 (1989).

Kelly, N., 'Guidelines for Women's Asylum Claims', 6 *IJRL* 517 (1994).

Kennedy, D., 'International Refugee Protection', 8 *HRQ* 1 (1986).

Kirişçi, K., 'Asylum Seekers and Human Rights in Turkey', 10 *Neth.Q.H.R.* 447 (1992).

Kiss, A., 'La convention européenne et la clause de la nation la plus favorisée', *Ann. Fr.* 478 (1957).

Kjaerum, M., 'Temporary Protection in Europe in the 1990s', 6 *IJRL* 444 (1994).

Kjær, K. U., 'The Abolition of the Danish *de facto* Concept', 15 *IJRL* 254 (2003).

Klug, A., 'Harmonization of Asylum in the European Union—Emergence of an EU Refugee System?' 47 *German Yearbook of International Law* 594 (2004).

Krill, F., 'The ICRC's Policy on Refugees and Internally Displaced Civilians', *International Review of the Red Cross*, No. 843, 607 (2001).

Lahav, G., 'Immigration and the State: The Devolution and Privatisation of Immigration Control in the EU', 24 *Journal of Ethnic and Migration Studies* 675 (1998).

Lambert, H., 'The EU Asylum Qualification Directive, Its Impact on the Jurisprudence of the United Kingdom and International Law', 55 *ICLQ* 161 (2006).

Lambert, H., 'The European Convention on Human Rights and the Protection of Refugees: Limits and Opportunities', 24 *RSQ* 39 (2005).

Lambert, H., 'Protection against *Refoulement* from Europe: Human Rights Law comes to the Rescue', 48 *ICLQ* 515 (1999).

Lambert, H., 'The European Court of Human Rights and the Right of Refugees and Other Persons in Need of Protection to Family Reunion', 11 *IJRL* 427 (1999).

Landgren, K., 'Safety Zones and International Protection: A Dark Grey Area', 7 *IJRL* 436 (1995).

Lauterpacht, E. & Bethlehem, D., 'The Scope and Content of the Principle of *Non-Refoulement*: Opinion' in Feller, Türk, & Nicholson, eds., *Refugee Protection in International Law*, 87.

Lauterpacht, H., 'The Universal Declaration of Human Rights', 25 *BYBIL* 354 (1948).

Lauterpacht, H., 'The Law of Nations and the Punishment of War Crimes', 21 *BYIL* 58 (1944).

Lautze, S., Jones, B., & Duffield, M., 'Strategic Humanitarian Co-ordination in the Great Lakes Region, 1996–1997: An Independent Assessment', Policy, Information and Advocacy Division, Office for the Co-ordination of Humanitarian Affairs, United Nations, New York, March 1998.

Lawand, K., 'The Right to Return of Palestinians in International Law', 8 *IJRL* 532 (1996).

Lawyers Committee for Human Rights 'Review of States' Procedures and Practices relating to Detention of Asylum Seekers', (Sept. 2002).

Lee, L. T., 'The Declaration of Principles of International Law on Compensation to Refugees: Its Significance and Implications', 6 *JRS* 65 (1993).

Lee, L. T., 'The Right to Compensation: Refugees and Countries of Asylum', 80 *AJIL* 532 (1986).

Legomsky, S. H., 'Secondary Refugee Movements and the Return of Asylum Seekers to Third Countries: The Meaning of Effective Protection', 15 *IJRL* 567 (2003).

Legomsky, S. H., 'The Detention of Aliens: Theories, Rules, and Discretion', 30 *Inter-American Law Review* 531 (1999).

Legomsky, S. H., 'Political Asylum and the Theory of Judicial Review', 73 *Minnesota L.R.* 1205 (1989).

Lewis, C., 'UNHCR's Contribution to the Development of International Refugee Law: Its Foundations and Evolution', 17 *IJRL* 67 (2005).

Liddy, J., 'The Concept of Family Life under the ECHR' [1998] *European HR L Rev* 15.

Lillich, R. B. 'Notes and Comments: The *Soering* Case', 85 *AJIL* 128 (1991).

Lillich, R. B., 'Civil Rights', in Meron, T., ed., *Human Rights in International Law* 15 (1984).

Luca, D., 'Questioning Temporary Protection, together with a Selected Bibliography on Temporary Refuge/Temporary Protection', 6 *IJRL* 535 (1994).

Luca, D., 'La notion de "solution" au problème des réfugiés', *Revue de droit international*, janv–mars 1987, 1.

Mahmoud, S., 'The Schengen Information System: An Inequitable Data Protection Regime', 7 *IJRL* 179 (1995).

Mandal, R., 'Protection Mechanisms outside of the 1951 Convention ("Complementary Protection")', UNHCR Legal and Protection Policy Research Series, PPLA/2005/02 (Jun. 2005).

Mangala Munuma, J., 'Le partage de la charge des réfugiés quand l'urgence s'impose', *Revue du droit des étrangers*, 2001, n° 113, 183.

Martin, D. A., 'Reforming Asylum Adjudication: On Navigating the Coast of Bohemia', 138 *University of Pennsylvania Law Review* 1247 (1990).

Martin, D. A., 'Effects of International Law on Migration Policy and Practice', 23 *Int. Mig. Rev.* 547 (1989).

Mathew, P., 'Australian Refugee Protection in the Wake of the Tampa', 96 *AJIL* 661, (2002).

Marx, R., 'The Criteria of Applying the "Internal Flight Alternative" Test in National Refugee Status Determination Procedures', 14 *IJRL* 179 (2002).

Mawani, N., 'Introduction to the Immigration and Refugee Board of Canada Guidelines on Gender-Related Persecution', 5 *IJRL* 240 (1993).

McAdam, J., 'The Refugee Convention as a Rights Blueprint for Persons in Need of International Protection Status', UNHCR, *New Issues in Refugee Research*, Research Paper No. 125, Geneva 2006.

McAdam, J., 'Seeking Asylum under the Convention on the Rights of the Child: A Case for Complementary Protection', 14 *International Journal of Children's Rights* 251 (2006).

McAdam, J., 'Complementary Protection and Beyond: How States Deal with Human Rights Protection', UNHCR, *New Issues in Refugee Research*, Working Paper No. 118, Geneva, August 2005.

McAdam, J., 'The European Union Qualification Directive: The Creation of a Subsidiary Protection Regime', 17 *IJRL* 461 (2005).

McAdam, J., 'Alternative Asylum Mechanisms: The Convention against Torture and Other Cruel, Inhuman or Degrading Treatment or Punishment', 27 *International Journal of Law and Psychiatry* 627 (2004).

McAllister, D. M., 'Refugees and Public Access to Immigration Hearings in Canada: A Clash of Constitutional Values', 2 *IJRL* 562 (1990).

McCallin, M., 'Living in Detention: A Review of the Psychological Well-Being of Vietnamese Children in the Hong Kong Detention Centres', Geneva: International Catholic Child Bureau, 1992.

McCallin, M., 'The Convention on the Rights of the Child: An Instrument to Address the Psychosocial Needs of Refugee Children', 2 *IJRL Special Issue—September 1990*, 82.

McCourt, K. & Lambert, M., 'Interpretation of the Definition of Torture or Cruel, Inhuman or Degrading Treatment or Punishment in the Light of European and International Case Law', OMCT Europe, 30 Oct. 2004.

McKean, W. A., 'The Meaning of Discrimination in International and Municipal Law', 44 *BYIL* 177 (1970).

McLeod, M., 'Legal Protection of Refugee Children separated from their Parents: Selected Issues', 27 *International Migration* 295 (1989).

McNair, Lord, 'Extradition and Exterritorial Asylum', 28 *BYIL* 172 (1951).

Médecins sans Frontières/Artsen zonder Grenzen, 'Awareness Survey: Rohingya Refugee Camps, Cox's Bazar District, Bangladesh, 15 March 1995', The Netherlands, 1995.

Meindersma, C., 'Population Exchanges: International Law and State Pratice—Part 1', 9 *IJRL* 335; 'Part 2', 9 *IJRL* 613 (1997).

Melander, G., 'Refugee Policy Options—Protection or Assistance', in Rystad, G., ed., *The Uprooted: Forced Migration as an International Problem in the Post-War Era*, 137, (1990).

Melander, G., 'The Two Refugee Definitions', Raoul Wallenberg Institute of Human Rights and Humanitarian Law, *Report No. 4* (Lund 1987).

Mendiluce, J. M., 'War and disaster in the former Yugoslavia: The limits of humanitarian Action,' in United States Committee on Refugees, *World Refugee Survey—1994*, 16.

Meron, T., 'On a Hierarchy of International Human Rights', 80 *AJIL* 1 (1987).

Merrills, J. G., 'Interim Measures of Protection in the Recent Jurisprudence of the International Court of Justice', 44 *ICLQ* 90 (1995).

Messina, C., 'Refugee definitions in the countries of the Commonwealth of Independent States', in Nicholson & Twomey, eds., *Refugee Rights and Realities*, 136.

Milner, D., 'Exemption from Cessation of Refugee Status in the Second Sentence of Article 1C(5)/(6) of the 1951 Refugee Convention', 16 *IJRL* 91 (2004)

Miranda, C. O., 'Haiti and the United States during the 1980s and 1990s: Refugees, Immigration, and Foreign Policy', 32 *San Diego Law Review* 680 (1995).

Mirdal, G. M., 'The Interpreter in Cross-Cultural Therapy', 26 *Int. Mig.* 327 (1988).

Mole, N., 'Asylum and the European Convention on Human Rights', Council of Europe H/Inf (2002).

Mooney, E. D., 'In-country protection: out of bounds for UNHCR?', in Nicholson & Twomey, *Refugee Rights and Realities* 200, (1999).

Mooney, E. D., 'Presence, *ergo* Protection? UNPROFOR, UNHCR and the ICRC in Croatia and Bosnia and Herzegovina', 7 *IJRL* 407 (1995).

Moore, J., 'From Nation State to Failed State: International Protection from Human Rights Abuses by Non-State Agents', 31 *Columbia Human Rights Law Review* 81 (1999).

Morgenstern, F., 'The Right of Asylum', 26 *BYIL* 327 (1949).

Morin, J.-Y., 'La zone de peche exclusive du Canada', 2 *Can YBIL* 77 (1967).

Morris, N., 'Refugees: Facing Crisis in the 1990s—A Personal View from within UNHCR', 2 *IJRL Special Issue—September 1990*, 38.

Morrison, J., and Crosland, B., 'The Trafficking and Smuggling of Refugees: The End Game in European Asylum Policy', *New Issues in Refugee Research*, Working Paper No. 39, (UNHCR Geneva, 2001).

Mowbray, A., 'A New Strasbourg Approach to the Legal Consequences of Interim Measures', 5 *Human Rights Law Review* 377 (2005).

Mowbray, A., 'Duties of Investigation under the European Convention on Human Rights', 51 *ICLQ* 437(2002).

Mtango, E.-E., 'Military and Armed Attacks on Refugee Camps', in Loescher & Monahan, eds., *Refugees and International Relations* (1989), 87.

Musalo, K., 'Claims for Protection based on Religion or Belief', 16 *IJRL* 165 (2004).

Musalo, K., 'Revisiting Social Group and Nexus in Gender Asylum Claims: A Unifying Rationale for Evolving Jurisprudence', 52 *De Paul Law Review* 777 (2003).

Musalo, K., 'Irreconcilable Differences? Divorcing Refugee Protections from Human Rights Norms', 15 *Michigan Journal of International Law* 1179 (1994).

Mushkat, R., 'Implementation of the CPA in Hong Kong: Compatibility with International Standards?', 5 *IJRL* 559 (1993).

Mushkat, R., 'Hong Kong as a Country of Temporary Refuge: An Interim Analysis', 12 *Hong Kong LJ* 157 (1982).

Nagy, B., 'Asylum Seekers and Refugees: Hungarian Dilemmas,' 34 *Acta Juridica Hungarica*, No. 1–2, 27 (1992).

Nagy, B., 'Before or After the Wave? The Adequacy of the New Hungarian Refugee Law', 3 *IJRL* 529 (1991).

Noll, G., 'Seeking Asylum at Embassies: A Right to Entry under International Law?', 17 *IJRL* 542 (2005).

Noll, G., 'Visions of the Exceptional: Legal and Theoretical Issues Raised by Transit Processing Centres and Protection Zones', 5 *EJML* 303 (2003).

Noll, G., 'Prisoners' Dilemma in Fortress Europe: On the Prospects for Equitable Burden-Sharing in the European Union', 40 *German Yearbook of International Law* 405 (1997).

Note, 'The Indefinite Detention of Excluded Aliens: Statutory and Constitutional Justifications and Limitations', 82 *Michigan Law Review* 61 (1983).

O'Donnell, D., 'Resettlement or Repatriation: Screened-out Vietnamese Child Asylum Seekers and the Convention on the Rights of the Child', 6 *IJRL* 382 (1994).

OAU/UNHCR, 'The Addis Ababa Symposium 1994,' 7 *IJRL Special Issu—Summer 1995* (1995).

Okoth-Obbo, G., 'Thirty Years On: A Legal Review of the 1969 OAU Refugee Convention Governing the Specific Aspects of Refugee Problems in Africa', 20 *RSQ* 79 (2001).

Oliver, P., 'The French Constitution and the Treaty of Maastricht', 43 *ICLQ* 1 (1994).

Oloka-Onyango, J., 'The Place and Role of the OAU Bureau for Refugees in the African Refugee Crisis', 6 *IJRL* 34 (1994).

Oloka-Onyango, J., 'Human Rights, the OAU Convention and the Refugee Crisis in Africa', 3 *IJRL* 453 (1991).

Oosterveld, V. L., 'The Canadian Guidelines on Gender-Related Persecution: An Evaluation', 8 *IJRL* 569 (1996).

Osborne, M., 'The Indochinese Refugees: Causes and Effects', *International Affairs*, 1980, 37.

Pallis, M., 'Obligations of States towards Asylum Seekers at Sea: Interactions and Conflicts between Legal Regimes', 14 *IJRL* 329 (2002).

Pejic, J., 'Minority Rights in International Law', 19 *HRQ* 666 (1997).

Perluss, D. & Hartman, J. F., 'Temporary Refuge: Emergence of a Customary Norm', 26 *Virginia JIL* 551 (1986).

Perruchoud, R., 'Persons falling under the Mandate of the International Organization for Migration, to Whom the Organization may Provide Migration Services', 4 *IJRL* 205 (1992).

Perruchoud, R., 'From the Intergovernmental Committee for European Migration to the International Organization for Migration', 1 *IJRL* 501 (1989).

Petrasek, D., 'New Standards for the Protection of Internally Displaced Persons: A Proposal for a Comprehensive Approach', 14 *RSQ*, Nos. 1 & 2, 285 (1995).

Phuong, C., 'The Concept of "Effective Protection" in the Context of Irregular Secondary Movements and Protection in Regions of Origin', *Global Migration Perspectives* No. 26 (April 2005).

Piotrowicz, R., '*Lay Kon Tji v Minister for Immigration and Ethnic Affairs*: The Function and Meaning of Effective Nationality in the Assessment of Applications for Asylum', 11 *IJRL* 544 (1999).

Piotrowicz, R. & van Eck, C., 'Subsidiary Protection and Primary Rights', 53 *ICLQ* 107 (2004).

Plender, R., 'The Legal Basis of International Jurisdiction to Act with regard to the Internally Displaced', 6 *IJRL* 345 (1994).

Pompe, C. A., 'The Convention of 28 July 1951 and the international protection of refugees', HCR/INF/42 (May 1958); originally published in Dutch in *Rechtsgeleerd Magazyn Themis* (1956), 425.

Prunier, G., 'La crise rwandaise: Structures et déroulment', 13 *RSQ*, Nos. 2 & 3, 13 (1994).

Pugash, J. Z., 'The Dilemma of the Sea Refugee: Rescue without Refuge', 18 *Harv. ILJ* 577 (1977).

Pugh, M. & Cunliffe, S. A., 'The Lead Agency Concept in Humanitarian Assistance: The Case of the UNHCR', *Security Dialogue*, Vol. 28(1), 17 (1997).

Rafiqul Islam, M., 'The Sudanese Darfur Crisis and Internally Displaced Persons in International Law: The Least Protection for the Most Vulnerable', 18 *IJRL* 354 (2006).

Ramcharan, B. G., 'Early Warning at the United Nations: The First Experiment', 1 *IJRL* 379 (1989).

Rasulov, A., 'Criminals as Refugees: The "Balancing Exercise" and Article 1F(b) of the Refugee Convention', 16 *Georgetown Immigration Law Journal* 815 (2002).

Reale, E., 'Le droit d'asile', 63 Hague *Recueil* 473, (1938-I).

Reale, E., 'Le problème des passeports', 50 Hague *Recueil* 89, (1934-IV).

Reville, A., '*L'abjuratio regni*: histoire d'une institution anglaise', *Revue historique*, 1, (1892).

Rhys Jones, D. & Smith, S. V., 'Medical Evidence in Asylum and Human Rights Appeals', 16 *IJRL* 381 (2004).

Rikhof, J., 'War Crimes, Crimes against Humanity and Immigration Law', (1993) 19 *Imm. L.R.* (2d) 18.

Riveles, S., 'Diplomatic Asylum as a Human Right: The Case of the Durban Six', 11 *HRQ* 139 (1989).

Rodier, C., '«Emigration illégale»: une notion à bannir', *Libération*, 13 juin 2006.

Rogers, N., 'Minimum Standards for Reception', 4 *EJML* 215 (2002).

Röhl, K., 'Fleeing Violence and Poverty: Non-refoulement Obligations under the European Convention of Human Rights', UNHCR *New Issues in Refugee Research*, Working Paper No. 111, Geneva, Jan. 2005.

Røsæg, E., 'Refugees as Rescuees: The Tampa Problem', *Scandinavian Institute of Maritime Law Yearbook* 2002, 295.

Rothwell, D., 'The Law of the Sea and the M/V *Tampa* incident: Reconciling Maritime Principles with Coastal State Sovereignty', 13 *Public Law Review* 118 (2002).

Ruiz, H. A., 'Early Warning Is Not Enough: The Failure to Prevent Starvation in Ethiopia, 1990', 2 *IJRL Special Issue—September 1990*, 83.

Russell, S., 'Unaccompanied Refugee Children in the United Kingdom', 11 *IJRL* 126 (1999).

Rusu, S., 'The Role of the Collector in Early Warning', 2 *IJRL Special Issue—September 1990* 65.

Rusu, S., 'The Development of Canada's Immigration and Refugee Board Documentation Centre', 1 *IJRL* 319 (1989).

Rutinwa, B., 'Prima Facie Status and Refugee Protection', UNHCR *New Issues in Refugee Research*, Working Paper No. 69 (Oct. 2002).

Rwelamira, M., '1989—An Anniversary Year: The 1969 OAU Convention on the Specific Aspects of Refugee Problems in Africa,' 1 *IJRL* 557 (1989).

Salomon, K., 'UNRRA and the IRO as Predecessors of UNHCR', in Rystad, G., ed., *The Uprooted: Forced Migration as an International Problem in the Post-War Era* 157 (1990).

Samuels, H., 'The Detention of Vietnamese Asylum Seekers in Hong Kong: *Re Pham Van Hgo and 110 Others*', 41 *ICLQ* 422 (1992).

Sarooshi, D., 'The Legal Framework Governing United Nations Subsidiary Organs', 67 *BYIL* 413 (1996).

Saul, B., 'Cultural Nationalism, Self-Determination and Human Rights in Bhutan' 12 *IJRL* 321 (2000).

Schabas, W. A., 'Canada and the Adoption of the Universal Declaration of Human Rights', 43 *McGill Law Journal* 403 (1998).

Schachter, O., 'Human Dignity as a Normative Concept', 77 *AJIL* 848 (1983).

Schaffer, R. P., 'The Singular Plight of Sea-Borne Refugees', 8 *Australian Yearbook of International Law* 213 (1978–80).

Schiratzki, J., 'The Best Interests of the Child in the Swedish Aliens Act', 14 *International Journal of Law, Policy and the Family* 206 (2000).

Schnyder, F., 'Les aspects juridiques actuels du problème des réfugiés', 114 Hague *Recueil* (1965-I) 339.

Schoenholtz, A. I. & Jacobs, J., 'The State of Asylum Representation: Ideas for Change', 16 *Georgetown Immigration Law Journal* 739 (2002).

Shah, P., 'Rewriting the Refugee Convention: The *Adan* Case in the House of Lords', 12 *Immigration & Nationality Law & Practice* 100 (1998).

Shoyele, O., 'Armed Conflicts and Canadian Refugee Law and Policy', 16 *IJRL* 547 (2004).

Sianni, A., 'Interception Practices in Europe and Their Implications', 21 *Refuge* 25 (2003).

Sicilianos, L.-A, 'The Classification of Obligations and the Multilateral Dimension of the Relations of International Responsibility', 13 *EJIL* 1125 (2002).

Simma, B. & Alston, P., 'The Sources of Human Rights Law: Custom, *Jus Cogens*, and General Principles', 12 *Australian Yearbook of International Law* 82 (1988–89).

Sitaropoulos, N., 'Refugee: A Legal Definition in Search of a Principled Interpretation by Domestic Fora', 52 *Revue hellénique de droit international* 151 (1999).

Smith, M., 'Warehousing Refugees: A Denial of Rights, A Waste of Humanity', in US Committee for Refugees, *World Refugee Survey 2004*, 38.

Stahn, C., 'International Territorial Administration in the former Yugoslavia: Origins, Development and Challenges Ahead', 61 *Zeitschrift für offentliches Recht und Volkerrecht* 107 (2001).

Statewatch, 'The fallacies of the EU-Africa dialogue on immigration: EU-African ministerial conference on immigration, 10–11 July 2006': <www.statewatch.org/news/2006/jul/06rabat.htm>.

Stavropoulou, M., 'Bosnia and Herzegovina and the Right to Return in International Law', in O'Flaherty, M. & Gisvold, G., eds., *Post-War Protection of Human Rights in Bosnia and Herzegovina*, The Hague: Kluwer Law International, 123 (1998).

Steinbock, D. J., 'The Refugee Definition as Law: Issues of Interpretation', in Nicholson & Twomey, eds., *Refugee Rights and Realities*, 13 (1999).

Storey, H., 'The Right to Family Life and Immigration Case Law at Strasbourg', 39 *ICLQ* 328 (1990).

Storey, H., 'The Internal Flight Alternative Test: The Jurisprudence Re-examined', 10 *IJRL* 499 (1998).

Storey, H. & Wallace, R., 'War and Peace in Refugee Jurisprudence', 95 *AJIL* 349 (2001).

Suhrke, A., Barutciski, M., Sandison, P., & Garlock, R., *The Kosovo Refugee Crisis: An Independent Evaluation of UNHCR's Emergency Preparedness and Response* (UNHCR Evaluation and Policy Analysis Unit, Geneva, Feb. 2000).

Suntinger, W., 'The Principle of *Non-Refoulement*: Looking Rather to Geneva than to Strasbourg?', 49 *Austrian Journal of Public International Law*. 203 (1995).

Sztucki, J., 'Who is a Refugee? The Convention Definition: Universal or Obsolete?', in Nicholson & Twomey, *Refugee Rights and Realities* (1999), 55.

Sztucki, J., 'The Conclusions on the International Protection of Refugees adopted by the Executive Committee of the UNHCR Programme', 1 *IJRL* 285 (1989).

Takkenberg, L., 'The Protection of Palestine Refugees in the Territories Occupied by Israel', 3 *IJRL* 414 (1991).

Tang Lay Lee, 'Refugees from Bhutan: Nationality, Statelessness and the Right to Return', 10 *IJRL* 118 (1998).

Tang Lay Lee, 'Stateless Persons and the Comprehensive Plan of Action–Part 1: Chinese Nationality and the Republic of China (Taiwan)', 7 *IJRL* 201 (1995).

Taran, P. A., 'Human Rights of Migrants: Challenges of the New Decade', 38 *International Migration* 7 (2000).

Taylor, S., 'Protection Elsewhere/Nowhere', 18 *IJRL* 283 (2006).

Thomas, D. Q. & Beasley, M. E., 'Domestic Violence as a Human Rights Issue', 15 *HRQ* 36 (1993).

Thorburn, J., 'Transcending Boundaries: Temporary Protection and Burden-Sharing in Europe', 7 *IJRL* 459 (1995).

Tiberghien, F., 'L'expulsion des réfugiés: Problèmes legislatifs et jurisprudentiels', *Doc. réf.*, no. 73, 5/14 mars 1989, Suppl., CJ, 1–8.

Tomuschat, C., 'A Right to Asylum in Europe', 13 *HRLJ* 257 (1992).

Towle, R., 'Human Rights Standards: A Paradigm for Refugee Protection?', in Bayefsky & Fitzpatrick, eds., *Human Rights and Forced Displacement*, 381 (2000).

Trenholme, N. M., 'The Right of Sanctuary in England', 1 *University of Missouri Studies*, No. 5 (1903).

Troeller, G., 'UNHCR Resettlement: Evolution and Future Direction', 14 *IJRL* 85 (2002).

Troeller, G., 'UNHCR Resettlement as an Instrument of International Protection', 3 *IJRL* 564 (1991).

Tuitt, P., 'Rethinking the refugee concept', in Nicholson & Twomey, eds., *Refugee Rights and Realities*, 106 (1999).

Türk, V., 'Forced Migration and Security', 15 *IJRL* 113 (2003).

Türk, V., 'Non-State Agents of Persecution', in Chetail & Gowlland-Debbas, V., eds., *Switzerland and the International Protection of Refugees*, 93 (2002).

Türk, V., 'The Role of UNHCR in the Development of International Refugee Law', in Nicholson & Twomey, *Refugee Rights and Realities*, 153 (1999).

UNHCR, 'Towards a Common European Asylum System', in de Sousa & de Bruycker, P., *The Emergence of a European Asylum Policy*, 249 (2004).

United Kingdom, House of Lords/House of Commons Joint Committee on Human Rights, 'Counter-Terrorism Policy and Human Rights: Terrorism Bill and Related Matters', (3rd Report of Session 2005–06), vol. 2, HL Paper 75-II, HC 561-II Ev 2.

United Kingdom, House of Lords/House of Commons Joint Committee on Human Rights, 'The UN Convention against Torture (UNCAT)', (19th Report of Session 2005–06), vol. 1, HL Paper 185-I, HC 701-I (May 2006).

United Kingdom, House of Lords European Union Committee, 'Fighting Illegal Immigration: Should Carriers Carry the Burden?' 5th Report of Session 2003–04, HL Paper 29, 2004.

United Kingdom, House of Lords European Union Committee, 'Handling EU Asylum Claims: New Approaches Examined', HL Paper 74, 11th Report of Session 2003–04).

United Kingdom, House of Lords/House of Commons Joint Committee on Human Rights, 'The Nationality, Immigration and Asylum Act 2002 (Specification of Particularly Serious Crimes) Order 2004', HL Paper 190/HC1212, 2004.

United Kingdom, House Lords Select Committee on the European Union, 'Proposals for a European Border Guard', Session 2002–03, 29th Report.

United Kingdom, House of Lords Select Committee on the EU, 'Minimum Standards of Reception Conditions for Asylum Seekers', 8th Report, 27 November 2001.

United Kingdom, House of Commons Select Committee on International Development 'Kosova: The Humanitarian Crisis', 3rd Report, 1999, HC 422.

US Department of State, Reports on Human Rights Practices: <http://www.state.gov/g/drl/rls/hrrpt/>.

US Committee for Refugees and Immigrants, *World Refugee Survey (2005)*, Washington, D.C (2005).

US Committee for Refugees, 'Transition in Burundi: The Context for a Homecoming,' Washington, D.C., Sept., 1993.

van den Wyngaert, C., 'Applying the European Convention on Human Rights to Extradition: Opening Pandora's Box?' 39 *ICLQ* 757 (1990).

Vedsted-Hansen, J., 'Non-admission Policies and the Right to Protection: Refugees' Choice versus States' Exclusion?', in Nicholson & Twomey, eds., *Refugee Rights and Realities*, 274 (1999).

Verdirame, G., 'Testing the Effectiveness of International Norms: UN Humanitarian Assistance and Sexual Apartheid in Afghanistan', 23 *HRQ* 733 (2001).

Verdirame, G., 'The Genocide Definition in the Jurisprudence of the *Ad Hoc* Tribunals', 49 *ICLQ* 578 (2000).

Vidal, M., ' "Membership of a Particular Social Group" and the Effect of *Islam* and *Shah*', 11 *IJRL* 528 (1999).

Virally, M., 'Review Essay: Good Faith in Public International Law', 77 *AJIL* 130 (1983).

von Sternberg, M. R., 'Political Asylum and the Law of Internal Armed Conflict: Refugee Status, Human Rights and Humanitarian Law Concerns', 5 *IJRL* 153 (1993).

von Sternberg, M. R., 'Emerging Bases of "Persecution" in American Refugee Law: Political Opinion and the Dilemma of Neutrality', 13 *Suffolk Transnational Law Journal* 1 (1989).

Ward, I., 'The Story of M: A Cautionary Tale from the United Kingdom', 6 *IJRL* 194 (1994).

Weil, P., 'Towards Relative Normativity in International Law?' 77 *AJIL* 413 (1985).

Weinman, S. C., '*INS v. Stevic*: A Critical Assessment', 7 *HRQ* 391 (1985).

Weis, P., 'The Draft Convention on Territorial Asylum', 50 *BYIL* 176 (1979).

Weis, P., 'Convention Refugees and De Facto Refugees', in Melander, & Nobel, *African Refugees and the Law*, (1978), 20.

Weis, P., review of Mutharika, *The Regulation of Statelessness under International and National Law: Texts and Documents* (1977), 72 *AJIL* 680 (1978).

Weis, P., 'The Legal Aspects of the Problems of *de facto* Refugees', in International University Exchange Fund, *Problems of Refugees and Exiles in Europe* (1974).

Weis, P., 'Human Rights and Refugees', 1 *Israel Yearbook on Human Rights* 35 (1971).

Weis, P., 'The United Nations Declaration on Territorial Asylum' 7 *Can. YIL* 92 (1969).

Weis, P., 'The 1967 Protocol relating to the Status of Refugees and Some Questions of the Law of Treaties', 42 *BYIL* 39 (1967).

Weis, P., 'Territorial Asylum', 6 *Indian Journal of International Law* 173 (1966).

Weis, P., 'The United Nations Convention on the Reduction of Statelessness', 11 *ICLQ* 1073 (1962).

Weis, P., 'The Convention relating to the Status of Stateless Persons', 10 *ICLQ* 255 (1961).

Weis, P., 'The Concept of the Refugee in International Law', *Journal du droit international* (1960) 1.

Weis, P., 'The International Protection of Refugees', 48 *AJIL* 193 (1954).

Weis, P., 'Legal Aspects of the Convention of 28 July 1951 relating to the Status of Refugees,' 30 *BYIL* 478 (1953).

Weisman, N., 'Article 1F(a) of the 1951 Convention relating to the Status of Refugees', 8 *IJRL* 111 (1996).

Wilde, R., 'The Extraterritorial Application of the Human Rights Act' in Holder, J. & O'Cinneide, C., eds., *Current Legal Problems 2005* (2005).

Wilde, R., 'Legal "Black Hole"? Extraterritorial State Action and International Treaty Law on Civil and Political Rights', 26 *Michigan Journal of International Law* 739 (2005).

Wilde, R., 'The "Legal Space" or "*Espace Juridique*" of the European Convention on Human Rights: Is it Relevant to Extraterritorial State Action?', 2 *European Human Rights Law Review* 115 (2005).

Wilde, R., 'Representing International Territorial Administration: A Critique of Some Approaches', 15 *EJIL* 71 (2004).

Wilde, R., 'From Danzig to East Timor and Beyond: The Role of International Territorial Adminstration', 95 *AJIL* 583 (2001).

Wilde, R., '*Quis custodiet ipsos custodes?* Why and How UNHCR governance of "Development" Refugee Camps Should be Subject to International Human Rights Law', 1 *Yale Human Rights & Development Law Journal* 108 (1998).

Wilsher, D., 'Non-State Actors and the Definition of a Refugee in the United Kingdom: Protection, Accountability or Culpability?' 15 *IJRL* 68 (2003).

Yeo, C., 'Agents of the State: When is an Official of the State an Agent of the State?' 14 *IJRL* 509 (2002).

Zambelli, P., 'Procedural Aspects of Cessation and Exclusion: The Canadian Experience', 8 *IJRL* 144 (1996).

SELECTED UNITED NATIONS DOCUMENTS

A Study of Statelessness: UN doc. E/1112 and Add. 1 (1949).

Aga Khan, Sadruddin, *Study on Human Rights and Mass Exoduses*: UN doc. E/CN.4/1503 (1981).

Boutkevitch, V., 'Working Paper on the Right to Freedom of Movement and Related Issues', UN doc. E/CN.4/Sub.2/1997/22, (19 July 1997).

Capotorti, F., *Study on the Rights of Persons belonging to Ethnic, Religious and Linguistic Minorities* (1978): UN doc. E/CN/4/Sub. 2/384/Rev. 1.

Commission on Human Rights, 'Civil and Political Rights, including the Questions of Disappearances and Summary Executions: Extrajudicial, Summary or Arbitrary Executions: Report of the Special Rapporteur, Philip Alston', UN doc. E/CN.4/2005/7 (22 Dec. 2004).

Daes, E.-I., 'Study of the Individual's Duties to the Community and the Limitations of Human Rights and Freedoms under Article 29 of the Universal Declaration of Human Rights': UN doc. E/CN.4/Sub.2/432/Rev.1 (1980).

Deng, F., 'Internally Displaced Persons'. Report of the Representative of the Secretary-General: UN doc. E/CN.4/1994/44 (1994).

Deng, F., 'Comprehensive Study on the Human Rights Issues relating to Internally Displaced Persons': UN doc. E/CN.4/1993/35 (1993).

Eide, A. & Mubanga-Chipoya, 'Conscientious Objection to Military Service': UN doc. E/CN.4/Sub.2/1983/30/Rev.1.

Elimination of All Forms of Religious Intolerance. *Note* by the Secretary-General: UN doc. A/8330 (1971).

Elles, Baroness, 'International Provisions protecting the Human Rights of Non-Citizens': UN doc. E/CN.4/Sub.2/392/Rev.1 (1980).

Ingles, J., 'Study of Discrimination in Respect of the Right of Everyone to Leave Any Country, including his Own, and Return to his Country': UN doc. E/CN.4/Sub.2/229/Rev.1 (1964).

Internally Displaced Persons. *Analytical Report* of the Secretary-General: UN doc. E/CN.4/1992/23, (14 Feb. 1992).

International Law Commission, 'Articles on the Responsibility of States for Internationally Wrongful Acts', annexed to UNGA res. 56/83 (12 Dec. 2001).

International Law Commission, Draft Statute of the International Criminal Court (1994): Text in *Report of the International Law Commission*, (1994), UN GAOR, 49th Sess., Suppl. No. 10 (A/49/10).

International Law Commission, Draft Articles on the Draft Code of Crimes against the Peace and Security of Mankind: UN doc. A/46/405 (11 Sept. 1991).

International Law Commission, 'International Liability for Injurious Consequences arising out of acts not prohibited by international law': UN doc. A/36/10 (1981).

Martinez Cobo, J. R., 'Study of the Problem of Discrimination against Indigenous Populations': UN doc. E/CN.4/Sub.2/L.707 (1979).

Mazowiecki, T., Special Rapporteur on former Yugoslavia of the UN Commission on Human Rights: UN docs. E/CN.4/1992/S-1/9 (28 Aug. 1992); E/CN.4/1992/S-1/10 (27 Oct. 1992).

Report of the Group of Governmental Experts on International Co-operation to Avert New Flows of Refugees: UN doc. A/41/324 (May 1986).

Report of the Secretary-General, 'Strengthening of the Coordination of Humanitarian and Disaster Relief Activities': UN doc. A/50/203; E/1995/79 (14 June 1995); also Add.1 (27 June 1995).

Report of the Secretary-General, 'The Role of Youth in the Promotion and Protection of Human Rights, including the Question of Conscientious Objection to Military Service': UN doc. E/CN.4/1989/30 (20 Dec. 1988).

Report of the Secretary-General on the Meeting on Refugees and Displaced Persons in South East Asia, Geneva, 20–1 July 1979, and Subsequent Developments: UN doc. A/34/627 (1979).

Report of the Secretary-General on Methods of Fact-Finding: UN docs. A/5694 (1964); A/6228 (1966).

Report of the UN Conference on the Human Environment: UN doc. A/CONF.48/ 14/Rev. 1 and Corr. 1 (1972).

Ruhashyankiko, N., 'Study of the Question of the Prevention and Punishment of the Crime of Genocide': UN doc. E/CN.4/Sub.2/416 (1978).

Stavenhagen, R., 'Report of the Special Rapporteur on the Situation of Human Rights and Fundamental Freedoms of Indigenous People': UN doc. E/CN.4/2006/78 (16 Feb. 2006).

UNHCR, 'Declarations and Reservations to the 1967 Protocol relating to the Status of Refugees', Geneva, March 2006.

UNHCR, 'Declarations and Reservations to the 1951 Convention relating to the Status of Refugees', Geneva, March 2006.

UNHCR, Department of International Protection, *Resettlement Handbook*, Geneva, 2004.

UNHCR, 'Procedural Standards for Refugee Status Determination under UNHCR's Mandate', Geneva, 2004.

UNHCR, 'Guidelines on International Protection: Religion-Based Claims under Article 1A(2) of the 1951 Convention and/or the 1967 Protocol relating to the Status of Refugees', HCR/GIP/04/06, (28 Apr. 2004).

UNHCR, 'Guidelines on Internal Flight or Relocation Alternative within the Context of Article 1A(2) of the 1951 Convention and/or 1967 Protocol relating to the Status of Refugees', HCR/GIP/04/06, (23 Jul. 2003).

UNHCR, 'Guidelines on International Protection: Application of the Execution Clauses: Article 1F of the 1951 Convention relating to the Status of Refugees', HCR/GIP/ 03/05, (4 Sept. 2003).

UNHCR, 'Guidelines on International Protection: Cessation of Refugee Status under Article 1C(5) and (6) of the 1951 Convention relating to the Status of Refugees', HCR/GIP/03/03, (10 Feb. 2003).

UNHCR, 'Declaration of States Parties to the 1951 Convention and/or its 1967 Protocol relating to the Status of Refugees', HCR/MMSP/2001/09 (16 Jan. 2002).

UNHCR, 'Guidelines on International Protection: Gender-Related Persecution within the Context of Article 1A(2) of the 1951 Convention and/or its 1967 Protocol Relating to the Status of Refugees': HCR/GIP/02/01, (7 May 2002).

UNHCR, 'Guidelines on International Protection: "Membership of a Particular Social Group" within the Context of Article 1A(2) of the 1951 Convention and/or its 1967 Protocol Relating to the Status of Refugees': HCR/GIP/02/02, (7 May 2002).

UNHCR, 'Policy on Refugee Women and Guidelines on Their Protection: An Assessment of Ten Years of Implementation.' An independent assessment by the Women's Commission for Refugee Women and Children, (May 2002).

UNHCR, 'Note on the Applicability of Article 1D of the 1951 Convention relating to the Status of Refugees to Palestinian refugees', Geneva, (Oct, 2002), text in 14 *IJRL* 450 (2002).

UNHCR, 'Selected Bibliography on Refugee Women, 1990—June 2005', update to the Select Bibliography Section of the Special Issue on Refugee Women, 21 *Refugee Survey Quarterly* (2002).

UNHCR, 'Interpreting Article 1 of the 1951 Convention relating to the Status of Refugees', Geneva, (Apr. 2001).

UNHCR, 'Safeguards for Asylum Seekers and Refugees in the Context of Irregular Migration into and within Europe: A Survey of the Law and Practice of 31 European States', (Jun. 2001).

UNHCR, 'New Directions for Resettlement Policy', UN doc. EC/51/SC/INF.2, (14 June 2001), 13 *IJRL* 690 (2001).

UNHCR, 'Guidelines on Policies and Procedures in dealing with Unaccompanied Children seeking Asylum', (Feb. 1997).

UNHCR, 'International Legal Standards applicable to the Protection of Internally Displaced Persons: A Reference Manual for UNHCR Staff', Geneva, (1996).

UNHCR, 'Protection Aspects of UNHCR Activities on behalf of Internally Displaced Persons', UN doc. EC/1994/SCP/CRP.2, (4 May 1994).

UNHCR, 'Overview of Re-Admission Agreements in Central Europe', (Sept. 1993).

UNHCR, *Handbook on Procedures and Criteria for Determining Refugee Status under the 1951 Convention and the 1967 Protocol relating to the Status of Refugees* UN doc. HCR/IP/4/Eng/Rev.1, Geneva, 2nd edn., (1992).

UNICEF & UNHCR, *Evacuation of Children from Conflict Areas: Considerations and Guidelines*, Geneva, (1992).

United Nations, *Humanitarian Response Review*, Office for the Coordination of Humanitarian Affairs, New York, Geneva, (Aug. 2005).

United Nations, 'Report of the Policy Working Group on the United Nations and Terrorism': UN doc. A/57/273, S/2002/875, (6 Aug. 2002).

United Nations, *A Selected Bibliography on Territorial Asylum*: UN doc. ST/GENEVA/LIB.SER.B/Ref.9 (1977).

United Nations, 'Study of Discrimination in the Matter of Religious Rights and Practices', UN doc. E/CN.4/Sub.2/300/Rev.1 (1960).

United Nations, *Multilateral Treaties deposited with the Secretary-General*, regularly updated in the series UN doc. ST/LEG/SER.E/.

Index

abduction, 397
abuse of rights, 2, 191, 374, 283, 388–90, 458
accelerated procedures, 222, 392, 400, 31, 541
access, 369–71, 409–12,
  procedures, 222, 370, 390–1, 539, 540
  UNHCR, 487, 540, 541
  see also refugee status determination
ACP, 503–4
acquired rights, 496, 554
actors of persecution, 87n, 99
Ad hoc Committee on Refugees, 35, 51n, 64n,
  67n, 101, 152n, 163, 164, 203–4, 235n,
  277, 362n, 507, 513–15, 518, 519n, 520,
  525, 526
administrative assistance, 512–15
admissibility, 397
admission, 382
adoption, 478–80
Ador, G., 421
affidavits, 512–15
Afghanistan, 31, 194, 228, 495
Africa, 25–6, 40, 71, 208, 230, 288, 341, 416
African Union, 37, 39, 444
agents of persecution, 41n, 61, 98–100
  State responsibility and, 99–100
  see also persecution
aggression, 30, 37, 38, 165–6, 185, 194
Ago, R., 451
aid and development, *see* assistance
airline liaison officers, 371–2, 379n, 385–6
Albania, 162n, 220n
Algeria, 428, 490n
Ambionese, 510
amnesty, 174, 493, 496
Amnesty International, 103n, 229, 407,
  411–12, 446
Angola, 509n, 511n
apartheid, 30, 71n, 132–3, 167
appeal and review, 262–4, 392–3, 403, 463–5,
  529, 530–1, 533, 535–7, 541
  suspensive effect, 403
  see also due process; refugee status
    determination
Arafat, Y., 160n
arbitration, 434
Argentina, 222, 260n, 510n
Aristide, Pres. J. B., 247
armed attacks, 471–2
armed conflict, 5, 30, 38, 40, 94–7, 476

Arusha Conference 1979, 205n
Asian–African Legal Consultative Committee,
  39, 212–13
asilado, 37–8
assistance, 15, 29, 31, 265, 293, 439, 483,
  500–1
  development, 500–1
asylum, 15, 32, 41, 149–51, 199–418, 410–1,
  552–3, and *passim*
  concept, 355–417
  diplomatic, 356–7
  discretion and, 58, 88, 172, 262, 414–15
  meaning, 225, 355–8, 368n
  obligation and, 359–65
  obstructing, 369–80
  regional, 366–9
  right of, 36n, 203, 223, 355–65
  right to seek, 4, 38, 203, 223, 358–9,
    370–1, 383, 487
  territorial, 38
asylum seekers, 28, 39n, 232–3, 265, 443, and
  passim,
Australia, 42, 46n, 47n, 59–60, 91–2, 171,
  175, 188–9, 221, 226, 238–40, 251–2,
  255–4, 265n, 268n, 270, 274, 276,
  280–4, 285n, 308–9, 350n, 351, 358n,
  359–60, 377, 385, 386n, 403–5, 452n,
  464n, 498n, 548–9
  Pacific Strategy, 255–7, 408, 403
  TPVs, 140n, 290n, 340n
Austria, 17, 69, 383n, 402n, 423, 498n, 509n
aut dedere aut judicare, 177, 259

Bahamas, 509n
balance of probabilities, *see* refugee status
    determination, proof
balancing, 56n, 120, 165, 172, 178, 192n,
  239–41, 317–21
  context and proportionality, 180–4
Bangkok Principles, 29, 212–13
Bangladesh, 26n, 229, 488n, 495n, 508n
Barry, J., 182n
Bastarache, J., 175n, 188n, 190n
Beaumont, J., 351n
Belgium, 48n, 62n, 101, 146, 148, 149, 173n,
  206n, 220, 227, 235n, 328, 358n, 379n,
  422, 452n, 489n, 508, 509n, 514, 515,
  520n, 521
Belize, 45